Handbook of
GROUP COUNSELING
and
PSYCHOTHERAPY

With love to my "Handbook support group": my husband, Bruce;
my children, Erik and Olivia; and my mother, Mary

—Maria

To my own little support group: my husband, Kevin, and my daughters
Jessica Lynn and Kellie Kathleen

—Debbie

To my parents with love and respect

—Cyndee

To my parents, the leaders of my "first group"

—Janice

Handbook of
GROUP COUNSELING and PSYCHOTHERAPY

Edited by

Janice L. DeLucia-Waack
University at Buffalo, SUNY

Deborah A. Gerrity
University at Buffalo, SUNY

Cynthia R. Kalodner
Towson University

Maria T. Riva
University of Denver

SAGE Publications
International Educational and Professional Publisher
Thousand Oaks ■ London ■ New Delhi

For information:

Sage Publications, Inc.
2455 Teller Road
Thousand Oaks, California 91320
E-mail: order@sagepub.com

Sage Publications Ltd.
6 Bonhill Street
London EC2A 4PU
United Kingdom

Sage Publications India Pvt. Ltd.
B-42, Panchsheel Enclave
Post Box 4109
New Delhi 110 017 India

Printed in the United States of America

Library of Congress Cataloging-in-Publication Data

Handbook of group counseling and psychotherapy / edited by
Janice L. DeLucia-Waack . . . [et al.].
    p. cm.
Includes bibliographical references and index.
ISBN 0-7619-2469-8 (cloth)
  1. Group psychotherapy. 2. Group counseling. I. DeLucia-Waack, Janice L.
RC488.H353 2004
616.89′152—dc22

                              2003017030

This book is printed on acid-free paper.

03   04   05   06   10   9   8   7   6   5   4   3   2   1

Acquisitions Editor:	Arthur T. Pomponio
Editorial Assistant:	Veronica K. Novak
Production Editor:	Denise Santoyo
Copy Editors:	Carla Freeman/Barbara Coster
Typesetter:	C&M Digitals (P) Ltd.
Indexer:	Will Ragsdale
Cover Designer:	Janet Foulger

TABLE OF CONTENTS

INTRODUCTION

JANICE L. DeLUCIA-WAACK, DEBORAH A. GERRITY,
CYNTHIA R. KALODNER, AND MARIA T. RIVA

In considering the development of this handbook, we approached our task with some key beliefs and values that guided our decision-making and editing processes. First, we strongly believed that this book should have a comprehensive coverage of groups, including history and theory, research, and practice, and also topics across the life span, diverse cultures, a variety of clinical problems, and different settings. Second, and connected to the first, was a view that the field of group counseling and psychotherapy would be better served with an increased collaboration between group researchers and practitioners. The research on groups has certainly increased, as has the number and types of groups that are conducted in a variety of diverse settings. Research has guided our thinking in areas such as how groups are led, the effective components that operate within groups, and how group progress is measured. We also know that there are many group practicioners who have expertise in numerous areas that, if tapped, could provide us with additional guidance on a variety of issues, including how to organize a group, select group members, facilitate exercises and interventions, and provide a therapeutic ending to a group. Information from group practitioners is harder to obtain, and many research studies are conducted regularly without any input from experienced leaders. One primary consideration was that this handbook would include the voices of researchers, group counseling educators, and group facilitators and that each chapter would be written with this collaboration in mind. To that end, we invited both experienced group leaders and researchers to write chapters for us. Typically, past books on group counseling and psychotherapy have emphasized either the empirical research or the practice of leading small groups, to the exclusion of the other view. We attempted to integrate these two important group knowledge delivery systems.

Another value that provided a foundation for this handbook is that group counseling and psychotherapy are multicultural and that group leaders and researchers need to be sensitive and competent to work with multicultural group clients and research participants. There is a section in the handbook dedicated to multicultural groups, along with many other chapters addressing issues of diversity and culture in groups.

Another driving force was the importance of ethical considerations that relate specifically to group counseling and psychotherapy. The majority of information written about ethical behavior focuses on individual psychotherapy. Given that group formats are much more complex than individual psychotherapy, it was essential that chapters address ethical implications of different types of groups and also discuss the contra-indications of group work if applicable to a specific chapter. It was our intention to provide the best practices gleaned from theory and research and the most up-to-date information possible. Group counseling and psychotherapy have expanded in many different types of settings, with different populations, and for people who represent the entire continuum of age and a large variety of problems. We attempted to respond to the wealth of ways that groups are used presently and also take a look into the future to see how groups might evolve.

The development of this handbook was a dynamic process that changed as we had conversations about the sections and the content and worked with our authors to further develop and refine their ideas. The evolution occurred at every level, from a change in our title to the organization of the sections and the chapters that were pertinent for each section. The seven sections, 47 chapters, and appendices in this handbook are the culmination of these efforts. As editors, our knowledge and appreciation of group counseling and psychotherapy have certainly increased and expanded, and we hope that this book will inform and inspire others to see the immense power and value of therapeutic groups.

ACKNOWLEDGMENTS

We would like to thank all the people who have contributed to this project from the beginning to the end. The contributing authors have written highly informative chapters, and we thank each person for the way in which they handled all our requests for modifications. We hope that all these authors find the chapters in this book to be state-of-the-art in group counseling and psychotherapy. We acknowledge Nancy Hale's role in the beginning of the process and Art Pomponio's dedication to getting this book finished. We have taken time from our academic duties at our universities to work on this project, and we thank our colleagues and students for their understanding when we were busier than usual. Finally, each of us acknowledge the role of our families—four husbands and eight children—who tolerated our absences while we edited these chapters.

ABOUT THE EDITORS

Janice L. DeLucia-Waack is Associate Professor in the Department of Counseling, School, and Educational Psychology at the University at Buffalo, SUNY. She is the program director for the School Counseling Master's program, and teaches two courses, Advanced Group Counseling Theory and Practice and Group Work in the Schools, related to groups for graduate students. She received a Bachelor's degree in Psychology from Eisenhower College, a Master's degree in Family Studies from the University of Maryland, and a Ph.D. in Counseling Psychology from Pennsylvania State University after completing a predoctoral internship in psychology at the University of Buffalo, SUNY Counseling Center. She began her academic career teaching group counseling courses at Purdue University. Her counseling and research interests include groups, eating disorders and body image, children of divorce, supervision, and multicultural counseling. She is the author of two books, *Multicultural Counseling Competencies: Implications and Challenges for Practice* and *Using Music in Children of Divorce Groups: A Session-by-Session Manual for Counselors,* and coauthor of another two books, *Group Work Experts Share Their Favorite Activities: A Guide to Choosing, Planning, Conducting and Processing* and *The Practice of Multicultural Group Work: Visions and Perspectives From the Field.* She is a former editor of the *Journal for Specialists in Group Work.* She has authored or coauthored more than 50 journal articles, book chapters, and journal editorials. She was also the recipient of the 2001 Association for Specialists in Group Work President's Award and was also made a Fellow by the same association in 1998. Also in 1998 she received the Distinguished Counselor Educator Award in the state of Indiana and the Association for Specialists in Group Work Professionals Advancement Award. In 1994, she received the Outstanding Research Article Award in the *Journal for Specialists in Group Work* and the Association for Specialists in Group Work President's Award.

Deborah A. Gerrity is Assistant Professor in the Department of Counseling, School, and Educational Psychology at the University at Buffalo, SUNY. She is a faculty member in the Counseling Psychology, Counselor Education, and School Counseling programs. She teaches the Introduction to Group Counseling course for the master's students in School and Rehabilitation Counseling and the doctoral students in Counseling Psychology. Her Bachelor's degree in Psychology, Master's in Community Counseling, Ph.D. in Counseling Psychology, and doctoral internship were all completed at the University of Maryland at College Park. Her counseling and research interests are in the areas of group counseling and women's issues, including sexual abuse, sexual harassment, infertility, and gender role socialization. She has authored or coauthored 20 journal articles, research reports, manuscripts, and book chapters. In 2002, she received the Outstanding Research Article on Groups Award from the Association for Specialists in Group Work.

Cynthia R. Kalodner is Associate Professor in the Department of Psychology at Towson University in Towson, Maryland. She is Director of the Master's program in Counseling Psychology and works closely with post-master's students seeking licensure as a Licensed Clinical Professional Counselor. She teaches Advanced Group Counseling and supervises students on practicum and internship placements throughout Maryland, Washington, D.C., and northern Virginia. She received a Bachelor's degree in Psychology from Rutgers University, and a Master's degree in Counselor Education and a Ph.D. in Counseling Psychology from Pennsylvania State University. She completed her internship at the Counseling Center at the University of Texas, Austin. She began her academic career at the University of Akron, completed a postdoctoral experience at Johns Hopkins University in the School of Public Health, and directed the Counseling Psychology program at West Virginia University for 7 years before moving to Towson. Her counseling and research interests lie primarily in the area of eating disorders and group counseling and psychotherapy; the intersection of these topics is her academic passion. She is the author of a book, *Too Fat or Too Thin: A Reference Guide to Eating Disorders*. She has authored or coauthored more than 40 book chapters and journal articles and made numerous presentations at national meetings focused on eating disorders, cognitive-behavioral counseling theory and practice, and a variety of topics as diverse as health care issues in Appalachia to burnout among graduate students. She continues to conduct research on predictors of the development of eating disorders and media literacy groups focused on the prevention of eating problems in girls and women.

Maria T. Riva is Associate Professor and Chair of the Counseling Psychology program at the University of Denver. She received her B.A. in Psychology from Illinois Wesleyan University, her M.S. in Behavior Modification from Southern Illinois University, and her Ph.D. from the University of Pittsburgh in Counseling Psychology in 1990. She has been actively involved in facilitating many types of counseling and psychotherapy groups over the past 20 years. She teaches both Group Counseling and Advanced Group Counseling courses, and her teaching style is strongly influenced by group and leadership theory. In 2001 she was awarded the University of Denver Distinguished Teaching Award. She has numerous publications on group counseling and psychotherapy. She belongs to the Association for Specialists in Group Work (ASGW, Division of ACA) and Group Psychology and Psychotherapy (Division 49 of APA). She was on the editorial board of the *Journal for Specialists in Group Work (JSGW)* for 6 years and currently serves as its Associate Editor. She is a Fellow of ASGW and in 1997 coedited a special issue on group research for *JSGW*.

LIST OF CONTRIBUTORS

Gregory Alexander
Northport VA Medical Center

Michael P. Andronico
Individual Practice, Somerset, NJ
University of Medicine and Dentistry
of New Jersey, Robert Wood Johnson
Medical School

Sally H. Barlow
Brigham Young University

Karen H. Bridbord
University at Buffalo, SUNY

Matthew M. Burg
VA Connecticut Healthcare System

Gary M. Burlingame
Brigham Young University

Lucille A. Cardella
The Abacus Group

Rita Chi-Ying Chung
George Mason University

Marvin W. Clifford
Ochsner Clinic Foundation

Robert K. Conyne
University of Cincinnati

Janelle W. Coughlin
Johns Hopkins University

David W. Cramer
Private Practice

Lori Brown Crutchfield
Clemson University

Michael D'Andrea
University of Hawaii

Janice L. DeLucia-Waack
University at Buffalo, SUNY

Liane Dornheim
Florida International University

Timothy R. Elliott
University of Alabama at Birmingham

Denise Emer
Daemen College

James Fauth
Antioch New England Graduate School

Laurie B. Fleckenstein
University of Georgia

Amelia Fleming
Bowling Green State University

Addie J. Fuhriman
Brigham Young University

Michael Tlanusta Garrett
Western Carolina University

Michael A. Gass
University of New Hampshire

Deborah A. Gerrity
University at Buffalo, SUNY

H. L. "Lee" Gillis
Georgia College & State University

Samuel T. Gladding
Wake Forest University

Les R. Greene
VA Connecticut Healthcare System

Alaina L. Haub
University of Denver

Donna A. Henderson
Wake Forest University

Stacey E. Holmes
University of Maryland at College Park

Arthur M. Horne
University of Georgia

Sharon G. Horne
University of Memphis

Keith Humphreys
Stanford University

Jennifer Johnson
Brigham Young University

Cynthia R. Kalodner
Towson University

Nathalie Kees
Colorado State University

Elizabeth A. Kincade
Indiana University at Pennsylvania

Dennis M. Kivlighan Jr.
University of Maryland at College Park

Elena Klaw
San Jose State University

Kathryn Kominars
Florida International University

Kenin M. Krieger
Indiana University

Gina B. Lasky
University of Denver

Nancy Leech
University of Colorado–Denver

Heidi M. Levitt
University of Memphis

Michele Litchy
Pittsburg Sate University

Rebecca R. MacNair-Semands
University of North Carolina at Charlotte

Laura Marshak
Indiana University of Pennsylvania

Andrew W. Meisler
VA Connecticut Healthcare System

Robert D. Morgan
Texas Tech University

D. Keith Morran
*Indiana University
Purdue University at Indianapolis*

John S. Ogrodniczuk
University of British Columbia

Sherlon P. Pack-Brown
Bowling Green State University

Betsy J. Page
Kent State University

Trica L. Peterson
University at Buffalo, SUNY

Loan T. Phan
University of New Mexico

David Pilkey
VA Connecticut Healthcare System

William E. Piper
University of British Columbia

Lynn S. Rapin
Private Practice
University of Cincinnati

Angie H. Rice
FamilyStrength

Maria T. Riva
University of Denver

Patricia Rivera
University of Alabama at Birmingham

Jonathan P. Schwartz
Louisiana Tech University

Milton Seligman
University of Pittsburgh

Zipora Shechtman
University of Haifa

Brian C. Sirois
Kaiser Permanente

Rex Stockton
Indiana University

Edil Torres Rivera
University at Buffalo, SUNY

James P. Trotzer
ETC³ Professional Services,
Hampton, NH

Emily Tucker
University of Alabama at Birmingham

Maximillian Wachtel
Mental Health Corporation of Denver

Michael Waldo
New Mexico State University

Donald E. Ward
Pittsburg State University

Susan A. Wheelan
GDQ Associates, Inc.

Martyn H. Wittingham
Indiana University

Tow Yee Yau
University of Pittsburgh

Part I

CURRENT AND HISTORICAL PERSPECTIVES ON THE FIELD OF GROUP COUNSELING AND PSYCHOTHERAPY

Introduction

MARIA T. RIVA

Group counseling and psychotherapy has had a rich and intricate historical road to its present place in the field of counseling and psychology. It is currently a popular and widely practiced method not only because it is efficient (once thought to be the primary strength of group formats) but also because it is *effective.* The transformation of group counseling and psychotherapy over the past 100 years has been truly amazing. The complex and interpersonal nature of group dynamics, which allows for the healing of many relational problems, also has resulted in numerous difficulties for researchers who have attempted to study these processes. Over the years, group counseling and psychotherapy has become more sophisticated and is used to treat a larger array of clinical problems and people across all age ranges. Over time, research and statistical methods have also improved, making it easier to assess not only group outcomes but also group process components. The journey to the present is an intriguing one that provides information about how groups have changed over time and what we currently know.

Part I, "Current and Historical Perspectives on the Field of Group Counseling and Psychotherapy," is a fascinating look at the many contributions and contributors that have made group counseling and psychotherapy a vital and potent treatment method. This section begins with a chapter on "The History of Group Counseling and Psychotherapy," by Sally Barlow, Addie Fuhriman, and Gary Burlingame. This chapter outlines 35 years of group counseling review articles (1962 to 1997), cites meta-analyses that compare the effectiveness of group treatment with individual treatment (1980 to 2003), and describes the evolution of group themes over the past 100 years.

Therapeutic factors that operate within group counseling and psychotherapy have been a

2 • HANDBOOK OF GROUP COUNSELING AND PSYCHOTHERAPY

strong focus for practice and research alike since at least the 1960s. The second chapter, "The Importance of Therapeutic Factors: A Typology of Therapeutic Factors Studies," by Dennis Kivlighan Jr. and Stacey Holmes, describes the essential nature of the therapeutic factors and addresses how they have been studied, what has been found, and problems in the way studies have looked at these factors. Many researchers have attempted to determine which therapeutic factors are most important given the stage of the group (e.g., beginning vs. middle) or the type of setting (e.g., inpatient vs. outpatient), although no clear consensus has been gained by these results. Using cluster analysis, Kivlighan and Holmes propose an alternative approach to understanding the past literature on therapeutic factors.

The third chapter addresses the leadership of group counseling and psychotherapy. This chapter, "Effective Leadership in Group Counseling and Psychotherapy: Research and Practice," by Maria T. Riva, Maximillian Wachtel, and Gina B. Lasky, provides an overview of the research on group leadership characteristics and behaviors that have been found to be critical in the facilitation of a group. Fortunately, over the years, many studies have investigated leadership variables and rather consistently point to some beneficial and destructive leadership behaviors. Less is known about coleadership or effective methods of training effective group leaders. These two areas of leadership are crucial to the field of group counseling and psychotherapy and are also addressed briefly in this chapter.

The final chapter in this section is titled "Process and Outcome in Group Counseling and Psychotherapy: A Perspective," by Gary Burlingame, Addie Fuhriman, and Jennifer Johnson. This chapter provides a broad perspective of the group counseling and psychotherapy process and outcome research, identifies the important components that have been studied over the years, and discusses how these components have evolved. For group leaders and group researchers, understanding group process and group outcome has been complex and often elusive. This chapter increases our understanding of process and outcome literature and uses a classification system to determine the strength of the research for specific variables.

1

THE HISTORY OF GROUP COUNSELING AND PSYCHOTHERAPY

SALLY H. BARLOW
Brigham Young University

ADDIE J. FUHRIMAN
Brigham Young University

GARY M. BURLINGAME
Brigham Young University

Over the last century, an energetic, oftentimes uneven history of group counseling has taken place. Of course, the informal study of groups has occurred ever since humans began to congregate! But the written history of groups really only began at the fin-de-siècle of the 19th century (Ruitenbeek, 1969). Certainly, earlier social scientists and philosophers recounted the power of the group: Kierkegaard (1944) referred to it as the dangerous "crowd"; Marx and Engels (1848) touted its incredible power to move human history forward. But for our purposes, we will view the enormous power of groups to change individuals through the careful lens of psychology. How the psychological study of groups has evolved can be recounted from a review of both research and application found in a number of relevant domains, from psychoeducation to psychoanalysis.

In addition, much of the advancement in group counseling has come to us via the excellent research in social psychology (often blurring the boundary between group psychology and group psychotherapy).

Do we all envision the same entity when we say "group therapy"? As little as a decade ago, this might have called to mind the traditional process group written about so elegantly by Yalom (1975, 1985) and often caricatured in situation comedies on television. But today, the term conjures up a host of models, tapping myriad applications and treating an enormous array of human issues, from medical "self-help" groups to the more traditional psychotherapy groups for adults with problems in living (Dagley, Gazda, Eppinger, & Stewart, 1994). A comprehensive definition of group therapy includes groups used for prevention, guidance, counseling, and training (Dagley et al., 1994). In 1905, when Dr. John Pratt began treating his tuberculosis patients in his "thought control classes," he likely could not have imagined the amazing scope of group treatments available by 1995! (For a more complete review, see Fuhriman & Burlingame, 1994). And if some of the forecasters are accurate (Goodman & Jacobs, 1994), by 2005, a mere 100 years after Pratt, the total application of groups to a variety of issues will be astonishing. This chapter will review this interesting history along the lines of various applications, theoretical developments, and efficacy of group psychotherapy as a change agent. We will address some troublesome issues, including meta-analysis as well as the enormous complexity group research presents— all in an effort to help us understand more fully the rich background of one of mental health's most viable interventions.

Historians will warn us that any in-depth examination of past events will no doubt be shaped by the method of examination we employ; and when anyone conducts a literature search using the various descriptors, *group counseling* and/or *group psychotherapy,* the results can look "conglomerate, complex, confabulatory, and conflictual," just as Anthony (1971, p. 4) described. It is but one view or angle from which to appreciate the development of group treatments. Fortunately, a number of authors have helped organize this once unwieldy field (Burlingame, MacKenzie & Strauss, in press; Dies, 1993; Fuhriman & Burlingame 1994; Kaul & Bednar, 1986; MacKenzie, 1992; Piper, Rosie, Joyce, & Azim, 1996). In particular, Fuhriman and Burlingame (1994) in their book *Handbook of Group Psychotherapy: An Empirical and Clinical Synthesis* organized the field further with their in-depth review of 90 years of methodological and conceptual work, including summaries of group outcome (as assessed by individual clients or group members, subgroups, and therapists or group leaders). They also examined therapeutic components of the group. These topics included the group as an ecosystem, important notions about development (stages that groups appear to move along), therapeutic factors (which have undergone an interesting history themselves!), and others that were carefully tracked and tallied into tables for clearer understanding.

Five more years of additional data have been added (see Barlow, Fuhriman, & Burlingame, 2000). Finally, studies from 2001 through 2002 were also culled from a library search, just as with the original literature review, including but not limited to Psychlit, Medline, and Social Science Index. These data were integrated into existing tables on the various issues of group psychotherapy, clinical application, and research, thus taking us into the new century.

A HISTORICAL REVIEW

Just who started group counseling is still subject to conjecture (see Dreikurs, 1969a, 1969b; Fuhriman & Burlingame, 1994; Horne & Rosenthal, 1997; McGrath, 1993; Sadock & Kaplan, 1983). Perhaps as with the invention of the combustion engine, it occurred in several places at once. Sigmund Freud might warrant the credit with his now famous Wednesday night meetings at 19 Berggasse Street in Vienna, Austria (Kanzer, 1983). Or it could be credited to John Pratt, whose treatment of tuberculin patients in group "classes" in the United States more closely aligns with what is considered group treatment. (He worked with medically ill patients, whereas Freud was meeting with his students.) Freud (1922), Adler (1955), and Moreno and Whitin (1932) published accounts influenced from individual therapy about the likely theoretical underpinnings of the group "cure." The beauty of their simultaneous efforts is that it set the stage for contributions from diverse theories (from psychoanalytic to psychodrama) and methodologies (from empirical to anecdotal). This "essential tension" (Kuhn, 1977) created an enormous fount of energy that foreshadowed the incredible power attributed to groups by the 1930s for solving the world's problems (e.g., Lewin, 1936). Psychoeducation as well as milieu therapy for inpatients (Lazell, 1921; Marsh, 1931, 1933, 1935, respectively) clearly broke ground for the treatment of mental illness. Adler (1955) and his disciple Dreikurs (1932, 1956) continued this more humane approach by adding knowledge about the power of group member influence. A cascade of exciting developments followed: here-and-now focus (Syz, 1928); group analysis (Burrows, 1927,

1928); re-creation of the primary group (Schilder, 1939; Wender, 1936); group treatment for children (Slavson, 1943); and even credentialing for this "new" area of expertise (Wolf, 1949). By the time Moreno and Whitin (1932) actually applied the title "Group Therapy" to this treatment endeavor, it had clearly come of age. The contributions from social work, clinical psychology, counseling and educational psychology, psychiatry, nursing, organizational behavior, and education added depth and breadth to this powerful phenomenon. And once it had been named, it could be studied.

GROUPS WORK: THE EMPIRICIST CLAIM

The efficacy of group psychotherapy has been undeniably established in the research literature. An enormous range of empirical studies over the decades has been conducted that address a progression of topics, from concerns about leadership, to members, to interactions, and finally to the complicated group processes that appear to result from these previous factors (i.e., therapeutic factors). These various topics have been assessed throughout the preceding century with an equally diverse set of methodologies, from simple tallies to much more complex statistical methods, such as hierarchical linear modeling. Clearly, these methodologies have become increasingly sophisticated to match the mind-boggling complexity inherent in a system that attempts to track member-to-member, leader-to-member, subgroup-to-leader or member, and member-to-leader interactions, plus the passage of time. Calculating the error variance alone for such complex data sets becomes exponentially challenging (and financially prohibitive in many cases, as a number of group researchers will attest). One of the troubling aspects of group research designs is the problem of unit of analysis (independent vs. dependent data), which has required some innovative strategies to overcome. Fortunately, enough dedicated group researchers have persisted, and their work has yielded increasingly more robust data. Initial studies (Burchard, Michaels, & Kotkov, 1948; Thomas, 1943) were hampered by a number of problems (e.g., groups that were not equivalent; Cook & Campbell, 1979). But by the 1960s, studies were including the necessary information to make fair comparisons. This allowed for statements of positive and negative outcome to be determined and hence efficacy or lack of efficacy to be determined as well. Table 1.1 includes these reviews of overall efficacy, 22 from the Fuhriman and Burlingame (1994) original chapter, as well as additional reviews covering 1992 to 2002. Although not exhaustive, these reviews are clearly representative of the empirical directions taken by researchers in the preceding decades. Table 1.1 highlights therapy orientation, the number of studies in each review, what group treatment was compared with to determine its overall efficacy, the particular population treated, and a brief description of outcome conclusions. As can be seen, reviews from the 1960s covered an array of treatments, from traditional analysis to large groups. The studies of Rickard (1962) and Pattison (1965) illustrate some of the problems inherent in studies of multiple between- and within-group phenomenon, such as accurately accounting for variance. Stotsky and Zolik (1965), Kreiger and Kogan (1964), Mann (1966), and Anderson (1968) presented general findings, though there was a range in their respective levels of caution, that groups are helpful adjuncts or complementary forms of treatment to other main therapy strategies. Given the types of patients and the nonequivalence of comparison groups, these data represent only tentative support for efficacy. The very absence of data suggests the newness of this domain of study. In addition, the popular National Training Laboratory (NTL) movement, whose methods found their way into the training "t" or sensitivity group movement in Bethel, Maine, and the Esalen Institute in California, occurred in this decade. Even though this particular movement was designed generally for personal growth, it still had an enormous impact on the later development of therapy group techniques, and at the time, they were not known for their rigorous empirical methods.

Reviews from 1971 to 1980, however, depict a different representation. The eight studies shown in Table 1.1 benefit from research designs with appropriate control treatments and/or comparison groups. The results offer more encouraging findings (Emrick, 1975;

(Text continues on page 10)

Table 1.1 Group Psychotherapy Review Articles

Author	Treatment Orientation	# of Studies	Comparison				Sample	Conclusions
			WLC	OT	I	COM		
Rickard (1962)	Nondirective, psychoanalytic, psychodrama	22	X	X	X	X	Mixed inpatient & outpatient	Too much variability among patients, therapists, and measures for comparison to be more than tentative. Efficacy of group remains to be empirically validated.
Pattison (1965)	Psychodrama, milieu, analytic	U					Inpatient, prison, addict, delinquent	Group activity is therapeutic using behavioral criteria, disappointing with psychometric criteria, and promising with construct criteria. Notes that the research on individual psychotherapy and small-group research has yet to be effectively incorporated into group psychotherapy research.
Stotsky & Zolick (1965)	Psychodrama, round table, & heterogeneous group	U	X	X	X	X	Psychotics	The results of controlled experimental studies do not offer clear support for using group therapy as an independent modality, but they do support group as an adjunctive or helpful intervention when combined with other treatments (drugs, individual, etc.).
Mann (1966)	Psychodrama, nondirective	41	X	X		X	Mixed diagnosis, adult & children, most institutionalized	Group therapy produces change in behavior, attitude, and personality regardless of orientation, method of comparison, or instruments.
Anderson (1968)	Counseling groups	6	X	X		X	Elementary students	Group counseling associated with higher GPA and personality change when compared with control. No difference when compared with other treatment combined.
Meltzoff & Kornreich (1970)	Heterogeneous, expressive, nondirective, systematic desensitization, behavior, analytic	6	X		X	X	Hospitalized adults, adult outpatients, children	80% of adequately controlled studies reviewed showed primarily positive results with both individual and group therapy. Six studies that made direct comparisons between group and individual found equivalent outcomes with a slight tendency for individual to be more effective.
Bednar & Lawlis (1971)	Heterogeneous, group psychotherapy, self-help, activity, milieu, work, insight	38	X	X	X	X	Mixed inpatient, seven outpatient, delinquents, alcoholics, sex offenders, students	Group therapy is valuable in treating neurotics, psychotics, and character disorders. It is a two-edged sword that can facilitate client deterioration.

(Continued)

Table 1.1 (Continued)

Author	Treatment Orientation	# of Studies	Comparison WLC	OT	I	COM	Sample	Conclusions
Luborsky, Singer, & Luborsky (1975)	Heterogeneous	12	X		X	X	Unspecific	Majority of comparisons showed no significant differences between group and individual treatment. There was a tie in nine comparisons, group was better in two comparisons, and individual was better in two comparisons.
Grunebaum (1975)	Unspecified	U			X		Heterogeneous	Only meager data exist comparing group and individual therapy, and the evidence suggests that they are equally effective in most instances. Some findings suggest that benefits may be disorder specific, such as phobias better treated by individual therapy and group more effective for schizophrenic outpatients.
Emrick (1975)	Heterogeneous	384	X		X	X	Alcoholics	Found a general trend for both individual and group to be effective in treating alcoholism.
Lieberman (1976)	Heterogeneous, psychotherapy, & personal growth groups	47	X		X		College students, adults	Group consistently produced favorable outcome over controls. Reported no outcome differences in studies that compared group with individual format. Noted that the indices used to measure outcome are relatively insensitive to the potentialities of different treatment contexts, such as group and individual psychotherapy.
Parloff & Dies (1977)	Heterogeneous, psychotherapy groups	39	X	X	X	X	Psychoneurotic, schizophrenic, addiction, legal offenders	Group has no unique advantage over other treatments with schizophrenic patients; no firm conclusions can be drawn with psychoneurosis, and limited support for effectiveness with addicts.
Bednar & Kaul (1978)	Heterogeneous, behavioral, TA, unspecific group therapy, & encounter groups.	21		X	X	X	College students, delinquents, prisoners, psychiatric patients	Group treatments have been more effective than no treatment, placebo, and other recognized psychological treatments.
Solomon (1983)	Psychodynamic, aversion	2		X	X	X	Alcoholics	Combined individual and group related to poorest outcome, while individual and group as independent treatment showed equivalent outcomes.

(Continued)

Table 1.1 (Continued)

Author	Treatment Orientation	# of Studies	WLC	OT	1	COM	Sample	Conclusions
			Comparison					
Kanas (1986)	Heterogeneous	32	X	X			Outpatient & inpatient schizophrenic	Group therapy proved to be superior to controls in 67% of inpatient and 80% of outpatients studied, with long-term therapy being the best.
Kaul & Bednar (1986)	Experimental psychotherapy groups	17	X	X			Primarily adult mixed diagnosis	Mixed but favorable outcomes for the efficacy of group psychotherapy.
Toseland & Siporin (1986)	Heterogeneous	32	X		X		Heterogeneous	Results of this review indicated that group treatment was as effective as individual treatment in 75% of the studies included and was more effective in 25%. In the 32 studies reviewed, there was no case in which individual treatment was found to be more effective than group treatment.
Bostwick (1987)	Unspecified	13			X	X	Unspecified	Individual treatment had less premature termination than group, while combined individual and group treatment proved superior in reducing dropouts over either modality.
Oesterheld, McKenna, & Gould (1987)	Heterogeneous, (e.g., behavioral, insight, cognitive-behavioral, dynamic)	18	X	X	X		Bulimia	Group seems to be helpful, but methodological limitations preclude robust conclusions.
Zimpfer (1987)	Heterogeneous: (e.g., group counseling, multimodal, growth, insight)	19	X	X			Elderly	Group seems to be helpful, but methodological limitations preclude robust conclusions.
Freeman & Munroe (1988)	Cognitive-behavioral, eclectic, supportive, didactic	13	X	X	X	X	Bulimia	Neither drug nor group as effective as individual, but all are more effective than placebo. Group most cost-effective, and combined group and individual was most effective of all treatment.
Cox & Merkel (1989)	Heterogeneous	32	X		X	X	Bulimia	In a review of 15 groups and 17 individual studies (only one study provided a comparison between the two modalities, the rest were inferential) it was concluded that there was no support for the two treatments having any differential effectiveness.

(Continued)

Table 1.1 (Continued)

Author	Treatment Orientation	# of Studies	Comparison				Sample	Conclusions
			WLC	OT	I	COM		
Zimpfer (1990)	Cognitive-behavioral, psychoeducational behavior	31	X	X			Bulimia	Regardless of treatment type and outcome criteria, group was shown to be an effective treatment.
Piper & McCallum (1991)	Self-help, consciousness, cognitive restructuring, behavioral skills, dynamic	5	X	X	X	X	Grief	Group treatment has not been adequately tested to determine its efficacy.
Vandorvoot & Fuhriman (1991)	Cognitive-behavioral, psychodynamic, cognitive	12	X	X			Outpatient, depression	Group efficacious in treating depression with little evidence for differences between individual and group.
Piper & Joyce (1996)	Behavior 30%, cognitive behavior 26%, interpersonal/ psychodynamic 14%, didactic 1%	86	X	X	X	X	Lifestyle problems, medical conditions, mixed psychiatric disorders, mostly adults	Preview of a variety of patient problems treated in interactive therapy groups for 6 months or less were examined for evidence of efficacy, applicability and efficiency of time-limited, short-term group therapy (TSGT). Strong evidence for all three factors was found. Of 50 studies that had TSGT vs. control comparison, 48 provided evidence of benefit of group treatment. A difference in benefit was found for the 6 studies that used TSGT vs. individual.
Hoag & Burlingame (1997)	60% behavioral or cognitive-behavioral	56	X	X	X	X	Male and female children and adolescents (4-18), primarily problems of disruptive behavior, self-esteem	Review of studies from 1974-1997 of group interventions for children and adolescents (including preventative, psychotherapy, guidance) revealed that treatments occurred mostly in school settings and groups were beneficial.

SOURCE: From *Handbook of group psychotherapy: An empirical and clinical synthesis*, by A. Fuhriman and G. Burlingame (Eds.), 1994, New York: John Wiley. Adapted with permission.

NOTE: WLC = wait list control or comparable control group; OT = other group treatment comparison including pharmacotherapy; I = individual therapy comparison groups; COM = combined treatment group (e.g., group plus individual or group plus inpatient ward treatment).

Lieberman, 1976; Luborsky, Singer, & Luborsky, 1975; Meltzoff & Kornreich, 1970). These reviews began to distinguish what types of groups might be best for certain kinds of patients (Bednar & Lawlis, 1971), although, of course, healthy disagreement existed (Grunebaum, 1975). In addition, researchers began to delineate possible mechanisms for change or group processes that came to be labeled "curative factors" (Bednar & Kaul, 1978; Parloff & Dies, 1977). Thus, by the decade of the 1980s, the serious search for these therapeutic factors was under way. Researchers began in earnest to attempt to connect these process variables with outcomes. While it became more and more clear that group treatments were effective in comparison with inactive treatments (Freeman & Munro, 1988; Kanas, 1986; Kaul & Bednar, 1986), it also became clear that group therapy was comparable or even superior to other active treatments (Cox & Merkel, 1989; Oesterheld, McKenna, & Gould, 1987; Solomon, 1983; Toseland & Siporin, 1986; Zimpfer, 1987).

These important comparisons continued into the 1990s and the early beginnings of this century (e.g., Burlingame, Fuhriman, & Mosier, 2003; Vandervoort & Fuhriman, 1991; Zimpfer, 1990). With few exceptions, the general conclusion to be drawn from an enormous number of studies, covering an even larger number of clients or group members, is that groups work. Those exceptions had to do with self-help groups (Barlow, Burlingame, Nebeker, & Anderson, 2000) in which change was not any greater than wait-list controls. Generally, groups work for an ever-increasing number of client complaints, using a dizzying array of methods or treatment models. At the beginning of the 21st century, the advances in methodology and the robustness of the studies were highlighted in a special issue of one of the main outlets for group research (Forsyth, 2000). Along with the good news, there was, of course, some bad or at least cautionary news.

With the 1977 Smith and Glass publication, the statistical method of meta-analysis burst onto the empirical scene and offered researchers a way to essentially compare oranges and apples. As long as studies included means and standard deviations, comparisons could be made

that yielded an effect size. This rendered previously disparate pieces of information comprehensible at an overview level. Still, having an estimate of the average amount of change one could expect from a given treatment has both positive and negative consequences. On one hand, it allows researchers and consumers to directly compare certain kinds of treatments. On the other hand, a number of excellent qualitative studies and/or N of 1 studies are generally left out of this database. In addition, as scientific journals generally only publish statistically significant results, even studies that included the traditional methods of statistical analysis but confirmed the null hypothesis are generally excluded from research journals. Thus, it has been argued by some that meta-analyses represent only a certain type of investigation. A harsh evaluation of meta-analysis as "junk science" has even been leveled at researchers by some authors (Mullen, Driskell, & Salas, 1998).

Nevertheless, it is important to review what significant empirical studies are actually in the literature. By reviewing the studies in Table 1.2, one can see that group-versus-individual as well as active group-versus-inactive group treatments have been included. Careful examination of each individual study yields rich intricacies that are sometimes lost at the "bottom-line" level afforded by the effect size communicated in the final result of a meta-analysis (Dush, Hirt, & Schroeder, 1983; Miller & Berman, 1983; Nietzel, Russel, Hemmings, & Gretter, 1987; Robinson, Berman, & Neimeyer, 1990; Shapiro & Shapiro, 1982; Smith, Glass, & Miller, 1980; Tillitski, 1990). In addition, many of these meta-analyses contradict each other. Horne and Rosenthal (1997) have attempted to help understand this apparent conundrum of ostensibly contradictory findings. They state,

Although there have been exceptions associated with these findings, Fuhriman and Burlingame (1994) suggested that individual treatment had been shown to be more effective only in studies in which the group format was simply a convenient and economic way to present material. The specific strengths of group were not measured. The basic efficacy of groups has been established across an array of disorders and treatment models. (p. 235)

Table 1.2 Group vs. Individual Meta-Analyses

Author	Treatment Orientation	Group Characteristics	Sample	Conclusions
Smith, Glass, & Miller (1980)	Heterogeneous	Variable	Heterogeneous	The mode in which therapy was delivered made no difference in its effectiveness. Indeed, the average effects for group and individual therapy are remarkably similar. The average effect size was 0.87 for individual therapy and 0.83 for group therapy. Of the studies reviewed, 43% were individual, and 49% were group.
Shapiro & Shapiro (1982)	Heterogeneous	Average time spent in therapy was 7 hours	Heterogeneous	This refined meta-analysis of the one conducted by Smith and Glass (1977) reported that although individual therapy appeared the most effective mode ($M = 1.12$), it was closely followed by the predominant group mode ($M = 0.89$), and the only striking treatment mode finding was for couple/family therapy ($M = 0.21$).
Miller & Berman (1983)	Cognitive-behavioral	Duration of treatment relatively short	Adolescents and adults, student/community volunteers & outpatients, anxious and/or depressed	This meta-analysis of 48 studies reported that cognitive behavior treatment was equally effective in group and individual formats when compared with a nontreatment group (individual = 0.93/group = 0.79) and when compared with other treatment controls (individual = 0.31/group = 0.18); it should be noted that none of the studies in the review directly compared individual with group treatment within a single study.
Dush, Hirt, & Schroeder (1983)	Cognitive-behavioral self-statement modification	Mean weeks of treatment were 5.9 with a range of 1-26	Approximately ¼ of studies used outpatients, ¼ used community volunteers, & ½ used undergraduate depressed and anxious volunteers	Treatment modality was highly influential, with the mean effect for individual therapy nearly double that of group therapy across all comparisons. When compared with no-treatment controls, the effect size was 0.93 for individual and 0.58 for group, and when compared with placebo controls was 0.71 for individual and 0.36 for group.
Nietzel, Russel, Hemmings, & Gretter (1987)	Cognitive, behavioral, & other	Mean number of hours in treatment was 16.3, with a range of 3-69	Individuals with unipolar depression, adults	Reports a reliable difference between individual and group treatment, with group treatment being less effective. Clients treated with group ($M = 12.47$) reported more

(Continued)

11

Table 1.2 (Continued)

Author	Treatment Orientation	Group Characteristics	Sample	Conclusions
		(distribution between group and individual hours not made)		depressive symptoms than clients receiving individual treatment (M = 0.06).
Robinson, Berman, & Neimeyer (1990)	Included treatments with a prominent verbal component (i.e., cognitive, cognitive-behavioral, behavioral, & general verbal therapy)	Number of clients per group ranged from 3 to 12 (M = 7)	Depressed individuals	Analysis indicated that both group and individual therapy produced more improvement than no treatment and that the effects of the two approaches were comparable. The 16 studies that compared individual/group therapy with a wait-list control and the 15 studies that compared group with a wait-list control produced nearly equal effect sizes (0.83 and 0.84, respectively).
Tillitski (1990)	Therapy, counseling, psychoeducational	Heterogeneous	Adults, adolescents, children diagnostically heterogeneous	In this reexamination of a subset of the studies looked at by Toseland and Siporin (1986), Tillitski reports finding the same average effect size for both group and individual treatment (1.35), and states that this effect was consistently greater than that of controls (0.18). Also, group counseling was found to be almost twice as effective as either therapy or psychoeducation, recent studies produced larger effect sizes, group tended to be better for adolescent and individual tended to be better for children.
Hoag & Burlingame (1997)	60% behavioral or cognitive-behavioral	79% took place in school groups (focused primarily on disruptive behavior, social skills, self-esteem). Average group size was 5-9. Average treatment length: 14 sessions.	Male and female children and adolescents (4-18)	56 outcome studies from 1974-1997 of group interventions (including preventative, psychotherapy, guidance) revealed effect size of 0.61 for group treatment over wait-list and placebo controls.
McRoberts, Burlingame, & Hoag (1998)	Cognitive, behavioral, dynamic, supportive, eclectic	Average groups of 16 sessions, lasting 90 minutes each,	Adult outpatients with heterogeneous diagnoses	In this meta-analysis of group vs. individual, the general finding was overall equivalence (0.01), though under certain circumstances individual therapy fared better (depression with

(Continued)

Table 1.2 (Continued)

Author	Treatment Orientation	Group Characteristics	Sample	Conclusions
		44% had cotherapists		cognitive-behavioral approach 0.16); and in other circumstances group fared better (with circumscribed problems, researcher's allegiance to format, attendance of member.)
McDermut, Miller, & Brown (2001)	95% behavioral or cognitive-behavioral; 5% interpersonal, psychodynamic, or nondirective	Highly diverse clinical settings, typical group 12 sessions, once a week, variety of therapists	Male (30%) and female (70%) outpatient adults with diagnosis of depression (mean age 44)	48 studies from 1970 to 1998 examined group therapy for depression. Patients showed clinically meaningful improvement compared with untreated controls, although their BDI scores were still higher than normal. Of studies that compared group to individual, slightly more reported individual to be superior.
Burlingame, Fuhriman, & Mosier (2003)	Cognitive, behavioral, dynamic, supportive, eclectic	University, correctional and outpatient mental health settings	Adult outpatients with heterogeneous diagnoses	20 years of studies examined. Patient diagnosis resulted in differential effects, homogeneous groups outperformed those in groups with mixed symptoms, and behavioral faired better than eclectic orientation.

This is especially helpful guidance when one considers that this method of meta-analysis has expanded beyond adults to children and adolescents (Hoag & Burlingame, 1997; McRoberts, Burlingame, & Hoag, 1998), who are potentially more vulnerable, and that the ramifications of effect sizes may mean governmental funding for treatments that reach the level of empirically validated or supported therapies. Some recent meta-analyses, which have compared long- and short-term treatment as well as specific formats, highlight another kind of potential confusion (de Jong & Gorey, 1996; Reeker, Ensing, & Elliott, 1997). When researchers are scrambling for limited grant money, the ideal study would favor a specified (e.g., manualized) treatment for a shorter amount of time (encouraging reimbursement strategies of many HMOs.) But these meta-analyses found no difference for specific formats or treatment lengths.

Another confusing issue is that many studies combine group therapy with other treatments. This complicates the issue of efficacy. Which active treatment is helping, pharmacotherapy, individual therapy, group therapy, or the combination? A number of reviews in Table 1.1 examine individual and group treatment. One of the reliable findings of 40 years of research is that the combination of individual and group therapy results in superior outcomes (Bostwick, 1987; Freeman & Munro, 1988; Pattison, Brissenden, & Wohl, 1967), though, as always, there are those who weigh in with a different perspective (cf. Anderson, 1968; Stotsky & Zolik, 1965). The field has received some help from Ormont and Strean (1978) and others (e.g., Porter, 1980) who suggested an innovative combination of treatments in their books, thus clarifying the difference between conjoint and combined treatment. This has led to interesting iterations of group treatment in the overall scheme of mental health strategies. Perhaps two of the most exciting iterations have to do with group therapy as the treatment strategy (Burlingame et al., 2002; Piper et al., 1996). The long-term effect of such broadly applied programs remains to be seen, although initial findings have been positive.

GROUP THEMES: CONTENT AND METHODOLOGY, INCREASING COMPLEXITY

It makes sense that the initial themes of group research in the early years reflected clinicians' burgeoning awareness of the power of group. Also, two important though sometimes differentiating areas, group psychology and group psychotherapy, emerged as contributors. If one follows the themes of their respective endeavors, overlap can be seen (see Tables 1.3 and 1.4). The themes that were addressed in group psychology included interpersonal influence and problem solving and expanded later into group climate, group structure, models or approaches, and leadership. Group psychotherapy researchers examined these as well but also included client populations, therapeutic factors, therapeutic relationships, client outcomes, ecosystems, and interaction analysis. Perhaps because of the related as well as different foci, a kind of synergistic theory building occurred, particularly in the area of leadership and interaction models. This combined data (based on analogue as well as therapy groups) created a certain kind of "essential tension" (Kuhn, 1977) that actually drove the research ahead. Increasing methodological sophistication also moved the research forward. Researchers moved from simple tallies to advanced statistical models and from single case studies to carefully controlled methods of investigation. In fact, an entire issue of the American Psychological Association's (APA) Division 49 journal (*Group Dynamics: Theory, Research, and Practice*) was dedicated to these new methodologies (Forsyth, 1998).

The difference between the number of journal articles on group counseling in the early decades of the 20th century compared with the later decades is enormous. In the main, the areas or themes these articles address include depression, children and adolescents, criminal populations, clients with physical and/or medical disorders, eating disorders, and an array of inpatient problems (see Table 1.5). An array of models or approaches was used with these populations, although the majority of studies were

Table 1.3   Small-Group Psychology: Thematic Evolution

	1900-1910	1911-1920	1921-1930	1931-1940	1941-1950	1951-1960	1961-1970	1971-1980	1981-1990	1991-2002
Models/approaches						X	X	X		X
Interpersonal influence	X				X	X	X	X	X	X
Problem solving/ Decision making	X		X	X	X			X	X	X
Group structure				X	X		X	X	X	X
Group climate				X	X	X	X	X	X	X
Leadership						X	X	X	X	X

SOURCE: From *Handbook of Group Psychotherapy: An Empirical and Clinical Synthesis*, by A. Fuhriman and G. Burlingame (Eds.), 1994, New York: John Wiley. Adapted with permission.

Table 1.4   Group Psychology: Thematic Evolution

	1900–1910	1911–1920	1921–1930	1931–1940	1941–1950	1951–1960	1961–1970	1971–1980	1981–1990	1991–2002
Formats/theories/models	X	X	X	X	X	X	X	X	X	X
Patient/client populations	X	X	X	X	X	X	X	X	X	X
Therapeutic relationship			X	X	X	X	X	X	X	X
Therapist variables							X	X	X	X
Therapeutic factors	X	X	X	X	X	X	X	X	X	X
Structure							X	X	X	X
Interaction analysis							X	X	X	X
Client outcomes						X	X	X	X	X
Ecosystem	X	X	X		X		X	X	X	X

SOURCE: From *Handbook of Group Psychotherapy: An Empirical and Clinical Synthesis*, by A. Fuhriman and G. Burlingame (Eds.), 1994, New York: John Wiley. Adapted with permission.

Table 1.5 Substantive Themes by Clinical Population

Models/Approaches	Child/Adolescent	Medical	Depressed	Eating Disorder	Substance Abuse	Criminal	Inpatient	Family/Marital	Elderly	Out patient	Schizo-phrenic	Sexual Abuse	Personality Disorder	Not Specified	Other[a]
Cognitive-behavioral	X	X	X	X	X	X	X	X	X	X		X	X	X	X
Short-term	X	X	X				X	X	X	X		X	X	X	
Rogerian										X					X
Gestalt											X			X	
Personal growth						X								X	
Psychodrama	X					X	X								
Therapist variables	X	X	X	X	X	X	X	X	X	X	X		X	X	X
Directiveness			X									X		X	
Interpretation												X		X	
Therapeutic factors	X	X	X	X	X	X	X	X	X	X	X	X	X	X	X
Structure	X	X	X	X	X	X			X	X		X		X	
Development						X				X				X	
Pregroup training								X		X				X	
Interaction	X	X	X	X	X	X	X	X	X	X	X	X		X	X

SOURCE: From *Handbook of Group Psychotherapy: An Empirical and Clinical Synthesis*, by A. Fuhriman and G. Burlingame (Eds.), 1994, New York: John Wiley. Adapted with permission.

NOTE: The topical and methodological themes of the 1980s and 1990s were derived from the approximately 500 articles about group psychotherapy. A bibliographic listing of the selected literature may be obtained from the authors.

a. Various nontherapeutic designations.

generally some form of cognitive-behavioral, short-term therapies. Therapist variables (studies that deliberately measured a therapist or leader attitude or behavior) were based almost entirely on secondary or post hoc results. The exceptions examined therapist effects explicitly (Barlow, Burlingame, Hardman, & Behman, 1997; Burlingame & Barlow, 1996; Kivlighan & Jauquet, 1990; Piper et al., 1996) and generally involved complicated statistical analyses that bear repeating if we are to truly understand therapist effects on client process and outcome.

Therapeutic (neé curative) factors also have been assiduously studied, although the majority of studies used only one source for measuring (client self-report). This potentially potent area for connecting process variables to outcome variables is still understudied, and when it is included in the research, few authors use the multiple-measure strategy first recommended by Cook and Campbell (1979) and echoed by others (Burlingame et al., in press). The matter of structured versus nonstructured treatment was studied far more than pregroup training or group development. This is unfortunate, because the effects of developmental stage, the impact of pregroup training on member role functioning, and later positive client outcome are important areas to study. Finally, the interaction category in Table 1.5 represents studies that used a process analysis system to tap interaction between members and between members and leaders. Because this interactional category is so critical to understanding group counseling efficacy, it bodes well that these studies appear to be on the rise.

CONCLUSIONS

Humans gather together to give and receive help, both formally and informally. If we had access to other sources in addition to the empirical articles reviewed here (journals, nonempirical studies, or qualitative group studies, etc.), we would have an even richer picture of the power of those gatherings. For our purposes, however, the empirical research on formal groups is clear: The human group phenomena titled "group counseling" or "psychotherapy" clearly has a set of recognizable factors (skilled leaders or therapists, appropriately referred clients or group members, defined goals, etc.) that create positive outcomes.

How have we come to know this? Initially, studies examined disparate variables in somewhat nonsystematic ways (approximately 1900-1950). With increasing methodological and statistical techniques used to track the huge complexities in group phenomenon, we began to understand group variables in much more controlled ways (1950-1970). Accounting for variance within a number of important domains allowed us to examine main effects and interaction effects of such important variables as leader/member contribution to positive results and to make definitive statements about efficacy compared with other treatment modalities as meta-analyses yielded reliable effect sizes (1970-1990). We were more able to predict who would do well in which kind of group led by which kind of leader (1990-2000). These are important steps. Little by little, we can make more sense out of myriad models and approaches, the innumerable theories of interpersonal influence and communication, and the elusive epiphenomenon of group "climate" as we move into the next chapter of group psychotherapy research.

Who knows what the history of group counseling will be at the end of the next century? No doubt, it will be even richer and better. This will be especially true if we are able to account for variance (the static "measures" of analysis of variance, etc.) as well as track the sequence of variables (the dynamic "measures" of structural equation modeling) as they modify each other and at what level of impact (individual, dyad, group-as-a-whole). For instance, what a triumph it would be if we could understand the exact influence of levels of cohesion in different stages of a therapy group on certain kinds of personality styles in interaction with differing coleader styles over the life of the group, as well as at 6-month follow up. Given the direction in which we are headed, this just may be possible. And why does this matter? Because the human condition will always include, at any given time, experiences of suffering, mental disorder, lack of adequate education, and the like. Group counseling is an intervention that can ameliorate many of these ills.

REFERENCES

Adler, A. (1955). *The practice and theory of individual psychology* (2nd ed.). (P. Radin, Trans.). London: Routledge & Paul.

Anderson, A. (1968). Group counseling. *Review of Educational Research, 33,* 209-226.

Anthony, E. J. (1971). The history of group psychotherapy. In H. Kaplan and B. Sadock (Eds.), *Comprehensive group psychotherapy* (1st ed., pp. 4-31). Baltimore, MD: Williams & Wilkins.

Barlow, S., Burlingame, G., Hardman, J., & Behrman, J. (1997). Therapeutic focusing in time-limited group psychotherapy. *Group Dynamics: Theory, Research, and Practice, 1,* 254-266.

Barlow, S., Burlingame, G., Nebeker, R., & Anderson, E. (2000). Meta-analysis of medical self-help groups. *International Journal of Group Psychotherapy, 50*(1), 53-70.

Barlow, S., Fuhriman, A., & Burlingame, G. (2000). The Therapeutic application of groups: From Pratt's "thought control classes" to modern group psychotherapy. *Group Dynamic: Theory, Research, and Practice, 4,* 115-134.

Bednar, R., & Kaul, T. (1978). Experiential group research: Current perspectives. In A. Bergin & S. Garfield (Eds.), *Handbook of psychotherapy and behavior change* (2nd ed.). New York: John Wiley.

Bednar, R., & Lawlis, G. (1971). Empirical research in group psychotherapy. In A. Bergin & S. Garfield (Eds.), *Handbook of psychotherapy and behavior change.* New York: Wiley.

Bostwick, G. (1987). Where's Mary? A review of the group treatment dropout literature. *Social Work with Groups, 10*(3), 117-132.

Burchard, E., Michaels, J., & Kotkov, B. (1948). Criteria for the evaluation of group therapy. *Psychosomatic Medicine, 10*(3), 257-274.

Burlingame, G., & Barlow, S. (1996). Outcome and process differences between professional and nonprofessional therapists in time-limited group psychotherapy. *International Journal of Group Psychotherapy, 46*(4), 455-478.

Burlingame, G. M., Earnshaw, D., Hoag, M., Barlow, S. H., Richardson, E. J., Donnell, A. J., Villani, J. (2002, October). A systematic program to enhance clinician group skills in an inpatient psychiatric hospital. *International Journal of Group Psychology 52*(4), 555-587.

Burlingame, G., Fuhriman, A., & Mosier, J. (2003). Differential effectiveness of group psychotherapy: A meta-analytical perspective. *Group Dynamics: Theory, Research, and Practice, 7*(1), 3-12.

Burlingame, G., MacKenzie, K. R., & Strauss, B. (in press). Small group treatment: Evidence for effectiveness and mechanisms of change. In M. Lambert (Ed.), *Handbook of psychotherapy and behavior change.*

Burrows, T. (1927). The group method of analysis. *Psychoanalytical Review, 10,* 268-80.

Burrows, T. (1928). The basis of group analysis or the analysis of the reactions of normal and neurotic individuals. *British Journal of Medical Psychology, 8,* 198-206.

Cook, T., & Campbell, D. (1979). *Quasi-experimentation: Design and analysis issues for field settings.* Boston, MA: Houghton Mifflin.

Cox, G., & Merkel, W. (1989). A qualitative review of psychosocial treatments for bulimia. *The Journal of Nervous and Mental Disease, 177*(2), 77-84.

Dagley, J., Gazda, G., Eppinger, S., & Stewart, E. (1994). Group psychotherapy research with children, preadolescents, and adolescents. In A. Fuhriman & G. Burlingame (Eds.), *Handbook of group psychotherapy* (pp. 340-369). New York: John Wiley.

de Jong, T. L., & Gorey, K. (1996). Short-term versus long-term group work with female survivors of childhood sexual abuse: A brief meta-analytic review. *Social Work With Groups, 19*(1), 19-27.

Dies, R. (1993). Research on group psychotherapy: Overview and clinical applications. In A. Alonso & H. Swiller (Eds.), *Group therapy in clinical practice.* Washington, DC: American Psychiatric Press.

Dreikurs, R. (1932). Early experiments with group psychotherapy. *American Journal of Psychotherapy, 13,* 882-891.

Dreikurs, R. (1956). The contribution of group psychotherapy to psychiatry. *Group Psychotherapy, 9*(2), 115-125.

Dreikurs, R. (1969a). Early experiments with group psychotherapy: A historical review. In H. Ruitenbeek (Ed.), *Group therapy today.* New York: Atherton.

Dreikurs, R. (1969b). Group psychotherapy from the point of view of Adlerian psychology. In H. Ruitenbeek (Ed.), *Group therapy today.* New York: Atherton.

Dush, D., Hirt, M., & Schroeder, H. (1983). Self-statement modification with adults: A meta-analysis. *Journal of Consulting and Clinical Psychology, 94,* 408-422.

Emrick, C. (1975). A review of psychologically oriented treatment of alcoholism. *Journal for the Study of Alcoholism, 36*(1), 88-108.

Forsyth, D. (Ed.) (1998). Special issue: Research methods. *Group Dynamics: Theory, Research, and Practice, 4*(2).

Forsyth, D. (Ed.). (2000). Special issue: 100 years of research. *Group Dynamics: Theory, Research, and Practice, 4*(1).

Freeman, C., & Munro, J. (1988). Drug and group treatments for bulimia/bulimia nervosa. *Journal of Psychosomatic Research, 32*(6), 647-660.

Freud, S. (1922). *Group psychology and the analysis of the ego.* New York: Boni.

Fuhriman, A., & Burlingame, G. (Eds.). (1994). *Handbook of group psychotherapy: An empirical and clinical synthesis.* New York: John Wiley.

Goodman, G., & Jacobs, M. (1994). The self-help, mutual support group. In A. Fuhriman & G. Burlingame (Eds.), *Handbook of psychotherapy: An empirical and clinical synthesis* (pp. 489-526). New York: John Wiley.

Grunebaum, H. (1975). A soft-hearted review of hard-nosed research on groups. *International Journal of Group Psychotherapy, 25*(2), 185-197.

Hoag, M., & Burlingame G. M. (1997). Evaluating the effectiveness of child and adolescent group treatment: A meta-analytic review. *Journal of Clinical Child Psychology, 26,* 234-246.

Horne, A. M., & Rosenthal, R. (1997). Research in group work: How did we get where we are? *The Journal for Specialists in Group Work, 22,* 228-240.

Kanas, N. (1986). Group psychotherapy with schizophrenics: A review of controlled studies. *International Journal of Group Psychotherapy, 36,* 339-351.

Kanzer, M. (1983). Freud: The first psychoanalytic group leader. In H. Kaplan & B. Sadock (Eds.), *Comprehensive group psychotherapy* (2nd ed.). Baltimore, MD: Williams & Wilkins.

Kaul, T., & Bednar, R. (1986). Experimental group research: Results, questions & suggestions. In S. Garfield & A. Bergin (Eds.), *Handbook of psychotherapy and behavior change.* New York: John Wiley.

Kierkegaard, S. (1944). *Attack upon Christendom* (W. Lowrie, Trans.). Princeton, NJ: Princeton University Press.

Kivlighan, D., & Jauquet, C. (1990). Quality of group member agendas and group session climate. *Small Group Research, 21,* 205-219.

Kreiger, M., & Kogan, W. (1964). A study of group processes in the small therapeutic group. *International Journal of Group Psychotherapy, 14,* 178-188.

Kuhn, T. (1977). *The essential tension.* Chicago: University of Chicago Press.

Lazell, E. W. (1921). The group treatment of dementia praecox. *Psychoanalytical Review, 8,* 168-179.

Lewin, K. (1936). *Principles of topological psychology.* New York: McGraw-Hill.

Lieberman, M. (1976). Change induction in small groups. *Annual Review of Psychology, 27,* 217-250.

Luborsky, L., Singer, B., & Luborsky, L. (1975). Comparative studies of psychotherapy. *Archives of General Psychiatry, 32,* 995-1008.

MacKenzie, K. R. (1992). *Classics in group psychotherapy.* New York: Guilford.

Mann, J. (1966). Evaluation of group psychotherapy. In J. Moreno (Ed.), *International handbook of group psychotherapy.* New York: Philosophical Library.

Marsh, L. C. (1931). Group treatment for the psychoses by the psychological equivalent of the revival. *Mental Hygiene, 15,* 328-349.

Marsh, L. C. (1933). An experiment in group treatment of patients at Worchester State Hospital. *Mental Hygiene, 17,* 396-416.

Marsh, L. C. (1935). Group therapy and the psychiatric clinic. *Journal of Nervous & Mental Disorders, 82,* 381-393.

Marx, K., & Engels, F. (1948). (Centenary ed.). *The communist manifesto.* London: The Communist Party.

McDermut, W., Miller, I, & Brown, R. (2001). The efficacy of group psychotherapy for depression: A meta-analysis and review of empirical research. *Clinical Psychology: Science and Practice, 8*(1), 98-116.

McGrath, P. (1993). Historical development of group psychotherapy. In K. Dwivedi (Ed.), *Groupwork with children and adolescents: A handbook.* London: Jessica Kingsley.

McRoberts, C., Burlingame, G., & Hoag, M. (1998). Comparative efficacy of individual and group psychotherapy: A meta-analytic perspective. *Group Dynamics: Theory, Research, and Practice, 2,* 101-117.

Meltzoff, J., & Kornreich, M. (1970). *Research in psychotherapy.* New York: Atherton.

Miller, R., & Berman, J. (1983). The efficacy of cognitive behavior therapies: A quantitative review of research evidence. *Psychological Bulletin, 94,* 39-53.

Moreno, J., & Whitin, E. (1932). *Application of the group method to classification.* New York: National Commission on Prison and Prison Labor.

Mullen, B., & Driskell, J., & Salas, E. (1998). Meta-analysis and the study of group dynamics. *Group Dynamics: Theory, Research, and Practice, 2,* 213-229.

Nietzel, M., Russel, R., Hemmings, K., & Gretter, M. (1987). Clinical significance of psychotherapy for unipolar depression: A meta-analytic approach to social comparison. *Journal of Consulting and Clinical Psychology, 55*(2), 156-161.

Oesterheld, A., McKenna M., & Gould, N. (1987). Group psychotherapy of bulimia: A critical review. *International Journal of Group Psychotherapy, 37*(2), 163-187.

Ormont, L., & Strean, H. (1978). *The practice of conjoint therapy: Combining individual and group treatment.* New York: Human Science Press.

Parloff, M., & Dies R. (1977). Group psychotherapy outcome research. *International Journal of Group Psychotherapy, 27,* 281-319.

Pattison, E. (1965). Evaluation studies of group psychotherapy. *International Journal of Group Psychotherapy, 15*(3), 382-397.

Pattison, E., Brissenden, A., & Wohl, T. (1967). Assessing specific effects of inpatient group psychotherapy. *International Journal of Group Psychotherapy, 17,* 283-297.

Piper, W., & Joyce, A. (1996). A consideration of factors influencing the utilization of time-limited, short-term group therapy. *International Journal of Group Psychotherapy, 46*(3), 311-328.

Piper, W., & McCallum, M. (1991). Group interventions for persons who have experienced loss: Description and evaluative research. *Group Analysis, 24,* 363-373.

Piper, W., Rosie, J., Joyce, A., & Azim, H. (1996). *Time-limited day treatment for personality disorders: Integration of research and practice in a group program.* Washington, DC: American Psychological Association.

Porter, K. (1980). Combined individual and group psychotherapy: A review of the literature.

International Journal of Group Psychotherapy, 30(1), 107-114.

Reeker, J., Ensing, D., & Elliott, R. (1997). A meta-analytic investigation of group treatment outcomes for sexually abused children. *Child Abuse and Neglect, 21,* 669-680.

Rickard, H. (1962). Selected group psychotherapy evaluation studies. *Journal of General Psychology, 67,* 35-50.

Robinson, L., Berman, J., & Neimeyer, R. (1990). Psychotherapy for the treatment of depression: A comprehensive review of controlled outcome research. *Psychological Bulletin, 108*(1), 30-49.

Ruitenbeek, H. (1969). *Group therapy today.* New York: Atherton.

Sadock, B., & Kaplan H. (1983). History of group psychotherapy. In H. Kaplan & B. Sadock (Eds.), *Comprehensive group psychotherapy* (2nd ed.). Baltimore, MD: Williams & Wilkins.

Schilder, P. (1939). Results and problems of group psychotherapy in severe neuroses. *Mental Hygiene, 23,* 87-98.

Shapiro, D., & Shapiro, D. (1982). Meta-analysis of comparative therapy outcome studies: A replication and refinement. *Psychological Bulletin, 92,* 581-604.

Slavson, S. R. (1943). *An introduction to group therapy.* New York: Commonwealth Fund.

Smith, M., & Glass, G. (1977). Meta-analysis of psychotherapy outcome studies. *American Psychologist, 32,* 752-760.

Smith, M., Glass, G., & Miller, T. (1980). *The benefits of psychotherapy.* Baltimore, MD: John Hopkins University Press.

Solomon, S. (1983). Individual versus group therapy: Current status in the treatment of alcoholism. *Advances in Alcohol and Substance Abuse, 2*(1), 69-86.

Stotsky, B., & Zolik, E. (1965). Group psychotherapy with psychotics. *International Journal of Group Psychotherapy, 15*(3), 321-344.

Syz, H. C. (1928). Remarks on group analysis. *American Journal of Psychiatry, 85,* 141-148.

Thomas, G. (1943). Group psychotherapy: A review of recent literature. *Psychosomatic Medicine, 5,* 166-180.

Tillitski, L. (1990). A meta-analysis of estimated effect sizes for group versus individual versus control treatments. *International Journal of Group Psychotherapy, 40*(2), 215-224.

Toseland, R., & Siporin, M. (1986). When to recommend group treatment. *International Journal of Group Psychotherapy, 36,* 172-201.

Vandervoort, D., & Furhiman A. (1991). The efficacy of group therapy for depression. *Small Group Research, 22*(3), 320-338.

Wender, L. (1936). The dynamics of group psychotherapy and its application. *Journal of Nervous and Mental Disorders, 84,* 54-60.

Wolf, A. (1949) The psychoanalysis of groups. *American Journal of Psychotherapy, 3,* 525-558.

Yalom, I. D. (1975). *The theory and practice of group psychotherapy* (2nd ed.). New York: Basic Books.

Yalom, I. D. (1985). *The theory and practice of group psychotherapy* (3rd ed.). New York: Basic Books.

Zimpfer, D. (1987). Groups for the aging: Do they work? *Journal for Specialists in Group Work, 12,* 85-92.

Zimpfer, D. (1990). Group work for bulimia: A review of outcomes. *Journal for Specialists in Group Work, 15,* 239-251.

2

THE IMPORTANCE OF THERAPEUTIC FACTORS

A Typology of Therapeutic Factors Studies

DENNIS M. KIVLIGHAN JR.

University of Maryland at College Park

STACEY E. HOLMES

University of Maryland at College Park

How does group therapy help patients? If we can answer this seemingly naive question with some measure of precision and certainty, we shall have at our disposal a central organizing principle by which to approach the most vexing and controversial problems of psychotherapy.

—Yalom (1995)

YALOM'S THERAPEUTIC FACTORS

Yalom (1995) succinctly identified the most pressing problem facing group therapists and group therapy researchers. Over the years, Yalom has attempted to answer this question and explain the process of group therapy by describing therapeutic factors that operate in groups. While Yalom was not the first researcher or theorist to use the concept of therapeutic factors, his seminal work has had an enormous influence on group therapy theory and research. An excellent history of the development of conceptions of therapeutic factors can be found in Crouch, Bloch, and Wanlass's (1994) chapter, "Therapeutic Factors: Interpersonal and Intrapersonal Mechanisms." Of Yalom's many contributions to group therapy theory, research, and practice, his delineation and description of 11 therapeutic factors as the essential elements of group-promoted change is arguably the single most influential aspect of

Table 2.1   Description of Therapeutic Factors

Therapeutic Factors (Yalom, 1995)	Definition
Instillation of hope	Member recognizes other members' improvement and that group can be helpful; member develops optimism for his or her own improvement.
Universality	Member perceives that other members share similar feelings or problems.
Imparting information	Advice giving by therapist or fellow members.
Altruism	Member gains a positive view of himself or herself through extending help to others in group.
Corrective recapitulation of primary family group	Member experiences the opportunity to reenact some critical familial incident with members of the group in a corrective manner.
Development of socializing techniques	Group provides members with an environment that allows the member to interact in a more adaptive manner.
Interpersonal learning-input	Member gains personal insight through other members' sharing his or her perception of the member.
Interpersonal learning-output	Group provides members with an environment that allows the member to interact in a more adaptive manner.
Cohesiveness	Feeling of togetherness provided and experienced by the group.
Catharsis	Member releases feelings about past or here-and-now experiences; this release leads to member feeling better.
Existential factors	Member ultimately accepts that he or she has to take responsibility for his or her own life.
Imitative behavior	Member learns through the observation of others' learning experiences.

his theoretical and research endeavors. Yalom's (1995) compendium of therapeutic factors is built on earlier writings of group theorists and practitioners and on his research into important change mechanisms in group therapy. Although Yalom (1995) provided descriptions of the 11 therapeutic factors or processes that constitute the framework of his group therapy approach, he has not provided a comprehensive conceptual definition of the therapeutic factors construct. Bloch and Crouch (1985), however, defined a therapeutic factor as "an element of group therapy that contributes to improvement in a patient's condition and is a function of the actions of the group therapist, the other group members, and the patient himself" (p. 4).

Yalom's approach to group counseling is organized around these 11 therapeutic factors or processes defined in Table 2.1. Yalom believes that these elements provide a comprehensive list of the operations and mechanisms that lead to

therapeutic change in groups. Although Yalom's compendium of therapeutic factors is widely accepted and used, several authors have criticized Yalom's therapeutic factors structure. For example, Crouch et al. (1994) suggest that the factors are (a) unbalanced in their content (self-understanding is a broader construct than self-disclosure) and (b) overlapping in their content. Despite these criticisms, the contribution of Yalom's factor structure has been important for furthering both understanding and research in the area of group psychotherapy.

Not only did Yalom define and describe 11 therapeutic factors, he developed a research paradigm that has had a major influence on how researchers have examined therapeutic factors in group settings. In a now classic study, Yalom and his colleagues (Yalom, Tinklenberg, & Gilula, 1968) developed a 60-item therapeutic factors Q-sort by writing five items that corresponded to each of the 11 factors described by Yalom

(12 factors were used because Interpersonal Learning was split into Interpersonal Learning Input and Interpersonal Learning Output categories). Twenty successfully treated group therapy adult clients ranked the 60 therapeutic factors Q-sort items in categories ranging from *Least helpful to me in group* to *Most helpful to me in group*. From this data, Yalom et al. (1968) derived a ranking of the relative importance of the therapeutic factors as perceived by successfully treated clients. Specifically, the clients in Yalom et al.'s study provided the following ranking, from most to least important, of the therapeutic factors: (1) Interpersonal Learning (Input), (2) Catharsis, (3) Cohesiveness, (4) Self-Understanding, (5) Interpersonal Learning (Output), (6) Existential Factors, (7) Universality, (8) Instillation of Hope, (9) Altruism, (10) Family Reenactment, (11) Guidance, and (12) Identification.

Yalom's paradigm for examining the importance of the therapeutic factors has spawned a large number of studies of therapeutic factors in group therapy. It is interesting to note that Yalom's therapeutic factors Q-sort has been used infrequently in these studies, probably because Q-sort methodology can be time-consuming to administer and because Q-sort data are ipsative rather than normative, limiting researchers' statistical options. Recent studies of therapeutic factors in group therapy have used Likert-type scales developed from Yalom's Q-sort items or have employed Critical Incidents Questionnaires and Bloch, Reibstein, Crouch, Holroyd, and Themen's (1979) Therapeutic Factors classification scheme for assessing therapeutic factors in group therapy. Regardless of methodology, group researchers have now amassed a number of studies that identify clients' ranking of the therapeutic factors across a number of different settings and patient populations. The implicit goal of these studies is to identify the most and least important therapeutic factors in various forms of group treatment.

Reviewers of studies that rank therapeutic factors have used various heuristics to try to make sense of the diverse, and at times contradictory, findings reported in this literature. For example, Crouch et al. (1994) used a less disturbed (outpatient) versus more disturbed (inpatient) distinction to provide a framework for organizing the results across the studies that rank order the importance of therapeutic factors. They concluded that self-understanding, learning through interpersonal interaction, and self-disclosure/catharsis were relatively more important for less disturbed group clients and cohesiveness, altruism, universality, and instillation of hope were relatively more important for more disturbed group clients. Yalom (1995) also used the outpatient-versus-inpatient heuristic and reached a similar conclusion in reviewing studies examining the relative importance of the therapeutic factors. He suggests that outpatients tend to value catharsis, self-understanding, and interpersonal learning most highly and cohesiveness and universality secondarily. According to Yalom, inpatients tend to value a wider range of therapeutic factors when compared with outpatients. However, inpatients seem to place a greater emphasis on hope and existential factors than do outpatients.

In a recent review of the therapeutic factors literature, Kivlighan, Coleman, and Anderson (2000) noted the broad range of therapeutic factors that were seen as most helpful by members of both inpatient and outpatient groups. They tried using Crouch et al.'s (1994) and Yalom's (1995) outpatient-versus-inpatient distinction to make sense of the therapeutic factors studies but could identify no discernable pattern in the most recent studies ($N = 12$, 1976-1997). In part, many of the groups examined in therapeutic factors studies did not fit neatly into the inpatient and outpatient categorization. This is because increasingly, client issues that used to be treated in inpatient settings are now likely to be treated in day treatment or community settings. Kivlighan et al. contended that the inpatient-versus-outpatient dimension proposed by both Yalom and Crouch et al. is not a useful heuristic for classifying studies examining the relative importance of therapeutic factors.

Kivlighan et al. (2000) found little evidence of consistent differences across various types of settings or types of groups in clients' relative ranking of therapeutic factors. Therefore, examination of the relative importance of group therapeutic factors is hampered by the lack of an articulated organizing theoretical structure to guide analysis of the disparate studies.

Researchers have compared the relative rankings of therapeutic factors across various groups and client populations without specifying a theoretical rationale for why these groups or client populations may differ in the action of the therapeutic mechanisms. This has resulted in a literature composed of contradictory and atheoretical findings that has added little to the practice and theory of group counseling. Reviewers of these studies are in an equally precarious position, applying post hoc, atheoretical classification schemes that have not served to advance our understanding of the therapeutic factors literature. Despite a large body of literature examining the relative importance of therapeutic factors, we are not much closer to answering Yalom's initial question: How does group therapy help patients? This question does not take into account the complexities of client, therapist, and group variables that contribute to group therapy effectiveness.

In this chapter, an alternative approach to understanding the literature examining the relative importance of therapeutic factors is proposed and, by extension, a new answer to Yalom's question. Rather than applying a deductive post hoc schema to explain why the relative importance of therapeutic factors differs across studies, an inductive approach was designed to uncover similarities among different therapeutic factors studies. Specifically, a cluster analysis was used to examine the underlying structure of the studies that have examined the relative importance of therapeutic factors. Cluster analysis uses a mathematical algorithm to search for similarities among group objects, in this case, therapeutic factors studies. Our goal is to use cluster analysis to meta-analytically combine data from studies examining the relative rankings of therapeutic factors to form a *typology* of groups based on their therapeutic mechanisms.

EXAMINING THERAPEUTIC FACTORS STUDIES

Literature Search Procedures

Two methods were used to locate empirical studies of therapeutic factors in group psychotherapy. First, a thorough computer literature search was conducted, surveying the PsychINFO and Medline databases. Search terms such as *therapeutic factors* or *curative factors* combined *with group therapy* were used. There was no time of publication limit placed on the search. Second, the reference sections of articles found through the database search that met criteria for this study were screened to determine other articles that might meet criteria.

Criteria for Including Studies

To be included in the current cluster analysis, studies had to be empirically based research in which the importance of therapeutic factors was examined. Studies had to use all or most (at least 9) of the 11 therapeutic factor categories described by Yalom (1995). The studies selected either had participants rank order the factors that they perceived as most important in their treatment or report the relative importance of therapeutic factors that were most salient in group therapy. Specifically, the authors had to be able to construct a ranking of the importance of the therapeutic factors for the study to be included in the analysis. Studies that used a significantly different taxonomy of therapeutic factors were not included. Patient population and problem type were not limited. Therefore, the studies used in this analysis are representative of a broad scope of group therapy patients.

Search Outcome

Search results initially identified 24 separate empirical articles that met criteria for inclusion. These articles are listed in the reference section and denoted by an asterisk. The dates of the studies ranged from 1975 to 2000. Within the 24 studies, there was often more than one sample that was reported to have provided information regarding salience of therapeutic factors. For example, some articles examined importance of therapeutic factors from the perspective of the therapists and from the perspective of the clients, creating two data sets. For this reason, the authors felt that dividing the articles into the various samples would provide the most comprehensive review and clustering of the therapeutic factors. The result of the divisions was 39 samples of reported data regarding the importance of therapeutic factors. However, some samples were not used in every analysis because of missing data. Therefore, reported N's vary from 37 through 39. Both group members' and group leaders' responses were used.

Coding of Studies

The studies were coded on several characteristics including (a) the rank order of each of the therapeutic factors, (b) type of population (inpatient versus outpatient), (c) treatment length, (d) number of clients, (e) number of therapists, (f) type of measurement method (e.g., Q-sort, ranking), (g) number of men in the sample, (h) number of women in the sample, and (i) average age of the group participants.

Data Analysis

Developing a taxonomy of studies examining the relative ranking of therapeutic factors requires finding the natural subgroupings within the data set. Cluster analysis provides an appropriate data reduction technique that reveals "homogeneous subtypes within a complex data set" (Borgen & Barnett, 1987, p. 460). Hierarchical clustering methods are the most widely used type of cluster analysis (Borgen & Barnett, 1987). These methods use successive steps of analysis that reveal a hierarchical structure of the data with groups linked in a tree or dendogram. Hierarchical clustering begins with each object (a discrete sample within the data set) forming its own cluster and then builds higher-order structures by a process where, step by step, similar objects (discrete samples based on rankings of therapeutic factors) are grouped into progressively larger and larger nested clusters (Borgen & Barnett, 1987). Ward's linkage method (Ward, 1963) was used in this investigation. This method of analysis has been widely used and has been found to adequately minimize the variance within clusters at each stage of grouping. Recent comparative studies indicate that Ward's method is one of the more effective methods for recovering underlying structure of multivariate data (Borgen & Barnett, 1987).

Types of Groups (Based on Therapeutic Factors Rankings)

As noted above, a comprehensive system for categorizing therapeutic factors research does not exist. Developing a taxonomy for describing groups in terms of therapeutic factors is an important first step for the systematic investigation of the role of therapeutic factors in group treatments. A taxonomy is defined as a categorization of a larger construct into smaller homogenous components. Categorization allows for ease of comparison and the ability to distinguish between similar and dissimilar concepts. The taxonomy thus allows the investigator to try to find empirical evidence of the various categories that make up the classification scheme. A taxonomy of groups based on therapeutic factors provides a structured system from which subsequent research and theory can be based.

The Ward (1963) method of cluster analysis was used to categorize the data from the studies examining the comparative ranking of therapeutic factors. Rankings for the 12 therapeutic factors (dividing Interpersonal Learning into Input and Output categories) were used in this clustering process. Each of the 39 sets of ranking data was initially regarded as a cluster. Through an iterative procedure, the number of clusters was systematically reduced. The error term (semipartial R^2 values) was used to decide the optimal number of clusters to retain. An increase in the error term indicated a decrease in the proportion of variance accounted for when two clusters were joined. An abrupt increase in the error term occurred when five clusters were collapsed into four clusters. Because there were no other marked increases in the error term, the four-cluster solution was retained. Ultimately, only 37 sets of therapeutic factors rankings were clustered because of missing data in 2 sets of rankings.

Table 2.2 contains the means and standard deviations for the therapeutic factors for the four clusters. To aid interpretation, Figure 2.1 graphically displays the mean proportions for the 12 therapeutic factors for the four clusters. For example, the affective support groups have peaks at Guidance and Vicarious Learning and valleys at Acceptance and Catharsis. Since smaller numbers reflect greater endorsement, the valleys indicate factors that were most

Table 2.2   Mean Ranking of Therapeutic Factors for the Affective Support Groups, Affective Insight Groups, Cognitive Support Groups, and Cognitive Insight Groups

Therapeutic Factor	Cluster	N	Mean	Std. Deviation
Acceptance	1	8	2.56	0.98
	2	8	2.19	2.14
	3	15	5.19	2.52
	4	6	7.00	3.22
	Total	38	4.29	2.86
Altruism	1	8	7.19	2.42
	2	8	3.94	1.86
	3	15	7.09	1.55
	4	6	7.33	2.16
	Total	38	6.49	2.27
Catharsis	1	8	2.00	1.60
	2	8	5.19	1.96
	3	15	6.19	2.94
	4	6	6.75	2.75
	Total	38	5.18	2.96
Guidance	1	8	10.00	1.51
	2	8	8.63	2.20
	3	15	8.94	1.52
	4	6	2.50	1.22
	Total	38	8.08	2.95
Hope	1	8	7.63	1.41
	2	8	3.69	2.37
	3	15	7.13	2.38
	4	6	3.83	0.75
	Total	38	5.99	2.62
Corrective recapitualization of the primary family group	1	7	9.29	2.81
	2	6	9.33	2.34
	3	3	11.00	0.00
	4	5	5.30	3.35
	Total	21	8.60	3.14
Interpersonal learning	1	8	4.25	2.49
	2	8	7.44	1.68
	3	15	3.09	2.23
	4	6	6.83	1.33
	Total	38	4.84	2.73
Self-disclosure	1	8	5.13	2.23
	2	8	7.88	3.27
	3	13	5.69	1.88
	4	5	4.80	2.28
	Total	34	5.94	2.55
Self-understanding	1	8	3.88	2.01
	2	6	5.33	3.67
	3	13	2.46	1.61
	4	6	9.83	2.93
	Total	33	4.67	3.54

(Continued)

Table 2.2 (Continued)

Therapeutic Factor	Cluster	N	Mean	Std. Deviation
Universality	1	8	7.88	1.46
	2	8	3.94	1.78
	3	15	4.59	2.64
	4	6	8.33	1.21
	Total	38	5.74	2.72
Vicarious learning	1	8	11.13	1.64
	2	8	10.38	2.13
	3	15	3.47	1.26
	4	6	3.33	3.83
	Total	38	6.51	4.18
Existential factors	1	7	5.86	2.34
	2	7	7.14	2.04
	3	3	10.00	0.00
	4	5	11.80	0.45
	Total	22	8.18	2.92

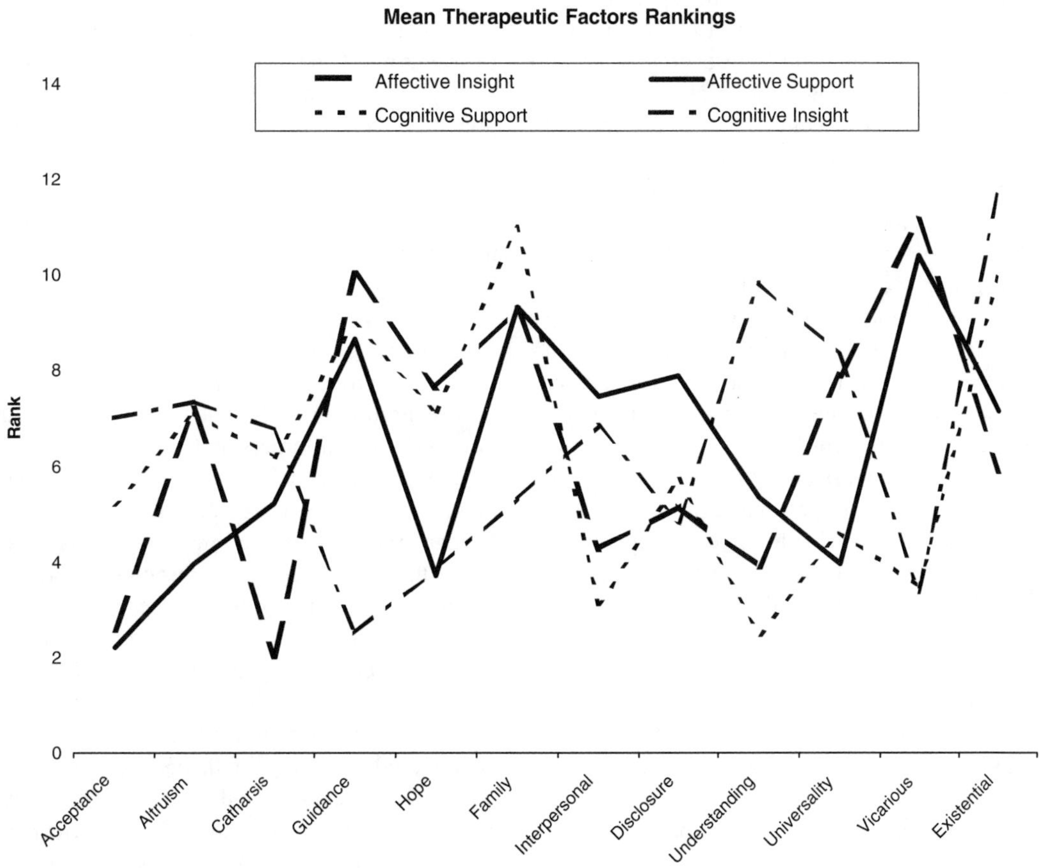

Mean Therapeutic Factors Rankings

Figure 2.1 Mean Therapeutic Factors Rankings

important for a given cluster of groups. Therefore, Acceptance and Catharsis were highly endorsed in the affective support group, and Guidance and Vicarious Learning were not seen as important. The four clusters that emerged from the analysis were named by noting the therapeutic factors that were the highest and lowest in each cluster.

The groups in Cluster 1 ($n = 8$), relative to groups in the other clusters, had the strongest endorsement for four therapeutic factor categories. Acceptance and Catharsis had the highest endorsement within Cluster 1, and Interpersonal Learning and Self-Understanding had the next-highest endorsement, indicating that these factors were most valued by the participants or leaders in these groups. This endorsement pattern of having two to four factors that stand out is consistent with patterns displayed by groups in the other clusters. Acceptance, Catharsis, Interpersonal Learning, and Self-Understanding seem to represent factors that would be valued in a classic growth group. It is possible that these groups would emphasize emotional expression, since both Catharsis, which is emotional expression, and Acceptance, which is a desired result of expression, were the most valued in this cluster. Bloch et al. (1979) regarded Acceptance and Catharsis as emotionally oriented therapeutic factors, which supports the role of affective expression. Also, it is interesting to note that group members in this cluster tended to rank both Guidance and Vicarious Learning as relatively unimportant. This suggests less of a focus on passive learning from others (Guidance and Vicarious Learning) and more of a focus on active learning (Interpersonal Learning) to promote insight in addition to affective expression. Because of the endorsement pattern present in this cluster, we labeled these groups *affective insight groups.*

The groups in Cluster 2 ($n = 8$) ranked Acceptance From Others as the most important therapeutic factor, with Instillation of Hope and Universality as the next most important factors. This combination of factors suggests a pattern of seeking hope and acceptance from others and valuing the feeling that one is not alone in his or her experience or emotion, which also suggests an affective component. These factors grouped together seem to represent a supportive and encouraging affective atmosphere. Group members and leaders from this cluster's groups, as in Cluster 1, ranked Guidance and Vicarious Learning as having the least importance and Interpersonal Learning as being only moderately important. This indicates that the members or leaders of groups in this cluster had little focus on learning either actively or passively, but were more invested in experiencing affective support and encouragement. For this reason, we have named these groups *affective support groups.*

The groups in Cluster 3 ($n = 15$) had relatively high ranks for both Vicarious Learning and Guidance. In addition, the members or leaders from these groups reported a relatively low importance of Self-Understanding. Both Vicarious Learning and Guidance involve a focus on gaining information from outside rather than inside the self, which is further supported by the lack of emphasis on Self-Understanding in these groups. Also, Vicarious Learning and Guidance are primarily cognitive factors, which generally lack an affective component. Therefore, these group members seemed to define their most important experiences in terms of what they could cognitively learn from getting advice from others or observing others, and they seemed to have relatively little interest in gaining insight into themselves. Overall, they valued obtaining cognitive support from others, and for this reason, we labeled this cluster *cognitive support groups.*

The groups in Cluster 4 ($n = 6$) had high rankings for Interpersonal Learning, Self-Understanding, and Vicarious Learning as the most valued therapeutic factors. Interestingly, Guidance was one of the lowest-ranked factors. While the group members in this cluster seemed to appreciate learning from observing others, unlike those in Cluster 3, they were less interested in receiving advice. Rather, they focused on actively learning from interpersonal interactions and using their group experiences to gain a greater understanding of themselves. In addition, both Acceptance and Catharsis were only moderately ranked, indicating that an affective component to the group was not as important as insight and learning. Compared with Cluster 1, this group was more focused on cognitively gaining insight rather than emotionally. This combination of factors suggests an emphasis on active learning, passive learning (through observation), and the acquisition of insight without a strong focus on emotion. Therefore, we have labeled this cluster *cognitive insight groups.*

Cluster Structure

As depicted in the tree diagram, the four clusters that emerged from this analysis fit into a broader pattern of rankings of the therapeutic factors. The affective support groups and the affective insight groups were contained under one major branch of the tree diagram, while the cognitive support groups and the cognitive insight groups formed the other major branch of the tree diagram. This suggests that group members or leaders tend to emphasize either cognitive or affective therapeutic factors. Therefore, groups seem to have two major routes of promoting therapeutic change. It is unclear from this data, however, how this differential valuing of therapeutic factors is brought about. Do the clients or leaders in affectively oriented groups value affective factors because affective factors are the foci of the leaders? Or do clients or leaders in affectively oriented groups see affective factors as most valued even though they are exposed to a wide range of therapeutic factors?

The therapeutic factors literature is almost mute in terms of the group leaders' influence on group members' endorsement of therapeutic factors. An exception to the lack of research on leadership and therapeutic factors is a recent study by Lieberman (2002). He found that group leader behavior was differentially related to therapeutic factor endorsement, with group members of more affectively oriented group leaders endorsing more affectively oriented therapeutic factors (e.g., support) and group members of more cognitively oriented group leaders endorsing more cognitively oriented therapeutic factors (e.g., self-understanding). Lieberman found that the group leaders' major influence was on the type of therapeutic factors that group members endorsed. Member outcome was related to the types of therapeutic factors endorsed. Therefore, it appears that leaders' influence on member outcome operates through the leaders' differentially emphasizing the therapeutic factors. Unfortunately, Lieberman's study is one of the few studies examining the relationship between group leader behavior and the endorsement of therapeutic factors. This is a critical area to address in future research.

The affective and cognitive branches of the cluster tree each split into two branches. There are supportive and insight-oriented clusters under both the affective and the cognitive branches of the cluster diagram. Group members seem to value either the stabilization that they receive through acceptance, hope, guidance, and vicarious learning or the challenge they receive through interpersonal learning and self-understanding. The support-versus-insight distinction in the derived therapeutic factors clusters is reminiscent of the supportive-therapy versus expressive-therapy distinction seen in the psychodynamic literature (see, for example, Gelso & Hayes's, 1998, discussion of levels of treatment). Expressive approaches seek to promote changes in psychic structures through interpretation, confrontation, feedback, and insight. The high levels of Self-Understanding and Interpersonal Learning seen in the affective insight groups and the cognitive insight groups seem to represent the results of an expressive therapeutic approach. Supportive approaches seek to bolster psychic structures through "suggestions, reassurance, advice and reinforcement" (Gelso & Hayes, 1998, p. 166). The high levels of Acceptance and Hope seen in affective support groups and of Guidance and Vicarious Learning seen in cognitive support groups seem to represent the results of two different, but related, supportive therapeutic approaches. Whether the group members experience relatively more support or insight as a result of their group experience is dependant on the leader's approach (Lieberman, 2002).

Types of Cluster Groups and Study Characteristics

We wanted to see whether the four types of groups that emerged from the clustering of therapeutic factors rankings were related to characteristics of the studies used in deriving the clustering results. As described above, studies were coded for type of population (e.g., inpatient, outpatient), treatment length, number of clients, number of therapists, type of measurement method (e.g., Q-sort, ranking), whether the rankings came from clients or therapists, number of men in the sample, number of women in the sample, average age of the group participants, and whether the rankings were obtained from group members or therapists. While it makes sense to see whether the stated goals of the group fit the cluster titles, unfortunately, most of the studies were not explicit enough about the theoretical structure to use it as a classifying variable. A series of ANOVAs (analysis of variance) and chi-square analyses (depending on whether the dependent variable was interval or categorical) were performed with the type of group (affective support groups, affective insight groups, cognitive support groups, and cognitive insight groups) as the independent variable and study characteristic as the dependent variable. In each case, the results of these analyses were not significant at the alpha = .05 level. Therefore, there was no relationship between the type of population studied (inpatients, outpatients, prisoners, students, and incest survivors) and group type. These empirical results support Kivlighan et al.'s (2000) qualitative analysis suggesting that the inpatient-versus-outpatient heuristic was not a useful model for understanding the operation of therapeutic factors in group treatments. In addition, the results of the ANOVA and chi-square analyses suggest that there are no relationships between factors such as treatment length, source of ranking data (client vs. therapist), client gender, or client age and the four group types derived from the cluster analysis of therapeutic factors rankings at the alpha = .05 level.

IMPLICATIONS FOR RESEARCH AND PRACTICE

As summarized above, much of the research on therapeutic factors in group therapy has stayed at a simplistic and atheoretical level. Researchers seem to search for a new client population (e.g., eating-disorder groups, groups for children of alcoholics) and then produce a ranking of therapeutic factors for that particular population. Because these new client populations are not chosen on theoretical grounds, therapeutic factors research has produced a dizzying array of specific rankings from studies of specific groups with no conceptual framework for organizing across the various studies. Also, as noted above, the inpatient-versus-outpatient heuristic that reviewers have attempted to apply to these studies has not proven to be useful either conceptually or practically.

Our cluster analysis suggests that there is a conceptually appealing taxonomic structure that appears to undergrid the varied studies obtaining client and therapist rankings of therapeutic factors. The derived taxonomy is not based on characteristics of the patient population, but rather on the impacts of group therapy operations. The derived taxonomy has intuitive appeal. The major distinction among therapeutic factors rankings involves a cognitive-versus-affective focus. That group and other treatments vary in their relative emphasis on affective-versus-cognitive learning and experiences is obvious from a quick perusal of the group therapy literature. The cognitive-versus-affective dimension revealed in the cluster analysis reflects the differing emphasis on cognition and affect seen in the group counseling literature. Secondarily, therapeutic factors rankings differed in terms of their focus on insight versus support. As noted above, this support-versus-insight distinction is also well grounded in the empirical and theoretical literature. We hope that the four-category typology derived from the cognitive-versus-affective and the support-versus-insight dimensions will provide a useful way for researchers and practitioners to view therapeutic groups. In the future, researchers cannot see each new client population as potentially producing a unique set of therapeutic factors rankings. Rather, researchers can begin to look at a common set of therapeutic impacts that operate across various client diagnoses and client and group factors.

Implied in the discussion above is our belief that continuing to identify specific client populations or types of treatment groups and creating yet another ranking of therapeutic factors is not going to be a beneficial strategy for enhancing our knowledge about the role of therapeutic factors in group treatments. The cluster analysis of the therapeutic factors studies suggests that there is a structure to the various rankings and that this structure can be used to advance our research endeavors in this area. We believe that identifying the underlying structure of therapeutic factors rankings allows researchers to ask and attempt to answer more interesting and therapeutically meaningful questions. Specifically, attempting to identify which clients will benefit the most from affective support groups, affective insight groups, cognitive support groups, and cognitive insight groups is an important question for researchers to tackle. Alternatively, it will also be important for researchers to identify group leader characteristics and behaviors that are related to clients experiencing affective support groups, affective insight groups, cognitive support groups, and cognitive insight groups. Research like that suggested above has the potential to generate knowledge that would be readily applicable in practice settings.

Currently, the therapeutic factors research confirms what most practitioners suspect, that group clients do not have a uniform reaction to the group counseling experience. Clients and groups of clients do differ in the therapeutic experiences that they find the most helpful. As noted above, however, current research provides little guidance as to which clients will benefit from which type of therapeutic experience. Two studies, however, examined the endorsement of therapeutic factors as a function of client individual differences. Both studies examined Yalom's (1995) and Kiesler's (1983) hypothesis that group members will benefit the most from experiences that are dissimilar to their typical way of interacting or experiencing the world.

Kivlighan and Mullison (1988) examined the relationship between group members' interpersonal style (along the dimensions of affiliation and control) and members' rating of therapeutic factors. Their results indicated that affiliative (friendly) group members found Self-Understanding most helpful, while nonaffiliative (hostile) members rated Self-Disclosure, Learning Through Interpersonal Action, and Altruism as most helpful. Kivlighan and Goldfine (1991) conducted a similar study also assessing group participants' interpersonal style along the dimensions of affiliation and dominance. Kivlighan and Goldfine found that affiliative (friendly) participants valued Universality and Vicarious Learning, while nonaffiliative (hostile) participants valued Interpersonal Learning and Acceptance.

The Kivlighan and Mullison (1988) and Kivlighan and Goldfine (1991) studies suggest that interpersonal theory shows promise for predicting which type of group experiences will be the most helpful for clients with differing interpersonal orientations. Specifically, the research suggests that group participants benefit from a group experience that encourages them to interact or experience the group in ways that are contrary to their normal interpersonal styles. For example, nonaffiliative (hostile) group members may value factors such as Self-Disclosure and Acceptance because they typically do not make themselves vulnerable (through self-disclosure) in their relationships outside of the group and consequently do not experience much acceptance from others. Group therapy is helpful to hostile individuals to the extent that they are encouraged to self-disclose and feel accepted.

Extrapolating from Yalom's (1995) and Kiesler's theories and the Kivlighan and Mullison (1988) and Kivlighan and Goldfine (1991) studies, it is proposed that client affiliation (friendly versus unfriendly) is an important construct for distinguishing between clients who will benefit from an affective or cognitive approach to group therapy. The control (dominant versus submissive) dimension is important for distinguishing between clients who will benefit from a supportive or insight-oriented group therapy experience. Specifically, we offer four hypotheses about the relationship between client interpersonal orientation and types of group experiences that will be most helpful to these clients:

1. Affiliative (friendly) dominant clients will derive the most benefit from group experiences that emphasize cognitive support.

2. Affiliative (friendly) submissive clients will derive the most benefit from group experiences that emphasize cognitive insight.

3. Nonaffiliative (hostile) dominant clients will derive the most benefit from group experiences that emphasize affective support.

4. Nonaffiliative (hostile) submissive clients will derive the most benefit from group experiences that emphasize affective insight.

We hope that these hypotheses will stimulate research that links client characteristics to the four-group typology described in this chapter.

Another small but robust group of studies has examined how the relative importance of therapeutic factors changes over time in group. Yalom (1995) hypothesized that the value that members place on therapeutic factors will vary across stages of group development. The Kivlighan and Mullison (1988) and Kivlighan and Goldfine (1991) studies also examined changes in the relative importance of therapeutic factors across stages of group development. Kivlighan and Mullison found that Universality was more highly valued in early stages of group development, while Learning Through Interpersonal Actions was more valued in later group sessions. Kivlighan and Goldfine found that Universality and Hope decreased and Catharsis increased across three stages of group development. Thus, it appears that Universality and Instillation of Hope are relatively more important in early group development and that Catharsis, Insight, and Learning Through Interpersonal Action increase in importance during later stages of group life.

Yalom's theory and the results of the Kivlighan and Mullison (1988) and Kivlighan and Goldfine (1991) studies provide a basis for linking the types of therapeutic factors experienced by group members to stages of group development. Our hypotheses linking stages of group development to types of group experiences are derived from Tuckman's (1965) synthesis of theories of group development. His synthesis articulated four stages of group development, which he labeled *forming, storming, norming,* and *performing.* Using Tuckman's stages of group development, four hypotheses related to therapeutic factors are offered:

1. Cognitive support experiences will be predominant in the forming stage of group development.

2. Affective support experiences will be predominant in the storming stage of group development.

3. Cognitive insight experiences will be predominant in the norming stage of group development.

4. Affective insight experiences will be predominant in the performing stage of group development.

As noted above, research is also needed examining the link between leader style and characteristics to members' experiences of groups as offering affective support, affective insight, cognitive support, or cognitive insight. Unfortunately, theory and research are even more lacking in this area than in the area of client characteristics. It may be that there is a direct and simple relationship between leader characteristics and group members' experience of therapeutic factors. For example, Hill and O'Grady (1985) developed a list of therapist intentions to describe the cognitive aspect of therapeutic technique. Hill and O'Grady (1985) defined an intention as "the cognitive component that mediates the [therapist's] choice of intervention" (p. 3). Specifically, they have stated that intentions "refer to *why,* whereas interventions and techniques refer to *what* the therapist does" (p. 3; italics in original). Within their comprehensive list of therapist intentions are the intentions labeled *support, insight, cognitions,* and *feelings.* It may well be, for example, that a group leader's high use of feeling and insight intentions is related to group members experiencing their groups as emotionally insight oriented. We believe, however, that group members' experience of group as emotionally insight oriented involves a complex interaction of group leader personal characteristics (affiliation and control), therapist intentions, and therapist technique. The exact specification of this complex relationship between group leadership and group members' experience of therapeutic factors awaits future research and theory.

THERAPEUTIC FACTORS: AN AFTERWORD

We have concentrated our review and analysis on studies that have examined the relative ranking of therapeutic factors in different patient populations and different types of groups at one point in time, or on studies assessing the relative ranking of therapeutic factors at different stages of development within the same group. These studies, however, do not constitute the entirety of research done on therapeutic factors in groups. We chose to concentrate on studies examining the rankings of therapeutic factors because (a) these studies represent the bulk of studies of therapeutic factors in groups and (b) we believed a fresh look at this area of research could help clarify a confusing and contradictory set of findings and point the way to new areas of research. It is important, however, to highlight the other areas of research in group therapeutic factors. A number of researchers have examined the operation of a single therapeutic factor in group settings. For example, there have been studies of feedback in group therapy. Both Crouch et al. (1994) and Kivlighan et al. (2000) provide reviews of studies that have examined isolated group therapeutic factors.

In summary, the results of the cluster analysis reported in this chapter suggest that there is a meaningful and, we hope, heuristic way to group studies examining the relative ranking of therapeutic factors. Specifically, group clients and therapists see therapeutic factors operating to produce four different types of therapeutic experience: *affective support, affective insight, cognitive support,* or *cognitive insight.* We have offered hypotheses that link these four types of group experience to client characteristics and stages of group development. Future research and theory will determine whether this derived typology is useful for stimulating research and theory about the role of therapeutic factors in group treatments.

BIBLIOGRAPHY

References marked with an asterisk indicate studies included in the cluster analysis.

Bloch, S., & Crouch, E. (1985). *Therapeutic factors in group psychotherapy.* Oxford: Oxford University Press.

Bloch, S., & Reibstein, J. (1980). Perceptions by patients and therapists of therapeutic factors in group psychotherapy. *British Journal of Psychiatry, 137,* 274-278.

*Bloch, S., Reibstein, J., Crouch, E., Holroyd, P., & Themen, J. (1979). A method for the study of therapeutic factors in group psychotherapy. *British Journal of Psychiatry, 134,* 257-263.

*Bonney, W., Randall, D. A., & Cleveland, J. D. (1986). An analysis of client-perceived curative factors in a therapy group of former incest victims. *Small Group Behavior, 17,* 303-321.

Borgen, F. H., & Barnett, D. C. (1987). Cluster analysis. *Journal of Counseling Psychology, 34,* 456-467.

*Brabender, V., Albrecht, E., Sillitti, J., Cooper, J., & Kramer, E. (1983). *Hospital and Community Psychiatry, 34,* 643-644.

*Colijn, S., Hoencamp, E. Snijders, H., Van Der Spek, M., & Duivenvoorden, H. (1991). A comparison of curative factors in different types of group psychotherapy. *International Journal of Group Psychotherapy, 41,* 365-378.

Crouch, E. C., Bloch, S., & Wanlass, J. (1994). Therapeutic factors: Interpersonal and intrapersonal mechanisms. In A. Fuhriman & G. M. Burlingame (Eds.), *Handbook of group psychotherapy.* New York: John Wiley.

*Falk-Kessler, J., Momich, C., & Perel, S. (1991). Therapeutic factors in occupational therapy groups. *The American Journal of Occupational Therapy, 45,* 59-66.

Gelso, C. J., & Hayes, J. A. (1998). *The psychotherapy relationship: Theory, research, and practice.* New York: John Wiley.

*Goldberg, F. S., McNiel, D. E., & Binder, R. L. (1988). Therapeutic factors in two forms of inpatient group psychotherapy: Music therapy and verbal therapy. *Group, 12,* 145-156.

Hill, C. E., & O'Grady, K. E. (1985). List of therapist intentions illustrated in a case study and with therapists of varying theoretical orientations. *Journal of Counseling Psychology, 32,* 3-22.

*Hobbs, M., Birtchnell, S., Harte, A., & Lacey, H. (1989). Therapeutic factors in short-term group therapy for women with bulimia. *International Journal of Eating Disorders, 8,* 623-633.

Kiesler, D. J. (1983). The 1982 Interpersonal Circle: A taxonomy for complementarity in human transactions. *Psychological Review, 90,* 185-214.

*Kilic, C., Ozbayrak, K., Ulusahin, A., & Ustun, B. (1996). Therapeutic factors in interactional inpatient groups: Results from a Turkish sample. *Group, 20,* 241-249.

Kivlighan, D. M. Jr., Coleman, M. N., & Anderson, D. C. (2000). Process, outcome and methodology in group counseling research. In S. D. Brown & R. W. Lent (Eds.), *Handbook of counseling psychology* (3rd ed., pp. 767-796). New York: John Wiley.

*Kivlighan, D. M. Jr., & Goldfine, D. C. (1991). Endorsement of therapeutic factors as a function of stage of group development and participant interpersonal attitudes. *Journal of Counseling Psychology, 38,* 150-158.

*Kivlighan, D. M. Jr., & Mullison, D. (1988). Participants' perception of therapeutic factors in group counseling: The role of interpersonal style and stage of group development. *Small Group Behavior, 19,* 452-468.

*Leszcz, M., Yalom, I. D., & Norden, M. (1985). The value of inpatient group psychotherapy: Patients' perceptions. *International Journal of Group Psychotherapy, 35,* 411-433.

Lieberman, M. A. (2002). Leader behavior as perceived by cancer patients in professionally directed support groups and outcomes. *Group Dynamics: Theory, Research and Practice, 6,* 267-276.

*Long, L. D., & Cope, C. S. (1980). Curative factors in a male felony offender group. *Small Group Behavior, 11,* 389-398.

*Lovett, L., & Lovett, J. (1991). Group therapeutic factors on an alcohol inpatient unit. *British Journal of Psychiatry, 159,* 365-370.

*Macaskill, N. D. (1982). Therapeutic factors in group therapy with borderline patients. *International Journal of Group Psychotherapy, 32,* 61-73.

*MacKenzie, K. R. (1987). Therapeutic factors in group psychotherapy: A contemporary view. *Group, 11,* 26-34.

*MacNair-Semands, R. R., & Lese, K. P. (2000). Interpersonal problems and the perception of therapeutic factors in group therapy. *Small Group Research, 31,* 158-174.

*Marcovitz, R. J., & Smith, J. E. (1983). Patients' perceptions of curative factors in short-term group psychotherapy. *International Journal of Group Psychotherapy, 33,* 21-39.

*Maxmen, J. S. (1973). Group therapy as viewed by hospitalized patients. *Archives of General Psychiatry, 28,* 404-408.

*Morgan, R. D., Ferrell, S. W., & Winterowd, C. L. (1999). Therapist perceptions of important therapeutic factors in psychotherapy groups for male inmates in state correctional facilities. *Small Group Research, 30,* 712-729.

*Mushet, G. L., Whalan, G. S., & Power, R. (1989). Inpatients' views of the helpful aspects of group psychotherapy: Impact of therapeutic style and treatment setting. *British Journal of Medical Psychology, 62,* 135-141.

*Shaughnessy, P., & Kivlighan, D. M. (1995). Using group participants' perceptions of therapeutic factors to form client typologies. *Small Group Research, 26,* 250-268.

Tuckman, B. W. (1965). Developmental sequence in small groups. *Psychological Bulletin, 63,* 384-399.

*Yalom, I. D. (1995). *The theory and practice of group psychotherapy* (4th ed.). New York: Basic Books.

Yalom, I., Tinklenberg, J., & Gilula, M. (1968). *Curative factors in group therapy.* Unpublished manuscript.

Ward, J. H. (1963). Hierarchical grouping to optimize objective function. *Journal of the American Statistical Association, 58,* 236-244.

3

EFFECTIVE LEADERSHIP IN GROUP COUNSELING AND PSYCHOTHERAPY

Research and Practice

MARIA T. RIVA
University of Denver

MAXIMILLIAN WACHTEL
Mental Health Corporation of Denver

GINA B. LASKY
University of Denver

Group counseling and psychotherapy has consistently been found to be effective with a broad range of problem areas and clients (e.g., Hoag & Burlingame, 1997; McRoberts, Burlingame, & Hoag, 1998). An essential component related to the effectiveness of therapeutic groups is the leadership. The leader plays a vital role in both the dynamics of the group and the outcomes of its members. Although much is unknown about effective group facilitation, several leader characteristics and behaviors are correlated with group effectiveness.

This chapter will begin with an overview of the research on group leadership characteristics and behaviors that have been shown to provide benefit to group counseling process and outcome. The second section will address coleadership, a common practice in group counseling and psychotherapy yet one that has received limited research attention. The next section will consider what is known about experienced group leaders, how they differ from novice leaders, and what these differences mean for leading groups effectively. Recommendations for group leaders based on theory, research, and practice will be included throughout the chapter. This chapter will concentrate specifically on group counseling and group psychotherapy, and these terms will be used interchangeably.

Overview of the
Research on Group Leadership

This section discusses several group leadership characteristics and behaviors that have been identified as affecting group process and outcome. Although these characteristics will be presented separately, the variables are not mutually exclusive and, rather, work together in a complex interplay. Six components have been chosen because besides having adequate research support, the leader either initiates them or the leader plays an essential role in carrying them out in the context of the group. The components include (a) group member selection, (b) pregroup preparation, (c) positive leader-member relationship, (d) leader's use of structure, (e) group cohesion, and (f) leader communication and feedback.

Selection of Group Members

The American Counseling Association *Code of Ethics and Standards of Practice* (1997) set as a criterion the need for group counselors to "select group members whose needs and goals are compatible with the goals of the group, who will not impede the group process, and whose well-being will not be jeopardized by the group experience" (p. 2). Yet as Piper and McCallum (1994) pointed out, the group literature provides little guidance to leaders as to which selection variables aid in the identification of clients who might benefit from group counseling or, for that matter, which type of group format is the best option. Corey and Corey (1997) suggested that most selection methods are highly subjective and based primarily on leader intuition. This view was supported in a national survey of 75 group leaders who almost exclusively used clinical judgment to determine whether the client possessed some specific behavior or characteristic that would be beneficial for group membership (Riva, Lippert, & Tackett, 2000). This survey data also suggested that although leader intuition is used in place of any standardized assessment instrument, "The most commonly used procedure for deciding whether someone was appropriate for a group was whether the person fit the specific group theme"

(Riva et al., 2000, p. 162). In other words, rather than selecting members because of specific personality characteristics that would increase the likelihood for them and other group members of having a successful group experience, a person with an eating disorder would be referred to an eating-disorder group.

Two areas that have received some attention and support in the selection of criteria literature are the interpersonal and intrapersonal characteristics of potential group members. It seems reasonable to argue the need for assessing relational characteristics during the selection process given the power of group interactions within therapeutic groups. Piper and McCallum (1994), for example, cited as beneficial inclusion criteria a moderate amount of social ability and frustration tolerance and a commitment to changing interpersonal behaviors. Surprisingly, little research has focused on these interpersonal behaviors at the time of selection and how they relate to positive outcomes for group members. Kew (1975) designed the Group Psychotherapy Evaluation Scale (GPES) to assess whether potential clients have the skills and characteristics to be successful in group therapy. This measure considers variables such as the amount and quality of communication and the capacity for change, which have some relationship with positive group outcomes. Some studies have found that group dropouts and completers can be distinguished on relational variables, such as amount of participation in a group for depression (Oei & Kazmierczak, 1997); difficulties trusting and relating to others (Blouin et al., 1995); and other interpersonal behaviors, such as introversion, shyness, loneliness, difficulties with friends (MacNair & Corazzini, 1994), and social inhibition (MacNair-Semands, 2002).

Intrapersonal variables that have promise as selection criteria are psychological mindedness and the potential group member's expectations about the benefits of group treatment. Lower levels of psychological mindedness (McCallum & Piper, 1990) and angry hostility (MacNair-Semands, 2002) have been shown to predict who will drop out of group. A positive correlation has also been found between psychological mindedness and the amount of work a member does in group (McCallum, Piper, & O'Kelly, 1997). Moreover, there is support for a positive relationship between a client's expectation that group will be beneficial and the actual benefits gained (Pearson & Girling, 1990). More research needs to be conducted in this important area so that group leaders can be informed by certain criteria in the selection of group members. Until more specific selection criteria are identified and formal selection instruments are developed, group leaders may want to ask questions during the selection process that address potential members' relationships with others (e.g., "Describe your behavior and participation in past or current social or therapeutic groups"); their expectations that the group will help them (e.g., "How much do you expect this group to be beneficial to you?"); and the ability to be self-reflective or psychologically minded (e.g., "Describe some of your behaviors that you find difficult to understand").

Pregroup Preparation

A strong case can be made for preparing group members for their entrance into a therapeutic group. Pregroup preparation, sometimes called pregroup training, has been shown to be related to the development of group cohesion (Santarsiero, Baker, & McGee, 1995) and may be associated with group member satisfaction and decreased risk of dropout (Piper & Perrault, 1989). In their review of the group literature, Bednar and Kaul (1994) suggested that pregroup training was a potent factor in successful treatment groups. Although the actual strength of this relationship is unknown, several studies suggest a connection between pregroup training and clients' later positive group behaviors (Bowman & DeLucia, 1993; Connelly & Piper, 1989; Piper & Marrache, 1981).

From a practical standpoint, leaders can use the preparation time to address much of the procedural information prior to the first session and help all group members begin with the same knowledge about how the group will function. This is particularly important when the composition of the group combines members who have previously not been in a group with members who have other group counseling experience. There is no standard method of preparation, yet Couch (1995) suggested a helpful four-step model, which includes identifying

the clients' needs, expectations, and commitment; challenging any myths and misconceptions; conveying information; and screening the person for group fit.

Burlingame, Fuhriman, and Johnson (2001) described pregroup preparation as one of their six empirically supported principles regarding the therapeutic relationship. Related to what Couch (1995) described as the third stage (conveying information), Burlingame et al. stated that "pregroup preparation sets treatment expectations, defines group rules, and instructs members in appropriate roles and skills needed for effective group participation and group cohesion" (p. 375). Preparation prior to the beginning of group is certainly a leader behavior that requires a facilitator who understands group dynamics and can articulate a sense of hope, trust, and safety to group members while also decreasing their anxiety about what group counseling and psychotherapy will be like, a common concern for new members. Additional resources that address information covered in the preparation of potential group members and (sometimes under sections on informed consent) are Association for Specialists in Group Work *Best Practice Guidelines for Group Workers* (ASGW, 1998); Corey (2000); and Gazda, Ginter, and Horne (2001).

Positive Leader-Member Relationship

Research firmly supports the view that group leaders are crucial in the development of a positive group climate and that for group members, a supportive relationship with the leader is necessary for client change (Dies, 1994). Group members who have a favorable view of their leaders are more likely to make substantial progress (e.g., Antonuccio, Davis, Lewinson, & Breckenridge, 1987). It is not surprising that group leaders who are warm, supportive, and genuinely interested in individual members, as well as the group as a whole, have group members who make more positive gains. In a review of 135 studies, Dies (1994) concluded that,

> Group members favor and seem to benefit more
> from a positive style of intervention, and that as
> leaders become more actively negative, they

increase the possibility that participants will not only be dissatisfied, but also potentially harmed by the group experience. (p. 139)

The finding that a group leader's negative behavior can be damaging to group members is consistent with those of Smokowski, Rose, and Bacallao (2001), who found that group casualties were related to some specific leader behaviors, such as when leaders became overly confrontational and prematurely pressured group members to self-disclose.

McCallum, Piper, Ogrodniczuk, and Joyce (2002) found that even as early as the third session, group therapists rated members who later dropped out as "less likeable, less desirable as friends, and having less significance as a group member" (p. 251) compared with those who completed group. The authors posited that group leaders may have been responding to group members' behavior that signaled disconnection from the group or that leaders may have responded less positively to certain members due to countertransference feelings. In this study, it is unclear whether the group leader's reactions translated into negative behavior toward the group member and contributed to group member dropout, but the question is an essential one to consider in future research. Group leaders who feel less positively about some group members need to consider that these reactions very likely will be translated to those group members, resulting in them distancing from the group cohesion and potentially dropping out altogether. The findings that a positive leadership style is more effective and that a negative leader can actually damage members underscores the importance of the selection process, when group leaders should monitor their own reactions to potential group members and select those with whom they can show support and genuine caring. Likewise, supervision should be used when group leaders find themselves feeling negatively about members in their group. ASGW *Best Practices Guidelines* (1998) state that "group workers seek consultation and/or supervision regarding ethical concerns that interfere with effective functioning as a group leader" (p. 241). For more information on the supervision of group leaders, see DeLucia-Waack and Fauth, in this volume (Chapter 10).

Use of Structure by the Leader

Structure is a broad term that encompasses many different techniques and interventions that have as their primary goal the development and maintenance of a healthy therapeutic group. For example, structure is conveyed when the group leader discusses the norms of the group. Some typical norms include the importance of attendance and what members should do if they are unable to attend, how communication occurs (not interrupting, using "I" statements, an expectation about participation), and clear norms about confidentiality and its limits. Group facilitators also provide structure by pointing out group themes, intervening in destructive communications between group members, underscoring their positive interactions, and in other ways providing safety and helping members understand the meaning of their reactions and behaviors.

The leader's role in structuring the group has received much attention (Burlingame & Fuhriman, 1994). It is a complex discussion given that how much, when, and how to structure a group are all important leader considerations. Dies (1994) reviewed studies that looked at therapist variables and their relationship to treatment outcomes. In a very broad sense, when group leaders provided structure, groups fared better than those with less directive leadership. Structure has been associated with increased self-disclosure, cohesion, and risk taking in groups, and there is enough evidence to suggest that group leaders "pay close attention to structuring tactics because of the positive effect such tactics can be expected to have on the content and process of group counseling" (Gazda et al., 2001, p. 39).

Group literature typically focuses on the leader's intentional use of structure in the initial sessions of a group. Almost 30 years ago, Bednar, Melnick, and Kaul (1974) theorized that group facilitators need to use high levels of structure in the initial sessions to handle procedural concerns, such as confidentiality, attendance, and participation, and to clarify the goals of the group and individual members. Bednar et al. also suggested that the amount of structure should be reduced gradually to help the members become more responsible for their own behavior change. Several studies have supported the need for initial structure, such as Stockton, Rohde, and Haughey (1992), who found that highly structured exercises used in the initial sessions led to more relevant behaviors for group members. Too little structure, then, is problematic for the group, particularly in the early sessions, yet too much structure also may be detrimental for spontaneity between group members and deter them from becoming active participants in their own goal attainment. Too much structure has been related to participants who do not feel an ownership of their group (Fuehrer & Keys, 1988) and develop an overdependence on the leader (Yalom, 1995).

In addition to group leaders needing to provide an ample amount of structure, the type of structure is also pivotal. In the classic study by Lieberman, Yalom, and Miles (1973), they described two types of structure used by group leaders: meaning attribution and executive function. They defined *meaning attribution* as the act of "providing concepts for how to understand, explaining, clarifying, interpreting, and providing frameworks for how to change" (p. 238). Dies (1994) argued that meaning attribution provides structure for the group in that it helps group members understand and make sense out of their actions and the actions of others. *Executive function* provides the limits, rules, and norms so that the group can operate. Lieberman et al. found that both of these functions are important in a group, although meaning attribution led to better outcomes. More recent findings have found similar results (e.g., Coche, Dies, & Goettelman, 1991), suggesting that a high level of meaning attribution and a moderate level of executive function are beneficial in therapeutic groups.

Group Cohesion

For Yalom (1995), the most important leadership role is the building and maintaining of a therapeutic group climate, often discussed as the cohesiveness of the group. Group cohesion is one of the most-studied variables related to leader behavior. The majority of research concludes that there is a strong positive correlation between cohesion and therapeutic group outcomes (e.g., Marziali, Munroe-Blum, & McCleary, 1997;

Tschuschke & Dies, 1994). An essential leader behavior is to foster a group climate that is safe, positive, and supportive yet strong enough to at times withstand highly charged emotions, challenges, and interactions between members.

Several recent articles include in-depth discussions of group cohesion. For example, Dion (2000) discussed the historical underpinnings and multiple dimensions of cohesion as it is used across many disciplines, while Burlingame et al. (2001) provided an overview of cohesion specifically in group psychotherapy. Burlingame et al. discussed the three important relational components in the development of cohesion as member to member, member to group, and member to leader. These multiple dimensions make group counseling and psychotherapy much more complicated than individual psychotherapy and require a group facilitator who can track and respond to all three areas. For groups to be most effective, group leaders need to encourage an environment in which group members are able to respond to, learn from, and support each other. Group members are less likely to drop out when they feel a certain amount of attraction to the group and thus feel more connected to the group as a whole (MacKenzie, 1994), and groups with less attrition have better outcomes (Hoag & Burlingame, 1997). Therefore, cohesion seems to be what Yalom (1995) called the "glue" of the group, by keeping group members connected until other group influences begin to operate.

Although often studied at one time period, cohesion seems to be a dynamic process that changes over the life of the group and needs continual attention from the leader. MacNair-Semands and Lese (2000), for example, found that regardless of the group stage or the perceived importance attributed to cohesion by members, cohesion ratings increased as a function of length of time spent in the group. Other authors have suggested that the relationship may be other than a positive correlation. Castongauy, Pincus, Agras, and Hines (1998) found that for binge eaters who made the most gains, early group climate was rated as *supportive,* whereas the middle stage was rated as *negative.* The authors argued that it was the positive group climate that initially allowed the members to tolerate the intense work that was necessary in the middle stage. Other research points to variables such as personality characteristics or the theme of the group as contributors to how cohesion evolves. For instance, Schwartz and Waldo (1999) found that cohesion occurred very slowly for the members of their spouse abuse groups due to their difficulty in trusting each other and the group process. Although future research needs to consider the longer-term trajectory of cohesion, measuring it at several points and accounting for its variability depending on the type, membership, and length of the group, there is no dispute about the importance and power of group cohesion.

Based on theory and research, the following are recommendations to facilitate group cohesion. Leaders should carefully select members for their groups, since even one member who deviates from the group norms or is not a good fit for the group will interfere with the development of group cohesion. Leaders need to be positive and supportive to each member. Providing information about what to expect in the group through pregroup preparation and initial group session structure will help members feel safe and encourage a feeling of trust. The early emphasis on safety is important so that members are not using their energy to feel anxious about what the group will be like (what Yalom, 1995, terms "extrinsic anxiety") instead of concentrating on their goals for behavior change. Research also suggests that homogeneous groups become cohesive more quickly (e.g., Perrone & Sedlacek, 2000), which is particularly critical in brief groups.

Leader Communication and Feedback

Research indicates that certain types of leader communication and feedback are more beneficial than others. In a review of the literature, Morran, Stockton, Cline, and Teed (1998) found that corrective feedback from the leader and other group members may be extremely important in providing a different perspective, but it is generally hard for group members to hear. Group members are more receptive to negative feedback if it follows positive feedback or is sandwiched between two positive comments. Also, feedback is much more beneficial when it is specific and behavioral rather than global and emotional (Morran, Stockton, & Harris, 1991). For example, a leader might comment to a group member, "You provided some very positive support for Gwen and Bill today when you pointed out their strengths. I wonder what stops you from seeing your own strengths? You seem to see them so easily in others."

Group members' receptivity to negative feedback is also related to the stage of the group. In initial group sessions, positive feedback is accepted more readily and should be the emphasis, while groups that are more developed can handle corrective feedback with less difficulty. At these later stages, group leaders can provide more of a balance between positive and corrective feedback. Group leaders can also evaluate the readiness and receptivity of the receiver prior to providing corrective feedback (Morran et al., 1998).

Group facilitators will want to consider not only the type and timing of feedback but also how much of the feedback is leader driven. Since much of the power of group counseling and psychotherapy occurs between the members, group leaders will want to model effective positive and corrective feedback and encourage members to exchange beneficial feedback (Morran et al., 1998). Morran, Robison, and Stockton (1985) and Flowers (1979) found that feedback from group leaders was less accepted than feedback given by group members, even though leader feedback was rated as higher quality (Morran et al., 1985). This finding emphasizes the need for the leader to develop a cohesive group so that members can begin to receive feedback from other group members and not just from the leader.

GROUP COLEADERSHIP

Coleadership is common in counseling and psychotherapy groups. For example, in the 1994 review by Dies, half of the 135 groups studied used a cotherapy leadership model. Group leaders often argue that cotherapy is better than individually led groups for a variety of reasons, such as efficiency (e.g., the group can still continue if one leader is sick or unavailable); effectiveness (e.g., two leaders can track group members more easily); supervision and training of new group therapists; or as a way to model healthy communication patterns (e.g., male/female interactions) between coleaders in front of the group members (Dies, 1994; Shapiro, 1999). Unfortunately, none of these potential benefits of cotherapy have been studied.

The hypothesis that coleaders who model appropriate interaction between themselves, such as resolving disagreements or compromising, will have group members who demonstrate better skills in these areas is intriguing. Unfortunately, McNary and Dies (1993) found that coleaders hardly ever talk to each other during group sessions. Although the hypothesis that coleader modeling could be used to teach specific member skills makes intuitive sense, no study has intentionally varied the type or amount of modeling that occurs between coleaders and then looked at the effect of leader modeling on group member interactions.

Currently, "There is no evidence that the presence of two therapists enhances the quality of efficacy of therapeutic outcome, but the limited findings suggest that co-leadership may complicate group process unless the leaders manage their relationship effectively within the sessions" (Dies, 1994, p. 141). It seems that to avoid the possibility of negatively affecting the group, cotherapists should be compatible in their views of how groups work and have a willingness to discuss their cotherapy relationships. It seems crucial to the health of the group for coleaders to be open, willing to share and listen to different points of view, and to discuss and resolve difficulties that may arise between them.

Several psychologists, psychiatrists, and social workers throughout the past 25 years have described the development of the cotherapy relationship. Thus far, these descriptions have been anecdotal and based on personal experience, yet they share some striking similarities. Two of these theorists compared husband-wife teams (Lazarus, 1976; Low & Low, 1975), while others wrote of meeting their cotherapists for the first time shortly before starting the group (Brent & Marine, 1982; McMahon & Links, 1984). Still others used previous group theory to form a theoretical perspective on cotherapist relationship development (Dick, Lessler, & Whiteside, 1980; Weiss, 1988). One theorist

used personal experiences, along with examples from supervision and observation over a period of a few years, to create her stage theory (Winter, 1976). Finally, Dugo and Beck (1997) outlined a nine-phase model based on their experience of supervising coleaders.

Two components discussed in all the models cited above are that (a) cotherapists must come to agreement on the basic structural issues of the group and (b) there must be an awareness of one's own personal concerns that might lead to feelings of competition with the cotherapist, anxiety about one's own performance, or the need to fight over power and control in the group. These models also emphasize that it is essential to communicate these concerns, along with one another's strengths and weaknesses, in order to work through them and move to a point where they do not negatively affect the group. Wheelan (1997) stated that "given the needs of new groups for direction and safety, a united front, clarity of purposes, a consistent approach, and a shared plan of action on the part of the co-therapists are essential" (p. 308).

At the present time, little is known about coleadership in therapeutic groups. Pinpointing the unique qualities of coleadership versus one leader or studying the components of an effective coleadership team compared with ineffective coleaders would be a beneficial direction for future investigation. While awaiting guidance from research studies, coleaders may want to consider some of these recommendations from the literature and from our own experience. First, it seems prudent to *select* a coleader. Many coleaders join together because they are interested in the theme of the group, but fail to discuss their respective styles and views of leadership. Two potential group leaders may want to interview each other to discuss the strengths and weaknesses they bring to the relationship, their views of group counseling, and how they will resolve differences when they occur. Second, it seems prudent to schedule some time before and after the group sessions to discuss the group members *and* the cotherapy relationship. In our experience, few cotherapy dyads make time to discuss the process or the progress of their groups (Riva, Wachtel, & Butcher, 2000; Wachtel, 2001). One additional point that has become evident in our discussions with group coleaders is that few of them receive supervision on their groups. If supervision is available, some attention is given to the specific clients in a group, but very little attention is given to the group process, and even less emphasis is put on the functioning of the coleadership relationship. DeLucia-Waack (2002) suggested a written format for coleaders to help them organize their observations and perceptions of group sessions prior to meeting for planning and supervision.

The Road to Effective Group Leadership

Several professional organizations (e.g., ASGW; American Group Psychotherapy Association, or AGPA) discuss the ethical responsibility of group leaders to be competent, yet exactly which characteristics are associated with competent group leadership is still not entirely clear. Training, an essential component of developing competent group leaders, unfortunately has received very little attention (Fuhriman & Burlingame, 2001; Weinstein & Rossini, 1998). The leadership of groups has been directly related to member outcomes, underscoring the need for knowledgeable and skillful group facilitators. Research on individual psychotherapy has found that therapist experience and competence are instrumental in client gains, and although it seems highly likely that this would be the same for group leadership, it has not been studied (Dies, 1994).

Group research has begun to investigate what variables distinguish advanced from novice group leaders. Hines, Stockton, and Morran (1995) found that novice and expert group leaders think differently about their groups. Three thought categories were positively correlated with the experience level of the group leaders: (a) interpretation of group process (e.g., the leader thinks, "Group members just changed the topic to avoid dealing with the anger that is present in the group today"); (b) internal questions regarding a member (i.e., "What else has he tried?"); and (c) interpretation of a member (e.g., "Juan's body language is saying he is disappointed"). Therapeutic value judgments (i.e., thoughts evaluating whether group interactions

are therapeutic or not) were negatively correlated with leader experience, suggesting that the less experienced the leader, the more thoughts he or she had about whether a group transaction was therapeutic. Interpretation of group process was the single most important thought category to predict the experience level of leaders. Group leaders with more experience interpreted group process, asked internal questions about members, and interpreted member behavior more often than did less experienced leaders, who more often tended to have thoughts about therapeutic value judgments.

Similarly, Kivlighan and Quigley (1991) found that, compared with novice leaders, experienced leaders had more complex views of group members and their interactions. Novice group leaders tended to perceive group members in two dimensions: dominant/submissive and rate of participation. Experienced leaders, on the other hand, used three dimensions to conceptualize group members: dominant/submissive, friendly/unfriendly, and supporting therapeutic work/hindering therapeutic work. Thus, not only did experienced leaders use more dimensions when thinking about group members, they also used different dimensions to conceptualize group members.

Both studies that compared experienced with novice group leaders (Hines et al., 1995; Kivlighan & Quigley, 1991) found that complexity of thinking about the group process distinguished experienced from less experienced group leaders. These studies suggest that experienced group leaders have more knowledge and a deeper cognitive understanding of the group process. Taking this a step further, it would seem reasonable to hypothesize that this appreciation of group dynamics would also lead to an increased ability to effectively intervene in the group as a whole. The importance of a group leader's attention to the group process, even potentially more important than a focus on individual group member change, has been well documented (Kivlighan & Tarrant, 2001; Yalom, 1995). Yet little empirical energy has gone into methods of teaching group leaders to increase their knowledge and skill in addressing the group process.

Toth, Stockton, and Erwin (1998) proposed a six-stage skill-based model for learning specific group leader techniques. The stages include Experiential 1, Didactic, Observational 1, Role Play, Observational 2, and Experiential 2. The model also uses a pretraining videotape of trainees' group leadership, which is then compared with posttraining abilities with the aim of increasing students' self-confidence. In a rare empirical study, Toth and Stockton (1996) tested the model and found that students who participated in the six-step model of training demonstrated a significant increase in their execution of here-and-now interventions from pretest to posttest when compared with a control group.

Despite the lack of research on essential components, ASGW has outlined training standards. These standards have established two levels of training: core training and specialist training (Conyne, 1996). *Core training* includes a cognitive and experiential component to aid in learning basic knowledge and skills. The distinction made between core training and specialized training recognizes the fact that therapeutic groups are wide ranging and diverse. This increased diversity means that different types of groups (e.g., task/work, guidance, psychoeducational, counseling, and psychotherapy groups) with different goals and emphases will require different skills.

Credentialing organizations have been developed to provide some assurance of group leader effectiveness. The AGPA has established the National Registry of Certified Group Psychotherapists (NRCGP), and the American Board of Professional Psychology (ABPP) created a Diplomate of Group Psychology. According to Bernard (2000), the two organizations have different goals: The NRCGP is designed to identify individuals who meet a minimal level of competence, while the ABPP is more interested in identifying individuals who demonstrate advanced competence in group treatment. Because the goals are different, the criteria for certification varies for these organizations. The ASGW standards, credentialing organizations, and some models of training provide a starting point for providing some standardization to the training of competent group leaders. Research on training of group leaders and deciphering the elements that relate to effective group leadership is much overdue and deserves a higher priority than it has so far received.

CONCLUSIONS

It is clear that counseling groups are effective across populations and problem areas (e.g., Bednar & Kaul, 1994; Hoag & Burlingame, 1997; McRoberts et al., 1998). It is also apparent that effective leadership requires certain knowledge and behaviors about group counseling and psychotherapy. For example, leaders will want to be positive, supportive, provide sufficient structure, attend to developing group cohesion, allow group members to take ownership of their group, and provide a meaningful context for what occurs in the group. Although the facilitation of groups is paramount, little research exists to guide the training of group leaders. Similarly, cotherapy is practiced widely in group counseling and psychotherapy, with little information on the best or even effective models. There is clear evidence that groups are highly effective and are a mainstay in all types of clinical settings. The more that is known about effective group leadership and training models, the greater will be the benefit to the field of group counseling and psychotherapy and to the group members that it serves.

REFERENCES

American Counseling Association. (1997). *Code of ethics and standards of practice.* Alexandria, VA: Author.

Antonuccio, D. O., Davis, C., Lewinson, P. M., & Breckenridge, J. S. (1987). Therapist variables related to cohesiveness in a group treatment for depression. *Small Group Behavior, 18,* 557-564.

Association for Specialists in Group Work. (ASGW). (1998). Association for Specialists in Group Work best practice guidelines. *Journal for Specialists in Group Work, 23,* 237-244.

Bednar, R. L., and Kaul, T. K. (1994). Experiential group research: Can the cannon fire? In A. E. Bergin & S. L. Garfield (Eds.), *Handbook of psychotherapy and behavior change* (4th ed., pp. 631-663). New York: Wiley.

Bednar, R. L., Melnick, J., & Kaul, T. J. (1974). Risk, responsibility and structure: A conceptual framework for initiating group counseling and psychotherapy. *Journal of Counseling Psychology, 21,* 31-37.

Bernard, H. S. (2000). The future of training and credentialing in group psychotherapy. *Group, 24,* 167-175.

Blouin, J., Schnarre, K., Carter, J., Blouin, A., Tener, L., Zuro, C., & Barlow, J. (1995). Factors affecting dropout rate from cognitive-behavioral group treatment for bulimia nervosa. *International Journal of Eating Disorders, 17,* 323-329.

Bowman, V. E., & DeLucia, J. L. (1993). Preparation for group therapy: The effects of preparer and modality on group process and individual functioning. *Journal for Specialists in Group Work, 18,* 67-79.

Brent, D. A., & Marine, E. (1982). Developmental aspects of the co-therapy relationship. *Journal of Marital and Family Therapy, 4,* 69-74.

Burlingame, G. M., & Fuhriman, A. (1994). Epilogue. In A. Fuhriman & G. M. Burlingame (Eds.), *Handbook of group psychotherapy: An empirical and clinical synthesis* (pp. 559-562). New York: Wiley.

Burlingame, G. M., Fuhriman, A., & Johnson, J. E. (2001). Cohesion in group psychotherapy. *Psychotherapy, 38,* 373-379.

Castongauy, L. G., Pincus, A. L., Agras, W. S., & Hines, C. E. (1998). The role of emotion in group cognitive-behavioral therapy for binge-eating disorder. When things have to feel worse before they get better. *Psychotherapy Research, 8,* 225-238.

Coche, E., Dies, R. R., & Goettelman, K. (1991). Process variables mediating change in intensive group therapy training. *International Journal of Group Psychotherapy, 41,* 379-397.

Connelly, J. L., & Piper, W. E. (1989). An analysis of pretraining work behavior as a composition of variables in group psychotherapy. *International Journal of Group Psychotherapy, 39,* 173-189.

Conyne, R. K. (1996). The Association for Specialists in Group Work training standards: Some considerations and suggestions for training. *The Journal for Specialists in Group Work, 21,* 155-162.

Corey, G. (2000). *Theory and practice of group counseling* (5th ed.). Belmont, CA: Wadsworth/Thomson.

Corey, M. S., & Corey, G. (1997). *Groups: Process and practice* (5th ed.). Pacific Grove, CA: Brooks/Cole.

Couch, R. D. (1995). Four steps for conducting a pregroup screening interview. *Journal for Specialists in Group Work, 20,* 18-25.

DeLucia-Waack, J. (2002). A written guide for planning and processing group sessions in anticipation of supervision. *Journal for Specialists in Group Work, 27,* 341-357.

Dick, B., Lessler, K., & Whiteside, J. (1980). A developmental framework for co-therapy. *International Journal of Group Psychotherapy, 30,* 273-285.

Dies, R. R. (1994). Therapist variables in group psychology research. In A. Fuhriman & G. M. Burlingame (Eds.), *Handbook of group psychotherapy: An empirical and clinical synthesis* (pp. 114-154). New York: Wiley.

Dion, K. L. (2000). Group cohesion: From "field of forces" to multidimensional construct. *Group Dynamics: Theory, Research, & Practice, 4,* 7-26.

Dugo, J. M., & Beck, A. P. (1997). Significance and complexity of early phases in the development of the co-therapy relationship. *Group Dynamics: Theory, Research, and Practice, 1*(4), 294-305.

Flowers, J. V. (1979). Behavioral analysis of group therapy and a modal for behavioral group therapy. In D. Upper & S. M. Ross (Eds.), *Behavioral group therapy, 1979: An annual review* (pp. 5-37). Champaign, IL: Research Press.

Fuehrer, A., & Keys, C. (1988). Group development in self-help groups for college students. *Small Group Behavior, 19,* 325-341.

Fuhriman, A., & Burlingame, G. M. (2001). Group psychotherapy training and effectiveness. *International Journal of Group Psychotherapy, 51,* 399-416.

Gazda, G. M., Ginter, E. J., & Horne, A. M. (2001). *Group counseling and group psychotherapy: Theory and Application.* Needham Heights, MA: Allyn & Bacon.

Hines, P. L., Stockton, R., & Morran D. K. (1995). Self-talk of group therapists. *Journal of Counseling Psychology, 42,* 242-248.

Hoag, M. J., & Burlingame, G. M. (1997). Evaluating the effectiveness of child and adolescent group treatment. *Journal of Clinical Child Psychology, 26,* 234-246.

Kew, C. E. (1975). A pilot study of an evaluation scale for group-psychotherapy patients. *ETS Test Collection (Set A).* Princeton, NJ: Educational Testing Services. (Tests in Microfiche No. 004944)

Kivlighan, D. M. Jr., & Quigley, S. T. (1991). Dimensions used by experienced and novice group therapists to conceptualize group process. *Journal of Counseling Psychology, 38,* 415-423.

Kivlighan, D. M. Jr., & Tarrant, J. M. (2001). Does group climate mediate the group leadership-member outcome relationship? A test of Yalom's hypotheses about leadership priorities. *Group Dynamics: Theory, Research, and Practice, 5,* 220-234.

Lazarus, L. W. (1976). Family therapy by a husband-wife team. *Journal of Marriage and Family Counseling, 20,* 225-233.

Lieberman, M. A., Yalom, I. D., & Miles, M. B. (1973). *Encounter groups: First facts.* New York: Basic Books.

Low, P., & Low, M. (1975). Treatment of married couples in a group run by a husband and wife. *International Journal of Group Psychotherapy, 25,* 54-66.

MacKenzie, K. R. (1994). Group development. In A. Fuhriman & G. M. Burlingame (Eds.), *Handbook of group psychotherapy: An empirical and clinical synthesis* (pp. 559-562). New York: Wiley.

MacNair, R. R., & Corazzini, J. G. (1994). Client factors influencing group therapy dropout. *Psychotherapy, 31,* 352-362.

MacNair-Semands, R. R. (2002). Predicting attendance and expectations for group therapy. *Group Dynamics: Theory, Research, and Practice, 6,* 219-228.

MacNair-Semands, R. R., & Lese, K. P. (2000). Interpersonal problems and the perception of therapeutic factors in group therapy. *Small Group Research, 31,* 158-174.

Marziali, E., Munroe-Blum, H., & McCleary, L. (1997). The contribution of group cohesion and group alliance to the outcome of group psychotherapy. *International Journal of Group Psychotherapy, 47,* 475-497.

McCallum, M., & Piper, W. E. (1990). A controlled study of effectiveness and patient suitability for short-term group psychotherapy. *International Journal of Group Psychotherapy, 40,* 431-452.

McCallum, M., Piper, W. E., Ogrodniczuk, J. S., & Joyce, A. S. (2002). Early process and dropping out from short-term group therapy for complicated grief. *Group Dynamics: Theory, Research, and Practice, 6,* 243-254.

McCallum, M., Piper, W. E., & O'Kelly, J. (1997). Predicting patient benefit from a group-oriented, evening treatment program. *International Journal of Group Psychotherapy, 47,* 291-314.

McMahon, N., & Links, P. S. (1984). Co-therapy: The need for positive pairing. *Canadian Journal of Psychiatry, 29,* 385-389.

McNary, S. W., & Dies, R. R. (1993). Cotherapist modeling in group psychotherapy: fact or fantasy? *Group, 17*(3), 131-142.

McRoberts, C., Burlingame, G. M., & Hoag, M. J. (1998). Comparative efficacy of individual and group psychotherapy: A meta-analytic perspective. *Group Dynamics: Theory, Research and Practice, 2,* 101-117.

Morran, D. K., Robison, R. F., & Stockton, R. (1985). Feedback exchange in counseling groups: An analysis of message content and receiver acceptance as a function of leader versus member delivery, session and valence. *Journal of Counseling Psychology, 32,* 57-67.

Morran, D. K., Stockton, R., Cline, R. J., & Teed, C. (1998). Facilitating feedback exchange in groups: Leader interventions. *Journal for Specialists in Group Work, 23,* 257-268.

Morran, D. K., Stockton, R., & Harris, M. (1991). Analysis of group leader and member feedback messages. *Journal of Group Psychotherapy, Psychodrama, and Sociometry, 44,* 126-135.

Oei, T. P. S., & Kazmierczak, T. (1997). Factors associated with dropout in a group cognitive behaviour therapy for mood disorders. *Behavior Research and Theory, 35,* 1025-1030.

Pearson, M. J., & Girling, A. (1990). The value of the Claybury Selection Battery in predicting benefit from group psychotherapy. *British Journal of Psychiatry, 157,* 384-388.

Perrone, K. M., & Sedlacek, W. E. (2000). A comparison of group cohesiveness and client satisfaction in homogenous and heterogenous groups. *Journal for Specialists in Group Work, 25,* 243-251.

Piper, W. E., & Marrache, M. (1981). Selecting suitable patients: Pretraining for group therapy as a method of patient selection. *Small Group Behavior, 12,* 459-476.

Piper, W. E., & McCallum, M. (1994). Selection of patients for group interventions. In H. S. Bernard & K. R. MacKenzie (Eds.), *Basics of group psychotherapy* (pp. 1-34). New York: Guilford.

Piper, W. E., & Perrault, E. L. (1989). Pretherapy preparation for group members. *International Journal of Group Psychotherapy, 39,* 17-34.

Riva, M. T., Lippert, L, & Tackett, M. J. (2000). Selection practices of group leaders: A national survey. *Journal for Specialists in Group Work, 25,* 157-169.

Riva, M. T., Wachtel, M. A., & Butcher, G. (2000, March). *Understanding group co-therapy relationships: A developmental approach.* Paper presented at the American Counseling Association Annual Conference, Washington, D.C.

Santarsiero, L. J., Baker, R. C., & McGee, T. F. (1995). The effects of cognitive pretraining on cohesion and self-disclosure in small groups: An analog study. *Journal of Clinical Psychology, 51,* 403-409.

Schwartz, J. P., & Waldo, M. (1999). Therapeutic factors in Duluth Model spouse abusers group treatment. *Journal for Specialists in Group Work, 24,* 197-207.

Shapiro, E. (1999). Cotherapy. In J. R. Price & D. R. Hescheles (Eds.), *A guide to starting psychotherapy groups* (pp. 53-61). San Diego: Academic Press.

Smokowski, P. R., Rose, S. D., & Bacallao, M. L. (2001). Damaging experiences in therapeutic groups: How vulnerable consumers become group casualties. *Small Group Research, 32,* 223-251.

Stockton, R., Rohde, R. I., & Haughey, J. (1992). The effects of structured group exercises on cohesion, engagement, avoidance, and conflict. *Small Group Research, 23,* 1555-1568.

Toth, P. L., & Stockton, R. (1996). A skill-based approach to teaching group counseling interventions. *The Journal for Specialists in Group Work, 21,* 101-109.

Toth, P. L., Stockton, R., & Erwin, W. J. (1998). Application of a skill-based training model for group counselors. *Journal for Specialists in Group Work, 23,* 33-49.

Tschuschke, V., & Dies, R. R. (1994). Intensive analysis of therapeutic factors and outcome in long-term inpatient groups. *International Journal of Group Psychotherapy, 44,* 185-208.

Wachtel, M. A. (2001). Exploring group co-therapist relationship development and the impact of training on the relationship. Doctoral dissertation, University of Denver. *Dissertation Abstracts International: Section B: The Sciences & Engineering, 62*(7-B), Feb 2002, pp. 3393.

Weinstein, M., & Rossini, E. D. (1998). Academic training in group psychotherapy in clinical psychology doctoral programs. *Psychological Reports, 82,* 955-959.

Weiss, J. C. (1988). The D-R model of coleadership of groups. *Small Group Behavior, 19*(1), 117-125.

Wheelan, S. A. (1997). Co-therapists and the creation of a functional psychotherapy group: A group dynamics perspective. *Group Dynamics: Theory, Research, and Practice, 1,* 306-310.

Winter, S. K. (1976). Developmental stages in the roles and concerns of group co-leaders. *Small Group Behavior, 7,* 349-362.

Yalom, I. D. (1995). *The theory and practice of group psychotherapy* (4th ed.). New York: Basic Books.

4

PROCESS AND OUTCOME IN GROUP COUNSELING AND PSYCHOTHERAPY

A Perspective

GARY M. BURLINGAME
Brigham Young University

ADDIE J. FUHRIMAN
Brigham Young University

JENNIFER JOHNSON
Brigham Young University

Group psychotherapy presents itself as a complex and dynamic endeavor designed to aid those who are in chronic or acute psychological distress. Over the past 50 years, researchers and clinicians have focused on the dynamics of this complexity, specifically, in terms of understanding its effectiveness—Does group counseling and psychotherapy work?—and in terms of its operations—What are the core therapeutic processes? The contributors to the theory, practice, and research in group work come from a variety of backgrounds, disciplines, and theoretical orientations that have influenced the approaches taken to answering these critical questions. The entity itself is also diverse, operating on various levels and engaging multiple players, goals, roles, and relationships, each contributing a singular influence, all shaping an interactive effect. We previously concluded, regarding the complexity of group (Fuhriman & Burlingame, 1994),

We have a system in which diverse categories of phenomena have the potential to develop simultaneously, and in which there is always a concern as to what constitutes a singular, cumulative, or collective phenomenon. Adding to this multiplicity, the group is a moving, evolving system, comprised of interlocking parts from which, predictably, emerges a catalytic process. The finality of this complexity is that the process and the group can never go back. (p. 7)

As well, the empirical journey toward understanding these process and outcome questions reflects the multiple perspectives of the researchers and the contexts of the specific groups involved. Understandably, the journey through this landscape has been neither direct nor systematic. Nevertheless, the effort has been constant and, today, presents the field with not only a clearer understanding of the effectiveness of group treatment and the processes involved but also more refined questions regarding the relationship of group processes to successful client change.

The purpose of this chapter is to provide a broad perspective of the group psychotherapy process and outcome research, identify the substantive components studied, and illustrate how these components have evolved or changed over time. Changes over the years can be seen not only in the focus (both content and population) and methodology taken by researchers but also in the results and conclusions derived from their analyses. First, we will describe the outcome and process findings from before 1990. Next, we will describe the recent outcome and process findings, including research on group structure, verbal interaction, therapeutic relationship, and therapeutic factors. Finally, we will provide commentary on the current state of the process-outcome literature as a whole.

Historical Perspective on Group Psychotherapy Process and Outcome Research

Outcome: Pre-1990s

Prior to 1960, the majority of the outcome research was based on case studies and anecdotal reports. Although authors voiced value for group treatment, they were aware of the difficulty of making conclusive statements regarding its comparative efficacy. The 1960s saw an increase in the use of more rigorous experimental methods, with results showing group therapy

in a strong complementary role to more robust therapies but only tentative support for it as an effective independent treatment. Research during this period focused primarily on institutional patients, limiting generalizability. During the 1970s, the results were more definitive, indicating that group treatment was more effective than control groups and comparable to individual and alternative psychological treatments, although there was some indication that other treatments might be better with certain disorders. Even though the conclusions were positive regarding outcome, the research designs were not able to pinpoint the therapeutic mechanisms that accounted for patient improvement, making the linking of process to outcome a future empirical issue. Studies in the 1980s were much more specific, particularly regarding patient populations and multiple comparison experiments. Group results from this decade showed significant client improvement over inert comparisons and comparable or superior outcomes to other active treatments, providing the strongest evidence to date for the efficacy of group treatment.

Capping this decade, researchers applied the new review procedure of meta-analysis to group studies. Results of seven reviews comparing group with individual treatment showed four with no reliable differences, one with a slight but nonsignificant difference favoring individual, and two indicating superior improvement when compared with individual treatment. Further analysis of these contradictory results led to an interpretation supportive of the concern regarding the importance of linking process with outcome. Studies in which group treatment was less successful than individual treatment found that no attempt was made by the researchers "to incorporate or capitalize on unique properties deemed therapeutic to the group format . . . most of the investigations that support the comparable efficacy of group therapy appear to highlight one or more of the unique properties of the group format" (Fuhriman & Burlingame, 1994, p. 16). More specifically, it appeared that researchers who paid attention to cohesion and group dynamics (e.g., member-to-member interaction patterns) reported more favorable outcomes than studies that used the group as a convenient and cost-effective vehicle for treatment delivery. In the latter case, the group treatment more closely approximated individual therapy in a group. The authors then concluded,

> Thus, when group is used as the format to capitalize on unique therapeutic factors operative in a group environment, it is associated with larger effects than when it is considered as a format to deliver a singular, specific type of treatment (e.g., cognitive-behavioral). (Fuhriman & Burlingame, 1994, p. 16)

The remaining question of outcome efficacy during these three decades is related to the efficacy of group therapy as an adjunct to other treatments. The accumulation of strong evidence over this period indicates superior outcome of combining both group and individual treatment in comparison to independent effects of either modality (cf. Bostwick, 1987; Freeman & Munro, 1988). With such strong support, empirical interest then shifted to a more specific focus on how best to combine group with alternate forms of treatment.

Process: Pre-1990s

The topical themes in the empirical process literature also evolved throughout the decades. Prior to the 1980s, these themes were considered in broad areas relating to models and approaches, client populations, the therapeutic relationship, curative factors, and the ecosystem (i.e., group-as-a-whole). Psychoanalytic and psychodrama received the most attention initially, but then empirical attention expanded to include other theoretical models. The approaches could broadly be categorized as intrapersonal, interpersonal, or integral (ecosystem) by nature and were applied and examined in separate fashion.

The empirical attention on client population shifted from general population observations (e.g., inpatient, specifically those who were chronic, psychotic, and schizophrenic) to much more specific combinations of client characteristics (e.g., Setting x Disorder x Age) in the 1980s. The therapeutic-relationship theme also evolved from a singular perspective of the patient's transference relationship to the therapist,

to other aspects of the client-therapist relationship (i.e., the therapeutic relationship), to a tripartite relationship in group (i.e., client-to-client, client-to-therapist, client-to-group relationships), indicating that in group treatment, the multiple relationships may be important and critical to the success of the client and the group.

One of the most-examined topics in group literature, *curative factors* (later designated as *therapeutic factors* or *mechanisms*) was built on a conceptual framework of the 1950s and 1960s and further facilitated by Irwin Yalom's development of a curative factor questionnaire (Crouch, Bloch, & Wanlass, 1994). In most studies, these 12 factors (e.g., cohesion, insight, catharsis, interpersonal input, etc.) were ranked in order of their helpfulness by group patients across multiple settings. Results confirmed that some factors (e.g., cohesion, catharsis, insight) are universally valued as helpful across populations, while others are valued by specific populations (e.g., instillation of hope and universality are more valued by inpatients than outpatients; cf. Crouch et al., 1994). The methodological limitation with therapeutic-factor research is the reliance on client self-report alone, leading some to question whether the complexity of the therapeutic process is being adequately captured (cf. Burlingame, MacKenzie, & Strauss, 2003).

Although some attention was given to issues relating to the ecosystem, or the group-as-a-whole, this area essentially remained untapped, at least to the degree necessary to discover the *interactive* processes involved in group treatment. Most representative of this ecological focus were studies that explored the development of the group over time and the verbal interaction of the members. Both group development and interaction highlight the moving and transitional aspects of the group and demonstrate the importance of moment-to-moment analyses, a difficult and tedious measurement undertaking. Nonetheless, the 1980s revealed that some interactional styles are more beneficial than others to personal, interpersonal, and group progress and that the leader's interactional style has the capacity to affect patient verbal style. Not only do leader and patient process variables interact, the ideal levels of several process variables appear to change over time. For example, the

Table 4.1   Quality of Evidence From 1990s to the Present: Group Treatment Outcome Research X
Patient Population

Use of Group Treatment	Very Good to Excellent	Promising to Good	Mixed to Untested
Group as primary	Bulimia nervosa Social phobia	Panic disorder Obsessive-compulsive disorder	Mood disorders Elders

Group as adjunct	SPMI—schizophrenia
	Medical—cancer
		Medical—HIV
		Personality disorder—
		  homogenous
		Sexual abuse victim
			Domestic violence
			Substance-related
			  disorders

ideal levels of interdependence, interpersonal intimacy, cohesion, autonomy, and openness all seem to change during the course of a group (MacKenzie, 1994).

Recent Outcome and Process Findings

To provide a broad perspective on the recent outcome and process literature, findings are organized using a two-dimensional scheme recently applied to the outcome literature (Burlingame et al., 2003). The first dimension, *How,* describes whether group treatment was used as the *primary* modality to address client goals or as an *augment* to other concurrent treatments. Examples of group as the primary are replete throughout the literature (e.g., depression), while group as augment is typically driven by setting (e.g., medical) or severity of the client disorder (e.g., schizophrenia).

The second dimension classifies *What* evidence is available using three categories. *Very Good to Excellent* evidence is associated with treatment gains supported by two or more randomized clinical trials (RCTs), or meta-analytic studies. *Promising to Good* evidence reflects limited RCT support or uncontrolled pre-post improvement. *Mixed* evidence represents literature where contradictory evidence abounds and patient improvement in active group treatment and control conditions is equivalent. If empirical examinations of existing protocols were not located, we classified them as *Untested.* In short, this dimension classifies available evidence based on both the quality/rigor of the research design (i.e., experimental vs. pre-post) and extant findings (e.g., consistent support of group efficacy over studies vs. contradictory findings from two or more studies).

Outcome Findings: 1990s to the Present

Table 4.1 reflects the crossing of the *How* and *What* dimensions and classifies the aggregate findings of more than 100 studies and 14 meta-analyses that tested the effectiveness of group treatment protocols (cf. Burlingame et al., 2003). Thirteen disorders or populations had a sufficient number of studies to summarize general trends. A heartening conclusion from Table 4.1 is that a sufficient number of studies exist that focus on answering the question: Which treatment works for whom and under what conditions? The available evidence suggests that the answer depends upon which population one examines.

Very Good to Excellent Evidence. Two disorders using group as primary had very good to excellent support in the literature. The effectiveness of group treatment for bulimia nervosa (BN) is buttressed by both meta-analytic (e.g., Hartmann, Herzog, & Drinkmann, 1992) and rigorous individual studies (e.g., Wilfley et al., 1993). The evidence for cognitive-behavioral protocols is excellent, although interpersonal models also show equivalent effects (Wilfley et al., 2003). In addition, those diagnosed with social phobia have also been found to be effectively treated with group protocols. Improvement has been associated with groups guided by cognitive-behavioral, exposure, and psychoeducational change strategies, although the evidence for cognitive-behavioral is particularly compelling.

Very good evidence for the effectiveness of group was found for two challenging populations. Schizophrenia illustrates the diversity of available group protocols. Specifically, four distinct group approaches exist in the literature: social skills, psychoeducation, cognitive information processing, and cognitive-behavioral. The most researched and effective approach is social skills groups, posting strong improvement on measures of social skills, assertiveness, and hospital discharge rates (e.g., Benton & Schroeder, 1990). Beneficial effects also have been associated with psychoeducational (e.g., Atkinson, Coia, Gilmour, & Harper, 1996), cognitive information processing rehabilitation (e.g., Spaulding, Reed, Sullivan, Richardson, & Weiler, 1999) and cognitive-behavioral groups (e.g., Wykes, Parr, & Landau, 1999). A similarly extensive literature exists for cancer patients with a wide array of protocols (e.g., psychoeducation, time-limited therapy, and support) that have shown improvements in emotional distress, coping, and other disease-related factors (e.g., quality of life, knowledge of disease, etc.).

Promising to Good Evidence. The majority of diagnostic groupings were classified in the promising to good evidence category. Models for panic disorder are most likely to be cognitive-behavioral, although others exist (supportive, behavioral, process), with client improvement found on a variety of symptoms compared with wait-list controls and group members at the beginning of treatment (e.g., Martinsen, Olsen, Tonset, Nyland, & Aarre, 1998; Scheibe, Albus, Walther, & Schmauss, 1993). Promising but less definitive evidence exists for the effectiveness of group (primarily behavior therapy) for obsessive-compulsive patients (e.g., Van Noppen, Pato, Marsland, & Rasmussen, 1998), due primarily to the paucity of experimental studies.

Tests of the effectiveness of groups for patients diagnosed with HIV/AIDS proliferated in the 1990s, with most addressing preventative goals with a psychoeducational framework. Prevention in this instance relates to the behavior that would infect others or exacerbate existing symptoms. Evaluative studies (e.g., Choi et al., 1996) showed group members decreasing at-risk behaviors (unprotected sex, number of sexual partners) and increasing protective factors (knowledge, coping, self-efficacy, treatment expectancies). Other models focusing on the psychological distress experienced by HIV/ AIDS patients demonstrated similar improvement (Kelly et al., 1993).

The strongest evidence for group treatment of personality disorders involves homogeneous groups, particularly those that focus on borderline personality disorders. A variety of models can be found in the literature (interpersonal, cognitive-analytic, experiential, dialectical behavior, psychodynamic, client centered), although many of the studies rely upon uncontrolled pre-post comparisons. Significant reductions in depression and suicidal tendencies and increases in interpersonal functioning and life satisfaction led in part to the *Promising* classification. Finally, much of the literature on group treatment for those victimized by sexual abuse consists of testimonials, untested protocols, and case studies rather than controlled investigations. Nonetheless, the most promising group of studies focus upon victims (adult women abused as children is the most frequently studied population) rather than perpetrators and child victims. The latter two populations are in need of further study in future research.

Mixed or Untested. The empirical legacy of group protocols for depressive and substance-related disorders is impressive, and in some cases, individual studies easily meet the criteria for good evidence. While nearly two thirds of the investigations dominated by cognitive-behavioral models produced beneficial effects for mood-disordered patients, four (Bright, Baker, & Neimeyer, 1999; Burlingame & Barlow, 1996; Kuhns, 1997; Ravindran et al., 1999) did not establish that group treatment provided any additional benefit beyond that realized by patients in control (placebo) or comparison groups (nonprofessional treatment). A similar pattern of results emerge with the substance-related studies. Formal change theories are effective (e.g., Kaminer, Burleson, Blitz, Sussman, & Rounsaville, 1998), but the differential effectiveness of group and individual is mixed (e.g., Weinstein, Gottheil, & Sterling, 1997), and improvement associated with 12-step groups rivals traditional group treatment (Crits-Christoph et al., 1999).

The absence of well-articulated models for victims and perpetrators of domestic violence, the paucity of controlled studies, and the weak support for effectiveness of existing protocols led to a mixed classification. Finally, there is an enormous literature associated with the group treatment of elders summarized by four meta-analyses that provide conflicting conclusions (Engels & Vermey, 1997; Gorey & Cryns, 1991; Pinquart, 1998; Scogin & McElreath, 1994). Two studies suggest that group protocols may be less effective than the individual format for this population, one suggests equivalence, and the last did not test this issue.

Process Findings: 1990s to the Present

We have argued elsewhere (Fuhriman & Burlingame, 1990) that the group format includes mechanisms of change (or processes) that add to the salubrious effects of formal change theories. In short, the interactive interpersonal environment of group provides unique and powerful change mechanisms. Although challenged by some (Hill, 1990), recent tests of this proposition have found support. For instance, Holmes and Kivlighan (2000) found that critical incidents reported by group clients reflected interpersonal and relationship mechanisms of change, while clients in individual treatment endorse intrapersonal mechanisms of change (i.e., insight, catharsis, problem solving). Complementary differences in client and therapist verbal behavior have also been found (Shectman & Ben-David, 1999). More specifically, in individual therapy, therapists disclosed more, and clients more frequently focused on problem solving, asking for advice, and dealing with the therapeutic relationship. In the group format, therapists were more directive, and clients focused more on the here and now.

SUBSTANTIVE PROCESS COMPONENTS

To highlight some of the unique features of the group format, this chapter focuses on four process components—structure, verbal interaction, therapeutic relationship, and therapeutic factors—that repeatedly appear in major reviews (Bednar & Kaul, 1994; Fuhriman & Burlingame, 1994). Although ordered along the same two dimensions used for the outcome, most studies are correlational, making causal conclusions impossible.

Structure

The structural features of the group format are defined by three processes: pregroup preparation, early in-session structure, and composition. Pregroup orientation (setting expectations, establishing group procedures, role preparation, skill building) has been positively associated with cohesion (Santarsiero, Baker, & McGee, 1995), members' satisfaction, and comfort with the group (Couch, 1995). While some (Bednar & Kaul, 1994) view pregroup preparation as one of the most potent factors in successful groups, others question the magnitude of effect claimed for pregroup preparation in the literature (Piper & Perrault, 1989). We view it as having the strongest empirical support of structural components (see Table 4.2).

Higher levels of structure in the early phases of a group experience are best articulated by the "risk, responsibility, and structure" model introduced nearly 30 years ago (Bednar, Melnick, & Kaul, 1974). These authors argued that structured activities in the early sessions led to lower levels of anticipatory anxiety and subsequently higher levels of interpersonal risk (e.g., member self-disclosure). While a number of studies support this model's predictions (Kaul & Bednar, 1994), the model is not supported in its entirety (e.g., Santarsiero et al., 1995). Alternative arguments (e.g., Dies, 1994) suggest that highly structured groups in general are related to good outcomes. The *Promising* rating (see Table 4.2) reflects historical findings, with recent literature moving it toward the *Mixed* category.

Knowledge regarding group composition resides primarily in the conceptual realm (Burlingame, Fuhriman, & Johnson, 2002). While some have advocated for making groups homogeneous in terms of gender (Wright & Gould, 1996) or members' ability to tolerate anxiety (Dacey, 1989), others promote heterogeneity to foster

Table 4.2   Quality of Evidence: Empirical Support Associated With Select Group Processes

Use of Group Treatment	Very Good to Excellent to Very Good	Promising to Good	Mixed to Untested
Group structure		Pregroup preparation Early group structure	Composition
Verbal interaction	Interpersonal feedback	Leader verbal style	Member self-disclosure
Therapeutic relationship	Alliance	Group climate	Cohesion
Therapeutic factors		Differential patient value X setting	Dynamic interplay

cohesion (De Bosset, 1991) or patient outcomes (Waltman & Zimpfer, 1988). In general, no clear empirical evidence exists to support either argument leading to the *Mixed* classification. However, one promising exception to this potpourri of findings comes from a recent meta-analysis of 111 studies (Burlingame, Fuhriman, & Mosier, 2003) that found greater improvement with homogeneous groups across a large number of studies. However, in this meta-analysis, setting (outpatient) and orientation (behavior therapy) also covaried with homogeneity, confounding a straightforward interpretation on the effect of composition.

Verbal Interaction

The interpersonal environment of the group is considered a powerful and unique vehicle for patient change (Yalom, 1995), and at least three aspects have been emphasized in the empirical literature: member and leader verbal style, member self-disclosure, and interpersonal feedback (see Table 4.2). Verbal style is a concrete manifestation of the group's interpersonal environment, and leaders are advised to carefully track its evolution (Fuhriman & Burlingame, 1994). Unfortunately, the different systems for tracking verbal interaction produce mixed findings that are challenging to integrate (Beck & Lewis, 2000). Nonetheless, there is limited correlational support to suggest that higher levels of patient improvement and cohesion can result when group interaction focuses on *member-member* and *member-group* relationship themes (Fuhriman, Seaman, Barlow, & Burlingame, 1999). However, style of interaction may also

matter, since member turn taking has been related to poorly functioning groups (Karterud, 1988) and leader directiveness and affiliation may result in higher levels of cohesion (Kivlighan, Mullison, Flohr, Proudman, & Francis, 1989). Although the diversity of methodologies makes integration of findings between studies nearly impossible, the consistency across studies led to the *Promising* classification.

The advent and ascendancy of more structured group protocols (cognitive-behavioral) have eclipsed the earlier import given to member self-disclosure. While disclosure continues to enjoy a high degree of theoretical importance in some group protocols, recent findings have produced mixed empirical support. The early literature found a positive association between outcome (Flowers, Booraem, & Hartman, 1981), interpersonal closeness (Bunch, Lund, & Wiggins, 1983), and self-disclosure. More recently, its relationship core processes (e.g., cohesion) have produced mixed results (Slavin, 1993, 1995), leading some (Crouch et al., 1994) to view it from a more conservative perspective.

Finally, giving and receiving interpersonal feedback has a long and substantial history as a unique process of the group format (Bednar & Kaul, 1994). It has been linked to increased motivation for change, greater insight into how one's behavior affects others, increased comfort with taking interpersonal risks, higher ratings of satisfaction with the group experience, and increased capacity for intimacy (Widra & Amidon, 1987). The literature on feedback is mature enough to yield empirically supported principles to guide clinical practice (see Morran,

Stockton, & Teed, 1998), making it one of the strongest process variables in the literature.

Therapeutic Relationship

Therapeutic relationships in group encompass multiple structural possibilities: member-member, member-leader, member-group, leader-group, and leader-leader relationships. In addition, there are multiple ways of looking at these relationships. A recent review of the group therapeutic relationship literature (Burlingame et al., 2002) identified the three most frequent constructs used to capture aspects of the therapeutic relationship in group treatment: group climate, cohesion, and alliance (see Table 4.2). The Group Climate Questionnaire (GCQ) is the dominant measure of group climate in the empirical literature. While the majority of studies (e.g., Castonguay, Pincus, Agras, & Hines, 1998) have found higher levels of member engagement to predict better member outcomes, results are not uniformly positive (e.g., MacKenzie & Tschuschke, 1993). Some have suggested that this may be because the GCQ asks about the behavior of "group members" rather than oneself, and it may be possible to see the other group members as working together and still not feel a part of the good things happening in the group (MacKenzie & Tschuschke, 1993). Recent research (Johnson, Burlingame, Olsen, Davies, & Gleave, 2002) also proposes changes in the factor structure of the instrument (e.g., the Engagement subscale combines items that tap a sense of belonging and work in the group into a single factor). The positive findings coupled with a clear direction for future research lead to our *Promising* classification.

A closely related construct, cohesion, has also had mixed success predicting outcome. This mixed success is undoubtedly linked to the multitude of measures in the literature. We (Burlingame et al., 2002) recently identified 23 different measures of cohesion in 31 studies. While higher levels of cohesion have been empirically linked to better outcomes (e.g., Tschuschke & Dies, 1994), other studies have found more tenuous links (Budman et al., 1989). The mixed findings and lack of conceptual and measurement clarity (cf. Burlingame, Kircher, & Taylor, 1994) lead to our mixed rating (see Table 4.2).

Finally, alliance in group psychotherapy can refer to alliances of group members with the group therapist or with one another (Glatzer, 1990). Group members' alliances with the therapist have consistently been found to predict better outcomes (e.g., Budman et al., 1989). Furthermore, at least one study (Marziali, Munroe-Blum, & McCleary, 1997) found that although cohesion and group alliance independently contributed to outcome, alliance appeared to account for more variance. The consistency of findings in this literature (cf. Burlingame et al., 2002) led us to rank alliance as one of the two strongest process variables (see Table 4.2).

Therapeutic Factors

Unraveling the therapeutic factors that thread group process continues to capture the attention of both clinicians and researchers. The main body of research has relied on Yalom's self-report instrument, which describes the value group members give to his therapeutic factors (instillation of hope, universality, imparting of information, altruism, recapitulation of primary family, development of socializing techniques, imitative behavior, interpersonal learning, cohesion, catharsis, existential factors; cf. Yalom, 1995). One study (Colijn, Hoencamp, Snijders, van der Spek, & Duivenvoorden, 1991) found that group members tended to value catharsis, self-understanding, interpersonal learning, and cohesion the most of the therapeutic factors, and to value family reenactment and identification the least. These results appeared to be the same across groups regardless of age, sex, treatment, or group type, and they are similar to those found by the majority of previous studies on therapeutic factors. Regrettably, the results typically are not related to outcome.

Other means of identifying therapeutic processes are strengthening this research area, most notably the inclusion of significant-event methodology. Using group member and therapist statements describing helpful and harmful events, Dierick and Litaer (1990) found content themes that overlapped the therapeutic factors of Yalom. These collapsed into three broad categories: relational climate and structural aspects of the group, specific interventions by group members and the therapist, and processes used by each group member (e.g., personal involvement, self-exploration, interpersonal exploration). Kivlighan, Multon, and Brossart (1996) report similar factors: relational-climate, other versus self-focus, emotional awareness-insight, and problem solving-behavior change.

Focusing on the moment-by-moment interaction, Hurley (1997) measured self and other acceptance and found positive relationships between aspects of leader and group climate that accelerated over time. Cohesion (e.g., acceptance, belonging) was found to be correlated with here-and-now (versus there-and-then) disclosure. These recent studies affirm the presence of therapeutic mechanisms and the necessity of connecting them to other features of the group (e.g., leadership, development). This study's more advanced methodology initiates a much-needed conceptual clarity to the therapeutic factor literature. We hope that improved instruments and sequential measurement will reap significant effects.

GENERAL REFLECTIONS

This broad perspective on outcome and process findings leads to three general observations with attendant recommendations. First, the group literature is in a much better position as it enters the new millennium, in contrast to reviewer conclusions a decade ago (e.g., Bednar & Kaul, 1994). Efficacious protocols are evident for specific populations and for different applications of group (primary & augment). Moreover, protocols classified within the *Promising* or *Mixed* categories outline the empirical work needed in the future. The evidence for the effectiveness of the group format has never been better, due primarily to the vast majority of recent group literature that focuses on tests of protocols for specific patient populations.

Parallel advances in the general psychotherapy literature have also created a new and compelling perspective for interpreting these positive developments. As empirically supported treatments have received greater attention in the past decade (Chambless & Hollon, 1998), researchers have carefully scrutinized factors that might explain the patient improvement associated with such (see

Lambert & Ogles, 2003). Over a decade ago, Crits-Christoph and colleagues (1991) showed that differences between individual therapists accounted for far more patient improvement than did the particular brand of treatment (e.g., cognitive-behavioral, psychodynamic, etc.). This viewpoint has been systematically studied by Wampold (2001), who recently declared that 9 times more of the variability in patient improvement is attributable to common factors across all treatments than the ingredients found in specific models of treatment (Hyun-nie & Wampold, 2001). We see no reason why Wampold's individually based research would not apply to group treatment. In fact, this research underscores the importance of specifying and studying the group properties and processes that may account for improvement—that is, ultimately account for client common factors in the group format.

Wampold's research provides evidence that experiments aimed at testing the efficacy of specific group treatment protocols can lead us back to the need for focused process studies, research that operationalizes and tests "common factors." Unfortunately, while the importance of process studies has grown, there has been a precipitous drop in the number of such studies being published in recent years (Burlingame et al., 2003). In retrospect, the emphasis on testing group outcome over process may be akin to "majoring in the minors." Although knowledge that a treatment works is essential, understanding the components of its effect may be more important (ie., indicator or mechanisms of change).

The second observation relates to the extant process literature. In our view, studies of the therapeutic relationship (alliance, cohesion, and climate) remain as one of the strongest areas of process evidence. This is noteworthy since the therapeutic relationship in the individual therapy literature appears in most operationalizations of the common factors (Weinberger, 1995) and continues to be highly predictive of outcome in general (Martin, Garske, & Davis, 2000). The indistinguishable definitions of constructs invoked to describe the therapeutic relationship in group therapy provide a clarion call for empirical effort that might clarify this conundrum of concepts.

Our final observation relates to a topic that has lost ground in the past decade of research:

process-outcome studies. The call for process-outcome research has been repeatedly issued by reviewers spanning decades of group research (cf. Burlingame et al., 1994). While there are stellar exceptions, the emphasis on outcome research over the past decade may have attenuated the number of such studies. We add our voice to past calls for more process-outcome studies that link group and theory-specific mechanisms of action to our ultimate goal, improving patient outcomes.

The group process and outcome literature has matured over the past decade. However, the oft-cited counsel to understand history to avoid repeating past mistakes seems to be a particularly apt warning for the group literature. If we do not heed past admonitions to conceptually and empirically focus on common and specific mechanisms of change, we will be doomed to repeat past mistakes and be left with empirical support for efficacious group protocols with little to no understanding regarding the underlying change mechanisms.

NOTE

1. We are aware of the active discussions regarding criteria for empirically supported treatments in the United States and evidence-based treatment in the United Kingdom and Germany. The unsettled nature of this debate led to our own criteria, which reflect our clinical and empirical understanding of the literature. The more liberal criteria have shortcomings (e.g., category overlap, reliability), but as we have argued elsewhere (Fuhriman & Burlingame, 1994), we believe the empirical group literature lags behind the individual psychotherapy literature and thus believe a more generous stance is appropriate.

REFERENCES

Atkinson, J., Coia, D. A., Gilmour, W. H., & Harper, J. P. (1996). The impact of education groups for people with schizophrenia on social functioning and quality of life. *British Journal of Psychiatry, 168,* 199-204.

Beck, A. P., & Lewis, C. M. (Eds.). (2000). The process of group psychotherapy: Systems for analyzing change. Washington, DC: American Psychological Association.

Bednar, R. L., & Kaul, T. J. (1994). Experiential group research: Can the cannon fire? In A. E. Bergin & S. L. Garfield (Eds.), *Handbook of psychotherapy and behavior change* (4th ed., pp. 631-663). New York: John Wiley.

Bednar, R., Melnick, J., & Kaul, T. (1974). Risk, responsibility and structure: Ingredients for a conceptual framework for initiating group therapy. *Journal of Counseling Psychology, 21,* 31-37.

Benton, M. K., & Schroeder, H. E. (1990). Social skills training with schizophrenics: A meta-analytic evaluation. *Journal of Consulting and Clinical Psychology, 58*(6), 741-747.

Bostwick, G. (1987). Where's Mary? A review of the group treatment dropout literature. *Social Work with Groups, 10*(3), 117-132.

Bright, J. I., Baker, K. D., & Neimeyer, R. A. (1999). Professional and paraprofessional group treatments for depression: A comparison of cognitive-behavioral and mutual support interventions. *Journal of Consulting and Clinical Psychology, 67*(4), 491-501.

Budman, S. H., Soldz, S., Demby, A., Feldstein, M., Springer, T., & Davis, S. (1989). Cohesion, alliance and outcome in group psychotherapy. *Psychiatry, 52,* 339-350.

Bunch, B. J., Lund, N. L., & Wiggins, F. K. (1983, May). Self-disclosure and perceived closeness in the development of group process. *Journal for Specialists in Group Work,* 59-65.

Burlingame, G. M., & Barlow, S. H. (1996). Outcome and process differences between professional and nonprofessional therapists in time-limited group psychotherapy. *International Journal of Group Psychotherapy, 46*(4), 455-478.

Burlingame, G., Fuhriman, A., & Johnson, J. (2002). Cohesion in group psychotherapy. In J. C. Norcross (Ed.), *A guide to psychotherapy relationships that work.* Oxford, England: Oxford University Press.

Burlingame, G., Fuhriman, A., & Mosier, J. (2003). The differential effectiveness of group psychotherapy: A meta-analytic perspective. *Group Dynamics: Theory, Research & Practice, 7*(1), 3–12.

Burlingame, G. M., Kircher, J. C., & Taylor, S. (1994). Methodological considerations in group psychotherapy research: Past, present, and future practices. In A. Fuhriman & G. M. Burlingame (Eds.), *Handbook of group psychotherapy: An empirical and clinical synthesis* (pp. 41-80). New York: John Wiley.

Burlingame, G. M., MacKenzie, K. R., & Strauss, B. (2003). Evidence-based small group treatments. In M. Lambert, A. E. Bergin, & S. L. Garfield (Eds.), *Handbook of psychotherapy and behavior change* (5th ed.). (pp. 647-696). New York: John Wiley.

Castonguay, L. G., Pincus, A. L., Agras, W. S., & Hines, C. E. (1998). The role of emotion in group cognitive-behavioral therapy for binge-eating disorder: When things have to feel worse before they get better. *Psychotherapy Research, 8,* 225-238.

Chambless, D., & Hollon, S. (1998). Defining empirically supported treatments, *Journal of Consulting and Clinical Psychology, 66*(1), 7-18.

Choi, K. H., Lew, S., Vittinghoff, E., Catania, J. A., Barrett, D. C., & Coates, T. J. (1996). The efficacy of brief group counseling in HIV risk reduction among homosexual Asian and Pacific Islander men. *AIDS, 10*(1), 81-87.

Colijn, S., Hoencamp, E., Snijders, H., van der Spek, M., & Duivenvoorden, H. (1991). A comparison of curative factors in different types of group psychotherapy. *International Journal of Group Psychotherapy, 41,* 365-378.

Couch, D. R. (1995). Four steps for conducting a pre-group screening interview. *Journal for Specialists in Group Work, 20,* 18-25.

Crits-Christoph, P., Baranackie, K., Kurcias, J. S., Beck, A. T., et al. (1991). Meta-analysis of therapist effects in psychotherapy outcome studies. *Psychotherapy Research, 1,* 81-91.

Crits-Christoph, P., Siqueland, L., Blaine, J., et al., (1999). Psychosocial treatments for cocaine dependence: National Institute on Drug Abuse Collaborative Cocaine Treatment Study. *Archives of General Psychiatry, 56*(6), 493-502.

Crouch, E., Bloch, S., & Wanlass, J. (1994). Therapeutic factors: Interpersonal and intrapersonal mechanisms. In A. Fuhriman & G. M. Burlingame (Eds.), *Handbook of group psychotherapy: An empirical and clinical synthesis* (pp. 269-315). New York: John Wiley.

Dacey, C. M. (1989). Inpatient group psychotherapy: Cohesion facilitates separation. *Group, 13,* 23-30.

De Bosset, F. (1991). Group psychotherapy in chronic psychiatric outpatients: A Toronto model. *International Journal of Group Psychotherapy, 41,* 65-78.

Dierick, P., & Litaer, G. (1990). In G. Litaer, J. Rombauts, & R. Van Balen (Eds.), *Client-centered and experiential psychotherapy in the nineties.* Leuven, Belgium: Leuven University Press.

Dies, R. (1994). Therapist variables in group psychotherapy research. In A. Fuhriman & G. M. Burlingame (Eds.), *Handbook of group psychotherapy: An empirical and clinical synthesis* (pp. 114-154). New York: John Wiley.

Engels, G. I., & Vermey, M. (1997). Efficacy of nonmedical treatments of depression in elders: A quantitative analysis. *Journal of Clinical Geropsychology, 3*(1), 17-35.

Flowers, J. V., Booraem, C. D., & Hartman, K. A. (1981). Client improvement on higher and lower intensity problems as a function of group cohesiveness. *Psychotherapy: Theory, Research, and Practice, 18,* 246-251

Freeman, C., & Munro, J. (1988). Drug and group treatments for bulimia/bulimia nervosa. *Journal of Psychosomatic Research, 32*(6), 647-660.

Fuhriman, A., & Burlingame, G. M. (1990). Consistency of matter: A comparative analysis of individual and group process variables. *The Counseling Psychologist, 18,* 6-63.

Fuhriman, A., & Burlingame, G. M. (1994). *Handbook of group psychotherapy: An empirical and clinical synthesis.* New York: John Wiley.

Fuhriman, A., Seaman, S. W., Barlow, S. H., & Burlingame, G. M. (1999, June). *Validating a behavioral measure of catharsis, cohesion, and insight in group therapy.* Paper presented at the International meeting of the Society for Psychotherapy Research, Braga, Portugal.

Glatzer, H. T. (1990). Psychoanalytic group psyc of group psychotherapy. In I. L. Kutash & A. Wolf (Eds.), *The group psychotherapist's handbook: Contemporary theory and technique* (pp. 46-60). New York: Columbia University Press.

Gorey, K. M., & Cryns, A. G. (1991). Group work as interventive modality with the older depressed client: A meta-analytic review. *Journal of Gerontological Social Work, 16*(1-2), 137-157.

Hartmann, A., Herzog, T., & Drinkmann, A. (1992). Psychotherapy of bulimia nervosa: What is effective? A meta-analysis. *Journal of Psychosomatic Research, 36*(2), 159-167.

Hill, C. E. (1990). Is individual therapy process really different from group therapy process? The jury is still out. *The Counseling Psychologist, 18,* 126-130.

Holmes, S., & Kivlighan, D. (2000). Comparison of therapeutic factors in group and individual treatment processes. *Journal of Counseling Psychology, 47,* 478-484.

Hurley, J. (1997). Interpersonal theory and measures of outcome and emotional climate in 111 personal develop groups. *Group Dynamics: Theory, Research, and Practice, 1*(1), 86-97.

Hyun-nie, A., & Wampold, B. (2001). Where oh where are the specific ingredients? A meta-analysis of component studies of counseling and psychotherapy. *Journal of Counseling Psychology, 48,* 251-257.

Johnson, J. E., Burlingame, G. M., Olsen, J., Davies, D. R., & Gleave, R. L. (2002, August). Clarifying relationships in group psychotherapy. Paper presented at the annual meeting of the American Psychological Association, Chicago, IL.

Kaminer, Y., Burleson, J. A., Blitz, C., Sussman, J., & Rounsaville, B. J. (1998). Psychotherapies for adolescent substance abusers: A pilot study. *The Journal of Nervous and Mental Disease, 186*(11), 684-690.

Karterud, S. (1988). The influence of task definition, leadership, and therapeutic style on inpatient group cultures. *International Journal of Therapeutic Communities, 9,* 231-247.

Kaul, T. J., & Bednar, R. L. (1994). Pretraining and structure: Parallel lines yet to meet. In A. Fuhriman & G. M. Burlingame (Eds.), *Handbook of group psychotherapy: An empirical and clinical synthesis.* New York: John Wiley.

Kelly, J. A., Murphy, D. A., Bahr, G. R., Kalichman, S. C., Morgan, M. G. Stevenson, L. Y., Koob, J. J., Brasfield, T. L., & Bernstein, B. M. (1993). Outcome of cognitive-behavioral and support group brief therapies for depressed, HIV-infected persons. *American Journal of Psychiatry, 150*(11), 1679-1686.

Kivlighan, D. M., Mullison, D. D., Flohr, D. F., Proudman, S., & Francis, A. M. (1989, August). *The interpersonal structure of "good" versus "bad" group counseling sessions.* Paper presented at the annual meeting of the American Psychological Association, New Orleans, LA.

Kivlighan, D. M., Multon, K. D., & Brossart, D. F. (1996). Helpful impacts in group counseling: Development of a multidimensional rating system. *Journal of Counseling Psychology, 43*(3), 347-355.

Kuhns, M. L. (1997). Treatment outcomes with adult children of alcoholics: Depression. *Advanced Practical Nursing Quarterly, 3*(2), 64-69.

Lambert, M., & Ogles, B. (2003). The efficacy and effectiveness of psychotherapy, In M. Lambert (Ed.), *Bergin & Garfield handbook of psychotherapy & behavior change* (pp. 139-193). New York: John Wiley.

MacKenzie, K. R. (1994). Group development. In A. Fuhriman & G. M. Burlingame (Eds.), *Handbook of group psychotherapy: An empirical and clinical synthesis* (pp. 223-268). New York John Wiley.

MacKenzie, K. R., & Tschuschke, V. (1993). Relatedness, group work, and outcome in long-term inpatient psychotherapy groups. *Journal of Psychotherapy Practice and Research, 2,* 147-156.

Martin, D., Garske, J., & Davis, M. (2000). Relation of the therapeutic alliance with outcome and other variables: A meta-analytic review. *Journal of Consulting and Clinical Psychology, 68,* 438-450.

Martinsen, E. W., Olsen, T., Tonset, E., Nyland, K. E., & Aarre, T. F. (1998). Cognitive-behavioral group therapy for panic disorder in the general clinical setting: A naturalistic study with 1-year follow-up. *Journal of Clinical Psychiatry, 59*(8), 437-442.

Marziali, E., Munroe-Blum, H., & McCleary, L. (1997). The contribution of group cohesion and group alliance to the outcome of group psychotherapy. *International Journal of Group Psychotherapy, 47,* 475-497.

Morran, D. K., Stockton, R., & Teed, C. (1998). Facilitating feedback exchange in groups: Leader interventions. *Journal for Specialists in Group Work, 23,* 257-268.

Pinquart, M. (1998). Wirkungen psychosozialer und psychotherapeutischer Interventionen auf das Befinden und das Selbstkonzept im höheren Erwachsenenalter B Ergebnisse von Meta-analysen. *Zeitschrift für Gerontologie und Geriatrie, 31,* 120-126.

Piper, W. E., & Perrault, E. L. (1989). Pretherapy preparation for group members. *International Journal of Group Psychotherapy, 39,* 17-34.

Ravindran, A. V., Anisman, H., Merali, Z., Charbonneau, Y., Telner, J., Bialick, R. J., Wiens, A., Ellis, J., & Griffiths, J. (1999). Treatment of primary dysthymia with group cognitive therapy and pharmacotherapy: Clinical symptoms and functional impairments. *American Journal of Psychiatry, 156*(10), 1608-1617.

Santarsiero, L. J., Baker, R. C., & McGee, T. F. (1995). The effects of cognitive pretraining on cohesion and self-disclosure in small groups: An analog study. *Journal of Clinical Psychology, 51,* 403-409.

Scheibe, G., Albus, M., Walther, A. U., & Schmauss, M. (1993). Gruppenpsychotherapie bei Patienten mit Panikstoerung und Agoraphobie [Group psychotherapy in patients with panic disorders and agoraphobia]. *Psychotherapie, Psychosomatik, Medizinische Psychologie, 43,* 238-244.

Scogin, F., & McElreath, L. (1994). Efficacy of psychosocial treatments for geriatric depression: A quantitative review. *Journal of Consulting and Clinical Psychology, 62*(1), 69-67.

Shechtman, Z., & Ben-David, M. (1999). Individual and group psychotherapy of childhood aggression: A comparison of outcomes and processes. *Group Dynamics: Theory, Research & Practice, 3*(4), 263-274.

Slavin, R. L. (1993). The significance of here-and-now disclosure in promoting cohesion in group psychotherapy. *Group, 17,* 143-150.

Slavin, R. L. (1995). "Here-and-now" and "there-and-then" disclosures on cohesion and on students' attitudes toward specific courses. *Psychological Reports, 76,* 111-121.

Spaulding, W. D., Reed, D., Sullivan, M., Richardson, C., & Weiler, M. (1999). Effects of cognitive treatment in psychiatric rehabilitation. *Schizophrenia Bulletin, 25*(4), 657-676.

Tschuschke, V., & Dies, R. R. (1994). Intensive analysis of therapeutic factors and outcome in long-term inpatient groups. *International Journal of Group Psychotherapy, 44,* 185-208.

Van Noppen, B. L., Pato, M. L., Marsland, R., & Rasmussen, S. A. (1998). A time-limited behavioral group for treatment of obsessive-compulsive disorder. *Journal of Psychotherapy Practice and Research, 7*(4), 272-280.

Waltman, D. E., & Zimpfer, D. G. (1988). Composition, structure, and duration of treatment: Interacting variables in counseling groups. *Small Group Behavior, 19,* 171-184.

Wampold, B. (2001). *The great psychotherapy debate: Models, methods & findings.* Mahwah, NJ: Lawrence Erlbaum.

Weinberger, J. (1995). Common factors are not so common: The common factors dilemma. *Clinical Psychology: Science & Practice, 2,* 45-69.

Weinstein, S. P., Gottheil, E., & Sterling, R. C. (1997). Randomized comparison of intensive outpatient vs. individual therapy for cocaine abusers. In E. Gottheil & B. Stimmel (Eds.), *Intensive outpatient treatment for the addictions* (pp. 41-56). New York: Haworth.

Widra, J. M., & Amidon, E. (1987). Improving self-concept through intimacy group training. *Small Group Behavior, 18,* 269-279.

Wilfley, D. E., Agras, W. S., Telch, C. F., Rossiter, E. M., Schneider, J. A., Cole, A. G., Sifford, L., & Raeburn, S. D. (1993). Group cognitive-behavioral therapy and group interpersonal psychotherapy for the nonpurging bulimic individual: A controlled comparison. *Journal of Consulting and Clinical Psychology, 61*(2), 296-305.

Wilfley, D. E., Welch, R. R., Stein, R. I., Spurrell, E. M., Cohen, L. R., Saelens, B. E., Dounchis, J. Z., Frank, M. A., Wiseman, C. V., & Matt, G. E. (2002). A randomized comparison of group cognitive-behavioral and group interpersonal psychotherapy for the treatment of overweight individuals with binge eating disorder. *Archives of General Psychiatry, 59*(8), 713-772.

Wright, F., & Gould, L. J. (1996). Research on gender-linked aspects of group behaviors: Implications for group psychotherapy. In B. DeChant (Ed.), *Women and group psychotherapy: Theory and practice* (pp. 333-350). New York: Guilford.

Wykes, T., Parr, A. M., & Landau, S. (1999). Group treatment of auditory hallucinations: Exploratory study of effectiveness. *British Journal of Psychiatry, 175,* 180-185.

Yalom, I. D. (1995). *The theory and practice of group psychotherapy* (4th ed.). New York: Basic Books.

Part II

BEST PRACTICES IN GROUPS

Introduction

MARIA T. RIVA

P art II of the handbook includes seven chapters that outline the best practices in group counseling and psychotherapy. Best practices are drawn from research, theory, and group counseling experience and are intended to provide group leaders and researchers with the most current and best practices in conducting group counseling and psychotherapy. In this section, the first four chapters are linked together by their focus on specific skills and interventions that are critical to effective group leadership. They take a closer look at specific leader interventions and behaviors and provide rich examples and recommendations for training group leaders: guidelines for choosing and using group activities; effective leader interventions around safety, encouraging participation, and group member feedback; and methods to process group material. The final three chapters take a more global perspective, outlining the best practices for measuring and assessing group

counseling and psychotherapy, the supervision of group leaders, and the ethical and legal guidelines for conducting effective groups.

Chapter 5, "An Overview of Current Research and Best Practices for Training Beginning Group Leaders," is written by Rex Stockton, D. Keith Morran, and Kenin Kreiger. They address the best practices for training beginning group leaders. This is a critical chapter because although training of group leaders is so essential for the practice of group counseling and psychotherapy, research in this area is limited. These authors not only review the research but also provide best practices based on many years of experience of training beginning group leaders.

Activities are commonly used in groups to activate the group, encourage members to take risks, and provide a learning experience that moves the group members. Group activities can be potent learning tools. Chapter 6, "Conducting a Group: Guidelines for Choosing and Using Activities," by James Trotzer, addresses the many considerations in selecting and using group activities effectively and ethically.

D. Keith Morran, Rex Stockton, and Martyn Whittingham focus on specific leader interventions that are related to more effective groups and better group member outcomes. Chapter 7, "Effective Leader Interventions for Counseling and Psychotherapy Groups," addresses leader interventions that are critical at different stages of the group. For example, the chapter outlines leader interventions that need to occur during the beginning stage of the group, such as those that promote safety, provide reassurance, encourage participation, and help group members feel connected with each other.

In Chapter 8, Donald Ward and Michele Litchy took on a complex task of defining group process, describing how it became integral to group counseling and psychotherapy, and providing best practice guidelines for how to effectively process group material. In "The Effective Use of Process in Groups," the authors illuminate their discussion of group process with many examples and conclude the chapter with 18 recommendations for group processing.

Assessing the progress of individual members and of the group as a whole is often an afterthought or neglected altogether for those who conduct group counseling and psychotherapy in the field. In Chapter 9, "Measures of Group Process, Dynamics, Climate, Leadership Behaviors, and Therapeutic Factors: A Review," Janice DeLucia-Waack and Karen Bridbord direct group leaders and group researchers to reliable and valid measures that can be used in screening and the selection of group members, the assessment of group leadership behaviors and skills, the assessment of group climate and therapeutic factors, and the ratings of in-session group behavior.

Chapter 10, "Effective Supervision of Group Leaders: Current Theory, Research, and Implication for Practice," authored by Janice DeLucia-Waack and James Fauth, reviews theory, research, and best practices related to the supervision of group leaders. They include best practices for different formats of supervision delivery and discuss the development of individual group leaders and the development of the coleadership relationship, two critical considerations for supervisors.

The section on best practices concludes with Chapter 11, written by Lynn Rapin, titled "Guidelines for Ethical and Legal Practice in Counseling and Psychotherapy Groups." In this chapter, she highlights key ethical definitions, decision-making models, and the best practice guidelines and their application to group counseling and psychotherapy. This chapter provides the most current and best practices for conducting groups ethically and can be a resource for group facilitators and researchers as they contemplate ethical decisions.

5

AN OVERVIEW OF CURRENT RESEARCH AND BEST PRACTICES FOR TRAINING BEGINNING GROUP LEADERS

REX STOCKTON

Indiana University

D. KEITH MORRAN

Indiana University

Purdue University at Indianapolis

KENIN M. KRIEGER

Indiana University

The origin of formal group counseling and psychotherapy is often traced to 1905, when Joseph Pratt, a physician, used a group or "class" format to assist patients with tuberculosis (Gazda, Ginter, & Horne, 2001). Throughout the remainder of the 20th century, groups emerged as an increasingly popular mode of intervention in psychotherapy and counseling settings. Today, group methods are popular across a wide variety of settings to assist clients who present with a diverse range of goals and concerns.

Group counseling is generally considered to be a treatment mode that is equal in effectiveness to individual counseling (Fuhriman & Burlingame, 1994; Kivlighan, Coleman, & Anderson, 2000; McRoberts, Burlingame, & Hoag, 1998). The effectiveness of group counseling, combined with its economical advantages, have made it an increasingly important treatment format in this age of managed care and third-party payments (Greene, 2000). However, despite the popularity of group work, research studies that focus on specific mechanisms that lead to positive change

---

Author's Note: Special appreciation is given to Martyn Whittingham for his valuable assistance with this chapter.

have been limited, and even less research has specifically addressed the role and function of the group leader in promoting desirable client outcomes.

The development of any training in group counseling and therapy that does not provide group leaders with a solid understanding of the dynamics that make groups therapeutic is a futile effort. For example, the best technically developed training package that fails to prepare group leaders to understand and respond to the unique needs of their groups at various developmental stages misses a critical point. Successful training programs must enable trainees to gain a thorough understanding of group processes, how these processes relate to outcomes, and how the leader may intervene to influence these dynamics. The importance of a research base to provide guidance for leadership training cannot be overemphasized. The purpose of this chapter is to review the research, models, and best practices related to training beginning group leaders. Training models and methods need to be informed by the research on effective group leadership, and therefore the first section will review the existing knowledge base in this area. The second section will look at existing models, including those focused on group process, skills acquisition, and a combination of the two. After reviewing the three approaches, a model that attempts to incorporate best practices across all three approaches is presented. A final section looks at professional standards and the potential ethical dilemma of dual relationships that often arises in the training of group leaders.

Before focusing on specific training approaches, it is important to review the existing knowledge base in this area. The next section of this chapter will review literature both on topics of counselor training and others related to it.

RESEARCH ON GROUP LEADERSHIP

In 1980, Stockton noted that while growth in the group work literature had been impressive, literature on the training of group leaders was not extensive. In his review, he concluded that most of the literature concerning the supervision of group leaders was anecdotal and focused on global concepts. Although there has been progress in this area, unfortunately, more than two decades later, this conclusion is still largely accurate.

Not surprisingly, there are a variety of approaches to research. It is beyond the boundaries of this chapter to hold an extended discussion on methodology, but it is important to note that researchers have most frequently used experimental and quasi-experimental designs that attempt to control for extraneous variables when researching outcomes of deliberate interventions. Thus, if it can be demonstrated statistically that the intervention has had an effect, conclusions can then be drawn and generalizations (with appropriate caveats) made. The Kivlighan et al. (2000) review provides good examples of studies of this type of outcome research as well as process research, which will be discussed next.

Because of the complexity, it is important for researchers to use a wide variety of approaches to capture "truth"; however, researchers have to keep in mind Polkinghorne's (1983) comments that "knowledge is understood to be the best understanding that we have been able to produce thus far, not a statement of what is ultimately real" (p. 2). Let us now focus on various studies that have relevance to the training of group leaders.

PROCESS AND OUTCOME RESEARCH ON GROUP LEADERSHIP AS A FOUNDATION FOR TRAINING

It is our belief that it is important to train leaders in efficacious behaviors. In an early study, Powdermaker and Frank (1953) used a form of process research in which segments from the written narratives of each group session were selected on the bases of what were believed to be the cause-and-effect elements of therapeutic significance. By comparing segments that had similar antecedents but different endings, they were able to make inferences about process elements that were positively related to change. They concluded that the ability of group leaders to face attack from group members without being defensive was the key factor in distinguishing episodes that were successful from those that were judged to be unsuccessful. This point has often been suggested, but this was the first research to support the common belief that group leaders must be able to assume a nondefensive stance when confrontation occurs in the group.

A later, but still early, systematic study of group leadership by Lieberman, Yalom, and Miles (1973) illustrated outcome research. They identified four styles of leadership, including executive function, emotional stimulation, caring, and meaning attribution. *Executive function* refers to a range of activities, including limit setting, managing time, establishing group norms, and other group maintenance functions. *Emotional stimulation* puts emphasis on the members' expressing feelings and revealing their personal attitudes and beliefs. This style of leadership encourages frequent participation as well as challenging and confronting group members at a higher level than other styles. Leaders who exhibit a *caring* style demonstrate warmth and a concern for group members. They emphasize feedback exchange and provide praise and encouragement. Finally, *meaning attribution* refers to the style of leadership that is characterized by interpreting and providing frameworks for the change process.

According to Lieberman et al. (1973), the most effective leadership style consists of leaders "who are moderate in Stimulation, high in Caring, utilize Meaning-Attribution, and are moderate in expression of Executive Functions" (p. 240). Meaning attribution emerged as an especially important aspect of this research. This leadership style highlights the importance of a cognitive element within group counseling. By attending to this element, leaders and members are able to make sense of what is occurring in the group and to consider implications for members both within and outside the group setting. Furthermore, this study demonstrated that there are qualities of leadership that are detrimental to the group as well as qualities that are beneficial. Less effective leaders in the Lieberman et al. (1973) study are "very low or very high in Stimulation, low in Caring, do very little Meaning-Attribution, and display too little or too much Executive behavior" (p. 240). Thus, it becomes important to identify leader behaviors that when used appropriately, will be efficacious (Fuhriman & Burlingame, 1990).

While both the Powdermaker and Frank (1953) and Lieberman et al. (1973) studies can be criticized today because of their relatively unsophisticated methodology, they nevertheless have influenced practice and have provided a format for other studies to follow. In two comprehensive reviews, Dies (1983, 1994) highlighted the results of studies that make evident the importance of a positive therapist-client relationship. He cites investigations that addressed open-ended or "nonmanualized" leadership approaches that correlated with process-outcome variables. Included in this are important aspects of the therapeutic change process, including providing a context or framework that is meaningful for clients, having the proper amount of structure in the therapeutic sessions as it relates to group members' clinical problems, and ensuring a safe climate for change. These leadership styles can promote the therapeutic conditions for productive member interactions and lead to positive treatment outcomes.

Fuhriman and Burlingame (1990) also noted the importance of the therapeutic relationship, stressing its complexity. They include the therapist, group members, and members' interactions as well as in-therapy feelings, attitudes, and behaviors. They suggest that the therapeutic relationship includes the alliance or bond, which can be facilitated through therapeutic interventions, and therapeutic factors, such as processes, which contribute to overall clinical change. Although this is one of the most recent major contributions in the area of group work, other researchers in the field have also commented on the role of the leader in group counseling.

Based on a long career as a researcher as well as clinician, Yalom (1995) provided a clear description of the group leader's purpose in therapy. He described an effective leader as one who allows group members to interact with each other, thereby acknowledging the importance of naturally occurring therapeutic forces. Thus, the leader's role is to aid the group in the maximization of these therapeutic forces through the use of specific interventions and techniques at appropriate times during the course of the group. Dies (1983), after reviewing a large body of literature, similarly concluded that while the role of the leader is important, interaction among group members has the most impact on individual change. Therefore, a critical task of the leader is to encourage and facilitate meaningful member interaction. Another article by Dies (1994) outlined a summary of leadership and group research that sheds light on the fact that certain therapeutic elements, such as the need for leaders to provide a climate for change, to define treatment goals, and to recognize the impact of client behaviors, all provide some answers as to what is occurring therapeutically in the group.

Group cohesion seems to be an important foundational element to a successful group experience. Once it is established, leaders may then be able to develop other therapeutic factors that require more member risk taking, including catharsis and insight-oriented elements. Also, group cohesion and the working alliance seem to be closely related elements of therapeutic change within groups. Kivlighan et al. (2000) discussed the research on leadership styles and concluded that less controlling leaders tended to have more cohesive groups. One caveat to this finding pertains to myriad variables and therapeutic elements that contribute to an overall successful group. Any one element contributes to a partial understanding but does not describe the entire picture.

One area of obvious importance is the *cognitions* of the group leader as they choose to use any particular intervention, understanding that they have a great variety of possibilities. It also follows that making one intervention may preclude being able to make another. Thus, it is important to examine the cognitions of group leaders as they choose their interventions. In individual counseling research, Morran, Kurpius, and Brack (1989) concluded that counselor and client cognitions affect the behavior of both the counselor and the client and also affect the outcomes of therapy. In a later study, Hiebert, Uhlemann, Marhsall, and Lee (1998) found that increased levels of negative therapist self-talk were related to increased anxiety and decreased effectiveness of therapist interventions. Unfortunately, there is only a small base of research related to the cognitions of group counselors; however, there is a growing interest.

Kivlighan and Quigley (1991) found that the conceptualizing of group process by experts was significantly more complex than that of inexperienced leaders; however, the study did not directly examine the cognitions of individual leaders. Nutt-Williams and Hill (1996) determined that negative self-talk by group leaders was related to leaders' perceiving group members as being critical of their performance.

Hines, Stockton, and Morran (1995) conducted a study that examined the cognitions of novice and expert group leaders. After viewing several video vignettes, leader cognitions were recorded and sorted into 17 thought categories. It was found that two of the cognitively complex categories, group process and internal questioning regarding member interpretation, accounted for 56% of the variance in leader experience level.

Several other studies are part of an overall research effort by Stockton and Morran in the identification of leader cognitions. These studies are under way or are very near completion. It is hoped that these and others will ultimately result in more definitive knowledge concerning this research area. Ultimately (given enough research and development), it is possible to assist novices as they are contemplating interventions. Of course, this possibility is a long way from fruition today.

An additional skill that is important for the group leader to be able to facilitate and manage is *interpersonal feedback*. Feedback that occurs between members of a group is essential for both group development and the interpersonal growth of the members. The self-reflection and insight that is promoted through feedback exchange allows members to better understand themselves and what is necessary for personal growth and behavior change (Morran, Robison, & Stockton, 1985; Morran, Stockton, Cline, & Teed, 1998; Stockton & Morran, 1981).

Feedback occurs when both members and leaders share, with each other, their personal reactions and insights about one another. Morran et al. (1998) reviewed a series of studies on feedback exchange and concluded that in early sessions, positive feedback should be emphasized, with a balancing of both corrective and positive occurring in later sessions. When feedback is delivered, a positive-corrective or positive-corrective-positive sequence of delivery is recommended. These exchanges should focus on observable and specific behaviors, while considering the readiness and openness of the receiver. Last, group leaders should also model feedback exchange to group members as they encourage them to engage in the process. The process of feedback exchange affords members with the opportunity to view their behavior from new perspectives and to make meaningful behavior change in the context of the group, thereby ideally promoting the transfer of this interpersonal insight into everyday life. Group leaders should therefore be knowledgeable about the role of feedback exchange as an underlying potentially therapeutic factor if done properly.

MODELS FOR LEADER TRAINING

It is important to note that standards and general guidelines for the training of group leaders have been developed by organizations such as the Association for Specialists in Group Work (ASGW, 2000), the Council for Accreditation of Counseling and Related Educational Programs (CACREP, 2001), and the American Group Psychotherapy Association (AGPA). Within the training standards of ASGW, basic competencies have been explicated that include both core group competencies and advanced group competencies (Conyne et al. 1992; Conyne, Wilson, Kline, Morran, & Ward, 1993). These standards suggest that knowledge and skill development should proceed from basic group work proficiency toward expertise required for specialty groups. They also recommend that training experiences focus on three areas: knowledge competencies, skill competencies, and clinical experience competencies.

The training of group leaders has typically been conceptualized across three domains, including group process, skill acquisition, and a combination of the two (Robison, Jones, & Berglund, 1996). The *group process model* of training emphasizes the importance of a process-oriented approach. This viewpoint is represented in the work of Yalom and his colleagues (Lieberman et al., 1973; Yalom, 1995). This process orientation asserts that specific therapeutic elements have been found to have a positive impact on outcome, thus students should first understand what occurs in groups and subsequently learn what to do as group leaders.

While Yalom (1995) notes the importance of didactic and methodological readings, he emphasizes in leadership training that the neophyte have an opportunity to serve, in effect, an apprenticeship with more experienced clinicians. He also recommends postsession meetings to give feedback, providing trainees with a group member experience and teaching trainees to maintain a here-and-now, interactional focus.

DeLucia, Bowman, and Bowman (1989) supported the notion of having trainees participate as group members in their early training. They contend that the transfer of knowledge from supervised group experiences can enhance the identification by the trainees of process level issues in the group. By clarifying these process issues, a trainee's self-confidence and intervention skills are increased.

Corey and Corey (2002), in their model, highlight the importance of focusing on three domains, which include thinking, feeling, and behaving. They begin their instruction with an experiential theme-oriented class (Corey, 2001). At each stage of the group process, the leader may focus on the thinking, feeling, and behaving of group members, while using an existential approach that consists of individual choice and responsibility. Finally, they conclude by describing the importance of fostering cohesion and trust in the group, as well as client readiness, when choosing interventions.

Skill acquisition approaches emphasize the importance of acquiring intervention behaviors that are specific to group counseling. The student is taught selected interventions as they pertain to member behavior and interpersonal issues that are occurring in the group. Skill-based approaches have been successfully used to prepare counselors in individual psychotherapy since the 1960s (Baker, Daniels, & Greeley, 1990; Ivey, 1994). Supporters of this approach within the group leader training area include Harvill, Masson, and Jacobs (1983), who adopted Ivey's microcounseling approach to training leaders. First, students observe the skill to be learned, through videotape or live interaction, and then practice the skill.

Smaby, Maddux, Torres-Rivera, and Zimmick (1999) outlined their model, called the skilled group counseling training model (SGCTM). This model focuses on "deliberately and systematically teaching group counselors both low-level and high-level skills, particularly decision-making and contracting skills for taking action" (p. 153). Therefore, students who experience their 36-hour training sequence are taught exactly how to apply general techniques in a group format through the use of both basic and higher-level counseling skills. They contend that the students who are in this program are better able to adapt to counseling situations with live clients. There is only one study reported thus far, but it shows promise.

Rather than using role play, Harvill et al. (1983); Toth, Stockton, and Erwin (1998); and Toth and Stockton (1996) involved students in brief small-group experiences. These small-group experiences differ from role play in that students do not have scripted scenarios to discuss, but instead engage in nonthreatening interaction that begins to activate the dynamic group process. Experiences such as these provide students with the security of a laboratory environment while giving them an interpersonal experience that simulates a real group session. Experiences such as these may prove to be an important aspect of skill acquisition (Toth et al., 1998).

While learning microskills, therapeutic conditions, and the components of effective leadership, the didactic components of training may overlook organizing such valuable skills and processes into an overall conceptual framework. By providing students with an overall understanding of the role of the leader that addresses the importance of the therapeutic conditions and how to facilitate such conditions, in addition to basic definitions and simulations, students will begin to understand the complexity of group processes and how to positively affect treatment outcomes at each stage of the group.

It is important to note that in practice, didactic knowledge, the group process (including experiential components), or skill acquisition approaches are not solely focused on by most training programs. Rather, they differ in terms of the degree to which they focus on these areas. Other theorists have stressed a need to combine process and skill-based approaches into a single integrated theoretically driven training model (Stockton, 1992). This speaks to the importance of using a combination of approaches in the training of group leaders.

Caffaro (2001) describes an integrated development sequence for group therapy, which begins with an initial 9 weeks of dyadic instruction as well as a "learning group" experience. Students progress into another 9-week segment, an in-class process group with the instructor providing consultation. This approach outlines the importance of developing a basic understanding about the group as well as the importance of participating in an experiential component in training.

Stockton (1992) proposed that instruction and training for group leaders should focus on these same three related dimensions: (a) perceiving, (b) selecting, and (c) risking. Though presented as separate training steps, an important caveat to this model is the understanding that this process, in actuality, is nonlinear and overlapping. The components are viewed as instructional targets that must be attended to within each didactic or experiential training activity. The processes of helping trainees learn to effectively perceive group dynamics, select appropriate interventions, and develop the courage to actually intervene in a group situation, for example, are recycled over and over as the trainee progresses toward new or more advanced skills.

The model assumes that group leaders begin with a basic understanding of individual counseling and related knowledge areas that are typically taught in counselor education programs. The importance of then building conceptual maps on top of these basic competencies and prior experiences is crucial. Although students may be eager to learn techniques, a sound grasp of schemata to understand groups and group dynamics is also important. Therefore, exploring, through didactic and other means, group dynamics, therapeutic factors, and other core principles that underlie all groups is essential.

The next step is to address techniques and microskills that are specific group interventions. These should include areas such as feedback, processing, protecting, and blocking. At this point, it is also important to reintegrate theory to allow the techniques to rest upon a solid foundation, allowing for later appropriate, purposeful selection. Without this integration of the two, choice of technique becomes problematic, and leaders end up making arbitrary choices in selecting interventions. Thus, theory helps inform the conceptual base, which allows leaders to select appropriate interventions.

An important thing to understand about beginning group leaders is that with this kind of learning comes accompanying anxiety. Dreyfus and Dreyfus (1986) highlighted the fact that in mastering any area, individuals go through several stages of cognitive and emotional development, each of which has its own process. Part of the process of mastering group leadership skills is the reduction of anxiety in those who have reached a point in training and experience, so they can appropriately select interventions.

The idea of leading a group is a very intimidating one for most neophytes. Instructors should be aware of this normal level of anxiety. To meet this need, students are provided the opportunity to discuss and practice specific leader intervention skills within the safety of small student groups. These small groups are used to engage students in discussing their apprehensions about being a group leader while also providing experience as a group member. As a parallel process, another key component of this training model is the supervised leadership experience that involves the student actually leading or coleading a group. This experience typically occurs in an advanced group course or as part of a practicum experience and includes observation by a supervisor, who provides immediate feedback upon completion of each session.

Stockton and Toth (1996) emphasize that trainees' ability to perceive group dynamics, select appropriate interventions, and risk making interventions are inextricably intertwined in both practice and training. For example, as trainees read and discuss the elements of group process, they can also be exposed to a wide range of leader interventions that are designed to influence group development. Such knowledge, in turn, can increase trainees' confidence that they can effectively lead a group. Similarly, classroom groups can offer an opportunity for trainees to discuss their anxieties about leading a group as well as help them crystallize the understanding of group processes that were acquired through reading and discussion. Having considered a variety of comprehensive models, it is now important to take these models and apply them within the context of the constraints of academic training programs.

As was noted earlier, significant gaps still exist on the best methods for training both beginning and advanced group leaders. However, the research findings and training models reviewed in this chapter do suggest a number of elements and activities that should be considered in designing a group leader training approach. However, it is important to remember that novice leaders are not "empty vessels" who simply need to absorb knowledge and experiences. Before developing a curriculum for leadership, instructors should pay attention to general principles of learning as well as the emotional aspects associated with acquiring new knowledge.

Even though theorists sometimes differ on which aspects of training are most significant, there is still convergence on what are considered to be the basic training components for group counselors; these include (a) theoretical and practical knowledge through the accumulation of didactic material, (b) opportunities to observe groups in action and to learn and practice specific group skills before actually leading a group, (c) participation in a personal growth group experience to promote personal development and to provide trainees with the opportunity to observe group development from a members' perspective, and (d) practice in leading or coleading a group under close supervision (Stockton & Toth, 1996).

While there is general agreement about the necessary components for group leader instruction, there are differences in emphasis. At this point in time, we simply don't have answers to the proper sequencing of (didactic) information and experiential learning. Clearly, leaders benefit by having comprehensive knowledge about what goes on in groups, thereby allowing them to make appropriate interventions. Some of this will be gained through didactic means, and some will be gained through practice, whether it is simulated or in an actual group. There are a number of issues that confront those who supervise experiential group training. The one most frequently discussed is the problem of dual relationship when a supervisor of an experiential group has the responsibility of evaluating the trainee (Anderson, Gariglietti, & Price, 1998; Gumaer & Martin, 1990; Lloyd, 1990; Merta & Sisson, 1991). The next section will discuss this dilemma in detail and provide possible solutions.

ETHICAL DILEMMAS IN EXPERIENTIAL GROUPS

The current ASGW Professional Standards for Training of group workers (2000), which are based on the 1994 CACREP standards, require that "Core training shall include a minimum of 10 clock hours (20 clock hours recommended), observation of and participation in a group experience as a group member and/or as a group leader" ("Experiential Requirements" section). Consistent with CACREP standards for accreditation, the supervised experience provides the student with direct experiences as a participant in a small group and may be met either in the basic course in group theory and practice or in a specially conducted small group designed for the purpose of meeting this standard (CACREP, 1994, Standard II.D). In arranging for and conducting this group experience, care must be taken by program faculty to assure that the American Counseling Association (ACA) ethical standard for dual relationships and ASGW standards for best practice are observed.

Thus, as can be seen, there is always a fine line between providing for experiential activities and safeguarding against learning information that may be used in an evaluative capacity. In commenting on this, Lloyd (1990) stated, "If participating in counseling demonstrations, group activities and supervision experiences (which include some elements of counseling) are the best training methods available, should the student be denied this opportunity because of the possibility of a dual relationship ethical violation?" Ethical guidelines as they apply to this issue are, without doubt, extremely complex. This type of training has similarities with the role of counselor-educator as a clinical supervisor, whether it be individual or group counselor training. Both roles require constant monitoring of boundaries, dual relationships, and maneuvering through the fine distinctions that may become blurred. It is critically important that those in a position of power (by definition supervisors) understand that they have special ethical obligations to adhere to so that training opportunities will be ethical and efficacious.

The ACA standards (2001), particularly Standard F.3.b on self-growth experiences, state that "Evaluative components of experiential training experiences explicitly delineates predetermined academic standards that are separate and do not depend on the student's level of self-disclosure." Some of the dilemmas in this situation can be resolved. Forester-Miller and Duncan (1990) suggest four possible solutions. First, there is the possibility of using students who are post-master's as supervisors (the implication here is that these students would not be in a power position). Second, the instructor may use a system in which the students make observations about the group process they have taken part in and use numbers as identification on the written assignment. Third, instructors require trainees to participate in a counseling group run by a group leader external to the training program. Fourth, they suggest using role play.

Merta, Wolfgang, and McNeil (1993) offer other alternatives, including simulated exercises, having a self-directed group, and having a leader observe but not lead a group. Instructors may also choose to use group leadership training videos whereby after viewing, students can actively participate in discussions. The first author of this chapter often focuses on specific vignettes after the students have had the chance to view an entire videotape. There are a number of group leader training videotapes available. ASGW has sponsored several of these. Videotapes can be purchased through the ACA or commercial publishers. It is most important that students do have numerous opportunities to interact with others regarding the various roles that are present in actual counseling groups. This may be achieved through small group simulations, class discussions, and other didactic materials. What is important is that students feel comfortable with themselves and in their interactions with others. Group experiences can enhance this and should be encouraged in a variety of ways.

CONCLUSION

Those designing group-training curricula are also faced with limitations, including resources, time, and others, which vary by program. It is important for instructors to realize that effective group leadership will not be taught in a one-semester course. However, having only one course can provide very effective group leader instruction. It depends on how the rest of the curriculum is constructed and sequenced and what other opportunities present themselves to the beginning leader. Depending on the resources, both human and material instruction can address a variety of approaches that will help to ensure that best practices are incorporated into leadership training. Further research may well reveal an "ideal" method for constructing curricula; however, the vagaries of real-world constraints will always impinge on these and continue the need for reflexive and adaptive planning. The concept of multiple means to achieve the same end is an important concept.

Although this chapter has focused on training beginners in group leadership skills, there is also clearly a need for a focus on how to move from beginner status to intermediate and advanced levels of practice. These training experiences should allow for the chance to develop specialized skills, techniques, and theory bases that encourage trainees to both deepen and broaden their skill base. For example, developing support groups for adolescents or addictions groups requires integration of specialized skill and knowledge bases to overlay onto preexisting conceptual schemata.

Therefore, to develop and work toward expert status, trainees should also be moved toward a model in which they have opportunities for informed, reflective practice. The need for supervisory feedback to help integrate new knowledge bases with underlying conceptual bases is arguably the most important piece of the process of moving to expert status. Without this reflection and questioning, group leaders run the risk of falling into conceptual and cognitive ruts that result in inflexible and unresponsive practice. Without opportunities to learn from emotional and cognitive responses to new situations and ways to integrate previous schemas, the dangers of stagnation are clear.

REFERENCES

American Counseling Association (ACA). (2001). *ACA code of ethics and standards of practice.* Alexandria, VA: Author.

Anderson, R. D., Gariglietti, K. P., & Price, G. (1998). A model for training group counselors. (Report No. CG-028-412). Lawrence: University of Kansas. (ERIC Document Reproduction Service No. ED 420 817)

Association for Specialists in Group Work (ASGW). (2000). Association for Specialists in Group Work: Professional standards for the training of group workers. *The Journal for Specialists in Group Work, 25,* 327-342.

Baker, S., Daniels, T. G., & Greeley, A. T. (1990). Systematic training of graduate-level counselors: Narrative and meta-analytic review of three major programs. *The Counseling Psychologist, 18,* 355-421.

Caffaro, J. V. (2001, August). *Group therapy training in a doctoral program.* Unpublished paper presentation at the American Psychology Association, San Francisco, CA.

Conyne, R. K., Dye, H. A., Kline, W. B., Morran, D. K., Ward, D. E., & Wilson, F. R. (1992). Context for revising the Association for Specialists in Group Work training standards. *The Journal for Specialists in Group Work, 17,* 10-11.

Conyne, R. K., Wilson, F. R., Kline, W. B., Morran, D. K., & Ward, D. E. (1993). *Training group workers: Implications of the new ASGW training standards for training and practice* (4th ed.). Pacific Grove, CA: Brooks/Cole.

Corey, G. (2001, August). *Group training for undergraduates.* Unpublished paper presentation at American Psychological Association, San Francisco, CA.

Corey, M. S., & Corey, G. (2002). *Groups: Process and practice.* Monterey, CA: Brooks/Cole.

Counsel for the Accreditation of Counseling and Related Educational Programs (CACREP). (1994). *CACREP accreditation standards and procedures manual.* Alexandria, VA: Author.

Counsel for the Accreditation of Counseling and Related Educational Programs (CACREP). (2001). *CACREP accreditation standards and procedures manual.* Alexandria, VA: Author.

DeLucia, J. L., Bowman, V. E., & Bowman, R. L. (1989). The use of parallel process in supervision of group counseling to facilitate counselor and client growth. *The Journal for Specialists in Group Work, 14,* 232-238.

Dies, R. R. (1983). Clinical implications of research on leadership in short-term group psychotherapy. In R. R. Dies & K. R. MacKenzie (Eds.), *Advances in group psychotherapy: Integrating research and practice.* New York: International Universities Press.

Dies, R. R. (1994). Therapist variables in group psychotherapy research. In A. Fuhriman & G. M. Burlingame (Eds.), *Handbook of group psychotherapy: An empirical and clinical synthesis.* New York: John Wiley.

Dreyfus, H. L., & Dreyfus, S. E. (1986). Five steps from novice to expert. In H. L. Dreyfus (Ed.), *Mind over machine: The power of human intuition and expertise in the era of the computer* (pp. 16-51). New York: Free Press.

Forester-Miller, H., & Duncan, J. A. (1990). The ethics of dual relationships in the training of group counselors. *Journal for Specialists in Group Work, 15,* 88-93.

Fuhriman, A., & Burlingame, G. M. (1990). Consistency of matter: A comparative analysis of individual and group process variables. *The Counseling Psychologist, 18,* 6-63.

Fuhriman, A., & Burlingame, G. M. (1994). Group psychotherapy: Research and practice. In A. Fuhriman & G. M. Burlingame (Eds.), *Handbook of group psychotherapy. An empirical and clinical synthesis.* New York: John Wiley.

Gazda, G. M., Ginter, E. J., & Horne, A. M. (2001). *Group counseling and group psychotherapy: Theory and application.* Boston: Allyn & Bacon.

Greene, L. R. (2000). Process analysis of group interaction in therapeutic groups. In A. P. Beck & C. M. Lewis (Eds.), *The process of group psychotherapy: Systems for analyzing change.* Washington, DC: American Psychological Association.

Gumaer, J., & Martin, D. (1990). Group ethics: A multimodal model for training knowledge and skill competencies. *Journal for Specialists in Group Work, 15,* 94-103.

Harvill, R., Masson, R. L., & Jacobs, E. E. (1983). Systematic group leader training: A skills development approach. *Journal for Specialists in Group Work, 8,* 226-232.

Hiebert, B., Uhlemann, M. R., Marhsall, A., & Lee, D. Y. (1998). The relationship between self-talk, anxiety, and counselling skill. *Canadian Journal of Counselling, 32,* 163-71.

Hines, P. L., Stockton, R., & Morran, K. D. (1995). Self-talk of group therapists. *Journal of Counseling Psychology, 42,* 242-248.

Ivey, A. E. (1994). *Intentional interviewing and counseling.* Pacific Grove, CA: Brooks/Cole.

Kivlighan, D. M., Coleman, M. N., & Anderson, D. C. (2000). Process, outcomes and methodology in group counseling research. In S. D. Brown & R. Lent (Eds.), *Handbook of counseling psychology* (3rd ed.). New York: John Wiley.

Kivlighan, D. M., & Quigley, S. T. (1991). Dimensions used by experienced and novice group therapists to conceptualize group process. *Journal of Counseling Psychology, 38,* 415-423.

Lieberman, M. A., Yalom, I. D., & Miles, M. B. (1973). *Encounter groups: First facts.* New York: Basic Books.

Lloyd, A. P. (1990). Dual relationships in group activities: A counselor education/accreditation dilemma. *Journal for Specialists in Group Work, 15,* 83-87.

McRoberts, C., Burlingame, G. M., & Hoag, M. J. (1998). Comparative efficacy of individual and group psychotherapy: A meta-analytic perspective. *Group Dynamics: Theory, Research and Practice, 2*(2), 101-177.

Merta, R. J., & Sisson, J. A. (1991). The experiential group: An ethical and professional dilemma. *Journal for Specialists in Group Work, 16,* 236-245.

Merta, R. J., Wolfgang, L., & McNeil, K. (1993). Five models for using the experiential group in the preparation of group counselors. *Journal for Specialists in Group Work, 18,* 200-207.

Morran, D. K., Kurpius, D. J., & Brack, G. (1989). Empirical investigation of counselor self-talk categories. *Journal of Counseling Psychology, 36,* 505-510.

Morran, D. K., Robison, F. F., & Stockton, R. (1985). Feedback exchange in counseling groups: An analysis of message content and receiver acceptance as a function of leader versus member delivery, session, and valence. *Journal of Counseling Psychology, 32,* 57-67.

Morran, K. D., Stockton, R., Cline, J. R., & Teed, C. (1998). Facilitating feedback exchange in groups: Leader interventions. *The Journal for Specialists in Group Work, 23,* 257-268.

Nutt-Williams, E., & Hill, C. E. (1996). The relationship between self-talk and therapy process. *Journal of Counseling Psychology, 43,* 170-178.

Polkinghorne, D. (1983). Narrative knowing and the human sciences. Albany: State University of New York Press.

Powdermaker, F. B., & Frank, J. D. (1953). Group psychotherapy: Studies in methodology of research and therapy. Cambridge, MA: Harvard University Press.

Robison, F. F., Jones, E. N., & Berglund, D. E. (1996). Research on the preparation of group counselors. *The Journal for Specialists in Group Work, 21,* 172-177.

Smaby, M. H., Maddux, C. D., Torres-Rivera, E., & Zimmick, R. (1999). A study of the effects of a skills-based versus a conventional group counseling training program. *Journal for Specialists in Group Work, 24,* 152-163.

Stockton, R. (1980). The education of group leaders: A review of the literature with suggestions for the future. *Journal for Specialists in Group Work, 5,* 55-62.

Stockton, R. (Presenter). (1992). Association for Specialists in Group Work (Producer). Developmental aspects of group counseling [Videotape]. (Available from the American Counseling Association, Alexandria, VA)

Stockton, R., & Morran, D. K. (1981). Feedback exchange in personal growth groups: Receiver acceptance as a function of valence, session, and order of delivery. *Journal of Counseling Psychology, 28,* 490-497.

Stockton, R., & Toth, P. (1996). A skill-based approach to teaching group counselor interventions. *Journal for Specialists in Group Work, 21,* 101-109.

Toth, P. L., & Stockton, R. (1996). A skill-based approach to teaching group counseling interventions. *The Journal for Specialists in Group Work, 21,* 101-109.

Toth, P. L., Stockton, R., & Erwin, W. J. (1998). Application of a skill-based training model for group counselors. *Journal for Specialists in Group Work, 23,* 33-49.

Yalom, D. I. (1995). The theory and practice of group psychotherapy (4th ed.). New York: Basic Books.

6

CONDUCTING A GROUP

Guidelines for Choosing and Using Activities

JAMES P. TROTZER

ETC³ Professional Services, Hampton, NH

ACTIVITIES: THE GROUP LEADER'S TOOL CHEST

If group leaders were carpenters, they would have tool chests that would accompany them to every site where they applied their leadership talents, skills, and functions. In that tool chest would be a host of activities that could be pulled out and used in different types of groups (task, psychoeducational, counseling, therapy), in diverse settings, with a wide variety of clients, for a multitude of purposes. Every skilled carpenter knows the tools that are needed for the job, why and how they work, and when to use them. In addition, dedicated carpenters take great pains to keep the tools of their trade sharp, in good condition, and up to date so that the final result does not display poor craftsmanship or shoddy labor. In other words, the tools are used to make their mark—but not leave their mark on the finished product. The same is true of activities that leaders use in groups. Activities are tools of a group leader's trade, but they are only tools and must be used in a manner that produces a group experience and result that is not flawed by the evidence a particular activity leaves in the aftermath of its use. To that end, this chapter is included to help group leaders stock their tool chests with activities (choose their tools), select them in an appropriate manner, and use them effectively.

THE NATURE OF ACTIVITIES

Structured group activities have many labels but are distinguished from leadership skills, functions, or roles by characteristics that make them entities unto themselves, with specific traits that define their nature. They have been called procedures, techniques, human relations, or communication activities, exercises, and even "catalysts" (Bates, Johnson, & Blaker, 1982). However, the traits that define their nature are as follows:

1. Group activities have specific instructions and parameters that give group members a format and focus for interaction.

2. Materials and props (pencils, paper, paint, music, etc.) may typically be used in the conduct of the activity.

3. Activities can be standardized and adapted with a minimum of alteration for use across groups and members so that a common framework can be replicated (Trotzer, 1999, p. 388).

As such, the main features of activities are technical and mechanical, having parameters and directions that make them merely tools. What they are used for and how they are integrated into the fabric of a group are facets that depend entirely on the group leader. They are not intended to be ends in and of themselves, but rather are to be the means by which specific objectives are reached. They should not be used to entertain or exploit group members and are only valid if selected and used in the context of effective group process and a defined group purpose. The intention of this chapter is to provide an overview of considerations attendant to selecting and using group activities ethically, appropriately, and effectively. The chapter will describe a model for assessing the nature of group activities, considerations for choosing them, and guidelines for using them. In addition, family theory as a group resource and the use of creative arts in groups will be discussed as particular sources of activities that are becoming more prominent in group practice and that require additional guidelines for appropriate use. Emphasis will be on developing a basis for effective use of activities in accordance with the *Association for Specialists in Group Work Best Practice Guidelines,* which state: "Group workers apply and modify knowledge, skills and *TECHNIQUES* (including activities) appropriate to group type and stage and to the unique needs of various cultural and ethnic groups" (Rapin & Keel, 2000, p. 2).

A MODEL FOR ASSESSING THE NATURE OF ACTIVITIES

Group activities can be categorized on the basis of focus and type of communication involved. The focus of activities is either *intrapersonal* or *interpersonal,* and the type of communication is either *verbal* or *nonverbal:*

Intrapersonal activities are designed to help people engage in the introspective process that leads to greater self knowledge. They stress personal learning about the subject of self. Interpersonal activities are designed to help people explore, understand, develop and improve their relationships with others. Their focus is on the social self and human relationships. (Trotzer, 1999, p. 389)

When these activities are conducted through the medium of expressed words, they are verbal activities, and when the activities rely on other means of communication, they are nonverbal activities. Consequently, all group activities fall into the following categories.

1. *Verbal Intrapersonal Activities:*
   Example: Group members draw pictures representing their own world and use them as props to introduce themselves verbally to the group.

2. *Verbal Interpersonal Activities:*
   Example: Introduction dyads are formed where partners are given the task of getting to know and then introducing each other to the group.

3. *Nonverbal Intrapersonal Activities:*
   Example: Guided imagery is used to induce relaxation and relieve anxiety and tension.

4. *Nonverbal Interpersonal Activities:*
   Example: Group members are directed to mill around the room making eye contact without speaking as a means of connecting with the other group members.

An additional feature is that many activities have both a nonverbal and a verbal component, as in the case where a member first does a self-assessment task, nonverbally, alone, and then verbally discloses what was experienced or learned. Regardless of the nature of the activity, it is imperative that all activities be processed verbally in the group no matter what the inherent nature of the experience. DeLucia-Waack (1997) stated that effectiveness of group activities "is greatly increased when the intervention *(activity)* is processed *(verbally)* at the individual *(intrapersonal)* and group *(interpersonal)* level" (p. 3). Consequently, effective leaders always incorporate a verbal sharing and processing component into any activity that is used.

Two additional features of the model for assessing the nature of group activities are *risk* and *leader control*. Every activity has a personal risk factor inherent in its nature and as an interactive feature of its impact on individual members and the group. A leader must evaluate this factor before using the activity. The risk dimension varies with the nature of the group, the members, and the stage in the group process. For example, nonverbal and intrapersonal activities may be more threatening for some members, while verbal and interpersonal activities may seem more risky to others. Verbal and interpersonal activities are more accessible and visible to group leader observation, thereby reducing risk and providing a basis for response or intervention if necessary.

Generally, leaders have more control over verbal and interpersonal activities than over nonverbal and intrapersonal activities. Again, the reason is related to being able to track what is actually happening rather than relying on second-hand accounts that emerge in the processing.

Effective group leaders develop a tool chest of activities that reflect the above-described traits and characteristics and continue to add to their repertoire over time.

Although a leader's personal style, theoretical orientation, and philosophy will affect the extensiveness and type of activities accumulated, their use is predicated on the nature of the group members, the characteristics of the group process, and the goals of the group.

CHOOSING ACTIVITIES IN GROUPS: MINDING YOUR P'S

Effective group work relies on the existence of a psychological framework or paradigm that serves as the foundation for what the leader does. How the leader carries out leadership roles and functions in a particular group is determined by three interacting factors that create the fabric and milieu of a group. These three factors are the *Persons* who make up the group, the *Process* that evolves in the group, and the *Purpose* for which the group is convened. As such, "group work is a bowl of P's," and effective group leadership is a matter of "minding your P's" (Trotzer, 2000, p. 9). With regard to choosing activities, leaders must consider the individual personality of each member, account for the interpersonal process in the group, and address the purpose for which the group is meeting.

The Person Component

Groups are composed of individual members, each of whom brings a personality, cultural background, and lifestyle into the group that must be considered (Trotzer, 2000). Activities must be selected that are appropriate to the nature of each person, both from a commonality (how members are alike) and a diversity (how members are different and unique) perspective. Certain activities may be more effective for persons with extroverted personalities, and others may be more appropriate for introverted individuals. Cultural values and traits may distinguish members from one another and must also be considered. For example, an activity that facilitates verbal interaction between members of the opposite sex may be acceptable for a man who has a religious orientation that forbids physical contact with the opposite sex in an interpersonal situation, whereas an activity that involves physical touch would not.

In addition to personality and cultural characteristics, each member enters the group with different needs that must be considered. Knowing and using a paradigm such as Maslow's hierarchy of motivational needs to determine the appropriateness of an activity is highly recommended. Maslow (1962) identified a sequential hierarchy of needs, including physiological, safety, love and belonging, esteem, and self-actualization, which have a direct relationship to the nature and characteristics of activities that can be chosen. These needs reflect the propensity of a member to respond positively, negatively, or indifferently to a proposed activity. For example, physiological needs (hunger, thirst, fatigue), if not met prior to group interaction can become a distraction during the conduct of structured activities. Physical safety, an aspect of the safety need, must be assured when using physical activities in groups. Other aspects of the safety need, such as interpersonal trust and self-confidence (the need to trust self) along with the need for love and belonging and esteem needs, can be directly addressed through the use of activities that help members meet those needs in the group. As members find that their lower-order needs are met in the group, they become more open and responsive to activities that relate to their higher-order needs, right up to the point where their need for self-actualization mobilizes energy to grow, change, or work at the highest level of individual functioning.

The Process Component

Every group develops a process pattern that characterizes the interpersonal dynamics of the group. Effective groups develop channels of contact that include self-disclosure and feedback as integral components of their relating process. The essential and ultimate impact of this process is to create a relating space where information is shared in such a way that all the resources of the group can be brought to bear on the task at hand, whether it is clinical and personal, as in counseling and psychotherapy groups, or informational and work oriented, as in psychoeducational and task groups. The climate of the group determines the ease of interaction, and all groups develop norms that relate to risk, privacy, and confidentiality, which are crucial to their effectiveness. Consequently, activities must be selected that enhance the group process *and* reflect the group process. For example, getting-acquainted activities are very useful early in the group, when members are building trust and forging cohesiveness, but might stymie or distract the group if introduced when the group is cohesive and work oriented.

Embedded in this process is the developmental nature of the group. Knowing the stages of group development and associated tasks is a crucial dimension of a group leader's competence. Although there are many developmental group models (Clark, 1992; Corey, 1995; Trotzer, 1999, 2001; Tuckman, 1965, 1977), the key is knowing and using at least one model to assess and determine a group's progress. In that regard, activities must be chosen that are commensurate with the stage of development and dynamics of the group. Jones and Robinson (2000) emphatically stated that "group activities must be appropriately timed in consideration of

the group stage" (pp. 356-357). They refer to the construct of "intensity" as a crucial dimension of choosing activities. The inherent intensity of activities increases as the group moves from the beginning to the middle or working stage and then recedes as the ending stage approaches. For example, groups that are in the middle or work stage benefit from activities that enhance their drive to be productive or help them iron out kinks in their process effectiveness. Choosing activities that are appropriate to the group's stage of development and reflect the intensity level of the group is a key skill that an effective group leader develops over time.

The Purpose Component

The basis for every group's existence is established by its purpose for being. Consequently, group activities must be chosen that address the purpose and move the group toward accomplishing its goals and objectives. Two types of activities are useful relative to purpose: (a) activities that enhance the process of the group and make it more efficient and (b) activities that promote the content of the group and make it more effective (Hulse-Killacky, Killacky, & Donigian, 2001). For example, a structured activity designed to help members attend to one another via active listening might help a group that is bogged down because members are reacting to input rather than understanding messages before responding. Or an activity designed to help identify priorities might be relevant for a group that is commissioned for the purpose of strategic planning.

Leaders who choose activities based on considerations of person, process, and purpose find that relevance and impact is increased and less energy is used in resistance and distraction. Appropriate choices are confirmed by the resonance of the group and its members, thus reinforcing the leader's decision making, competence, and effectiveness.

USING ACTIVITIES IN GROUPS: PROCESS FUNCTIONS AND PURPOSES

Once the nature of activities is determined and the choice of a particular activity is made based on the above-noted criteria, the actual implementation of activities in a group can ensue. Every group session is a prototype of the entire group process to the extent that it has a beginning, middle, and ending phase. Within that generic framework, the leader uses activities in one of three ways: *to initiate, to facilitate,* or *to terminate/ culminate* group interaction (Trotzer, 1999). Each method has advantages and disadvantages, and the way leaders use activities usually reflects their leadership styles and indicates their propensity toward structure and control.

Using Activities to Initiate

Activities can be used to initiate the focus and interaction of a group at the beginning of the overall group process, at the start of an individual session, or to interject a new or different direction in the group. When activities are used to initiate interaction, members are given a format to follow and a structure to guide them. Members realize a sense of security, and ambiguity is resolved because the leader takes the initiative. Extensive research has confirmed the value of using activities to initiate. McMillon (1994) found that "intentionally structured groups" that used task- and process-oriented activities had a positive impact on problem solving and interpersonal communication among a population of underprepared, first-year minority college students. Hetzel, Barton, and Davenport (1994) found that structured activities significantly enhanced the beginning of their men's groups, but discovered that using more than one activity per session produced a tendency for the men to become dependent. Stockton, Rohde, and Haughey (1994) found that activities initiated at the beginning of each session resulted in participants being significantly more satisfied with their group experience. They also found that groups did significantly less regressing process-wise when activities were used to initiate interaction. Shechtman (2001) found that activities helped children to express themselves and self-disclose when instituted at the beginning of group sessions.

Another reason to use activities to initiate interaction is to orient the group to a topic or subject that is to be the focus of the group. This purpose is particularly applicable to psychoeducational groups in which a predetermined topic of relevance to the participants is selected and activities are designed to introduce a subject, teach a lesson, pass on information, or demonstrate a skill (Brown, 1998). All the articles in the *Journal for Specialists in Group Work* mini–special issue on psychoeducational groups (Ward, 2000) described and advocated for the use of activities to initiate interaction. For example, Furr (2000) explicates an excellent model for designing psychoeducational groups and then gives extensive detail on how to design exercises to implement them. In addition, most prevention groups, a particular form of psychoeducational group, rely heavily on using activities to initiate focus and interaction (Conyne & Horne, 2001).

One drawback to initiating activities is that the activity provides members with a target for resistance. That may not be a disadvantage, however, since the activity becomes the forum in which members test boundaries and ferret out the leader's reactions rather than directly confronting the leader. Group leaders who use activities to initiate interaction gain the benefit of control but risk creating dependency, because members may begin to rely on leader initiatives to generate interaction. This is less of a problem in psychoeducational groups but can become problematic in counseling and psychotherapy groups in which one of the objectives is to help members take responsibility for action in the group and in their own lives. However, effective processing can defuse the tendencies to rely on the leader for direction, and the normal emergence of self-initiative that arises when groups get rolling also mitigates against dependency.

Using Activities to Facilitate

The primary purpose of using activities to facilitate interaction is to mobilize the group's resources. Facilitating "activities should be derived from or suggested in response to a situation or dynamic that has emerged in the group. [They] help groups clarify problem situations, present alternatives, alleviate anxiety producing circumstances, and break through impasses that occur in groups" (Trotzer, 1999, p. 396). The key to the effective use of activities to facilitate interaction is the leader's sensitivity, spontaneity, and perceptiveness in here-and-now situations. As the group process unfolds, the leader's tracking and scanning skills are helpful in deciphering what is happening, when to suggest an activity, and how to carry it out.

Facilitating activities are intended to be catalytic, stimulating, and enhancing to group interaction without creating a noticeable structure that detracts from the group process. For that reason, facilitating activities often enjoy ready acceptance and generate enthusiasm. The only limitation is the leader's own resources. However, if a leader has an extensive tool chest, there are usually plenty of options available.

Using Activities to Terminate/Culminate

Activities are useful at the end of individual group sessions, when individual members terminate, and when the total group is disbanded. In all cases, the major effects are to consolidate and integrate what has been experienced in the group and to generate closure (Trotzer, 1999). Activities serve a transitional purpose in helping members move on in their lives. A term I have been using recently to refer to culminating activities is the "accountability catapult." The idea is to view ending as a dynamic process that helps members say goodbye to the group and propels them on in their life with vigor and forward momentum. Combining a series of activities that help members confirm and affirm personal growth and change, give feedback to each other and the group leader, say goodbye, and plan a follow-up contact produces an impact that inspires the ending process and helps members celebrate closure as a kind of commencement exercise.

Resources for activities to use in group work abound. Some examples are DeLucia-Waack, Bridbord, and Kleiner (2002); Gladding (1997, 1998); Halverson (1996); Jacobs (1992); Jacobs, Harvill, and Masson (1988); Johnson (1981); Johnson and Johnson (1997); Morganette (1990, 1994); Pfeiffer and Jones (1969-1985); Rosenthal (1998); and Trotzer (1999). While familiarity with a wide range of structured activities is a preparatory step, selection and implementation of specific activities in a group are the bailiwick of the group leader.

Consequently, the rest of this chapter will consider guidelines, precautions, and suggestions for ethical and effective use.

GUIDELINES FOR SELECTING AND USING ACTIVITIES

Once activities have been assembled, chosen for implementation according to appropriate criteria, and the means of introducing them determined, effective use is still subject to certain considerations that ensure their effectiveness. The objective of this section is to identify and define parameters and guidelines that will assist leaders in effectively using activities in groups. First, process objectives for using activities will be reviewed, and general guidelines that relate to all activities will be noted.

Then, considerations for using family-based activities derived from family theory and the systems perspective and the creative arts in groups will be discussed. Finally, research and clinical practice literature in support of activities will be presented.

General Guidelines for Using Activities

Jacobs et al. (1988) suggested seven generic reasons or purposes for using activities in groups. These objectives generate dynamics that are conducive to healthy and productive group interaction. Activities can be used as follows:

1. To generate discussion and participation

2. To get the group focused on a common topic or issue

3. To shift or deepen the focus

4. To provide opportunity for experiential learning

5. To increase comfort level

6. To provide the leader with useful information

7. To provide fun and relaxation

These goals relate to the impact of activities and as such give them intrinsic validity.

The above-stated purposes coupled with a list of guidelines for using activities that have been in practice and in print for some time

Table 6.1   The Dynamic Dozen Guidelines for Selecting Activities in Groups

1. Select activities on the basis of their purposes, relevance, and desired outcomes.

2. Select activities that have a solid conceptual framework and rationale relative to human growth and development and interpersonal communication.

3. Select activities that are familiar and comfortable for you to use.

4. Select activities that are primarily verbal rather than physical.

5. Select activities that do not rely on jargon or labels and that can be presented in terms that do not stereotype, stigmatize, or raise negative connotations.

6. Select activities that are commensurate with the maturity level of group members.

7. Select activities that are compatible with and adaptable to the physical setting in which the group is meeting.

8. Select activities that allow for maximum member participation.

9. Select activities that allow members to control their own levels of involvement and disclosure.

10. Select activities that will result in outcomes you are confident that the group and you as a leader can handle.

11. Select activities that can be culminated in the time frame available to the group.

12. Select activities that are easy to process and integrate effectively into the flow of group interaction.

SOURCE: Adapted from *The Counselor and the Group: Integrating Theory, Training and Practice* (pp. 399-403), by J.P. Trotzer, 1999, Philadelphia: Accelerated Development.

(Trotzer, 1999; Trotzer & Kassera, 1973) create a general framework for implementing activities. The guidelines, referred to here as "The Dynamic Dozen," stipulate the technical aspects or mechanics of using activities in groups. Leaders must be cognizant of both the process implications and the mechanics when using activities in order to recognize the subtleties that sometimes attend to structuring group interaction via activities. The guidelines listed in Table 6.1 serve as an operational "umbrella" that leaders can refer to as checkpoints when activities are used. Individually and together, the guidelines integrate many of the elements necessary to promote constructive dynamics in group interaction.

When the process impact is clear and the mechanics for implementation are conducive to use, activities are helpful tools in the hands of a group leader. Keep these general guidelines in mind as two specific sources of activities in groups are discussed: activities derived from family theory (systems dynamics) and the creative arts.

Using Family-Based Activities in Groups

The relevance of family theory and systemic thinking to counseling in general and group work in particular is well established (Becvar, 1982; Couch & Childers, 1989; Trotzer, 1988a, 1988b, 1999; Yalom, 1995). The fact that members manifest the impact of their families of origin and systemic background in groups is unquestioned (Satir, 1972; Teyber, 1997; Yalom, 1995). The utility of thinking systemically, which has proven merit in all counseling and psychotherapy, is particularly valid relative to process and content in groups (Trotzer, 1988b; 1999). However, the impact of family theory as a source of activities that can be used in groups is burgeoning. An ever-increasing reference to family-based activities is emerging in group literature (Hage & Nosanow, 2000; Lawson, 1988; Mathis & Tanner, 2000; Pan, 2000; Schwartz & Ward, 1986; Vacha-Haase, Ness, Dannison, & Smith, 2000; Vinson, 1995). For this reason, special consideration is given here to activities that derive from and promote a family or systemic perspective in groups.

Family-based group activities have great relevance and appeal because they provide a focus that authenticates each person's individuality, uniqueness, and expertise (i.e., "No one can speak with more authority on my family than I can") while at the same time providing input that is inherently stimulating and interesting to other members (i.e., "Other families are always intriguing if only for comparative purposes"). As group members share their family experiences, other members tend to reflect on how their own families are similar and different. This produces what Mathis and Tanner (2000) call "a safe group forum for understanding and accepting family differences (and) helps prevent cultural encapsulation and promote(s) appreciation of cultural diversity" (p. 91). Because of the prepotent power of these activities and the subsequent potential to engage participants rapidly and intensely, group leaders who use family-based activities must choose and use them wisely and carefully. Family-based activities are relatively easy to develop and use given the broad range of systemic perspectives. Therefore, it is important that leaders use them in a manner that promotes healthy interaction while preserving personal privacy and protecting the vulnerability of group members. Table 6.2 presents five crucial guidelines and precautions for leaders to adhere to in order to assure best results when using family or systems-based group activities.

The overarching principle that governs the use of family-based activities in groups is that *the content and nature of the activity from a systemic perspective must be directly relatable to group dynamics in such a way that results can be integrated into the group process relative to purpose, focus, and experience* (Trotzer, 1988b). For example, asking members to make a list of spoken and unspoken rules they grew up with in their family of origin can be an effective means of introducing the importance, usefulness, and necessity of ground rules in the group. The content and discussion subsequent to such an activity is invaluable in forming ground rules, anticipating members' boundary concerns, and getting

a sense of how members will respond to group rules and expectations.

Another example is using members' ordinal position in their family constellation as a means of introducing themselves to the group and soliciting feedback via members' perceptions (Trotzer, 2000). Members simply state their name and position in their family without further explanation (e.g., "My name is Jim, and I am the oldest of three with a younger sister and brother."). Group members are then invited to share their thoughts about Jim based on their own experiences of being or relating to "oldest" persons. The focus member simply listens and then responds by affirming, modifying, disconfirming, or expanding on the members' comments. This activity provides useful information for the group members interpersonally and emphasizes the relationship of self-disclosure and feedback, because the focus person has the last say in responding to members' comments.

Finally, the use of an activity like "Draw Your Childhood Table" (Trotzer, 1998) in a training group for hospice caregivers can be useful in helping them come to grips with the impact of the death of a family member on a person's life. Members are asked to draw a table with all family members around it when they were at a certain age (usually between 6 and 16). First, they describe each member of the family (including themselves) as they remember them at that age and the family atmosphere. Then, they pass their pictures to the persons on their right, who are instructed to put an X through one member of the family and return the pictures to their owners. The task of each member is to think about, share, and discuss the following question: "If the person who is marked had died when you were that age, (a) how would you be different today? and (b) how would your family be different today?" The discussion usually addresses the systemic impact of death and makes the members aware of these dynamics in clients they are working with. The key in each of these examples is that the content and focus of the family-based activity is directly relevant to group dynamics, is compatible with content (purpose), and enhances the process of the group.

Table 6.2   Family-Based Group Activities

Guidelines and Precautions

   1. ***Remember the loyalty factor.*** Whenever individuals are invited or induced to discuss their families, an automatic loyalty conflict is created—particularly if negative information is involved. When using family-based activities, leaders must learn and use the skill of *multi-directed partiality* (Boszormenyi-Nagy & Krasner, 1986). This skill enables the leader to be partial and empathic to both the discloser's side (viewpoint) and the family's side (viewpoint) without taking sides. This enables a constructive dialogue to ensue that assists the member and the group in exploring both perspectives in the safety of the group context without invading, intruding, or violating family loyalty dynamics. Raising the family's side of a group member's perspective helps the member to disclose without feeling like a traitor, because the leader and group members demonstrate fairness and caring not only for the member but also his or her family.

   2. ***Seek resources, not skeletons.*** The purpose of family-based activities is to generate material that will provide understanding of the individual member and assistance in helping the member deal with his or her problems or concerns. While family material can be extremely enticing from an interest perspective, leaders must avoid getting distracted by family storytelling. If the information emerging cannot be directly related to the group process, purpose, and focus, measures should be taken to redirect the discussion.

   3. ***Avoid meddling in families.*** A basic premise of counseling and psychotherapy groups is that the group process can directly affect only the person in the group. This fact must be recognized and continually affirmed when using family-based activities. Leaders must avoid doing long-distance family therapy or turning group members into therapists for their own families. The tendency to meddle in families must be avoided and curtailed. Keeping the focus on the person in the group rather than the family when processing family-based activities will circumvent the tendency to dabble in family dynamics without a clear purpose with respect to the individual member.

   4. ***Build family-based techniques from concepts rather than content.*** Privacy relative to family information is a generic value for most people. This is particularly true in certain cultures and ethnic groups. Group activities should be created out of a sound conceptual framework and not merely for the purpose of eliciting particular information. The structure of the activity should be such that members do not feel threatened by the content of the desired disclosure. Apprise members of the construct undergirding the activity that relates to all group members and the purpose of the group so that they will feel comfortable supplying the subsequent information.

   5. ***Use care in selecting family-based activities that elicit highly emotional or traumatic disclosures.***[a] Family encounters often produce the most painful emotional reactions. Psychological pain garnered in the context of family relationships tends to produce emotional responses, whether they represent recent or old wounds. Leaders must be sensitive to the traumatizing potential in family-based activities, discard high-risk activities, and modify instructions to temper the level of emotional impact.

SOURCE: Reprinted and adapted from *The Counselor and the Group: Integrating Theory, Training and Practice* (pp. 427-428), by J.P. Trotzer, 1999, Philadelphia: Accelerated Development.

a. In psychotherapy groups with members who have experienced intrusive acts in a family context (e.g., incest or sexual, physical, emotional abuse or trauma), this guideline does not constitute avoidance, but rather a monitoring of disclosures to maintain a pace and focus that facilitates working through such experiences in a therapeutic manner (Courtois & Leehan, 1982).

Using the Creative Arts in Groups

   Sam Gladding (1997, 1998), author of *Counseling as an Art: The Creative Arts in Counseling,* is a leading proponent of using the creative arts in groups. He advocates their use because "the arts can do much to enrich and enliven any type of group" (Gladding, 2000, p. 7). Creative arts encompass processes and products that are "primarily visual (e.g., painting), auditory (e.g., music), moving (e.g., dance), and verbal (e.g., reading/writing/drama)" (Gladding, 2000, p. 7). Shechtman and Perl-Dekel (2000) include drawing, painting, photography, and sculpture as art techniques used in their art therapy groups. Williams, Frame, and Green (1999) use the full gamut of creative arts, including art, music, dance, imagery, journaling, and rituals in conducting African American spirituality groups.

Many group leaders use creative writing in the form of journals or logs as a useful tool in their groups (Riordan & White, 1996). Such methods have wide-ranging utility and support. Yalom (1995) was an early advocate of writing as a therapeutic adjunct to the group process. He wrote summaries of sessions and distributed them to group members. Members have traditionally been prompted to write in a journal as an addendum to their group experiences. Riordan and White (1996) discuss the use of logs in groups but raise the caution that member-leader exchanges can lead to a form of triangulation that must be noted and addressed if it interferes with the therapeutic process. Parr, Haberstroh, and Kottler (2000) suggest a model of journaling that counters this tendency. They use a procedure whereby journals are exchanged in all directions (leaders and members) and part of the session is devoted to processing material that emerges as members read and reflect on the entries outside the group. Leaders use their journal entries to promote and describe the stages of the group process as well as reflect on the intrapersonal, interpersonal, and interactional dynamics they observe in the group. In this way, members benefit from leader input with respect to both process and content.

The creative arts, like other activities, must take into account the person, process, and purpose components of group work and can be introduced and used at any stage or phase of the group process. They can be adapted and modified to account for age differences and used with all group members regardless of individual creative ability or talent. Gladding (2000) identifies the generic advantages of using the creative arts in Table 6.3. In concert, he views them as one of the most versatile means of drawing out members in groups and stimulating meaningful group interaction. The arts provide another channel for expression that weaves greater variety into the fabric of the group milieu. The positive energy of creativity invites members to reveal and use all aspects of their

Table 6.3 Advantages of Using Creative Arts in Groups

1. They are multicultural.
2. They energize.
3. They promote insight and self-awareness.
4. They communicate messages on multiple levels.
5. They are playful and nonthreatening.
6. They open up options.

SOURCE: From "Group Work Practice Ideas: The Use of the Creative Arts in Groups," by S.T. Gladding, 2000, *The Group Worker 28*(2), p. 8.

personhood to interact. It introduces the language of creativity as a viable means of individual expression and interpersonal access to one another. Shechtman and Perl-Dekel (2000) view art as helpful in engaging group clients during the early stages of group development and throughout the process. They posit that art therapy enhances group therapy and promotes interpersonal learning.

Finally, the use of art, particularly that of drawing, has been invaluable in groups for children who have experienced trauma, are terminally ill, or are grieving (DeSpelder & Strickland, 2002). Bereavement groups, groups for children of divorce, groups for patients with life-threatening or terminal illnesses (Gore-Felton & Spiegel, 1999), and groups for victims of physical, sexual, and emotional abuse (Loewy, Williams, & Keleta, 2002) all make extensive use of drawing. In addition, crisis intervention groups for children and adolescents advocate the use of drawing and collages in helping them cope with violence, natural disasters, accidental deaths, and death by suicide (DeSpelder & Strickland, 2002). In all cases, the guidelines and cautions noted regarding use of activities apply.

Despite the advantages of using the creative arts, there are also some drawbacks that leaders must take into account. These limitations emanate from the inherent nature of the tools and call on leaders to exercise common sense. Gladding (2000) lists the reservations for using the creative arts as follows:

1. They may be inappropriate in some situations.
2. They may become gimmicky.

3. They are not effective when applied with most artists.

4. They may not be useful for group members who are emotionally labile.

5. They may take up too much time that could be more productively used in other ways.

6. They may lead group members to be too self-occupied and introspective (p. 9).

However, in most cases, these factors will manifest themselves quite quickly in groups, so leaders can take appropriate action to modify or redirect the group. Resources for activities that use the creative arts, in addition to Gladding's (1998) book, are Jacob's (1992) *Creative Counseling Techniques: An Illustrated Guide* and Trotzer's (1999) *The Counselor and the Group: Integrating Theory, Training and Practice.*

RESEARCH AND CLINICAL SUPPORT FOR ACTIVITIES

An abundance of professional literature attests to the fact that structured activities are an endemic part of the group work field. Research studies are typically designed to test the generic hypothesis that structured activities enhance the group process and produce positive results in divergent settings with varied populations and from multiple theoretical perspectives. These studies provide formats, designs, and procedures that can be replicated to reinforce validity and expand applicability, or modified to explore variations that might produce significant results. Examples of studies that directly test the effect of structured activities are Hetzel et al. (1994); McMillon (1994); Shechtman (2001); Stockton et al. (1994); and Pan (2000). All found significant positive effects of structured activities. Many research studies have been designed to test the generic hypothesis that groups work effectively when they incorporate structured activities in their treatment procedures. Therefore, when significant results are attained, a concurrent implication is that the structured activities are effective in producing the results. The specific activities are often described in the treatment plan, and anecdotal evaluative comments are typically made regarding their impact, effectiveness, and importance. Examples of studies that embed structured activities in the treatment process are Barr, Emer, and Keller (2001); Claypoole, Moody, and Peace (2000); Daniels, D'Andrea, Omizo, and Pier (1999); Huss and Ritchie (1999); Shechtman and Perl-Dekel (2000); and Sells, Giordano, and King (2002).

Numerous articles describe in detail a specific group method, technique, or activity identifying parameters as to why, when, where, and how to implement them. More articles are appearing that present activities and then discuss how they can be applied and adapted for a wide range of settings, populations, and purposes. For example, Carmichael (2000) describes using a metaphor (the "Wizard of Oz" story) in groups with disaster survivors. Van Lone, Kalodner, and Coughlin (2002) expound on the use of short stories as an activity in eating-disorder groups. Garrett, Garrett, and Brotherton (2001) provide a detailed description of the "inner circle/outer circle" technique from a Native American perspective in a group process context. Brenner (1999) promotes the use of "process-play," a simulation activity that enhances group work training. Asner-Self and Feyissa (2002) describe the use of poetry in pyschoeducational groups with multicultural-multilingual clients; and Loewy et al. (2002) explicate the *Kaffa* ceremony as a group counseling technique with traumatized East African women in the United States.

Many articles that describe group counseling or psychotherapy programs and psychoeducational groups include structured activities as an integral part of their agendas and protocol. In most cases, structured activities are the core tools used to help group members address the purpose, topics, and focus of the group. In fact, models for developing group programs for practice, training, and psychoeducational purposes specifically call for the use of structured activities as inherent features of their organizational formats (Furr, 2000; Jones & Robinson, 2000; Kulic, Dagley, & Horne, 2001). Specific protocols for *group counseling and psychotherapy* (Gore-Felton & Spiegel, 1999; Loewy et al., 2002; Portman & Portman, 2002; Samide & Stockton, 2002, Stanko & Taub, 2002; Williams et al., 1999); *psychoeducational groups* (Akos, 2000; Asner-Self & Feyissa, 2002; Daignault,

2000; Hage & Nosanow, 2000; Martin & Thomas, 2000; Sommers-Flanagan, Barrett-Hakanson, & Sommers-Flanagan (2000); Vacha-Haase et al., 2000); and *training/teaching groups* (Brenner, 1999; Cummings, 2001; Kees & Leech, 2002; Marotta, Peters, & Paliokas, 2000; Smaby, Maddux, Torres-Rivera, & Zimmick, 1999) delineate structured activities as part and parcel of their formats.

CONCLUSION

In one sense, perusal of the literature might well result in a conclusion that use of structured activities in groups is rampant and dominates the group work field. For that reason alone, it is important to diligently maintain this chapter's proffered perspective that structured activities in group work are merely tools. Losing sight of that fact will endanger the integrity of both the group process and the activity itself. The meaning, impact, and relevance of any activity are derived from the context, not from the activity. Consequently, it is critical that each leader who uses activities does so with an awareness of the ethical, professional, and technical ramifications that are presented in this chapter. Doing so will ensure effectiveness and circumvent obstacles that can distort or distract the group process, and will make activities a valued resource in the hands of a skilled and competent group leader.

REFERENCES

Akos, P. (2000). Building empathic skills in elementary school children through group work. *Journal for Specialists in Group Work,* 214-223.

Asner-Self, K. K., & Feyissa, A. (2002). The use of poetry in psychoeducational group with multicultural-multilingual clients. *Journal for Specialists in Group Work, 27,* 136-160.

Barr, K., Emer, D., & Keller, P. (2001). Teaching group process to mentally ill adult clients: Effect on client ratings of self-esteem and psychological well-being. *Journal for Specialists in Group Work, 26,* 48-65.

Bates, M., Johnson, C. D., & Blaker, K. E. (1982). *Group leadership: A manual for group counseling leaders* (2nd ed.). Denver: Love.

Becvar, D. (1982). The family is not a group—Or is it?. *Journal for Specialists in Group Work, 7,* 88-95.

Boszormenyi-Nagy, I., & Krasner, B. (1986). *Between give and take: A clinical guide to contextual therapy.* New York: Brunner/Mazel.

Brenner, V. (1999). Process-play: A simulation procedure for group work training. *Journal for Specialists in Group Work, 24,* 145-151.

Brown, N. W. (1998). *Psychoeducational groups.* Philadelphia: Accelerated Development.

Carmichael, K. D. (2000). Using a metaphor in working with disaster survivors. *Journal for Specialists in Group Work, 25,* 7-15.

Clark, A. J. (1992). Defense mechanisms in group counseling. *Journal for Specialists in Group Work, 17,* 151-160.

Claypoole, S. D., Moody, E. E. Jr., & Peace, S. D. (2000). Moral dilemma discussions: An effective group intervention for juvenile offenders. *Journal for Specialists in Group Work, 25,* 394-411.

Conyne, R. K., & Horne, A. M. (2001). Special issue: The use of groups for prevention. *Journal for Specialists in Group Work, 26*(3).

Corey, G. (1995). *Theory and practice of group counseling* (4th ed.). Monterey, CA: Brooks/Cole.

Couch, R. D., & Childers, J. H. Jr. (1989). A discussion of differences between group therapy and family therapy: Implications for counselor training and practice. *Journal for Specialists in Group Work, 14,* 226-231.

Courtois, C. A., & Leehan, J. (1982). Group treatment for grown-up abused children. *Personnel and Guidance Journal, 60,* 564-566.

Cummings, A. L. (2001). Teaching group process to counseling students through the exchange of journal letters. *Journal for Specialists in Group Work, 26,* 7-16.

Daignault, S. D. (2000). Body talk: A school-based group intervention for working with disordered eating behaviors. *Journal for Specialists in Group Work, 25,* 191-213.

Daniels, J., D'Andrea, M., Omizo, M., & Pier, P. (1999). Group work with homeless youngsters and their mothers. *Journal for Specialists in Group Work, 24,* 164-185.

DeLucia-Waack, J. L. (1997). The importance of processing activities, exercises and events to group work practitioners. *Journal for Specialists in Group Work, 22,* 82-84.

DeLucia-Waack, J. L., Bridbord, K. H., & Kleiner, J. S. (Eds.). (2002). *Group work experts share their favorite activities: A guide to choosing, planning, conducting and processing.* Association for Specialists in Group Work. (Available from J. L. DeLucia-Waack, Department of Counseling, School and Educational Psychology, University at Buffalo, SUNY, 403 Baldy Hall, Buffalo, NY 14260)

DeSpelder, L. A., & Strickland, A. L. (2002). *The last dance: Encountering death and dying* (6th ed.). Boston: McGraw-Hill.

Furr, S. R. (2000). Structuring the group experience: A format for designing psychoeducational groups. *Journal for Specialists in Group Work, 25,* 29-49.

Garrett, M. T., Garrett, J. T., & Brotherton, D. (2001). Inner circle/outer circle: A group technique based on Native American healing circles. *Journal for Specialists in Group Work, 26,* 17-30.

Gladding, S. T. (1997) The creative arts in groups. In H. Forester-Miller & J. A. Kottler (Eds.), *Issues and challenges for group practitioners* (pp. 81-99). Denver: Love.

Gladding, S. T. (1998). *Counseling as an art: The creative arts in counseling.* Alexandria, VA: American Counseling Association.

Gladding, S. T. (2000). Group work practice ideas: The use of the creative arts in groups. *The Group Worker, 28*(2), 7-9.

Gore-Felton, C., & Spiegel, D. (1999). Enhancing women's lives: The role of support groups among breast cancer patients. *Journal for Specialists in Group Work,* 274-287.

Hage, S. M., & Nosanow, M. (2000). Becoming stronger at broken places: A model for group work with young adults from divorced families. *Journal for Specialists in Group Work, 25,* 50-66.

Halverson, S. (1996). *55 group-building activities for youth.* Nashville, TN: Abingdon.

Hetzel, R., Barton, D. A., & Davenport, D. S. (1994). Helping men change: A group counseling model for male clients. *Journal for Specialists in Group Work, 19,* 52-64.

Hulse-Killacky, D., Killacky, J., & Donigian, J. (2001). *Making task groups work in your world.* Upper Saddle River, NJ: Prentice Hall.

Huss, S. N., & Ritchie, M. (1999). Effectiveness of a group for parentally bereaved children. *Journal for Specialists in Group Work, 24,* 186-196.

Jacobs, E. E. (1992). *Creative counseling techniques: An illustrated guide.* Sarasota, FL: Psychological Assessment Resources.

Jacobs, E. E., Harvill, R. L., & Masson, R. L. (1988). *Group counseling: Strategies and skills.* Monterey, CA: Brooks/Cole.

Johnson, D. W. (1981). *Reaching out: Interpersonal effectiveness and self-actualization.* Englewood Cliffs, NJ: Prentice-Hall.

Johnson, D. W., & Johnson, F. P. (1997). *Joining together: Group theory and group skills* (6th ed.). Englewood Cliffs, NJ: Prentice Hall.

Jones, K. D., & Robinson, E. H. III. (2000). Psychoeducational groups: A model for choosing topics and exercises appropriate to group stage. *Journal for Specialists in Group Work, 25,* 343-355.

Kees, N. L., & Leech, N. L. (2002). Using group counseling techniques to clarify and deepen the focus of supervision groups. *Journal for Specialists in Group Work, 27,* 7-15.

Kulic, K. R., Dagley, J. C., & Horne, A. M. (2001). Prevention groups with children and adolescence. *Journal for specialists in Group Work, 26,* 211-218.

Lawson, D. M. (1988). Using family sculpting and choreography in a student growth group. *Journal for Counseling and Development, 66,* 246-278.

Loewy, M. I., Williams, D. T., & Keleta, A. (2002). Group counseling with traumatized East African refugee women in the United States. *Journal for Specialists in Group Work, 27,* 173-191.

Marotta, S. A., Peters, B. J., & Paliokas K. L. (2000). Teaching group dynamics: An interdisciplinary model. *Journal for Specialists in Group Work, 25,* 16-28.

Martin, V., & Thomas, M. C. (2000). A model psychoeducational group for shy college students. *Journal for Specialists in Group Work, 25,* 79-88.

Maslow, A. H. (1962). *Toward a psychology of being.* Princeton, NJ: Van Nostrand.

Mathis, R. D., & Tanner, Z. (2000). Structured group activities with family-of-origin themes. *Journal for Specialists in Group Work, 25,* 89-103.

McMillon, H. G. (1994). Developing problem solving and interpersonal communication skills through intentionally structured groups. *Journal for Specialists in Group Work, 19,* 43-47.

Morganette, R. (1990). *Skills for living: Group counseling activities for young adolescents.* Champaign, IL: Research Press.

Morganette, R. (1994). *Skills for living: Group counseling activities for elementary students.* Champaign, IL: Research Press.

Pan, P. J. D. (2000). The effectiveness of structured and semistructured Satir model groups on family relationships with college students in Taiwan. *Journal for Specialists in Group Work, 25,* 305-319.

Parr, G., Haberstroh, S., & Kottler, J. (2000). Interactive journal writing as an adjunct in group work. *Journal for Specialists in Group Work, 25,* 229-242.

Pfeiffer, D. C., & Jones, J. E. (1969-1985). *A handbook of structured experiences for human relations training* (Vols. 1-10). San Diego, CA: University Associates.

Portman, T. A. A., & Portman, G. L. (2002). Empowering students for social justice (ES² J): A structured group approach. *Journal for Specialists in Group Work, 27,* 16-31.

Rapin, L., & Keel, L. (March, 2000). Best practice guidelines. In *Association for Specialists in Group Work professional standards for the training of group workers; principles for diversity-competent group workers; best practice guidelines for group workers* (pp. 1-4). Alexandria, VA: Author.

Riordan, R. J., & White, J. (1996). Logs are therapeutic adjuncts in group. *Journal for Specialists in Group Work, 21,* 94-100.

Rosenthal, H. G. (Ed.). (1998). *Favorite counseling and therapy techniques: 51 therapists share their most creative strategies.* Bristol, PA: Accelerated Development.

Samide, L. L., & Stockton, R. (2002). Letting go of grief: Bereavement groups for children in the school setting. *Journal for Specialists in Group Work, 27,* 192-204.

Satir, V. (1972). *Peoplemaking.* Palo Alto, CA: Science and Behavior Books.

Schwartz, K., & Ward, C. (1986). Leaving home: A semistructured group experience. *Journal for Counseling and Development, 65,* 107-115.

Sells, J. N., Giordano, F. G., & King, L. (2002). A pilot study in marital group therapy: Process and outcome. *The Family Journal: Counseling and Therapy for Couples and Families, 10,* 156-166.

Shechtman, Z. (2001). Prevention groups for angry and aggressive children. *Journal for Specialists in Group Work, 26,* 228-236.

Shechtman, Z., & Perl-Dekel, O. (2000). A comparison of therapeutic factors in two group treatment modalities: Verbal and art therapy. *Journal for Specialists in Group Work, 25,* 288-304.

Smaby, M. H., Maddux, C. D., Torres-Rivera, E., & Zimmick, R. (1999). A study of the effects of a skills-based versus a conventional group counseling training program. *Journal for Specialists in Group Work, 24,* 152-163.

Sommers-Flanagan, R., Barrett-Hakanson, T., & Sommers-Flanagan, J. (2000). A psychoeducational school-based coping and social skills group for depressed students. *Journal for Specialists in Group Work, 25,* 170-190.

Stanko, C. A., & Taub, D. J. (2002). A counseling group for children of cancer patients. *Journal for Specialists in Group Work, 27,* 43-58.

Stockton, R., Rohde, R. I., & Haughey, J. (1994). The effects of structured group exercises on cohesion, engagement, avoidance and conflict. *Journal for Specialists in Group Work, 23,* 155-168.

Teyber, E. (1997). *Interpersonal process in psychotherapy: A relational approach* (3rd ed.). Pacific Grove: CA: Brooks/Cole.

Trotzer, J. P. (1988a). Group and family interface. *Together, 16,* 6,8.

Trotzer, J. P. (1988b). Family theory as a group resource. *Journal for Specialists in Group Work, 13,* 180-185.

Trotzer, J. P. (1998). Draw your family table/family-o-gram. In H. G. Rosenthal (Ed.), *Favorite counseling and therapy techniques: 51 therapists share their most creative strategies* (pp. 179-181). Bristol, PA: Accelerated Development.

Trotzer, J. P. (1999). *The counselor and the group: Integrating theory, training and practice.* Philadelphia: Accelerated Development.

Trotzer, J. P. (2000). Group work practice ideas: Problem solving procedures in group work. *The Group Worker, 29,* 9-12.

Trotzer, J. P. (2001). Problem solving group therapy. In R. Corsini (Ed.), *Handbook of innovative therapy* (2nd ed., pp. 501-513). New York: John Wiley.

Trotzer, J. P., & Kassera, W. J. (1973). Guidelines for selecting communication techniques in group counseling. *The School Counselor, 20,* 299-301.

Tuckman, B. W. (1965). Developmental sequences in small groups. *Psychological Bulletin, 63,* 384-399.

Tuckman, B. W. (1977). Stages of group development revisited. *Group and organizational studies, 2,* 419-427.

Vacha-Haase, T., Ness, C. M., Dannison, L., & Smith, A. (2000). Grandparents raising children: A psychoeducational group approach. *Journal for Specialists in Group Work, 25,* 67-78.

Van Lone, J. S., Kalodner, C. R., & Coughlin, J. W. (2002). Using short stories to address eating disturbances. *Journal for Specialists in Group Work, 27,* 59-77.

Vinson, M. L. (1995). Employing family therapy in group counseling with college students. *Journal for Specialists in Group Work, 20,* 240-252.

Ward, D. E. (2000). Introductions: A new associate editor and psychoeductional groups mini-special issue. *Journal for Specialists in Group Work, 25*(1).

Williams, C. B., Frame, M. W., & Green, E. (1999). Counseling groups for African American women: A focus on spirituality. *Journal for Specialists in Group Work, 24,* 260-273.

Yalom, I. D. (1995). *The theory and practice of group psychotherapy* (4th ed.). New York: Basic Books.

7

EFFECTIVE LEADER INTERVENTIONS FOR COUNSELING AND PSYCHOTHERAPY GROUPS

D. KEITH MORRAN

Indiana University

Purdue University at Indianapolis

REX STOCKTON

Indiana University

MARTYN H. WHITTINGHAM

Indiana University

When leaders employ a given intervention during the course of a group session, there is the implicit assumption that their behavior will have a positive impact on individual members and/or on the processes and outcomes of the group. Relatively few group research studies have investigated the impact of specific leader behaviors on the group and its members. However, some recent research findings have indicated that group dynamics and outcomes are influenced by general factors such as the leader's interaction style, personal characteristics, and attitudes. For example, researchers have found that leaders who are less controlling,

who exhibit warmth/caring, and who set and reinforce clear norms are more likely to have cohesive groups (Antonuccio, Davis, Lewinson, & Breckenridge, 1987; MacKenzie, Dies, Coche, Rutan, & Stone, 1987; Phipps & Zastowny, 1988). Increased cohesiveness, in turn, has been found to be positively related to a variety of group treatment outcomes (e.g., Kivlighan & Lilly, 1997; Marziali, Munroe-Blum, & McCleary, 1997).

Dies (1994) reviewed the findings of 51 group studies that focused on the leader's level of activity within the group session. He reported that leaders who were more active and directive and provided more structure in terms of guiding group sessions had groups with more favorable outcomes in 78% of the studies reviewed. Other studies have linked more structured leader styles with increased group cohesiveness, especially during early group stages (e.g., Fuehrer & Keys, 1988; Robison & Hardt, 1992).

Although some leader behaviors have been linked to improved outcomes, others have been linked to negative outcomes. Fuehrer and Keys (1988), for example, concluded that structuring by group leaders can have both positive and negative effects. Too little structure may lead to ineffective member interactions, and too much structure may lead members to feel they have no ownership of group accomplishments. Leader passivity, in terms of protecting and supporting group members, also has been linked to negative outcomes, such as premature termination and damaging group experiences (Dies, 1994; Smokowski, Rose, Todar, & Reardon, 1999).

We have described only a few of the studies that link leader behaviors to either positive or negative group outcomes. The findings of these and similar studies, however, offer support that group leaders do have the potential to influence group dynamics and, in turn, to influence member outcomes. Thus, if leaders are able to step in and apply the right intervention at the right time, group effectiveness can be enhanced.

The remainder of this chapter will review a variety of group leader interventions that have been recommended by practitioners, theorists, and researchers in the group work field. Many of these interventions can be used in task or psychoeducational groups; however, our focus will be on what is commonly termed *group counseling* or *group therapy,* where the primary purpose of the group is for members to disclose information, gain insight, and pursue positive personal/social change. Within such therapy groups, leaders must seek to energize members in a manner that promotes meaningful self-disclosure and self-reflection while also intervening at critical points to protect members and preserve a climate of safety. Through the careful selection and application of interventions, group leaders can promote a balance of safety and challenge within the group.

The group therapy literature frequently refers *to group leader interventions* or simply *group interventions;* however, these terms are seldom defined in any specific manner. Group interventions range from relatively spontaneous leader actions, such as blocking or drawing out group members, to more formal and planned exercises, such as structured feedback exchange (Jacobs, Masson, & Harvill, 1998). Leader interventions may also focus on individual members, a subgroup of members, or the entire group and, in addition, may be intended to achieve either process or outcome goals.

Given the wide range of possibilities available to the group leader, it seems useful to characterize "group intervention" in broad terms. Accordingly, we have defined group interventions as purposeful actions of the leader to ensure safety and/or to initiate, energize, or enhance the therapeutic factors operating within the group setting. Thus, leaders typically intervene to promote therapeutic factors such as altruism, security, reality testing, interpersonal learning, cohesiveness, ventilating emotions, and many others that have consistently been recognized as critical dimensions of successful groups (e.g., Corey & Corey, 1997; Corsini & Rosenberg, 1955; Hill, 1957; Yalom, 1995).

The following sections of this chapter will present a total of 10 specific group interventions and will include related research and clinical support for each intervention skill. The first 3 interventions are grouped under the category of protecting group members/promoting safety and include protecting, blocking, and supporting. These interventions are typically most useful in the leader's efforts to provide a group climate that is conducive to trust, openness, and cohesion. The remaining interventions are grouped under the category of energizing/involving group members and include drawing out, modeling, linking, processing, interpreting, self-disclosing, and feedback. These interventions are most often used to stimulate forward progress, increase member participation, and enhance interpersonal learning.

Many group interventions are more appropriate, or at least more typical, during some group phases than others. Therefore, the presentation of each intervention will also include consideration of its relative appropriateness for various group development stages. The concept of group stages or group development is critical for leaders and suggests that the group and its members change in some manner over time

(MacKenzie, 1994). Thus, effective leaders must accurately assess where the group and its members are in the developmental process and select interventions that are geared to members' levels of readiness.

Almost any intervention can be appropriate at almost any group stage, provided that it is appropriately geared to the readiness of members and the issues being dealt with at that point in the group. However, even though the stages of a group are often indistinct and overlapping, there are certain predictable differences in group atmosphere, and therefore, some interventions may be more advisable in one stage and less advisable in another.

Many group leader interventions or skills are common to both individual and group therapy situations. Examples include active listening, reflecting, summarizing, and clarifying. Our focus, however, will be on interventions that are relatively exclusive to groups or that may have unique applications or purposes within the group setting.

Protecting Group Members/Promoting Safety

Protecting

Protecting (or protecting members from indiscreet self-disclosure) refers to a broad category of leader interventions aimed at preventing members from taking unnecessary psychological risks in the group (Capuzzi & Gross, 2002). Members of a group will often vary widely in terms of risk-taking readiness, and some members may feel pressure, whether from themselves or others, to share too much or too soon. It is then that the leader should intervene to protect the member from sharing too much and subsequently feeling regret or possibly withdrawing emotionally from the group. The importance of protecting members has been noted by a number of group work experts (Clark, 1995; Lieberman, Yalom, & Miles, 1973; Yalom, 1995), and research has indicated that members who are dissatisfied with their group experiences often implicate the group leader for negligence in providing adequate protection (Dies, 1983). Smokowski, Rose, and

Bacallo (2001), for example, interviewed 33 group members who were identified as having had damaging experiences in therapeutic groups. They reported that 82% of these group members felt a lack of support and protection from their leaders.

Protecting interventions may be valuable at any point in the group but should be particularly useful in promoting a feeling of safety during the initial stage, when members are uncertain about their roles, and in helping them deal with the conflict that is prevalent in the transition stage. During later stages, as members seek to take greater risks, protection may also be quite useful at times.

Protecting can sometimes be indirect and might include member selection/exclusion procedures, the establishment of appropriate group norms, or the modeling of caring for group members. More direct protecting interventions might take the form of intervening to stop a member who is self-disclosing too much or at a level that is significantly more intimate than the rest of the members. The following two examples illustrate the leader's use of protection interventions in situations that are typical of early group sessions:

Leader: Paul, you've shared a great deal about your recent marriage problems. At this point it might be good for you to think about the comments you've heard from others and perhaps share more with us after you've had time to reflect on things a bit.

Leader: (To Ed, who has begun to share details about his depression and alcohol use during the first group session). I really appreciate your willingness to share, but I think it would be best to wait and tell us more when we have all gotten a chance to know each other and can be more helpful.

Another example demonstrates the use of protection in a situation that might be more typical of later counseling stages:

Andrea: (Who has attended and actively participated in every session since the group began 12 weeks ago and who has often expressed appreciation for help she received from others. She has talked for a few minutes about her infant daughter who died shortly after birth, 2 years ago). This is the first time I ever talked about this with anyone except my husband and my mother.... (Looks very distraught and begins crying) I think it will help me to talk about this, but now I'm not sure I can do it, it just brings back so much pain that I feel numb....

Leader: Andrea, I'm really pleased that you trusted the group enough to share this with us. If you feel like sharing more that will be fine, but it's also okay to wait and share more when you feel ready.

This leader response provides protection by giving the client permission to either stop or to continue if she feels ready.

Blocking

Blocking is a specific type of protection that is used to stop a member from storytelling, rambling, or otherwise talking in a manner that runs counter to the purposes of the group. Blocking is often used to protect group members when one member is inappropriately probing, gossiping, or invading the privacy of others (Corey & Corey, 1997; Trotzer, 1989). In their study of members who had been identified as "group casualties," for example, Smokowski et al. (2001) found evidence that members frequently attributed their damaging experiences to undue confrontation, criticism, and pressure to self-disclose by other members. In an earlier study, Smokowski et al. (1999) concluded that damaging group experiences were almost 6 times more likely to occur if leaders were passive in respect to protecting members. Thus, it would seem essential that leaders use blocking and related interventions to protect potentially vulnerable group members.

Blocking interventions, sometimes referred to as "cutting off" (Jacobs et al., 1998) or "intervening" (Dyer & Vriend, 1980), must be used with both sensitivity and directness so that the best interests of the group and its members are served but without attacking or embarrassing the member whose dialogue is being blocked. This may be accomplished in a variety of ways, such as a simple hand gesture to cue the member

that it is time to move on or a question that helps the member become more focused.

Blocking will typically be most useful during the transition stage of the group, when members sometimes engage in scapegoating or demonstrate other problematic interpersonal behaviors. It is at this point that the leader must intervene to stop any behaviors that could create undue anxiety and thus delay the group's progress toward the working stage. Blocking may also be necessary at later stages, when sensitive issues tend to emerge.

The following example of blocking demonstrates how the leader can intervene to stop a member who is rambling:

Kyle: (Who has spent several minutes complaining about his family while other group members are displaying increasing frustration) And my sister is another one who blames me for her problems. . . .

Leader: Let me stop you for a second. You've told us a lot about your family, but I'm wondering about you. Tell us more about the kind of help you want from the group.

Another example illustrates how the leader might employ blocking in the form of a question to prevent a member from monopolizing:

Anna: (Who frequently jumps in to gain the group's attention at the beginning of each session and thus receives a disproportionate amount of therapy time) I'll go first tonight, I had another argument with my son and I need some help.

Leader: Okay, Anna has something she would like to work on at some point. But let's first see what other issues also need our attention. What about the rest of the group (gesturing to the whole group)? What would each of you like to work on tonight?

Supporting

Supporting is a leader intervention designed to directly reassure members and thus encourage and reinforce their appropriate participation (Capuzzi & Gross, 2002; Jacobs et al., 1998; Trotzer, 1989). Because members are sometimes worried about how they may be viewed by other group members, they may withhold their participation to avoid saying something that could be viewed as "wrong" or "weird." In such situations, the leader may choose to directly support the member's effort to reveal scary feelings or sensitive information to the group.

Supporting interventions may be particularly useful during the initial and transition stages of the group. During these stages, members are often too uncertain or fearful to take even small risks, and such support can provide valuable encouragement. During the working stage, members may need leader support as they seek to go deeper with their self-understanding and self-challenging efforts. This type of support may be appropriate when a member is facing a crisis, venturing into frightening territory, struggling to break old behavior patterns, or is feeling uncertain about making changes (Corey & Corey, 1997). Care should be taken, however, not to offer support to members before they have had a chance to experience their own conflict and deal with it independently. Premature or excessive supporting interventions may foster dependency on the leader and be detrimental to the individual and the group (Corey & Corey, 1997). When timed appropriately, however, supporting interventions can provide just enough encouragement to help a group member move forward and become involved in the group interaction.

The following example shows how a leader might intervene to support a member who wants to share but is fearful:

Tonya: I know I'm the only one who hasn't talked about their problem yet; I want to share but it's really hard for me to do this in a group this large.

Leader: I think it's scary for all of us to share things that we have usually kept private. But I think you just took an important first step and I want to assure you that we are here to be helpful rather than critical.

ENERGIZING/INVOLVING GROUP MEMBERS

Drawing Out

Drawing out occurs when the leader directly invites comments or involvement from one or more group members. It is often used to encourage participation from members who find it hard to share with others or with those who share on a surface level but avoid deeper issues. Drawing out can be contrasted with the skill of blocking, which serves the opposite function by stopping or redirecting unhelpful comments or member behaviors. In their text, Jacobs et al. (1998) stated, "If cutting off is the most essential skill a leader needs to know then drawing out is probably the second most important skill" (p. 162).

Drawing out can be appropriate during the initial group stage if used cautiously. Jacobs et al. (1998) recommend that leaders attempt to get all members to talk during the early part of the group, since the longer a shy or silent member waits to participate, the harder it becomes. The ability to draw out members may be even more important during the transition and working stages, since silent or shy members will tend to limit the potential for members to help each other. In addition, members may need such encouragement before they will openly exchange feedback or engage in other therapeutic interactions that are vital to successful working-stage interactions.

When using drawing-out interventions, leaders should seek to encourage participation, while still allowing members to choose their own levels of sharing. That is, an invitation to participate can allow for the opportunity to not share at the present time if it is followed by an option to pass or is directed at more than a single group member. Furthermore, the leader should consider the reasons for a member's silence before deciding how or whether to intervene. The member who is silent due to a lack of trust in the group may need to be dealt with differently than the member who is simply quiet by nature.

The following example shows how drawing out could be used when several group members find it difficult to contribute but seem on the edge of saying something:

Leader: Mark, Jenny, and Jay, you all seem like you have something to say about that last subject. I wonder if any of you can share.

Another example demonstrates how the leader can encourage one member to give feedback to another:

Leader: Gloria, you seem to be hinting that you had a strong reaction to what Trenna just said. Could you give her your feedback more directly?

As Jacobs et al. (1998) outlined, drawing out can be accomplished nonverbally (making eye contact or gesturing for someone to contribute), verbally (such as through a question), or using a variety of structured techniques that might include dyads, rounds, or set activities designed to elicit one or more members' comments. As an example of multiple means to achieve the same end, one of the authors recently ran a group for international students in which drawing out was achieved by the members literally "drawing out" their acculturation experience on paper and then using this as a means to facilitate personal disclosure and group discussion.

Modeling

Modeling occurs when leaders demonstrate the skills, attitudes, and other characteristics they hope to engender within group members (Trotzer, 1989). Thus, leaders may encourage by example things such as respect and caring for others, appropriate self-disclosure, giving and receiving feedback, openness, and many other traits that are desirable for group members. Many social cognitive theorists (Bandura, 1977, 1986; Rosenthal & Zimmerman, 1978) propose that modeling operates at a metalevel within the group. That is to say, it is a common factor of nearly all interventions, since members naturally observe group leaders and tend to imitate what they see demonstrated. Therefore, leader modeling is not only useful but is essential at every group stage.

A number of research studies have found that behaviors displayed by the therapist, including interpersonal behaviors, feedback delivery and acceptance, and here-and-now communications, lead to increases in those same behaviors by group members (Barlow, Hansen, Fuhriman, & Finley, 1982; Kanas, Barr, & Dossick, 1985; Linehan & O'Toole, 1982). Dies (1994), in his review of therapist variables in group psychotherapy research, concluded that leader-modeling effects are present in counseling and therapy groups and suggests that therapists be

aware of the potential effects of their own behavior and how it influences group members. As a whole, these studies suggest that leaders can use modeling interventions to help shape positive group dynamics; however, care should be exercised to avoid the unintentional modeling of undesirable behaviors.

The following example demonstrates how a leader might model self-disclosure to members:

Leader: At this point I would like for each of us to take turns and describe what we see as our best personal qualities. I'll begin the process and you will be able to see how it works. I think my best personal qualities are . . .

A second example depicts the leader modeling nondefensive responding to an angry member who has issued a challenge:

Jeff: (To the leader) I am really angry with you for always seeming like you are above the rest of us. What are you trying to prove?

Leader: Jeff, I appreciate your feedback. I did not realize you perceived me that way. Perhaps we can explore together what I am doing that comes across in that manner.

Linking

Linking is an intervention often used to connect what one group member is saying or doing with the concerns of one or more other members. It encourages interaction among group members and promotes the development of facilitative relationships that have been found to be essential for effective group functioning (Dies, 1983). This intervention has received much support in the group literature (Banawi & Stockton, 1993; Corey & Corey, 1997; Dies, 1983; Yalom, 1995), and leaders may find linking interventions to be particularly useful in promoting member cohesion and interaction during the transition and working stages of groups. It may also be quite useful during the initial group stage, when feelings of universality and the identification of common ground are important.

The following example shows how a leader might link two members who share similar concerns:

Maria: I want to be close to my stepdaughter but she always finds ways to let me know that I don't measure up to her real mother. When she does this, I get defensive and everything goes wrong.

Leader: Maria, this seems to be very painful for you. Since Todd has also talked about difficulties with his two stepchildren, I wonder if the two of you could discuss your concerns here in the group, and others can join in as well.

Linking may also be used to give direction to the group by focusing on themes that have emerged over the course of the group. That is, it serves to bring a variety of themes common to the group or individuals together in a way that can give focus and organization to the group process. This helps not only with universality but also with a sense of group purpose, motivation, and therapeutic direction, as well as building cohesion. The following example shows how themes might be linked:

Leader: Although it has been stated in a variety of ways, I think all of you are saying that you want to be more direct in dealing with conflicts in your relationships. If we focus for a few minutes on what scares us about conflict, perhaps we can help each other.

Finally, linking interventions by the leader also serve to model social and cognitive skills for group members. In demonstrating how to bring ideas and people together with unifying themes, the leader is sharing a thought process that some group members may begin to imitate. Creating this new set of cognitive schemata with which to view the world can therefore help members use the same set of cognitive skills in their own lives.

Processing

Processing occurs when the group leader and members capitalize on significant happenings to help members reflect on the meaning of their experience; better understand their own thoughts, feelings, and actions; and generalize what is learned to situations outside of the group (Glass & Benshoff, 1999; Stockton,

Morran, & Nitza, 2000). A variety of planned and unplanned events occur in any given group and often provide golden opportunities for members to gain insight about themselves and how others perceive them, as well as to learn about current group dynamics.

Yalom (1995) emphasizes that simply experiencing events or critical incidents is not sufficient for growth, but must be augmented by processing that provides a framework for retaining, integrating, and generalizing the experience. This is supported by research findings that have identified a positive relationship between higher levels of group processing and greater outcome gains related to both group productivity and individual member achievement (Johnson, Johnson, Stanne, & Garibaldi, 1990; Yager, Johnson, Johnson, & Snider, 1986). In addition, research findings have suggested that processing should go beyond emotional insight and also focus on cognitive dynamics or meaning attributions to help members frame and understand their emotional experiences (Coche, Dies, & Gottelman, 1991; Lieberman et al., 1973; Richardsen & Piper, 1986).

Effective processing of critical incidents requires that members engage in a process of sharing and exploring among themselves. This is important during all group stages but is particularly critical during the working and ending stages. During early group stages, processing is likely to be initiated by the leader, but in later sessions may sometimes occur spontaneously.

Conyne (1997) noted that without systematic processing, learning opportunities may go unknown or be mistaken or only partially understood. Therefore, it is imperative that leaders recognize the occurrence of critical incidents and intervene in a manner that helps members derive meaning from their experiences. Stockton et al. (2000) provide a general cognitive map designed to help leaders effectively initiate and guide group processing. Their four-step model includes identifying critical incidents of importance to group members, examining the event and member reactions, deriving meaning and self-understanding from the event, and applying new understandings toward personal change. The following leader statements are examples of how a leader might intervene to promote or guide processing:

Leader: I'm wondering what each of you learned about yourself from the exercise we just completed.

Leader: Tonya just shared some very emotional experiences, and we responded by giving her lots of advice. Let's take a moment and examine whether or not our advice was helpful to her.

Leader: Don, you just received feedback from several of us about your tendency to exaggerate setbacks in your life. What have you learned, and how can you apply it outside of the group?

Interpreting

Corey and Corey (1997) defined interpreting as "offering possible explanations for certain behaviors or symptoms" (p. 71). Because such interventions go beyond a surface level, leaders must have an understanding of members' deeper-level feelings, patterns of behavior, and motivations. Thus, interpreting is most likely to be successfully used during the working and ending group stages.

During the working and ending stages, members typically experience interactions, either directly or vicariously, that provide the opportunity to learn more about themselves. Such insight, however, may be difficult for the member to acquire without some cognitive framework being provided by the leader. In such situations, the leader can assist group members by providing a tentative interpretation that can be discussed and considered in the group.

In two separate reviews, Dies (1983, 1994) identified a total of 29 studies that investigated group leader interpretations along with other meaning attribution dynamics. He concluded that leader interpretations helped members to integrate complex personal and group-related events, thus encouraging their investment in the group experience. He also concluded that interpretations were beneficial when they facilitated generalization from group experiences to personal experiences outside the group. Flowers and Booraem (1990) studied four types of interpretations offered during psychodynamic and cognitive-behavioral groups. These included interpretations concerning the client's impact on

his or her environment, patterns of behavior, motives for behavior, and historical causes of behavior. They concluded that interpretations about the client's impact on the environment and his or her patterns of behavior were most associated with client change.

Although interpreting can be a powerful intervention for promoting member insight and meaning attribution, leaders should carefully consider several factors. If leader interpretations are made too frequently, for example, group members may soon place the leader in an expert role and not attempt to make their own interpretations. Leaders should also remain tentative in the interpretations they offer, perhaps offering them in the form of hypotheses that the client can consider and discuss with the group. This, of course, allows more room for alternative perspectives and serves to enhance group interaction. Finally, the leader must consider a given member's readiness before offering an interpretation, and the readiness of the group to meaningfully engage in the processing that follows. The following examples illustrate interpretations that are directed to either the group or to individual members:

Leader: For the past 30 minutes, the group has jumped around between topics without really focusing on anything in particular. Maybe we're just trying to keep things at a surface level where everyone is safe.

Leader: Greg, I've noticed several times that when someone in the group is getting corrective feedback from others, you step in and defend them. I wonder if this could be your way of saying that you don't want others to give you feedback.

Self-Disclosing

Leader self-disclosure is an intervention whereby therapists reveal their personal feelings, experiences, or here-and-now reactions to group members. The sharing of personal information allows therapists to reveal enough of themselves so that members gain a sense of their leader as a person (Corey & Corey, 1997). Used too early or too often, however, this type of self-disclosure may lessen the leader's credibility with the group. Leader self-disclosure of here-and-now reactions to the group process can be valuable when used to model sharing for the members or to enhance the group process. As a general rule, leaders should self-disclose only when the information or reaction is directly related to what is happening in the group or models a behavior for members, or where a direct benefit to the group is anticipated (Yalom, 1995). Leaders should avoid self-disclosures that are designed only to impress members, gain sympathy, or unburden personal problems.

Studies of group therapist self-disclosure (or transparency) have been limited and the findings somewhat inconsistent. There is evidence to suggest that leader self-disclosure does foster increased openness among group members (Fromme, Dickey, & Schaefer, 1983; Linehan & O'Toole, 1982), though no consistent links with treatment outcome have been established (Dies, 1993). Clinical knowledge, however, generally supports the use of leader self-disclosure when it provides opportunities for interpersonal learning or is directed toward helping members attain their goals (Corey & Corey, 1997; Yalom, 1995). Thus, it may be best for leaders to carefully consider the purpose of a given self-disclosure and to monitor and assess group member reactions before sharing too much.

Leader modeling is particularly important during the initial and transition stages of the group. At an early point, the leader may want to model appropriate self-disclosure, and during the transition stage, it will be critical that the leader model how to deal directly and nondefensively with conflict. During the working stage, leaders will often find it useful to model behavior such as the appropriate giving and receiving of feedback and other insight-oriented interventions.

In the following example, the leader self-discloses to gently challenge a member's intellectualization and avoidance of grief. This may also allow other members to risk talking about their own, deeper feelings, after having seen the therapist take the risk first:

Jack: (Distancing himself from his feelings) People sometimes just want to deal with loss by getting on with their lives. There is no need to spend hours crying about it.

Leader: I hear what you are saying, Jack. When my mother died, I just wanted to throw myself back into my work. The thing was, those feelings were still there, just buried under the surface, and they ended up coming out "sideways," and I broke down and cried over the death of my goldfish and losing a favorite pen.

As noted earlier, leader self-disclosure may also be useful when here-and-now reactions are shared, to help members better understand themselves or the group process. Examples of this type of self-disclosure are illustrated below:

Leader: At this point, I am feeling that the group has been pretty hard on Lori. She is getting a great deal of criticism, and I think she has actually made some good progress.

Leader: (To Gary who is exploring how he is perceived by others) I see you as one who is generally easygoing and friendly; however, you come across to me as very intense, almost angry, when someone disagrees with you.

Feedback

Feedback is the sharing of one's own observations or reactions regarding the behavior, thoughts, or feelings of another. This process provides recipients with the opportunity for reflective self-appraisal and represents one of the most direct avenues for group members to learn from each other (Morran, Stockton, Cline, & Teed, 1998). Positive feedback is generally useful as a means of reinforcing appropriate behaviors at any group stage. Corrective (or negative) feedback, however, tends to arouse group member anxiety, especially when delivered by the leader, who may be looked upon as an authority figure during early sessions. Corrective leader feedback is generally most useful during the working and ending stages of the group but may also be useful during the transition stage to help the group identify blocks to progress.

The efficacious outcomes from feedback have been well documented in research literature. It has been linked to increased motivation for change (Davies & Jacobs, 1985; Robison, Stockton, Morran, & Uhl-Wagner, 1988), greater insight into how one's behavior affects others (Rothke, 1986), greater comfort in interpersonal risk taking (Coche et al., 1991), and group members rating their experience more positively (Jacobs, Jacobs, Gatz, & Schaible, 1973).

To maximize the potential benefits of group feedback exchange, leaders must successfully intervene on two levels. On one level, the leader must effectively give and receive feedback within the group. At the second level, leaders must engage group members in effectively sharing feedback with each other. A study by Flowers (1979) emphasized the value of member-to-member feedback, finding that feedback messages from other members were valued over feedback from the leader during middle and later group stages.

Research findings have identified a number of general guidelines for successful feedback exchange. These guidelines suggest emphasizing positive feedback in early group sessions, with a balance of positive and corrective feedback during middle and later sessions (Morran, Stockton, & Harris, 1991; Stockton & Morran, 1981). In addition, feedback delivery should follow a positive-corrective or positive-corrective-positive sequence of delivery (Davies & Jacobs, 1985; Schaible & Jacobs, 1975), while focusing on specific and observable behaviors rather than focusing on the giver's emotional response (Jacobs, Jacobs, Cavior, & Burke, 1974). Though less established by research findings, it is also recommended that careful consideration be given to the readiness of the receiver before delivering corrective feedback, since closed or defensive group members may be more likely to deny or distort the feedback message (Schaible, 1970). Examples of leader interventions designed to either deliver feedback or promote member-to-member feedback are given below.

Leader: Carlos, for the last several sessions I have seen you make great strides toward your goal of being more self-accepting. Today, however, I see you slipping back into your old pattern of self-criticism.

Leader: Everyone seemed very careful about what they shared in our first two meetings, but today everyone seems much more willing to open up. Let's take a few minutes and share with others what you think they did that allowed this to happen.

Many feedback interventions may be relatively spontaneous, as in the examples above. However, it is sometimes helpful to instruct members on the principles of effective feedback giving and receiving and/or to use structured exercises that provide a format for feedback exchange. These types of planned experiences are designed as "icebreakers" that can lead to more naturally occurring member-to-member feedback in future sessions. Morran et al. (1998) suggest that structured feedback exchange exercises be introduced during the third or fourth group session as a general rule. While such exercises may take on a variety of forms, Morran et al. recommend a written feedback exercise. This exercise involves members privately writing one or more positive feedback messages for each of the other group members on index cards. When members and leader(s) have completed their writing, turns are taken in orally delivering the feedback messages (and/or handing the written messages to the recipient) and allowing time for recipients to respond or ask questions. This process is then repeated with the exchange of corrective feedback. Morran et al. caution that members should be encouraged—but not forced—to participate in this exercise. They also recommend that following the entire exercise, the leader engage the group in processing and learning from the experience.

CONCLUSION

Before employing a given intervention, leaders should carefully consider factors such as the type of group, the characteristics of group members, the stage of the group, the goals of group members, and the intensity level of the exercise or intervention. A few experts have recommended general guidelines related to the appropriateness of interventions. Capuzzi and Gross (2002), for example, suggest that initial group interventions should be nonthreatening and that more intensive interventions are likely to be most effective during the group's working stage. They further recommend that ending-stage interventions should address cognitive learning and skill building as well as feelings associated with the conclusion of the group. Jones and Robinson (2000) emphasize the importance of carefully assessing the intensity level of activities and their appropriateness for early, middle, or ending stages of the group.

The interventions described in this chapter represent only a small sample of the many possibilities. As noted earlier, we attempted to select interventions that were relatively specific to group counseling or that had unique applications or purposes in the group. Leaders should not, however, ignore basic listening, responding, challenging, and goal-setting skills that are essential in promoting therapeutic relationships and preparing members for change. Put simply, even the best group intervention will have little impact if delivered within a nontherapeutic environment. It should also be noted that we have not attempted to identify interventions related to every leader function in the group. Many group experts, for example, believe that leaders must intervene even before the first meeting to help ensure the success of the group. During this time, issues must be addressed that relate to selecting members, deciding on the level of structure for the group, and the pre-training of members (Corey & Corey, 1997; Kaul & Bednar, 1994).

Although we have presented group interventions as discreet entities in this chapter, there is, in fact, significant overlap and interaction among them. Protecting and blocking, for example, share some of the same elements even though we have artificially separated them for clarity of presentation. Also, one leader intervention often engenders another. For example, a member's self-disclosure may elicit feedback from others that, in turn, calls for processing by the group. Thus, while it is useful to conceptualize the various interventions as separate and distinct, it should be anticipated that they might blend together and operate interactively in actual practice.

Another critical point for leaders to remember is that group interventions are not the exclusive domain of the leader. The leader's input is, of course, vital for creating a meaningful learning environment in the group but does not take the place of interpersonal sharing and validation among members (Dies, 1994). To a great extent, the group as a whole is the primary agent of change, a distinction that clearly separates group therapy from individual therapy (Yalom,

1995). Leaders must, therefore, not only use interventions effectively but also model their appropriate use for group members, who will gradually assume more and more responsibility for helping each other.

REFERENCES

Antonuccio, D. O., Davis, C., Lewinson, P. M., & Breckenridge, J. S. (1987). Therapist variables related to cohesiveness in a group treatment for depression. *Small Group Behavior, 18,* 557-564.

Banawi, R., & Stockton, R. (1993). Islamic values relevant to group work, with practical applications for the group leader. *Journal for Specialists in Group Work, 18,* 151-160.

Bandura, A. (1977). *Social learning theory.* Englewood Cliffs, NJ: Prentice Hall.

Bandura, A. (1986). *Social foundations of thought and action: A social-cognitive theory.* Englewood Cliffs, NJ: Prentice Hall.

Barlow, S., Hansen, W. D., Fuhriman, A. J., & Finley, R. (1982). Leader communication style: Effects on members of small groups. *Small Group Behavior, 13,* 518-531.

Capuzzi, D., & Gross, D. R. (2002). *Introduction to group counseling* (3rd ed.). Denver, CO: Love.

Clark, A. J. (1995). Modification: A leader skill in group work. *Journal for Specialists in Group Work, 20,* 14-17.

Coche, E., Dies, R. R., & Gottelman, K. (1991). Process variables mediating change in intensive group therapy training. *International Journal of Group Psychotherapy, 41,* 379-397.

Conyne, R. (1997). A developing framework for processing experiences and events in group work. *Journal for Specialists in Group Work, 22,* 167-174.

Corey, M. S., & Corey, G. (1997). *Groups: Process and practice* (5th ed.). Pacific Grove, CA: Brooks/Cole.

Corsini, R., & Rosenberg, B. (1955). Mechanisms of group psychotherapy: Processes and dynamics. *Journal of Abnormal & Social Psychology, 51,* 406-411.

Davies, D., & Jacobs, A. (1985). Sandwiching complex interpersonal feedback. *Small Group Behavior, 16,* 387-396.

Dies, R. R. (1983). Clinical implications of research on leadership in short-term group psychotherapy.

In R. R. Dies & K. R. MacKenzie (Eds.), *Advances in group psychotherapy: Integrating research and practice* (pp. 27-78) (American Group Psychotherapy Association Monograph Series). New York: International Universities Press.

Dies, R. R. (1993). Research on group psychotherapy: Overview and clinical applications. In A. Alonso & H. I. Swiller (Eds.), *Group therapy in clinical practice* (pp. 473-518). Washington, DC: American Psychiatric Press.

Dies, R. R. (1994). Therapist variables in group psychotherapy research. In A. Fuhriman & G. M. Burlingame (Eds.), *Handbook of group psychotherapy: An empirical and clinical synthesis* (pp. 114-154). New York: John Wiley.

Dyer, W., & Vriend, J. (1980). *Group counseling for personal mastery.* New York: Sovereign.

Flowers, J. V. (1979). Behavioral analysis of group therapy and a model for behavioral group therapy. In D. Upper & S. M. Ross (Eds.), *Behavior group therapy, 1979: An annual review* (pp. 5-37). Champaign, IL: Research Press.

Flowers, J. V., & Booraem, C. D. (1990). The frequency and effect on outcome of different types of interpretation in psychodynamic and cognitive-behavioral group psychotherapy. *International Journal of Group Psychotherapy, 40,* 203-214.

Fromme, D. K., Dickey, G. V., & Schaefer, J. P. (1983). Group modification of affective verbalizations: Reinforcement and therapist style effects. *Journal of Clinical Psychology, 39,* 893-900.

Fuehrer, A., & Keys, C. (1988). Group development in self-help groups for college students. *Small Group Behavior, 19,* 325-341.

Glass, J. S., & Benshoff, J. M. (1999). PARS: A processing model for beginning group leaders. *Journal for Specialists in Group Work, 24,* 15-26.

Hill, W. F. (1957). Analysis of interviews of group therapists' papers. *Provo Papers, 1,* 1.

Jacobs, A., Jacobs, M., Cavior, N., & Burke, J. (1974). Anonymous feedback: Credibility and desirability of structured emotional and behavioral feedback delivered in groups. *Journal of Counseling Psychology, 21,* 106-111.

Jacobs, E. E., Masson, R. L., & Harvill, R. L. (1998). *Group counseling: Strategies & skills.* Pacific Grove, CA: Brooks/Cole.

Jacobs, M., Jacobs, A., Gatz, M., & Schaible, T. (1973). Credibility and desirability of positive and negative structured feedback in groups. *Journal of Consulting and Clinical Psychology, 40,* 244-252.

Johnson, D. W., Johnson, R. T., Stanne, M. B., & Garibaldi, A. (1990). Impact of group processing on achievement in cooperative groups. *Journal of Social Psychology, 130,* 507-516.

Jones, K. D., & Robinson, E. H. (2000). Pschoeducational groups: A model for choosing topics and exercises appropriate to group stage. *Journal for Specialists in Group Work, 25,* 356-365.

Kanas, N., Barr, M. A., & Dossick, S. (1985). The homogeneous schizophrenic inpatient group: An evaluation using the Hill Interaction Matrix. *Small Group Behavior, 16,* 397-409.

Kaul, T. J., & Bednar, R. L. (1994). In A. Fuhriman & G. M. Burlingame (Eds.), *Handbook of group psychotherapy: An empirical and clinical synthesis* (pp. 155-188). New York: John Wiley.

Kivlighan, D. M. Jr., & Lilly, R. L. (1997). Developmental changes in group climate as they relate to therapeutic gain. *Group Dynamics: Theory, Research, and Practice, 1,* 208-221.

Lieberman, M. A., Yalom, I. D., & Miles, M. B. (1973). *Encounter groups: First facts.* New York: Basic Books.

Linehan, E., & O'Toole, J. (1982). Effect of subliminal stimulation of symbiotic fantasies on college student self-disclosure in group counseling. *Journal of Counseling Psychology, 29,* 151-157.

MacKenzie, K. R. (1994). Group development. In A. Fuhriman & G. M. Burlingame (Eds.), *Handbook of group psychotherapy: An empirical and clinical synthesis* (pp. 223-268). New York: John Wiley.

MacKenzie, K. R., Dies, R. R., Coche, E., Rutan, J. S., & Stone, W. N. (1987). An analysis of AGPA Institute groups. *International Journal of Group Psychotherapy, 37,* 55-74.

Marziali, E., Munroe-Blum, L., & McCleary, L. (1997). The contribution of group cohesion and group alliance to the outcome of group psychotherapy. *International Journal of Group Psychotherapy, 47,* 475-497.

Morran, D. K., Stockton, R., Cline, R. J., & Teed, C. (1998). Facilitating feedback exchange in groups: Leader interventions. *Journal for Specialists in Group Work, 23,* 257-268.

Morran, D. K., Stockton, R., & Harris, M. (1991). Analysis of group leader and member feedback messages. *Journal of Group Psychotherapy, Psychodrama, and Sociometry, 44,* 126-135.

Phipps, L. B., & Zastowny, T. R. (1988). Leadership behavior, group climate and outcome in group psychotherapy: A study of outpatient psychotherapy groups. *Group, 12,* 157-171.

Richardsen, A. M., & Piper, W. E. (1986). Leader style, leader consistency, and participant personality effects on learning in small groups. *Human Relations, 39,* 817-836.

Robison, F. F., & Hardt, D. A. (1992). Effects of cognitive and behavioral structure and discussion of corrective feedback outcomes on counseling group development. *Journal of Counseling Psychology, 39,* 473-481.

Robison, F. F., Stockton, R., Morran, D. K., & Uhl-Wagner, A. (1988). Anticipated consequences of communicating corrective feedback during early counseling group development. *Small Group Behavior, 19,* 469-484.

Rosenthal, T. L., & Zimmerman, B. J. (1978). *Social learning and cognition.* San Diego: Academic Press.

Rothke, S. (1986). The role of interpersonal feedback in group psychotherapy. *International Journal of Group Psychotherapy, 36,* 225-240.

Schaible, T. (1970). *Group cohesion, feedback acceptance, and desirability: Functions of the sequence and valence of feedback.* Unpublished master's thesis, West Virginia University, Morgantown.

Schaible, T., & Jacobs, A. (1975). Feedback III: Sequence effects: Enhancement of feedback acceptance

and group attractiveness by manipulation of the sequence and valence of feedback. *Small Group Behavior, 6,* 151-173.

Smokowski, P. R., Rose, S. D., & Bacallo, M. L. (2001). Damaging experiences in therapeutic groups: How vulnerable consumers become group casualties. *Small Group Research, 32,* 223-251.

Smokowski, P. R., Rose, S. D., Todar, K., & Reardon, K. (1999). Post-group casualty status, group events and leader behavior: An early look into the dynamics of damaging group experiences. *Research on Social Work Practice, 9,* 555-574.

Stockton, R., & Morran, D. K. (1981). Feedback exchange in personal growth groups: Receiver acceptance as a function of valence, session and order of delivery. *Journal of Counseling Psychology, 28,* 490-497.

Stockton, R., Morran, D. K., & Nitza, A. G. (2000). Processing group events: A conceptual map for leaders. *Journal for Specialists in Group Work, 25,* 342-355.

Trotzer, J. P. (1989). *The counselor and the group: Integrating theory, training and practice* (2nd ed.). Muncie, IN: Accelerated Development.

Yager, S., Johnson, R. T., Johnson, D. W., & Snider, B. (1986). The impact of group processing on achievement in cooperative learning groups. *Journal of Social Psychology, 126,* 389-397.

Yalom, I. D. (1995). *The theory and practice of group psychotherapy* (4th ed.). New York: Basic Books.

8

THE EFFECTIVE USE OF PROCESSING IN GROUPS

DONALD E. WARD

Pittsburg State University

MICHELE LITCHY

Pittsburg State University

The term *processing* evokes a sense of familiarity in the minds of group leaders, facilitators, trainers, counselors, and therapists, hereafter all referred to as "group workers," except where differentiation is necessary. Indeed, a process orientation may be considered to be a common characteristic of modern professional group work. However, the complexity of the phenomenon and the traditional emphasis upon an idiosyncratic, intuitive understanding of the term have challenged group workers in their efforts to develop a clear, common definition from which to empirically investigate and systematically apply processing in their work.

Processing may be narrowly defined as an activity in which individuals and groups regularly examine and reflect upon their behavior in order to extract meaning, integrate the resulting knowledge, and thereby improve functioning and outcome. However, as with many other cherished and familiar concepts common in the field, it would be useful to revisit and examine the term and its use in group work to clarify its meaning and increase its utility. This represents a step toward combining an intuitive, artistic application with a more planful, systematic application that combines the best of art and science in working with groups (Ward, 2002). In this chapter, the origins and current status of group processing will be highlighted in a brief history, models that have been proposed for how to process will be described, and finally, general recommendations for the effective use of processing in group work will be presented.

ORIGINS AND CURRENT STATUS

Modern group work had its most prominent origins in the development of the T-group by Kurt Lewin and his colleagues, and the deliberate use of the term *processing* also has its roots in this movement (Yalom, 1975). Lewin's emphasis on the importance of experiential learning or "learning by doing" was the fundamental premise upon which this influential, heuristic approach to group work began. By emphasizing experience and discussion in the *here and now,* including shared perceptions of personal, interpersonal, and group-as-a-whole behavior through the use of *feedback,* the foundation of *process groups* and the deliberate use of processing in groups was established. Especially important was the event that occurred in 1946 known as "The Accident," during which group members, at their own request, were allowed to observe the first meeting for analyzing the groups and planning the next activities by the weekend coordinators, trainers or leaders, and researchers. In retrospect, it is not surprising that these members, who were instructed not to interact but only to observe, very quickly became vocally active in the discussion, bringing a new perspective to the analysis of what had happened and its meaning. That Lewin and his colleagues immediately recognized the incredible potential value of this shared interaction and analysis at a time when the demarcations between leaders and members and their respective roles were much more formal and rigid is a testament to their genius, as well as to the fact that Lewin lived his philosophy of learning by doing and through his commitment to action research in the field (Lewin, 1951).

From this innovative weekend group experience for the Connecticut Interracial Commission in New Britain, Connecticut, came the establishment of the National Training Laboratory (NTL) in Bethel, Maine. Following Lewin's unexpected death in 1947 shortly after the original T-group weekend, professionals from diverse backgrounds developed a wide variety of revisions and applications of this new and exciting approach to group work. Over the following quarter of a century, adaptations of the T-group model arose quickly in forms such as sensitivity-training groups, encounter groups, personal growth groups, and process groups. These groups were applied in a wide variety of settings, including business in the form of organizational development; in counseling and psychotherapy, particularly as *group work for normals* to enhance their levels of functioning

personally and in relationships and groups; and especially with the advent of funding by the National Defense Education Act in the 1960s for intensive counselor-training programs to increase the number of school counselors in the United States.

Central to these groups, which often differed in a number of ways in form or context, was an emphasis, to a greater or lesser degree, upon the importance of what the members and leaders did with one another in the group, how they did it, their relationships with each other, and the functioning of the groups as whole units. Providing personal feedback to one another and personal reactions about group development and seeking to extract meaning from the experience became crucial characteristics. A number of scholars conducted important research studies and proposed models to identify, define, and describe some of the key group dynamics or group process features of group work (Bales, 1950; Benne & Sheats, 1948; Cartwright & Zander, 1968; Golumbiewski, 1961; Hill, 1965; Schutz, 1958, 1966; Tuckman, 1965; Tuckman & Jensen, 1977). However, most groups conducted at that time emphasized experiential learning and deemphasized linear thinking to such an extent that the use of cognitive models to examine and extract meaning from the process was uncommon. Group workers, for the most part, emphasized the facilitation of group interaction and intuitive, experiential learning, but few models existed to help members examine, cognitively understand, and extract broader meaning from their experiences.

The social climate in the United States during the 1960s allowed and encouraged a dramatic proliferation of groups for training, personal growth, counseling, and psychotherapy. This increased interest in and respect for group counseling and psychotherapy marked the beginning of the reversal of the negative attitude toward the efficacy of group work that was strongly adhered to by most of the psychoanalytic community at that time. The professional knowledge base, primarily acquired through participation and observation, was most often directed only at what Yalom (1995) describes as "the first tier of the here and now" or process focus, in which members are helped to work and relate in the here and now. Therefore, although the establishment of a group climate in which members spontaneously describe their perceptions of the ongoing group experience itself is critical, the other fundamental requirement for the development of powerful group culture, systematic reflecting upon and extracting meaning from the experience, which Yalom called the "second tier," was not regularly met.

Many counselors and therapists who engaged in group work at this time were either left conducting some type of T-group or one of its derivations, such as personal growth and encounter groups, or were left attempting to use theories developed primarily for therapeutic work with individuals. One unfortunate consequence was that in the first case, mixed or inadequate outcomes of group counseling and therapy resulted from methods designed for work with "normals." On the other hand, in the case of applying theories of therapy designed for work with individuals, group work often became individual counseling in a group setting and focused primarily on the intrapsychic activity of the individual members, rather than on the potential power of the relationships in the group itself.

During the 1970s, an important trend began to influence the field of group work, especially in regard to the conceptualization of group work and of the nature of processing itself. A marker event that punctuated this trend was the publication of the first edition of Yalom's (1970) classic book, *The Theory and Practice of Group Psychotherapy*. Based partially on findings from comprehensive content analyses of both encounter groups and therapy groups summarized in *Encounter Groups: First Facts* (Lieberman, Yalom, & Miles, 1973), Yalom presented a systematic, comprehensive model for incorporating a here-and-now group process application in group therapy. His premise was that if all the potential for working in groups were to be harnessed, group workers needed to facilitate the development of 11 therapeutic or curative factors, the most central and necessary of which are *group cohesiveness* and *interpersonal learning*. Leader facilitation skills that had been derived from a quarter of a century of exploration and development by proponents of the T-group movement were necessary to develop and establish the importance of here-and-now relationships and

cohesiveness in the group. However, cohesiveness and here-and-now activity alone would not often lead to lasting, long-term change. To unleash and harness the powerful interpersonal-learning change mechanisms available in group work, groups must be helped to establish *process illumination* as a norm to "recognize, examine, and understand the process. It must examine itself and its own transactions; it must transcend pure experience" (Yalom, 1995, pp. 129-130). Thus, in addition to working in the here and now, the group "doubles back on itself; it performs a self-reflective loop and examines the here-and-now that has just occurred" (Yalom, 1995, p. 130). The articulation of this two-tier process was one of Yalom's seminal creative contributions. He postulated that once the here-and-now norm had been established, members were often able to maintain this focus themselves, but that the process commentary for reflection and meaning extraction often had to be initiated and guided by the leader.

Other major publications providing information and models for helping to establish and use within-group relationships and group-as-a-whole features began to appear after the first edition of Yalom's (1970) book. Pfeiffer and Jones (1972-1980) published a series of annual handbooks describing a wide variety of structured exercises and lectures, and a series of books of structured exercises (1977) to help group workers facilitate group development and extract meaning from it. Lieberman et al. (1973) described their comprehensive study of encounter groups, in which they identified the four major functions of effective leaders: caring, meaning attribution, executive function, and emotional stimulation. From this study, Yalom concluded that for significant learning to occur as a result of group process, leaders must also attend to cognitive elements by helping members to understand and extract meaning from their here-and-now group experiences. Shaffer and Galinsky (1974) published the first edition of their book describing models of group therapy, and Gazda (1971) described a developmental model to guide group work in the first edition of his book. Both described initial attempts at models that could be used to facilitate the development of cognitive processing of the experiential aspects of group activity.

RATIONALE FOR GROUP PROCESSING

This deliberate shift of attention to cognitive as well as affective and experiential levels of group work marked the beginning of another phase in the use of group processing. The within-group discussions of group level norms and interpersonal interaction or first tier of here-and-now activation and processing, including leader and member feedback, required focus upon process illumination and the meaning of those processes to members to facilitate maximum successful outcome (Yalom, 1995). As Lieberman et al. (1973) concluded,

> The absence of Meaning-Attribution appears to spell the difference between the relatively low levels of success of the leader with high caring behavior and greater success of another who carries on high caring behavior, and provides a cognitive framework as well. (p. 240)

They concluded that in the encounter groups they investigated, high levels of leader affective characteristics, which they labeled *caring,* must be integrated with high levels of emphasis upon cognitive activity, or *meaning attribution,* to achieve maximum outcome in group work (Lieberman et al., 1973).

Yalom believed that much of the first tier of processing in groups involving here-and-now experiential interaction and feedback can be shared by members and leaders, but the second tier, *process commentary,* is primarily a leader responsibility. Another implication of the Lieberman et al. (1973) research is that cognitive processing to help members learn from their experience is a critical function of all effective groups directed at personal change, learning, and growth, from encounter groups to therapy groups (Yalom, 1995). For the most powerful group dynamics to be set in motion, the second tier of the processing of the here-and-now experience must be established. An example of the second tier of processing follows:

Member: I am having difficulty listening and staying focused on the group discussion right now.

Leader: Stacy, I remember your having this same reaction at other points in the group. I wonder if we can talk about what it is

that the group is doing now and at these other points when you have this reaction. Perhaps others can also share their perceptions and reactions to the group's discussion and process.

This expanded emphasis upon using processing in groups is not limited to groups directed at bringing about personal change. Conyne (1997a) advocated the use of processing with all types of groups identified in the Association for Specialists in Group Work (ASGW) spectrum: task, psychoeducational, counseling, and psychotherapy groups (ASGW, 1990). Conyne's rationale is as follows:

> (a) all these groups involve complex interaction, (b) all these groups are intentional in execution and in their expected outcomes, and (c) all these groups involve the application of learning. Processing allows leaders and members alike to make sense of group dynamics, events, and experiences that otherwise might remain unknown, mistaken or only partially understood. The resulting translation of observation and experience into understanding and meaning affords participants an increased capacity for learning and change, and it is the most important phase of group experience (Kees & Jacobs, 1990). (p. 168)

Chalofsky and Bates (1984) advocated the use of a process facilitator in addition to a group leader to increase task force effectiveness. Johnson and Johnson (1991) also advocated the use of group processing in cooperative-learning groups in school settings at all levels, citing two studies that yielded empirical support for the use of processing in these task groups (Johnson, Johnson, Stanne, & Garibaldi, 1993; Yager, Johnson, Johnson, & Snider, 1986).

In 1993, Wiggins and Carroll concluded from surveys they conducted among 2,270 school counselors that group processing skills were absent from the repertoires of school counselors. Although a majority of the school counselors in this sample were able to identify important group dynamic variables and interactions, their understanding of the act of processing seemed almost unrelated to their knowledge of the concept. Conyne, Wilson, and Ward (1997) stressed the importance for group leaders to be able to process and extract meaning themselves from the sometimes overwhelming amount of information in a group before they are able to assist members to process relevant information and extract meaning for personal learning, change, and growth. DeLucia-Waack (1997) concurred and stated, "The processing of critical events and issues is critical to all forms of group work. Even if events are unplanned, they often must be processed to clarify group interactions and assure interpersonal learning" (p. 82).

The importance of group processing has been so well established that it is included throughout the most recent version of the ASGW *Professional Standards for the Training of Group Workers* (2000) and in the ASGW *Best Practice Guidelines* (1998). They state, "Group workers process the workings of the group with themselves, group members, supervisors, or other colleagues, as appropriate" (ASGW, 1998, p. 243), and they go on to recommend that group workers engage in *reflective practice* by engaging in regular internal processing of group dynamics and interaction and their relationships to individual learning and group development, based upon the concept of the *reflective practitioner* described in Conyne et al. (1997). The widespread acceptance of the critical value of processing is echoed in the descriptions of group work for specific purposes, including processing group exercises (Jacobs, Masson, & Harvill, 2002; Kees & Jacobs, 1990) and training group leaders (Corey, 1981; Glass & Benshoff, 1999; Stockton, Morran, & Nitza, 2000; Trotzer, 1999; Werstlein & Borders, 1997) and with a variety of specific populations, including working with children and adolescents (Smead, 1995), with survivor groups using feminist principles (Rittenhouse, 1997), and in international settings (Conyne, Wilson, & Tang, 2000).

The critical importance of effective processing in group work is nearly universally accepted and has received increasing attention in recent years. Most professionals agree that highly effective group work requires processing "because it is making sense of the interaction or event that is the critically important variable," and it is this process of making sense of or extracting meaning from the interactions and events that "can be integrated and then be applied outside the group" (Conyne, 1997b, p. 153). If this is the case, why is the presentation of the concept so uneven in basic textbooks and training programs and its use unsystematic and sometimes counterproductive?

CURRENT STATUS OF EFFECTIVE GROUP PROCESSING: CLARIFYING THE COMPLEXITY

The primary restraints upon the more effective use of processing in all modern group work are a result of the complexity of the terms *group process* and *group processing* themselves and the lack of clear, common definitions for their use by group work scholars, educators, and practitioners. Therefore, this is an appropriate time in the development of group work to examine the definitions and meanings used to describe "group processing." By clarifying the meanings, it may be possible to improve their conceptualization and to increase the effectiveness of the application of processing to group work.

The second edition of the *Oxford English Dictionary* includes four pages of definitions of the words *process* and *processing* (Simpson & Weiner, 1989). Group workers and mental health professionals in general have applied a number of these definitions in their work, resulting in confusion concerning what is meant when discussing group processing.

Another reason for the confusion and uneven application of processing in group work is the nonsystematic way in which the idea of "techniques" is treated in the broader field of counseling and psychotherapy. As with many terms in common use, processing has been used to describe group leader and member behavior at various levels of complexity aimed at a variety of targets, and has not been used to describe a clearly articulated set of behaviors. It will be used here in the broadest sense to refer to a set of skills or a strategy or intervention that may be applied at various levels of complexity, may be directed at various targets, and may include a variety of microskills, conditions, and behaviors.

Professional group workers, then, use various specific skills at multiple levels of complexity when they engage in processing. In addition, group workers direct their processing efforts at various targets in the group. Some of these include the processing of (a) process or content; (b) process (affective, relationship, cohesiveness-building, and maintenance functions) or task (cognitive-behavioral, goal-oriented functions); (c) external behavior, events, communication patterns or internal feelings, thinking, attitudes, values, or processing itself; or (d) individual member, member-member interpersonal interaction and communication patterns, or group-as-a-whole dynamics and patterns of behavior. Even this list may not identify all targets of group worker processing efforts. Another complication is that some descriptions emphasize leader internal processing or processing with a coleader, supervisor, or in a supervisory team, while others primarily describe processing in the group itself. Processing in the group can emphasize leader processing, or it can include members sharing in the processing activity, both through giving feedback and through more general processing activity. Processing may also be directed at the individual member to promote individual learning and change or at the interpersonal and group-as-a-whole levels to promote positive group development toward a cohesive, collaborative working group that enhances the quality and amount of group productivity. Yalom (1995) recognized the multiple levels of activity at which effective processing is often directed when he stated that it can also focus primarily on bringing about a here-and-now focus or upon adding the critically important second tier of process commentary to bring about illumination of the process.

Yalom (1995) defines processing as leader or therapist behavior that helps the group to "recognize, examine, and understand process . . . examine itself . . . study its own transactions" and "transcend pure experience and apply itself to the integration of that experience," and he believes that its use is necessary to bring about the powerful therapeutic factor of interpersonal learning (pp. 129-130). Posthuma (1999) based her definition on that of Conyne (1997a) by stating that although processing involves following group dynamics and events on an ongoing basis, "It is not enough to only perceive what is occurring in the group; the leader must also help the members acquire some cognitive understanding of the process in order for them to benefit from

the experience" (p. 120). Hansen, Warner, and Smith (1980) stated, "The purpose of a process intervention is to focus on what is happening in the group. The leader may intervene to clarify, make suggestions, or share his or her feelings in the group" (p. 125).

More recently, Stockton et al. (2000), consistent with Yalom (1995), asserted that although members can learn through exchanging feedback and examining interpersonal events with the help of the leader, significant personal growth results when leaders help the group "to recognize, articulate, and reflect on the experiences that result from these events" (p. 343). They also refer to Cohen and Smith's (1976a) description of a group's integration of experiences as *critical-incident processing.* Glass and Benshoff (1999) contend that processing or "helping group members identify and examine what happened in the group and their individual experience of the event, as well as how the event occurred and how different members responded to it" (p. 16) is essential for group experience to have maximum impact on members. They warn, however, that, without a sound understanding of group dynamics theory, processing skills will not effectively increase member and group understanding and outcome. Gazda, Ginter, and Horne (2001) include processing in their list of 12 characteristics displayed by effective leaders and define it as follows:

> The leader references and processes group data in a manner to enhance members' understanding and ability to clarify their own behavior and thoughts as well as to develop the ability to interpret interpersonal and intrapsychic interventions without the leader's assistance. (p. 36)

As it relates to specific aspects of group work, Jacobs, Masson, and Harvill (2002) contend that processing, or "spending time discussing thoughts, feelings, and ideas that result from closing the exercise," is "by far the most important phase of any exercise" (p. 243). In their discussion of the importance and purpose of group processing, Johnson and Johnson (1991) present a definition and purpose statement of group processing in cooperative learning task groups:

Reflecting on a group session to (1) describe what member actions were helpful and unhelpful and (2) make decisions about what actions to continue or change. The purpose of group processing is to clarify and improve the effectiveness of the members in contributing to the collaborative efforts to achieve the group's goals. (p. 203)

The ASGW training standards (2000) emphasize the importance of several aspects of group processing, and it is one of the three headings used to organize the ASGW *Best Practice Guidelines* (1998). Standard C.1. calls for the systematic use of processing:

Group workers process the workings of the group with themselves, group members, supervisors, or other colleagues, as appropriate. This may include assessing progress in group and member goals, leader behavior and techniques, group dynamics and interventions, as well as developing understanding and acceptance of meaning. Processing may occur both within sessions and before and after each session, at time of termination and later follow-up, as appropriate. (p. 243)

These descriptions and definitions all have potential relevance for group work. Processing may be considered to be a desirable activity in which individuals and groups regularly examine and reflect upon their behavior to extract meaning, integrate the resulting knowledge, and improve functioning and outcome. Although members may engage in intrapsychic processing of their thoughts, feelings, and behavior at any time, including during group sessions themselves, one of the major goals of individual and group psychotherapy is to increase the use of this type of processing as a regular, naturally occurring, productive activity. It is also essential that professional mental health workers engage in internal processing in their work to help them to understand the complex patterns of behavior in which clients and group members engage and to plan and effectively intervene to maximize understanding, learning, change, and growth. In all cases, the use of processing in groups should enhance group functioning and the functioning of individual members both in the group and in their everyday lives.

Because here-and-now communication and systematic examination of interpersonal experience are atypical of natural conversation, it is difficult for members to process their relationships and whole-group activity themselves (Hansen et al., 1980; Stockton et al., 2000; Yalom, 1995). In groups where the conditions are conducive for the establishment and use of processing to enhance group productivity and outcome, the leader must assume responsibility for the facilitation of here-and-now interaction and deeper reflective processing as a norm of group activity. In addition to the facilitation of this level of activity, in which part of the group's natural activity is to engage in here-and-now activity and feedback, the leader must also use group processing intervention skills to direct members to focus upon, examine, and learn from their own personal behavior, interpersonal interactions and relationships, and whole-group activity. At this level, processing can also serve to increase the level of functioning of the group itself, leading to increased collaborative productivity and higher levels of positive outcome on the group's task or goals.

Group leaders, then, facilitate the development of an atmosphere in which processing is expected and natural. Once processing has been established as a natural, ongoing group activity, effective group leaders direct their efforts in order to intervene deliberately and judiciously to assist the group to focus upon, examine, and extract meaning from its activity. They then assist members to apply that meaning to improve individual, interpersonal, and group level functioning both inside and outside of the group, as well as to improve the functioning and productivity of the group itself. There is consensus among experts that without a solid understanding of individual interpersonal and group dynamic theory and a sense of timing for when and how it is most helpful to focus the group's attention, leader attempts to involve the group in deeper processing may be ineffective or even harmful (Conyne, 1997a; Glass & Benshoff, 1999; Jacobs et al., 2002; Stockton et al., 2000; Yalom, 1995).

MODELS THAT DESCRIBE STEPS IN PROCESSING OR "HOW TO PROCESS"

Although the actual process of group processing or how to process has been relatively neglected, additional models have been proposed since Yalom's seminal work in 1970. It is important that further efforts be directed toward clearly explicating conceptual steps and interventions to expand these models and toward research investigation of their effectiveness so that they are more effective in describing and guiding the differential application of group processing. Kees and Jacobs (1990) also emphasized the importance of processing in groups:

> Without adequate processing, the leader cannot be sure what learning has taken place. If done correctly, processing can provide members with additional learning about themselves and other members of the group. Through processing, members may also develop a plan of action for transferring this learning to their lives outside of the group. (p. 23)

Ward (1982, 1994, 1996) stated that the most complex and powerful use of processing is enhanced when groups develop into interactive, cohesive, collaborative working units.

General Group Processing Models

Yalom's Processing Approach

At the first level of Yalom's (1995) two-tiered processing model, the group therapist gives attention during the early phases of the group to encouraging member-member interpersonal interaction in order to activate a here-and-now orientation. By establishing a norm of member-member feedback, the basic foundation for a process-oriented group is established. Since Yalom's emphasis is upon therapy groups, here-and-now feedback exchange is only the first step. The leader must then assume overall responsibility for establishing process illumination as an important norm. The leader continually observes the relationship messages being communicated with the content of member verbal interaction, selects those that are most relevant to each member's therapeutic goals, and helps the members to focus upon, understand, and integrate the learning into their everyday patterns of behavior. This is accomplished by escorting the member through the following sequence:

1. *Here is what your behavior is like.* Through feedback and later through self-observation, members learn to see themselves as seen by others.

2. *Here is how your behavior makes others feel.* Members learn about the impact of their behavior on the feelings of other members.

3. *Here is how your behavior influences the opinion others have of you.* Members learn that as a result of their behavior, others value them, dislike them, find them unpleasant, respect them, avoid them, and so on.

4. *Here is how your behavior influences your opinion of yourself.* Building on the information gathered in the first three steps, patients formulate self-evaluation; they make judgments about their self-worth and their lovability. (Yalom, 1995, p. 166)

The resulting new knowledge can lead to significant change in the member's everyday world, with continuing effort and work by both the member and the leader to integrate the insights from examining the member's behavior in the group with the member's past history and usual behavioral style. The following is an example of a leader processing statement in a therapy group making use of the four parts of Yalom's model:

Leader: Kristen, let me see if I can summarize what you have learned about your tendency to talk a great deal and monopolize the conversation. It seems to me that other members have begun to react with disinterest when you begin a lengthy speech and that you believe that they do not want to listen and even resent your taking up so much of the group's time with stories that do not seem to lead anywhere. As you perceive their reactions, you feel rejected and believe that this rejection confirms your negative self-concept. Then the anxiety you feel about this view of yourself results in your talking even more to relieve stress, which simply begins the same process again. Is that accurate?

Yalom (1995) also advocated the use of *mass group process commentary,* or identifying, examining, and discussing the relevance and meaning of whole-group themes and trends. Although Yalom uses mass group process commentary to help members understand their behavior in a system, he stated that the more important use of the leader drawing attention to group-as-a-whole interaction is to prevent group forces that may impede effective therapy by removing "some obstacle that has arisen to obstruct the progress of the entire group" (p. 178), primarily in the form of anxiety-laden leader issues and antitherapeutic norms. The following might be an example in a therapy group:

Leader: Before we continue very much longer with this new topic of how stressful life is today, I would like to check something. Scott, how are you feeling?

Scott (hesitant and subdued): I don't know. I guess I am OK.

Leader: You're not really certain about your feelings now. Maybe I can ask the same question of Michael. Can you describe your feelings now, Michael?

Michael: Yes, I'm frustrated.

Leader: Can you identify the source of your frustration?

Michael: It seems like whenever Scott and I begin to talk directly to each other about our feelings toward women, we don't get to finish.

Leader: Yes, that is what I noticed. I think that it is important that you, Michael and Scott, have the opportunity to discuss and work through your strong differences on the topic of

women. I also wonder if this tendency of the group to begin an enthusiastic discussion of a new topic whenever strong tension arises between members is something that we should discuss.

Yalom (1975) emphasized that specific incidents that are potentially most productive for processing vary from group therapist to group therapist and group to group. However, he believes that the key to the effective use of group processing in therapy groups is the therapist's continuing effort to identify and make use of examination of in-group behavior to identify and then help members to transfer meaning to their self-concepts and out-of-group behavioral styles. Therefore, Yalom stresses the importance of the leader function of meaning attribution to process the relationship implications of the member's interpersonal interactions in the group and to help the members transfer their learning to their everyday lives.

Cohen and Smith's Model

Cohen and Smith (1976a, 1976b) developed a model to help leaders classify and choose effective leader interventions when processing critical incidents in groups. This model consists of three levels of interventions, each with three sublevels:

The level of intervention, i.e., whether the focus is on group, interpersonal, or individual behavior; the *type of intervention,* i.e., whether the intervention is conceptual, experiential, or structural; and the *intensity of intervention,* i.e., the degree to which the choice of response is directed at the emotional center of the target issue on a continuum from *low* to *medium* to *high.* These three response dimensions are conceptualized as the Intervention Cube. (Cohen & Smith, 1976a, pp. 87-88)

Conyne's Model

For a number of years, Conyne has been interested in and worked to develop a processing model or cognitive map to facilitate processing in groups and to teach to students learning to lead groups (Ward, 1993). He believes that the complexity of group work can confuse members and leaders and "this confusion makes the effective processing of group experiences and events impossible" (Conyne, 1997a, p. 167). His model is called the "grid for processing experiences in group," and it consists of three dimensions: the level of focus ("I" or intrapsychic, "You" or other, "We" or the interpersonal, and "Us" or the group as a whole unit), the content ("What"), and the process ("How") (Conyne, 1997a, pp. 169-171). Conyne recommended explaining the grid to members and asking them to join the leader in examining and extracting meaning from group experience by focusing on the "What" (content) and the "How" (process) at specific levels of experience.

Glass and Benshoff's PARS Model

Glass and Benshoff (1999) describe the PARS model (process, activity, relationship, and self) for use in processing. The model is displayed as a three-by-three cell matrix. The processing dimension has three stages: reflecting on what happened by tracing the steps, understanding the meaning of what happened, and applying the meaning to member behavior outside the group. They also present an appendix with three pages of sample questions to use when processing activity within each cell. These questions can be applied to process the activities or events themselves, the relationships or how things evolved and their meaning in the group, or the self to examine the implications of each member's roles and behaviors. For example, if a member were to state, "I am confused, because we are talking about Jeremy's graduation rather than the topic of unfairness that I brought up," the leader might suggest that the group engage in the first level of processing in the PARS model, or *reflecting-activity,* to track the activities or events that had occurred, by saying, "I wonder if we can put our current discussion on hold and trace the steps we took to get from Monica's topic of unfairness to Jeremy's graduation. Is that all right with you, Jeremy?" After the events have been traced and the group has some consensus about what has happened, the leader might stimulate a discussion by focusing on the PARS processing dimension of *understanding-relationships* with the following statement,

"It seems to me that Jeremy and Monica may be able to benefit if we discuss their shift from Monica's initiation of an intellectual topic to Jeremy's personalizing the discussion by focusing on his feelings about the unfairness of the current economic climate and lack of job opportunities, and what it means about their attitude and feelings toward each other."

Stockton, Morran, and Nitza's Cognitive Map

Stockton, Morran, and Nitza (2000) define processing as "a formal attempt by the leader to help members derive meaning from specific events that occur in the group" (p. 345). They describe four steps in processing: identifying critical incidents, examining the event and member reactions, deriving meaning and self-understanding from the event, and applying new understanding toward personal change. Although they contend that a description of an organized set of counselor skills or behaviors for processing has not been satisfactorily developed, use of their four-step model can be implemented through leader encouragement of member-member feedback exchange and by sharing hypotheses to model the processing function in order to help develop a reflective processing norm in which members and leaders can engage. In addition to focusing on direct member involvement in a critical incident, all group members can be invited to participate in processing in the manner of a *reflection team* used in family work.

Models for Processing With Specific Populations

Models have been described for group processing with specific populations. Examples presented have included processing group exercises, processing training experiences for group workers, working with children and adolescents, and working in multicultural and international situations.

Processing Group Exercises

Kees and Jacobs (1990) described guidelines for processing group exercises. Much of their work is now included in and expanded upon in Jacobs et al. (2002), in which processing is considered to be the most important aspect of using group exercises. The goals of processing include (a) stimulating sharing and discussion about topics or issues, (b) stimulating members to delve deeper into thoughts and feelings, and (c) stimulating sharing and discussion of the group dynamics and process (Jacobs et al., pp. 243-244). They identify the most important leader skills for processing as good empathy skills, questioning skills, and the ability to hold, deepen, and shift the focus, as appropriate, and they provide a number of excellent brief examples of effective and ineffective group verbal interactions involving processing.

Teaching and Using Processing in Group Leader Training Programs

Conyne et al. (1997) stressed the importance of teaching group leaders to attend to both content and process and to use processing skills as they learn to lead groups. Examples of how processing skills are used and taught in a number of exemplary counselor education programs are provided.

Corey (1981) described a group leadership practicum course taught over two weekends. Throughout the entire course, process commentary was used to help students process their ongoing group experiences as leaders and members. Processing questions for learning included variations on the following:

- How can you incorporate the theories in a personal way into your own leadership style?
- How can members be best prepared for a group?
- In what ways can coleaders resolve differences of opinion in a respectful manner?
- What are some constructive approaches for dealing with difficult group members?
- How can confrontation be done in a caring and effective manner?
- How can techniques be used in a way to enhance group work, and how can these techniques become an integral part of the style of leading of the student interns? (pp. 104-105)

Shortly after Corey described the use of processing in his training model, Anderson (1982) presented a training module for group facilitators with processing as one of four steps in each round of the activity. After the trainer modeled specific leader behavior to the entire group or class, small groups interacted in a discussion. The third step in each of these interactions is processing, with the leader and group members focusing upon issues such as the leader giving feedback to each group member about their involvement in the task, and focusing on which members most influenced the group and how. The fourth step in each cycle, critiquing the leader, is actually a form of processing, since members discussed and shared their perceptions of leader behavior with the leader.

Kane (1995) described the topics upon which she focused the total group processing session in her use of the fishbowl technique for training group leaders. After half the class observed the other half engaging in small-group activity, she invited the entire class to ask questions and give feedback. Her emphasis was on the process or relationships and group dynamics more than on content. In her summary description of the major dynamics upon which the processing usually focused, Kane cited critical elements that had been identified by other authors:

> During the total group processing, students were able to comment on the various leadership styles and group members' responses to them (Boy, 1990), the effect of greater versus less structure from the leaders, the power of a here-and-now focus, the occurrence of transference and countertransference among group members and leaders, the stages of group development, and the effect of certain member behaviors, such as dominance or silence, on the group, as well as possible interventions (Behr, 1990; Dinkmeyer, 1991). (p. 186)

Processing in Groups for Children and Adolescents

Smead (1995) describes guidelines for processing in groups of children and adolescents. She views processing as one of the most important group leader skills and especially emphasizes its use at the end of each group session. During this processing phase, members are helped to review various elements of the session, identify what they learned, and identify ways in which they can use the learning outside of the group. Smead recommends processing the objective, cognitive, and behavioral, as well as content dimensions of the group activity, at four levels: (a) the intrapersonal dimension; (b) the interpersonal dimension; (c) new thoughts, feelings, and behavior; and (d) use and application of new knowledge. She also provides excellent examples of processing questions for use at each level, as well as an example of a specific value-sharing activity making use of processing questions. The following might be an example of a counselor processing statement in a counseling group for low-achieving high school students:

Leader: I think that it would be helpful if we pause and talk about how our meetings have been going up until now. I am very interested in knowing how you view what we have done, what it means to us as a group, and how we can use it to work together better and to help each of us to be more successful in school.

DeLucia-Waack (2001) has written a book describing the innovative use of music in groups of children of divorce; it is accompanied by an audiotape of songs for young people (Conley, 1994). She presented a plan for an 11-session group, with specific topics and guidelines for each meeting, using the songs from the audiotape in each session. She states that "the most common mistake in group work is insufficient processing of activities" (DeLucia-Waack, 2001, p. xiii). She also provides sample questions for use with each activity for processing with each child and the group as a whole, and to enhance the application of new learning.

Multicultural International Group Work

Several models emphasizing the importance of the use of processing in groups with multicultural membership have been identified (Conyne, 1997a; DeLucia, Coleman, & Jensen-Scott, 1992; DeLucia-Waack, 1999; Ivey, Pederson, & Ivey, 2001). Working with groups in China, Conyne (1999) used a specific between-sessions leader processing model consisting of five steps: (a) transposing, (b) reflecting, (c) discovering, (d) applying, and (e) evolving. He and his colleagues emphasized that increased patience

must be exercised when group workers from the United States apply these five steps of group processing, because cultural norms in China require a more moderate pace (Conyne et al., 2000). Although he stressed that general processing skills and questions may be used in cross-cultural international work, he also contended that leaders must give special attention to reflecting upon and adapting processing to be effective and compatible with this and other salient cultural characteristics of the members.

GENERAL RECOMMENDATIONS FOR GROUP PROCESSING

The origins and current status, rationale, definitional challenges, and models that have been developed for how to process in groups have been addressed. It is clear that group processing is a complex topic that needs systematic attention by group work theorists, researchers, and practitioners to maximize the effectiveness of its use in facilitating group development and individual and group functioning and productivity.

What can be concluded concerning the effective use of group processing at this time? The following is a modest set of recommendations for consideration in regard to processing in groups:

1. Processing is critical to and synonymous with sophisticated modern group work. As Yalom (1995) and Conyne (1997a, 1997b) contend, the development of an interactive, here-and-now, systemic, collaborative group that reflects upon its activity is an extremely powerful mechanism for learning and growth.

2. Leaders themselves should always engage in internal processing during and between sessions to maximize their understanding of and work in groups.

3. Counseling, therapy, and other group approaches directed at psychological learning and change almost always lend themselves to and are enhanced by intrapersonal, interpersonal, and group processing, except in cases where conditions require an emphasis on the external management of behavior or direct instruction.

4. For individual members, the purpose of engaging in processing is to help them make sense of and extract meaning from their group experience, as well as to apply this meaning to their everyday lives.

5. The development of collaborative functioning leading to high levels of productivity for the group itself can be enhanced by processing, or by facilitating client or member focusing upon, reflecting upon, extracting meaning from, and applying learning from individual, interpersonal, and group level activity and relationships.

6. Effective group processing focuses both upon the content or the "What" of group activity as well as upon the "How" of group dynamic and relationship processes.

7. An important assumption in the mental health field is Paul's (1966) dictum that techniques and theories of counseling and psychotherapy must be carefully selected and differentially applied by considering the specific characteristics of a variety of salient factors, such as the client, the therapist, and the goals of treatment. This is consistent with the group work literature on processing, because although general skills and models for use in group processing have been developed, one of the most important principles that may be extracted from a survey of the literature is that to be effective, processing must be differentially applied according to a variety of factors. These include the type of group, the specific characteristics and needs of the members, the personal and professional skills and style of the leader, the developmental stage and goals of the group, and other cultural-environmental influences.

8. Processing involves a here-and-now focus upon what happens in a group and often on highly personal thoughts and feelings, which can involve an intensity of interaction that may be threatening to members and to the group structure. Therefore, it is best used differentially in gradations as strong, supportive, facilitative leader-member and member-member relationships, as well as group cohesiveness, are established. Effective group leaders also understand when not to engage in group processing.

9. A single comprehensive model for group processing has not been developed. Since there are differences in the working models thus far presented in the literature and since different variations and approaches appear to be effective, a constructivist perspective is the most realistic position to describe the use of group processing models and skills at this point. In other words, the logical and sensitive application of processing skills consistent with member needs, group setting, and leader knowledge and style can be effective using a number of models. So long as the processing is perceived as relevant by clients and leads to their ability to learn and generalize from their activity and interactions in the group, it may be effective.

10. There are valid reasons for the lack of substantive research to establish empirical support for the widespread belief in the efficacy and use of processing in group work. Despite the challenges, researchers should increase their efforts to work toward the goal of providing evidence to guide group workers in the differential application of processing at various levels of complexity and directed at various targets.

11. The use of the personal characteristics and natural interpersonal style of the leader, integrated with professional knowledge and skills, is critical for the effective use of group processing. Because processing so often involves the examination of strongly held thoughts and intense feelings and because it can be directed at the leader's own performance, a sound personal self-concept consisting of psychological openness, comfort with intimacy, and strength to deal effectively with challenging and powerful personal, interpersonal, and group issues internally and in the public forum are ideal characteristics of effective group leaders.

12. Effective group workers, therefore, know themselves and have adopted a processing approach in their own personal and professional experiences. Although obsessive self-examination can be overused and become problematic in itself, a healthy balance between experience and processing for self-awareness is the ideal for psychosocial health and effective professional functioning as a group leader.

13. To incorporate the effective use of processing, leaders need to learn as much about human development, psychological and interpersonal functioning, counseling theory and skills, group dynamics theory, a multicultural perspective and cross-cultural counseling theory, and professional group leadership skills and theory as possible. They seek understanding at all levels of mastery, from abstract to specific, and learn to be open to, to be aware of, and to work at multiple levels of experience and knowledge simultaneously.

14. Effective leaders are guided by processing models that are consistent with their professional developmental levels, theoretical and professional styles, and the needs and goals of the specific group members and types of groups with which they work.

15. These leaders are open to learning and to expanding their models and styles as a result of processing itself. Personal and professional growth should be a rewarding and meaningful by-product of the effective use of processing in working with groups.

16. Belief in the immense value of developing and working with an interactive, collaborative systems model of group work and in sharing the responsibility for process and outcome with group members, where appropriate, characterizes those who are effective group processors.

17. It is always an important responsibility of the professional group leader to decide the extent to which the responsibility for processing should be assumed primarily by the leader or be shared with group members. This decision should be based upon a number of variables, such as the psychological maturity and motivation of the members for the specific group purpose, the nature and characteristics of the task, time available, group stability or continuity of membership, group size, and external influences.

18. Cherished adages of modern group workers include "trust the process" and trust the "collaborative process of processing" itself (Conyne, 1997b). Effective leaders work to develop the openness, flexibility, strength, and courage to work collaboratively in groups and to model the use of processing for others.

REFERENCES

Anderson, W. (1982). A training module for preparing group facilitators. *The Journal for Specialists in Group Work, 7,* 119-124.

Association for Specialists in Group Work (ASGW). (1990). *Professional standards for the training of group workers.* Alexandria, VA: Author.

Association for Specialists in Group Work (ASGW). (1998). ASGW best practice guidelines. *Journal for Specialists in Group Work, 23,* 237-244.

Association for Specialists in Group Work (ASGW). (2000). *Professional standards for the training of group workers.* Alexandria, VA: Author.

Bales, R. F. (1950). *Interaction process analysis: A method for the study of small groups.* Reading, MA: Addison-Wesley.

Behr, H. (1990). Block training: The influence of the modified setting on the group-analytic process. *Group Analysis, 23,* 347-352.

Benne, K. D., & Sheats, P. (1948). Functional roles of group members. *Journal of Social Issues, 4,* 41-49.

Boy, A. V. (1990). The therapist in person-centered groups. *Group Analysis, 23,* 347-352.

Cartwright, D., & Zander, A. (Eds.). (1968). *Group dynamics: Research and theory* (3rd ed.). New York: Harper & Row.

Chalofsky, N., & Bates, R. (1984). Using group process techniques to increase task force effectiveness: A case study. *Journal for Specialists in Group Work, 9,* 93-98.

Cohen, A. M., & Smith, R. D. (1976a). *The critical incident in growth groups: A manual for group leaders.* La Jolla, CA: University Associates.

Cohen, A. M., & Smith, R. D. (1976b). *The critical incident in growth groups: Theory and technique.* La Jolla, CA: University Associates.

Conley, D. (1994). *If you believe in you* [Cassette]. New York: Treehouse Music.

Conyne, R. K. (1997a). Developing framework for processing experiences and events in group work. *Journal for Specialists in Group Work, 22,* 167-174.

Conyne, R. K. (1997b). Group work ideas I have made aphoristic (for me). *Journal for Specialists in Group Work, 22,* 149-156.

Conyne, R. K. (1999). *Failures in group work: How can we learn from our mistakes?* Thousand Oaks, CA: Sage.

Conyne, R. K., Wilson, F. R., & Tang, M. (2000). Evolving lessons from group work involvement in China. *Journal for Specialists in Group Work, 25,* 252-268.

Conyne, R. K., Wilson, F. R., & Ward, D. E. (1997). *Comprehensive group work: What it means and how to teach it.* Alexandria, VA: American Counseling Association.

Corey, G. (1981). Description of a practicum course in group leadership. *Journal for Specialists in Group Work, 6,* 100-108.

DeLucia, J. L., Coleman, V. D., & Jensen-Scott, R. L. (1992). Cultural diversity in group counseling. *Journal for Specialists in Group Work, 17,* 194-195.

DeLucia-Waack, J. L. (1997). The importance of processing activities, exercises, and events to group work practitioners. *Journal for Specialists in Group Work, 22,* 82-84.

DeLucia-Waack, J. L. (1999). Exploring multicultural group work from a variety of perspectives. *Journal for Specialists in Group Work, 24,* 339-341.

DeLucia-Waack, J. L. (2001). *Using music in children of divorce groups: A session-by-session manual for counselors.* Alexandria, VA: American Counseling Association.

Dinkmeyer, D. (1991). Encouragement: Basis for leader training and participative management. *Individual Psychology, 47,* 504-508.

Gazda, G. M. (1971). *Group counseling: A developmental approach.* Boston: Allyn & Bacon.

Gazda, G. M., Ginter, E. J., & Horne, A. M. (2001). *Group counseling and group psychotherapy: Theory and application.* Boston: Allyn & Bacon.

Glass, J. S., & Benshoff, J. M. (1999). PARS: A processing model for beginning group leaders. *Journal for Specialists in Group Work, 24,* 15-26.

Golumbiewski, R. (1961). *The small group.* Chicago: University of Chicago Press.

Hansen, J. C., Warner, R. W., & Smith, E. J. (1980). *Group counseling: Theory and process* (2nd ed.). Chicago: Rand McNally.

Hill, W. F. (1965). *HIM: Hill Interaction Matrix.* Los Angeles: University of Southern California, Youth Studies Center.

Ivey, A. E., Pedersen, P. B., & Ivey, M. B. (2001). *Intentional group counseling: A microskills approach.* Belmont, CA: Brooks/Cole.

Jacobs, E. E., Masson, R. L., & Harvill, R. L. (2002). *Group counseling: Strategies and skills* (4th ed.). Australia: Brooks/Cole.

Johnson, D. W., & Johnson, F. P. (1991). *Joining together: Group theory and group skills* (4th ed.). Upper Saddle River, NJ: Prentice Hall.

Johnson, D. W., Johnson, R. T., Stanne, M. B., & Garibaldi, A. (1993). Impact of group processing on achievement in cooperative groups. *The Journal of Social Psychology, 130,* 507-516.

Kane, C. M. (1995). Fishbowl training in group process. *The Journal for Specialists in Group Work, 20,* 183-188.

Kees, N. L., & Jacobs, E. (1990). Conducting more effective groups: How to select and process group exercises. *Journal for Specialists in Group Work, 15,* 21-29.

Lewin, K. (1951). *Field theory in social science.* New York: Harper.

Lieberman, M. A., Yalom, I. D., & Miles, M. (1973). *Encounter groups: First facts.* New York: Basic Books.

Paul, G. L. (1966). *Insight versus desensitization in psychotherapy: An experiment in anxiety reduction.* Stanford, CA: Stanford University Press.

Pfeiffer, J. W., & Jones, J. E. (Eds.). (1972-1980). *The annual handbook for group facilitators* (Vols. 1-9). La Jolla, CA: University Associates.

Pfeiffer, J. W., & Jones, J. E. (Eds.). (1977). *A handbook of structured experiences for human relations training* (Vols. 1-6). La Jolla, CA: University Associates.

Posthuma, B. W. (1999). *Small groups in counseling and therapy: Process and leadership* (3rd ed.). Boston: Allyn & Bacon.

Rittenhouse, J. (1997). Feminist principles in survivor's groups: Out-of-group-contact. *Journal for Specialists in Group Work, 22,* 111-119.

Schutz, W. C. (1958). *FIRO: A three-dimensional theory of human behavior.* New York: Rinehart.

Schutz, W. C. (1966). *The interpersonal underworld.* Palo Alto, CA: Science and Behavior.

Shaffer, J. B. P., & Galinsky, M. D. (1974). *Models of group therapy.* Englewood Cliffs, NJ: Prentice-Hall.

Simpson, J. A., & Weiner, E. S. C. (Eds.). (1989). *The Oxford English dictionary* (2nd ed., Vol. 12). Oxford, England: Clarendon.

Smead, R. (1995). *Skills and techniques for group work with children and adolescents.* Champaign, IL: Research Press.

Stockton, R., Morran, D. K., & Nitza, A. G. (2000). Processing group events: A conceptual map for leaders. *Journal for Specialists in Group Work, 25,* 343-355.

Trotzer, J. P. (1999). *The counselor and the group: Integrating theory, training, and practice* (3rd ed.). Philadelphia: Accelerated Development.

Tuckman, B. W. (1965). Developmental sequence in small groups. *Psychological Bulletin, 63,* 384-399.

Tuckman, B. W., & Jensen, M. A. C. (1977). Stages of small group development revisited. *Group and Organizational Studies, 2,* 419-427.

Ward, D. E. (1982). A model for the more effective use of theory in group work. *Journal for Specialists in Group Work, 7,* 224-230.

Ward, D. E. (1993). An interview with Bob Conyne. *Journal for Specialists in Group Work, 18,* 99-108.

Ward, D. E. (1994). *Principles in group work* (2nd ed.). Pittsburg, KS: Pittsburg State University Bookstore.

Ward, D. E. (1996). Factors influencing the development and quality of cooperative teamwork in groups. In S. T. Gladding (Ed.), *New developments in group counseling* (pp. 115-120). Greensboro, NC: ERIC Clearinghouse on Counseling & Student Services.

Ward, D. E. (2002). Like old friends, old familiar terms and concepts need attention. *Journal for Specialists in Group Work, 27,* 119-121.

Werstlein, P. O., & Borders, L. D. (1997). Group process variables in group supervision. *Journal for Specialists in Group Work, 22,* 120-136.

Wiggins, J. D., & Carroll, M. R. (1993). Back to the basics: Perceived and actual needs of group leaders. *Journal for Specialists in Group Work, 18,* 24-28.

Yager, S., Johnson, R. T., Johnson, D. W., & Snider, B. (1986). The impact of group processing on achievement in cooperative learning groups. *Journal of Social Psychology, 126,* 389-397.

Yalom, I. D. (1970). *The theory and practice of group psychotherapy.* New York: Basic Books.

Yalom, I. D. (1975). *The theory and practice of group psychotherapy* (2nd ed.). New York: Basic Books.

Yalom, I. D. (1995). *The theory and practice of group psychotherapy* (4th ed.). New York: Basic Books.

9

MEASURES OF GROUP PROCESS, DYNAMICS, CLIMATE, LEADERSHIP BEHAVIORS, AND THERAPEUTIC FACTORS

A Review

JANICE L. DELUCIA-WAACK

University at Buffalo, SUNY

KAREN H. BRIDBORD

University at Buffalo, SUNY

Group counseling and therapy have been shown to be effective in changing problematic attitudes, emotions, and behaviors (Fuhriman & Burlingame, 1994; Kaul & Bednar, 1986; Lieberman, 1976; Toseland & Siporin, 1986). In addition, the efficacy of psychoeducational groups designed to teach specific skills and behaviors has been supported in research studies (Cooper & Stoltenberg, 1987; Shechtman, 1994). The focus has shifted from the question, "Do groups work?" to the question of what makes groups effective.

Leading group theorists have long hypothesized that process variables such as group climate, dynamics, and therapeutic factors contribute to change in group member behavior, regardless of type of group or group members' specific problems. Only recently have researchers begun to systematically study the process of group

counseling and therapy. One slowdown in group process research has been the lack of reliable and valid measures. More reliable and valid outcome measures exist (e.g., anxiety, depression, social skills) than group process instruments.

Measures with demonstrated reliability and validity have only begun to be consistently used; typically, researchers constructed their own measures of group process (Riva & Smith, 1997). Several issues have contributed to the difficulties of creating reliable and valid measures of group process. One is a lack of definitional consensus. For example, what exactly is group cohesiveness? Various definitions abound, making it difficult to operationalize and measure. Another issue relates to the reliability of the measure used. Group process is a dynamic construct, and instruments used to assess process variables need to be sensitive to small and large changes within and across group sessions. Furthermore, with only a limited number of reliable and valid measures of group process, it is difficult to establish convergent validity for new measures.

This chapter will review measures related to group process, dynamics, interventions, therapeutic factors, and leadership behaviors. The focus will be on reliable and valid measures used to assess group process variables. A brief description of the measure and subscales, reliability, and validity information will be provided. Relevant research that uses the measure will also be included. Measures of group process that appear promising will also be noted briefly.

SCREENING AND SELECTION INSTRUMENTS

This section will describe measures used to select group members. These measures assess attitudes toward groups and/or interpersonal behavior that may affect group members' ability to function successfully in psychoeducational, counseling, and therapy groups.

Elements

Schutz (1992) based his instrument, *Elements (Es),* on his interpersonal relations theory called *fundamental interpersonal relations orientation-behavior* (FIRO), which asserts that there are three basic feelings: significance, competence, and likeability. Es is derived from the revision, evolution, and development of his FIRO theory and his instrument, the FIRO Inventory, over the course of 37 years. Schutz's theory and two versions of the FIRO are widely used in business and industry and counseling groups to assess leadership style and potential. Es is a combination of the two earlier instruments: FIRO-Behavior, now Element B; FIRO-Feelings, now Element F; and a new scale, Self-Concept (S).

Element B encompasses three behavioral areas of interpersonal interaction: Inclusion, Control, and Affection. Element F assesses feelings on the dimensions Significance, Competence, and Likeability. In Self-Concept, people assess how they feel about themselves in the following areas: Aliveness (self-inclusion), Self-Determination (self-control), Self-Awareness (self-openness), Self-Significance, Self-Competence, and Self-Like.

All three subscales have a dynamic relationship to each other; together, they measure dimensions of individual, interpersonal, team, and organizational dynamics (Schutz, 1992). The content of the items within the three scales was given to judges to ensure logical agreement between the item content and the definition of the scale. Refer to Schutz (1992) for the complete listing of norms for each subscale and a discussion of differences between populations.

Es is useful for measuring interpersonal behavior and predicting interaction between people (Schutz, 1992) These three instruments measure areas with respect to expressed and wanted behavior (i.e., how an individual acts, and how an individual wishes others to act interpersonally). Compatibility is determined by computing how the expressed behavior of an individual fits with the behavior desired by his or her partner. The FIRO-B and FIRO-F and now Es often have been used to predict task and work group effectiveness, leader and member compatibility, and leadership style (e.g., Armstrong & Priola, 2001; Fisher, Macrosson, & Semple, 2001; Tullett & Davies, 1997).

Group Psychotherapy Evaluation Scale

The Group Psychotherapy Evaluation Scale (GPES) (Kew, 1975) was originally an eight-question instrument designed to assess whether potential group members have the necessary skills to participate successfully in group psychotherapy. The form, completed by the group leader after an initial interview, assesses the behavior of the potential member in the following categories: Amount of Communication (participation), Quality of Relatedness and Communication, Quality of Content in Communication and Relatedness, Capacity for Change, Involvement, Amount of Therapist Verbal Activity, and Direction of Therapist Verbal Activity. This instrument taps factors pertaining to client behavior and ego functioning and also recognizes that therapist behavior can affect client outcome in group therapy (Kew, 1975). After an initial interview, potential group members are rated on a 5-point scale ranging from 0 = *low emphasis* to 4 = *high emphasis*. The total score ranges from 0 to 24, and those scoring over 10 were considered most suitable for group psychotherapy; those between 7 and 9 represented a middle segment; and those least suitable for group psychotherapy scored 6 or less (Kew, 1975). In the sample Kew used, the mean score was 8.07, with a standard deviation of 3.8 based on 12 therapists leading 14 therapy groups with 114 members total. Group leaders completed the GPES initially and then again after 2 years on each group member to assess group member progress. Kew examined each component criterion and determined that the relationship between component items and the total scale score were strongly related to the overall prediction of client suitability for group therapy. Intercorrelations among component items of the GPES indicated that 6 items related to client behavior showed a positive association with measures of success. To make for a more complete instrument, Van Dyck (1980) suggested replacing the items related to the therapist with client willingness to discuss problems openly, client-stated commitment to change, and client identification of goals and specificity of goals. Cronbach's alpha on this revised 10-item questionnaire ranged from .84 to .94, with a median value of .91, indicating high inter-item consistency using a sample of 31 college students (Van Dyck, 1980).

Group Therapy Survey

The Group Therapy Survey (GTS) (Slocum, 1987) is the only measure with some empirical support that assesses misperceptions about group therapy. The GTS has 25 items rated on a 4-point scale from *strongly agree* to *strongly disagree*. Slocum suggested that the items were based on three categories of unfavorable expectations: *It is unpredictable, It is not as effective as individual therapy,* and *It can be detrimental.* Internal consistency of the GTS was reported as .59 using a sample of 96 college students with a mean age of 20.2 (range 16 to 50). Later, Broday, Gieda, Mullison, and Sedlacek (1989) conducted a factor analysis using a sample of 147 college students with a mean age of 18 and suggested three slightly different factors using only 15 items. These 15 items predicted 41% of the variance with a Cronbach's alpha of .59 (individual variance predicted in parentheses): Positive Attitudes (7 items; 20%), Self-Disclosure Fears (4 items; 13%), and Misconceptions (4 items; 8%).

Recently, Carter, Mitchell, and Krautheim (2001) revised the GTS by replacing the term *group therapy* with *group counseling,* modifying the wording of a few items, and using a 5-point scale, with 1 = *strongly agree* to 5 = *strongly disagree,* with high scores indicating more positive attitudes. A factor analysis of the Group Therapy Survey-Revised (GTS-R), with a sample of 212 college students (mean age of 20, range from 17 to 50) indicated 3 subscales using 20 of the 25 items that together predicted 41% of the total variance (individual variance predicted in parentheses): Efficacy (27%), Myths (8%), and Vulnerability (6%). The internal consistency of the overall GTS-R as measured by Cronbach's alpha was .88; and for the individual subscales, it was .78 for Efficacy, .77 for Myths, and .75 for Vulnerability. The 2-week test-retest reliability coefficient for the overall GTS-R was .79 for a different sample of 93 college students with a mean age of 23. Reported means were 3.66 for Efficacy, 3.69 for Myths, and 3.43 for Vulnerability, suggesting neutral to positive attitudes toward group counseling from college students who presented for counseling.

The GTS is one of the few group measures that has been examined with regard to cultural influences. Leong, Wagner, and Kim (1995) found that attitudes toward group counseling were predicted by level of acculturation for Asian American students. Using a sample of 134 Asian American college students, a hierarchical multiple regression indicated that the integration subscale of the Acculturation Attitudes Scale (Kim, 1988) positively and significantly correlated with the Positive Attitudes subscale ($r = .35, p < .01$).

Hill Interaction Matrix-B

The Hill Interaction measures were among the first group process measures developed. The Hill Interaction Matrix was developed and refined to "measure the therapeutic quality of group participant interactions" (Fuhriman & Burlingame, 2000, p. 135). Hill (1965) introduced the Hill Interaction Matrix-B instrument

(HIM-B) to classify interactional styles of prospective group members. The HIM-B is a 64-item, self-report instrument based on the Hill Interaction Matrix, consisting of statements that describe Content Style and Work Style interactions. Content Style categories predict group members' preferred topics within a group: Topic Centered (topics, group) or Member Centered (personal relationship). Work Style categories predict group members' preferred level of work (interactional style) within the group, Pre-Work (responsive, conventional, assertive) or Work (speculative or confrontational) (Hill, 1973). Potential group members rate their reactions to each item on a 6-point continuum. A factor analysis suggested three factors: Pre-Work Interactional Styles, Work Interaction and Styles, and General Willingness to Interact in a Group (Stockton, Robison, & Morran, 1983). Stockton et al. (1983) also concluded that the HIM-B was useful to predict prospective group members' willingness to engage in high or low levels of therapeutic work. The HIM-A is identical in structure to the HIM-B but uses simpler language, making it more appropriate for children, adolescents, and those with reading or vocabulary difficulties. Other versions are discussed in later sections.

ASSESSMENT OF GROUP LEADERSHIP BEHAVIOR AND SKILLS

Measures have been developed to assess and rate group leaders' skills as part of training and to understand the relationship between group leadership behaviors and effective groups. Specific leadership behaviors and self-efficacy related to group leadership behaviors have been included. While many measures are widely used to provide feedback and for evaluation purposes in training, few have been systematically evaluated and used for research purposes.

Skilled Group Counseling Scale

The Skilled Group Counseling Scale (SGCS) (Smaby, Maddux, Torres-Rivera, & Zimmick, 1999) consists of 18 group leadership skills, 6 for each of 3 stages, Exploring, Understanding, and Acting, based on the skilled group counseling training model (Smaby et al., 1999). The Exploring stage focuses on appropriate eye contact, body language, verbal tracking skills, accurate open-ended questioning, paraphrasing, and summarizing skills. The Understanding stage consists of succinctly stating the feeling and content of a problem; self-disclosing a related experience, asking for specific and concrete expression; recognizing immediate feelings expressed when discussing the problem; identifying the general problem situation, actions taken when facing the problem, and feelings about self after taking action; and confronting in a caring way. The Acting stage focuses on deciding to change or not to change; choosing a course of action and recognizing the immediate implications of taking a course of action; delineating long-term consequences of the decision, reaching agreements about actions to take for solving the problem; setting action deadlines; and reviewing goals and the results of actions taken for resolving the problem (Smaby et al., 1999). Each item is scored on a 5-point scale from 1 = *not at all* to 5 = *always,* with high scores indicating a greater level of that skill.

Internal consistency using 3 raters for 78 group counseling sessions was greater than .99 (Smaby et al., 1999). These authors found significant differences on all 3 subscales as a result of intensive group skills training. For students who had not received intensive group training, their means ranged from 20.87 to 29.93 on the three subscales; for those who had received intensive group training, their means ranged from 88.25 to 89.67. Downing, Smaby, and Maddux (2001) further examined the application of group counseling skills training to actual group leadership using 13 students completing their master's level internships. For most of the 18 skills, students maintained the levels of leadership behavior attained at the end of the intensive skills training. Only those skills related to Action tended to decline, suggesting that further training, experience, and supervision are necessary to develop such advanced skills.

Trainer Behavior Scale

The Trainer Behavior Scale (TBS) (Bolman, 1971) comprises 28 items rated on a 5-point scale, ranging from *strongly agree* to *strongly disagree,* to measure seven dimensions of group leadership behavior: Affection (e.g., he/she shows considerable affection for most members of the group), Conditionality (e.g., he/she gives the impression that he/she likes some kinds of behaviors better than others), Congruence-Empathy (e.g., he/she seems to be in close touch with how members of the group are feeling), Openness (e.g., he/she seems to hold back from expressing his/her own reactions to what is happening in the group), Perceptiveness (e.g., he/she misinterprets what people say), Dominance (e.g., he/she exerts considerable influence over the direction the group takes), and Conceptual Input (e.g., when he/she calls attention to something, he/she gives a theoretical explanation of why it occurred). The higher the score, the more of that specific leadership behavior displayed. Kivlighan and Shaughnessy's (1993) factor analysis suggested two general dimensions: Control and Affiliativeness, which together accounted for 72% of the predicted variance. Congruence-Empathy, Openness, and Affection loaded on the Affiliativeness dimension, while Conditionality, Perception, Dominance, Security, and Conceptual Input loaded on the Control dimension. Coefficient alphas for all subscales ranged from .87 to .94 (Kivlighan, Jauquet, Hardie, Francis, & Hershberger, 1993). In addition to being used quite extensively to assess group leader behavior, the TBS has also been used in other ways. For example, Kivlighan, Marsh-Angelone, and Angelone (1994), using the TBS, suggested that group members project their own personality characteristics onto their group leaders in a study of training groups, while Kivlighan (1997) reported a positive correlation between later session ratings of Congruence/Empathy with outcome, and a positive correlation between early session ratings of Conditionality and outcome.

Other Promising Measures

Corrective Feedback Self-Efficacy Instrument. The Corrective Feedback Self-Efficacy Instrument (CFSI) (Page & Hulse-Killacky, 1999) is a 16-item instrument to measure group leaders' self-efficacy for giving corrective feedback within counseling groups. The instrument is based on the premise that "by giving corrective feedback in groups, the giver learns to communicate honestly and openly with others as well as to provide opportunities for receivers to learn about themselves" (Page & Hulse-Killacky, 1999, p. 38); they may also have significant anxiety about giving feedback in a group, and this hesitancy varies by the type of feedback to be given. Each item is rated on a 6-point scale. A factor analysis indicated two subscales, Therapeutic Efficacy (9 items) and Fears Efficacy (7 items), which together accounted for 47.8% of the variance (Page & Hulse-Killacky, 1999). Convergent validity was demonstrated by significant correlations with the Counselor Self-Estimate Inventory subscales (Larson et al., 1992), while discriminant validity was demonstrated by nonsignificant correlations with the Neuroticism Extraversion Openness (NEO) subscales (Costa & McCrae, 1992). Internal consistency measured by a Cronbach's alpha was .84. Test-retest reliability over a 2-week period was .74 (Page & Hulse-Killacky, 1999).

Group Counselor Behavior Rating Form. The Group Counselor Behavior Rating Form (GCBRF) (Corey & Corey, 1987) is a 28-item, 7-point Likert-type scale to assess group leadership skills. Each item is rated from 1 = *an extremely low degree* to 7 = *an extremely high degree,* with higher scores indicating greater levels of a specific skill. The Guttman split-half reliability coefficient and the equal-length Spearman-Brown reliability coefficient were both .97 (DeLucia & Bowman, 1991). DeLucia and Bowman's factor analysis revealed four factors that predicted 58.9% of the variance (individual variance is indicated in parentheses): Interventions (44.8%), Facilitative Conditions (5.8%), Application of Theory (4.3%), and Professionalism (4%). "Group leaders can use it as a self-evaluation device, supervisors can use it to evaluate group leaders' training, group leaders can evaluate their co-leaders with it, and group members can use it to evaluate their leader" (Corey & Corey, 1987, p. 65).

Group Leadership Self-Efficacy Instrument. The Group Leadership Self-Efficacy Instrument (GLSI) (Page, Pietrzak, & Lewis, 2001) is a

36-item scale measuring self-efficacy of group leadership skills. Each item is rated on a 6-point Likert scale, from 1 = *strongly disagree* to 6 = *strongly disagree,* with higher scores indicating higher self-efficacy for the skill described. Cronbach's alpha for the entire scale was .95 (Page et al., 2001), with 2-week test-retest reliability of *r* = .72. Two factor analyses indicated support for a 1-factor solution for the GLSI that accounted for 38.7% and 37.7% of the total variance. Discriminant validity was demonstrated with nonsignificant correlations between the NEO (Costa & McCrae, 1992) and the S scale of the STAI (Spielberger, 1983). Page et al. (2001) reported a mean of 171.8 (*SD* = 19.6, range of 36 to 216) for group trainees.

Leadership Characteristics Inventory. The Leadership Characteristics Inventory (LCI) (Makuch, 1997) measures group leadership characteristics, specifically, compatibility of style between coleaders, linking leadership style with efficacy and enabling leaders to adjust their leadership styles according to the group's feedback. This 56-item measure comprises 10 subscales: Direction Focus, Content Focus, Expression Focus, Immediacy Preference, Structure Preference, Directiveness, Confrontation, Transparency, Verbal Activity, and Empathy. The higher a score on a given subscale, the greater the extent to which that specific group leadership behavior is exhibited. Findings supported the creation of separate norms for ratings by leaders, supervisors, and members. Scale means on members' ratings of leaders are as follows: Group Directed Style (18.96); Individual Directed Style (12.96); Group Process Focus (16.69); Group Topic Focus (13.17); Cognitive Focus (13.41); Affect Focus (19.82); Immediacy Preference (17.43); Structure Preference (14.09); Directiveness (10.70); Transparency (16.09); Verbal Activity (19.04); Confrontation (16.89); and Empathy (21.43) (Makuch, 1997).

ASSESSMENT OF GROUP CLIMATE

Two measures of group climate and environment have been used extensively with counseling and psychotherapy groups.

Group Climate Questionnaire-Short

The Group Climate Questionnaire-Short (GCQ-S) (MacKenzie, 1983, 1990) measures group members' perceptions of the *importance of cohesion,* their *reluctance to take responsibility for change,* and *interpersonal friction and distrust.* Originally, the GCQ consisted of 32 items and eight subscales. However, after extensive clinical use, MacKenzie concluded that because major shifts in group climate dimensions occur from one session to the next, the GCQ must be sufficiently short to be administered after every session. Consequently, the GCQ-S consists of 12 items rated on a 6-point scale, from 1 = *not at all* to 6 = *extremely,* and can be completed by both group leaders and members. High scores indicate higher perceived levels of that construct. Engaging is the degree of cohesion and work orientation of the group and consists of the subscales Cohesion, Self-Disclosure, and Willingness to Confront. Avoiding is the degree to which individuals rely on group members and leaders, consisting of subscales of Conformity, Superficiality, and Denial of Responsibility. Conflict consists of the subscales Friction, Distrust, and Mutual Withdrawal. "In more successful groups, clients perceived the climate as more engaging and characterized by more conflict and anxiety and less avoiding" (Kivlighan & Angelone, 1992, p. 469).

MacKenzie (1983) suggested that the GCQ-S provides leaders with information regarding group members' perspectives; specifically, the GCQ-S may identify members who view their groups so differently from their peers that they end up being scapegoats. The GCQ-S may also be helpful in assessing the developmental stage of the group. In support of the validity, Kivlighan and Goldfine (1991) reported similar levels of group climate as reported between the group members in their personal growth groups and those in MacKenzie's psychotherapy groups.

Group Environment Scale

The Group Environment Scale (GES) (Moos, 1986) assesses group functioning and the social environment of groups, such as task-oriented, social, psychotherapy, or mutual support groups

(Littlepage, Cowart, & Kerr, 1989). This measure is used to assess group member perception of climate both over time and after individual sessions. The GES consists of 90 items rated as *true* or *false*. Ten subscales, comprising nine questions each, assess three underlying dimensions: Relationship, Personal Growth, and Systems Maintenance/Systems Change. Higher scores indicate greater levels of that subscale. The Relationship dimension includes the subscales Cohesion, Leader Support, and Expressiveness. The Personal Growth dimension includes the subscales Independence, Task Orientation, Self-Discovery, and Anger and Aggression. The System Maintenance/System Change dimension includes the subscales Order and Organization, Leader Control, and Innovation.

Cronbach's alpha for the 10 subscales ranged from .62 to .86, with a median of .76 (Moos, 1986); 1-month interval test-retest reliabilities ranged from .65 to .87. Support for the construct validity of the GES has been reported by Evans and Jarvis (1986), who noted that cohesion was highly correlated with group attraction in members of personal growth groups, while Rose and Bednar (1980) reported that cohesion was significantly related to quality of group interaction. Furthermore, observers' ratings of the amount of positive interpersonal behavior in a support group were correlated with participants' perceptions of the group as cohesive, expressive, and oriented toward independence and self-discovery (Shadish, 1984).

For members of psychotherapy groups, Moos (1986) reported mean scores as follows: Cohesion = 4.90 (*SD* = 1.77); Leader Support = 5.23 (*SD* = 1.46); Expressiveness = 5.88 (*SD* = 1.36); Independence = 6.32 (*SD* = .91); Task Orientation = 4.84 (*SD* = 1.43); Self-Discovery = 4.78 (*SD* = 1.66); Anger and Aggression = 4.54 (*SD* = 2.10); Order and Organization = 3.94 (*SD* = 1.72); Leader Control = 3.06 (*SD* = 1.41); and Innovation = 5.10 (*SD* = 1.49).

The GES has been used in various capacities since its inception. Consultants and program evaluators have used the GES to assess how well groups are functioning and to better understand group social climate. These groups have ranged from interdisciplinary rehabilitation treatment teams to psychotherapy, training groups, and supervision groups, including such diverse groups as teaching skills to mothers of developmentally challenged children (e.g., Hudson, 1982) to classrooms (e.g., Hartsough & Davis, 1986) to computer support groups (e.g., Kruger & Struzziero, 1997).

ASSESSMENT OF GROUP THERAPEUTIC FACTORS

Yalom (1995) suggested that 12 therapeutic factors form the basis for what makes groups effective. The 12 factors are Altruism, Catharsis, Cohesiveness, Existentiality, Family Reenactment, Guidance, Hope, Identification, Interpersonal Learning Input (feedback), Interpersonal Learning Output (new behavior), Self-Understanding, and Universality. Several instruments have been designed to assess therapeutic factors in groups. Studies over the years have assessed ratings of therapeutic factors and yielded inconsistent results. These inconsistencies may be due to differences in the groups surveyed or the methods used to assess therapeutic factors. In an effort to make sense of the inconsistent findings, Kivlighan and Holmes (see Chapter 2, this volume) used a cluster analysis of studies that ranked or rated the importance of therapeutic factors. Four clusters emerged from the analysis based on the therapeutic factors that were highest and lowest in each cluster. Cluster 1, *Affective Insight Groups,* rated Acceptance, Catharsis, Interpersonal Learning, and Self-Understanding as the most-valued factors. These groups also rated both Guidance and Vicarious Learning as relatively unimportant. Cluster 2, *Affective Support Groups,* rated Acceptance, Installation of Hope, and Universality as the most important group factors. Similar to Cluster 1, members of the groups in Cluster 2 rated Guidance and Vicarious Learning as relatively unimportant. Cluster 3, *Cognitive Support Groups,* rated Vicarious Learning and Guidance as highly valued, while Self-Understanding was rated much lower. Cluster 4, *Cognitive Insight Groups,* rated Interpersonal Learning, Self-Understanding, and Vicarious Learning as the most-valued therapeutic factors.

Therapeutic Factors Scale

The Therapeutic Factors Scale (TFS) (Yalom, 1985; Yalom, Tinklenberg, & Gilula, 1968) contains 60 items, 5 for each therapeutic factor, and can be rated using either a Likert scale (from 1 = *not helpful at all* to 7 = *extremely helpful*), with higher scores indicating greater importance of a factor, or a Q-sort (statements are sorted into categories from *not helpful at all* to *extremely helpful*). Yalom et al. (1968) originally found that members of 20 therapy groups using the Q-sort ranked the factors in the following order, from most to least important: Interpersonal Learning (output), Catharsis, Cohesiveness, Self-Understanding, Interpersonal Learning (input), Existential Factors, Universality, Instillation of Hope, Altruism, Family Reenactment, Guidance, and Identification. While often used in group research, no studies of reliability and validity have been conducted.

Curative Factors Scale and the Curative Factors Scale-Revised

The Curative Factors Scale (CFS) (Lieberman, Yalom, & Miles, 1973) assesses the 12 therapeutic factors in counseling and therapy groups and, more recently, was adapted for use in professional training groups. The original CFS contains 14 items, 2 items for Cohesiveness and Self-Understanding and 1 item for each of the remaining 10 scales, and was initially used extensively with encounter groups. Stone, Lewis, and Beck (1994) modified the CFS for use with task and psychoeducational groups. They deleted the Altruism and Family Reenactment items; added two items, Skill Development and Insight into Professional Rules and Responsibilities; and reworded one Self-Understanding item to include Personal and Professional difficulties. Stone et al.'s factor analysis with two different samples revealed three factors: Affective Arousal (Self-Disclosure, Identification, Insight, Self-Understanding, Interpersonal Output, Universality, Hope); Cognitive Mastery (Skill Development, Insight Into Professional Roles and Responsibilities); and Behavior Change (Guidance). Although frequently used, no reliability or validity has been conducted.

Critical Incidents Questionnaire

The Critical Incidents Questionnaire (CIQ) (Kivlighan & Goldfine, 1991) assesses important therapeutic factor(s) for group members during a specific session. Group members are asked to describe the most important event in a given session and explain why it was important. Several versions of this instrument have been used in group research (Berzon, Pious, & Parson, 1963; MacKenzie, 1990).

The critical-incident data obtained by group members are then rated on one of two criteria. The first is Bloch and Crouch's (1985) definition of therapeutic factors that include Insight (self-understanding), Learning From Interpersonal Actions (interaction), Acceptance (cohesiveness), Self-Disclosure, Catharsis, Guidance, Universality, Altruism, Vicarious Learning, and Instillation of Hope.

The CIQ can also be scored using the Group Counseling Helpful Impact Scale (GCHIS) (Kivlighan Multon, & Brossart, 1996). The GCHIS is a 28-item scale that combines adaptive items from three different rating systems: Elliott's (1985) Taxonomy of Helpful Impacts, Mahrer and Nadler's (1986) Good Moments System, and Bloch and Reibstein's (1980) Therapeutic Factors Rating System. The rating scale is a 5-point scale (0 = *not all* to 4 = *very much*) that approaches therapeutic factors from a broader perspective. The 28 items of the GCHIS have been subdivided into four dimensions: Emotional Awareness-Insight; Relationship-Climate; Other-Focus vs. Self-Focus; and Problem Definition-Change. Interrater reliability for the four dimensions ranged from .61 to .99 (Holmes & Kivlighan, 2000). Validity was established by examining the relationship between the four dimensions and group members' ratings of leadership dimensions (Kivlighan, Multon, & Brossart, 1996). As predicted, more technical leadership was related to the Emotional Awareness-Insight and Problem Definition-Change factors, whereas more personal leadership was related to the Relationship-Climate and Other-Focus vs. Self-Focus components. Also, a more engaged group climate was positively correlated with Problem Definition-Change (Holmes & Kivlighan, 2000).

Research using the CIQ has provided some important findings. Using the ratings of the CIQ on the GCHIS, no differences between group stages were found; however, significant differences between individual and group counseling were noted. Holmes and Kivlighan (2000) reported that "components of Relationship-Climate and Other- vs. Self-Focus are more prominent in group psychotherapy, whereas Emotional Awareness-Insight and Problem Definition-Change are more central to the processes of individual treatment" (p. 482).

Kivlighan and Goldfine (1991) additionally used the CIQ to classify group therapeutic factors into three categories: Affective (Acceptance/Group Cohesion, Catharsis, Installation of Hope), Behavioral (Altruism, Learning From Interpersonal Actions/Interpersonal Learning, Self-Disclosure), and Cognitive (Guidance, Self-Understanding, Universality, and Vicarious Learning). When examining the relationship between group stage and therapeutic factors, Hope and Universality predominated the initial stage of group development. Catharsis increased across the stages, reaching its highest level during the working stage and then decreasing in termination. Guidance increased, achieving its highest level during the working stage. The authors concluded that Acceptance is important in all stages of group; members not only need acceptance when exploring personal issues but also when making an initial commitment to the group. Levels of Self-Understanding, Vicarious Learning, Learning From Interpersonal Actions, Altruism, and Self-Disclosure were not related to stage of group development.

The CIQ has been used with a variety of populations and ages. It has been used with middle school children in Israel (Shechtman, Bar-El, & Hadar, 1997) and 7th grade students in an alternative middle school in the United States (Horrocks & DeLucia-Waack, 2003) to assess important therapeutic factors. Schwartz and Waldo (1999) used the CIQ to examine the relationship between therapeutic factors and group stage development for group treatment of spousal abuse. Shechtman and Perl-Dekel (2000) examined perceptions of therapeutic factors of adult inpatient group members for both verbal and art group therapies.

Another Promising Measure: The Therapeutic Factors Inventory

The Therapeutic Factors Inventory (TFI) (Lese & McNair-Semands, 2000) assesses group members' perceptions of the degree to which the therapeutic factors as described by Yalom (1995) are present in a particular group, with each therapeutic factor as a subscale. The TFI is a 99-item instrument rated on a 7-point Likert scale, from 1 = *strongly disagree* to 7 = *strongly agree,* based on item analysis and internal consistency analysis. McNair-Semands and Lese (2000) also reported moderate to high alpha reliabilities for the 9-item scales, ranging from .70 to .89. Test-retest reliability after 1 week ranged from .60 to .93, with the exception of the corrective reenactment of primary family group, which had an *r* of .28.

RATINGS OF IN-SESSION GROUP BEHAVIOR

Some of the oldest instruments used to analyze and assess therapeutic groups are those that rate in-session group leader and member behavior based on videotapes, audiotapes, or transcripts of actual group sessions.

> Interactional analysis attempts to unravel and understand the dialogue of the participants through observational techniques. Basically, the rating systems functioned as coding schemes, assigning behavior to predetermined categories deemed important by the clinician or researcher . . . overall patterns can be recognized either within a single session, or over the entire length of the group. Such patterns lend contextual meaning . . . are more likely to capture the dynamic properties of the process. (Fuhriman & Barlow, 1994, p. 192)

Groups Sessions Rating Scale

The Groups Sessions Rating Scale (GSRS) (Cooney, Kadden, Litt, & Getter, 1991; Getter, Litt, Kadden, & Cooney, 1992) was designed to assess the use of different therapeutic interventions by both group leaders and members of psychoeducational and counseling groups. It was constructed as a process measure to test the differences between two types of groups: coping-skills training and short-term interactional group therapy (Kadden, Cooney, Getter, & Litt, 1989). The seven categories included four related to coping skills: Education/ Skill Training, Problem Solving, Role-Playing, and Identifying High-Risk Situations; and three were related to interactional therapy: Interpersonal Learning, Expression/Exploration of Feelings, and Here-and-Now Focus. Getter et al. (1992), using a sample of 96 adult group members in alcohol and drug abuse groups, reported interrater reliability of three raters. Cronbach's alpha ranged from .83 to 97. Internal consistency for all four coping-skills items was .60 and .81 for the interactional therapy items. The authors suggested selecting a 15-minute section from the first half of the session and another 15-minute section from the second half of the group session, then analyzing them in 1-minute time blocks.

Kadden, Litt, Cooney, Kabella, and Getter (2001) reported significant differences between cognitive-behavioral and interactional therapy groups for alcoholic abuse. As predicted, the four coping-skill interventions occurred significantly more often in the cognitive-behavioral groups, and the interactional interventions occurred significantly more in the interactional therapy groups.

DeLucia-Waack (2003) used the GSRS to rate critical incidents after Sessions 2, 5, and 7 of an 8-week psychoeducational group for children of divorce to determine the effective group elements. Preliminary results using 81 children in 14 groups suggest a differential rating of interventions at different times during the group. All group members consistently identified the highest number of critical incidents related to *education/skill training, problem solving,* and *expression/exploration* of feelings. In addition, education/skill training was identified most often after Session 2 and then significantly less often after Sessions 5 and 7 (but still significantly more than any other skill). For interpersonal learning and exploration/expression of feelings, the differences between sessions were similar to education/skill training. In contrast, problem solving was consistently identified as important throughout all three sessions.

Hill Interaction Matrix

The Hill Interaction Matrix (HIM) (Hill, 1965, 1973) statement-by-statement approach was designed to help "beginning group workers make sense of the bewildering bombardment of group interaction" (Hill, 1973, p. 159). All verbal statements made during a group session are categorized into 16 cells of a matrix divided into four quadrants, which focus on interpersonal interaction and discussion skills. The four quadrants, containing combinations of content and work categories, are (a) Topic Centered (topics or group) by Pre-Work (responsive, conventional, or assertive), (b) Topic Centered by Work (speculative or confrontational), (c) Member Centered (personal relationship) by Pre-Work (responsive, conventional, or assertive), and (d) Member Centered (personal relationship) by Work (speculative or confrontational). Hill has suggested that each statement be rated with regard to which cell it falls into and then a weighting be assigned to it based on two therapeutic values: interpersonal threat and member centeredness. Fuhriman and Burlingame (2000) noted that the weighting system is based on a theoretical framework that has not yet been empirically validated. They also commented that sometimes cell totals are used to derive scores but it makes more sense theoretically and empirically to use quadrant scores. Therapeutic potential and higher-quality verbal interaction are presumed to increase from Quadrant 1 to Quadrant 4 (Hill, 1965).

Because of the time-consuming nature and problems with interrater reliability of the statement-by-statement version of the HIM, Hill (1973) suggested using the HIM-G. The HIM-G is a 72-item scale completed by observer or group leader after viewing a group session, watching a videotape, listening to an audiotape, or reading a transcript of a group session. Four items (2 for the leader, 2 for the members) represent each of the 16 Work by Content cells, and then 4 items represent other categories: Silence, Resistance, Group Laughter, and Total Volume of Participation of Leader. Each item is rated from 0 = *not all* to 6 = *40 to 100% of the time*. The HIM-G has been used to assess the group environment with a variety of groups, from inpatient psychiatric hospitals to career counseling groups to marriage enrichment groups.

Interaction Process Analysis

Interaction Process Analysis (IPA) (Bales, 1950) measures task and social-emotional interpersonal behavior using 12 categories that emphasize problem-solving behavior. Data from observers form two profiles: (a) a summary of the number of behavioral acts and (b) responses in the 12 categories and subcategories. The IPA was designed to systematically study the interaction in groups, specifically task-oriented and "self-analytic groups," but Bales considered his observation system to be applicable to all types of groups. Bales postulated that episodes of task-oriented activity alternate with episodes of short socioemotional interventions that restore group solidarity. Positive Reactions consists of *shows solidarity, shows tension release,* and *shows agreement.* Negative Reactions consists of *shows disagreement, shows tension,* and *shows antagonism.* These are both socioemotional categories. The Task-Oriented categories include *attempted answers* (gives suggestions, gives opinion, asks for suggestions) and *questions* (asks for information, asks for opinion, asks for suggestions).

Much research has used the IPA to analyze groups, particularly work groups (e.g., Bell, 2001; DeGrada, Kruglanski, Mannetti, & Pierro, 1999; Mpofu et al., 1998). Responses are coded into one of the four categories, and those categories are used as scores (DeGrada et al., 1999). Kelly (2000) discusses current research using the IPA related to task groups. The IPA has been used to assess group interaction in many different types of groups, from business and industry to classrooms and counseling groups.

Systems for Multiple Level Observation of Groups

Systems for Multiple Level Observation of Groups (SYMLOG) (Bales, Cohen, & Williams, 1979) focuses on interpersonal behavior and values. The behavior of each group member is rated on 26 items organized into three dimensions: Dominant-Submissive, Unfriendly-Friendly, and Instrumentally Controlled–Emotionally Expressive. Bales et al. (1979) suggested that for diagnostic purposes, it is important for raters to rate all possible combinations of the three dimensions and for group members to receive as feedback information regarding their behavior for each of the 26 items. Rywick (1987) suggested that for research participants, detailed feedback is not necessary; thus, the shorter 6-item and 8-item forms may be appropriate because they have adequate reliability and correlate strongly with the longer version. SYMLOG has been used to categorize group interactions in task and work groups in business and industry settings, as well as counseling groups (e.g., Herzog, Kronmuller, Hartmann, Bergmann, & Kroger, 2000; Kecharananta & Baker, 1999).

Other Promising Measures

Group Observer Form. The Group Observer Form (GOF) (Romano, 1998; Romano & Sullivan, 2000) provides cofacilitators with structured and unstructured feedback about the group dynamics and leaders' use of skills observed during the group session. Responses are rated by an independent rater or a supervisor on a 7-point Likert-type scale, with anchors from *low* to *high, past* to *present, little* to *much,* and *intellectual* to *feelings*, with high scores indicating more interactive group behavior. A preliminary factor analysis yielded three factors accounting for 69% of the variance: Group Cohesiveness, Here-and-Now Focus, and Group Conflict. Data from the three subscales support group stage characteristics (Romano & Sullivan, 2000). Group Cohesion increased during the first two stages and remained constant over the last two stages, with means of 4.47 to 5.80. Here-and-Now Focus increased from Stage 1 (initial) to Stage 2 (transition) (4.04 to 5.36) and then remained constant in Stages 2 and 3 (working) and Stage 4 (termination). Conflict peaked during Stage 2 (3.08 to 4.42 to 2.96 to 2.94).

Group Cohesiveness Scale. The Group Cohesiveness Scale (GCS) (Budman & Gurman, 1988) defines cohesion as "group connectedness, demonstrated by working together toward a common therapeutic goal, constructive engagement around common themes, and openness to sharing personal material" (Budman, Soldz, Demby, Davis, & Merry, 1993, p. 202). The scale consists of five subscales and a global scale. The global scale is called Global Fragmentation vs. Global Cohesiveness. The subscales are Withdrawal and Self-Absorption vs. Interest and Involvement, Mistrust vs. Trust, Disruption vs. Cooperation, Abusiveness vs. Expressed Caring, and Unfocused vs. Focused. Observers rate 30-minute group segments on each scale continuum along a 10-point measure from − 5 (*very strong*) for the negative aspect to +5 (*very strong*) for the positive aspect of the scale. Budman et al. (1987, 1989) reported that the GCS was positively correlated with group member outcome. Budman et al. (1993) concluded that there was a strong correlation between Cohesion and the number of different kind of statements made by group members in early sessions (1-5); an even stronger relationship between the two variables during the middle sessions (6-10); and no significant correlation during later sessions (11-15).

Individual Group Member Interpersonal Process Scale. The Individual Group Member Interpersonal Process Scale (IGIPS) (Soldz, Budman, Davis, & Demby, 1993) "elucidates the therapeutically significant behaviors of individual patients in the group setting, measures change in patient behavior over the course of the group, and illuminates the interactional functioning of the group as a whole" (Soldz et al., 1993, p. 552). Each statement made by group leaders and members is rated on 12 items on the presence/absence of a behavior (e.g., discusses own issues), locational and object designations (to whom the behavior is directed and whether the topic is related to in-group or out-of-group issues), and intensity or significance of the behavior using a 9-point Likert format. A principal component analysis indicated five factors that accounted for 74% of the variance: Activity, Interpersonal Sensitivity, Comfort With Self, Self-Focus, and Psychological Mindedness.

CONCLUSIONS

It is important that studies evaluate the effectiveness of group interventions using instruments that are reliable and valid. It is also important that there is some uniformity and consensus about what instruments are used so that some comparisons can be made across studies. While there are some established instruments that assess group process, dynamics, interventions, and interactions, it is essential for further development and validation of such instruments to occur. Too often, instruments are created specifically for a particular study, and thus, it is difficult to compare results from study to study.

There has been an increased interest in and effort directed at the development of reliable and valid instruments to measure group process, dynamics, and leadership skills. Instruments have begun to become more sophisticated, more practitioner-friendly, and have more demonstrated construct validity. The next step is to develop clearly established norms that can be used to compare specific samples and act as a baseline for future studies.

Furthermore, it is apparent that instruments that appear to be based on the same construct may sometimes be measuring different dimensions or constructs. It also seems apparent that perspective influences the data. Several instruments have been designed to be used by group leaders, group members, supervisors, and even observers. Some studies have shown significant differences between these perspectives for the same instrument. Much is to be gained by the reliable and consistent examination of the group processes and dynamics that make groups effective.

REFERENCES

Armstrong, S. J., & Priola, V. (2001). Individual differences in cognitive style and their effects on task and social-orientation of self-managed work teams. *Small Group Research, 32,* 283-312.

Bales, R. F. (1950). *Interaction process analysis: A method for the study of small groups.* Cambridge, MA: Addison-Wesley.

Bales, R. F., Cohen, S. P., & Williams, S. A. (1979). *SYMLOG: A system for the multiple level observation of groups.* New York: Free Press.

Bell, L. (2001). Patterns of interaction in multidisciplinary child protection teams in New Jersey. *Child Abuse & Neglect, 25,* 65-80.

Berzon, B., Pious, C., & Parson, R. E. (1963). The therapeutic event in group psychotherapy: A study of subjective reports by group members. *Journal of Individual Psychology, 19,* 204-212.

Bloch, S., & Crouch, E. (1985). *Therapeutic factors in psychotherapy.* Oxford: Oxford University Press.

Bloch, S., & Reibstein, J. (1980). Perceptions by patients and therapists of therapeutic factors in group psychotherapy. *British Journal of Psychiatry, 137,* 274-278.

Bolman, L. (1971). Some effects of trainers on their T-groups. *Journal of Applied Behavioral Science, 7,* 309-325.

Broday, S. F., Gieda, M. J., Mullison, D. D., & Sedlacek, W. E. (1989). Factor analysis and reliability of the Group Therapy Survey. *Educational & Psychological Measurement, 49,* 457-459.

Budman, S. H., Demby, A., Feldstein, M., Redondo, J., Scherz, B., Bennett, M. J., Koppenall, G., Sabin Daley, B., Hunter, M., & Ellis, J. (1987). Preliminary findings on a new instrument to measure cohesion in group psychotherapy. *International Journal of Group Psychotherapy, 37,* 75-94.

Budman, S. H., & Gurman, A. S. (1988). *The theory and practice of brief therapy.* New York: Guilford.

Budman, S. H., Soldz, S., Demby, A., Davis, M., & Merry, J. (1993). What is cohesiveness? An empirical examination. *Small Group Research, 24,* 199-216.

Budman, S. H., Soldz, S., Demby, A., Feldstein, M., Springer, T., & Davis, M. (1989). Cohesion, alliance, and outcome in group psychotherapy: An empirical examination. *Psychiatry, 52,* 339-350.

Carter, E. F., Mitchell, S. L., & Krautheim, M. D. (2001). Understanding and addressing clients' resistance to group counseling. *Journal for Specialists in Group Work, 26,* 66-80.

Cooney, N. L., Kadden, R. M., Litt, M. D., & Getter, H. (1991). Matching alcoholics to coping skills or interactional therapies: Two-year follow-up results. *Journal of Consulting & Clinical Psychology, 59,* 598-601.

Cooper, A., & Stoltenberg, C. D. (1987). Comparison of a sexual enhancement program and a communication training program on sexual and marital satisfaction. *Journal of Counseling Psychology, 34,* 309-314.

Corey, M. S., & Corey, G. (1987). *Group counseling: Process and practice* (3rd ed.). Monterey, CA: Brooks/Cole.

Costa, P. T., & McCrae, R. R. (1992). Professional manual: revised NEO personality inventory and (NEO PI-R) and NEO five-factor inventory (NEO-FFI). Odessa, FL: Psychological Assessment Resources.

DeGrada, E., Kruglanski, A. W., Mannetti, L., & Pierro, A. (1999). Motivated cognition and group interaction: Need for closure affects the contents and processes of collective negotiations. *Journal of Experimental & Social Psychology, 35,* 346-365.

DeLucia, J. L., & Bowman, V. E. (1991). Internal consistency and factor structure of the Group Counselor Behavior Rating Form. *Journal for Specialists in Group Work, 16,* 109-114.

DeLucia-Waack, J. L. (2003). *Therapeutic factors in psychoeducational groups for children of divorce.* Manuscript in preparation.

Downing, T. K. E., Smaby, M. H., & Maddux, C. D. (2001). A study of the transfer of group counseling skills from training to practice. *Journal for Specialists in Group Work, 26,* 155-167.

Elliott, R. (1985). Helpful and nonhelpful events in brief counseling interviews: An empirical taxonomy. *Journal of Counseling Psychology, 32,* 307-322.

Evans, N., & Jarvis, P. (1986). The Group Attitude Scale: A measure of attraction to group. *Small Group Behavior, 17,* 203-216.

Fisher, S. G., Macrosson, W. D. K., & Semple, J. H. (2001). Control and Belbin's team roles. *Personnel Review, 30,* 578-588.

Fuhriman, A., & Barlow, S. H. (1994). Interaction analysis: Instrumentation and issues. In A. Fuhriman & G. M. Burlingame (Eds.), *Handbook of group psychotherapy: An empirical and clinical synthesis* (pp. 191-222). New York: John Wiley.

Fuhriman, A., & Burlingame, G. M. (1994). Measuring small group process: A methodological application of chaos theory. *Small Group Research, 25,* 502-519.

Fuhriman, A., & Burlingame, G. M. (2000). Hill Interaction Matrix: Therapy through dialogue. In A. P. Beck & C. M. Lewis (Eds.), *The process of group psychotherapy: Systems for analyzing change.* Washington, DC: American Psychological Association.

Getter, H., Litt, M. D., Kadden, R. M., & Cooney, N. L. (1992). Measuring treatment process in coping skills and interactional group therapies for alcoholism. *International Journal of Group Psychotherapy, 42,* 419-430.

Hartsough, C. S., & Davis, J. M. (1986). Dimensions of the Group Environment Scale. *American Journal of Community Psychology, 14,* 371-376.

Herzog, W., Kronmuller, K. T., Hartmann, M., Bergmann, G., & Kroger, F. (2000). Family perception of interpersonal behavior as a predictor in eating disorders: A prospective, six-year follow-up study. *Family Process, 39,* 359-374.

Hill, W. F. (1965). *Hill Interaction Matrix.* Los Angeles: University of Southern California.

Hill, W. F. (1973). Hill Interaction Matrix (HIM) conceptual framework for understanding groups. In J. W. Pfeiffer & J. E. Jones (Eds.), *The 1973 annual handbook for group facilitators* (pp. 159-176). San Diego: University Associates.

Holmes, S. E., & Kivlighan, D. M. Jr. (2000). Comparison of therapeutic factors in group and individual treatment processes. *Journal of Counseling Psychology, 47,* 478-484.

Horrocks, S., & DeLucia-Waack, J. L. (2003). *An examination of the therapeutic factors of a year-long group for alternative middle school students.* Manuscript in preparation.

Hudson, A. (1982). Training parents of developmentally handicapped children: A component analysis. *Behavior Therapy, 13,* 325-333.

Kadden, R. D., Cooney, N. L., Getter, H., & Litt, M. D. (1989). Matching alcoholics to coping skills or interactional therapies: Post treatment results. *Journal of Consulting & Clinical Psychology, 57,* 698-704.

Kadden, R. M., Litt, M. D., Cooney, N. D., Kabella, E., & Getter, H. (2001). Prospective matching of alcoholic clients to cognitive-behavioral or interactional group therapy. *Journal of Alcohol Studies, 62,* 359-369.

Kecharananta, N., & Baker, H. G. (1999). Capturing entrepreneurial values. *Journal of Applied Social Psychology, 29,* 820-833.

Kelly, J. (2000). Interaction process analysis in task performing groups. In A. P. Beck & C. M. Lewis (Eds.), *The process of group psychotherapy: Systems for analyzing change.* Washington, DC: American Psychological Association.

Kew, C. E. (1975). A pilot study of an evaluation scale for group-psychotherapy patients.

ETC Test Collection (Set A). Princeton, NJ: Educational Testing Services. (Tests in Microfiche No. 004944)

Kim, U. (1988). *Acculturation of Korean immigrants to Canada: Psychological, demographic, and behavioral profiles of emigrating Koreans, non-emigrating Koreans, and Korean Canadians.* Unpublished doctoral dissertation, Queens University, Kingston, Canada.

Kivlighan, D. M. Jr. (1997). Leader behavior and therapeutic gain: An application of situational leadership theory. *Group Dynamics, 1,* 32-38.

Kivlighan, D. M. Jr., & Angelone, E. O. (1992). Interpersonal problems: Variables influencing participants' perception of group climate. *Journal of Counseling Psychology, 39,* 468-472.

Kivlighan, D. M. Jr., & Goldfine, D. C. (1991). Endorsement of therapeutic factors as a function of stage of group development and participant interpersonal attitudes. *Journal of Counseling Psychology, 38,* 150-158.

Kivlighan, D. M. Jr., Jauquet, C. A., Hardie, A. W., Francis, A. M., & Hershberger, B. (1993). Training group members to set session agendas: Effects on in-session behavior and member outcome. *Journal of Counseling Psychology, 40,* 182-187.

Kivlighan, D. M. Jr., Marsh-Angelone, M., & Angelone, E. O. (1994). Projection in group counseling: The relationship between members' interpersonal problems and their perceptions of the group leader. *Journal of Counseling Psychology, 41,* 99-104.

Kivlighan, D. M. Jr., Multon, K. D., & Brossart, D. F. (1996). Helpful impacts in group counseling: Development of a multidimensional rating system. *Journal of Counseling Psychology, 43,* 347-355.

Kivlighan, D. M. Jr., & Shaughnessy, P. (1993). *Dimensions of group leader behavior.* Unpublished manuscript, University of Missouri, Columbia.

Kruger, L. J., & Struzziero, J. (1997). *Journal of Educational & Psychological Consultation, 8,* 75-90.

Larson, L. M., Suzuki, L. A., Gillespie, K. N., Potenz, M. T., Bechtel, M. A., & Toulouse, A. L. (1992). Development and validation of the counseling self-estimate inventory. *Journal of Counseling Psychology, 39,* 105-120.

Leong, F. T. L., Wagner, N. S., & Kim, H. H. (1995). Group counseling expectations among Asian

American students: The role of culture-specific factors. *Journal of Counseling Psychology, 42,* 217-222.

Lese, K. L., & McNair-Semands, R. R. (2000). The Therapeutic Factors Inventory: Development of the scale. *Group, 24,* 303-317.

Lieberman, M. (1976). Change induction in small groups. *Annual Review of Psychology, 27,* 217.

Lieberman, M., Yalom, I., & Miles, M. (1973). *Encounter groups: First facts.* New York: Basic Books.

Littlepage, G. E., Cowart, L., & Kerr, B. (1989). Relationships between group environment scales and group performance and cohesion. *Small Group Behavior, 20,* 50-61.

MacKenzie, K. R. (1983). The clinical application of a group climate measure. In. R. R. Dies & K. R. MacKenzie (Eds.), *Advances in group psychotherapy: Integrating research and practice* (pp. 159-170). New York: International Universities Press.

MacKenzie, K. R. (1990). *Introduction to time-limited group therapy.* Washington, DC: American Psychiatric Press.

Mahrer, A. R., & Nadler, W. P. (1986). Good moments in psychotherapy: A preliminary review, a list, and some promising research avenues. *Journal of Consulting & Clinical Psychology, 54,* 10-15.

Makuch, L. (1997). *Measuring dimensions of counseling and therapeutic group leadership style: Development of a leadership characteristics inventory.* Unpublished doctoral dissertation, Indiana University.

McNair-Semands, R. R., & Lese, K. L. (2000). Interpersonal problems and the perception of therapeutic factors in group therapy. *Small Group Research, 31,* 158-174.

Moos, R. H. (1986). *Group environment scale manual.* Palo Alto, CA: Consulting Psychologists Press.

Mpofu, D. J., Lanphear, J., Stewart, T., Das, M., Ridding, P., & Dunn, E. (1998). Facility with the English language and problem-based learning group interaction: Findings from an Arabic setting. *Medical Education, 32,* 479-485.

Page, B. J., & Hulse-Killacky, D. (1999). Development and validation of the corrective feedback self-efficacy instrument. *Journal for Specialists in Group Work, 24,* 37-54.

Page, B. J., Pietrzak, D. R., & Lewis, T. F. (2001). Development of the group leader self-efficacy

instrument. *Journal for Specialists in Group Work, 26,* 168-184.

Riva, M. T., & Smith, R. D. (1997). Looking into the future of group research: Where do we go from here? *Journal for Specialists in Group Work, 22,* 266-276.

Romano, J. L. (1998). Simulated group counseling: An experiential training model for group work. *Journal for Specialists in Group Work, 23,* 119-132.

Romano, J. L., & Sullivan, B. A. (2000). Simulated group counseling for group work training: A four-year research study of group development. *Journal for Specialists in Group Work, 25,* 366-375.

Rose, G., & Bednar, R. (1980). Effects of positive and negative self-disclosure and feedback on early group development. *Journal of Counseling Psychology, 27,* 63-70.

Rywick, T. (1987). SYMLOG rating for reliability. *International Journal of Small Group Research, 3,* 119-125.

Schutz, W. C. (1992). Beyond FIRO-B—Three new theory driven measures—Element B: Behavior, Element F: Feelings, Element S: Self. *Psychological Reports, 70,* 915-937.

Schwartz J. P., & Waldo, M. (1999). Therapeutic factors in spouse-abuse group treatment. *Journal for Specialists in Group Work, 24,* 197-207.

Shadish, W. R. (1984). Intimate behavior and the assessment of benefits in clinical groups. *Small Group Behavior, 15,* 204-221.

Shechtman, Z. (1994). Group counseling-psychotherapy as a school intervention to enhance close friendships and preadolescent. *International Journal of Group Psychotherapy, 44,* 377-391.

Shechtman, Z., Bar-El, O., & Hadar, E. (1997). Therapeutic factors in counseling and psychoeducation groups for adolescents: A comparison. *Journal for Specialists in Group Work, 22,* 203-213.

Shechtman, Z., & Perl-Dekel, O. (2000). A comparison of therapeutic factors in two group treatment modalities: Verbal and art therapy. *Journal for Specialists in Group Work, 25,* 288-304.

Slocum, Y. S. (1987). A survey of expectations about group therapy among clinical and non-clinical populations. *International Journal of Group Psychotherapy, 37,* 39-54.

Smaby, M. H., Maddux, C. D., Torres-Rivera, E., & Zimmick, R. (1999). A study of the effects of a skills-based versus a conventional group counseling training program. *Journal for Specialists in Group Work, 24,* 152-163.

Soldz, S., Budman, S., Davis, M., & Demby, A. (1993). Beyond the interpersonal circumplex in group psychotherapy: The structure and relationship to outcome of the individual group member interpersonal process scale. *Journal of Clinical Psychology, 49,* 551-563.

Spielberger, C. D. (1983). *State-trait anxiety inventory.* Palo Alto, CA: Mind Garden.

Stockton, R., Robison, F. F., & Morran, D. K. (1983). A comparison of the HIM-B with the Hill Interaction Matrix model of group interaction styles: A factor analytic study. *Journal of Group Psychotherapy, Psychodrama & Sociometry, 36,* 102-113.

Stone, M. H., Lewis, C. M., & Beck, A. P. (1994). The structure of Yalom's Curative Factors Scale. *International Journal of Group Psychotherapy, 44,* 239-245.

Toseland, R., & Siporin, M. (1986). When to recommend group treatment: A review of the clinical and group literature. *International Journal of Group Psychotherapy, 36,* 171.

Tullett, A. D, & Davies, G. B. (1997). Cognitive style and affect: A comparison of the Kirton Adaption-Innovation and Schutz's Fundamental Interpersonal Relations Orientation-Behaviour Inventories (KAI and FIRO-B). *Personality & Individual Differences, 23,* 479-485.

Van Dyck, B. J. (1980). An analysis of selection criteria for short-term group counseling clients. *The Personnel & Guidance Journal, 59,* 226-230.

Yalom, I. D. (1985). *The theory and practice of group psychotherapy* (3rd ed.). New York: Basic Books.

Yalom, I. D. (1995). *The theory and practice of group psychotherapy* (4th ed.). New York: Basic Books.

Yalom, I. D., Tinklenberg, J., & Gilula, M. (1968). *Curative factors in group psychotherapy.* Unpublished manuscript.

10

EFFECTIVE SUPERVISION OF GROUP LEADERS

Current Theory, Research, and Implications for Practice

JANICE L. DELUCIA-WAACK

University at Buffalo, SUNY

JAMES FAUTH

Antioch New England Graduate School

Why do you look at the speck in your brother's eye, but pay no attention to the log in your own eye? How can you say to your brother, "Please, brother, let me take that speck out of your eye," yet cannot see the log in your own eye? . . . First take the log out of your own eye, and then you will be able to see clearly to take the speck out of your brother's eye.

—Luke 6:41-44

The essence of supervision for group leaders is to help them remove the "logs" (e.g., anxiety, insufficient skills, limited awareness of self or group process) from their own eyes so that they might intervene more effectively (i.e., help group members to take the specks out of their eyes as well). Of course, given the complexity and intensity of group leadership, there is no shortage of potential logs to dislodge in the eyes of both beginning and experienced group leaders (DeLucia-Waack, 1999; Hayes, 1995). Clearly, the supervision of group leaders is of paramount importance to the field of group leadership.

The purpose of this chapter is to review the theory, research, and best practices related to the supervision of group leaders. The focus is primarily on the aspects of supervision that are unique to working with groups. First, the importance and focus of effective supervision for group leaders are described. Second, the critical events identified in the literature on the supervision of group leaders, and unique to the supervision of group leadership, are highlighted: anxiety, skill development, parallel process, and countertransference. Third, various modalities (i.e., individual, coleader, and group) and models for supervising group leadership are discussed. The final section concludes with specific recommendations for best practices for the supervision of group leadership.

IMPORTANCE AND FOCUS OF SUPERVISION FOR GROUP LEADERS

The Association for Specialists in Group Work's (ASGW) *Professional Standards for the Training of Group Workers* (2000) specifies a minimum level of 1 hour a week of planning time for group leaders (either individually or with a coleader). According to these standards, leading effective groups demands constant assessment of leader skills and interventions, group development, and individual progress of group members. Thus, the supervisor and group leaders must understand the unique characteristics of the group being led in order to provide effective supervision (ASGW, 2000). Furthermore, the ASGW *Best Practice Guidelines* (1998) consistently emphasize the importance of supervision and/or consultation with other group leaders as an integral part of effective and ethical group leadership. Specifically, these standards state that group leaders must act as follows:

> Process the workings of the group with themselves, group members, supervisors or other colleagues, as appropriate. This may include assessing progress on group and member goals, leader behaviors and techniques, group dynamics and interventions, and developing understanding and acceptance of meaning. Processing may occur both within sessions and before and after each session, at time of termination, and later follow up, as appropriate (p. 4).

Unfortunately, other than ASGW, no professional organization has suggested guidelines for the supervision of group leaders. Furthermore,

the field of supervision has paid little attention to the supervision process of group leaders (Kleinberg, 1999), although current research on the supervision of individual counseling and psychotherapy suggests that a positive supervisory relationship is helpful and important for trainee development and effective in improving client outcome (Bernard & Goodyear, 1998; Lambert & Ogles, 1997; Worthen & McNeil, 1996).

What little research has been done specific to supervision of group leaders suggests the importance of supervision. Ebersole, Leiderman, and Yalom (1969) reported that without supervision, group therapists were not able to identify mistakes and generate new plans of action; instead, they became stuck in a cycle of repeated ineffective interventions. Furthermore, Leszcz and Murphy (1994) found that complaints about technical difficulties, such as recruiting and retaining group membership, did not distinguish satisfied from unsatisfied beginning group leader trainees. Rather, the quality of the supervision relationship was the chief variable associated with training satisfaction. Specifically, dissatisfied group leader trainees reported feeling "unheard," "criticized," and "unhelped," whereas satisfied trainees reported feeling "supported" and "empathized with" (p. 100). In an attempt to identify the effective elements of group supervision, Marshall (1999), through a survey of group leaders, noted four important variables: acceptance and support (e.g., I can talk about mistakes and it is okay); play (e.g., We have a lot of fun); tolerance and enjoyment of primary process (e.g., When I could feel and act as dysfunctional as the client, the whole case turned around); and resolution of intergroup conflict (e.g., When we have our differences, we are able to talk about them).

CRITICAL EVENTS IN THE SUPERVISION OF GROUP LEADERS

Supervising group leadership is much more complicated than supervising individual counseling because of the multiple participants and relationships involved in both group membership and leadership (DeLucia, Bowman, & Bowman,

1989; Yalom, 1995). In effect, supervision of group leadership must attend not only to relationships with individual group members but also with subgroups and the group as a whole. The stage of the group and the experience level of the group leader(s) dictates the focus of supervision, ranging from skill development and decreasing anxiety to awareness of group process and dynamics to discussion of countertransference. This complicated nature of group leadership often elicits complex events and reactions for group leaders and their supervisors, such as anxiety, parallel process, and countertransference. Thus, the following section will focus on these three key themes as they relate to the supervision of group leaders and the development of group leadership skills.

Anxiety

Leszcz and Murphy (1994) identified several sources of anxiety for group leaders, including the fear of losing control, appearing incompetent, becoming overwhelmed by the sheer volume of material, contributing to premature terminations, and exposing personal and professional weaknesses. Supervision may help group therapists alleviate some of these fears. For instance, in their qualitative investigation of neophyte group therapy trainees, Murphy, Leszcz, Collings, and Salvendy (1996) noted that intense anxiety seemed to be a universal experience among trainees. Furthermore, empathic uncovering and exploration of anxiety in supervision seemed to help group therapists to appropriately manage anxiety and decrease negative affect. Overall, they suggested that effective supervision could contain and reframe the anxiety.

Christensen and Kline (2000, 2001) conducted two qualitative studies of beginning group leaders' experience of receiving supervision in a group format. In both studies, they found that "participant anxiety" (i.e., emotional reactions, thoughts, and behavioral choices related to anxiety in group supervision) permeated the experience of the group leaders in supervision. In the earlier study (Christensen & Kline, 2000), they found that the group leaders were initially anxious and thus hesitant to participate in supervision. As the level of trust and

support in the supervision group increased, however, anxiety became a motivating aspect of group supervision, fueling feedback and group interaction, especially when anxiety was perceived as facilitating learning (i.e., If I am anxious, then it is because I need to ask for help in supervision to learn a new skill or approach) rather than when it was related to the fear of being perceived as incompetent. In their 2001 study, Christensen and Kline found that the result of coping with participant anxiety included enhanced insight regarding relationships with their coleaders and significant others, increased understanding and development of group facilitation skills, and improved interpersonal interactions.

Starling and Baker (2000) and Newman and Lovell (1993) provided support for the importance of dealing with anxiety in the group supervision of group leaders. Specifically, Starling and Baker's qualitative analysis revealed that decreased anxiety and confusion enhanced group supervision of group leaders. In addition, Newman and Lovell, based on a case study, suggested that "significant and difficult moments in group supervision were often inseparable because the successful resolution of challenges often left favorable impressions" (p. 29).

Parallel Process

Although definitions of parallel process vary, the common element among them is the reenactment of the counseling relationship within supervision, focusing on impasses, resistance, and other distortions in the counseling relationship. Because there are so many opportunities for relationships at different levels to affect other relationships, parallel process becomes more complex and important to attend to in the supervision of group leaders (DeLucia et al., 1989). DeLucia et al. noted, "As the counselor explores conflicts and blocks, the supervisory relationship itself becomes the source of learning and growth about the counseling relationship, thus facilitating adaptive counselor interactions with clients" (p. 232). Psychodynamic theorists have consistently emphasized the importance of parallel process in groups. For example, Spotnitz (1958) pointed out that experienced group therapists engaged in group supervision were no more immune to the complex phenomenology of parallel process in the supervisory group than were the patients in their groups. In addition, Etgar (1996) provided clinical examples of parallel process that occurred between therapy groups for adolescent sex offenders and the supervision group for the leaders. She suggested that parallel processes are likely to emerge during times of stress in treatment (e.g., mandated treatment or member relapses), times of client resistance (e.g., absenteeism), times of shared affect between client and therapist (e.g., feelings of isolation), and times when therapists and clients share an important context (e.g., when both therapists and clients view a particular event as not helpful).

Holmes, Stader, Swaim, Haigler, and Myers's (1998) qualitative analysis of the journals of group therapists in group supervision revealed a clear similarity between the needs of group members and the needs of group leader interns in group supervision. Specifically, they noted parallels of information giving and problem focus during the initial stage, a focus on skill development and identity development during the middle stage, and closure and consolidation of skills and knowledge during the ending stage of group for both group leaders in supervision and group members in their groups.

Two clinical examples provide further evidence of the importance of parallel process in the supervision of group work. Rosenberger, Fauth, and Gehlert (2003) described two group facilitators of a men's therapy group engaged in an unconscious struggle for control of the direction of the group, thereby leading to a "stalemate" in both the group and in supervision. After several weeks, this dynamic was finally made explicit and discussed at the prompting of the supervisor during their supervisory session. In the group session immediately following this discussion, the members challenged the leaders for the first time, the successful handling of which ultimately led the group to enter the working stage. Friedman and Handel (2002) presented the concept of "reverse parallel process," which occurs in supervision groups by containing and working through difficult emotions disowned by the therapy group and subsequently results in changes in the functioning of both the supervision and therapy groups. In essence, they were naming the process whereby

in supervision, group leaders examine and work through the parallel process that has occurred from their group to the supervisory group; and thus, they are able to affect their counseling group based on insight gained from the supervisory group.

Countertransference

Countertransference is postulated to increase exponentially when working with groups (Hayes, 1995). Although definitions of countertransference abound, current scholars who distinguish between therapists' "real" and "unreal" reactions define *countertransference* as irrational reactions emanating from therapists' unresolved personal issues (Corey & Corey, 2002; Fauth & Hayes, 2002; Gelso & Carter, 1985; Yalom, 1995). Unfortunately, countertransference has been virtually ignored in the research on group counseling and supervision of group therapy (Hayes, 1995). Thus, supervisors are in the unfortunate position of extrapolating from research on countertransference in individual therapy to the supervision of group leadership. This section has been arranged according to four components of group countertransference identified by Hayes: origins, triggers, manifestations, and management.

Countertransference *origins* are therapists' unresolved personal issues (Hayes, 1995). Countertransference origins likely to be evoked in group therapy include reactions to authority, conflict, and anger; narcissistic needs; cultural values; excessive need for control; family issues; and separation-individuation issues (Halperin, 1989; Hayes et al., 1998; Slavson, 1953; VanWagoner, 2000). Countertransference *triggers* are the therapy events and/or client characteristics that evoke therapists' unresolved conflicts (Hayes, 1995). Group leadership, due to its complex, interactive, and affective nature, is probably even more likely than individual therapy to trigger therapists' unresolved conflict (DeLucia-Waack, 1999; Hayes, 1995; Van-Wagoner, 2000). Therapists could have their personal reactions triggered by individual group members or their cotherapists as well as the group as a whole (Hayes, 1995). Specific countertransference triggers in group tend to be related to conflict, competition, resistance, intense affect, dependency, termination, and cultural values (Flapan & Fenchel, 1984; Halperin, 1989; Hayes, 1995; Slavson, 1953; VanWagoner, 2000).

Countertransference *manifestations* are myriad cognitive, emotional, and behavioral reactions that therapists exhibit when countertransference is triggered (Hayes, 1995). When therapists' personal issues are triggered, their countertransference manifestations typically take on either a positive or negative valence (Fauth & Hayes, 2002; Friedman & Gelso, 2000; Hayes et al., 1998) and are manifested in many idiosyncratic ways (e.g., overly critical behavior, anxiety, boredom, avoidance, overinvolvement) (Halperin, 1989; Hayes, 1995). Regardless of the specific form it takes, the hallmark of countertransference manifestations is that they are extreme in some way or represent some departure from normal clinical practice (Hayes, 1995).

To cope with their countertransference, group therapists may employ one or more countertransference *management* strategies, such as denial, repression, personal therapy, and (ideally) supervision (Hayes, 1995). Group theory posits that one of the greatest benefits of supervision of group leaders may be to help manage (rather than necessarily prevent) and normalize countertransference (Flapan & Fenchel, 1984; Halperin, 1989, Vannicelli, 1991). Identification and exploration of countertransference in the context of a safe and supportive supervisory relationship is touted as probably the most effective countertransference management strategy for group therapists (Kleinberg, 1999; Murphy et al., 1996; VanWagoner, 2000).

For example, Cohen, McGrath, and Sharpe (1991) reported two case studies that emphasized the importance of supervision for successfully identifying and managing group countertransference. In both cases, the discussion of countertransference in supervision resulted in recognition of how it had blocked important information about and reactions to group members based on the group leaders' unresolved family issues that were displaced on to group members. Cohen et al. postulated that discussion and recognition of the countertransference resulted in changes in group leader behavior and impact within group sessions. In sum, the scant empirical evidence on individual counseling as well as current group theory suggests that countertransference can have positive or negligible effects on therapy outcome if successfully managed, but deleterious effects if unrecognized or poorly managed. Thus, an imperative task in the supervision of groups is to help group leaders identify, discuss, work through, and successfully manage their countertransference reactions in group.

MODELS FOR SUPERVISION OF GROUP LEADERSHIP

Several models of the supervision of group leaders, each with distinct advantages, have been developed. Supervision of group leaders occurs in various modalities, including supervision of an individual group leader or coleaders, supervision by one member of a coleadership dyad by the more experienced coleader (dyadic supervision), and group supervision of multiple group leaders. Variations as to how supervision is delivered will be discussed in this chapter. Furthermore, several authors have proposed theoretical models of supervision for group leaders designed for a specific modality and include different tasks for different developmental stages. These models follow, along with relevant research.

Models of Supervision for Individual/Coleaders

Supervision of a Group Leader

Little has been written about supervision of one group leader conducting a group, although it probably occurs quite often in counseling practice. What can be inferred from the individual supervision literature is the importance of emphasizing three areas in supervision: case conceptualization, development of skills, and resolution of personal reactions that interfere with successfully intervening in group situations (Bowman & DeLucia, 1993). Case conceptualization includes discussion of group dynamics and interactions between members. Development of skills focuses on the implementation of counseling skills to facilitate group discussion, support, and feedback between members. Resolution of personal issues includes discussion of potential parallel process and countertransference. DeLucia-Waack (2002) described a writing activity that can be used to help beginning group leaders organize the information about their groups and plan for future sessions, including sections on case conceptualization, analysis of effective and noneffective interventions, and reactions to group members and events. She suggested sharing these planning and processing sheets with a supervisor prior to supervision.

Dyadic Supervision

Leszcz and Murphy (1994) defined dyadic supervision as an "apprenticeship model in which a more experienced group leader co-leads with an inexperienced trainee" (p. 99). This senior-junior group leadership model is quite common. Bridbord (2003) found that in her national sample of 51 coleadership pairs, 29% of them were composed of senior-junior leadership teams. Leszcz and Murphy stated,

> Benefits of such a model include the trainee's opportunity to observe directly how an experienced leader conducts group psychotherapy. Similarly, the junior leader may be able to receive direct feedback from the supervising leader about his or her therapeutic style and use of therapeutic interventions. (p. 110)

Tuckman and Finkelstein (1999) suggested several dilemmas that may arise for the more experienced coleader: choosing to have a group therapeutic impact versus supervisee-training impact, the unidimensionality of the analysis of countertransference, choosing to discuss the supervisor's countertransference versus overwhelming the new trainee, managing the balance of interventions in session by both coleaders, and idealization of the supervisor by the new trainee.

Triadic Supervision

Triadic supervision consists of both members of a coleadership team and a supervisor. The advantages of triadic supervision include the provision of comprehensive reporting about the group in supervision as each cotherapist serves to correct each other's blind spots (Leszcz & Murphy, 1994). Their ability to give one another feedback and together examine the group process, transference, and countertransferential developments within the group and the interpersonal processes can provide significant amounts of support and information.

> However, the cotherapy team is subject to its own process and dynamics, and supervision needs to address issues that invariably arise, including issues of competence, dependency, and rivalry. How the co-therapy relationship develops influences dramatically how the group will function. (Leszcz & Murphy, 1994, p. 112)

Nakkula and Watts (1997) suggested that a uniqueness of supervising group coleaders is the focus on their relationship, the "friendship-in-the-making" as they refer to it, which requires an interpersonal focus for supervision (p. 145).

The benefits of coleadership are often described in the literature, though little research has been conducted on any aspect of it. There have been several proposed models of group coleader development (e.g., Brent & Marine, 1982; Gallogly & Levine, 1979; McMahon & Links, 1984; Stempler, 1993) that are relevant as a background for discussing triadic supervision. While previous models of group leadership development vary in the number and emphasis of stages, Dugo and Beck (1997), drawing from earlier models in the literature, suggested a coleadership model of development that consisted of nine phases. In Phase 1, "Creating a Contract," the coleaders establish a foundation by creating formal norms for the critical aspects of their relationship and for the conduct of the group. In Phase 2, "Forming an Identity," cotherapists establish an initial identity as a team and form the structure of their relationship. In Phase 3, "Building a Cooperative Team," the cotherapists have made basic structural decisions and are ready to move into the information gathering that can set up a collaborative working relationship. In Phase 4, "Developing Closeness," the cotherapists establish a deeper interest and attraction based an actual working knowledge of one another. In Phase 5, "Defining

Strengths and Limitations," the important task is for the cotherapists to develop realistic perceptions of their strengths and limitations in their own relationship and as therapists in the group. In Phase 6, "Exploring Possibilities," there is a reworking of the cotherapy contract that allows for exploring new behavior in the personal realm and greater flexibility in role behavior as leaders in the group. In Phase 7, "Supporting Self-Confrontation," leaders challenge their own personal and professional frontiers, confronting the issues that interfere with growth. In Phase 8, "Integrating and Implementing Changes," the personal insights and changes resulting from self-confrontations in Phase 7 must now be integrated. In Phase 9, "Closing," the need for closure exists with discussion of how the relationship worked and what they learned from each other. Dugo and Beck emphasize that the first stage, "Creating a Contract," is essential to becoming an effective cotherapy team and insist that cotherapists should not lead a group together unless they have at least reached Phase 3, "Building a Cooperative Team."

Often, working with a coleader greatly enhances the effectiveness of group work interventions but necessitates more time and attention to the coordination of joint leadership efforts (Yalom, 1995). This additional attention also carries over in triadic supervision. While acknowledging the benefits of triadic supervision, Stempler (1993) cautioned that it is not easy to create an appropriate balance of power where "both co-leaders can simultaneously learn from each other, grow from the experience, and model a healthy balance of authority and intimacy for their groups" (pp. 97-98).

Leszcz and Murphy (1994) made several recommendations that are relevant for triadic supervision:

> Supervision ideally encourages the development of an effective relationship between the co-leaders without siding with one in any conflict. A systemic view of the contributions of the group, the co-therapy team, the supervision, and the multiple levels of relationships both empowers the supervision and illuminates the impact of interpersonal and group process. . . . Whenever possible, linking the co-therapy process to the group process may help

resolve difficulties between the co-therapists, as the only real supervisory leverage present is what is in the best interest of the treatment. (p. 113)

DeLucia et al. (1989) presented a model for supervising coleaders that was based on the developmental tasks proposed by a group stage model and emphasized the parallel processes that occur in the development of the group and coleader relationships. They suggested that for group leaders to facilitate the attainment of tasks by group members at each group stage, they must have first worked through those tasks as a dyad. For example, as group leaders learn how to give each other constructive feedback, they are more encouraging of similar behavior in their group members. Specifically, DeLucia et al. (1989) suggested,

> [The] stages of group process are parallel to stages of co-leadership development; thus, successful resolution of issues and tasks for the leaders result in heightened ability to help group members resolve similar issues and facilitates movement through the stages of group development. Counselors are able to facilitate resolution of similar tasks with their clients to the extent they have addressed those tasks in the supervisory relationship. (p. 233)

Initially, coleaders, like new group members, may be anxious or uncomfortable about self-disclosing deeply in supervision, taking risks, and trying different behaviors because of the newness of the supervisory relationship. Thus, DeLucia et al. (1989) postulated that it is important to acknowledge and successfully manage this anxiety and discomfort in supervision. To facilitate this process, a structure must be created for coleaders to feel safe and understand the boundaries of supervision, so that they can take risks and honestly assess the success of their interventions in an effort to promote new and effective behaviors in future sessions. It is also important for coleaders to explore their relationship in terms of session planning and processing, giving and receiving constructive feedback (to each other and the group members), and helping members formulate and achieve individual goals.

As group members move out of the beginning orientation stage, DeLucia et al. (1989)

hypothesized that it is essential for the coleaders to establish a relationship that encourages continuous evaluation of each coleader's specific interventions, strengths, and weaknesses. During transition, coleaders must learn to give each other constructive feedback, disagree respectfully, and resolve differences in a manner in which each coleader feels comfortable. As coleaders experience the value and benefit of resolving the conflict successfully, they are then able to encourage such resolutions within their group. In the working stage, coleaders have established a working relationship in which they feel comfortable giving each other feedback and discussing personal reactions related to the group. As termination draws near, coleaders must begin to prepare for termination by talking about their feelings of grief and loss, how they normally say goodbye, and how this may affect their group's termination. Acknowledgement of such affect then theoretically allows the coleaders to encourage such discussion in their group.

DeLucia-Waack (2002) extended DeLucia et al.'s (1989) model with suggestions for facilitating the developmental tasks of each stage in supervision with group coleaders. Supervision tasks and interventions are identified as the coleader relationship progresses in supervision. Three major tasks for supervisors are identified for a new supervisory relationship. The first task is to revisit major sources of information about supervision and group leadership (e.g., ASGW, 1998, 1999, 2000; Bernard & Goodyear, 1992). The second task is to gather information about the specific type of group the supervisees will be leading, such as foci, goals, and interventions. The third task is to examine the supervisor's specific beliefs, theoretical orientation, and expectations about supervision in order to be able to articulate these to new supervisees. According to DeLucia-Waack (2002), the middle stage of supervision is focused on the evaluation of the effectiveness of group interventions. At this stage of supervision, coleaders reflect on what happens in group sessions in terms of critical events, interventions, leader and member reactions, and member progress in an effort to evaluate effective leader behaviors, plan for future sessions, and explore new behaviors, interventions, and strategies. At this stage, case

conceptualization, techniques and interventions, and personal reactions are the foci.

DeLucia-Waack (2002) suggested a format for each supervision session that allows time for discussion, planning, and processing. She included the following five steps: (a) *reporting* of what specifically happened in the last session in terms of critical events, member behavior, and leader interventions; (b) *reflection* on what happened in the last session, specifically in terms of what worked and what did not work, and what produced emotional reactions from coleaders and members; (c) *integration* of events in group sessions with theoretical perspectives on group stages, therapeutic factors, leader interventions, member psychosocial development, and progress toward member goals; (d) *planning* for what needs to happen in the next session in terms of content and process, group interventions, and interventions directed at specific members; and (e) *evaluation* of what was learned during the supervision session and how it will be applied. The format is postulated to provide structure and reduce anxiety for group leaders as well as to allow them to reflect on what was effective (and what was not) in order to plan for future group sessions. Conyne (1999) and Brown, Spenser, and Dlin (1990) have also suggested similar outlines for supervision sessions of group leaders.

Several authors have suggested formats for written notes used by coleaders as part of the supervision process. DeLucia-Waack (2002) suggested the use of "Planning and Processing Sheets" to initially guide the group leaders as they reflect on their group sessions and to provide the supervisor with information prior to supervision. Brown et al. (1990) suggested a similar schema, titled the "Group Recording Form." Bloch, Brown, Davis, and Dishotsky (1975) also emphasized the use of a written summary of each group session dictated by coleaders as a narrative account of the meeting that provides the supervisor with more time to focus on particularly striking elements of a group session, including critical process events, dynamics of patients, and intervention strategies. Aveline (1986) advocated the use of written reports in brief-group-psychotherapy training focusing on the following questions: (a) What themes were present in the session?

(b) How would these themes be tackled in the group? (c) How were these themes tackled by the leader? and (d) How were members involved in the session?

Models of Group Supervision for Group Leaders

Group supervision of group leaders is cost-efficient in that several students can be supervised at one time, with the added benefit of having multiple viewpoints and feedback exchanges. Newman and Lovell (1993) noted the advantages of group supervision for group leaders as being an "excellent forum for obtaining feedback, encouraging healthy coleadership relationships, enhancing group facilitation skills, and fostering counselor-in-training self-awareness" (p. 22) as well as gaining valuable insights into group process.

Almost all models of group supervision of group leaders emphasize the application of group dynamics and vicarious learning principles to the supervisory relationship. Werstlein and Borders (1997) emphasized the importance of "group process to enhance learning" (p. 2), although the incorporation of group process into supervision groups is used infrequently in actual practice (Riva & Cornish, 1995).

A majority of the models emphasize the usefulness of parallel process events and countertransference reactions in learning effective group leadership skills. For example, Leszcz and Murphy (1994) concluded that a group model of supervision "most directly realizes group process and provides participants with firsthand exposure to group dynamics through actual group participation" (p. 107).

Altfeld and Bernard (1997) suggested that several important dynamics related to group leadership are most effectively dealt with in group supervision: competitiveness, dependency, and the advantages of collaborating in a "lonely profession." VanWagoner (2000) noted anger and aggression as essential elements in groups, thus making these inevitable topics in supervision for group leaders.

Group supervision of group leaders offers unparalleled opportunities for emotional and intellectual learning. The presence of fellow group leaders who are emotionally responsive to others

"acts as a powerful solvent for countertransference resistance, and the group itself offers rich learning inherent in the frequent re-enactment of the dynamics of the treatment situation" (Altfeld & Bernard, 1997, p. 390). Glatzer (1971) noted,

> The use of the group process is particularly appropriate in the supervision of analytic group therapy because the subtle nuances of group transferences, multiple resistances, and interlocking mechanisms of defense can be illustrated and that experiencing their own fears of exposure to the group, their own competition for and with the supervisor, and their own rivalry with one another helps group trainees empathize with the members of their own groups. (p. 436)

She also emphasized that the supervisor has the opportunity to model key aspects of the group leader role, from forming the group through termination. This modeling also includes in vivo resistance recognition, exploration, and resolution at individual, subgroup, and group-as-a-whole levels.

Within supervisory groups, group leaders' "resistance to cooperative functioning with each other and with the group leader are permitted to emerge, be studied, and be resolved" (Rosenthal, 1999, pp. 211-212). Cooper and Gustafson (1985) provided two case examples of how to explore countertransference by discussing the parallel process that occurred in group supervision. One example relevant to parallel process focused on the supervisor commenting that the pressure that he felt to provide answers to the supervisees was equal to the pressure that the supervisees were feeling from some of their more difficult clients. This comment thus freed up the supervisor and supervises to discuss responsibility felt toward group members and how to provide support and feedback rather than solutions, resulting in different interactions in supervision and group sessions.

Aronson (1990) suggested that the effectiveness of group supervision of counselors, paralleling the effectiveness of group counseling and therapy, is dependent upon three factors: (a) the contributions of the leader, (b) the group members' interactions with the leader and with each other, and (c) the benefits derived from belonging to a valued group.

Kleinberg (1999) suggested three major areas of intervention. The first area of intervention is the balance between the experiencing and reflecting egos. He summed it up eloquently by saying,

A strong supervisory alliance makes it possible for the supervisor, perhaps assisted by one or two of the supervisees, to step up on the perch and place the events of the treatment group in a dynamic perspective. The climate in which all this takes place can enhance the receptivity of the supervisees to what is being offered to them from the supervisory team. (p. 161)

Kleinberg's (1999) second emphasis was creativity. He believed that clients would experience textbook-derived responses as wooden; therefore, he believed that supervisees should work to translate supervisors' and peers' ideas into their own personal therapy styles. The third area was assessment of the group leader's "clinical skills, knowledge of psychodynamic theory, knowledge of group-dynamics theory, self-reflective capacity, consultation skills, and supervisory capacity" (p. 163).

Using a case study, Newman and Lovell (1993) developed a model of group supervision for group leaders that focuses on the needs of the group leaders based on the stage of the supervision group and the counseling groups being led. During the initial stage, the major tasks of the group supervisor are to set norms to create safety within the group, encourage individual goal setting, and initiate a collaborative group atmosphere. During transition, control issues are important. The major tasks for the group supervisor focus on encouraging independence through immediacy skills and helping to resolve client differentiation struggles. During the working and final stages, the major topics are affect and termination. The focus includes taking ownership of the group and planning for termination.

Altfeld and Bernard (1997) presented an experiential model of group supervision emphasizing concepts from object relations, group-as-a-whole dynamics, and gestalt theory, based on the following assumptions: (a) The group leader is discussing his or her group in supervision because he or she wants help with the case, is

stuck in some way, and is not seeing clearly what is going on in the therapy; (b) the group leader's countertransference feelings being expressed will begin a parallel process in the supervisory group; (c) all reactions in the group are considered valuable countertransference responses to the case material; and (d) group-as-a-whole phenomenon exist and are a crucial part of the process. The supervision group "will unself-consciously, and probably unconsciously, begin functioning as a holding environment for the unaware feelings, thoughts, and experiences the therapist is experiencing with the patient, but with regard to which he (or she) has not yet achieved understanding" (Altfeld & Bernard, 1997, p. 386).

Rosenthal's (1999) model, which is based on multiple-level interactions and parallel process, suggested that the major aspects of group supervision include (a) resolution of countertransference resistance; (b) demonstration of group leader interventions (i.e., setting the climate, contracting, integrating new members, preserving the integrity of the group as a learning modality, and managing and resolving the whole variety of resistances that inevitably emerge); and (c) discussion of the parallel process to illustrate resistance, transference, and countertransference to facilitate effective interventions.

Rosenthal's (1999) model focused specifically on resistance. She defines *resistance* as follows:

The very same measures patients used in the face of psychological exigency in order to maintain psychological equilibrium in their very first groups, their families. Resistance is seen as serving a vital function of communicating life history and is therefore elicited and welcomed. . . . Attempts to forcibly wrest resistance from patients cause them to cling to the resistance even more desperately and also raise the danger of forcing the patient to use even more primitive defenses. (p. 201)

Her interventions to deal with resistance include modeling support and joining with nondestructive resistance, such as restricting presentations to successful sessions or interventions, competitiveness with the supervisor, and argumentativeness with fellow members, a task she views as essential.

The divergently genuine feeling responses of the other members tend to offer the specific emotional experience [that] is needed to meet previously unmet developmental needs. This collective feedback plays a more significant role in the working through process than the explanations offered by the therapist. (Rosenthal, 1999, p. 210)

Most of the models suggested for group supervision of group leaders have been based on theory and clinical experience. Many of the writings include case examples of group supervision. However, almost no research has been done to date to test the effectiveness of models of supervision. Riester (1991), in one of the few evaluation studies of group supervision, focused on group leaders of inpatient children's groups. Riester reported that cohesiveness, trust, and supervision group size were the most important factors influencing communication, followed by the desire for both experiential and didactic materials, the importance of clearly stated goals and expectations initially, and the importance of the supervisor as a model. Hunter and Armstrong (1994) examined the efficacy of a group supervision seminar focused on discussion of group processes, the development of cotherapy relationships, and the training of beginning group leaders. Overall, group leaders in the group supervision seminar reported that the seminar leaders, the group, and the choice of readings were helpful. These studies used small selected samples and self-report questionnaires or interviews. Thus, it is essential that more research be conducted to evaluate the effectiveness of group supervision in general and the comparative efficacy of different models of group supervision of group leaders.

SUGGESTIONS FOR BEST PRACTICES FOR THE SUPERVISION OF GROUP LEADERSHIP

In this section, the most clinically relevant suggestions for best practices for the supervision of group leaders that have emerged from the literature review are presented. The section is organized to reflect the three primary topics reviewed above: importance and ingredients of successful supervision of group leaders, critical themes in the supervision of group leaders, and models for supervising group leaders.

Critical Themes in the Supervision of Group Leaders

Supervisors of group leaders can help their trainees prevent, identify, and successfully manage their anxiety, parallel process, and countertransference (Corey & Corey, 2002; Gladding, 1999; Hayes, 1995). The key to preventing these events from affecting leadership negatively seems to be to increase awareness of the leaders' personal feelings and reactions in group and supervision (Corey & Corey, 2002; Hayes, 1995; Yalom, 1995). Thus, supervisors of group leaders need to be empathically attuned to their trainees' personal and emotional experiences in group, which are likely to be quite prevalent and intense, instead of just their technical skills (Murphy et al., 1996). Ideally, supervisors should strive to establish a positive supervisory alliance early in the supervision process; indeed, most trainees will explore such sensitive topics only within an extremely safe and supportive supervisory context (Kleinberg, 1999; Murphy et al., 1996; Yalom, 1995).

Group supervisors of group leaders can help identify trainees' anxiety, parallel process, and countertransference reactions by attending to trainees' affective, behavioral, and cognitive reactions in their group and supervisory sessions (DeLucia et al., 1989; DeLucia-Waack, 1999; Halperin, 1989). Supervisors can use live observation, audiotapes, or videotapes to assess group therapist-trainees' behavior in group, while process notes and discussion in supervision can help identify trainees' emotional and cognitive reactions to group (Fauth & Hayes, 2002; Halperin, 1989). For example, group leaders who exhibit excessively positive reactions toward member(s) of their group (e.g., excitement, happiness) might be in danger of becoming enmeshed with the group, whereas group leaders who experience overly negative reactions might withdraw or become overly critical toward group members (Fauth & Hayes, 2002).

Supervisors also should be alert to their own reactions that are stimulated in the supervisory sessions (DeLucia et al., 1989; Yalom, 1995). DeLucia et al. noted that parallel process in group supervision includes reenactment of the group counseling relationship within supervision (or vice versa) and focusing on impasses, resistances, and other distortions in the counseling relationship. As such, it is an important vehicle for illuminating potential countertransference processes (in both the supervisory and group contexts) (Yalom, 1995). Once group leader countertransference is identified via parallel process, supervisors have an opportunity to model effective interpersonal skills, make the connection between the two relationships, separate realistic from unrealistic reactions, and discuss potential future intervention strategies (DeLucia et al., 1989; DeLucia-Waack, 1999).

Group leaders can then use their realistic reactions in crafting effective group interventions (e.g., interpersonal feedback). However, interventions emanating from anxiety or countertransference are likely to be countertherapeutic in nature (Yalom, 1995). At times, simple exploration and self-reflection in supervision will clarify the intent of the intervention. When exploration fails to illuminate the intent, however, the primary means for separating real from unreal reactions is consensual validation, which is available from up to four sources: supervisor, peers (when supervision is conducted in a group format), cotherapists (when group is conducted in a cotherapy format), and group members. For instance, a group leader who is feeling frustrated and critical toward a group member might elicit reactions from his or her cotherapist, supervisor, and other group members. When others share similar reactions, the reaction is more likely based in reality (and can be used to give interpersonal feedback to that member). However, when others' reactions are dissimilar, the reaction is more likely based in the group leader's anxiety, countertransference, or parallel process.

Types of Supervision for Group Leadership

Several suggestions for best practices in the supervision of group leaders can be made on the basis of this review of the literature. First, supervision is essential to effective group leadership. Second, skill development; the relationship between group leaders, group members, and supervisor; and personal reactions must all be topics of supervision. Third, different

modalities of supervision provide different benefits and emphases for group leaders.

Yalom (1985) reported the importance of supervision for group leaders in continuing to increase their repertoire of effective group interventions and to prevent them from getting stuck in a cycle of ineffective inventions. Each model of supervision reviewed previously suggested the importance of evaluating group leader interventions in terms of their effectiveness for individual members and the group as a whole, and then based on these evaluations, planning for future group sessions. All models emphasized the importance of the development of trust in the supervisory relationship not only between the supervisor and the group leader(s) but also between coleaders. This trust is needed to facilitate honest feedback and a collaborative working relationship.

While many of the models of supervision, particularly those based on psychodynamic theory, emphasize the necessity of analyzing parallel process and countertransference, most also emphasize the need for discussion of specific skills interventions and application of group theory. Beginning group leaders need help developing certain skills, specifically confrontation, here-and-now interventions, and relating group events to individual group members' goals. They also need help in moving beyond their initial stage of providing individual therapy within a group context. Thus, supervision must focus on skill development and also personal reactions that may be affecting group facilitation skills.

Different modalities of supervision have also been postulated to have different advantages. A coleadership model in which an inexperienced group leader coleads with a more experienced group leader provides the advantages of the shared group experience and the apprentice being able to experientially observe and learn from the coleader. A triadic model of supervision in which a supervisor supervises a coleadership team has the advantage of objectively being able to intervene in the coleader relationship as well as providing a different perspective on group events. Group supervision of group leaders provides the opportunity to experience group process, observe models of group leadership, and receive feedback from multiple perspectives.

CONCLUSION

Supervision is critical to enhancing the effectiveness of group leader training and counseling practice. Although research on the supervision of group leaders is still preliminary, it does suggest that supervision is important. Furthermore, due to the complexity of group leadership, leader anxiety, countertransference, and parallel process will occur frequently and are essential to consider in supervision. Numerous models of supervision have been developed reflecting the various potential modalities (e.g., individual, coleader, and group), with different formats, foci, and interventions suggested. More research is needed, both quantitative and qualitative, that assesses the effectiveness of group supervision of group leaders in general, the efficacy of specific models of supervision, and critical interventions within supervision groups.

REFERENCES

Altfeld, D. A., & Bernard, H. S. (1997). An experiential group model for group psychotherapy supervision. In C. E. Watkins Jr. (Ed.), *Handbook of psychotherapy supervision* (pp. 381-399). New York: John Wiley.

Aronson, M. L. (1990). A group therapist's perspectives on the use of supervisory groups in the training of psychotherapists. *Psychoanalysis & Psychotherapy, 8,* 88-94.

Association for Specialists in Group Work (ASGW). (1998). Association for Specialists in Group Work best practice guidelines. *Journal for Specialists in Group Work, 23,* 237-244.

Association for Specialists in Group Work (ASGW). (1999). Association for Specialists in Group Work principles for diversity-competent group workers. *Journal for Specialists in Group Work, 24,* 7-14.

Association for Specialists in Group Work (ASGW). (2000). Association for Specialists in Group Work professional standards for the training of group workers. *Journal for Specialists in Group Work, 25,* 327-342.

Aveline, A. (1986). The use of written reports in a brief group psychotherapy training. *International Journal for Group Psychotherapy, 36,* 477-482.

Bernard, J. M., & Goodyear, R. K. (1992). *Fundamentals of clinical supervision.* Needham Heights, MA: Allyn & Bacon.

Bernard, J. M., & Goodyear, R. K. (1998). *Fundamentals of clinical supervision* (2nd ed.). Boston: Allyn & Bacon.

Bloch, S., Brown, S., Davis, K., & Dishotsky, N. (1975). The use of a written summary in group psychotherapy supervision. *American Journal of Psychiatry, 132,* 1055-1057.

Bowman, V. E., & DeLucia, J. L. (1993). Preparation for counseling revisited: New applications to meet the goals of brief counseling. *Crisis Intervention & Time-Limited Treatment, 2,* 255-266.

Brent, D. A., & Marine, E. (1982). Developmental aspects of the co-therapy relationship. *Journal of Marital & Family Therapy, 8,* 69-75.

Bridbord, K. H. (2003). *Co-therapy teams: The effects of personality, temperament, compatibility, and therapeutic/leadership style on co-therapy relationship satisfaction.* Unpublished doctoral dissertation, University at Buffalo, SUNY.

Brown, R. A., Spenser, A., & Dlin, R. (1990). Formulation in groups, or understanding what is going on. *Group, 14*(2), 69-79.

Christensen, T. M., & Kline, W. B. (2000). A qualitative investigation of the process of group supervision with group counselors. *Journal for Specialists in Group Work, 25,* 376-393.

Christensen, T. M., & Kline, W. B. (2001). Anxiety as a condition for learning in group supervision. *Journal for Specialists in Group Work, 26,* 385-396.

Cohen, V., McGrath, P., & Sharpe, J. (1991). Countertransference and therapist change: An aspect of supervision. *Group Analysis, 24,* 53-63.

Conyne, R. K. (1999). *Failures in group work: How we can learn from our mistakes.* Thousand Oaks, CA: Sage.

Cooper, L., & Gustafson, J. P. (1985). Supervision in a group: An application of group therapy. *The Clinical Supervisor, 3*(2), 7-24.

Corey, M. S., & Corey, G. (2002). *Groups: Process and practice* (6th ed.). Monterey, CA: Brooks/Cole.

DeLucia, J. L., Bowman, V. E., & Bowman, R. L. (1989). The use of parallel process in supervision and group counseling to facilitate counselor and client growth. *Journal for Specialists in Group Work, 14,* 232-238.

DeLucia-Waack, J. L. (1999). Supervision for counselors working with eating disorder groups: Countertransference issues related to body image, food, and weight. *Journal of Counseling & Development, 77,* 379-388.

DeLucia-Waack, J. L. (2002). A written guide for planning and processing group sessions in anticipation of supervision. *Journal for Specialists in Group Work, 27,* 341-357.

Dugo, J. M., & Beck, A. P. (1997). Significance and complexity of early phases in the development of the co-therapy relationship. *Group Dynamics: Theory, Research, & Practice, 1,* 294-305.

Ebersole, G., Leiderman, P., & Yalom, I. D. (1969). Training the nonprofessional group therapist. *Journal of Nervous & Mental Disorders, 149,* 385.

Etgar, T. (1996). Parallel processes in a training and supervision group for counselors working with adolescent sex offenders. *Social Work with Groups, 19,* 57-69.

Fauth, J., & Hayes, J. A. (2002, August). *Therapists' stress appraisals as predictors of countertransference with men.* Paper presented at the annual meeting of the American Psychological Association, Chicago, IL.

Flapan, D., & Fenchel, G. H. (1984). Countertransference in group psychotherapy. *Group, 8,* 17-29.

Friedman S. M., & Gelso, C. J. (2000). The development of the inventory of countertransference behavior. *Journal of Clinical Psychology, 56*(9), 1221-1235.

Friedman, R., & Handel, O. (2002). Facilitating individuation processes in supervision groups comprised of co-therapists conducting group therapy with bereaved parents. *Group, 26,* 95-105.

Gallogly, V., & Levine, B. (1979). Co-therapy. In B. Levine (Ed.), *Group psychotherapy: Practice and development* (pp. 296-305). Englewood Cliffs, NJ: Prentice Hall.

Gelso C. J., & Carter, J. A. (1985).The relationship in counseling and psychotherapy: Components, consequences, and theoretical antecedents. *Journal of Counseling Psychology, 13,* (2), 155-243.

Gladding, S. T. (1999). *Group work: A counseling specialty* (3rd ed.). Columbus, OH: Merrill.

Glatzer, H. (1971). Analytic supervision and group psychotherapy. *International Journal of Group Psychotherapy, 21,* 436-443.

Halperin, D. A. (1989). Countertransference and group psychotherapy: The role of supervision. In D. A. Halperin (Ed.), *Group psychodynamics: New paradigms and new perspectives* (pp. 62-75). Chicago: Year Book Medical Publishers.

Hayes, J. A. (1995). Countertransference in group psychotherapy: Waking a sleeping dog. *International Journal of Group Psychotherapy, 45,* 521-535.

Hayes, J. A., McCracken, J. E., McClanahan, M. K., Hill, C. E., Harp, J. S., & Carozzoni, P. (1998). Therapist perspectives on countertransference: Qualitative data in search of a theory. *Journal of Counseling Psychology, 45,* 468-482.

Holmes, G. R., Stader, S. R., Swaim, K. F., Haigler, E. D., & Myers, deRosset Jr. (1998). Adolescent group psychotherapy supervision in a group format: An emerging model. *Journal of Child & Adolescent Group Therapy, 8,* 197-206.

Hunter, D. S., & Armstrong, H. (1994). Establishing group supervision within a group psychotherapy program. *Journal of Child & Youth Care, 9,* 51-62.

Kleinberg, J. L. (1999). The supervisory alliance and the training of psychodynamic group psychotherapists. *International Journal of Group Psychotherapy, 49,* 159-179.

Lambert, M. J., & Ogles, B. M. (1997). The effectiveness of psychotherapy supervision. In C. E. Watkins (Ed.), *Handbook of psychotherapy supervision* (pp. 421-446). New York: John Wiley.

Leszcz, M., & Murphy, L. (1994). Supervision of group psychotherapy. In S. E. Greben & R. Ruskin (Eds.), *Clinical perspectives on psychotherapy supervision* (pp. 99-120). Washington, DC: American Psychiatric Press.

Marshall, R. J. (1999). Facilitating cooperation and creativity in group supervision. *Modern Psychoanalysis, 24,* 181-186.

McMahon, N., & Links, P. S. (1984). Co-therapy: The need for positive pairing. *Canadian Journal of Psychiatry, 29,* 385-389.

Murphy, L., Leszcz, M., Collings, A. K., & Salvendy, J. (1996). Some observations on the subjective experience of neophyte group therapy trainees. *International Journal of Group Psychotherapy, 46,* 543-552.

Nakkula, M. J., & Watts, C. L. (1997). The particulars of pairs supervision. In R. L. Selman, C. L. Watts, & L. H. Schultz (Eds.), *Fostering friendship: Pair therapy for treatment and prevention. Modern applications of social work.* (pp. 145-164). New York: Aldine de Gruyter.

Newman, J. A., & Lovell, M. (1993). Supervision: A description of a supervisory group for group counselors. *Counselor Education & Supervision, 33,* 22-31.

Riester, A. E. (1991). Supervision and support structures for group leaders working with children and adolescents. In S. Tuttman (Ed), *Psychoanalytic group theory and therapy: Essays in honor of Saul Scheidlinger.* American Group Psychotherapy Association monograph series (Monograph No. 7, pp. 211-219). Madison, CT: International Universities Press.

Riva, M. T., & Cornish, J. A. E. (1995). Group supervision practices at psychology predoctoral internship programs: A national survey. *Professional Psychology: Research & Practice, 26,* 523-525.

Rosenberger, E. W., Fauth, J., & Gehlert, K. (2003). *Blood, sweat, and tears: Process-oriented therapy groups for college men.* Manuscript submitted for publication.

Rosenthal, L. (1999). Group supervision of groups: A Modern analytic perspective. *International Journal of Group Psychotherapy, 49,* 197-213.

Slavson, S. R. (1953). Sources of countertransference and group-induced anxiety. *International Journal of Group Psychotherapy, 3,* 373-388.

Spotnitz, H. (1958). Resistance reinforcement in the affect training of analytic group therapists. *International Journal of Group Psychotherapy, 8,* 395-402.

Starling, P. V., & Baker, S. B. (2000). Structured peer group practicum supervision: Supervisee's perceptions of supervision theory. *Counselor Education & Supervision, 39,* 163-176.

Stempler, B. L. (1993). Supervisory co-leadership: An innovative model for teaching the use of social group work in clinical social work training. *Social Work With Groups, 16,* 97-110.

Tuckman, A., & Finkelstein, H. (1999). Simultaneous roles: When group co-therapists also share a supervisory relationship. *Clinical Supervisor, 18,* 185-201.

Vannicelli, M. (1991). Dilemmas and countertransference considerations in group psychotherapy with adult children of alcoholics. *International Journal of Group Psychotherapy, 41,* 295-312.

VanWagoner, S. L. (2000). Anger in group therapy, countertransference and the novice group therapist. *Journal of Psychotherapy in Independent Practice, 1,* 63-75.

Werstlein, P. O., & Borders, L. D. (1997). Group process variables in group supervision. *Journal for Specialists in Group Work, 22,* 120-136.

Worthen, V., & McNeil, B. W. (1996). A phenomenological investigation of "good" supervision events. *Journal of Counseling Psychology, 43,* 25-34.

Yalom, I. D. (1985). *The theory and practice of group psychotherapy* (3rd ed.). New York: Basic Books.

Yalom, I. D. (1995). *The theory and practice of group psychotherapy* (4th ed.). New York: Basic Books.

11

GUIDELINES FOR ETHICAL AND LEGAL PRACTICE IN COUNSELING AND PSYCHOTHERAPY GROUPS

LYNN S. RAPIN

Private Practice

University of Cincinnati

Ethical dilemmas and choice points occur in every phase of group counseling and psychotherapy planning, performing, and processing. Group facilitators need to navigate an ethical course while providing for the therapeutic needs of group members. Formal training programs in counseling and psychology may offer core and/or specialty training in groups that includes training in theoretical approaches, models of group process, leader and member skills, specific techniques and activities, and structured and unstructured group formats. Ongoing professional education, supervision, and consultation in group facilitation afford opportunities for further skill development.

This chapter will include a review of key ethics definitions, decision-making models, and best practice guidelines and their applications to group counseling and group psychotherapy. The first section will include a review of ethics codes, moral principles, and ethical decision-making models. Reviews of the literature follow

on ethical and legal considerations in psychology and in their specific applications to counseling and psychotherapy group practice. This chapter will conclude with the demonstration of specific best practice guidelines designed to reduce ethical and legal risks in delivering counseling and psychotherapy groups.

GUIDING DOCUMENTS

Codes of Ethics and Standards of Practice

One of the defining tenets of a profession is that it has a code of ethics. Central to the effective execution of any group method or technique is the assumption of moral and ethical behavior. In governing professional practice, the term *ethical* refers specifically to documents that mandate or prohibit behavior (Acuff et al., 1999). These documents guide professions or encompass codes of ethics adopted by specific professional and state or provincial licensing boards. Membership in professional associations such as the American Counseling Association (ACA, 1997) and the American Psychological Association (APA, 2002) requires strict adherence with formal ethical codes of conduct and standards of practice. Because such documents are reflective of developing knowledge and are revised periodically, "They often fail to address or anticipate current or emerging issues" (Hansen & Goldberg, 1999, p. 497).

Parts of ethical documents are aspirational in nature (for example, APA *Ethical Principles*) and not enforceable, while other sections require strict professional adherence (for example, APA and ACA *Code(s) of Ethics*). Group facilitators need to be aware of the distinctions in the documents of their professional associations. Group specialty organizations such as the Association for Specialists in Group Work (ASGW), a division of ACA; Group Psychology and Group Psychotherapy, Division 49 of APA; and the American Group Psychotherapy Association (AGPA, 1991) follow the ethical codes and standards of practice of the parent organizations of their members. AGPA parent organizations include, for example, psychology, counseling, social work, and psychiatry. In addition, ASGW provides guidance to group practitioners through aspirational best practice guidelines (ASGW, 1998), group work training standards (ASGW, 2000), and guidelines for diversity-competent group work (ASGW, 1999). In many cases, group practitioners may belong to several professional associations, each with a set of ethical principles and standards that guide professional conduct. Furthermore, group facilitators must abide by the laws and regulations in the states where they practice. In some cases, ethical codes and state legal requirements may be in conflict. In these situations, professionals are held to the higher standard.

Ethics Code References to Group Counseling and Psychotherapy

While professional codes of ethics in counseling and psychology are general in nature, they contain key components that address groups directly. The ACA (1997) *Code of Ethics and Standards of Practice* references several specific areas of responsibility related to therapeutic groups. Section A9, concerning the counseling relationship, includes group member screening and protection of clients. Confidentiality in groups and families is specifically addressed in subsection B2a. The section on peer relationships in teaching, training, and supervision (F2e) delineates protections required of students or supervisees assigned to lead counseling groups or of those who provide supervision to peers. Parallel references are noted in the *Standards of Practice* companion document, which identifies minimum expected behaviors related to the code. The APA *Ethical Principles of Psychologists and Code of Conduct* (2002) includes a new specific reference to group therapy in Ethical Standard 10.03, "Group Therapy," which states that "when psychologists provide services to several persons in a group setting, they describe at the outset the roles and responsibilities of all parties and the limits of confidentiality." Otherwise, the APA document guides the broad practice of psychology.

KEY ETHICAL CONCEPTS

Ethical practice is more than the execution of lists of requirements or prohibitions. As practice options have become more complex, technology has burgeoned, and access to mental health services has increased, psychologists and counselors are challenged in daily practice to think and act on moral principles. Ethical issues in group practice have become more intricate.

The counseling and psychology ethics literature has grown over the last several decades as understanding of the complexities of ethical decision making has deepened. A number of authors have discussed ethical and moral practice, the role of values in ethics, professional ethical decision-making models, and more specific applications of ethical principles and best practice guidelines to groups. There is a healthy and ongoing debate about the essence of ethical decision making. Group facilitators are challenged to better define the essential elements of ethical thinking and to measure the presence of ethical behavior in group counseling and psychotherapy. Continuing discussion and research will further clarify the professional responsibilities of ethical action and the legal burdens of ethical practice in groups.

Moral Principles

Acuff et al. (1999) defined *ethical decisions* as those that pertain to overarching moral principles, such as doing good for others (beneficence), and doing no harm (nonmaleficence). Kitchener (1984) viewed ethical practice as a complex process influenced by the moral principles of autonomy, beneficence, nonmaleficence, justice, and fidelity executed through defined ethical guidelines. Forester-Miller and Davis (1996) provided an overview of these five generally accepted moral principles and their application to counseling.

Application of Moral Principles to Groups

Values and value-based decisions are influenced by the contexts in which they occur. Thus, moral principles have to be considered carefully as they are applied to the ethical practice of group counseling and therapy. Each of the five moral principles is briefly described here and demonstrated through an example in group practice.

Autonomy allows the individual freedom of choice and participation. Autonomy is also based on the assumption that the client or group member has the ability to make such sound decisions. In considering group counseling and therapy, issues of client autonomy are multiplied by the numerous layers of participation and choice points available to leaders and members. For example, a silent group member may be exercising autonomy in level of participation at a particular time during the life of the group. Alternately, the silent member may be demonstrating resistance. A skilled group facilitator can invite the silent member to participate without coercion and assist in educating group members to variations in style of participation.

Nonmaleficence, the concept of doing no harm, involves both protection from intentional harm and refraining from actions that would risk harm. Choices of activities, structuring and pacing of counseling and therapeutic events, levels of disclosure, modeling, and member selection are but a few areas of group practice influenced by this moral principle. For example, some group members may cry while talking about difficult subjects. Other members of the group may feel coerced by this informal norm to display their emotions in similar fashion. This could result in members disclosing too much personal information too soon or at an uncomfortable level. Too much disclosure too soon can result in members withdrawing from further discussion. A group facilitator sensitive to this pressure would routinely reinforce a message that group members can choose the level of emotional expression in the group and that members can elect to stop disclosing when they need to do so.

Beneficence, that principle of doing good for others, reflects a proactive and harm prevention perspective. For example, group psychotherapy and counseling facilitators can demonstrate beneficence in responding to a discussion of depression symptoms in a therapy group by assisting members in identifying common experiences and helpful coping strategies. Many issues related to confidentiality and its limits in groups relate to harm prevention. Because the principle of confidentiality is owned by the individual client, group disclosures are not protected as privileged communication. Group facilitators are bound by the requirements of confidentiality, but members of groups are not. Ethical codes of both APA and ACA, as well as state laws, specify these limits and also other limits on confidentiality (child abuse, elder abuse, and imminent danger to self and others, for examples).

Justice reflects uniqueness and individuality in the treatment of others. Clear rationales need to be considered whenever an individual is treated uniquely. Issues of diversity, leader and member experience, levels of participation, targeted group treatments, and homogeneity versus heterogeneity in group composition present opportunities to apply the justice principle. For example, if there is a group member whose first language is not English, the facilitator could assist in ensuring that the member understands the meaning of idioms other group members may use ("I was *so* happy with my father," meaning

I was so upset with my father, understood by the member and some of her peers but confusing to others who might take it more literally).

Fidelity, referring to honor, faithfulness, and loyalty, requires trust in the therapeutic process and in those who execute it. Group interventions require a careful balance to preserve trust. Group facilitators can increase trust by modeling good group member behaviors and reinforcing those behaviors as they are demonstrated by group members. For example, the leader can reflect and summarize common experiences expressed by members with social anxiety, thereby assisting the members in understanding the similarities in their experiences and fostering a climate in which members can learn from each other.

Hansen and Goldberg (1999) suggested that some authors, most notably Meara, Schmidt, and Day (1996), have promoted virtue ethics on the basis of these moral principles. Meara et al. provided additional definitional distinction to the terms *virtue ethics* and *principle ethics* in their foundational lead article in a special issue on ethics in *The Counseling Psychologist*. Virtue ethics were defined as character traits and ideals, for example, prudence, integrity, respectfulness, and benevolence, which promote ethical practice.

In a response to Meara et al., Kitchener (1996) agreed that both virtue and character are factors that need to be better understood and integrated into ethical practice. She also agreed that principle ethics are insufficient to guide ethical behavior. Individuals may know the right or principled response but may not respond appropriately because of personal shortcoming; or people may act out of principle with little regard for the consequences of those actions. For example, a colleague in an informal social situation may ask a counseling group facilitator about how a specific person he or she referred is doing in group. The facilitator may not resist the temptation to reveal confidential information in an inappropriate setting. A better response would be to redirect the colleague to discuss case-specific information about any individual in a professional setting and with the appropriate disclosure permission in place. Kitchener concluded that while principles provide a means of evaluating virtues and actions, neither principles nor virtues are absolute guarantees of ethical responses. Vasquez (1996) recommended that attention be devoted to the processes by which a profession and its members develop the valued virtues.

ETHICAL/LEGAL DECISION-MAKING MODELS

Principle- and Practice-Based Models

Based on moral principles, a number of ethical decision-making and problem-solving models exist to assist counselors and psychologists through ethical questions and dilemmas in broad areas of practice. While it is beyond the scope of this chapter to review each of these models in detail, it is relevant to provide an overview of congruencies among them. See Cottone and Claus (2000) for an exhaustive review of theoretical and practice-based ethical decision-making models published between 1984 and late 1998. As with character traits and values, no one decision-making tool is adequate to guarantee ethical practice.

In Kitchener's theoretical model (1984), a two-stage decision-making process involves intuitive responses to the facts of a situation and ordinary moral sense. If the first stage is insufficient to resolve a dilemma, a second critical-evaluative level of response involves employing ethical theory, ethical principles, ethical codes of conduct, and legal sources. This model has served as a stimulus for later model development.

A number of practice-based ethical decision-making models (Corey, Corey, & Callanan, 2003; Forester-Miller & Davis, 1996; Haas & Malouf, 1995; Paradise & Siegelwaks, 1982) have been developed to provide a sequential process for identifying and resolving ethical issues in practice situations. While there is some variability in the format of each decision model, they contain several common elements, including (a) assessment of the problem situation and its contexts, (b) definition of the potential ethical conflict(s), (c) consultation and application of codes of ethics and relevant statutes, (d) generation of alternative responses to the situation, (e) assessment of the consequences of potential responses, (f) implementation of the selected course of action, and (g) evaluation of the final action taken. Each of these models has wide applicability to all forms of counseling and psychology intervention, and all can assist group leaders in evaluating ethical dilemmas.

Adding Legal Threads to Ethical Decision Making

While these decision-making models all reflect codes of ethics, values, and moral reasoning, they do not emphasize legal issues that have had an increasing influence on the ethical aspects of group practice. As Cooper and Gottlieb (2000) observed, the model by Haas and Malouf (1995), as well as the majority of those cited here, did not address the legal ramifications of ethical decision making. In some cases, an ethical decision may not be legal, and in other cases, a legal obligation may not seem ethical. Careful attention to and clarification of both sets of expectations will increase the performance of ethical practice in counseling and psychotherapy groups. When questions of conflict arise between ethics and the law, consultations with colleagues, with state professional associations and boards, with ethics committees, or with attorneys who are familiar with psychology and counseling are recommended.

Hansen and Goldberg (1999) presented an integrated matrix of seven strands to assist in ethical and legal decision making. A significant addition to previous models, this model addressed with some specificity factors affecting legal considerations. These include (a) the moral principles and personal values identified by Kitchener (1984) as a foundation for moral choices; (b) clinical and cultural factors, including clinical skills, consultation with colleagues, and relevant literature; (c) professional codes of ethics; (d) agency or employer policies; (e) federal, state, and local statutes, all of which are subject to legislative action and which vary with locale; (f) rules and regulations that may accompany federal, state, or local ordinances or statutes; and (g) case law, including federal and state court rulings. While the last three categories on this list may seem intimidating or confusing, there are resources available to assist in understanding and applying them. State laws and rules are published and are also available on

the Internet. For example, the state of Ohio has a set of laws and rules governing the practice of counseling and social work, and another set of laws and rules governing the conduct of psychologists and school psychologists, both available in print or from the State of Ohio Web site. The laws are enacted by the state legislature, and the rules set out the standards by which professional conduct is monitored. One example of available information to guide professional conduct is an August 2002 reminder to psychologists published on the State of Ohio Web site concerning the legal limits of confidentiality and the requirement to inform clients of those limits. Case law documents situations in which specific laws have been tested in court (for example, malpractice actions).

Group facilitators are governed not only by codes of ethics, formal laws, and rules of professional practice but also by institutional rules. Numerous agency and employer issues, including the independence in selection of group members, the formats used for counseling and psychotherapy groups, the ownership of group data, the identified client, and documentation requirements can result in ethical conflicts. Many of these concerns can be identified and modified in the planning process.

Hansen and Goldberg (1999) presented two excellent case illustrations using the APA ethics code and some state licensing laws. One of the cases dealt with complex relationships that occurred between an individual therapist, the therapist's client, and a separate therapy group relationship between the therapist and the significant other of the client. The case demonstrated how unanticipated events pose ethical and legal issues. The APA has published a series of state-specific books to assist mental health professionals in understanding applications of mental health law in their states of residence.

Applications to Managed Care Settings

As managed care has become a more dominant factor in the delivery of mental health services, agency and individual provider contracts with managed care companies greatly affect, and often restrict, the range of individual choices available in treatment planning and execution.

Cooper and Gottlieb (2000) said in identifying expected trends in managed care, "It is expected that practitioners will be doing more group therapy, especially psychoeducational groups (e.g., stress reduction)" (p. 229). Therefore, it is imperative that group facilitators be aware of managed care contracts that affect the delivery of psychotherapy and counseling groups.

Acuff and colleagues (1999), members of the APA task force on Ethical Practice in Organized Systems of Care, identified a number of applications of ethical decision making to managed care relationships. The authors provided a list of questions for practitioners to ask regarding personal ethics in managed care settings. These queries include whether an ethical dilemma exists, the stakeholders involved, applicable ethical and legal codes, and the development of alternate responses. No specific dilemmas related to groups were identified.

Authors of two articles on ethical and legal issues within managed care settings (Cooper & Gottlieb, 2000; Daniels, 2001) identified a number of managed care issues facing counseling psychologists and counselors. The concerns presented are relevant to group counseling and psychotherapy as well as to individual modes of treatment. The ethical challenges reviewed within the APA ethical guidelines included those for informed consent, confidentiality, competence, integrity, human welfare, abandonment, conflict of interest, record maintenance, business relationships, and conflicts between ethics and organizational demands. Daniels (2001) reviewed the Cooper and Gottlieb (2000) article related to the APA ethics code and adapted the managed care situations to the ACA ethics code. The ethics codes of the two associations emphasize very similar responsibilities. For example, limits of confidentiality, while already unenforceable for group interventions, are further confounded by managed care organization and insurance requirements for five-axis diagnoses and releases of information whenever an insurance claim is filed. Utilization and care planning, ownership of group treatment records, upcoding (using a more severe diagnosis to ensure treatment) and downcoding (using a less severe diagnosis to protect the client) of diagnoses, conflicts of care for group members, and practicing in areas of competence greatly affect group planning and continuity of service provision in multisession group interventions. The authors of both articles encourage psychologists and counselors to be vigilant in their monitoring of managed care issues, mindful in applying a decision-making model and appropriate codes of ethics, and proactive in their education on these emerging challenges.

FINDINGS FROM ETHICS RESEARCH

General Research Findings on Ethics

Formal research on ethical practice of psychologists and counselors is relatively sparse in comparison with theoretical material on ethical principles and models. Ethical research on group practice is even more limited. Therefore, a great deal of interpolation is required of group psychotherapy and counseling facilitators in translating the general findings to group situations.

Pope, Tabachnick, and Keith-Spiegel (1987) studied a national sample of 1,000 psychologists in the Psychotherapy Division of APA. Psychologists rated 83 behaviors for occurrence in their practice and the degree to which they considered each behavior to be ethical. None of the behaviors related specifically to group work. Raters then compared 14 resources for guiding or regulating practice. Results were discussed using seven principles for coordinating and applying ethical guidelines and other standards to practice and case situations. These principles, consistent with the material presented in the "Moral Principles" section of this chapter, are (a) do no harm, (b) practice only with competence, (c) do not exploit, (d) treat people with respect for their dignity as human beings, (e) protect confidentiality, (f) act only with informed consent, and (g) promote equity and justice. Pope et al. concluded that the behaviors and beliefs of this general sample should be used to inform our ethical deliberations but not determine them. When looking at the results of the 14 resources, published works of colleagues were rated as most effective, with high ratings for APA *Ethical Principles* and the APA Ethics Committee. Significantly lower ratings were given for state and local ethics committees.

Pope and Bajt (1988) surveyed 100 senior psychologists, of whom 57% reported that they had violated a formal ethical principle or law intentionally in light of a client's welfare or other deeper value. This is an example of the potential conflicts between moral principles and codes of ethics. Of these described violations, 48% related to issues of confidentiality. In considering decision-making steps, 50% consulted someone before taking action, and 68% discussed the situation after taking action. Beneficial results of the actions taken were reported by 91% and ill effects by 11%. In some cases, both positive and negative effects were reported. About 75% of those studied responded that psychologists would sometimes violate formal legal and ethical standards. Only 18% reported that the conflicts between values and formal legal and ethical obligations were adequately addressed in education, training, and supervision. In addition, only 22% said professional literature adequately addresses these conflicts.

In a more recent review, Betan and Stanton (1999) found a "discrepancy between what psychologists define as the appropriate ethical decision and their intention to implement the decision toward ethical action" (p. 295). Betan and Stanton concluded that documentation of ethical violations reflects the power of contextual considerations. Furthermore, they emphasized that ethical commitment is enhanced when practitioners recognize and act on emotions related to the welfare of their clients. Most powerfully, they concluded about the state of ethics awareness,

> We suggest that psychologists are making inadequate decisions about ethical dilemmas in part because they are not well attuned to the influential role of emotions, values, and contextual concerns in ethical discourse. Consequently, anxiety or other concerns can impede the ability to implement the ethical course of action. By contrast, those who are more aware of personal emotions and values may be better able and willing to intervene ethically. (Betan & Stanton, 1999, p. 299)

Ethical transgressions of psychology graduate students were studied in a survey of clinical and counseling psychology training directors (Fly, van Bark, Weinman, Kitchener, & Lang,

1997). Results showed that most identified ethical errors committed by graduate students occurred in the areas of dual-role relationships and confidentiality, areas similar to those reported by more experienced professionals. The authors recommended more focused attention to ethics education in training programs.

Research on Ethics in Groups

There has been consistency in the ethical areas of concern associated with group interventions over the last 20 years. Key ethical issues cited since 1980 include member screening and orientation, voluntary and involuntary membership, group facilitator preparation and behaviors, protection of members, confidentiality, and dual relationships (Berg, Landreth, & Fall, 1998; Capuzzi & Muffett, 1980; Corey et al., 2003; Paradise & Siegelwaks, 1982; Posthuma, 2002). Issues of multiculturalism and diversity (Corey et al., 2003; Posthuma, 2002) as well as the role of leader values (Corey et al., 2003) appear in more recent discussions of ethical behavior in groups.

Research conducted on ethics in groups has reflected the common issues identified above and how group practitioners respond in practice to these critical ethical areas. Gumaer and Duncan (1982) reported results of a random survey of ASGW members regarding ethical practices and standards for group facilitators. Two sets of ethical guidelines were designed by the authors: a set of 21 ethical guidelines for group leaders and a set of 13 ethical guidelines for using group exercises. The surveys measured the degree of agreement with each set of guidelines and the degree to which leaders actually implemented the guidelines in practice. Results demonstrated that those surveyed were living by their ethical beliefs by putting into practice actions consistent with the ethical guidelines and with the guidelines for conducting group activities. Women respondents were more consistent in their responses to ethical guidelines than were men, by indicating higher levels of agreement and implementation of the guidelines. An interesting additional finding was that group practitioners holding doctorates had more variability in their responses to both sets of ethical guidelines than did group facilitators without doctorates. This difference may reflect the effects of experience and values considerations developed over time, for example, moving a facilitator from following a specific list of prescriptions and prohibitions to a formulation of ethical decisions based on values and the nuances of a particular situation.

Gumaer and Scott (1986) conducted a survey of ASGW members employing modified vignettes on the ASGW ethical guidelines. The researchers found that years of experience and training provided no significant difference in the ethical decision making of those surveyed. They suggested that group leaders take an active, reflective, and consultative stance in considering their actions and responses to group events by recommending that the leader ask,

> How would I feel in this person's position? What would I want the leader to do? What can I do to contribute to the individual member's personal growth? Will the behavior also positively affect other group members? Will my behavior demonstrate that I am genuinely concerned with group members or worried about myself? Is no action better than intervening poorly? (Gumaer & Scott, 1986, p. 149)

In a content analysis, Lakin (1994) reviewed the 1992 APA ethics code revision for its application to group and family therapies. He made several general observations about the applicability of the code to group therapy and raised issues regarding the elaborate contexts in which ethical decisions are made in groups. Competence, a central issue in group practice, is an aspirational principle in the current APA code, thus leaving open to group leaders' judgment their scope of group practice. The practice of informed consent is complicated by multiple layers of communication and participants' concerns about being accepted. Lakin asserted that issues of mutual help and interdependency, assumed in the nature of counseling and therapy groups, can be both positive sources of therapeutic change and ethical risk. Group interactions cannot always be anticipated and controlled. Group cohesion and diversity present ethical challenges in groups as pressures on members and among members to conform to the therapeutic plan may be contradicted by outlying points of view or experience.

Burlingame, Fuhriman, and Johnson (2001) outlined six empirically supported therapeutic principles that foster best practice in group treatment. These principles concentrate on the power of the group leader's behaviors in fostering cohesion and relationship building in groups. Leaders (a) conduct pregroup preparation to establish treatment expectations, define group rules, and instruct members in appropriate roles and skills needed for effective group participation and group cohesion; (b) establish clarity regarding group processes in early sessions, because higher levels of structure probably lead to higher levels of disclosure and cohesion; (c) model real-time observations, guide effective interpersonal feedback, and maintain a moderate relationship-building process; (d) consider the timing and delivery of feedback as they facilitate this relationship-building process; (e) serve as models to members in demonstrating the importance of managing their emotional presence; and (f) facilitate group members' emotional expression, the responsiveness of others to that expression, and the shared meaning derived from such expression.

Both general ethics research and more specific research on ethical behavior in group treatments suggest that ethics codes provide only broad guidelines for professional conduct. Codes cannot dictate ethical practice in the extremely complex interactions that take place in group counseling and therapy settings (ASGW, 1998; Betan & Stanton, 1999; Kitchener, 1996; Kottler, 1982; Pope & Bajt, 1988). Group facilitators who have more training and experience have not been found to make more ethical choices than those less advanced. Different definitions of ethical behavior may be reflected in varying experience levels. For example, those with more training and experience may be more likely to identify contextual issues that influence ethical responses.

APPLYING BEST PRACTICE GUIDELINES TO COUNSELING AND PSYCHOTHERAPY GROUPS

ASGW Best Practice Guidelines

ASGW has modified its governing documents to reflect changing technologies and ethical practice since its inception as an organization in 1973. The variety of settings and the potential complexities faced by group facilitators demand that group leaders understand the parameters of their work and the principles available to guide effective and ethical practice. Two special issues of the *Journal for Specialists in Group Work* have enhanced and stimulated the understanding of ethical concerns in groups (Forester-Miller, 1990; Kottler, 1982).

The ASGW *Best Practice Guidelines* (1998) replaced earlier versions that were written as independent ethical guidelines for group counselors (see ASGW 1989 revision; ASGW, 1990). The current guidelines are organized into planning, performing, and processing sections. The *Best Practice Guidelines* reflect the four broad types of groups identified in the ASGW training standards as task, psychoeducation, counseling, and psychotherapy (ASGW, 2000) and therefore govern ethical best practice in all phases of group interventions.

The ASGW *Best Practice Guidelines* can provide structure to the planning, performing, and processing tasks required for effective and ethical practice in counseling and psychotherapy groups. (The ASGW *Best Practice Guidelines* are reprinted as an Appendix at the end of this handbook.) Because the areas of responsibility for ethical practice are similar for psychologists and counselors, the guidelines can provide a general source of assistance to professionals in both fields. The guidelines incorporate the use of ethics codes and standards of practice as integral elements and include many of the contextual issues that have been identified in the literature as crucial to ethical conduct in group practice.

Best Practice in Planning

Preparation can reduce, but not eliminate, the likelihood of some ethical concerns and legal issues. The *Best Practice Guidelines* can prompt thinking about potential choice points and provide opportunities for planned responses in anticipation of common dilemmas. The guidelines can also be used to promote reflective examination of the values, moral dilemmas, and varieties of influences that underlie any choice point. Nine areas have been identified for best practice in planning. These are professional context and regulatory requirements, scope of practice and conceptual framework, assessment, program development and evaluation, resources, professional disclosure statement, group and member preparation, professional development, and trends and technological changes. A few case examples demonstrate some of the myriad choice points.

Professional Context. An experienced, licensed psychologist or counselor in an agency setting is planning a 10-session counseling or therapy group for a specific emotional situation (for example, depression). In considering professional context and regulatory requirements, the staff member reviews the relevant code(s) of ethics and standards of practice and confirms how the professional code is reflected in the licensing laws and regulations in the practitioner's state. State statutes are periodically revised, as are the professional documents, and need to be reviewed routinely. Furthermore, any special agency requirements that govern the counseling and therapy groups are consulted. If this agency uses insurance reimbursement or some subsidy for payment, there may be specific requirements that have to be met for a particular group. For example, specific treatment guidelines for depression are mandated by many managed care organizations. Agency guidelines may permit or prohibit groups with 10 sessions. Settings that emphasize short-term treatment may have restrictions on the length of interventions. In some cases, shortening a group plan may meet agency requirements but not meet the treatment needs of its members. In this situation, the group plan would have to be modified to maintain both compliance with organization guidelines and remain an ethically sound intervention.

Voluntary/Involuntary Participation. Group facilitators employed in treatment units often work within a structure that requires group participation of all clients. Day treatment programs, for example, are composed of a series of required group counseling or group therapy sessions. Group members need to understand what choices they have in participating and what consequences will occur if they refuse. If participation in therapeutic events (for example, singing aloud with others in music therapy) is documented in case notes, clients must know in advance that their behavior will be documented, because level of participation may directly influence length of treatment or other therapeutic events.

Scope of Practice. The group facilitator's scope of practice would determine whether a counseling group with a predominantly here-and-now orientation for individuals or a therapy group with a more remedial focus and more severe or chronic maladjustment is most appropriate. Assuming that the group facilitator is adequately trained in both counseling and therapy groups, the specific type of group is chosen for the best fit for the agency's clients (ASGW, 2000; Wilson, Rapin, & Haley-Banez, 2000).

The group facilitator should develop a theoretical framework that provides a consistent template for an upcoming group. The leader can articulate the origins of the framework and assess how this framework will reflect personal values, experiences, and fit with the cultural and situational demands of the potential group (Rapin & Conyne, 1999). For example, a group facilitator with a cognitive-behavioral orientation would incorporate elements of monitoring specific behaviors, homework, and practice into a therapy group for anxiety sufferers.

Professional Disclosure and Informed Consent. Two key ethical issues identified consistently in the group literature are informed consent and confidentiality within groups (Berg, Landreth, & Fall, 1998; Capuzzi & Muffett, 1980; Corey et al., 2003; Lakin, 1994; Paradise & Siegelwaks, 1982; Posthuma, 2002). Informed consent can be viewed as a process variable during the course of the group, affected by individual member disclosures and opportunities for varied levels of participation. Informed consent is aided by full oral or written disclosure. A professional disclosure statement can assist in a number of information areas related to training, group focus, and information about confidentiality and its limitations. Depending on credentials and state of employment, such a professional disclosure statement may be required by law (see, for example, the State of Ohio counselor licensure). For an example of such a

disclosure statement, see Rapin and Conyne (1999).

Careful planning can assist in reducing errors related to confidentiality and informed consent. An evaluation plan designed before the group begins and provided to members can identify key evaluation components (appropriateness, adequacy, effectiveness, efficiency, side effects, and effort) and serve as a baseline for later progress (e.g., how progress will be defined and assessed). Measures (for example, amount of reduction in depression scores) and data sources (for example, postmeeting reaction forms) for formative and summative evaluations can be identified in advance and built into the format of the group. Institutional requirements (for example, outcome measures) can be integrated into the plan to meet quality assurance standards.

Supervision arrangements and coleader conferences demonstrate examples of informed consent and confidentiality. Plans established for coleader conferences or supervision between group sessions should be known by all members of the group in advance of the initial session. For example, such preparation might include a coleader (if there are two) discussion of issues of theoretical approach, leader disclosure, complementarity of styles, specific techniques that may be appropriate for the group, whether the group is structured or not, and if so, what form the structure will take. Informed consent requirements may also vary with state regulations. Again, taking the time to know the legal requirements of practice will enhance the level of ethical conduct with the group.

Group Member Screening and Preparation. Group facilitators need to be competent at group member selection and screening. Prescreening for fit with the counseling or therapy group assists potential members in understanding member roles and expectations for the experience. Riva, Lippert, and Tackett (2000) found in a survey on selection practices of group leaders that the primary variable for selecting members was fit with the group theme. While this straightforward and frequently employed selection process would match a potential group member with a counseling or therapy theme (for example, depression), theme alone would not take into account personality characteristics that might suggest a poor therapy group match. Therefore, knowledge of who might most benefit from a particular type of group and group format is central to ethical practice. In addition, screening is an essential protection both for members and leaders. For example, in a therapy group designed for depression, a group facilitator may elect to screen out those with bipolar disorder or depression with psychotic features and refer them to a different intervention. Potential members with therapeutic needs greater than those designed for the group can be harmed if they are not a good fit for the group.

Working with minors poses many more potential ethical dilemmas. Ritchie and Huss (2000) and Hines and Fields (2002) discussed special considerations for recruitment and screening of minors to counseling groups. Ritchie and Huss suggest that it would be reasonable to screen first and seek permission if the minor fits the screening criteria for the group, although the risk is that parents may not want their children assessed at all. Hines and Fields reflected that it may be frustrating to preselect minors for balanced counseling groups only to have permission later withheld by parents. This consideration depends upon the setting of the counseling or therapy group. In a school setting, group facilitators would have access to potential members for pre-screening and often have contact with potential group members and their parents over time. In a community setting, care must be taken to ensure compliance with state law. In some states (e.g., Ohio revised code, 1998), minors can be seen for a specific number of sessions without prior parental consent. This is a case of potential conflict between legality and ethics, because intervention directly with the minor may put the child at risk with his or her family. Ritchie and Huss (2000) and Hines and Fields (2002) also discussed considering the options of individual or group interviews, prescreening interviews as part of a team staffing, and screening through written questionnaire and other technologies. Some group experts prefer individual interviews (Couch, 1995; Jacobs, Masson, & Harvill, 1998) to protect confidentiality of potential members and to provide information about the child's background and presenting concerns.

Couch (1995) suggests four steps for pregroup interviews, each of which assists in providing informed consent. First, the leader identifies prospective member needs, expectations, and commitment to change. Second, potential myths and misconceptions about counseling or therapy group activities are clarified. Third, accurate information about the group is provided, including limits to and advantages of confidentiality, stages of group development, procedures to be expected during the group from inception to termination, and leader and member roles. Fourth, potential group members are screened for fit with the group treatment.

Confidentiality Limits in Groups. In the ethics codes of both APA (2002) and ACA (1997), specific references are made to clarify the limits of confidentiality within group treatments. The legal principle of privileged communication that may exist in some states between an individual therapist and client generally does not apply to group counseling and psychotherapy (Anderson, 1996). Furthermore, because confidentiality is owned by the client or group member, participation with other individuals in a group setting opens up the communications of all members to out-of-group contacts. While a group facilitator may not disclose any information about members of the group, the facilitator cannot guarantee that individuals in the group do not talk about their in-group experiences. When other members breach confidentiality, personal experiences, diagnoses, and histories of other group members may be revealed. Very innocent contacts can lead to a loss of confidentiality. For example, members of a group may encounter each other in public and introduce each other to friends with reference to the group. Personal and/or diagnostic information may be revealed merely in saying a person is in the same treatment group. Therefore, the group facilitator's efforts to inform group members about confidentiality can assist each member in making a personal determination about how much to reveal during the group.

There are specific situations in which confidentiality cannot be guaranteed. As soon as treatment plans are written, insurance preauthorization is granted, or insurance claims filed, confidentiality of group member information is out of the control of the group leader(s) and agency. Many clients do not realize that agreement to use insurance benefits comes with a waiver of confidentiality, verified when the client signs the claim form for insurance reimbursement. Managed care companies, insurance companies, and national data banks have access or potential access to client information. Furthermore, state statutes and codes of ethics identify situations in which the safety of group members or other individuals imposes limits upon confidentiality. Confidentiality of interactions among group members cannot be guaranteed or protected by most statutes.

New Technologies Affecting Ethical Group Practice. Professional development is an ongoing responsibility. Theoretical advances, individual skill development, consultation, supervision, and attention to personal issues are examples of professional development opportunities. It is difficult to anticipate what advances in technology may bring to the practice of group work. Ten years ago, the tremendous impact that the Internet and distance technologies would have on group training and practice was unknown. A chapter in this handbook is devoted to technology and cutting-edge trends. Certainly, most of the issues of ethical concern to group leaders are multiplied in Internet technologies (Humphreys, Winzelberg, & Klaw, 2000).

Best Practice in Performing

The performing phase of group work encompasses the intricate applications of self-knowledge, values, and ethical decision making to the dynamic interactions within group. Effective efforts at the planning stage provide theoretical and practical frameworks for the leader(s) and members to follow during the performing stage of group. Other chapters in this handbook address specific techniques, process issues, and best practices in the performing stage of specific group counseling and therapy groups.

Leader Preparation. Strengths and weaknesses of the facilitators can be monitored throughout the progress of the group in before-group planning meetings, after-group debriefing and supervision sessions, and in summary group evaluations.

These preparation sessions are crucial to the effective performance stage and can be used to identify content for professional development of group skills. Timing, choice of technique, responses to group members, encouragement of participation, and distributed leadership between leaders and members are just a few examples of potential ethical decision points.

Knowledge of core competencies in group work is complemented by advanced training and experience in specific group types. Leaders conducting counseling or therapy groups must be adequately prepared or work under supervision. Leader participation in counseling or therapy group experiences and participation in training groups provide situations for the active enhancement of the leader's level of self-knowledge.

Group and member goals influence the choice of techniques to be employed during each stage of the group's development. Furthermore, choices are limited by competency or supervisory opportunities if new techniques are considered for implementation. The positive power of group may inappropriately influence an enthusiastic leader to attempt interventions "on the fly." These are the very times to stop, reflect on the potential outcomes of an intervention, and have a good reason for proceeding, thereby reducing ethical risk.

No plan, however well developed, is likely to be implemented without significant modification. Group counseling and therapy leaders need to assess which parts of their initial plans can be implemented as designed, which parts need to be modified, or which parts need to be redesigned or discarded. Most ethical transgressions occur because the clinician didn't see ahead of time that a sticky issue might arise. Awareness of possible problems is essential to ethical implementation. When choice points arise, it is helpful to assess how the facilitator feels about the situation, upon what principles the facilitator is operating, and how particular responses will affect individuals in the group. As Betan and Stanton (1999) suggested, potential emotional responses may vary from feeling good to embarrassment, anxiety, discomfort, and anger. These events, and the questions that they prompt, occur in a multitude of forms during the active life of a group. Challenges emerge as group members become better acquainted.

Some members may appear more likeable than others, prompting differential responses from other members. Other individuals in the group may have styles that provoke the group. Levels of self-disclosure, risk taking, and opportunities for out-of-group contacts are but a few additional variables that may affect the leader's response to members. Consistent ethical vigilance of leader effects is never wasted.

Diversity. Diversity is demonstrated in group composition and cultural perspective. Ethical practitioners continuously strive to understand the nuances of diversity and their effects on group members. Sensitivity to diversity can be reflected in the group facilitator's choice of responses to member interactions. The use of idioms, for example, may reflect a particular regional or cultural bias not uniformly understood by all group members. Another example may be demonstrated in the carefully considered use of homogeneous or heterogeneous group composition for certain counseling and psychotherapy topics (for example, with eating disorders). See the multicultural section (Part III) of this handbook for chapters addressing these issues.

Best Practice in Group Processing

The events in counseling and psychotherapy groups can occur with such speed that it is impossible to respond to all activities during each group session. As one follows the *Best Practice Guidelines,* a general plan for within-group, between-group, and termination processing should be established prior to the start of the group. Once the group is under way, processing between facilitator and group and between coleaders is necessary to understand what has occurred, how the group events can be understood, and how the progress of the group can be monitored and enhanced through the plan for subsequent sessions. For example, if a group is progressing well, there may be temptation for coleaders or leader and supervisor to skip a between-session meeting. Planning time is often treated as if it were optional when the pressure of other assignments weighs heavily. It is crucial that this time be preserved to assess the relative effectiveness of the session and to draw deeper meaning from the group events (Rapin & Conyne, 1999).

Reflective practice occurs as the group leader integrates the observations, ethical choice points, decisions made, and ultimate effects of the group plan and its components. This reoccurring pattern provides ample information for ongoing planning, improvement, and revision of the group plan. Learning can be documented, compared with other group results, used for revision of the counseling or therapy group, and can potentially add to the professional literature.

Evaluation. Evaluation occurs in every session as part of the monitoring of group progress. Postgroup evaluation at termination should be conducted as part of the original group plan to measure long-term gains. Summative components such as overall member satisfaction with the counseling or therapy group, level of member involvement, and goal accomplishment can be reviewed. Classic evaluation questions (Craig, 1978) of appropriateness, adequacy, effectiveness, efficiency, side effects, and effort can be applied to each group component.

As part of ethical responsibility to group members and to the profession, group leaders initiate appropriate opportunities for consultation and training both within and outside of their work organizations. Opportunities include learning experiences via course work, conference, and workshop attendance. Experienced group leaders have many opportunities for enhancing legal and ethical group practice. In serving on planning teams to design or evaluate group offerings; by participating in training and supervision opportunities in agency, community, institution, or professional settings; and in contributing to the professional literature, group facilitators increase visibility of ethical practice.

Ethical and legal decision making in counseling and therapy groups is enhanced by the implementation of available professional resources. Familiarity with professional codes of conduct and models of decision making in complex situations can be executed through the use of best practices. Continued practitioner growth will enhance the ethical and effective practice of group work.

REFERENCES

Acuff, C., Bennett, B. E., Bricklin, P. M., Canter, M. B., Knapp, S. J., Moldawsky, S., & Phelps, R. (1999). Considerations for ethical practice in managed care. *Professional Psychology: Research and Practice, 30,* 563-575.

American Counseling Association (ACA). (1997). *Code of ethics and standards of practice: As approved by governing council, April, 1997.* Alexandria, VA: American Counseling Association.

American Group Psychotherapy Association (AGPA). (1991). *Guidelines for ethics.* New York: American Group Psychotherapy Association.

American Psychological Association (APA). (2002). *Ethical principles of psychologists and code of conduct.* Washington, DC: American Psychological Association.

Anderson, B. S. (1996). *The counselor and the law* (4th ed.). Alexandria, VA: American Counseling Association.

Association for Specialists in Group Work (ASGW). (1990). Ethical guidelines for group counselors: ASGW 1989 revision. *Journal for Specialists in Group Work, 15,* 119-126.

Association for Specialists in Group Work (ASGW). (1998). Association for Specialists in Group Work best practice guidelines. *Journal for Specialists in Group Work, 23,* 237-244.

Association for Specialists in Group Work (ASGW). (1999). Principles for diversity-competent group workers. *Journal for Specialists in Group Work, 24,* 7-14.

Association for Specialists in Group Work (ASGW). (2000). Association for Specialists in Group Work: Professional standards for the training of group workers, 2000 revision. *Journal for Specialists in Group Work, 25,* 327-342.

Berg, R. C., Landreth, G. L., & Fall, K. (1998). *Group counseling concepts and procedures* (3rd ed.). Philadelphia: Taylor and Francis.

Betan, E. J., & Stanton, A. L. (1999). Fostering ethical willingness: Integrating emotional and contextual awareness with rational analysis. *Professional Psychology: Research and Practice, 30,* 295-301.

Burlingame, G. M., Fuhriman, A., & Johnson, J. E. (2001). Cohesion in group psychotherapy. *Psychotherapy: Theory/Research/Practice/ Training, 38,* 373-379.

Capuzzi, D., & Muffett, L. (1980). An overview of ethical standards for group facilitators. *Journal for Specialists in Group Work, 5,* 98-106.

Cooper, C. C., & Gottlieb, M. C. (2000). Ethical issues with managed care: Challenges facing counseling psychology. *The Counseling Psychologist, 28,* 179-236.

Corey, G., Corey, M. S., & Callanan, P. (2003). *Issues & ethics in the helping professions* (6th ed.). Pacific Grove, CA: Brooks/Cole.

Cottone, R. R., & Claus, R. E. (2000). Ethical decision-making models: A review of the literature. *Journal of Counseling and Development, 78,* 275-283.

Couch, R. D. (1995). Four steps for conducting a pregroup screening interview. *Journal for Specialists in Group Work, 20,* 18-25.

Craig, D. P. (1978). *Hip pocket guide to planning and evaluation.* Austin, TX: Learning Concepts.

Daniels, J. A. (2001). Managed care, ethics, and counseling. *Journal of Counseling and Development, 79,* 119-122.

Fly, B. J., van Bark, W. P., Weinman, L., Kitchener, K. S., & Lang, P. R. (1997). Ethical transgressions of psychology graduate students: Critical incidents with implications for training. *Professional Psychology: Research and Practice, 28,* 492-495.

Forester-Miller, H., & Davis, T. (1996). *A practitioner's guide to ethical decision making.* Alexandria, VA: American Counseling Association.

Forester-Miller, H. E. (Ed.). (1990). Ethical and legal issues in group work (Special Issue). *Journal for Specialists in Group Work, 15*(2).

Gumaer, J., & Duncan, J. A. (1982). Group workers' perceptions of their philosophical ethical beliefs and actual ethical practices. *Journal for Specialists in Group Work, 7,* 231-237.

Gumaer, J., & Scott, L. (1986). Group workers' perceptions of ethical and unethical behavior of group leaders. *The Journal for Specialists in Group Work, 11,* 139-150.

Haas, L. J., & Malouf, J. L. (1995). *Keeping up the good work: A practitioner's guide to mental health ethics* (2nd ed.). Sarasota, FL: Professional Resource Exchange.

Hansen, N. D., & Goldberg, S. G. (1999). Navigating the nuances: A matrix of considerations for ethical-legal dilemmas. *Professional Psychology: Research and Practice, 30,* 495-503.

Hines, P. L., & Fields, T. H. (2002). Pregroup screening issues for school counselors. *Journal for Specialists in Group Work, 27,* 358-376.

Humphreys, K., Winzelberg, A., & Klaw, E. (2000). Psychologists' ethical responsibilities in Internet-based groups: Issues, strategies, and a call for dialogue. *Professional Psychology: Research and Practice, 31,* 493-496.

Jacobs, E., Masson, R., & Harvill, R. (1998). *Group counseling: Strategies and skills.* Pacific Grove, CA: Brooks/Cole.

Kitchener, K. S. (1984). Intuition, critical evaluation and ethical principles. *The Counseling Psychologist, 12,* 43-55.

Kitchener, K. S. (1996). There is more to ethics than principles. *The Counseling Psychologist, 24,* 92-97.

Kottler, J. A. (Ed.). (1982). Special issue: Ethical issues in group work. *Journal for Specialists in Group Work, 7*(3).

Lakin, M. (1994). Morality in group and family therapies: Multiperson therapies and the 1992 ethics code. *Professional Psychology: Research and Practice, 25,* 344-348.

Meara, N. M., Schmidt, L. D., & Day, J. D. (1996). Principles and virtues: A foundation for ethical decisions, policies, and character. *The Counseling Psychologist, 24,* 4-77.

Paradise, L., & Siegelwaks, B. J. (1982). Ethical training for group leaders. *Journal for Specialists in Group Work, 7,* 162-166.

Pope, K. S., & Bajt, T. R. (1988). When laws and values conflict: A dilemma for psychologists. *American Psychologist, 43,* 828.

Pope, K. S., Tabachnick, B. G., & Keith-Spiegel, P. (1987). Ethics of practice: The beliefs and behaviors of psychologists as therapists. *American Psychologist, 42,* 993-1006.

Posthuma, B. W. (2002). *Small groups in counseling and therapy: Process and leadership* (4th ed.). Boston: Allyn & Bacon.

Rapin, L. S., & Conyne, R. K. (1999). Best practices in group counseling. In J. P. Trotzer (Ed.), *The counselor and the group: Integrating theory, training, and practice* (3rd ed., pp. 253-276). Philadelphia: Accelerated Development/Taylor and Francis.

Ritchie, M., & Huss, S. N. (2000). Recruitment and screening of minors for group counseling. *Journal for Specialists in Group Work, 25,* 146-156.

Riva, M. T., Lippert, L., & Tackett, M. J. (2000). Recruitment and screening of minors for group counseling. *Journal for Specialists in Group Work, 25,* 146-156.

Vasquez, M. J. T. (1996). Will virtue ethics improve ethical conduct in multicultural settings and interactions? *The Counseling Psychologist, 24,* 98-104.

Wilson, F. R., Rapin, L. S., & Haley-Banez, L. (2000). *Group work training standards for the new millennium.* Paper presented at the National Conference of the Association for Specialists in Group Work, Deerfield Beach, FL.

Part III

MULTICULTURAL GROUPS

Introduction

JANICE L. DELUCIA-WAACK

Diversity is an essential issue in counseling and psychological training. Multicultural competencies have been suggested by several professional organizations over the years, but it is only recently that the issue of multicultural competency as related to group practice has received much attention. In 1999, the Association for Specialists in Group Work approved *The Principles for Diversity-Competent Group Workers,* which clearly specified three areas of emphasis: attitudes and beliefs, knowledge, and skills for both group leaders and group members. Arredondo (1999) emphasized that multicultural-competence skill development consists of three domains: (1) counselor's awareness of personal beliefs and attitudes, and knowledge and skills for effective practice; (2) counselor's understanding of beliefs and attitudes, and knowledge he or she holds about the worldview of the client; and (3) counselor's ability to provide ethical and culturally relevant counseling with appropriate interventions and techniques.

DeLucia-Waack and Donigian (2003) provide specific recommendations for the development of multicultural group counseling competencies and skills. They first suggest the development of an awareness of different cultural worldviews and the subsequent impact on group work interventions. Second, they suggest a focus on group leader self-awareness, particularly racial identity and personal and cultural worldviews. Their third recommendation focuses on the development of a repertoire of culturally relevant group work interventions. To do this, they suggest learning about group interventions shown to be effective with specific cultural groups as well as culturally specific healing rituals. The chapters in Part III were chosen with these guidelines and recommendations in mind.

Several chapters were written with the goal of providing group leaders with essential information about different cultural groups and their worldviews, perceptions of groups, naturalistic healing methods, suggested group interventions, and implications for groups. They include the chapters by Michael Garrett on groups for Native Americans, Sherlon Pack-Brown and Amelia Fleming on groups for African Americans, Rita Chi-Ying Chung on groups for Asians, and Edil Torres Rivera on groups with Latinos. In addition, we have included two chapters that focus on other disempowered groups in our society. Sharon Horne and Heidi Levitt wrote the chapter on counseling groups with gay, lesbian, bisexual, and trangendered (GLBT) clients; Milton Seligman and Laura Marshak wrote the chapter on groups for disabled persons. The issue of how to work with international college students, addressing bicultural issues, led to the inclusion of a chapter by Tow Yee Yau on guidelines for groups with this population. These chapters provide an overview for group leaders of potential group members' worldviews, issues related to racial and cultural identity development, how these values may inhibit or enhance group members' willingness to participate in groups, and suggestions for groups that include members of these cultural or lifestyle groups.

Consistent with the *Principles for Diversity-Competent Group Workers* (1999), our goal is to emphasize that group leaders' racial identity development and awareness of their own cultural worldviews are essential to the provision of effective multicultural group interventions. The chapter by Michael D'Andrea explores the impact of racial identity of both group leaders and group members on their willingness to participate in groups, their ability to interact with others, and the effectiveness of the group. In addition, the chapter by Loan Phan and Edil Torres Rivera examines the impact of language on group processes for both members and leaders. Finally, the chapter by Edil Torres Rivera, Michael Garrett, and Lori Crutchfield describes the naturalistic group healing methods used by many cultures, which may at times be appropriate for use in heterogeneous, as well as homogeneous, multicultural groups.

REFERENCES

Arredondo, P. (1999). Multicultural counseling competencies as tools to address oppression and racism. *Journal of Counseling & Development*, *77*, 102-108.

Association for Specialists in Group Work. (1999). Association for specialists in group work principles for diversity-competent group workers. *Journal for Specialists in Group Work, 24*, 7-14.

DeLucia-Waack, J. L., & Donigan, J. (2003). *The practice of multicultural group work: Visions and perspectives from the field*. Monterey, CA: Wadsworth.

12

SOUND OF THE DRUM

Group Counseling With Native Americans

MICHAEL TLANUSTA GARRETT

Western Carolina University

Hoop Dancer
It's hard to enter
circling clockwise and counter
clockwise moving no
regard for time, metrics
irrelevant to this dance
where pain is the prime number

and soft stepping feet
praise water from the skies:

I have seen the face of triumph
the winding line stare down all moves
to desecration: guts not cut from arms,
fingers joined to minds,
together Sky and Water
one dancing one
circle of a thousand turning lines
beyond the march of gears—
out of time, out of
time, out
of time.

—Paula Gunn Allen (1991)

This poem by Paula Gunn Allen (1991), Laguna Pueblo/Lakota, shows the movement, stamina, and skill of the hoop dancer, considered widely by many to be one of the most difficult and most revered of the Native dance styles on the powwow circuit. However,

169

the poem also illustrates a number of concepts central to the experience of Native people in general, with an extraordinary emphasis on the harmony and balance required to survive and thrive. For Native people, the balance of multiple identities, pressures, and expectations can take on a new meaning as it relates to the metaphorical movements of the hoop dancer.

Native Americans consist of more than 2.4 million people, with a population that is steadily growing (U.S. Bureau of the Census, 2001). Although this number represents only 1% of the total population of the United States, Native people have been described as representing "50% of the diversity" in our country (Hodgkinson, 1990). Across the United States, there are more than 557 federally recognized and several hundred state-recognized Native American nations (Russell, 1998). Given the wide-ranging diversity of this population, it is important to understand that the term *Native American* encompasses the vastness and essence of tribal traditions represented by hundreds of Indian nations. Navajo, Catawba, Shoshone, Lumbee, Cheyenne, Cherokee, Apache, Lakota, Seminole, Comanche, Pequot, Cree, Tuscarora, Paiute, Creek, Pueblo, Shawnee, Hopi, Osage, Mohawk, Nez Perce, Seneca—these are but a handful of the hundreds of Indian nations that exist across the United States.

Native Americans represent a wide-ranging diversity illustrated, for example, by approximately 252 different languages. At the same time, a prevailing sense of "Indianness" based on common worldview and common history seems to bind Native Americans together as a people of many peoples. Although acculturation plays a major factor in Native American worldview, there tends to be a high degree of psychological homogeneity, a certain degree of shared cultural standards and meanings, based on common core values that exist for traditional Native Americans across tribal groups (Garrett, 1999; Heinrich, Corbine, & Thomas, 1990). Because approximately 50% of the Native American population resides in urban areas, the degree of traditionalism versus the degree of acculturation to mainstream American values and cultural standards for behavior is an important consideration in counseling Native people (Garrett & Pichette, 2000).

This chapter explores the world of a Native client and the meaning of group work from a Native perspective. The purposes of this chapter are to discuss (a) Native traditions, such as Harmony Ethic, noninterference, and the symbolism of the Eagle feather, (b) what it means to enter the Circle from both a traditional Native perspective and contemporary therapeutic perspective, and (c) specific implications and recommendations for group practice with Native clients.

NATIVE TRADITIONS: WHERE POWER MOVES

Harmony Ethic: Together We Stand

The Native cultural value of harmony in interpersonal relationships as well as in one's relationship with the environment speaks to the essence of Native tradition (Four Worlds Development Project, 1984). This traditional value has been referred to as the *Harmony Ethic* (Garrett & Garrett, 1996; Neely, 1991). The Harmony Ethic guides both the beliefs and behaviors of Native people in the communal spirit of cooperation and contribution as a way of maintaining the natural harmony and balance that exists within oneself and with the world around oneself. The basic tenets of the Harmony Ethic are as follows:

1. A nonaggressive and noncompetitive approach to life. If the goal of competition is to benefit the family, clan, tribe, or community, then competition is considered acceptable. Intertribal sports competitions can become quite aggressive in nature. Competition or aggression for personal gain, however, is frowned upon.

2. Intermediaries are used as a way of minimizing face-to-face hostility and disharmony in interpersonal relations. This involves the conscious avoidance of interpersonal conflict in an attempt to maintain reciprocally harmonious relations with "all one's relations." This is a common strategy in the traditional way for resolution of conflict without upsetting the natural balance of things. For example, a respected person in the community who is not related by

family or clan to either of the parties in conflict might serve as a go-between in helping the two reach a mutually agreeable resolution.

3. Reciprocity and the practice of generosity. This occurs even when people cannot afford to be generous. The acts of respectfully giving and of receiving are believed to be necessary to maintain the proper functioning of the community. Being able to share unselfishly frees the individual to learn important lessons that are offered in life.

4. A belief in immanent justice. This relieves people from feelings of needing to control others through direct interference. There is a natural order to things, and sometimes there are situations or experiences that are "out of our hands." It is important to be able to release rather than harm oneself or others with destructive emotions, thoughts, or actions. There is an old Indian saying that one should never speak ill against another for the wind will carry it to that person, and, eventually, the ill will returns on the wind, 7 times stronger.

The Harmony Ethic is a system based upon caring for fellow human beings through the expression of deep respect and kindness. It is a system based upon harmonious survival among people in their social and environmental communities. It also emphasizes the importance of choice. To the people of many Native nations, a person has equal choice to create harmony or to create disharmony and social disruption.

Noninterference: Path of Peace

From a traditional Native view, all things are alive and possess intrinsic worth. Native American worldview and spirituality focus on the harmony and balance that comes from connection with all parts of the universe, in which everything has the purpose and value exemplary of "personhood." Within this view lies the most powerful sense of belonging and connectedness, as well as a deep respect for "all our relations." Spiritual "being" essentially requires only that we seek our place in the universe; everything else will follow in good time. Because everyone and everything was created with a specific purpose to fulfill, no one has the power on a universal

level to interfere with or to impose upon others concerning their paths.

In the Medicine Way, the significance of relationship lies in a balance struck between an all-encompassing sense of belonging and connectedness with one's relations and the practice of noninterference. The highest form of respect for another person is respecting his or her natural right to be self-determining. This means not interfering with another person's ability to choose, even when it would keep them from doing something foolish or dangerous. Noninterference means caring in a respectful way, and it is the way of "right relationship." Every experience holds a valuable lesson— even in death, the spirit carries forth valuable learning. There are lessons to be learned through the making of choices and certain truths to be experienced through respect for the autonomy and presence of all living things. The following anecdote illustrates this:

> I think it is time you knew of Tagoona, the Inuit. Last year one of our white men said to him, "We are glad you have been ordained as the first priest of your people. Now you can help us with their problem." Tagoona asked, "What is a problem?" and the white man said, "Tagoona, if I held you by your heels from a third-story window, you would have a problem." Tagoona considered this long and carefully. Then he said, "I do not think so. If you saved me, all would be well. If you dropped me, nothing would matter. It is you who would have the problem." (Craven, 1973, p. 74)

Interfering with the activity of others, by way of aggression, for example, cannot and should not be encouraged nor tolerated. This is not only disrespectful but also violates the natural order of harmony and balance in which each being has to learn and experience life in his or her own way. Each person, each living being on Mother Earth, has his or her own Medicine that should not be disrupted or changed without that person choosing it. This is part of learning. What moves the Circle is choice, and what nourishes the Circle is kindness and respect for the natural flow of life energy.

According to Good Tracks (1973), patience is the number-one virtue governing Indian relationships. Respect often demands patience of us, since things rarely go the way that we expect. Yet we have the tendency to want to change *how things are,* rather than change *what we expect.* From a traditional way, "pain" is really nothing more than the difference between *what is* and *what we want it to be.* To be respectful of all things, we sometimes must sacrifice expectation.

Sacred space is more than just physical space. It consists of all Four Directions, in the realm of mind, body, spirit, and natural environment. Just as we have all had the experience of someone bumping into us and not saying that they were sorry, we have all had the experience of someone telling us what to do, pressuring us, criticizing us, or manipulating us, and not giving us the choice or the chance. All these things take away choice, disrespect choice, and show little sign of "regarding with interest, deference, and admiration." And we have done the same to others as well. No one wants to feel that his or her choice is being violated. Such things as asking intrusive questions, interrupting, speaking for others, telling others what to do, arguing, blaming, using sarcasm, sulking, being condescending, nit-picking, or using threats (both spoken and unspoken) are all fairly common occurrences, and they violate the natural laws of Creation. It does not matter why we do it, what matters are the consequences of such actions that result in disharmony and discord.

Noninterference stresses the importance of always asking permission and not making unnecessary assumptions about others. It reminds us to always be thankful for what we have and not "expect" more than that, but rather, show "respect" for what we do have, and for the Greater Circle of which we are all part.

Above all, "respect" for others through patience, openness, and flexibility ultimately shows respect for oneself and one's community. It is not uncommon in the traditional way for the group to allow or accept a person's withdrawal without question or expectation. In addition, that person is to be welcomed back into the group without a required explanation for his or her absence. There is no need to interfere by asking what is wrong or by offering solutions. Respect for another dictates that when a person is ready to share information, he or she will do so. Likewise, if a person is in need of assistance or advice, he or she will ask.

The same philosophy applies, in a traditional way, to our relation with nature, in which permission must be asked before taking and thanks must be expressed by giving back in some way. This could be as simple as a small prayer giving thanks. It might mean sprinkling a little tobacco as an offering of gratitude for whatever has been received. Noninterference may take many different forms depending on the tribe and specific Native person, but the essence of respectful intent remains the same.

Eagle Feather: Balancing Winds

Eagle feathers are considered to be infinitely sacred among Native Americans, who make use of the feathers for a variety of purposes, including ceremonial healing and purification. Eagle Medicine represents a state of presence achieved through diligence, understanding, awareness, and a completion of "tests of initiation," such as the Vision Quest (Lake, 1991) or other demanding life experiences. Highly respected elder status is associated with Eagle Medicine and the power of connectedness and truth. It is through experience and patience that this Medicine is earned over a lifetime. And it is through understanding and choice that it is honored.

The Eagle feather, which represents duality, tells the story of life. It tells of the many dualities or opposites that exist in the Circle of Life, such as light and dark, male and female, substance and shadow, summer and winter, life and death, peace and war (Garrett & Myers, 1996). The Eagle feather has both light and dark colors, dualities and opposites. Though one can make a choice to argue which of the colors is most beautiful or most valuable, the truth is that both colors come from the same feather, both are true, both are connected, and it takes both to fly. The colors are opposite, but they are part of the same truth. The importance of the feather lies not in which color is most beautiful, but in finding out and accepting what the purpose of the feather as a whole may be. Traditionally, one earns the Eagle feather through enormous acts of courage, understanding, compassion, and generosity. Through acts such as these, a recognition of universal "oneness" or truth occurs, and universal learning takes place. An honoring of underlying meanings, choice, and the interrelationship of all things in the Circle of Life emerges. As one Native elder puts it,

> The Eagle feather teaches us about the Rule of Opposites, about everything being divided into two ways. The more one is caught up in the physical, or the West, then the more one has to go in the opposite direction, the East, or the spiritual, to get balance. And it works the other way too—you can't just focus on the spiritual to the exclusion of the physical. You need harmony in all Four Directions. (J. T. Garrett, 1991, cited in Garrett & Myers, 1996, p. 101)

ENTERING THE CIRCLE: HEARTBEAT OF NATIONS

> You have noticed that everything an Indian does is in a circle, and that is because the Power of the World always works in circles, and everything tries to be round. . . . The sky is round, and I have heard that Earth is round like a ball, and so are all the stars. The wind, in its greatest power, whirls. Birds make their nests in circles, for theirs is the same religion as ours. . . . Even the seasons form a great circle in their changing, and always come back again to where they were. The life of a person is a circle from childhood to childhood, and so it is in everything where power moves. (Niehardt, 1959, cited in Garrett, 1998, p. 75)

Historically, group counseling has used the circle as a means of facilitating open communication and the sense of equity that each member possesses upon entering the circle. Native Americans have long used the circle to celebrate the sacred interrelationship shared with one another and with our world. Old Western movies conjure up images of the "Indians" sitting together in council, sitting together in the Circle, while they make decisions about whether or not to go to war with the "White man." But the Circle is more far-reaching than portrayed in the movies. The idea of council or "Talking Circle," as well as the "Healing Circle," permeates the traditions of Native Americans to this day in that it symbolizes an entire approach to life and to the universe in which each being participates in the Circle, and

each one serves an important and necessary function that is valued no more or no less than that of any other being (Wilbur, 1999a, 1999b).

Group Work: The Medicine of Healing

As group leaders, we have the responsibility and privilege of being able to serve as facilitators and guides for our Native clients as they walk their own Medicine paths, seeking their own visions. Archie Fire Lame Deer, Lakota Medicine Man, described the role of the caretaker through the following words:

> To be a Medicine person, you have to experience everything, live life to the fullest. If you don't experience the human side of everything, how can you help teach or heal? To be a good Medicine person, you've got to be humble. You've got to be lower than a worm and higher than an eagle. (Padilla, 1994, cited in Garrett, 1998, p. 41)

Though it is not the group leader's job to be a Medicine person, they do walk a parallel path as another form of helper. Though not Medicine persons, they create some of the same healing, just in a different cultural context and perhaps in different ways.

The process of healing in the traditional way varies from tribe to tribe, but there are some general commonalities. First of all, someone seeking a Medicine person might never have any direct contact with that person, but rather communicate through a mediator (maybe a relative or mutually trusted person) who goes between helper and helpee. It is generally true that someone seeking a Medicine person will make an offering of some kind to the Medicine person as sign of respect and good intent, and this offering is done without expectation of anything in return, although it is a request for help. The Medicine person might pray about the situation and make a decision about whether to help, and if so, how to help. Often, a form of ceremony will be implemented. The Medicine person might talk at length with the helpee or might not talk at all. A specific task might be given to the helpee for completion. Regardless, personal cleansing is usually a given. Two very important things the Medicine person will often include as part of the healing process are (a) the support system for the person, such as family, friends, or other trusted persons, and (b) some type of ceremony or ritual (sometimes including a family or communal meal) that helps restore the person and his or her environment to harmony and balance. Finally, there is the philosophy with which the Medicine person approaches the entire process of healing, as best summarized by Godfrey Chips, Lakota Medicine Man: "I'm the spirit's janitor. All I do is wipe the windows a little bit so you can see out for yourself" (cited in Garrett, 1998, p. 145). Somewhat parallel is that in group work, sometimes being the most skilled group leader may involve simply getting out of the way so the group can do the work that it is capable of doing. Sometimes, it means helping people see things in a way that they might never have seen things before. Sometimes less is more when one is dealing with the essence of the human experience.

Sweat Lodge: Metaphor for Group Work

As a Native tradition that has been practiced since ancient times, the Sweat Lodge Ceremony honors the process of growth and healing central to the modern-day practice of group counseling. The Sweat Lodge Ceremony is a widely accepted and practiced tradition by many tribes that serves to purify those undergoing transformation or healing (Brown, 1972; Heinrich et al., 1990). It is interesting to note that many cultures have at one time or another had some ritual similar to the Sweat Lodge (Lake, 1991). In fact, the whole notion of "group counseling" originated in the Sweat Lodges of ancient cultures such as Native American and European tradition. Perhaps the idea of coming together in a group for purification and healing is more universal than we think.

Native Americans have always believed that healing and transformation should take place in the presence of the group because all are related to one another in very basic ways and can always use the support and insight of fellow brothers and sisters to move away from something and toward something else. In this way, the Sweat Lodge Ceremony has served a very sacred function through the ritual healing or cleansing of body, mind, and spirit, while also serving as a way of bringing people together.

Native American traditionalists believe that to ensure harmony, balance, and wellness, one must participate in the ritualized cleansing of the mind, body, and spirit provided through ceremony. The Sweat Lodge Ceremony provides a time for purifying oneself by joining with the powers of Mother Earth and those of the Universal Circle, for giving thanks, and for asking that oneself and others be blessed (Brown, 1972; Garrett & Osborne, 1995).

Through sweating, the body naturally cleanses itself of impurities, such as toxins in the blood, and stabilizes or balances body temperature to survive demanding conditions. In a like manner, the Sweat Lodge Ceremony uses this natural process to purify not only the body but also the mind and the heart or spirit. It provides a time for "collecting" oneself and for healing.

Traditionally, the Sweat Lodge Ceremony was conducted on many different occasions, such as preparation for the hunt; a form of schooling for the young, who would be taught their history, heritage, language, culture, myths, and religion; physical doctoring; spiritual training; or celebration at the time of the new moon (Lake, 1987). First, a sacred place in which to conduct the ceremony is sought out, usually in close proximity to a creek, river, pond, or lake. Careful attention is practiced with methods emphasizing the law of Reciprocity, in which something is given for everything that is respectfully taken, to honor and maintain the harmony and balance of interrelationship (Garrett, 2001). Lake (1987) elaborates on the Native American belief,

> [That] each piece, part, or element contributes a special life force and spirit to the ceremony, that all things are alive and possess a spirit, and everything in nature is a form of medicine if one knows how to recognize and use it. Each rock, for example, has its own form of communication and vibratory level which affects its energy pattern and frequency; hence it is alive. The same can be said for the trees which are not just dead wood but "energy forces" combined with the rocks and natural elements to create a special kind of physical and spiritual energy. (p. 20)

The Sweat Lodge itself, usually a small turtle-shaped dwelling, is constructed by searching out and asking permission from the various materials of Mother Earth for their willing participation in the ceremony (e.g., tree saplings, wood, bark, rocks). The rock pit is formed in the center of the designated sacred spot, around which the Lodge is constructed from materials placed in relation to the Four Directions—east, south, west, and north—and covered with animal hides, blankets, woven mats, or bark and sod (Lake, 1987).

Meanwhile, the Fire Keeper, usually a young apprentice, has the responsibility of tending the sacred fire in which the ceremonial rocks are being heated. Participants in the ceremony strip themselves of clothing and any personal belongings, such as jewelry, and enter the Sweat Lodge or "womb of Mother Earth" one by one, usually on their hands and knees to show humility and respect for the Earth. Inside, participants sit in the sacred Circle, representing the Circle of Life. Next, the rocks are brought into the Lodge, arranged to represent the Four Directions, and the flap or door opening is sealed shut. The darkness in the Lodge represents the darkness of the spirit, our ignorance, which requires purification in order to have light (Brown, 1972).

After making an invocation to the Great Spirit, Mother Earth, the Four Directions, the spirits, and all the relations in nature, special water or an herbal mixture is poured over the heated rocks, producing a purifying steam that fills the Lodge. The Pipe (or Medicine object) is passed from person to person, usually in a clockwise direction, imitating the path of the sun, moving from the east around to the west and back around to the east again. This is repeated several times. Participants pray for their families, friends, each other, and themselves, asking for strength, healing, protection, blessing, or forgiveness for any harm committed against any living creature in nature. In addition, songs might be sung, rites and rituals performed, or problems discussed. Herein, the Talking Circle serves as a form in which traditional "group counseling" takes place. As Lake (1987) emphasized,

The Sweat Lodge becomes a type of counseling center and place for group therapy; marriage and family problems [are] analyzed and remedied, personal problems discussed, inter-family conflicts [are] resolved, and problems involving fears,

anxieties, and depressions [are] dealt with in a group way. (p. 8)

Following the completion of the ceremony, participants emerge from the Sweat Lodge to bathe in the cooling waters of the nearby creek, river, pond, or lake. Afterward, the participants take time to reflect with one another on their experience (Lake, 1987).

Though techniques for the Sweat Lodge Ceremony vary from tribe to tribe, the Ceremony serves an important function through purification and healing for all who participate in it. From the skin, bodily toxins and negative energy are released. Similarly, from the mind and spirit, toxins such as anger, frustration, hurt, or anxiety are released. Ways of dealing with various situations, with others, and with oneself are talked about within the framework of the Universal Circle represented by the Sweat Lodge and its sacred Ceremony.

The Sweat Lodge Ceremony centers around helping people work toward change in and with the group (Colmant & Merta, 1999). People who enter the group process want to work on change and are willing to help others to do the same. This is an approach drawing upon our humanity through the processes of learning, experiencing, and growing in a supportive environment. Please refer to Garrett and Osborne (1995) for more discussion of a four-phase group process drawing on the symbolism of the Sweat Lodge Ceremony.

The Talking Circle

The Circle is a sacred symbol reminding us of the importance of our unique place in the universe and relation with all things. In a traditional Native American "coming-together" such as the Sweat Lodge Ceremony, the Talking Circle fulfills an important purpose by ensuring that relations are conducted in a very respectful manner. The Talking Circle traditionally serves as a forum for the expression of thoughts and feelings in a context of complete acceptance by group members (Garrett, 1998).

To begin, participants form a circle together, leaving an opening in the direction of the east, which is where the sun rises, bringing with it clarity and honesty. A traditional chant with music, rattle, or drumming may be used for relaxation and clearing of mind, body, and spirit as people enter the circle. When everyone has gathered, initial greetings are made. The "talking stick"—a wooden stick embellished with symbolic carvings or paintings—is used in the group as a sacred object representing truth and understanding as powerful agents of healing. The "Medicine object," as it is sometimes called, by way of whoever holds it, signifies permission to speak. It should be noted here that other sacred objects may also serve as the "Medicine object" or "talking stick," such as the Eagle feather, pipe, sacred stone (e.g., crystal), and others, as a way of signifying that whoever holds the object is bound by truth and humility.

The leader begins by picking up the talking stick to share feelings or concerns with the group. When the leader has spoken, the talking stick is passed clockwise (left) to the next person, who may speak if he or she wishes or choose to remain silent. During the circle, questions may be asked with verbal exchanges taking place but only by permission of whoever is holding the stick. Another member wishing to speak about something not related to what the "stick holder" is talking about must wait his or her turn. The leader is free to ask questions or make clarifying statements, but only by permission of the one who holds the stick. It is made clear that the stick holder may not be interrupted or criticized. Statements directed to other members are encouraged to be framed as "I statements," using feelings or ideas. In this way, an atmosphere of patience and respect is cultivated, freeing members to experience transformation and healing in the group.

When the talking stick has made at least two or three go-arounds, it can be laid in the center of the circle to be picked up by anyone wishing to speak further. When all those who want to speak are finished, the Talking Circle can be brought to a close with a traditional chant, prayer, or blessing as a way to give thanks for the "coming-together." It is understood that what was said in the circle remains in the circle to demonstrate respect for all members and to protect the sacredness of the experience.

GROUP WORK WITH NATIVE AMERICANS: THROUGH THE EYES OF THE HAWK

To say that research on group counseling with Native clients is limited would be an understatement. One of the underlying reasons for this is the difficulty in getting Native clients to participate in counseling. More than 50% of Native clients do not return after the initial session (Herring, 1999). To combat this high rate of dropout, more settings are turning to group work as the mode of therapeutic intervention with Native clients (Dufrene & Coleman, 1992). Although group work tends to be more congruent with Native clients' cultural frame of reference, the disadvantage lies in the potential for Native clients to be reluctant with self-disclosure and a tendency to use noninterference with their fellow group members. In addition, Merta (1995) cited the emphasis placed on the traditional Native value of group harmony and cooperation as a potential barrier in the sense that many traditional Native clients might consider group conflict unacceptable as a part of the process. Several authors have documented the effectiveness of group counseling as the "treatment of choice" when working with Native clients. LaFromboise, Berman, and Sohi (1994) documented the effectiveness of using Talking Circles or Healing Circles that were led by Alaska Native women with their grandchildren in teaching them how to talk about their feelings through role-playing and modeling. Similarly, Ashby, Gilchrist, and Miramontez (1987) discussed the selection of the Talking Circle as "the most helpful and useful activity" (p. 29) in a group conducted with Native female survivors of sexual abuse. Heilbron and Guttman (2000) also highlighted the effective combination of cognitive therapy with the traditional Healing Circle for working with Ojibway women. Weaver & Brave Heart (1999) described the positive effects of group work on shaping cultural identity of Native clients and providing an outlet for discussion of historical trauma.

A number of authors have discussed the effectiveness of using group work with Native youth. For example, Appleton and Dykeman (1996) presented a model using art in group counseling with Native youth representing different ages and tribal affiliations. Marsiglia, Cross, and Mitchell-Enos (1998) concluded that culturally grounded group work with Native students was a vital tool for increasing pride, self-esteem, interpersonal skills, and for strengthening cultural identity. Likewise, Husted, Johnson, and Redwing (1995) discussed the positive effects of groups with Native youth who were significantly more likely to remain in school and progress academically. Colmant and Merta (1999) discussed the use of the sweat lodge ceremony with Navajo boys at a Navajo-owned residential treatment center. Finally, Vick, Smith, and Iron Rope Herrera (1998) cited the use of the Healing Circle as a primary factor in creating an effective program of recovery for Lakota adults dealing with alcoholism.

Several authors have presented models of group work based on Native traditions, ceremonies, or techniques. For example, Garrett and Crutchfield (1997) presented a model of group work with children and adolescents that combined the Talking Circle format with activities and exercises based on Native cultural traditions. Roberts-Wilbur, Wilbur, Garrett, and Yuhas (2001) provided evidence of the effectiveness of using Talking Circles in a group format with peer educators at the college level. Running Wolf and Rickard (2003) suggested a format for using the Talking Circle as an experiential, process-based approach with undergraduate and graduate students in the university setting. Garrett, Garrett, and Brotherton (2001) offered a process-based intervention called "Inner Circle/Outer Circle" that combines the Native tradition of Healing Circles with a contemporary approach to group work. Likewise, Garrett, and Garrett (2002) presented a group technique called "Ayeli," based on the Native tradition of honoring the Four Directions as a way of seeking harmony and balance both within the group and within the lives of individual members. The Torres-Rivera, Garrett, and Crutchfield chapter (21) in this volume also discusses culture-specific traditional methods of healing in modern-day group work.

IMPLICATIONS FOR PRACTICE: ALL OUR RELATIONS

There are a number of implications for practice of group work with Native clients. Several authors have suggested that racially homogeneous groups representing Native clients from a variety of acculturation levels may be ideal (Herring, 1999; Merta, 1995). Counselors who understand the impact of acculturation as a reflection of historical events or circumstances and life choices that shape the worldview of Native American clients will be able to see the clients as they see themselves: through their hopes, their dreams, their struggles, their pain, their strength, their relations, their history, and their perceptions of what is real and meaningful in life.

Walking the Path Together

When working with a Native client, it is important to get a sense of that person's level of acculturation by informally assessing (a) values (traditional, marginal, bicultural, assimilated, pan-traditional); (b) geographic origin/residence (reservation, rural, urban); and (c) tribal affiliation (tribal structure, customs, beliefs) (for further discussion of formal and informal assessment of Native American acculturation, see Garrett & Pichette, 2000). Both verbal and nonverbal cues will give counselors a good sense of a Native American client's level of acculturation. If questions remain, it is important to pose them in a respectful, unobtrusive way. Moreover, with a client who seems to have more traditional values and beliefs, it may be particularly helpful to suggest that family or other significant persons (e.g., a Medicine man or Medicine woman) participate in the process to support the client as he or she moves through important personal transitions and any subsequent personal cleansing.

For many Native people, the potential for cultural conflicts due to differing values within the context of the larger society is evident. Native clients can be encouraged to talk about the personal meaning of family, clan, or tribe as a way of exploring worldview, especially in light of intergenerational differences or the effects of oppression as contributing factors in issues being presented. Therefore, group work can be approached as a developmental process of helping Native American clients come to a better understanding of themselves, others, community, society, and life.

Second, having a general understanding of Native American worldview and spiritual traditions does not prepare one to participate in or conduct Native ceremonies as part of the counseling process (Garrett & Wilbur, 1999; Matheson, 1996). That is the responsibility of those who are trained as Medicine persons (i.e., traditional spiritual healers, Medicine men or Medicine women, Indian doctors, etc.), individuals who can serve as important resources to counselors working with Native clients. However, having this understanding does prepare one to recognize culturally specific meanings and practices that may play a critical role in understanding not only the client's issues and appropriate ways of dealing with these but also in understanding the very world in which the client lives.

Once the group counselor has some general information concerning the client's cultural background and traditions, he or she has a better understanding of what may or may not be considered appropriate with and for the client. The following recommendations offered in Garrett (1999) are intended as culturally responsive ways for working with a traditional Native client:

1. *Greeting.* For traditional Native Americans, a gentle handshake is the proper way of greeting. Sometimes, there is no handshake at all, just a word of greeting or nonverbal acknowledgment, such as a head nod. To use a firm handshake, as is expected in mainstream American society as a sign of confidence and enthusiasm, is considered an insult in the traditional way because it is interpreted as an aggressive show of power. It may be important to follow, rather than lead, the client.

2. *Hospitality.* Given the traditional emphasis on generosity, kindness, and "gifting" as a way of honoring the relation, hospitality is an important part of Native American life. Therefore, it is helpful to be able to offer or share a beverage or snack as a sign of good relations with traditional

Native clients. In the traditional way, to not offer hospitality to a visitor or guest is to bring shame on oneself and one's family. In the group setting, the sharing of a snack or beverage at the beginning would be a way to honor the value of hospitality and sharing.

3. *Silence.* In the traditional way, when people meet, very little may be said between them during the initial moments of the encounter. Therefore, quiet time at the beginning of a session is an appropriate way of transitioning into the therapeutic process by giving both counselor and clients a chance to orient themselves to the situation, get in touch with themselves, and experience the "presence" of the other person.

4. *Space.* Taking care to respect physical space is an extension of the importance in traditional Native culture that one need not always fill relational space with words. In Native tradition, both the physical form and the space between the physical are considered sacred. In group counseling, it is important to respect the physical space of Native clients by not sitting too close in a way that unintentionally communicates intrusion. The burning of sage, cedar, or sweetgrass (a method of spatial cleansing for many tribal nations, commonly known as "smudging") should only be done at the request or with permission of the Native client.

5. *Eye contact.* Native American clients with traditional values (and possibly those who are marginal or bicultural) may tend to avert their eyes as a sign of respect. To subtly match this level of eye contact is respectful and shows an understanding of the client's way of being. The eyes are considered to be the pathway to the spirit; therefore, to consistently look someone in the eye is to show a level of entitlement or aggressiveness. It is good to glance at someone every once in a while, but listening, in the traditional way, is something that happens with the ears and the heart.

6. *Intention.* One of the most important issues with many Native clients in the counseling relationship is trust. This should come as no surprise given the history of broken promises and exploitation survived by many tribal nations. Typically, an Indian client will "read" the counselor's nonverbals fairly quickly to

determine whether the counselor is someone to be trusted or not. Therefore, group counselors can focus on honoring the mental space between counselor and client by seeking to offer respect and humility in the counseling process. Acceptance by the counselor means not trying to control or influence the client. This is considered "bad Medicine."

7. Collaboration. In counseling, more traditional clients may welcome (or even expect) the counselor to offer helpful suggestions or alternative ways of dealing with things. From a traditional perspective, respect for choice is utmost, but healing is a collaborative process. Therefore, offer suggestions without offering directions; this applies to group facilitators as well as members. The group can talk about when and how they prefer to offer feedback to each other, and practice it beforehand. With traditional Native American clients, actions will always speak louder than words. Furthermore, contrary to the popular stereotype that Native people are stoic and unemotional, laughter and teasing is a good sign of connecting. If a group of Native clients uses humor, then that can be a indication a greater level of trust is being attempted or has developed and should therefore be encouraged.

For group leaders, establishing "trustworthiness" with a Native client means being attentive, respectful, and culturally responsive to the client, and giving appropriate structure and direction to the process while also being flexible enough to incorporate helpful resources or interventions. Showing respect could also mean being open to or suggesting the possibility of client consultation with a traditional healer. In fact, "linking" services could prove to be very effective if counselors encourage that such services be provided by traditional healers in conjunction with counseling or therapy. This would be a clear demonstration of respect for traditional ways while providing a more comprehensive service to Native clients in need. Another way of demonstrating respect for the traditional way is to encourage extended family members to participate in the healing process (Attneave, 1985). Working in the presence of a group, giving people a choice about the best way

to proceed with the process, and encouraging the participation of family members and friends are all natural components of the traditional healing way. Of course, this must and can be done while also respecting confidentiality of clients. The key is collaboration.

Recommendations

In addition to contemporary counseling interventions and treatment modalities, counselors can incorporate tribal-specific interventions as well as social advocacy to meet the cultural and spiritual needs of specific Native clients. The following are practical recommendations offered by Garrett and Carroll (2000) for working with Native clients.

Sociodemographics: Native clients can reconnect with a sense of purpose by finding ways to combat the high rates of unemployment, inadequate housing, low educational levels, poverty-level incomes, and isolated living conditions. Participation in community-wide volunteer programs to help those in need has proven to be a successful part of healing for many Indian people.

Physiology: Native people should be encouraged to get regular physical check-ups and have blood tests done to monitor any difficulties regarding blood sugar or any other physiological difficulties.

Historical Context: A critical component of counseling could include a psychoeducational piece or dialogue designed to provide insight concerning many historical factors, such as exploitation of Native people through discrimination, assimilation through boarding schools and relocation programs, and disruption of traditional cultural and familial patterns. This could provide important topics for discussion, as well as helping Native clients explore their own levels of cultural identity development.

Acculturation/Identity: Native clients can be assisted with exploration of cultural identity issues by focusing on the cultural themes of belonging, mastery, independence, and generosity. Counselors can use the following general questions for each of the four respective areas: (a) Where do you belong? (b) What are you good at? What do you enjoy doing? (c) What are your sources of strength? What limits you? (d) What do you have to offer or contribute?

Isolation/Social Connections: Participation in other social events, such as family gatherings and powwows, to name but a couple, allows Native clients to experience social cohesion and social interaction in their communities. Moreover, some Native clients can benefit from a sense of reconnection with community and traditional roles. This could be, and has been, accomplished through the revival of tribal ceremonies and practices (e.g., Talking Circles, sweat lodges, powwows, peyote meetings, and so on), reestablishing a sense of belonging and communal meaningfulness for Native people "returning to the old ways" or at least integrating many of these ways into modern-day life.

Generational Splits: Native clients of all ages can benefit from acting as or learning from elders serving as role models or teachers for young people. This, too, has become more commonly practiced by tribal nations across the country in therapeutic programs as well as in the schools.

Coping Mechanisms: Native clients can learn other methods of dealing with stress, boredom, powerlessness, and the sense of emptiness associated with acculturation and identity confusion. Consultation with or participation of a Medicine person (i.e., traditional Native healer) may prove very helpful.

Noninterference: The avoidance behavior of community members to maintain respect is something that can be addressed with the Native client as well as with community members to the extent that the behavior may be destructive. Carol Attneave's (1969, 1985) Network Therapy has been very effective with Indian clients as a way of working with individuals in family and community contexts.

From a traditional Native American perspective, being well means "walking in step with the universe." This highlights the cultural importance of understanding, participating in, maintaining, and revering the importance of relationships and the art of relation. Indeed, counselors are trained as professionals to use that same "Medicine" of relation for healing and helping people. It is in everything where power moves. . . .

CONCLUSION: CIRCLES WITHIN CIRCLES

As you hear the sound of the drum rumbling low to the sharp, impassioned cries of the singers, the vibration moves through you like a storm that rises in the distance, building slowly in the azure sky, then unloading in a rhythmic yet gentle pounding of the soil. Anyone, Native or non-Native, who has ever had the opportunity to experience the colors, movement, sounds, tastes, and smells of the powwow understands the feeling that passes through you. It is different for every person, but if you really experience the feeling, you know that it is connection. For some, it is a matter of seeing old friends or making new ones. For some, it is the image of the dancers moving in seemingly infinite poses of unity and airy smoothness to every flowing pound of the drum. For some, it is the laughter and exchange of words and gestures. For some, it is silent inner prayer giving thanks for another day of life. For some, it is the delicious taste of your second and third helping of that piping hot fry-bread. Whatever it is, in the end, it is coming together in one way or another and walking in step with the Greater Circle. And just when you think you have seen all there is to see, the hoop dancer quietly emerges from the crowd and enters the Circle. . . .

REFERENCES

Allen, P. G. (1991). Hoop dancer. In A. R. Velie (Ed.), *American Indian literature: An anthology* (p. 235). Norman: University of Oklahoma.

Appleton, V. E., & Dykeman, C. (1996). Using art in group counseling with Native American youth. *Journal for Specialists in Group Work, 21,* 224-231.

Ashby, M. R., Gilchrist, L. D., & Miramontez, A. (1987). Group treatment for sexually abused American Indian adolescents. *Social Work with Groups, 10,* 21-32.

Attneave, C. L. (1969). Therapy in tribal settings and urban network intervention. *Family Process, 8,* 192-210.

Attneave, C. L. (1985). Practical counseling with American Indian and Alaska Native clients. In

P. Pedersen (Ed.), *Handbook of cross-cultural counseling and therapy* (pp. 135-140). Westport, CT: Greenwood.

Brown, J. E. (1972). *The sacred pipe: Black Elk's account of the seven rites of the Oglala Sioux.* New York: Penguin.

Colmant, S. A., & Merta, R. J. (1999). Using the sweat lodge ceremony as group therapy for Navajo youth. *Journal for Specialists in Group Work, 24,* 55-73.

Craven, M. (1973). *I heard the owl call my name.* New York: Laurel.

Dufrene, P. M., & Coleman, V. D. (1992). Counseling Native Americans: Guidelines for group process. *Journal for Specialists in Group Work, 17,* 229-235.

Four Worlds Development Project. (1984). *The sacred tree: Reflections on Native American spirituality.* Wilmot, WI: Lotus Light.

Garrett, J. T. (2001). *Meditations with the Cherokee: Prayers, songs, and stories of healing and harmony.* Rochester, VT: Bear & Company.

Garrett, J. T., & Garrett, M. T. (1996). *Medicine of the Cherokee: The way of right relationship.* Santa Fe, NM: Bear & Company.

Garrett, M. T. (1998). *Walking on the wind: Cherokee teachings for harmony and balance.* Santa Fe, NM: Bear & Company.

Garrett, M. T. (1999). Understanding the "Medicine" of Native American traditional values: An integrative review. *Counseling & Values, 43,* 84-98.

Garrett, M. T., & Carroll, J. (2000). Mending the broken circle: Treatment and prevention of substance abuse among Native Americans. *Journal of Counseling & Development, 78,* 379-388.

Garrett, M. T., & Crutchfield, L. B. (1997). Moving full circle: A unity model of group work with children. *Journal for Specialists in Group Work, 22,* 175-188.

Garrett, M. T., & Garrett, J. T. (2002). Ayeli: Centering technique based on Cherokee spiritual traditions. *Counseling & Values, 46,* 149-158.

Garrett, M. T., Garrett, J. T., & Brotherton, D. (2001). Inner circle/outer circle: Native American group technique. *Journal for Specialists in Group Work, 26,* 17-30.

Garrett, M. T., & Myers, J. E. (1996). The rule of opposites: A paradigm for counseling Native Americans. *Journal of Multicultural Counseling & Development, 24,* 89-104.

Garrett, M. T., & Osborne, W. L. (1995). The Native American sweat lodge as metaphor for group work. *Journal for Specialists in Group Work, 20,* 33-39.

Garrett, M. T., & Pichette, E. F. (2000). Red as an apple: Native American acculturation and counseling with or without reservation. *Journal of Counseling & Development, 78,* 3-13.

Garrett, M. T., & Wilbur, M. P. (1999). Does the worm live in the ground? Reflections on Native American spirituality. *Journal of Multicultural Counseling & Development, 27,* 193-206.

Good Tracks, J. G. (1973). Native American noninterference. *Social Work, 17,* 30-34.

Heilbron, C. L., & Guttman, M. A. J. (2000). Traditional healing methods with First Nations women in group counselling. *Canadian Journal of Counselling, 34,* 3-13.

Heinrich, R. K., Corbine, J. L., & Thomas, K. R. (1990). Counseling Native Americans. *Journal of Counseling & Development, 69,* 128-133.

Herring, R. D. (1999). *Counseling with Native American Indians and Alaska Natives: Strategies for helping professionals.* Thousand Oaks, CA: Sage.

Hodgkinson, H. L. (1990). *The demographics of American Indians: One percent of the people; fifty percent of the diversity.* Washington, DC: Institute for Educational Leadership.

Husted, J., Johnson, T., & Redwing, L. (1995). Multidimensional adolescent treatment with American Indians. *American Indian & Alaska Native Mental Health Research, 6,* 23-30.

LaFromboise, T. D., Berman, J. S., & Sohi, B. K. (1994). American Indian women. In L. Comez-Diaz & B. Greene (Eds.), *Women of color: Integrating ethnic and gender identities in psychotherapy.* (pp. 30-71). New York: Guilford.

Lake, M. G. (1987). The sweat lodge: An ancient medicine for modern sicknesses. *Self Discovery Magazine.* Unpublished manuscript.

Lake, M. G. (1991). *Native healer: Initiation into an ancient art.* Wheaton, IL: Quest Books.

Marsiglia, F. F., Cross, S., Mitchell-Enos, V. (1998). Culturally grounded group work with adolescent American Indian students. *Social Work with Groups, 21,* 89-102.

Matheson, L. (1996). Valuing spirituality among Native American populations. *Counseling & Values, 41,* 51-58.

Merta, R. J. (1995). Group work: Multicultural perspectives. In J. G. Ponterotto, J. M. Casas, L. A. Suzuki, & C. M. Alexander (Eds.), *Handbook of multicultural counseling* (pp. 567-585). Thousand Oaks, CA: Sage.

Neely, S. (1991). *Snowbird Cherokees: People of persistence.* Athens: University of Georgia Press.

Roberts-Wilbur, J., Wilbur, M., Garrett, M. T., & Yuhas, M. (2001). Talking circles: Listen or your tongue will make you deaf. *Journal for Specialists in Group Work, 26,* 368-384.

Running Wolf, P., & Rickard, J. A. (2003). Talking circles: A Native American approach to experiential learning. *Journal of Multicultural Counseling and Development, 31,* 39-43.

Russell, G. (1998). *American Indian facts of life: A profile of today's tribes and reservations.* Phoenix, AZ: Russell.

U.S. Bureau of the Census. (2001). *2000 Census counts of American Indians, Eskimos, or Aleuts and American Indian and Alaska Native areas.* Washington, DC: Author.

Vick, R. D. Sr., Smith, L. M., & Iron Rope Herrera, C. (1998). The healing circle: An alternative path to alcoholism recovery. *Counseling & Values, 42,* 132-141.

Weaver, H. N., & Brave Heart, M. Y. H. (1999). Examining two facets of American Indian identity: Exposure to other cultures and the influence of historical trauma. *Journal of Human Behavior in the Social Environment, 2,* 19-33.

Wilbur, M. P. (1999a). Finding balance in the winds. *Journal for Specialists in Group Work, 24,* 342-353.

Wilbur, M. P. (1999b). The rivers of a wounded heart. *Journal of Counseling & Development, 77,* 47-50.

13

AN AFROCENTRIC APPROACH TO COUNSELING GROUPS WITH AFRICAN AMERICANS

SHERLON P. PACK-BROWN

Bowling Green State University

AMELIA FLEMING

Bowling Green State University

I am because we are; and because we are, therefore I am.

—Mibiti

Much of the multicultural counseling research has pointed out the need for counselors to become culturally competent to appropriately address the needs of a diverse community. Traditional psychology and psychotherapy have been based on theoretical and diagnostic standards established with a select group of client characteristics and have expanded their interventions in recent years to emphasize and utilize client diversity. Group approaches have been even slower to incorporate psychological, emotional, and spiritual factors of cultural groups, especially when related to group work from an African American perspective. While it is true that African American cultural dynamics may influence the character of the group, common misconceptions abound about the nature and function of an Afrocentric approach to groups. Ethical considerations in organizing and implementing group work with African Americans are warranted; however, fostering positive attitudes about forming groups based on an Afrocentric approach and European approach to group work with African Americans is of the essence.

African Americans bring, in some form or another, their traditions to groups. These traditions can naturally enhance the process and dynamics of groups and/or be barriers to participation. African American culture has typically provided a network of support systems through community resources such as familial, church, and/or fraternity and sorority relationships. African Americans generally minimize the use of professional counseling services due to the cultural mistrust stemming from the devaluation and negative imaging that White European American society has historically perpetrated against people of African descent.

Group leaders are influenced by their theoretical orientations. Yet little attention has been given to the client perspective of what is helpful and desired in counseling and therapy, particularly those clients who do not come from the Eurocentric culture. When working with African Americans within the group context, it is important to integrate client perspectives by examining African American preferences, worldviews, and expectations; appreciate the dynamics of African American culture and its influence on optimal mental health; recognize thematic cultural beliefs and values; and understand the impact of such beliefs and values on group work.

Upon this foundation, four questions are posed to assist readers in strengthening their helping foundations for competent group leadership. Practical applications are presented for culturally competent leading of groups with African American membership. We then discuss diversity-competent group workers and African Americans, followed with an explanation of the Afrocentric approach to group work and a brief discussion of two models of an Afrocentric approach to group work with African Americans. We conclude the chapter with a preliminary framework that highlights group counseling competencies for work with African American group members.

Cultural Beliefs, Issues, and Values That Affect Groups for African Americans

African American (Black) culture is distinct from the European American (White) culture. Given this reality, diversity-competent group leaders are ethically bound to hear and recognize the cultural beliefs common to the African American and European American cultures. Furthermore, group leaders must understand the impact of both the Afrocentric and Eurocentric cultural beliefs on groups and the subsequent impact on members. When working with African American group members, for example, the following emphases must be taken into

account (Boykin, 1986, 1994, as cited in Hill, Block, & Buggie, 2000).

African-Centered Values

Spirituality

Belief in a Supreme Being who has power to determine what happens in people's everyday lives is commonly accepted among African American populations. Traditional counseling often negates or trivializes this practice, failing to utilize a source of empowerment and vitality and excluding a moral code that promotes altruism, fairness, and justice (Helms & Cook, 1999). Spirituality may positively affect groups by enhancing group cohesiveness. The shared belief that group members are not meeting together by accident—rather, divine design—may create an atmosphere of acceptance, engagement, and heightened group purpose. Groups may be negatively affected when a member disregards or devalues spiritual input. Because spirituality is personal, offense may be taken when spiritual beliefs radically differ among the membership, and the capacity to listen to and value these differences may be inhibited.

Movement

Personal conduct is organized through movement (Helms & Cook, 1999). Movement may be expressed in terms of getting out of one's seat or gesturing of hands, neck, and other body parts while engaging in discussion. It can positively affect the group by allowing an avenue of freedom of expression, more intense involvement in group exercises, and a greater sense of comfort when speaking. This movement can negatively affect the group process if it is perceived as threatening or invades personal space of other members. Groups that are restrictive in motion may inhibit this process for African American members.

Affect

Enthusiasm or passion for a topic may be reflected by a group member's raised volume, pitch, and/or deepened intonation. When this is perceived as anger, group members may withdraw, verbally attack, or in some other way negatively react to the display of affect. Strong displays of affect can be misinterpreted as confrontational, dramatic, and/or overemotional.

Communalism

Defining one's self in relation to one's group contributes to communalism. Group success may be emphasized, while individual objectives are generally set aside for the realization of group goals.

Orality

Rhythmic communication that is filled with symbolism and is expressed in multidimensional (cognitive, affective, and/or behavioral) levels (Helms & Cook, 1999) is commonplace. Knowledge is gained and transmitted orally; however, those who are the most effective communicators may enhance the group process by fostering clarity or hinder the group by domination and/or manipulations.

Socially Defined

This refers to physical, emotional, cognitive, and spiritual behaviors that are defined and measured by meaningful events and customs. These behaviors may elicit reactions that are not common to (thematic within) a particular group of people and their cultural worldview.

Time Perspective

Group process may be affected by members' personal involvement in, knowledge of, and/or commitment to various socially significant occurrences from a historical perspective.

Cooperation

This value emphasizes power associated with being interdependent as African Americans build and maintain community and relationships. There is a belief in the extended self as represented in the statement: "I am because we are, we are therefore I am." An impact on group

work is that African American group members embracing this value and belief are culturally appreciative of the power of being a member of a group. One benefit is that as group members, they are positioned to embrace a group therapeutic approach to healing.

Mutual Respect

Reciprocity exhibited within relationships is held in high esteem. Two guidelines important to how members relate are (a) deferential regard for others and (b) avoidance of intrusion on others. The importance of recognizing and understanding the cultural merits of collective survival and inherent dimensions is emphasized. An important belief for many African Americans is that members are appreciated and regarded for their worth because they are members of the whole (the community). An impact of this value and belief system on groups is in part dependent on how group leaders hear, interpret, and act on the idea of mutual respect. If, for example, mutual respect is operationalized from an individualistic perspective ("I respect what you have to say") rather than a collectivistic perspective ("We respect what each of us has to say"), an African American group member believing in mutual respect may feel separated from the group. If, however, the group leader hears the African American member take a collectivistic stance, interprets the "We" statement as a cultural value, and affirms the empowerment received from interdependence and mutual respect, the group member may feel validated and part of the group.

Emotional Vitality

An appreciation for and interpersonal expression of feelings is valued. Verbal and nonverbal language are animated and often direct, however, not personalized in part because values such as cooperation and mutual respect are held in esteem. African American group members espousing the value of emotional vitality may believe that group members are free to express positive and negative emotions directly with group members. The effectiveness of groups is dependent on the leader's cultural competence and ability to encourage and understand free expressions of emotions as a tool to facilitate growth during the group process.

The next two characteristics (racial identity and gender identity) will be discussed in more detail than the previous values. While all are important to consider in group dynamics and process, specific values and beliefs inherent to racial identity and gender are critical to understanding how African Americans, individually and collectively, construct and make meaning of their world. Group leaders must understand that the values and cultural beliefs specific to racial identity and gender may differentially impact group work with African Americans.

Racial Identity

A focus on acculturation, ethnicity, and race in African American group work is critical. In general, a strong racial identity is often related to high self-esteem, self-clarity, and appreciation for differences in others (Helms, 1984; Helms & Cook, 1999; Pack-Brown, Whittington-Clark, & Parker, 1998). However,

for African Americans who have made less progress in racial identity development (RID), the opposite may be true (Helms & Cook, 1999).

It is assumed that the reader has fundamental knowledge of RID. Thus, due to space limitations, racial identity will not be discussed in depth. For those needing more discussion of racial identity development, Cross (1971), Hargrow (2001), and Helms and Cook (1999) provide in-depth discussions particularly as it relates to African Americans. The D'Andrea chapter (19) in this volume also discusses the impact of group leader and member RID on group interactions and dynamics.

This section presents a brief discussion of (a) each of the RID stages, (b) how the various stages influence group members' behaviors, and (c) potential issues that might occur in group. The Helms racial identity model (1984) uses four statuses to classify how African Americans progress through racial identity states. These statuses influence African American group members' cognitive, emotional, and physical behaviors and create potential group issues.

Status	Influence on Behavior (African American Perspective)	Potential Issues in Group
Preencounter	Black culture is denied or rejected. Blacks are viewed as inferior to White culture.	Do not see my Blackness. See me only as a person! Preference for group comprised of predominately or all White group members.
Encounter	Group member may begin to question how he/she has been treated as a racial person.	Have I ever been treated equally? Depending on the level of encounter, low encounter—preference for group comprised mostly of Whites; high encounter—preference for group comprised of little to no White members.
Immersion Emersion	Extreme identification with Blacks and denigration of Whites.	White people are devils. Anger at White culture. Preference for an all-Black group.
Integration	Incorporates positive aspects of White culture into personal identity; able to discern and confront racist behavior. Embraces a positive Black identity.	Dark, medium, or light-skinned African Americans are equally valued. Black is okay, and I am able to overcome oppression!

An area within the African American community in which discrepancy in skin color, hair preference, and facial features may be most prominent is that of Black identity in the biracial

(Black/White) and African American communities. Issues of racial awareness are evident, and people notice similarities and differences in hair texture, facial features, and skin color. This awareness begins in childhood and expands to adulthood. Labels and categories are used to define the differences and similarities among African Americans. While some of the labels connote a positive reality and are meant to send messages of affirmation, other labels connote a less positive reality and do not affirm. Regardless of the intent of the messages, they carry psychological and emotional implications that have an impact on African American mental health. For example, labels such as "light skinned," "high yellow," "tar baby," "Mulatto," "pretty brown baby," "good hair," and "bad hair" are descriptors. The life experiences of Tammra and Alisha, two sisters, illustrate this point.

Tammra and Alisha share many commonalities, including envy of each other. Although they are only 2 years apart and have the same mother and father, their biological features are distinctly different. Tammra has always felt inferior to Alisha. As children, friends and strangers commented on how pretty Alisha was, often ignoring Tammra. Even as adults, men seem to prefer Alisha's light skin tone over Tammra's chocolate brown complexion. The employment market seemed to reward Alisha also, because while Tammra has consistently outperformed Alisha in scholastics and performance reviews, Alisha continues to land the desirous "up-front" marketing positions. Tammra thinks that everything has come so easily for Alisha. Hair care is even a chore for Tammra. She must spend excessive amounts of money for professional treatments or resort to personally straightening or relaxing her neck-length hair, which in turn often breaks off; Alisha just washes her hair that falls midway down her back and curls it with her fingers or brushes it up into a style.

Alisha, on the other hand, has issues with Tammra. Her parents preferred to leave Tammra in charge in their absence, although Alisha was older. They trusted Tammra's judgment and valued her opinion but questioned Alisha's motives and downplayed her abilities. Men treat Tammra with respect, according to Alisha. They engage in meaningful conversation with Tammra, not always quick to get physical or use her and throw her away like a toy.

Tammra and Alisha could benefit from an Afrocentric inhale/exhale group experience such as the following, which taps into feelings and perceptions associated with a variation in hue. The group leader tapes a piece of paper with a shade of blackness (chocolate brown to high yellow) on chair bottoms before the group assembles. Each group member is asked to image his or her skin tone as it reflects the shade written. An object (e.g., a talking stick) is passed to determine who speaks. The person with the object describes personal and individual feelings and thoughts about the perceptions of others.

Gender Issues

Although African Americans share historical and cultural contexts, gender issues are often unique and necessitate distinct emphasis. Historically, unlike the European American male counterpart, achieving masculine privileges in the United States has not been a birthright for the African American male (Franklin & Pack-Brown, 2001). Issues confronting African American men include (but are not limited to) negative attitudes of authority figures, low levels of educational attainment, discriminatory hiring practices, increased activity in violence and substance abuse, and disproportionate involvement in the criminal justice system. To provide a framework for counseling African American males, a number of important issues need to be considered (Franklin & Pack-Brown, 2001): racism, programs of aggression and control, cultural alienation, self-esteem, dependency, and help-seeking attitudes and behaviors. In many instances, African American men are referred for counseling by some societal agent—judge, social worker, or probation officer—after they have committed some offense against the social order (Franklin & Pack-Brown, 2001). Counseling, therefore, becomes for these men a forced process, and the implicit goal is rehabilitation or punishment. Thus, counseling seems to be just one more infringement on African American manhood. For example, an African American male group member has been referred to counseling by his probation officer. The member questions his White group leader's ability to understand the Black male experience in a racist legal system. The group member attempts to protect himself by cautiously sharing information in group. The leader perceives the group member as resistant to group process (without regard for or understanding of the potential cultural and racial influences). In fact, the group member is hesitant (not resistant) due to a historical distrust that many African Americans have of the White European American culture and its power within the legal system. While some men may deem the counseling process beneficial, others may present with an unresponsive and inattentive front. They may seek opportunities to challenge the leaders and/or sabotage group goals.

African American women, on the other hand, who present for counseling bring a double burden. One is the burden of race in a racist society. The other is being burdened with the problems of being a woman in a male-dominated society that does not fully value the feminine perspective. In addition, African American women, like Tammra, must contend with long-standing negative, stereotypical images of being Black and female. Factors affecting the lives of African American women encompass racial identity, cultural mistrust, self-esteem, and empowerment (Jordan, 1991; Pack-Brown et al., 1998). To compensate for their "second-class" status in a male-dominated society, women in groups may be affected by a desire to control the group setting. Discussions may easily and often be diverted to topics devoted to "male bashing."

DIVERSITY-COMPETENT GROUP LEADERS

"Culturally effective, ethical, and competent group workers strive to understand the life experiences and worldviews of group members."

"Workers seek to create a caring, accepting and nonjudgmental group environment that fosters the development of a therapeutic relationship so that trust is quickly established and a climate for growth and change is evident."

"Group workers treat group members with dignity and respect."

These quotations are familiar rhetoric among group leaders and those training and supervising group workers. However, when provided opportunities to explain what these words mean and how to operationalize them within a cultural context, many become restrained. They hold back from acting in a professional manner that promotes change and repress behaviors that encourage development.

Group leaders possess beliefs, values, and behaviors that have a cultural foundation and have an impact on their effectiveness as leaders. Corey, Corey, and Callanan (1998) posited that counselors respect the rights of their clients to hold different sets of values. In response, professional associations have offered competencies and principles to promote diversity competence among their members. The Executive Board of the Association for Specialists in Group Work (ASGW) endorsed a document in 1999, *Association for Specialists in Group Work Principles for Diversity-Competent Group Workers,* which specifies personal and professional responsibilities for members serving as diversity-competent professionals, such as group leaders.

We propose that characteristics of culturally competent helping professionals include the following:

- *Beliefs and Attitudes:* Awareness of personal beliefs, attitudes and biases about the African American population and sensitivity to how these may influence one's work with African American clients; the development of an appreciation for the African American culture; and an attitude of comfort, challenge, and satisfaction when working with African American clients.

- *Knowledge:* Understanding of the history, traditions, and values of African American culture; an awareness of African-centered views of mental health, life adjustment, and helping; sensitivity to institutional barriers and prejudices that impinge on African American clients, and thus, implementation of therapeutic approaches that match the needs and backgrounds of African American clients.

- *Skills:* Flexibility in utilizing approaches that are compatible with African American clients; effective communication with African

American clients by using appropriate language and nonverbal behaviors; and familiarity with referral sources, agencies, and programs that are appropriate for African American clients (Arredondo et al., 1996; Sue & Sue, 1999).

AN AFROCENTRIC APPROACH TO GROUP WORK: A MODEL

The African American community often presents a challenge to group leaders who are unfamiliar with the African American worldview and life experiences. Sometimes the challenge is clear, and other times it is clouded. Nevertheless, the challenge exists. The purpose of this section is to offer an approach that helps group leaders, educators, and supervisors provide healing opportunities to African Americans, which is (a) based on a collective culture and ethnic background and (b) more congruent with African American life experiences.

The Afrocentric approach to groups is a diversity-competent mechanism that is recommended for both heterogeneous (multiracial and multiethnic) and homogeneous African American groups. This approach (a) is culture centered and practical, (b) is grounded in African-centered psychology, and (c) provides a set of therapeutic tools and culturally appropriate knowledge necessary to understand worldview and reality. Diversity and multicultural issues such as race, ethnicity, and gender are central themes within group process and dynamics. The Afrocentric approach to groups builds on a cultural base, demonstrates a collectivistic approach to life and helping, and focuses on group members finding their success and happiness in a multicultural and diverse society that operates from a communal worldview.

The following guidelines are offered to assist in identifying and using culturally appropriate skills that promote a safe environment for African American group members as they strive toward their individual and collective goals. It is important to remember that group members tend to follow the leader's manner of leadership, so that effective group leaders possess specific characteristics and behaviors that promote rather than impede group members' maturation and development.

EXAMINING WORLDVIEW: THE TWO PERSPECTIVES OF THE GROUP LEADER AND GROUP MEMBER

Worldview is the way a person views and interacts with the world. The Eurocentric worldview guides the work of mental health professionals. Typically, within a group context, leaders operate from an individualistic perspective, with individual members' needs and concerns as the primary focus. Select thematic values include the following:

Individualism: The primary force is independence. Autonomy, and individual responsibility are guiding forces. Individual group members are encouraged to be in control of their environments.

Competition: The primary force for group members is to win and overcome at any cost.

Religion: The primary force is a Christian base.

Action orientation: The primary force is a group member taking action to control his or her life and life circumstances.

Group leaders:
- Help members to live more fully by identifying and using interventions that focus on the individual.
- Help individuals to take charge of their lives.
- Encourage the use of verbal skills, self-disclosure, and eye contact.
- Promote insight and awareness as tools to enhance maturation and change.

While the Eurocentric worldview is often a viable tool to promote mental health and psychological well-being, this approach may not be in the best interests of African American group members. Many scholars of African American psychology propose that mental health professionals are not well positioned to provide helping services to African Americans if they do not understand mental health from an African American psychological perspective.

For group leaders operating from an Afrocentric worldview (a collectivistic approach to group work), two factors affect the ability to accurately analyze worldview. The first factor is the way in which the group leader personally and professionally interacts in a world that struggles with "ism" and difference. For example, a Puerto Rican American group leader personally fears African Americans because she was taught (in school and at home) that African Americans were angry and aggressive people. When faced with African Americans (males in particular), her biases included tough, ghetto, and loud people. The group leader psychologically and emotionally struggles with her personal biases and their impact on treating African American clients the same way she would treat other clients of color. Another example of a group leader's ability to accurately analyze worldview due to personal and professional interaction with "isms" is that of a Mexican American female group leader who has experienced both racism and sexism. From elementary school through college, she has been oppressed in one way or another due to her gender and her race. She has been fortunate to come from a family of individuals strong in their own racial and ethnic identities and united in ensuring her academic success. During group, an African American female shares her experiences of racism and gender. The group leader hears the group member's experiences and validates them as real in a society that struggles with race and gender. She encourages the group to share ways they have experienced oppression, racism, and/or sexism and to identify effective coping strategies.

The second factor is the way in which the world around the group leader responds to her as a multicultural and diverse person and to her culture. To illustrate, when he was a young child, a Chinese American group leader's mother was killed by an African American man. This death created a general sense of distrust and anger toward African American males that the group leader carried into his adult life. His family distrusts African Americans; they believe all African Americans dislike Chinese people; and they encourage the group leader to distance himself from African Americans because they are evil people. He runs a group for male sexual abusers compromising diverse racial and ethnic group members. Because of his past experience with an African American, the group leader experiences strong negative thoughts and feelings about an African American male group member that distorts his ability to accurately analyze worldview.

Another example is a Chinese American group leader who attended high school with African Americans. The group leader discovered that he and his family had several core values similar to those of many African Americans in his high school, such as the importance of family and elders. The group worker was comfortable with African Americans throughout his personal and professional life, and he found African Americans to embrace him and his family. When leading a group that included African Americans, the group leader drew upon his personal experiences and understanding of African American values and used his worldview and experiences with African Americans as tools to engage and validate the African American group member as a result of his ability to more accurately analyze worldview. While it is important for group leaders to analyze their own worldviews, it is equally important for group leaders to analyze the worldviews of group members.

Worldview information provides a framework from which to work and a sense of group dynamics and process. That is, group leaders must consider how cultural, racial, and ethnic differences and similarities may interface during group dynamics and process.

The following are select questions that group leaders might use to initiate a worldview examination from an Afrocentric approach:

What are each group member's desires for group?

What are possible cross-cultural issues that may evidence in group?

What are possible thematic cultural value/belief system differences and similarities that may evidence in group?

What is my personal level of racial identity development?

How will I assess each group member's racial identity development?

What is my personal theory of effective group work with diverse and multicultural populations?

For a worldview assessment to be accurate, group leaders must possess a working understanding of and appreciation for the Afrocentric worldview and value system. Pack-Brown et al. (1998) discussed the Afrocentric worldview and

Table 13.1   Level of Personal Awareness: Values and Life Experiences of African Americans

Rate yourself from 1-4 on each item. Rating scale: 1 = Not true at all for me. 4 = Absolutely true for me.

	Ranking			
	Not True for Me			*Absolutely True for Me*
I am aware of and understand the core Afrocentric value system.	1	2	3	4
I am aware of the major differences between a Eurocentric value system and an Afrocentric value system.	1	2	3	4
I avoid seeing differences.	1	2	3	4
I believe all people are the same, simply because we are all human beings.	1	2	3	4
When I look at an African American, I don't see color, I see the person.	1	2	3	4
I understand the concept of a collectivistic worldview.	1	2	3	4
I believe the individual is the building block of society.	1	2	3	4
I understand the concept of an Afrocentric approach to group work.	1	2	3	4
I use an Afrocentric approach in my work.	1	2	3	4
I have a number of African American friends, associates, and/or colleagues.	1	2	3	4
I understand the concept of racism.	1	2	3	4
I have experienced discrimination.	1	2	3	4
I am a racist.	1	2	3	4
Total Possible Score:	13	26	39	52
Actual Score:				

value system and its application to groups with African American women. They assisted in assessing the worldviews of individual and collective African American group members working to better understand what it means to be an individual and a member of the collective African American community. Table 13.1 provides a tool to help group leaders identify their awareness of common values and life experiences of African Americans. Group leaders may use information obtained from Table 13.1 to tap into their awareness of similarities and differences in the Afrocentric and Eurocentric value systems as they identify treatment modalities for groups with African Americans. Finally, group leaders may increase their awareness of personal biases and stereotypes that affect how they hear and interpret the life experiences of African Americans.

The Afrocentric worldview is collectivistic rather than individualistic. Immediately, group members are taught to identify how their cultural and individual realities affect the issues they bring to group, as well as group process and dynamics. Group leaders help members to see how cultural and individual realities are guided by a set of social standards and codes of conduct that have an African value orientation. Maulana

Table 13.2 An Afrocentric Worldview (Select African-Centered Values and Questions for Group Leaders)

African-Centered Values	Select Questions for Group Leaders Working With African American Group Members
Interconnectedness	How do group members individually and collectively relate to each other from a self-in-relation perspective?
Group	What individual concerns and needs affect other African Americans?
Collectivism	How are interdependence and collective responsibility manifested in group and in the lives of African American members? What spiritual harmony is evidenced relative to nature and other African Americans?
Communication	How is bilingualism expressed by African American group members?
Time	Are African American group members relaxed and spontaneous? Is there an appreciation for the present and how the present affects the past and future?
History	Grounded in the "minority" experience in the U.S.
Power	What is the power of personal existence and God's love? Do group members receive power through God's love within their lives?
Respect	Elders valued, expression of feelings, assertive behavior, family orientation.

Karenga (1997) proposed a set of principles (*Nguzo Saba*) as guides for African Americans to live by. The following is a description of each principle:

Umoja (oo-MOH-jah) means harmony and unity. Encourages striving for unity in family, community, nation, and race.

Kujichagulia (koo-ji-chah-goo-LEE-ah) means self-determination. Encourages self-identity as a people and an individual.

Ujima (oo-JEE-mah) means collective work and responsibility. Encourages collectively building and maintaining the African American community and making the burdens of African American males and females those of the African American people and community.

Ujama (oo-JAH-mah) means cooperative economics. Encourages building and maintaining African American businesses and profiting from those businesses.

Nia (NEE-ah) means purpose and direction. Encourages doing whatever possible to create beauty in the community.

Kuumba (koo-OO-mbah) means creativity. Encourages freedom to become empowered to be creative and identify a new reality for African Americans (individually and collectively).

Imani (ee-MAH-nee) means faith. Encourages belief in African American people, parents, teachers, leaders, righteousness, and the victory of the African American struggle.

Table 13.2 reflects core values of the Afrocentric worldview and suggests questions that group leaders might ask themselves as they identify group treatment modalities appropriate for African American group members. The reader is reminded that no one group is homogeneous and that this table provides a foundation for group leaders to build on as they ascertain the African perspective held by individual and collective African American group members.

A group leader might use these questions to (a) guide individual and group diagnosis of problems or issues and (b) identify treatment modalities more in-line with the African American worldview. Two examples are provided to give insight into how questions may be posed and responded to. The first example is that of a group leader addressing the African-centered value of *interconnectedness*. In trying to determine the problem, the group leader asks the question, "How do group members individually and collectively relate to each other from a self-in-relation perspective?" After reflecting on the group experience, the group leader determines that one African American group member distances herself from other African American group members and actively denies her racial and ethnic heritage. However, the group member brings issues of racism in her work environment and social life to the group. To address this problem, the group leader identifies a treatment intervention to help the group member obtain a healthier racial identity and consciousness. The group leader emphasizes interconnectedness among African American people and the strengths therein related to dealing with "isms." During group, the leader selects a treatment modality that encourages interconnectedness among all group members, particularly among African American group members. A second example is a group leader addressing the value of *power.* In determining how group members address their problems, the group leader asks, "Do group members receive power through God's love within their lives?" Upon reflection of past group sessions, the leader notices that many of the African American group members refer directly or indirectly to the power of God and prayer in solving their problems. The group leader recognizes spirituality as a common African American value and encourages group members to use prayer (power of God) as a treatment intervention, when appropriate, during group.

Afrocentric group leaders work to balance the individual as well as the cognitive, emotional, and behavioral themes of the group. Afrocentric group leaders view mental health as interdependence, place a value on cooperation, help group members identify, appreciate, and empower their collective and individual strengths, and use multiple helping tools (e.g., educate, facilitate, challenge, reward) to achieve balance and empowerment.

Two core values that group leaders adhere to are spirituality and community. These values are critical to effective group work with African Americans. They may be operationalized via implementing exercises and seizing opportunities for group members to experience the power of the "spirit" (a force outside self) and of cooperation within and outside of group. An exercise to

include the power of the "spirit" in group is to have group members listen to spiritual music, such as Yolanda Adams's "Talk to Me." After the song is over, group members are invited to reflect on their individual and collective thoughts and feelings related to the lyrics of the song. Processing questions include the following:

- How does this song speak to your spirit?
- How is the idea of interconnectedness of things reflected in the song? What are the implications for your life as an individual and member of the African American community
- How has the "spirit" shown power in your life?

The second core value, community, may be operationalized by leaders promoting the use of language that reflects a collectivistic approach to life (we, our) rather than an individualistic (I, me) approach. When language emphasizing the extended self (e.g., us) and interdependence (e.g., our) is used, the leader affirms and reinforces the power within. Affirming statements that leaders may offer include the following:

- "I hear you emphasizing interdependence as a core value and that interdependence empowers you and those you love."
- "It sounds as if cooperation and collective responsibility are powerful in your life."
- "There seems to be a communal spirit here and it is reflected in your words 'I am because we are, we are therefore I am.'"

GOALS FOR GROUP LEADERSHIP

Several goals are inherent to the Afrocentric approach to groups when working with African Americans. The following is a select set of goals for group leaders as they work with African American group members:

To facilitate both individual self-esteem and group pride among group members. An example of how to achieve this goal is to help group members enhance their awareness of self as an individual at multiple levels (cognitively, affectively, and physically). At the same time, the group leader helps individual African American group members heighten their awareness of who they are as individuals and as members of the African American community as experienced within a society that struggles with racism.

To empower group members by enhancing their understanding of the interplay of culture, race, and ethnicity on life realities in a society struggling with social and cultural issues.

To engage in ongoing self-assessment by asking, "Through whose lenses am I looking?" as I hear, perceive, and relate to individual and collective African American group members.

To recognize personal values, beliefs, and attitudes about the African Americans in group and the subsequent implications for group leadership. Table 13.2 reflects select values and life experiences that may assist in identifying your level of awareness about the African American community and areas needing personal attention.

To enhance personal and professional knowledge about the African American culture and worldview as it relates to the individual and collective African Americans in group.

To listen for and identify the African American group members' support systems (e.g., church, religion, extended family, social groups, etc.).

To recognize the possibility of needing to change both the individual and the system within which the individual group member is interacting.

To enhance personal awareness and knowledge of African Americans by interacting with African Americans via immersion within the African American community (e.g., attend a church service, participate in a community affair).

To obtain ongoing training in the use of skills that will create a group environment and climate that fosters the growth and maturation of African American group members.

African American members of counseling groups are searching, as are other group members, for life meaning and self-affirmation. However, for African Americans, race is an additional factor that affects this search. While many African Americans are proud of who they are as racial beings, they live in a world that struggles with racial differences. These struggles cut across educational and socioeconomic levels.

Regardless of the amount of education and/or money, as African Americans seek ways in which to live life more successfully and happily, their racial characteristics have an impact. So many African Americans have similar questions and need guidance particularly related to their race and accompanying characteristics. How do I determine what is empowering? In a society that struggles with race and difference, where can I find a place(s) of affirmation?

GROUP ACTIVITIES TO PROMOTE UNDERSTANDING AND ACCEPTANCE OF DIFFERENT WORLDVIEWS

Exercise One: A Communal Collage

One way to help group members to (a) identify their personal and collective worldviews and values and (b) immediately operate as a collective and better understand and experience community is the creation of a group collage. This collage can take on a number of themes, such as unity, purpose, and collective responsibility. A communal collage cut from magazines that reflect African Americans can be particularly effective as it uses helping modalities that embrace the Nguzo Saba (e.g., Umoja, Ujima, and Nia).

The following questions may help with processing:

- What does your contribution to the collage reflect about you as an individual? As a member of your community? As a member of this group?
- What values do you see reflected in the collage?
- What do these values tell you about the group members?
- What impact might these values have on group unity, purpose, and collective work and responsibility?

This exercise is an excellent introduction to group process and dynamics and begins to give a flavor of the differences and similarities of group members and the subsequent impact on group process and dynamics.

Two Group Models

The next section introduces two models for group work with African Americans based on an Afrocentric approach. The first is described in a video that provides theory and practice for using an Afrocentric group approach. The title of the video is *"I Am Because We Are!" Afrocentric Approaches to Group Work* (Pack-Brown & Whittington-Clark, 2002). The second is a text titled *Images of Me: A Guide to Group Work with African American females* (Pack-Brown et al., 1998).

"I Am Because We Are!" An Afrocentric Approach to Group Work: A Training Video

In this video, group leaders work to balance the individual, the group, and the themes of group members as they promote healing and a better quality of life. Specific group mechanisms are being generated for members of diverse racial, ethnic, and cultural backgrounds. Sample mechanisms include drumming and the puzzle exercise. Both techniques offer group members an opportunity to engage in a collectivistic effort, thereby experiencing self-in-relation to others. Both techniques are briefly described below.

Drumming. Group members are instructed to beat a drum (e.g., an African drum). The group leader initiates the drumming process and invites members to join in as each emotionally and psychologically experiences the rhythm and spirit of the moment. Drumming offers group members an opportunity to engage in a collectivistic effort toward unity and responsibility. Via beating of drums, group members gain a deeper understanding and experience of "self" as a member of the collective/group. The beat of the drums promotes a communal spirit that empowers both individual and collective strengths.

Puzzle Exercise. Group members are instructed to collectively complete a puzzle. Members are instructed to observe their own as well as others' physical behaviors as they put the puzzle together. In addition, group leaders and members are instructed to attend to their emotional and spiritual experiences as they complete the exercise. Upon completion, group members and leaders are instructed to reflect on the puzzle experience and discuss implications for (a) themselves as individuals as well as members of the group and (b) group process.

Images of Me: A Guide to Group Work With African American Females

The book *Images of Me: A Guide to Group Work With African American Females* (Pack-Brown et al., 1998) reflects individual and collective self-images that group members hold of Black women, as well as images of Black women in society and the communities in which they live and work. Group leaders assist Black women in giving their lives direction and pose this quest for meaning and purpose within the Afrocentric principle of Nia. Group leaders focus on the individual and cultural actions and subsequent consequences of these actions in a society that does not fully understand or appreciate the racial and gender dimensions of Black womanhood. For example, many Black women are perceived by society as aggressive and "in your face." A statement reflective of this perception is "Black women say what they think and say what they feel." Inherent to this perception are cultural and individual values and actions. To illustrate, emotional vitality is a value held in high esteem by African Americans (Pack-Brown et al., 1998; Parham, 1993; Sue & Sue, 1999). A value held in high esteem by women is the expression of emotions (Pack-Brown et al., 1998). Combined, culturally and in terms of gender, an African American woman may experience and interpret life affectively (with emotion). A physical behavior that may reflect this experience is to directly and with intensity say what you think and feel. Numerous Black women in *Images of Me* groups voiced at least one experience of being perceived as aggressive and "in your face." Group leaders were challenged to promote an understanding of and appreciation for the interplay of individual and cultural values for African Americans and African American women. Several interventions were found effective within *Images of Me* groups. One intervention was educating group members about cultural and gender values.

Another intervention was role-playing how different cultural values (e.g., control of emotions and expression of emotions) may be perceived and interpreted within a cultural context. Of significance was reminding group members that what may be perceived as normal in one culture (e.g., expression of emotions with intensity) may be interpreted as abnormal (out of control) in another culture.

Group members were empowered and unified via Afrocentric principles of Umoja (harmony and unity) and Kujichagulia (self-determination). Group leaders promoted Imani (faith) in the cultural values held by Black women with an African heritage. Leaders help group members self-identify (Kujichagulia) and draw strength from collective work and responsibility (Ujima) (Franklin & Pack-Brown, 2001).

One question woven throughout the fabric of *Images of Me* groups that affects strength and collective work and responsibility is: "Am I crazy, or is this what's happening?" Group members directly or indirectly express feeling out of touch with reality. Personal and cultural affirmation and recognition are factors in this confusion that affect strength and collective work and responsibility. African American group members are particularly affected by race and culture as they work individually and collectively within the group context, so an emphasis may be placed on how tenets of the African American culture and worldview play out while living in a world guided by tenets of a different culture and worldview. To illustrate, an African American professor (Binta) shares thoughts in a faculty meeting about her program's direction. She is passionate, direct, and descriptive; yet no one recognizes her. Within 2 minutes, a White male colleague (John) shares a proposal in almost the same words as Binta's. The group dialogues with John, and Binta asks herself, "Am I crazy or is this what's happening?" She chooses not to address her confusion in the meeting. Instead, Binta shares with a friend to check reality and ensure that she is not merely reading something into what happened, such as race or gender bias. After dialoguing with her friend, they conclude that Binta's experience was real and had undertones of racial and gender bias.

Conclusions

Group leaders working with African Americans must begin the group process with a philosophy viewing the African way of being as positive and healthy. This permits African Americans to lay a firm foundation for success and places them on the road toward holistically embracing who they are, individually and collectively. Karenga (1997) suggests that as African Americans embrace themselves, they revisit their African roots and use the past as a firm foundation to assist them in constructing their future. To do this, group leaders striving to effectively provide group work to African Americans engage as follows:

1. Are initially challenged to understand within-group similarities and differences and how these similarities and differences affect mental health from an African American psychological and emotional perspective.

2. Are challenged to understand, in addition to being male in general, the perceptions and past experiences of counseling and the subsequent impact thereof on mental health from an African American male psychological and emotional perspective.

3. Are challenged to understand, in addition to issues of women in general, the burden of being Black and female in a racist and sexist society and images (personal, collective, and societal) of Black womanhood and femininity and the subsequent impact thereof on mental health from an African American female psychological and emotional perspective.

The transition from theory to practice cannot be attained simply by reading about applications; therefore, we made an effort to present the material in such a way that it explicitly encourages your active involvement. We entreat you to formulate your own ideas as you read the material presented, because it is self-discovery that narrows the gap between cultural inattentiveness and cultural competency. As you embark on your journey toward cultural competency, approach each challenge as an opportunity to pioneer into relatively uncharted territory. It is our hope that your adventure will be an interesting and exciting one for you and a rewarding, affirming one for your African American group participants. Please find a tool in the Appendix at the end of this chapter titled "Group Counseling Competencies for Working With African American Group Members (A Preliminary Framework)." This tool is designed to help group leaders identify areas of competence in working with African Americans. This framework is a modified version of the Association for Multicultural Counseling and Development *Multicultural Competencies* (1996). It is designed to capture the essence of the ideas discussed in this chapter on group work with African Americans.

REFERENCES

Arredondo, P., Toporek, R., Brown, S. P., Jones, J., Locke, D. C., Sanchez, J., & Stadler, H. (1996). Operationalization of the multicultural counseling competencies. *Journal of Multicultural Counseling & Development, 25,* 42-78.

Association for Multicultural Counseling and Development (1996). *Multicultural competencies.* Alexandria, VA: American Counseling Association.

Association for Specialists in Group Work (ASGW). (1999). Association for Specialists in Group Work principles for diversity-competent group workers. *Journal for Specialists in Group Work, 24,* 7-14.

Corey, G., Corey, M., & Callanan, P. (1998). *Issues and ethics in the helping professions.* (5th ed.). Pacific Grove, CA: Brooks/Cole.

Cross, W. E. (1971). The Negro-to-Black conversion experience: Toward a psychology of black liberation. *Black World, 20*(9), 13-27.

Franklin, R., & Pack-Brown, S. P. (2001). TEAM BROTHERS: An Afrocentric approach to group work with African American male adolescents. *Journal for Specialists in Group Work, 26,* 237-245.

Hargrow, A. M. (2001). Racial identity development: The case of Mr. X, an African American. *Journal of Mental Health Counseling, 23,* 222-238.

Helms, J. E. (1984). Toward a theoretical explanation of the effects of race on counseling: A Black and White model. *The Counseling Psychologist, 12,* 153-165.

Helms, J. E., & Cook, D. A. (1999). *Using race and culture in counseling and psychotherapy: Theory and process.* Needham Heights, MA: Allyn & Bacon.

Hill, O. W., Block, R. A., & Buggie, S. E. (2000). Culture and beliefs about time: Comparisons among Black Americans, Black Africans, and White Americans. *The Journal of Psychology, 134*(4), 443-462.

Jordan, J. M. (1991). Counseling African-American women: Sister-friends. In C. Lee & B. Richardson (Eds.), *Multicultural issues in counseling: New approaches to diversity* (pp. 49-63). Alexandria, VA: American Association for Counseling and Development.

Karenga, M. (1997). *Kwanzaa philosophy.* Retrieved from www.itskwanzaatime.com/meaning.html.

Pack-Brown, S. P., & Whittington-Clark, L. E. (2002). *"I am because we are!" Afrocentric approaches to group work (A diversity competent model).* Farmingham, MA: Microtraining Associates. (www.emicrotraining.com)

Pack-Brown, S. P., Whittington-Clark, L. E., & Parker, W. M. (1998). *Images of me: A guide to group work with African-American women.* Needham, MA: Allyn & Bacon.

Parham, T. A. (1993). *Psychological storms: The African-American struggle for identity.* Chicago: African-American Images.

Sue, D. W., & Sue, D. (1999*). Counseling the culturally different: Theory and practice.* (3rd ed.). New York: John Wiley.

Appendix: Group Counseling Competencies for Working With African American Group Members (A Preliminary Framework)

Diversity-Competent Awareness:

As a diversity competent group leader working with African American group members, I . . .	Competencies	Ranking	Not at All	Very Much
1. Am aware of the way in which my cultural background, experiences, attitudes, value and biases influence my group work with African American group members.	1	2	3	4
2. Have moved from being unaware of the African American worldview and common life experiences to being aware of the African American worldview and common life experiences.	1	2	3	4
3. Am comfortable with differences that exist between myself and African American group members in terms of race, culture, beliefs, values, and communication styles.	1	2	3	4
4. Believe in the value of African American psychological perspective.	1	2	3	4
5. Believe that cultural differences can enhance group process and dynamics.	1	2	3	4
6. Am aware of my stereotypes and preconceived notions about African Americans and subsequent influence these may have on my ability to effectively facilitate maturation of African American group members.	1	2	3	4
7. Am knowledgeable about communication style differences between me and African Americans and how these differences may clash with or foster the group process and dynamics.	1	2	3	4

Diversity-Competent Knowledge:

As a diversity-competent group leader working with African American group members, I . . .				
1. Have familiarized myself with relevant research and latest findings regarding group work with African Americans.	1	2	3	4
2. Possess specific knowledge of African American cultural values, life experiences, and worldviews.	1	2	3	4
3. Understand the principles of the Nguzo Saba and how they apply to individual and collective African Americans.	1	2	3	4
4. Understand the potential impact of spirituality and the extended self on African American group members.	1	2	3	4
5. Understand the idea of mental health emerging from an African-centered worldview.				
6. Know the potential consequences of using a Eurocentric group approach when working with African Americans.	1	2	3	4
7. Understand the importance of knowing the African American group member as an individual and a member of the African American community.	1	2	3	4
8. Understand within-group differences among African				

American group members and subsequent
impact on group work.

Diversity-Competent Skills:

As a diversity competent group leader working with African American group members, I . . .	*Competencies*	*Ranking*	*Not at All*	*Very Much*
1. Have the ability to differentiate between African American group members who espouse Afrocentric worldviews and Eurocentric worldviews.	1	2	3	4
2. Have the ability to use cultural knowledge and sensitivity for appropriate group diagnosis and treatment planning, particularly when working with African American group members.	1	2	3	4
3. Have the ability to interpret the ACA *Code of Ethics* and ASGW *Guidelines for Best Practice* within the African American cultural context.	1	2	3	4
4. Am aware of some institutional and/or agency barriers that may inhibit African Americans from partaking of group counseling services.	1	2	3	4
5. Have training and experience in using an Afrocentric approach to group work.	1	2	3	4
6. Have participated in African American cultural and social events, such as attending church, community events, etc.	1	2	3	4
7. Take responsibility for collaborating with African American leaders, mental health professionals, and others who know and understand the African American worldview and have life experience about unique knowledge and skills for the benefit of African American group members.	1	2	3	4

14

GROUP COUNSELING WITH ASIANS

RITA CHI-YING CHUNG

George Mason University

The Asian American population is one of the fastest-growing ethnic groups in the United States. At present, this group represents 4.1% of the total U.S. population (U.S. Bureau of Census, 1996). It is projected that by 2030, Asians will increase to 7.0% and that by 2050, this population will exceed 32 million (9.3%) of the total U.S. population, a 245.2% increase from 1999. With the growth of the Asian American population, there is an increasing likelihood that counselors will encounter Asian clients.

It is important to keep in mind that Asian Americans come from collectivistic cultures that value interconnectedness with family and community. It is particularly relevant to emphasize the therapeutic factors of universality, altruism, the corrective recapitulation of the primary family group, and development of socializing techniques identified by Yalom (1995), as well as love, as identified by Bemak and Epp (1996). Therefore, group work may be an appropriate and effective mental health intervention for this population.

Asian Americans are one of the most diverse groups in the United States, consisting of more than 40 groups (Sandhu, 1997). To work effectively with Asian Americans as individuals in groups, it is critical that group counselors be aware of, understand, and acknowledge the diversity between and within the Asian American population. The main groups within this category are Chinese, Japanese, Koreans, Filipinos, Vietnamese, Cambodians, and Laotians. In addition, understanding and appreciation of the different historical, sociopolitical, and cultural values of each group and how these factors affect mental health and behavior is imperative. Although there is extensive literature on Asian Americans and mental health issues in general, literature regarding Asian Americans in group counseling is lacking. Therefore, this chapter will begin with an overview and a brief discussion of cultural values. A discussion of the major issues and challenges in working with Asian Americans in groups will be presented, followed by recommendations and strategies.

GENERAL CONSIDERATIONS ABOUT ASIAN AMERICANS

Intergroup Differences

Given the heterogeneity of Asian Americans, it is critical for counselors not to assume that all Asians are the same. Each group has its own distinct historical and sociopolitical backgrounds, languages, identity issues, cultures, and challenges encountered in the mainstream society (Lee, 1998; Uba, 1994). For example, unique to Japanese Americans is the intergenerational effect of the World War II internment trauma (Ina, 1997; Nagata, 1998). Interned Japanese Americans present very different issues and dynamics in a group compared with Chinese Americans, whose ancestors migrated to the United States to become laborers and never faced internment. Another example can be seen with Southeast Asian refugees who first arrived in the United States after the fall of Saigon in 1975. This group is at risk for experiencing serious psychological problems due to their pre-migration trauma experiences (e.g., Chung, 2001; Chung, Bemak, & Okazaki, 1997; Chung & Kagawa-Singer, 1993; Kinzie, Frederickson, Ben, Fleck, & Karls, 1984; Mollica, Wyshak, & Lavelle, 1987). In a group environment, they would present very differently from Filipino Americans, who may have voluntarily migrated to the United States to pursue a better quality of life and not faced the hardship of war or pre-migration trauma.

Furthermore, Asian Americans have often been stereotyped as the "model minority," with low rates of crime, delinquency, and poverty and high academic and career achievement (Hsia & Peng, 1998). However, the model minority myth is not totally accurate (Root, 1997). Although many Asians have achieved high academic performance, this is not the case for all Asian American groups. While many Chinese, Japanese, and Korean students may be succeeding academically, the same is not true for Cambodian, Filipino, Laotian, and Hmong students (Hsia & Peng, 1998; Root, 1997). Furthermore, Chung, Walkey, and Bemak (1997) found that although Chinese students had achieved high levels of academic performance, they also reported low self-esteem. This suggests that academic achievement should not be the sole measure of psychological well-being.

Asian Americans have also been reported to have low rates of poverty and welfare dependency, yet it has been found that Southeast Asian refugees are the highest ethnic group in the United States to be welfare dependent (Chung & Bemak, 1996; Ong, 1993). Crime and delinquency rates among Asian Americans have also been reported to be low; however, in the past years, there has been national attention on the increase of Asian youth gang activities (Dao, 1992). Furthermore, in the last decade, there has been an increase in Asian runaways associated with an increase in gang membership (Louie, Joe, Lu, & Tong, 1991).

Intergroup Conflict

Group counselors also need to be aware of potential intergroup conflicts between Asian groups. For example, the author was asked to consult in a school situation where a teacher assumed she was displaying cultural sensitivity by placing Chinese and Japanese students together to work on a class project. The teacher was confused when the students refused to work together. Given the sociopolitical and historical background between China and Japan, this was not surprising. The Japanese attacks on China during World War II have had an intergenerational impact and may result in tension between Chinese and Japanese students. Another example is the sometimes strained relationship between Chinese and Vietnamese or Koreans and Japanese, again due to historical and sociopolitical backgrounds between these countries. Therefore, placing all Asians together does not display cultural sensitivity and eliminate cultural differences, but instead has the potential to create tension that affects group dynamics. Examples of challenges in working with groups that comprise individuals from different Asian groups are discussed in Chung (in press).

Intragroup Differences

Although it is important to acknowledge intergroup differences, it is just as important to understand intragroup differences within Asian cultural groups. Southeast Asian refugees in the United States, for example, consist of five main groups. There are similarities among each of the groups because they are refugees from the same geographical region with similar cultural and religious values. However, they differ in their premigration and postmigration experiences. For example, the first wave of Southeast Asian refugees tended to experience fewer adjustment problems in the United States compared with subsequent waves of refugees, due to the differences in education, English proficiency, and premigration trauma experiences (Chung & Okazaki, 1991). Differences are also found within the subsequent waves of Southeast Asian refugees (Chung & Kagawa-Singer, 1993). For example, the Cambodians experienced the genocide orchestrated by the Pol Pot regime, in which it has been estimated that 1 to 3 million of Cambodia's 7 million died (Chung, 2001), while Vietnamese boat people encountered brutal attacks by Thai pirates, in which it has been estimated that 77% of the boats were attacked and more than 50% of the boat people were subjected to severe violence, rape, and sexual abuse (Chung & Okazaki, 1991).

There are also gender differences in postmigration adjustment between and within the Southeast Asian groups (Chung & Bemak, 2002; Chung, Bemak, & Kagawa-Singer, 1998). In general, Southeast Asian refugee women experienced more psychological distress than their male counterparts. Gender differences were found within and between groups in the predictors of stress. For example, for Vietnamese women, the predictors of distress were that someone else had made the decision to leave Vietnam and fewer years in the United States. For Vietnamese men, the predictors of distress were large family size in the United States and multiple premigration traumatic experiences. In further contrast, the distress predictor for Cambodian women was their personal decision to leave Cambodia, while for the Cambodian men it was a greater number of years spent in a refugee camp. Differences have also been found within the Chinese American population in terms of their home countries and how they identify themselves. For example, due to the sociopolitical and historical background of China and Taiwan, group counselors may offend their Chinese clients and risk premature termination by assuming that they are from mainland China when they are in fact from Taiwan.

CULTURAL CONSIDERATIONS FOR ASIAN AMERICANS IN GROUP WORK

Cultural Values

Although there are marked cultural differences among the 40 Asian groups, there are also many shared similarities. This section will discuss cultural values that can be generalized across Asian cultures. It is important to note that differences among Asian cultures are too vast and complex to present in this paper.

Collectivistic vs. Individualistic. In general, the Asian populations come from collectivistic cultures that emphasize family, community, and interdependent relationships. Priority is given to collective goals over personal goals so as to maintain harmony with their in-groups. For Asians, *in-group* refers to the extended family and community. In contrast, individualistic cultures, such as the United States and other Western cultures, focus on individualism, independence, competitiveness, personal goals over group goals, feelings of distinction from their social networks, the acceptance of confrontation with in-groups, and defining oneself independently from the in-group to which they belong (Markus & Kitayama, 1991; Rhee, Uleman, & Lee, 1996; Yamaguchi, Kuhlman, & Sugimori, 1995). Members of a collectivistic culture are more likely to describe themselves in social and collective terms compared with individualistic members who describe themselves independently from others using a variety of abstract terms (Triandis, 1989).

Loss of Face. Asians have been found to have a greater tendency to be highly sensitive to rejection and embarrassment and are stronger self-monitors compared with White Americans (Gudykunst, Gao, & Franklyn-Stokes, 1996; Triandis, 1989; Yamaguchi et al., 1995). Asians are very concerned with "face" and use shame as a mechanism for social control. According to Yeh and Huang (1996), "Face includes the positive image, interpretation, or social attributes that one claims for oneself or perceives others to have accorded one. If one does not fulfill expectations of the self, then one loses face" (p. 651).

The shame associated with losing face is strongly felt not only by the individual but also by the collective to which the individual belongs. Therefore, the prospect of losing face means loss of support and threat of ostracism from one's in-group. For this reason, individuals with strong concerns about face are more likely to conform to interpersonal expectations and to threaten others and themselves with shame to influence others' and their own behaviors (Shon & Ja, 1982). Therefore, Asians have developed intricate and very subtle ways of communicating with each other as a means of allowing all parties involved to maintain face. If one does not fulfill expectations of the self, then one loses face (Yeh & Huang, 1996). It is thus important to keep saving face in mind when doing group work. For example, a school counselor facilitating a group would not directly point out that an Asian member is failing in a course, but instead would discuss assignments, study habits, and homework.

Family Structure and Filial Piety. Family interactions are governed by prescribed roles defined by family hierarchy, obligation, and duties. Independent behavior or expressions of emotions that might disrupt familial harmony are discouraged. The family is patriarchal; males, particularly the father and eldest son, have dominant roles. Spousal relationships are secondary to the parent-child relationship. Filial piety, or responsibility to family, is a major Asian cultural value that involves many obligations. Especially important is the obligation and duty that children have for their parents. Parents expect to be taken care of by their children in their old age and never experience the "empty nest" syndrome (Lin, 1985; Osako & Lui, 1986). For American parents, the emphasis is on what parents should do for their children, whereas for Asians, the emphasis is on what children should do for their parents (Hsu, 1973). Grandparents and other extended family members also significantly influence family life. Old age for Asians is a sign of status and symbolizes honor, authority, respect, and custodians of the cultural heritage (Cheung, Cho, Luan, Tang, & Yan, 1980; Lum, Cheung, Cho, Tang, & Yau 1980; Nagasawa, 1980). These traditional values regarding family

are essential to understand within the context of groups.

As Asian families become more acculturated in the United States, there is a shift from the traditional family structure of extended family to a more nuclear family, where functional relations apply instead of household structure (Lee, 1997). The traditional patriarchal family may be transformed to a diarchal system, where a mother shares decision making with the father. Successful child rearing is measured mostly by the children's academic and career achievements, and family earning power is no longer solely the father's, but is shared with other adult family members (Lee, 1997).

Help-Seeking Behavior

Sue and Sue (1985) reported that Asian American parents tend to promote emotional self-reliance and restraint and view seeking outside help as being weak and dependent. Strong emotional expression has been discouraged because it is seen as a threat to the order and unity of the family and community. Therefore, disclosing of personal problems and displaying emotions openly brings stigma and shame to family members and community (Ho, 1984). Many Asian American college students report that they turn to family members, such as parents and siblings, for help (Atkinson, Whiteley, & Gim, 1990) or practice "self-reliance." Furthermore, mental health problems are seen as a genetic disorder and therefore affect the entire family, past and future generations. Distress is often described in terms of physical complaints through somatization (Cheung, 1989; Chung & Kagawa-Singer, 1995), hence the preference for discussing academic or career-related problems rather than personal problems (Gim, Atkinson, & Whiteley, 1991).

Acculturation

Acculturation, the process and the degree to which individuals adopt mainstream society's values and behaviors (Berry, 1980), should be considered in group work with Asian clients. Studies have found a relationship between acculturation and psychological problems

(Padilla, Wagatsuma, & Lindholm, 1985; Sodowsky & Carey, 1988). Berry's (1980, 1983) model of acculturation suggests that an integration of the individual's traditional culture and that of the mainstream society leads to a healthy person. The acculturation process differs among Asian Americans depending on whether they are foreign born or U.S. born, as well as the number of generations living in the United States. Level of acculturation has an impact on the effectiveness of therapeutic techniques. It has been found that Asian Americans who are highly acculturated tend to have more positive attitudes toward seeking professional psychological help and group counseling (Leong, Wagner, & Kim, 1995).

Racial/Ethnic Identity

It is also important for group leaders to be aware of the racial/ethnic identity of members. Racial identity theory provides an understanding of the developmental process of coping with societal racism and developing a healthy self-conception within a racial heterogeneous society (Helms, 1995). Each identity status is characterized by unique affective, cognitive, and behavioral reactions to race and racism. Individuals can develop more than one status and be in multiple statuses (Helms, 1995).

Knowledge and understanding of racial/ethnic identity is a valuable asset in multiethnic groups in assisting the group toward positive interethnic group relations and tolerance for diversity. Group leaders must be willing to work through differences with members and serve as role models in the exploration and acceptance of ethnic and cultural differences. Group leaders must model openness to cultural and ethnic differences and the willingness to integrate a variety of cultural experiences in the group process. This modeling prevents the group from polarizing along racial or cultural lines. For example, an Asian member may be in the immersion/emersion status and therefore may value everything that is Asian, while denigrating other cultures. It is critical that group counselors be aware of and understand the Asian member's racial identity status and work within that framework to help that person come to terms with resentment and anger toward other cultures. For further information on racial and ethnic identity, please refer to the chapter (19) by D'Andrea in this volume.

MAJOR CHALLENGES IN GROUP WORK WITH ASIANS

Group Goals and Culture

Corey (2000) listed the goals of group counseling as follows:

> a) to become more sensitive to the needs and feelings of others; b) to learn to confront others with care, concern, honesty, and directness; c) to achieve self-knowledge and the development of a unique sense of identity; d) to live by one's own expectations; and e) to increase self-direction, autonomy, and responsibility toward oneself and others. (pp. 7-8)

These goals are based on Western cultural perspectives and may not always apply to diverse group members. Asian culture, in general, tends to emphasize groups rather than individuals. Therefore, Asian clients may benefit more from group than individual counseling. However, in the emphasis of traditional group counseling upon verbalization and confrontation of internal and interpersonal conflict, individuation and autonomy may cause anxiety and confusion in Asian clients (Leong, 1992; Sue, 1996).

A goal of Western group counseling is to build a sense of trust and openness so that individual members feel safe to explore feelings and thoughts (Corey, 1995). In contrast, Asian culture emphasizes humility and modesty, such that openly expressing feelings and possibly drawing attention to oneself may be contradictory to cultural values and may create anxiety (Sue & Morishima, 1982; Uba, 1994). Many Asian Americans are uncomfortable with more direct types of communication, especially challenge, confrontation, interruption, and assertiveness (Chu & Sue, 1984). Thus, the emphasis on honest communication may not be applicable for many Asian clients. Traditional group skills and interventions need to be redefined, modified, and reformulated.

Personality and Culture

Many Asian group members remain quiet and withdrawn, even when language proficiency is not an issue. They may be too polite to participate, avoid self-disclosure with polite nods or smiles, or attempt to focus upon the trivial as a way of participating without violating cultural norms. Group members and leaders may become frustrated by the failure of initial attempts to engage Asian members and may make erroneous assumptions based on Asian stereotypes. Simultaneously, Asian members may be perceived as sitting pleasantly through session after session, hiding frustration and perhaps anger about feeling alienated from the group.

Alternatively, the Asian member may become extraordinarily verbose, talking superficially with little reference to the therapeutic work of the group. Such members may be viewed as monopolizing, unsophisticated, and obstructionistic (Tsui & Schultz, 1988). Instead of patiently listening, the group leader may attempt to set limits with such clients, redirect or restructure their comments, or interpret them in such a way that they will fit in with the current focus of the group. Rather, a leader's goal should be culturally sensitive interventions aimed at appropriately addressing this behavior within the context of the group. Furthermore, group counselors must be aware that if Asian clients appear to be overly pessimistic, this is a cultural phenomena and not a display of negativity or pathology (Chang, 2002).

The Mysterious Member Syndrome. Given these group dynamics, Asian members may increasingly feel alienated and out of place, resulting in withdrawal and silence. Group members may react by projecting unwanted qualities upon this "mysterious" group member. Generalized frustration with non-Asian members may turn into displaced anger directed at silent Asian clients. Given the Asian's courteous, nonconfrontative demeanor compounded by the "mysterious member syndrome," Asian members may become scapegoats. If the group leader is unaware of this process and ignores the event, it may result in negative group experiences for Asian clients and a continuation of an image of Asian members as helpless, unemotional, dysfunctional, mysterious, and unreachable. Once again, a culturally sensitive

assessment for the context of the behavior and a culturally appropriate intervention illuminating cultural differences, styles, and tolerance within the group setting are recommended.

Unconscious Racism in Group Dynamics. The issues of power relations, that is, in-group versus out-group, majority versus minority, and the struggle of inclusion, are inevitable in a multiethnic group. The members' attitudes and behaviors toward each other are a reflection of race relations in the United States. Hence, group dynamics may consist of stereotyping, scapegoating, displacement, intellectualizing, intolerance of differences, and, ultimately, polarization of the group along cultural and racial lines (Tsui & Schultz, 1988). The group may become polarized with the members divided into different camps, resulting in unconscious racism. This situation may be harmful in that group members consciously and unconsciously respond in a racial manner toward each other. They may use overt or covert racial jokes, mimic the Asian members' accents, speak and overprotect Asian members, bully Asian members through inaccurate interpretations, attribute nonexistent thoughts and feelings to Asian members, and/or alienate Asian members from the rest of the group. It is crucial that group leaders honestly identify these issues within the group and assist in facilitating their resolution.

Expectations of the Group Leader(s)

For Asian clients, the group leader is seen as an authority figure, an adviser, a teacher, an information giver, and a problem solver. This perception is not necessarily negative. Instead, it represents the group leader as an expert with credability, solid professional qualification, and/or leadership qualities, such as maturity, sophistication, calmness, insight, knowledge, wisdom, and the skill to provide clients with direction and guidance (Tsui & Schultz, 1988). These values cannot be ignored in group dynamics (Yamaguchi, 1986). It may be difficult for Asian clients to relate to the group leader as a facilitator of the group process rather than as an authority figure who will behave in a parental fashion. Given the importance of the role of group leaders, their permissiveness may enable clients to accept their own imperfections. It has been found that Asian clients were frequently more comfortable disclosing personal information in groups than in individual counseling sessions (Yamaguchi, 1986). Subsequently, it is important that group leaders are mindful that promoting clients' premature disclosure, comments on group process, or requests to provide feedback to other members about delicate issues may be perceived by Asians as demands related to the group leader's power and privileges.

SUGGESTIONS FOR EFFECTIVE IMPLEMENTATION OF GROUP WORK WITH ASIAN AMERICANS

Community Resources

To gain knowledge and understanding of the complexities and dynamics of the Asian American population, group leaders should use community leaders and members as resources. Community leaders and members can be critical in educating group leaders about cultural values, communication styles, and general issues affecting Asians clients' participation in group. Community leaders and members can also act as a cultural bridge in understanding hesitation displayed by Asian group members in participating and disclosing in group, as well as assisting group leaders in developing culturally sensitive communication and skills in working with Asian clients.

When are Homogenous Groups Most Effective?

Although culturally homogeneous specific groups are perceived as having less conflict, being more cohesive and better attending, and providing more support and more rapid relief of symptoms than are multiethnic heterogeneous groups (Merta, 1995), there are concerns that homogeneous groups may be at risk for being more superficial and less creative and productive (Johnson & Johnson, 1994; Yalom, 1995). Research has found that members of certain

racial/ethnic groups, Asian Americans being one such group, benefit more from ethnically homogeneous groups (Fukuyama & Coleman, 1992; Lee, 1988; Kinzie, Leung, Bui, & Ben, 1988; Sue, 1996). It is erroneous, however, to assume that for Asians, a homogeneous group will eliminate conflict and cultural biases. Given the long-standing sociopolitical history of these groups, problems can arise in placing different Asian groups together, such as the example mentioned previously regarding historical tension between Chinese and Japanese students.

Thus, because of the heterogeneity within Asian cultures, it is important to initially acknowledge inter- and intragroup differences that may have some bearing on group dynamics. This may mean that in early stages of Asian groups, there is a psychoeducational component focusing on historical and sociopolitical differences, which can then evolve into a therapeutic mode. Topics in early developmental stages of psychoeducational groups might include inter- and intragroup differences, historical and sociopolitical issues of various Asian populations as represented in the group, information regarding migration, generation and acculturation levels, and reports of racism and discrimination and crimes against Asian populations.

Furthermore, Asian homogeneous groups with mixed genders could also be problematic because Asian culture is male oriented. In some traditional Asian cultures, men do most of the talking, and women are not encouraged to speak unless given permission by men. Women often defer to men, suggesting that men and women should be divided into two separate groups to promote female participation (Kinzie et al., 1988). Respect for age is also a factor influencing homogeneous Asian group interactions. Older members tend to have greater authority than younger members and often talk more and dominate the activities (Kinzie et al., 1988).

Considerations on Level of Acculturation

Acculturation is a major factor that needs to be considered. For example, a homogeneous group may consist of all Chinese clients. It is essential that group leaders working with Asian group members are aware and understand the complexity of acculturation (Berry, 1980). The group leader should ascertain whether group members are foreign born versus American born and/or how they identify themselves. For example, do they characterize themselves as Chinese or Chinese American? These acculturative differences are essential to understand when working with what may appear to be a homogeneous group. Those who have just arrived in the country may still hold strong traditional Asian values compared with those who may be foreign born but have lived most of their lives in the United States. Thus, an all-Chinese group may comprise individuals who identify themselves as Chinese American, Taiwanese, Malaysian Chinese, or as being from mainland China, each with different levels of acculturation and perceptions about their Chinese peers in the group, resulting in profound differences among group members despite similar Chinese backgrounds.

For Asians, similar to other immigrant groups, there are significant psychological struggles involved in the acculturation process and issues arising from pressure to either acculturate or to maintain traditional values. Studies have suggested that Asians who have high levels of acculturation are more open to group counseling than are their counterparts who have low or no levels of acculturation (Chu & Sue, 1984; Leong, 1992). Group leaders can assess the level of acculturation and adapt their leadership styles by asking a series of questions, such as whether members speak English as a second language; whether they speak an Asian language and how often they speak it; whether their friends are Asians; their preferences of music and food, and so on. These questions are based on the Suinn-Lew acculturation measure for Asian Americans (Suinn, Rickard-Figueroa, Lew, & Vigil, 1987). However, a word of caution: The Suinn-Lew measure is a unidimensional measure and by no means provides a complete assessment picture, necessitating further in-depth examination of acculturation. Given the importance of acculturation, it is essential that group counselors assess acculturation levels of individual Asian members and avoid making the mistake of assuming that all Asian group members are at the same level.

Consideration of the Structure and Format of the Group

An important step in the beginning of the first group session is the acknowledgement of the different ethnic and cultural backgrounds of the group leader and members. This is less important in psychoeducational groups given the emphasis on information and education and a more clearly defined role of the group facilitator. By acknowledging ethnic and cultural differences, leader and members validate the unique life experience arising from the interplay between ethnic clients' cultural heritages and challenges, such as a person of color living in a White-majority society. This step must be taken to prevent the group from treating ethnic and cultural differences as irrelevant and therefore avoiding talking about sensitive race issues. However, group counselors must take care not to rely on Asian clients to answer all questions regarding their culture or make them the spokespeople for their entire ethnic group. Treating Asian American clients as cultural representatives devalues their own unique life experiences.

Given the stereotype of Asians as not disclosing personal feelings, it is critical that group leaders acknowledge that Asian members make significant contributions to the group. To encourage group cohesiveness and exploration of ethnic differences, group leaders may focus on the universality of personal problems and emotional reactions to these problems, such as reactions to loss, separation, and family conflict. When the Asian client's behavior becomes "problematic," for example, silent, withdrawn, or argumentative, group leaders need to be cognizant of cultural influences. However, they must do what they normally do with any other clients, that is, facilitate the group's endeavors to understand, interpret, and confront the phenomenon. Working with Asian group members to explore and reflect on how their cultural values influence their behavior is important in the therapeutic process.

Considerations for Culturally Responsive Interventions Within the Group

Group leaders should become neither overprotective of the Asian client nor overly confrontational. Unnecessary protection of an Asian client can cause reactivation of group members' stereotypes of Asian clients, for instance, as helpless, fragile, and inarticulate. Such behavior encourages other group members to treat the overprotected clients in the same manner or to ignore and devalue them. Excessive confrontation can result when the group leader becomes anxious, frustrated, or unable to draw the client into the group or establish any meaningful participation. At times, group leaders who may think they are culturally responsive to Asian clients may be patronizing. For example, a group counselor who continually tells the group that it is acceptable for an Asian member to remain silent because she comes from a reserved culture may be overly protective and patronizing.

Although seeking collective help is part of Asian culture, specific group counseling techniques, as discussed previously, are foreign to Asian clients. It is important for group leaders to discuss the goals and the process of group counseling. Having an open discussion about expectations of the group eliminates potential problems and dynamics arising from misunderstandings and generates a set of group norms that is, by and large, constant with the varying cultural and ethnic backgrounds and personal expectations of the group. The role of the group leader is to educate group members as to the purpose of the group, expected behavior, and the nature of members' relationships to the group leader and other group members. This type of education and norm setting is best addressed in the first group session and may be periodically revisited and explored as the therapeutic process evolves.

Racial/Ethnic Identity of Group Leaders

It is important for group leaders to be aware of their own and their members' racial/ethnic identities and how racial/ethnic identity affects the group dynamics and process. Thus, group leaders must undergo an in-depth analysis of their own racial/ethnic identities, honestly examining personal prejudices, stereotypes, and biases. This calls for an assessment of their socialization and conditioning with regard to their attitudes, beliefs, perceptions, prejudices, biases, and stereotypes of other racial or ethnic groups. They must be aware of, understand, acknowledge, and accept issues of racism, discrimination, and oppression, as well as the concept of White privilege. To be effective, group leaders must be able to identify stages of White/Racial identity and the relationship to themselves and group members (Helms, 1995). This requires that group leaders be able to identify and be aware of countertransference issues (Bemak & Epp, 2002). For example, female group leaders may face problems with Asian men who come from male-dominated cultures, requiring that they address their own feelings about men. In turn, Asian men may be conflicted and uncomfortable with having a woman in a leadership position. If these issues are not understood and addressed, group interaction may be inhibited. The D'Andrea chapter in this volume also discusses the impact of group leader and member racial identity development on group process.

Considerations for the Role of the Group Leader

To be effective with this population, the role of group leader may require modification. The group counselor may need to be in the role of an expert, educator, problem solver, information giver, analyzer, as well as provide suggestions and initiate alternatives. In a psychoeducational group in which the group leader is in a role of a teacher and information giver, the role of the Asian member is clearly defined and in-line with cultural norms. In group counseling, the roles of both group leader and member may be more ambiguous and not as clearly defined, resulting in Asian members having to define their roles to a greater degree. This may require greater structure with more directness, rather than a passive leadership role. Open-ended questions can be used; however, the group leader may find that in many situations, Asian clients expect straightforward statements from the group leader. Asian clients may feel anxiety due to the vagueness of many open-ended questions.

Expression of emotions is not easy for Asian clients, and they may be inhibited in expressing feelings, even during the later stages in the group process. Since the group would be considered by Asians as being in a public setting, it is critical that group leaders create a nonthreatening and safe group environment and assist Asian clients in gaining a sense of acceptance and security. It is thus essential to let Asian clients know that it is acceptable to explore personal feelings, both positive and negative. A norm for this level of openness must be clearly established during the first session. Consistent with self-disclosure is establishing confidentiality, which must also be presented and discussed in the first session. Confidentiality is important in reducing Asian members' fear that their personal stories might someday be exposed outside the group, and it is essential for each member to understand his or her personal obligation to protect all other group members' right of privacy as a way to achieve a safe environment. The formation of a mutually supportive and respectful atmosphere is a critical task of the group leader in working with Asian group members.

Even if a safe environment is created, Asian members may still be constrained from openly sharing within the group. To assist Asian members in feeling more comfortable, group leaders may disclose personal information to model and facilitate openness (Sue, 1996). This should be done intentionally throughout the group meetings to reinforce the norm of openness and assist clients in learning how to be respectful about others' feelings as well as express their own feelings. A byproduct of personal sharing by the group leader is fostering the Asian client's confidence and trust in the group leader. However, a word of caution is necessary: If group counselors self-disclose, they must do so with authenticity. By self-disclosing, they are fostering both achieved and ascribed credibility and thus avoiding premature termination and dropout (Sue & Zane, 1987). *Ascribed credibility* is credibility counselors have due to their status as a counselor, whereas *achieved credibility* is determined by the counselor's cultural responsiveness. A group counselor may have ascribed credibility; however, Asian clients may drop out of group if counselors do not demonstrate achieved credibility.

When working with Asian clients, there must be a fine balance regarding self-disclosure. If the Asian group member feels pressured to tell some family or personal stories, anxiety may accumulate and the sense of withdrawal may intensify or even prevail. It is essential to set a tone that helps each Asian member understand that although they are encouraged to share personal feelings and thoughts, it is not a requirement. This cultivates a safe and trustful environment so that Asian members' psychological needs and interests to share and communicate would arise naturally. However, group leaders must also be mindful of the resistant Asian client who may use culture as an excuse not to disclose or to participate. Group leaders must therefore have an in-depth knowledge of Asian culture and skills to determine whether the lack of participation is cultural or individual.

CONCLUSION

In summary, group leaders must acknowledge that many goals and techniques used with groups are based on Western values and may be inappropriate for, or of no value to, Asian group members. Furthermore, it is erroneous for group leaders to assume that Asians will not benefit in group counseling and psychotherapy due to their difficulties with self-disclosure. Asian members will personally share given the "right" environment. To be effective with Asian clients, group leaders must not only have the multicultural competencies to work with this population but also understand the effects and impact of culture on their clients. They must have skills and be creative in using, modifying, and altering traditional skills and techniques to be effective with this population. To truly understand the complexities of the Asian American population, group leaders must assess Asian community resources as a context for group work. Since group is viewed as a public setting for Asian clients and therefore has the potential for Asian members to be inhibited in expressing themselves, it is critical that group leaders not only create a safe environment but also model self-disclosure.

Group leaders who truly understand Asian culture and have the multicultural competencies required to work with ethnic groups will be able to create a safe environment for each member's personal growth and facilitate effective groups.

REFERENCES

Atkinson, D. R., Whiteley, S., & Gim, R. H. (1990). Asian-American acculturation and preference for help providers. *Journal of College Student Development, 31,* 156-161.

Bemak, F., & Epp, L. (1996). The 12th curative factor: Love as an agent of healing in group psychotherapy. *Journal of Specialists in Group Work, 21,* 118-127.

Bemak, F., & Epp, L. (2002). Countertransference in the development of graduate student group counselors: Recommendations for training. *Journal for Specialists in Group Work, 26,* 305-318.

Berry J. W. (1980). Acculturation as varieties of adaptation. In A. M. Padilla (Ed.), *Acculturation: Theory, model, and some new findings* (pp. 9-25). Boulder, CO: Westview.

Berry, J. W. (1983). Acculturation: A comparative analysis of alternative forms. In R. J. Samuda & S. L. Woods (Eds.), *Perspectives in immigrant and minority education* (pp. 65-78). Lanham, MD: University Press.

Chang, E. C. (2002). Cultural differences in psychological distress in Asian and Caucasian American college students: Examining the role of cognitive and affective concomitants. *Journal of Counseling Psychology, 49,* 47-60.

Cheung, F. (1989). The indigenization of neurasthenia in Hong Kong. *Cultural Medicine and Psychiatry, 13,* 956-959.

Cheung, L. Y. S., Cho, E. R., Luan, D., Tang, T. Y., & Yan, H. B. (1980). The Chinese elderly and family structure: Implications for health care. *Public Health Reports, 95,* 491-495.

Chu, J., & Sue, S. (1984). Asian/Pacific Americans and group practice. *Social Work With Groups, 7,* 23-36.

Chung, R. C-Y. (2001). Psychological adjustment of Cambodian refugee women: Implications for mental health counseling. *Journal of Mental Health Counseling, 23,* 115-126.

Chung, R. C-Y. (in press). Reactions to group work: An Asian perspective. In J. L. DeLucia-Waack & J. Donigian (Eds.), *The practice of multicultural group work: Visions and perspectives from the field.* Belmont, CA: Wadsworth.

Chung, R. C-Y., & Bemak, F. (1996). The effects of welfare status on psychological distress among Southeast Asian refugees. *The Journal of Nervous & Mental Disease, 184,* 346-353.

Chung, R. C-Y., & Bemak, F. (2002). Revisiting the California Southeast Asian mental health data: An examination of refugee ethnic and gender differences. *Journal of Counseling & Development, 80,* 111-119.

Chung, R. C-Y., Bemak, F., & Kagawa-Singer, M. (1998). Gender differences in psychological distress among Southeast Asian refugees. *Journal of Nervous & Mental Disease, 186,* 112-119.

Chung, R. C-Y., Bemak, F., & Okazaki, S. (1997). Counseling Americans of Southeast Asian descent: The impact of the refugee experience. In C. C. Lee (Ed.), *Multicultural issues in counseling: New approaches to diversity* (2nd ed., pp. 207-232). Alexandria, VA: American Counseling Association.

Chung, R. C-Y., & Kagawa-Singer, M. (1993). Predictors of psychological distress among Southeast Asian refugees. *Social Science & Medicine, 36,* 631-639.

Chung R. C.-Y., & Kagawa-Singer, M. (1995). Interpretation of symptom presentation and distress: A Southeast Asian refugee example. *Journal of Nervous & Mental Disease, 183,* 639-648.

Chung, R. C-Y., & Okazaki, S. (1991). Counseling Americans of Southeast Asian descent: The impact of refugee experiences. In C. C. Lee & B. L. Richardson (Eds.), *Multicultural issues in counseling: New approaches to diversity* (pp. 107-124). Alexandria, VA: American Counseling Association.

Chung, R. C-Y., Walkey, F. H., & Bemak, F. (1997). A comparison of achievement and aspirations of New Zealand Chinese and European students. *Journal of Cross-Cultural Psychology, 28,* 481-489.

Corey, G. (1995). *Theory and practice of group counseling* (4th ed.). Pacific Grove, CA: Brooks/Cole.

Corey, G. (2000). *Theory and practice of group counseling* (5th ed.). Belmont, CA: Wadsworth.

Dao, J. (1992, April 1). Asian street gangs emerging as new underworld. *The New York Times,* p. B2.

Fukuyama, M. A., & Coleman, N. C. (1992). A model for bicultural assertion training with Asian-Pacific American college students: A pilot study. *The Journal for Specialists in Group Work, 17,* 210-217.

Gim, R. H., Atkinson, D. R., & Whiteley, S. J. (1991). Asian American acculturation, counselor ethnicity and cultural sensitivity, and rating of counselors. *Journal of Counseling Psychology, 38,* 57-62.

Gudykunst, W. B., Gao, G., & Franklyn-Stokes, A. (1996). Self-monitoring and concerns for social appropriateness in China and England. In J. Pandey, D. Sinha, & D. P. S. Bhawuk (Eds.), *Asian contributions to cross-cultural psychology* (pp. 255-267). New Delhi, India: Sage.

Helms, J. (1995). An update of Helm's White and people of color racial identity model. In J. G. Ponterotto, J. M. Casas, L. A. Suzuki, & C. M. Alexander (Eds.), *Handbook of multicultural counseling* (pp. 181-198). Thousand Oaks, CA: Sage.

Ho, M. K. (1984). Social group work with Asian/Pacific-Americans. *Social Work With Groups, 7,* 49-61.

Hsia, J., & Peng, S. S. (1998). Academic achievement and performance. In L. C. Lee & N. W. S. Zane (Eds.), *Handbook of Asian American psychology* (pp. 325-358). Thousand Oaks, CA: Sage.

Hsu, F. (1973). Kinship is the key. *Center Magazine, 6,* 4-14.

Ina, S. (1997). Counseling Japanese Americans: From internment to reparation. In C. C. Lee (Ed.). *Multicultural issues in counseling: New approaches to diversity* (2nd ed., pp. 189-206). Alexandria, VA: American Counseling Association.

Johnson, D. W., & Johnson, F. P. (1994). *Joining together: Group theory and group skills* (5th ed.). Boston: Allyn & Bacon.

Kinzie, D., Frederickson, R. H., Ben, R., Fleck, J., & Karls, W. (1984). Posttraumatic stress disorder among survivors of Cambodian concentration camps. *American Journal of Psychiatry, 141,* 645-650.

Kinzie, J. D., Leung, P., Bui, A., & Ben, R. (1988). Group therapy with South East Asian refugees. *Community Mental Health Journal, 24,* 157-166.

Lee, E. (1988). Cultural factors in working with Southeast Asian refugee adolescents. *Journal of Adolescence, 11,* 167-179.

Lee, E. (1997). *Working with Asian Americans: A guide for clinicians.* New York: Guilford.

Lee, S. M. (1998). Asian Americans: Diverse and growing. *Population Bulletin, 53*(2), 1-40.

Leong, F. T. L. (1992). Guidelines for minimizing premature termination among Asian American clients in group counseling. *The Journal of Specialists in Group Work, 17,* 218-228.

Leong, F. T. L., Wagner, N. S., & Kim, H. H. (1995). Group counseling expectations among Asian American students. The role of culture-specific factors. *Journal of Counseling Psychology, 42,* 217-222.

Lin, C. (1985). *Intergenerational relationships among Chinese immigrant families: A study of filial piety.* Unpublished doctoral dissertation, University of Illinois, Chicago.

Louie, L., Joe, K., Lu, M., & Tong, B. (1991, August). *Chinese American adolescent runaways.* Paper presented in the convention of the Asian American Psychological Association, San Francisco, CA.

Lum, D., Cheung, L. Y. S., Cho, E. R., Tang, T. Y., & Yau, H. B. (1980). *The psychological needs of the Chinese elderly. Social Casework, 61,* 100-106.

Markus, H. R., & Kitayama, S. (1991). Culture and the self: Implications for cognition, emotion, and motivation. *Psychological Review, 98,* 224-253.

Merta, R. J. (1995). Group work: Multicultural perspectives. In J. G. Ponterotto, J. M. Casas, L. A. Suzuki, & C. M. Alexander (Eds.), *Handbook of multicultural counseling* (pp. 567-585). Thousands Oaks, CA: Sage.

Mollica, R. F., Wyshak, G., & Lavelle, J. (1987). The psychosocial impact of war trauma and torture on Southeast Asia refugees. *American Journal of Psychiatry, 144,* 1567-1572.

Nagasawa, R. (1980). *The elderly Chinese: A forgotten minority.* Chicago: Pacific/Asian American Mental Health Research Center.

Nagata, D. (1998). Internment and intergenerational relations. In L. C. Lee & N. W. S. Zane (Eds.), *Handbook of Asian American psychology* (pp. 433-456). Thousand Oaks, CA: Sage.

Ong, P. (1993). *Beyond Asian American poverty: Community economic development policies and strategies.* Los Angeles: Leadership Education for Asian Pacifics.

Osako, M. M., & Liu, W. T. (1986). Intergenerational relations and the aged among Japanese Americans. *Research on Aging, 8,* 128-155.

Padilla, E. R., Wagatsuma, Y., & Lindholm, K. J. (1985). Acculturation and personality as predictors of stress in Japanese and Japanese-Americans. *Journal of Social Psychology, 125,* 285-305.

Rhee, E., Uleman, J. S., & Lee, H. K. (1996). Variations in collectivism and individualism by ingroup and culture: Confirmatory factor analyses. *Journal of Personality & Social Psychology, 71,* 1037-1054.

Root, M. M. (1997). *Filipino Americans: Transformation and identity.* Thousand Oaks, CA: Sage.

Sandhu, D. S. (1997). Psychocultural profiles of Asian and Pacific Islander Americans: Implications for counseling and psychotherapy. *Journal of Multicultural Counseling & Development, 25,* 7-22.

Shon, S., & Ja, D. (1982). Asian families. In M. McGoldrick, J. Pearce, & J. Giordano (Eds.), *Ethnicity and family therapy* (pp. 208-229). New York: Guilford.

Sodowsky, G. R., & Carey, J. C. (1988). Relationships between acculturation-related demographics and cultural attitudes of an Asian-Indian immigrant group. *Journal of Multicultural Counseling & Development, 16,* 117-135.

Sue, D. (1996). Asian men in groups. In M. P. Andronico (Ed.), *Men in groups: Insights, interventions, and psychoeducational work* (pp. 69-80). Washington DC: American Psychological Association.

Sue, D., & Sue, W. (1985). *Counseling the culturally different: Theory and practice.* New York: John Wiley.

Sue, S., & Morishima, J. K. (1982). *The mental health of Asian Americans.* San Francisco: Jossey-Bass.

Sue, S., & Zane, N. (1987). The role of culture and cultural techniques in psychotherapy: A critique and reformulation. *American Psychologist, 42,* 37-45.

Suinn, R. M., Rickard-Figueroa, K., Lew, S., & Vigil, P. (1987). The Suinn-Lew Asian self-identity acculturation scale: An initial report. *Educational & Psychological Measurement, 47,* 401-407.

Triandis, H. (1989). The self and social behavior in differing cultural contexts. *Psychological Review, 96,* 596-520.

Tsui, P., & Schultz, G. L. (1988). Ethnic factors in group process: Cultural dynamics in multiethnic therapy groups. *American Journal of Orthopsychiatry, 58,* 136-142.

Uba, L. (1994). *Asian Americans: Personality patterns, identity, and mental health.* New York: Guilford.

U.S. Bureau of Census. (1996). *Current population reports: Population projections of the United States by age, race and Hispanic origin: 1995 to 2050* (pp. 25-1130). Washington, DC: U.S. Government Printing Office.

Yalom, I. D. (1995). *The theory and practice of group psychotherapy* (4th ed.). New York: Basic Books.

Yamaguchi, T. (1986). Group psychotherapy in Japan today. *International Journal of Group Therapy, 36,* 567-578.

Yamaguchi, T., Kuhlman, D. M., & Sugimori, S. (1995). Personality correlates of allocentric tendencies in individualist and collectivist cultures. *Journal of Cross-Cultural Psychology, 26,* 658-672.

Yeh, C., & Huang, K. (1996). The collectivistic nature of ethnic identity development among Asian American college students. *Adolescence, 31,* 645-661.

15

PSYCHOEDUCATIONAL AND COUNSELING GROUPS WITH LATINOS

EDIL TORRES RIVERA

University at Buffalo, SUNY

W hile much progress has been made in the field of counseling and psychotherapy in working with ethnic minorities in the United States (Aponte & Wohl, 2000; Sue & Sue, 2003), nearly all the work has concentrated on individual counseling rather than group work (Arcaya, 1996; Corey & Corey, 2002; Yalom, 1995). Most of the research on group dynamics and group process with regard to particular ethnic minority populations has concentrated on American Indians and African Americans (Garrett & Crutchfield, 1997; Garrett, Garrett, & Brotherton, 2001; Garrett & Osborne, 1995; Han & Vasquez, 2000; Pedersen & Carey, 1994; Sue & Sue, 2003). Even though the need for more empirical data about groups with particular ethnic minorities has been identified (DeLucia-Waack, 1996; Kees, 1999), the primary focus has remained on behavioral techniques and psychopathology (Aponte & Wohl, 2000; García & Zea, 1997; Padilla, 1995; Paniagua, 1994; M. Ramirez, 1999). Not to undermine the value of these foci,

but these approaches often do not consider the needs and basic cultural beliefs and conflicts of ethnic populations with Euro-American models of counseling, and perpetuate the intrapsychic model of treatment (García & Zea, 1997).

This chapter will use the term *Latino* rather than the term *Hispanic,* as Latino is an inclusive term that has been used by people of Latin/Hispanic descent to empower themselves in political arenas, humanities, and literature (Oboler, 1995; Shorris, 1992; Torres-Rivera, Wilbur, Roberts-Wilbur, & Phan, 1999). Latino is also preferred by more liberal, more politically correct people, as it affirms their native pre-Hispanic identity (Comas-Díaz, 2001). Furthermore, in accordance with the *Spaniard Real Academic* (Real Academia Española, 2001), the word Latino is an inclusive term that refers to both males and females. Although it is not our attempt to lump all Latinos into one group, based on the latest census bureau statistics, this chapter will focus on three Latino groups: (a) people of Mexican descent or

Mexicans, (b) Puerto Ricans, (c) and Cubans. Approximately 33 million Americans are Latinos. Sixty-six percent of all Latinos are Mexicans or Mexican descendents, 9% are Puerto Ricans, 4% are Cubans, and 21% belong to other Latino groups, which include Central and South American descendents (U.S. Bureau of the Census, 2000).

To address the social, racial, political, and demographic issues of Latinos in the United States, mental health professionals must observe and understand the experiences, cognitions, and behaviors of Latinos from a multicultural perspective as an alternative to the current intrapsychic, Euro-American approaches to group counseling and therapy (Torres-Rivera, Smaby, & Maddux, 1998; Torres-Rivera, Wilbur, & Roberts-Wilbur, 1998). In 1981, Betz, Wilbur, and Roberts-Wilbur and Wilbur, Roberts-Wilbur, and Betz had developed, proposed, and published a very similar typology of three group modalities: task-process groups; socio-process groups (called "psychoeducational groups" by ASGW, 2000); and psycho-process groups (called "counseling and therapy groups" by ASGW, 2000). By using the modalities and types of groups mentioned above, it is possible to develop a culturally sensitive approach that is not only effective when working with Latino clients in group settings but also, and foremost, is effective when used in combination with language and family variables. For this chapter, our focus will be Latinos in psychoeducational and counseling groups, as they are currently the most-employed group modalities with Latinos (e.g., Belitz & Valdez, 1997; Gloria, 1999).

This chapter will discuss general characteristics of Latinos in the United States, including culture-specific attitudes, values, beliefs, and language use and their impact on receptiveness and participation in psychoeducational and counseling groups. Also, suggestions for group leader preparation, effective group leadership behavior, and interventions will be provided.

GENERAL CHARACTERISTICS OF LATINOS

Latinos can be found in every state of the United States, with the largest concentration in the Southwestern states (García & Marotta, 1997).

More than 87% of all Latinos are concentrated in California, Texas, New York, Florida, New Jersey, Arizona, New Mexico, Colorado, Massachusetts, and Illinois (U.S. Census Bureau, 2000). Many differences exist among Latino groups, and these differences could be as simple as what one group calls "buses" in Spanish (for example, in Puerto Rico, buses are called "guaguas," while in Mexico they are call "autobus"). Marked differences may include how they celebrate particular religious events (for example, "El día de los muertos" in Mexico is a big celebration, while in the Dominican Republic, there is acknowledgment but not in the same manner or with the same rituals). However, similarities exist among Latinos in the United States, with the most important similarities being (a) the use of the Spanish language; (b) Catholicism, the main religion among Latinos (even though about 25% of all Latinos are Protestant, mainly Pentecostals) (Hugen, 2001); (c) *familismo,* which indicates family members' loyalty for family, including *compadres* and *comadres* (coparents); (d) *respecto,* meaning respect for authority, family, and tradition; (e) *personalismo,* which is the inclination of Latinos to prefer personal contacts over detached or institutional ones; (f) *machismo,* which is related to male superiority and the ability to achieve sexual conquest; (g) *marianismo,* referring to "the cult of female spiritual superiority which teaches that women are semi-divine, morally superior to, and spiritually stronger than men" (Stevens, 1973, p. 315); and (h) *simpatia,* which refers to an interpersonal style that focuses on lowering conflict and promotes agreement. These culture-specific variables occur in combination with the following variables: (a) attitudes, values, and beliefs of Latinos; (b) bilingualism/biculturalism; (c) family and community issues; (d) group leader preparation; (e) mental set; (f) structure; (g) resistance; (h) intervention; and (i) behavioral change.

Attitudes, Values, and Beliefs of Latinos

Several issues must be taken into consideration as one tries to understand life from the Latino perspective. First, Latinos, on average, are younger than the general United States population. Seventy-five percent of all Latinos are 39 years old or younger, in contrast with 60% for the total United States population (U.S. Bureau of the Census, 2000). Second, socioeconomically, 23% of all Latino households are below the poverty level. More than 87% of all Latinos are employed in service-, support-, or labor-type jobs. Third, although the gender proportions of Latinos in the United States are equal, the unemployment level for men is 6.2% versus 7.7% for women—and 3.6% for non-Latino males (U.S. Bureau of the Census, 2000). Fourth, there is a gap of 2.73% in education attainment between Latinos and dominant-culture males (Smith, 2001). These statistics suggest potential issues related to the inability of Latino males to support and provide for their families, one of the most important means used by Latino men to define their masculinity and manhood, which may lead to increased counseling and group work needs among Latino men and their families (Torres-Rivera et al., 1999).

Research has suggested that the cultural dynamics, issues, and discussion topics of truly relevant and common concern among Latino group members include time, money, relationships, friendship, intimacy, love, sexuality, parenting, commitment and responsibility, center of focus, communication and negotiation, thought, logic, decision making, power, rules, product and process, and morality (Fernández Bauzó, 1992; Torres-Rivera et al., 1999; Vázquez Muñoz, Macksound López, & Cantera Espinosa, 1992). Torres-Rivera et al. (1998) noted that the ways Latinos describe, think, and feel about leadership, communication, logic, and morality significantly differ from those of the dominant culture in the United States.

Time. For the majority of Latinos, time is not absolute or concrete. For many, it may mean being present when they are needed. For instance, a mechanic shop in a Latino barrio may have a sign that indicates that the shop is open from 9:00 a.m. until 5:00 p.m.; however, the shop rarely opens at 9:00 a.m., nor does it close until the last car in the shop is fixed.

On the other hand, the majority culture in the United States believes that the numbers on the clock are real, emphasizing the importance of being "on time" (Schaef, 1985). Also in contrast

with the Latino perspective of time is the American middle-class value of "future" as the most important aspect of time, rather than the present or past, while Latinos seems to stress the past as the primary worldview of time (Torres-Rivera et al., 1999). Group leaders who do not have an understanding of how Latinos view time may label them as irresponsible or unmotivated if they are late or absent from group sessions. Furthermore, if a group leader ends the group session without allowing the Latino group member to feel "complete" or "done," it could lead to early termination and/or emotional withdrawal from the group, because it invalidates clients' experiences.

Intimacy and Love. Latinos (men in particular) approach emotional intimacy via sexual and physical avenues. The area of intimacy is also more gender-specific than cultural. For instance, many Latino males establish a relationship with a woman assuming that the relationship will lead to sexual intercourse (París Alicea, 2000; R.L. Ramírez, 1999), which may be similar to many dominant-culture male beliefs as stated by Schaef (1985). Latino males also have the tendency to assume that they will have complete control of the relationship, and this may or may not be similar with the dominant-culture male beliefs, but for Latino males, this is not a matter of choice. Folklore dictates some behaviors for men and women that are related to their gender, such as machismo and marianismo (Laird, 1998; Torres-Rivera et al., 1999). Nevertheless, intimacy is approached in an emotional manner as well (Bourgeois, 1995; Hassid, Colpaert, & Anders, 1994; Thomas & Nava, 1995). Latinas are not immune to this characteristic, for they oftentimes establish emotional intimacy initially, which then may lead to physical intimacy (Torres-Rivera et al., 1999). This type of behavior can be seen in victims of traumatic events, particularly in victims of colonialism, which Latinos are familiar with (Duran & Duran, 1995; Torres-Rivera & Phan, 2002). That is, people who have been exposed to catastrophic events find themselves closer to those with similar experiences.

Therefore, it will be important for the group leader to become a compadre or comadre (coparent) to Latino clients (this is an indication of the commitment of the group leader to become part of the Latino family). Latinos may sometimes appear superficial during group sessions though they express intense feelings during individual sessions with the group leader (Arcaya, 1996; Torres-Rivera et al., 1999). This type of behavior should not be perceived as an indication of group member sabotage or resistance, but rather as a Latino expression of intimacy and trust toward the group leader. Group leaders need to follow a nondirect but firm approach to reach respect and trust and overcome this behavior. In addition, as it will be explained latter, discussing the client's family is also highly recommended: for example, asking the group about their mothers or grandmothers without making eye contact with anyone in the group.

One last important point to mention about intimacy and love is that Latinos oftentimes express intense doubt, confusion, and questioning regarding the existence and meaning of love (París Alicea, 2000; R.L. Ramírez, 1999). Despite the fact that romanticism and the idealization of love are common among Latinos (Garcia-Preto, 1998), and love, intimacy, and relationships with the opposite sex are important within the Latino culture (Torres-Rivera, Phan, Wilbur, & Maddux, 2001), when Latinos find themselves in an unfamiliar culture, they often develop doubts and a distorted sense of what it means to love and to be loved or to be romantic. Moreover, these beliefs about love and romanticism may be at variance with the majority culture, which often believes that love can be "defined" and proven by doing specific things, such as remembering anniversaries and giving presents (Schaef, 1985). Thus, many Latinos may experience incongruity and confusion about the meaning of love and relationships. Group leaders may need to realize that such confusion and doubt are a result of cultural differences and not a lack of commitment to significant people or to relationships in Latinos' lives.

Logic and Data Processing. Latinos usually process information from more of an emotionally oriented perspective, which may include mistrust of people and society (Torres-Rivera et al., 1999). Therefore, it may not be uncommon

for Latinos to express a great deal of dissonance with regard to their own beliefs and behaviors, divided between self- and social identity issues (Bacigalupe, 2000; Brice, 2002; Flores-Ortiz, 2000). This could manifest itself in members contradicting themselves and sometimes making statements, one after the other, that directly contradict each other. A good example of such contradictions is when, in group, a group member has just expressed fear of dying and a second later, tells the group that he is not afraid of dying. Thus, group leaders might want to assist Latinos to be less emotionally involved with their attitudes and values during the early stage of the group, by developing a cognitive discussion of the topic and their exploration of different perceptions, influences, beliefs, and conflicts.

According to the dominant culture, logical and linear thinking are ideas that provide people security and predictivity (Masterpasqua & Perna, 1997; Torres-Rivera et al., 1998). For Latinos, on the other hand, security often stems from and depends upon their ability to stay alive (survival). Group leaders who are unaware of this particular characteristic may impose logical, linear, and security-based thinking onto Latinos and deny their realities of survival in a hostile and chaotic world. Consequently, group leaders must be careful not to impose a linear worldview onto Latinos.

Responsibility. Latinos customarily approach responsibility by trusting those around them, by doing what they need to do, and by making decisions based on collateral influence. Most often, decision making will be delegated to the person or persons that Latinos believe possess more experience and intelligence to deal with the matter at hand. In contrast, members of the majority culture generally blame others for failures or ineffective decision making by means of established "accountability" procedures (Schaef, 1985). Taking this into consideration in the group setting, group leaders working with Latinos need to understand that trust and collateral influence are part of Latino culture and neglecting these important aspects of responsibility and decision making may create unnecessary distance between group leaders and Latinos.

Morality. Morality is defined as the quality of being that should be in agreement with standards of what is good or right behavior. Although this definition rings true for Latinos, how it is viewed creates a completely different paradigm. For the majority of Latinos, morality is viewed as a private issue (Torres-Rivera et al., 1999) that is only discussed within the family circle. For the majority culture, morality is more often viewed as a public issue that is frequently mandated and controlled through legislation (i.e., the protective marriage law voted in Nevada received more than 80% support). It is necessary to discuss how Latinos view morality, because for most Latinos (Torres-Rivera et al., 1999), the issues discussed in counseling and psychotherapy are viewed as moral issues.

Rules. Latinos perceive rules as a tool of control to limit others' and one's own behavior (Schaef, 1985; Torres-Rivera et al., 1999). The all-or-nothing belief among many members of the majority culture is that the use of rules, order, and power to control the negative and destructive influences in society is necessary to protect and preserve the American middle-class "way of life" (Schaef, 1985) and without rules and order, there is chaos. Among many Latinos, however, chaos is not necessarily negative, but sometimes a new beginning or an opportunity (Daniels, Young, Olmos, & Olmos, 1992).

For Latinos, responsibility and rules are probably critical when working in a group setting. Because group leaders, in particular those who belong to the dominant culture, are often seen as authority figures (rather than compadres) representing the rules of the system, Latinos will most likely view the process as oppressive and freedom limiting. Therefore, group work with this population requires the establishment of relationships from a more humanistic, less authoritarian position to prevent such self-defeating perceptions.

Communication and Negotiation. Latinos use their language in a genuine attempt to understand others and to get closer, rather than to control or dominate the communication (Sue & Sue, 2003). For example, if a group member or the leader is being controlling or dominating the dynamics, it would not be atypical for a Latino group member to withdraw from the interaction. The Latino group member may even use an abstraction or metaphor to tell a story that may or may not be directly related to the focus of the current discussion (Torres-Rivera et al., 1999). This example illustrates a different pattern of communication compared with that of the majority culture, which tends to be more controlling and linear in communication and negotiation patterns (Torres-Rivera et al., 1998).

Group leaders who are unable to comprehend and accept this pattern and purpose of communication among Latinos as a cultural variable may not be able to establish themselves as trustworthy and knowledgeable. This could lead to further misunderstanding, as the leader may define the Latino members' desires and attempts to understand as negative, when in actuality, what Latino members expect from communication is greater understanding and connection instead of control, negotiation, or prediction (Sue & Sue, 2003).

Leadership. Being in control and having answers for all problems is characteristic of how the majority culture defines leadership and how expertise and competence are measured by status, credentials, and economic possessions (Schaef, 1992; Torres-Rivera et al., 1998). For Latinos, leadership involves egalitarian relationships with importance placed in responding to people equally and with respect (Padilla, 1995). A group leader who does not acknowledge this difference may be imposing his or her values onto Latino group members and by doing so may be perpetuating existing variance in perceptions of leadership.

Differences in Being Bilingual/Bicultural

Although there may be different sentiments regarding the levels of effectiveness of bilingual mental health professionals and monolingual counselors, Delgado (1997), Santiago-Rivera and Vazquez (2000), and Santiago-Rivera (1995) maintain that bilingualism is as important and at times even more essential than being bicultural. Regardless of the differing views about bilingualism, it is critical that mental health professionals who work with Latinos in groups have some knowledge of the language in order to break barriers with Latinos whose primary language at home was and/or is Spanish. In other words, if the Latino clients are recent immigrants, second- or third-generation immigrants living in Latino barrios, their earlier experiences as well as their most traumatic moments have been associated with Spanish language (Santiago-Rivera & Vazquez, 2000). Therefore, the ability to assess those emotions and/or feelings decreases dramatically when the intervention is conducted in a language other than Spanish. The use of the language is improved immensely when used within the cultural bounds of the specific Latino culture (Mexicans, Puerto Ricans, Cubans, etc.), such as *dichos* or *refranes* (proverbs) during the counseling intervention (Santiago-Rivera & Vazquez, 2000). For example, a group leader will be seen as a friend by greeting the group with "y la familia como está," meaning "How is the family doing?" Other examples of openings or "backdoor" interventions, such as "No se puede tapar el cielo con la mano," meaning that a person cannot cover the sky with their hand, can be used when a group member is in denial and does not want to see the reality of his or her problem(s); "lo que no mata engorda," meaning that what does not kill you makes you stronger, can be used when a group member needs motivation to move forward despite the obstacle ahead.

Community Involvement/Familial Ties

For most Latinos, the primary source of self-definition and self-esteem, as well as the structure and support for the individual, is the family (Arredondo, 1996). Consequently, since most issues in mental health are seen as moral issues for Latino clients, such as issues dealing with family or intimacy (Torres-Rivera et al., 1998), mental health professionals who want to work effectively with Latino clients need to become part of the Latino family to reach the working stage in the group process. That is, they need to establish trust and gain the Latino clients' loyalty, almost as if the counselor were a compadre, or coparent, of the Latino clients. Mental health professionals who are unable to recognize this important variable during group sessions with Latino clients are perceived as violating the client's right for human dignity and privacy. In addition, families should be included when dealing with Latinos clients, implying that mental health professionals are working with a significant number of people (Gushue & Sciarra, 1995). This is known as familismo and is accomplished through a series of steps that lead to accepting the mental health professional, in a sense, as a member of the "Latino family." To become a member of the family, a mental health professional should invest time in participating in community activities, such as *quinceñeras* (when a young girl celebrates entering into womanhood), weddings, and other religious/community celebrations. *Respecto* is perhaps one of the most important elements of Latino culture. Counselors working with Latino clients need to be knowledgeable about cultural matters without being seen as a *pendante,* which means pretentiously displaying how much book knowledge they have. This is a difficult balance to achieve, but a necessary ingredient if *respecto* is to be fully accomplished (Maples et al., 2001; R.L. Ramírez, 1999). Group leaders need to be humble but firm in their approaches when working with Latinos and use what is known in Spanish as *la peleita monga,* which means to reach the clients without being overly intrusive and all knowing, but rather allowing the client to make his or her own decisions and simultaneously providing the means for the decision making of the client.

GROUP WORK WITH LATINOS

Pregroup Planning

Group leaders need to be culturally competent by having an awareness of their own mental sets, as well as the specific knowledge of rituals, ceremonies, and other healing practices used by the different Latino cultures. The chapter (19) by D'Andrea in this volume emphasizes the importance of group leaders' self-awareness as cultural beings and its impact on group dynamics. Torres-Rivera et al. (1998) and Flores and Carey (2000) provide helpful tools for understanding the complexity of the Latino cultures, interventions, and rituals applicable to group counseling. Also, group leaders need to know when and how to perform the necessary interventions, as the timing of the intervention is oftentimes more important than the intervention itself when working with Latino clients. It is important for group leaders working with Latinos to be familiar with the specific charge of group leaders in psychoeducational group modality and how it is different from the group counseling modality, as one modality is more intimate than the other.

Group Size. It is important that most groups of Latino clients remain small. Some Latinos have the tendency to speak all at the same time. Therefore, by limiting the number of interactions, group leaders will be able to maximize their intervention effectiveness. It is our experience that 10 group members with a cofacilitator is an optimal number of Latinos in one group. It is also important to understand that in the psychoeducational group modality, due to its structured nature, the number could be bigger (11-12), but for counseling groups, because of the intimacy and emotional disclosure, keeping the number of members to a maximum of 10 is very important to ensure the effectiveness of the interventions.

Resistance. Resistance is part of the regular movement of the group between "stages," or change, in the group members. However, with Latino group members, different from members of the dominant culture, resistance may be manifested in the form of honest expression of feelings and hostility toward the group leader(s) at a later stage of the group development. Group leaders who engage in the open expression of Latino client feelings will be able to help them move forward toward resolution and, by doing so, help the group to deal with group stage tasks and dynamics.

Resistance is also encountered at the beginning of group if group members' think that the group is "therapeutic," as many Latinos believe that "therapy" is only for "crazy" people. Therefore, sometimes to help minimize this kind of resistance, group leaders use the word *counseling* or just *group*. This type of resistance is more common in counseling groups than in psychoeducational groups. Also, while the use

of food is sometimes used in group settings to increase familiarity among group members and to decrease hostility in psychiatry group settings, it is not a good idea while working with Latinos. However, if food is to be used, it is best that it be used during an informal setting, as part of a familial activity.

Leader Culture-Specific Knowledge and Self-Knowledge. A group leader's "mental set" refers to attitudes, values, beliefs, perceptions, opinions, and ideas that person brings to the group (Wilbur et al., 1981), as well as their biases, prejudices, and expectations about the group, group leaders, and other group members. In the Latino mental set, the group leader is expected to (a) know how to modify his or her technique to reflect the cultural differences of the client, (b) know how to deal with difficulties during the group process/dynamics due to cultural differences between the client and the group leader, and (c) understand how culturally different people conceptualize and resolve their problems that are bound in cultural patterns (for more details about groups leader training and preparation, see DeLucia-Waack (2003). For example, a group leader who has been trained without a culture-specific component that addresses self-awareness may not be able to distinguish between a Latino client who is quiet because he or she needs an invitation from the leader from someone who is resistant. Group leaders may want to become familiar with movies such as *Mi Familia* (Thomas & Nava, 1995) and *Mi Vida Loca* (Hassid et al., 1994) and textbooks such as *Family Therapy With Hispanics: Toward Appreciating Diversity* (Flores & Carey, 2000), *In Search of Respect: Selling Crack in El Barrio* (Bourgeois, 1995), and *Psychological Interventions and Research With Latino Populations* (García & Zea, 1997).

Preparation of Members

Group leaders need to prepare members with regard to member expectations and behaviors, depending on the type of group and the culture-specific attitudes, values, and beliefs of each particular Latino group. The effectiveness of the preparation of group members to function in both group modalities depends on the ability of the group leader(s) to deal with the variables of *personalismo* (by conveying egalitarian approach), *familismo* (by using *compadrazgo,* or acting as coparent, as mentioned earlier), *marianismo* (by knowing how this particular characteristic plays into religion and machismo when working with Latinas), machismo (similar to *marianismo*, although this characteristic can be overstated in the United States), *dignidad* (again refers to attitudes, values, and beliefs, particularly to aspects such as responsibility, decision making, gender-specific topics, etc.), and *respecto* (similar to *dignidad*, this particular variable is tied to responsibility, morality, rules, leadership, and gender-specific roles).

Interventions

Because it is imperative for Latinos to understand and accept the conflict between their beliefs and experiences, only when group counselors engage in some specific techniques, including effective listening, analyzing, and responding from a multicultural perspective in the group setting (Torres-Rivera et al., 1999), will this conflict lessen.

Listening. In a group setting, Latino clients need to tell their stories, accounts, and life events in order to be heard. This is accomplished through informing, orienting, and educating group members as they interact and receive support from the group. That is, listening to the specific events of the group members' lives and validating those experiences will result in congruency between their beliefs, behaviors, and experiences. This is critical for a real multicultural understanding. The problem is that many mental health professionals are unaware of their subscription to the beliefs of White middle-class American society, thus leaving them unable to provide the necessary listening and validation of Latinos' experiences and beliefs.

Understanding and Responding. A group leader's explanation of Latinos' beliefs as being in conflict with those of the dominant culture provides Latinos with a cognitive framework for a better understanding of how and why they were traumatized by the immigration experience. This realization helps them to view their divergent beliefs as normal rather than "crazy" when compared with the normative beliefs of the majority culture.

This intervention not only assists Latinos in separating their disparate beliefs from those of the majority but also helps them to accept their beliefs as part of their reality rather than attempting to deny, distort, or delete them. This separation and acceptance of their minority beliefs results in less emotionalism, stress, and self-defeating behavior and an increased ability to perform normative tasks and behaviors in the dominant culture.

Behavioral Change

While many approaches to mental health interventions clearly call for specific, measurable changes in behavior, when working with Latinos in group settings and depending on the specific type of group (task, psychoeducational, etc.), the changes in the group members range from talking about a specific set of values, attitudes, and beliefs in a different/new tone of voice to modifying behavior completely. Latinos who, during the process of the group session, begin to listen, speak, and share their perspectives or become willing to see things differently are considered to be showing an indication of behavioral change when working with that particular intervention. In other words, change must be seen from a culture-specific perspective and not only as a quantitative, absolute behavior modification on the part of the client. In many Latino cultures, raising consciousness is considered significant change (Vázquez Muñoz et al., 1992). Therefore, group leaders must be observant and realistic in regard to the particular changes that group members are to accomplish.

CONCLUSIONS AND DISCUSSION

The change in demographics of the United States of America indicates that Latinos are increasing in numbers and needs, meaning that it is highly probable that group leaders in any system will encounter Latino clients. However, many Latinos still struggle to understand how discrimination and immigration in the United

States have affected and changed them. Such issues need to be better investigated, understood, and treated from the perspective of the Latino experience, as well as the Latino cultural perspective.

Therefore, as group leaders, we must continue to increase awareness of our own attitudes, values, and beliefs, in addition to our awareness of those who suffer oppression in our country (Sue & Sue, 2003). When working with Latinos or any minority group, it is important to understand our own personal biases, stereotypes, and assumptions. Many of these assumptions and biases are based on a universalist focus that does not address differences in experiences and beliefs or the effects of oppression (McGoldrick, 1998). Such biases, stereotypes, and assumptions may unintentionally lead group workers to misdiagnosis and to inequality in treatment. There also is a need for more societal awareness about discrimination in general and Latino clients in particular. Most counseling and group work texts devote little or no attention to Latino clients, ignoring their unique issues (Arredondo, 1996). Thus, group leaders need to be educated about the issues of their Latino members and applicable group work models.

REFERENCES

Aponte, J. F., & Wohl, J. (Eds.). (2000). *Psychological interventions and cultural diversity.* Needham Heights, MA: Allyn & Bacon.

Arcaya, J. M. (1996). The Hispanic male in group psychotherapy. In M. P. Andronico (Ed.), *Men in groups: Insights interventions and psychoeducational work* (pp. 151-163). Washington, DC: American Psychological Association.

Arredondo, P. (1996). MTC theory and Latina(o)-American population. In D. W. Sue, A. E. Ivey, & P. B. Pedersen (Eds.), *A theory of multicultural counseling and therapy* (pp. 217-235). Pacific Grove, CA: Brooks/Cole.

Association for Specialists in Group Work (ASGW). (2000). Professional standards for training group workers. *Journal for Specialists in Group Work, 25,* 327-342.

Bacigalupe, G. (2000). El Latino: Transgressing the macho. In M. T. Flores & G. Carey (Eds.),

Family therapy with Hispanics: Toward appreciating diversity (pp. 29-57). Needham Heights, MA: Allyn & Bacon.

Belitz, J., & Valdez, D. M. (1997). A sociocultural context for understanding gang involvement among Mexican-American male youth. In J. G. Garcia & M. C. Zea (Eds.), *Psychological interventions and research with Latino populations* (pp. 56-72). Needham Heights, MA: Allyn & Bacon.

Betz, R. L., Wilbur, M. P., & Roberts-Wilbur, J. (1981). A structural blueprint for group facilitators: Three group modalities. *Personnel & Guidance Journal, 60,* 31-36.

Bourgeois, P. (1995). *In search of respect: Selling crack in el barrio.* New York: Cambridge University Press.

Brice, A. E. (2002) *The Hispanic child: Speech, language, culture and education.* Boston: Allyn & Bacon.

Comas-Díaz, L. (2001). Hispanics, Latinos, or Americanos: The evolution of identity. *Cultural Diversity & Ethnic Minority Psychology, 7,* 115-120.

Corey, M. S., & Corey, G. (2002). *Groups: Process and practice* (6th ed.). Pacific Grove, CA: Brooks/Cole.

Daniels, S., Young, R. M., & Olmos, E. J. (Producers) & Olmos, E. J. (Director). (1992). *American me* [Film]. Available from Universal Studios, 70 Universal City Plaza, Universal City, CA 91608.

Delgado, M. (1997). Hispanics/Latinos. In J. Philleo & L. Brisbane (Eds.), *Cultural competence in substance abuse prevention* (pp. 33-54). Washington, DC: NASW Press.

DeLucia-Waack, J. (1996). *Multicultural counseling competencies: Implications for training and practice.* Alexandria, VA. American Counseling Association.

DeLucia-Waack, J. (2003). Training multicultural group workers. In J. DeLucia-Waack & J. Donigian (Eds.), *The practice of multicultural group work: Eleven visions.* Belmont, CA: Wadsworth.

Duran, E., & Duran, B. (1995). *Native American postcolonial psychology.* Albany: State University of New York Press.

Fernández Bauzó, E. (1992). Crítica de la sección a nivel grupal. In I. Serano-García & W. Rosario Collazo (Eds.), *Contribuciones Puertorriqueñas a la psicología social-communitaria* (pp. 457-464). Rio Piedras, Puerto Rico: Editorial de la Universidad de Puerto Rico.

Flores, M. T., & Carey, G. (Eds.). (2000). *Family therapy with Hispanics: Toward appreciating diversity.* Needham Heights, MA: Allyn & Bacon.

Flores-Ortiz, Y. (2000). La mujer Latina: From margin to center. In M. T. Flores & G. Carey (Eds.), *Family therapy with Hispanics: Toward appreciating diversity* (pp. 597). Needham Heights, MA: Allyn & Bacon.

García, G. J., & Marotta, S. (1997). Characterization of the Latino population. In J. G. García & M. C. Zea (Eds.), *Psychological interventions and research with Latino populations* (pp. 1-14). Needham Heights, MA: Allyn & Bacon.

García, G. J., & Zea, M. C. (Eds.). (1997). *Psychological interventions and research with Latino populations.* Needham Heights, MA: Allyn & Bacon.

Garcia-Preto, N. (1998). Latinas in the United States: Bridging two worlds. In M. McGoldrick (Ed.), *Re-visioning family therapy: Race, culture and gender in clinical practice* (pp. 330-344). New York: Guilford.

Garrett, M. T., & Crutchfield, L. B. (1997). Moving full circle: A unity model of group work with children. *Journal for Specialists in Group Work, 22,* 175-188.

Garrett, M. T., Garrett, J. T., & Brotherton, D. (2001). Inner circle/outer circle: A group technique based on Native American healing circles. *Journal for Specialists in Group Work, 26,* 17-30.

Garrett, M. T., & Osborne, W. L. (1995). The Native American sweat lodge as metaphor for group work. *Journal for Specialists in Group Work, 20,* 33-39.

Gloria, A. M. (1999). Apoyando estudiantes Chicanas: Therapeutic factors in Chicana college student support groups. *Journal for Specialists in Group Work, 24*(3), 246-259.

Gushue, G. V., & Sciarra, D. T. (1995). Culture and families: A multidimensional approach. In J. G. Ponterotto, J. M. Casas, L. A. Suzuki, & C. M. Alexander (Eds.), *Handbook of multicultural counseling* (pp. 586-606). Thousand Oaks, CA: Sage.

Han, A. L., & Vasquez, M. J. T. (2000). Group intervention and treatment with ethnic minorities. In J. F. Aponte & J. Wohl (Eds.), *Psychological interventions and cultural diversity* (2nd ed., pp. 110-130). Needham Heights, MA: Allyn & Bacon.

Hassid, D., Colpaert, C. J. (Producers), & Anders, A. (Director). (1994). *Mi vida loca: My crazy life* [Film]. (Available from HBO Video, 1100 Avenue of the Americas, New York, NY 10036)

Hugen, B. (2001). Spirituality and religion in social work practice: A conceptual model. In M. Van Hook, B. Hugen, & M. Aguilar (Eds.), *Spirituality within religious traditions in social work practices* (pp. 9-17). Pacific Grove, CA: Brooks/Cole Publishing.

Laird, J. (1998). Theorizing culture: Narrative ideas and practice principles. In M. McGoldrick (Ed.), *Re-visioning family therapy: Race, culture and gender in clinical practice* (pp. 20-36). New York: Guilford.

Kees, N. L. (1999). Women together again: A phenomenological study of leaderless women's groups. *Journal for Specialists in Group Work, 24,* 288-305.

Maples, F. M., Dupey, P., Torres-Rivera, E., Phan, L. T., Vereen, L., & Garrett, M. T. (2001). Ethnic diversity and the use of humor in counseling: Appropriate or inappropriate. *Journal of Counseling and Development, 79,* 53-60.

Masterpasqua, F., & Perna, P. A. (Eds.). (1997). *The psychological meaning of chaos: Translating theory into practice.* Washington, DC: American Psychological Association.

McGoldrick, M. (Ed.). (1998). *Re-visioning family therapy: Race, culture, and gender in clinical practice.* New York: Guilford.

Oboler, S. (1995). *Ethnic labels, Latino lives: Identity and the politics of (re)presentation in the United States.* Minneapolis: University of Minnesota Press.

Padilla, A. M. (Ed.). (1995). *Hispanic psychology: Critical issues in theory and research.* Thousand Oaks, CA: Sage.

Paniagua, F. A. (1994). *Assessing and treating culturally diverse clients: A practical guide.* Thousand Oaks, CA: Sage.

París Alicea, D. (2000). *Hechos y derechos: Consideraciones en torno a los hombres y su desarrollo.* Rio Piedras, Puerto Rico: Ediciones Juissa.

Pedersen, P. B., & Carey, J. C. (1994). *Multicultural counseling in the schools: A practical handbook.* Needham, MA: Allyn & Bacon.

Ramirez, M. III (1999). *Multicultural psychotherapy: An approach to individual and cultural differences* (2nd ed.). Needham Heights, MA: Allyn & Bacon.

Ramírez, R. L. (1999). *What it means to be a man: Reflection on Puerto Rican masculinity* (R. E. Casper & P. J. Guarnaccia, Trans.). New Brunswick, NJ: Rutgers University Press. (Original work published 1993)

Real Academia Española. (2001, November). *Diccionario 2001.* Retrieved November 29, 2001, from http://www.rae.es/.

Santiago-Rivera, A. L. (1995). Developing a culturally sensitivity treatment modality for bilingual Spanish-speaking clients: Incorporating language and culture in counseling. *Journal of Counseling and Development, 74,* 12-17.

Santiago-Rivera, A. L., & Vazquez, L. (2000). *Culturally competent counseling & therapy, Part III: Innovative approaches to counseling Latin/o.* North Amherst, MA: Microtraining Associates.

Schaef, A. W. (1985). *Women's reality: How you can reach your full potential.* New York: Harper.

Schaef, A. W. (1992). *Beyond therapy, beyond science: A new model for healing the whole person.* San Francisco: HarperCollins.

Shorris, E. (1992). *Latinos: A biography of the people.* New York: Avon Books.

Smith, J. P. (2001). Race and ethnicity in the labor market: Trends over the short and long term. In N. J. Smelser, W. J. Wilson, & F. Mitchell (Eds.), *American becoming: Vol. II. Racial trends and their consequences* (pp. 52-97). Washington, DC: National Academic Press.

Stevens, E. P. (1973). The prospect for a women's liberation movement in Latin America. *Journal of Marriage & the Family, 35,* 313-320.

Sue, D. W., & Sue, D. (2003). *Counseling the culturally different: Theory and practice* (4th ed.). New York: Wiley-Interscience Publication.

Thomas, A. (Producer), & Nava, G. (Director). (1995). *Mi familia* [FILM]. (Available from New Line Video, http://www.newline-shop.com)

Torres-Rivera, E., & Phan, L. T. (2002, March). *Che Guevarra, Don Pedro Albizú Campos, Paulo Freire, and the revolution of counseling: Revisioning social justice when counseling Latino clients.* Paper presented at the meeting of the American Counseling Association, New Orleans, LA.

Torres-Rivera, E., Phan, L. T., Wilbur, M. P., & Maddux, C. (2001). Definiendo los conflictos de género sexual en los hombres puertorriqueños: Una comparación multicultural. *Revista Profesional de la Asociación Puertorriqueña de Consejería Profesional, 1,* 26-31.

Torres-Rivera, E., Smaby, M., & Maddux, C. D. (1998). Attitudes, values and beliefs of Latino men: Implications for counselors. *Journal of Psychological Practice, 4,* 77-87.

Torres-Rivera, E., Wilbur, M. P., & Roberts-Wilbur, J. (1998). The Puerto Rican prison experience: A multicultural understanding of values, beliefs, and attitudes. *Journal of Addictions & Offender Counseling, 18,* 63-77.

Torres-Rivera, E., Wilbur, M. P., Roberts-Wilbur, J., & Phan, L. (1999). Group work with Latino clients. *Journal for Specialists in Group Work, 24,* 383-404.

U.S. Bureau of the Census. (2000). *Profile of general demographics characteristics: 2000.* Retrieved September 10, 2001, from http://www.census.gov/prod/cen2000/index.html.

Vázquez Muñoz, M., Macksound López, S., & Cantera Espinosa, L. (1992). El grupo de discusión como método de concientización y su aplicación con grupos de mujeres divorciadas. In I. Serano-García & W. Rosario Collazo (Eds.), *Contribuciones Puertorriqueñas a la psicología social-communitaria* (pp. 399-426). Rio Piedras, Puerto Rico: Editorial de la Universidad de Puerto Rico.

Wilbur, M. P., Roberts-Wilbur, J., & Betz, R. L. (1981). Leader and member behaviors in three group modalities: A typology. *The Journal for Specialists in Group Work, 6,* 224-234.

Yalom, I. D. (1995). *The theory and practice of group psychotherapy* (4th ed.). New York: Basic Books.

16

Psychoeducational and Counseling Groups With Gay, Lesbian, Bisexual, and Transgendered Clients

Sharon G. Horne
University of Memphis

Heidi M. Levitt
University of Memphis

Although group work with gay, lesbian, bisexual and transgendered (GLBT) clients is commonplace in large metropolitan cities and on university campuses, research discussing group dynamics, processes, and outcomes of group work with GLBT populations is scarce. DeBord and Perez's (2000) review revealed only six relevant research articles (Everaerd et al., 1982; Hedge & Glover, 1990; Mulder et al., 1994; Quadland, 1985; Reece, 1981/1982; Russell & Winkler, 1977), all of which focused solely on men, and five of which focused upon either sexual dysfunction or HIV-positive men. Only two were published as recently as the early 1990s. Seven research studies investigating cognitive-behavioral skills training, stress management, culturally appropriate brief group therapy, and cognitive-behavioral therapy in combination with medication have since been published (Choi et al., 1996; Lee, Cohen, Hadley, & Goodwin, 1999; Roffman et al., 1997; Roffman, Beadnell, Ryan,

& Downey, 1995; Roffman, Downey, Beadnell, & Gordon, 1997; Roffman, Ficciano, Bolan, & Kalishman, 1997; Schneiderman, 1999). Again, all studies focused on men and HIV prevention and treatment.

There have been a few theoretical articles based on case studies of group work with gay, lesbian, and bisexual (GLB) populations (e. g., Chojnacki & Gelberg, 1995). In addition to DeBord and Perez's (2000) chapter on group therapy with GLBT individuals, which focused primarily on Yalom's therapeutic factors (1995), Norsworthy and Horne (1994) discussed groups with HIV-positive men, Perez (1996) provided guidelines for the development of groups for HIV-positive university students, and Baum and Fishman (1994) described a group treatment approach for sexually compulsive gay men. More recent contributions include case studies of male sexual abuse survivor groups of mixed sexual orientation (Meyer, 2000), accounts of gay men discussing their experiences as participants in a support group (Blye, 1999), a therapist's description of a process-oriented therapy group with women of diverse sexual identities (Firestein, 1999), and a discussion of eating-disorder groups with students of mixed sexual orientations (Krentz & Arthur, 2001). No articles discussed group work specific to trans- gendered or bisexual individuals, with the exception of one that included a section on bisexual clients (i.e., Firestein, 1999).

Although it is commonly acknowledged that GLBT individuals access therapeutic services to a significant degree (Bradford, Ryan, & Rothblum, 1994; Liddle, 1996; Morgan, 1992), much less is known about GLBT group work. Groups commonly advertised in GLBT community newspapers and on university cam- puses include HIV support groups, coming-out groups, and more recently, gay and lesbian par- enting groups. Group counseling is beneficial to GLBT individuals in a number of ways. Given the isolation that many GLBT people experi- ence due to the stigmatization of their sexual and gender identities, groups can offer an atmosphere conducive to sharing universality of experience (Yalom, 1995). Because many GLBT individuals experience disruptions in their families of origin during the coming-out process, groups can also provide instillation of hope for members to work through changing relationships. Groups also provide an opportu- nity to observe and imitate other members' skills and strategies for integrating and disclos- ing sexual and gender identities to significant others. Finally, groups for GLBT individuals allow for interpersonal learning among members, the development of socializing tech- niques that are necessary for successful integra- tion of a new identity, and the imparting of vital information about GLBT concerns to group members (DeBord & Perez, 2000).

The purpose of this chapter is to outline important issues to consider when leading groups that include or focus upon GLBT clients. In general, the dynamics and process in groups with GLBT clients are similar to group work in general. However, this chapter highlights the differences that are important within this type of group. Because GLBT clients face issues of discrimination and isolation that may be unique, it is important for counselors to be sensitized to

these experiences. Throughout the chapter, insights from the authors' clinical experience and the professional literature will serve to highlight the main points.

GENERAL CONSIDERATIONS RELEVANT TO GROUP WORK WITH GLBT CLIENTS

Coming Out

Facilitators for GLBT groups need an aware- ness of the issues and challenges that GLBT individuals regularly face. Generally, GLBT individuals go through a "coming-out" process that involves disclosing to self and significant others their sexual or gender identities (Brown & Rounsley, 1996; Cass, 1979). During this process, many individuals are faced with uncer- tainty, fear, and anxiety, which can contribute to clinical depression and social isolation. Groups can serve to foster positive self-identity by exposing group members to the varied develop- mental processes of others. Members with solid GLBT identities can model positive identity development to emerging GLBT members. Group leaders should be aware, however, that for many people, the coming-out process is lengthy and nonlinear; at times, individuals will fluctuate from being very comfortable with their GLBT identities but then can be set back by a negative self-disclosure or event.

Discrimination Based on Sexual or Gender Orientation

In most states, there is no protection for GLBT individuals against employment discrim- ination, meaning that mere participation in a GLBT group could jeopardize job security if confidentiality is breached. Many states and municipal governments discriminate against GLBT people by denying custody of children, refusing adoption to GLBT individuals (e.g., Florida's anti-adoption policy), and limiting access to housing (Barón & Cramer, 2000). In addition to overt discrimination, GLBT individ- uals are at risk for losing social support of family members, friends, or religious affilia- tions if their sexual or gender identity is made known (Savin-Williams, 1998). Even in a progressive environment, where there are ample supports and legislature supporting GLBT rights, individuals may be vulnerable to subtle discrimination, such as deprived health care and poor service, should their GLBT status become public (Douglas, Kalman, & Kalman, 1985). Being raised in a heterosexist society and being aware of cases of verbal and physical harassment, as well as highly publicized gay bashings and murders, many clients will not be able to escape feelings of insecurity or fear related to the disclosure of their sexual or gender orientations. Therefore, members may require differing degrees of security and comfort in group settings. Members who have come out and have taken significant risks in their personal and professional lives may not take into consideration the fear and concerns that those members who are not out are facing. A discussion about the experience of personal safety is important to consider in any group.

Structuring Effective Group Work With GLBT Clients

Group Facilitator Personal Preparation

Group facilitators should have examined their own biases and assumptions regarding sexual and gender orientation. Because heterosexist attitudes and norms are prevalent in the United States, most people harbor some heterosexist beliefs and assumptions regarding GLBT individuals. Heterosexual group leaders can explore their attitudes and beliefs by spending time and asking questions of GLBT friends and acquaintances, reading GLBT narratives and fiction, and visiting GLBT Web sites (e.g., www.glsen.org, www.pflag.org). GLBT facilitators should examine and consider their own possible internalized homophobia while seeking out accurate information about unfamiliar GLBT groups. At the same time, facilitators should not commit an alpha bias in relation to GLBT individuals (the belief that enduring differences in problems and concerns characterizes heterosexuals and GLBT individuals, thereby exaggerating dissimilarities and dichotomizing orientations) nor a beta bias (minimizes and dismisses concerns unique to GLBT individuals) (Hare-Mustin & Marecek, 1988).

Group facilitators should also be aware of their own developmental processes, whether heterosexual or GLBT identified. Chojnacki and Gelberg (1995) described a parallel process of coming out for heterosexual group leaders and GLBT individuals. The process encompasses confusion for the counselor who is just becoming aware of the oppression of GLBT individuals and is engaged secretly in GLBT work; fear and anxiety about becoming a GLBT ally; increasing activism and advocacy on the part of the GLBT community; pride concerning their roles as advocates while experiencing increased alienation from homophobic colleagues; and finally, a sense of professional and personal integration as the leader's values become more congruent with their relationships and activities as advocates and allies. Many individuals find it helpful to participate in groups that include only GLBT individuals in order to explore and understand issues unique to their communities. Group facilitators may find that the initial structure of the group has a great influence on the ensuing process and outcome. When forming a group, facilitators may wish to consider issues such as consent, confidentiality, members' out-of-group contact, disclosure, group purpose and theme, and membership. Considerations relevant to groups that include GLBT members as well as for homogeneous GLBT groups are discussed.

Recruitment of Members: Informed Consent

A clear purpose of the group statement is to recruit members and build group cohesion. It is also important to indicate in any advertisements that the group is affirmative toward GLBT individuals. Despite the ethical guidelines put forth by official organizations of helping professionals (e.g., American Psychological Association, American Counseling Association, etc.) that explicitly repudiate therapies who attempt to convert same-sex identified individuals to heterosexual identities (conversion and reparative therapies), these therapists proliferate throughout the United States. GLBT individuals are aware of these conversion efforts and will be more inclined to follow up with an ad that states at the outset that the group is affirmative in its approach to GLBT individuals. The advertisement should also describe the theme of the group (e.g., transgendered support group, safe-sex psychoeducational group, etc.). A screening interview should be arranged with each potential member. During this interview, the group leaders should discuss group goals, session expectations, fees, and other concerns. By encouraging individuals to articulate their needs in individual interviews, counselors can ensure that members' goals are compatible with the group's purpose. Providing information such as purpose of the group, number of sessions, and information about facilitators and their backgrounds allows clients to give informed consent to participate. Because GLBT supports are lacking in many areas, some individuals may join a group that is not appropriate for their needs in order to feel a sense of belonging. As a result, leaders may wish to have referral sources or community resources available to those potential members who are not suitable for a group.

CONFIDENTIALITY: STRUCTURING A SAFE ENVIRONMENT

For GLBT groups in particular, there is no more important issue than establishing and maintaining confidentiality. Group leaders should state the limits of confidentiality, making members fully aware of the consequences of breaching confidentiality agreements (e.g., expulsion from the group). Group members should determine what course of action to take if members and leaders are encountered outside of group or if group members' names are mentioned by a nongroup member. These rules should be clearly established, and consensus reached among members.

Facilitators should not assume that all members of groups have the same respect and level of concern about confidentiality. For example, some GLBT individuals maintain that being out about one's sexual or gender orientation in all spheres of life is essential for mental health and well-being. Such group members may believe that "outing" members who are closeted would be beneficial to their psychological adjustment. Such a practice could be extremely damaging to members who are at risk if their identities are revealed; therefore, this possibility should be discussed as a group. Preinterview screening is vital to ensuring that

all members will be equally sensitive to the importance of maintaining group confidentiality. Individuals who are accepted to join a group should sign a statement of confidentiality that describes the limits and value of confidentiality and asks all group members to adhere to this value. The implications of breaches of confidentiality should be described to members. Leaders may ask the group to explore the consequences of breaking confidentiality. Confidentiality should be discussed periodically in the group, as the need arises.

Issues Around Out-of-Group Contact

Members should negotiate about what to do if they meet outside the group context by chance and come to a consensus on whether they wish to have relationships among group members outside of group sessions (e.g., social meetings, Internet exchanges, etc.) or to contain their interactions within the group setting. Holahan and Gibson (1994) caution that the likelihood of interaction outside of the group is generally quite high, given the small size of GLBT communities, even in large cities; thus, group members need to decide if the restriction of outside-group contact is a realistic or desired goal. Again, it will be important that all group members agree to the final decision, which may include a timeline for acceptable contact after the group's termination. For psychoeducational and coming-out groups (many individuals join coming-out groups to make their initial contacts with the GLBT community), limiting outside contact may not be beneficial or even reasonable for group members. However, with counseling and psychotherapy groups, facilitators should prioritize group discussion and consensus on outside contact due to the nature of the group.

Group Facilitators' Orientations and Disclosure

Leaders of groups should be expected to disclose their sexual/gender orientations during the initial screening interview. By doing so, leaders can enhance trust and model openness. If leaders are heterosexual, an immediate disclosure in combination with a description of the development of their interest in and support for GLBT issues can help to avoid suspicion and build group cohesion. Chojnacki and Gelberg (1995) suggested that this process of sharing development as a GLBT ally by heterosexual counselors fosters an alliance among participants and counselors. Heterosexual leaders can be important in creating a sense of affirmation for GLBT individuals and generate a sense of alliance against heterosexism. For example, heterosexual allies and GLBT clients share many limitations imposed by heterosexism. Social sanctions against emotional intimacy between heterosexual male friends (which also places burdens on heterosexual women to exclusively meet emotional needs of heterosexual men) is rooted in the stigmatization and fear of gay men, similar to the social intolerance of shared public affection by gay men and lesbian women.

TYPES OF GLBT GROUPS

Psychoeducational vs. Counseling

Although psychoeducational and counseling groups can be distinguished by their respective goals, these aims may overlap in homogeneous GLBT groups. The goal of psychoeducational groups is to impart information that promotes personal growth and the prevention of specific problems through here-and-now interaction with group members who may be at risk for the particular identified problem (ASGW, 1998; Gazda, Ginter, & Horne, 2001). In contrast, a counseling group is one in which facilitators use theoretical strategies to address interpersonal development issues with members who may be experiencing temporary adjustment issues or are interested in personal enhancement. At times, psychoeducational groups will need to take on aspects of a counseling group even though psychoeducation remains the primary focus. For example, in an HIV prevention group that is providing information on safe-sex procedures, a member may need to discuss the loss of a partner who would not engage in new relational safe-sex rules. Likewise, during a counseling group, if a member were to share lack of knowledge concerning safe-sex practices, leaders and members might share information and concerns about safe-sex practices.

Group Topic: Theme-Specific and General Interpersonal Groups

If group members are highly verbal and self-aware, the group may not need a great deal of direction to function smoothly. These groups typically consist of individuals who have worked through their coming-out processes and are engaged in considerations of career, relationships, and meaning.

Some counseling groups work best, however, with weekly themes, either leader or member generated. These groups often consist of members who are early in their coming-out processes, such as adolescents or university students. Usually, members welcome structure as long as the group is flexible to emerging concerns that should take precedence over weekly themes (e.g., the concerns of a young lesbian who is kicked out of her home when her sexual identity is revealed to her family should be prioritized over a weekly theme such as dating). Weekly themes can increase participation by group members with topics that generally are avoided in general interpersonal groups, such as hate crimes, safe sex, and intimacy.

Membership: Men vs. Women

The literature discusses a variety of GLBT groups, some consisting of mixed groups of men and women and others that favor homogeneous gender groups (Perez, DeBord, & Brock, 1999). The purpose of the group should determine gender makeup. Obviously, a psychoeducational group focusing on issues of conception and fertility clinic usage would typically include lesbian and bisexual women, whereas a "considering parenthood" group could include both men and women. Increasingly, parenting groups are including both men and women together as gay and bisexual fathers become more common. At the adolescent and university age level, mixed groups often are beneficial. They highlight universal concerns of GLBT men and women and help increase support networks at a vulnerable developmental stage.

Membership: Gay, Lesbian, Bisexual, or Transgendered

Differences among GLBT individuals are important to consider when working with groups. For example, transgendered individuals may seek support in understanding and living with their gender identity, which may or may not involve sexual identity concerns. Likewise, many bisexual individuals feel unwelcomed or misunderstood in traditional gay and lesbian groups because they may have other-sex relationships, an option not typically available or favored by gay and lesbian individuals and one that might be viewed as discrediting their group membership. On university campuses, GLBT groups often include members of all four identities; however, as sexual and gender identity develops, such mixed groups may be less appropriate. The issues and concerns that are important for gay men in their 30s can be dramatically different from those for lesbian women at that age. Similarly, transgendered individuals later in life may be making other decisions (real-life test to live as the genetically other sex, sex-reassignment surgery, hormone treatment, etc.) rather than dealing with coming-out issues, which are common themes for university and college groups.

GROUP PROCESS ISSUES

Identity Formation: Respecting the Developmental Process

There is great diversity within GLBT populations in the ways individuals understand and discuss their sexual and gender orientations. While some group members may be quick to identify themselves in one category, others may be reluctant to label themselves or may be struggling with identity issues. Appreciating the gradual process of building a sexual and gender identity will allow leaders to recognize and accept clients as they explore these themes.

Facilitators should be familiar with stage models of sexual identity development (e.g., Brady & Busse, 1994; Brown, 1995; Cass, 1979; Coleman, 1987; McCarn & Fassinger, 1996; Troiden, 1989). These models describe processes of GLBT identity acceptance, synthesis with other identities, and increasing GLBT group affiliation. An awareness of these models can help leaders understand and normalize differences among members' own development.

At the same time, these models should be used as guides and should not blind facilitators to the idiosyncratic processes of development among group members (for a critique of the application of contemporary sexual identity models, see Fassinger, 2000). Based on research on a sexual identity group that did not employ a GLBT title, Horne, Levitt, and Leitner (2003) asserted that groups can be more inclusive of GLBT members if they reflect the diversity represented within these stage models of identity. Many individuals would not identify as GLBT until they fell into later stages or phases of the various sexual identity models. If groups assume that a coherent GLBT identity is already formed prior to beginning a group, they may exclude those members who are most in need of supportive exploration, such as clients who are unsure or ambivalent about their identities.

Not Being "Label-Ready." In initial stages of sexual identity development, group members may not be ready to assume labels describing their gender or sexual identities. They may be sexually inexperienced, hold internalized homophobic beliefs or attitudes, or may fear external reactions. Adopting a title for a counseling group that does not assume a fixed identity, such as "Exploring Sexual Identity," invites members at earlier stages to join. In a postcounseling qualitative interview (Horne et al., 2003), one member of one such university group reported, "I don't think I would have attended a group, at that point, named 'les/gay/bi.' I just wouldn't have wanted to identify. . . . And even if I had decided to come, I wouldn't have started the conversations I did with other people—I wouldn't have been saying, 'I'm going to this GLBT group,' you know, whereas I could say, 'I'm going to this sexual identity exploration group'" (p. 13).

Active Rejection of Labels. Group leaders may encounter many members who object to categorizing themselves within a sexual or gender identity label. To allow group members freedom to explore and shape their own identities, leaders will need to accept the ambiguity that this represents. They may wish to overtly encourage members to take their time in coming to sexual or gender identities congruent with their self-identities and acknowledge that identities can be fluid and changing. Also, groups may need to give permission for members to develop identities that are not defined by gender or sexual orientation labels. Another participant from the Horne et al. (2003) study stated, "I am just more of an individual, I think. . . . And so being that forward about my sexuality, if it comes up, you know, I can say it any other way without using a label, because they might have all these preconceived ideas that I don't want them putting on me" (p. 15). Not requiring a label for the group or using a more fluid terminology to describe the group will allow leaders to include these individuals who dislike labels but are engaging in same-sex behaviors or attractions. It is suggested that group facilitators model a supportive and accepting environment for same-sex desires and feelings, irrespective of identity labels. For example, facilitators could refer to friends or acquaintances who have same-sex relationships or attractions without using identifying GLBT labels.

Coming Out. Counselors should be aware of the complexity of the coming-out process for group members. Often, the initial disclosure to family or friends is the beginning of a long and involved process. Multiple layers of emotion may be triggered, such as relief, anxiety, fear, and pride, which can be explored in a group setting. Leaders need to be careful that the group does not "push" or use "peer pressure" to get members to come out. The dangers and the risks need to be fully explored and assessed, both on a general societal level and on a personal level. Group members can help prepare one another to come out, if this is a shared goal. Role-playing disclosure and sharing experiences of coming out can be beneficial in a member's preparation. A client who has just come out may require the group's attention and support for the majority of a group session to come to terms with their changing relationships. It may be important to check for safety concerns, especially with GLBT youth who are at increased risk of familial rejection and homelessness. Because family and friends also go though their own process in reaction to a member's coming out, leaders may wish to prepare members to expect reactions to shift over time, in either positive or negative

directions. Leaders may find themselves confronted with different emotional reactions from the same group members from week to week as they negotiate changing relationships.

After one group member shares a coming-out story, other group members may experience heightened anxiety about their own coming-out processes. Leaders may invite group members to share their personal reactions and reflect upon the way these affect their own stories. They can discuss the process of coming out in a prospective sense as well, as individuals may have to make decisions about coming out repeatedly throughout their lives. Members can discuss pros and cons to coming out in different situations and can share strategies that they use to assess safety concerns and weigh them in against personal and political needs to be visible.

DIVERSITY AND SPECIAL GROUPS WITHIN GLBT POPULATIONS

DeLucia-Waack (1996) pointed out the erroneous belief that groups are ever homogeneous, given the numerous ways group members can differ multiculturally, such as age, ethnicity, and socioeconomic backgrounds. Leaders should be prepared to address diversity issues within any GLBT group they organize. Members of culturally diverse groups may experience oppression on multiple levels. Helping members to negotiate the intersection of these identities is an important part of group work. Important spheres of difference to consider include race, age, spirituality, class, and disability. Leaders of any type of group may wish to make available contact information for organizations that provide resources and support for diverse subgroups within the GLBT community.

GLBT Youth Issues: Needing Support. Organizing a group for GLBT youth requires preliminary research into the state laws about parental consent and providing counseling to youth. States have different laws about the necessity of consent when it places a child at risk; however, many youth do not feel safe enough to disclose their sexual orientations to parents. To provide needed services for GLBT youth, counselors may act as facilitators for peer support or straight-gay alliances in schools. These groups are typically psychoeducational and supportive in nature and allow GLBT youth visibility and safety in one of the environments in which GLBT youth often report feeling most unsafe: school. Typically, one or two GLBT-affirming adults serve as facilitators or faculty sponsors for the groups, which usually comprise both GLBT youth and their heterosexual allies. The Gay Lesbian Straight Education Network is a good place to start for information on such groups (*www.glsen.org*). These alliances have generally been upheld as constitutional in cases that have gone before the courts (e.g., Romer v. Evans, 1996).

In addition to the same developmental concerns that all adolescents face, GLBT adolescents' lives can also be complicated by a number of severe stressors. Much research has documented the elevated rates of depression and anxiety that GLBT youth experience (e.g., D'Augelli & Hershberger, 1993). They are at high risk for substance abuse (e.g., Grossman & Kerner, 1998), physical and verbal harassment by family members (e.g., Pilkington & D'Augelli, 1995), homelessness (Kruks, 1991), HIV-positive status (e.g., Rotheram-Borus, Hunter, & Rosario, 1994), and suicide attempts (Garofolo, Wolf, Kessel, Palfrey, & DuRant, 1998). Facilitators should screen carefully for suicidal ideation, depression, and anxiety before the group starts, as well as periodically throughout the group. Although group members may need to discuss challenges unique to their sexual or gender identities, they often want to discuss normal developmental concerns, such as career, dating, and social relationships.

For youth in particular, it can be important to respect the process of negotiating labels. Hollander (2000) stressed the importance of supporting "questioning" youth by not superimposing rigid developmental models on their growth, and providing them with school support programs that build alliances among youth regardless of sexual identity or orientation. Facilitators' modeling of comfort is important, as the youth may be seeking clues about life as an adult, especially if the leader is GLBT. They may be inquisitive and may use humor to try to learn about the leader's life choices and day-to-day life. Leaders may decide to self-disclose by describing examples from their own lives but should be clear that there are varieties of ways healthy GLBT adults structure their lives and that a broader view is also helpful.

Also, leaders should have consistent boundaries about self-disclosure and its potential impact on youth. They should refrain from providing overly personal information and from framing their own choices as sole alternatives. For instance, a group leader who identifies as lesbian may want to make clear she views all other identities as equally valid, as well as the process of coming to an identity or the decision not to identify using a sexual orientation label.

Age. Aging can be an isolating experience, in particular for GLBT individuals. Research suggests that gay men may determine self-worth according to chronological age more so than lesbians or heterosexual individuals (Kimmel & Sang, 1995) and that such self-estimations lead to "accelerated aging," the defining of oneself as old earlier than one's chronological age (Friend, 1987). Facilitators can counter and discourage statements that suggest members are "past their prime." As older GLBT individuals become more visible in public life, this tendency toward accelerated aging may decrease.

At present, there are few resources for senior GLBT community members. Elderly GLBT individuals may feel hesitant about using resources that are not clearly GLBT-friendly, especially after being raised in an era that was more heterosexist. At the same time, facilitators should be aware of "cohort effects," the influences of various political and historical conditions that affect identity formation across generations. Many GLBT individuals who are older than 70 grew up during a time of very limited openness about sexual orientation and may actually experience discomfort in participating in activities labeled for GLBT individuals. Facilitators should take historical context into consideration for older adult GLBT individuals when it comes to identity discussion and formation (Barón & Cramer, 2000). It may also be challenging for senior GLBT individuals to ensure legal safeguards for medical care, long-term partner care, and death and dying issues if they are not accustomed to discussing sexual or gender orientation with health care and legal professionals. Groups can be a place where senior GLBT members can share their aging concerns and forge new connections with others. Although retirement communities for GLBT individuals are increasing in number, there is no information to date about the types of groups offered in these communities or whether these groups are beneficial to the psychological well-being of older adults. Given that many GLBT individuals retire to communities that are primarily heterosexual, further exploration of group work with senior GLBT clients in both GLBT and non-GLBT communities is a worthy area of future study.

Race/Ethnicity. Therapists who are in tune with the ways oppression shapes minority clients' identities and who possess multicultural counseling competencies will be better prepared to guide group members to integrate their GLBT identities with their racial and ethnic identities. The decision to disclose sexual or gender identity to racial group members may be more threatening for GLBT people of color, as they may risk rejection from their racial group, in addition to other forms of discrimination. According to Morales (1989), LGB people of color balance three identities, "the gay/lesbian community, the ethnic minority community, and the predominantly white, mainstream society" (p. 217).

GLBT members who are part of a minority racial or ethnic group may face additional conflicts, as aspects of their minority identities or cultures may conflict with their sexual or gender identities. Adopting a gay identity, for example, may therefore mean relinquishing one's ties to one's ethnic community. Similarly, claiming an ethnic identity within a dominantly White GLBT community may leave individuals feeling as if part of their identity is not supported, and they may experience oppression within the GLBT community. In the group context, raising the topic of multiple oppressions can give members permission to share experiences of racism in relation to heterosexism and to explicate cultural differences within the group. GLBT group members of color may be able to share with White group members their strategies for managing oppression in their daily lives and contribute to the group's resources, as well as broaden group members' perspectives on oppression.

Some ethnic minority people who engage in same-sex behavior do not adopt GLBT identities because the adoption of such an identity may be seen as assimilation into White culture (Tsang, 1994; Zamora-Hernandez & Patterson, 1996). Group facilitators should be cautious about encouraging members to adopt labels that are not congruent with their sense of self.

Spirituality. Contrary to popular accounts of dissonance between religious beliefs and GLBT identities, recent research (Noffsinger-Frazier & Horne, 2003) suggests that many GLBT individuals reconcile their spirituality and sexual orientations. In group contexts, it can be important for group members to share the different ways their faith beliefs can change as they adopt a positive sexual or gender identity. It has been found that gay men are quicker to come out when they have integrated their spiritual beliefs with their sexual identities (Wagner, Serafini, Rabkin, Remien, & Williams, 1994). It can be very painful, however, for many members to sever attachments to their faith or congregation in search of an affirming place of worship. The group process can be used to help members identify their spiritual needs and to become aware of a broader set of options available to them within their communities (Horne & Noffsinger-Frazier, 2003).

Class. There is very little research available on class and sexual and gender orientation (Barón & Cramer, 2000). GLBT groups are often provided through university counseling centers, and thus, clients of lower socioeconomic status (SES) and education may not have easy access to these services and may not feel comfortable attending groups in these settings. Group leaders should be aware that GLBT groups with different SES status may have different cultural characteristics. For instance, "butch-femme" identities historically have been associated with lower-SES communities, with upper-class neighboring lesbian communities blending into heterosexual models of femininity (Faderman, 1991), although this trend may be changing (see Levitt & Horne, 2002). There can be differences in group members' abilities to access community or mental health resources based on their financial demands. For example, rural lower-income GLBT individuals will have fewer resources at their disposal, and the costs (e.g., transportation) for accessing services in nearby cities may be prohibitive.

Disability. Disability creates additional stressors for GLBT clients to manage. For the physically disabled, it may be more difficult to access resources and information to support their sexual or gender identities (Caitlin & Futterman, 1997). Boden (1992) suggested that the shame surrounding disability could compound the shame associated with sexual or gender differences. However, Ketz and Horne (2003) found that lesbians with disabilities reported better sexual self-concepts than heterosexual disabled women, suggesting that a lesbian identity could be a mitigating factor that helps to reduce shame-based sexual self-constructs induced by disability status in an able-bodied world. The emphasis in many lesbian communities on sexual self-acceptance and respect for diversity may serve as a buffer for stigma associated with disability status. Group leaders should talk to potential group members in preinterviews about accessibility and participation needs (e.g., American Sign Language interpreters or wheelchair accessibility). They should promote an atmosphere that dispels myths about disability and encourages disabled members to communicate their sexual and social needs.

Bisexual and Transgender Identity: Difference Doubled. Bisexual and transgendered individuals often face double marginalization. Bisexual clients can experience rejection within heterosexual society because of their potential for same-sex attractions. At the same time, they may face discrimination within gay and lesbian communities because of the misconceptions that bisexuals should commit to a gay or lesbian identity or that bisexuality itself is not a "genuine" orientation. To ensure safety in group contexts, bisexual clients will need to have their acceptance guaranteed, whether they are involved with same-sex or other-sex partners. It will be important to discuss the acceptance of group members' sexual diversity in all preinterviews.

Transgendered individuals may find it difficult to use GLB resources because of their nontraditional gender status. They may identify as heterosexual but be seeking support for their cross-gender presentation. Alternatively, they may identify as homosexual and have a gender presentation that is consistent with a GLB identity, such as "drag queen." It is important for facilitators to determine an individual's needs. If clients are seeking the resources that are being offered by the group, they should be incorporated as members. Therapists should discuss with these clients in a preinterview the amount of disclosure they desire. If needed, facilitators should refer them to an appropriate group but do so with attention to the many different identities that are subsumed by the broad rubric *transgender.* For instance, many cities have transitioning female-to-male groups, but a masculine-appearing lesbian who identifies as butch may be misplaced in such a group and should be given other alternatives to explore her gender identity (e.g., Levitt & Bigler, 2003). It can be important for leaders to realize that although some transgendered individuals may wish to undergo sex-reassignment surgery and hormone treatments to change their bodies to match their internal experiences, others may be looking to develop healthy and positive identities without any interest in medical intervention.

HIV-Positive Groups. Although HIV (human immunodeficiency virus) and AIDS (acquired immune deficiency syndrome) are blind to sexual orientation and gender, this illness has caused particular devastation within the male gay and bisexual community. Different types of group interventions have been developed specifically for this population, including support, psychoeducational, and prevention groups.

The stigma facing individuals with HIV/AIDS remains a formidable obstacle for individuals seeking diagnosis and treatment. Berger, Ferrans, and Lashley (2001) suggested that HIV/AIDS stigma is made up of four components: personalized stigma, concerns about disclosure, self-image, and concern with public attitudes toward HIV individuals. Issues relating to stigma will be important topics of conversation as individuals work to retain or develop a positive sense of self and their homosexual histories.

Because of this stigma, support groups for HIV/AIDS-infected individuals differ from groups for other diseases. Although there have been many promising developments in the treatment of HIV and AIDS and life expectancy has been extended considerably, there still is no cure for the virus, and so individuals struggle with existential as well as social issues. The opportunity to come together with others who share similar struggles with the virus can be empowering, educational, and may lead to activism. Supportive therapy can be effective not only for individuals with HIV/AIDS but also for those mourning the loss of AIDS victims (e.g., de Ridder, 1999).

There have been many varieties of psychoeducational group formats that have been developed to prevent HIV/AIDS within specific populations. Telephone groups have targeted closeted men (e.g., Roffman, Beadnell, et al., 1995), and hip-hop groups have been created for African American adolescents (Stephens, Braithwaite, & Taylor, 1998). In addition to ethnicity, groups have targeted sexually compulsive men having difficulty implementing safety precautions in their sexual practices (Baum & Fishman, 1994). Choi et al. (1996) identified four main goals of prevention group work: the development of self-identity and social support, safe-sex education, the eroticization of safe sex, and the negotiation of safe sex. Research indicates that these groups do appear to promote safer-sex practices and greater awareness of risk (e.g., Sorenson, London, & Morales, 1991).

It may be most efficacious to form groups that are exclusive in terms of the stage of illness, risk behaviors, and gender of members (see Siebert & Dorfman, 1995). At initial stages of HIV/AIDS, individuals have to come to terms with integrating this illness into their own identities. Initially, group members will need to bolster one another's sense of hope, which may be difficult if confronted with other members in the latter stages of AIDS. Similarly, it may be difficult for members who have later-stage AIDS and are negotiating physical and treatment stressors to have a sense of group cohesion with members who are asymptomatic. For end-stage AIDS, in the case of victims who may not be able to come together physically, Rittner and Hammons (1992) discussed the use of group telephone therapy. These conversations can allow members a place to discuss issues related to impending death, interpersonal disengagement, frustration with the medical community, and living with illness. With the increasingly popular use of the Internet as a therapeutic tool, online groups may be another possible solution for clients with end-stage AIDS.

The risk factors that lead to the development of HIV/AIDS can be used to guide the formation of groups as well. Heterosexual individuals who have HIV/AIDS may have to deal with the stigma of having this illness but without the same attribution of blame that gay men face (Herek & Capitanio, 1999). Individuals who contracted HIV/AIDS through drug use may require group support to resist continued addiction risks. By designing groups specific to risk group, the challenges facing members may be explored more deeply and without comparison to other processes.

It can be advantageous to restrict groups by gender as well. HIV/AIDS may hold different meanings for women and men (see Green, 1996; Siebert & Dorfman, 1995). Women may require their own groups to reshape their sense of gender and sexuality; and group supports may be important for women with HIV/AIDS with children to explore their experiences and concerns in mothering (e.g., Edell, 1998).

Heterogeneous Groups With GLBT Group Members. In addition to the concerns above, there are other concerns relevant for group facilitators who are conducting mixed groups of heterosexual and GLBT clients. In the screening interview, leaders should ask GLBT clients if they are comfortable self-disclosing their sexual orientations or gender identities within the group. Similarly, group leaders should inquire of potential heterosexual members their comfort level with diversity and varied sexual identities. Facilitators should screen these members for signs of heterosexism or overt homophobia, although it may not necessarily keep a potential member from joining, as acquaintanceships with GLBT individuals can be one of the most effective ways to counter heterosexism (Mohr & Sedlacek, 2000). The inclusion of these members does mean that facilitators will need to create a safe environment for the GLBT individual, however, and advocate on his or her behalf. Therefore, individuals whose biases would be overly disruptive or irreconcilable should not be admitted into the group. When GLBT members are included in a group with non-GLBT members, helping members to build upon universal aspects of their experiences will be important. For example, when one of the authors cofacilitated a group with women who had post-traumatic stress disorder while serving in the military, it was helpful to stress the shared emotions, such as anger and shame, that the women had felt in relation to both their other-sex and same-sex partners when their PTSD symptoms caused difficulties in their relationships. Likewise, it is important to appreciate the differences between members' experiences. For instance, a lesbian who experiences the loss of her partner may suffer unique stressors when the significance of her loss is not legitimized by familial, legal, or medical systems.

CONCLUSION

Although in most respects, working with GLBT clients will be similar to working with heterosexual clients, it is important for counselors to be prepared to deal with unique issues and concerns that operate in tandem with oppression that many GLBT individuals experience. Because the source of difference for GLBT clients can be invisible, clients may not have terms to describe their experiences. Because GLBT experiences are usually not raised within a context of other minority groups, individuals may have internalized a great deal of heterosexist prejudices without buffers or role models from family and community. Group leaders will need to form, shape, and conduct groups with an eye to revealing the biases within the culture at large and within group members themselves. By allowing for the discussion of oppression at multiple levels and valuing the differences between group members, group facilitators can allow members to shape identities that are congruent with their experiences and to become resilient in the face of future obstacles.

REFERENCES

Association for Specialists in Group Work. (ASGW). (1998). ASGW best practice guidelines (Prepared by L. Rapin & L. Keel). *Journal for Specialists in Group Work, 23,* 237-244.

Barón, A., & Cramer, D. W. (2000). Potential counseling concerns of aging lesbian, gay, and bisexual clients. In R. M. Perez, K. A. DeBord, & K. J. Beischke (Eds.), *Handbook of counseling and psychotherapy with lesbian, gay, and bisexual clients* (pp. 207-224). Washington, DC: American Psychological Association.

Baum, M. D., & Fishman, J. M. (1994). AIDS, sexual compulsivity, and gay men: A group treatment approach. In S. A. Cadwell & R. A. Burnham (Eds.), *Therapists on the front line: Psychotherapy with gay men in the age of AIDS* (pp. 255-274). Washington, DC: American Psychiatric Press.

Berger, B. E., Ferrans, C. E., & Lashley, F. R. (2001). Measuring stigma in people with HIV: Psychometric assessment of the HIV Stigma Scale. *Research in Nursing & Health, 24,* 518-529.

Blye, F. W. (1999). Searching for support and community: Experiences in a gay men's psychoeducational group. *Canadian Journal of Counselling, 33,* 127-141.

Boden, R. (1992). Psychotherapy with physically disabled lesbians. In S. H. Dworkin & F. J. Gutierrez (Eds.), *Counseling gay men and lesbians: Journey to the end of the rainbow* (pp. 157-174). Alexandria, VA: AACD Press.

Bradford, J., Ryan, C., & Rothblum, E. D. (1994). National lesbian health care survey: Implications for mental health care. *Journal of Consulting & Clinical Psychology, 62,* 228-242.

Brady, S., & Busse, W. J. (1994). The gay identity questionnaire: A brief measure of homosexual identity formation. *Journal of Homosexuality, 26*(4), 1-22.

Brown, L. S. (1995). Lesbian identities: Concepts and issues. In A. R. D'Augelli & C. J. Patterson (Eds.), *Lesbian, gay, and bisexual identities over the lifespan: Psychological perspectives* (pp. 3-23). New York: Oxford University Press.

Brown, M. L., & Rounsley, C. A. (1996). *True selves: Understanding transsexualism.* San Francisco: Jossey-Bass.

Caitlin, R., & Futterman, D. (1997). *Lesbian and gay youth: Care and counseling.* Philadelphia: Hanley & Belfus.

Cass, V. C. (1979). Homosexual identity formation: A theoretical model. *Journal of Homosexuality, 4,* 219-235.

Choi, K., Lew, S., Vittinghoff, E., Catania, J. A., Barrett, D. C., & Coates, T. J. (1996). The efficacy of brief group counseling in HIV risk reduction among homosexual Asian and Pacific Islander men. *AIDS, 10,* 81-87.

Chojnacki, J., & Gelberg, S. (1995). The facilitation of a gay/lesbian/bisexual support therapy group by heterosexual counselors. *Journal of Counseling & Development, 73,* 352-354.

Coleman, E. (1987). Assessment of sexual orientation. *Journal of Homosexuality, 14*(1/2), 9-24.

D'Augelli, A. R., & Hershberger, S. L. (1993). Lesbian, gay, and bisexual youth in community settings: Personal challenges and mental health problems. *American Journal of Community Psychology, 21,* 1-28.

DeBord, K. A., & Perez, R. M. (2000).Group counseling theory and practice with lesbian, gay, and bisexual clients. In R. M. Perez, K. A. DeBord, & K. J. Bieschke (Eds.), *Handbook of counseling and psychotherapy with lesbian, gay, and bisexual clients.* (pp. 183-206). Washington DC: American Psychological Association.

DeLucia-Waack, J. L. (1996). Multiculturalism is inherent in all group work. *Journal for Specialists in Group Work, 21,* 218-223.

de Ridder, N. F. (1999). HIV/AIDS in the family: Group treatment for latency-age children affected by the illness of a family member. In N. B. Webb (Ed.), *Play therapy with children in crisis: Individual, group, and family treatment* (2nd ed., pp. 341-355). New York: Guilford.

Douglas, C. J., Kalman, C. M., & Kalman, T. P. (1985). Homophobia among physicians and nurses: An empirical study. *Hospital & Community Psychiatry, 36,* 1309-1311.

Edell, M. (1998). Replacing community: Establishing linkages for women living with HIV/AIDS—A group work approach. *Social Work With Groups, 21,* 49-62.

Everaerd, W., Dekker, J., Dronkers, J., an der Rhee, K., Staffeleu, J., & Wiselius, G. (1982). Treatment of homosexual and heterosexual sexual dysfunction in male-only groups of mixed sexual orientation. *Archives of Sexual Behavior, 11,* 1-10.

Faderman, L. (1991). *Odd girls and twilight lovers: A history of lesbian life in twentieth-century America.* New York: Columbia University Press.

Fassinger, R. (2000). Applying counseling theories to lesbian, gay, and bisexual clients: Pitfalls and possibilities. In R. M. Perez, K. A. DeBord, & K. J. Bieschke (Eds.), *Handbook of counseling and psychotherapy with lesbian, gay, and bisexual clients* (pp. 107-132). Washington, DC: American Psychological Association.

Firestein, B. A. (1999). New perspectives on group treatment with women of diverse sexual identities. *Journal for Specialists in Group Work, 24*(3), 306-315.

Friend, R. A. (1987). The individual and social psychology of aging: Clinical implications for lesbians and gay men. *Journal of Homosexuality, 14*(1/2), 307-331.

Garofolo, R., Wolf, R. C., Kessel, S., Palfrey, J., & DuRant, R. H. (1998). The association between health risk behavior and sexual orientation among a school-based sample of adolescents. *Pediatrics, 101,* 895-902.

Gazda, G. M., Ginter, E. J., & Horne, A. M. (2001). *Group counseling and group psychotherapy: Theory and application.* Needham Heights, MA: Allyn & Bacon.

Green, G. (1996). Stigma and social relationships of people with HIV: Does gender make a difference? In L. Sherr & C. Hankins (Eds.), *AIDS as a gender issue: Psychosocial perspective* (pp. 46-63). Philadelphia: Taylor & Francis.

Grossman, A. H., & Kerner, M. S. (1998). Support networks of gay male and lesbian youth. *Journal of Gay, Lesbian, & Bisexual Identity, 3,* 27-46.

Hare-Mustin, R. T., & Marecek, J. (1988). The meaning of difference: Gender theory, postmodernism, and psychology. *American Psychologist, 43,* 455-464.

Hedge, B., & Glover, L. F. (1990). Group intervention with HIV seropositive patients and their partners. *AIDS Care, 2,* 385-396.

Herek, G. M., & Capitanio, J. P. (1999). AIDS stigma and sexual prejudice. *American Behavioral Scientist, 42,* 1130-1147.

Holahan, W., & Gibson, S. A. (1994). Heterosexual therapists leading lesbian and gay therapy groups: Therapeutic and political realities. *Journal of Counseling & Development, 72,* 591-594.

Hollander, G. (2000). Questioning youths: Challenges to working with youths forming identities. *School Psychology Review, 29,* 173-179.

Horne, S., Levitt, H., & Leitner, D. (2003). *Conducting a sexual identity group for women.* Manuscript submitted for publication.

Horne, S. G., & Noffsinger-Frazier, N. (2003). Reconciling with religion/exploring spirituality. In J. S. Whitman & C. J. Boyd (Eds.), *The therapist's notebook for lesbian, gay, and bisexual clients* (pp. 202-209). Binghamton, NY: Haworth.

Ketz, F., & Horne, S. (2003). *An examination of sexual self-concept and body image in predominantly Caucasian lesbian and heterosexual women with physical disabilities.* Manuscript submitted for publication.

Kimmel, D. C., & Sang, B. E. (1995). Lesbians and gay men in midlife. In A. R. D'Augelli & C. J. Patterson (Eds.), *Lesbian, gay and bisexual identities over the lifespan* (pp. 190-214). New York: Oxford University Press.

Krentz, A., & Arthur, N. (2001). Counseling culturally diverse students with eating disorders. *Journal of College Student Psychotherapy, 15,* 7-21.

Kruks, G. (1991). Gay and lesbian homeless/street youth: Special issues and concerns. *Journal of Adolescent Health, 12,* 515-518.

Lee, M. R., Cohen, L., Hadley, S. W., & Goodwin, F. K. (1999). Cognitive-behavioral group therapy with medication for depressed gay men with AIDS or symptomatic HIV infection. *Psychiatric Services, 50,* 948-952.

Levitt, H., & Horne, S. (2002). Explorations of lesbian-queer genders. *Journal of Lesbian Studies, 6*(2), 25-39.

Levitt, H. M., & Bigler, M. (2003). Facilitating lesbian gender exploration. In J. S. Whitman & C. J. Boyd (Eds.), *The therapist's notebook for lesbian, gay, and bisexual clients* (pp. 183-196). Binghamton, NY: Haworth.

Liddle, B. J. (1996). Therapist sexual orientation, gender, and counseling practices as they relate to ratings of helpfulness by gay and lesbian clients. *Journal of Counseling Psychology, 43,* 394-401.

McCarn, S. R., & Fassinger, R. E. (1996). Revisioning sexual minority identity formation: A new model of lesbian identity and its implication for counseling and research. *The Counseling Psychologist, 24,* 508-534.

Meyer, P. A. (2000). Variety is the spice: Survivor groups of mixed sexual orientation. In J. Cassesse (Ed.), *Gay men and childhood sexual trauma: Integrating the shattered self* (pp. 91-106). Binghamton, NY: Haworth.

Mohr, J. J., & Sedlacek, W. (2000). Perceived barriers to friendship with lesbians and gay men among university students. *Journal of College Student Development, 41,* 70-80.

Morales, E. S. (1989), Ethnic minority families and minority gays and lesbians. *Journal of Homosexuality, 17,* 217-239.

Morgan, K. S. (1992). Caucasian lesbians' use of psychotherapy. *Psychology of Women Quarterly, 16,* 127-130.

Mulder, C. L., Emmelkamp, P. M. G., Antoni, M. H., Mulder, J. W., Sandfort, T. G. M., & de Vries, M. J. (1994). Cognitive-behavioral and experiential group psychotherapy for HIV-infected homosexual men: A comparative study. *Psychosomatic Medicine, 56,* 423-431.

Noffsinger-Frazier, N., & Horne, S. G. (2003). *Resolution of religious conflict among gay, lesbian, bisexual, and transgendered individuals: The influence of religious orientation on depression and internalized homonegativity.* Manuscript submitted for publication.

Norsworthy, K. L., & Horne, A. M. (1994). Issues in group work with HIV-infected gay and bisexual men. *Journal for Specialists in Group Work, 19,* 112-119.

Perez, R. M. (1996). Group counseling for HIV+ students: Issues and considerations. *Journal of College Student Psychotherapy, 11,* 11-26.

Perez, R. M., DeBord, K. A., & Brock, K. J. (1999). Group counseling for lesbian, gay, and bisexual students. In V. A. Wall & N. J. Evans (Eds.), *Toward acceptance: Sexual orientation and today's college students.* Washington, DC: American College Personnel Association.

Pilkington, N., & D'Augelli, A. R. (1995). Victimization of lesbian, gay, and bisexual youth in community settings. *Journal of Community Psychology, 23,* 33-56.

Quadland, M. C. (1985). Compulsive sexual behavior: Definition of a problem and an approach to treatment. *Journal of Sex & Marital Therapy, 11,* 121-132.

Reece, R. (1981/1982). Group treatment of sexual dysfunction in gay men. *Journal of Homosexuality, 7*(2-3), 113-129.

Rittner, B., & Hammons, K. (1992). Telephone group work with people with end stage AIDS. *Social Work with Groups, 15,* 59-72.

Roffman, R. A., Beadnell, B., Ryan, R., & Downey, L. (1995). Telephone group counseling in reducing AIDS risk in gay and bisexual males. In G. A. Lloyd & M. Kuszelewicz (Eds.), *HIV disease: Lesbians, gays and the social services* (pp. 145-157). New York: Harrington Park/Haworth.

Roffman, R. A., Downey, L., Beadnell, B., & Gordon, J. R. (1997). Cognitive-behavioral group counseling to prevent HIV transmission in gay and bisexual men: Factors contributing to successful risk reduction. *Research on Social Work Practice, 7,* 165-186.

Roffman, R. A., Ficciano, J. F., Bolan, M., & Kalishman, S. (1997). Factors associated with attrition from an HIV-prevention program for gay and bisexual males. *AIDS and Behavior, 1,* 125-135.

Roffman, R. A., Ficciano, J. F., Ryan, R., Beadnell, B., Fisher, D., Downey, L., & Kalishman, S. C. (1997). HIV prevention group counseling delivered by telephone: An efficacy trial with gay and bisexual men. *AIDS and Behavior, 2,* 137-154.

Romer v. Evans, 116 S. Ct. 1620 (1996).

Rotheram-Borus, M. J., Hunter, J., & Rosario, M. (1994). Suicidal behavior and gay-related stress among gay and bisexual male adolescents. *Journal of Adolescent Research, 9,* 498-508.

Russell, A., & Winkler, R. (1977). Evaluation of assertiveness training and homosexual guidance service groups designed to improve homosexual functioning. *Journal of Consulting & Clinical Psychology, 45,* 1-13.

Savin-Williams, R. (1998). The disclosure to families of same-sex attractions by lesbian, gay, and bisexual youths. *Journal of Research on Adolescence, 8,* 49-68.

Schneiderman, N. (1999). Behavioral medicine and the management of HIV/AIDS. *International Journal of Behavioral Medicine, 6,* 3-12.

Siebert, M. J., & Dorfman, W. L. (1995). Group composition and its impact on effective group treatment of HIV and AIDS patients. *Journal of Developmental & Physical Disabilities, 7,* 317-334.

Sorensen, J. L., London, J., & Morales, E. S. (1991). Group counseling to prevent AIDS. In J. L. Sorensen & L. A. Wermuth (Eds.), *Preventing AIDS in drug users and their sexual partners* (pp. 99-115). New York: Guilford.

Stephens, T., Braithwaite, R. L., & Taylor, S. E. (1998). Model for using hip-hop music for small group HIV/AIDS prevention counseling with African American adolescents and young adults. *Patient Education & Counseling, 35,* 127-137.

Troiden, R. R. (1989). The formation of homosexual identities. *Journal of Homosexuality, 17*(1/2), 43-73.

Tsang, D. C. (1994). Notes on queer n'Asian virtual sex. *Amerasia Journal, 20,* 117-128.

Wagner, C., Serafini, J., Rabkin, J., Remien, R., & Williams, J. (1994). Integration of one's religion and homosexuality: A weapon against internalized homophobia? *Journal of Homosexuality, 26,* 91-110.

Yalom, I. D. (1995). *The theory and practice of group psychotherapy* (4th ed.). New York: Basic Books.

Zamora-Hernandez, C. E., & Patterson, D. G. (1996). Homosexually active Latino men: Issues for social work practice. In J. F. Longres (Ed.), *Men of color: A context for service to homosexually active men* (pp. 69-91). New York: Harrington Park.

17

Group Approaches for Persons With Disabilities

Milton Seligman

University of Pittsburgh

Laura Marshak

Indiana University of Pennsylvania

Much has changed for persons with disabilities over the years. Technology has increased longevity and improved lifestyles, especially for those with chronic illness and disability. Legislation has altered children's educational opportunities, and accessibility for children and adults has widened the world of opportunity for those with disabilities. Language changes have evolved from descriptors such as "defective," "handicapped," and "disabled" to person-first language such as "a person with a disability." Together, technology, legislation, and improved language have combined to bring those with disabilities into the mainstream of society. However, stigma toward people with disabilities continues to be a significant problem. In fact, stigma creates social barriers (handicaps) that pose larger obstacles than do physical limitations.

As the reader will see later in the chapter, groups for persons with disabilities have distinct functions. They have been reported to help overcome powerlessness, isolation, depression,

and powerful challenges to one's sense of self. They provide support, information, encouragement, and guidance. They can play a role in relapse prevention and help calm fears when facing painful and difficult medical procedures. They provide a fellowship of like-challenged individuals pursuing some measure of stability, identity, and a positive future. All in all, such groups provide participants with numerous advantages to help them endure and overcome the challenges brought on by illness and disability.

Social attitudes along with other concomitants of the illness and disability experience necessitate that the professional community continue to provide services and treatment for those who endure these challenges. The chapter begins with a brief history of group treatment for those with disabilities. It then discusses relevant therapeutic factors and group themes and describes the self-help group movement that has become a salient force in the disability area. This chapter also explores the group leader's reactions to disability, practical considerations, and the emergence of groups for specific populations and circumstances.

HISTORY

According to Spira (1997), group therapy with persons who have illnesses or disabilities has only recently received the attention it deserves. This is an interesting observation because the seeds for group therapy are often acknowledged to have been Pratt's group meetings with tuberculosis patients, circa 1905 (Pratt, 1907). The chronicity of tuberculosis as well as its cyclical nature alerted Pratt to the discouragement and depression that accompanied the illness. It is to Pratt's credit that he observed the psychological concomitants of this illness and prescribed a group procedure that turned out to be appropriate to this special patient population. Spira asserted that historically, group work has been primarily directed at treating people with psychological issues rather than illness or disability-related concerns. Of course, some would argue that for many coping with chronic illness or disability, psychological concerns such as depression and anxiety can interfere with progress toward a successful rehabilitation.

World War II spurred the development of groups and the training of group leaders in response to overwhelming numbers of war casualties. The need for psychological services outpaced their availability, and therefore, group therapy was considered an efficient treatment designed to serve more veterans. Groups were established for those suffering from trauma and other psychological reactions to the war, but they were also formed to address the issues brought about by permanent disabilities.

The current interest in groups for persons with disabilities has been encouraged by the surge of studies linking psychosocial factors to health outcome and showing health improvement for patients in group therapy treatment (Spira, 1997). Spira also reported that group therapy effectiveness in combination with cost- and time-efficiency "are responsible for the sudden popularity of this mode of treatment" (p. 4).

The research that attests to the effectiveness of group therapy in general (Fuhriman &

Burlingame, 1994) and specifically to this population (Johnson & Johnson, 1991; Halstead & Halstead, 1983; Rose, West, & Clifford, 2000; Rothenberg, 1994; Spira, 1997) argues that groups are now employed out of both an efficiency and effectiveness rationale. Unlike the post–World War II period when efficiency was paramount, group therapy, including groups for persons with disabilities and chronic illness, is now employed more for the profound changes made in one's coping abilities, interpersonal relationships, and symptom levels.

Groups provide an important opportunity to address social and emotional issues often intensified by a disability. These include coping with major life transitions, existential issues, and prejudice. In addition, persons with disabilities (especially newly acquired ones) often have heightened issues around changes in body image and functioning, as well as social relationships. The issues are not unique to persons with disabilities, but are often amplified when disabilities are suddenly acquired.

Specific groups for those with an illness or disability are helpful for persons who are not well suited to intensive, insight-oriented, long-term individual psychotherapy (Spitz & Spitz, 1999). A further justification and value of such groups is the extent to which they can help prevent or reduce relapse, a goal that can be central to a number of conditions, such as groups for victims of cancer or poststroke.

The remainder of this chapter will address issues that are especially germane to persons with disabilities. Although in many respects, the conduct of group work for those with disabilities or chronic illness proceeds in ways similar to that of persons who are challenged by other life circumstances, this chapter will discuss the unique considerations that characterize these populations. For the most part, groups for this population tend to have both therapeutic and psychoeducational components.

GROUP THEMES

Persons with disabilities may worry about whether the disability or illness will essentially stay the same, improve, or worsen (Rolland,

1994). A fear noted by Goodheart and Lansing (1997) is whether and how one can live in an altered state, for example, in a wheel chair, or with a disfigurement. Groups offer information about coping strategies (e.g., stress reduction techniques) and cognitive interventions (e.g., suggesting other perspectives on the disability/ illness), as well as feedback from others who share an individual's plight.

It is well established that changes or transitions in one's life can lead to stress. For persons with disabilities or chronic illness, numerous and powerful changes are confronted by the introduction of a life-altering illness or disability. According to Falvo (1999), the following represent threatened areas that people with disabilities may face that can be the focus of group meetings:

- Life and physical well-being
- Body integrity and comfort as a result of the illness or disability and concerns about diagnostic procedures or treatment
- Independence, privacy, autonomy, and control
- Self-concept and fulfillment of customary roles
- Life goals and future plans
- Relationships with family, friends, and colleagues
- Ability to remain in familiar surroundings
- Economic well-being (p. 2)

Thus, according to Falvo, the goal of psychotherapy is the stability of self and identity in the face of the aforementioned threats. Goodheart and Lansing (1997) noted that any successful intervention should address two related factors: (a) the internal disorganization that threatens the structure of the self and identity and (b) the reorganization and reconsideration of self and identity based on a changed reality (p. 5).

Anxieties can center around whether one will be able to return to work or school, be able to walk and adjust to a wheelchair, have and enjoy sex, and so forth (Goodheart & Lansing, 1997). Existential issues such as changes in self-image, how patients spend time, a reevaluation of priorities, and a consideration of life in the face of dying may also arise. For many, just being able to verbally release in the group private worries that have plagued them can help to reduce

anxiety and depression. Group members can articulate their thoughts and fears and receive support and information on how others have dealt with similar concerns.

Group leaders need to be alert to the issues mentioned in this section. Denial can be present in groups, but it is the leader's task to help group members broach the issues that brought them to the group. However, due to the isolation found in the lives of some persons with disabilities, the leader must also recognize the essential connecting function of "small talk." A balance between socialization and actively confronting challenging issues is the hallmark of a well-functioning group.

DISABILITY AND THERAPEUTIC FACTORS IN GROUPS

Although we don't want to explore in depth the therapeutic factors (Yalom, 1995) because they are discussed elsewhere in this volume (for a detailed description of therapeutic factors in groups, see Kivlighan & Holmes, Chapter 2), we will discuss those factors that are especially germane to groups of persons with disabilities. From our experiences, we believe that the following therapeutic factors are especially relevant in disability-oriented groups.

1. *Imparting information.* For example, clients may be helpful to others in the group by revealing where certain services are available or where relevant job opportunities exist. For example, they may share information about professionals that have a track record of treating persons with disabilities and who offer specific expertise, empathy, and support. Group members can also share with each other how they have dealt with unkind, prejudiced people and awkward situations in public places. Didactic instruction may be used by the leader or invited experts to inform group members of medical processes or psychological concerns characteristic of a particular illness or disability. Leaders can also educate and provide information on a variety of health issues and help participants understand and cope with identity concerns, anger, and the grieving process (Jacobs, Harvill, & Masson, 1988).

2. *Instillation of hope.* In seeing the progress of others in the group, a member may feel encouraged that positive changes can occur. To perceive improvement in others who have overcome considerable adversity is a particularly hopeful sign to other group members. It is also reassuring when a member's progress is noted and affirmed in the group.

3. *Universality.* Group members discover that others with similar conditions face similar challenges. Universality is a powerful group dynamic that reassures and confirms that one is not alone. The group provides relief that there are others who can truly understand by virtue of their experience. Group members can learn that others can cope with the disability and, indeed, can lead productive lives. A major benefit of groups is to understand from others that individuals should not allow disabilities to define their existence or to substantially hinder them from their goals.

4. *Altruism.* Contributing to another's well-being can be an important source of self-esteem. Group members are encouraged to reach out and be supportive and empathic toward other group members. Since some members of counseling groups suffer from low self-esteem or depression, the process of helping others can be an ego-strengthening experience. Many persons with disabilities are cast in the dependent role of receiving most of the time. Being in the giving role promotes elevated self-esteem, a sense of accomplishment, and the realization that one has something to offer to others.

5. *Development of socializing behaviors.* Loneliness and withdrawal can be reduced by learning behaviors that promote prosocial interactions. Participants learn strategies that can help them feel more comfortable and competent when interacting with professionals, family members, friends, and strangers. Role play can help by enacting interpersonal behaviors that facilitate communication and decrease isolation. For example, a shy person can learn to speak out to his physicians so that he feels heard and acquires the information he needs. A defensive, angry person with a disability can learn to be more open and less hostile, thereby creating more gratifying relationships.

Group leaders should be knowledgeable about therapeutic factors and actively promote them when they do not develop naturally. For example, in terms of altruism, the leaders should encourage group members to reach out to others and explain that by helping, one can be thrust into the role of an active, contributing, and knowledgeable person. Also, more active strategies (e.g., role play) can help group members learn behaviors that will enable them to have positive relationships and feel more in control of their environment. In groups with persons who are disabled or chronically ill, the leader can encourage members to offer their knowledge of a particular condition. Most important, the leader can invite experts to the group to explain and comment on coping attitudes and behaviors. Thus, imparting information, a prominent therapeutic factor in such groups, becomes an important component that the leader should promote.

MEDICAL CRISIS GROUP COUNSELING

There is an approach to helping persons with chronic medical illness that involves a structured, short-term group intervention focused on several issues. This modality, called medical crisis counseling (MCC), was developed by Irene Pollin in the late 1970s. The impetus for MCC came from her experience of raising and then losing two children to illness (Pollin, 1995).

Pollin's personal experience led her to obtain a professional degree and eventually to develop MCC. She went on to establish a clinic for persons with chronic illnesses in Washington, D.C. In 1994, the Linda Pollin Institute was established at the Harvard Medical School, supporting postgraduate training and conducting research on the MCC model.

MCC groups have been offered to persons with a variety of chronic illnesses, for example, lupus, heart disease, cancer, and AIDS. The approach asserts that the principal psychosocial issues across illness are the same, no matter the condition. The groups focus the content of the sessions on the following fears:

1. Loss of control

2. Loss of self-image

3. Dependency

4. Stigma

5. Abandonment

6. Expressing anger

7. Isolation

8. Death

According to Pollin (1995), these issues often occur in sequence, but the order can vary. More than one concern can occur at the same time, and they can reemerge. These concerns form the basis of the MCC model and determine what is discussed in the sessions.

Before proceeding with the MCC model, the reader will note the overlap of some of the central issues for persons with disability or chronic illness noted by Pollin (1995), Falvo (1999), and Goodheart and Lansing (1997). We believe that the central concerns noted by these authors provide considerable grist to the group endeavor. We would like to synthesize those factors that by virtue of our literature search and personal experience reflect salient concerns people with disabilities or chronic illness experience:

1. Mourning losses

2. Self-esteem issues

3. Fear of the future

4. Threats to important relationships

5. Threats to independence, fear of dependency

6. Threats to issues of control

7. Threats to body integrity

8. Existence of depression and anxiety

9. Issues related to stigma and acceptance from others

10. Job and financial viability

11. Accessibility

12. Issues of isolation and abandonment

These challenges caused by illness or disability in persons reflect common themes in group work. They constitute many, though not all, of the central issues that are discussed in group treatment.

In terms of forming a group, Pollin's (1995) MCC model advocates including members who have the same illness and are at similar stages of the disease, making trust and empathy easier to attain. According to Pollin, strict homogeneity is the ideal in groups to foster alliances and rapid identification among the participants. Persons readily identify with the issues faced by others that they share. Such groups tend to be less psychodynamic and more supportive and educational. The benefits of such groups include symptomatic relief over a short period of time, better cohesion, better attendance, less conflict, fewer cliques, and less resistance (Furst, 1960; Yalom, 1995). Yalom noted that heterogeneous groups are better suited for more intensive interaction and for altering character structure. Heterogeneous groups take longer to coalesce but offer a richer variety of issues from which to learn and a diverse membership, with problems and concerns that are similar and others that are different. The concepts of heterogeneity and homogeneity can be misleading in that a group of cancer patients may share the illness, but they may be different ages, single or married, and have different concerns about the cancer.

In selecting members, a first step for the leader is to ascertain the motivation and commitment of prospective members. The leader must be sure that a group member doesn't face obstacles, perhaps brought on by a serious medical condition, that mitigate group participation. Relatedly, Pollin (1995) stated,

> Given the number of possible combinations short of the ideal (which is strict homogeneity), all that can be said here by way of advice is that the greater the specificity, the greater the group's chance of being effective. In general, the group leader should avoid combining people who are in the very early stages of a condition with those in advanced stages of the same condition; confronting the manifestations of an illness at an advanced stage can be very disheartening for people in its early stage. (p. 140)

As the reader can readily determine, the MCC model puts considerable emphasis on member selection and group composition. Thus, group leaders need to consider the many variables that can potentially affect the group experience, such as disability type, stage of illness or disability, age, gender, race, personality, and so on. While extolling the virtues of homogeneity, Pollin (1995) acknowledges that member identification can be a source of an excessively intense experience. She reports on a group composed of wheelchair-bound women in their 20s with advanced-stage multiple sclerosis (MS). The experience proved to be too traumatic for these women, who saw themselves in other members. This forced them to confront the harsh reality of being young, female, and significantly impaired. This was too painful for the women, and the group disbanded.

For the group leader, then, it is important to be cognizant of group variables such as stage of illness or disability, central focus (e.g., terminal vs. chronic phase vs. adjusting to diagnosis), or disability type. According to the MCC model, the leader should embrace homogeneity as the main goal in group composition. Our experience does suggest, however, that selecting group members is a challenging and unpredictable endeavor. Groups that appear to be ideal in terms of certain selection criteria can, by virtue of a number of characteristics, turn out to be failures. And at times, when we believe that a group will fail based on group composition, we are surprised to find a cohesive, productive working group. At times, the personalities of group members appear to be a more critical variable than illness, disability, and stage of illness.

Groups for Persons With Acute Medical Illness

As noted, there is great value in being with others who are "insiders" to a shared disabling condition, because life experiences and concerns differ so much from others. Persons in need of organ transplantation fall in this category. As described by Abbey and Farrow (1998), "Transplant candidates and their families face potentially opposing tasks, preparing to die should they not receive a transplant, and

fighting to live and make preparations to adjust following a successful transplant" (p. 175).

Abbey and Farrow's (1998) work with groups for organ transplantation patients provides a description of how a range of group structures and goals can be developed to meet the needs of individuals who share a similar life-threatening disorder. Their work also elucidates the value of a mutuality of concerns. According to Abbey and Farrow (1998),

The vast majority of transplant candidates are waiting for a cadaveric organ, that is, someone has to die and the bereaved family donate their loved one's organs for transplant to be possible. This leads to feelings of guilt and sadness that their opportunity for life requires someone else's death. With increasing desperation for transplantation, either in terms of deteriorating medical status or increased time on the waiting list, some individuals begin actively wishing for an organ and may make comments that others at a distance may find macabre or upsetting (e.g. "hopefully this holiday weekend will bring my transplant with everyone out drinking and boating"). Group members are often relieved to find that they are not the only ones with such thoughts. (p. 177)

As with other groups for members with a specific disability, organ transplantation patients share many general concerns, but their individual issues differ by stage of treatment and/or recovery. Abbey and Farrow (1998) describe the group therapy work at Toronto Hospital Multi-Organ Transplantation Program, which is based on a pyramidal structure. The hospital has a range of groups for persons coping with different aspects and periods of time in the transplant process. The base of the pyramid comprises groups that are primarily psychoeducational in nature; toward the top of the triangle are more emotionally intensive groups focused on interaction and emotional expression. The overall group program was developed with the expectation that some participants will develop the abilities to move up the pyramid and benefit from more insight-oriented group work after gaining group experience. Others may not be interested in, need, or benefit from groups that are more intensive in terms of focusing on insight and emotional expression.

GROUP THERAPY AND COGNITIVE DISABILITIES

Group therapy also holds great benefits for persons with disabilities that affect their cognitive abilities. Its use for social skills training is common in many treatment programs for persons with mental retardation, traumatic brain injury, or many other disorders that affect intellectual functioning. Many practitioners overlook the potential for group counseling as a means to help individuals with cognitive disabilities address concerns of an emotional nature (in contrast to skills training). Our focus in this section is to provide readers with a glimpse of some additional ways in which group counseling can be used with persons whose disabilities affect their cognition. Toward this end, we turn to a brief discussion of group counseling and mental retardation.

Rothenberg (1994) provides an excellent illustration of the creative use of group counseling with bereavement groups for persons with developmental disabilities. It was developed to help these young adults cope with their grief over the sudden death of an important and loved member of the clients' network. Group members had a range of developmental delays in areas of cognition, language, motor abilities, and/or social development. The group was conceptualized as "intended to facilitate the group of participants through a planned grieving process, based on knowledge of the stages of grieving, and the special needs of the population" (p. 62). This is an important model because emotional needs of persons with cognitive limitations are often overlooked due to the stereotype that they are "like children." Consequently, they often struggle with adult emotions with little support.

The value and viability of group counseling for persons with mental retardation is also emphasized by Tomasulo, Keller, and Pfadt (1995) in their discussion of the use of an interactive-behavioral model. It shares a similarity with the work by Rothenberg (1994) in that it focuses on traditional psychotherapeutic factors more so than skills training. The authors describe group facilitators as needing to do what they termed "cognitive networking." They define this concept as follows:

This is an effort to establish basic interactions between and among the group's members by having them repeat and acknowledge or otherwise support what was said by another member of the group. Physically orienting towards the person speaking, looking at them and echoing back what was heard are central elements to cognitive networking. (p. 3)[1]

The interested reader is encouraged to review this article because it provides a fund of knowledge about how to handle some of the difficulties in applying group counseling techniques to persons who are mentally retarded.

The group counseling literature is also beginning to address the needs of persons with traumatic brain injuries and cognitive impairments not accompanied by mental retardation. Stein (1996) wrote of the importance of modifying traditional group counseling techniques to compensate for the fact that persons with brain injuries often have problems with language and conversational exchange. He provides very practical advice, which includes the following:

Given that some group members may have problems tracking the flow of conversation, the clinician should make a special effort to regularly summarize the gist of the discussion verbally or by means of points written on a blackboard. For those patients who have difficulty organizing their approach to problems, the therapist can help by structuring the group process to highlight steps in an orderly problem-solving process. Other patients with poor social judgment and poor error monitoring can be helped by eliciting concrete information about their perceptions and their plans by inviting other members to provide constructive feedback. (Stein, 1996, p. 271)

Stein also writes about the importance of reducing emotional intensity and modifying the use of ambiguous language, if necessary, along with providing greater structure than in groups comprising members without cognitive impairments. These all represent relatively simple modifications of group counseling technique that can make the benefits of group counseling available to a wider range of persons with disabilities.

GROUP DYNAMICS WHEN A SINGLE MEMBER HAS A DISABILITY

It is also useful for group therapists to be aware of additional dynamics that may occur in a group when there is only one member with a disability. This type of group composition is clearly valuable and provides rich opportunities for growth; however, it is important to be aware of distortions in interaction and perception that are likely to arise. The first has to do with what has been termed "interactional strain" (Davis, 1972). It has been clearly documented that persons without disabilities often, at least initially, interact in a less natural manner with persons who have disabilities (Marshak & Seligman, 1993; Safilos-Rothschild, 1970). Initial encounters are often described as stilted, somewhat uncomfortable, less intimate, less candid, and terminated relatively quickly (Freund & McGuire, 1999; Kleck, Ono, & Hastorf, 1966). These difficulties arise in part because many people without disabilities view those with disabilities as being very different from themselves in terms of their interests, needs, and daily concerns (Marshak & Seligman, 1993). The interactional strain is also partially due to people with disabilities who worry about saying the "wrong thing" that may offend. Often, this involves unnecessary monitoring of one's speech in order not to say something like "Do you see my point?" to someone without vision. Actually, this type of verbal vigilance is in itself problematic, whereas these casual phrases are acceptable by persons with disabilities.

The phenomenon of "inferred emotional consequences" may result in stereotypical ways in which others view the group member who has a disability. Persons who overlook the growth-promoting aspects of living with a disability assume that they would feel overwhelmed with bitterness, depression, or feelings of inferiority. Often, these negative emotions are projected onto the member with a disability.

By the same token, group members with disabilities may also find that they misperceive others. They may be overly sensitive to some issues and profit from group experiences in which they have an opportunity to process interactions in a group setting. For example, we have worked in therapy with several individuals who have felt repeatedly excluded by others due to their disabilities. Sometimes this is accurate; however, it is not uncommon that the perceived exclusion is actually the result of their own withdrawal from interactions. This withdrawal may result from fear of rejection or doubts that they had anything useful to contribute, problems with self-worth, or reactions from past negative interactions. For these individuals, valuable insights about their roles in social exclusion can be gained within a heterogeneous group of disabled and nondisabled persons. The insight gained from such an experience can be generalized outside the group.

Questions regarding "politically correct" speech are often raised regarding verbal references to disability. There is a great deal written on this topic and some on the importance of watching one's speech. Our position is that it is important to avoid phrases that have the potential to be offensive or contribute to stereotypes of persons with disabilities. For these reasons, we suggest avoiding phrases such as "the disabled" or "the handicapped" because they obscure the individuality of persons with disabilities. In specific, their disabilities are a single aspect of their lives, not the defining characteristic. We also believe that it is important to watch the use of clichés that portray persons with disabilities as unusually courageous, brave, and "gifted" to compensate for their disabilities. Similarly, references to persons as "victims" of disorders should be avoided.

It is important that group leaders work to decrease misperceptions of or overreactions to the group member's disability. Of particular importance is the encouragement of normalized interactions with other group members. It is not unusual for people to subscribe to what has been called "the norm to be kind" when interacting with someone who has a severe disability (Hastorf, Northcraft, & Picciotto, 1979). This term pertains to the withholding of useful but negative feedback because of pity and the desire to spare someone "more pain." Actually, the feedback is often what is needed to promote personal growth and should be present in group counseling to function as the powerful treatment modality that it can be.

SELF-HELP GROUPS

Any discussion of group work for persons with disabilities or chronic illness must include some observations about self-help groups (SHGs). SHGs represent a major resource for persons with disabilities or chronic illness and enjoy considerably more popularity than traditional psychotherapy groups. Such groups exist for just about any condition or life circumstance (Barlow, Burlingame, Nebeker, & Anderson, 2000; Lieberman, 1990; Seligman & Marshak, 1990).

SHGs for persons with a variety of life circumstances and psychological issues have a long history. Lieberman (1990) offers the following definition:

[Self-help groups are] composed of members who share a common condition, situation, heritage, symptom, or experience. They are largely self governing and self regulating. They emphasize self reliance and generally offer a face-to-face or phone-to-phone network that is available and accessible without charge. They tend to be self supporting rather than dependent on external funding. (p. 2)

With the popularity of the Internet and the capacity for interaction through e-mailing, "virtual" support groups have become accessible. An interesting research question is whether groups that are not face-to-face are as effective as groups held in a church, community building, or a person's home. The anonymity and accessibility of the Internet may benefit some (e.g., those that live in a remote area or are homebound), but it may not be as helpful for others where person-to-person interaction can help to combat isolation, alienation, and anomie.

Originally, the "purest" model (using only lay members and leaders) was preeminent, because it was created by people for people, without the inclusion of professionals. In fact, some SHGs held a certain amount of disdain toward professionals whom they deemed to have failed them. This would fit into Lieberman's (1990) view of SHGs as an alternate service delivery system: one that meets one's needs, is accessible, free, and in addition to or instead of a professional delivery system.

Some would argue that by referring to such gatherings as SHGs is a misnomer. In many cases, these are professionally led support groups. According to Barlow et al. (2000), patient-led SHGs are "apparently neither valid nor acceptable any longer" (p. 54). These authors cite a survey of 2,000 SHGs in California and found that 84% of the groups had professional involvement. They noted further that there are opportunities for professionals to get involved in establishing, coleading, and consulting. Goodman and Jacobs (1994) also observed that some professionals are involved in starting SHGs. It seems the group title remains, but its definition and makeup have altered recently.

Since professionals are involved in SHGs, how do their roles differ from leaders who conduct psychotherapy groups? One difference might be that some professional leaders share the disability or illness of the group members. Furthermore, groups for persons with chronic illnesses or disabilities tend to eschew psychodynamic group models or models that promote intense, here-and-now interaction. Group members may be less likely to join a more dynamically oriented group, perhaps believing that such groups are designed for persons with more serious psychological problems. SHG members' needs tend to be more directed at exchanging information, gaining support from others in similar situations, and acquiring knowledge to heighten feelings of control and competence. The members' needs tend to be less intrapsychic or interpersonal, generally speaking, yet there are emotional needs related to members' relationships with family members, professionals, and in some instances, a hostile and prejudiced society.

Because SHGs are more concerned with being supportive, cathartic, and educational, there may not be a pressing need to have extensive training in psychodynamics, group dynamics, or group leadership. And yet like any therapeutic group (we believe that SHGs have a therapeutic purpose and outcome), some rudimentary knowledge or training pertaining to group dynamics, managing problems, and providing safety should be a prerequisite for group leadership. We suspect that peer leaders do not generally have fundamental training or experience in group leadership, which may account for the increased number of professional leaders. This is a concern because safety and management issues can arise in these groups.

One of the authors was invited to a session of a parent group in which the requirement for membership was the loss of a child. The group had recently lost their peer leader and felt rudderless. They also wanted "tips" from an experienced group leader, such as what themes to look for during the group's interaction; how to cope with an overly aggressive, verbose, or shy member; and when it is helpful to intervene and when to remain silent. This SHG wanted competent lay leadership to keep the members safe, especially in light of their traumatic losses. They already felt vulnerable and in need of support.

As we know, SHGs tend to be specific to a condition, an illness, or a disability (Ciechoski, 2000). Therefore, we believe that in addition to some exposure to group dynamics, a leader should be knowledgeable about the disability that is the group's focus. In the absence of direct knowledge, the leader should be aware of agencies or professionals in the community that can provide information and accurate knowledge. The group leader may be a social worker or psychologist, but what the group may need on occasion is a medical professional who can be invited to a group meeting.

As noted, some SHGs are led by members, some by professional leaders who share the disability, and still others by professionals, such as counselors, psychologists, or social workers, who do not share the disability. Group members seek a supportive, therapeutic environment that also has an educational component. We believe that leaders need to recognize that persons with disabilities do not by virtue of their condition have problems beyond the restrictions of the disabilities themselves or those imposed by society. However, the leader needs to be aware that preexisting or coexisting mental health problems may be present along with the disability. Generally speaking, groups should be supportive, educative, and interpersonal. The leader needs to encourage interpersonal exchanges and facilitate openness when the group is in denial. However, in-depth psychotherapy is less likely to be the goal of a prospective group member who is attempting to cope with a major alteration in his or her life.

THERAPIST REACTION TO DISABILITY

Disability is a personal characteristic that often has the power to elicit reactions from others. It has been well documented that initial interactions with a person with a disability often draw out stereotypes, altered interpersonal patterns, and personal fears (Wright, 1988). It has been established that professionals can share the same misconceptions of the general public regarding persons with disabilities (Elston & Snow, 1986; Marshak & Seligman, 1993). Group leaders are prone to a number of misconceptions and stereotypes commonly held by the general public.

One of the stereotypes that most significantly affects participation in group therapy is the concept of *inferred emotional consequences.* The phenomenon of inferred emotional consequences has been described by Wright (1988) as referring to the general tendency to assume that persons with disabilities will almost invariably experience negative personality and emotional effects by virtue of the difficulties inherent in living with a disability. Although the research on adjustment to disability does not support this common stereotypical belief, it persists (Coleman, 1977; Marshak & Seligman, 1993; Wright, 1988). This has the potential to affect group experiences in more than one significant way. First, group leaders may assume that the member's emotional problems are directly due to having a disability. As one person with cerebral palsy stated about her counseling experience, "The therapist always wanted to talk about my disability, and that was not what I was there for." Because the disability is only one characteristic of the individual, problems with adjustment may or may not be related to the disability. Furthermore, if there is a relationship between having a disability and emotional and/or adjustment problems, the effects of the disability may be much more indirect than what group members and leaders assume. Persons unfamiliar with the disability experience often assume that some of the main problems with having a disability have to do with direct impact of the impairment itself or functional limitations of the disability per se. They tend to overlook that it is often the societal context of disability that is most disturbing, such as problems due to stigma, discrimination, and environmental barriers.

Interactions with persons who have severe disabilities often trigger personal fears, particularly when the disability has been acquired through illness or injury. Such interactions are reminders of one's own vulnerability to disability or illness, and this is often accompanied by an increase in anxiety. This phenomenon, termed *distressed identification,* and described by Siller (1976), often results in attempts to introduce "psychological distance" as a way to manage this anxiety. This reaction is exacerbated by the common stereotype that persons with disabilities lead tragic lives. Consequently, group leaders may find they are initially less comfortable and less well engaged with some individuals for this reason.

Group leaders serve as models for members regarding a congenial attitude with persons who have disabilities. Toward this end, it is important that group leaders increase their familiarity with the lives of persons with disabilities, because this tends to increase one's comfort. When it is understood that the majority of persons with disabilities rate their lives as being as high in satisfaction as does the general population, the tendency toward pity and avoidance is diminished (Marshak & Seligman, 1993). For those with disabilities, life is often reported as "more difficult"; however, it is important to note that this does not necessarily preclude life as being very satisfying. Contact in real life is clearly the best educator. However, if this is not feasible, familiarity can also be gained through reading autobiographies of persons with disabilities. Another method is to try to sweep away preconceived notions by being aware of one's stereotypes and by focusing on the individual, not the disability. By using these strategies, stereotyped thinking will diminish. Group leaders should ensure that the member with a disability is not marginalized in the group. The best way to accomplish this is to be aware of one's prejudices, be conversant with the disability literature on stigma, read about persons with disabilities, and become more comfortable with this minority population through direct contact.

Practical Considerations

Some practical considerations are necessary to consider when accommodating members with a chronic illness or disability in groups. Patterson, McKenzie, and Jenkins (1995) provide one of several sources of information on this topic. Their discussion includes specific guidelines that are important to follow but cannot be covered in depth here. Their recommendations include remembering when having a dialogue with someone who uses a wheelchair to take a seated position and to proceed on eye level. This is important because of the perception of being "talked down to," a common experience in the lives of person with mobility impairments. Understanding common principles for communicating with someone with a hearing impairment is necessary. Some of these principles include speaking without exaggerated tones and remembering that persons who lip-read need an unobstructed view; this requires others to be careful not to place their hands in front of their lips and to be aware of matters such as lighting and glare from windows. Accommodating a person with blindness requires other accommodations, such as making such group members identify themselves when speaking (as necessary) and simple mobility assistance. Mobility assistance generally takes the form of letting a blind person take another person's arm or elbow for guidance. The counselor can serve as a role model so that other members know more about these procedures, as well as to increase their comfort level with persons with disabilities. Ignorance of what to do breeds much of the discomfort in group members.

Considerations Regarding Group Composition

As noted earlier, one of the most important considerations for a discussion on group work and disability is the question of heterogeneous versus homogenous group placement. The benefits available to the individual with a disability through participation in counseling and support groups differ depending on whether the group composition is heterogeneous or homogenous with respect to disability. However, a review of the literature on group counseling and disability (as well as our experience in the field) makes it clear that the initial professional reaction is to assume that it is best to place persons with disabilities in homogenous groups. This makes as much sense as routinely placing members of other minority groups with persons who are similar in terms of racial or ethnic background. Addressing this point, Patterson et al. (1995) stated,

> The appropriateness of disability-specific or disability-focused groups for individuals with disabilities who are addressing adjustment issues related to their disability is not disputed; however, it is important to remember that disability represents only one facet of any person. Individuals with disabilities also represent cultural diversity. There are individuals with disabilities who are incest survivors, older adults, and children whose parents have alcohol or substance abuse issues. People with and without disabilities have interpersonal, marital, career, social, and transition concerns that can be addressed in a group setting. (p. 76)

As has been discussed in this chapter, great benefits can be available through homogenous groups; however, this should be an *option,* not an automatic practice. Brown (1995) sheds light on routinely including persons with disabilities in groups composed primarily of persons without disabilities. Raising the interesting observation that the general exclusion of persons with disabilities in traditional therapy groups reflects society's general reactions to persons with disabilities, she wrote,

> Group work, as a microcosm of society, provides a place where the richness of democracy is represented and the evolution of civil rights has been demonstrated. In recent years, group workers have given a great deal of attention to the inclusion of members of both sexes as well as those of a different race, color, ethnicity, and national origin. Additionally, we have examined the use of group work with homogenous groups of members with a specific disability. Little attention has been given to the inclusion of people with disabilities into the mainstream of group work. Group work seems to reflect society's neglect of including persons with disabilities into the mainstream of the workforce. (Brown, 1995, p. 71)

A final yet provocative thought on the issue of inclusion of persons with disabilities into

heterogeneous groups can be found in Brown's observations on the legal aspects of inclusion: "A disability cannot be used as the sole criterion for exclusion from group work" (p. 73).

A second major consideration regarding group composition pertains to gender. As described by Tepper (1999), disability "is experienced in the context of gender" (p. 37); for this reason, same-sex group composition may sometimes prove to be advantageous. One aspect of the interface between disability and gender is well illustrated by Tepper:

> Men arrive at rehabilitation with all the baggage society, culture, the media, parents, friends, and religion packed for us. We were socialized to be strong and self-reliant, successful, manly and sexual performers. We learned the same myths and fantasy model of sex as our peers. What happens when we are faced with the loss of strength and self-reliance, loss of sexual prowess, and loss of success? (p. 45)

There is little written in the professional literature about group work for men with physical disabilities and illnesses; however, the potential benefits should not be overlooked. It counteracts the tendency of men in rehabilitation to attempt to try to go through the rehabilitation process on their own, in a silent, stoic manner, without expressing their feelings or fears (Tepper, 1999). The group setting can provide access to role models of men with disabilities who have been successful in establishing and maintaining positive self-images that incorporate their disabilities, masculinity, and sexuality.

About 20 years ago, Kriegsman and Celotta (1981) described the use of group counseling for women with disabilities; there have been few similar discussions in the literature since that time. Kriegsman and Celotta noted that their groups were very diverse in terms of types of disabilities, marital status, socioeconomic status, age, and vocational status, yet they found "the common threads of womanhood and general feelings about disability" bound the groups together (p. 37). Similarly to men with disabilities, women experience difficulties stemming from sex role expectations that permit little deviation from that role. In addition, they often experience unusually high rates of unemployment and underemployment (even compared with men with disabilities); victimization, including domestic violence, also occurs at exceedingly high rates. These and other concerns are often well addressed in a group setting. Whereas Kriegsman and Celotta (1981) highlighted the commonalities with other women's groups, there are some important differences that argue for the use of groups that are homogenous for the presence of disability for some women. This is reflected in the comment of one woman as reported by these authors, "I've never felt free to share my feelings about being a woman with a physical disability before" (p. 36).

CONCLUSION

In this chapter, we have endeavored to comment on a number of issues pertaining to group work with persons who have chronic illnesses or disabilities. It is evident that groups add an important and, in some cases, essential intervention to the variety of medical and psychosocial services currently offered. The anxieties and sometimes dramatic alterations attendant to the disability experience can at least in part be ameliorated through supportive, informative, and emotionally therapeutic groups. For persons who are ill or disabled, group counseling has become a powerful tool in helping the rehabilitative process.

NOTE

1. From Tomasulo, Keller, and Pfadt (1995). Reprinted with permission from: http:thearc.org/faqs/group.html, pp. 1-9.

REFERENCES

Abbey, S., & Farrow, S. (1998). Group therapy and organ transplantation. *International Journal of Group Psychotherapy, 48, 2,* 163-185.

Barlow, S. H., Burlingame, G. M., Nebeker, R. S., & Anderson, E. (2000). Meta-analysis of medical self help groups. *International Journal of Group Psychotherapy, 50,* 53-69.

Brown, B. (1995). Group process considerations for inclusion of people with disabilities in group work. *The Journal for Specialists in Group Work, 20,* 76-82.

Ciechoski, M. A. (2000). Sharing the experience of ALS: Patient and family support groups. In H. Mitsumoto and T. L. Munsat (Eds.), *Amyotropic lateral sclerosis: A guide for patients and families* (pp. 261-268). New York: Demos.

Coleman, L. M. (1977). Stigma. An enigma demystified. In L. J. Davis (Ed.), *The disability studies reader* (pp. 216-231). New York: Routledge.

Davis, F. (1972). Deviance disavowal: The management of strained interaction by the visibly handicapped. In F. Davis (Ed.), *Illness, interaction, and the self* (pp. 133-149). Belmont, CA: Wadsworth.

Elston, R., & Snow, B. (1986). Attitudes toward people with disabilities as expressed by rehabilitation professionals. *Rehabilitation Counseling Bulletin, 6,* 284-286.

Falvo, D. R. (1999). *Medical and psychosocial aspects of chronic illness and disability.* Gaithersburg, MD: Aspen.

Freund, P. E. S., & McGuire, M. B. (1999). *Health, illness and social body* (3rd ed.). Upper Saddle River, NJ: Prentice Hall.

Fuhriman, A., & Burlingame, G. M. (1994). *Handbook of group psychotherapy.* New York: John Wiley.

Furst, W. (1960). Homogeneous versus heterogeneous groups. *Topical Problems in Psychotherapy, 2,* 170-173.

Goodheart, C. D., & Lansing, M. H. (1997). *Treating people with chronic disease.* Washington, DC: American Psychological Association.

Goodman, G., & Jacobs, M. K. (1994). The self-help, mutual support group. In A. Fuhriman & G. M. Burlingame (Eds.), *Handbook of group psychotherapy* (pp. 489-526). New York: John Wiley.

Halstead, L. S., & Halstead, K. (1983). Disability SAR's and the small group experience: A conceptual framework. *Sexuality and Disability, 6,* 183-196.

Hastorf, A. H., Northcraft, G. B., & Picciotto, S. R. (1979). Helping the handicapped: How realistic is the performance feedback received by the physically handicapped? *Personality & Social Psychology Bulletin, 5,* 373-376.

Jacobs, E. E., Harvill, R. L., & Masson, R. L. (1988). *Group counseling: Strategies and skills.* Pacific Grove, PA: Brooks/Cole.

Johnson, C. L., & Johnson, J. A. (1991). Using short-term group counseling with visually impaired adolescents. *Journal of Visual Impairment and Blindness, 85,* 166-170.

Kleck, R., Ono, H., & Hastorf, A. H. (1966). Effects of physical deviancy upon face-to-face interactions. *Human Relations, 19,* 425-436.

Kriegsman, K. H., & Celotta, B. (1981). A program of group counseling for women with physical disabilities. *Journal of Rehabilitation, 43*(7), 36-39.

Lieberman, M. (1990). A group therapist's perspective on self help groups. In M. Seligman & L. E. Marshak (Eds.), *Group psychotherapy: Interventions with special populations* (pp. 1-18). Boston: Allyn & Bacon.

Marshak, L. E., & Seligman, M. (1993). *Counseling persons with disabilities: Theoretical and clinical perspectives* (pp. 185-213). Austin, TX: Pro-Ed.

Patterson, J. B., McKenzie, B., & Jenkins, J. (1995). Creating accessible groups for individuals with disabilities. *The Journal for Specialists in Group Work, 20,* 76-82.

Pollin, I. (1995). *Medical crisis counseling.* New York: Norton.

Pratt, J. H. (1907). The class method of treating consumption in the homes of the poor. *JAMA, 49,* 755-759.

Rolland, J. S. (1994). *Families, illness, and disability.* New York: Basic Books.

Rose, J., West, C., & Clifford, D. (May-June, 2000). Group interventions for anger in people with intellectual disabilities. *Research in Developmental Disabilities, 21,* 171-181.

Rothenberg, E. D. (1994). Bereavement interventions with vulnerable populations. *Social Work With Groups, 17,* 61-75.

Safilos-Rothschild, C. (1970). *The sociology and social psychology of disability and rehabilitation.* New York: Random House.

Seligman, M., & Marshak, L. E. (1990). (Eds.). *Group psychotherapy: Intervention with special populations.* Boston: Allyn & Bacon.

Siller, J. (1976). Attitudes towards disability. In H. Rusalem & D. Malikin (Eds.), *Contemporary vocational rehabilitation* (pp. 67-68). New York: University Park Press.

Spira, J. L. (1997). *Group therapy for medically ill patients.* New York: Guilford.

Spitz, H. I., & Spitz, S. T. (1999). *A pragmatic approach to group psychotherapy.* Philadelphia: Brunner/Mazel.

Stein, S. M. (1996). Group psychotherapy and patients with cognitive impairment. *Journal of Developmental and Physical Disabilities, 8,* 263-273.

Tepper, M. S. (1999). Letting go of restrictive notions of manhood: Male sexuality, disability and chronic illness. *Sexuality and Disability, 17,* 37-51.

Tomasulo, D. J., Keller, E., & Pfadt, A. (1995, May/June). The healing crowd: Process, content, and technique issues in group counseling for people with mental retardation. *The Habilitative Mental Healthcare Newsletter, 14*(3), 1-9.

Wright, B. A. (1988). Attitudes and the fundamental negative bias: Conditions and correction. In H. E. Yuker (Ed.), *Attitudes toward persons with disabilities* (pp. 3-21). New York: Springer.

Yalom, I. D. (1995). *The theory and practice of group psychotherapy* (4th ed.). New York: Basic Books.

18

GUIDELINES FOR FACILITATING GROUPS WITH INTERNATIONAL COLLEGE STUDENTS

TOW YEE YAU

University of Pittsburgh

There is an increasing need for administrators and counseling service providers at institutions of higher education to address the unique concerns facing the growing population of international students in the United States. According to the annual report in *Open Doors,* by the Institute of International Education (2001), 547,867 international students were enrolled in colleges and universities in the United States for the 2000/2001 academic year. This was the largest enrollment increase (6.4%) since 1999/2000. The Institute of International Education (2001) further reported that for the third year in a row, China (10.9%) sent the most international students to the United States, followed by India (10.0%), Japan (8.5%), Republic of Korea (8.3%), Taiwan (5.2%), Canada (4.6%), and Indonesia (2.1%). Among the international students in the United States, Asian students comprised 55% of international student enrollment, followed by European students (15%), Latin American students (12%), Middle Eastern students (7%), African students

(6%), and Northern American and Oceanian students (6%).

The majority of Asian students come from (a) East Asia (China, Hong Kong, Mongolia, Japan, Korea, Macao, and Taiwan); (b) South and Central Asia (Bangladesh, Bhutan, India, Kazakhstan, Kyrgyzstan, Pakistan, Nepal, Republic of Maldives, Sri Lanka, Tajikistan, Turkmenistan, and Uzbekistan); and (c) Southeast Asia (Brunei, Cambodia, Indonesia, Laos, Malaysia, Myanmar, Philippines, Thailand, Singapore, and Vietnam).

Another group of international students who are from cultures different from the American and Western culture are students from (a) Latin America (Caribbean, Anguilla, Antigua, Aruba, Bahamas, Barbados, Cayman Islands, Cuba, Dominica, Dominican Republic, Grenada, Guadeloupe, Haiti, Jamaica, Leeward Islands, Martinique, Montserrat, Netherlands Antilles, St. Kitts-Nevis, St. Lucia, St. Vincent, Trinidad and Tobago, Turks and Caicos Islands, and Windward Islands; (b) Central America/Mexico

(Belize, Costa Rica, El Salvador, Guatemala, Honduras, Mexico, Nicaragua, and Panama); and (c) South America (Argentina, Bolivia, Brazil, Chile, Colombia, Ecuador, Falkland Islands, French Guiana, Guyana, Paraguay, Peru, Suriname, Uruguay, and Venezuela). Furthermore, Middle Eastern international students come from Bahrain, Cyprus, Iran, Iraq, Israel, Jordan, Kuwait, Lebanon, Oman, Palestinian Authority, Qatar, Saudi Arabia, Syria, Turkey, United Arab Emirates, and Yemen.

The majority of African international students come from (a) East Africa (Burundi, Comoros, Djibouti, Eritrea, Ethiopia, Kenya, Madagascar, Malawi, Mauritius, Mozambique, Reunion, Rwanda, Seychelles, Somalia, Tanzania, Uganda, Zambia, and Zimbabwe); (b) Central Africa (Angola, Cameroon, Central African Republic, Chad, Congo, Equatorial Guinea, Gabon, Sao and Principe, Zaire, and Congo); (c) North Africa (Algeria, Egypt, Libya, Morocco, Sudan, Tunisia, and Western Sahara); (d) Southern Africa (Botswana, Lesotho, Namibia, South Africa, and Swaziland); and (e) West Africa (Benin, Burkina Faso, Cape Verde, Cote d'Ivoire, Gambia, Ghana, Guinea, Guinea-Bissau, Liberia, Mali, Mauritania, Niger, Nigeria, Senegal, Sierra Leone, St. Helena, and Togo).

INDIVIDUAL COUNSELING OF INTERNATIONAL STUDENTS

Who are these international students? International students can be defined as individuals who are culturally different from the host culture and are temporary residents in pursuit of educational goals. Another salient characteristic is the difference in sociopolitical factors that influence the experiences of international students and American students (Jacob & Greggo, 2001; Paige, 1990). In addition, these international students experience many adjustment problems, and their need for counseling is great. However, cultural values may either accentuate or impede their use of counseling services, and groups in particular.

During their sojourns in the host country, international students have to adjust to Western lifestyles and value systems. However, many international students maintain their own cultural values and beliefs that are different from the United States and other Western cultures. The differences in cultures often result in culture shock for these students (Alexander, Klein, Workneh, & Miller, 1981; Fernandez, 1988; Furnham & Bochner, 1982; Surdam & Collins, 1984; Thomas & Althen, 1989). A host of problems encompass culture shock and include academic adjustments (i.e., language barrier and examination structure), psychological distress (i.e., depression and paranoia), and personal problems (i.e., racial discrimination and role conflict) (Barratt & Huba, 1994; Church, 1982; Leong, 1984, 1986; Pedersen, 1991; Perkins, Perkins, Guglielmino, & Reiff, 1977; Sandhu, 1994; Surdam & Collins, 1984; Stafford, Marian, & Salter, 1980).

Based on myriad problems faced by the international students, one might expect counseling centers to be flooded with them. Unfortunately, international students are generally reluctant to initiate counseling for a number of reasons: (a) lack of information regarding counseling services and (b) lack of understanding of the usefulness of the counseling process (Idowu, 1985; Sue, McKinney, Allen, & Hall; 1974; Sue & Sue, 1977).

How to provide appropriate counseling to international students with diverse cultures and values is less clear. There is a controversy among authors regarding the adoption of a "universalist or a culture-specific approach to counseling culturally different individuals" (Leong & Chou, 1996). The universalist approach maintains that due to the diversity of cultures, counselors identify universal themes and values to be applied sensitively across cultures (Fukuyama, 1990; Leong & Chou, 1996). The culture-specific approach, in contrast, attains culture-specific knowledge and information to work sensitively with specific groups of international students (Cadieux & Wehrly, 1986; Leong & Chou, 1996; Locke, 1990; Sue & Sue, 1990). An integrative model of the culture-specific and universalist approaches can be culturally effective and sensitive in providing individual counseling to international students. The field of multicultural counseling has begun to focus on and advance the understanding of effective individual counseling models and interventions with international students. There is general agreement that a directive or problem-solving approach is effective with and preferred by international students from the South and South East Asian countries (Alexander et al., 1981; Atkinson, Maruyama, & Masui, 1978; Exum & Lau, 1988; Thomas & Althen; 1989; Yuen & Tinsley, 1981). However, Sodowsky (1991) and Yau, Sue, and Hayden (1992) noted that the global statement that international students would prefer a problem-solving or directive approach over a nondirective approach may not always be true.

Research on multicultural group work with international students is lacking. As stated by Pedersen (1991), "Lack of grounded theory has been a major factor inhibiting research about international students" (p. 14). There is little or no training that provides psychologists and counselors with a working framework on how to lead groups with international students. Furthermore, there is yet no professional consensus or conceptual clarity regarding the appropriate focus of groups with international students. Hence, the objectives of this chapter are (a) to provide a review of the current literature on psychoeducational and counseling groups and (b) to provide guidelines for conducting groups with international students.

LITERATURE REVIEW RELATED TO INTERNATIONAL STUDENTS AND GROUPS

Goals of Counseling

International students generally underutilize counseling services, and to reduce help-seeking thresholds, helping professionals in general have stressed the importance of developing counseling programs designed specifically for international students (Brinson & Kottler, 1995; Brislin & Pedersen, 1976; Jacob & Greggo, 2001; Lin & Yi, 1997; Westwood, Lawrence, & Paul, 1986). These programs are designed to meet the different needs of international students at different stages of their stay in the United States. Sue (1981) stated that international students' cultural adjustment follows a developmental course, with the needs of incoming students

being very different from students who are preparing to leave the United States.

For incoming international students who are unfamiliar with the host culture, preventive programs are effective to learn skills to adapt successfully during their transitional phase in the United States. Such international students may require programs to assist them to learn about the host culture's (a) academic system (e.g., classroom behaviors), (b) social roles (e.g., friendships), (c) living environment (e.g., housing), (d) financial system (e.g., banking), and (e) values (e.g., individualism versus collectivism).

On the other hand, international students who have been in the United States for a period of time and are preparing to leave for their home countries tend to have different needs, for example, programs to help them successfully integrate back into their home countries. They need programs to learn about (a) reentry cultural shock (e.g., newly acquired independence that is resented in their home countries), (b) career prospects (e.g., career information and career networking), and (c) building social networking in their own countries.

Generally, the advancement of groups with people of color in the United States has been slow (DeLucia, Coleman, & Jensen-Scott, 1992; Helms, 1990; Merta, 1995), especially as related to international students. There is a dearth of research studies on group counseling, support groups, or psychoeducational group programming with international students. Due to the large number of students from different countries and cultures involved, "It seems quite clear that the practice of counseling international students cannot wait for the fruits of scientific research" (Leong & Chou, 1996, p. 238). Hence, this section will summarize the literature relevant to psychoeducational workshops and support groups with international college students.

Psychoeducational Workshops

Lin and Yi (1997) proposed a four-stage model of programs to facilitate successful adjustments of Asian international students into the new environment. The four-stage model of adjustment stages includes (a) prearrival adjustment, (b) initial adjustment, (c) ongoing adjustment, and (d) return-home adjustment.

In the *prearrival adjustment stage,* the main goal is to assist international students in reducing their anxiety and culture shock. This is done before the arrival of students by providing information about the host culture, educational system, housing information, and financial requirements. Brochures on these materials are sent to the international students prior to their arrival into the United States. In addition, question-answer sessions are organized by the alumni or students currently visiting home to provide information about studying and living in the United States.

During the *initial adjustment stage* (from arrival to first 6 months), orientation programs are implemented to further reduce culture shock (e.g., meeting students at the airport and orienting students to the environment to increase their sense of safety and reduce stress). Ongoing orientation programs to U.S. customs and traditions, academic system, classroom behaviors, counseling services, and so on help to inform international students about the cultural and academic differences. For example, workshops on cross-cultural communication, cultural values, and classroom behaviors are helpful to international students.

In addition, the main goal of the *ongoing adjustment stage* (after the first 6 months to graduation) is to "help international students with bi-cultural conflicts to achieve a balance between participating in the new culture and maintaining their own cultural identities" (Lin & Yi, 1997, p. 478). For example, social support groups can include people with the same nationality as well as American students. This provides great opportunity for the international students to learn more about the American culture. The authors further stressed the importance of helping international students who are going back to their own countries to learn resumé writing and job-hunting skills. For example, international students can learn about different effective ways to explore job prospects in their own countries.

Last, the *return-home adjustment stage* generally starts upon graduation and lasts for 6 months after returning to home. The goal is to help international students to anticipate the adjustment issues related to returning to their home countries, for example, offering group workshops addressing potential family adjustments they may face due to newly acquired, liberal ideas that may be different from their family members'. During their sojourn in the host country, international students have acquired certain host cultural values. According to Adler (1985), an international student is called a "multicultural person," who has gained new experiences abroad and is different from the person who left the country of origin. So what are the problems of just going back home? Going home must bring feelings of happiness and excitement because students have missed their loved ones, friends, and local cuisine.

However, going home is not that simple. As Westwood et al. (1986) indicated,

> It is assumed that because the student is returning home that they know what to expect, how to act, and, in short, be comfortable in "their" home culture. But for most students, much time has passed and through their experiences, they have changed and have learned to accept and value new ways of thinking and doing things. They often discover that things at home have changed or that their expectations of return have been inaccurate. (p. 223)

Returning international students are faced with feelings, thoughts, and behaviors modified by the host culture and may be resented by their family members, friends, and society. For example, the newfound sense of independence may cause problems with their own cultures that value interdependence and collectivism.

Westwood et al. (1986) developed a group program for international students returning back to their home countries. The goal of this program is to help international students anticipate possible negative events and use the group to generate possible ways to resolve these situations. Returning international students are involved in small-group discussion about their possible negative adjustments, and this process allows a greater flow of information among group members. For the international students to feel comfortable in self-disclosure, structured activities or exercises are built into the group process. For example, they are asked to share about their first impressions of the host country. This exercise is nonthreatening because it allows them to share their similar and different views of the host country. Moreover, this activity allows international students to feel included and be part of the group.

The next structured activity is to involve the international students in a guided visualization exercise in which group members are asked to visualize about going back to their home countries. The students are asked to visualize (a) the date of their arrival, (b) the people who are meeting them at the airport, and (c) the first place they would go when they arrive at home. Furthermore, they are asked to explore some of the possible difficulties in adjustments back home. Finally, the group leaders facilitate the group members to generate solutions to their adjustment problems. For example, the group members are to find different ways to deal with their family members and friends who do not understand their value for independence.

International students who participated in this group program for reentry stated "the value it had in helping them to concretize or vivify what had been until then an abstraction . . . and they felt benefited by the group's problem solving ability through which new perspectives and strategies were shared" (Westwood et al., 1986, p. 229). The students further reported that the guided visualization exercise helped them to anticipate possible negative events, which helped them to reduce anxiety and deal with the actual negative situations more effectively.

Support Groups

Jacob and Greggo (2001) developed a cultural exchange program (CEP) model to provide ongoing adjustment support to international students and, specifically, to broaden their social support networks with American students. In addition, the CEP also aims to transmit direct multicultural awareness and knowledge of international students' experiences to the counseling graduate students in practicum. This program was collaborated between the Department of Counseling and Human Services in the Counselor Training Center (CTC) and the Office of International Student Affairs.

During the orientation, incoming international students were encouraged to participate in the CEP. Counseling graduate students doing their practicum in the CTC were to attend the international students' picnics, club meetings, gatherings, or business meetings. In addition, counseling graduate students assisted in the international students' orientation, which provided information on locating housing, shopping, community resources, and understanding U.S. culture so as to reduce culture shock. The counseling students were asked to reflect their experiences back to the group supervision class.

The CEP also involved international students and counseling graduate students together in a focus group to examine various adjustment concerns faced by international students. The focus group concerns were (a) cultural/social, (b) environment, (c) language, (d) classroom, (e) social, and (f) contact with counseling students (Collins, Simons, Bamford, & Blazes, 1994). For example, as for cultural/social concerns, international students indicated the importance of understanding the "dos" and "don'ts" in the American culture. Jacob and Greggo (2001) concluded,

> Counseling students saw the CEP as a mutual and growth-producing learning relationship through the opportunity to engage in cultural and social events with international students and their families while the program also acted as a resource to international students in understanding U.S. culture. (p. 82)

Another successful approach involving international students as cofacilitators in an international support group is the Intercultural Communications Workshop (ICW; Brislin & Pedersen, 1976). In the ICW, the goals are to involve a small group of equal numbers of international students and U.S. students from different cultural backgrounds to have deeper understanding, appreciation, and acceptance of cultural similarities and differences. These objectives are accomplished through the following methods: (a) intercultural communication research readings, (b) role-playing exercises to allow group participants to rehearse one another's role in conflict situations, (c) analyzed critical-incident case scenarios describing conflicting needs, and (d) communication exercises to facilitate the exchange of ideas across cultures and help to develop cross-cultural communication skills.

The beginning stage of this support group is the emerging awareness of other cultures through the understanding of the similarities and differences. International students are asked to share their initial experiences in the United States, or American students give their initial impressions of foreign countries. It is the task of the group facilitator to use the ideas generated in the group to discuss the underlying cultural differences and similarities. Helping group members tolerate and respect differences among individuals of other cultures and finding different ways of intercultural understanding further develop group members' cohesion. Group leaders must be sensitive and skillful in helping international students from cultures that focus on maintaining group harmony to be comfortable in discussing personal experiences and feelings. For example, group leaders could ask the international students their opinions of an American student's self-disclosure and what would allow them to feel comfortable in sharing their own personal experiences.

GUIDELINES TO LEADING GROUPS WITH INTERNATIONAL STUDENTS

The basic questions faced by group leaders at university counseling centers are (a) what types of groups or programs are beneficial to international students, (b) how to run a group counseling or group work with international students, (c) what must be considered to prevent premature termination, and (d) when is it appropriate to use groups with international students. Thus, this section will discuss the guidelines of group interventions with international students in a group setting. First, a case study will be presented.

Case Study: Academic Support Group

A counseling psychologist recently developed a strong interest in providing an ongoing support group for Asian international students. Despite her enthusiasm, she found it difficult to recruit international students to participate voluntarily in her "Academic Support Group." She had made many contacts with all the international students organizations, faculty, and staff regarding this ongoing support group. Five participants attended her first group meeting (two students from the People's Republic of China and students from Japan, Hong Kong, and Taiwan). During the group meeting, she asked the group members to express their feelings of difficulty adjusting to the American academic system. She was able to get responses from the students from Hong Kong and Taiwan but not from students from the People's Republic of China and Japan. Being a skilled group facilitator, she then acknowledged the other group members who were quiet by saying, "Qinping, you are rather quiet. . . . How do you feel about your difficulty adjusting to the different academic system?" In the next session, she was surprised that students from People's Republic of China and Japan did not return, with no reasons given.

Having discussed with other colleagues who had experienced working with Asian international students, she realized that she may have made several mistakes: (a) assuming that Asian international students shared similar values and would be able to respond similarly to the question, (b) using a Western model of group counseling that aims for free exchange of feelings and thoughts among group members, and (c) using reflection of feelings such as "You are rather quiet" as a technique to "draw out" the reticent group participant.

Leong (1992) asserted, "Many therapeutic problems are created when value conflicts generated by cultural differences among racial and ethnic minorities in group counseling situations are not recognized and addressed early in the group experience" (p. 218). These problems have led to premature termination among Asian international students and students of color (Leong, 1992; Sue et al., 1974).

This brief case study illustrates the difficulty and challenges of providing group counseling to

Asian international students for a number of reasons. First, Asian international students come from diverse sociopolitical, linguistic, cultural, and historical backgrounds. (For a more detailed discussion of groups for Asian clients and group differences, see Chapter 14, by Chung, in this volume.) Second, due to the diverse backgrounds of international students, it is difficult to develop coherent individual counseling theories and group work models for working with international students. Third, acculturation levels, language proficiency, exposure to counseling, and counseling-style preferences are important mediating factors but not yet well understood in counseling of international students (Leong, 1992). Last, numerous authors strongly advocate the importance of providing creative outreach and preventive programs for international students (Hayes & Lin, 1994; Lin & Yi, 1997; Leong & Chou, 1996; Locke & Velasco, 1987; Marks, 1987; Pedersen, 1991), but few provide guidelines on groups for international students. Hence, in the next section, the author shares his personal perspectives from being a graduate international student from Singapore and clinical experience as a counseling psychologist, to suggest guidelines in conducting academic support groups with incoming international students.

ACADEMIC SUPPORT GROUPS WITH INTERNATIONAL STUDENTS

As indicated earlier, international students face adjustment problems in understanding the educational system and classroom behaviors of the host culture that are different from their own countries. For instance, professors in U.S. college classrooms expect students to participate freely by (a) asking questions, (b) challenging or rebuking the professors' point, or (c) carrying ongoing discussions among fellow classmates. However, the international students tend to take much more passive roles because they perceive the professors to be experts and it is therefore inappropriate to challenge their ideas or views. Furthermore, international students are less assertive and confident about their English language than are American students, which prevents them from speaking freely in the classroom.

Hence, many international students have voiced a need for and interest in educational and classroom behavior training workshops or discussion groups. To be effective working with international students, certain topics need to be addressed by the group facilitator: (a) cultural sensitivity, (b) awareness of one's own cultural identity and values, (c) outreach and recruitment, (d) pregroup meetings, (e) first group meetings, and (f) group structure and process.

Cultural Sensitivity

Counseling professionals must be sensitive to the general values, beliefs, attitudes, and behaviors of international students. Leong (1992) has provided an excellent account of the cultural variables in group counseling with Asian American clients, which are similar to the Asian international students. For instance, both the Asian Americans and Asian international students have been socialized to value restraint of emotional expression, humility, and modesty in social interactions (Ho, 1984; Leong, 1992; Sue & Sue, 1990). Hence, Asian international students may be modest about expressing their feelings and thoughts as a form of deferential behavior.

However, this value is directly in conflict with the primary goal of the Western model of group counseling, which is to create a supportive environment that allows group participants to have an "open and free exchange of feelings and thoughts about any topic" (Shertzer & Stone, 1974, p. 352). Group counselors should be aware that forcing international students to express their emotions directly, especially negative emotions, will meet with "resistance and be counterproductive" (Sue & Sue, 1990, p. 84). Instead, group leaders must be sensitive and able to focus on the behaviors that are indirect forms of expression. For example, Caucasian Americans generally express their love to their parents by saying, "I love you," whereas Chinese students tend to express their feelings of love to their parents by doing well in their academic achievements.

Other important cultural values of Asian international students are the collective self versus individual self and the need to maintain harmonious relationships in groups (Ho, 1984;

Leong, 1992). Such collective social orientation results in little distinction between personal and family problems of the Asian international students. Hence, self-disclosure of personal problems at the expense of family issues can be difficult or unacceptable (Leong, 1992). The aim is to maintain harmonious relationships and avoid bringing shame or "loss of face" to family members (Ho, 1984; Sue & Sue, 1990). Hence, it is also important for group leaders to avoid direct confrontation in regard to self-disclosure of problems to prevent bringing shame to the Asian international students and family members.

Group leaders must also demonstrate understanding of the cultural differences in the group to be perceived by the international students as credible and competent (Zhang & Dixon, 2001). Furthermore, Sue and Sue (1990) have stressed the importance of understanding the worldviews of multicultural clients. Moreover, group leaders must understand the within-group differences among international students. For example, students from Taiwan and People's Republic of China may have different academic adjustment concerns.

Self-Awareness

Multiculturally competent group leaders must first examine their own values, theoretical orientations, and assumptions about group work to prevent the risk of imposing their values onto the group participants. Moreover, Leong (1992) asserted that group leaders must be sensitive to culturally different clients and not assume that "one's value system is best or better than others" (p. 220). An example is when group leaders hold the value that emotional openness is better than emotional inhibition in a group process. As mentioned in the case study, students from People's Republic of China and Japan may not be comfortable expressing their feelings, because they value harmony and respect for authorities. Therefore, they might be reluctant to share feelings or opinions openly that are in opposition with group members. In group, the author will ask the group member, "How would your peers from your country deal with this issue?" This line of questioning would give permission to the international students to talk about sensitive issues from a

"we" standpoint that prevents any "loss of face." (For a discussion of group leader and member racial identity development, see Chapter 19, by D'Andrea, in this volume.)

Group leaders must have tolerance for an indirect way of interpersonal communication. This communication style is a form of respect to the listener, so as not to bring shame or loss of face to that person. For example, in the brief case study above, the group leader used a direct way of communication by indicating to the group member that he was being quiet. The international student perceived that he had done something "wrong" in the group and probably felt embarrassed. What might have been helpful and effective would be to have said, "Qinping, others have shared their views and would like to hear from you what you and your peers feel about the difficulty in adjusting to the academic system here in the United States." Moreover, international students may find that Americans' direct confrontation, verbal assertiveness, and interrupting of others are counter to their preferred modes of communication (Chu & Sue, 1984).

Outreach and Recruitment

Recruitment of international students to participate in group counseling or support groups has been very difficult and challenging for helping professionals in counseling centers. Group leaders must be aware that international students enter counseling in less formal ways than American students. International students can be reached in a less formal manner through outreach into the different student organizations, such as the International Students Association, Chinese Students and Scholars Association, Indian Students Society, and Hong Kong Students Society. The purpose of such outreach is to first establish and build friendships with international students. International students feel much more comfortable when they see the helping professional as someone who is trustworthy and credible in an informal setting.

International students from non-Western countries tend to underutilize the counseling services or delay getting counseling for emotional problems because the term *counseling* is alien to them. Hence, it is helpful to refer to the group counseling program as a "workshop" or "discussion group." This is because international students are much more ready to attend workshops to learn skills that will enhance their social and academic adjustment in the host culture than they are to attend group counseling. International students from non-Western countries may not be familiar with counseling due to a lack of awareness of the benefits of counseling and the cultural mistrust of the counseling process (Alexander et al., 1976; Idowu, 1985; Locke & Velasco, 1987; Sue & Sue, 1977).

Another successful outreach strategy is to work collaboratively with international student advisors in the international students' office at the university. Both the helping professionals from the counseling center and international students' office can have a great impact on helping students deal with adjustment issues during the orientation program. It is important to offer a series of topical workshops to international students, such as communication, cultural diversity, academic system, networking, and stress management, as follow-up orientation programs. Many times, international students feel frustrated that they are being left alone to deal with adjustment issues after the initial orientation program. At the orientation, counseling professionals can gather useful information regarding the needs and concerns of international students to aid in design of workshop topics.

Another way to successfully recruit international students into workshops is to work closely with campus networks of resource people who are cross-culturally sensitive to the needs of such students (e.g., faculty members, administrators, residence advisors, and campus police) (Jacob & Greggo, 2001; Leong & Chou, 1996; Lin & Yi, 1997; Locke & Velasco, 1987). Leong and Sedlacek (1986) found that international students were more likely to seek help for academic and personal problems from faculty members and counselors. This implies that they tend to use formal sources to get help, and thus designated personnel can work effectively with international students.

Pregroup Meetings

At a pregroup meeting, a 30-minute individual meeting is conducted with prospective group members who are interested in (a) understanding the American academic system, (b) learning classroom behaviors, and (c) learning studying skills for success. During this time, there is an opportunity to assess, select, screen, and prepare international students for group work. This preinterview allows group leaders to assess the English language proficiency, acculturation levels, and within-group differences of the international students. Furthermore, it allows group leaders to assess the appropriateness of a group for these individuals. For example, the leader can inform the international students that a one-to-one session may better fit their needs, if necessary. The leader can also explain the membership, structure, duration of workshop, expectations of group members, and group process.

Homogeneous membership (i.e., country of origin or culture) is not important to the smooth operation of the group. Leong (1992) indicated that with proper screening and preparation, Asian American clients could benefit in a heterogeneous group. The author has found that international students from different countries tend to feel at ease as they realize that they are not the only people from their countries having academic adjustment issues. In addition, the international students are informed of the various educational and classroom behavioral training topics that are being covered in the workshop.

First Group Meetings

In the first meeting, the group leader discusses the purpose of the workshop, the topics that will be covered in the semester, and the techniques that will be employed. Group leaders also stress the importance of confidentiality. The group can start by using "icebreaker" activities, to get the international students to know each other better, and then personal introductions, beginning with the leader to serve as model. Moreover, group members share their goals in coming into the workshop. Structure is provided by indicating who will go next so as to reduce their anxiety. Group members receive a copy of the program that describes the different topics that will be covered in the semester: (a) orientation, (b) classroom behaviors, (c) group projects, (d) time management, (e) lectures and note taking, (f) reading and studying, (g) test taking, (h) writing papers, and (i) campus resources.

Group Structure and Process

In each psychoeducational workshop and support group, the group should consist of 8 to 10 international students. The format of the group is both psychoeducational and process oriented. The first half hour of the group is to provide skills for international students to be effective in adjusting to the U.S. academic system. The second hour is to allow group members to share their views regarding the differences of educational and classroom behaviors in the American university. The aim is to allow international students to share their problems in classroom settings and to receive support from the group members' problem-solving strategies.

As indicated earlier, group members expect the group leader to be an expert and authority. Thus, it is important to establish rapport with the international students by maintaining hierarchical relationships with them during the first few group sessions. During the sessions, group facilitators can be appropriate cultural role models regarding the dynamics of group process (i.e., sharing of experience and receiving feedback). Once the group members have learned the group process behaviors, they will be more comfortable in moving from hierarchical to egalitarian relationships. However, keep in mind that the international students respond differently to egalitarian relationships because of their acculturation levels with respect to Western group process. Thus, group counselors must be patient and not expect group members to share their feelings and concerns quickly in group setting.

Hence, group participants feel enriched by the support of the group, and the goals of the workshop are being accomplished through a variety of methods: (a) role-playing exercises that allow the international students to rehearse oral presentation and classroom behaviors, (b) critical-incidents studies to help participants problem solve and provide solutions to the issues, (c) skills to assist them to be effective learners in an American academic system, and (d) communication exercises to facilitate the exchange of ideas across cultures and help participants to develop necessary new skills.

CONCLUSIONS

This chapter has provided some guidelines that are effective in offering group interventions with international students. To be successful in providing group services to international students, counseling professionals must (a) be able and willing to study the universal and specific cultural values and customs, (b) apply culturally appropriate and therapeutic group techniques, and (c) create a safe group culture.

Furthermore, groups can serve as an excellent social support for international students who are faced with transitional adjustment problems and issues in foreign cultures. The most common advantages to groups include (a) creating a sense of belonging among students facing common issues associated with American university life, (b) experiencing support from one another through sharing common experiences and concerns, and (c) learning coping behaviors in dealing with stressful life changes in an unfamiliar environment.

REFERENCES

Adler, P. (1985). The multicultural man. In L. Samovar & L. Porter (Eds.), *Intercultural communication* (2nd ed., pp. 410-426). Belmont, CA: Wadsworth.

Alexander, A. A., Klein, M. H., Workneh, F., & Miller, M. H. (1981). Psychotherapy and the foreign student. In P. Pedersen, J. Draguns, W. Lonner, & J. Trimble (Eds.), *Counseling across cultures* (2nd ed., pp. 227-243). Honolulu: University of Hawaii Press.

Atkinson, D. R., Maruyama, M., & Matsui, S. (1978). Effects of counselor race and counseling approach on Asian Americans' perceptions of counselor credibility and utility. *Journal of Counseling Psychology, 25,* 76-83.

Barratt, M. F., & Huba, M. E. (1994). Factors related to international undergraduate student adjustment in an American community. *College Student Journal, 28,* 422-436.

Brinson, A. J., & Kottler, J. (1995). International students in counseling: Some alternative models. *Journal of College Student Psychotherapy, 9,* 57-70.

Brislin, R. S., & Pedersen, P. B. (1976). *Cross-cultural orientation programs.* New York: Gardner.

Cadieux, R. A., & Wehrly, B. (1986). Advising and counseling the international student. In K. R. Pyle (Ed.), *New directions for student services: Guiding the development of foreign students* (pp. 51-63). San Francisco: Jossey-Bass.

Chu, J., & Sue, S. (1984). Asian/Pacific-Americans and group practice. *Social Work With Groups, 7,* 23-36.

Church, A. T. (1982). Sojourner adjustment. *Psychological Bulletin, 91,* 540-572.

Collins, T. M., Simons, M., Bamford, S., & Blazes, J. (1994). *A multicultural counseling practicum on a majority White campus.* Paper presented at the annual convention of the American Counseling Association, Minneapolis, MN.

DeLucia, J. L., Coleman, V. D., & Jensen-Scott, R. L. (1992). Cultural diversity in group counseling. *Journal for Specialists in Group Work, 17,* 194-195.

Exum, H., & Lau, E. (1988). Counseling style preference of Chinese college students. *Journal of Multicultural Counseling & Development, 16,* 84-92.

Fernandez, M. S. (1988). Issues in counseling South East-Asian students. *Journal of Multicultural Counseling & Development, 16,* 157-166.

Fukuyama, M. A. (1990). Taking a universal approach to multicultural counseling. *Counselor Education & Supervision, 30,* 6-17.

Furnham, A., & Bochner, S. (1982). Social difficulty in a foreign culture: An empirical analysis of culture shock. In S. Bochner (Ed.), *Cultures in contact* (pp. 161-198). New York: Pergamon.

Hayes, R. L., & Lin, H.-R. (1994). Coming to America: Developing social support systems for international students. *Journal of Multicultural Counseling & Development, 22,* 7-16.

Helms, J. E. (1990). Generalizing racial identity interaction theory to groups. In J. E. Helms (Ed.), *Black and White racial identity: Theory, research, and practice* (pp. 187-204). Westport, CT: Greenwood.

Ho, M. K. (1984). Social group work with Asian/Pacific Americans. *Social Work With Groups, 7,* 49-61.

Idowu, A. K. (1985). Counseling Nigerian students in United States colleges and universities. *Journal of Counseling & Development, 63,* 506-509.

Institute of International Education. (2001). *Open doors.* Retrieved from www.opendoorsweb.org.

Jacob, E. L., & Greggo, J. W. (2001). Using counselor training and collaborative programming strategies in working with international students. *Journal of Counseling & Development, 29,* 73-88.

Leong, F. T. L. (1984). *Counseling international students* (Searchlight plus: Relevant resources in high interest areas No. 56+). Chapel Hill, NC: Education Resources Information Center Counseling and Personnel Services Clearinghouse.

Leong, F. T. L. (1986). Counseling and psychotherapy with Asian Americans: A review of the literature. *Journal of Counseling Psychology, 33,* 196-206.

Leong, F. T. L. (1992). Guidelines for minimizing premature termination among Asian American clients in group counseling. *Journal for Specialists in Group Work, 17,* 218-228.

Leong, F. T. L., & Chou, E. L. (1996). Counseling international students. In P. Pedersen, J. G. Draguns, W. J. Lonner, & J. E. Trimble (Eds.), *Counseling across cultures* (4th ed., pp. 210-242). Thousand Oaks, CA: Sage.

Leong, F. T. L., & Sedlacek, W. E. (1986). A comparison of international and U.S. student preferences for help sources. *Journal of College Student Development, 27,* 426-430.

Lin, G., & Yi, J. K. (1997). Asian international students' adjustment: Issues and program suggestions. *College Student Journal, 31,* 473-479.

Locke, D. C. (1990). A not so provincial view of multicultural counseling. *Counselor Education & Supervision, 30,* 18-25.

Locke, D. C., & Velasco, J. (1987). Hospitality begins with the invitation: Counseling foreign students. *Journal of Multicultural Counseling & Development, 15,* 115-119.

Marks, M. S. (1987). Preparing international students in the United States for reentering the home country. *Journal of Multicultural Counseling & Development, 15,* 120-128.

Merta, R. J. (1995). Group work: Multicultural perspectives. In J. G. Ponterotto, J. M. Casas, L. A. Suzuki, & C. M. Alexander (Eds.), *Handbook of multicultural counseling* (pp. 567-585). Thousand Oaks, CA: Sage.

Paige, R. M. (1990). International students: Cross-cultural psychological perspectives. In R. W. Brislin (Ed.), *Applied cross-cultural psychology* (pp. 161-185). Newbury Park, CA: Sage.

Pedersen, P. (1991). Counseling international students. *The Counseling Psychologist, 19,* 10-58.

Perkins, C. S., Perkins, M. L., Guglielmino, L. M., & Reiff, R. F. (1977). A comparison of the adjustment problems of three international student groups. *Journal of College Student Personnel, 18,* 382-388.

Sandhu, D. S. (1994). An examination of the psychological needs of the international student: Implications for counseling and psychotherapy. *International Journal for the Advancement of Counseling, 17,* 229-239.

Shertzer, B., & Stone, S. C. (1974). *Fundamentals of counseling.* Boston: Houghton-Mifflin.

Sodowsky, G. R. (1991). Effects of cultural consistent counseling tasks on American and international student observers' perception of counselor credibility: A preliminary investigation. *Journal of Counseling & Development, 69,* 253-256.

Stafford, T. H., Marian, P. B., & Salter, M. L. (1980). Adjustment of international students. *NASPA Journal, 18,* 40-45.

Sue, D. W. (1981). *Counseling the culturally different: Theory and practice.* New York: John Wiley.

Sue, D. W., & Sue, D. (1977). Barriers to effective cross-cultural counseling. *Journal of Counseling Psychology, 24,* 420-429.

Sue, D. W., & Sue, D. (1990). *Counseling the culturally different: Theory and practice* (2nd ed.). New York: John Wiley.

Sue, S., McKinney, H., Allen, D., & Hall, J. (1974). Delivery of community mental health services to Black and White clients. *Journal of Consulting & Clinical Psychology, 42,* 794-801.

Surdam, J. A. C., & Collins, J. R. (1984). Adaptation of international students: A cause for concern. *Journal of College Student Personnel, 25,* 240-245.

Thomas, K., & Althen, G. (1989). Counseling foreign students. In P. B. Pedersen, J. G. Draguns, W. J. Lonner, & J. E. Trimble (Eds.), *Counseling across cultures* (3rd ed., pp. 205-241). Honolulu: University of Hawaii Press.

Westwood, M. J., Lawrence, W. S., & Paul, D. (1986). Preparing for re-entry: A program for sojourning students. *International Journal for the Advancement of Counseling, 9,* 221-230.

Yau, T. Y., Sue, D., & Hayden, D. (1992). Counseling style preference of international students. *Journal of Counseling Psychology, 39,* 100-104.

Yuen, R. K., & Tinsley, H. (1981). Brief reports: International and American students' expectancies about counseling. *Journal of Counseling Psychology, 28,* 66-69.

Zhang, N., & Dixon, D. N. (2001). Multiculturally responsive counseling: Effects on Asian students' ratings of counselors. *Journal of Multicultural Counseling & Development, 29,* 253-262.

19

THE IMPACT OF RACIAL-CULTURAL IDENTITY OF GROUP LEADERS AND MEMBERS

Theory and Recommendations

MICHAEL D'ANDREA

University of Hawaii

USING RACIAL-CULTURAL IDENTITY THEORY IN MULTICULTURAL GROUP COUNSELING SETTINGS

Group counselors need to transcend their own ethnocentric thinking about the content and process of group counseling and psychotherapy to respectfully and ethically address the needs and perspectives of persons who come from cultural-racial backgrounds that are different from their own. The present chapter specifically addresses the use of racial-cultural identity development (RCID) theories to facilitate effective multicultural groups.

The importance of incorporating RCID theories into group counseling practice is highlighted by several considerations. The first consideration relates to the results of the 2000 Census, which substantiate what multicultural experts have stressed for the past two decades. That is, the United States is rapidly undergoing an unprecedented transformation in its demographic makeup: from a country that has been historically comprised of a majority of persons from White, Western European, English-speaking backgrounds to a nation in which most of its citizens will come from a variety of non-White, non-European, non-English-speaking groups and backgrounds (D'Andrea & Daniels, 2001).

Second is the increasing pressure on mental health practitioners to acquire new counseling competencies that will enable them to work more effectively, respectfully, and ethically with persons from diverse racial groups and backgrounds (Lewis, Lewis, Daniels, & D'Andrea, 2003; Sue & Sue, 2003).

A HISTORIC OVERVIEW OF THE MULTICULTURAL COUNSELING COMPETENCY MOVEMENT

Division 17 (The Society for Counseling Psychology) of the American Psychological

Association (APA) became the first professional mental health organization to develop a set of 11 cross-cultural counseling competencies in January 1981 (Sue et al., 1982).

Ten years later, the Association for Multicultural Counseling and Development (AMCD), a division in the American Counseling Association (ACA), expanded the original 11 competencies and formally endorsed a new set of 31 multicultural counseling competencies (Sue, Arredondo, & McDavis, 1992). Since that time, six other divisions in ACA have formally endorsed the AMCD competencies. The Association for Specialists in Group Work (ASGW) has built on the earlier work of AMCD by publishing the *Principles for Diversity-Competent Group Workers* (Haley-Banez, Brown, & Molina, 1999).

Most recently, APA gave its formal organizational endorsement for a new expansive set of multicultural guidelines that were developed in a joint project undertaken by leaders in Division 17 (The Society for Counseling Psychology) and Division 45 (The Society for the Psychological Study of Ethnic Minority Issues). This expanded set of guidelines was formally endorsed at the annual APA convention held in August 2002, in Chicago, Illinois (APA, 2003). The APA multicultural guidelines are built on and greatly extend the earlier multicultural competency efforts to understand the cultural awareness, knowledge, and skills needed to provide effective individual and group interventions (D'Andrea, 2000; Sue et al., 1998).

Culturally competent group counselors strive to (a) increase their understanding of the impact that race, culture, and ethnicity have on the development of clients who come from cultural-racial groups that are different from their own, (b) be mindful of their own cultural-racial-ethnic development in the process, and (c) consider how clients' cultural-racial backgrounds may influence their preferences for particular types of groups, approaches to group counseling, and group leaders (Ivey, Pedersen, & Ivey, 2001).

Over the past 20 years, several multicultural researchers have described a complex dimension of human development that is generically referred to as *racial and cultural identity development.* This chapter is designed to serve a threefold purpose: (a) increase familiarity with the RCID theories, (b) examine how interpersonal interactions that take place within multicultural group counseling settings affect group dynamics, and (c) foster new thinking about how to work more effectively and respectfully within racially and culturally heterogenous groups.

DEFINING TERMS AND CLARIFYING CENTRAL ISSUES

The rapid cultural-racial diversification of the United States heightens the likelihood that counselors will increasingly be called upon to provide group services to persons of diverse cultural-ethnic-racial backgrounds. "Multicultural group counseling" (D'Andrea & Daniels, 1996, p. 1) refers to such groups. "Racially heterogenous groups" (Merta, 1995, p. 570) more specifically refers to groups comprising persons from two or more different racial backgrounds. An example of a racially heterogenous group is one made up of a White group counselor, three White clients, one Asian American client, one Latino, and one Latina client. For the purpose of this chapter, the terms *multicultural group counseling, racially heterogenous groups,* and *racially and culturally heterogenous groups* are used interchangeably.

To work effectively and ethically in multicultural groups, it is essential for group counselors to be knowledgeable of the unique "between-group differences" that characterize the psychological development of persons who come from diverse racial-cultural backgrounds in our society. While attention has historically been directed toward the types of between-group differences that commonly exist in racially heterogenous groups, it is equally important for group counselors to accurately identify and effectively address the "within-group differences" that characterize persons who come from similar racial-cultural backgrounds (Lewis et al., 2003). One way that group counselors can expand their thinking about the types of within-group differences that distinguish persons from similar cultural-racial backgrounds is to reflect on information that is contained in identity development theories in general and RCID theories in particular.

IDENTITY DEVELOPMENT AND RACIAL CULTURAL IDENTITY DEVELOPMENT

Identity development relates to the process by which individuals answer the universal question "Who am I?" linked to the thoughts (e.g., self-concept) and feelings a person has about oneself (e.g., one's sense of self-esteem). Erikson's (1963, 1987) psychosocial identity theory acknowledges that a host of environmental factors influence an individual's psychological development. This includes experiences one has in his or her family, at school, work, and within the community. While Erikson's theory has received much appeal in the past, it is important to note that it generally fails to address the significant impact of cultural-racial factors on identity development (Cross, 1991; Helms, 1995; Sue & Sue, 1999, 2003).

Although Cross (1991), Helms (1995), and Sue and Sue (1999, 2003) presented different ideas about the process of RCID, their theoretical models are all based on a similar set of assumptions. The five points presented below represent shared assumptions that cut across all RCID theories. The sixth point has been added to emphasize the implications of these theories for group counseling.

1. Members of the dominant racial-cultural group in the United States (White, English-speaking persons of Western European descent) continue to disproportionately benefit from a host of social, educational, economic, and personal privileges and advantages that individuals from racially disempowered minority groups do not (Cross, 1995; D'Andrea & Daniels, in press; Helms, 1995; Scheurich, 1993; Scheurich & Young, 1997).

2. A number of sociopolitical factors have been identified as playing key roles in maintaining the social inequities that continue to exist in the United States, including racism, racial stereotyping, discrimination, and cultural oppression (Jones, 1997).

3. The complex problems of racism, racial stereotyping, discrimination, and cultural oppression that continue to be perpetuated in our contemporary society not only help to sustain unfair and racially disempowered structural societal arrangements but also impact the psychological development of White and non-White persons in the United States (D'Andrea & Daniels, in press).

4. According to most RCID theorists, people victimized by racism and cultural oppression usually rely on others within their own racial-cultural group for psychological support and assistance to cope with the stressors of life and make sense of who they are. This results in the development of a *group-referenced identity:* a unique identity that often provides persons from minority groups with a heightened sense of personal power and support that is linked to the collective survival and progress of their group and fosters the development of healthy individual racial-cultural identities (Helms, 1990, 1995).

5. Differences in RCID reflect within-group psychological differences that characterize persons who come from the same cultural-racial background (Sue & Sue, 2003).

6. To lead racially heterogeneous groups in an effective, respectful, and ethical manner, group counselors need to accurately assess how their group members' and their own levels of RID affect the counseling process (D'Andrea, Brown, Locke, & Parker, 1996; Helms, 1995).

RACIAL-CULTURAL IDENTITY DEVELOPMENT THEORY

The RCID theories that have emerged over the past 30 years can help group counselors more accurately understand some of the unique within-group differences that underlie the different attitudes and behaviors that racially and culturally similar group members exhibit in racially heterogenous groups. To gain a more in-depth understanding of this area, readers are encouraged to review the works on Black identity (Cross, 1971, 1985, 1991, 1995; Helms, 1984, 1990, 1995), Asian identity (Kim, 1981; Sue & Sue, 1999, 2003), and Latino/Latina identity development theories (Bernal & Knight, 1993). Recognizing the similarities in these models, Sue and Sue (1999) developed a theoretical framework that they refer to as the racial cultural identity development (R/CID) model, which integrates the ideas outlined by other RID theorists. In describing their R/CID theory, Sue and Sue (1999) emphasize that it is not offered as

> A comprehensive theory of personality, but rather as a conceptual framework to aid therapists in understanding their racially and culturally different clients' attitudes and behaviors. The model defines five stages of psychological development that oppressed people experience as they struggle to understand themselves in terms of their own race and culture, the dominant cultural group, and the oppressive relationship that exists between these groups. . . . At each level or stage of RCID, individuals typically exhibit four corresponding attitudes and beliefs about (a) the self, (b) other members of the same minority group, (c) persons from other minority groups, and (d) individuals in the dominant racial-cultural group in the United States. (p. 128)

Sue and Sue (2003) refer to the five stages that comprise the R/CID framework as the *conformist, dissonance, resistance and immersion, introspection,* and *integrative awareness stages.* The following sections of this chapter provide (a) a brief description of key characteristics associated with each stage, (b) an overview of ways that various dimensions of a person's RCID might be manifested in group counseling settings, and (c) guidelines for working with group members operating from different stages of the R/CID model.

The Conformist Stage

The complex and pervasive ways in which racism, racial stereotyping, discrimination, and cultural oppression are manifested in our society create a host of psychological stressors for minority group persons. Sue and Sue (2003) note that these stressors lead many culturally and racially diverse persons to (a) adapt a White Euro-American worldview, (b) disavow the reality of their own racial-cultural backgrounds, and (c) internalize negative aspects of the various forms of racism and White superiority that continue to be played out in both explicit and subtle ways.

At the conformist stage, persons from marginalized cultural-racial groups develop what

Helms (1995) refers to as an "externalized self-identity" (p. 186). They (a) internalize negative attitudes and beliefs about one's own cultural-racial background, (b) construct a host of negative thoughts and feelings toward other members of their own racial-cultural groups, as well as persons who are associated with other devalued and disempowered groups, and (c) idealize all aspects of the dominant racial-cultural group in the United States (Sue & Sue, 2003).

1. *Attitudes and beliefs toward self:* These persons often internalize the negative racial-cultural attitudes and beliefs that the dominant cultural group perpetuates about them. As a result,

> Physical and cultural characteristics identified with one's own racial-cultural group are perceived negatively, as something to be avoided, denied, or changed. Physical characteristics (e.g., Black skin color, slant-shaped eyes of Asians), traditional modes of dress and appearance, and behavioral characteristics associated with the minority group are a source of shame. There may be attempts to mimic what are perceived to be White mannerisms, speech patterns, dress, and goals. (Sue & Sue, 1999, p. 131)

2. *Attitudes and beliefs toward members of the same cultural-racial group:* At this stage, the negative and depreciating attitudes and beliefs described above are generalized to other members of one's own racial-cultural group. In doing so, persons at this developmental stage thus refuse to give much credence to how racism and cultural oppression adversely affect the psychological health and personal well-being of many persons in the group. Instead, they tend to place the blame for problems that other members of their racial-cultural group experience entirely on these persons themselves; oftentimes, individuals at the conformist stage use racial-cultural stere types perpetuated by the dominant group to explain the difficulties these people encounter. As Sue and Sue (1999) explain,

> In the case of Hispanics, for example, individuals operating from the conformist stage may believe that other members of his or her group have high rates of unemployment because they are lazy, uneducated, and unintelligent. Little thought or validity is given to other viewpoints, such as unemployment

being a function of job discrimination, prejudice, racism, unequal opportunities, and inferior education. Because persons in the conformity stage find it psychologically painful to identify with these negative traits, they divorce themselves from their own group. The denial mechanism most commonly used is: "I am not like them; I've made it on my own; I'm the exception." (p. 132)

3. *Attitudes and beliefs toward members of other minority groups:* Persons functioning at the conformist stage of the R/CID framework may express discriminatory and stereotypic thoughts and feelings toward individuals from other disempowered minority groups because they have adapted many of the negative attitudes and beliefs that the dominant racial-cultural group perpetuates about other minorities in our nation (Helms & Cook, 1999; Sue & Sue, 1999). From this vantage point, "Minority groups most similar to White cultural groups are viewed more favorably, while those most different are viewed less favorably" (Sue & Sue, 1999, p. 132).

4. *Attitudes and beliefs toward members of the dominant group:* Conformist stage persons not only avoid thinking about the sociopolitical factors that underlie the way our contemporary society is organized, but "members of the dominant group are admired, respected, and emulated. White people are believed to possess superior intelligence and other personal attributes" (Sue & Sue, 1999, p. 132).

5. *Considerations for group counseling:* Because of their beliefs about the superiority of the White Euro-American worldview, conformist stage persons are likely to exhibit very positive reactions to group counselors who come from the dominant cultural-racial group and a host of negative thoughts and feelings toward non-White group counselors (Parham, 2002).

In addition, conformist stage group members are generally not interested in participating in group discussions that focus on cultural-racial issues. Sue and Sue (2003) note that these clients are likely to prefer traditional task-oriented and problem-solving counseling approaches that do not include an exploration of cultural-racial considerations.

The Dissonance Stage

The dissonance stage of the R/CID model is characterized by a heightened sense of confusion about one's racial-cultural identity. On one hand, there is considerable societal pressure to accept the notion that "White is best." On the other hand, dissonance stage persons have begun to question why they place such a high value on the dominant cultural-racial group (Helms, 1995). Cognitive dissonance is often triggered by unfair and discriminatory racial-cultural experiences to which these persons have repeatedly been subjected over the course of their lives.

1. *Attitudes and beliefs toward self:* At the dissonance stage, individuals experience a growing awareness that racism and cultural oppression continue to exist in the United States and that not all aspects of minority or majority culture are good or bad (Sue & Sue, 2003). Although negative feelings about one's racial-cultural background persist, dissonance stage persons begin to entertain the possibility that there are positive factors associated with their racial-cultural heritages. As a result of the mixed thoughts and feelings that characterize this newly emerging sense of self, they may appear uncertain and confused about their own thoughts and feelings when racial-cultural issues are discussed.

2. *Attitudes and beliefs toward members of the same cultural-racial group:* Persons at this stage are further distinguished from those at the conformist stage in that they typically exhibit dissonant thoughts and feelings, including adherence to both group-depreciating and group-appreciating views of other racially similar individuals. This dissonance propels them to question negative stereotypes that they have historically held about other individuals who come from their racial-cultural groups.

3. *Attitudes and beliefs toward members of other minority groups:* Dissonant stage individuals also begin to reflectively question some of the discriminatory and stereotypic attitudes and beliefs they hold about persons from other devalued and marginalized groups. Upon examining the stereotypes and negative views

promoted by the dominant cultural-racial group, dissonant stage individuals begin to find aspects of other minority cultures personally appealing to them (Sue & Sue, 2003).

4. *Attitudes and beliefs toward members of the dominant group:* While dissonant stage persons continue to exhibit many appreciating attitudes and beliefs about the dominant cultural-racial group, they experience "a growing awareness that not all of the values of the dominant group are beneficial to him/her" (Sue & Sue, 1999, p. 133), leading to a growing interest in discussing cultural-racial issues.

5. *Considerations for group counseling:* Movement to the dissonance stage is marked by gradual psychological changes as individuals begin to question both the superiority of a White, Western European worldview and their willingness to accept the personal costs that go along with fully assimilating into the dominant cultural-racial group. Group counselors should provide opportunities to explore these individuals' thoughts and feelings about various cultural and racial topics in supportive and confidential group settings. Recognizing that RCID is a gradual developmental process that necessitates the processing of intense emotional reactions toward racism, discrimination, and cultural oppression (Sue & Sue, 2003), group counselors must (a) listen carefully to verbal responses of dissonance stage group members and (b) closely observe their nonverbal reactions to group discussions that focus on cultural-racial issues to gauge their clients' overall readiness to express their thoughts and feelings about various cultural-racial issues. Culturally competent group counselors avoid moving too quickly when fostering in-depth and emotionally laden discussions of such topics (D'Andrea & Daniels, 1996; Parham, 2002; Sue & Sue, 2003), because they recognize the risk of stimulating an excessive amount of anxiety, anger, guilt, and frustration that may inhibit further development and cause some persons functioning at the dissonance stage to regress to the conformist stage.

The Resistance and Immersion Stage

This developmental stage is marked by two fundamental opposing themes held conjointly by persons from minority racial-cultural groups, "the idealization of people of color and the denigration of Whites" (Helms, 2003, p. 47).

1. *Attitudes and beliefs toward self:* A heightened self-acceptance as a racial-cultural being reflects a growing sense of psychological liberation (Martin-Baro, 1994) fueled by a surge of interest in self-discovery and leading to an immersion in their own racial-cultural heritage, values, beliefs, and history. Consequently,

> Cultural and racial characteristics that once elicited feelings of shame and guilt now become symbols of pride and honor. The individual moves into this stage primarily as he/she asks the question: "Why should I be ashamed of who and what I am?" (Sue & Sue, 1999, p. 134)

2. *Attitudes and beliefs toward members of the same cultural-racial group:* Resistance and immersion stage individuals express strong feelings of connection with other persons of the same racial-cultural group. However, these persons not only exhibit a high level of admiration and respect for other members of their own racial-cultural group but also, as noted above, manifest an almost total rejection of everything and everyone that is associated with the dominant group (Helms, 1995; Sue & Sue, 2003).

3. *Attitudes and beliefs toward members of other minority groups:* While individuals at this developmental stage display strong positive attitudes about their own cultural-racial group, many also demonstrate an increasing sense of care and empathy for persons in other disempowered racial-cultural groups who are also subjected to cultural oppression, racism, and discrimination. Resistance and immersion stage individuals often form alliances with persons from other minority groups for political reasons (Sue & Sue, 1999), with such alliances being purposefully formulated to combat the various forms of racism and cultural oppression that continue to be perpetuated in our contemporary society.

4. *Attitudes and beliefs toward members of the dominant group:* Resistance and immersion stage individuals view members of the dominant group as oppressors responsible for the

unfair and unwarranted treatment that continues to be unjustly imposed on their own racial-cultural groups. Consequently, individuals at this stage are generally suspicious and distrustful of anyone seen as part of the dominant cultural-racial group as well as those minority group members who are supportive of it (e.g., persons operating from the conformist stage).

5. *Considerations for group counseling:* It is important to consider how group leaders' own cultural-racial characteristics affect the dynamics of a group at this stage. In light of the heightened levels of distrust and hostility that resistance and immersion stage individuals commonly exhibit toward persons in the dominant cultural-racial group, having one or both group leaders come from White, Western European backgrounds is likely to produce heightened interpersonal tensions from the onset of the group (Parham, 2002). Thus, culturally competent group counselors exercise care in selecting group leaders to work with multicultural counseling groups comprising group members functioning from the resistance and immersion stage. One recommendation is to include at least one group leader who comes from the same racial-cultural background as the group member(s) operating from the resistance and immersion stage.

However, it is overly simplistic and not appropriate to suggest that the selection of group counselors to work in groups with resistance and immersion stage group members should be primarily based on matching phenotypes (physical characteristics). It is equally important to think about how group counselors' own levels of RCID may affect group dynamics and, specifically, interactions with group members at the resistance and immersion stage. Interpersonal conflicts are likely to ensue in groups comprising one or more group members operating from the resistance and immersion stage and a non-White group counselor who is functioning from the conformist stage.

It is recommended that at least one group cofacilitator (in a group comprising resistance and immersion stage members) be operating from a more highly developed stage of the R/CID model (e.g., the introspection or integrative awareness stages), because group leaders who have developed a more mature sense of their own racial-cultural identities are better positioned to (a) effectively address the kinds of emotionally charged, racial-cultural questions and concerns that resistance and immersion stage persons typically manifest in group counseling settings and (b) provide the sort of support and challenge that these clients need to develop new and more complex ways of thinking about these questions and concerns.

The Introspection Stage

Cross (1995) suggests that as individuals work through the strong and emotionally charged attitudes, beliefs, feelings, and behaviors that mark the resistance and immersion stage, they frequently experience a growing discontent with the rigid ways of thinking that characterize this developmental phase. In addition, these individuals become increasingly tired of the intense psychic energy output they exert in resisting continued racism, discrimination, and cultural oppression (Sue & Sue, 2003).

1. *Attitudes and beliefs toward self:* In attempting to deal with their growing discontent over the rigid racial thinking and the psychic energy drain that characterizes persons at the resistance and immersion stage of the R/CID model, individuals enter the introspection stage motivated to explore new psychological issues related to their own sense of personal independence and autonomy as racial-cultural beings. This self-reflection process encourages a better understanding of how personal independence and autonomy can be compromised when one rigidly adheres to generalized positive beliefs about one's own racial-cultural group and negative thoughts and feelings about all members of the dominant racial-cultural group. Thus, one of the major developmental challenges introspection stage persons face involves learning how to balance a genuine sense of responsibility and allegiance to their own racial-cultural groups with an increasing interest in developing more psychological autonomy and personal independence when it comes to analyzing and making sense of racial-cultural issues.

272 • MULTICULTURAL GROUPS

2. *Attitudes and beliefs toward members of the same cultural-racial group:* Persons at the introspection stage demonstrate a shift from the unequivocal acceptance of one's own racial-cultural group to more self-evaluative ways of thinking about racial-cultural issues in general and one's own cultural-racial group in particular. While introspection stage individuals continue to maintain strong personal allegiance to their own cultural-racial groups, they become increasingly frustrated and resentful over the ways in which others try to pressure them to make decisions that are not consistent with their own personal values, beliefs, and worldviews.

3. *Attitudes and beliefs toward members of other minority groups:* Introspection stage persons commonly demonstrate an increased interest in learning about people who come from cultural-racial groups that historically have been devalued and unjustly treated by the dominant group in the United States. This interest is stimulated in part by a continued distrust in White persons in general and a growing uneasiness with the strong, negative, and ethnocentric attitudes and beliefs manifested by persons from their own cultural-racial groups who operate from a resistance and immersion stage mentality. As a result, introspection stage persons are more comfortable discussing cultural and racial issues with individuals from other minority backgrounds in group counseling settings in comparison with group members who operate from less developed R/CID stages.

4. *Attitudes and beliefs toward members of the dominant group:* Introspection stage individuals continue to harbor some general feelings of distrust for members in the dominant cultural-racial group. Rather than looking at this generalized sense of distrust as a psychological liability or problem to be changed, culturally competent group counselors view this psychological perspective as an important psychological strength and coping strategy that persons in minority groups use to survive in a society that continues to perpetuate racism and cultural oppression (Helms, 1990; Sue & Sue, 1999, 2003). It is important to note that the heightened sense of distrust and overt hostility that is manifested at the resistance and immersions stage of the R/CID framework are greatly tempered as

individuals move to the introspection stage. Sue and Sue (2003) suggest that this change reflects a growing discomfort and dissatisfaction that introspection stage persons manifest when pressed to maintain highly depreciating attitudes, beliefs, and feelings about all members of the dominant racial-cultural group. In contrast with other stages of the R/CID model, introspection stage individuals demonstrate a greater willingness to try to balance feelings of trust and distrust for White European Americans.

5. *Considerations for group counseling:* It is important to consider whether introspection stage individuals have a preference for group counselors' racial-cultural backgrounds. In commenting on this issue, Sue and Sue (1999) point out that "clients at the introspection stage may continue to prefer a therapist of their own race, but they are also receptive to help from therapists of other cultures as long as the therapist understands their worldview" (p. 140).

It is also important to note that interpersonal conflicts are likely to repeatedly occur within racially heterogenous groups comprising members at different R/CID stages and statuses. Numerous negative group interactions may take place in group settings, as resistant and immersion stage clients are likely to mistakenly view the reflective questions that introspection stage clients bring to the group as a sign of "selling out to the system." While these group members are likely to engage in heated discussions regarding what it means to "sell out to the system," conformist stage group members may simply disengage from such discussions because they (a) are genuinely not interested in talking about such issues and (b) do not think such discussions appropriate for group counseling.

The Integrative Awareness Stage

Cross (1995) explained that as individuals move toward a more complex, internalized, and integrated racial identity, they often report feeling "totally changed, with both a new worldview and a revitalized personality" (p. 114). This sense of personal revitalization as they move to the integrative awareness stage is tied to a growing knowledge and appreciation for the unique aspects of their own and other cultural-racial groups in our society, including an increased understanding and appreciation for various aspects of the dominant cultural-racial group.

1. *Attitudes and beliefs toward self:* In comparison to persons who are operating at the other stages of the R/CID model, individuals at the integrative awareness stage have developed more expansive and positive self-images based on a strong and growing sense of self-worth and personal confidence. The unique sense of personal confidence that marks persons functioning at this developmental stage is rooted in a more fully integrated self-concept that involves a deep and genuine sense of racial pride in their own cultural-racial heritage, on one hand, and a heightened sense of personal autonomy and psychological independence, on the other (Sue & Sue, 2003).

2. *Attitudes and beliefs toward members of the same cultural-racial group:* Although persons at the integrative awareness stage experience a genuine sense of connection with and respect for other members of their cultural-racial groups, they do not feel pressured to unequivocally accept all the values and attitudes espoused by these persons. "Strong feelings of empathy with other members of their group are coupled with an awareness that each member of the group is also an individual" (Sue & Sue, 1999, p. 136). People who exhibit the personal confidence and empathic understanding that characterize the integrative awareness stage can provide interpersonal stability within racially heterogenous groups. This is possible because integrative awareness stage persons have developed the personal competencies necessary to respectfully communicate with persons at other stages of the R/CID framework who exhibit conflicting attitudes, beliefs, and feelings about cultural-racial issues in group counseling settings.

3. *Attitudes and beliefs toward members of other minority groups:* A more consistent effort to reach out to members of other minority groups is also noted. This outreach is largely precipitated by a growing desire to learn more about the values, worldviews, attitudes, beliefs, and feelings of persons from different cultural-racial

groups. "Support for all oppressed people, regardless of similarity to the individual's own group, tends to be emphasized" (Sue & Sue, 1999, p. 137).

4. *Attitudes and beliefs toward members of the dominant group:* Persons operating from the integrative awareness stage demonstrate a more positive and open-minded attitude toward members of the dominant cultural-racial group. These individuals are very cognizant of the many ways in which White people perpetuate racism and cultural oppression in our society, both intentionally through their actions and unintentionally through their inaction (D'Andrea, 1996, 2002). They are also aware that these social pathologies not only adversely affect individuals from disempowered minority groups but also have a tremendous negative psychological impact on persons in the dominant cultural-racial group as well (Sue & Sue, 2003).

5. *Considerations for group counseling:* Given their complex cognitive abilities as well as the positive and confident attitudes that integrative awareness stage persons commonly exhibit in discussions about cultural-racial issues, they can be very helpful in facilitating constructive discussions about these topics in groups comprising group members operating from different stages of the R/CID model. For this reason, it would be very helpful to have minority group counselors functioning at this developmental stage as leaders of racially and culturally heterogenous groups.

EFFECT OF GROUP COUNSELORS' RACIAL IDENTITY DEVELOPMENT

White RID

It is also essential for white group counselors to consider how their own levels of racial identity development (RID) may affect group process and interventions for several reasons. First, the vast majority of mental health practitioners in the United States come from White Western European backgrounds. Second, as members of the dominant cultural-racial group in the United States, White European American group counselors enjoy many psychosocial, political, and economic privileges that are not made available to members of disempowered minority groups in this country (Jones, 1997; West, 1999). One of the problems that results from the widespread and unfair phenomenon comm-only referred to as "White privilege" (Neville, Worthington, & Spanierman, 2001) is the negative and distrustful attitudes that many minority group persons harbor toward White European Americans in general and especially toward individuals who are oblivious to their privileged status within our racially and culturally stratified society. It is important that White European American group counselors examine (a) the ways in which their membership in the dominant racial-cultural group in the United States affects their own identity development and (b) the impact that their racial-cultural status and privileges have on persons from disempowered minority backgrounds who participate in counseling groups.

Helms's Theory of White Racial Identity Development (WRID)

White racial identity development (WRID) theory is a relatively recent development in the fields of counseling and psychology. Advancements in thinking about WRID are largely influenced by the work of Dr. Janet Helms (1984, 1990, 1995, 2003), who notes that most White persons do not consider how their own racial backgrounds, histories, and life experiences affect their psychological development. She also argues that because White persons (regardless of their socioeconomic status) have greater privilege and power relative to persons from other racial groups in our society, "they can more readily avoid working through issues of RID than other groups" (Helms, 1995, p. 49).

Given (a) the rapid cultural-racial transformation of U.S. society, (b) the need for White group counselors to be knowledgeable of their own RID, and (c) the importance of understanding how this variable affects group counseling, Helms's WRID theory represents an important and welcomed contribution to the mental health profession. One of the ways her theory is distinguished from other racial-cultural identity theories relates to the terms she uses to describe the qualitatively different changes White people commonly exhibit in their RID. Rather than using the term *stages* to describe these changes, Helms uses the term *statuses* when referring to the different attitudes, beliefs, and feelings White persons manifest at various points in their RID. More specifically, the term *psychological status* refers to an identifiable set of developmental changes that White persons undergo as they become more or less conscious of the ways in which their racial background and experiences influence their constructions of the world, persons from other racial groups, and themselves (D'Andrea, 2002).

Helms describes WRID as a process marked by six psychological statuses. According to Helms, White persons are capable of moving from simply avoiding or denying the sociopolitical implications that race has on their own and others' development to a much more complex psychological disposition characterized by more comprehensive and accurate thinking about the impact of racial-cultural factors on human development. According to Helms (1995), the increased level of cognitive complexity that occurs as individuals move toward a more mature White identity status is a major factor that leads individuals in the dominant racial-cultural group to realize a more humanistic and nonracist identity.

The six racial identity statuses that comprise Helms's model include *contact, disintegration, reintegration, pseudoindependence, immersion/emersion,* and *autonomy statuses.* Table 19.1 provides an overview of key characteristics of the psychological statuses that make up Helms's theoretical framework. Following a brief description of these statuses are statements that reflect the thinking of persons functioning at each status of her model. If you are a White counselor or psychologist, you are strongly encouraged to take time to think about which status or statuses of Helms's framework you think you generally operate as you review the information provided in Table 19.1.

USING RCID THEORIES TO UNDERSTAND MULTICULTURAL GROUP INTERACTIONS

When working in multicultural groups, group counselors will notice that some interactions are

Table 19.1   Helms's White Racial Identity Ego Statuses

Contact Status: Individuals operating from this status exhibit satisfaction with the existing racial status quo in the United States, obliviousness to racism in general, and one's unintentional participation in it in particular. If racial factors influence life decisions, they are generally thought to do so in a simplistic manner.

Example: "I'm a White woman. When my grandfather came to this country, he was discriminated against, too. But he didn't blame Black people for his misfortunes. He educated himself and got a job; that's what Blacks ought to do. If White callers (to a radio station) spent as much time complaining about racial discrimination as your Black callers do, we'd never accomplished what we have. You all should just ignore it."

Disintegration Status: White persons who are functioning at this status commonly experience a heightened sense of disorientation and anxiety as a result of facing unresolvable racial dilemmas. Becoming aware of these racial dilemmas forces White persons operating from this status to choose between one's own racial group loyalty and a broad commitment to humanist values and beliefs about racial issues. They are also noted to be stymied by life situations in which racial issues come into direct conflict with the moral beliefs and standards by which they try to live.

Example: "I myself try to set a nonracist example [for other Whites] by speaking up when someone says something blatantly prejudiced. My biggest challenge in these situations is to learn how to do this without alienating people so they will no longer take me seriously."

Reintegration Status: This WRID status couples an idealization of one's socioracial group with the denigration and intolerance of persons from other racial groups.

Example: "So, what if my great-grandfather owned slaves. He didn't mistreat them and besides, I wasn't even here then. I never owned slaves. So, I don't know why Blacks expect me to feel guilty for something that happened before I was born. Nowadays, reverse racism hurts Whites more than slavery hurts Blacks. My brother can't even get a job with the police department because they have to hire less qualified Blacks. That [expletive] happens to Whites all the time."

Pseudoindependence Status: White persons who operate from this status have been noted to intellectualize a strong commitment to their own socioracial group and, as Helms (1995) points out, commonly exhibit a deceptive and patronizing tolerance for non-White individuals.

Example: "Am I the only person left in America who believes that the sexual mingling of the races is a good thing . . . that it can help erase cultural barriers and leave us all a lovely shade of tan? . . . Racial blending is inevitable. At the very least, it may be the only solution to our dilemmas of race."

Immersion/Emerison Status: At this point in their RID, White people are motivated to search for a greater understanding of the personal meaning of racism and cultural oppression. In doing so, they demonstrate a willingness to thoughtfully consider some of the ways that they benefit from being a part of the dominant racial-cultural group in the United States. Life choices for these persons may include racial activism.

Example: "It's true that I personally did not participate in the horror of slavery, and I don't even know whether my ancestors owned slaves. But I know that because I am White, I continue to benefit from a racist system which stems from the slavery era. I believe that if White people are ever going to understand our role in perpetuating racism, then we must begin to ask ourselves some hard questions and be willing to consider our role in maintaining a hurtful system. Then, we must try to do something about it."

(Continued)

Table 19.1 (Continued)

Autonomy Status: Persons functioning primarily from this status demonstrate an informed and positive commitment to ameliorate various forms of racism and cultural oppression that continue to exist in our society. In doing so, they rely on the use of internal standards for self-definition and demonstrate a genuine willingness to relinquish the privileges of racism that go along with being a member of the dominant cultural-racial group in this country.

Example: "I live in an integrated [Black-White] neighborhood and I read Black literature and popular magazines. So I understand that the media presents a very stereotypic view of Black culture. I believe that if more of us White people made more than a superficial effort to obtain accurate information about racial groups other than our own, then we could help make this country a better place for all people that live here regardless of their racial background."

SOURCE: From "An Update of Helm's White and People of Color Racial Identity Models," by J.E. Helms, 1995, in J.G. Ponterotto, J.M. Casas, L.A. Suzuki, & C.M. Alexander (Eds.), *Handbook of Multicultural Counseling* (pp. 181-191), Thousand Oaks, CA: Sage. Adapted with permission.

helpful in building an increased sense of trust and cohesiveness within the group, while other interactions have negative effects on group members. The next section of this chapter explores unique interactions that are likely to occur in multicultural group counseling settings. This is followed by excerpts from a multicultural group that involves persons operating from different stages/statuses of the R/CID and WRID models described above.

Four Types of Racial-Cultural Interactions That Occur in Multicultural Counseling Groups

Helms (1995) noted that multicultural group counseling sessions are commonly affected by four types of interpersonal interactions. These interactions can have both positive and negative effects on the group process. Helms (1995) refers to these interactions as *parallel, progressive, regressive,* and *crossed racial-cultural interactions.*

Parallel racial-cultural interactions are manifested when two or more group members operating from similar R/CID or WRID stages/statuses express similar thoughts and feelings about racial-cultural issues. Because parallel interactions are rooted in similar constructions of racial-cultural issues, they can increase the sense of understanding, trust, and support that these group members experience toward one another within the group setting.

Another type of interpersonal interaction that takes place in multicultural group counseling

settings involves what Helms refers to as a *progressive racial-cultural group interaction* or, more simply, *progressive group interaction.* This occurs when a group member expresses views about racial and cultural issues that are indicative of more fully developed R/CID stages and WRID statuses, in comparison with other members who are functioning at less developed stages/statuses of these developmental models. Progressive group interactions can potentially stimulate new and more complex ways of thinking among some of the group members who, although operating at a less developed stage or status of RCID, are open to reframing different aspects of their thinking about racial and cultural issues (as is the case among persons who operate from the dissonance and introspection stages of the R/CID model and the disintegration and pseudo-independence WRID statuses).

In sharp contrast are *regressive racial-cultural interactions.* According to Helms (1995), regressive interactions occur when group members functioning from less mature psychological statuses express their thoughts and feelings about racial-cultural issues to other group members operating from more mature and sophisticated understanding of such issues; their comments can easily foster negative interpersonal dynamics (e.g., feelings of frustration, resentment, anger, etc.) that undermine a sense of trust and cohesiveness within the group.

Crossed racial-cultural interactions occur when group members exhibit attitudes and beliefs about racial-cultural issues that are directly opposed to one anther. This group interaction frequently occurs when individuals functioning at the contact status of the WRID model interact with resistance and immersion stage persons about racial and cultural issues. When these interactions are allowed to persist in group counseling settings, they will predictably result in highly antagonistic interpersonal relationships among persons who manifest substantially different perspectives regarding racial-cultural issues (D'Andrea, 1996, 2002). Like the regressive racial-cultural interactions, crossed interactions can seriously undermine the potential benefits that members might otherwise derive from racially heterogenous groups and even promote the premature termination of some persons in the group.

How These Interactions Affect Group Counseling

Table 19.2 provides excerpts of a multicultural group counseling session in which several persons functioning at different stages/statuses of the R/CID and WRID models were involved in a discussion that focused on one of the member's concerns about working with two White group counselors, one female and one male. Three of the group members were African Americans (two males and one female), and the remaining member was a Mexican American female.

This group was organized to serve two general purposes. First, it provided an opportunity for adults experiencing serious mental health problems to explore various factors that contributed to their overall sense of psychological distress. Second, the group was designed to assist clients in learning new cognitive and behavioral strategies to cope more effectively with personal difficulties (D'Andrea & Daniels, 1994).

Table 19.2 includes (a) statements made by the group leaders and members in the first group meeting immediately following the White male counselor's opening comments about the roles and responsibilities of the group leaders and members and issues related to confidentiality, (b) an identification of the R/CID stage or WRID status that characterize comments made by the group leaders and members, (c) a description of the different types of racial-cultural

group interactions that ensued from the statements made by the participants (e.g., parallel, progressive, regressive, and crossed interactions), (d) a brief discussion of the impact that these different statements/interactions had on the group, and (e) suggestions for creating a greater sense of respect and trust in the group so that positive psychological outcomes might ensue.

SUMMARY AND RECOMMENDATIONS

The R/CID and WRID models were presented in this chapter to foster a greater understanding of within-group differences that affect the psychological development of persons from similar racial-cultural backgrounds. By becoming familiar with the different stages and statuses of these theoretical models, group counselors can better understand how various within-group and between-group differences can affect group dynamics and interactions.

Group counselors are encouraged to avoid organizing groups comprising persons whose R/CID and WRID would promote tense and antagonistic interpersonal group dynamics. As noted above, the psychological differences that characterize the development of persons at the immersion/emersion and autonomy statuses of the WRID framework and individuals manifesting conformist stage characteristics of the R/CID are likely to promote crossed-group interactions when racial-cultural issues are discussed in group counseling settings. More antagonistic and volatile interactions are likely to occur in situations where group members are evenly divided among persons functioning from the resistance and immersion stage of the R/CID model and individuals operating primarily from contact status of the WRID framework.

One way to avoid including such configurations is to take time to conduct pregroup screening interviews with all prospective group members. By raising questions designed to elicit clients' thoughts and feelings about racial-cultural issues in pregroup counseling screening interviews, leaders are better able to organize groups comprising persons who are likely to become engaged in positive and growth-producing interactions (e.g., parallel and progressive racial-cultural group interactions).

Table 19.2 Excerpt From a Multicultural Group Counseling Session Comprised of Persons From Diverse Racial Backgrounds

Group Member	Comment	R/CID Stage—White Racial Identity Development (WRID) Status
Black Male Client	"Yeah, I understand how this group is going to work, but as I sit here and look around the room, I see two white counselors, three black clients, and a Mexican. I don't know how the rest of you feel (nodding to the other clients), but I can honestly say I don't know of any white person I really trust and don't think I want to share a lot of personal stuff with the two of you (gesturing to the counselors).	R/CID Stage = Resistance and Immersion Stage
Second Black Male Client	(In a frustrated tone of voice) "I don't know why you would want to bring that up now. I hate it when people try to make such a big deal about other people's race. I really don't like it. It sounds like you just don't like them (gesturing to the counselors). I have to admit that most of the black people I know just have a big chip on their shoulders when it comes to white people. But when I look at their lives I see that they are not honest; they don't have jobs; they are lazy; and they really don't seem to want to make a better life for themselves. Maybe you could learn some things from white people who are successful? I wish you would give these two counselors more of a chance. They seem like fine people to me.	R/CID Stage = Conformist Stage

** Please note: The interaction that occurred between these two clients was reflective of a crossed group interaction. Group counselors need to be mindful of these interactions (especially when they occur at the very beginning of the group process) before they lead to heightened antagonism between group members.

| White Female Counselor | I have to admit that I am surprised by what you just said (gesturing to the 1st black male client). I mean I have never done anything to intentionally harm another black person or any one who is different from me in terms of their race. I wish you would just give me a chance and get to know me before you start judging me. | WRID Status = Contact Status |

** Please note: While these statements help foster a regressive interaction between the white female counselor and the first black male client, they simultaneously represent a parallel interaction between the white female counselor and the second black client.

| Mexican American Client | Well, I want to say that I really know what you are saying (pointing to the first black male client). My family members and I have all had very bad experiences with white people. Not just once or twice, but all the time. If I am to be very honest I would have to say that I don't trust white people either. But lately, I have been thinking about one white guy I know that isn't like all the rest. He does a lot of work in our community that tries to deal with racism and | R/CID Stage = Introspection Stage |

other problems my community is facing. A lot of people think he is weird and wonder what he is really trying to do. But I think he is really trying to do the right thing. So recently I have been saying to myself, "Maybe all white people aren't bad. Maybe some can be trusted. I don't know. It is kind of confusing but. . . ." (long pause)

** Please note: Although these statements might potentially lead to crossed group interactions between this client, the 2nd black client, and the white female counselor; they constitute a progressive interaction between this client and the 1st black male client who spoke up at the beginning of this group session.

| White Male Counselor | I want to say that I think this is an important discussion and the type of conversation that can help to "make" or "break" a group that is made up of people who come from so many different backgrounds. I think I understand the different things everyone has said so far and in a strange kind of way I would have to say that I agree with a lot that has been said by everyone so far. I don't know if or how well we may learn to trust each other in this group. I do think that if we are going to learn to trust one another, we will have to not only talk about very difficult issues like racism, but we will also need to be honest about the ways that we all might be affected by it. I also think we are going to have to recognize that there will be times that we agree on things that are said in this group and other times when we strongly disagree with other things that might be said here. That is what I like about what you have done (Gesturing to the 1st black male who started this discussion). You took a big chance, said what you really think and feel, and are giving the rest of us an opportunity to tell you what we think and feel. | WRID Status = Integrative Awareness Stage |

Please note: These statements may be said to represent a progressive racial-cultural group interaction between the white male counselor, the 2nd black client, and the Mexican client. These statements can, however, also result in a crossed racial-cultural group interactions between the 1st black male client and the white male counselor.

| First Black Male Client | So am I supposed to trust you now? Talk about my personal feelings and think that you can understand what it is like to be a black man? I don't think so. (His voice gets stronger.) | R/CID Stage = Resistance and Immersion Stage |
| White Male Counselor | No, I don't expect you to automatically trust me or even like me. In fact, given your past experiences with white people and my limited understanding of the many ways that racism continues to exist in this country, I think you are pretty smart not to trust white people. But I also think that we both could probably teach each other new things and learn from each other. I do believe that I can learn a lot from you and specifically what it "means to be a black man" from your perspective. I hope we all will give this group a chance to do that . . . . but . . . I respect your feelings about being here right now. | WRID Status = Integrative Awareness Status |

** Please note: These comments reflect a progressive interaction between the counselor and the 1st black client who was functioning at the resistance and immersion stage of the R/CID model.

An important area of research that has particular relevance for multicultural group counseling includes numerous studies that direct attention to the impact that cultural/ethnic/racial similarities have in the helping process (Atkinson, Bui, & Mori, 1995; Atkinson & Lowe, 1995; Flaskerud, 1991; Ricker, Nystul, & Waldo, 1999; Russell, Fujino, Sue, Cheung, & Snowden, 1996; Sue, Fujino, Hu, Takeuchi, & Zane, 1991). These studies suggest that similarities in clients' and group counselors' cultural/ethnic/racial backgrounds affect four major areas that have relevance for group counseling: (a) clients' preference for counselors, (b) counselor credibility, (c) service utilization rates, and (d) counseling outcomes.

Empirical findings clearly suggest that clients from non-White, non-European minority groups generally prefer to work with counselors from similar cultural/ethnic/racial backgrounds (Atkinson et al., 1995). Other studies indicate that clients also give higher professional credibility ratings to counselors from similar cultural/ethnic/racial backgrounds (Atkinson & Lowe, 1995). Collectively, these research findings underscore the importance of recruiting greater numbers of non-White, non-European persons into the fields of counseling and psychology so that the professional preferences and needs of an increasingly diverse client base can be better addressed in the United States.

In addition, it has been noted that psychotherapeutic service utilization rates and counseling outcomes are both positively affected by cultural/ethnic/racial similarity matchings between clients and counselors. In this regard, clients (a) use counseling and psychotherapeutic services more frequently (Flaskerud, 1991; Sue et al., 1991) and (b) demonstrate more positive psychological outcomes when they participate in counseling and psychotherapy situations in which the counselor/psychologist comes from the same cultural/ethnic/racial background as themselves (Ricker et al., 1999; Russell et al., 1996).

In closing, it is acknowledged that the information presented in this chapter only begins to scratch the surface in terms of describing the complex challenges that group counselors face when working with multicultural groups. Nonetheless, it is hoped that upon reading this chapter, group counselors might become more (a) sensitive to the complexity of multicultural counseling groups, (b) respectful of the between- and within-group differences that may be manifested in racially and culturally heterogenous groups, (c) inclined to assess clients' RCID during pregroup screening interviews, (d) motivated to learn more about effective group interventions so that they can effectively address racial-cultural issues in future group counseling situations, and (e) willing to conduct research that will help expand group counselors' understanding of the complex issues associated with multicultural group counseling.

REFERENCES

American Psychological Association. (2003). Multicultural guidelines: Education, research, and practice. *American Psychologist, 58,* 377-402.

Atkinson, D. R., Bui, U., & Mori, S. (1995). Multiculturally sensitive supported treatments—An oxymoron? In J. G. Ponterotto, J. M. Casas, L. A. Suzuki, & C. M. Alexander (Eds.), *Handbook of multicultural counseling* (pp. 542-574). Thousand Oaks, CA: Sage.

Atkinson, D. R., & Lowe, S. (1995). The role of ethnicity, cultural knowledge, and conventional techniques in counseling and therapy. In J. G. Ponterotto, J. M. Casas, L. A. Suzuki, & C. M. Alexander (Eds.), *Handbook of multicultural counseling* (pp. 387-414). Thousand Oaks, CA: Sage.

Bernal, M. E., & Knight, G. P. (1993). *Ethnic identity: Formation and transmission among Hispanics and other minorities.* Albany: State University of New York Press.

Cross, W. E. (1971). The Negro-to-Black experience. *Black World, 20,* 13-27.

Cross, W. E. (1985). Black identity: Rediscovering the distinction between personal identity and reference group orientation. In M. B. Spencer, G. K. Brookins, & W. R. Allen (Eds.), *Beginnings: The social and affective development of Black children* (pp. 155-171). Hillsdale, NJ: Lawrence Erlbaum.

Cross, W. E. (1991). *Shades of Black.* Philadelphia: Temple University Press.

Cross, W. E. (1995). The psychology of nigrescence: Revising the Cross model. In J. G. Ponterotto,

J. M. Casas, L. A. Suzuki, & C. M. Alexander (Eds.), *Handbook of multicultural counseling* (pp. 93-122). Thousand Oaks, CA: Sage.

D'Andrea, M. (1996). White racism. In P. B. Pedersen & D. C. Locke (Eds.), *Cultural and diversity issues in counseling* (pp. 55-58). Greensboro, NC: ERIC/CASS Publications.

D'Andrea, M. (2000). Postmodernism, social constructionism, and multiculturalism: Three forces that are shaping and expanding our thoughts about counseling. *Journal of Mental Health Counseling, 22,* 1-16.

D'Andrea, M. (2002, October). *Dealing with racism in counselor education: Promoting a social justice training framework.* Paper presented at the Association for Counselor Education and Supervision National Conference. Park City, UT.

D'Andrea, M., Brown, S., Locke, D. C., & Parker, M. (1996, January). *The challenges of multicultural group work.* A preconvention workshop presented at the annual meeting of the Association for Specialists in Group Work, Athens, GA.

D'Andrea, M., & Daniels, J. (1994). Group pacing: A developmental eclectic approach to group counseling. *Journal of Counseling & Development, 72,* 585-590.

D'Andrea, M., & Daniels, J. (1996). What is multicultural group counseling? Identifying its potential benefits, barriers, and future challenges. *Counseling & Human Development, 28,* 1-16.

D'Andrea, M., & Daniels, J. (2001). Facing the changing demographic structure of our society. In D. C. Locke, J. E. Myers, & E. L. Herr (Eds.), *The handbook of counseling* (pp. 529-539). Thousand Oaks, CA: Sage.

D'Andrea, M., & Daniels, J. (in press). *Multicultural counseling: Empowerment strategies for a diverse society.* Pacific Grove, CA: Brooks/Cole.

Erikson, E. H. (1963). *Childhood and society.* New York: Norton.

Erikson, E. H. (1987). *A way of looking at things.* New York: Norton.

Flaskerud, J. H. (1991). Effects of Asian client-therapist language, ethnicity, and gender match on utilization and outcome of therapy. *Community Mental Health Journal, 22,* 127-141.

Haley-Banez, L., Brown, S., & Molina, B. (1999). Association for Specialists in Group Work: Principles for diversity-competent group workers. *Journal for Specialists in Group Work, 24,* 7-14.

Helms, J. E. (1984). Toward a theoretical explanation of the effects of race on counseling: A Black and White model. *The Counseling Psychologist, 12,* 153-165.

Helms, J. E. (1990). *Black and White identity: Theory, research, and practice.* New York: Greenwood.

Helms, J. E. (1995). An update of Helm's White and people of color racial identity models. In J. G. Ponterotto, J. M. Casas, L. A. Suzuki, & C. M. Alexander (Eds.), *Handbook of multicultural counseling* (pp. 181-191). Thousand Oaks, CA: Sage.

Helms, J. E. (2003). Racial identity in the social environment. In P. B. Pedersen & J. C. Carey (Eds.), *Multicultural counseling in schools: A practical handbook* (2nd ed., pp. 44-58) Boston: Allyn & Bacon.

Helms, J. E., & Cook, D. A. (1999). *Using race and culture in counseling and psychotherapy: Theory and process.* Boston: Allyn & Bacon.

Ivey, A. E., Pedersen, P. B., & Ivey, M. B. (2001). *Intentional group counseling: A microskills approach.* Belmont, CA: Wadsworth/Thomson.

Jones, J. M. (1997). *Prejudice and racism* (2nd ed.). New York: McGraw Hill.

Kim, J. (1981). The process of Asian American identity development: A study of Japanese-American women's perspectives of their struggle to achieve personal identities as Americans of Asian ancestry. *Dissertation Abstracts International, 42,* 1551A. (University Microfilms No. 81-18080)

Lewis, J. A., Lewis, M. D., Daniels, J. A., & D'Andrea, M. (2003). *Community counseling: Empowerment strategies for a diverse society* (3rd ed.). Pacific Grove, CA: Brooks/Cole.

Martin-Baro, I. (1994). *Writings for a liberation psychology.* Cambridge, MA: Harvard University Press.

Merta, R. J. (1995). Group work: Multicultural perspectives. In J. G. Ponterotto, J. M. Casas, L. A. Suzuki, & C. M. Alexander (Eds.), *Handbook of multicultural counseling* (pp. 567-585). Thousand Oaks, CA: Sage.

Neville, H. A., Worthington, R. L., & Spanierman, L. B. (2001). Race, power, and multicultural counseling psychology: Understanding White privilege and color-blind racial attitudes. In J. G. Ponterotto, J. M. Casas, L. A. Suzuki, &

C. M. Alexander (Eds.), *Handbook of multicultural counseling* (2nd ed., pp. 257-288). Thousand Oaks, CA: Sage.

Parham, T. (Ed.). (2002). *Counseling persons of African descent: Raising the bar of practitioner competence.* Thousand Oaks, CA: Sage.

Ricker, M., Nystul, M., & Waldo, M. (1999). Counselors' and clients' ethnic similarity and therapeutic alliance in time-limited outcomes of counseling. *Psychological Reports, 84,* 674-676.

Russell, G., Fujino, D. C., Sue, S., Cheung, M. K., & Snowden, L. R. (1996). The effects of psychotherapist-client ethnic match in the assessment of mental health functioning. *Journal of Cross-Cultural Psychology, 27,* 598-615.

Scheurich, J. J. (1993). Toward a discourse on White racism. *Educational Researcher, 22,* 5-10.

Scheurich, J. J., & Young, M. D. (1997). Coloring epistemologies: Are our research epistemologies racially biased? *Educational Researcher, 26,* 4-16.

Sue, D. W., Arredondo, P., & McDavis, R. J. (1992). Multicultural counseling competencies and standards: A call to the profession. *Journal of Counseling & Development, 70,* 477-486.

Sue, D. W., Bernier, J. B., Durran, M., Feinberg, L., Pedersen, P., Smith, E., & Vasquez-Nuttall, E. (1982). Position paper: Cross-cultural counseling competencies. *Counseling Psychologist, 10,* 45-52.

Sue, D. W., Carter, R. T., Casas, J. M., Fouad, N. A., Ivey, A. E., Jensen, M., LaFromboise, T., Manese, J. E., Ponterotto, J. G., & Vasquez-Nutall, E. (1998). *Multicultural competencies: Individual and organizational development.* Thousand Oaks, CA: Sage.

Sue, D. W., & Sue, D. (1999). *Counseling the culturally different: Theory and practice* (3rd ed.). New York: John Wiley.

Sue, D. W., & Sue, D. (2003). *Counseling the culturally diverse: Theory and practice* (4th ed.). New York: John Wiley.

Sue, S., Fujino, D. C., Hu, L., Takeuchi, T. D., & Zane, N. (1991). Community mental health services for ethnic minorities: A test of the cultural responsiveness hypothesis. *Journal of Consulting & Clinical Psychology, 59,* 533-540.

West, C. (1999). *The Cornel West reader.* New York: Basic Civitas Books.

20

THE IMPACT OF LANGUAGE ON DYNAMICS IN COUNSELING AND PSYCHOTHERAPY GROUPS

LOAN T. PHAN

University of New Mexico

EDIL TORRES RIVERA

University at Buffalo, SUNY

While little has been written about the impact of language and communication patterns on group dynamics and group process when working with ethnic minority populations, it is an important variable in group work that can no longer be neglected (Axelson, 1999; Orasanu, Fischer, & Davison, 1997; Toseland & Rivas, 2001). Language and communication patterns are strongly related to people's worldviews and thinking patterns, which may directly affect how people behave in group settings and group dynamics and process (Gross & Miller, 2002). The U.S. Bureau of the Census (1990) indicated that 13.82% of the total United States population speak languages other than Standard English as their first language, with about 17 million people fluent in at least two languages. Approximately 7.52% of the U.S. population speaks Spanish, while another 6.3% speaks 25 other languages, which include

French, German, Italian, Chinese, Tagalog, Polish, Korean, Vietnamese, Portuguese, Japanese, Greek, Arabic, Hindu, Russian, Yiddish, Thai, Persian, French Creole, Armenian, Navaho, Hungarian, Hebrew, Dutch, Mon-Khmer, and Gujarathi (U.S. Bureau of the Census, 2000). The remaining 86.18% of the United States population speaks only Standard English. Standard English is defined as the language acceptable and normative among reputable people in reputable circumstances, the prestige dialect recognized throughout the area (Wilson, 1993).

Language differences, communication patterns, and the implications of language when working with ethnic minorities are mentioned in only a few group counseling textbooks (i.e., Carroll, Bates, & Johnson, 1997; Corey & Corey, 1997; Forsyth, 1999; Gladding, 1999; Yalom, 1995). Furthermore, they typically note only the complexity of language briefly without providing specific suggestions about how to address this issue in groups. In addition, the topic of counseling and therapy groups performed in languages other than English is not addressed. Also absent is the topic of bilingual groups. The small amount of information found about multilingual groups concentrates on helping clients feel comfortable in speaking English, rather than helping clients express themselves in their native languages (Asner-Self & Feyissa, 2002).

Research has indicated that accents may be positive because they may produce cohesiveness in groups with people who speak English as a second language (Fuertes, 1999). In contrast, there is also evidence suggesting that clients who are not proficient in Standard English may be misdiagnosed and receive incorrect treatment from counselors (Gopaul-McNicol & Thomas-Presswood, 1998). The problem becomes compounded in groups because a translator may not be a plausible option. Even if it is an option, the dynamics of a group grow increasingly complex with the addition of a translator who is an "outsider" (Posthuma, 1996).

Furthermore, the theme of language as a major form of subtle oppression among linguistically different groups has been largely ignored by many social scientists. The dynamics of language have been used in the United States as a vehicle to impose, disseminate, and maintain the status quo of the "dominant culture" (Urciuoli, 1996). For example, definitions of normality, acceptable or appropriate behavior, as well as suitable language are dictated without considering input from those who do not use Standard English. Consequently, group leaders may not be immune to dominant culture ideas about language and unintentionally perpetuate negative attitudes toward clients whose primary language is not English (Locke, 1992).

This chapter will first discuss language and communication patterns as important variables to consider in group settings with ethnic minorities, then provide suggestions for groups. Specifically, this chapter will concentrate on language variations, worldviews, and communications styles and their impact on group facilitation. The following sections of this chapter address language as a communication tool in groups, with a focus on language variation among the different ethnic groups and implications of communication dynamics. Although language is an immensely complex and extensive subject, the purpose of this chapter is to assist group leaders of psychoeducational and counseling groups to understand and become familiar with language dynamics in order to increase effectiveness with linguistically and culturally different clients.

IMPACT OF LANGUAGE ON GROUPS

Language is the primary means of providing help by group leaders in the United States, with talk therapy being the major source of treatment for clients (Wiener, 2001). It is also the most important method of communicating and understanding others in this culture. This importance magnifies with culturally different people whose first language is not English, because language variation can mean the difference between receiving or not receiving the appropriate services or any services at all. For example, Sue and Sue (1999) reported that the majority of ethnic minorities do not seek mental services because most providers speak only English.

Language also influences how people think and communicate in writing and verbally (Torres-Rivera, Smaby, & Maddux, 1996; Wehrly, 1995). That is, the language in which the culture communicates determines the thinking process and patterns of processing information, in particular when thinking about abstract concepts such as time, love, relationships, and other concepts that are often discussed in psychoeducational and/or counseling groups (Boroditsky, 2001). For instance, most English speaking people are linear thinkers, while most people who speak Semitic languages are more complex and far from linear in their languages as well as in their thinking. Similarly, Asian languages are indirectional, and romance languages are curvilinear (Torres-Rivera, Wilbur, Saracini-Frank, & Roberts-Wilbur, 1999). Therefore, the implications of miscommunication based on language variation are more complicated than simple misunderstandings, with results such as the misdiagnosing and misapplication of treatment. For example, Sue (1995) described a Caucasian doctor instructing a Filipino nurse to perform a particular type of medical procedure. The Filipino nurse nodded her head as a sign of agreement. Later, the doctor returned to see if the nurse was performing the procedure correctly and discovered that the nurse had continued to do the procedure incorrectly. Sue (1995) later explained that the Filipino nurse believed that to tell the doctor that she did not understand his instructions may have been seen as a sign of disrespect, because communicating such a message may have conveyed that the doctor was a bad teacher. The following sections will discuss specific issues related to the impact of language on groups.

Language and Worldview

Ethnographic studies suggest that how people talk about language, race, ethnicity, class, gender and how they share their life experiences depends greatly on who interprets language (Torres, 1997). For example, an English-speaking motivational speaker used the term *crisis* and stated that in the Chinese language, the word means danger and opportunity. This translation can be confusing to Chinese clients in therapy because the real meaning of the word *crisis* in the Chinese language means danger but not necessarily opportunity (Adams, 2002).

Linguistic prejudices are usually understood as a concrete and linear concept. For instance, a person who speaks with an accent may be viewed as having little or no education, rather than the accent being seen as a normal result of speaking a foreign language. As a result, language is objectified along with the people using the language, which makes them a convenient target for discrimination. Later in this chapter, under the subheading of "Socioeconomic Status and Language," an example of this objectification is provided. Linguistic studies support the notion that the language in which a person is thinking has a direct impact on his or her thought process (Boroditsky, 2001). For example, when a person speaks in English about a table, he or she refers to the table as an "it." If the same person changes from English to Spanish and continues the conversation, the table now becomes female and the context of

the conversation would change completely because the table is no longer an "it" but rather a "she" (Gross & Miller, 2002). The implication for group leaders is that females and males have role characteristics attached to their gender, and culturally speaking, each one of these role characteristics is prescribed by the culture. For example, females in many cultures are supposed to be nurturing and emotionally supportive, while males are supposed to be strong, unemotional, and virile. Therefore, if the language used in a group session (i.e., Spanish, Chinese, etc.) calls something "male" or "female," as mentioned in the example of the table, the role characteristics implied in the language will affect the message that is being said about that object.

Since their arrival in the United States, many ethnic minority groups in the United States have endured exclusion because of the languages they speak, the color of their skin, and their socioeconomic status. Prejudice and racism are displayed as important actions that occur in everyday social transactions such as greetings and casual conversations. Therefore, one can say that verbal communication is a complex system of significant social transactions (Urciuoli, 1996). Communication is a political phenomenon, because how the spoken and written language is interpreted depends greatly upon the people holding the political power. Language is action, and thus language concepts are reality and not simply concepts. Many people do not see language as an influential and powerful force in their lives. However, counselors need to look at language as a process that plays a role in understanding how power is gained and maintained as it relates to oppression and prejudice. For all ethnic minority groups, this variable is an important one; their reality is shaped by the conditions that limit where and how they live, work, earn money, and send their children to school. Ultimately, their lives, present and future, lie in the hands of those who control the power (Draguns, 2001; Fischman, 1999; Preciado & Henry, 1997). A good example of how this plays out in psychoeducational and counseling groups can be seen in the recent article that appeared in the *Journal for Specialists in Group Work* (Asner-Self & Feyissa, 2002): While the intention of this article is to help people feel comfortable during their initial cultural shock, the subtle messages in it may give immigrants the idea that English is the preferred way of communication (Asner-Self & Feyissa, 2002). The message conveyed by the group leaders is that one language is better than the other and that how their clients communicate may have an impact on their future in this country.

Socioeconomic Status and Language

Similarly, people also attribute languages with different hierarchical positions based on socioeconomic status. This phenomenon is not limited to the negative assessment of Spanish-speaking people, but it seems to be less derogatory to Western European languages (i.e., French, English, German, etc.) (Horsman, 1981). For example, if someone goes to a fast-food restaurant and the server speaks with a Spanish accent, he or she might think that the server is uneducated. On the other hand, if the same person goes to a French restaurant and the server speaks with a French or English accent, the belief might be that the server is educated and possesses "culture" (Torres, 1997). In the United States, language objectification customarily places Spanish and non–Western European languages in an inferior position to English. Examples of this objectification can be found in negative interpretations of accents, mistakes, and/or incorrect grammar as signs of ignorance (Flores, Attinasi, & Pedraza, 1981; Zentella, 1988). This kind of interpretation is based primarily on assumptions about class and race made by those who have power and control over how language should be conveyed, such as its appropriateness and delivery. It is not limited to Spanish-speaking people but is also projected toward many non-White ethnic minority groups who do not speak Standard English, such as African Americans, low-socioeconomic-status Asian Americans, and bilingual Native Americans (Liang, Fuller, & Singer, 2000).

In contrast, low-socioeconomic-status bilingual Latinos in the United States use Spanish and English fluidly and move from one language to another without much difficulty and without the belief that one language is better or has more value than the other (Santiago-Rivera, 1995).

As stated earlier, group leaders may be influenced by dominant culture ideas and consequently may be imposing their attitudes, values, and beliefs on linguistically different clients. For example, during one supervisory group, one of the counselors-in-training seemed frustrated with one of the clients because he was speaking in broken English and was difficult to understand. The supervisor eventually asked the counselor-in-training how he was feeling. The counselor-in-training responded "that people should learn English, if they want to live in this country."

Within-Language Variations

African American Language Variations. African Americans who speak Black English or Ebonics follow different rules in phonology, syntax, and semantics than those who speak Standard English (Ogbu, 1999). For example, many African Americans who use Black English do not discriminate between syllables and produce many sounds that Standard English speakers are not familiar with in order to make sense of the message that is being sent to them (for example, *test* is pronounced "tes" and *He is going* is pronounced "He goin"). Similarly, Black English speakers tend not to use Standard English subject-verb agreement, negation, articles, and tenses. Last but not least is the tendency of Black English speakers to use the verb *to be* differently than those using Standard English (Gopaul-McNicol & Thomas-Presswood, 1998). These differences create difficulties for group leaders who are not familiar with this type of language and/or the communication style that is usually attached to it. Also, Black English is spoken with affect and animation, versus Standard English, which is spoken loudly, quickly, and unemotionally. Black English communication in group settings goes far beyond simple semantics, because the client's language system does not occur in a vacuum. To ensure effective communication during the group session, the client must feel connected and understood by the counselor. Without that connection, the meaning of the client's statement will be lost (Harper, Braithwaite, & LaGrande, 1998). As a consequence, group leaders need to be aware of this type of language use and also be aware that because of societal pressures to conform to Standard English demands, many African American clients may feel the use of Black English is inappropriate during the group sessions (Koch, 2000). This removes the benefits of originality and expressiveness during the session and may serve as a put-down, which in turn results in an ineffective group session and may even be more harmful than helpful.

Asian Americans Language Variations. Even though many Asian American parents encourage their children to learn and use Standard English as their primary means of communication in public, it is important to understand that the primary language of the family may continue to be their native language (i.e., Vietnamese, Korean). A common assumption made by many counselors is that because the Asian American client is proficient in conversational English, his or her thinking patterns are similar to those whose primary language is English. For the most part, Asian languages are high context, relying heavily on nonverbal communication. For example, in the Japanese language, the focus of the communication among people is often concentrated on reflection, other-centeredness, indirection, indecision, and apology. This is important to recognize because Japanese relationships are often based on the above characteristics (Lee & Zane, 1998), emphasizing the interdependence of the Japanese culture. For example, during a group session facilitated by one of the authors of this chapter, the group leader, employing an egalitarian leading style, was trying to "force" definitions onto a Japanese group member. The group leader assumed that because the group member was fluent in English, providing direction and structure was the best way to help the group member understand group dynamics. As the group progressed, the apparent indecision of the Japanese member increased along with her noticeable discomfort with the direct approach used by the group leader. Afterward, the group leader realized that perhaps if he had allowed the indirection and indecision from the Japanese group member to flourish, then she may have better understood and grasped the group dynamics and process.

Group leaders who understand Asian American language structure, such as indirectionality, syntax, communication styles, and word terminology, have a greater ability to apply effective interventions during group work with Asian Americans. Specifically, knowing the dynamics of the language could result in understanding patterns of thought processes among group members, which could mean the difference between being helpful or not. Group counselors working with Asian Americans could benefit from watching movies such as *The Joy Luck Club* (Wang, Tan, Bass, Markey, & Wang, 1993) and *Heaven and Earth* (Stone, Milchan, Kline, Ho, & Stone, 1993) and from observing Leong, Iwamasa, and Sue (2000) performing a counseling session with an Asian American client. DeLucia-Waack and Donigian (2003) present a list of popular movies, training videos, and books that may be useful in learning about other cultures.

Native American/Indian People Language Variations. A great deal of misunderstanding about Native American languages and traditions seems to be the norm in the counseling field. Many people seem to automatically associate Native Americans with spirituality (Duran & Duran, 1995; Irwin, 2000). While it is true that spirituality is a strong presence in Native American traditions, the idea that all Native Americans are spiritual is as nonsensical as saying that all White people are not spiritual. Another myth and/or misconception is one of the "noble savage" (Garrett & Wilbur, 1999). Who doesn't remember watching John Wayne's movie in which the "Good Chief" welcomed the great American hero with the following greeting: "Me Chief Rattlesnake is happy to help you." Moreover, group counselors with some experience in the addictions field and familiarity of the Big Book cannot refute that the last part of the Big Book mocks the way in which Native Americans use Standard English by using broken English to present the Native American story. Although the intention is to assist Native Americans with alcohol problems, inadequate knowledge of Native American language variations maintains misconceptions that may impede the application of effective interventions.

The bilingualism of Native Americans in the United States has survived staunch efforts by the church and the government to eliminate not only their language but also Native American religion and culture (Irwin, 2000). More than 150 Native American languages are spoken in the United States today, supporting the reality that Native Americans are bilingual people (i.e., Navaho, Washoe, Apache, etc.). Although many differences exist among the tribes or Nations and languages in Native American cultures, there are some common characteristics that may help group leaders who work with bilingual Native American clients. The language and thought processes of Indian people indicate interconnectedness (Garrett, 1998). Consequently, group leaders need to understand that the Native American belief that everything is alive, everything has a purpose, and all things are interconnected is reflected in their language. For example, when working with Native American clients in a group setting, metaphors such as the "Legend of the Rock" or taking the "Red Road" could result in a more effective approach, because according to Native American tradition, every living and nonliving thing has a soul and is therefore part of our human interconnectedness. Also, it may be beneficial to remember the Native American notions that the spoken word is powerful and oral tradition is magical.

Latino/Hispanic Language Variations. Spanish-speaking people are the largest linguistically different group in the United States. According to Baruth and Manning (2003), 50.8% of all Latinos speak Spanish skillfully but do not speak English proficiently. When looking at the three largest Spanish-speaking groups in the United States (Mexicans, Puerto Ricans, and Cubans), it is clear that the percentages of people in the United States using Spanish to perform their daily transactions is great (Baruth & Manning, 2003). Spanish, as with other languages, is very different from English because of its nonlinearity, syntax, phonology, and semantics. Semantics also differ among Spanish-speaking people, such that an individual of Mexican descendent may use *carnal* to refer to his brother, in comparison with an individual of Cuban descendent who uses *hermano*. To illustrate this point, one of the authors of

this chapter had an interesting experience during one of his first psychoeducational groups with high school children of Mexican descent. The group was run completely in Spanish, as the group leader is Puerto Rican and his native language is Spanish. During one of the group sessions, the group leader pointed at an object and asked one of the group members to "Vete y coje aquello que esta alli," meaning "Go and get the object that is there." The group leader noticed that the group members became very excited and frantically pointed at each other telling one another, "No tu, no tu," which means "No you, no you." The group leader could not understand what all of the commotion was about and asked his cofacilitator, who was of Mexican descendent, for some assistance. The Mexican descent cofacilitator calmly informed the group leader that in the Mexican culture, *coje* (take) means having sexual contact: thus, the members' reluctance to obey the request.

Language Alternation

There are two different types of language alternation: code switching and code mixing. This is a common phenomenon among bilingual speakers and is defined by the ability of a speaker to move from one language to the other during the construction of a sentence (Brice, 2002). This ability is the reason that a number of linguists believe that the majority of bilingual people are creative, meaning that they will find creative ways of communicating their messages to others (Boroditsky, 2001). For example, it would not be out of the ordinary for bilingual people to use their hands, facial expressions, metaphors, and examples to convey their messages during a conversation. Latino bilingual clients are not an exception to that creativity, as illustrated by their ability to move from one language to the other (fluidity).

Group leaders need to understand this fluidity to capitalize on the creativity and adaptability of Latino bilingual clients. They also need to realize that code switching may be seen as inappropriate in formal counseling sessions given that the stigma of broken English is a reality for Latino clients and for all other linguistically different groups. This is an important distinction because formal counseling is similar to going to school, where following the rules, in this case speaking Standard English, is intended to help linguistically different people understand the rules of the dominant culture (Straussner, 2001). Code switching and code mixing may occur during a group session when the clients do not understand the meaning of what is being stated, strong feelings arise, or when they try to convey an important message to other group members or the leader (Brice, 2002).

Communication Patterns

African American. African American communication patterns can be described as high context, depending more on the situation and the person than on the content of the message (Sue & Sue, 1999). High-context communication relies on nonverbal and group identification to understand the message being delivered. English-speaking countries such as the United States, on the other hand, function with low-context communication that focuses more on the verbal component of the message and the explicit expression of words, whether written or spoken (Hall, 1976; Sue & Sue, 1999). For example, when working with high-context communication groups, silence is used more than long verbal exchanges. It is important to emphasize that it is a function of the language and not necessarily of the culture. Interestingly, some research has been conducted at Stanford University that looks at how language affects thought processes (Boroditsky, 2001; Gross & Miller, 2002). These studies concluded that language is a strong variable in shaping thought in the abstract domain and a person's native language has a powerful contribution in the shaping of one's habitual thinking patterns.

Asian American. Many Asian Americans seem to speak softly, indirectly, and in a low-key manner. Silence does not usually give an invitation for someone else to speak, but rather allows time for the speaker to collect his or her thoughts to convey a message (Leong et al., 2000). It is also important to remember that many Asian cultures do not promote open expression and display of feelings, as this sometimes is seen as a sign of immaturity and lack of

wisdom (Lee & Zane, 1998). In addition, many Asian Americans may feel uneasy with direct confrontation, challenges, and interruptions during communication discourses (Baruth & Manning, 2003).

Native American/Indian People. Native American people's communication styles are very similar to those of Asian American people. Native Americans tend to be soft-spoken, indirect, and at times share long narratives to convey a point. Also, levels of verbal engagement may depend on the level of acculturation. For instance, while conducting a workshop at the Pyramid Lake Paiute Indian reservation, one of the authors of this chapter noticed that during a group exercise, tribal members who disclosed that they rarely leave the reservation appeared to be less engaged than tribal members who lived in the city. This behavior was consistent with a prior visit to the reservation during a workshop for Native Americans parents. In contrast, the majority of the Native American students coming from large urban areas in California who attended graduate courses at large Western universities where both of the authors teach appeared to be more engaging, direct, and confrontational during verbal exchanges in the classes. While it is important not to stereotype this behavior, it is also important to be observant of the levels of acculturation and the behaviors presented by each group. In other words, more highly acculturated group members may communicate in styles that are more similar to dominant-culture communication than do those who are more traditional (LaFromboise, 1995).

Latino/Hispanic. As a more expressive language, Spanish is considered to be a high-context language. For example, in Spanish, the word *amor* has a meaning that extends beyond the simple translation of love. It can mean an expression of oneself, including beliefs, emotions, doubts, questioning, and confusion. Of equal importance for group leaders working with bilingual Latino clients is the awareness of different narrative forms of communication in the Spanish used by Puerto Ricans, which tends to be more historically present and dramatic than the narrative forms of Spanish communication that Mexicans and Chileans use (Torres, 1997). Puerto Ricans like to tell stories that are based on the past when they talk with each other, while Mexicans and Chileans have more direct communication styles.

Implications of Communication Dynamics

As explained earlier, the communication process is a complex one. Traditionally, communication has been simplified as having two components, with at least six subcomponents that influence the process. For instance, in a situation involving two communicators, one is the source of the message, and the other is the receiver. The process is simplified as an idea, or the need to communicate arouses the source communicator. The source communicator makes the choice to communicate the idea using verbal means and past experiences to find the exact symbols to communicate the idea to the receiver. The receiver communicator is aroused by aural stimuli or the need to communicate, and receives symbols in a distorted form. The receiver communicator then uses memory and past experiences to give meaning to the symbols, stores the information, and finally sends feedback to the source communicator (Torres, 1997).

While the process appears simple enough, complications still exist as other influential variables affect the communication process. Let us assume that other variables related to this process are included, such as the physical state of the participants, past and present experiences, mental sets, socioeconomic status, formal education, expectations, cultural influences, and the channel used to send the message (for example, the environment in which the communication takes place). With the inclusion of these variables, the communication process no longer appears to be a simple exchange of symbols, but rather a powerful process. In other words, let us assume that the group leader has learned to use some common phrases in one language but lacks proficiency in the meaning of the language and the appropriate use of the phrases (Vazquez, Santiago-Rivera, & Orjuela, 2000). The group leader, while confident in her or his ability to deliver the appropriate intervention with the bilingual group, feels uncomfortable with using "unknown" terms in the session. These added variables introduce increased tension for the group leader to deliver his or her interventions to a group of non-English speakers, and at the same time, non-English-speaking clients may feel pressured to grasp the information and/or help that the group leader attempts to put forth. The group leader holds the position of an expert, while the expectation of the group member involves his or her performance and evaluation. In this example, the dynamics of bilingualism comes into play as an important role in the group dynamics and process. When people feel pressured to perform, the natural tendency to immerse themselves in familiar territory (native language) occurs. People from different cultures address problems according to their worldviews, which are deeply rooted in their cultures. Some cultures use a direct approach, while others use an indirect or non-confrontational approach to solve a problem. Members of U.S. society, for the most part, use a direct confrontational approach to deal with problems, while Asian Americans, Latinos, and Indian people prefer an indirect approach.

The following examples illustrate the indirect approach of two different ethnic groups. First, Sue (1995) described an interaction between himself and his father in which he was expressing his anxiety about an upcoming examination to his father. His father responded to him, "Derald, just don't think about it." Second, in a conversation with a Native American friend, one of the authors of this chapter was expressing frustration about the racism and sexism she was experiencing in her graduate program. The Native American friend's response was, "So what can you really do about it?" Although in both examples, the responses appeared to be invalidating, the message of both responses involves dealing with problems in a nondirect way rather than using a direct approach.

Even though the complexity of bilingualism in group work may seem daunting, the ability to apply this understanding and knowledge is viable. Some bilingual experts contend that group leader professionals must be proficient in the language of the client to deliver quality care. The relationship between the client and the group leader professional who is not bilingual suffers a great deal because symptoms could be misinterpreted. Negative outcomes due to invalidating clients' experiences have been well documented with clients suffering from post-traumatic stress disorders (Friedman & Marsella, 1996; Marsella, Friedman, Gerrity, & Scurfield, 1996). Thus, the primary implication for group leaders who are not bilingual is that lack of integration between affect and the experience of their clients does not mean that some type of pathology exists in the client. Rather, the language in which the client is forced to deliver the message may not accurately convey the message, feelings, and affect that the client truly wishes to express. Comprehension of the complexity of different language and communication patterns is essential in group work with ethnic minority populations.

The authors have found that becoming familiar with controversial yet powerful movies and/or songs can help group leaders and counselors in general to acquire an understanding of how language and thinking patterns work. For example, rap music can be a powerful tool that allows inner-city African American adolescents to express their inner feelings, as well as providing a vehicle to create cohesiveness in group sessions. Similarly, movies such as *Black Is . . . Black Ain't* (Riggs, Atkison, Badgley, Paris, & Riggs, 1996), *Smoke Signals* (Estes, Rosenfelt, & Eyre, 1998), *The Joy Luck Club* (Wang et al., 1993), and other similar movies appear to offer counselors a greater knowledge of language dynamics and thought processes.

CONCLUSIONS

An understanding of how language and communication patterns are used in a specific culture is vital for the comprehension of the language. As it has been presented throughout this chapter, language shapes experience, and experience shapes language. In groups, language predetermines modes of observation and interpretation of experiences, re-creating experiences and empowering group members to imagine and create new experiences (Okun, Fried, & Okun, 1999). Therefore, it is important that group leaders have a clear understanding of cultural and linguistic differences of their clients as well

as in themselves. Although generalizations have been the rule in this chapter, group leaders must understand that individual differences do exist and that differences within the various ethnic minority groups are also important to consider.

SUGGESTIONS FOR BEST PRACTICES

The following are suggestions for group leaders who work with linguistically different clients:

1. Group leaders should try to learn or become familiar with a language other than English.

2. Group leaders should be aware of their own linguistic biases and be able to understand where these biases come from.

3. Movies and ESL textbooks are very helpful in providing a basis for understanding the thinking process of linguistically different people.

4. Familiarity with ethnic neighborhoods will provide counselors with an understanding of how people communicate in their own languages.

5. Learning and knowing important phrases in the clients' language help counselors establish credibility and respect with linguistically different clients.

6. Finally, flexibility and comfort with ambiguity are important when working with linguistically different clients. This will allow clients to create their own structures during group sessions.

In closing, since psychoeducational and counseling groups generally concentrate on the abstract parts of the client's life (i.e., relationships and self-esteem), the strong empirical evidence indicating that native language influences the way people think about these abstract domains further necessitates group leaders to address language as an essential component for effective group work (Boroditsky, 2000, 2001). Accordingly, group workers who are not aware of such relationship aspects and are unable to use different metaphors, language analogies, and other structural alignment may render themselves ineffectual due to miscommunication or the inability to help clients understand.

REFERENCES

Adams, C. (2002). *The straight dope.* Retrieved June 15, 2002, from http://www.straightdope.com/columns/001103.html.

Asner-Self, K. K., & Feyissa, A. (2002). The use of poetry in psychoeducational groups with multi-cultural-multilingual clients. *The Journal for Specialists in Group Work, 27,* 136-160.

Axelson, J. A. (1999). *Counseling and development in a multicultural society* (3rd ed.). Pacific Grove, CA: Brooks/Cole.

Baruth, L. G., & Manning, M. L. (2003). *Multicultural counseling and psychotherapy: A lifespan perspective* (3rd ed.). Upper Saddle River, NJ: Prentice Hall.

Boroditsky, L. (2000). Metaphoric structuring: Understanding time through spatial metaphors. *Cognition, 75,* 1-28.

Boroditsky, L. (2001). Does language shape thought? Mandarin and English speakers' conceptions of time. *Cognitive Psychology, 4,* 1-22.

Brice, A. E. (2002). *The Hispanic child: Speech, language, culture and education.* Boston: Allyn & Bacon.

Carroll, M., Bates, M., & Johnson, C. (1997). *Group leadership: Strategies for group counseling leaders* (3rd ed.). Denver, CO: Love.

Corey, M. S., & Corey, G. (1997). *Groups: Process and practice* (5th ed.). Pacific Grove, CA: Brooks/Cole.

DeLucia-Waack, J., & Donigian, J. (Eds.). (2003). *The practice of multicultural group work: Visions and perspectives from the field.* Belmont, CA: Wadsworth.

Draguns, J. G. (2001). Toward a truly international psychology: Beyond English only. *American Psychologist, 56,* 1019-1030.

Duran, E., & Duran, B. (1995). *Native Americana postcolonial psychology.* New York: State University of New York Press.

Estes, L., Rosenfelt, S. (Producers), & Eyre, C. (Director). (1998). *Smoke signals* [Film]. United States: Miramax Home Entertainment.

Fischman, G. E. (1999). Challenges and hopes: Multiculturalism as revolutionary praxis. *Multicultural Education, 6,* 32-34.

Flores, J., Attinasi, J., & Pedraza, P. (1981). La carreta made a U-turn: Puerto Rican language and culture in the United States. *Daedalus, 110,* 193-217.

Forsyth, D. R. (1999). *Group dynamics* (3rd ed.). Belmont, CA: Wadsworth.

Friedman, M. J., & Marsella, A. J. (1996). Posttraumatic stress disorder: An overview of the concept. In A. J. Marsella, M. J. Friedman, E. T. Gerrity, & R. M. Scurfield (Eds.), *Ethnocultural aspects of posttraumatic stress disorder: Issues, research, and clinical applications* (pp. 11-32). Washington, DC: American Psychological Association.

Fuertes, J. N. (1999). Asian Americans' and African Americans' initial perceptions of Hispanic counselors. *Journal of Multicultural Counseling and Development, 27,* 122-135.

Garrett, M. T. (1998). *Walking on the wind: Cherokee teaching for harmony and balance.* Santa Fe, NM: Bear and Company.

Garrett, M. T., & Wilbur, M. P. (1999). Does the worm live in the ground? Reflections on Native American spirituality. *Journal of Multicultural Counseling and Development, 27,* 193-206.

Gladding, S. T. (1999). *Group work: A counseling specialty* (3rd ed.). Upper Saddle River, NJ: Prentice Hall.

Gopaul-McNicol, S., & Thomas-Presswood, T. (1998). *Working with linguistically and culturally different children: Innovative clinical and educational approaches.* Boston: Allyn & Bacon.

Gross, T., & Miller, D. (Executive Producers). (2002, January 19). *Fresh air* [Radio series]. Philadelphia: WHYY-FM.

Hall, E. T. (1976). *Beyond culture.* New York: Anchor.

Harper, F. D., Braithwaite, K., & LaGrande, R. D. (1998). Ebonics and academic achievement: The role of the counselor, *Journal of Negro Education, 6,* 25-34.

Horsman, R. (1981). *Race and manifest destiny: The origins of American racial Anglo-Saxonism.* Cambridge, MA: Harvard University Press.

Irwin, L. (2000). Freedom, law, and prophecy: A brief history of Native American religious resistance. In L. Irwin (Ed.), *Native American spirituality: A critical reader* (pp. 295-316). Lincoln: University of Nebraska Press.

Koch, L. M. (2000). Attitudes towards Black English and code-switching: A variable in interracial perceptions. *Dissertation Abstracts International, 60,* 12-B.

LaFromboise, T. D. (1995). *Counseling and therapy with Native Americans.* North Amherst, MA: Microtraining Associates.

Lee, L. C., & Zane, N. W. S. (1998). *Handbook of Asian American psychology.* Thousand Oaks, CA: Sage.

Leong, F., Iwamasa, G., & Sue, D. W. (2000). *Culturally-competent counseling & therapy. Part II: Innovative approaches to counseling Asian-American people.* North Amherst, MA: Microtraining Associates.

Liang, X., Fuller, B., & Singer, J. (2000). Ethnic differences in child care selection: The influence of family structure, parental practices, and home languages. *Early Childhood Research Quarterly, 15,* 357-384.

Locke, D. C. (1992). *Increasing multicultural understanding: A comprehensive model.* Thousand Oaks, CA: Sage.

Marsella, A. J., Friedman, M. J., Gerrity, E. T., & Scurfield, R. M. (Eds.). (1996). *Ethnocultural aspects of posttraumatic stress disorder: Issues, research, and clinical applications.* Washington, DC: American Psychological Association.

Ogbu, J. U. (1999). Beyond language: Ebonics, proper English, and identity in a Black-American speech community. *American Educational Research Journal, 36,* 147-184.

Okun, B. F., Fried, J., & Okun, M. L. (1999). *Understanding diversity: A learning-as-practice primer.* Pacific Grove, CA: Brooks/Cole.

Orasanu, J., Fischer, U., & Davison, J. (1997). Cross-cultural barriers to effective communication in aviation. In C. S. Grandrose & S. Oskamp (Eds.), *Cross-cultural work groups* (pp. 134-160). Thousand Oaks, CA: Sage.

Posthuma, B. W. (1996). *Small groups in therapy settings* (3rd ed.). Boston: Allyn & Bacon.

Preciado, J., & Henry, M. (1997). Linguistic barriers in health education and services. In J. G. Garcia & M. C. Zea (Eds.), *Psychological interventions and research with Latino populations* (pp. 235-254). Boston: Allyn & Bacon.

Riggs, M. T., Atkison, N., Badgley, C., Paris, B. (Producers), & Riggs, M. T. (Director). (1996). *Black is . . . Black ain't* [Film]. United States: Independent Television Service.

Santiago-Rivera, A. L. (1995). Developing a culturally sensitivity treatment modality for bilingual Spanish-speaking clients: Incorporating language and culture in counseling. *Journal of Counseling and Development, 74,* 12-17.

Stone, O., Milchan, A., Kline, R., Ho, K. A. (Producers), & Stone, O. (Director). (1993).

Heaven and earth [Film]. United States: Warner Brothers.

Straussner, S. L. A. (2001). Ethnocultural issues in substance abuse treatment: An overview. In S. L. A. Straussner (Ed.), *Ethnocultural factors in substance abuse treatment* (pp. 3-28). New York: Guilford.

Sue, D. W. (1995). *Counseling Asian Americans clients.* North Amherst, MA: Microtraining Associates.

Sue, D. W., & Sue, D. (1999). *Counseling the culturally different: Theory and practice* (3rd ed.). New York: John Wiley.

Torres, L. (1997). *Puerto Rican: A sociolinguistic study of a New York suburb.* Mahwah, NJ: Lawrence Erlbaum.

Torres-Rivera, E., Smaby, M., & Maddux, C. D. (1996). Chaos theory and computers. *Computers in the Schools, 12,* 55-61.

Torres-Rivera, E., Wilbur, M. P., Saracini-Frank, J., & Roberts-Wilbur, J. (1999, February). *Identidad Liquidad.* Paper presented at the meeting of the Puerto Rican Branch of the American Counseling Association, Ponce, Puerto Rico.

Toseland, R. W., & Rivas, R. F. (2001). *An introduction to group work practice* (4th ed.). Boston: Allyn & Bacon.

Urciuoli, B. (1996). *Exposing prejudice: Puerto Rican experiences of language, race and class.* Boulder, CO: Westview.

U.S. Bureau of the Census. (1990). *Language use: 1990.* Retrieved January 23, 2003, from www.census.gov/population/www/socdemo/lang_use.html.

U.S. Bureau of the Census. (2000). *Profile of general demographics characteristics: 2000.* Retrieved June 4, 2002, from http://www.census.gov/prod/cen2000/index.html.

Vazquez, L., Santiago-Rivera, A., & Orjuela, E. (2000). *Culturally-competent counseling & therapy. Part III: Innovative approaches to counseling Latina/o people.* North Amherst, MA: Microtraining Associates.

Wang, W., Tan, A., Bass, R., Markey, P. (Producers), & Wang, W. (Director). (1993). *The joy luck club* [Film]. United States: Hollywood Pictures.

Wehrly, B. (1995). *Pathways to multicultural counseling competence: A development journey.* Pacific Grove, CA: Brooks/Cole.

Wiener, D. J. (Ed.). (2001). *Beyond talk therapy: Using movement and expressive techniques in clinical practice.* Washington, DC: American Psychological Association.

Wilson, K. G. (1993). *The Columbia guide to Standard American English.* Retrieved March 31, 2002, from http://www.bartleby.com/68/3/5703.html.

Yalom, I. D. (1995). *The theory and practice of group psychotherapy* (4th ed.). New York: Basic Books.

Zentella, A. C. (1988). Language politics in the USA: The English only movement. In B. J. Craige (Ed.), *Literature, language and politics in the 80s* (pp. 39-53). Athens: University of Georgia Press.

21

Multicultural Interventions in Groups

The Use of Indigenous Methods

Edil Torres Rivera

University at Buffalo, SUNY

Michael Tlanusta Garrett

Western Carolina University

Lori Brown Crutchfield

Clemson University

The Power of the World always works in circles, and everything tries to be round. . . . The sky is round, and I have heard that Earth is round like a ball, and so are all the stars. The wind, in its greatest power, whirls. Birds make their nests in circles. . . . Even the seasons form a great circle in their changing, and always come back again to where they were. The life of a person is a circle from childhood to childhood, and so it is in everything where power moves.

—Black Elk, cited in Garrett (1998)

In general, traditional counseling practices are predicated on the needs and values of the European American dominant culture, failing to integrate theories and methods pertaining to the useful and effective naturalistic helping methods in other cultures (Parham & Ajamu, 2000). As professionals in a multicultural society, we must look to all the resources of our differing and rich cultural traditions for valuable insight and methods to promote individual and group wellness (Garrett & Crutchfield, 1997). There is much to be gained from understanding cultures that value collectivist ideals within the context of designing group work experiences that reflect inclusion of and appreciation for clients of all cultures.

For many ethnic minority clients, the reality of oppression as a part of their experience in the world brings an added need due to the possible sense of isolation, cultural alienation, mistrust of institutions, and the struggle to maintain or reconcile cultural identity in the face of adversity (Robinson & Howard-Hamilton, 2000). Groups targeting personal growth and development may be ideal to help clients move beyond society's imposed limitations and pressures (Omizo, Omizo, & D'Andrea, 1992). Recognizing this need, the *Principles for Diversity-Competent Group Workers* (ASGW, 1999) emphasizes group leaders' responsibility to provide services that are culturally responsive (see Appendix B in this volume). The American Counseling Association (ACA) as well as the American Psychological Association (APA) have also developed and endorsed guidelines when working with ethnic minority clients (APA, 1993; Arredondo et al., 1996).

When considering the use of culturally based interventions in groups, one is likely to note two seemingly divergent applications. The first application is the use of interventions with members of culturally homogeneous groups that are culturally responsive. Many authors have discussed the importance of working effectively with racially or ethnically homogeneous groups to specifically address issues and concerns of people from those specific populations (i.e., Appleton & Dykeman, 1996; Franklin & Pack-Brown, 2001; Santiago-Rivera & Vazquez, 2000). The second application is the integration of indigenous practices into psychoeducational and counseling groups that may not be racially/ethnically homogeneous or focused on cultural issues. This approach consists of a synthesis of contemporary group counseling techniques and traditional wisdom.

The purpose of this chapter is to discuss the implications of implementing culture-specific interventions when working with both culturally homogeneous and heterogeneous groups to meet the therapeutic needs of both majority and minority group members. First, culture-specific interventions will be examined relating to working with African Americans, Asian Americans, Latino/a Americans, and Native Americans within groups. This section is not meant to be extensive, but rather to provide a context for understanding traditional cultural methods and approaches to healing within different cultures. The hope is that this discussion will provide a backdrop for the following sections, which will provide suggestions for how to incorporate naturalistic healing interventions within multicultural groups. Implications for group practice will be discussed, and practical considerations for the adaptation of culture-specific interventions to non-culture-specific groups will be offered.

CULTURE-SPECIFIC INTERVENTIONS

In the recent literature, there has been much discussion of culture-specific group interventions (e.g., Brinson & Fisher, 1999; Chen & Han, 2001; Colmant & Merta, 1999; Haley-Banez & Walden, 1999; Kim, Omizo, & D'Andrea, 1998; Torres-Rivera, Wilbur, Roberts-Wilbur, & Phan, 1999) Chapters specific to group work with diverse groups are also included in this handbook in this section, "Part III: Multicultural Group Work." Recommendations to majority culture group leaders on how to best serve group members of a particular culture are the focus of much of this literature. Suggestions are offered about enhancing groups by using approaches, techniques, indigenous approaches, and rituals that are familiar to and accepted by specific cultural groups. These techniques and interventions are based on the traditional values of each cultural group, how they view healing, and how groups are used within the traditional framework of their cultures.

African Americans

Some of the traditional values identified for African Americans include an emphasis on being group focused, sensitivity to interpersonal matters, hard work and education, sense of community, cooperation, interdependence, and commitment to religious values, church, and familial bonds (Sue & Sue, 1999). The literature indicates that group counseling with African Americans has great value from a cultural point of view because it complements the sense of communal bonding and work. Nothing exemplifies this value better than the Black church as a source of community for African Americans. The church affords opportunities for spiritual development and expression within the context of a community that provides social connections and fosters cultural pride (Morris & Robinson, 1996).

In discussing group counseling for African American women, Williams, Frame, and Green (1999) discussed the importance of including issues of spirituality with this population. They posited that for Black women, spirituality is "woven into everyday experience" (p. 262), and recommended the use of homogenous groups with a focus on spirituality and empowerment for promoting growth for African American women. In such groups, three main elements of spirituality are advocated: the archaic (collective archetypes), the cultural (daily practices of religion), and the personal (one's own individual practices of faith). Through the use of ritual, the group facilitator addresses each of these elements during each group. One activity for empowerment and connection was "calling out," taken from rituals of African American worship services:

> One person calls out those concerns that cause despair. She elicits keening and moaning responses from other group members. The facilitator was the caller for the group, calling out: "Ohhh, my mother, ohhh, my father, help me to love myself. Ohhh, my father, ohhh, my mother, help me to honor myself. . . ." This ritual was followed by a deep silence in the group, punctuated with statements like, "Wow! That was really powerful!" Some women had tears in their eyes. (Williams et al., 1999, p. 266)

With this ritualized activity, members are able to become reacquainted with their inner spiritual selves and release some of their sadness, anger, and pain. This type of bonding over shared historical and cultural experiences provides group members the impetus to strive to lift each other up and forge a lasting support network. Others have also provided examples

(Brown, Lipford-Sanders, & Shaw, 1995; Franklin & Pack-Brown, 2001; Parham & Ajamu, 2000). These interventions reinforce traditional group counseling values in that they foster the exploration and establishment of group norms that are necessary to facilitate group development. Ultimately, this is important because it leads to the cohesiveness that the membership needs to achieve group goals. As the group environment becomes a cohesive and supporting place, members are likely to realize therapeutic factors (e.g., universality, altruism, catharsis) (Yalom, 1995) and take the risks needed to support their own growth. Pack-Brown and Fleming in this volume (Chapter 13) suggest other culturally related group interventions for African American group members.

Asian Americans

Although the term *Asian American* actually encompasses many diverse groups within that category, certain common traditional values have been identified, including the emphasis on respect; loyalty; honor versus shame; deference to authority; emotional restraint; specified roles within family, community, and society; hierarchical family structure; gender-specific roles; and the importance of extended family (Sue & Sue, 1999). With regard to the value of group counseling, the notion of communal ties and family responsibilities becomes both a potential area for exploration and an opportunity to draw on cultural values.

Culturally based interventions within Asian cultures might include a highly structured and didactic approach to leadership, as this expectation of leaders as experts is often present (Conyne, Wilson, & Tang, 2000). For example, when involving the group in an "icebreaker," the leader in a group of Asian American clients might be most successful by setting up a specific structure for the process, rather than leaving it open-ended and expecting group members to be comfortable with participating freely, because it is common for Asian children to be cautioned against appearing too talkative or seeking control in a group setting.

In a recent example of culture-specific approaches, Queener and Kenyon (2001)

focused on group work with Southeast Asian adolescent girls. The authors recommended that group leaders maintain a structured, highly directive stance during the initial session, to clearly communicate group goals and expectations to the members. While this is a common approach to an initial session, particularly with children, in this instance it was stressed even more strongly that the "group leaders did most of the talking and had to be directive most of the session by asking specific questions" (p. 358). In later sessions, they went on to discuss matters related to cultural identity development, with a focus on issues such as the importance of family and gender issues with Asian culture. Given the values noted previously, these topics might feel risky to Asian clients. Therefore, keeping this discussion structured in group with ongoing active leadership by the facilitator(s) may help facilitate discussion. For example, a group leader may begin by stating, "We have a few sessions left before the group ends, therefore I would like for each one of you to take some time to talk about some things you have wished to talk about but haven't had the courage or the opportunity to do so. I know that it's risky, but it is important to give it a try" (Chen & Han, 2001). Others have also provided examples (Leong, 1992; Leong, Iwamasa, & Sue, 2000; Pope, 1999; Yu & Gregg, 1993).

Latino Americans

A common core of traditional values exists for Latino Americans, which centers around the importance of family. The specific values tend to be an emphasis, respect for, and loyalty to family, cooperation, interpersonal relationships, strictness of child rearing, religiosity, and Catholicism (Sue & Sue, 2003). "Family unity (*familismo*) is seen as very important, as are respect for and loyalty to the family" (Sue & Sue, 2003, p. 346). The fact that the family is of central importance for Latino/a Americans makes this a value upon which group counseling can build through the sense of family and cohesion that can be developed in the group. In an example of culture-specific approaches, Gloria (1999) described a homogenous support group for Chicana college students, and she noted two important dimensions for group work

with this population: tradition (type of cultural values held) and acculturation (level of attachment to these cultural values in the face of adjusting to the dominant culture). She suggested assessing these dimensions for each member and for the group as a whole through an activity called a "cultural collage," pictorial displays of their own cultural worldviews, which are then shared with the group.

Gloria (1999) enumerated several traditional Chicana values that may be evidenced in this type of group. She noted, for example, that *familiarismo* (placing high value on supporting and relying on family members) is a core Chicana value. One way to encourage group cohesiveness would be to promote this value through the concept of the group members as an extended family. Gloria suggested that group facilitators should actively participate in cultural events within the Chicana community to better understand their culture and increase the likelihood of acceptance into the "extended family." Several other authors have also provided examples of culture-specific interventions with Latino/a Americans (Baca & Koss-Chioino, 1997; Santiago-Rivera, Arredondo, & Gallardo-Cooper, 2002; Santiago-Rivera & Vazquez, 2000; Torres-Rivera et al., 1999; Torres-Rivera, Wilbur, & Roberts-Wilbur, 1998).

Torres-Rivera et al. (1998) pointed out that when working with Latinos, five elements seem to be more in disagreement with the majority culture and other ethnic minority groups. These elements are not only relevant to the success of group interventions with this population but are also necessary when attempting to gain familiarismo with Latinos. The five elements are how Latinos define or perceive leadership, communication, logic, morality, and time. These elements combined with the necessary knowledge of language are important ingredients in producing effective interventions with Latinos (Santiago-Rivera et al., 2002).

Specifically, leadership for most Latinos is viewed as more egalitarian. Latinos believe that it is important to respond to people as equals to gain their respect. Therefore, it is important that group leaders are aware of how to facilitate the group process and to be sure that everyone is included during the session (Torres-Rivera et al., 1998). For example, in a group session, if one of the group members is not participating much, the group leader might want to ask something like, "¿Que tu piensas de eso Juan?" ("What do you think about that, Juan?").

In regard to communication patterns, Latinos seem to communicate indirectly through storytelling. Counselors leading groups with Latinos who are not knowledgeable of this characteristic of the Latino culture may not be able to establish themselves as trustworthy and knowledgeable in the eyes of Latino clients. The directness of the English language could push Latino clients into a defensive mode and undermine the safe atmosphere necessary for an effective counseling relationship (Torres-Rivera et al., 1998). Phan and Torres Rivera in this volume (Chapter 20) discuss the impact of language on group dynamics and processes.

Logic is something that may be confusing and difficult to understand for some Latinos. Latinos' logic in many instances is based on their ability to survive, to bring food to the home, and to gain and retain the respect of their family members. Consequently, counselors who lead groups with Latino clients and overrely on strictly logical analysis of clients' problems may estrange Latino clients who are more responsive to affective and intuitive approaches to life experiences. It is important to remember that this is more the case for less assimilated, less formally educated Latinos and that as Latinos assimilate dominant-culture attitudes, values, and beliefs, their interpretation of logic becomes more like that of the dominant culture (Torres-Rivera et al., 1998).

Native Americans

Native Americans have been estimated to comprise more than 50% of the diversity that exists in this country (Garrett & Carroll, 2000), with vast differences between members of the 557 tribes that exist in the United States. Nevertheless, a common core of traditional values has been identified for Native Americans, including the importance of community contribution, sharing, acceptance, cooperation, harmony and balance, noninterference, extended family, attention to nature, immediacy of time, awareness of the relationship, and a deep respect for elders (Garrett, 1998). Of central importance

in many Native traditions is the family, clan, and tribe/nation. The importance of a group approach to working with Native clients cannot be overemphasized as a way of respecting the cultural traditions from which many of these people may come.

Across tribal nations, there are many different ceremonies used for healing, giving thanks, celebrating, clearing the way, and blessing (Garrett & Garrett, 2002). The underlying goal of these ceremonies, from a Native perspective, is to offer thanks for, create, and maintain a strong sense of connection through harmony and balance of mind, body, and spirit with the natural environment. The main purpose of healing ceremonies is to "keep oneself in good relations," which can mean honoring or healing a connection with oneself, between oneself and others (relationships, i.e., family, friends, community), between oneself and the natural environment, or between oneself and the spirit world. Among the various traditions of healing ceremonies used by Native people, the most well-known examples include sweat lodge, vision quest, clearing-way ceremony, blessing-way ceremony, pipe ceremony, sunrise ceremony, sundance, and the powwow.

Garrett and Garrett (2002) described a group-centering technique, called Ayeli, based on Cherokee healing ceremonies. With this intervention, group members call out to each of the four directions as a way of seeking harmony and balance in their lives and in the context of the group process. The following examples drawn from Ayeli describe areas that group members explore with each other as a way of working toward harmony and balance:

East (belonging): "Where do you belong (or not belong); who's your family/clan/tribe?"

South (mastery): "What do you do well; what do you enjoy doing?"

West (independence): "What are your (sources of) strengths; what limits you?"

North (generosity): "What do you have to offer; what do you receive?"

Several authors have provided other examples of culture-specific interventions with

Native people or using Native traditions (Appleton & Dykeman, 1996; Colmant & Merta, 1999; Garrett & Carroll, 2000; Garrett & Garrett, 2002; Garrett, Garrett, & Brotherton, 2001; Roberts-Wilbur, Wilbur, Garrett, & Yuhas, 2001). Garrett in this volume (Chapter 12) also provides a more detailed discussion of this topic.

Adapting Culture-Specific Interventions to Non-Culture-Specific Groups

This section will examine and discuss considerations for adapting these types of interventions for use with non-culture-specific groups. Group composition, group structure, group leadership, and specific interventions will be discussed.

Group Composition

According to Sue and Sue (1999), "A minority individual's reaction to counseling, the counseling process, and to the counselor is influenced by his/her cultural/racial identity" (pp. 123-124). In general, cultural identity development signifies movement through stages of cognitive/emotional awareness regarding the relation of one's self as a cultural being to one's cultural group and the dominant culture. These stages begin with naïveté, move through encounters with discrimination and the naming of such, to the reflection on one's own cultural being, and on to acceptance and internalization. It is an ongoing process, with constant recycling through the stages in response to new situations (Cheatham et al., 2002). D'Andrea in this volume (Chapter 19) provides a detailed discussion of the impact of group leaders' and members' racial identity development on group process and dynamics.

The necessity or desirability of working in homogeneous or heterogeneous groups is based almost entirely on group goals (Corey, 1999; Gladding, 1998). Cultural identity development should be considered when planning a group and screening members. Clients who are highly self- and other-aware may benefit from the mirroring of society that can come out of heterogeneous group composition across racial, ethnic,

and social lines. However, a number of authors advocate the need for working with culturally homogeneous groups to effectively deal with the specific issues and concerns of minority clients from those populations (Holahan & Gibson, 1994). It has been argued that culturally homogeneous groups provide a safe and supportive environment for minority clients to work on self-esteem, cultural identity, cultural conflicts, acculturation, and relationship issues by being able to openly discuss their experiences with both external and internalized oppression (Holahan & Gibson, 1994).

In contrast, since trust is an underlying issue, some assert that a culturally heterogeneous group facilitated by a culturally responsive leader can provide opportunities for minority clients to explore the very same issues from multiple perspectives yet still feel supported. Others would argue that a group without some conflict and tension between members might not effectively stimulate the kind of growth that groups purport to offer and would not offer the microcosm of society within which members could work out some of their difficulties.

In addition, the logistical problem of small numbers of minority group members can make it difficult to work with homogeneous groups. There are very real pros and cons to both sides of the issue. In the end, the group leader must decide what is possible, what is necessary, and what is desirable given the purpose of the group, the setting, and the needs of potential clients.

Group Structure

It has been posited that group structure issues should be most thoroughly addressed with groups of ethnic minority clients, because with many of these ethnic/cultural groups, a strong allegiance to one's family members is key. Topics such as confidentiality and boundary issues should be clarified at the start and continuously throughout the process, to set group members' minds at ease about participation in the group. For example, morality is an important issue for Latinos because it is viewed as a private issue; this means that among Latino clients, moral issues can be discussed only with family members. The implications for counselors who want to work effectively with Latino clients are important, because the need to become part of the Latino family cannot be missed. The group leader needs to establish trust and gain the Latino clients' loyalty by becoming part of the family (Morrissey, 2002).

Concerns related to trust, confidentiality, and privacy, while highlighted well by considering how they affect work with this population, are not unique to ethnic minority group members; they relate to group work across cultures, as well. Group counseling in university counseling centers and group supervision in graduate programs, for example, may involve extra caution in addressing confidentiality. Even in larger communities, when groups are composed of members with little outside social support, issues such as out-of-group socialization may pose some dilemmas for members and leaders.

Leadership

Leadership factors should also be considered. Clients are likely to make assumptions about the leader's attitudes and biases regarding cultural characteristics such as race, ethnicity, gender, age, and sexual orientation. There are mixed opinions in the literature as to whether or not leaders of culturally homogeneous or heterogeneous groups must share cultural characteristics in common with members to be able to function effectively in the therapeutic role with those clients (Berg-Gross, Graig, & Wessel, 2001; Corey & Corey, 2002; Stewart & Shapiro, 2000). Several authors have suggested that what makes leaders effective and creates trustworthiness, more than sharing common characteristics with members, are leaders' accurate cultural knowledge, sense of awareness of their cultural meanings and personal biases, comfort level with difficult cultural and social issues, sensitivity to and respect for differences, and willingness to confront oppression and inequality (Lee, 2001, 2002). Given that most ethnic minority group members most often end up in ethnically heterogeneous groups, it is crucial to speak directly to meeting their diverse cultural needs within the group (Chen & Han, 2001). It is suggested that in the case of dominant-culture group leaders, those who possess the highest level of competency in multicultural counseling skills (awareness, culture-specific

knowledge, and culture-specific skills) are the ones who have also moved through the stages of their own White ethnic identity development, thus having a positive, accepting view of other cultures (Helms & Cook, 1999).

For example, when working with Asian group members in the early phases of ethnic identity development, it would be important for group leaders to use a more directive leadership approach. This might involve giving self-disclosing feedback in reaction to one group member's cultural insensitivity to the Asian client's needs and values, in the following manner:

> Tatiana, when you told Grace to forget about what others might think of her and just go ahead and say what was in her guts, I felt saddened by your lack of consideration for Grace's dilemma. I would feel disrespected if I were in Grace's position. During this session, Grace has shared with us how her behaviors are sanctioned by her cultural values. I wish we would have more respect for her boundaries. (Chen & Han, 2001, p. 118)

The White group leader in this example consciously selected this more directive intervention to convey a sense of directive leadership to the Asian client, thus paving the way for a more harmonious relationship with that client and also a more fruitful group experience. Particular interventions depend on which type of group (i.e., task, psychoeducational, counseling, or psychotherapy) is being conducted, as well as the group members (i.e., African Americans, Latinos, Native Americans, or a heterogeneous group). The following section includes examples of different activities that dominant-culture group leaders can put to use with heterogeneous groups. In addition, as mentioned earlier, group leaders who have a good grasp of their own identity development and are familiar with the competencies can adapt and are able to use existing interventions without imposing their own worldviews onto group members.

Interventions

The nature of the intervention chosen should be based on the type of group, goals of the group, as well as the nature of group membership. The intervention chosen, whether it be culture specific or otherwise, should be based on helping members achieve their therapeutic goals. For culturally homogeneous groups, an intervention might be chosen that is consistent with the cultural needs and expectations of the members of that group. For culturally heterogeneous groups, when culture-specific interventions are chosen, it becomes increasingly important to justify a rationale for that intervention over any other, not only to oneself but also to the group members. It is important to allow members to have a say in what happens in the group regardless of the type of intervention chosen and to be committed as a group to the process that will follow from such an intervention.

For example, Garrett and Crutchfield (1997) proposed a wellness group for children of all cultural backgrounds. Their holistic, developmental approach to group work draws from Native American culture and tradition, yet it does not specifically target groups of Native American children. Rather, it is presented as a model that can be useful with all children, regardless of race or ethnicity. The model complements the underlying philosophy of our profession by emphasizing the importance of facilitating the natural human processes of growth and development concerning how one feels about oneself, how one develops one's potential, how one experiences one's physical presence, and how one sees or defines oneself. They used a Native American cultural tradition of the "talking circle" to help group members interact in a harmonious manner:

> The "talking stick"—a wooden stick embellished with carvings, paintings, or items from nature—is used as an object representing truth and understanding as powerful agents of learning, change, and growth. Possession of the talking stick signifies permission to speak (Garrett & Osborne, 1995). Thus, use of the talking stick gives each group member a chance to speak and encourages each member to listen more carefully without need for competition. Traditionally in many Native American tribes, people used the talking stick during council meetings to discuss issues or concerns peacefully by "speaking from the heart," and by listening intently to what others had to say. (Garrett and Crutchfield, 1997, p. 7)

In another attempt to incorporate Native American cultural teachings into groups for all populations, Garrett et al. (2001) discussed the concept of the healing nature of concentric circles. The "inner circle/outer circle" places focus on connectedness, relation with significant others, and orientation in time and space. In its use of three concentric circles, it captures the complexity and unity of our social support systems in a very meaningful way. A person in the inner circle shares sensory perceptions in the first person, while people in the outer circle serve as supportive guides, helping the person in the inner circle express himself or herself. Those in the community circle also provide support and protection, but in a less direct way. It is a powerful demonstration of the complexities of interconnectedness often found at the heart of human existence. The goal of this activity is to create awareness and bring cohesiveness among group members. Thus, this activity might be used in multicultural groups to aid group members in developing a greater sense of universality and similarities among different ethnic groups.

Roberts-Wilbur et al. (2001) also used the principle of the talking stick to train heterogeneous groups of undergraduate students as peer counselors for drug and alcohol issues. The principles that they used are the sacredness of the circle, connectedness, relationships with others, orientation in time and space, and respect for each other's spoken word. Roberts-Wilbur et al. bring symbols and ritual into the training as part of the complexities of interconnectedness often found at the heart of human existence. The format for this type of training is a pyschoeducational modality in which the goal is to promote participation and expression from all members; facilitate discussion by promoting an atmosphere of mutual listening and hearing of all opinions, understanding, support, and feedback; discourage members' judgments of others' attitudes, values, and beliefs; and strive for a variety of attitudes, values, and beliefs. A similar approach has been used to work with younger group members in school settings (J. Roberts-Wilbur, personal communication, February 2, 2003).

The sweat lodge can also be used with heterogeneous groups in which group leaders belong to the dominant culture. This type of group could be useful with Latino group members who identify with their Native American roots (Warren, 2001). The sweat lodge exercise as well as the talking stick can be used for all stages of group development (orientation, transition, working stage, etc.). The goal (or focus) of the sweat lodge is similar to the goals of the talking stick, mentioned above, promoting participation and expression from all members.

> Though techniques for the sweat lodge ceremony vary from tribe to tribe, the ceremony serves an important function through purification and healing for all who participate in it. From skin, bodily toxins and negative energy are released. Similarly, from the mind and spirit, toxins such as anger, frustration, hurt, or anxiety are released. Ways of dealing with various situations, with others, and with oneself are talked about within the framework of the Universal Circle represented by the sweat lodge and its sacred Ceremony. (Garret & Osborne, 1995, p. 35)

Pack-Brown (2002) also described activities that can be used with heterogeneous groups in which the leaders can be White. Drumming is an Afrocentric exercise based on the collectivist worldview of the Afrocentric theory:

> Drumming is an Afrocentric approach to group work. It is a diversity competent exercise espousing a collective view of groups built around the African values of Umoja (oo-MOH-jah) which means unity and Ujima (oo-JEE-mah) which means collective responsibility. The foundation upon which this group activity is constructed is the reality of "I am because we are." Group work leaders continuously build on the African value of Kujichagulia (koo-ji-chah-goo-LEE-ah), which means self empowerment, to promote "self-in-relation" among and between group members. Group members are taught to perceive "self" as a member of the community (the group) and to assume responsibility for promoting both individual and collective self-esteem and empowerment within group process and dynamics. (Pack-Brown, 2002, p. 183)

The goals for this group intervention are to encourage emotions between the individual and the group, cultivate connections between members, develop community knowledge, and empower the group as an agent for communal spirit.

Choice of the Activity

It is the experience of the authors that when working with children and adolescents, almost all suggested activities get a warm reception. On the other hand, adult group members appear to be more resistant to unfamiliar activities. The group composition and the leader experience also make a difference with regard to the type of activity. For example, while working with a group of high school Latinos and Native American adolescents, the talking stick activities in combination with drumming allowed the group to rapidly reach the working stage and also helped group members to reach a safety zone in which they felt accepted and valued as a group member. On the other hand, when working with adults in a heterogeneous group setting using activities that are more traditional in nature, the activity is typically received with more resistance by group members with the lowest levels of identity development. Thus, it is recommended to begin with the most structured activities (i.e., talking stick).

Introduction of the Activity

An explanation of the principles of the activity and its purpose serves to lower anxiety and creates comfort among group members. In addition, the use of words such as *ritual, sacredness,* and *connectedness,* and the power of the spoken word add seriousness and credibility to the activity. Some people also use music, sage burning or incense to begin the activity, when appropriate and to create the rules of the activity.

Cautions

There are some precautions to observe for each of the specific ethnic/cultural groups discussed in this chapter, and many that pervade across all groups. A history of oppression may hold great sway over African American and Native American group members. Often with Latino/a group members, language issues may emerge as central concerns for success in the group process. With Asian American group members, reticence to freely express personal issues may inhibit group participation. Still, the main underlying consideration when working with culturally diverse groups is the need for awareness of the group members' levels of cultural identity development. D'Andrea in this volume (Chapter 19) focuses on this issue.

No matter how carefully chosen by the group leader, no intervention will be completely successful without each group member's consent. The group is the circle, the microcosm of life, where power moves. For this reason, it may be suggested that the group format is the most effective approach to serving the needs of minority clients. Whether it be in homogenous (culture-specific) groups or heterogeneous groups, culturally based interventions can be powerful tools for moving people toward a stronger sense of wellness in their lives.

Finally, incorporating naturalistic rituals into group work will help group leaders establish their credibility regardless of their ethnicity or background, and in addition, trust in group treatment across groups will increase by word of mouth. Also, naturalistic or indigenous forms of group therapy not only offer multiple belief systems but also incorporate a spiritual and humane form of helping that is in harmony with the different ethnic groups.

REFERENCES

American Psychological Association. (1993). Guidelines for provider of psychological services to ethnic, linguistic, and culturally diverse populations. *American Psychologist, 48,* 45-48.

Appleton, V. E., & Dykeman, C. (1996). Using art in group counseling with Native American youth. *Journal for Specialists in Group Work, 24,* 224-231.

Arredondo, P., Toporek, R., Brown, S. P., Jones, J., Locke, D. C., Sanchez, J., & Stadler, H. (1996). Operationalization of the multicultural counseling competencies. *Journal of Multicultural Counseling & Development, 24,* 42-78.

Association for Specialists in Group Work (ASGW). (1999). Principles for diversity-competent group workers. *Journal for Specialists in Group Work, 24,* 7-14.

Baca, L., & Koss-Chioino, J. (1997). Development of a culturally responsive group counseling model for Mexican American adolescents. *Journal of Multicultural Counseling & Development, 25,* 130-141.

Berg-Gross, L., Graig, K., & Wessel, T. (2001). Multiculturalism at historically black colleges and universities: A case study of Howard University. In J. G. Ponterotto, J. M. Casas, L. A. Suzuki, & C. M. Alexander (Eds.), *Handbook of multicultural counseling* (pp. 849-870). Thousand Oaks, CA: Sage.

Brinson, J., & Fisher, T. A. (1999). The Ho'oponopono group: A conflict resolution model for school counselors. *Journal for Specialists in Group Work, 24,* 369-382.

Brown, S. P., Lipford-Sanders, J., & Shaw, M. (1995). Kujichagulia—Uncovering the secrets of the heart: Group work with African American women on predominantly White campuses. *Journal for Specialists in Group Work, 20,* 151-158.

Cheatham, H., D'Andrea, M., Ivey, A. E., Ivey, M. B., Pedersen, P., Rigazio-DiGilio, S., Simek-Morgan, L., & Sue, D. W. (2002). Multicultural counseling and therapy I: Metatheory—Taking theory into practice. In A. E. Ivey, M. D'Andrea, M. Bradford Ivey, & L. Simek-Morgan (Eds.), *Theories of counseling and psychotherapy: A multicultural perspective* (5th ed., pp. 291-328). Boston: Allyn & Bacon.

Chen, M., & Han, Y. S. (2001). Cross-cultural group counseling with Asians: A stage-specific interactive approach. *Journal for Specialists in Group Work, 26,* 111-128.

Colmant, S. A., & Merta, R. J. (1999). Using the sweat lodge ceremony as group therapy for Navajo youth. *Journal for Specialists in Group Work, 24,* 55-73.

Conyne, R. K., Wilson, F. R., & Tang, M. (2000). Evolving lessons from group work involvement in China. *Journal for Specialists in Group Work, 25,* 252-268.

Corey, G. (1999). *Theory and practice of group counseling* (5th ed.). Belmont, CA: Wadsworth.

Corey, G., & Corey, M. S. (2002). *Groups: Process and practice* (6th ed.). Monterey, CA: Brooks/Cole.

Franklin, R. B., & Pack-Brown, S. (2001). TEAM BROTHERS: An Afrocentric approach to group work with African-American male adolescents. *Journal for Specialists in Group Work, 26,* 237-245.

Garrett, M. T. (1998). *Walking on the wind: Cherokee teachings for harmony and balance.* Santa Fe, NM: Bear & Company.

Garrett, M. T., & Carroll, J. (2000). Mending the broken circle: Treatment and prevention of substance abuse among Native Americans. *Journal of Counseling & Development, 78,* 379-388.

Garrett, M. T., & Crutchfield, L. B. (1997). Moving full circle: A unity model of group work with children. *Journal for Specialists in Group Work, 22,* 175-188.

Garrett, M. T., & Garrett, J. T. (2002). Ayeli: Centering technique based on Cherokee spiritual traditions. *Counseling & Values, 46,* 149-158.

Garrett, M. T., Garrett, J. T., & Brotherton, D. (2001). Inner circle/outer circle: A group technique based on Native American healing circles. *Journal for Specialists in Group Work, 26,* 17-30.

Garrett, M. T., & Osborne, W. L. (1995). The Native American sweat lodge as metaphor for group work. *Journal for Specialists in Group Work, 20,* 33-39.

Gladding, S. T. (1998). *Group work: A counseling specialty.* Upper Saddle River, NJ: Prentice Hall.

Gloria, A. M. (1999). Apoyando estudiantes Chicanas: Therapeutic factors in Chicana college student support groups. *Journal for Specialists in Group Work, 24,* 246-259.

Haley-Banez, L., & Walden, S. L. (1999). Diversity in group work: Using optimal theory to understand group process and dynamics. *Journal for Specialists in Group Work, 24,* 405-422.

Helms, J. E., & Cook, D. A. (1999). *Using race and culture in counseling and psychotherapy: Theory and process.* Needham Heights, MA: Allyn & Bacon.

Holahan, W., & Gibson, S. A. (1994). Heterosexual therapists leading lesbian and gay therapy groups: Therapeutic and political realities. *Journal of Counseling & Development, 72,* 591-594.

Kim, B. S. K., Omizo, M. M., & D'Andrea, M. J. (1998). The effects of culturally consonant group counseling on the self-esteem and internal locus of control orientation among Native American adolescents. *Journal for Specialists in Group Work, 23,* 145-163.

Lee, C. C. (2001). Defining and responding to racial and ethnic diversity. In D. C. Locke, J. E. Myers, & E. L. Herr (Eds.), *The handbook of counseling* (pp. 581-588). Thousand Oaks, CA: Sage.

Lee, C. C. (Ed.). (2002). *Multicultural issues in counseling: New approaches to diversity* (3rd ed.). Alexandria, VA: American Counseling Association.

Leong, F., Iwamasa, G., & Sue, D. W. (2000). Innovative approaches to counseling Asian-American People. *Cultural-competence counseling & therapy.* North Amherst, MA: Microtraining Associates.

Leong, F. T. (1992). Guidelines for minimizing premature termination among Asian American clients in group counseling. *Journal for Specialists in Group Work, 17,* 218-228.

Morris, J. R., & Robinson, D. T. (1996). Community and Christianity in the Black church. *Counseling & Values, 41,* 59-69.

Morrissey, M. (2002, June 25). Ethics in professional counseling. *Counseling Today.* Retrieved December 17, 2002 from http://www.counseling.org/ctonline/archives/epc.htm.

Omizo, M. M., Omizo, S. A., & D'Andrea, M. J. (1992). Promoting wellness among elementary school children. *Journal of Counseling and Development, 71,* 194-202.

Pack-Brown, S. (2002). Drumming (Drum circle). In J. L. DeLucia-Waack, K. H. Bridboard, & J. S. Kleiner (Eds.), *Group work experts share their favorite activities: A guide to choosing, planning, conducting, and processing* (p. 183). Alexandria, VA: Association for Specialists in Group Work.

Parham, T., & Ajamu, A. (2000). Innovative approaches to counseling African descent people. *Cultural-competence counseling & therapy.* North Amherst, MA: Microtraining Associates.

Pope, M. (1999). Applications of group career counseling techniques in Asian cultures. *Journal of Multicultural Counseling & Development, 27,* 18-30.

Queener, J. E., & Kenyon, C. B. (2001). Providing mental health services to Southeast Asian adolescent girls: Integration of a primary prevention paradigm and group counseling. *Journal for Specialists in Group Work, 26,* 350-367.

Roberts-Wilbur, J., Wilbur, M., Garrett, M. T., & Yuhas, M. (2001). Talking circles: Listen or your tongue will make you deaf. *Journal for Specialists in Group Work, 26,* 368-384.

Robinson, T. L., & Howard-Hamilton, M. F. (2000). *The convergence of race, ethnicity, and gender: Multiple identities in counseling.* Upper Saddle River, NJ: Merrill.

Santiago-Rivera, A. L., Arredondo, P., & Gallardo-Cooper, M. (2002). *Counseling Latinos and la familia: A practical guide.* Thousand Oaks, CA: Sage.

Santiago-Rivera, A. L., & Vazquez, L. (2000). Innovative approaches to counseling Latina/o. *Culturally-competence counseling & therapy.* North Amherst, MA: Microtraining Associates.

Stewart, M. M., & Shapiro, D. L. (2000). Selection based on merit versus demography: Implications across race and gender lines. *Journal of Applied Psychology. 85,* 219-231.

Sue, D. W., & Sue, D. (1999). *Counseling the culturally different: Theory and practice* (3rd ed.). New York: John Wiley.

Sue, D. W., & Sue, D. (2003). *Counseling the culturally different: Theory and practice* (4th ed.). New York: John Wiley.

Torres-Rivera, E., Wilbur, M. P., & Roberts-Wilbur, J. (1998). The Puerto Rican prison experience: A multicultural understanding of values, beliefs, and attitudes. *Journal of Addictions & Offender Counseling, 18,* 63-77.

Torres-Rivera, E., Wilbur, M. P., Roberts-Wilbur, J., & Phan, L. (1999). Group work with Latino clients: A psychoeducational model. *Journal for Specialists in Group Work, 24,* 383-404.

Warren, J. W. (2001). *Racial revolutions: Antiracism and Indian resurgence in Brazil.* Durham, NC: Duke University Press.

Williams, C. B., Frame, M. W., & Green, E. (1999). Counseling groups for African American women: A focus on spirituality. *Journal for Specialists in Group Work, 24,* 260-273.

Yalom, I. D. (1995). *The theory and practice of group psychotherapy* (3rd ed.). New York: Basic Books.

Yu, A., & Gregg, C. H. (1993). Asians in groups: More than a matter of cultural awareness. *Journal for Specialists in Group Work, 18,* 86-93.

Part IV

GROUPS ACROSS SETTINGS

Introduction

CYNTHIA R. KALODNER

Part IV, "Groups Across Settings," includes examples of psychoeducational, counseling, and psychotherapy groups in a variety of settings. Groups exist in schools, the Veterans Administration (VA) system, university counseling centers, and others described in this section. The goal of this section of this book is to present readers with a look at the diverse settings within which a variety of different types of groups are used. Each chapter in this section provides theoretical and empirical support for group psychoeducation, counseling, and psychotherapy.

The first chapter in the section, by Maria Riva and Alaina Haub, focuses on groups in the school setting. Group formats are heavily used in the schools to address social competence, children of divorce, at-risk youth, and prevention topics (i.e., unsafe sexual behaviors, adolescent drug abuse, high school dropout). Chapter 23, led by Les Greene and coauthored by six clinicians employed in the VA system,

provides comprehensive coverage of the vast uses of groups in the VA system, including outpatient group work for veterans with posttraumatic stress disorder, day treatment programs focused on substance abuse, groups with the chronically mentally ill in inpatient units, and groups that focus on health promotion, such as smoking cessation and stress management. Chapter 24, presented by Tim Elliott, Patricia Rivera, and Emily Tucker, provides a framework for the use of support, educational, psychoeducational, counseling, and task groups in behavioral health and medical settings and includes a large number of examples of these groups used after the onset of a disabling condition or following a medical diagnosis. Chapter 25, written by Denise Emer, focuses on groups in inpatient settings and reviews the challenges associated with group work in psychiatric facilities. Her chapter, based on several theoretical models, highlights unique challenges associated with conducting groups in inpatient settings.

In Chapter 26, Elizabeth Kincade and Cynthia Kalodner provide information about the use of groups on college and university counseling centers, including the history of groups in this setting. In Chapter 27, David Cramer presents suggestions for the development of groups in a private practice setting. In Chapter 28, Robert Morgan focuses on the groups used with offenders and mandated clients. He provides a depth of understanding about this difficult population, covering structured psychoeducational groups on topics unique to this setting as well as those that appear in other kinds of settings. In Chapter 29, Susan Wheelan reviews the use of groups in the workplace. This chapter focuses on task groups (referred to as *work groups* or *teams*) established to accomplish organizational goals, and psychoeducational groups (referred to as *skills*

training groups) that serve to help task groups increase productivity. The final chapter, by Marvin Clifford, reviews different types of psychoeducational, counseling, and psychotherapy groups used in community mental health settings. Organized by the age of the participants, Clifford reviews some of the more frequently used groups and highlights the large assortment of groups in this setting.

Although groups may exist in other settings, these nine examples are known for their use of group interventions. The breadth of the impact of group interventions is impressive. Clearly, groups are well used in a variety of settings for people of diverse ages with different presenting problems. Research suggests that groups in general are effective and that different types of groups meet different group member needs and goals.

22

GROUP COUNSELING
IN THE SCHOOLS

MARIA T. RIVA

University of Denver

ALAINA L. HAUB

University of Denver

The research regarding counseling groups for children and adolescents lags behind that for adults, yet the results concerning positive outcomes are similar (Dagley, Gazda, Eppinger, & Stewart, 1994). In a meta-analysis examining the effectiveness of group treatment for children and adolescents, Hoag and Burlingame (1997) found that group treatments (broadly described as group counseling, guidance, and training groups) were significantly better than wait-list or placebo control groups, with an effect size of .61, meaning that the average child or adolescent participating in group treatment was "better off than 73% of those treated in a control group" (p. 234). Of the 54 studies included in this meta-analysis, 39, or almost 74%, were in school settings.

Schools face an enormous array of challenges in addressing the educational, social, cultural, and economic needs of children and adolescents. Increasingly, research supports the implementation of comprehensive guidance and counseling programs (e.g., Borders & Drury, 1992; Lapan,

Gysbers, & Petroski, 2001; Whiston & Sexton, 1998). Lapan et al. found that effective guidance programs consisted of school counseling activities that included the following:

> (a) spending more time in classrooms, (b) assisting students with personal problems as well as educational and career plans, (c) consulting with parents and school personnel, (d) providing individual and group counseling services, (e) referring students as needed, and (f) communicating to others both within the school and local community about the goals and aims of the guidance program. (p. 327)

In most descriptions of comprehensive guidance and counseling programs, group counseling is an essential component, partially due to the efficiency of delivering information and treatment in a group format but also because groups have been found to be effective for many types of concerns.

"Very often, group formats are the treatment of choice for the delivery of school based interventions" (Kalodner, Alfred, & Hoyt, 1997, p. 253). "In this setting, children are naturally organized in groups and perceive group interventions as part of their daily routine" (Shechtman, 2002, p. 296). During the past several decades, research on groups for children and adolescents has shifted to schools and away from psychiatric institutions as the primary research setting (Dagley et al., 1994). Schools continue to be the setting where the majority of research on groups with children and adolescents are conducted (Hoag & Burlingame, 1997; Prout & Prout, 1998). The inclusive view of school-based group treatments suggested by recent research reviews and meta-analyses, which include prevention, guidance, counseling, and training groups, also underpins this chapter.

Therapeutic groups in the schools span a wide array of topics and formats. Most recently, prevention groups have increased in school settings, commonly focusing on topics such as substance abuse, sexually transmitted diseases, and violent/aggressive behavior (Vera & Reese, 2000). Some groups provide counseling to eliminate or reduce an existing behavior, while others are directed toward enhancing competencies and promoting resiliency. In general, the bulk of the research on counseling and psychotherapy groups in the schools tends to fall into four primary areas: social competence deficits, adjustment to parent divorce, behavior problems, and learning disabilities. The format for groups is most often behavioral or cognitive-behavioral, brief (10-15 weeks), structured, homogeneous, and problem, rather than prevention, focused (Dagley et al., 1994; Hoag & Burlingame, 1997).

In a recent comprehensive review (Whiston & Sexton, 1998), two meta-analyses on school counseling outcomes (Prout & DeMartino, 1986; Prout & Prout, 1998), and a meta-analysis on group counseling for children and adolescents in a variety of settings (Hoag & Burlingame, 1997), school-based group counseling has received consistent support. These results and descriptions of school-based groups provide only a small glimpse of the therapeutic groups conducted in school settings. There are numerous other psychoeducational and counseling interventions occurring in school settings that are not being studied. In other words, groups are

a mainstay of the mental health services provided in schools.

SPECIFIC TYPES OF GROUPS

Social Competence Problems

Within the past 20 years, there has been an emphasis on and a broadening of the concept and interventions directed toward social skills training. In the past, social difficulties were most often seen as deficits in social skills. It is now acknowledged that there are several other reasons why social interaction problems occur for children and adolescents, making the broader term, *social competence* (instead of *social skills*) more inclusive (Beelmann, Pfingsten, & Losel, 1994).

At least four theoretical conceptions have emerged for social competence training (SCT). Several authors are proponents of the social skills approach, or deficit model, which assumes that children lack the knowledge of suitable behaviors for appropriate social interaction (Goldstein, 1973; Lazarus, 1971; Oden & Asher, 1977). This approach focuses on providing children with adequate cognitive and social competencies as well as teaching appropriate behavioral responses to social interaction. In comparison, the other three conceptions assume that children have the social skills in their repertoire but do not appropriately apply them. The social problem-solving approach focuses on training consequential thinking and problem solving (Spivack & Shure, 1974), whereas social perspective taking is concerned with children's abilities to perceive and evaluate someone else's perspective (Chandler, 1973). Finally, self-control training promotes children's abilities to perceive and evaluate their own impulses prior to acting (Camp, Blom, Hebert, & van Doorninck, 1977).

The results of recent meta-analyses indicated that SCT is most often conducted in a group format. The majority of these groups are psychoeducational and counseling groups, and the rest are educational groups that occur in the classroom setting (Beelmann et al., 1994; Schneider, 1992). For example, Schneider's (1992) meta-analysis of social competence training programs included 79 studies that were published between 1942 and 1987. Of these studies, 56 used a counseling and/or psychoeducational small-group format, 14 used a psychoeducational classroom group, while only 6 of the studies delivered skills training individually. Children 8 to 10 years old are most often targeted for SCT, although children 5 to 17 years have also been studied. Most groups consist of 6 to 10 members, and research assistants have most frequently led the groups, although some studies have incorporated school counselors or teachers as group leaders. The number of sessions has varied widely, with almost an equal number of groups having up to 10, 11 to 15, or more than 20 sessions. The majority of SCT studies involved groups with both boys and girls. Although there were studies with exclusively male participants, rarely has the group composition been exclusively female.

In general, SCT has been shown to be quite effective with children and adolescents, although information about what specific components are effective and whether the effects are long-term remain less clear (Beelmann et al., 1994; Caplan, Weissberg, Grober, & Sivo, 1992; Romer, White, & Haring, 1996; Schneider, 1992). A meta-analysis of research published between 1981 and 1990 suggests that multimodal groups predominate in SCT (Beelmann et al., 1994). Multimodal groups incorporate a variety of techniques that may address behaviors, affective processes, sensations, images, cognitions, and/or interpersonal relationships with the goal of teaching a skill or lesson (Colman, 2001). Multimodal programs may also address different contexts of the group member's life, such as family, peer group, and school (Prout, 1999). More specific in their focus, monomodal groups address one context (school) and target one aspect of the group member, such as his or her behavior.

The meta-analysis conducted by Beelmann et al. (1994) provided some directions for the field of SCT. Compared with monomodal programs, multimodal SCT programs have been found to have better generalization of treatment effects, although generalization of effects beyond the target behaviors (e.g., social adjustment, popularity, etc.) and training setting is generally poor. Multimodal social problem-solving programs were found to have particularly positive

effects on social cognitive and social interaction skills, with a small but significant longer-term effect. Self-control procedures showed promise in modifying social adjustment and self-related cognition/affect, at least in the short-term. Consistent with another meta-analysis (Baer & Nietzel, 1991), self-control training had positive effects on externalizing behaviors, such as aggression and conduct problems. Beelmann et al. were surprised to find that simple behavioral training, instead of a multimodal program, was highly effective for socially withdrawn children. Multimodal programs were most effective for children older than 6, and monomodal programs worked better for the younger age group. To increase potency of treatment, these authors concluded that "the future task in developing SCT programs for children is to search for programs that fit the specified social deficits of the clients and bring about not only narrowly defined, short-term modification, but also more comprehensive, long-term changes" (Beelmann et al., 1994, p. 268).

Schneider (1992) found that SCT was more effective for students who were withdrawn rather than aggressive or diagnosed as behaviorally disordered, although research has shown that social skills training still results in positive gains for emotionally disturbed students. Singh, Deitz, Epstein, and Singh (1991) conducted a meta-analysis of interventions aimed at improving the social behavior of seriously emotionally disturbed students. Of these studies, 68% took place in school settings. The majority of the studies reviewed were found to be effective in controlling or improving the behaviors of seriously emotionally disturbed children.

This chapter has focused on research that has looked at SCT groups conducted in the schools. Educators and school administrators have become increasingly aware of the need for SCT in school settings and the efficiency and effectiveness of this type of intervention. Their popularity is evident by the plethora of social competence programs available for implementation on a school-wide basis. Many are targeted toward prevention. Several social competence programs marketed specifically for use in the schools are accessible on the World Wide Web. Some of the programs found at the time of publication were The CONNECTIONS

Series *(www.buildingrelationshipskills.org);* RQ: Relationship Intelligence *(www.freeteens. org);* Building Relationship: Developing Skills for Life *(www.lifeinnovation.com);* and the PEERS (Practical Exercises Enriching Relationship Skills) for Schools Program *(www.smartmarriages. com/school.html).* Most of these programs are designed for use with adolescents aged 13 to 18 in classroom or small-group settings. Even though these programs are readily available, research on their effectiveness is often limited or nonexistent.

Two programs that have been extensively investigated and show positive results are Shure's (1992) I Can Problem Solve (ICPS) and Goldstein and McGinnis's (1997) Skillstreaming Curriculum. ICPS uses a social skills training and social problem-solving approach with children in kindergarten through sixth grade. ICPS groups consist of 6 to 10 children learning up to 59 lessons over a period of approximately 3 months. ICPS has been shown to reduce impulsivity, increase participation, and improve problem-solving skills with children in pre-school, kindergarten, and first grade (Feis & Simons, 1985; Shure, 1992; Youngstrom et al., 2000). Skillstreaming began in 1973 and has been effective with diverse training groups and for diverse target behaviors (Goldstein & McGinnis, 1997). There are several versions of Skillstreaming (i.e., young children, elementary age children, and adolescents), which use modeling, role play, performance feedback, and generalization as techniques to improve prosocial skills and reduce aggression. Skillstreaming is based on a social skills deficit model in which 50 skills are available to be taught depending on the group's deficiencies. The manual suggests groups consist of six to eight members, which are co-led for 45- to 50-minute sessions two times weekly.

Groups for Children of Divorce

The sudden increase in the divorce rate during the 1970s resulted in a body of research that studied the effects of divorce on children (e.g., Emery, 1982; Felner, Farber, & Primavera, 1980; Hetherington, 1979; Wallerstein & Kelly, 1979). These findings suggested that children of divorce were at risk for one or more of the

following characteristics: loss of appetite, aggression, anxiety, anger, sadness, inability to sleep at night, daydreaming, guilt feelings, lower academic achievement, depression, diminished self-concepts, insecurity, or a loss of self-identity (Omizo & Omizo, 1987).

Dagley et al. (1994) stated in their review of group psychotherapy that specifically designed intervention programs for children's and adolescents' adjustment to divorce had become quite popular in schools. The U.S. Bureau of the Census (1999) reported that each year during the past decade, over one million children experienced the divorce of their parents. These numbers are particularly concerning for counselors, because children with divorced parents have been found to have poorer outcomes on variables such as academic achievement, psychological well-being, and social relationships when compared with children whose parents are married (Amato, 2001; Amato & Keith, 1991).

During the late 1970s and early 1980s, many recommendations were proposed to help children of divorce. Wilkinson and Bleck (1977) specifically made suggestions for implementing divorce groups in elementary schools. In their review of the literature, Kalter, Pickar, and Lesowitz (1984) found only 10 published reports in 7 years using group treatment for children of divorce. The majority of the research on divorce groups was conducted during the 1980s and 1990s, yet there has been a dearth of studies in the past 5 years.

Several types of groups have been included in research on divorce interventions in schools. Omizo and Omizo (1987) found that fourth-through sixth-grade children of divorce had reduced levels of anxiety, higher levels of aspiration, a greater sense of control, and felt more accepted by others than the control group following 10 weeks of treatment in a support group. A commonly studied format for divorce group intervention is a multimodal group. This model incorporates activities such as role play, discussion about feelings, puppetry, and teaching relationship skills. These activities are intended to use cognitive, emotional, sensorial, and kinetic dimensions of the group members. Anderson, Kinney, and Gerler (1984) studied the effects of an eight-session multimodal group for 52 third through sixth graders. Children in the divorce group had improved attitudes toward divorce, better conduct grades, and improved classroom behavior ratings following group treatment compared with children in the control group.

The Children of Divorce Intervention Program (CODIP), developed by Pedro-Carroll and Cowen (1985), is an example of a multimodal group. CODIP involves support, skill building, anger control, and an emphasis on feelings related to the divorce and uses discussion, filmstrips, and role play. Research on CODIP has included fourth through sixth graders in 10 to 11 weekly hour-long groups (Pedro-Carroll & Cowen, 1985; Pedro-Carroll, Cowen, Hightower, & Guare, 1986) as well as second and third graders in 16 weekly sessions of 45 minutes in length (Alpert-Gillis, Pedro-Carroll, & Cowen, 1989). Results showed that effective components differed for age. Older CODIP participants were less shy or anxious, had reduced learning problems, more positive attitudes toward divorce and self, and increased adaptive assertiveness and tolerance for frustration (Pedro-Carroll et al., 1986). Younger CODIP participants displayed significant improvements in their ability to assess their feelings about self and family as well as an increased ability to cope with problems (Alpert-Gillis et al., 1989).

The overall purpose of CODIP is as follows:

[To] create a supportive group atmosphere in which children can share divorce-related feelings, clarify common misconceptions, and reduce feelings of isolation.... [It also] builds competence by teaching problem-solving, communication, and anger control skills to help children cope adaptively with challenges posed by parental divorce. (Pedro-Carroll & Cowen, 1985, p. 603)

The program is divided into three blocks. Sessions 1 through 3 consist of the affective component in which the goal is to reduce children's feelings of isolation, stigma, and being different. Techniques used to accomplish this goal are skits and role play to facilitate the expression of feelings.

In the cognitive skills component that occurs in Sessions 4 through 6, children are taught self-statements and a five-step sequence for resolving interpersonal problems. They are given homework assignments, which are later used as role play in subsequent sessions. A clear distinction is emphasized between problems that are within and beyond the children's control.

The last block of the program deals with anger expression and control. In Sessions 7 through 9, the group discusses circumstances that precipitate anger. The children are asked how they identify anger in themselves and others. The children describe actual anger experiences they have had and then discuss appropriate and inappropriate ways of expressing anger and the possible consequences of angry reactions. Positive anger management skills are taught and role-played by the group.

In the 10th and final session, an informal evaluative experience of the group occurs. Group members are encouraged to express their feelings about the group ending and provide feedback about positive and negative aspects of the experience. A final discussion is held about how to continue friendships made in the group and ways to feel supported outside of the group.

Due to the challenges of scheduling groups in school settings, brief groups for children of divorce have been studied. Gwynn and Brantley (1987) studied an 8-week group intervention led by an individual counselor with fourth through sixth graders. At the end of the eighth week, participants in the treatment group had reduced levels of depression and anxiety and were more knowledgeable about divorce compared with children in the control group. Effects were maintained at a 2-month follow-up. Crosbie-Burnett and Newcomer (1990) also found positive results using a brief 6-week group. This group was designed for sixth graders and led by two facilitators using a multimodal approach. The group displayed significantly improved beliefs about parental divorce, reduced depression, and an increase in scholastic competence following group therapy. This research suggests that brief groups, as few as six sessions, can be effective in reducing the symptoms for children of divorce. This is positive news for school settings in which brief groups are more feasible given school calendars and the logistics of working out several students' schedules.

Some research is based on the hypothesis that there is a relationship between quality of family interaction and children's adjustment to divorce. Stolberg and Garrison (1985) investigated the differential effects of four conditions: a children's support group alone (CSG), a single-parent's support group alone (SPSG), a group incorporating both CSG and SPSG, and a no-treatment control group. Participants included 82 divorced mothers and their 7- to 13-year old children. Groups consisted of 12 weekly 1-hour sessions co-led by trained facilitators. The CSG group was significantly better than the combined and the no-treatment groups at increasing children's self-concept at posttest and adaptive social skills at a 5-month follow-up. The SPSG group significantly increased parents' adjustment compared with the CSG/SPSG combined group, but neither group had an effect on children's functioning. This study demonstrated that children of divorce groups can benefit children on variables such as self-concept and social competence. Unfortunately, due to nonrandom assignment of mothers, this study was not able to provide guidance on whether the inclusion of a parent support group would enhance student gains even further. Mothers in the combined group had been separated longer, had lower employment status, and reported that the noncustodial fathers spent less time with their children than mothers of children participating in the CSG-alone condition. It seems reasonable to assume that parent involvement would increase positive outcomes for children, and in keeping with multimodal treatments, this hypothesis needs to be studied further.

Skitka and Frazier (1995) conducted a program evaluation of Rainbows for Children, a group intervention for children of divorce that has been used with more than 140,000 school children. Previous evaluations of the program reported positive changes in the participants' self-esteem and self-concept (Kavanagh, 1991), but no comparison group was used. When Skitka and Frazier compared groups composed of 67 first through sixth graders with 28 wait-list controls, they found no significant improvement for either the treatment or the control group. The implication of this study is that school programs can become widely available and regularly implemented before rigorous assessments are conducted. Because programs can be costly and time-consuming, there should be an emphasis on the selection of programs with strong research support.

Currently, there are several divorce group programs being used in school systems. DeLucia-Waack (2001) developed a manualized divorce group, which incorporates music as a therapeutic intervention. Some other structured programs in use are Banana Splits (Nugent, 1990); Kids in the Middle *(www.kidsinthemiddle.org);* Rainbows for All Children (Skitka & Frazier, 1995); Spectrum (Skitka & Frazier, 1995); and CODIP (Pedro-Carroll & Cowen, 1985), described earlier.

When reviewing the research, there appear to be common characteristics of divorce groups conducted in the schools. Groups have typically focused on children whose parents voluntarily give consent for their children to participate. This group of children on average comprises students who are functioning reasonably well in school. While children of divorce have been found to display a range of symptoms, the divorce groups studied do not generally include students who have severe problems, and results may not generalize to a more troubled population.

Most studies have included students in fourth through sixth grades. Yauman (1991) suggested that when organizing divorce counseling groups for children, developmental level should be considered both in the grouping of children and in the selection of activities for the group. Most groups reviewed had 6 to 16 weekly sessions for 30 to 60 minutes with either individual or co-leadership. Groups for children up to age 13 typically consisted of both boys and girls. Information on divorce groups for adolescents is extremely limited; future research is needed to provide empirically based recommendations for the structure and format of adolescent divorce groups. Effective divorce group interventions involved children whose parents had been separated or divorced for 1 month to 4 years. A variety of group models were shown to be effective, including multimodal, psychoeducational, and support groups.

It is important to note several limitations in the research on group therapy with children of divorced parents. Many studies used measures without reliability or validity or exclusively used self-report measures. Another limitation is the homogeneity of the samples in most studies. Generalizations cannot necessarily be made about these research findings to older adolescents, early elementary children, a more diverse group of children, or clinical samples.

Groups for At-Risk Youth

The category *at risk* is used typically to describe students experiencing some type of difficulty that is thought to lead to more serious problems later. The umbrella, at risk, is a broad one that includes a wide variety of problems and life circumstances. In the group literature with school age children and adolescents, at risk has been used with students who display truancy, teenage pregnancy, low academic achievement, substance abuse, low socioeconomic levels, disruptive and aggressive behavior, and social isolation, to name a few. Behavior problems and learning disabilities are two areas in which group treatment research has been targeted.

Group counseling has been shown to be effective in treating aggressive behavior and discipline problems in children and adolescents (e.g., Bauer, Sapp, & Johnson, 2000; Briggs, Mackay, & Miller, 1995; Nelson, Dykeman, Powell, & Petty, 1996; Omizo, Hershberger, & Omizo, 1988). Omizo et al. found that cognitive-behavioral techniques, modeling, role play, and positive reinforcement significantly decreased aggressive behaviors in children. Bauer et al. compared 9 weeks of cognitive-behavioral group counseling with supportive group counseling for 30 at-risk rural adolescents aged 14 to 18 years. The cognitive-behavioral group scored significantly higher on self-esteem and academic self-concept, while the support group did significantly better at reducing detentions. It is worth noting that supportive group counseling reduced detentions from a mean of 3.21 times per student for the 10 weeks prior to treatment to a mean of .64 for the 10 weeks following treatment, suggesting a statistically significant and clinically important reduction in detentions that lasted over several weeks. Neither group made an impact on grade point average (GPA). Nine weeks of treatment might be too few to increase GPA for such students, but it is certainly possible that as they decrease their behavior problems, other students, teachers, and administrators may feel more positively about them and they may begin to see school as a more supportive environment.

Research has also looked at group counseling for students with learning and academic problems (e.g., McCollum & Anderson, 1974;

Omizo & Omizo, 1988a, 1988b; Palisano, 1989). Several studies that include students with learning disabilities and academic problems investigate group interventions that address other concomitant problems, such as self-esteem and social competence, and are less likely to target learning problems directly. For example, Utay and Lampe (1995) found that a cognitive-behavioral group counseling game enhanced social competence of children with learning disabilities. The treatment condition also was significantly better at improving academic-related skills, such as listening and attending to assigned tasks, compared with the control and placebo conditions. Shechtman, Gilat, Fos, and Flasher (1996) studied 142 low-achieving elementary school students in Israel. All students were receiving assistance with their academic problems, but half of these students also participated in group therapy that focused on listening and self-expression. Students in group therapy did significantly better than the control group on academic achievement, self-concept, social acceptance, and locus of control measures. These studies suggest that targeting behaviors such as self-concept and social competence can also result in gains in achievement. Fewer group studies address the academic skills and learning problems directly by providing psychoeducational groups on study skills, problem solving, or specific content areas such as math or science. It may be that these skills groups would also be effective in increasing achievement in children and adolescents who are struggling academically.

Prevention Groups

In the past decade, several commissions and task forces have concluded that school-based or school-linked mental health programs offer the best opportunity to affect the physical and mental health of children and adolescents (Hughes & Cavell, 1999). School-based prevention programs are particularly appealing given their potential to interrupt the development or progression of deviant behavior and are more cost-effective than interventions aimed at already-established emotional problems (Felner, 1999). Prevention programs have the advantages of targeting behavior problems before they become crystallized, are able to reach large numbers of students through a group format delivery, often are more easily accessible for families compared with community-based mental health clinics, and can be less stigmatizing than psychological services in the community (Hughes & Cavell, 1999).

Durlak and Wells (1997) defined primary prevention as "an intervention intentionally designed to reduce the future incidence of adjustment problems in currently normal populations as well as efforts directed at the promotion of mental health functioning" (p. 117). Kulic, Dagley, and Horne (2001) argued that "prevention and groups are a natural combination to use in enhancing the health of children and adolescents" (p. 217). Although prevention programs are most often delivered in small or large groups, descriptions of group dynamics have rarely occurred. What is known is that prevention groups are numerous, especially in school settings, and appear to be promising.

In a meta-analysis of prevention studies with children and adolescents, Durlak and Wells (1997) included 177 studies that spanned from 1955 to 1991. The mean age of the participants was 9.3 years, with only 13% of the 177 studies including adolescents 13 years or older. Similar to other meta-analyses with children and adolescents, the large majority of studies ($n = 129$, 72.9%) were conducted in school settings, once again showing the large number and variety of therapeutic programs that are conducted in schools. This meta-analysis indicated that most types of prevention programs resulted in significant positive outcomes, with effect sizes ranging from .24 to .93 suggesting that as a group, the participants in the prevention programs exceeded the performance of 59% to 82% of the control group.

Prevention groups have addressed a variety of different behaviors. For example, primary prevention groups in school settings have attempted to reduce the risk for anxiety disorders (Dadds, Spence, Holland, Barrett, & Laurens, 1997); conduct problems (Conduct Problem Prevention Research Group, 1999; Reid, Eddy, Fetrow, & Stoolmiller, 1999); AIDS and unsafe sexual behaviors (McDermott, 1998); dating violence (Macgowan, 1997); adolescent drug abuse and high school dropout (Eggert, Thompson, Herting, Nicholas, & Dicker, 1994); suicide (Eggert, Thompson, & Herting, 1995;

LaFromboise & Howard-Pinney, 1995); and violence (Bosworth, Espelage, DuBay, Daytner, & Karageorge, 2000).

Common denominators for successful group-based prevention programs for school age children and adolescents include (a) theoretical models and extant research that guide the design and interventions, (b) the use of multiple-measure evaluation strategies, (c) matching techniques to the developmental level of the students, and (d) using a multilevel comprehensive approach that often includes students, teachers, parents, school administrators, and other community agencies. For example, a study using Fast Track, a prevention program for conduct problems based on a developmental model, employed multisite, multiple-component preventative strategies for young children. Interventions included classroom programs, social skills training, academic tutoring, parent training, and home visits (Conduct Problem Prevention Research Group, 1999). Given the complexity of and numerous pathways to emotional problems, it is only reasonable that prevention programs for these types of problems will need to be comprehensive and carefully select participants. For less severe behaviors or preventative measures aimed at increasing competencies, the programs will be less complex and usually target larger numbers of students. Group theory and methods, whether referring to counseling in small groups, classroom formats, or larger seminars, have an important role to play in the dissemination of information and intervention techniques geared toward primary prevention.

CONTRAINDICATIONS OF GROUPS IN THE SCHOOLS

Group treatment is not suitable for all children and adolescents, and not all school settings are conducive to group counseling and psychotherapy. Due to the many logistical challenges of conducting groups in school settings, teachers and administrators need to have an appreciation for the *effectiveness,* and not just the *efficiency,* of group counseling. Some of the logistical challenges include arranging a time for group that does not or only minimally conflicts with students' class schedules, and finding an available, private, and comfortable group room. It is crucial for group leaders to understand the limits of confidentiality between group members and in school systems where the student body has close contact. It is important for a climate to exist in the school that can support the changes that occur in therapeutic groups. It is possible, for example, that even if students become more socially competent in group counseling, the behavior of other students will not change toward them unless there is an intervention in the larger school context that prohibits teasing, bullying, and harassing behavior.

Some students may not be candidates for group counseling. Students who are extremely anxious or shy may find a group format too stressful. Those who are truant may interfere with the progress of the group. Research also suggests that group treatment for early adolescents with deviant behavior may serve to inadvertently reinforce these behaviors (Dishion, McCord, & Poulin, 1999). The power of peer influences and modeling that occur within the group format increases the likelihood that adolescents will learn more deviant behaviors. Strategies found to be effective include combining prosocial and problem youth in a treatment group instead of including only problem youth, as well as mobilizing parents and adult caregivers as part of the treatment program (Dishion et al., 1999).

CONCLUSION

Therapeutic groups play a vital role in the counseling services offered in school settings. Group formats, whether aimed at prevention or remediation, have accumulated considerable empirical support. Dagley et al. (1994) stated that the majority of research studies implementing group treatment had shifted to schools. This trend continues to be true. For example, more than 72% of the 177 studies cited in a recent prevention meta-analysis were in school settings (Durlak & Wells, 1997), and in a meta-analysis of child and adolescent counseling groups, more than 73% were conducted in schools (Hoag & Burlingame, 1997). Prout and Prout (1998) and Whiston and Sexton (1998) found that in their reviews of counseling in school settings, the majority were delivered in group formats.

Group research with children and adolescents continues to lag behind studies on adult populations, and research on groups is less developed than research on individual treatment. Yet recent comprehensive reviews and several meta-analyses have pointed to some interesting findings. In general, therapeutic groups are typical components of comprehensive school guidance and counseling programs (Lapan et al., 2001). Multimodal treatment programs that address different aspects (i.e., social, emotional, cognitive, etc.) and contexts (i.e., family, peer, school, etc.) of group members' lives appear to be more beneficial. Children are most often the focus of group counseling and therapy, with very little emphasis on adolescents. Given the scheduling problems inherent in school settings, groups are usually brief, between 6 to 15 sessions, and rarely include follow-up evaluations to determine whether the change in behavior is maintained. Groups are also structured, cognitive-behavioral, and have homogeneous membership. Similar to conclusions from the group literature on adult populations, it is clear that groups with children and adolescents are effective, although the research is only beginning to tease out the essential ingredients.

Several authors have expressed the need for developmental theory to guide the composition of group members and the leader techniques chosen. Dagley et al. (1994) stated,

> Although groups work, we have yet to implement all that is known to expand the power of group intervention in the lives of children, preadolescents, and adolescents, and to make more effective use of our knowledge of human development and of small group dynamics. (p. 363)

The obstacle here is that some group leaders receive very little training that specifically targets children and adolescents in group formats, and their training with adults does not generalize well to the younger age group. Besides some information about different age groups, little is known about what works best for children and adolescents who are culturally diverse, or for females and males. Similarly, information is lacking on how group composition, group size, and leader characteristics affect group outcomes.

One last point relates to whether group research in school settings can be generalized to treatment settings such as community clinics and residential treatment facilities. Students represent a unique, albeit heterogeneous, population, yet they also differ considerably from outpatient and inpatient clients. Weisz, Donenberg, Han, and Weiss (1995) distinguished between the characteristics of research therapy and clinic therapy. Many of these distinctions apply to research in schools. School groups are often composed of recruited clients who have less severe problems than the referred clients in other settings. Group counseling in schools is brief compared with the longer-term treatment in clinic settings and uses cognitive-behavioral interventions, whereas treatment in clinic settings is nonbehavioral and less structured and group members are more diverse with regard to problem areas and personality characteristics. These differences suggest that generalization of results obtained from school groups to community-based mental health groups is unwarranted. Although this may seem problematic, the real benefit of school-based treatment is that it can potentially reach many students before they need remedial counseling for more serious mental health problems.

References

Alpert-Gillis, L. J., Pedro-Carroll, J. L., & Cowen, E. L. (1989). The children of divorce intervention program: Development, implementation, and evaluation of a program for young urban children. *Journal of Consulting and Clinical Psychology, 57,* 583-589.

Amato, P. R. (2001). Children of divorce in the 1990s: An update of the Amato and Keith (1991) meta-analysis. *Journal of Family Psychology, 15,* 355-370.

Amato, P. R., & Keith, B. (1991). Parental divorce and the well-being of children: A meta analysis. *Psychological Bulletin, 110,* 26-46.

Anderson, R. F., Kinney, J., & Gerler, E. R. (1984). The effects of divorce groups on children's classroom behavior and attitudes toward divorce. *Elementary School Guidance and Counseling, 19,* 70-76.

Baer, R. A., & Nietzel, M. T. (1991). Cognitive and behavioral treatment of impulsivity in children: A meta-analytic review of outcome literature. *Journal of Clinical Child Psychology, 20,* 400-412.

Bauer, S. R., Sapp, M., & Johnson, D. (2000). Group counseling strategies for rural at-risk high school students. *The High School Journal, 83,* 41-50.

Beelmann, A., Pfingsten, U., & Losel, F. (1994). Effects of training social competence in children: A meta-analysis of recent evaluation studies. *Journal of Clinical Child Psychology, 23,* 260-271.

Borders, L. D., & Drury, S. M. (1992). Comprehensive school counseling programs: A review for policymakers and practitioners. *Journal of Counseling & Development, 70,* 487-498.

Bosworth, K., Espelage, D., DuBay, T., Daytner, G., & Karageorge, K. (2000). Preliminary evaluation of a multimedia violence prevention program for adolescents. *American Journal of Health Behavior, 24,* 268-280.

Briggs, W., Mackay, T., & Miller, S. (1995). The Edinbarnet Playgroup Project: Changing aggressive behavior through structured intervention. *Educational Psychology in Practice, 11,* 37-44.

Camp, B. W., Blom, G. E., Hebert, F., & van Doorninck, W. J. (1977). "Think aloud": A program for developing self-control in young aggressive boys. *Journal of Abnormal Child Psychology, 5,* 157-169.

Caplan, M., Weissberg, R. P., Grober, J. S., & Sivo, P. J. (1992). Social competence with inner-city and suburban young adolescents: Effects on social adjustment and alcohol use. *Journal of Consulting and Clinical Psychology, 60,* 56-63.

Chandler, M. J. (1973). Egocentrism and antisocial behavior: The assessment and training of social perspective-taking skills. *Developmental Psychology, 9,* 326-337.

Colman, A. M. (2001). *A dictionary of psychology.* Oxford: Oxford University Press.

Conduct Problem Prevention Research Group. (1999). Initial impact of the Fast Track prevention trial for conduct problems: I. The high-risk sample. *Journal of Consulting and Clinical Psychology, 67,* 631-647.

Crosbie-Burnett, M., & Newcomer, L. L. (1990). Group counseling children of divorce: The effects of a multimodal intervention. *Journal of Divorce, 13,* 69-78.

Dadds, M. R., Spence, S. H., Holland, D. E., Barrett, P. M., & Laurens, K. R. (1997). Prevention and early intervention for anxiety disorders: a controlled trial. *Journal of Consulting and Clinical Psychology, 65,* 627-635.

Dagley, J. C., Gazda, G. M., Eppinger, S. J., & Stewart, E. A. (1994). Group psychotherapy research with children, preadolescents, and adolescents. In A. Fuhriman & G. M. Burlingame (Eds.), *Handbook of group psychotherapy: An empirical and clinical synthesis.* New York: John Wiley.

DeLucia-Waack, J. L. (2001). *Using music in children of divorce groups: A session-by-session manual for counselors.* Alexandria, VA: American Counseling Association.

Dishion, T. J., McCord, J., & Poulin, F. (1999). When interventions harm: Peer groups and problem behavior. *American Psychologist, 54,* 755-764.

Durlak, J. A., & Wells, A. M. (1997). Primary prevention mental health programs for children and adolescents: A meta-analytic review. *American Journal of Community Psychology, 25,* 115-152.

Eggert, L. L., Thompson, E. A., & Herting, J. R. (1995). Reducing suicide potential among high-risk youth: Tests of a school-based prevention program. *Suicide and Life Threatening Behavior, 25,* 276-296.

Eggert, L. L., Thompson, W. A., Herting, J. R., Nicholas, L. J., & Dicker, B. G. (1994). Preventing adolescent drug abuse and high school dropout through an intensive school-based social network development program. *American Journal of Health Promotion, 8,* 202-215.

Emery, R. E. (1982). Interpersonal conflict and the children of discord and divorce. *Psychological Bulletin, 92,* 310-330.

Feis, C. L., & Simons, C. (1985). Training preschool children in interpersonal cognitive problem-solving skills: A replication. *Prevention in Human Services, 3,* 59-70.

Felner, R. D. (1999). An ecological perspective on pathways of risk, vulnerability, and adaptation: Implications for preventive interventions. In S. W. Russ & T. H. Ollendick (Eds.), *Handbook of psychotherapies with children and families* (pp. 483-503). New York: Plenum.

Felner, R. D., Farber, S. S., & Primavera, J. (1980). Children of divorce, stressful life events, and transitions: A framework for preventive efforts. In R. H. Price, R. F. Ketterer, B. C. Bader, &

J. Monahan (Eds.), *Prevention in mental health: Research, policy and practice* (pp. 81-108). Beverly Hills, CA: Sage.

Goldstein, A. P. (1973). *Structured learning therapy.* New York: Academic.

Goldstein, A. P., & McGinnis, E. (1997). *Skillstreaming the adolescent: New strategies and perspectives for teaching prosocial skills.* Champaign, IL: Research Press.

Gwynn, C. A., & Brantley, H. T. (1987). Effects of a divorce group intervention for elementary school children. *Psychology in the Schools, 24,* 161-164.

Hetherington, E. M. (1979). Divorce: A child's perspective. *American Psychologist, 34,* 851-858.

Hoag, M. J., & Burlingame, G. M. (1997). Evaluating the effectiveness of child and adolescent group treatment: A meta-analytic review. *Journal of Clinical Child Psychology, 26,* 234-246.

Hughes, J. N., & Cavell, T. A. (1999). School-based interventions for aggressive children. In S. W., Russ & T. H. Ollendick (Eds.), *Handbook of psychotherapies with children and families* (pp. 419-446). New York: Plenum.

Kalodner, C. R., Alfred, A. R., & Hoyt, W. T. (1997). Group research in applied settings: Examples and recommendations. *Journal for Specialists in Group Work, 22,* 253-265.

Kalter, N., Pickar, J., & Lesowitz, M. (1984). School-based developmental facilitation groups for children of divorce: A prevention intervention. *American Journal of Orthopsychiatry, 54,* 613-623.

Kavanagh, J. A. (1991). *Rainbows for all God's children: A case study.* Report prepared for the Rainbows for All God's Children, Inc., Chicago, IL.

Kulic, K. R., Dagley, J. C., & Horne, A. M. (2001). Prevention groups with children and adolescents. *Journal for Specialists in Group Work, 26,* 211-218.

LaFromboise, T., & Howard-Pinney, B. (1995). The Zuni Life Skills Development curriculum: Description and evaluation of a suicide prevention program. *Journal of Counseling Psychology, 42,* 479-486.

Lapan, R. T., Gysbers, N. C., & Petroski, G. F. (2001). Helping seventh graders be safe and successful: A statewide study of the impact of comprehensive guidance and counseling programs. *Journal of Counseling & Development, 79,* 320-330.

Lazarus, A. A. (1971). *Behavior therapy and beyond.* New York: McGraw-Hill.

Macgowan, M. J. (1997). An evaluation of a dating violence prevention program for middle school students. *Violence and Victims, 12,* 223-234.

McCollum, P. S., & Anderson, R. P. (1974). Group counseling with reading disabled children. *Journal of Counseling Psychology, 21,* 150-155.

McDermott, R. (1998). Adolescent HIV prevention and intervention: A prospect theory analysis. *Psychology, Health, & Medicine, 3,* 371-385.

Nelson, J. R., Dykeman, C., Powell, S., & Petty, D. (1996). The effects of a group counseling intervention on students with behavioral adjustment problems. *Elementary School Guidance & Counseling, 31,* 21-33.

Nugent, P. (1990). Children of divorce. *The American School Board Journal, 177,* 31.

Oden, S., & Asher, S. R. (1977). Coaching children in social skills for friendship making. *Child Development, 48,* 495-506.

Omizo, M. M., Hershberger, J. M., & Omizo, S. A. (1988). Teaching children to cope with anger. *Elementary School Guidance and Counseling, 22,* 241-246.

Omizo, M. M., & Omizo, S. A. (1987). Group counseling with children of divorce: New findings. *Elementary School Guidance and Counseling, 22,* 46-52.

Omizo, M. M., & Omizo, S. A. (1988a). Group counseling's effects on self-concept and social behavior among children with learning disabilities. *Journal of Humanistic Education and Development, 26,* 109-117.

Omizo, M. M., & Omizo, S. A. (1988b). The effects of group counseling on classroom behavior and self-concept among elementary school learning disabled children. *Exceptional Child, 34,* 57-64.

Palisano, R. J. (1989). Comparison of two methods of service delivery for students with learning disabilities. *Physical and Occupational Therapy in Pediatrics, 9,* 79-99.

Pedro-Carroll, J. L., & Cowen, E. L. (1985). The children of divorce intervention program: An investigation of the efficacy of a school-based prevention program. *Journal of Consulting and Clinical Psychology, 53,* 603-611.

Pedro-Carroll, J. L., Cowen, E. L., Hightower, A. D., & Guare, J. C. (1986). Prevention intervention with latency-aged children of divorce: A replication study. *American Journal of Community Psychology, 14,* 277-290.

Prout, H. T. (1999). Counseling and psychotherapy with children and adolescents: An overview. In H. T. Prout & D. T. Brown (Eds.), *Counseling and psychotherapy with children and adolescents: Theory and practice for school and clinical settings.* New York: John Wiley.

Prout, H. T., & DeMartino, R. A. (1986). A meta-analysis of school-based studies of psychotherapy. *Journal of School Psychology, 24,* 285-292.

Prout, S. M., & Prout, T. (1998). A meta-analysis of school-based studies of counseling and psychotherapy: An update. *Journal of School Psychology, 36,* 121-136.

Reid, J. B., Eddy, J. M., Fetrow, R. A., & Stoolmiller, M. (1999). Description and immediate impacts of a preventive intervention for conduct problems. *American Journal of Community Psychology, Special Issue: Prevention Science, Part 1, 27,* 483-517.

Romer, L. T., White, J., & Haring, N. C. (1996). The effect of peer mediated social competence training on the type and frequency of social contracts with students with deaf-blindness. *Education and Training in Mental Retardation and Developmental Disabilities, 31,* 324-338.

Schneider, B. H. (1992). Didactic methods for enhancing children's peer relations: A quantitative review. *Clinical Psychology Review, 12,* 363-382.

Shechtman, Z. (2002). Child group psychotherapy in the school at the threshold of a new millennium. *Journal of Counseling and Development, 80,* 293-299.

Shechtman, Z., Gilat, I., Fos, L., & Flasher, A. (1996). Brief group therapy with low-achieving elementary school children. *Journal of Counseling Psychology, 43,* 376-382.

Shure, M. (1992). *I can problem solve (ICPS): An interpersonal cognitive problem solving program for children.* Champaign, IL: Research Press.

Singh, N. N., Deitz, D. E., Epstein, M. H., & Singh, J. (1991). Social behavior of students who are seriously emotionally disturbed. *Behavior Modification, 15,* 74-94.

Skitka, L. J., & Frazier, M. (1995). Ameliorating the effects of parental divorce: Do small group interventions work? *Journal of Divorce and Remarriage, 24,* 159-178.

Spivack, G., & Shure, M. B. (1974). *Social adjustment of young children: A cognitive approach to solving real-life problems.* San Francisco: Jossey-Bass.

Stolberg, A. L., & Garrison, K. M. (1985). Evaluating a primary prevention program for children of divorce. *American Journal of Community Psychology, 13,* 111-124.

U.S. Bureau of the Census. (1999). *Statistical abstract of the United States 1999, 19th edition.* Washington, DC: U.S. Government Printing Office.

Utay, J. M., & Lampe, R. E. (1995). Use of a group counseling game to enhance social skills of children with learning disabilities. *Journal for Specialists in Group Work, 20,* 114-120.

Vera, E. M., & Reese, L. E. (2000). Preventive interventions with school-age youth. In S. D. Brown & R. W. Lent (Eds.), *Handbook of counseling psychology* (pp. 411-434). New York: John Wiley.

Wallerstein, J. S., & Kelly, J. B. (1979). Children and divorce: A review. *Social Work, 24,* 468-475.

Weisz, J. R., Donenberg, G. R., Han, S. S., & Weiss, B. (1995). Bridging the gap between laboratory and clinic in child and adolescent psychotherapy. *Journal of Consulting and Clinical Psychology, 63,* 688-701.

Whiston, S. C., & Sexton, T. L. (1998). A review of school counseling outcomes research: Implications for practice. *Journal of Counseling & Development, 76,* 412-426.

Wilkinson, G. S., & Bleck, R. T. (1977). Children's divorce groups. *Elementary School Guidance & Counseling, 11,* 205-213.

Yauman, B. E. (1991). School-based group counseling for children of divorce: A review of the literature. *Elementary School Guidance and Counseling, 26,* 130-138.

Youngstrom, E., Wolpaw, J. M., Kogos, J. L., Schoff, K., Ackerman, B., & Izard, C. (2000). Interpersonal problem solving in preschool and first grade: Developmental change and ecological validity. *Journal of Clinical Child Psychology, 29,* 589-602.

23

Psychological Work With Groups in the Veterans Administration

Les R. Greene
VA Connecticut Healthcare System

Andrew W. Meisler
VA Connecticut Healthcare System

David Pilkey
VA Connecticut Healthcare System

Gregory Alexander
Northport VA Medical Center

Lucille A. Cardella
The Abacus Group

Brian C. Sirois
Kaiser Permanente

Matthew M. Burg
VA Connecticut Healthcare System

That World War II marked the big-bang beginning of group psychotherapy is perhaps no better documented than in the early writings by clinicians working with veterans in the 1,300 hospital and clinic megalopolis known formally as the Department

Table 23.1 Small-Group Work Within the VA: The Clinical and Research Literature

Decade	N^a	PTSD	Substance Abuse	Chronic and Severe Mental Illness	Health Psychology	Other[b]
1940s and 50s	26	19[c]	4	8	8	61
1960s	10	0	20	0	0	80
1970s	29	3	45	17	14	21
1980s	53	55	15	11	8	15
1990s	55	47	13	16	4	20

a. Number of articles in refereed journals.

b. Primarily studies of group process in heterogeneous groups and, more recently, group therapy for geriatric patients.

c. Percentages may be greater than 100% when articles focus on two or more primary categories, such as PTSD (post-traumatic stress disorder) and substance abuse.

of Veterans Affairs, but more colloquially as the VA. Rather unceremoniously, group therapy was born of necessity, an "emergent" matter of supply and demand, with too many soldiers returning wounded in spirit and mind from the war and too few therapists to treat them individually. Like all innovative techniques, group therapy was a trial, an experiment with a clinical rationale that had, at least, face validity: Bring together soldiers with a common recent history in a safe environment, and maybe some healing will happen. These pioneering efforts, documented in early writings, introduced nascent ideas about the ways in which these groupings can in fact alleviate symptoms and facilitate readjustment into civilian life (Ackerman, 1945; Grotjahn, 1947; Hadden, 1947; Schwartz, 1945). Many of these early writings laid the groundwork for the subsequent, and now well-established, classification systems by Corsini and Rosenberg (1955) and Yalom (1995), which identify core mediators and moderators of therapeutic change in groups, such as the instillation of hope, universality, and catharsis.

Not all the early work in group therapy within the VA system focused on war trauma. An exhaustive search of both PsychLit and Medline databases, using keywords of *veterans, Veterans Administration,* and *veterans hospitals* each crossed with *group therapy, group psychotherapy,* and *group counseling,* revealed that early writings contained seminal articles on treating a variety of disorders in small-group settings. Many papers in the decades of the 1940s and 1950s seemed intent on establishing the legitimacy of group therapy

per se, which meant, in those years, the application of psychodynamic psychotherapeutic principles in heterogeneous groups of patients with neurotic level and character level psychopathology. A few other efforts, however, focused on working with diagnosis-specific homogeneous groupings. Thus, there are rudimentary efforts at describing how group therapy can be applied to veterans' suffering from specific medical diseases and alcoholism. A few brave souls were even attempting to explore the uses of group therapeutic approaches in treating the severest forms of mental illness—this, in the pre-Thorazine era. Included here were the initial works by Florence Powdermaker and Jerome Frank (1948), developing their still impressive, though long-lost, qualitative method for studying how group therapy heals—situation analysis—and paving the way for their classic volume *Group Psychotherapy* (1953), on the psychotherapeutic treatment of schizophrenic patients. Table 23.1 summarizes the published works on group therapy within the VA across the decades, organized by categories that reflect the natural clusterings of articles found in the literature. The table and this chapter focus on psychological work only within small-group settings; a variety of large-group and milieu therapies have also been implemented within the VA system (cf. Greene & Johnson, 1987) but are beyond the scope of the present work.

The sections that follow are written by experienced frontline clinicians who continue the traditions established in these very beginnings of group work within the VA. These contributions—on posttraumatic stress disorder (PTSD), substance abuse, chronic and severe forms of psychopathology in inpatient settings, and the burgeoning field of behavioral medicine—mirror contemporary trends in the field as a whole (cf. Fuhriman & Burlingame, 1994) as group therapy shifts away from more psychodynamically oriented work and toward cognitive-behavioral techniques in theme-focused groups. We examine how these groups are implemented across a variety of settings within the VA system: Andrew Meisler describing the ever-widening array of outpatient group techniques for PTSD veterans, David Pilkey exploring the use of group work in a day treatment setting dedicated to treating substance abuse, Gregory Alexander illuminating psychosocial work in treating the severely and chronically mentally ill on inpatient units, and the shared efforts of Lucille Cardella, Brian Sirois, and Matthew Burg in attending to the physical health needs of veterans via group interventions. The first author, Les Greene, attempts to place these specific approaches into historical perspective as well as into the contemporary mental health treatment context.

POSTTRAUMATIC STRESS DISORDER (PTSD)

It can be argued that even more than World War II, Vietnam and its aftermath served as the major impetus for the growth of group work within the VA system. Rooted in the development of "rap" groups and other nascent group efforts for returning Vietnam soldiers in the early 1970s and clearly reflected in the literature in the past 20 years (see Table 23.1), there is a major commitment to implementing effective group therapies for veterans with PTSD in the VA system. These efforts became more formalized in 1989 with the development of specially designed and funded inpatient and outpatient treatment programs throughout the VA. In the year 2000, the VA supported 140 specialized programs nationwide, serving more than 50,000 veterans with PTSD (Fontana, Rosenheck, Spencer, & Gray, 2001).

Because group therapy is considered to offer several advantages over other treatment modalities, it has come to serve as the core of most treatment programs for Vietnam era veterans

(e.g., Ford & Stewart, 1999). First, a group provides the most efficient and cost-effective way to treat and educate clients. Second, a group of individuals with similar difficulties borne of similar recent histories can provide a supportive environment for change. Often, the knowledge that others share similar experiences and distress—what Yalom (1995) terms "universality"—is helpful, as clients often feel isolated, embarrassed, and misunderstood prior to entering treatment. The group context can offer a safe environment for self-disclosure and reassurance. Finally, the group setting serves to counteract and confront the socially avoidant and isolative tendencies common in PTSD by providing a much-needed forum for social reintegration and rehabilitation of social skills.

Group therapy for PTSD within the VA system is not monolithic. As shown below, it comprises many different approaches and orientations, some tried-and-true, some innovative, all aimed at alleviating sequelae of war trauma. The clinical subtleties of conducting effective group therapy for veterans with PTSD are beyond the scope of this overview; the reader is referred to Ford and Stewart (1999) for a more detailed review. Group treatment of PTSD in the VA may be accomplished in a self-help or support group format, in trauma-focused work, through cognitive-behavioral and skills training groups, as well as through several other ancillary group therapy formats. The following sections review these modalities.

Supportive Group Therapies

Group therapies for veterans with PTSD have often involved informal gatherings where veterans can talk about their experiences, both past and present, and receive social support from others. These groups, "rap groups" as they were called, were prominent within the VA especially in the early years following Vietnam and, in particular, at the Vet Centers run by the Veterans Readjustment Counseling Service (Sipprelle, 1992; Walker, 1983). Although such peer counseling appears to have helped many and still represents one component of treatment, many veterans seeking treatment require more intense, focused, and professionally led therapies. Today, most support groups are led by mental health professionals who assist in providing direction and facilitating a supportive group atmosphere. Although such groups may discuss traumatic material, they focus more often on current, day-to-day stressors and optimum ways to manage these situations given veterans' underlying stress-related problems.

Trauma-Focused Group Therapy

Trauma-focused or exposure therapy is a behavioral treatment based on conditioning principles in which veterans are exposed repeatedly to reminders or "cues" of their trauma in order to desensitize them to these cues. Some studies have found that exposure therapy is an effective treatment for combat-related PTSD in Vietnam veterans (e.g., Keane, Fairbank, Caddell, & Zimering, 1989), and group exposure therapy has been shown to be highly effective in treating victims of civilian trauma (e.g., Foa et al., 1999). VA investigators have recently completed a large multisite controlled study of trauma-focused group therapy (TFGT) for Vietnam veterans (Schnurr, Friedman, Lavori, & Hsieh, 2001). Ten participating VA sites conducted three cohorts of TFGT compared with matched cohorts of present-centered, supportive group therapy. Veterans in the TFGT participated in exposure sessions during group and in homework assignments, learned active coping strategies, and received group support. Although findings have not yet been published, preliminary data suggest that such treatment plays an important role in helping veterans with PTSD and may have particular benefit in treating avoidance symptoms. Its advantages, however, over present-centered treatment are not clear at this time.

Cognitive-Behavioral and Skills-Training Approaches

Cognitive-behavioral therapy (CBT) encompasses a wide variety of treatment approaches that together serve as the linchpin in many VA treatment programs for PTSD. These modalities include traditional cognitive therapy adapted from Beck (cf. Beck & Emery, 1985), designed to challenge maladaptive cognitions and help clients think more positively and realistically.

Resick and colleagues have demonstrated the efficacy of such therapy adapted specifically for group treatment of trauma survivors with PTSD (e.g., Resick & Schnicke, 1992). CBT also includes training in self-management skills, such as relaxation training and anger management, which incorporate both cognitive and physiological components. Because of the central importance of such skills, many PTSD treatment programs have begun to incorporate alternative methods for improving these skills, including the use of meditation, yoga, and tai chi. Other skills-training methods include problem-solving therapies (e.g., D'Zurilla, 1986) and assertiveness training. At many VA facilities, an integrated package of psychoeducation, self-management, cognitive therapy, and graded exposure (e.g., "stress inoculation training"; Meichenbaum, 1977) serves as the core of PTSD treatment.

Dual-Diagnosis Treatment

Alcohol and other substance use disorders accompany PTSD in as many as 75% of those seeking treatment in the VA (Keane, Gerardi, Lyons, & Wolfe, 1988; Meisler, 1999). Yet only recently have systematic and integrative approaches to treatment been developed for these dual disorders. Until quite recently, patients suffering from both PTSD and substance abuse were often caught between two different and split-off treatment systems with differing philosophies. Fortunately, the past 10 to 15 years have seen significant growth in treatments of the dually diagnosed (e.g., Drake & Noordsy, 1996), approaches that emphasize working with the "whole person" rather than the partitioning into separate psychiatric and substance abuse components. This integrative approach has formed the basis for the development of the Substance Use PTSD Teams (SUPTs) within the VA system. At present, there are seven SUPTs and one inpatient PTSD Substance Unit (PSU) operating nationwide. Group therapy serves as the cornerstone of treatment in these settings, with a focus on psychiatric symptom treatment and management, substance abstinence and "harm reduction" (i.e., the reduction in the frequency and extent of substance use to minimize negative biopsychosocial consequences;

cf. Marlatt, Larimer, Baer, & Quigley, 1993), and relapse prevention focused on both PTSD and substance use simultaneously. Because PTSD symptoms such as irritability or hyperarousal often serve as triggers for substance abuse, education about the interplay of these two disorders and the "self-medication" aspect of substance use is a critical component of effective treatment (Meisler, 1999).

Creative and Expressive Arts Therapies

Many PTSD programs incorporate creative, visual, or dramatic arts as an element of treatment. The underlying rationale for these modalities is that individuals with PTSD often suffer impairments in their ability to experience or express emotions, a condition known as *alexithymia.* Expressive art therapies provide a structured medium for veterans with PTSD to express emotions in a safe and therapeutic way. Although there are relatively few outcome studies on these treatments compared with more traditional psychotherapeutic interventions, anecdotal evidence suggests they can play an important role in the multimodal group therapy of individuals with PTSD.

Summary

Group therapy represents the cornerstone of treatment for veterans with PTSD within the VA. As the need for effective treatment of PTSD in the VA has grown over the past 30 years, so too has the range of group therapies designed to meet the many and complex needs of this patient population. Effective group treatment programs provide a panoply of therapies ranging from specific trauma-focused exposure therapy to meditation, art, music, and supported work therapies. Given the importance of PTSD within the VA system—not only clinically but politically—the development and implementation of new group therapies for PTSD is certain to remain a top priority in the years to come. At present, few studies have examined the effectiveness of such group therapy for PTSD within the VA, due largely to the complexities inherent in conducting well-controlled research in this area (Schnurr et al., 2001). Additional research on the most effective group therapy approaches for this veteran population is sorely needed.

SUBSTANCE ABUSE

The group treatment of alcohol and drug problems within the VA has grown significantly over the years, although as described above and implied in Table 23.1, it is increasingly likely to be integrated into the treatment of a comorbid psychiatric condition such as PTSD or depression. Today, the VA is innovating a variety of group-oriented programs designed to address substance abuse problems. One of the most salient of these group approaches is the intensive group-oriented day treatment program. The typical substance abuse day program (SADP), as it is referred to, is aimed at treating veterans who have severe substance use and a high likelihood of relapse, nonsupportive recovery environments, and/or mild to moderate comorbid psychiatric disorders. In a recent study on readiness to change, veterans in the SADP at VA Connecticut Healthcare System, West Haven Campus, were found to meet an average of 8.9 of 9 criteria for alcohol abuse and dependence by their treating clinicians (Pilkey, 2000). This severity of substance use disorder leads to numerous other quality of life problems, including homelessness, often as high as 50% to 60% of the SADP population (Pilkey, 2000, 2001), and unemployment, ranging from 50% to 90% of SADP patients (Cooney, Pilkey, Cooney, & Kranzler, 2000; Pilkey, 2001). In addition, most of these substance-abusing patients have inadequate social supports and limited leisure activity repertoires. Thus, effective treatment must be geared toward meeting these multiple needs.

The SADP at VA Connecticut Healthcare System, typical of most, is a short-term, 21-day treatment program primarily using group therapies; it is designed as an integrative, group-based approach to address the multifarious needs of a clinical population with relatively severe substance use disorders. Groups vary in approach from highly structured and didactic to psychoeducational to more process oriented. In addition, while the crux of the program is informed by cognitive-behavioral theory, 12-step participation is encouraged throughout treatment. Groups are led by a multidisciplinary staff of registered nurses, addiction therapists, social workers, and psychologists. Core components of SADP are as follows.

Cognitive-Behavioral Group Therapy

The cornerstone of the SADP is a cognitive-behavioral coping-skills group based on the work of Monti, Abrams, Kadden, and Cooney (1989) in which the goal is the complete abstinence from alcohol and other substances. This core group meets 5 times a week in 45-minute sessions. The work in these sessions focuses on the identification of high-risk situations and the development of skills to manage these situations. High-risk situations include both internal states, such as cravings or negative affects, and external triggering situations, such as the offering of substances by one's peers or the observing of cues that remind one of past use. Core skills are selected from the clinical literature (cf. Kadden et al., 1995), covering ways of coping with cravings, strategies for refusing substances, problem-solving techniques, anger and stress management training, planning for emergencies, and dealing with lapses. Additional psychoeducational topics presented in the group might include adaptive assertiveness training and managing negative thoughts.

Psychoeducational Groups

In addition to the cognitive-behavioral group, veterans are provided with a range of other, more theme-focused and more highly structured psychoeducational groups. The life skills training is conducted as a topic-oriented discussion group with themes on affiliation, productivity, and leisure. This group provides the members with opportunities for learning about (a) their support networks and whether these networks support or hinder efforts toward abstinence, (b) their attitudes about work and meaningful time-structuring activities, such as volunteering, and (c) how to implement skills acquired in leisure skills group.

An education group didactically presents material relevant for those with substance use disorders. In this context, patients can learn about the medical consequences of substance use, including information about HIV and hepatitis, the biochemistry of addiction, and associated health risks. For example, participants are taught about the potential impact of substance use on liver functioning, cognitive functioning, and the nervous system. They may also receive information about current pharmacotherapy for substance use disorders. In another formal setting known as the "speakers' group," graduates of SADP who have achieved 6 months or more of abstinence present their experiences with treatment and how they have maintained abstinence. This group is designed to provide its current members with the sense of hope that they too may achieve similar abstinence. In many instances, invited speakers also facilitate involvement in 12-step participation through discussing their own experiences in Alcoholics, Cocaine, or Narcotics Anonymous.

Leisure skills and recreation groups focus on participants' repertoire of leisure activities. Many individuals with substance use disorders have a limited range of leisure activities, and such activities are likely to be associated with substance use. Thus, a leisure skills group identifies and encourages activities independent of substance use. Through group participation, veterans might return to long-abandoned hobbies, develop new activities, or engage in familiar activities while abstinent for the first time in many years. A recreation group provides participants with the opportunity to try out these activities in vivo with the support of staff and other group members.

As with any group-oriented program, the overriding organizational aim is to integrate its various small groups into a meaningful whole. Within the SADP, this synthesis is achieved by means of a daily community meeting in which participants discuss new events and experiences in their lives, progress toward their individual treatment goals, and their struggles to remain abstinent. In this go-around, participants are encouraged to offer and receive feedback from peers as well as from treatment staff. Frequently, feedback from other group members, both supportive and confrontational, serves as a catalyst to change or to increased receptivity for treatment.

In this meeting and throughout the program, the staff attempts to monitor and promote group cohesiveness, which is difficult to achieve because of the rolling admissions into the program. To facilitate group cohesiveness, treatment staff works at fostering a culture of abstinence within the participant community. Reinforcing this cultural standard begins with the intake procedure of soliciting a commitment to abstain for the duration of SADP and an acceptance of a goal of long-term abstinence. Within all the groups, clinicians maintain the focus on achieving and maintaining abstinence as the primary value. Through this focus, group members come to acculturate new participants to the norm of abstinence and abstinence-oriented behavior. The effectiveness of this kind of group-based program is revealed by preliminary outcome data generated in the SADP at VA Connecticut Healthcare System (Pilkey, 2001): About 70% of the veterans successfully complete the treatment and are abstinent at discharge. Typically, these patients are referred to less intensive outpatient groups to continue the ongoing psychological work of abstaining from substances.

INPATIENT GROUP THERAPY

Despite the considerable downsizing on inpatient psychiatry services both within and outside the VA, along with steadily decreasing lengths of stay and greater emphasis on psychopharmacological approaches, psychosocial treatments are still considered core aspects of the treatment in many VA inpatient units (Buchanan, Dixon, & Thyer, 1997; Johnson, Lubin, & Corn, 1999). Typical of many psychiatric wards in the VA system, the two general admissions units at the Northport, New York, VA, have a variety of groups designed to work in integrative fashion for the veterans who carry a wide range of diagnoses, though primarily affective disorders, substance abuse, and schizophrenia. These inpatient groups include a number of task-focused, psychoeducational groups, such as stress management, dual diagnosis, and discharge planning. Following Yalom (1983), the psychotherapy groups are constituted on the basis of functional status with a more open-ended "process" group for higher-functioning patients and a more formally structured "focus" group for the lower-functioning veterans.

Challenges to Inpatient Group Psychotherapy

There are several unique aspects to inpatient group psychotherapy in the VA system, some useful for the therapeutic work, others problematic. As described above, perhaps the most salient feature of group therapy at the VA is the immediate identification among the veterans as veterans, fellow soldiers in arms sharing a common bond that holds across many sociodemographic and clinical differences, such as age and diagnosis. It also seems to override real differences in military status parameters, such as service era (i.e., World War II, Korean War, Vietnam War, or peacetime eras), service-connected disability status, and level of combat experience. Thus, while the therapy group in general potentiates feelings of community and is often experienced by its members as a family (Earley, 2000), this cohesion tends to be redoubled in groups within the VA system. Of course, this is a mixed blessing, since cohesion, as the research literature on group therapy processes reveals (Fuhriman & Burlingame, 1994), often serves as a therapeutic factor but can also function as resistance to the work of the group, a banding together to fight or flee from the task of the group. For example, a group member may be covertly invited by the whole group to serve as its "fight leader," a spokesperson tasked with confronting the group therapists about some clinical decision or policy. In this "us versus them" dynamic of patients vis-à-vis the staff authorities, individual differences are usually obscured, and patients alternately feel victimized and empowered; the therapeutic task of self-exploration and change is typically lost in the context of this emotionally charged group process.

Equally complicated in terms of therapeutic value within the inpatient group is the potential for exaggerated dependency dynamics. With its service-connected financial, health, and insurance benefits and other "entitlements," the VA is a "total institution" that can elicit dependency, counterdependency, and parental-authority transference dynamics in many veterans (cf. Parson, 1986). Such processes may be a continuation of the veteran's experiences in the highly hierarchical and authoritarian structure of the military. The cognitive and affective reactions to the VA as a whole, in contrast to the "outside," clearly infiltrate all components of the system of an inpatient unit, including the therapy group.

A third salient, distinguishing feature of VA groups is that most of the patients who compose them are male. The role of gender, sexuality, and aggressiveness (cf. Lanza, Satz, Stone, & Kayne, 1996), heightened within the typical context of all-male veteran patients treated predominantly by female nurses, can powerfully affect, again for better or worse, the processes within the inpatient group. Working on "men's issues" can prove fruitful for this population, but the blind enactment of culturally held male stereotypes can interfere with the work.

Finally, the brevity of veteran inpatients' hospitalization—with a current mean length of stay of 2.5 weeks at Northport—precludes the use of closed-ended groups. Due to the rapid turnover of the patient population, most groups on the unit remain in the first or "formative" developmental stage, in which a core task is to establish the group qua group, a bounded and cohesive entity founded on identifications between and among group members, widening to subgroups and ultimately identifications with the group-as-a-whole (Brabender & Fallon, 1993; Whitaker, 2001). As discussed above, this task is made easier by the common military backgrounds of the veterans but must be furthered by observing, exploring, and commenting upon similarities by both the therapist and patients themselves.

An approach with a proven track record in fostering cohesion is an emphasis on the problems and issues of most immediate concern to the patients, namely, their symptoms and experiences of the events leading up to hospitalization. Focusing on these topics has immediate "face validity" and gives patients the support to start from "where they are." This model is closest to an "educative" one (Maxmen, 1978, 1984) and challenges patients to learn about their "triggers," stressors, and patterns of relapse and regression and to develop and use improved coping techniques and resources. The encouragement of patient-patient interaction in this model, the "giving and receiving of feedback," as it is called in the group, tends to reduce dependence on both the therapist and on the VA system as a whole. Countering this "double dependency" has been a major factor in the evolution of the inpatient therapeutic approach. Thus, after initially preparing each new patient for group therapy by reviewing the purposes and rules, it is very helpful to let patients dictate

the content of the group and to regard whatever emerges as "grist for the mill." The only content that is directly challenged or confronted is "small talk."

While there are drawbacks to the open-ended structure of these groups characterized by rapid patient turnover, these features also create important therapeutic opportunities. For example, encouraging the ongoing members to orient and acculturate a new group member to ward life allows them to experience altruism and a sense of social responsibility. Yalom (1983) cites the power of altruism in groups to counter demoralization and low self-esteem, so salient in depressed and chronically self-negating patients. Similarly, inviting the patient who is leaving to review "what worked" is challenging and inviting to those left behind to try new, adaptive behaviors. Focusing on comings and goings of patients in the context of a single-session temporal perspective, as espoused by Yalom (1983), helps make the group process clinically meaningful and relevant to the overall mission of the contemporary short-term psychiatric ward.

Therapeutic Processes and Techniques

Much of the research on inpatient groups has focused on exploring Yalom's therapeutic factors. Typical of this approach, Maxmen (1978, 1984) identified the instillation of hope, cohesiveness, altruism, and universality as those factors most valued by inpatients. For example, combating demoralization, which is widespread among our patients, is a process that needs to be reinforced in the groups. It is a task jointly shared by the group members and the therapist and is especially helpful to substance-abusing, dual-diagnosis patients, with their frequent relapses, and to the chronically mentally ill patients who experience many decompensations. The experience of altruism as a curative factor is often mentioned by patients when they leave the unit. As Yalom (1983) has observed, it can work to counter patients' demoralization based on low self-esteem and overabsorption in their own problems. Learning that "I'm not alone" in psychiatric emergencies, decompensations, relapses, family problems, and losses—the experience of universality—also seems profoundly therapeutic. Another therapeutic factor to add to this list is catharsis. While the research on its helpfulness has been mixed (Brabender & Fallon, 1993), clinical experience with veterans suggests that this is often the most helpful part of inpatient group therapy. "Letting it all out" or "getting my feelings out on the table" is often mentioned as one factor that patients perceive to be beneficial and important in the groups.

Over time, several techniques have worked well with veteran inpatients. While emphasizing that the here and now is of central value in patients' discovering of new experiences, balancing this focus with discussions on the past and future seems useful. Being able to discuss past trauma is especially important for patients suffering from PTSD, whether these are based on childhood, military, or other experiences. Many veteran inpatients have experienced childhood physical, verbal, emotional, and sexual abuse and raise these memories in the flow of group explorations, sometimes triggered by perceptions of and associations with authority figures on the unit (cf. Lubin & Johnson, 2000).

Striking a balance between the individual and the group is also technically important. Given the considerable identification with each other among veterans, lapsing into the "we" is a common phenomenon in the groups. Encouraging "I" statements facilitates the assumption of responsibility for one's role and behavior in any problem being discussed. This norm also tends to short-circuit the role development of group spokesmen who give voice to the collective feelings and reactions of the group.

As in many psychotherapy groups in which group members' mutual identifications are high, content themes readily develop during the meetings. Although it is the therapist's task to observe and clarify themes as they emerge, such as social isolation, recovering from psychic wounds, and the many faces of depression, patients are able to do so when asked. Group themes can be revisited in later groups, especially with the same core group, in a manner described as "a kind of deepening spiral" (Whitaker, 2001, p. 127) characteristic of the "established phase" of group development. The sounding of group themes aids cohesiveness and can assist quieter members to disclose.

While "vicarious learning" or "spectator therapy" is recognized as another therapeutic

factor in group psychotherapy (Yalom, 1995), so that even the quieter or silent patient can presumably benefit from the group process, at some point it is helpful for most inpatients to become more actively engaged. Gentle commenting on observations of their behaviors in the group is especially productive. Behavioral observations (e.g., "You've been very quiet in the group so far," or "It looked like you had a response to John, when you moved forward in your chair a moment ago") invariably lead to some self-disclosure, even if brief. These interventions seem to validate a person's quiet presence in the group and provide support to become more verbal. They may also stimulate other patients to express interest in the quiet or silent group member.

In addition to working with the silent patients, identifying and commenting on roles that patients take in the group, often irrational or maladaptive, can help them in understanding the meaning of such roles and, paradoxically, in moving them out from such limiting scripts. Among the typical roles that are enacted in the inpatient groups are the critic or cynic, the caretaker of other patients (but not of self), the scapegoat, the child, the father or grandfather figure, the monopolist, the group spokesman, and unique to the VA system, "Sarge."

The research literature on the effectiveness of inpatient group therapy within the VA network is scarce. What does exist shows empirical findings for relatively homogeneous groups composed of patients with specific diagnoses or problems. The largest clusters of reports focus on inpatient groups for PTSD (Daniels & McGuire, 1998; Goodman & Weiss, 1998; Johnson, Lubin, & Corn, 1999; Lubin & Johnson, 2000; Stewart, 1995) and schizophrenia (Brown & Mumford, 1983; Kanas & Smith, 1990; Nightingale & McQueeney, 1996). Other studies can be found that focus on inpatient groups for substance abuse (Verinis & Taylor, 1994), childhood abuse (Zaidi, 1994), and aggression (Lanza, Satz, Stone, & Kayne, 1995). While these reports fail to isolate and study the separate treatment components within an inpatient unit, when coupled with clinical experience, they strongly suggest the therapeutic benefits of these inpatient groups.

HEALTH PROMOTION GROUPS

It is well-known that lifestyle factors play a significant role in many chronic medical conditions, such as heart disease, diabetes, cancer, chronic obstructive pulmonary disease, and HIV (Brannon & Feist, 2000). By learning the role that these lifestyle factors play in both the onset and progression of various diseases, patients can become motivated to improve self-care skills. Once motivated, patients can learn skills to reduce or eliminate disease risk factors and improve their quality of life. Throughout the VA network, a variety of health promotion, group-oriented programs are offered, all designed to provide effective help for veterans interested in changing health behaviors and improving health status. The three core group-based programs at VA Connecticut Healthcare System, West Haven, are weight management, smoking cessation, and stress management. Our health promotion groups attempt to gauge the stage in which patients are starting (Prochaska & Norcross, 1994), provide appropriate interventions designed to advance them to the action stage, and then offer specific skills along with group support to assist them in modifying health risk behaviors.

Healthy Lifestyles Weight Management

Healthy Lifestyles is a comprehensive psychoeducational group program for veterans who desire to make lifestyle changes in nutrition, eating habits, and physical activity levels. The emphasis is in making long-lasting changes in day-to-day habits. While most patients view changes and intervention as short-term and remedial (i.e., going on and off a diet; Grommet, 1997), we attempt to reframe change as a lifestyle venture. The complex etiology of obesity necessitates a comprehensive approach (Grommet, 1997). Commonly, there is an interaction of causal agents, including poor eating habits, lack of physical activity, genetics, metabolic complications, and negative emotional states. During each of the 12 sessions of the Healthy Lifestyles group, several factors involved in weight management are addressed, including improving nutrition, increasing physical activity, modifying eating habits, and sustaining motivation for behavior change. A group format is used because weight management groups have been shown to be both cost-effective and superior to other approaches (Wadden, 1993), especially closed groups, because they can enhance cohesiveness and the influence of social support and may consequently reduce attrition rates.

Typically referred by their primary care physicians, patients enter the program by first completing the Weight Loss Readiness Test (Brownell, 2000) to assess their degree of readiness to change in relevant areas. Knowledge of patients' stage of change is extremely important in treatment planning. Precontemplators and contemplators may derive limited benefit and drop out of treatment should insufficient attention be given to motivational enhancement. Many obese patients may not be ready to take action (Greene, Rossi, Reed, Willey, & Prochaska, 1994). Because most of our patients tend to be in the contemplation stage, we rely on several motivational enhancements in our group work, including using the decision matrix to explicate pros and cons of changing lifestyles (Dimeff & Marlatt, 1995), addressing significant practical barriers (Miller, 1995), using a menu approach (Miller, 1995), clarifying goals (Miller, 1995), and assessing the value, readiness, and self-confidence in making specific behavior changes (Rollnick, Mason, & Butler, 1999).

The action phase of the program incorporates many general principles of behavior treatment, including a focus on modifiable factors and health-related behaviors as well as the functional analysis of behavior (Grommet, 1997). Intervention strategies within the group are keyed to specific changes of health behavior, such as reducing fat intake and incorporating physical activity into one's lifestyle. Moreover, treatment centers on developing behavioral coping strategies for managing visual, emotional, and social triggers of eating behavior. Stimulus control techniques, self-monitoring, and the use of cognitive-behavioral strategies are some of the central strategies taught (Brownell, 2000). For example, stimulus control techniques include eating only at the kitchen table, refraining from engaging in other activities while eating, and leaving the table immediately after eating.

The method of learning these strategies is process oriented, client centered, and collaborative in order to empower individual patients to manage their chronic conditions. To that end, the first 30 minutes of each 90-minute group session is devoted to reviewing behavior change implementation accompanied by exploration and clarification of individual needs. In this portion of each session, collective problem solving focuses on the refinement of strategies and addressing barriers to change.

Treatment for obesity often fails—with patients regaining one third of weight lost within a year of treatment (Wadden, 1993)—because it does not adequately equip the patient to cope with ongoing physiological processes that compensate for weight loss and negative psychological reactions that result from inability to sustain weight loss (Perri & Nezu, 1993). Thus, relapse prevention is a critical aspect of our groups. Relapse is presented as an expected part of the change process, with emphasis on making plans to minimize relapse. During final sessions of the groups, patients learn to identify and examine high-risk situations that became lapses and frame them as learning experiences. Group leaders facilitate the process of troubleshooting when difficulties arise and help patients cope with high-risk situations. Follow-up by the leaders is also important. Perri and colleagues (1990) found that the combination of relapse prevention training and posttreatment contact was the only condition in which patients did not suffer significant relapse over a 12 month follow-up. Our approach aims to reduce the patients' sense of hopelessness as they cope with managing lifestyle changes.

The efficacy of these groups is measured via a comparison of pre- and posttreatment assessments. The diet of patients is assessed (Brownell, 2000), as well as physical activity level and body weight. The Perceived Stress Scale (Cohen, Kamarack, & Mermelstein, 1983) and the Beck Depression Inventory (Beck, 1996) are used to assess global perceptions of stress and depressive symptoms, respectively. Unpublished data collected over the past 6 months from a small sample of 25 patients indicate that 73% were classified in the contemplation stage and 27% in the action stage with regard to motivation and attitudes. Of these patients, 65% lost weight during the 12-week program, with an average weight loss of 9.8 pounds. These preliminary data are encouraging and consistent with reports from similar programs (cf. Wadden, 1993), suggesting that comprehensive, stage-appropriate, group-based interventions can be successful in assisting patients directly with weight issues.

Smoking Cessation

The Smoking Cessation program is a two-phase group intervention based on the *stages of change model* (Prochaska & DiClemente, 1983), which also uses group leader support and encouragement, group process, problem-solving and coping-skills training, and nicotine replacement therapy. These groups are designed especially for veterans who have attempted to quit smoking on their own but have had little success; most have either a variety of illnesses associated with smoking or a wish to avoid developing them. Typically, veterans are referred by their primary care providers and are assessed for readiness to participate. Interested patients are invited to attend weekly group sessions in the first phase of the program. Because the first phase is designed as an open group, the number of patients attending varies week to week. Patients can attend as many of these 60-minute sessions as they require to progress to the second phase of the program, although a minimum of two sessions is encouraged.

Matching group interventions to patients' stage of readiness and even helping patients progress just one stage can double their chances of cessation 6 months later (Prochaska & Goldstein, 1991). Recognizing that patients attending the first phase of the group are at varying stages in terms of their readiness to change smoking behaviors, we administer to all new participants a questionnaire that assesses their current stages, similar to that used in the Healthy Lifestyles program. Information is also collected regarding level of nicotine addiction, health history, social support, and confidence regarding quitting behaviors. Information on stage of change is also collected at weekly group sessions to monitor patient progress.

For veterans found to be in the precontemplation stage, education is provided regarding the health risks of smoking, the benefits of quitting, and the addictive properties of nicotine. Financial, social, and personal motivators that might induce patients to consider smoking a problem are introduced into the group. For that greater number of veterans who start the group in the contemplation stage, decision matrix exercises (Dimeff & Marlatt, 1995) are employed that help patients weigh personal inducements for smoking versus desire to quit. The group therapists also work with the veterans at this stage to resolve ambivalence about the need to change. Patients might also be asked to monitor how much they actually smoke as well as the times and reasons that they smoke to get a better understanding of their specific smoking habits.

Once patients have decided that smoking is a problem and a habit that they wish to break, self-paced, action-oriented goals are set. Helping patients move into this action stage is critical because patients in this stage are twice as successful at quitting as those in the contemplation stage (Rohren et al., 1994). The group therapists assist clients to set attainable weekly goals, which include changing habits related to smoking, reducing environmental triggers, and moving toward the second phase, namely, the "Nicotine Patch Group." Inclusion criteria for this group are that patients should be smoking less than one pack of cigarettes per day, have switched to cigarette brands with the lowest amount of nicotine, and have attempted a 24-hour quit period.

The Nicotine Patch Groups are formed when at least two to three patients have reached this stage of readiness. In the general population, use of the nicotine patch in conjunction with group therapy has been found to significantly increase success rates, almost doubling the rate of sustained smoking cessation at 6-month follow-up (Fiore et al., 1994). These highly structured groups are typically led by one therapist, run for four sessions every 2 weeks, plus a final check-in once patients are off the nicotine patch. In the first meeting, personal motivation for quitting is reviewed along with the dangers of smoking and the benefits of quitting. The role of social support and the means to obtain it are discussed. The relationship between caffeine and nicotine is reviewed, and

patients are encouraged to decrease caffeine consumption. Tips for breaking smoking habits are presented, and patients are encouraged to choose strategies to use in dealing with urges to smoke. Finally, preparation for quitting smoking and starting the patch are discussed, and participants are asked to sign a behavioral contract that sets the date of the next group meeting as their quit date.

At the second session, progress is monitored, the ability to cope with urges is processed by the group, and health benefits and urge reduction strategies are reviewed. Patients are congratulated for reaching their quit dates. They receive education about the nicotine patch as well as about withdrawal symptoms they may experience. In the third session, strategies for handling urges and health benefits of quitting are again reviewed, and any problems with nicotine patches are discussed. Lapses are discussed and reframed as learning experiences. The role of thoughts in behavior change is also reviewed, and patients discuss ways to use their thoughts to view themselves as nonsmokers and to avoid urges. The fourth session focuses primarily on maintenance, involving a review on managing lapses, an exploration of tempting situations and various coping techniques for these situations, and a focus on positive changes that group participants have noticed since quitting.

Given the many health risks related to smoking and the difficulty patients experience in quitting, efforts should be made to assist patients who express their readiness to become nonsmokers. While assistance should, at minimum, consist of health care provider evaluation, advice, and education, psychoeducational and behavioral groups along with nicotine replacement therapy can significantly benefit patients in stopping their smoking and remaining free of tobacco use. The use of stage-matched interventions such as the ones used in our VA program are particularly effective. Recent unpublished outcome data from our program show that approximately 50% of the veterans who had quit smoking at the end of the program remained nonsmokers at a 1-year follow-up and reported a high level of satisfaction with the program (Cardella, Sirois, & Burg, 2001).

Stress Management

Stress management groups focus on assisting patients in coping with the multiple stressors associated with chronic medical conditions. Such stressors include making urgent and critical decisions, facing arduous treatments and their side effects, experiencing changes in self-image, dealing with the effects of illness on family members, and having fears of uncertainty and death (Fawzy, Fawzy, Hyun, & Wheeler, 1997). Groups are designed to help patients learn to cope effectively with this series of stressors, following the psychoeducational processes outlined by Tunks and Bellissimo (1991). The specific group process incorporates four elements: (a) emphasizing the importance of patient-provider collaboration, (b) exploring the stressors within patients and their environments, (c) supporting health-promoting activities, and (d) learning from one's own experiences and developing one's own coping skills. To this end, the eight 90-minute group sessions incorporate basic knowledge about the stress response, cognitive and behavioral coping and problem-solving techniques, and specific relaxation-training procedures.

Patients are educated on the distinction between the stress reaction, a state of hyperarousal that can lead to long-term physiological dysregulation, and the stress response, involving adaptive coping strategies (Kabat-Zinn, 1990). Cognitive coping skills are then introduced as a major component of our stress management groups. These cognitive coping approaches attempt to alter maladaptive images and inappropriate beliefs and expectations, including so-called catastrophic thinking and negative self-talk (Tunks & Bellissimo, 1991).

When exposed to a potentially stressful situation, individuals appraise the event and make judgments about the level of threat it presents and then assess available resources to handle the stressors (Baum, Gatchel, & Krantz, 1997). Patients are taught about this process and how to increase their available resources. In this vein, active behavioral coping strategies are introduced, such as increasing the involvement of patients in their own care; improving communication with health care providers, family, and friends; seeking instrumental or emotional support from others; and pacing oneself in undertaking activities. The group leaders offer a menu of relaxation procedures from which patients can choose the best fit for their coping styles and needs. Instruction centers on both physical relaxation techniques (i.e., progressive muscle relaxation) and imaginal exercises (i.e., autogenic training, guided visual imagery, meditation). Based on the specific needs of each group, other topics may be raised, such as anger, time, and job stress management skills, sleep hygiene, healthy nutrition, and exercise. This flexibility is important in matching coping strategies to the needs of group members as well as enhancing their coping resources and expectations for positive change.

As with the other health groups, outcomes are measured via pre- and posttreatment comparisons, using the State-Trait Anxiety Inventory (Speilberger, Gorsuch, & Lushene, 1970), the Perceived Stress Scale (Cohen et al., 1983), and the Beck Depression Inventory (Beck, 1996). In addition, informal assessments of everyday life stress and physical symptoms of stress are undertaken. Similar to smoking and obesity, stress has a negative impact on health not only through direct physiological mechanisms but also through its association with poor health behaviors. In fact, smoking, poor diet, and lack of physical activity are common behavioral manifestations in patients experiencing high levels of stress. Given this relationship, elements of stress management are taught in all the health promotion groups, and stress management should be considered for any patient who identifies stress as a primary barrier to their making and maintaining behavioral changes of any kind. By teaching veterans adaptive, healthy coping skills, they are not only better able to manage their health issues but can also use these strategies in all aspects of their lives, as documented in the research literature (Murphy, 1996.)

SUMMARY

Some 50 years after the explosive beginnings of group therapy in the VA system, the preceding efforts attest to its continued application in the treatment of a wide range of psychological and medical maladies. Group counseling is most prominent in the rehabilitation of veterans afflicted with war trauma and addictions, continues to serve a vital role within the inpatient psychiatry setting, and is showing promise as a psychosocial intervention in the treatment of psychosomatic disease. Its contribution goes beyond the four areas described in this chapter, as suggested by the "Other" column in Table 23.1. Veterans are an integral part of our society, and they suffer from those signs-of-the-times illnesses that afflict other parts of contemporary society— struggles with growing old, pathological gambling, violence, and abuse, to name a few. While predictions about future trends are always a risky business, it seems likely that group therapy will remain alive and well within the VA system for the next 50 years.

REFERENCES

Ackerman, N. W. (1945). Psychiatric disorders in service-men and veterans. *American Journal of Orthopsychiatry, 15,* 352–360.

Baum, A., Gatchel, R., & Krantz, D. (1997). *An introduction to health psychology* (3rd ed.). New York: McGraw-Hill.

Beck, A. (1996). *Beck Depression Inventory* (2nd ed.). San Antonio, TX: Psychological Corporation.

Beck, A. T., & Emery, G. (1985). *Anxiety disorders and phobias.* New York: Basic Books.

Brabender, V., & Fallon, A. (1993). *Models of inpatient group psychotherapy.* Washington, DC: American Psychological Association.

Brannon, L., & Feist, J. (2000). *Health psychology: An introduction to behavior and health.* (4th ed.). Belmont, CA: Wadsworth/Thompson.

Brown, M., & Mumford, A. (1983). Life skills training for chronic schizophrenics. *Journal of Nervous and Mental Disease, 181,* 466–70.

Brownell, K. (2000). *The LEARN program for weight management.* Dallas, TX: Lifestyle Company.

Buchanan, J. P., Dixon, D. R., & Thyer, B. A. (1997). A preliminary evaluation of treatment outcomes at a veterans' hospital's inpatient psychiatry unit. *Journal of Clinical Psychology, 53,* 853–858.

Cardella, L., Sirois, B., & Burg, M. (2001). [Smoking cessation follow-up data]. Unpublished raw data.

Cohen, S., Kamarack, T., & Mermelstein, R. (1983). A global measure of perceived stress. *Journal of Health and Social Behavior, 24,* 385–396.

Cooney, J. L., Pilkey, D. T., Cooney, N. L., & Kranzler, H. R. (2000, February). *Acute nicotine withdrawal and depressive symptomatology in alcoholic smokers.* Presented at the 6th annual meeting of the Society for Research on Nicotine and Tobacco, Washington, DC.

Corsini, R., & Rosenberg, B. (1955). Mechanisms of group psychotherapy: Processes and dynamics. *Journal of Abnormal and Social Psychology, 51,* 406–411.

Daniels, L., & McGuire, T. (1998). Dreamcatchers: Healing traumatic nightmares using group dreamwork, sandplay and other techniques of intervention. *Group, 22,* 205–226.

Dimeff, L., & Marlatt, G. A. (1995). Relapse prevention. In R. Heister & W. Miller (Eds.), *Handbook of alcoholism treatment approaches: Effective alternatives* (2nd ed., pp. 176–194). Boston: Allyn & Bacon.

Drake, R. E., & Noordsy, D. L. (1996). Case management for people with coexisting severe mental disorder and substance use disorder. In N. Miller (Ed.), *Addiction psychiatry.* New York: W.B. Saunders.

D'Zurilla, T. J. (1986). *Problem-solving therapy: A social competence approach to clinical intervention.* New York: Springer.

Earley, J. (2000). *Interactive group therapy.* Philadelphia: Brunner/Mazel.

Fawzy, I., Fawzy, N., Hyun, C., & Wheeler, J. (1997). Brief coping-oriented therapy for patients with malignant melanoma. In J. Spira (Ed.), *Group therapy for medically ill patients* (pp. 133–164). New York: Guilford.

Fiore, M. C., Kenford, S. L., Jorenby, D. E., Wetter, D. W., Smith, S. S., & Baker, T. B. (1994). Two studies of the clinical effectiveness of the nicotine patch with different counseling treatments. *Chest, 105,* 524–533.

Foa, E. B., Dancu, C. V., Hembree, E. A., Jaycox, L. H., Meadows, E. A., & Street, G. P. (1999). A comparison of exposure therapy, stress inoculation training, and their combination for reducing posttraumatic stress disorder in female assault victims. *Journal of Consulting and Clinical Psychology, 67,* 194–200.

Fontana, A., Rosenheck, R., Spencer, H., & Gray, S. (2001). *The long journey home, IX: Treatment of PTSD in the Department of Veterans Affairs: Fiscal year 2000 service delivery and performance.* West Haven, CT: Northeast Program Evaluation Center and National Center for PTSD.

Ford, J. D., & Stewart, J. (1999). Group psychotherapy for war-related PTSD with military veterans.

In B. H. Young and D. D. Blake (Eds.), *Group treatment for post-traumatic stress disorder: Conceptualization, themes, and processes* (pp. 75–100). Philadelphia: Taylor & Francis.

Fuhriman, A., & Burlingame, G. M. (Eds.). (1994). *Handbook of group psychotherapy: An empirical and clinical synthesis.* New York: John Wiley.

Goodman, M., & Weiss, D. (1998). Double trauma: A group therapy approach for Vietnam veterans suffering from war and childhood trauma. *International Journal of Group Psychotherapy, 48,* 39–54.

Greene, G., Rossi, S., Reed, G., Willey, C., & Prochaska, J. (1994). Stages of change for reducing dietary fat to 30% of energy or less. *Journal of the American Dietetic Association, 94,* 1105–1110.

Greene, L. R., & Johnson, D. R. (1987). Leadership and the structuring of the large group. *International Journal of Therapeutic Communities, 8,* 99–108.

Grommet, J. (1997). Weight management: Framework for changing behavior. In S. Dalton (Ed.), *Overweight and weight management* (pp. 332–347). Gaithersburg, MD: Aspen.

Grotjahn, M. (1947). Experience with group psychotherapy as a method for treatment of veterans. *American Journal of Psychiatry, 103,* 637–643.

Hadden, S. B. (1947). Post-military group psychotherapy with psychoneurotics. *Mental Hygiene, 31,* 89–93.

Johnson, D. R., Lubin, H., & Corn, B. (1999). Course of treatment during a cohort-based inpatient program for posttraumatic stress disorder. *Group, 23,* 19–35.

Kabat-Zinn, J. (1990). *Full catastrophe living.* New York: Bantam.

Kadden, R., Carroll, K., Donovan, D., Cooney, N., Monti, P., Abrams, D., Litt, M., & Heister, R. (1995). *Cognitive-behavioral coping skills therapy manual: A clinical research guide for therapists treating individuals with alcohol abuse and dependence* (Monograph Series Vol. 3). Rockville, MD: National Institute on Alcohol Abuse and Alcoholism Project MATCH.

Kanas, N., & Smith, A. (1990). Schizophrenic group process: A comparison and replication using the HIM-G. *Group, 14,* 246–252.

Keane, T. M., Fairbank, J. A., Caddell, J. M., & Zimering, R. T. (1989). Implosive (flooding) therapy reduces symptoms of PTSD in Vietnam combat veterans. *Behavior Therapy, 20,* 245–260.

Keane, T. M., Gerardi, R. J., Lyons, J. A., & Wolfe, J. (1988). The interrelationship of substance abuse and post-traumatic stress disorder: Epidemiological and clinical considerations. In M. Galanter (Ed.), *Recent developments in alcoholism* (Vol. 6). New York: Plenum.

Lanza, M. L., Satz, H., Stone, J., & Kayne, H. L. (1995). Assessing the impact of group treatment for aggressive inpatients. *Group, 19,* 195–219.

Lanza, M. L., Satz, H., Stone, J., & Kayne, H. L. (1996). Developing psychodynamic group treatment methods for aggressive male inpatients. *Issues in Mental Health Nursing, 17,* 409–426.

Lubin, H., & Johnson, D. R. (2000). Interactive psychoeducational group therapy in the treatment of authority problems in combat-related post-traumatic stress disorder. *International Journal of Group Psychotherapy, 50,* 277–269

Marlatt, G. A., Larimer, M. E., Baer, J. S., & Quigley, L. A. (1993). Harm reduction for alcohol problems: Moving beyond the controlled drinking controversy. *Behavior Therapy, 24,* 461–504.

Maxmen, J. (1978). An educative model for inpatient group therapy. *International Journal of Group Psychotherapy,. 28,* 321–338.

Maxmen, J. (1984). Helping patients survive theories: The practice of an educative model. *International Journal of Group Psychotherapy, 34,* 355–368.

Meichenbaum, D. (1977). *Cognitive-behavior modification: An integrative approach.* New York: Plenum.

Meisler, A. W. (1999). Group treatment of PTSD and comorbid alcohol abuse. In B. H. Young and D. D. Blake (Eds.), *Group treatment for post-traumatic stress disorder: Conceptualization, themes, and processes* (pp. 117–136). Philadelphia: Taylor & Francis.

Miller, W. (1995). Increasing motivation for change. In R. Heister & W. Miller (Eds.), *Handbook of alcoholism treatment approaches: Effective alternatives* (2nd ed., pp 89–104). Boston: Allyn & Bacon.

Monti, P. M., Abrams, D. B., Kadden, R. M., & Cooney, N. L. (1989). *Treating alcohol dependence: A coping skills training guide.* New York: Guilford.

Murphy, L. R. (1996). Stress management in work settings: A critical review of health effects. *American Journal of Health Promotion, 11,* 112–135.

Nightingale, L., & McQueeney, D. (1996). Group therapy for schizophrenia: Combining and expanding the psychoeducational model with supportive psychotherapy. *International Journal of Group Psychotherapy, 46,* 517–533.

Parson, E. R. (1986). Transference and post-traumatic stress: Combat veterans' transference to the Veterans Administration Medical Center. *Journal of the American Academy of Psychoanalysis, 14,* 349–375.

Perri, M., McKelvey, W., Schein, R., Renjilian, D., Viegener, B., & Nezu, A. (1990). *Relapse prevention training versus frequent therapist contacts as weight-loss maintenance strategies.* Paper presented at the annual meeting of the Association for Advancement of Behavior Therapy, San Francisco, CA.

Perri, M., & Nezu, A. (1993). Preventing relapse following treatment for obesity. In A. J. Stunkard & T. A. Wadden (Eds.), *Obesity: Theory and therapy* (2nd ed., pp. 287–299). New York: Raven.

Pilkey, D. T. (2000). *Contemplating readiness to change: Relationship to underreporting and defensiveness.* Unpublished doctoral dissertation, Syracuse University, Syracuse, New York.

Pilkey, D. T. (2001). [Homelessness and other quality of life problems in SADP patients]. Unpublished raw data.

Powdermaker, F. B., & Frank, J. D. (1948). Group psychotherapy with neurotics. *American Journal of Psychiatry, 105,* 449–455.

Powdermaker, F. B., & Frank, J. D. (1953). *Group psychotherapy: Studies in methodology of research and therapy.* Cambridge, MA: Harvard University Press.

Prochaska J., & DiClemente, C. C. (1983). Stages and processes of self-change in smoking: Toward an integrative model of change. *Journal of Consulting and Clinical Psychology, 40,* 432–440.

Prochaska, J., & Goldstein, M. G. (1991). Process of smoking cessation. Implications for clinicians. *Clinical Chest Medicine, 12,* 727–735.

Prochaska, J., & Norcross, J. (1994). *Systems of psychotherapy: A transtheoretical analysis* (3rd ed.). Pacific Grove, CA: Brooks/Cole.

Resick, P. A., & Schnicke, M. K. (1992). Cognitive processing therapy for sexual assault victims. *Journal of Consulting and Clinical Psychology, 60,* 748–756.

Rohren, C. L., Croghan, I. T., Hurt, R. D., Offord, K. P., Marusic, Z., & McClain, F. L. (1994). Predicting smoking cessation outcome in a medical center from stage of readiness: Contemplation versus action. *Preventive Medicine, 23,* 335–344.

Rollnick, S., Mason, P., & Butler, C. (1999). *Health behavior change: A guide for practitioners.* Edinburgh, Scotland: Churchill Livingstone.

Schnurr, P. P., Friedman, M. J., Lavori, P. W., & Hsieh, F. Y. (2001). Design of Department of Veterans Affairs cooperative study No. 420: Group treatment of posttraumatic stress disorder. *Controlled Clinical Trials, 22,* 74–88.

Schwartz, L. A. (1945). Group psychotherapy in the war neuroses. *American Journal of Psychiatry, 101,* 498–500.

Sipprelle, R. C. (1992). A vet center experience: Multievent trauma, delayed treatment type. In D. W. Foy (Ed.), *Treating PTSD: Cognitive-behavioral strategies.* New York: Guilford.

Smart, J. (2001). *Disability, society and the individual.* Gaithersburg, MD: Aspen.

Speilberger, C., Gorsuch, R., & Lushene, R. (1970). *The State-Trait Anxiety Inventory manual.* Palo Alto, CA: Consulting Psychologists Press.

Stewart, J. (1995). Reconstruction of the self: Life-span-oriented group psychotherapy. *Journal of Constructivist Psychology, 8,* 129–148.

Tunks, E., & Bellissimo, A. (1991). *Behavioral medicine: Concepts and procedures.* New York: Pergamon.

Verinis, J., & Taylor, J. (1994). Increasing alcoholic patients' aftercare attendance. *International Journal of the Addictions, 29,* 1487–1494.

Wadden, T. (1993). *The treatment of obesity: An overview.* In A. J. Stunkard & T. A. Wadden (Eds.) *Obesity: Theory and therapy* (2nd ed., pp. 197–217). New York: Raven.

Walker, J. I. (1983). A comparison of "rap" groups with traditional group therapy in the treatment of Vietnam combat veterans. *Group, 7,* 48–57.

Whitaker, D. S. (2001). *Using groups to help people* (2nd ed.). Philadelphia: Taylor & Francis.

Yalom, I. D. (1983). *Inpatient group psychotherapy.* New York: Basic Books.

Yalom, I. D. (1995). *The theory and practice of group psychotherapy* (4th ed.). New York: Basic Books.

Zaidi, L. (1994). Group treatment of adult male inpatients abused as children. *Journal of Traumatic Stress, 7,* 718–27.

24

GROUPS IN BEHAVIORAL
HEALTH AND MEDICAL SETTINGS

TIMOTHY R. ELLIOTT

University of Alabama at Birmingham

PATRICIA RIVERA

University of Alabama at Birmingham

EMILY TUCKER

University of Alabama at Birmingham

The use of therapeutic groups in behavioral health has attracted considerable attention for many years. Group approaches are used in health care settings because they are time- and cost-efficient (Spira, 1997). The flexibility of group formats can be used advantageously to address a wide array of concerns specific to a health condition or unique to a given population (Roback, 1984). Groups are often conducted in a variety of health care settings, including certain inpatient units, outpatient clinics, and community centers, schools, and churches. In most of these groups, participation is voluntary, but in some programs, groups are an integral part of the treatment program, and attendance may be expected (e.g., pain rehabilitation programs).

Specific group formats observed in health care settings include support, educational, psychoeducational, counseling, and task groups. In this chapter, we will define the salient, distinguishing features and the primary dynamics of these groups that may be particularly therapeutic. We will also discuss issues regarding the openness of the format to new members, time commitment, confidentiality issues, and role of the facilitator. We will also note important

Author's Note: This chapter was supported in part by the National Institute on Disability and Rehabilitation Research Grant #H133B980016A and by Grant #R49/CCR403641, USDHHS, Centers for Disease Control and Prevention, National Center for Injury Prevention and Control to the University of Alabama at Birmingham. Its contents are solely the responsibility of the authors and do not necessarily represent the official views of the funding agencies.

findings from the extant literature concerning each format.

THERAPEUTIC GROUP FACTORS AND BEHAVIORAL HEALTH

The therapeutic properties of groups are well suited to address the many issues that accompany health-related problems. Soon after the onset of a disabling condition or following the initial medical diagnosis, individuals typically want detailed information and may benefit from intensive discussions with professionals knowledgeable about the condition. It is often helpful to hear from others who have lived with the condition, learn how these persons handle various aspects of the condition, manage symptoms, solve problems they encounter, and prepare for certain events, procedures, or surgeries. Group contact may provide opportunities for people to learn of impending or associated difficulties that may be otherwise unanticipated, such as managing negative reactions or treatment from health care personnel, family members, and friends. They may also learn much about uncontrollable aspects of a particular condition or potential side effects of a medication. Observing others who have adjusted well or who live with conditions that may impose greater impairment and severity is another benefit gained from group participation. We have often observed people who have recently incurred a physical disability react positively to an individual who lives with the same condition and maintains an active lifestyle and exhibits a high degree of well-being.

Groups can effectively and efficiently provide participants with valuable and detailed information relevant to any health problem. The educational properties of a group may be the most rudimentary function of therapeutic group work. For that reason, psychoeducational groups also fit well in the behavioral health setting. These formats are used to teach participants specific information about a condition, its symptoms, and various ways to cope with a condition. For health care professionals, education may be construed in terms of facts and details about a condition and its management, but participants may find the shared life experiences conveyed by other members in the group helpful and enlightening.

In this manner, participants have an opportunity to learn the information presented by the facilitators, and they also have an opportunity to learn from other participants in the group as they share their experiences about coping with their health. Yalom (1995) stipulates that groups help members by instilling a sense of hope and optimism. In groups, participants can develop new patterns of interacting with others, imitate behavior modeled by others, and see themselves as part of a larger group of people (thus gaining greater perspective on their own personal situations). Groups also offer members opportunities to help and assist others. Participants often offer helpful suggestions to each other, and at times, these are based on their own personal experiences. Advice can range from tips on assertively interacting with an insensitive health care professional or family member to ideas about changes in diet that might be helpful in managing side effects of a medication or treatment.

Unfortunately, groups possess an equal capacity for harm, as these same dynamics can affect great distress (Forsyth & Elliott, 1999). The elements that offer potential for accurate information and social support and model adaptive behavior can be tainted by misinformation, negative interactions, and interpersonal rejection and model maladaptive, destructive behaviors. It is important that therapists carefully consider these issues when developing strategic group interventions for use in behavioral health. As we shall see, there are many situations in which education and peer interaction can effectively facilitate support groups. However, in other formats, it is imperative that a trained facilitator with clinical acumen and a firm grasp of factual information work within the group.

SPECIFIC FORMATS OF GROUPS

Support Groups

As a result of managed care and reduced health care expenditures, support groups have become increasingly popular in the United States. The 12-step approach, begun in 1935 with the founding of Alcoholics Anonymous, is one model that provides inexpensive and positive support to a specific population. More informal models of support exist for persons dealing with almost every health or psychosocial condition experienced. Goals such as problem solving, coping, education, and fellowship are typical.

One of the most obvious benefits of support group participation is the universal accessibility of such a treatment modality. Meetings that are consumer oriented and community based are often held in churches, schools, health care centers, or private homes. Meeting times and attendance vary, with national organizations such as the Alzheimer's Association or the American Cancer Society offering meetings at almost any time of the day in chapters in large urban areas. In addition, absence of fees makes support group participation one of the most cost-effective treatment options available. Finally, because support groups are typically open to the public, attendance is strictly voluntary and consumers are encouraged to participate in different groups to find one that is best suited for their individual needs. These principles hold true for "closed" meeting formats as well, with the only requirement being that the participant meet the diagnostic or conditional criteria of concern.

Yalom (1995) identified the therapeutic qualities of support groups. The installation of hope, the provision and exchange of information, the belief that one is not alone, and the giving and receiving of advice are factors contributing to the beneficial effects of support group participation. Because membership is typically open, the benefits of a support group may differ with length of membership. In one study of participants in a breast cancer support group, newer members valued the medical information they learned in the group; however, established members reported coping skills and a sense of community from the group as being most helpful (Stevens & Duttlinger, 1998). Participants who reported a sense of empowerment and affiliation with other participants experienced more benefits from a support group of persons with AIDS (Kates, 1998). Those individuals who reported having enough support did not attend the groups. This self-selection is a feature that works well in the support group tradition, as it assures that those in attendance have a desire to participate fully in the therapeutic experience.

Despite high degrees of consumer-reported satisfaction with support group attendance,

empirical evidence for their effects on well-being is mixed. In an attempt at identifying the mechanism of benefit in women with newly diagnosed breast cancer, Helgeson, Cohen, Schulz, and Yasko (2001) reported that women who lacked emotional support or reported negative support from their partners benefited from peer-led support groups. Alternatively, women who reported satisfaction with the emotional support from their partners at the beginning of their participation in a peer-led support group subsequently reported dissatisfaction with their partners over time. The authors concluded that peer-led support groups redefined the meaning of social support in these women such that they were no longer satisfied with their previous interactions. Other research has found that support groups conducted by trained facilitators had more beneficial effects on emotional adjustment and interpersonal support among depressed persons with HIV when compared with a cognitive-behavioral group (Kelly et al., 1993).

Educational Groups

The purpose of an educational group is to disseminate specific information to participants. Typically, a leader or coleaders will provide specific information to group members. The group leader may be a professional or paraprofessional employed by a medical institution, or a member of the community who has knowledge in the area of focus. Educational groups are often a part of interdisciplinary treatment programs (e.g., pain management), and in these situations, any team member may at times conduct group sessions (Johansson, Dahl, Jannert, Melin, & Andersson, 1998). This may include counselors, nurses, nutritionists, pharmacists, and occupational therapists. For example, in a treatment program for women with fibromyalgia, the group leader—a physical therapist—provided information about the disease, the role of stress in symptom management, coping skills, relaxation exercises, and problem-solving techniques (Burckhardt, Mannerkorpi, Hedenberg, & Bjelle, 1994).

Educational groups are commonly used for several reasons. First, in some settings, a health care professional can disseminate valuable medical information to several patients at once. Second, patients may benefit from contact with others who have experienced similar injuries or medical conditions. Third, family members may also observe, participate, and establish contact with other patients and caregivers.

Educational groups allow individuals to learn in a group environment, receive emotional support, and provide cost-effective means for addressing medical and related emotional concerns. Educational groups can take place in an institution such as a hospital, school, university, or a church. Commonly, educational seminars and group meetings are held to provide information to patients with specific illness, or they may be used as preventative measures promoting wellness and health care. Educational groups provide an opportunity for health care professionals to convey techniques and ideas such as stress management, coping skills, and health promotion (Spira, 1997). Evidence indicates that educational groups can effectively augment interdisciplinary treatment programs. Participants in an inpatient pain management program featuring group education sessions had significant improvements over time in activity levels, physical fitness, and occupational training and decreases in medication use, sick leave, and distress compared with patients who did not receive these group sessions (Johansson et al., 1998).

The specific structure of each educational group varies depending on the personality and competency of the group leader, the material used, and the content of information provided. Interest of group members, level of participation, and group composition are among factors that contribute to the unique definition and substance of every educational group (Benson, 2001). According to Benson, group leaders may choose whatever time limit they deem appropriate. In certain settings, such as a hospital, time constraints may be a consideration due to scheduling of various treatments, therapies, and appointments. In such a setting, the educational group may be limited in time and frequency of meetings. Typically, an educational group in a traditional rehabilitation facility or hospital extends to a maximum of 1 hour and may meet anywhere from weekly to daily. Group leaders and facilitators establish time and meeting standards that are suitable to the program and the institution in which they are developed.

Most educational groups are open in nature, with meetings lasting from one to many sessions (Spira, 1997). At times, educational groups may also be designed as "closed" to limit the number of group members. Childbirth preparation classes, for example, typically have a closed membership to limit the number of participants, and these groups also address a set number of topics in a sequential fashion. In other clinical situations, potential group members may even be screened depending upon the sensitivity of the material involved in the educational group. In groups designed to promote cautionary and safe-sex behaviors among persons at risk for HIV, it is often important to interview potential members before initiating the group, because confidentiality and respect for other participants are important issues. Most of the extant literature describes educational groups with adults, but there is also evidence that educational groups can be successfully conducted with children as young as 4 years old (e.g., teaching safety behaviors to young children; Wurtele, 1990).

Childbirth preparation courses, which were first developed in the 1940s, exemplify the basic tenets of educational groups. In these "classes," expectant parents learn detailed information about pregnancy and childbirth. Health maintenance, nutrition, labor and delivery, and instruction in relaxation and breathing techniques are typically discussed in these classes (Hart & Foster, 1997). Although the data concerning the relation of preparation courses to actual birth outcomes are inconsistent, there is evidence that beneficial experiences occur for many participants (e.g., less pain medication during labor, greater satisfaction with childbirth, increased sense of self-control; Hart & Foster, 1997).

In the educational group, self-disclosure is neither a necessity nor a requirement. As the level of self-disclosure in a group increases, concern for group adherence to confidentiality increases as well. Ideally, the focus of the group is on the exchange of educational information. Personal self-disclosure of group members may certainly complement the educational material; however, in some groups, members are not encouraged to divulge emotional reactions. Nevertheless, educational groups can have pronounced effects on personal adjustment.

Participation in educational groups had greater effects in reducing personal distress than a peer discussion group among women with breast cancer (Helgeson, Cohen, Schulz, & Yasko, 1999). In particular, women who reported more personal difficulties at the beginning of the educational group benefited more from the educational intervention than women with fewer difficulties. Furthermore, there may be times when educational groups are more suitable for participants than are psychoeducational or counseling groups. For example, participants with fibromyalgia in an education and discussion group had significant improvements in fear reduction and coping skills compared with others in a cognitive-behavioral group (Vlaeyen et al., 1996). It is possible that the education and discussion group was more strategic and direct in addressing participant needs than the counseling group.

Educational groups can incorporate cognitive-behavioral ideas to provide participants with helpful information about coping with certain aspects of a condition. For example, programs offering education and basic information about problem-solving principles have been developed for family caregivers of cancer patients in accessible sites within communities (e.g., churches; Bucher, Houts, Nezu, & Nezu, 1999).

Psychoeducational Groups

This format has much in common with the essential features of educational groups: Both share an emphasis on providing participants with accurate information about a specific topic. Both can provide opportunities for therapeutic interaction between participants. Goals of this type of group, much like behavioral objectives, are attainable, specific, and tailored to the needs of the members. Unlike educational groups—which function primarily to convey useful information to members—psychoeducational groups address psychological content, and leaders are sensitive to the potential effects of this content on members. Skill building is an important element of this group format.

Typically, these groups are structured in that they address a specific theme or topic; they usually have a closed membership and are time limited. They may be very brief (consisting of a single session lasting an hour or more) or extended over time (e.g., five sessions over several weeks). The format is ideal for increasing awareness and teaching skills in health promotion and prevention. Other topics often include interpersonal skills, coping skills, anger management, time management, and relaxation techniques. Participants should have a reasonable awareness and expectation of group goals upon entering the group; assessment may or may not be conducted, depending upon the theme and the intensity of the process.

Group content usually features some didactic presentation of information, but participants will also engage in guided therapeutic exercises to augment learning and heighten the therapeutic experience. These exercises may include activities such as imagery, role play, group tasks, homework assignments, relaxation techniques, physical exercises, and diaries. These elements were used successfully in a study of psychoeducational group effects among women with fibromyalgia (Keel, Bodoky, Gerhard, & Muller, 1998) and with caregivers of persons with dementia (Gallagher-Thompson, 1994). In sessions like these, group members have ample opportunity to discuss their experiences and feelings within the therapeutic milieu. Effective facilitators are knowledgeable about the topic, offer information, and possess considerable clinical skill in leading the group through exercises and subsequent process. However, the primary emphasis of the format is on the educational experience, requiring that exercises and interactions be relevant to the topic and conducive to the overall learning experience of the group.

Psychoeducational groups can be conducted in inpatient, outpatient, and community settings. This format can be effectively adapted to serve culturally diverse populations (e.g., in Spanish; Gallagher-Thompson, Arean, Rivera, & Thompson, 2001). Psychoeducational groups are popular with interdisciplinary teams, and groups often feature experts from different fields working as cofacilitators (e.g., a nutritionist with a counselor, a nurse with a psychologist) to ensure that detailed and complex information is provided to participants. In some cases, this interdisciplinary approach is highly desirable, as some health conditions require accurate information and extensive changes in everyday routine to maintain health, promote quality of life, and prevent further complications.

For example, to enhance adjustment among persons with Type I diabetes, counselors often work with nurse specialists and diabetes educators. This pairing facilitates the presentation of information about diabetes, its complications, and the ways to adhere to insulin guidelines, as well as promoting recommended nutritional and lifestyle changes that uphold glycemic control (Snoek, van der Ven, & Lubach, 1999). While many persons with diabetes have adequate information about their condition and its management, they do not make the recommended changes to their lifestyle or diet (Glasgow et al., 1999). Thus, it becomes necessary to train participants in the behavioral components of coping, problem solving, and stress management (including relaxation; Snoek et al., 1999). Groups that train members in coping skills relevant to their health condition were found to have beneficial effects in lowering distress, enhancing a sense of self-efficacy and decreasing the severity of problems encountered when compared with support groups (among cancer patients; Telch & Telch, 1986).

Psychoeducational groups are ideally suited for helping individuals acquire new skills pertinent to their conditions and situations. For example, structured group experiences can help older persons with osteoarthritis learn effective pain management skills, decrease pain behavior, and decrease their sense of impairment (Keefe et al., 1990). Persons with physical disabilities and other mobility impairments can learn assertiveness and other social skills in psychoeducational groups (Dunn, Van Horn, & Herman, 1981). Moreover, assertion skill training may enhance a participant's sense of meaning and positive acceptance following disability (Glueckauf & Quittner, 1992).

Individuals with chronic health conditions may be at risk for ongoing complications of distress due to the deteriorating aspects of the disease (e.g., multiple sclerosis) or the recurrent problems with psychosocial restrictions and mobility impairments (e.g., spinal cord injury). Psychoeducational groups can be very effective in enhancing the coping skills prerequisite for adjustment among persons with these conditions. These effects may be seen in improved coping skills and a heightened sense of well-being (Schwartz, 1999) and in decreasing feelings of depression and anxiety (King & Kennedy, 1999). Thus, there is evidence that psychoeducational groups—though designed to target specific issues and to train participants in specific domains—may have beneficial, higher-order effects on appraisal activities, and the acquisition of certain competencies may parallel effects on a person's sense of purpose, meaning, and well-being.

Cognitive-behavioral psychoeducational groups emphasize skill acquisition and behavior change and usually anticipate and address negative emotional reactions and counterarguments to therapeutic content. Furthermore, facilitators skilled in cognitive-behavioral techniques work to establish a warm, empathic therapeutic milieu so that members feel safe, respected, and heard. These are critical elements in any therapeutic encounter, and they are essential features in effective cognitive-behavioral interventions. In this group format, facilitators are able to anticipate and address participant reactions to information presented during the group. In some situations, participants may develop negative attitudes and harbor counterarguments to specific information presented in an educational group, and these reactions can thwart the beneficial effects of the group. For example, participants in a substance abuse treatment program reported many negative reactions and counterarguments during an educational group on HIV risk and precautionary behaviors, and these negative reactions were predictive of their disinclination to engage in precautionary behaviors (MacNair, Elliott, & Yoder, 1991). Psychoeducational groups guided by a cognitive-behavioral perspective should anticipate possible negative reactions to information presented during the group and address these issues in such a way that the group experience is enhanced.

Counseling Groups

By definition, these groups are more interpersonally oriented than other formats and require the skills of a facilitator extensively trained in psychological assessment and group counseling techniques. These groups rarely focus on educational content germane to a specific condition, although such a context is certainly relevant to members. This background information is a prerequisite to a group, and the focus is usually on the psychological and social issues that impede and complicate adjustment. Thus, these groups are problem centered, and prospective members are screened and evaluated to determine eligibility, commitment, and ability to appropriately contribute to the group process. Typically, these groups have a closed membership (although this may not be the case in certain inpatient settings) and may or may not be time limited.

The direction, goals, and process of the group will be dictated by the theoretical orientation of the facilitators. Some groups may have an *interpersonal* process approach, derived in part from psychoanalytic theory (Yalom, 1995). Similar techniques may be used to conduct groups with a more existential focus and may be more appropriate with individuals who have more personal resources and a shared diagnosis (e.g., terminal cancer) to facilitate group cohesion.

Counseling groups are sometimes preferred when therapists wish to help group members process emotional reactions or personality issues that may be apparent to the group. The group process allows for the exploration of different perspectives of the other participants and facilitates an objective awareness of abilities, deficits, and emotional reactions over time (Prigatano, 1986). One elegant study found that women with metastatic breast cancer in a psychotherapy group reported beneficial effects on traumatic stress and negative mood compared with women participating in a control group (Classen et al., 2001). Group counseling can also help participants prepare for specific health-related events. For example, pregnant women who had at least one risk factor for postpartum depression and who participated in a counseling group designed to address these issues were significantly less likely to develop postpartum depression than other at-risk women receiving standard medical treatment (Zlotnick, Johnson, Miller, Pearlstein, & Howard, 2001).

Groups embedded in cognitive-behavioral models have been popular in health care settings. These kinds of groups are attractive for several reasons. Cognitive-behavioral models provide testable explanations of behavior and behavioral change, so they can be easily studied and examined in correlational and outcome research. They provide clear directives for affecting change in individual and group interventions. It is also fairly easy to put therapeutic procedures for a cognitive-behavioral group into a standardized protocol that can be adapted for use across settings, with people who have various conditions and diagnoses. These features lend credibility to the supportive research, increasing generalizability and the likelihood of replication. Furthermore, there is evidence that cognitive-behavioral groups are cost-efficient (in promoting prevention behaviors among persons at risk for HIV; Holtgrave & Kelly, 1996).

Cognitive-behavioral therapy groups have been used to target specific behavioral styles that are associated with certain medical diagnoses, with beneficial effects that can be observed on related psychophysiological markers. For example, cognitive-behavioral groups reduced depressive symptomology among persons with Type 2 diabetes, with corresponding improvement in glycemic control (Lustman, Griffith, Freedland, Kissel, & Clouse, 1998). Similarly, this format is effective in reducing hostility among men with coronary heart disease, with corresponding reductions in diastolic blood pressure (Gidron, Davidson, & Bata, 1999).

Significant increases in health-promotive behaviors learned in cognitive-behavioral group interventions have been maintained up to 8 months later (safe-sex behaviors among gay men; Kelly, St. Lawrence, Hood, & Brasfield, 1989). Benefits from cognitive-behavioral group therapy for chronic low back pain have been found one year after participation (Turner & Clancy, 1988). This therapeutic approach to pain management appears to be more effective than treatment options emphasizing increased activity, awareness of pain behaviors, and communication training (Kerns, Turk, Holzman, & Rudy, 1986; Turner & Clancy, 1988). Nevertheless, it may be important for facilitators to carefully assess prospective members, because preexisting affective disturbance may impair effective participation in groups of this nature (Dworkin et al., 1994).

Cognitive-behavioral groups are often a treatment of choice for many psychological disorders that may be associated with medical problems incurred under traumatic circumstances. Exposure to traumatic events is associated with increased health complaints, decreased functioning, and greater psychiatric comorbidity. The elements of safety, commonality, and trust evoked in a group setting are ideal for trauma survivors. The telling of one's story to an audience of empathic peers facilitates the expression of emotions that allows for the refocusing on the present and current symptoms, rather than reliving past memories. Exposure therapy is a form of cognitive-behavioral therapy for the treatment of post-traumatic stress and is conducted in a group format. Through the careful use of repeated imagining of the traumatic experience within the controlled safety of the group, the survivor can learn to gain control of the overwhelming emotions associated with the event. In addition to the retelling of the trauma, group members are exposed to and taught coping skills such as cognitive restructuring, stress inoculation, relapse prevention, and social skills (Foy et al., 2001).

The results are mixed as to the value of incorporating family members into groups with participants. This is an important issue among persons with chronic conditions, because individual health may be directly associated with family interaction patterns and family member coping behavior. Individuals with recent spinal cord injury showed greater benefit from a cognitive-behavioral group when a family member participated than those who did not participate with a relative (Moore, 1989). Among persons with rheumatoid arthritis, initial differences found between groups with and without family members participating were not evident at a 2-month follow up (Radojevic, Nicassio, & Weisman, 1992). Other work found no significant effect for family member participation (Moore & Chaney, 1985). It is possible that the success of family member participation in a cognitive-behavioral group may hinge on the relevance of the group focus to their perspectives and experiences and the degree to which they are involved as full members in the group process.

Task Groups

Certain task groups can be used to obtain valuable information from health care professionals and consumers of health care services. Focus groups are used to collect information from participants who share certain characteristics of the population they represent. Information acquired from focus groups can help counselors and administrators develop and evaluate service delivery programs. Focus groups have several advantages over individual assessment procedures (Krueger, 1994; Morgan, 1997). Focus groups may enhance social facilitation processes for the group members and make shared experiences and perspectives salient among participants. The subsequent dialogue between group members might approximate interaction that could occur between these individuals in more naturalistic settings. Although some participants might feel uncomfortable in a group situation, the procedural rules of a structured approach serve to solicit new information from members in a way that individual interview methods do not (Krueger, 1994; Morgan, 1997). Moreover, the information gathered from a focus group is framed in the perspectives, and actual language, of individuals who have daily experience with these issues.

The Nominal Group Technique (NGT; Delbecq, Van de Ven, & Gustafson, 1975) is a way to conduct a structured focus group so that social facilitation processes on a given task may be optimized. The NGT is based on the presentation of a specific, relevant question to the group for their reactions and feedback. Questions posed to a focus group should be framed so participants can generate information that sufficiently conveys their understanding of the issue under consideration (Delbecq et al., 1975; for an alternative method for conducting focus groups in a health care setting, see Seal, Bogart, & Ehrhardt, 1998).

The depersonalized format of the NGT is ideal for promoting creative and meaningful disclosures about personally important issues that would less likely be expressed in other types of focus groups. The NGT essentially harnesses group facilitation processes in a manner that structures group interaction on specific tasks to achieve a specific goal. This structure actually serves to minimize group cohesion that results in uniformity in responses at the expense of broad and diverse reactions. Because information is generated impartially from each participant and weighted equally, the data obtained with the

NGT tend to provide a valid representation of the implicit views of the group. The NGT can be used to solicit information from consumers and providers of health care services in a manner that can have direct implications for service delivery and program development (for an excellent demonstration of the NGT for this purpose, see Pollard, 1994-1995).

Prior research illustrates the utility of structured focus groups in identifying the self-care issues of persons with chronic disease and their family members. Miller and colleagues (Miller, Shewchuk, Elliott, & Richards, 2000) found that persons living with diabetes were most concerned about developing complications in their extremities, managing their blood glucose levels at night, and getting adequate exercise. In contrast, family members expressed concerns about inheritability of the disease, personal diet, and specific worries about their loved one driving alone. Both groups shared concerns about managing progression of the disease. This information can be used to direct programs in assisting individuals to engage in daily self-care regimens, find suitable exercises to promote health, and manage their blood glucose levels.

Focus groups structured with the NGT have also highlighted important therapeutic issues between family members who provide ongoing caregiving tasks for a loved one who has a traumatic brain injury (Willer, Allen, Liss, & Zicht, 1991) or a spinal cord injury (Elliott & Shewchuk, 2002). Many of the concerns identified by these individuals are interpersonal issues, anxieties, and worries about self-care behaviors and regimens, mobility and independence, and management of symptoms. These are problems that may be best addressed by strategic group interventions.

SUMMARY AND IMPLICATIONS

When selecting an appropriate group format, counselors take into account the needs of the clientele and the best judgment of staff or treatment team at a particular clinic. In some cases, these perspectives may not be complementary. For example, many persons who incur spinal cord injuries (SCI) and other severe physical disabilities will eventually encounter problems adhering to complex self-care regimens, being assertive in awkward and tense social situations, and having access to accurate and sensitive information about sexual functioning. Most rehabilitation teams routinely conduct educational groups for persons with recent-onset SCI to address issues of coping, self-care, social skills, and sexuality.

Over the years, our psychology staff has documented that most participants with recent-onset SCI do not actively participate in many educational sessions during the inpatient rehabilitation program. In subsequent follow-up interviews, we have learned that many participants were preoccupied with other rehabilitation tasks, their personal discomfort, or other life stressors. Some have stated that they never received information about sexuality, while others have reported that the relevance of the content in these sessions was realized after they had encountered real-life situations. We have yet to find any association between group attendance and any salient outcome indicative of health and adjustment following discharge (e.g., life satisfaction, acceptance of disability, depression, pressure sore occurrence).

Groups are more effective when members have common goals for the group and when they have a clear and shared sense of how these goals will be attained (Higginbotham, West, & Forsyth, 1988, pp. 226-230). When these conditions are met, group cohesion is more likely to occur. In some health care settings, however, members may have little more in common than the health condition or medical diagnosis and thus may share few, if any, goals for the group experience. Thus, in an inpatient program for persons with recent-onset SCI, individuals who have a history of health-compromising behavior and a lack of appreciation for psychological issues may not be initially receptive or concerned about the array of social and personal issues they will face upon their return to the community (Craig & Hancock, 1994). Groups in which participants join on their own initiative and that have a stated purpose valued by the participants are more likely to be effective than groups in which members are expected to attend primarily because of a shared diagnosis and that have goals not shared by the participants.

In light of these observations, we recommend that counselors carefully assess the degree of congruence between the aims and scope of a group format and the needs of the clientele. Matching the format and content with consumer needs and expectations may result in a more beneficial group experience. We also believe that the timing of the intervention is essential in order to work with participants who are sufficiently motivated to learn new information and acquire new skills. Much of the information in an educational sequence may be more relevant after individuals have realized a personal need for it. This may occur at any time as persons live with a chronic health problem or face sudden changes in their health.

From our focus group work, we have learned that many community-residing individuals with chronic health problems want educational and support groups (Elliott & Shewchuk, 2002; Miller et al., 2000). Yet mobility restrictions, time constraints, and geographic distances limit access and success of support groups for persons with severe health problems and their family members. Some research suggests that telephone adaptations can be used to effectively develop support groups for family caregivers in rural areas (Brown et al., 1999). Other computer-based applications may also prove promising (e.g., online support groups).

Groups have encountered some degree of controversy in health care settings. One study reported that participation in group counseling was related to increased survival rates among women with metastatic breast cancer (Spiegel, Bloom, Kraemer, & Gottheil, 1989). Recent research has failed to replicate this finding (Cunningham et al., 1998; Goodwin et al., 2001). However, this work has found that group counseling participants experienced less distress and less pain than those who received standard care (Goodwin et al., 2001). Other data indicate that participation in group counseling may be related to improved basal endocrine and immune response values among women with early-stage breast cancer (van der Pompe et al., 2001). These functions are believed to be vital processes in the treatment and recovery of breast cancer.

Short-term group counseling has been effective in reducing physical symptoms and in reducing costs associated with services to patients with multiple health complaints (52% net savings in health care charges among patients with somatization disorder; Kashner, Rost, Cohen, Anderson, & Smith, 1995). This study also found that participants who attended more sessions had greater benefit. "Booster sessions" may be necessary to help participants who live with a chronic health condition (e.g., breast cancer; Hosaka et al., 2001) or who have difficulty maintaining health promoting behaviors (among gay and bisexual men; Roffman et al., 1998), as initial beneficial effects of group counseling may wane over time. There are also situations in which individual approaches may be preferred over group counseling: Depressed persons with multiple sclerosis (MS) seem to respond better to individual cognitive-behavior counseling than to group counseling, for example (Mohr, Boudewyn, Goodkin, Bostrom, & Epstein, 2001). The unique and degenerative symptoms of MS may be better addressed in individualized treatments. In all of these scenarios, a thorough knowledge of the clinical issues surrounding these conditions and expert assessment of individual needs of candidates will be essential in developing and offering appropriate group interventions in health care settings.

REFERENCES

Benson, J. F. (2001). *Working more creatively with groups.* (2nd ed.). New York: Routledge.

Brown, R., Pain, K., Berwald, C., Hirschi, P., Delehanty, R., & Miller, H. (1999). Distance education and caregiver support groups: Comparison of traditional and telephone groups. *Journal of Head Trauma Rehabilitation, 14,* 257-268.

Bucher, J. A., Houts, P. S., Nezu, C. M., & Nezu, A. M. (1999). Improving problem-solving skills of family caregivers through group education. *Journal of Psychosocial Oncology, 16*(3-4), 73-84.

Burckhardt, C. S., Mannerkorpi, K., Hedenberg, L., & Bjelle, A. (1994). A randomized, controlled clinical trial of education and physical training for women with fibromyalgia. *Journal of Rheumatology, 21,* 714-720.

Classen, C., Butler, L., Koopman, C., Miller, E., DiMiceli, S., Giese-Davis, J., Fobair, P., Carlson, R., Kraemer, H., & Spiegel, D. (2001). Supportive-expressive group therapy and distress with metastatic breast cancer. *Archives of General Psychiatry, 58,* 494-501.

Craig, A., & Hancock, K. (1994). Difficulties in implementing group cognitive behaviour therapy for spinal cord injury persons: A clinical discussion. *Australian Psychologist, 29*(2), 98-102.

Cunningham, A. J., Edmonds, C., Jenkins, G., Pollack, H., Lockwood, G., & Warr, D. (1998). A randomized controlled trial of the effects of group psychological therapy on survival in women with metastatic breast cancer. *Psycho-Oncology, 7,* 508-517.

Delbecq, A. L., Van de Ven, A. H., & Gustafson, D. H. (1975). *Group techniques for program planning: A guide to nominal group and delphi processes.* Glenview, IL: Scott, Foresman.

Dunn, M., Van Horn, E., & Herman, S. (1981). Social skills and spinal cord injury: A comparison of three training procedures. *Behavior Therapy, 12,* 153-164.

Dworkin, S. F., Turner, J. A., Wilson, L., Massoth, D., Whitney, C., Huggins, K., Burgess, J., Sommers, E., & Truelove, E. (1994). Brief group cognitive-behavioral intervention for temporomandibular disorders. *Pain, 59,* 175-187.

Elliott, T., & Shewchuk, R. (2002). Using the nominal group technique to identify the problems experienced by persons who live with severe physical disability. *Journal of Clinical Psychology in Medical Settings, 9,* 65-76.

Forsyth, D. R., & Elliott, T. (1999). Group dynamics and psychological well-being: The impact of groups on adjustment and dysfunction. In R. Kowalski & M. R. Leary (Eds.), *The social psychology of emotional and behavioral problems: Interfaces of social and clinical psychology* (pp. 339-361). Washington, DC: American Psychological Association.

Foy, D. W., Schnurr, P., Weiss, D., Wattenberg, M., Glynn, S., Marmar, C., & Gusman, F. (2001). Group psychotherapy for PTSD. In J. P. Wilson & M. J. Friedman (Eds.), *Treating psychological trauma and PTSD* (pp. 183-202). New York: Guilford.

Gallagher-Thompson, D. (1994). Clinical intervention strategies for distress caregivers: Rationale and development of psychoeducational approaches. In E. Light, G. Neiderehe, & B. Lebowitz (Eds.), *Stress effects on family caregivers of Alzheimer's patients: Research and interventions.* (pp. 260-279). New York: Springer.

Gallagher-Thompson, D., Arean, P., Rivera, P., & Thompson, L. (2001). A psychoeducational intervention to reduce stress in Hispanic caregivers. *Clinical Gerontologist, 23*(1-2), 17-32.

Gidron, Y., Davidson, K., & Bata, I. (1999). The short-term effects of a hostility-reduction intervention on male coronary heart disease patients. *Health Psychology, 18,* 416-420.

Glasgow, R. E., Fisher, E. B., Anderson, B., LaGreca, A., Marrero, D., Johnson, S. B., Rubin, R., & Cox, D. J. (1999). Behavioral science in diabetes. *Diabetes Care, 22,* 832-843.

Glueckauf, R. L., & Quittner, A. L. (1992). Assertiveness training for disabled adults in wheelchairs: Self-report, role-play, and activity pattern outcomes. *Journal of Consulting and Clinical Psychology, 60,* 419-425.

Goodwin, P. J., Leszcz, M., Ennis, M., Koopmans, J., Vincent, L., Guther, H., Drysdale, E., Hundleby, M., Chochinov, H., Navarro, M., Speca, M., & Hunter, J. (2001). The effect of group psychosocial support on survival in metastatic breast cancer. *New England Journal of Medicine, 345,* 1719-1726.

Hart, M. A., & Foster, S. N. (1997). Couples' attitudes toward childbirth participation: Relationship to evaluation of labor and delivery. *Journal of Perinatal and Neonatal Nursing, 11*(1), 10-26.

Helgeson, V., Cohen, S., Schulz, R., & Yasko, J. (1999). Education and peer discussion group interventions and adjustment to breast cancer. *Archives of General Psychiatry, 56,* 340-347.

Helgeson, V., Cohen, S., Schulz, R., & Yasko, J. (2001). Long-term effects of educational and peer discussion group interventions on adjustment to breast cancer. *Health Psychology, 20,* 387-392.

Higginbotham, H. N., West, S., & Forsyth, D. R. (1988). *Psychotherapy and behavior change.* New York: Pergamon.

Holtgrave, D., & Kelly, J. A. (1996). Preventing HIV/AIDS among high-risk urban women: The cost-effectiveness of a behavioral group intervention. *American Journal of Public Health, 86,* 1442-1445.

Hosaka, T., Sugiyama, Y., Hirai, K., Okuyama, T., Sugawara, Y., & Nakamura, Y. (2001). Effects of a modified group intervention with early-stage breast cancer patients. *General Hospital Psychiatry, 23,* 145-151.

Johansson, C., Dahl, J., Jannert, M., Melin, L., & Andersson, G. (1998). Effects of a cognitive-behavioral pain management program. *Behaviour Research and Therapy, 36,* 915-930.

Kashner, T. M., Rost, K., Cohen, B., Anderson, M., & Smith, G. (1995). Enhancing the health of somatization disorder patients: Effectiveness of short-term group therapy. *Psychosomatics, 36,* 462-470.

Kates, T. D. (1998). The use of support groups by families with members with AIDS. *Dissertation Abstracts International: Section B: The Sciences and Engineering, 58.*

Keefe, F., Caldwell, D., Williams, D., Gil, K., Mitchell, D., Robertson, C., Martinez, S., Nunley, J., Beckham, J., Crisson, J., & Helms, M. (1990). Pain coping skills training in the management of osteoarthritic knee pain: A comparative study. *Behavior Therapy, 21,* 49-62.

Keel, P. J., Bodoky, C., Gerhard, U., & Muller, W. (1998). Comparison of integrated group therapy and group relaxation training for fibromyalgia. *Clinical Journal of Pain, 14,* 232-238.

Kelly, J. A., Murphy, D. A., Bahr, G., Kalichman, S., Morgan, M., Stevenson, L., Koob, J., Brasfield, T., & Bernstein, B. (1993). Outcome of cognitive-behavioral and support group brief therapies for depressed, HIV-infected persons. *American Journal of Psychiatry, 150,* 1679-1686.

Kelly, J. A., St. Lawrence, J. S., Hood, H., & Brasfield, T. (1989). Behavioral intervention to reduce AIDS risk activities. *Journal of Consulting and Clinical Psychology, 57,* 60-67.

Kerns, R. D., Turk, D., Holzman, A., & Rudy, T. (1986). Comparison of cognitive-behavioral and behavioral approaches to the outpatient treatment of chronic pain. *Clinical Journal of Pain, 1,* 195-203.

King, C., & Kennedy, P. (1999). Coping effectiveness training for people with spinal cord injury: Preliminary results of a controlled trial. *British Journal of Clinical Psychology, 38,* 5-14.

Krueger, R. A. (1994). *Focus groups: A practical guide for applied research* (2nd ed.). Thousand Oaks, CA: Sage.

Lustman, P., Griffith, L., Freedland, K., Kissel, S., & Clouse, R. (1998). Cognitive behavior therapy for depression in type 2 diabetes mellitus. *Annals of Internal Medicine, 129,* 613-621.

MacNair, R. R., Elliott, T., & Yoder, B. (1991). AIDS prevention groups as persuasive appeals: Effects on attitudes about precautionary behaviors among persons in substance abuse treatment. *Small Group Research, 22,* 301-319.

Miller, D., Shewchuk, R., Elliott, T., & Richards. J. S. (2000). Nominal group technique: A process for identifying diabetes self-care issues among patients and caregivers. *The Diabetes Educator, 26,* 305-314.

Mohr, D. C., Boudewyn, A., Goodkin, D., Bostrom, A., & Epstein, L. (2001). Comparative outcomes for individual cognitive-behavioral therapy, supportive-expressive group psychotherapy, and sertraline for the treatment of depression in multiple sclerosis. *Journal of Consulting and Clinical Psychology, 69,* 942-949.

Moore, J. E., & Chaney, E. F. (1985). Outpatient group treatment of chronic pain: Effects of spouse involvement. *Journal of Consulting and Clinical Psychology, 53,* 326-339.

Moore, L. I. (1989). *Behavioral changes in male spinal cord injured following two types of psychosocial rehabilitation experience.* Unpublished doctoral dissertation, St. Louis University.

Morgan, D. L. (1997). Focus groups as qualitative research. In *Sage University series on qualitative research,* Vol. 16. Newbury Park, CA: Sage.

Pollard, R. Q. Jr. (1994-1995). Mental health services and the deaf population: A regional consensus planning approach [Special issue]. *Journal of the American Deafness and Rehabilitation Association, 28*(3), 1-47.

Prigatano, G. P. (1986). Psychotherapy after brain injury. In G. P. Prigatano, D. J. Fordyce, H. K. Zeiner, J. Roeche, M. Pepping, & B. Woods (Eds.), *Neuropsychological rehabilitation after brain injury* (pp. 29-50). Baltimore, MD: Johns Hopkins University.

Radojevic, V., Nicassio, P., & Weisman, M. (1992). Behavioral intervention with and without family support for rheumatoid arthritis. *Behavior Therapy, 23,* 13-30.

Roback, H. (1984). *Helping patients and their families cope with medical problems.* San Francisco: Jossey-Bass.

Roffman, R. A., Stephens, R. S., Curtin, L., Gordon, J., Craver, J., Stern, M., Beadnell, B., & Downey, L. (1998). Relapse prevention as an intervention model for HIV risk reduction in gay and bisexual men. *AIDS Education and Prevention, 10,* 1-18.

Schwartz, C. E. (1999). Teaching coping skills enhances quality of life more than peer support:

Results of a randomized trial with multiple sclerosis patients. *Health Psychology, 18,* 211-220.

Seal, D. W., Bogart, L. M., & Ehrhardt, A. A. (1998). Small group dynamics: The utility of focus group discussions as a research method. *Group Dynamics: Theory, Research, and Practice, 2,* 253-266.

Snoek, F. J., van der Ven, C. W., & Lubach, C. (1999). Cognitive behavioral group training for poorly controlled type I diabetes patients: A psychoeducational approach. *Diabetes Spectrum, 12,* 147-157.

Spiegel, D., Bloom, J. R., Kraemer, H., & Gottheil, E. (1989, November 18). Effect of psychosocial treatment on survival of patients with metastatic breast cancer. *Lancet, 2,* 1209-1210.

Spira, J. L. (1997). *Group therapy for medically ill patients.* New York: Guilford.

Stevens, M. J., & Duttlinger, J. (1998). Correlates of participation in a breast cancer support group. *Journal of Psychosomatic Research, 45,* 263-275.

Telch, C. F., & Telch, M. (1986). Group coping skills instruction and supportive group therapy for cancer patients: A comparison of strategies. *Journal of Consulting and Clinical Psychology, 54,* 802-808.

Turner, J. A., & Clancy, S. (1988). Comparison of operant behavioral and cognitive-behavioral group treatment for chronic low back pain. *Journal of Consulting and Clinical Psychology, 56,* 261-266.

van der Pompe, G., Antoni, M., Duivenvoorden, H., de Graff, A., Simonis, R., van der Vegt, S., & Heijnen, C. (2001). An exploratory study into the effect of group psychotherapy on cardiovascular and immunoreactivity to acute stress in breast cancer patients. *Psychotherapy and Psychosomatics, 70,* 307-318.

Vlaeyen, J. W. S., Teeken-Gruben, N., Goosens, M., Rutten-van Molken, M., Pelt, R., van Eek, H., & Heuts, P. (1996). Cognitive-educational treatment of fibromyalgia: A randomized clinical trial. I. Clinical effects. *Journal of Rheumatology, 23,* 1237-1245.

Willer, B. S., Allen, K., Liss, M., & Zicht, M. (1991). Problems and coping strategies of individuals with traumatic brain injury and their spouses. *Archives of Physical Medicine and Rehabilitation, 72,* 460-464.

Wurtele, S. K. (1990). Teaching personal safety skills to four-year-old children: A behavioral approach. *Behavior Therapy, 21,* 25-32.

Yalom, I. (1995). *The theory and practice of group psychotherapy* (4th ed.). New York: Basic Books.

Zlotnick, C., Johnson, S., Miller, I., Pearlstein, T., & Howard, M. (2001). Postpartum depression in women receiving public assistance: Pilot study of an interpersonal therapy-oriented group intervention. *American Journal of Psychiatry, 158,* 638-640.

25

THE USE OF GROUPS IN INPATIENT FACILITIES

Needs, Focus, Successes, and Remaining Dilemmas

DENISE EMER

Daemen College

Since the early 1980s, a plethora of articles has appeared regarding the use of groups with psychiatric inpatient populations. Interest in inpatient groups initially followed a shift in hospital care toward a focus on the acquisition of living skills, problem-solving techniques, coping mechanisms for daily existence, and reliance on social support systems for therapeutic success rather than on psychiatrists alone (Zimpfer, 1987). Although inpatient groups are cost-efficient, many practitioners are concerned about their efficacy. The large turnover of patients and staff makes only short-term groups possible, with some patients attending a maximum of one or two meetings (Bradlee, 1984; Clarke, Adamoski, & Joyce, 1998; White, 1987; Yalom, 1983). Actively psychotic and involuntary patients dealing with acute crises are placed in the same groups as voluntary patients with clearer cognitions about the self (Bradlee, 1984; White, 1987; Yalom, 1983). Functioning level across patients differs considerably, leading to significant differences in the motivation and self-reflection of group participants (Bradlee, 1984; Clarke et al., 1998; White, 1987; Yalom, 1983). Patients with different diagnoses are frequently placed within the same treatment group (Bradlee, 1984; White, 1987; Yalom, 1983). Staff members serve in numerous roles, causing interference with their effectiveness as group leaders (Bradlee, 1984; White, 1987; Yalom, 1983). Therapists have little time or authority to prepare and screen clients (Yalom, 1983). Clients are often confused by diverse group formats across sessions and ward groups (e.g., therapeutic vs. psychoeducational). The dynamics of the ward often interact with, and affect the dynamics of, any treatment groups being conducted (Bradlee, 1984; Klein & Kugel, 1981; White, 1987). In addition, "extra group contacts" (White, 1987) between patients, and patients and staff, can interfere with group success because the boundaries of the group are violated and group issues may be processed in inappropriate ways on the ward.

Practitioners of group work caution that inpatient groups must incorporate systems theory to evaluate the usefulness and efficacy of particular groups. The danger in an inpatient setting is that groups will serve nontherapeutic functions, such as occupying or distracting clients and generating additional revenue for other hospital functions (Satterley, 1995; White, 1987). When groups form to meet nontherapeutic needs, they are doomed to fail. Group leaders are often not adequately prepared or have little authority for making decisions about group composition and protocol. Leaders often rotate, which destroys group cohesion and progress. Resources needed to promote group efficacy are often not allocated to the group (e.g., adequate support for staff to prepare patients, encourage attendance, and protect group boundaries; White, 1987).

Despite concerns raised by practitioners, groups became a frequently practiced form of therapy within hospital settings in the 1980s, often serving as the most consistently used medium for therapeutic change ("New Model Proposed," 1982; Satterley, 1995). Inpatient group leaders borrowed from theories of outpatient group therapy. However, as Satterley (1995) noted, the inpatient group requires its own theoretical framework. The remainder of this chapter will review models of inpatient groups. In addition, the ways in which psychotherapeutic groups and psychoeducational groups are being used in current inpatient settings are discussed. Suggestions for further research regarding the use of inpatient groups and potential new uses of inpatient groups are provided.

INPATIENT GROUP MODELS: REVIEW AND CRITIQUE

Yalom's Model

Yalom (1983) provided the most comprehensive adaptation of traditional group therapy to the inpatient setting. Yalom suggested that group leaders treat the inpatient setting as a unique entity rather than transferring goals from outpatient groups. For example, engaging patients in the process of therapy is a central goal for inpatient groups in Yalom's model;

this engagement must involve interpersonal interaction. Inpatients can learn significant information about themselves and how they relate to others via group interaction. For example, this author once encountered a young woman diagnosed with borderline personality disorder and major depression who had a pervasive mistrust of individuals in her life, stemming primarily from her perception that her mother had abandoned her as a young child. In group sessions, this mistrust became evident in the young woman's interactions with other group members; she rejected them before they could do the same to her and remained extremely guarded in sharing herself with members of the group. Yalom's observations of various inpatient groups that existed in the 1980s suggested that none of the groups had an interactional focus. None of the groups worked in the here and now, and none of the groups promoted exchanges between members that could be used by patients to understand how they related to other people or how to generalize what was learned about the self to other experiences.

Yalom (1983) suggested that a major goal of an inpatient group should be to introduce patients to the potential benefit of therapy so that they will continue it after they are discharged. Among the group experiences that might help patients to realize the usefulness of therapy are (a) talking (because it provides immediate catharsis and initiates the change process), (b) interpersonal "problem spotting" (becoming aware of one's deficits in relating to others and maladaptive interpersonal behavior), and (c) the alleviation of the anxiety associated with the process of hospitalization (this makes patients more comfortable overall, which in turn allows them to participate more effectively in their own therapy). Yalom rejects the idea that inpatient groups should be used to solve problems or reduce the symptoms associated with severe and persistent mental illness. Rather, the inpatient group functions to make the patient aware of the self and how the self interacts with others, identify problems for further therapeutic investigation, and introduce the concept that therapy can be helpful in achieving a more functional state of living (see also White, 1987). A critical component of Yalom's model is that inpatient groups retain a "here-and-now" focus, that is, that each group session accomplishes the overall goals of the group and that the focus remain on the events of the immediate therapy session rather than on patients' life problems that exist outside the group. Yalom's model is based, first, on the assumption that psychopathology is at least to some degree interpersonally based, and second, that each patient's individual pathology will be revealed in his or her interactions within the group setting (Yalom, 1983).

Miller and Matthews (1988) conducted an inpatient group therapy intervention based on Yalom's suggestions. Prior to the group, patients underwent preparation experiences to ensure that they understood the purpose and goals of the group. Although Yalom recommends that the group be held daily, Miller and Matthews held the group twice weekly, given constraints on staff time and availability. Group sessions were structured as follows: (a) *pregroup therapist discussion* (15 minutes during which group leaders shared information, such as important events on the ward, issues concerning specific patients, and the warm-up exercises for group); (b) *introduction for new patients/warm-up* (10 minutes during which therapists restated the goals of the group for new members, emphasized the "here-and-now" focus, and outlined the structure and boundaries of the session; warm-up exercises included activities to build trust, reduce threat, and increase comfortableness); (c) *formulation of personal agendas and "work-on" items* (45 minutes during which patients selected a topic they each wanted to work on during the session, such as feeling closer to others; established "work-on" items that would bring the individual closer to that goal, such as shaking hands with each group member or seeking positive feedback from other group members; and carried out relevant tasks after they enumerated agenda items); (d) *summary and evaluation from group members and leaders* (5 minutes during which patients discussed whether or not they had completed their agenda items and positive and negative feedback were given about the group session as a whole); and (e) *postgroup therapist write-up and evaluation* (10 minutes during which therapists noted the themes and events that had occurred for individuals in the group and difficulties that needed to be addressed by leaders'

supervisors). Although the success of the group was not formally evaluated, feedback from group members and ward staff suggested that the group made a positive impact on participants, particularly in the area of social functioning (Miller & Matthews, 1988).

The Froberg and Slife Model

Although Yalom's model provides a needed framework for conducting inpatient group therapy, there are some potential difficulties with implementing it (see Froberg & Slife, 1987). Yalom suggested that a minimum of 75 to 90 minutes per session is necessary to meet the goals of the inpatient group. However, a session of this length might conflict with other scheduled activities that are deemed critical and would also be less possible for lower functioning patients. Furthermore, Yalom's model requires the processing of interpersonal experiences. However, patients routinely participate in various groups throughout the day that promote a more receptive attitude and might be confused by these "conceptual shifts" (Froberg & Slife, 1987). For example, this author has led groups for psychiatric inpatients who within the same day participated in interactive discussion groups, "lecture-type" psychoeducational groups, and groups in which they were expected to communicate with the leader, but not with one another. Finally, as Froberg and Slife noted, the "here-and-now" focus of Yalom's group might be undermined by the reality that in many inpatient settings, staff conducting the group do not have a full understanding of each group member's current interpersonal functioning. Froberg and Slife also pointed out that many patients might resist participation because they want to talk about past and current problems that brought them to the inpatient setting, problems that in a "here-and-now" focus are not addressed. Furthermore, patients seem to have difficulty engaging in the interpersonal paradigm; Slife, Froberg, Sasscer-Burgos, Barron, and Ellington (1986) found that inpatients were unable to translate their problems into interpersonal terms and were even threatened by the idea that more general problems relating to others were the sources of their particular dysfunctions.

Patients are not the only ones who resist the group format; therapists also resist because some believe that Yalom's approach does not address patients' most critical problems (Froberg & Slife, 1987). This belief is often combined with the therapist's inability to connect the interactional experience with the patient's individual problems (Froberg & Slife, 1987). Froberg and Slife also noted that patients have little understanding of the role of other group members and tend to treat the group leader as the individual toward whom they should direct their discussion. Finally, many patients, especially the lower-functioning patients, seem to lack the self-awareness and conceptual sophistication required to meaningfully process the importance of the interpersonal interaction; in Slife et al.'s (1986) research, patients parroted back the content of the interactions rather than the implications of the experiences. Delusional thinking might also prevent actively psychotic individuals within the group from processing the importance of interactions.

Froberg and Slife (1987) presented a modification of Yalom's model that involves (a) framing the agenda of the group in terms of interpersonal problems that have salient relevance to all group members; (b) continually pointing out to group members the differences between other groups they may be participating in (didactic groups) and the interpersonal group (process group); (c) planned, consistent intertherapist communication; (d) providing concrete, detailed examples from prior groups to orient patients to the focus and purpose of an interactional group and to decrease feelings of anxiety or perceived threat; (e) frequent reminders that the therapist is not the dispenser of truth and that his or her purpose is to help patients to help each other; (f) encouraging patients with lower functioning levels to set agendas that focus on improving interpersonal processing skills; and (g) teaching patients to recognize signals of emotional experience in themselves and others. Froberg and Slife recommend that therapist resistance be dealt with by providing therapists with training for using inpatient group therapy models, allowing staff to experience the power of "here-and-now" groups for themselves by acting as participants, and making examination and tracking of patients' interactional patterns a more regular part of patient assessment.

Problems With Froberg and Slife's Model and a Look at Additional Group Structures

Satterley (1995) suggested that Froberg and Slife's approach has a number of limitations. The main problem is that the model does not challenge Yalom's unrealistic assumption that the theoretical framework of outpatient models can be modified for use in inpatient settings (Satterley, 1995). One potential alternative to both Yalom's and Froberg and Slife's models is Sautter, Heaney, and O'Neill's (1991) rational "problem-solving" model. Sautter et al.'s model is composed of five stages (Satterley, 1995; Sautter et. al., 1991): (a) *problem discovery* (patient figures out what is dysfunctional in his or her attempts to deal with life problems); (b) *problem identification* (patient seeks to understand how dysfunctional behaviors lead to problems); (c) *alternative solutions* (patient tries to find new behaviors that will lead to functional living rather than problems); (d) *decision* (patient determines which of the alternative behaviors to select); and (e) *experience* (patient tries out the chosen behavior and decides whether it is the best alternative). Although this model is conceptually less complex than its counterparts and has the potential to change behavior in a relatively short time period, it does not take into account the reality that many inpatients are in acute phases of their illnesses and therefore are not capable of using a rational approach. Furthermore, the complexity of problems that require solutions will differ across patients; Sautter et al.'s model seems best suited to problems of minor complexity (e.g., finding more appropriate ways to ask another person if you can change the television channel on the ward television) but less useful for complex problems (e.g., a borderline personality patient who routinely self-mutilates).

Maxmen (1984) suggested that Yalom's "here-and-now" focus could be retained in an inpatient group setting if broad-ranging, concrete therapeutic goals specific to each patient were included. These goals should be "specific, achievable, and relate to life after discharge"

(White, 1987, p. 425). As White noted, the group should be a place where a patient can practice new behaviors with other members, hear how they were affected by something said or done by the patient, and observe the interactions of other group members to discern effective and ineffective problem-solving strategies. If the goal of the patient is "learning how to have a conversation," the patient could try different methods of initiating conversations with various group members, observe conversations across group members, and discuss what was difficult about initiating conversations with various group members (White, 1987). Since the length of the group in inpatient settings is relatively short, White (1987) suggested that the leader take on the responsibility of fulfilling some functions for the group, such as introducing new members, helping patients to see commonalties, and providing support. Leaders must also provide significant structure because some group patients may be disorganized in their thinking, withdrawn, or regressed (Bradlee, 1984; White, 1987). The inpatient group leader must clearly establish a reality orientation, set clear rules for the prevention of disruptive behaviors, and discourage the building of anxiety and/or frustration by limiting "silent periods" within the session. The leader must also be clear about the purpose of a particular group and flexible enough to use different modalities when necessary, such as active teaching, role play, and facilitating (Erickson, 1981). Since the group serves primarily a supportive function and serves to help patients practice behaviors they should continue after discharge, the leader must be a continual model of appropriate social behavior (Clarke et al., 1998; Maves & Schulz, 1985; White, 1987). In addition, the group leader should model more "authentic" communication, including candor, self-disclosure, appropriate use of parallel conversation, and paraphrasing (Pam & Kemker, 1993). Given the potential for high levels of leader burnout in inpatient groups, White (1987) recommended that the inpatient group use coleaders and peer group supervision.

Some practitioners have combined Yalom's suggestions with Maxmen's model for inpatient educational groups to yield various levels of groups for use in the inpatient setting. Griffin-Shelly

and Trachtenberg (1985) presented a model using three group types in a short-term inpatient setting: a low-level group (focus on concrete, specific, "here-and-now-oriented" material; main purpose is to provide opportunities for patient interaction with others); a medium-level group (interactional in nature, less structured, goals more abstract; discussions could include feelings about past events); and a high-level group (modeled on Yalom's approach, Gestalt oriented). The medium- and high-level groups provided opportunities for sharing and feedback, with responsibility resting with clients rather than on the group leader. Building on Maxmen's inpatient educative groups, Griffin-Shelley and Trachtenberg included groups at each of the three levels that focused on interpersonal skills, life skills, and creative expression (see also Griffin-Shelley & Wendel, 1988).

PSYCHOTHERAPEUTIC AND PSYCHOEDUCATIONAL GROUPS: SOME ILLUSTRATIVE EXAMPLES OF THEIR USE IN INPATIENT SETTINGS AND ASSOCIATED EVALUATIVE RESEARCH

Psychotherapy Groups

Leszcz, Yalom, and Norden (1985) found that inpatients consistently reported group psychotherapy to be among the most useful treatments they received. In most inpatient facilities today, group psychotherapy is viewed as an important addition to psychopharmacotherapy (Pollack, 1995b). Currently, psychotherapy groups are being used successfully in inpatient settings for patients with various diagnoses; the structure of these groups fall out of a number of different theoretical orientations, including cognitive, psychoanalytic, and behavioral approaches to the understanding and treatment of mental disorders.

Patients suffering from bipolar disorder often experience significant interpersonal disruption. Using a modification of Yalom's interactional model for higher-level inpatient therapy groups, Pollack (1990) established an interactional group for people with mood swings. Similar to the format used by Miller and Matthews, the interactional group involved 5 minutes of patient preparation for the group, an agenda go-around, the creation of agendas by group members, and therapist and patient discussion of the session. As suggested by Yalom, the single-session framework was followed. The purpose of Pollack's group was "to accomplish the goals of interpersonal learning, share information about bipolar disorder and associated treatment and medications, model the recovery process, and problem-solve in a supportive environment" (Pollack, 1990, p. 19). Pollack found that three dominant therapeutic goals emerged from the weekly sessions: information sharing, coping with the disorder, and improving interpersonal relationships. Although Pollack reported favorable outcomes, formal measures of the group's effectiveness were not taken. However, Pollack (1995a) reported that the therapeutic factors found to be most personally important to group participants were guidance, universality, and self-understanding; the core concepts that emerged were understanding bipolar disorder, relating to others, managing daily life, relating to self, and living in society. Furthermore, group patients reported that the groups were very helpful or somewhat helpful; no participant reported feeling that the group was harmful in any way.

Pollack's continued use of the interactional model, along with outcome research, formed the basis for a new model, which is based upon three factors (Pollack, 1995b): (a) the theme-centered interactional model (an experiential group format that combines psychoeducational, psychotherapeutic, and group dynamics); (b) group psychotherapeutic techniques tailored to inpatients with bipolar disorder; and (c) informational needs and activities of patients, as derived from research on the ward in which the model was being instantiated. In other words, the model includes opportunities for patients to get information they desire about their illness or about life activities that they need to manage as part of living with their illness (e.g., symptom information, information about what triggers relapse, information about the impact of medication on sexual experience). The central theme in this model is the *self-management* of bipolar disorder (Pollack, 1995b). The format of the self-management group includes preparation/orientation to the group, an introduction phase

for group members, a review and discussion of group rules, presentation of material relevant to group goals by the therapist, a group discussion, and discussion about the session by the patients and the therapist. The group leader maintains balance between the individual, group, and theme (Pollack, 1995b). Group members are provided with brief readings about their illness and complete assignments that engage them in thinking about why it is important to learn about their disorder and how to manage it. Pollack (1995b) reported that patient satisfaction with the self-management group was high and suggested that it might be a better approach than the original interactional group, because the themes that provide the structure of the self-management group were derived from research on the specific needs of the population being targeted by the group: inpatients suffering from bipolar disorder (for the specific informational needs identified by patients hospitalized for bipolar disorder, see Pollack, 1995a, 1996).

Pollack also discussed the use of group psychotherapy in inpatient settings for dealing with patients' problem-solving skill deficits. Pollack (1991) presented two problem-solving therapy groups based on cognitive-behavioral theory for use with both low-level and high-level patients (Yalom, 1983). The *problem-solving group* (PSG) was designed to allow patients functioning at a lower level to learn and apply basic problem-solving skills in their lives, such as defining a problem, thinking of alternatives, making a decision and a plan to act, taking a first step toward acting on the alternative, and evaluating the success and modifying accordingly. The problems presented by participating members were practical or interpersonal. Patients in the PSG group were generally psychotic, severely regressed, delusional, and hallucinatory. The *interpersonal problem-solving group* (IPSG) was primarily for patients functioning at a higher level and was designed to help patients apply problem-solving skills to specific relationship difficulties and recognize their roles in responses from people with whom they interact. Patients in the IPSG group were encouraged to identify a problem, clarify the nature of the problem, come up with alternatives or options, discuss how realistic the options were and what possible consequences could be, select the best option and role-play it, and give themselves a homework assignment based on the options. The problems presented in the sessions were relationship problems being experienced by members. Patients in the IPSG were not actively psychotic and were able to sustain focused attention and acknowledge psychological distress.

Following Yalom's suggestion for inpatient psychotherapy groups (Yalom, 1983), a single-session framework was used in both group types. In both groups, there was significant member interaction. For example (Pollack, 1991), after a group member presented a problem to be solved, alternatives for dealing with the problem were generated by group members and listed on a chalkboard. After members generated lists of alternatives, the patient was told it was up to him to take the first step; other group members were told to do the same within the next 48 hours for the problem they identified (low-functioning group). In the high-functioning group, the member who presented his problem chose the best alternative generated by the group, and then group members role-played the option. The member whose problem was discussed was told to assign himself a homework assignment based on the role play. Pollack noted that the successful implementation of these groups requires that the group leader be capable of many interventions, including teaching the problem-solving method didactically and experientially, helping patients generate solutions to problems, helping patients evaluate alternatives, addressing patients' cognitions and statements about themselves and their solutions, helping patients challenge false beliefs, providing information, providing positive reinforcement, and assigning homework. Pollack cautioned that the use of this model in the inpatient setting is not without potential problems, such as resistance, arguments between group members, and ridicule of members by other group members.

Groups for Borderline Personality Disorder

Inpatient group psychotherapy has been used successfully with individuals suffering from borderline personality disorder (BPD). Individuals suffering from BPD make up between 10% and 15% of inpatient psychiatric admissions (Springer & Silk, 1996) and experience considerable interpersonal difficulties often resulting in self-destructive behaviors. Some practitioners argue that finding an effective form of group therapy for inpatients suffering from BPD is critical because they may have difficulty with individual psychotherapy (Luboshitsky & Sachs, 1996). As noted by Springer and Silk, inpatient group therapy for BPD sufferers retains a "here-and-now" focus. However, groups with BPD patients concentrate on building ego strength by processing unconscious material that often causes the patient to internalize rather than externalize anger (Kibel, 1978, 1981; see also Kernberg 1975, 1984). In Kibel's approach, inpatients with BPD are encouraged to merge separate images of the self through the support of group members; patients are encouraged to express anger to group members (Springer & Silk, 1996). The group promotes ego strength and reinforces "'good' self-images" by encouraging group members to express shared conflicts (Springer & Silk, 1996).

Unfortunately, few studies specifically examine the effectiveness of inpatient psychotherapy groups for use with persons suffering from BPD. It is difficult to evaluate the handful of studies that have been done because (a) patients with various disorders were lumped together in the analyses, (b) group leaders were inexperienced either with group therapy in general or with the theoretical orientation upon which the therapeutic group was based, and (c) qualitatively different dependent variables were measured across studies. Studies conducted with patients suffering from BPD that were designed to determine which curative factors were believed by patients to be most helpful suggested that self-understanding and altruism were ranked highest (Macaskill, 1982). Macaskill suggested that one benefit of the inpatient group is that it provides opportunities for altruistic behavior among patients suffering from BPD (Springer & Silk, 1996), which could then lead to better interpersonal relationships.

In a comparison of three inpatient group structures, Luboshitsky and Sacks (1996) found that some models are more beneficial than others for enhancing self-concept, exploring disturbed interpersonal relationships, and reducing the anxiety of inpatients with BPD. Specifically, groups that used either "experiencing" (focus is on learning and application of what is being learned through practice; members are encouraged to express feelings and thoughts; members receive feedback without explanation/ clarification) or "process illumination" (focus is on the development of insight to increase self-understanding; free interactions and spontaneous expression of feelings are encouraged) contributed more to patients' self-understanding, catharsis, and interpersonal relationship success than did models that combine the two across different group phases. These findings are consonant with Yalom (1983), wherein it is suggested that inpatient psychotherapy groups require uniformity and consistency. Luboshitsky and Sachs note that uniformity and consistency might be especially important with patients who suffer from BPD, because they tend to become disorganized when under stress, which could be caused by a group setting in which processes change rapidly and require the patient to adapt to changes. Luboshitsky and Sachs suggest that perhaps group formats based upon the experiencing model, such as occupational, dance, and art therapy, could be used in inpatient settings in place of, or in addition to, classical psychotherapy groups.

One promising form of group therapy for inpatients suffering from BPD is *dialectical behavior therapy* (DBT) (Linehan, 1987a, 1987b, 1987c, 1993). The major assumption behind DBT is that people suffering from BPD cannot establish a unified self because they mentally represent the people in their lives in dichotomies. The distortions produced by the nondialectical, rigid thinking patterns of the person suffering from BPD results in overwhelming stress, which is dealt with through nonproductive, self-destructive coping behaviors, such as self-mutilation. The format of the DBT group is partially psychoeducational in nature: The therapist presents material to the patients, and homework is assigned to help them develop new skills and coping mechanisms and try out the new skills in their daily lives. Unlike Yalom's and Kibel's models, Linehan's DBT is not based upon a "here-and-now" focus. Linehan assumes that education about alternative ways to represent life experiences along with reinforcement from actual behavioral applications of these alternatives will help the patient reach a more functional state (see Springer & Silk, 1996). Available data on the effectiveness of DBT suggests that inpatients benefit from this form of treatment; both staff and colleagues report satisfaction with the approach and a significant reduction in the self-destructive behaviors committed by patients suffering from BPD (Barley et al., 1993).

Groups for Schizophrenia

Perhaps the diagnosis that presents the greatest amount of difficulty in an inpatient group setting is schizophrenia, because the presence of psychotic symptoms leaves the patient with disorganized thinking and impaired reality testing. Still, de Chavez, Gutierrez, Ducaju, and Fraile (2000) suggested that inpatient psychotherapy groups could be used effectively with inpatients who suffer from schizophrenia. The therapeutic team consists of four people: a designated "principal therapist" who tracks group dynamics, two cotherapists, and one observer (de Chavez et al., 2000). Following Yalom's suggestion, the group works in the here and now, and the main goals are to identify the patients' psychotic experiences through their interactions with group members and contributions to the group. de Chavez et al. suggest that patients be capable of exercising control over themselves, verbalizing their psychotic experiences, and listening to other persons present their experiences. Patients who are incapable of attending to anything outside their psychosis or are paranoid are not included in the group.

de Chavez et al. (2000) compared the therapeutic factors in the inpatient version of the psychotherapy group for persons suffering from schizophrenia with its outpatient counterpart. Findings suggested factors found to be most important in the inpatient setting were installation of hope, cohesiveness, and altruism, whereas in the outpatient setting, installation of hope, self-understanding, and universality were considered most critical. Both inpatients and outpatients rated the installation of hope as the most important therapeutic factor. These findings suggest what Yalom argued in his earlier writings on inpatient group therapy

(Yalom, 1983): One of the most important functions of an inpatient psychotherapy group may be that it allows patients who feel desperate and dehumanized to observe the improvement and success of others with similar symptoms. It is not until patients are discharged and able to maintain at least basic functioning on their own that other factors such as self-understanding become the focus of continuing group therapy. It is suggested by practitioners who engage in inpatient group therapy that focusing the group on self-knowledge may be counterproductive for patients hospitalized for psychotic disorders (de Chavez et al., 2000). Patients' inability to analyze their problems during psychotic states could lead to anxiety and frustration. A better way to ensure that inpatient groups will serve a therapeutic purpose for patients suffering from psychosis is to focus groups on instilling a sense of hope that progress is possible and to use groups to build a sense of togetherness among members who share similar experiences.

Psychoeducational Groups

Many inpatient groups educate patients either about symptoms and management of their illness or skills they need for successful reentry into the community. Some of the most important skills inpatients can learn prior to discharge are social skills. Social skills training groups have been shown to be effective for patients suffering from a variety of clinical syndromes, including severe and persistent mental illness (Wallace, Liberman, MacKain, Blackwell, & Eckman, 1992). The main goal of social skills training groups with inpatients is to teach specific interpersonal skills that can be generalized beyond the hospital setting and applied in daily living. Given myriad potentially stressful circumstances faced by patients in a hospital setting (see Waldo & Harman, 1999), it is critical that patients and staff maintain positive interpersonal interactions if patients are to learn social skills they can take with them once placed back in community settings.

Waldo and Harman (1999) conducted a pilot group program based on the methodology of relationship enhancement (RE) therapy (Guerney, 1977). Inpatients suffering from schizophrenia, mood disorders, or personality disorders participated in sessions that covered attitudes and skills such as conveying respect, honesty, and understanding through nonverbal communication and expressive speaking, empathic listening, and appropriate switching between speaking and listening (Waldo & Harman, 1999). Group leaders presented skills, and patients were encouraged to try out each skill with one another in pairs under the guidance of group leaders. Evaluation suggested that patients found the group to be helpful and that staff noted improvement in the patients who participated (e.g., improved relations between roommates, reduction of anger outbursts).

In addition to experiencing interpersonal conflict, hospitalized psychiatric patients often have problems maintaining self-esteem because being confined to a hospital seems inconsistent with any positive qualities (Klose & Tinius, 1992). As Klose & Tinius noted, feelings of low self-esteem interfere with inpatients' abilities to maintain positive relationships with others, advocate for themselves, and act in a productive manner. Furthermore, low self-esteem can contribute to social withdrawal, substance abuse, withdrawal from reality, and self-destructive behaviors (Klose & Tinius, 1992; Stuart & Sundeen, 1988).

Klose & Tinius (1992) discussed a self-esteem group in which patients acknowledge even their smallest accomplishments during their hospital stay. Patients must identify one event, action, or thought that occurred in the past few days that made them feel good about themselves. After group members share their positive experiences, a number of activities ensue that encourage members to become involved in group process, establish trust, and promote member interaction, such as group art tasks, poetry, pictures, and music, and "self-help" exercises, such as identifying and discussing irrational beliefs and self-defeating behaviors (e.g., "I must be loved by everyone" and continually trying convince someone to like us who does not share our views). Klose and Tinius reported that feedback from participants suggested that the group helped them to feel better about themselves and helped them to have a more successful transition into the community following discharge. However, the authors caution that the group did not work well with actively psychotic patients.

In addition to focusing on skill acquisition, psychoeducational groups also encourage the acquisition of information necessary for treatment success. The development of informational groups followed from research suggesting that patients have informational needs and resent the fact that little information is provided to them about their illness when they are hospitalized (McNiel & Binder, 1987). Pollack (1996) found that patients with bipolar disorder have a number of informational needs, including information regarding self-management of their disorder, understanding the symptoms and causes of their disorder, managing daily life, living in society, relating to others, and relating to the self. Numerous inpatient facilities include information-focused psychoeducational groups as a regular part of treatment protocol. It has become clear that education helps to combat patient failure to follow through on aftercare recommendations, which often results in readmittance to the hospital (Holmes, Ziemba, Evans, & Williams, 1994).

Patients with dual diagnoses present the greatest challenge to treatment facilities (and often get readmitted to hospitals numerous times) because they are simultaneously dealing with active symptoms of psychiatric illness and the process of addiction. Pollack and Stuebben (1998) reported on an addiction education group for inpatients with dual diagnoses. The purpose of the group was to educate people who had both substance abuse disorders and major mental disorders about how the process of recovery from addiction is affected by the symptoms associated with an additional diagnosis. The model of the group involved presentation of the topic of the session by the group leader (e.g., "denial," "relapse"), structured activities, discussion about the activity, summary of what was learned during the session, and patient evaluations.

Inpatient psychoeducational groups sometimes focus on experiences that are common to a number of individuals who have disparate diagnoses but have similar feelings and reactions based on the shared experience. For example, Allen, Kelly, and Glodich (1997) reported on a psychoeducational program for patients with trauma-related disorders. Patients who participated were inpatients in a trauma recovery program at an inpatient facility who had extensive trauma histories and severe psychiatric disorders.

The course was didactic in nature. The leader presented topics and encouraged group members to share personal experiences related to the topics (e.g., masochism, self-injury, and the desire to suffer). Discussion between group members was summarized and diagrammed on a blackboard, with many patients taking detailed notes.

An interesting example is the discussion that followed when the topic of "masochism" was introduced. Allen et al. (1997) noted that many of the patients had been called masochists by people they had encountered in their lives. For many patients, masochism translated into a "desire to suffer." This led to a discussion of self-injury and motivations for engaging in self-injurious behaviors. The list generated on the blackboard for motivations (e.g., self-injury is a means of expressing frustration and anger; self-injury spares others from the overt expression of anger; the aggression satisfies the need to be punished and reduces guilt feelings; Allen et al., 1997) and led to a challenge to the group leader from the patients: "Why should we give up self-injurious behavior?" This question led to patients' discussing some reasons why continuing the behavior could lead to further pain, tension, and guilt (e.g., it retraumatizes the self; it serves as an obstacle to positive interpersonal relationships).

Allen et al. (1997) noted that the group serves a variety of goals. First, it helps patients understand the rationale for various aspects of their treatment. Second, the course allows patients to become informed consumers of mental health services. Third, the group provides a sense of universality (Yalom, 1994) such that patients realize that others share their experiences and struggles; this is critical for patients who have experienced significant trauma, as it can decrease feelings of alienation that lead to self-harm (Allen et al., 1997). In addition, it fosters reflectiveness (thinking before acting) and provides patients with insight into their illness, which can relieve anxiety. Allen et al.'s program also confronts patients with the destructive consequences of their behavior in an intellectual environment, which can be less threatening than the milieu of a traditional psychotherapy group. Finally, the group empowers patients by allowing them to have an intellectual experience in which they figure things out together.

Some inpatient units combine the two types of psychoeducational groups discussed above: those that focus on the development of a particular skill and those that deliver information about a particular illness or treatment. Kopelowicz, Wallace, and Zarate (1998) presented a community reentry program for inpatients suffering from schizophrenia or schizoaffective disorder. Group sessions focused on helping patients to better understand their disorders and the medications necessary to control symptoms, develop an aftercare treatment plan, and address the skills needed to prevent relapse, enhance coping skills, and manage stress. Kopelowicz et al. found that inpatients who participated in the community reentry group program significantly improved their knowledge and performance of the skills taught in the sessions, compared with a control group who received standard occupational therapy.

Ascher-Svanum and Whitesel (1999) studied the efficacy of two types of group educational interventions for patients suffering from schizophrenia. The groups used a didactic format to cover topics regarding the characteristics and treatment of schizophrenia. Topics included diagnosis, prevalence, course, causes, prognosis, medication management, nonmedical treatments, stress factors, community resources, substance abuse, and legal issues. The groups differed in the format used to convey information; leaders in the discussion group encouraged active exchange of ideas among participants regarding specific topics, whereas leaders in the didactic group provided lectures, ran structured question-and-answer periods, provided media aids, and encouraged active discussion between group members. Analyses comparing how much information members of each group learned suggested that patients who participated in didactic groups made similar gains in knowledge about schizophrenia as patients who participated in discussion groups. Perhaps the exchange of information alone, whether it occurs in a structured format or primarily through interactions with group members, enhances patients understanding of their illness. What is clear from research on psychoeducational groups is that inpatients want information and learn when such information is provided.

BEYOND PSYCHOTHERAPY AND PSYCHOEDUCATION: EXPERIMENTAL GROUPS FOR THE INPATIENT SETTING

Before concluding, it is worthwhile to note that some inpatient facilities are experimenting with groups that do not clearly fall into either the traditional psychotherapy or psychoeducational category. These groups are designed to foster (a) creative expression and enjoyment, (b) skills necessary for effective participation in psychotherapy, (c) therapeutic opportunities for psychotic and disorganized patients, (d) catalysts for therapeutic discussions, or (e) opportunities to enhance adjustment. McGarry and Prince (1998) discussed an inpatient creativity group that was designed to encourage self-expression and was not meant to be therapeutic in nature. Patients expressed themselves through individual poetry, group poetry, storytelling, drawing and painting, or music. During each session, the facilitator "promoted group interaction and discussion, discouraged competition, and encouraged acceptance of differences" (McGarry & Prince, 1998, p. 20). The goals of the group were to allow patients to express feelings, allow patients to verbalize positive self-statements regarding their creative expression, and allow patients to verbalize positive statements about themselves in relation to experiences they had with other group members.

Other facilities are including improvisational drama groups in their protocol. Sheppard, Olson, Croke, LaFave, and Gerber (1990) discussed improvisational drama techniques including mime, word games, charades, free association, portrayal of fairy-tale creatures or famous people, poetry reading, role play, and role reversal skits that were used with psychiatric inpatients. Formal analysis revealed that patients who participated in the drama group demonstrated significant increases in the frequency of appropriate verbalizations, demonstrated high levels of creativity across sessions, and displayed positive emotions and thoughts about the self.

Houlding and Holland (1988) found that psychotic patients were able to express meaningful communications about their inner states through their involvement in a poetry writing group; patients seemed not only to be able to use the poetry as a means of organizing overwhelming experiences but also to connect with other patients. Dick (2001) reported that involving patients in a group mural intervention (acute patients collaborated on determining a theme for a mural and worked together to produce it) helped patients move toward an ability to focus externally in the here and now, instead of solely on their internal disorganization, and resulted in peer interaction.

Conclusions and Ideas for the Future Use of Groups in Inpatient Settings

As is clear from the preceding discussion, staff members at inpatient facilities try to meet the unique needs of psychiatric inpatients through a variety of group formats. As we go forward into the new millennium, it is prudent to keep in mind remaining challenges presented by the use of groups in inpatient settings, as well as potentially new uses for groups that could remedy some of the difficulties involved in inpatient group work.

First, the formation of task/work groups for staff members at inpatient facilities might help to coordinate individuals involved in the variety of activities going on inside ward groups, on the ward itself, and in the hospital system at large. As many practitioners of inpatient group work have suggested, the use of groups in an inpatient facility requires a coordinated approach. A work group might help to promote intertherapist communication and communication between therapists and other staff members; this is essential, since most hospitals invoke treatment teams to make decisions about individual patients and ward protocol. Furthermore, the coordination of various hospital personnel at all levels, both within the hospital setting and in affiliated outpatient facilities, is critical for the development of "care pathways" currently being discussed in the literature to facilitate treatment for severely mentally ill individuals (Jones, 2000; Jones & Kamath, 1998).

Second, a psychoeducational group for therapists might be a useful way to educate staff members with different levels of group preparation for carrying out psychotherapeutic groups effectively. As has been noted earlier in this chapter, persons with varying degrees of expertise and experience lead psychotherapy groups in inpatient settings. A psychoeducational group designed to educate the staff members who will be leading groups with inpatients could enhance the therapeutic potential of these groups.

Third, the problem of heterogeneous populations within the same group on an inpatient ward is one that still needs to be tackled. As Birckhead (1984) noted, the needs of psychotic clients can differ markedly from those of nonpsychotic clients; psychotic clients may require group strategies that are tailored to that population (for a model of analytic group therapy with psychotic clients, see Birckhead, 1984).

Fourth, special attention needs to be paid to the unique problems associated with termination in inpatient groups and potentially negative effects of the group process on psychiatric inpatients. As Brabender and Fallon (1996) noted, the fact that the inpatient group is embedded within the structure of the larger hospital system can influence the therapist's ability to effectively deal with group members' departures from the group. Erickson (1987) suggested that including patients in the same groups who are experiencing distinct levels of functioning and cognitive disorganization could potentially be harmful for some patients; for example, higher-functioning individuals might ridicule the bizarre behavior and speech of acutely psychotic group members.

Finally, further quantitative research is needed to determine which groups work best for specific inpatient populations (Lettieri-Marks, 1987). However, as both Leszcz et al. (1985) and Lettieri-Marks (1987) noted, conducting research in an inpatient facility is difficult because it is impossible to separate out the impact of various treatment approaches on individual patients. Patients who participate in a particular form of group treatment are also taking medication, living within a specific ward structure, and working with different therapists. Furthermore, the patient population is often too unstable to study; this is why so many inpatient group practitioners have advocated for a single-session format to accomplish treatment goals. Isolating the impact of a specific group on patient success, be it therapeutic, educational, or otherwise, will continue to be difficult to accomplish in the years to come.

REFERENCES

Allen, J. G., Kelly, K. A., & Glodich, A. (1997). A psychoeducational program for patients with trauma-related disorders. *Bulletin of the Menninger Clinic, 61,* 223-239.

Ascher-Svanum, H., & Whitesel, J. (1999). A randomized control study of two styles of group patient education about schizophrenia. *Psychiatric Services, 50,* 926-930.

Barley, W. D., Buie, S. E., Peterson, E. W., Hollingsworth, A. S., Griva, M., & Hickerson, S. C. (1993). Development of an inpatient cognitive-behavioral treatment program for borderline personality disorder. *Journal of Personality Disorders, 7,* 232-240.

Birckhead, L. (1984). Techniques for group psychotherapy on inpatient units. *Issues in Mental Health Nursing, 6,* 127-142.

Brabender, V., & Fallon, A. (1996). Termination in inpatient groups. *International Journal of Group Psychotherapy, 46,* 81-98.

Bradlee, L. (1984). The use of groups in short-term psychiatric settings. *Short-Term Treatment in Occupational Therapy,* 47-57.

Clarke, D. E., Adamoski, E., & Joyce, B. (1998). Inpatient group psychotherapy: The role of the staff nurse. *Journal of Psychosocial Nursing, 36,* 22-26.

de Chavez, M. G., Gutierrez, M., Ducaju, M., & Fraile, J. C. (2000). Comparative study of the therapeutic factors of group therapy in schizophrenic inpatients and outpatients. *Group Analysis, 33,* 251-264.

Dick, T. (2001). Brief group art therapy for acute psychiatric inpatients. *American Journal of Art Therapy, 39,* 108-112.

Erickson, R. C. (1981). Small-group psychotherapy with patients on a short-stay ward: An opportunity for innovation. *Hospital and Community Psychiatry, 32,* 269-272.

Erickson, R. C. (1987, November). The question of casualties in inpatient small group psychotherapy. *Small Group Behavior,* 443-458.

Froberg, W., & Slife, B. D. (1987). Overcoming obstacles to the implementation of Yalom's model of inpatient group psychotherapy. *International Journal of Group Psychotherapy, 37,* 371-388.

Griffin-Shelly, E., & Trachtenberg, J. (1985). Group psychotherapy with short-term inpatients: Further developments. *Small Group Behavior, 16,* 97-104.

Griffin-Shelley, E., & Wendel, S. (1988). Group psychotherapy with long-term inpatients: Application of a model. *Small Group Behavior, 19,* 379-385.

Guerney, B. G. Jr. (1977). *Relationship enhancement: Skill training programs for therapy, problem prevention, and enrichment.* San Francisco: Jossey-Bass.

Holmes, H., Ziemba, J., Evans, T., & Williams, C. A. (1994). Nursing model of psychoeducation for the seriously mentally ill patient. *Issues in Mental Health Nursing, 15,* 85-104.

Houlding, S., & Holland, P. (1988). Contributions of a poetry writing group to the treatment of severely disturbed psychiatric inpatients. *Clinical Social Work Journal, 16,* 194-200.

Jones, A. (2000). Implementation of hospital care pathways for patients with schizophrenia. *Journal of Nursing Management, 8,* 215-225.

Jones, A., & Kamath, P. D. (1998). Issues for the development of care pathways in mental health services. *Journal of Nursing Management, 6,* 87-95.

Kernberg, O. F. (1975). *Borderline conditions and pathological narcissism.* New York: Jason Aronson.

Kernberg, O. F. (1984). The couch at sea: Psychoanalytic studies of group and organizational leadership. *International Journal of Group Psychotherapy, 34,* 5-23.

Kibel, H. D. (1978). The rationale for the use of group psychotherapy for borderline patients on a short-term unit. *International Journal of Group Psychotherapy, 28,* 339-358.

Kibel, H. D. (1981). A conceptual model for short-term inpatient group psychotherapy. *American Journal of Psychiatry, 138,* 74-80.

Klein, R. H., & Kugel, B. (1981). Inpatient psychotherapy from a systems perspective: Reflections through a glass darkly. *International Journal of Group Psychotherapy, 31,* 311-328.

Klose, P., & Tinius, T. (1992). Confidence builders: A self-esteem group at an inpatient psychiatric hospital. *Journal of Psychosocial Nursing, 30,* 5-9.

Kopelowicz, A., Wallace, C. J., & Zarate, R. (1998). Teaching psychiatric inpatients to re-enter the community: a brief method of improving the continuity of care. *Psychiatric Services, 49,* 1313-1316.

Leszcz, M., Yalom, I. D., & Norden, M. (1985). The value of inpatient group psychotherapy: Patient's perceptions. *International Journal of Group Psychotherapy, 35,* 411-433.

Lettieri-Marks, D. (1987). Research in short-term inpatient group psychotherapy: A critical review. *Archives of Psychiatric Nursing, 1,* 407-421.

Linehan, M. N. (1987a). Dialectical behavior therapy: A cognitive approach to parasuicide. *Journal of Personality Disorders, 1,* 328-333.

Linehan, M. N. (1987b). Dialectical behavior therapy for borderline personality disorder. *Bulletin of the Menninger Clinic, 51,* 261-276.

Linehan, M. N. (1987c). Dialectical behavior therapy in groups: Treating borderline personality disorders and suicidal behavior. In C. M. Brody (Ed.), *Woman's therapy groups: Paradigm of feminist treatment* (pp. 145-162). New York: Springer.

Linehan, M. N. (1993). *Cognitive-behavioral treatment of borderline personality disorder.* New York: Guilford.

Luboshitsky, D., & Sachs, D. (1996). Structural models of psychotherapy groups and their effect on inpatients with borderline personality disorders: Patients' perceptions. *Group, 20,* 223-239.

Macaskill, N. D. (1982). Therapeutic factors in group therapy with borderline patients. *International Journal of Group Psychotherapy, 32,* 61-73.

Maves, P., & Schulz, J. (1985). Inpatient group treatment on short-term acute care units. *Hospital and Community Psychiatry, 36,* 69-73.

Maxmen, J. (1984). Helping patients survive theories: The practice of an educative model. *International Journal of Group Psychotherapy, 34,* 355-368.

McGarry, T. J., & Prince, M. (1998). Implementation of groups for creative expression on a psychiatric inpatient unit. *Journal of Psychosocial Nursing, 36,* 19-24.

McNiel, D. E., & Binder, R. L. (1987). Patients who bring weapons to the psychiatric emergency room. *Journal of Clinical Psychiatry, 48,* 230-233.

Miller, K., & Matthews, D. (1988). Setting up a ward-based group therapy programme for psychiatric inpatients. *British Journal of Occupational Therapy, 51,* 22-24.

New Model Proposed for Inpatient Group Therapy. (1982, March 19), *Psychiatric News, 9,* 32-34.

Pam, A., & Kemker, S. (1993). The captive group: guidelines for group therapists in the inpatient group. *International Journal of Group Psychotherapy, 43,* 419-438.

Pollack, L. E. (1990). Improving relationships: groups for inpatients with bipolar disorder. *Journal of Psychosocial Nursing, 28,* 17-22.

Pollack, L. E. (1991). Problem-solving group therapy: two inpatient models based on level of functioning. *Issues in Mental Health Nursing, 12,* 65-80.

Pollack, L. E. (1995a). Informational needs of patients hospitalized for bipolar disorder. *Psychiatric Services, 46,* 1191-1194.

Pollack, L. E. (1995b). Treatment of inpatients with bipolar disorders: a role of self-management groups. *Journal of Psychosocial Nursing, 33,* 11-16.

Pollack, L. E. (1996). Inpatients with bipolar disorder: Their quest to understand. *Journal of Psychosocial Nursing, 34,* 19-24.

Pollack, L. E., & Stuebben, G. (1998). Addiction education groups for inpatients with dual diagnoses. *Journal of the American Psychiatric Nurses Association, 4,* 121-127.

Satterley, J. A. (1995). Needed: A fresh start for psychiatric inpatient groups, *Social Work With Groups, 17,* 71-81.

Sautter, F. J., Heaney, C., & O'Neill, P. (1991). A problem-solving approach to group psychotherapy in the inpatient milieu. *Hospital and Community Psychiatry, 42,* 814-817.

Sheppard, J., Olson, A., Croke, J., LaFave, H. G., & Gerber, G. J. (1990). Improvisational drama groups in an inpatient setting. *Hospital and Community Psychiatry, 41,* 1019-1021.

Slife, B. D., Froberg, W., Sasscer-Burgos, J., Barron, D., & Ellington, S. (1986). *Group therapy processing as a function of depression.* Paper presented at the meeting of the Southwest Psychological Association, Fort Worth, TX.

Springer, T., & Silk, K. R. (1996, January/February). A review of inpatient group therapy for borderline personality disorder. *Harvard Review of Psychiatry, 3,* 268-278.

Stuart, G. W., & Sundeen, S. J. (1988). *Pocket nurse guide to psychiatric nursing.* St. Louis: C. V. Mosby.

Waldo, M., & Harman, M. J. (1999). Relationship enhancement groups with state hospital patients and staff. *Journal for Specialists in Group Work, 24,* 27-36.

Wallace, C. J., Liberman, R. P., MacKain, S. J., Blackwell, G., & Eckman, T. A. (1992). Effectiveness and replicability of modules for teaching social and instrumental skills to the severely mentally ill. *American Journal of Psychiatry, 149,* 654-658.

White, E. M. (1987). Effective inpatient groups: Challenges and rewards. *Archives of Psychiatric Nursing, 1,* 422-428.

Yalom, I. D. (1983). *Inpatient group psychotherapy.* New York: Basic Books.

Yalom, I. D. (1994). *The theory and practice of group psychotherapy* (4th ed.). New York: Basic Books.

Zimpfer, D. G. (1987, March). Group work with psychiatric patients. *Journal for Specialists in Group Work,* 49-56.

26

THE USE OF GROUPS IN COLLEGE AND UNIVERSITY COUNSELING CENTERS

ELIZABETH A. KINCADE

Indiana University of Pennsylvania

CYNTHIA R. KALODNER

Towson University

The history of psychoeducational, counseling, and therapy groups in university and college counseling centers reveals that group experiences have been an important part of therapeutic and prevention work with students for many years. In 1993, Golden, Corazzini, and Grady wrote that "group treatment has become a central component of the direct services offered by many university counseling centers" (p. 228). Groups continue to be used to reach a large number of students seeking psychological services. This chapter begins with a brief history of the use of groups in this setting and ends with a summary of the last comprehensive study of groups in higher educational settings. The developmental needs of college students are also explored. We describe the current use of psychoeducational, counseling, and therapy groups, focusing on the suggestions about the formation and function of various types of groups in counseling centers. Although not often published in journal articles

or book chapters, there is considerable expertise and anecdotal evidence of those working in the counseling center field. This chapter gives voice to those experts. As Kalodner, Alfred, and Hoyt (1997) indicated, it is important to give attention to the studies that are conducted within an applied setting with actual counseling center clients. Thus, we also highlight studies that have been done in the counseling center environment (e.g., Alfred, 1992; MacNair-Semands, 2002; Quintana, Kilmartin, Yesenosky, & Macias, 1991).

In 1972, Berman, Messersmith, and Mullens wrote that "the modal leader is a 35-year-old male who has held a doctorate for 3 years. On the average, he has had no significant postdoctoral group training, although it is likely that his graduate curricula provided sufficient coursework in group dynamics and group process. At present, he leads two groups, each comprised of eight members, meeting once a week for 2 hours. While the group is heterogeneous for sex and diagnosis, it is relatively homogeneous by age"

(p. 353). This profile was based on a study of 230 staff members of counseling centers. The study also revealed that 70% of respondents preferred to work with a cotherapist, a time-limited model was typically used, fees were rarely charged, and therapists usually met both before and after their group sessions for planning and consultation. Much of this description of groups in the 1970s is consistent with what currently exists in counseling centers. One interesting difference concerns the gender of the staff. In 1975, less than a quarter of the counseling center group therapists were female. However, since the majority of group leaders preferred to work with a female coleader, it was recommended that there be an active recruitment of female group leaders (Berman et al., 1972).

About the same time, Conyne, Lamb, and Strand (1975) noted that even though college and university counseling centers were a major source of group experiences, there was little written about this topic. In their survey of 129 counseling centers, there were 514 groups offered (about 4 groups per center). Larger counseling centers offered more groups than smaller centers; public institutions offered more groups than private institutions. The most important finding of this survey was that the majority of groups were categorized as adequacy enhancing (62%) with a personal growth and developmental-preventative focus. In the parlance of the Association for Specialists in Group Work (ASGW) (1998), these are psychoeducational groups. The members were well-functioning individuals, and the groups were designed to enhance their skills. Problem-reduction groups (38%), defined by ASGW (1998) as counseling or therapy groups, have a remedial focus. Members of these groups were not functioning well; thus the groups were designed to develop skills that were needed in the past that had not developed.

Golden et al. (1993) provided the most recent comprehensive study of groups in college and university counseling centers. They surveyed 148 directors of college and university counseling centers and found that 92% are actively using various types of groups, including structured groups, process-oriented psychotherapy groups, and support groups of various types. Golden et al. reported that the average counseling center groups are co-led. Groups meet once a week for 90 minutes in the afternoon or the evening. Coleaders often meet for 10 to 15 minutes before the group session and for an average of 30 minutes after the session. The mean number of members ranged from five to eight. The mean number of groups offered by a counseling center was 11. Larger counseling centers offered more groups (15) and smaller ones offered fewer (4). These data suggest a large increase in the role of groups, compared to the Conyne et al. (1975) study.

Referral to groups was accomplished primarily by individual therapists (90%), information provided at intake (80%), client request (79%), brochures, student newspaper, and outreach (76%, 71%, and 65%), and at the intake interview (62%) (Golden et al., 1993). Screening for the members was provided by 96% of the group leaders. Criteria for excluding members from group included severe psychopathology, lack of fit with other members, having a personality disorder, and being actively suicidal. Preparation for group counseling was provided by 76% of the sample. Preparation included some verbal description of the experience of group therapy, or less often a written explanation, or an in vivo or video preparation. As in the Conyne et al. (1975) study, the most common type of group was a time-limited structured topic group (66%; psychoeducational group). There were also a large number of time-limited process-oriented topic groups (35%; counseling). In addition, process-oriented psychotherapy groups (therapy groups) were offered by 59% of the centers.

Most centers rated their group programs as fairly successful or very successful, and indicated that the success of the program was enhanced by staff attitude and motivation, administrative support, and professional development (Golden et al., 1993). Even given all the data that suggest that groups are in demand and well used in college counseling centers, Golden et al. noted that only 20% of the clients were involved in group counseling. Furthermore, some group offerings may be absent, even when group counseling is considered a treatment of choice. For example, Sack, Graham, and Simmons (1995) noted that while almost all counseling centers offer individual counseling for clients who have a history of childhood sexual abuse, under 40% offer groups for this population.

Groups are effective in helping young adults deal with a broad range of issues from developmental concerns to severe psychopathology (Golden et al., 1993). In the 1990s and beyond, numerous articles have described specific types of groups on campus. As examples, there are descriptions of groups for gay/lesbian/bisexual/transvestite issues (Chojnacki & Gelberg, 1995; Welch, 1996), athletes (Fitch & Robinson, 1998), academic concerns (Halstead, 1998), alcohol education (Freeman, 2001), and African American student adjustment (Brown, Lipford-Sanders, & Shaw, 1995). Cornish and Benton (2001) presented an innovative therapeutic group that integrates interpersonal, brief dynamic and solution-focused interventions into an eight-session group on developing healthy relationships, which is used as an example later in this chapter.

An Introduction to College Student Development, Counseling Centers, and Group Experiences

Before providing descriptions of the types of groups offered in counseling centers, it is helpful to briefly review the developmental issues faced by college students. College students are at a unique place in their adult development. At this stage in life, they are coping with issues of forming their own identity, dependence versus interdependence and independence with friends, families, and partners, separation from parents, and choosing lifestyles and careers (Chickering & Reisser, 1993; Whitaker, 1992). Returning adult students also go through a similar developmental process as they are exposed to new ideas and ways of thinking about themselves (Chickering & Reisser, 1993). Many of these issues can best be addressed in both formal and informal group situations. For instance, college students seeking support in separating from parents and in formulating and owning their belief systems can try out new ideas and ways of being and receive feedback in a safe environment from students in similar situations. This may take place informally in residence halls and college coffee shops but also takes place formally through a variety of college-sanctioned activities.

College and university counseling mental health professionals began to use group interventions for personal growth in the 1960s. This was the heyday of the encounter group movement, and it seemed natural that groups would also be offered as part of the educational experience for college students. At this time, there was a great deal of excitement about the power of marathon and encounter groups. These were common weekend occurrences at many colleges and universities (Corey & Corey, 2002; Yalom, 1995). Studies of the period (Culbert, Clark, & Bobele, 1968) recorded moderate growth and improvement reported by students in these kinds of groups. However, the move toward group work in the college mental health environment was not merely a product of the zeitgeist of the 1960s and concepts of self-actualization. During the rapid growth of higher education in the 1960s, colleges and universities did not have concerns about staffing and costs of cocurricular activities. However, the 1970s found higher education in a different position. Even as support services (residence life staff, developmental educators, and mental health professionals) continued to expand on college campuses, those in charge of budgets sought ways to cut costs (Birnbaum, 1999). Personal growth and counseling groups were viewed as efficient uses of resources. A smaller number of mental health professionals could serve a greater number of clients through the use of groups. Thus, ongoing groups became a standard feature in the repertoire of college counseling center services.

Colleges and universities have continued to struggle with diminished budgets (Bishop, 1990). In order to be more accountable, counseling centers were advised to use short-term counseling, group therapy, and developmental and preventative interventions (Bishop, 1990). Colleges and universities are scrambling to find ways to do what they do best—academic and social/personal education—with fewer resources for students who are more diverse. There continues to be an increase in the demand for mental health services on campuses, and individual counseling cannot meet these demands (Bishop, 1990). Thus group treatment programs continue to be a cost-effective intervention for the multiple needs in counseling center environments.

Psychoeducational Groups

Psychoeducational groups are the most common groups offered on college campuses (Golden et al., 1993). These are often prevention focused rather than remedial in the sense that these skill- and awareness-building groups impart knowledge and thus serve an educative function. McWhirter (1995) indicated that there are four key elements important in psychoeducational groups: a common and focused theme, didactic teaching, personalizing the information, and teaching behavioral skills. Furthermore, this format may be useful for college students because it provides "emotional education" that supports the intellectual education of college students. In the college mental health environment, psychoeducational groups follow a general format of balancing content with discussion and support (Archer & Cooper, 1998).

Examples of psychoeducational counseling center groups are described on counseling center Web sites. For example, psychoeducational groups focused on academic issues are offered at many counseling centers. There is an Academic Probation Support at Keene State College Counseling Center (2001) designed to help students on academic probation deal with stress concerns, self-esteem issues, personal value, and identity. The goal of this group is to help students at academic risk revitalize their academic career. Another group identifies students at risk academically and provides a 5-week group with the following phases: (a) institution and professor bashing, (b) member confrontation and accepting responsibility, (c) implementation of success strategies, and (d) future pacing. The unique factor in this group is the first one: institution and professor bashing. Here students are given an opportunity to vent about their professors and the institution in a safe and supportive environment. The benefit to having students vent their frustration in a formal group is that the group leader can facilitate problem solving. The purpose of the group leader is to help students move beyond emotional venting to the skill-building components of the group (Halstead, 1998).

Psychoeducational groups focused on stress management and depression management are also common. These groups are time-limited and can run from 3 to 6 weeks, depending on the agency and the philosophy of the group leader. A stress management group is similar.

Psychoeducational groups may be targeted toward at-risk populations. At-risk can mean a number of different things in this context, including but not limited to substance abuse issues, poor coping skills, low self-esteem, inadequate social skills, lack of assertiveness, lack of academic preparedness, and experiencing developmental life events (e.g., death of a grandparent, leaving home for the first time, dissolution of the first serious relationship, sexuality and sexual orientation concerns, career and lifestyle choices). A description of a group developed for women who have been previously acquaintance raped and are identified as at risk for further assault includes a program of rape "inoculation"; this program showed moderate success in helping the women to develop self-esteem as an inoculation against repeat sexual assault (Himelein, 1999).

Psychoeducational groups can also be tailored to fit the specific college environment or cultural context. Student needs at small, private, religious colleges may not be the same as those at large public universities. One example of this is a psychoeducational group for devout Mormon students. The topic of the group is coping with self-defeating perfectionism. However, the interventions and content of the group weave together tenets of the students' faith in addition to purely academic content. In this case, students confront their perfectionism using religious imagery and religious bibliotherapy assignments. Discussions focus on religious concepts about perfectionism. Evaluation data suggest that participants scored lower on perfectionism and higher on self-esteem than prior to the group (Richards, 1993). Another group of a similar nature focuses on personal religious and spiritual concerns (Genia, 1990).

The staff members of counseling centers often conduct outreach or workshops on a variety of topics. Workshops are usually one-shot presentations that may be presented in classes or in the college community. The following topics are common workshops on college campuses: Time Management, Career Decision

Making, Learning Styles, Values Clarification, Test Anxiety, How to Get Off Academic Probation, Preparing for Graduate School, A Short Course in College Life, Beating the

Holiday Blues, Preparing for Finals, Creating Good Relationships, Coping With Change, Self-Esteem, and Stress Management and Relaxation.

An informal survey of college counseling and health centers found the following topics to be common psychoeducational groups:

- Dysfunctional Family Groups (Adult Child of Alcoholics, Children of Divorce, Children of Mental Illness, General Family Dysfunction)
- Enhancing or Building Self-Esteem
- Exploring Diversity and Multicultural Issues
- Speech Anxiety
- Self-Awareness Skills for Students in the Helping Professions
- Depression Management

- Stress Management/Relaxation Groups
- The Meditative Experience
- Meditation and Stress Reduction
- Facilitating Change
- When Anger Hurts Relationships
- Eating Disorder Support
- Obsessive-Compulsive Disorder
- Academic Probation Support
- Living a Healthy Lifestyle
- Counseling and Therapy Groups

Counseling groups focus on resolving problems in living or coping with developmental issues and concerns. In short, these are the problems that life gives us. Counseling groups seek to offer students new, healthier ways of thinking about problems so that they can make relational, social, career, and educational decisions in the future that lead to greater life satisfaction. From the college and university perspective, the goals of counseling groups are to increase coping skills and understanding of self and others. Students in counseling groups are urged to recognize the interpersonal nature of problems. They are provided a safe, confidential, and caring place where they can share their concerns with others.

Therapy groups are offered for students who have more significant psychological issues. On college campuses, this may be accomplished in a general therapy group format. According to Golden et al. (1993), this format of group was offered by 59% of counseling centers. The general therapy group on college campuses is strongly focused on improving interpersonal relationships. At one college, this group is described as one where you may "[l]earn about how others experience you and how to talk to others about how you experience them. The main goal of this group is to improve your level of happiness by improving satisfaction with

your relationships" (Oregon State University, Counseling and Psychological Services, n.d.). Another description is more content oriented: "General therapy groups are open to those wishing to explore a variety of issues, such as relationships, communication skills, family issues, academic stress, depression or anxiety" (Montana State University, Counseling and Psychological Services, 2001).

Counseling and therapy groups may also focus on specific issues or populations. A popular and usually well-attended example is the women's group. A description of a college women's group states, "This . . . is intended for women who are interested in gaining greater understanding of themselves and ways of relating more comfortably to others. . . . The format is open-ended and provides women with both mutual support and challenge in a respectful atmosphere" (Shippensburg University, The Counseling Center, n.d.). The majority of women's groups advocate exploring areas of relationships, career, academics, and other societal pressures in a nonthreatening milieu. Although women's groups on college campuses grew out of political discussion and self-awareness/consciousness-raising groups, the current philosophy is based in contemporary feminist psychological and linguistic theory. That is, given the dynamics of gendered communication and knowledge of male-female interpersonal relationships, women are more free of social pressures to be polite, to manage the emotions of others, to put their needs second, and so on, in a group of all women than in a group of men and women (Jordan, 1995; Tannen, 2001).

Men's groups are also emerging in college counseling centers. Many of the same issues about gendered communication and relational

styles that affect women are also problematic for men (Brooks, 1998). In addition, male psychologists have recently commented on "male" style interfering with men's ability to form meaningful connections and stay in relation with others, particularly with other men (Shem & Surrey, 1998). Men's groups seek to address this concern (Horne & Mason, 1991).

A number of counseling and therapy groups are commonly found in the college environment. The list below is representative of these groups:

- Groups for Students of Various Cultural/ Ethnic Heritage
- Sexual Assault Recovery
- Survivors of Sexual Abuse
- Groups for Sexual Orientation Concerns
- Women Loving Women
- Gay, Lesbian, Bisexual, Transsexual Support
- General Personal Growth Groups/General Group Therapy
- Personal Growth for Specific Populations (Adult Learners, Graduate

Students, Student Athletes, Spouses/Partners/Friends of Alcohol and Drug Users, Men, Women)
- Groups for Developmental/Life Issues
- Homesickness
- Grief/Loss
- AIDS/HIV
- Health Issues/Long-Term Illness
- Current Events Support Group
- Clinical and Practical Issues in Running College Counseling Groups

---

Although many of the issues confronting college and university counseling center staff are similar to those in other venues, differences exist. The facilitation of groups in a college environment is complex for a number of reasons. First is diversity. Although the majority of college students are traditional aged (defined as individuals between the ages of 18 and 25), an increasing number are nontraditional aged or returning adult students (Chickering & Reiser, 1993). Furthermore, students vary in terms of credits taken, lifestyles, culture, socioeconomic status, and physical ability. The individual and group psychological needs of these students vary.

It is beyond the scope of this chapter to address multicultural groups (see Part III: Multicultural Groups, in this volume). However, one study is especially relevant here. Leong, Wagner, and Kim (1995) studied the expectations for group counseling of Asian American college students and found that more acculturated Asian American students had more positive attitudes toward group treatment and seeking professional help. Groups may require modification for use with persons from diverse

backgrounds; for example, Fukuyama and Coleman (1992) report on assertion training with a focus on Asian-Pacific college students.

Another unique factor is the closed nature of the college environment. The most obvious and problematic result of this is that dual relationships abound between group members. College and university students attend classes together, belong to the same social groups, and live in the same residence halls. This is sometimes problematic in the classroom and can be even more problematic in groups run from a mental health perspective. Furthermore, dual relationships exist between members and leaders. For mental health professionals and paraprofessionals working in the college environment, dual relationships may be present. College and university counselors often teach, advise various groups, and are active members of the academic community. These two factors create problems and complications that may not exist in a community setting, and they influence the facilitation and leading of groups on college campuses.

Some other issues arise in the college milieu. For instance, scheduling of groups must coincide with students' course schedules. Unlike the greater community, college students have staggered schedules. Some students have classes in the morning, some in the late evening, and there are many other variations. In addition, small groups are preferable to large groups. This, of course, is true for other agencies as well. However, in the college environment, where many students attend classes that may be rather large, a group of five to nine members takes on greater significance. In a smaller group, students can be individuals. They are not known only by their Social Security or student identification number as they might be in large classes. In a small group, they become people interacting with other people. Thus, interpersonal concerns can be more effectively addressed.

Once students are screened and accepted into a group, additional issues have to be addressed. One that differentiates college students from the general population is the concept of commitment. Most colleges do not have class attendance policies, as college students are assumed to be adults who will act responsibly or accept the consequences if they do not. There are very few offices on campus that require students to have appointments for meetings. Thus, students are used to being in control of their own schedule and, other than classes, not having ongoing appointments. In addition, if they attend a college or university with large classes, they are not used to being "missed" if absent. In groups at the counseling center, however, students are expected to have a commitment to come weekly to sessions.

Fears about the lack of confidentiality are also evident. This issue differs in significance with regard to college size, with students at small colleges more concerned about privacy and confidentiality issues. As one college group worker put it, "When you have only one cafeteria, one student union, etc., and students frequently see each other on a daily basis outside group, they often are uncomfortable with revealing very personal information in group" (L. Lankin, personal communication, October 31, 2001). Issues of privacy and confidentiality emerge at larger colleges and universities as well. Often students may come from the same town, the same residence hall, be in the same major or in the same organized social group. At the college level,

potential group members may be more likely to know one another than at the larger community level. One college group worker reported that a sorority member enjoyed the ongoing women's group so much that she called the next semester and said she would be bringing five of her sorority sisters with her to group.

Although groups are potent modalities for college students, there are practical problems with running on-campus groups. College counselors indicate that recruiting group members is a concern. College students may not seek out groups on their own. College counselors offer numerous reasons for this, but research on it is scarce. In addition, potential group members may be referred to group by an individual therapist, a college professor or other college personnel. These students are less aware of what they want from or can gain from group work and often need additional background and information prior to beginning the group. One college counselor reports, "The challenge we struggle with . . . is what I call 'critical mass.'. . . It is often difficult to get 6-8 students ready to join a group at the same time. However, when we have tried to start a group with 3-4 students, . . . I think the implicit message is sent that this must not be very valuable because otherwise more people would be there" (J. Wade, personal communication, October 30, 2001).

Likewise, staff members at counseling centers may not refer appropriate clients to groups. Quintana et al. (1991) studied the referral decisions made by the staff and doctoral-level trainees at a university counseling center for 170 students. Of these students presenting for treatment, 106 were referred to individual counseling and 56 were referred to group treatment. Factors that differentiated between those referred to individual and group treatment were studied. The presenting problem was not such a factor, even though it is often considered to be a primary factor distinguishing between referral to individual or group modalities. Rather, pragmatic issues, such as long waiting lists (for group) or no group openings, financial considerations, and availability of an outside referral, led counselors to refer clients to individual rather than group counseling. Also, counselors who judged clients to be socially skilled and to have intimacy issues were more likely to be referred to group. More severely disturbed clients were referred to individual more often than to group. When a client expressed a preference for a focused psychoeducational group, counselors were likely to comply with that request if the client was suitable for group therapy and if the group had openings. Anecdotally, in college counseling centers that serve as training agencies, clients most appropriate for groups are also those most appropriate for trainees doing individual counseling. Thus, students may not be referred to group.

Quintana et al. (1991) also found that staff with expertise in group counseling referred more individuals to group counseling. This fits with what Corazzini (1994) found when he reported that there is some indication that in counseling centers where counselors/therapists value individual work over group work, groups will not fill with the required number of students. Jennings and Anderson (1997) also found that the more counselors trained specifically in groups, the more likely it is that the group program and the groups will be successful.

THE NUTS AND BOLTS OF RUNNING A GROUP IN A COUNSELING CENTER

The next section of this chapter reviews the formation of groups in the counseling center environment. Beginning with recruitment, screening, and preparation, we report on the commonly held assumptions about groups in this setting. Cornish and Benton's (2001) description of a group focused on interpersonal relationships is used as an example in this section. When there is research to support a practice, it is included here.

Recruitment. Recruiting members for groups may require considerable effort and should be part of the planning process. Cornish and Benton (2001) used eye-catching brochures, posters, and newspaper articles in the student newspaper to generate student interest in their group. The title of the group is important; often, group leaders seek more appealing names for groups oriented to college students. For example, one university's women's group is called Finding Our Way (Indiana University of Pennsylvania, Counseling and Student Development Center, 2001).

Screening. Potential members of groups should be screened by leaders. Golden et al. (1993) indicated that 96% of group leaders reported that they screened for their groups. Screening is identified as part of the ASGW "Best Practice Guidelines" (1998) in which group leaders are instructed to "identify members whose needs and goals are compatible with the goals of the group."

With regard to screening, questions frequently asked by college group workers are, How do you usually act in groups? If you are doing group work in a class, what is your role? Do you sit back and do your work as assigned? Are you the one who assigns the work? How do you feel when you perceive that people in your group are not doing the work? These questions are specific to college students and acknowledge that they already do group work as a normal course of their academic responsibilities. Thus, not only does this help the group worker assess how the student will perform in group, it also normalizes group counseling for the potential group member.

Cornish and Benton (2001) suggested that criteria for exclusion and inclusion be printed on the intake form to facilitate referrals to groups. They used these criteria for exclusion for their group on healthier relationships: current emotional crisis, low level of interpersonal insight, obvious antisocial, borderline, histrionic, and narcissistic personality features, and any characteristic that could lead to isolation (being the only client in the group who is involved in a same-sex relationship). It is as important to establish criteria for inclusion: high motivation to participate, commitment to attend the eight sessions, capacity and willingness to self-disclose and listen, experience at least one positive relationship, capacity for introspection, and an ability to articulate concrete problematic patterns in relationships (Cornish & Benton, 2001, p. 134).

The criteria for inclusion and exclusion seem to be based on clinical wisdom, rather than empirically derived. However, MacNair-Semands (2002) has been working to develop a screening tool to predict dropouts from group counseling. The Group Therapy Questionnaire is a tool to assess client motivation, goals, group roles, and interpersonal behaviors (MacNair-Semands, 2001; MacNair & Corazzini, 1994). This questionnaire is an important advance, since "making treatment decisions on the basis of empirical evidence about the likelihood of solid attendance and completion of the group has been almost impossible in our field thus far" (MacNair-Semands, 2001). In a study of 310 group therapy participants in two counseling centers over 7 years, MacNair-Semands (2002) reported that interpersonal factors of social phobia/inhibition and anger/hostility predicted poor attendance in group therapy. Clearly, group therapy may be difficult for those with social anxiety. In addition, those members with anger and hostility dynamics may set up a pattern that elicits anger from group members by missing group meetings, and when they return to the group, they experience the anger of the members. Substance abuse and somatic complaints were associated with less optimistic expectations for group therapy. Active substance abusers have a high rate of dropping out of groups (MacNair & Corazzini, 1994). On the other hand, clients who had previous experience in therapy had higher expectations about group therapy. These data fit with earlier findings (MacNair & Corazzini, 1994), which also indicated that dropouts were different than completers on variables such as alcohol and drug use, somatic symptoms, fighting, and introversion.

Preparation. As indicated earlier, preparation for group counseling was provided by 76% of the leaders in the Golden et al. (1993) study. Preparation may be a variable process that may include a variety of pregroup activities. Previous research recommends group preparation or role induction for counseling groups (Borgers & Tyndall, 1982; Bowman & DeLucia, 1993). Various formats are used for group preparation. The most common include verbal information given during the screening interview, handouts, information available on the agency Web site, and a pregroup meeting of members. These techniques can be used separately or in conjunction with each other. Information given usually includes the following: brief description of group counseling and why it works, including number of sessions, trust building, and issues of confidentiality. This is usually followed by a list of ground rules for groups. Some group leaders conceptualize these as the "rights and responsibilities of group." These ground rules include expectations for being in group, including attendance, arriving/leaving on time, and communication with the group leaders. Other "rules" encompass various behavioral and emotional expectations. For instance, group members are responsible for sharing their emotional concerns with the group but also have the right to not respond to a question if they wish. Group members are instructed that the group is a microcosm of the real world and a place where they can receive feedback about their beliefs and behaviors. They are encouraged to "experiment" or to take risks in this relatively safe environment in order to learn ways that they may change and grow (Miami University of Ohio, n.d.; SUNY University of Buffalo Counseling Services, n.d.).

Group Size and Leadership. It seems that the standard number of members in groups in counseling centers is five to eight (Golden et al., 1993). Cornish and Benton (2001) indicate that as many as 10 to 12 clients can be screened for a group, since there may be dropouts or no-shows. Most groups in counseling centers are co-led. Cornish and Benton (2001) describe the use of an apprenticeship model, where the group may be led by a staff member and a trainee. Using male and female coleaders continues to be recommended (see Berman et al., 1972) but is rarely studied. Alfred (1992) examined whether the sex of the leader affected group members' perceptions of therapist influence and effectiveness. Although the sex of the therapist was not statistically significant overall, there were certain groups in which perceptions varied widely. This may have been due to idiosyncratic issues such as the differential status of leaders (senior staff and trainees). Additional research on this topic is necessary.

Summary and Key Points

In summary, although there are challenges to using groups in college and university settings, groups are a part of the work of counseling centers and continue to be an efficient and effective way to provide psychological services on campuses.

The following points are important to remember:

- Counselors must value group experiences and not see them as secondary to individual therapy.
- Small groups are best, but too small is counterproductive.
- Advertising and marketing are essential. College mental health workers need alliances with numerous college personnel in order to have students understand the value of groups and seek out membership.
- Screening is important not only for therapeutic reasons but also to ensure confidentiality.
- College students are particularly sensitive to the opinions of their peers. Issues of confidentiality and privacy must be addressed.
- Preparation for group is imperative for the group's success.
- Pay attention to students' individual characteristics in group. Take issues of diversity into account for screening and group process issues.
- The student calendar is important to consider. Planning is important for the success of the group.
- Counselors need to remain flexible in their expectations for group and take into account the developmental issues and concerns of the group members.

References

Alfred, A. R. (1992). Members' perceptions of coleaders' influence and effectiveness in group psychotherapy. *Journal for Specialists in Group Work, 17,* 42-53.

Archer, J., & Cooper, S. (1998). *Counseling and mental health services on campus: A handbook of contemporary practices and challenges.* San Francisco: Jossey-Bass.

Association for Specialists in Group Work. (1998). Best practice guidelines. *Journal for Specialists in Group Work, 23,* 237-244.

Berman, A. L., Messersmith, C. E., & Mullens, B. N. (1972). Profile of group-therapy practice in university counseling centers. *Journal of Counseling Psychology, 19,* 353-354.

Bishop, J. B. (1990). The university counseling center: An agenda for the 1990s. *Journal of Counseling and Development, 68,* 408-413.

Borgers, D., & Tyndall, L. (1982). Setting expectations for groups. *Journal for Specialists in Group Work, 7,* 109-111.

Bowman, V., & DeLucia, J. (1993). Preparation for group therapy: The effects of preparer and modality on group process and individual functioning. *Journal for Specialists in Group Work, 18,* 67-79.

Brooks, G. (1998). *A new psychotherapy for traditional men.* San Francisco: Jossey-Bass.

Brown, S., Lipford-Sanders, J., & Shaw, M. (1995). Kujichagulia—Uncovering the secrets of the heart: Group work with African American women on predominantly white campuses. *Journal for Specialists in Group Work, 20,* 151-158.

Chickering, A., & Reisser, L. (1993). *Education and identity.* San Francisco: Jossey-Bass.

Chojnacki, J., & Gelberg, S. (1995). The facilitation of a gay/lesbian, bisexual support therapy group by heterosexual counselors. *Journal of Counseling and Development, 73,* 352-354.

Conyne, R., Lamb, D. H., & Strand, K. H. (1975). Group experiences in counseling centers: A national survey. *Journal of College Student Personnel, 16,* 196-200.

Corazzini, J. (1994). Staff beliefs which hinder the use of group treatment. In C. Sieber (Ed.), [Theme issue: Group Work in Counseling Centers] *Commission VII Counseling and Psychological Services Newsletter, 21,* 3.

Corey, M., & Corey, G. (2002). *Groups: Process and practice.* Pacific Grove, CA: Brooks/Cole.

Cornish, P. A., & Benton, D. (2001). Getting started in healthier relationships: Brief integrated dynamic group counseling in a university counseling setting. *Journal for Specialists in Group Work, 26,* 129-143.

Culbert, S., Clark, J., & Bobele, H. (1968). Measures of change toward self-actualization in two sensitivity training groups. *Journal of Counseling Psychology, 15*, 553-577.

Fitch, T., & Robinson, C. (1998). Counseling and development interventions with college athletes: A proposed model. *Journal of College Student Development, 39*(6), 623-627.

Freeman, M. S. (2001). Innovative alcohol education program for college and university judicial sanctions. *Journal of College Counseling, 4*, 179-186.

Fukuyama, M., & Coleman, N. (1992). A model for bicultural assertion training with Asian-Pacific American college students: A pilot study. *Journal for Specialists in Group Work, 17*(4), 210-217.

Genia, V. (1990). Psychospiritual group counseling for college students. *Journal of College Student Development, 31*, 279-280.

Golden, B. R., Corazzini, J. G., & Grady, P. (1993). Current practices of group therapy at university counseling centers: A national survey. *Professional Psychology: Research and Practice, 24*, 228-230.

Halstead, R. (1998). Academic success support groups. *Journal of College Student Development, 39*(5), 507-508.

Himelein, M. (1999). Acquaintance rape prevention with high risk women: Identification and inoculation. *Journal of College Student Development, 4*, 93-96.

Horne, A., & Mason, J. (1991, August). *Counseling men: A university campus experience.* Paper presented at the 99th annual meeting of the American Psychological Association, San Francisco, CA.

Jennings, M., & Anderson, K. (1997). Process groups: A survey of small college counseling center issues in solutions. *Journal of College Student Psychotherapy, 12*, 65-74.

Jordan, J. (1995). *Relational awareness: Transforming disconnection.* Wellesley, MA: Jean Baker Miller Training Institute.

Kalodner, C. R., Alfred, A. R., & Hoyt, W. T. (1997). Group research in applied settings: Examples and recommendations. *Journal for Specialists in Group Work, 22*, 253-265.

Keene State College Counseling Center. (2001, Fall). Current *Groups.* Retrieved October 30, 2001, from http://www.keene.edu/counseling/grouplist.cfm.

Leong, F. T. L., Wagner, N. S., & Kim, H. H. (1995). Group counseling expectations among Asian American Students: The role of culture-specific factors. *Journal of Counseling Psychology, 42*, 217-222.

MacNair, R. R., & Corazzini, J. G. (1994). Client factors influencing group therapy dropout. *Psychotherapy: Theory, Research, Practice and Training, 31*, 352-361.

MacNair-Semands, R. R. (2001, February). Assessment of group selection factors and therapeutic dynamics. In S. Taylor (Chair), *Current research in groups.* Symposium conducted at the annual meeting of the American Group Psychotherapy Association, Boston, MA.

MacNair-Semands, R. R. (2002). Predicting attendance and expectations for group therapy. *Group Dynamics, 6*, 219-228.

McWhirter, J. J. (1995). Emotional education for university students. *Journal of College Student Psychotherapy, 10*, 27-38.

Miami University of Ohio Student Counseling Services. (n.d.). *Group is often the best choice.* Retrieved October 30, 2001, from http://www.units.muohio.edu/saf/scs/services.html.

Montana State University Counseling and Psychological Services. (2001, Fall). *Groups for fall, 2001.* Retrieved October 30, 2001, from http://www.montana.edu/wwwcc/docs/groups-avai13.html.

Oregon State University Counseling and Psychological Services. (n.d.). *Groups.* Retrieved October 30, 2001, from http://www.oregonstate.edu/dept/counsel/groups.htm.

Quintana, S. M., Kilmartin, C., Yesenosky, J., & Macias, D. (1991). Factors affecting referral decisions in a university counseling center. *Professional Psychology: Research & Practice, 22*, 90-97.

Richards, P. S. (1993). A religiously oriented group counseling intervention for self defeating perfectionism: A pilot study. *Counseling and Values, 37*, 96-104.

Sack, R. T., Graham, M. F., & Simmons, K. P. (1995). Treatment groups for sexual abuse survivors on campus: Results of a national survey. *Journal of College Student Psychotherapy, 9*, 89-95.

Shem, S., & Surrey, J. (1998). *We have to talk: Healing dialogues between women and men.* New York: Basic Books.

Shippensburg University Counseling Center. (n.d.). *Group counseling.* Retrieved October 31, 2001, from http://www.ship.edu/~counstr/group.html.

State University of New York, University of Buffalo Counseling Services. (n.d.). *Group therapy at UB*. Retrieved October 30, 2001, from http://ub-counseling.buffalo.edu/aboutgroup.shtml.

Tannen, D. (2001). *You just don't understand: Women and men in conversation*. New York: Quill Paperbacks.

Welch, P. J. (1996). In search of a caring community: Group therapy for gay, lesbian and bisexual college students. *Journal of College Student Psychotherapy, 11*, 27-40.

Whitaker, L. (1992). Psychotherapy as a developmental process. In L. Whitaker & R. Slimack (Eds.), *College student development*. New York: Haworth.

Yalom, I. (1995). *The theory and practice of group psychotherapy* (4th ed.). New York: Basic Books.

27

BUILDING THE FOUNDATION FOR GROUP COUNSELING AND PSYCHOTHERAPY IN PRIVATE PRACTICE

DAVID W. CRAMER

Private Practice

Facilitating groups in private practice is similar to painting a landscape, limited only by the practitioner's imagination and ethical considerations. Each therapist can, using various mediums, paint a picture that represents his or her individual theoretical orientation. While serving the needs of the clientele, the group facilitator is also free to develop and offer groups that fit his or her individual interests. One can produce a sketch, such as creating and leading a group that meets on a single occasion, or one can establish a "work in progress," an ongoing group that meets for years upon end, with an ever-changing palette of members. This variety of canvasses and the freedom to create with few limits from an external organization is both the challenge and the reward of providing group psychotherapy services to a private clientele. Groups can be offered at various times of the week, can meet in the private office or can be arranged to be offered in community settings. This chapter presents and discusses the many critical issues that confront the private group practitioner, including the variety of group

structures, possible populations, and settings; facets that differentiate private practice from agency practice; and the fundamentals of developing a competent practice that uses group psychotherapy. A good way of introducing the reader to the many facets of this particular group practice is to present a vignette that captures many of these issues.

VIGNETTE

Two colleagues colead an ongoing psychotherapy group. Working together is a great pleasure for both of them. After starting the group several years ago, they did not raise their group fee for the first 5 years. At that time, they increased the fee for each group member by $5. Over time, they realized they were taking in much less money individually from this arrangement than they earn in the groups they conduct without a coleader. Two years after the initial increase, they informed the group members that the fee would increase another $15 per session.

As expected, there were many different reactions from group members. Several members began discussing the "greed" of the therapists and their anger about feeling attached to the group and valuing its benefit yet also feeling "trapped" into paying higher fees. Another member expressed her relief, as she had feared the leaders would build up resentment about their income, or worse yet, terminate the group due to the low financial intake. Yet another member acknowledged he had been considering leaving the group, because he was worried that the coleaders were not good examples of taking care of their own needs by having such a low fee in the group. Another member expressed similar concerns and acknowledged that secretly she had always yearned for a therapist who drove a Mercedes-Benz, which to her was a sign of success and competency. No one left the group as a result of this change. Instead, many new feelings were being brought to the surface. One member took on a part-time job to be able to stay in the group, and another member began to identify clear goals for himself and established a period of time for working on these goals in the group. The group leaders also began to understand more about their reluctance to charge a fee that would be more equivalent to others in their geographic location. For them, concerns about greed and self-interest had led them to charge a lower fee. In addition, one of the leaders was more anxious about handling client anger, and he realized that keeping his fee low was a way of undervaluing himself and "paying" his clients to not get angry with him.

Discussion of Vignette

Group therapists have the unique opportunity to learn about themselves through the conscious and unconscious ways in which they conduct their groups. Having standard policies around the fundamental issues of running a practice and facilitating groups aids the clinician evaluating his or her own process of leadership and helps to establish a safer place for group work to take place. For example, a set policy on fee increases on a regular basis (once a year, every other year, etc.) is one way of handling this issue. Clients can then be informed with enough notice to allow time for processing all the emotional overtones.

As this vignette indicates, there are multiple facets to creating and maintaining a group practice in the private setting (Cohen, 1993). It is primarily important that group leaders stay informed of their field. This edited handbook provides detailed and thorough information on the professional opportunities available that offer the clinician ongoing education, training, and access to research findings pertinent to group work. In addition, most major cities have professional organizations that can be a rich resource for attending to the educational and professional needs of the group practitioner. In general these organizations offer workshops, supervision, study groups, and an informal network of peers. Developing a sense of a community as a group therapist is of utmost importance in this work, as groups can be unpredictable and challenging entities. Group therapists will often find themselves dealing with a clinical issue that is confounding and/or frustrating. Using contacts with colleagues and supervisors for consultation will not only help foster the leader's growth and learning, but it can also minimize the burden of working alone. Much has been written about the power and input of group therapy on the individual member (Yalom, 1995), and this is often experienced and carried by the group therapist as well. Where else does the therapist have the good fortune and vulnerability of being in a room with several clients who will all have their individual transferences and projections at once? The growth of an ongoing psychodynamic group is dependent on the therapist's capacity to contain all the emotional vicissitudes of each member so that regression can be appropriately contained and working through can occur.

GROUP STRUCTURE, POPULATIONS, AND SETTINGS

The private practice group may be a long-term psychodynamic therapy group. While this is my orientation, it is only one form of group practice that can be conducted in this setting. The private practice environment is quite conducive to a wide array of group offerings. Time-limited groups that meet for a predetermined number of sessions are very amenable to this environment and usually will have a more structured or theme-oriented approach (MacKenzie, 1993). These may meet for 1 session or 10, depending on the topic, need of the clientele, and interests of the therapist. Examples of these types of groups are assertiveness training, anger management, depression, anxiety/panic, and divorce groups. Generally a combined educational and process blend makes up the group time, and the parameters often allow for outside group contact among members in order to encourage more supportive relationships among members. In addition, group therapists will need to be more active in their facilitation of these psychoeducational groups, which usually have a set curriculum of topics and exercises for each session (Drum & Lawler, 1988). Examples of these forms of groups are Smead's skill groups for children and young adults (Smead, 1990, 1994).

The client population may also define groups. Often a major attraction to a group for a client is a desire to "identify" with others, to feel a sense of belonging, safety, and likeness with others. Special populations groups became very popular in the 1970s and continue to be so, and can function as long-term psychotherapy groups or as a time-limited education/thematic group. These groups are often defined by a life experience (ACOA, battered spouses, refugees, death of one's child, Vietnam vets, divorce recovery, coping with loss and grief, loss of employment, survivors of the suicide of a loved one) or a specific identity (women's or men's groups, gay/lesbian/bisexual/transgendered groups, adolescents, the differently-abled, Hispanic women). Other groups in this category may be more defined by certain diagnoses or life problems (alcoholism and drug recovery, dissociation, panic disorders, PTSD, eating disorders). Others can be based more on specific interests or personal enrichment (spirituality groups, couples groups, supervision groups, and art therapy/dance/movement groups).

In general, these groups are most often conducted in the confidential setting of the private office. Yet the practitioner is not in any way limited to providing group services in this environment alone. The practitioner may also lead groups in other settings, such as schools, local hospitals and clinics, retreat settings (weekend groups), business settings (managerial training groups), religious institutions, or prisons. Again, the only limits are the desires and skills of the therapist. Each specific setting will require that the practitioner pay special attention to and address any restraints that each setting places on confidentiality and privacy. The degree of confidentiality available should also be discussed, as some settings are more conducive to greater confidentiality than others. Whatever limits exist should be acknowledged, so that all are aware of it, as confidentiality may be compromised in groups that are led outside the private office or with members who may know one another in other areas of their personal or work life.

What Differentiates the Private Group Practitioner?

Two variables that distinguish private practice from other settings are time and money. Private practitioners establish both their hours of work and fees. These are also important variables in conducting group therapy in this setting. When the group is offered, its length, the fee, and how fees are collected are important considerations likely to affect the course and purpose of group. Clinicians in early career stages would be well advised to learn about rates charged by established colleagues, as these vary widely across geographical areas. Fees, of course, can also vary based on the level of experience of the clinician. In general, it is customary to establish a set fee for all group members. However, some clinicians offer sliding scale fees based on ability to pay, and this can often provide a conduit to discussing money in the group, as different members may be paying different amounts based on their financial status. If the clinician accepts insurance, managed care, or other third-party payments, then various group members may pay a different co-pay for the group, and this too can be a good topic that facilitates the meaning of money in the group. These factors become opportunities to discuss important issues and dynamics that include responsibility, greed, envy, and power (Gans, 1992).

My personal policy includes the following parameters: groups are paid for a month in advance (this facilitates the dynamic of commitment), members pay for their seat even if they do not attend that session, payment is due at the beginning of each month, and bills are placed out openly at the first session of the month for group members to take. This process allows for all members to see what others are charged as well as what they have paid, which enhances the discussion of money in the group. Inevitably, how clients handle their fees will be reflective of important interpersonal dynamics for the clients, such as do they feel worthy, take time for their needs, or feel resentment about having to pay (need) the therapist. If a group member falls behind in payment, it is the responsibility of the therapist to address it as a clinical issue in the group. Many therapists find that dealing with money is a difficult issue, and they might be tempted to handle it one-on-one with the client. However, this would undermine the group by taking an important issue out of the group's awareness and not allowing the group to explore all the potential meanings and vicissitudes of this experience. Bringing up the issue directly at the beginning of group will usually lead to a fruitful process and model a healthy and open perspective concerning money.

Fundamental Principles and Suggestions

This section focuses on a number of suggestions that experience has proven to aid in the establishment of a successful group practice in the private sector. Many of these points are discussed earlier in this chapter but are mentioned again to highlight the importance of each item. These basic principles and suggestions include the areas of pregroup preparation (including informed consent), ethics, group maintenance, supervision, and therapist self-care. It is also extremely important that the therapist has had education and training in basic group theory and practice. Most graduate mental health degree programs offer courses on group work, and clinicians can get ongoing training through local group psychotherapy societies and at the national meetings of associations such as the American Group Psychotherapy Association, the Association for Specialists in Group Work, and others. In addition, I consider several books important for all clinicians considering the practice of group psychotherapy. These include Yalom (1995) and Rutan and Stone (2001), both

of which describe detailed theoretical views about group psychotherapy process.

Pregroup Interview

Screening members is an important aspect of ensuring a good fit between the goals and tasks of the group and each potential member. The pregroup interview is helpful in evaluating each referred member for a particular group. For example, an interpersonal short-term, psychoeducational group can include members from all walks of life, but due to its limited time period and focus on specific goals, it will generally require members with average or above intelligence and is often contraindicated for those with major depression or severe psychotic disorders. Rutan and Stone (2001) include other pertinent reasons why some individuals are not good candidates for group psychotherapy, including people in crisis, persons with very poor impulse control, and in certain instances, an individual who the therapist is simply too uncomfortable to work with. During the pregroup interview, the therapist can evaluate the client's background and inquire into the client's goals for his or her group psychotherapy experience.

I have found it helpful to ask about clients' interpersonal relationships, particularly assessing their attachment style, the quality of their relationships, and the manifestations of their needs within these relationships. Questions about the client's family dynamics and current interpersonal relationships can provide the therapist with an understanding of each group member's strengths and weaknesses in social interactions. I also inquire about the clients' connection to their parents, the strength and intimacy of other family and friendship relationships, and clients' interactions in various social settings, such as with colleagues and authority figures at work.

The use of preparatory materials during the pregroup interview can highly facilitate a group getting off to a good start and aid members in joining an ongoing group (Bowman & DeLucia, 1993). The American Group Psychotherapy Association has developed a brochure titled *A Consumer's Guide to Group Psychotherapy* (AGPA, 1995), which provides valuable information to the potential client on many facets of group psychotherapy. The brochure describes the purposes of group therapy, advantages of that particular form of treatment, information about evaluating a clinician's credentials, and some guidelines on what the client can expect from group psychotherapy. Clinicians can also develop forms pertaining to their specific group offerings and business guidelines. These forms can provide vital information to the potential member concerning the nature of the group, fees, confidentiality, the goals of the group, and the importance of attendance. In addition, this sheet can list any specific boundaries that are pertinent to the group. Some groups may allow and encourage outside member contact (thematic groups, for example), while others, such as long-term psychodynamic therapy groups, may discourage outside contact in order to keep the group process contained for exploration during the group meeting time. Two specific forms, one pertaining to general office practice information and one that discusses my approach to group therapy, are discussed in more detail below. In general, the use of preparatory material is encouraged as a way of promoting healthy decision making in aiding members in determining if the group may help them to meet their goals.

Office Policies and Information Form (See Chapter Appendix 1)

This form includes pertinent information about the general business policies of the clinician's practice, including the charge for services, the cancellation policy, and the limits of confidentiality. This information form clearly elucidates the policy for fees and collections. The specific conditions may vary widely from one therapist to the next, but it is important to fully inform all group clients of the requirements for payment and the possible consequences of nonpayment. Examples of fee arrangements include the following: (a) a single fee for each group session, (b) a set fee for each month of group sessions, (c) the same fee for each group member or a sliding scale fee based upon ability to pay, (d) acceptance of insurance or managed care arrangements and co-pays, (e) charges for each session regardless of attendance, (f) payment in full at the beginning of each month, and (g) use of collection agencies

for overdue charges. As is evident, the business side of group psychotherapy contains many elements of basic business practice. How a clinician handles payments and delinquencies in payments varies, based upon the clinician's theoretical orientation, personal comfort with dealing with money issues, and the type of group the clinician is conducting.

This form also clearly defines the present state of affairs pertaining to the legal limits of confidentiality. There are some occasions in which the law requires the clinician, in good judgment, to break confidentiality, and this includes the area of group work. Reviewing this consent forms allows the client to fully understand the nature and practice of psychotherapy and the extent that confidentiality may be offered. In addition, only the clinician is required to honor confidentiality. Thus it is important that members know that others in the group have agreed to the principle but it cannot be enforced legally.

Group Psychotherapy Process Form (see Chapter Appendix 2)

This form gives the potential client a clear understanding of some of the guidelines that help a particular type of group function in a healthy manner and can be used for an outpatient ongoing psychodynamic therapy group. This particular form addresses the behaviors of attendance, participation, confidentiality, team treatment with other clinicians, drug use and addictive behaviors, boundaries, and termination. A time-limited psychoeducational theme group might have very different guidelines, and this form could easily be adapted for use in that setting.

Ethics

Each segment of the mental health profession has developed its own ethical guidelines, most of which can be adapted well to group work. It is hoped that clinicians are well versed in the ethical guidelines of their profession and areas of specialty. In addition, the American Group Psychotherapy Association and the Association of Specialists in Group Work have each developed and published guidelines on ethics that practitioners are encouraged to integrate into their work. A thorough understanding of local, state, and federal laws pertaining to mental health issues is advisable. Confidentiality is of utmost importance in any psychotherapy medium and needs to be monitored carefully in the group setting in particular. Breaches in confidentiality by group members should be addressed quickly and intently to explore and determine the various possible meanings of the breach and to protect against future occurrences. If a member cannot maintain confidentiality, then the safety of the other group members is imperiled, and the offending member should be terminated from the group.

Starting a Group in Private Practice

Several considerations can facilitate getting a group started in this setting. Perhaps the primary factor for therapists contemplating starting a group is the attitude and beliefs of those therapists about group therapy. The more positive therapists are about group psychotherapy as a growth/healing medium, the more likely their clientele will respond favorably to the suggestion of joining a group. It behooves therapists to understand how the therapeutic aspects of a group work, so they can convey this in understandable terms to the potential client. I have found it helpful to have the consulting room arranged so that individual, couples, family, and group therapy all take place in the same setting. Clients in individual therapy see the group therapy furniture from their very first visit. Often, they ask about group on their own volition. In general, clinicians can start a group once they have three or four reliable members and then allow the group to grow over time to the desirable number of members. If the group is to reach a limit of eight, and starts with three initial members, it is advisable to have five empty chairs present to represent the members yet to join. Therapists can get referrals by announcing their services to other professionals, by attending and joining local group psychotherapy professional societies, and even by advertising in specific publications, such as local area health magazines.

Group Maintenance

This section focuses on important issues of ongoing group work that are of particular importance to the private practice setting. The particular areas discussed are boundaries, money/fees, managing absences and vacations, starting the group, supervision, and therapist self-care.

Boundaries

The leaders' role of facilitating the group, establishing trust, and aiding the progress of the group is greatly based on the level of consistency they display in running their practice and groups. Starting and ending each group on time is a primary action. Leaders who are late to group are likely to have difficulty dealing with members who attend sporadically. Discussing and emphasizing the importance of confidentiality also enhances a feeling of trust and safety, which is very important if members are to be expected to reveal themselves genuinely to one another. Enforcement of other "rules" pertinent to each group is to be observed. Two examples of these additional items include allowable group social contact and touch. A psychodynamic group model may discourage both touch and outside group contact among members in order to encourage verbal communication and exploration. Other groups, such as structured/thematic groups, movement-oriented groups, or bioenergetic groups, may encourage safe touch and allow outside group contact. The "rules" (such as those listed on the Group Psychotherapy Process Form) help define and promote the nature of each specific group and inherent goals of that group. Of course, it is important to understand and utilize the rules as a means of exploration and understanding a client's behavior. With few exceptions, the rules are not meant to be used to control, reward, or punish clients. Typically, clients may gain understanding of some part of their problems by exploring their reactions to specific rules. Why did the client "break" that particular rule and not other ones? Why is this rule being "violated" at this particular time? Some violations may result in withdrawing a client from group, but these are rare and extreme occasions. Clients who refuse to pay their bill, who attend very sporadically, or who refuse to honor the confidentiality of the other members may have to be removed in order for the group to function securely.

Money and Fees

Another variable has to do with how patients' bills are distributed. Are the statements mailed, handed to the client, distributed in group or outside of group? While personal preference of the leader may dictate how such matters are handled, a consistent and equal treatment to all members will enhance a more therapeutic group experience for the members. Informed consent is crucial. Private practice is, partially by definition, replete with interpersonal dynamics that pertain to issues relevant to money. It is important that self-employed clinicians focus on their own dynamics about money and about being self-supporting. Most graduate programs in mental health provide little or no training about the business side of running a practice. Again, colleagues in professional groups can be a great resource for the beginning group practitioner. There are a multitude of issues around money that clinicians must handle, such as raising fees, collecting payments, discussing money in the group, their reactions to underpayments or overpayments, balancing a healthy self-interest with greed, and whether to accept insurance and managed care co-pays.

Therapist Absences

From time to time the therapist may miss group sessions due to vacations and illnesses. In a time-limited group, it may be easy to simply have the group not meet while the therapist is not available. In ongoing groups, the leader has other options, which may be used based upon the clinician's judgment. For example, instead of canceling the group, leaders may want to bring in another therapist to facilitate the group during their absence. I have found that some of my groups benefit from continuing to meet during my absences with a female leader who has been substitute leading my groups for several years. Not only does it give the members a chance to experience a leader of a different gender, but the members also value the opportunity to explore their feelings about me outside my presence. Another option is to allow a group to meet leaderless, if in the leader's opinion the group is safe and mature. Of course, if no

therapist is present, then the services for that session are usually not charged.

Supervision and Training

Ongoing training through supervision and continuing education workshops will help the group therapist stay abreast of the field and develop peer and collegial relationships. Ongoing supervision can be particularly helpful for novice private practitioners, to aid them in establishing their group policies and digesting the many levels of information from a single group session. In addition, the clinician can inquire with local group psychotherapy societies about potential learning opportunities in study or supervision groups led by senior therapists. Some of the larger metropolitan areas have postgraduate courses of study that often include extensive group psychotherapy training.

Therapist Self-Care

Leading groups in private practice is a challenging and rewarding experience. Often, group leaders need a place to take their feelings about the work, and to detoxify or be better able to leave the burdens of the work at the office. Vicarious traumatization (McCann & Pearlman, 1990), the effect of ongoing exposure to the deep pain and traumas of our clients, can impede the therapist's capacity to work effectively and enjoy life fully. The therapist can invoke multiple strategies to help balance the may stresses of the work and prevent burnout (Kottler, 1999). Our work is best done with involvement from others (Courtois, 1993). Supervision and consultation can provide education, support, and help in strengthening boundaries between our personal and professional activities. Being careful to monitor our caseloads in terms of size and number of trauma cases can prevent depletion. Personal psychotherapy for the therapist is one valuable way of helping the therapist maintain a healthy lifestyle while working with clients and their difficulties. In addition, being a member of a psychotherapy group can also not only aid therapists' personal growth but also give them the valuable insight of what it is like to be a member of such a process.

CONCLUSION

This chapter has focused on many of the fascinating facets of independent practice that the reader will find helpful in conducting groups in a private setting. The mental health field in general has undergone major shifts and changes during the last decade. Many of these changes, including the growth and spread of managed care, will affect group psychotherapy and private practice in particular. The popularity of group psychotherapy has grown significantly, in part due to its cost-effective nature. Group therapy in general is far more affordable than individual psychotherapy. MacKenzie (2001) and Stone (2001) both speak to the changes that the group profession is undergoing. They predict that group services will continue to expand in the future. In particular, thematic and structured groups that treat specific diagnostic conditions will likely become more popular and be the treatment of choice for those conditions. Rosenberg and Zimet (1995) have shown the effectiveness of these group models in their review of a selected set of studies that evaluated the effectiveness of brief outpatient group therapy. The private practitioner who develops skills and training in group psychotherapy will be better able to offer a wide array of services and survive in a more competitive marketplace.

REFERENCES

American Group Psychological Association, Inc. (1995). *A consumer's guide to group psychotherapy*. New York: Author.

Bowman, V., & DeLucia, J. L. (1993). Preparation for group therapy: The effects of preparer and modality on group process and individual functioning. *Journal for Specialists in Group Work, 18,* 67-79.

Cohen, A. (1993). Establishing groups in an individual office practice. In A. Alonso & H. I. Swiller (Eds.), *Group therapy in clinical practice* (pp. 357-367). Washington, DC: American Psychiatric Press.

Courtois, C. (1993). Vicarious traumatization of the therapist. *NCP Clinical Newsletter, 3,* 8-9.

Drum, D., & Lawler, A. C. (1988). *Developmental interventions: Theories, principles and practice.* Columbus, OH: Merrill Publishing.

Gans, J. S. (1992). Money and psychodynamic group psychotherapy. *International Journal of Group Psychotherapy, 42,* 133-152.

Kottler, J. A. (1999). *The therapist's workbook: Self-assessment, self-care, and self-improvement exercises for mental health professionals.* Hoboken, NJ: John Wiley.

MacKenzie, R. (1993). Time-limited group therapy and technique. In A. Alonso & H. I. Swiller (Eds.), *Group therapy in clinical practice* (pp. 423-447). Washington, DC: American Psychiatric Press.

MacKenzie, R. (2001). An expectation of radical changes in the future of group psychotherapy. *International Journal of Group Psychotherapy, 51*(2), 175-180.

McCann, I. L., & Pearlman, L. A. (1990). *Psychological trauma and the adult survivor: Theory, therapy, and transformation.* New York: Brunner/Mazel.

Rosenberg, S., & Zimet, C. (1995). Brief group treatment and managed mental health care. *International Journal of Group Psychotherapy, 45,* 367-380.

Rutan, S., & Stone, W. (2001). *Psychodynamic group psychotherapy.* New York: Guilford.

Smead, R. (1990). *Skills for living: Group counseling activities for young adolescents.* Champaign, IL: Research Press.

Smead, R. (1994). *Skills for living: Group counseling activities for elementary students.* Champaign, IL: Research Press.

Stone, W. (2001). A retrospective of group therapy: A letter. *International Journal of Group Psychotherapy, 51,*169-174.

Yalom, I. (1995). *The theory and practice of group psychotherapy* (4th ed.). New York: Basic Books.

APPENDIX 1

Office Policies and Procedures

1. Office charges for therapy are based on a rate of \$_____ per 45-minute appointment. Group therapy is billed at \$_____ per 90-minute group. If the client is covered by a special insurance contract that Dr. Cramer participates in, those allowable fees and arrangements will be substituted.

2. All fees for individual, couples, and family therapy are payable at the time of the appointment unless specific alternate arrangements are made. If bills accrue for services, terms for payment should be made in advance. Fees for group therapy are billed at the beginning of the month in advance.

3. Any fees relating to foreseen or unforeseen legal actions that require Dr. Cramer to reproduce records or participate in depositions or court appearances will be the responsibility of the person signing below. Such fees are substantially higher than therapy fees and are not usually covered by insurance. This is without regard to who files the subpoena or initiates the legal action. It is the signer's responsibility to obtain reimbursement from any other party. These fees must be paid in advance.

4. A charge is made for all appointments unless cancelled 48 hours in advance. Cancellations made within 24 hours will be charged at 100% of the fee. Cancellations made between 24 and 48 hours will be charged at 50% of the fee. Group therapy sessions cannot be cancelled, and payment is required regardless of attendance. The client should be aware that insurance generally does not reimburse for late cancels or missed appointments. Certain circumstances, such as illness, are exempt from this charge.

5. Delinquent accounts may be turned over for collection to a collection agency, although every effort is made to avoid this action. If efforts to arrange payment are unsuccessful and the bill is sent to collection, the balance due will be increased by the total of all collection agency fees, plus a finance charge of 18% ANNUAL PERCENTAGE RATE (1.5% per month) on the unpaid account balance. The undersigned is also responsible for any/or all legal fees and court costs connected to collection.

6. In signing this form, you assign insurance benefits to Dr. Cramer for any charges that he submits to your insurance company. While filing for insurance is usually left to the client, some insurance companies require that Dr. Cramer do the filing. This form authorizes him to do so and to collect the fees from the carrier.

_____   _____

Signature of Responsible Party   Date

_____   _____

Home Address   City, State, & Zip Code

_____   _____

Home Telephone   Work Telephone

_____   _____

Social Security Number   Date

APPENDIX 2

Group Psychotherapy Process Form

While people seek psychotherapy for many different reasons, all have some problems in establishing and maintaining close and gratifying relationships with others. Often, they have wished that they understood relationships better and wished that they could be really honest about their positive and negative feelings with someone and get reciprocally honest feedback. The therapy group attempts to set up a situation where this type of honest, interpersonal exploration will occur.

Inevitably, members will experience others in the group similarly to the ways in which they experience intimate others outside the group, or similarly to the ways in which they experienced family members while they were growing up. All group members should be committed to learning about themselves and their relationships to others outside of therapy and how that all relates to their early relationships within their families. To this end, all group members must be committed to the instrumental goal of expressing all their thoughts and feelings as they occur within the group. The way in which members can learn the most in a group is by being honest and direct with their feelings in the group at that moment, especially feelings toward the other group members and the therapist. Members' thoughts and feelings in the present are the database from which group psychotherapy flows. The following guidelines will foster your personal growth in the group:

1. Members are asked to attend the group regularly for at least 3 months before making a decision about whether or not this is the group for them. It takes a minimum of 3 months for members to feel comfortable enough to begin to evaluate the usefulness of a particular group. The course of therapy is expected to be considerably longer than this.

2. Regular and timely attendance at all sessions is important. Members agree to try to be present each week, to arrive on time, and remain throughout the entire meeting. As a member, it is your responsibility to notify the group in advance when it is absolutely necessary for you to be away or to be late for a group.

3. Members have a commitment to share all feelings, reactions, and thoughts during the group meetings as a way of increasing their understanding of their interpersonal dynamics.

4. As a member, you are agreeing to work actively on the problems that brought you to the group. This will require all group members to take their fair share of group time. Members also have a commitment to talk about important issues in their lives that cause difficulty in relating to others or in living life fully. It is assumed that these difficulties will be reenacted within the group and will be available for exploration by group.

5. Members will treat matters that occur in the group with utmost confidentiality. To that end, members agree to keep confidential the names and identities of all group members.

6. While you must observe the utmost confidentiality relating to individuals that are not a part of your "treatment team," there are absolutely no secrets among members of your treatment team. Your treatment team consists of your group therapist, your individual and/or couples therapist, your psychiatrist, and all members of your psychotherapy group. Thus, what you share in the group or in individual and/or couples therapy or with your psychiatrist may be shared with other members of your treatment team when anyone feels that it is important for your treatment to do so.

7. The use of any illegal drugs, even when used recreationally, is strongly discouraged. Those who choose to drink alcohol, or to use an illegal substance, agree to try to abstain from usage on the day of the group meeting. Group members who are taking medication for physical or emotional concerns are asked to inform Dr. Cramer of their medication regimen.

8. Group members who are experiencing active addiction problems (food, alcohol, drugs, sex, etc.) may be asked to sign abstinence contracts. Supplemental support, self-help groups, 12-step programs, or other forms of treatment may be recommended to address particular types of problems. This will be assessed and implemented on an individual basis.

9. Members agree to use relationships in the group therapeutically—not socially. The group provides an opportunity for learning about one's problems in social relationships, and in general, outside contact hinders this exploration.

10. Members agree to discuss termination from the group several weeks in advance if they are considering leaving the group. It is important for everyone to have an opportunity to express and explore their feelings about the pending departure.

11. The fee for group is charged 1 month in advance. Members are responsible for payment for their space in group even on weeks that they are unable to attend.

I am committed to the above therapeutic goals and guidelines for group psychotherapy.

Signed _____

Date _____

28

GROUPS WITH OFFENDERS AND MANDATED CLIENTS

ROBERT D. MORGAN

Texas Tech University

A common mantra from correctional mental health professionals is "If you can facilitate groups in here, you can facilitate groups anywhere." The uniqueness of working with this population is a sentiment not only felt among penitentiary care providers, but is a truism, as we know that group treatment with offender and mandated client populations presents problems not typical of therapy groups in other settings (Coyne & Fabricatore, 1979; Morgan, Winterowd, & Ferrell, 1999). Unfortunately, there remains a paucity of published literature focusing on treatment strategies with offenders and other mandated clients (Riordan & Martin, 1993). Nevertheless, group psychotherapy with incarcerated offenders, including mandated clients, results in positive treatment gains across a range of outcome variables (e.g., Morgan & Flora, 2002).

The purpose of this chapter is to discuss strategies for the application of group therapy with offenders and mandated clients. This chapter discusses the types of groups applicable for these populations (i.e., psychoeducational groups, counseling groups, psychotherapy groups), treatment goals in group work, therapeutic strategies for working with these difficult clients, and the benefits of the group modality for working with these populations. Furthermore, this chapter concludes with a discussion of the need for further group counseling and therapy research and the barriers to such research with offenders and mandated clients.

It should be noted that for purposes of this chapter, offenders refers to people convicted of a crime and includes both incarcerated (i.e., housed in a secure correctional environment) and nonincarcerated (i.e., on parole, probation, etc.) offenders, whereas mandated clients refers to clients required to attend treatment services by a governing agency (e.g., a department of corrections, the judicial system, parole/probation officers, etc.).

TYPES OF OFFENDER AND MANDATED GROUPS

As indicated in previous chapters, group therapy can be categorized into four primary types of groups: task groups, psychoeducational groups, counseling groups, and psychotherapy groups. Group therapists in state correctional institutions facilitate a variety of groups (Morgan, Winterowd, & Ferrell, 1999) that fit broadly into these categories, with the lone exception being the task group. Few opportunities exist for the facilitation of task or work groups in correctional environments; however, psychoeducational groups, counseling groups, and psychotherapy groups appear readily available (and appropriate) for offenders and other mandated clients.

PSYCHOEDUCATIONAL GROUPS WITH OFFENDERS AND MANDATED CLIENTS

Psychoeducational groups incorporate educational and developmental strategies (ASGW, 2000) into the therapeutic process to facilitate growth and change. Research with offenders indicates that the most favorable results occur when cognitive-behavioral or behavioral approaches are incorporated into rehabilitation treatment programs (Andrews, Zinger et al., 1990; Garrett, 1985; Gendreau & Ross, 1981), including group treatment approaches (Morgan & Flora, 2002). It has been further documented that structure results in beneficial outcomes for this particular population (e.g., Leak, 1980; Morgan & Flora, 2002) and that group therapists also responded favorably when structure was incorporated into group work with offenders (e.g., Morgan, Winterowd, & Fuqua, 1999). Thus, structured psychoeducational groups may be a preferred treatment modality, particularly for new professionals, because this group treatment modality tends to require less clinical experience. Furthermore, the structure of psychoeducational groups may be particularly beneficial for therapists, given that co-leadership and group supervision are relatively uncommon with incarcerated offenders (Morgan, Winterowd, & Ferrell, 1999). In addition, there appears to be a trend to employ nondoctoral-level providers in state correctional facilities (Morgan, Winterowd, & Ferrell, 1999), and those who have received less formal education and training may feel more comfortable with the structure and educational components of the psychoeducational group.

Not surprisingly, many types of groups for offenders or mandated clients appear amenable to a structured psychoeducational modality, including anger or stress management, problem-solving skills, life skills, cognitive restructuring or criminal thinking errors, as well as recidivism-focused groups. Psychoeducational components can also be included in groups focused on substance abuse, sexual offending, and domestic violence. Functional outcomes of structured psychoeducational strategies include (a) decreased defensiveness compared to the more ambiguous group counseling and group psychotherapy models, (b) decreased need to test the group, the therapeutic boundaries, or the therapist, and (c) fewer hidden agendas (Shields, 1986). In addition, the structure provided in psychoeducational groups may provide direction and focus in early group sessions that is less prevalent in other types of group work (i.e., group counseling, group psychotherapy). This is particularly relevant for offender and mandated clients, as they are frequently resistant to the therapeutic process (Milgram & Rubin, 1992; Rappaport, 1982) and may actively pursue efforts to avoid engaging in treatment (Riordan & Martin, 1993). Increased focus and direction may also limit the clients' need to find meaning in the group (i.e., searching for the purpose of the group as it relates to them), thereby orienting the mandated client to focus on the topic at hand.

Based on a meta-analytic review of group treatment methods with inmates, out-of-group homework exercises resulted in improved outcomes compared to groups not utilizing such exercises (Morgan & Flora, 2002). Therefore, when facilitating psychoeducational groups with offenders and mandated clients, out-of-group homework exercises should be incorporated to improve outcomes. It should be noted, however, that offenders and mandated clients might be resistant to completing work outside of group sessions (e.g., Morgan, Winterowd, & Fuqua, 1999); thus, therapists will need to provide a solid rationale for the program and promptly address any lack of client compliance with assigned homework exercises.

Of particular interest for psychoeducational groups with offenders and mandated clients is the opportunity (and need) to develop group treatment programs aimed at helping these clients facilitate cognitive changes that may ultimately reduce the likelihood of future criminal behavior. Offenders think differently than do nonoffenders (Walters, 1990; Yochelson & Samenow, 1976). For example, offenders exhibit a cognitive pattern of "ownership" whereby they think that if they want something, it is theirs to have. Thus, therapy efforts need to address the cognitive thinking errors that are specific to offender populations to help them identify, evaluate, and modify the thinking errors that contribute to their antisocial problems. Preliminary efforts at designing such treatment programs have begun (e.g., Fox, 1999; Morgan, 2000; Morgan, Winterowd, & Fuqua, 1999); however, additional research is warranted to identify treatment programs that result in significant reductions in the number and occurrence of criminal thinking errors that result in unlawful or antisocial behavior.

Counseling Groups

Group counseling is typically preventative, with an educational, vocational, social, or personal focus aimed at enhancing growth (ASGW, 2000; Corey, 1995). An institutional adjustment group is one example of a counseling group with incarcerated offenders. This particular group is not aimed at remediation or personality restructuring; rather, it is aimed at assisting the offender to function at the highest possible level within the confines of a correctional environment. In fact, the social support received from counseling groups may allow incarcerated offenders to cope with the circumstances and problems of incarceration (Mathias & Sindberg, 1986). Other examples of counseling groups with offenders and mandated clients include vocational group counseling, relationship enhancement groups, and support groups, to name a few.

In spite of the increasing presence of mental illness among offenders in the criminal justice system (Condelli, Bradigan, & Holanchock, 1997; Hodgins, 1995; Steadman, Morris, & Dennis, 1995; Torrey, 1995), not all offenders or mandated therapy clients suffer from severe psychopathology. Rather, some offenders have engaged in poor life choices, and group counseling is sufficient for these clients to achieve an optimal level of functioning, both in the penitentiary setting as well as after released into society. The goal of group counseling with these clients is to increase self-awareness, identify attitudes, choices, and behaviors that led to problematic behavior, and promote prosocial decision making and behavior.

Rehabilitational groups focus on strategies aimed at reducing recidivism, particularly on prosocial integration back into society (Morgan, Winterowd, & Ferrell, 1999). As previously indicated, correctional rehabilitation necessitates a variety of treatment programs (Boudouris, 1984). Group therapy can contribute to the process of offender rehabilitation by offering groups focused on cognitive restructuring, criminogenic needs (dynamic factors, such as antisocial beliefs, inadequate work skills or anger/hostility, that contribute to recidivism (Andrews, Zinger et al., 1990), and recidivism issues. Groups may also serve to supplement other rehabilitative programs such as substance abuse, vocational, educational, and leisure programs.

Psychotherapy Groups

Unlike counseling groups, the focus of group psychotherapy with offenders and mandated clients is typically on the remediation of problematic behaviors and personality restructuring (ASGW, 2000; Corey, 1995). The goal of psychotherapy groups is to reduce future harmful behaviors and antisocial acts (both while incarcerated as well as when released into the free world). More specifically, the focus of group psychotherapy is on the "here and now" of dysfunctional interactions as they occur within the group (Yalom, 1995) with the goal of using these interactions to facilitate increased self-awareness and behavioral change (Dustin & George, 1973). In fact, developing functional peer relationships (possibly for the first time) is one of the primary benefits of group psychotherapy with offenders (Yong, 1971).

Typical problems presented by incarcerated offenders include depression, anger, psychoses, stress and anxiety, and substance abuse (e.g., Boothby & Clements, 2000; Morgan, Winterowd, & Ferrell, 1999), and general mental health groups for offenders focus on psychological problems that the group members are experiencing at the time with emphasis placed on symptom reduction and the development of adaptive coping skills (Morgan, Winterowd, & Ferrell, 1999). Group psychotherapy, with its focus on remediation and personality restructuring, offers an appropriate therapeutic milieu for addressing such problems.

Therapeutic Factors

Morgan and Winterowd (2002) reviewed how Yalom's (1995) therapeutic factors pertain to offender populations and provide specific suggestions for facilitating these factors with offender groups; however, it is noted that few studies have investigated the impact of the therapeutic factors in psychotherapy groups with offenders.

In general, offenders view the therapeutic factors similarly to other client populations (Long & Cope, 1980; Steinfeld & Mabli, 1974). In the first study to investigate the importance of Yalom's therapeutic factors with offenders, Steinfeld and Mabli (1974) utilized a 60-item Q-sort method and found that male offenders ranked insight, catharsis, and existential factors as the most helpful therapeutic factors. Long and Cope (1980) also utilized a 60-item Q-sort method and found that male offenders rated the therapeutic factors similarly to outpatient psychotherapy groups (i.e., Yalom, Tinklenberg, and Gilula, as cited in Yalom, 1995), with catharsis, cohesiveness, and interpersonal learning output as the most valued therapeutic factors. In a follow-up study, MacDevitt and Sanislow (1987) presented male offenders in differing levels of security restriction with 60-items using a Likert-type scale as an alternative to the Q-sort method and found that some therapeutic factors valued by offenders tend to vary with changes in the restrictiveness of the correctional environment (e.g., minimum to maximum security). For example, interpersonal learning was increasingly valued by inmates as the restrictiveness of the environment increased, whereas factors such as catharsis, existential awareness, and instillation of hope were consistently perceived as more important by inmates across security levels.

Of concern with regard to the therapeutic factors in group psychotherapy with offenders is that group therapists and offenders may differentially value some of these therapeutic factors (Morgan, Ferrell, & Winterowd, 1999). For example, catharsis and the existential factors were rated as less important than other therapeutic factors by group therapists (Morgan, Ferrell et al., 1999), whereas these factors were rated as important therapeutic factors by offender group participants (Long & Cope, 1980; MacDevitt & Sanislow III, 1987). In other words, although offender clients highly value the therapeutic factors of catharsis and existential factors, group therapists view these factors as less important. Although such differences between clients and therapists are of concern with any group (e.g., Randall, 1995), they may be particularly problematic for therapy groups with offenders and other mandated clients (Morgan, Ferrell et al., 1999). As already indicated, mandated clients are likely to be resistant to the therapeutic process, and indications that the therapist is working at cross-purposes may increase feelings of paranoia, suspicion, and concern regarding the perceived hidden agenda of the therapist. Furthermore, offenders and mandated clients may be presenting with needs that are unrecognized by group therapists (e.g., dealing with the existential issues of incarceration); thus, therapists must provide ample opportunity for mandated clients and offenders to explore the purpose of the group and their direction in life (regardless if they are living their life in a prison environment or as a free person in society).

These therapeutic factors are necessary but not sufficient for offenders and mandated clients to experience significant change. In fact, Yalom (1995) noted that it is the therapist's job to facilitate a therapeutic environment and focus on the interpersonal dynamics between and among group members as they occur (Yalom, 1995). Offenders are capable of developing a group environment whereby the group members are responsible for the therapeutic process, and interpersonally oriented group psychotherapy helps offenders (both voluntary and involuntary group participants) develop responsibility for the working of the group (Morgan, Winterowd, & Fuqua, 1999). Although this level of therapeutic responsibility and group participation is possible to achieve with offenders and mandated clients, it is not a natural skill for them. Therapists must work to establish a therapeutic environment by teaching clients appropriate group behavior (e.g., directing comments to other group members rather than just the therapist), modeling trust and authenticity (via appropriate self-disclosure and restraint), and reinforcing risk-taking behavior (for a more detailed description of the therapist's task in establishing a therapeutic environment for offender populations, the reader is referred to Morgan and Winterowd, 2002).

Here-and-Now Interaction

Although task groups, psychoeducational groups, and group counseling are applied in the context of "here-and-now" interactions (ASGW, 2000), focusing on dysfunctional interpersonal interactions of group members as they occur in the moment is the hallmark of group psychotherapy. Group psychotherapy with offenders and mandated clients is no different. The majority of offenders and mandated clients are not accustomed to evaluating their own behavior, particularly in an interpersonal context. Nevertheless, interpersonal problems are at the heart of offenders' and mandated clients' behavior. Hurting (emotionally or physically), manipulating, taking advantage of, and violating the rights of others, typical characteristics of offenders and mandated clients, are interpersonal problems. Thus, group psychotherapy affords offenders and mandated clients an opportunity to begin to learn about their behavior, and more important, how their behavior affects others. In turn, as they learn of the effect their behavior has on others, they discover that their behavior affects how others respond to them. Thus, the goal of this interpersonal focus with offenders and mandated clients is that they begin to accept responsibility for their interpersonal style, the impact this interpersonal style has on others, and how this contributes to their antisocial behaviors, as well as how their interpersonal style affects how other people respond to them (Morgan & Winterowd, 2002).

Correctional professionals have described the use of unstructured relationship-oriented groups as unhelpful to the rehabilitation of offenders (e.g., Andrews, Zinger et al., 1990). In fact, Andrews, Zinger et al. (1990) refer to dynamic, nondirective, or communicative groups as ineffective and potentially counterproductive to the rehabilitative process. However, these criticisms have attacked such groups from the framework of the group as the sole rehabilitative model, and offender rehabilitation does not occur within the scope of one treatment; rather, it is a process that requires several treatment approaches (Bourdais, 1984). Group psychotherapy that focuses on increased knowledge of one's interpersonal style will not likely, in and of itself, lead to a reformed offender or mandated client. However, when combined with other treatment programs (e.g., cognitive-behavioral interventions, vocational and educational programs, substance abuse programs), group psychotherapy may lead to improved overall functioning (i.e., increased prosocial behavior). Furthermore, any therapeutic program that facilitates the process of offenders accepting responsibility for themselves and their behavior (including responsibility for therapeutic progress as discussed in Morgan, Winterowd, & Fuqua, 1999) is certain to be beneficial toward the overall goal of increased social responsibility and a reduction of recidivism.

AN INTEGRATED GROUP MODEL

The distinction between the differing types of groups is ambiguous with much overlap, particularly when differentiating between group counseling and group psychotherapy (Corey, 1995; Gazda, Ginter, & Horne, 2001). Group work with offenders is no exception, and group therapists may frequently find themselves alternating among the three types of groups discussed previously (i.e., psychoeducational groups, group counseling, group psychotherapy). However, given the nature of the clientele, that is, antisocial personalities with a tendency for indirect harm to self and direct harm to others, group psychotherapy may become the treatment of choice with psychoeducational approaches integrated, as suggested by Morgan and Winterowd (2002). For example, it is not uncommon during a group psychotherapy session that a therapist may need to educate group members about various issues. Newly incarcerated offenders may be naïve to the structure and unwritten rules (i.e., inmate code) of the penitentiary environment (e.g., Demuth, 1995). A group therapist may temporarily alter the group psychotherapy format to provide education (via a didactic format) to newly incarcerated offenders about the unwritten rules of a penitentiary and to teach survival tactics.

Similarly, a group therapist leading a group for mentally ill offenders may need to educate group members about their mental illnesses followed by the implementation of counseling strategies to assist group members in the prevention of relapse. Such needs frequently arise in psychotherapy groups with offenders and mandated clients, and group therapists need to be flexible to adjust the style of leadership to meet the needs of the participants. This appears particularly relevant for group therapists working in a correctional environment in which practitioners provide services aimed at multiple and varied presenting problems with heterogeneous offender populations (Boothby & Clements, 2000).

GOALS OF GROUP THERAPY WITH OFFENDERS AND MANDATED CLIENTS

General group goals with offenders and mandated clients include learning more about themselves (Kahnweiler, 1978), increased awareness of values and opinions (Scott, 1993), improved relationships with others (Gendreau, 1996; Ionedes, 1962; Kahnweiler, 1978; Yong, 1971), modifying antisocial behaviors and attitudes (Walters, 1990; Wardrop, 1976; Yochelson & Samenow, 1976), lifestyle issues such as substance abuse, career development, and leisure interests (Gendreau, 1996; Walters, 1990), increased social support (French, 1981), and effective expression of feelings and emotions (e.g., Halleck, 1960). Given the tendency for group work with this population to be heterogeneous in nature (Boothby & Clements, 2000), group goals tend to be diverse and varied, dependent upon the needs of the group.

An understanding of universal and overarching goals with offenders and mandated clients, however, provides a conceptual framework from which group therapists can develop appropriate groups. Winterowd, Morgan, and Ferrell (2001) reported the results of a factor analysis resulting in eight overarching goals reported by group therapists working with incarcerated offenders. These goals include the following:

1. *Self-exploration and learning within a supportive group environment*: focuses on personal awareness and relational and coping skills within a cohesive and supportive group environment

2. *Group relationship building*: focuses on the development of interpersonal awareness and interpersonal dynamics

3. *Substance abuse*: focuses on substance abuse and issues surrounding addictive behaviors

4. *Learning healthier attitudes and behaviors*: focuses on the acquisition of behavioral skills (conflict resolution, social skills, anger management) and insight (personal growth)

5. *Conformity*: focuses on rule compliance (recidivism issues and institutional compliance)

6. *Prosocial behavior*: focuses on improved interpersonal functioning in relationships and preparing for life outside prison

7. *Lifestyle*: focuses on developing a healthy and productive lifestyle (e.g., career issues, diet, stress management, and the development of leisure activities)

8. *Institutional adjustment*: focuses on inmates' need to deal with prison life and includes relationships with inmates as well as prison staff, stress/anger/crisis management, and coping with the existential issues of incarceration

Although several of these goals are not unique to group work with offenders or mandated clients, several of these factors (i.e., prosocial behavior modification, conformity issues, and institutional adjustment issues) are unique to group work with these special populations. More important, these group goals are consistent with the criminogenic needs of offenders (Andrews & Bonta, 1994; Andrews, Bonta, & Hoge, 1990), which have been found to be critical to the effectiveness of treatment programming with offenders (Gendreau, 1996). Furthermore, these group goals can provide a framework and structure to the therapeutic milieu, which may be preferred by both inmates and group facilitators. In addition, these goals are conceptually broad so as to provide guidelines for a comprehensive group therapy rehabilitation program.

STRATEGIES FOR
WORKING WITH RESISTANT
OFFENDERS AND MANDATED CLIENTS

As previously noted, group psychotherapy with offenders and mandated clients presents unique problems not encountered by group therapists working with other populations (e.g., Coyne & Fabricatore, 1979). Of utmost concern is the potential for resistance to disrupt the therapeutic process. Unfortunately, offenders (and likely mandated clients) harbor negative attitudes toward treatment programs (particularly mandated treatment programs) (Rappaport, 1982) and exhibit lack of trust that may never be fully overcome (Mathias & Sindberg, 1985). Furthermore, the prison environment does not support inmate trust and self-disclosure (Halleck, 1960; Mathias & Sindberg, 1985), and the very nature of mandated treatment programs with required reporting of participation (e.g., brief reports to parole officers that the client is or is not regularly attending group sessions) creates barriers to the therapeutic process, as therapists may be viewed as "cops." Further complicating treatment in institutional settings is the possibility that offenders may be subjected to negative consequences from peers for actively participating in treatment (Kupers, 2001; Morgan & Winterowd, 2002).

Resistance in groups with mandated clients may be more prominent and intense, particularly in initial group sessions, compared to nonmandated therapy groups (Duan et al., 2001); nevertheless, resistance is as critical a developmental phase for these populations as it is for others. Resistance is a normal and functional response to self-exploration (Milgram & Rubin, 1992) and serves to protect oneself from discomfort (Fenchel & Flapan, 1985).

Morgan and Winterowd (2002) have identified difficult client characteristics that appear to be unique to offender and mandated groups. "Religious converts" are clients who will no longer engage in antisocial or criminal acts because they have found or renewed their faith in God, and believe that God will "save" them. These clients use spirituality or religion as a defense mechanism to avoid evaluating or accepting responsibility for their behavior. "Helper clients" are clients who avoid the therapeutic process by assuming a helper role for those less fortunate in the group (from the helper clients' perspective), rather than seeking help for themselves. This defense mechanism is similar to the "superior client" and is entrenched in narcissism, with the helper role used to avoid self-exploration. Challenging this behavior is likely to be unsuccessful unless done in a supportive and positive framework. For example, the therapist(s) may reframe the behavior as an effective method of the clients protecting themselves from having to look at their behavior; however, in doing so they may be neglecting themselves and losing an opportunity to benefit and learn from the group. Furthermore, Yalom (1995) suggested that it is beneficial to interpret the behavior as an interpersonal problem and explore how the behavior affects their relationships with others (the group serving as a social microcosm to the client's real world; thus, the behavior is not unique to the group experience). Not all offenders or mandated clients are difficult group clients; however, the involuntary client with no therapeutic goals or expectation of benefit from the group experience presents problems for the group facilitator.

Approximately 54% of offenders in state correctional facilities who participate in group therapy in state correctional facilities are mandated (i.e., not self-referred) to attend treatment (Morgan, Winterowd, & Ferrell, 1999), and 18% of an inmate sample participated in mandated treatment as an adult during a time when they were not incarcerated (Morgan, Rozycki, & Wilson, in press). Thus, the possibility exists that some group participants will enter treatment without identified therapeutic goals. Nevertheless, incarcerated offenders mandated to treatment have benefited from group therapy services in the same fashion as self-referred offenders (Morgan & Flora, 2002). Pregroup screening interviews are recommended to counter the manipulation and resistance associated with this particular client and to facilitate the development of therapeutic goals by the client (Morgan & Winterowd, 2002; Morgan, Winterowd, & Ferrell, 1999). In addition, the use of out-of-group homework has been found to result in improved treatment outcome with incarcerated offenders (Morgan & Flora,

2002); thus, homework exercises focusing on the identification of problematic behavior on the part of the client may help facilitate the development of therapeutic goals.

Rooney (1992) highlights the following three assumptions about attitude and behavior change that may assist therapists to help clients develop appropriate treatment goals. First, attitudes and behaviors that are inconsistent with deeply held beliefs are more likely to be changed by clients. In other words, cognitive dissonance will occur as clients become aware of inconsistencies in their behaviors and attitudes. They will begin to work to change their attitudes or behaviors. With incarcerated offenders, identifying antisocial behaviors and the effect of these behaviors on one's goal of remaining out of prison (or out of contact with the criminal justice system) may facilitate client motivation to change behaviors and develop treatment goals. Second, therapists should focus on how clients want to act and behave, rather than on how they want their life to be. Focusing on prosocial behavior in their current situation/environment, for example, is short term and immediate (i.e., good treatment goals), rather than focusing on long-term goals of avoiding recidivism. Third, clients typically adopt attitudes that are similar to people whom they respect and like as opposed to attitudes of those they do not value. Thus, as Yalom (1995) suggests, group members should be encouraged to "try on" the attitudes and behaviors of other group members, particularly group members who are actively working to make changes in their behavioral presentation.

Finally, clients with certain forms of psychopathology (e.g., psychopathy) are a particular concern in group work with offenders and mandated clients (Morgan, Winterowd, & Ferrell, 1999). Psychopathy is a severe personality disorder (Hare, 1993) characterized by aggression and an absence of interpersonal bonding (Meloy, 1988). Psychopathy may best be conceptualized as an extreme form of antisocial personality disorder and includes only the most manipulative and dangerous individuals. A client presenting with this type of psychopathology may not only sabotage the therapeutic environment (Morgan & Winterowd, 2002), but treatment may also be contraindicated (Hare,

1993, 1996). Furthermore, group work may not be an appropriate treatment modality for this type of client, in part because of the danger to other clients as well as potential damage to the therapeutic process. Therefore, group therapists working with these populations should carefully consider the ramifications of allowing offenders with certain forms of psychopathology into their groups and be prepared to immediately address any danger to the therapeutic culture and/or predatory behavior directed toward other group members.

BENEFITS OF GROUP THERAPY WITH OFFENDERS AND MANDATED CLIENTS

Group therapists in state correctional facilities provided a variety of therapy groups, and these therapists perceived these groups to be at least "fairly effective in achieving positive outcomes" (Morgan, Winterowd, & Ferrell, 1999, p. 601). Historically, treatment outcome research on the use of group therapy for offenders and mandated clients has been plagued by inconsistencies. Some studies have reported positive outcomes (e.g., Homant, 1976; Jew, Clanon, & Mattocks, 1972; Jew, Kim, & Mattocks, 1975; Leak, 1980; Serok & Levi, 1993; Stallone, 1993; Wolk, 1963), whereas others reported less positive results (e.g., Goldenberg & Cowden, 1977; Kassenbaum, Ward, & Wilner, 1971).

More recently, the results of a meta-analytic review provided compelling evidence regarding the utility of group psychotherapy with these special populations (Morgan & Flora, 2002). Positive treatment effects from group psychotherapy with incarcerated offenders were found across all outcomes assessed, including institutional adjustment (Mean Effect Size [ES] = 0.43), anger (Mean ES = 0.45), anxiety (Mean ES = 0.94), depression (Mean ES = 0.57), interpersonal relations (Mean ES = 0.36), locus of control (Mean ES = 0.64), and self-esteem (Mean ES = 0.31). Thus, the efficacy of group treatment for offender and mandated clients is no longer in question. Rather, the focus has shifted to identifying the most effective group therapy strategies and interventions, and the results of this meta-analysis indicated that the use of homework exercises significantly improves outcomes. In addition, there were trends for increased therapeutic outcomes when cognitive-behavioral strategies and a mix of structured and unstructured group formats were used.

In spite of these results, offenders continue to prefer individual therapy services to group services (Morgan, Wilson, & Rozycki, 2001), and the majority of mental health services for incarcerated offenders are provided via an individual format (Boothby & Clements, 2000). Nevertheless, increased focus on the use of the group modality with offenders appears to be a necessity (Morgan, Winterowd, & Ferrell, 1999), because to not do so is a "poor" use of psychological resources, given the large number of offenders requiring mental health services (Boothby & Clements, 2000). Therefore, it is not surprising that approximately 20% of incarcerated populations participate in group treatment programs (Morgan, Winterowd, & Ferrell, 1999) and that approximately one half of all offenders receiving mental health services (either voluntarily or mandated to attend) have participated in group services (Morgan et al., 2001). Clearly, group treatment remains a viable treatment option with potential increase in the use of this treatment method to reach a larger number of offenders and/or mandated clients. But what types of group programs are most appropriate?

From a rehabilitative perspective, any group treatment program geared toward the reduction of recidivism needs to address the cognitive thinking patterns that contribute to unlawful or criminal behavior. Furthermore, offenders participating in general mental health groups (as previously defined) also benefit from the inclusion of cognitive-behavioral strategies. It appears that the learning process for offenders (and mandated clients) is enhanced when strategies are aimed at maladaptive cognitive patterns and thought processes. Consistent with the beneficial effects of cognitive-behavioral approaches with this population is the benefit of structure in group work with offenders and mandated clients (e.g., Leak, 1980; Morgan & Flora, 2002); however, as indicated above, much may be gained by incorporating interpersonal or client-centered approaches into group work with these clients.

It is also worth noting that offenders mandated to attend group treatment fared no better or worse than did offenders volunteering to attend group treatment (Morgan & Flora, 2002). The finding that mandated clients were no less likely to benefit than were self-referred offenders suggests that policy makers, correctional administrators, and judges should continue to refer inmates to group treatment programming as an alternative to punitive strategies (e.g., incarceration without rehabilitative services), as it is clear that treatment is more effective than punishment alone (Andrews, Zinger et al., 1990; Gendreau, 1996).

FUTURE RESEARCH AND BARRIERS IN CORRECTIONAL RESEARCH

There is an unfortunate scarcity of research conducted in correctional facilities (Boothby & Clements, 2000; Morgan, Winterowd, & Ferrell, 1999); however, such activities are strongly encouraged (Andrews & Bonta, 1998; Bartol, 1999). Group counseling and therapy research necessitates further research (Morgan, Winterowd, & Ferrell, 1999). In particular, future research needs to focus on investigating the efficacy of differing theoretical approaches, strategies, and dynamics in group work with offenders. It is disconcerting that in a recent meta-analysis, only 11% (26 of 238) of published articles on group therapy with offenders focused on treatment outcome and met the empirically based inclusion criteria necessitated for meta-analytic review (Morgan & Flora, 2002). Clearly, increased focus on such studies is warranted to identify factors related to efficacious group treatment with offenders and other mandated clients. However, as evidenced by the number of reviewed studies in the Morgan and Flora (2002) meta-analyses, mere quantity without quality is not sufficient. Group treatment outcome studies with offenders and mandated clients need to incorporate appropriate measures to accurately assess client progress (e.g., DeLucia-Waack, 1997), assess intergroup relations as a measure of therapeutic progress (e.g., Marcus & Kashy, 1995; Shechtman & Yanov, 2001), as well as institutional behavior and postrelease follow-up. Although many are interested in the effectiveness of group therapy to reduce recidivism, recidivism may not be an appropriate measure of the effectiveness of group treatment (Reppucci & Clingempeel, 1978), particularly as rehabilitation programs aimed at reducing recidivism are comprehensive in nature with the inclusion of more than one treatment modality (Boudouris, 1984). Thus, the evaluation of group treatment programs should be specific and tailored to the goals and aims of the group, rather than to the issue of recidivism, as many factors contribute to offenders' postrelease success. Given recent advances and methodological improvements in our understanding of group therapy research (Burlingame, Kircher, & Taylor, 1994), it is hoped that increased empirical analyses will begin to elucidate those treatment factors and strategies related to improved outcome with this population.

Unfortunately, this optimism is clouded by the reality of the limitations to researchers' resources and efforts within correctional environments. Time restraints limit the research activities of correctional mental health professionals (Boothby & Clements, 2000). One strategy is to create partnerships between correctional mental health professionals who provide services and academic researchers (Boothby & Clements, 2000; Petersilia, 1996). This strategy has proven beneficial in other jurisdictions (see Motiuk, 1999), and a similar strategy may prove beneficial for increasing the group treatment research productivity in the United States. Many institutional barriers also limit the production of correctional research. For example, many correctional systems are closed to "outside" researchers with concerns regarding the use of data by nonaffiliated researchers. In addition, the necessary human rights protection afforded incarcerated offenders presents a time-consuming and lengthy review process. Conducting a correctional research-oriented doctoral dissertation or thesis is not time efficient. In addition, research may not be highly valued by prison officials and administrators, thereby limiting the availability of resources. Last, correctional facilities are frequently located in remote areas, limiting opportunities for the aforementioned partnerships. Nevertheless, offenders and mandated clients are high-need populations that have been understudied, and such research is of great social importance. Therefore, it is hoped that increased focus on research activity, particularly as it relates to the utilization of group work with offenders and mandated clients, will delineate the highest quality of group services available.

References

Andrews, D. A., Bonta, J., & Hoge, R. D. (1990). Classification for effective rehabilitation: Rediscovering psychology. *Criminal Justice and Behavior, 17,* 19-52.

Andrews, D. A., & Bonta, J. (1994). *The psychology of crime.* Cincinnati, OH: Anderson.

Andrews, D. A., & Bonta, J. (1998). *The psychology of criminal conduct* (2nd ed.). Cincinnati, OH: Anderson.

Andrews, D. A., Zinger, I., Hoge, R. D., Bonta, J., Gendreau, P., & Cullen, R. T. (1990). Does correctional treatment work? A clinically relevant and psychologically informed meta-analysis. *Criminology, 28,* 369-404.

Association for Specialists in Group Work. (2000, January). *Professional Standards for the Training of Group Workers.* Retrieved from http://asgw.educ.kent.edu/training_standards.htm.

Bartol, C. R. (1999). *Criminal behavior: A psychosocial approach.* Englewood Cliffs, NJ: Prentice Hall.

Boothby, J. L., & Clements, C. B. (2000). A national survey of correctional psychologists. *Criminal Justice and Behavior, 27,* 716-732.

Boudouris, J. (1984). Recidivism as a process. *Journal of Offender Counseling, Services, & Rehabilitation, 8,* 41-51.

Burlingame, G. M., Kircher, J. C., & Taylor, S. (1994). Methodological considerations in group psychotherapy research: Past, present, and future practices. In A. Fuhriman & G. M. Burlingame (Eds.), *Handbook of group psychotherapy: An empirical and clinical synthesis* (pp. 41-80). New York: John Wiley.

Condelli, W. S., Bradigan, B., & Holanchock, H. (1997). Intermediate care programs to reduce risk and better manage inmates with psychiatric disorders. *Behavioral Sciences and the Law, 15,* 459-467.

Corey, G. (1995). *Theory and practice of group counseling* (4th ed.). Pacific Grove, CA: Brooks/Cole.

Coyne, J. C., & Fabricatore, J. M. (1979). Group psychotherapy in a corrections facility: A case study of individual and institutional change. *Professional Psychology, 10,* 8-14.

DeLucia-Waack, J. L. (1997). Measuring the effectiveness of group work: A review and analysis of process and outcome measures. *Journal for Specialists in Group Work, 22,* 277-293.

Demuth, P. W. (1995). The relationship between maintenance of the Criminal Code and group denial in a substance abuse population: Its effects on treatment. *International Journal of Offender Therapy & Comparative Criminology, 39,* 77-81.

Duan, C., Murdock, N. L., Clark, J. M., Jones, L. N., Kraatz, B., & Murray, T. S. (2001, August). *Differences between voluntary and involuntary clients in counseling.* Poster presented at the annual convention of the American Psychological Association, San Francisco, CA.

Dustin, R., & George, R. L. (1973). *Action counseling for behavior change* (2nd ed.). Cranston, RI: Carroll.

Fenchel, G., & Flapan, D. (1985). Resistance in group psychotherapy. *Group, 9,* 35-47.

Fox, K. J. (1999). Changing violent minds: Discursive correction and resistance in the cognitive treatment of violent offenders in prison. *Social Problems, 46,* 88-103.

French, L. (1981). Correctional treatment: A note on student/inmate group counseling. *Corrective & Social Psychiatry & Journal of Behavior Technology, Methods & Therapy, 27,* 84-87.

Garrett, C. J. (1985). Effects of residential treatment on adjudicated delinquents: A meta-analysis. *Journal of Research in Crime and Delinquency, 22,* 287-308.

Gazda, G. M., Ginter, E. J., & Horne, A. M. (2001). *Group counseling and group psychotherapy: Theory and application.* Needham Heights, MA: Allyn & Bacon.

Gendreau, P. (1996). Offender rehabilitation: What we know and what needs to be done. *Criminal Justice and Behavior, 23,* 144-161.

Gendreau, P., & Ross, R. R. (1981). Correctional potency: Treatment and deterrence on trial. In

R. Roesch & R. R. Corrado (Eds.), *Evaluation and criminal justice policy* (pp. 29-57). Beverly Hills, CA: Sage.

Goldenberg, E., & Cowden, J. E. (1977). An evaluation of intensive group psychotherapy with male offenders in isolation units. *Corrective & Social Psychiatry & Journal of Behavior Technology, Methods & Therapy, 23,* 68-72.

Halleck, S. L. (1960). The criminal's problem with psychiatry. *Psychiatry, 23,* 409-412.

Hare, R. D. (1993). *Without conscience: The disturbing world of the psychopaths among us.* New York: Pocket Books.

Hare, R. D. (1996). Psychopathy: A clinical construct whose time has come. *Criminal Justice and Behavior, 23,* 25-54.

Hodgins, S. (1995). Assessing mental disorder in the criminal justice system: Feasibility versus clinical accuracy. *International Journal of Law and Psychiatry, 18,* 15-28.

Homant, R. J. (1976). Therapy effectiveness in a correctional institution. *Offender Rehabilitation, 1,* 101-113.

Ionedes, N. (1962). Group methods and the adult offender. *Group Psychotherapy, Psychodrama, & Sociometry, 15,* 144-146.

Jew, C. C., Clanon, T. L., & Mattocks, A. L. (1972). The effectiveness of group psychotherapy in a correctional institution. *American Journal of Psychiatry, 129,* 602-605.

Jew, C. C., Kim, L. I. C., & Mattocks, A. L. (1975). *Effectiveness of group psychotherapy with character disordered prisoners* (Research Report No. 56). Sacramento: California Department of Corrections.

Kahnweiler, W. (1978). Group counseling in a correctional setting. *Personnel and Guidance Journal, 57,* 162-164.

Kassenbaum, G., Ward, D., & Wilner, D. (1971). *Prison treatment and parole survival: An empirical assessment.* New York: John Wiley.

Kupers, T. A. (2001). Psychotherapy with men in prison. In G. R. Brooks & G. E. Good (Eds.), *The new handbook of psychotherapy and counseling with men: A comprehensive guide to settings, problems, and treatment approaches.* San Francisco: Jossey-Bass.

Leak, G. K. (1980). Effects of highly structured versus nondirective group counseling approaches on personality and behavioral measures of adjustment in incarcerated felons. *Journal of Counseling Psychology, 27,* 520-523.

Long, L. D., & Cope, C. S. (1980). Curative factors in a male felony offender group. *Small Group Behavior, 11,* 389-398.

MacDevitt, J. W., & Sanislow, C., III. (1987). Curative factors in offenders' groups. *Small Group Behavior, 18,* 72-81.

Marcus, D. K., & Kashy, D. A. (1995). The social relations model: A tool for group psychotherapy research. *Journal of Counseling Psychology, 42,* 383-389.

Mathias, R. E., & Sindberg, R. (1985). Psychotherapy in correctional settings. *International Journal of Offender Therapy and Comparative Criminology, 29,* 265-275.

Mathias, R. E., & Sindberg, R. M. (1986). Time limited group therapy in minimum security. *Journal of Offender Counseling, Services & Rehabilitation, 11,* 7-17.

Meloy, J. R. (1988). *The psychopathic mind: Origins, dynamics, and treatment.* Northvale, NJ: Jason Aronson.

Milgram, D., & Rubin, J. S. (1992). Resisting resistance: Involuntary substance abuse group therapy. *Social Work With Groups, 15,* 95-110.

Morgan, R. D. (2000, August). *The efficacy of an integrative group psychotherapy program for inmates.* Paper presented at the annual meeting of the American Psychological Association, Washington, DC.

Morgan, R. D., Ferrell, S. W., & Winterowd, C. L. (1999). Therapist perceptions of important therapeutic factors in psychotherapy groups for male inmates in state correctional facilities. *Small Group Research, 30,* 712-729.

Morgan, R. D., & Flora, D. B. (2002). Group psychotherapy with incarcerated offenders: A research synthesis. *Group Dynamics: Theory, Research, and Practice, 6,* 203-218.

Morgan, R. D., Rozycki, A. T., & Wilson, S. (in press). Inmate perceptions of mental health service. *Professional Psychology: Research and Practice.*

Morgan, R. D., & Winterowd, C. L. (2002). Interpersonal process-oriented group psychotherapy with offender populations. *International Journal of Offender Therapy and Comparative Criminology, 46,* 466-482.

Morgan, R. D., Winterowd, C. L., & Ferrell, S. W. (1999). A national survey of group psychotherapy services in correctional facilities. *Professional Psychology: Research and Practice, 30,* 600-606.

Morgan, R. D., Winterowd, C. L., & Fuqua, D. R. (1999). The efficacy of an integrated theoretical approach to group psychotherapy for male inmates. *Journal of Contemporary Psychotherapy, 29,* 203-222.

Motiuk, L. (1999, August). Role of psychology in applied correctional research. In C. B. Clements (Chair), *Correctional psychology in North America: New roles, new challenges.* Symposium conducted at the meeting of the American Psychological Association, Boston.

Petersilia, J. (1996). Improving corrections policy: The importance of researchers and practitioners working together. In A. T. Harland (Ed.), *Choosing correctional options that work: Defining the demand and evaluating the supply* (pp. 223-231). Thousand Oaks, CA: Sage.

Randall, D. A., Jr., (1995). Curative factor rankings for female incest survivor groups: A summary of three studies. *Journal for Specialists in Group Work, 20,* 232-239.

Rappaport, R. G. (1982). Group therapy in prison. In M. Seligman (Ed.), *Group psychotherapy and counseling with special populations* (pp. 215-227). Baltimore: University Park Press.

Reppucci, N. D., & Clingempeel, W. G. (1978). Methodological issues in research with correctional populations. *Journal of Consulting and Clinical Psychology, 46,* 727-746.

Riordan, R. J., & Martin, M. H. (1993). Mental health counseling and the mandated client. *Journal of Mental Health Counseling, 15,* 373-383.

Rooney, R. H. (1992). *Strategies for work with involuntary clients.* New York: Columbia University Press.

Scott, E. M. (1993). Prison group therapy with mentally and emotionally disturbed offenders. *International Journal of Offender Therapy and Comparative Criminology, 37,* 131-145.

Serok, S., & Levi, N. (1993). Application of gestalt therapy with long-term prison inmates in Israel. *Gestalt Journal, 16,* 105-127.

Shechtman, Z., & Yanov, H. (2001). Interpretives (confrontation, interpretation, and feedback) in preadolescent counseling groups. *Group Dynamics: Theory, Research, and Practice, 5*, 124 135.

Shields, S. A. (1986). Busted and branded: Group work with substance abusing adolescents in schools. *Social Work With Groups, 9*, 61-81.

Stallone, T. M. (1993). The effects of psychodrama on inmates within a structured residential behavior modification program. *Journal of Group Psychotherapy, Psychodrama and Sociometry, 46*, 24-31.

Steadman, H. J., Morris, S. M., & Dennis, D. L. (1995). The diversion of mentally ill persons from community-based services: A profile of programs. *American Journal of Public Health, 85*, 1630-1635.

Steinfeld, G., & Mabli, J. (1974). Perceived curative factors in group therapy by residents of a therapeutic community. *Criminal Justice Behavior, 1*, 278-288.

Torrey, E. F. (1995). Editorial: Jails and prisons: America's new mental hospital. *American Journal of Public Health, 85*, 1611-1613.

Walters, G. D. (1990). *The criminal lifestyle: Patterns of serious criminal conduct.* Thousand Oaks, CA: Sage.

Wardrop, K. (1976). Group therapy with adult offenders in Scotland. *International Journal of Offender Therapy & Comparative Criminology, 20*, 236-241.

Winterowd, C. L., Morgan, R. D., & Ferrell, S. W. (2001). Principal components analysis of important goals for group work with male inmates. *Journal for Specialists in Group Work, 26*, 406-417.

Wolk, R. L. (1963). The relationship of group psychotherapy to institutional adjustment. *Group Psychotherapy, 16*, 141-145.

Yalom, I. D. (1995). *The theory and practice of group psychotherapy* (4th ed.). New York: Basic Books.

Yochelson, S., & Samenow, S. E. (1976). *The criminal personality I: A profile for change.* New York: Jason Aronson.

Yong, J. N. (1971). Advantages of group therapy in relation to individual therapy for juvenile delinquents. *Corrective Psychiatry and Journal of Social Therapy, 19*, 34-39.

29

GROUPS IN THE WORKPLACE

SUSAN A. WHEELAN

GDQ Associates, Inc.

Groups figure prominently in today's workplace. While it is difficult to know with certainty the percentage of U.S. workers who participate in work-related groups, research has provided some reasonable estimates. A survey of Fortune 1000 companies reported that the percentage of companies utilizing problem-solving task groups increased from 74% in 1987 to 92% in 1993 (Lawler, Mohrman, & Ledford, 1995). Gordon (1992) reported that 82% of organizations employing 100 or more people used some kind of designated work groups or teams. Over half (53%) of the workers in these organizations were members of teams. Another study noted that 69% of larger organizations and 36% of smaller companies provide some form of training to help team members work together more effectively (Devine, Clayton, Philips, Dunford, & Melner, 1999).

Other kinds of group-based training are prevalent in the workplace as well. Internal and external professionals conduct technical training, psychoeducational or skills training, and personal growth groups. Also, other professionals often are called on to help task groups become more effective and productive. Finally, employee assistance providers, while primarily focused on providing employees psychological treatment outside the confines of the workplace, do offer some lunchtime workshops on a wide variety of mental health issues.

A major reason for the current emphasis on workplace task groups is the increasing complexity of work tasks. Product development or process improvement, for example, requires too much knowledge and too many different skills for any individual to successfully accomplish such tasks alone. As a result, most work tasks are undertaken by groups of employees. Collaboration and teamwork among employees, then, are essential in order to meet organizational goals. Collaboration and teamwork require employees to have effective group membership and leadership skills. Also, given the increased size of the service economy, employees need effective interpersonal and communication skills and the ability to work with an increasingly diverse population of coworkers and customers. Technical skills no longer suffice. Group-based psychoeducational training has emerged to support employees' efforts to enhance their interaction skills.

Today's workplace also requires employees to be active, creative contributors. Employees are expected to be aware of their talents and limitations and to actively engage in personal and professional development throughout their careers. Many companies provide technical, personal, and professional training to help employees meet these expectations.

This handbook focuses on four types of groups: task, psychoeducational, counseling, and therapy. Counseling and therapy groups are not conducted in the workplace. Companies that participate in Employee Assistance programs refer employees seeking treatment to certified Employee Assistance providers in the community. Therefore, this chapter focuses on a discussion of task groups, psychoeducational groups, and personal growth groups. Personal growth groups are akin to psychoeducational groups. However, they focus on individual self-awareness or attitude change rather than behavioral skill development.

TASK GROUPS

Task groups in the workplace are referred to as work groups or teams. A work group or team "has two or more people; it has a specific objective or recognizable goal to be attained; and coordination among the members of the team is required for the attainment of the team goal or objective" (Larson & LaFasto, 1989, p. 19). Work teams are "small groups of interdependent individuals who share responsibility for outcomes for their organizations" (Sundstrom, DeMeuse, & Futrell, 1990, p. 120). Team goals and tasks may relate directly to production or service. Groups also may be employed in planning, decision making, policy setting, and other activities related to organizational goals. Finally, teams may be ongoing or short-term project teams.

Research investigations have provided a reasonably consistent description of the characteristics of effective teams (e.g., Cummings, 1981; Dyer 1984; Friedlander, 1987; Hackman, 1989; Larson & LaFasto, 1989; Sundstrom et al., 1990; Wheelan, 1994, 1999). For example, Larson and LaFasto (1989, p. 8) found that effective teams shared the following characteristics:

- A clear, elevating goal
- A collaborative climate

- A results-driven structure
- Standards of excellence
- Competent team members
- External support and recognition
- Unified commitment
- Principled leadership

In a review of work team effectiveness, Sundstrom et al. (1990) found evidence to support the validity of the characteristics outlined by Larson and LaFasto. In addition, they noted that effective work groups are commonly found in organizations that support innovation and excellence. Such groups have the technical training, team training, and consulting resources necessary to do their jobs and sufficient autonomy to regulate and manage their own activities.

Team building, also known as team development, is the most common intervention employed to help work groups or teams to become more effective and productive (Salas, Rozell, Mullen, & Driskell, 1999). Team building interventions are difficult to define. The overall goal of team building is to improve team performance and productivity. Methods used to reach these goals vary widely, however. In general, there are two approaches to team building. The first approach is conducted by psychoeducators, who are called trainers in the workplace. Trainers conduct workshops with employees on a variety of topics that are thought to be related to effective group functioning. Training in communication, decision making, and conflict resolution skills might be provided. Other trainers may emphasize trust building or the development of interpersonal skills among group members. Some trainings focus on developing positive relationships between and among group members. Others focus on planning and problem solving, goal setting, or role clarification (Buller & Bell, 1986).

The second approach to team building is conducted by consultants. This approach requires a consultant to collect information about the group from group members via interviews, surveys, or questionnaires. Next, the consultant organizes and synthesizes the information and develops an intervention strategy designed to help group members to improve group functioning. Typically, the intervention includes feedback to group members about the results of the assessment and facilitation of a process in which group members develop a plan, based on the results of the assessment, to improve group effectiveness. As was the case with training, the focus of consultation also varies. Some consultants focus on improving relationships among individual group members and others focus on improving the group's processes and procedures such as goal setting, planning, role clarity, and the like.

GROUP DEVELOPMENT ACROSS TIME

Reviews of group development research (Tuckman & Jensen, 1977; Wheelan, 1994) supported the idea that all task groups move through five stages or phases. The initial stage of development focuses on issues of inclusion and dependency, where members attempt to identify behavior acceptable to the leader and other group members (e.g., Mann, Gibbard, & Hartman, 1967). These early group meetings also are characterized as a time of member anxiety (e.g., Slater, 1966).

The second stage is described as a period of counterdependency (e.g., Bennis & Shepard, 1956) and conflict (e.g., Yalom, 1995). Issues of power, authority, and competition are debated at this stage (e.g., Mills, 1964). A number of theories suggest that these early struggles regarding authority and status are prerequisites for subsequent increases in cohesion and cooperation (e.g., Tuckman & Jensen, 1977). If conflicts are adequately resolved, member relationships with the leader and each other become more trusting and cohesive (e.g., Deutsch, 1971). This phase also provides the opportunity to clarify areas of common goals and values, which increases group stability (Theodorson, 1962).

The third stage is devoted to the development of trust and more mature and open negotiation regarding goals, roles, group structure, and division of labor (e.g., Lundgren & Knight, 1978). This is followed by a work phase characterized by an increase in task orientation, more open exchange of ideas and feedback, and goal achievement (e.g., Bennis & Shepard, 1956). Groups that have a distinct ending point experience a fifth stage. Impending termination may cause disruption and conflict (e.g., Mann,

Gibbard, & Hartman, 1967). Increased expression of positive feelings also may occur (e.g., Lundgren & Knight, 1978), and separation issues are discussed (e.g., Braaten, 1974/1975).

A group's stage of development is related to that group's level of effectiveness and productivity. Work groups functioning at higher levels of group development generate more revenue than work groups functioning at lower levels (Wheelan, Murphy, Tsumura, & Fried Kline, 1998). More patients survive in intensive care units, in which staff groups are functioning at higher stages of group development (Burchill, 2001). A group's level of development clearly makes a difference.

Group development does not always proceed in a positive direction. Groups can get stuck at a particular stage for extended periods of time, resulting in long-term ineffectiveness and low productivity. Also, groups may fluctuate widely, based on the circumstances and forces affecting them at a given moment. Significant changes in membership, external demands, and internal conflicts can all affect the work of a group.

Furthermore, not all groups, of any type, achieve adequate levels of effectiveness and productivity. In fact, Gabarro (1987) found that between 75% and 90% of work groups have problems with performance at some point. The road to productivity is fraught with difficulties. It is for these reasons that efforts to help work groups increase their effectiveness and productivity have proliferated in the workplace.

Most team building interventions, however, do not take group development into account when working with teams (Sundstrom et al., 1990). Group trainers and consultants typically employ the same methods with all groups regardless of their developmental level. Research on group development, however, suggests that groups are able to focus on certain tasks at different stages of group development (Burnand, 1990). Thus, a new group might have difficulty with interventions focused on planning, problem solving, conflict resolution, or interpersonal issues but might benefit from goal and role clarification. Older groups might need help with conflict resolution, planning, or problem solving, since goal or role clarification issues were resolved at an earlier time (Wheelan, 1999). This suggests that team building strategies should be designed to meet the needs of groups at different stages of development.

The lack of attention to group development may account for the inconsistent findings of studies designed to determine the effects of team building on performance. While case studies often report positive effects (e.g., Halstead et al., 1986; Robinson-Kurpius & Keim, 1994), most research reviews and meta-analyses report mixed, poor, or no effects on team performance (e.g., Druckman & Bjork, 1994; Salas et al., 1999; Sundstrom et al., 1990; Tannenbaum, Beard, & Salas, 1992).

Guzzo, Jett, and Katzell (1985) conducted an analysis of 330 group intervention studies. They found that interventions that included goal setting and performance feedback had the most positive effects on group productivity. Interventions that take group development into account enhance these effects by targeting issues that are impeding developmental progress (Buzaglo & Wheelan, 1999). Finally, role clarification produces positive effects as well (Salas et al., 1999).

Based on these research results, the keys to successful group intervention include the following elements. First, an accurate, detailed assessment of a group's current developmental level is critical. Such information is difficult, if not impossible, to obtain from interviews. This is so because group members tend to frame group problems as interpersonal problems, which makes it difficult to discover more basic system problems.

For example, group members tend to believe that group problems are the result of an incompetent leader or member (Wheelan, 1996). However, in most cases, other factors, such as a lack of goal clarity, unclear decision-making procedures, and the like are inhibiting performance. Assessment disconfirms member beliefs, reduces blaming, and increases members' motivation to work at improving group performance. Therefore, successful intervention does not focus on individuals, personalities, or emotional issues. Instead, it focuses on the group as a system, how that system is functioning, and what members can do to improve the group's effectiveness and productivity.

Second, successful intervention is guided by information. That is, educating members about group development, the characteristics of effective teams, and the importance of taking a systemic, as opposed to an individual or interpersonal, view of group problems is an important step in the intervention process. Views that see individuals, or interpersonal relationships, as the reasons for group problems make positive change extremely unlikely. This is due to the fact that such views are taken personally, cause hurt or humiliation, and encourage retaliation. Cycles of blame, attacks, and counterattacks are the typical result. If members can take a systemic view, then they can work together to improve the functioning of the group system. No individual should fear being blamed or threatened in any way (Wheelan, 1999).

The third key to successful intervention is to devise a strategy that allows group members, not consultants, to decide what to change and how to change in identified areas. The more directive a consultant is with a group, the less likely that group is to change. The most likely result of a directive style would be that group members would become dependent on the consultant for guidance or resent and challenge the consultant's advice. In either case, the group's developmental progress would be impeded. Consultants who act as educators and design a process in which group members can make their own decisions will have better results (Schein, 1988).

A Case Example

The consulting process described above was implemented with an executive team working in health care. The team contained 13 members. Participants were physicians, accountants, executives, and a number of support personnel. The goal of the team was to design strategies to implement the decisions made by the executive team of the district. The team had met an average of two times a month for 6 months at the time the intervention was undertaken.

An initial assessment was conducted utilizing the Group Development Questionnaire (Wheelan & Hochberger, 1996). The assessment results suggested that the team had characteristics of Stage 2 (Counterdependency and Fight) of group development. The majority of members reported that dissension occurred in the group. At the same time, members reported that people were worried about personal safety and being liked by others in the group. Finally, the majority of members reported high levels of leader dependency, a hesitancy to address or confront the leader, and hostility toward the leader.

The core of this 1-day intervention with the team centered around educating members about group development and about how all task groups experience both dependent and hostile feelings toward the leader during the early stages of group development. During the intervention session, the team members realized that they could address issues of leadership by speaking about the impact of the leadership function, not about the leader himself.

This strategy was so successful that even the leader began using this method, in the presence of the members, to evaluate the kind of leadership that was needed in the group at the present time. Plans were made to distribute these leadership functions among group members. Team members also decided to focus in on one task that would unite the team. The chosen task was to devote a significant amount of energy to improving the effectiveness of their regional hospital.

Three months later, the team was reassessed. The results confirmed that the group had moved from Stage 2 to Stage 3 (Trust and Structure). It is of interest to note that the team was able to continue to improve its level of functioning and that member efforts with regard to the regional hospital were successful. Eight months after the intervention, the regional hospital received a national prize for excellence.

This case brings up an important point about the role of the consultant. Work groups have designated leaders, and consultants must be careful not to usurp the designated leader's role. Consultants conduct assessments and design intervention processes. They also educate teams about how effective groups function and facilitate the intervention process. However, they do not make decisions for the team or recommend plans of action. Instead, they encourage the team leader and team members to decide for themselves how to improve group functioning (Schein, 1988).

PSYCHOEDUCATIONAL GROUPS

Psychoeducational groups are referred to as skills training groups in the workplace. A skills training group is "a group established to teach such human relations skills as assertion, communication, management, or leadership in order to enhance personal and professional effectiveness" (Wheelan, 1990, p. 49). Nelson-Jones (1992) defined skills training groups as "time-limited structured groups in which one or more leaders use a repertoire of didactic and facilitative skills to help participants develop and maintain one or more specific life skills. Important features of training groups include: no assumption of psychological disturbance, systematic instruction, experiential learning-by-doing, and a high degree of participant involvement" (p. 6).

What are the skills that training groups in the workplace attempt to teach? Stress accompanies many work tasks. Skills that increase an individual's ability to manage stress include relaxation, time management, goal setting, and modifying one's thinking with regard to potentially stressful situations. A variety of training groups have been designed to teach these and other stress reduction skills (e.g., Bruning & Frew, 1987; Murphy & Hurrell, 1987).

Management skills are taught as well. Individuals who assume management roles require leadership, communication, and decision-making skills. The management role also requires the ability to facilitate team development, to motivate employees, and to organize materials, schedules, and personnel. Even this list does not begin to exhaust the set of skills required of managers in an increasingly competitive, diverse, and complex work environment. Many of these skills are required of employees as well. Management and employee training groups have proliferated rapidly in both private and public sector organizations. They have become an integral part of workplace practices and are the focus of significant research investigations to increase their effectiveness (e.g., Cohen & Sproull, 1996; Goldstein, 1989).

In contrast to consultation, psychoeducators or trainers need to be directive leaders and facilitators. They also must be supportive of members' efforts to acquire the skills being taught and they must be excellent role models capable of demonstrating those skills with confidence and ease (Silberman, 1990; Wheelan, 1994).

Skills training groups assume that individuals acquire life skills by

- Learning about these skills and how they can increase one's ability to function effectively in specific work situations
- Learning to differentiate when and when not to use specific skills
- Developing attitudes and beliefs that support skill acquisition
- Observing competent role models demonstrating the skills in clear, interesting, and unique ways
- Developing positive emotional attachments to those role models
- Mentally practicing the skills
- Discussing and verbally labeling the skills
- Overtly practicing the skills
- Personally assessing their performance
- Receiving feedback from others about their performance
- Receiving praise, encouragement, and support for their performance (Wheelan, 1994, p. 205)

A Case Example

A trainer was asked to conduct a 2-day training for physicians. The topic was effective communication with patients. As a result of a needs assessment conducted with potential participants, the trainer learned that

- The training was being offered to physicians who have been successfully sued by patients more than once. Experience suggests that suits are not always the result of incompetence but can be the result of ineffective communication with patients. Therefore, a medical society was offering training to doctors with a history of lawsuits.

- The physicians did not have to attend. They were volunteers. Most participants were white male surgeons or obstetricians between the ages of 40 and 50. They wanted to learn to communicate more effectively with patients. However, they were a bit embarrassed about attending a training in "remedial bedside manner"

and were worried that spending a lot of extra time with patients would interfere with the important parts of their job such as reviewing test results, planning with nurses and residents, and performing technical procedures. They were worried that hospital administrators would reprimand them if they saw fewer patients per day, since that would affect hospital finances.

- Participants from a number of hospitals were participating in the training. They were from all over the United States and, in general, did not know each other.

The needs assessment alerted the trainer to a number of design issues. First, training in assertive communication would be of use to the physicians. Second, the shame and embarrassment that participants were experiencing might interfere with learning. Therefore, strategies to reduce negative self-image and self-blame must be incorporated into the training from the outset. Third, extensive and time-consuming communication skills would be resisted, since the physicians were concerned about maintaining schedules and the quality of technical services to patients. Fourth, the physicians perceived themselves as scientists first and foremost. Therefore, including research evidence supporting the effectiveness of the skills being taught would be necessary. Fifth, the 2-day format did not provide sufficient time for group development to occur at a natural pace. Consequently, the design would need to be structured to allow safety and cooperation to occur more rapidly. Sixth, since participants were from different places, there would be no opportunity for them to support each other in utilizing learned skills after the group was over. Therefore, the design had to include time for individuals to plan ways to gain support for personal style changes in their particular work settings.

The training design for this population included

1. An introductory lecture in which the trainer made the following points:
   - Medical education emphasizes technical skills but does not usually adequately prepare physicians to communicate effectively with patients.
   - Communication skills are learned.

- Communication with patients is more difficult due to the stress of illness.
- Effective doctor-patient communication does not need to be time consuming.
- The acquisition of a limited set of communication skills can increase a physician's effectiveness as a communicator.
- There is significant research that assertive communication skills facilitates positive relationships, decreases misunderstandings, and creates an atmosphere of mutual respect (Fensterheim & Glazer, 1983; Wheelan & Bastas, 1979).

2. An activity in which participants introduce themselves in an assertive, nonassertive, or aggressive manner and state what they hope to learn from the workshop

3. A discussion of the nonverbal and verbal components of these three communication styles

4. Group discussions of the likely outcomes of using the different styles

5. Video examples of physicians employing the three styles in interactions with patients

6. Group discussion of the key behaviors employed in the video demonstrations of the three styles

7. Trainer demonstration of active listening skills

8. Group covert and overt practice of these skills utilizing case examples of doctor-patient interactions provided by the trainer

9. Trainer feedback to participants on their performance

10. Trainer demonstration of two basic assertive techniques

11. Group covert and overt practice of these skills utilizing cases generated by participants themselves based on their experience with patients

12. Trainer and member feedback on individual performance

13. Trainer demonstration of negative and positive assertion, negative and positive inquiry, free information and self-disclosure techniques

14. Group covert and overt practice of these skills

15. Trainer and member feedback to individuals about their performance

16. Individual and group planning sessions focused on implementing these skills in their practice and ways to gain support from others for utilizing assertive skills with patients

17. Discussion of participants' reactions to the training

18. Formal evaluation of the training experience

Participant reactions to the training were very positive. The physicians felt that the training was worthwhile and that they would employ the skills that they had acquired in interactions with patients. Whether that occurred or not, however, is not known. The outcomes of skills training generally are not evaluated on the job in any systematic way. However, there is research to suggest that skills training can produce benefits for employees and for companies (Goldstein, 1989; Quinones & Ehrenstein, 1997). Employees benefit from learning new skills necessary to cope with an increasingly complex workplace. Companies benefit from the increased efficiency of employees and increases in profits (Casio, 1991; Phillips, 1994). However, not all training designs produce these positive results. Those that do employ pretraining assessment (Silberman, 1990), follow-up in the work setting (Parry, 1994), and attention to group development issues (Wheelan, 1990).

In contrast to consultation, psychoeducators, or trainers, need to be directive leaders and facilitators. They also must be supportive of members' efforts to acquire the skills being taught and be excellent role models capable of demonstrating those skills with confidence and ease (Silberman, 1990; Wheelan, 1994).

PERSONAL GROWTH GROUPS

Personal growth groups are "intended to help relatively healthy people function better on a interpersonal level. . . . Such groups are developmental, in that they explore personal issues that most people struggle with at the various transition periods in life" (Corey & Corey, 1992, p. 12). Personal growth groups in the workplace are perhaps most accurately described as a subset of psychoeducational, or skills training, groups. While skills training groups are more common in the workplace because of their emphasis on the development of behavioral skills (Silberman, 1990), personal growth groups sometimes are employed when attitude change, self, or interpersonal development are the goals. For example, increased tolerance of diversity in the workplace, increased awareness of individual personality traits, work styles, or leadership styles are typical goals of personal growth groups. Likewise, increased awareness and acceptance of differences in personality, work, or leadership styles in coworkers often are goals.

Personal growth groups in the workplace differ from counseling groups in that they focus on development, not remediation (Corey & Corey, 1992). Also, personal growth groups are designed around a topic such as leadership style, personality types, and the like. As is the case with therapy groups, models and theoretical perspectives of personal growth group leaders vary widely.

A Case Example

Many employees have attended training based on the Myers-Briggs Type Indicator assessment instrument (Myers, 1962; Myers & McCaulley, 1985). Prior to the training, participants complete the Myers-Briggs Type Indicator assessment, which yields a profile of each participant's preferences with regard to gathering and processing information. Each person's profile details the extent to which he or she prefers to utilize sensations, intuition, objective facts and principles, or feelings to obtain and process information. Also, each participant's degree of introversion and extroversion is reported. The Myers-Briggs assessment has been applied to other topics as well. Career management (Zunker, 1994), team cohesion and collaboration (Hirsh, 1985), and diversity (Kirby & Barger, 1996) are all thought to be enhanced by awareness of one's own and one's colleagues' personality types.

In this case, the focus of the 1-day training was on understanding how one's preferences may help or hinder an employee in a supervisory or management role. First, the trainer helped the supervisors and managers to understand their profile. Next, group members discussed occasions when their preferences helped them in their role. This was followed by a discussion of occasions when their preferences led them to make mistakes in dealing with employees or in developing business strategies. Finally, participants were invited to think of ways to build on the strengths of their profiles and to think of ways to increase the use of underdeveloped aspects of their personality.

Research on the effectiveness of personal growth groups for the achievement of individual goals, however, has produced mixed results. Personal growth groups do not always contribute to positive changes in their members. In a review of 177 tests (reported in 91 studies) of the immediate effects of such groups, 54% reported positive changes in members. Only 28 of these studies did follow-up, and of these, only 33% found that positive changes endured over time (Smith, 1975, 1980). This leads to the conclusion that there is some evidence that positive change can occur in such groups. However, many of these changes tend to fade out with time. There are a number of reasons why studies of personal growth groups produce mixed results. Smith's review, for example, contained 91 different studies conducted in a variety of educational and work settings. The length of time that groups met varied, as did the follow-up time and methods of evaluation.

Differences in the ways studies are conducted and weaknesses in study designs account for some of the variability in results (Walck, 1996). The fact that group leaders employ different models and theories of change makes comparisons difficult as well (Shaffer & Galinsky, 1989). Also, human beings, who vary in their skill and competence to facilitate positive change, lead personal growth groups. Finally, many leaders are unaware of, or do not attend to, group process or development issues. For example, most workplace personal growth groups are of very short duration and participants come from different areas of the company. As a result, more structure may be needed to ensure that members feel included and safe enough to participate in the group. If teams of people who work together attend a personal growth group together, the stage of development that the team is in may affect outcomes.

Members of teams that are functioning at the higher stages of group development will be more supportive of each other and more eager to learn. Members of teams that are functioning at lower stages of development may feel inhibited about participating and sharing personal information. For these groups, a team-building intervention might be necessary before participation in personal growth or psychoeducational workshops.

Regardless of leader or member views concerning individual change or learning, this process is enhanced by participation in a well-functioning group. Therefore, a primary task of personal growth group leaders and members is to create an effective and supportive group environment. Leaders of personal growth groups are more directive than consultants and less directive than psychoeducators for this reason. This style is necessary, since the success of personal growth groups hinges on participants' willingness to share personal information with others (Lieberman, Yalom, & Miles, 1973).

KEY ISSUES FOR PRACTITIONERS AND RESEARCHERS

The previous descriptions of workplace groups brought to the surface a number of problematic issues for practitioners and researchers. Four key issues are discussed next. These are linking research and practice, ethical standards, professional preparation of trainers and consultants, and financial considerations.

Linking Research and Practice

Perhaps the clearest example of the poor linkage between research and practice in this area can be seen in the area of team building. While numerous studies, reviews, and meta-analytic studies (e.g., Salas et al., 1999) have concluded that most current methods of team building or team development have little or no effect on team performance, these methods continue to be employed.

Team-building interventions that include goal setting and performance feedback (Guzzo et al., 1985) and role clarification (Salas et al., 1999) and that take group development into account have the most positive effects on group productivity (Buzaglo & Wheelan, 1999). The plethora of other types of team-building interventions are not supported by research. Despite these findings, the majority of team-building interventions do not include attention to goal setting, performance feedback, group development, or role clarification.

The link between research and practice in psychoeducational groups also is tenuous. For example, research suggests that pretraining needs assessments (Silberman, 1990), follow-up in the work setting (Parry, 1994), and attention to group development issues (Wheelan, 1990) are positively associated with outcomes. Unfortunately, many psychoeducators do not incorporate these elements into their training designs.

The apparent disregard for the research in these areas is not necessarily intentional. Rather, it may be due to the lack of professional preparation of many trainers and consultants. This is addressed in a later section. Strengthening the connection between researchers and practitioners will be the key to improving the quality of workplace interventions.

Ethical Standards

Ethical practice is another area of concern. Unfortunately, all three of the intervention models described in this chapter can be, and are, misused. Most of the time, ethical violations occur out of ignorance, but sometimes boundary violations or financial considerations motivate improper actions.

For example, I have encountered hundreds of people over the past 25 years who were required to participate in group trainings and felt traumatized by the experience. The stories vary. Some report being ridiculed by coworkers for being introverts (as measured by one of many personality assessments used in work settings). Other people tell stories about how a trainer or consultant seemed to be acting like their therapist. These people felt that their privacy was invaded without their permission, but felt that they had to comply for fear of job loss or other consequences. Still others reported being identified as the team's "problem" and receiving a barrage of negative feedback that the trainer or consultant made no attempt to stop. Finally, many people report that a trainer or consultant routinely shared information about individual employees with those employees' bosses. In these cases, the employees thought that what was said in the group was confidential.

Most trainers and consultants are not psychologists and do not understand the ethical standards required of those who are. These people may innocently cross the boundaries between training or consulting and therapy in a misguided attempt to help. However, some of the boundary violators were trained as social workers, counselors, and psychologists. In these cases, it may be that they have not received sufficient training in the differences between the therapeutic context and the work context.

Some trainers and consultants have acknowledged using a method or accepting an assignment that they knew would not be successful. The rationale usually was that they did what the client wanted and they had to make a living.

There is a growing body of literature concerning the ethics of providing psychoeducational and consulting services in the workplace (e.g., Lowman, 1998; Rhodeback, Wen, & White, 1990). The problem is that many people in those roles are unaware of these resources.

Professional Preparation of Trainers and Consultants

Many of the individuals working as trainers and consultants have little or no educational preparation for those jobs. Many large consulting firms hire young, recent graduates from a variety of undergraduate majors as trainers and consultants. The company provides some training, but most training is on the job. Other companies recruit school teachers, who became corporate trainers for financial reasons. Still other organizations promote excellent employees to the role of trainer or consultant. Some trainers and consultants are social workers or psychologists but with little or no preparation for the training and consultation role in the workplace. Of course, there are some training and consulting professionals with excellent educational and practice credentials.

Unlike many other professions, training and consulting is not a unified field with one designated professional society. There is no unified code of ethics, no standard body of knowledge, and no required educational preparation. There are, however, many companies eager for help in improving organizational effectiveness and productivity. Unfortunately, their employees who are charged with finding good consultants and trainers often are at a loss as to how to go about doing so. The problem for companies is one of supply and demand. The need for psychoeducators and consultants in the workplace continues to grow, and the supply of qualified individuals that can be hired for reasonable cost has not kept pace.

Some established professional organizations are trying to address these issues. Collaboration among professional groups has begun, but much more needs to be done in the interest of consumer protection. There also are a number of graduate degree programs, at both master's and doctoral levels, that prepare professional workplace psychoeducators and consultants. What remains to be done is to educate business organizations about the value of hiring professionally prepared psychoeducators and consultants.

Financial Considerations

Companies and work organizations utilize trainers and consultants to increase productivity, competitiveness, and profitability. This does not mean that organizational leaders do not care about their employees' or teams' growth and development. In my experience, the majority of executives care deeply about their employees. However, business is business, as they say.

Trainers and consultants cost companies billions of dollars a year (Casio, 1991), and research suggests that the return on that investment is mixed. More research is needed to determine what interventions work best and how to increase the effectiveness of those that show promise. More collaboration between practitioners and researchers will be needed to accomplish this. More focus on the credentials and professional development of trainers and consultants is needed as well. Perhaps the best way to accomplish these goals is to create more educated consumers of these services. If workplace organizations begin to demand higher standards for training and consultation, efforts to meet that demand will be forthcoming.

Summary

The use of task groups in the workplace to accomplish organizational goals and tasks continues to grow. The use of psychoeducational training groups and group consultation to help those task groups become effective and productive has grown as well. A professional field of training and development is emerging. At present, however, this field is not unified. Its researchers are housed in departments of psychology, business, communications, social work, and education at universities throughout the world. This makes it difficult for seasoned researchers to stay current with the research in this area, since that research can be found in more than 50 different journals. One can only imagine the difficulties faced by practitioners as they search the literature for better training and consultation methods or for graduate programs in this area.

The American Society for Training and Development, the Organizational Development Network, the American Management Association, three APA divisions (Society for Industrial and Organizational Psychology, Group Psychology and Group Psychotherapy, and Consulting Psychology), and the Professional Organizational Development Network in Higher Education are just some of the professional groups that have a stake in this field's future. This makes credentialing and a unified code of ethics challenging to say the least.

It will take all the training and consultation skills of the leaders, both researchers and practitioners, of this emerging field to address the issues detailed in this chapter. With that said, as both a researcher and a practitioner, I cannot imagine a more fascinating, intellectually stimulating, useful, and rewarding profession in which to participate.

References

Bennis, W., & Shepard, H. (1956). A theory of group development. *Human Relations, 9,* 415-437.

Braaten, L. J. (1974/1975). Developmental phases of encounter groups: A critical review of models and a new proposal. *Interpersonal Development, 75,* 112-129.

Bruning, N. S., & Frew, D. R. (1987). Effects of exercise, relaxation, and management skills training on physiological stress indicators: A field experiment. *Journal of Applied Psychology, 72,* 515-521.

Buller, P. F., & Bell, C. H. (1986). Effects of team building and goal setting on productivity: A field experiment. *Academy of Management Journal, 29,* 305-328.

Burchill, C. (2001). *A study of the relationship between group development level and productivity: The intensive care unit and patient outcome.* Unpublished dissertation, Temple University, Philadelphia, PA.

Burnand, G. (1990). Group development phases as working through six fundamental human problems. *Small Group Research, 21,* 255-273.

Buzaglo, G., & Wheelan, S. (1999). Facilitating work team effectiveness: Case studies from Central America. *Small Group Research, 30,* 108-129.

Casio, W. F. (1991). Using utility analysis to assess training outcomes. In I. L. Goldstein (Ed.), *Training and development in organizations* (pp. 63-88). San Francisco: Jossey-Bass.

Cohen, M. D., & Sproull, L. S. (Eds.). (1996). *Organizational learning.* Thousand Oaks, CA: Sage.

Corey, M. S., & Corey, G. (1992). *Group process and practice* (4th ed.). Pacific Grove, CA: Brooks/Cole.

Cummings, T. G. (1981). Designing effective work-groups. In P. C. Nystrom & W. Starbuck (Eds.), *Handbook of organizational design* (Vol. 2) (pp. 250-271). Oxford, UK: Oxford University Press.

Deutsch, M. (1971). Toward an understanding of conflict. *International Journal of Group Tensions, 1,* 42-54.

Devine, D. J., Clayton, L. D., Philips, J. L., Dunford, B. B., & Melner, S. B. (1999). Teams in organizations: Prevalence, characteristics, and effectiveness. *Small Group Research, 30,* 678-711.

Druckman, D., & Bjork, R. A. (Eds.). (1994). *Learning, remembering, believing: Enhancing human performance.* Washington, DC: National Academy Press.

Dyer, J. L. (1984). Team research and team training: A state-of-the-art review. In F. A. Muckler (Ed.), *Human factors review* (pp. 285-323). Santa Monica, CA: Human Factors Society.

Fensterheim, H., & Glazer, H. I. (1983). *Behavioral psychotherapy.* New York: Brunner/Mazel.

Friedlander, F. (1987). The ecology of work groups. In J. W. Lorsch (Ed*.), Handbook of organizational behavior* (pp. 301-314). Englewood Cliffs, NJ: Prentice Hall.

Gabarro, J. J. (1987). The development of working relationships. In J. W. Lorsch (Ed.), *Handbook of organizational behavior* (pp. 172-189). Englewood Cliffs, NJ: Prentice Hall.

Goldstein, I. L. (Ed.). (1989). *Training and development in organizations.* San Francisco: Jossey-Bass.

Gordon, J. (1992). Work teams: How far have they come? *Training, 29,* 59-65.

Guzzo, R. A., Jett, R. D., & Katzell, R. A. (1985). The effects of psychologically-based intervention programs on worker productivity: A meta-analysis. *Personnel Psychology, 38,* 275-291.

Hackman, J. R. (1989). *Groups that work (and those that don't).* San Francisco: Jossey-Bass.

Halstead, L. S., Rintala, D. H., Kanellos, M., Griffin, B., Higgins, L., Rheinecker, S., et al. (1986). The innovative rehabilitation team: An experiment in team building. *Archives of Physical Medicine and Rehabilitation, 67,* 357-361.

Hirsh, S. K. (1985). *Using the Myers-Briggs Type Indicator in organizations: A resource book.* Palo Alto, CA: Consulting Psychologists Press.

Kirby, L. K., & Barger, N. J. (1996). Multicultural applications In A. L. Hammer (Ed.), *MBTI applications* (pp. 167-196). Palo Alto, CA: Consulting Psychologists Press.

Larson, C. E., & LaFasto, F. M. J. (1989). *Team work: What must go right/what can go wrong.* Newbury Park, CA: Sage.

Lawler, E. E., III, Mohrman, S. A., & Ledford, G. E., Jr. (1995). *Creating high performance organizations: Practices and results of employee involvement and total quality management in Fortune 1000 companies.* San Francisco: Jossey-Bass.

Lieberman, M., Yalom, I., & Miles, M. (1973). *Encounter groups: First facts.* New York: Basic Books.

Lowman, R. L. (1998). *The ethical practice of psychology in organizations.* Washington, DC: American Psychological Association.

Lundgren, D., & Knight, D. (1978). Sequential stages of development in sensitivity training groups. *Journal of Applied Behavioral Science, 14,* 204-222.

Mann, R., Gibbard, G., & Hartman, J. (1967). *Interpersonal style and group development.* New York: John Wiley.

Mills, T. (1964). *Group transformations: An analysis of a learning group.* Englewood Cliffs, NJ: Prentice Hall.

Murphy, L. R., & Hurrell, J., Jr. (1987). Stress management in the process of occupational stress reduction. *Journal of Managerial Psychology, 2,* 18-23.

Myers, I. B. (1962). *Manual: The Myers-Briggs Type Indicator.* Palo Alto, CA: Consulting Psychologists Press.

Myers, I. B., & McCaulley, M. H. (1985). *Manual: A guide to the development and use of the Myers-Briggs Type Indicator.* Palo Alto, CA: Consulting Psychologists Press.

Nelson-Jones, R. (1992). *Group leadership: A training approach.* Pacific Grove, CA: Brooks/Cole.

Parry, S. B. (1994). Using action plans to measure return on investment. In J. L. Phillips (Ed.), *Measuring return on investment* (Vol. 1). Alexandria, VA: American Society for Training and Development.

Phillips, J. L. (Ed.). (1994). *Measuring return on investment* (Vol. 1). Alexandria, VA: American Society for Training and Development.

Quinones, M. A., & Ehrenstein, A. (Eds.). (1997). *Training for a rapidly changing workplace: Applications of psychological research.* Washington, DC: American Psychological Association.

Rhodeback, M., Wen, B., & White, L. P. (1990). Ethical consideration in organization development: An empirical approach. *Organizational Development Journal, 8,* 40-49.

Robinson-Kurpius, S. E., & Keim, J. (1994). Team building for nurses experiencing burnout and poor morale. *Journal for Specialists in Group Work, 19,* 155-161.

Salas, E., Rozell, D., Mullen, B., & Driskell, J. E. (1999). The effect of team building on performance: An integration. *Small Group Research, 30,* 309-329.

Schein, E. H. (1988). Process consultation (Rev. ed.). Reading, MA: Addison-Wesley.

Shaffer, J., & Galinsky, M. D. (1989). *Models of group therapy* (2nd ed.). Englewood Cliffs, NJ: Prentice Hall.

Silberman, M. (1990). *Active training.* Lexington, MA: Lexington Books.

Slater, P. (1966). *Microcosm.* New York: John Wiley.

Smith, P. B. (1975). Controlled studies of the outcome of sensitivity training. *Psychological Bulletin, 82,* 597-622.

Smith, P. B. (1980). The outcomes of sensitivity training and encounter. In P. B. Smith (Ed.), *Small groups and personal change* (pp. 25-55). London: Methuen.

Sundstrom, E., DeMeuse, K. P., & Futrell, D. (1990). Work teams: Applications and effectiveness. *American Psychologist, 45,* 120-133.

Tannenbaum, S. I., Beard, R. L., & Salas, E. (1992). Team building and its influence on team effectiveness: An examination of conceptual and empirical developments. In K. Kelley (Ed.), *Issues, theory, and research in industrial/organizational psychology.* Amsterdam: Elsevier.

Theodorson, G. A. (1962). The function of hostility in small groups. *Journal of Social Psychology, 256,* 57-66.

Tuckman, B. W., & Jensen, M. A. C. (1977). Stages in small group development revisited. *Group and Organizational Studies, 2,* 419-427.

Walck, C. L. (1996). Management and leadership. In A. L. Hammer (Ed.), *MBTI applications* (pp. 55-79). Palo Alto, CA: Consulting Psychologists Press.

Wheelan, S. A. (1990). *Facilitating training groups: A guide to leadership and verbal intervention skills.* New York: Praeger.

Wheelan, S. (1994). *Group processes: A developmental perspective.* Boston: Allyn & Bacon.

Wheelan, S. (1996). An initial exploration of the relevance of complexity theory to group research and practice. *Systems Practice, 9*(1), 47-70.

Wheelan, S. (1999). *Creating effective teams: A guide for members and leaders.* Newbury Park, CA: Sage.

Wheelan, S., & Bastas, E. (1979). Should doctors be more assertive? *Behavioral Medicine,* August, 39-41.

Wheelan, S., & Hochberger, J. (1996). Validation studies of the group development questionnaire. *Small Group Research, 27,* 143-170.

Wheelan, S., Murphy, D., Tsumura, E., & Fried Kline, S. (1998). Member perceptions of internal group dynamics and productivity. *Small Group Research, 29,* 371-393.

Yalom, I. (1995). *The theory and practice of group psychotherapy* (4th ed.). New York: Basic Books.

Zunker, V. G. (1994). *Career counseling: Applied concepts of life planning* (4th ed.). Pacific Grove, CA: Brooks/Cole.

30

Group Counseling and Group Therapy in Mental Health Settings and Health Maintenance Organizations

Marvin W. Clifford

Ochsner Clinic Foundation

Group counseling and therapy are important treatment interventions in many mental health and health maintenance organization (HMO) settings. Mental health and HMO settings include but are not limited to mental health centers and clinics, departments of psychiatry in medical schools, centers, and hospitals, outpatient settings, day treatment programs, dual-diagnosis treatment programs, family service agencies, and child guidance clinics. This chapter highlights the most common groups used in these settings and includes information on psychoeducational, counseling, and therapy groups. Group techniques and research are discussed and case vignettes are included. This chapter describes how groups are used in mental health and HMO settings. This is followed by a discussion of specific issues related to the types of

groups specific to mental health and HMO settings.

Psychoeducational Groups

In mental health settings, psychoeducational groups offer an important method for teaching skills, knowledge, new ideas, and personal growth issues to clients. Although these groups vary in topics presented, the mutual goal for all groups is education and skill development. It is important to emphasize that psychoeducational groups are preventative by design. The major goals of these groups are to prevent the development of mental and emotional issues, learn coping skills, improve relationships, and build self-esteem (Conyne, 1996). Staff members often use these groups with structured approaches

(Niemann, 2002) focused on a specific topic or specific goals. Topics in psychoeducational groups include medication management, assertiveness training, self-esteem, anger management, relationships, coping skills, parenting, communication, decision making, using community resources, stress management, coping with trauma, loss, and grief, conflict resolution, child rearing, and caregiving.

Psychoeducational groups have been and continue to be popular in managed care settings due to their cost effectiveness. More people can receive services in a short period of time and may be reimbursed by health insurance. A targeted audience is important, and using a structured format is preferable. Having administrative support from the agency is imperative. The sessions are usually 1½ to 2 hours long and usually include 6 to 15 sessions (Corey & Corey, 2002).

Children. Groups that help children in these settings include those that deal with coping with divorce, building social skills, increasing self-esteem, achievement of educational goals, developing anger management skills, and learning life skills (Buchholz & Mishne, 1994; Rose, 1998; Rose & Edelson, 1987). Life skills groups use training to help individuals improve their lives by learning new skills and correcting ineffective skills (Gladding, 1999). An example of a life skills training group would be one that helps shy children learn to be more interested in others. The emphasis on the group is "how to" for life skills (Gladding, 1999). Another example is an antibullying group teaching children to not bully others, a serious problem in the schools (Halverson, 2002). A 12-week model can be used in schools or counseling settings, teaching children skills to deal with bullies, values that bullying is not acceptable, and how to get help from parents and adults (Wylie, 2000).

Children of divorce groups are generally short term, six to eight sessions, and last 1 hour per session (Rose, 1998). The goal is to help children learn coping skills when their parents divorce or separate. The optimum number of group members varies from four to nine depending on the age and needs of the children. The focus is to provide support, resolution, and expression of feelings, problem solving, and

coping skills (Rose, 1998). Some of the techniques in such groups include drawing, using puppets, storytelling, and discussions. Drawings can be used for children who have difficulty talking about their feelings (Cordell & Bergman-Meador, 1991; Rose, 1998).

Groups that educate, teach skills, and foster interaction for children are important, and games are commonly used as learning opportunities for children. For example, the Talking, Feeling, Doing Game (Gardner, 1973) and Fun and Games in Stepfamily Therapy (Keshet, 1995) emphasize learning concepts like communication, self-esteem, relationships, and expressing feelings.

Strategies that are helpful for children to be successful in psychoeducational groups include keeping the topic and activity relevant to the emotional and physical development of the children served (Halverson, 2002), selecting group members who have common learning needs, selecting topics for discussion that are pertinent to children (e.g., divorce, loss and grief, self-esteem, dealing with bullies, making friends, or dealing with siblings), and keeping the focus of the group on a preventive direction (Capuzzi & Gross, 1998). It is helpful to screen children for psychoeducational groups to determine appropriate goals and fit for each group. Meeting the child and parents before the group starts to make these decisions is good practice (Bergin, 1999). Group selection is important, and the children should share common goals for learning (Bergin, 1999). Size of the group is also an important factor. This can vary depending on the children, their problems, emphasis of the group, and skills of the leaders. Younger children 4 to 6 years of age should have fewer group members, four to five, while older children ages 7 to 12 can tolerate six to nine group members (Rose, 1998).

Adolescents. Groups can help adolescents make a successful transition from childhood to adulthood (Gladding, 1999). Psychoeducational groups for adolescents focus on their concerns relating to relationships, family, school, peers, self-esteem, drugs and alcohol, sexuality, dating, the future, and their feelings (Gladding, 1999). Bowman (1987) found five common topics discussed in adolescent groups: careers, communication skills, decision making, study skills, and self-concept. Similarly, Dansby (1996) found that the most frequently discussed topics in adolescent groups were college careers, study skills, decision making, and self-esteem.

Gouet (1994) stated that "prevention groups designed for high-risk young people can provide education about the disease or addiction, along with teaching the coping, social, and resistance skills necessary to ward off drug-using behavior" (p. 16). Williams (1990) has researched models that indicate that an educational format can be helpful for young people younger than 18 years of age to discuss and understand alcoholism. They can help prevent excessive alcohol use for youth from alcoholic families. Techniques used in adolescent psychoeducational groups include didactic education on the impact of drugs and alcohol on health (Smith, 1985), development of support from peers (Shields, 1986), and acquisition of problem-solving (Wodarski, 1990), self-esteem (Jensen, 1997), and anger management skills (Snyder, Kymissis, & Kessler, 1999).

An example of a psychoeducational group for adolescents in mental health clinics is one that focuses on drug and alcohol education for adolescents who have been exposed to or used/experimented with drugs or alcohol (Dryfus, 1990, 1993). These adolescents are believed to be at risk for possible drug or alcohol problems. The group meets for 1 hour for 12 weeks (Rose, 1998; Shields, 1986), and goals are to teach skills to say no, prevent use of drugs or alcohol, understand the impact of substances, and how to deal with family or peer issues. The group is led by adults trained in the areas of addictions, adolescents, and group methods.

Adults. Topics that often occur in mental health settings for adult psychoeducational groups include stress management, coping skills, medication, parenting skills, relationships, communication, grief and loss, anger management skills, divorce, self-esteem, and health or career areas. Most groups are very specific, goal oriented, and short term.

Training and educational groups are frequently used in mental health settings. One model combined mandated and voluntary patients into one group that met weekly. The focus of the group was on improving parenting skills. The group, designed to be outpatient and instructional (Family Service of Greater New Orleans, 2001), provided a source of information, support, and skill building for the parents. The group met weekly for 1 hour for 12 weeks and was led by two master's degree-level professionals. The leaders taught child and adolescent development skills and parenting techniques and skills, and then helped group members discuss their situations and get support from each other. Group workers received positive feedback from the referring case managers that parents reported positive results from attending the parents' group in their skills and effectiveness as parents.

Stress management is another good example of a psychoeducational group. Wakeman (2001) described a group titled Stress Management for Everyday Living that included managing stress, identifying sources of stress, job burnout, relaxation techniques, beliefs inventory, cognitive restructuring, worrying, self-esteem, assertiveness, communication, and taking care of yourself. The purpose was to teach and practice stress management skills with an emphasis on prevention aimed at educating oneself to deter illness, health problems, and burnout. The seminar met for six sessions of 2 hours each. Feedback from participants was that the group was helpful in improving coping skills that could be used in daily living with stress. Earlier research (Wakeman & Metayer, 1985) found this model effective in a day treatment program that provided stress management training and therapy to adults having stress symptoms and psychosomatic complaints. These patients reported decreased symptoms of stress and psychosomatic complaints as a result of attending stress management seminars.

Other examples of psychoeducational groups are medication management groups for clients on psychiatric medications. Clients are selected based on the need for common medications, similar disorders, and potential for group participation. This model serves many client populations and is popular in outpatient settings (Beltman, Chiles, & Carlin, 1984; Cohen & Amdur, 1981). It is more cost effective than one-to-one medication checks. One goal of this type of group is to have clients with similar emotional concerns, for example depression, be in a group to discuss their medications. Generally, a medical doctor (usually a psychiatrist) and a master's degree-level clinician, such as a social worker or licensed professional counselor, conduct the group. Clients are taught about their medications and appropriate dosages, side effects, and other aspects of the disorder. Clients have reported benefit from the support, guidance, and suggestions from the group leaders and members (Brooks, 1993). Groups usually meet for 1 to 1½ hours once every month or every 2 months and are limited to six to eight participants. Brooks wrote, "The group offered patients education, mutual support, an opportunity to practice socialization, decreased isolation, and a haven to express their feelings and reveal their fears without the worry of rejection" (p. 167). In general, patient satisfaction has been high (Diamond & Little, 1984; Larkin, 1982; Moffic, 1982).

COUNSELING GROUPS

Counseling groups are used regularly in mental health and HMO settings. These groups focus on skill building, improving skills for everyday living, relationships, and social and personal growth and development. For example, skills to deal with anxiety, cope with negative feelings, and improve relationships are often the focus (Gladding, 2003).

Counseling groups use the interaction among the members and leaders as a major medium for exchange, often emphasizing interpersonal relationships as a change agent (Gladding, 2003). Counseling groups are more often used for people experiencing difficult problems of everyday life as well as the usual problems of living (Gladding, 2003). Counseling groups are short term in length, usually 6 to 16 months (Gladding, 2003). Gladding states that "[c]ounseling groups are a more direct approach to dealing with troublesome behavior than are psychoeducational groups because they target specific behavior and are focused on problem solving instead of a world of general difficulties that may or may not be pertinent to every member's life. A major advantage of counseling groups is the interpersonal interaction, feedback, and contributions

group members experience from one another over time" (p. 29).

Children. Child and adolescent counseling groups are popular in mental health clinics, especially grief and loss groups and activity groups (Halverson, 2002; Rose, 1998). Children's grief, loss, or trauma groups are very therapeutic in helping group members cope with these tragedies (Samide, 2002). Tremendous support is given by the leaders to help children resolve their fears and conflicts and feel supported (Rose, 1998). Children's grief groups also provide relief from isolation, a safe place to share their feelings, validation of their experience, and help to deal with the grief process (Levine & Noell, 1995). Play therapy (Glazer & Myra, 1999) and guided imaging (Glazer, 1998) also can be helpful techniques, as well as using drawings to express feelings (Glazer, 1998). Education, discussions, and group sharing are also suggested (Keitel, Kopala, & Robin, 1998). When working with children, the leader is very active, and group members do a lot of sharing of their feelings and experiences (Rose, 1998; Shelby, 1994).

One group for latency boys ages 8 to 13 met weekly and emphasized a variety of topics for discussions and interactions, including school problems, family issues, self-esteem, parents, siblings, friends, and loss and grief (Clifford, 1991). One boy in the group discussed his feelings about his father not being in his life. He discussed missing his father and wanting him back. The group members gave support and acknowledgment of his feelings. Two other group members shared their father loss experiences as well. The group session focused on developing coping skills, finding adult male role models within and outside the family as people with whom to identify, and acknowledging the importance of fathers in boys' lives. Grief and loss were frequent themes in this group (Clifford, 1991; Rose, 1998).

Activity or social skill-building groups are very important for children (Frank, 1983). These counseling groups help children develop skills, resolve feelings, improve behavior, and develop self-esteem. They involve structured activities, games, discussion of themes, and interaction in real experiences (Fatout, 1996). Activity and social skill counseling groups emphasize the members' interactions as a primary focus for the group. The client populations are select groups with a specific problem, behavior, or emotional concern in common, and the purposes of the groups are growth oriented, remedial, and dealing with rough spots in the clients' lives (Gazda, Ginter, & Horne, 2001; Gladding, 2003). One activity useful in these groups is to have children draw a picture of their family and then share this with the group. Children learn about each other's families and problems, and it creates an environment for positive group interaction. It also offers counselors an opportunity to help the children identify or discuss family strengths, areas for improvement, and family conflicts. Activities in groups can help foster verbal interactions, develop problem solving, improve self-esteem, foster development, and improve relationships (Wright, 1999).

Adolescents. Adolescent counseling groups are also frequently used in mental health and HMO settings (Kraft, 1989). Examples include anger management, self-esteem building, and general adolescent counseling groups. Anger management and self-esteem groups are usually limited to 6 to 12 sessions and have very specific goals. For anger management groups, the major goal is to learn to manage anger effectively and safely and improve relationship and conflict resolution skills. Self-esteem groups improve adolescent self-esteem by developing relationship skills, increasing appropriate behaviors, and teaching peer, social, and problem-resolution skills (Azima & Richmond, 1989).

I have had extensive experience with adolescent anger management groups for court-mandated males ages 14 to 17. The groups meet for 1½ hours per week for 8 weeks with a specific topic for each week. These topics included:

Week 1 Introduction, goals, anger management

Week 2 Signs, symptoms, behavior, and consequences of anger

Week 3 Relationships and families

Week 4 Peer skills

Week 5 Self-esteem

Week 6 Conflict management

Week 7 Culture and spirituality

Week 8 Evaluating, discussion of progress, and termination

Sixty percent of the adolescents who started the 8-week program successfully finished it. The court counselors, probation officers, parents, and group members reported that the group assisted the adolescent group members in learning to manage anger more effectively. Counseling emphasized major adolescent issues, including concerns related to self-esteem, girlfriends, relationships and friendships, family and parents, sexuality, school, fears and anxieties about their lives, individualization/separation processes, and conflict resolution skills. The group used learning skills, breaks, time-outs, group interactions, role plays, and specific handouts. Success is strongly reinforced by praise, support, and acknowledgment. The leader is very active, the group members are expected to interact, and change is emphasized. Self-responsibility and appropriate skill building are the focus.

In most mental health settings, an example of the general adolescent group would be a coed group ages 14 to 17 meeting with the goals of building social skills, improving self-esteem, and fostering appropriate behavior in school, family, and community settings. The group may meet 1 hour per week and be ongoing. Clients make a 12-week commitment and can negotiate to stay longer if necessary. Considerable information is discussed in these groups, and the counselor provides a safe, confidential environment where adolescents can show their feelings, solve problems, and interact with each other (Kraft, 1989). Often this model uses cotherapists (Kymissis, 1993). The issues facing adolescents that can be addressed in this group include relationships, peers, dealing with feelings, self-esteem, families, school, sexuality, drug and alcohol concerns, fears, and adolescent development (Kraft, 1989). Counselors use varied methods and skills to enhance growth of the group members such as teaching, providing support, clarification, interpretation, and giving information (Kymissis, 1993). For example, in one adolescent session described by Kymissis, the members decided that they did not have anything important to talk about and that they would remain silent for the whole session. The leader asked the group to vote for one member to become the therapist for the next 15 minutes. This intervention broke the silence and allowed the group to move toward a productive session, during which they discussed their feelings about the leader and about authority.

Adults. Another type of group focuses on grief and loss resolution. Piper (1991) stated: "We have repeatedly been impressed with how quickly patients disclose and become effectively involved in loss groups. The presence of readily identifiable commonalities in multiple areas facilitates the process" (p. 420). These loss and grief groups are important because all group members have a common problem and can support each other. Generally these groups are short term and have a very specific theme of loss and grief (Piper, 1991). Research (McCallum & Piper, 1990; Piper, McCallum, & Azim, 1992) has found that short-term grief and loss groups help clients to reduce symptoms, improve psychosocial functioning, resolve grief, and improve coping skills. In their research, McCallum and Piper found that the long-term benefit of these groups for clients persisted 6 months after therapy. Adolph (1996) wrote that "our grief group meetings helped us understand that grief is a universal experience and that life does go on even when those who are dearest to us are no longer available" (p. 33). Group is one of the most effective approaches in helping people deal with grief and loss (Price, Dinas, Dunn, & Winterowd, 1995; Vernon, 2002).

Counseling groups can also help with the treatment of depression. Rice (2001) proposed a model for 12 weeks in which group members participate in a structured format with experiential and didactic components. For each session, time is allowed for group members to discuss their situation and express their feelings. Feedback and support are given within the group structure (Rice, 2001).

Severely and persistently mentally ill populations are also served in mental health clinics (Hellerstein & Meehan, 1987). A group model frequently used for this population is a combined psychoeducational and counseling group. The emphasis is on engaging the clients, providing voluntary service, using empowerment, and

involving them in planning the group program (Cohen, 1989). Among other dimensions, these groups usually focus on socialization skills (Toseland & Rivas, 2001) such as coping and interpersonal skills, knowledge of the community resources, stabilization and support, and making connections with people who have similar problems (Stone, 1993). The basic outpatient group model for severely and persistently mentally ill patients emphasizes a 45- to 75-minute session meeting weekly for 12 or more sessions (Stone, 1995) and focuses on communication skills, relationships, anger management, and so on (Lieberman, 1988; Stone, 1993, 1995). Some programs may include medication management as part of their structure. Some research suggests that these groups are more effective when they are time limited and highly structured (Videka-Sherman, 1986).

Group Psychotherapy

"Therapy groups help members change their behavior, cope with and ameliorate personal problems, or rehabilitate themselves after physical, psychological, or social trauma" (Toseland & Rivas, 2001, p. 26). The demands of managed care systems have forced mental health and HMO programs to be creative in developing short-term group work models. Therefore, to make services cost effective, group therapy in these settings is very short term, with a maximum of 12 to 15 sessions (Hoyt, 1995). Although the major factor is cost, counselors and therapists are concerned about the quality of services as well. Another adult counseling group used in mental health or HMO settings is a group for male batterers. For more information on groups for batterers, see Chapter 41 in this handbook.

Children. Most group work with children in this setting tends to be psychoeducational. However, group therapy is useful with children and is applicable in short-term presentations with specific problems or issues. Examples of therapy groups appropriate for children include groups that focus on attention-deficit/hyperactivity disorder (ADHD), behavior change (e.g., in-and-out-of-seat behavior, talking out of turn, aggressive behavior), and children who are abused sexually, physically, and/or emotionally.

The diagnosis of ADHD for a child usually involves a comprehensive treatment plan. Including group therapy can be helpful (Rose, 1998). A typical group for ADHD children meets 1 hour per week over a 12-week period (Clifford, 1991). The use of such a model has had good results with behavior improvement at school, with the family, and in peer settings. Very clear contracts are written before a group begins. The therapists develop the contract to state the behavior to be changed (Fatout, 1992). An example would read: "My contract is to control my angry feelings by taking breaks and time-outs when I am angry." The therapists would focus on this contract in the group sessions. A participant may have more than one goal. Contracts can be changed, added to, or modified according to the needs or progress of the child. Throughout the group, the leaders use a strengths-based approach, emphasize change, offer support, and give feedback. For progress, it is very important to acknowledge positive changes, small or large (Clifford, 1991). The group can develop a sense of belonging for members and foster healthy peer relationships (O'Rourke, 1990).

Similar to ADHD groups, behavioral change groups for children target specific behaviors. These behaviors include social skills, peer skills, anger management, and school or family relationships (Rose & Edelson, 1987). An identified behavior is agreed on by the child, the parents, and the counselor. A contract is written, reward systems are put in place at home, at school, and in the group, and therapy then proceeds. The counselors stay in close contact with parents and the school. A team approach can be very helpful to focus on change for a child or adolescent. Rewards are offered for meeting targeted behavioral goals. For example, Edward, age 9, had a behavior that was annoying to peers and adults. He often interrupted conversations so he could get attention. His family was frustrated with him, as were his teachers. He had difficulty maintaining friends. He was referred to group therapy and started in an ongoing boys' group for latency-aged boys. Edward's group was coordinated with the school and family interventions. Edward's goal was to stop interrupting other people's conversations and to learn appropriate

times to talk. He started the group being very disruptive to others' discussions. A time-out system was put in place to help him. Every time he was disruptive, he went to time-out. The same system was put in place at home and school. Also, varied rewards were given for not interrupting for specific periods of time. Over the length of the 12-week group, Edward went from 15 disruptions per group down to zero. The same outcome occurred at home and at school. He also learned about social and peer skills, conversational skills, and how to make and keep friends. Groups have been shown to be effective as a way for children to learn social and interpersonal skills (Shechtman & Bar-El, 1994).

Frequently, clinics and HMOs also offer group treatment for children or adolescents who have been abused sexually, physically, or emotionally (Hoyt, 1995). These groups generally are all male or all female, age specific, and focus on treatment of abuse issues. The groups are specific to the type of abuse (e.g., physical abuse). An example of the content for this type of group follows:

Session 1 Creating a safe place

Session 2 Identifying the group identity and counseling abuse themes

Session 3 Self-disclosure and sharing of one's abuse experience

Session 4 Discharging abuse-related feelings

Session 5 Defining and clarifying rights

Session 6 Clarifying issues of blame and responsibility

Sessions 7 & 8 Developing age-appropriate behaviors and assertiveness skills

Session 9 Feelings toward offenders

Session 10 Letting go: putting the trauma in the past

Sessions 11 & 12 Acknowledging progress and a sense of accomplishment and saying good-bye (Heiman & Ettin, 2001, pp. 269-297)

For more information about groups for survivors of sexual abuse, see Chapter 36 in this handbook.

Adolescents. Therapy groups for adolescents include hospital follow-up groups, depression groups, sexual abuse groups, substance abuse groups, and process groups. Hospital follow-up groups are generally 1½ hours per week for 10 to 12 sessions. These are mixed groups for boys and girls together. The group membership is composed of adolescents who were recently in psychiatric hospitals with various diagnoses. The group provides a supportive environment to learn and practice skills so that group members can successfully reenter the community after a hospitalization (Azima & Richmond, 1989).

The depression groups are for boys and girls meeting the criteria for an Axis I diagnosis of depression according to the *Diagnostic and Statistical Manual of Mental Disorders* (4th ed.) *(DSM-IV)* (American Psychiatric Association, 1994). Often, groups are 1 hour per week for 12 or more weeks, and boys and girls attend the same group. The purpose of these groups is to help members improve coping skills, decrease isolation, learn and use problem-solving skills, build peer and social skills, and discuss their situations, feelings, and lives. Often tremendous support is available in these groups (Azima & Richmond, 1989).

Sexual abuse groups for adolescents are generally same-gendered groups, which helps to improve trust and is less threatening to group members. The purpose of these groups is to heal emotional hurts, resolve anger and resentment, improve self-esteem, improve relationships, deal with guilt and shame, and recover from the trauma of abuse. Groups usually meet for 16 or more weeks for 1½ hours per week. Using cotherapists versus a single therapist has an advantage for these groups in that the work is intense, and using a team approach can help to prevent burnout, improve therapeutic effectiveness, and provide more support (Corey & Corey, 2002). For a more detailed discussion of groups for sexual abuse survivors, see Chapter 36 in this handbook.

Substance abuse therapy groups traditionally are not short-term groups. Programs need to be creative in managed care, mental health, and HMO settings to be cost effective. Corey and Corey (2002) give an example of a 30-week group for adolescents in recovery from substance abuse. Many treatment programs support a 1-year recovery program that includes group therapy. Usually these groups meet for 1 to 1½ hours per week for both boys and girls ages 14 to 17. The goals for these members are to remain clean and sober, receive education on substance abuse, build successes and cope with the challenges of recovery, prevent relapse, and change lifestyles to healthier options than chemical abuse or addictions (Corey & Corey, 2002).

Process groups for adolescents are popular in mental health settings for young people ages 14 to 17. The goal of an adolescent process group is to learn about their feelings, self-esteem, and the effect of their behavior on other people. For adolescents, peer social acceptance strongly affects self-esteem (Harter, 1990). A strong focus of these groups is on interpersonal relationships and skills. Groups can influence the positive development of self-esteem for adolescents (Shechtman & Bar-El, 1994). These groups generally run 15 or more weeks for 1½ hours per week. Many topics can be discussed; for example, school, peers, self-esteem, family, boyfriends, girlfriends, feelings, and behavior. The goals are on changing group process, improving behavior, and learning about self. The main focus of these adolescent process groups is to promote individual growth, personal learning, and personal problem solving (Halverson, 2002).

Adults. Typical adult psychotherapy groups in mental health and HMOs are related to themes such as depression, anxiety, men, women, and other topic-specific groups like sexual abuse or victims of violence groups. The focus is on changing and healing emotional or personality hurts or defects. There is more intensity and depth of focus in psychotherapy groups as compared to counseling and psychoeducational groups. Emotional closeness among members is one variable that has been found to be related to effectiveness in psychotherapy groups (Zastrow, 2001).

An adult depression group usually consists of six to eight members, meets weekly for 12 or more weeks, and focuses on the reduction of distress for group members. Often the group members may receive other therapies as well; for example, individual, marital, family, or medication management. The group focuses on an opportunity to resolve grief or loss, solve problems, make changes, and improve positive thinking. Generally, a variety of therapeutic modalities can be used with these groups. Research has clearly demonstrated that depression groups help depressed clients (Dykeman & Appleton, 2002).

Cognitive-behavioral groups have become popular as methods to help adults with depression, fears, anxieties, phobias, and worries (Clarke, Rohde, Lewinsohn, Hops, & Seeley, 1999). The clients' beliefs and their behaviors are addressed in the group setting to help achieve more positive outcomes.

Adult process groups for interpersonal therapy are popular. The groups focus on how people impact others. People express their feelings and learn more effective ways of relating to, behaving, and communicating with others. Clients with adjustment disorder or milder forms of Axis I disorders from the *DSM-IV* (American Psychiatric Association, 1994) may benefit from this group format (Mackenzie & Grabovac, 2001; Wifley, Mackenzie, Welch, Ayres, & Weissman, 2000). A major benefit for clients attending adult process or interpersonal groups is that of transferring their learning to their outside lives and improving their relationships (Wifley et al., 2000). Short-term process group therapy generally runs from 6 to 15 weeks (Wifley et al., 2000; Mackenzie & Grabovac, 2001).

Solution-focused therapy groups are gaining popularity in mental health clinics and HMO settings (Coe, 2001). These groups focus on very specific solutions to problems, emphasize strengths, do not uncover the past, and empower group members to use resources and skills they may already have (Selekman, 1997). See Metcalf (1998) for guidelines for the solution-oriented group therapy, which include recommendations such as helping the group members redefine their problems, emphasize exceptions to these problems, and focus on specific, solvable problems.

GUIDELINES FOR GROUPS IN MENTAL HEALTH AND HEALTH MAINTENANCE ORGANIZATIONS

This section focuses on specific issues regarding groups in settings of mental health programs and HMOs. The issues discussed are client selection and screening for group membership, short-term group work models, retaining clients and referral resources, billing and payment issues, and similarities and differences for psychoeducational, counseling, and therapy group work models. Information on current trends and future directions is also briefly discussed.

Client selection and screening for group membership are important procedures for all professional groups (Posthuma, 2002; Yalom, 1995). An in-depth screening interview that covers the potential group member's goals, expectations, strengths, reasons for joining the group, and relationship history is important for all groups and especially important for counseling and therapy groups (Yalom, 1995). In psychoeducational groups, the opportunities for screening may not always exist, as lectures may be presented to large audiences on specific educational topics and may be "grouped together because they work in the same office" (Gladding, 2003, p. 114). For counseling and psychotherapy groups, the more prepared that group members and the leader are, prior to the group starting, the lower the dropout rate, the better the communication, and the higher the group cohesion (Gladding, 2003; Yalom, 1995).

Clients should be selected based on having goals similar to those of other group members and the group as a whole (Yalom, 1995). For example, clients entering a group to help people with depression need to have the common goal of wanting to be less depressed. The goals that members choose to work on in groups "must be explicit, realistic, attainable, measurable, and verifiable" (Reid, 1997, p. 198). An example of an appropriate goal for someone joining an anger management group would be to handle angry feelings safely, appropriately, and responsibly. Safety, appropriateness, and responsibility could be broken down into specific behavioral expectations such as: "My goal is not to hit anyone or anything when angry. I will take a time-out or a break. I will not hurt myself, others, or property when angry."

The length of short-term groups varies from 8 to 25 sessions. Groups with more than 26 sessions are considered long-term groups (MacKenzie, 1997). Short-term groups are popular for several reasons. They are cost effective (Shapiro, 1978), clients can get in and out of therapy quickly, group members learn from each other (Shapiro, Peltz, & Bernadett-Shapiro, 1998), and clients with similar goals can help each other grow and change. Short-term groups need to "be carefully geared to specific limited goals, conducted by trained professional leaders, and structured to maximize factors such as cohesion, altruism, and other unique treatment advantages by employing a process focus" (Shapiro et al., 1998, p. 5).

When conducting groups, the counselors need referral sources from which to receive potential group members and methods for retaining group members in the groups. Referral sources include other counselors, agencies, other professionals, physicians, and previous clients. In managed care settings, clients may be referred by insurance panel case managers, nurse coordinators, employee assistance professionals, or care review managers. To keep groups full, the counselor needs reliable and varied referral sources (Yalom, 1995). Developing positive relationships with a variety of referral resources, marketing one's group well, and being on many managed care panels will help to ensure regular client flow for group therapy. Having successful groups where clients have positive experiences also helps, as these clients will tell other potential future clients of their successful experiences.

In HMOs, referrals to the group counselor or therapist often come from physicians. Connecting well with physicians is important. Family practice and internal medicine physicians tend to make general referrals for counseling, and the mental health professional determines the best course of treatment. Physicians who are specialists may refer for more specific treatments or types of group therapies.

In most settings, billing and payment issues are clarified before treatment begins. Generally with groups, payment is on a per session basis, with the client expected to attend a minimum number of sessions. The leader needs to be equally educated on how the payment and billing practice works in their setting. Groups are cheaper per session than other forms of counseling and therapy. In clinics, hospitals, and HMOs, a separate billing department generally collects fees and sends out monthly billing

statements. Counselors should work closely with their billing departments to be aware of problems any clients may have with payments. In most settings, clients pay week by week. However, in rare circumstances, clients may pay the full amount for an entire number of sessions in one payment.

CONCLUSION

The current and future predictions for group counseling and group therapy are bright. We will continue to need creative, cost-effective, short-term models of groups (Spitz, 1996). The issues that will confront groups in the next decade are having enough trained leaders, emphasizing diversity, and doing research to prove outcome effectiveness (Shapiro et al., 1998). Managed care looks like it is here to stay. The need for trained leaders with short-term group work skills will continue to be high (Spitz, 1996; Winegar, Bistline, & Sheridan, 1992).

Cognitive-behavioral, solution-focused, and other brief approaches will continue to dominate the field of group work. Newer modalities that involve the arts, music, poetry, writing, and movement will continue to be developed and implemented. Long-term models of group work will be less popular due to costs and market demands by consumers of the services. Specific groups for unique problems will be developed. For example, after the recent September 11, 2001, terror strikes against the United States, groups focused on trauma, crisis, and related services.

REFERENCES

Adolph, M. R. (1996). No longer an outsider: A social group worker as a client in a bereavement group for older women. *Social Work With Groups, 19,* 17-34.

American Psychiatric Association. (1994). *Diagnostic and statistical manual of mental disorders* (4th ed.). Washington, DC: Author.

Azima, C. F. J., & Richmond, L. H. (Eds.). (1989). *Adolescent group psychotherapy.* Madison, CT: International Universities Press.

Beltman, B. D., Chiles, J., & Carlin, A. (1984). The pharmacotherapy-psychotherapy triangle:

Psychiatrist, medical psychotherapist, and patient. *Journal of Clinical Psychiatry, 45,* 458-459.

Bergin, J. J. (1999). Small group counseling. In A. Vernon (Ed.), *Counseling children and adolescents* (2nd ed.) (pp. 300-332). Denver, CO: Love Publishing.

Bowman, R. P. (1987). Small group guidance and counseling in schools: A national survey of school counselors. *School Counselor, 34,* 236-262.

Brooks, B. W. (1993). Medication groups. In A. Alonso & H. Swiller (Eds.), *Group therapy for clinical practice* (pp. 155-169). Washington, DC: American Psychiatric Press.

Buchholz, E. S., & Mishne, J. M. (Eds.). (1994). *Group interventions with children, adolescents and parents.* Northvak, NJ: Jaron Aronson.

Capuzzi, D., & Gross, D. R. (1998). *Introduction to group counseling* (2nd ed.). Denver, CO: Love Publishing.

Clarke, G. N., Rohde, P., Lewinsohn, P. M., Hops, H., & Seeley, J. R. (1999). Cognitive-behavioral treatment of adolescent depression: Efficacy of acute group treatment and booster sessions. *Journal of the American Academy of Child & Adolescent Psychiatry, 38,* 272-279.

Clifford, M. (1991). A model for group therapy with latency age boys. *Group, 15,* 116-124.

Coe, D. M. (2001). Solution-oriented group counseling in community mental health: An outcome study. *Dissertation Abstracts International, 61,10A,* 3905.

Cohen, M., & Amdur, M. A. (1981). Medication group for psychiatric patients. *American Journal of Nursing, 81,* 343-345.

Cohen, M. B. (1989). Social work practice with homeless mentally ill people: Engaging the client. *Social Work, 34,* 505-509.

Conyne, R. K. (1996). The Association for Specialists in Group Work training standards: Some considerations and suggestions for training. *Journal for Specialists in Group Work, 21,* 155-162.

Cordell, A. S., & Bergman-Meador, B. (1991). The use of drawings in group interventions for children of divorce. *Journal of Divorce & Remarriage, 17,* 139-155.

Corey, M. S., & Corey, G. C. (2002*). Groups: Process and practice* (6th ed.). Pacific Grove, CA: Brooks/Cole.

Dansby, V. S. (1996). Group work within the school system: Survey of implementation and leadership

role issues. *Journal for Specialists in Group Work, 21,* 232-242.

Diamond, R. J., & Little, M. L. (1984). Utilization of patient expertise in medication groups. *Psychiatry Quarterly, 56,* 13-19.

Dryfus, J. G. (1990). *Adolescents at risk: Prevalence and prevention.* New York: Oxford University Press.

Dryfus, J. G. (1993). Schools as places for health, mental health, and special services. In R. Torkanishi (Ed.), *Adolescence in the 1990s.* New York: Teachers College Press.

Dykeman, C., & Appelton, V. E. (2002). Group counseling: The efficacy of group work. In D. Capuzzi & D. R. Gross (Eds.), *Introduction to group counseling* (3rd ed.) (pp. 114-119). Denver, CO: Love Publishing.

Family Service of Greater New Orleans (2001). *Parents group: Education and counseling* [Brochure]. New Orleans, LA: Author.

Fatout, M. F. (1992). *Models for change in social group work.* Hawthorne, NY: Aldine De Gruyter.

Fatout, M. F. (1996). *Children in groups. A social work perspective.* Westport, CT: Auburn House.

Frank, M. G. (1983). Modified activity group therapy with ego impoverished children. In E. S. Buckholz & J. M. Mishne (Eds.), *Ego and self psychology: Group interventions with children, adolescents, and parents* (pp. 145-155). New York: Jason Aronson.

Gardner, R. A. (1973). *The talking, feeling and doing game.* Cresskill, NJ: Creative Therapeutics.

Gazda, G. M., Ginter, E. J., & Horne, A. M. (2001). *Group counseling and group psychotherapy: Theory and application.* Boston: Allyn & Bacon.

Gladding, S. T. (1999). *Group work: A counseling specialty* (3rd ed.). Upper Saddle River, NJ: Prentice Hall.

Gladding, S. T. (2003). *Group work: A counseling specialty* (4th ed). Upper Saddle River, NJ: Merrill Prentice Hall.

Glazer, H. R. (1998). Expressions of children's grief: A qualitative study. *International Journal of Play Therapy, 7,* 51-65.

Glazer, H. R., & Myra, D. (1999). A family centered intervention in grieving preschool children. *Journal of Child & Adolescent Group Therapy, 9,* 161-168.

Gouet, M. M. (1994). *Counseling the adolescent substance abuser: School-based intervention programs and prevention.* Thousand Oaks, CA: Sage.

Halverson, S. (2002). Group counseling: Children and adolescents. In D. Capazzi & D. R. Goss (Eds.), *Introduction to group counseling* (3rd ed.) (pp. 377-405). Denver, CO: Love Publishing.

Harter, S. (1990). Self and identity development. In S. S. Feldman & G. R. Elliott (Eds.), *At the threshold: The developing adolescent* (pp. 352-387). Cambridge, MA: Harvard University.

Heiman, M. L., & Ettin, M. F. (2001). Harnessing the power of the group for latency-aged sexual abuse victims. *International Journal of Group Psychotherapy, 51,* 265-282.

Hellerstein, D. J., & Meehan, B. (1987). Outpatient group therapy for schizophrenic substance abusers. *American Journal of Psychiatry, 144,* 1337-1339.

Hoyt, M. F. (1995). *Brief therapy and managed care: Readings for contemporary practice.* San Francisco: Jossey-Bass.

Jensen, J. M. (1997). Risk and protective factors for alcohol and other drug use in childhood and adolescence. In M. Frasier (Ed.), *Risk and resilience in childhood* (pp. 117-139). Washington, DC: National Association of Social Workers/NASW Press.

Keitel, M. A., Kopala, M., & Robin, L. (1998). Loss and grief groups. In K. C. Stoiber & T. R. Kratochwill (Eds.), *Handbook of group intervention for children and families* (pp. 159-171). Needham Heights, MA: Allyn & Bacon.

Keshet, J. (1995, Spring). *Fun and games in stepfamily therapy. Stepfamilies.* Retrieved from http://www.saafamilies.org/education/articles/prof/Keshet.htm.

Kraft, I. A. (1989). A selective overview. In F. J. Cramer Azima & L. H. Richmond (Eds.), *Adolescent group psychotherapy* (pp. 55-68). Madison, CT: International Universities Press.

Kymissis, P. (1993). Group psychotherapy with adolescents. In H. T. Kaplan & B. J. Sadock (Eds.), *Comprehensive group psychotherapy* (3rd ed.) (pp. 522-524). Baltimore, MD: Williams & Wilkins.

Larkin, A. R. (1982). What's a medication group? *Journal of Psychosocial Nursing and Mental Health Services 20,* 35-37.

Levine, J., & Noell, D. (1995). Embracing fears and sharing tears: Working with grieving children. In S. C. Smith & M. Pennells (Eds.), *Interventions with bereaved children* (pp. 285-295). London: J. Kingsley.

Lieberman, R. P. (1988). Social skills training. In R. P. Lieberman (Ed.), *Psychiatric rehabilitation of chronic mental patients* (pp. 147-198). Washington, DC: American Psychiatric Press.

Mackenzie, K. R. (1997). *Time-managed group therapy: Effective clinical applications.* Washington, DC: American Psychiatric Press.

Mackenzie, K. R., & Grabovac, A. D. (2001). Interpersonal psychotherapy group (IPT-G) for depression. *Journal of Psychotherapy Practice and Research, 10,* 46-51.

McCallum, M., & Piper, W. E. (1990). A controlled study of effectiveness and patient suitability for short-term group psychotherapy. *International Journal of Group Psychotherapy, 40,* 431-452.

Metcalf, L. (1998). *Solution focused group therapy: Ideas for groups in private practice, schools, agencies, and treatment programs.* New York: Free Press.

Moffic, H. S. (1982). A preliminary report on effects of initiating medication: Groups at a mental health clinic. *Hospital Community Psychiatry, 33,* 387.

Niemann, S. H. (2002). Guidance/psychoeducational groups. In D. Capuzzi & D. R. Gross (Eds.), *Introduction to group counseling* (3rd ed.) (pp. 265-290). Denver, CO: Love Publishing.

O'Rourke, K. (1990). Recapturing hope: Elementary school support groups for children of alcoholics. *Elementary School Guidance and Counseling, 25,* 107-115.

Piper, W. E. (1991). Brief group psychotherapy. *Psychiatric Annals, 21,* 417-422.

Piper, W. E., McCallum, M., & Azim, H. F. A. (1992). *Adaptation to loss through short-term group psychotherapy.* New York: Guilford.

Posthuma, B. W. (2002). *Small groups in counseling and therapy: Process and leadership.* Boston: Allyn & Bacon.

Price, G. E., Dinas, P., Dunn, C., & Winterowd, C. (1995). Group work with clients experiencing grieving: Moving from theory to practice. *Journal for Specialists in Group Work, 20,* 159-167.

Reid, K. E. (1997). *Social work practice with groups: A clinical perspective* (2nd ed.). Pacific Grove, CA: Brooks/Cole.

Rice, A. (2001). Evaluating brief structured group treatment of depression. *Research on Social Work Practice, 11,* 53-76.

Rose, S. R. (1998). *Group work with children and adolescents: Prevention in school and community systems.* Thousand Oaks, CA: Sage.

Rose, S. R., & Edelson, J. L. (1987). *Working with children and adolescents in groups.* San Francisco: Jossey-Bass.

Samide, L. L. (2002). Letting go of grief: Bereavement groups for children in the social setting. *Journal for Specialists in Group Work, 27,* 192-204.

Selekman, M. D. (1997). *Solution focused therapy with children.* New York: Guilford.

Shapiro, J. L. (1978). *Methods of group psychotherapy and encounter: A tradition of innovation.* Itasca, IL: F. E. Peacock.

Shapiro, J. L., Peltz, L. S., & Bernadett-Shapiro, S. (1998). *Brief group treatment: Practical training for therapists and counselors.* Pacific Grove, CA: Brooks/Cole.

Shechtman, Z., & Bar-El, O. (1994). Group guidance and group counseling to foster social acceptability and self-esteem in adolescence. *Journal for Specialists in Group Work, 19,* 188-196.

Shelby, J. (1994). Psychological intervention with children in disaster relief shelters. *Child, Youth, & Family Services Quarterly, 17,* 14-18.

Shields, S. A. (1986). Busted and branded: Group work with substance abusing adolescents in schools. *Social Work With Groups, 8,* 61-81.

Smith, T. H. (1985). Group work with adolescent drug abusers. *Social Work With Groups, 8,* 55-64.

Snyder, K. V., Kymissis, P., & Kessler, K. (1999). Anger management for adolescents: Efficacy of brief group therapy. *Child and Adolescent Psychiatry 38,* 1409-1416.

Spitz, H. I. (1996). *Group psychotherapy and managed mental health care: A clinical guide for providers.* New York: Brunner-Mazel.

Stone, W. N. (1993). Group psychotherapy with the chronically mental ill. In H. L. Kaplan & B. J. Sadock (Eds.), *Comprehensive group psychotherapy* (3rd ed.) (pp. 418-429). Baltimore, MD: Williams & Wilkins.

Stone, W. N. (1995). Group therapy for the seriously mentally ill patients in a managed care system. In K. R. McKenzie (Ed.), *Effective use of group therapy for managed care* (pp. 67-74). Washington, DC: American Psychiatric Press.

Toseland, R. W., & Rivas R. F. (2001). *An introduction to group work practice* (4th ed.). New York: Allyn & Bacon.

Vernon, A. (2002). Group counseling: Loss. In D. Capuzzi & G. R. Gross (Eds.), *Introduction to group counseling* (3rd ed.) (pp. 321-349). Denver, CO: Love Publishing.

Videka-Sherman, L. (1986). *A meta-analytic study of services to the chronically mentally ill.* Albany: School of Social Welfare, State University of New York.

Wakeman, J. (2001). *Stress management workshops for everyday living* [Description of Program]. New Orleans, LA: Ochsner Clinic Foundation.

Wakeman, J. R., & Metayer, R. F., III. (1985). Stress-related disorders: Recent developments in hospital treatment. *Postgraduate Medicine, 77,* 189-196.

Wifley, D. E., Mackenzie, K. R., Welch, R. R., Ayres, V. E., & Weissman, M. M. (2000). *Interpersonal psychotherapy for groups.* New York: Basic Books.

Williams, C. N. (1990). Prevention and treatment approaches for children of alcoholics. In M. Windles & J. S. Searles (Eds.), *Children of alcoholics: Critical perspectives* (pp. 187-216). New York: Guilford.

Winegar, N., Bistline, J. R., & Sheridan, S. (1992). Implementing a group therapy program in a managed-care setting: Combining cost effectiveness and quality care. *Families in Society: Journal of Contemporary Human Services, 173,* 56-58

Wodarski, S. J. (1990). Adolescent substance abuse: practice implications. *Adolescence, 25,* 667-668.

Wright, W. (1999). The use of purpose in on-going activity groups: A framework for maximizing the therapeutic impact. *Social Work With Groups, 22,* 31-54.

Wylie, M. S. (2000). Teaching kids to care. *Family Therapy Networker, 24,* 26-35.

Yalom, I. D. (1995). *The theory and practice of group psychotherapy* (4th ed.). New York: Basic Books.

Zastrow, C. (2001). *Social work with groups* (5th ed.). Pacific Grove, CA: Brooks/Cole.

Part V

GROUPS ACROSS THE LIFE SPAN

Introduction

DEBORAH A. GERRITY

How people interact in groups and why they join a group changes across the life span. For children and adolescents, there are specific cognitive and developmental issues that affect group content and process. For many adults, the cognitive and developmental issues are much less of a concern, but socialization and interpersonal difficulties, specifically around gender, play an important part. Because other sections in this handbook discuss mixed gender groups, this one includes two separate chapters for the adult stage of the life span, one for female groups and the other for male groups. Finally, for the elderly, cognitive functioning may again become a focus, as well as existential issues centered on life review and generativity and a variety of health concerns. The goal of this part is to provide the reader with a sample of groups for each age. Theoretical, empirical, and practical information is provided for psychoeducational, counseling, and therapy groups.

Zipora Shechtman discusses groups for children and adolescents across therapeutic settings. She reviews the current clinical and research literature, as well as providing rich practical examples from the author's experience. Shechtman describes specific skills and techniques used by group leaders. Group formation, process, therapeutic factors, theoretical frameworks, specific types of groups, and implications for future research are covered.

Nathalie Kees and Nancy Leech focus on the philosophical background of group interventions, including cultural/contextual and feminist perspectives. The authors provide an overview of practice trends and discuss groups with a strong emphasis on meeting the needs of women from diverse perspectives. Examples include a focus group for American Indian women around breast cancer issues, group interventions with indigent African American mothers and their babies, a psychoeducational group for prostituted women, and personal empowerment and systemic change groups.

Chapter 33 by Michael P. Andronico and Arthur M. Horne describes men's groups as ways of understanding the societal and systemic pressures facing men and contravening the myths about male interactions in groups. They explore the range of problems that concern men, the processes that facilitate male participation in groups, the myths and misconceptions about men's groups, the roles of group leaders, and different groups designed just for men.

In Chapter 34, Donna A. Henderson and Samuel T. Gladding explain the special needs of older adults and how these affect counseling and therapeutic interventions. They discuss the types of groups, how they are implemented, the role of the group leader, and strengths and limitations. The authors briefly describe advocacy, remediation, and prevention groups for this population.

The utility and adaptability of group interventions across the life span is inspiring. These chapters describe an array of ways that groups are used, but also give the reader a lens through which to view the myriad applications that group interventions can address. Across the life span, group interventions are efficacious and the process is adaptable to suit the very different needs of children, adolescents, women, men, and the elderly.

31

GROUP COUNSELING AND PSYCHOTHERAPY WITH CHILDREN AND ADOLESCENTS

Current Practice and Research

ZIPORA SHECHTMAN

University of Haifa

The literature suggests that over 20% of all children under the age of 18 experience developmental, emotional, or behavioral problems (Kazdin & Johnson, 1994). In regard to adolescents, the numbers increase: 30% of 14- to 17-year-olds engage in multiple-problem high-risk behaviors (Dryfoos, 1997). Children and adolescents feel angry, sad, anxious, and depressed; they are lonely and rejected. Some are submissive, and others are aggressive and violent. They are troubled by poor interpersonal relationships at home and with peers. These problems are reflected in learning difficulties, as well as in their behavior (MacLennan, 2000).

Such an increasing need clearly calls for greater prominence of counseling for children and adolescents (Owense & Kulic, 2001). Moreover, these children need corrective interpersonal experiences not only with adults but also with peers—good experiences that can make life a bit easier for them. Such experiences are best provided in effective group work (Dies, 2000; MacLennan, 2000; Rose, 1998; Smead, 1995). Indeed, the high level of need has contributed to an increase of group work in the schools, and over 70% of children's groups are performed in that setting (Hoag & Burlingame, 1997; Kulic, Dagley, & Horne, 2001) (see Chapter 22 in this volume for more information on groups in school settings). Other groups are conducted in community centers, corrective institutions, hospitals, or private agencies (O'Rourk & Wortbyt, 1996; Rose, 1998; Schaefer, 1999).

Although groups with children and adolescents are long practiced, little is known scientifically about the outcomes and particularly the processes in such groups (Barlow, Burlingame, & Fuhriman, 2000). Considering developmental psychology, groups for children and adolescents are different from those of adult groups. Thus, the purpose of this chapter is to review the current clinical and research literature on groups for children and adolescents, as well as the author's experience with child and adolescent groups.

Several questions require consideration: How unique are child and adolescent groups? Who is the leader of such groups, and what are some qualifications he or she needs? What is the theory of working with children and adolescents in groups? What type of group is effective?

THE UNIQUENESS OF CHILD AND ADOLESCENT GROUPS

Developmental psychology suggests that children develop in cognitive, social, and emotional stages (Piaget, 1986). They have special needs at each stage, specific tasks to accomplish, and certain abilities suitable to their age. An understanding of normal child development is therefore essential for effective group treatment (Kymissis, 1996).

Preschool children show short attention span, a low level of abstract thinking, difficulties in verbal expression, limited perspective-taking skills, and difficulties in controlling their own behavior. For them, play would be the major instrument used in therapeutic groups. Slavson (1945) was probably the first to develop groups for young children. This activity-group therapy is based on psychoanalytic tenets, nondirective and devoid of verbal interventions. Play-therapy, puppets and dolls, storytelling, bibliotherapy, and pictures and drawings are all techniques to permit reexperiencing of earlier conflicts in a safe environment (Huth-Bocks, Schettini, & Shebroe, 2001).

Elementary-age children (Latency: 7-11) are industrious, eager to learn, and demonstrate abstract thinking and competent verbal skills. They are able to be empathic and self-aware. The peer group provides support in the beginning emancipation from the family and serves as a prime source of self-esteem. Games, sports, crafts, and writing become the building blocks for a sense of self-confidence and can be implemented in the group therapy process, along with other techniques (e.g., creative drama, storytelling) (Lomonaco, Sceidlinger, & Aronson, 2000).

Adolescents (age 12-18) struggle with separation from parents and the development of self-identity. Self-awareness and empathy are now developed, and permit close relationships and friendships. Peers become an extremely important source of support; therefore, groups become the treatment of choice for them (Dies, 2000). Commonality of problems leads to a sense of universality and permits the discussion and problem solving of many disturbing issues. Although adolescents appear to be best equipped for group work, they may also be the greatest challenge for group therapists. In their struggle for independence, they are often resistant to authority. Their struggle for a clear identity leads to inflexibility and intolerance. Although talk therapy is used at this stage, the therapist must structure the sessions and regulate the anxiety while allowing for freedom of expression (Kymissis, 1996; Nichols-Goldstein, 2001).

Developmental considerations suggest that therapy groups for children and adolescents require leaders with specific skills, yet most of such groups are led by group leaders who are not specifically trained for group work with children (Pollock & Kymissis, 2001) and are often inexperienced in group treatment with children (Dagley, Gazda, Eppinger, & Stewart, 1994).

GROUP LEADER'S TECHNIQUES AND SKILLS

It is important, first and foremost, that the group leader understand the developmental needs of children at their different stages of development. Adolescents may be more concerned with friendship issues than younger children, while young children may be more concerned with adjustment and behavior problems (Shechtman, 1997). These different needs dictate the group process, the topics for discussion, and the methods and tools used.

In a study of verbal responses in groups (Leichtentritt & Shechtman, 1998), most of the frequent self-disclosure by the children was initiated by structured activities and by the leader's questions. Thus, more structure and a greater variety of therapeutic games and activities for younger children are important. At the initial stage of the group process, activities aimed to break the ice, get to know each other,

The leader reads the book *The Soul Bird* (Snunit, 1999), where the soul encompasses a range of emotions, each locked in a special drawer, and group members are encouraged to open their drawers and become attuned to their emotions.

Leader: "Listen carefully to your bird. Sometimes the bird calls us and we don't listen. Too bad, because it wants to tell us about ourselves."

The 10-year-old girls are seated on the floor listening to music while the poem is read to them.

Dina: "For me, the secret drawer is the biggest. I have all types of secrets—blue, green—but the black secrets that belong to my family are the most difficult to open. I'm afraid that once I open this drawer, I will never be happy again."

Alice: "I know how you feel. I also have all kinds of secrets, but the worst is the drawer of anger. I believe that some of it was released in this group, thanks to you, Dina. You remember telling about your father's violence? [It was then] I realized that we have much in common and perhaps others have too. So you don't have to feel embarrassed, and perhaps we can help."

Dina: "I like to help others. Perhaps, when I grow up, I will be a counselor too."

The leader goes on reading:	"And when someone hugs us, our bird grows and grows until she covers all of us, so good she feels. So good is the hug."
Dina:	"My bird is very sad. Sometimes my bird is so lonely, and there is no one to hug her. He does not live with us anymore."
Leader:	"Is it your father?"

Dina stares at the floor.

Dina:	"He is never around when I need him. I invited him for my birthday, but he didn't show up. Mom said it is not that important and that I should enjoy the people that came, but I couldn't."
Leader:	"How do you feel about opening up your drawer a bit?"

Dina says she feels good, and goes on.

Dina:	*"I remember telling you I have a loving family. It was all a lie. I did not trust you."*
Another member:	"I don't think it's a lie. It's OK to keep private any personal information you want."

Dina looks relaxed. She gets up, pulls her head up, hands up as wings, to show how much it has freed her.

Another member:	"It did not change your life, so how come you feel so good?"
Dina:	"I am not so angry anymore."

The next session she reports calling her father, who apologized for not coming, but was happy to hear her voice.

Dina sums up:	"I was glad to talk to him, even though I know he will not change."

establish norms of support and inquiry, and promote self-expressiveness are helpful (see examples in Hanna, Hanna, & Keys, 1999; O'Rourke & Wortbyt, 1996; Shechtman, 1999; Smeat, 1995).

One method that has proven successful with young children is bibliotherapy, defined as the use of literature for therapeutic purposes (Gladding, 1995). It is a useful way to promote emotional responsiveness because of its indirect approach. Children identify with the characters introduced to them, and through the process of identification, they come a bit closer to understanding themselves. There are many ways to use the literature in the service of therapy. Sometimes literature provides metaphors that facilitate the talk process, as illustrated in the boxed group session on page 431, at the working stage, with a group of 10-year-old girls.

Much of Dina's self-disclosure was made possible by the metaphors presented in the story. However, another way to use bibliotherapy is to structure a program in which each story/poem serves as a unique goal in the process of change. Such is the treatment in an aggression program (Shechtman, 1999). It starts with iterature discussing anger and conflict and ends with self-control literature.

Other techniques from the expressive arts (e.g., art therapy) also help to keep the process going for children and adolescents.

In one session around holiday time (similar to Halloween), an adolescent group of 14-year-old girls prepared masks. One girl prepared a mask of a clown, saying, "This is how I present myself to the world, but let me show you who I really am." She took off her mask crying, explaining how difficult it is for her to constantly pretend that she is happy, and eventually shared with the group her poor relationships with her family. The mask was the trigger that helped her to express her disturbing secret.

A recent book (DeLucia-Waack, 2001) provides guidelines for the use of music and creative arts activities in groups for children. Specifically, songs are utilized to introduce a topic, suggest coping strategies, and channel energy. Music is used to encourage children to express their feelings, problem-solve, and brainstorm coping strategies. Music serves as a concrete reminder and reinforcer of what they have learned in group.

Therapeutic games are useful facilitative techniques as starters of sessions as well as throughout the group process. For example, rather than asking participants to verbalize a problem, they play the Fisher game and "fish" for their problems. They get into a mood of playing and hardly realize that they are in therapy. At termination, instead of verbalizing their gains following group treatment, children play the Traffic Signs game. Each participant selects two signs: one that represents his or her feelings at the beginning of the group process and the other at termination.

Tanya says, "At first, I used the No Entrance Sign, as I really did not trust you. . . . I told you that I have no problems and that I don't know what I am doing here. Now I use the Yield Sign, as I have learned that I appear bossy and that I need to give space to others."

Beyond understanding developmental needs and mastering methods, the leader of child and adolescent psychotherapy groups needs to possess strong skills of handling the group effectively, yet helping the individual child within the group. Children and adolescents often express their resistance to therapy in an immature, even aggressive manner, which requires special understanding and skills (Dies, 2000). Consider the next boxed example on page 433.

Research supports the premise of leader self-disclosure in children's groups. A study investigating client and leader verbal responses in the group process with children (Leichtentritt & Shechtman, 1998) found high rates of leader self-disclosure. This relatively high level of disclosure was attributed to the leader's attempt to model the behavior to the children and to legitimize it. Many of the reservations concerning the leader's self-disclosure in group (Yalom, 1995) hold true for children's groups as well, perhaps even more so. Disclosure of the leader's own problems may make him or her seem weak and unable to help, and children in particular need to be able to count on their leader for support. The question of what to disclose is not an easy one, and more research is needed to answer it.

The initial stage of a group of 13-year-old girls is very stormy, and the leader identifies Rita, an angry and aggressive child, as the most destructive group member. Meeting with Rita individually, the counselor quickly recognizes that she needs the girl's cooperation in order for the group to work, and so she decides to make Rita her assistant.

Once Rita sees that she is getting special attention, she becomes active and cooperative and the group moves to the working stage. However, one day, Rita is absent, and Albina, a group member who is rejected by others, takes the opportunity to blame Rita for some nasty behavior.

The next session, the seventh for this group, Rita is furious. How could someone talk behind her back? She cannot trust the group anymore; she is considering leaving.

The leader takes a few important steps to resolve the problem, one of which is her own self-disclosure. She shares with the group a past experience of group rejection that is still painful to her. They are surprised to hear that rejection has such a lasting effect, and, following the leader's self-disclosure, Rita describes in length how difficult it is for her to be rejected and says that now, although she is in a different place, she is still afraid of it. She eventually understands that rejecting Albina provides her with a sense of power that diminishes her own fear of rejection. Understanding this, she is more open to change her behavior.

GROUP FORMATION

The leader must also take into account some practical considerations in regard to group formation and structure, specifically, issues of composition and length of treatment. The most relevant variables in group composition are age, sex, problem, and size of group. Most practitioners recommend same-age and same-sex groups (Lomonaco et al., 2000; MacLennan & Dies, 1992). Considering developmental psychology, same-age groups seem logical. Children face similar developmental tasks, have common interests, and show similar emotional and cognitive abilities. Same-sex groups are often recommended to eliminate tension between the genders. Although it is easier to work with an all-girl group, it is also more difficult to work with an all-boy group. It may be preferred to work with heterogeneous groups, as girls can be good models for group interaction (Leichtentritt & Shechtman, 1998).

Type of problem or severity of problem is another issue of group composition. Many practitioners prefer focal groups, assuming that the commonality of the problem would facilitate the group process: children of divorce, anger management, aggression/ violence are a few examples. However, there is the danger of labeling that may strongly interfere with the process. Children of divorce may not want to be labeled as such, and may find a common ground in other groups as well. Moreover, in the case of aggressive/violent children, constructing an all-aggressive group can even be harmful (Dishion, McCord, & Poulin, 1999). Hence, it is suggested that children with varying strengths and assets should be combined when possible (Shechtman, 1994, 2001a).

Length of group refers to both length of session and treatment. Length of session depends on age, type of group, and context. Usually, groups for elementary-age children are based on 45-minute weekly sessions. For younger children, 30-minute twice a week sessions seems more appropriate. For adolescents, sessions usually last up to 90 minutes (MacLennan & Dies, 1992). Length of treatment depends on the group goals and the leader's theoretical orientation. Most of the groups with children and adolescents are short term, averaging 10 sessions (Hoge & Burlingame, 1997; Owense & Kulic, 2001); many are even shorter (Schaefer, 1999). However, longer groups are recommended in the literature. In one group that lasted 2 years, research showed that some children started working effectively only in the second year (Shechtman, Vurembrand, & Malajek, 1993).

Finally, the size of a group is determined by its purpose, age of participants, and severity of problem. Adolescent educational or counseling groups range from 10 to 15 members. Younger children work well in groups of 6 to 8 children (Gladding, 1995). Children with more severe problems (e.g., aggressive/violent) may require even smaller groups (Shechtman, 2001a).

Process Research

Research on the process of child and adolescent group psychotherapy is extremely limited (Barlow et al., 2000). We tend to transfer our knowledge from adult groups to children, disregarding the obvious fact that children's and adolescents' developmental needs and behavior patterns are so different from those of adults (DeLucia-Waack, 2000). What do we know about child and adolescent group psychotherapy?

Therapeutic Factors

The following illustrates an adolescent group session in which many of the therapeutic factors are present. The group was comprised of six 14-year-old boys and girls.

Many of the therapeutic factors known from adult groups appeared in this group of adolescents. There was catharsis, interpersonal learning, group cohesion, altruism, universality, and

---

The group is in its eighth session. Yan is absent, following an earlier stressful session for him. The leader, anxious about him, asks if anyone knows anything about him.

| After a long silence,
Tanya says: | "We are not close in school. It is only here that we got to know each other other. All I knew about him is that he is absent from school most of the time, and actually I was surprised that he attended all our sessions." |

This makes Tanya the focus of the group anger.

| *Maggie:* | "You don't know anyone except your best friends, which you change every day. You act like a queen, indifferent to the rest; no one is really important to you." |

| *Tanya:* | "Who are you to speak to me like this!" |

Maggie begins to cry.

| *Tanya:* | "You're crying already, using your parent's divorce to look miserable, to be excused of school tasks, to be weak. You're not the only one whose parents got divorced, you know, and you're not the only one who's upset." |

Shai, a very shy person who has hardly talked in the group, reaches out to help Maggie.

| *Shai shouts at Tanya:* | "Stop it! You don't care about anything but your appearance, and gossip, yes, and you are not frightening me at all with this look. It is time that someone told you what people think about you." |

| Turning to *Maggie,*
Shai continues: | "Why don't you fight back? You've cried so many times because of her. She calls you names, and gives you a hard time." |

After a long silence,

Maggie
responds: "I don't want to fight with anyone."

Shai: "What are you afraid of?"

Maggie: "I'm not afraid; I think Tanya has changed in the group. She is trying to be nice to me."

Tanya: "It's not worth it to be nice. Once you don't act properly, everyone jumps on you. You know that I kept our group secrets, even though it's not like me."

Shai does
not let up: "What can you tell about us—that her parents are disabled and mine are divorced? You have no right to talk about us because you have not revealed anything about yourself."

Leader (after
a very long
silence):   "There is a lot of anger in the group. Here you express your real emotions, while outside the group you act like strangers."

Tanya takes the challenge offered to her by the group and, encouraged by Maggie's positive feedback, shares the following.

Tanya: "You really think I have you in my mind all day? I feel tired, I have no energy to fight [looks very pale]. Yesterday I ate only one apple all day. All my friends look better than me. My mother nags me about eating, my boyfriend says he loves me, but I don't trust him. I can't believe he doesn't mind my appearance. I've learned that some drugs help you to lose weight, so I tried them. I had a difficult week and I am very nervous."

The next session, the children play a game in which they select a card that holds the name of an emotion and share the feeling with the group, explaining why they chose the card.

Shai selects
Surprise and
Embarrassment: "I have learned that you never really know people. I did not know the truth about Tanya and I regret having attacked her."

Maggie: "I feel so much closer to Tanya now. I'm really not afraid of her anymore."

Tanya: "I selected Anxiety because my boyfriend is about to join the army, which means that I may lose him."

hope. Yet, what does research tell us about the importance of therapeutic factors as perceived by children and adolescents? Shechtman, Bar El, and Hadar (1997) report on one study investigating therapeutic factors in adolescent groups. Results indicated that catharsis and interpersonal learning were the two most frequent factors mentioned by group members, which is congruent with the adult professional literature (Yalom, 1995). But the third factor was learning socializing techniques. Socializing techniques could be attributed to the developmental needs of adolescents, but could also reflect the individual leader's type of work in those groups. More research is clearly needed to establish the importance of factors in adolescent group therapy—and in group therapy for younger children as well. Also research needs to investigate gender differences in respect to the therapeutic factors.

Verbal Responses

Another process study investigated the verbal responses in elementary school-age counseling groups (Leichtentritt & Shechtman, 1998). The study was comprised of 10 small groups conducted in one school. Results suggested that self-disclosure is the most frequent verbal response that group members use, several times more frequent than other responses, and that self-disclosure starts very early in the stage of group development. These findings suggest that young children have a strong need and high ability to disclose and show limited reservations regarding self-disclosure.

Another study (Shechtman & Ben-David, 1999) of elementary-age children characterized as aggressive found the most frequent response in the group to be experiencing—defined as high expression of emotions while sharing personal information from in-group or out-of-group experiences. Experiencing was found to be even higher in group sessions than in individual treatment. Emotional experiencing and catharsis seem to be the basis for change in younger children, who mostly need a sense of relief. Moreover, relatively little use of interpretives, such as feedback, confrontation, and interpretation, were found in these groups (Leichtentritt & Shechtman, 1998).

A further study was specifically designed to measure the frequency and quality of interpretives used in children's groups. Interpretive interaction is very common in adult groups (Morran, Robison, & Stockton, 1985), and also considered pathways of change in groups for adolescents (Cramer Azima, 1989). The study included five groups of fifth- and sixth-grade students. The study investigated the effectiveness (the degree to which they were supportive, positive responses) and productiveness (the extent to which they led to positive behavior in the therapy process) of the interpretives. Results indicated that children tended to use more ineffective interpretives than effective ones. For example, the confrontation "You are always so childish" led to withdrawal, whereas the confrontation "You only say you don't want to see your mom, because you are so angry" led to further sharing and insight. Confrontation was the most frequent interpretive used by children, and it usually generated nonproductive responses. Only feedback, when provided in an effective way, produced productive responses. Interpretations were extremely rare (Shechtman & Yanuv, 2001). Thus, a process

based on feedback and confrontation, as the one illustrated in the adolescent group above, is less common among younger children, where the group process is characterized by self-expressiveness and support. The younger children do not seem to have the emotional strength necessary to handle confrontation. Rather, they seem to need to be heard and release some of the burdens they so unjustly carry. These process studies led to a proposed theory for group work with children and adolescents.

THE THEORY OF GROUP WORK WITH CHILDREN

The most popular theory for child and adolescent treatment is cognitive-behavioral (Barlow et al., 2000; Hoag & Burlingame, 1997; Kulic et al., 2001). This trend may be related to such factors as the structured nature of cognitive-behavioral interventions, and the fact that they tend to lend themselves to time-limited and short-term interventions. However, what emerges in the process studies as well as in practice is that children demonstrate a high need for self-expressiveness, cathartic experiences, social acceptance and support, and guidance and training in areas of social deficit. While cognitive-behavioral therapy is strong in offering guidance and training, it falls somewhat short in providing the needed opportunity for emotional experiencing.

An interactional approach that dominates adult groups seems to work better with adolescents than with younger children. As I have demonstrated in the case illustrations and research, younger children need to express themselves and to release some of the burdens that they carry. They are less interested or able to learn from others' feedback, particularly if that feedback is negative (Shechtman & Yanuv, 2001). Interpersonal interaction based on interpretives may even be harmful for children who have not yet developed some ego strength. Therefore, what is needed is a theoretical approach that addresses children's needs for emotional expressiveness, social support, and assistance with their everyday difficulties.

Such a theory has been recently suggested for adults with low psychological ability (McCallum, 1999; Piper, Joyce, McCallum, Azim, & Ogrodniczuk, 2002) and with physical illness (Spiegel, 2000). Expressive Supportive Therapy incorporates three fundamental approaches: emotional expression, social support, and cognitive management skills. Supportive psychotherapy is very different from interpretive psychotherapy. Some of the features of supportive therapy are to create a state of gratification in the session, relieve pressure on the patient to talk, provide noninterpretive interventions, focus on conscious processes, engage in structured problem solving, provide guidance and advice, and offer praise (Piper et al., 2002, p. 52). Its primary objective is to improve the patient's immediate adaptation to his or her life situation, build ego strength, and teach problem-solving skills (McCallum, 1999)—all of which are congruent with the definition of child group psychotherapy (Dagley et al., 1994).

It is easy to see the logic of using Expressive Supportive Theory with children. Some children are the product of a nonaccepting and critical climate and need corrective interpersonal experiences in order to change. They need to be heard with care and support and empowered in order to open up, learn to trust themselves and others, and develop some insight. Moreover, they need assistance with immediate emotional and instrumental difficulties (O'Rourke & Wortbyt, 1996).

Type of Group and Its Effectiveness

Child and adolescent group psychotherapy is defined as "any intervention designed to alleviate psychological distress, reduce maladaptive behavior, or enhance adaptive behavior through counseling, structured or unstructured interaction, a training program, or a predetermined treatment plan" (Weisz, Weiss, Alicke, & Klotz, 1987, p. 543) with multiple people under the age of 18. Such a comprehensive definition encompasses all types of group intervention: Guidance/Educational, Counseling/Interpersonal Problem Solving, and Psychotherapy/Personality Reconstruction (Gazda, Ginter, & Horne, 2001; Gladding, 1995).

Based on several literature reviews, a consensus seems to have been reached about the effectiveness of group psychotherapy for children and adolescents (Dagley et al., 1994; Gazda et al., 2001; Hoag & Burlingame, 1997; Kulic et al., 2001). Moreover, in a recent study comparing individual and group treatment for elementary-age aggressive children, no difference in outcomes was found for the two treatment modalities: in both interventions, children's level of aggression decreased following treatment compared to a control sample (Shechtman & Ben-David, 1999). Hence, group therapy is as effective as individual therapy and also cost-effective. With the increase of mental health problems among children and adolescents, group counseling and therapy become the appropriate response (MacLennan, 2000; Rose, 1998).

The issues normally addressed in such groups range from skill building and training in a variety of developmental areas (educational groups), to problem solving of a personal or interpersonal type (counseling groups), to a focus on personal problems and dysfunctional behavior of individuals (psychotherapy groups). The type of group dictates the goals, the population, the process, the leader's role, and the expected outcomes. Although an overlap between the types of groups is expected (Gazda et al., 2002; Gladding, 1995), it is extremely important to keep a clear distinction among the groups.

Guidance/educational groups are mainly used for primary prevention, targeted at the normal student population and essentially aimed at training in social skills. Primary prevention has increasingly become the focus of child and adolescent research over the past 25 years (Kulic et al., 2001). Given the amount of time children and adolescents spend with their peers both in and out of the classroom, the class is a logical choice for the delivery of prevention services. Such interventions have been found to reduce behavioral and social problems in children (Durlak & Wells, 1997). Although educational groups in the school are reviewed in Chapter 22 in this book, several outcomes of recent studies warrant mentioning.

The Life Skills Training (LST) program, conflict resolution skill groups, including the Young Negotiation (YN) program, and the Classroom Climate Program, are a few examples of educational primary prevention groups conducted mostly in the classroom. The LST program develops skills for living, such as self-identity, problem solving, decision making, social skills, and physical health. This particular program had been conducted in a variety of settings and with different populations, and has gained professional support for its effectiveness, particularly when conducted in small groups (Gazda et al., 2001). However, an evaluation study conducted in Israel (Shechtman, 2001b) on a nationwide scale and including close to 10,000 students found that the program did not meet its goals. Interestingly, though, the process variables indicated that the problem was in the implementation phase: although students and teachers alike appreciated the program, implementation was inconsistent and inefficient. The program was not delivered on a regular basis, and it was performed in groups that were overly large by ill-trained teachers. This is an important finding, as guidance programs are usually carried out on a large scale, and it is quite easy to lose control over the process of valid implementation.

Another example is the Classroom Climate program, which has proven effective in enhancing social relationships in the classroom, improving the social status of special needs students in junior high classes, and reducing adjustment problems among elementary school children (Shechtman, 1997). A comparison between the Classroom Climate program and small counseling groups (Shechtman & Bar-El, 1994) suggested that each has its unique contribution. While the educational program was more effective in developing positive behavior in the classroom, the counseling groups were more effective in developing self-esteem. These initial results suggest that different goals are met in different types of groups. More research is definitely needed to establish the specific goals met in each group. Furthermore, much more process research is needed to explain the lack of positive results of good programs.

Primary prevention through educational groups is not limited to the school or classroom arena. In fact, many of the life skills training programs mentioned earlier are conducted with small groups sponsored by community service agencies, vocational centers, corrective institutions, or religious institutions (Gazda et al., 2001). Perhaps the most common educational small groups are those designed to foster prevention of substance abuse and AIDS. These groups are led by mental health professionals. Audiovisual tools are combined with group discussion to provide relevant information and to foster desirable attitudes and habits (Lomonaco et al., 2000).

For example, Rose (1998) describes the kNOw DOPS group, developed in a small community following the death of a youngster because of overdrinking. The group was planned as an educational group, located in a community room in a shopping center. Nine boys and girls attended a short-term group that focused on education about substance use, misuse, abuse, and addiction. The leader promoted the development of self-control and assertiveness skills in avoiding the use of alcohol and other drugs. They role-played, listened to guest speakers, and made educational trips to treatment facilities.

Counseling groups are targeted at children and adolescents who experience some developmental or situational difficulties for which they need special assistance. Obviously, such needs must be addressed in small groups and led by mental health professionals who know how to use the group process in the service of the individual child. Counseling groups often focus on self-esteem, social difficulties, and school achievements (Dagley et al., 1994). While the literature reports positive results in these areas of study, the research needs to be broadened to include variables that are pertinent to the group process. For example, the measure of social difficulties is usually sociometric status or social acceptance. However, a variable that is even more relevant to group work is intimacy in friendship.

Intimacy is the ability to get along in a close relationship, and it is a unique variable distinguished from general interpersonal relationships. Intimacy is primarily related to trust of self and others, and therefore it is not just another skill that can be taught. Children and adolescents must reexperience positive relationships with people they can trust in order to carry over this sense of trust to a dyadic relationship outside the group. This need is effectively addressed in small counseling or psychotherapy groups characterized by intimacy and trust, the same ingredients that make up close friendships.

A series of studies have confirmed the claim that counseling groups increase intimacy in close friendships for both elementary school children (Shechtman, 1994) and adolescents in disadvantaged populations (Shechtman, Freedman, Kashti, & Sharabani, 2002). To achieve such gains, the counseling process should emphasize a nurturing and supportive group environment, close relationships, and self-disclosure. These components seem to establish the basis for trust, eventually transferred to close dyadic relationships outside of group.

Counseling groups for children of divorce have become quite popular and proved effective (Hage & Nosanow, 2000; Sanders & Riester, 1996). For example, Omizo and Omizo (1988) studied a group of adolescents with divorced parents. Adolescents who participated in group counseling showed higher scores in self-esteem and a more internal locus of control than those who did not participate in group.

These children often have no one with whom to share their concerns, fears, anger, loneliness, and sense of rejection. The small group provides a place for catharsis, an opportunity to increase understanding and insight, and a chance to learn new coping skills. Treatment modalities vary from highly structured groups that have a predetermined goal and plan, and focus on central issues of family of divorce (Morganett, 1990, 1994), to low-structured dynamic groups that are client centered and dynamic in nature, as illustrated below.

The group of six 9-year-old children is in its 13th session. Sagi initiates the disclosure of his conflict with his mother. He tells the group that his mother called, offered him a present for his upcoming birthday, but he refused. He sounds angry and hurt, but has difficulty expressing his true feelings. The leader suggests role-playing, and two girls volunteer, acting as him and his mother talking over the phone. It becomes obvious that his mother feels rejected and that he is very angry ("I don't want anything from you"). The group tries to bring up all the emotions that come up; some members are angry, others are sad and feel rejected. They all agree that his mother should have tried harder. Supported by the group, Sagi cries out, "She hasn't called in

months," and later says, "She doesn't love me." At this point the children share their ways of coping with this sense of rejection. They express a wide range of options, from no contact to direct expression of feelings to the mother. Together, they write a letter expressing all these emotions, and Sagi is asked to correct it, based on his own feelings. He agrees to most of the emotions, including feelings of longing and love, but admits that he is not ready to act yet. However, in summarizing the session, he says, "I am very happy, everyone was so helpful. I love the group so much that I feel like crying. And you know, it seems to me that I already miss her [Mom]."

In the course of the session, Sagi's anger seems to decrease and make room for his love to emerge. The counseling group provided him with a place for emotional relief, social support, and personal growth, and assisted him instrumentally in finding alternative ways of coping; the session did not include skills training.

An interesting counseling group conducted in a hospital in Israel is reported by Somer, Gilbar, and Dolgin (1999). This group was developed for siblings of children with cancer, aged 7 to 17, and planned as a short-term counseling group. The focus of the group was on children's reaction to the diagnosis, behavior of the ill child, medical information, and coping with changes in the family. Results indicated statistically and clinically significant improvement in interpersonal problems, intrapsychic preoccupation, disease-related communication, mood, and cancer-related knowledge.

Group psychotherapy is targeted at children and adolescents with adjustment and behavior problems. These groups must be very small, led by mental health experts, and are usually conducted in outpatient or inpatient clinics. One example is a group for anxiety disorders conducted in an inpatient clinic. A study conducted by Silverman and colleagues (1999) using cognitive-behavioral therapy indicated that the group was highly efficacious in producing and maintaining treatment gains. This particular study used parent groups in conjunction with the children's groups and followed Kendall's (1994) procedure, that is, teaching children to self-observe, self-talk, self-evaluate, and self-reward. Parents were encouraged to allow their children to use the self-control procedures.

Anger management and aggression control is one topic that has gained recent attention. Snyder, Kymissis, and Kessler (1999) studied the effect of a cognitive-behavioral short-term treatment with 50 adolescents in small groups in a psychiatric hospital. They used discussion, structured role play, and peer feedback. The program proved effective in reducing anger and aggression.

However, not all interventions with aggressive children and adolescents are of a cognitive-behavioral orientation. The complex nature of aggression gave rise to a multitheoretical approach. Lochman, Fitzgerald, and Whidby (1999) suggest dealing with the children's high level of arousal through the expression of emotions, using a variety of expressive techniques, before teaching them the correct information processing skills. They also reported positive results using this multiple approach.

Another example is a group developed for angry and aggressive children (Shechtman, 2001a). This intervention is based on an atheoretical approach, using the process of change developed by Prochaska (1999) as a basis. In general, it is a dynamic approach in which children are led to express emotions, develop motivation to change, and acquire alternative behavior to aggression. Bibliotherapy is used to facilitate the development of self-awareness, understanding, and empathy. Research has demonstrated the efficacy of such groups (Shechtman & Ben-David, 1999). Following is a case illustration of such a therapy group.

The small group is comprised of three 11-year-old children: Gad, the aggressor, Uri, the victim, and Gail, the role model.

The first sessions are characterized with a lot of confrontations between the aggressor and his victim, with Gale suggesting constructive ways to resolve their problems. Gad refuses to admit to his aggression. Following a story in which an aggressive father is presented, Gail suggests that the abused child talk to an adult. Gad responds to this: "I've never considered such a possibility." He never had a chance to, but now for the first time is ready to accept assistance from an adult and does not feel he has to fight his problems alone. At a later session, following a poem on loneliness, Uri shares with the group his sense of loneliness, when Gad says, "I am surprised that people can talk about their feelings this way." He responds with interest and empathy to Uri, and the bullying gradually lessens. Following this experience, Gad admits that he hits and bullies, but expresses his desire to make a change. A poem named "My Own Commander" is introduced, in which a boy decides to take control over his impulsive behavior. Gad identifies with the character in the poem and orders himself to be his Own Commander. At termination, he says he learned what to do when he gets angry, he learned it from the stories/poems, his group peers, but the most important thing was that "we could talk about ourselves."

In this illustration, we can see the change in group dynamics and process that can be attributed to the emotional experiencing through which Gad went and the climate of acceptance and support in which this process took place. However, stories/poems served as important facilitators in the process of change. Considering the difficulties that boys demonstrate in expressing feelings and developing self-awareness (Pollack, 1998), psychotherapy groups for high-risk children are clearly needed.

Groups are also conducted in psychiatric outpatient and inpatient clinics (MacLennan & Dies, 1992). There are short- and long-term groups, depending on the severity of the problems. In contrast to most of the groups for children and adolescents, these groups are open-ended, gender mixed, with a large age range, and led by more than one therapist. The focus of such groups is on understanding the nature of the mental illness, recognizing what precipitated the episode, and considering how to make an adequate adjustment when returning to the community. These groups are mostly supportive and nonconfrontational, and use the expressive arts (bibliotherapy, art therapy, music and dance therapy) as the major tool for intervention.

Other psychotherapy groups are held in community shelters and institutions for juvenile delinquents. Very few groups are conducted in private practice (MacLennan & Dies, 1992).

IMPLICATIONS FOR FUTURE RESEARCH

Although a consensus has been established regarding the effectiveness of child group psychotherapy, the number of studies based on rigorous research methods is relatively limited (Durlak & Wells, 1997; Hoag & Burlingame, 1997; Kulic et al., 2001). What is needed is research with an experimental design, a large sample, replication studies, varied multiple instruments, and follow-up measures (Division 17 Special Task Group, 1999).

Generalizing to children and adolescents results that point to the effectiveness of group work with adults may be misleading. There is little research on groups for young children, and most conclusions are based on findings for adolescent groups. Clearly, findings for adolescents should not be used to generalize about groups for younger children, who have different developmental needs and require somewhat different methods. Nor should results of one type of group be used to generalize about other types. Therapy groups are very different from educational groups; yet, in many of the reviews, the type of group is not specified. In several of the review studies (e.g., Hoag & Burlingame, 1997), the discussion includes all groups. The very broad definition of child group psychotherapy (Dagley et al., 1994) adds to the lack of distinction between the groups. More research focusing on specific types of interventions or comparing outcomes across types of intervention (Shechtman & Bar-El, 1994) is needed to produce more accurate conclusions.

Therapy groups are mentioned in the literature as more effective than educational groups (Hoag & Burlingame, 1997), yet they are the minority in group work with children. As illustrated in case samples and research

(Shechtman & Ben-David, 1999), it is clear that group therapy with children is possible and effective. More efforts should therefore be taken in this direction.

Notwithstanding the mentioned limitations regarding outcome studies, the field is more informed about outcomes than process in child and adolescent group psychotherapy. In fact, extremely little is known about these processes (Barlow et al., 2000) that need to be intensively explored to inform best practice (Lusky & Hayes, 2001). Actually, most of what is known about practical implications for group work (e.g., group composition, size of group, length of treatment) is drawn from clinical experience rather than from research. There is still a lot to learn about specific populations (e.g., children who experience loss), the leadership skills (e.g., types of verbal interaction, self-disclosure), and child characteristics (e.g., predictors of success and failure).

Two conclusions may be drawn from this review. First, group psychotherapy of all three types—educational, counseling, and psychotherapy—is effective with children and adolescents, provided that suitable goals are set for each. The three types of groups address primary, secondary, and tertiary prevention efforts, respectively, and together they offer a comprehensive approach to counseling services for children.

Second, process research is in its infancy. We know very little about how children interact in groups and what the leader's role is. More research on group process—both for young children and for adolescents—is strongly encouraged in order to help practitioners in selecting a theory and methods for working with such groups.

REFERENCES

Barlow, S. H., Burlingame, G. M., & Fuhriman, A. (2000). Therapeutic application of groups: From Pratt's "thought control classes" to modern group psychotherapy. *Group Dynamics, 4,* 115-134.

Cramer Azima, F. (1989). Confrontation, empathy, and interpretation: Issues in adolescent group psychotherapy. In F. Cramer Azima and L. H. Richmond (Eds.), *Adolescent group psychotherapy* (pp. 3-19). Madison, VI: International Universities Press.

Dagley, J. C., Gazda, G. M., Eppinger, S. J., & Stewart, E. A. (1994). Group psychotherapy research with children, preadolescents, and adolescents. In A. Fuhriman & G. M. Burlingame (Eds.), *Handbook of group psychotherapy* (pp. 340-370). New York: Wiley.

DeLucia-Waack, J. L. (2000). Effective group work in the schools. *Journal for Specialists in Group Work, 25,* 131-132.

DeLucia-Waack, J. L. (2001). *Using music in children of divorce groups: A session-by-session manual for counselors.* Alexandria, VA: American Counseling Association.

Dies, K. G. (2000). Adolescent development and a model of group psychotherapy: Effective leadership in the new millennium. *Journal of Child and Adolescent Group Therapy, 10,* 97-111.

Dishion, T. J., McCord, J., & Poulin, F. (1999). When interventions harm: Peer groups and problem behavior. *American Psychologist, 54,* 755-764.

Division 17 Special Task Group. (1999, August). *Principles of empirically supported intervention programs.* Paper presented at the APA annual conference, Boston, MA.

Dryfoos, J. (1997). The prevalence of problem behaviors: Implications for programs. In R. Weissberg, T. Gullotta, R. Hampton, B. Ryan, & G. Adams (Eds.), *Enhancing children's wellness* (pp. 17-46). Thousand Oaks, CA: Sage.

Durlak, J. A., & Wells, A. M. (1997). Primary prevention mental health programs for children and adolescents: A meta-analytic review. *American Journal of Community Psychology, 25,* 115-152.

Gazda, G. M., Ginter, E. J., & Horne, A. M. (2001). *Group counseling and group psychotherapy.* Boston, MA: Allyn & Bacon.

Gladding, S. T. (1995). *Group work: A counseling specialty* (2nd ed). Columbus, OH: Merrill.

Hage, S. M., & Nosanow, M. (2000). Becoming stronger at broken places: A model for group work with young adults from divorced families. *Journal for Specialists in Group Work, 25,* 50-66.

Hanna, F. J., Hanna, C. A., & Keys, S. G. (1999). Fifty strategies for counseling defiant, aggressive adolescents: Reaching, accepting, and relating. *Journal of Counseling & Development, 77,* 395-404.

Hoag, M. J., & Burlingame, G. M. (1997). Evaluating the effectiveness of child and adolescent group treatment: A meta-analysis review. *Journal of Clinical Child Psychology, 26,* 234-246.

Huth-Bocks, A., Schettini, A., & Shebroe, V. (2001). Group play therapy for preschoolers exposed to domestic violence. *Journal of Child and Adolescent Group Therapy, 11,* 19-34.

Kazdin, A. E., & Johnson, D. W. (1994). Advances in psychotherapy for children and adolescents: Interrelations of adjustment, development, and intervention. *Journal of School Psychology, 32,* 217-246.

Kendall, P. C. (1994). Treating anxiety disorders in children: Results of a randomized clinical trial. *Journal of Consulting and Clinical Psychology, 62,* 200-210.

Kulic, K. R., Dagley, J. C., & Horne, A. M. (2001). Prevention groups with children and adolescents. *Journal for Specialists in Group Work, 26,* 211-218.

Kymissis, P. (1996). Developmental approach to socialization and group formation. In P. Kymissis and D. A. Halperin (Eds.), *Group therapy with children and adolescents* (pp. 21-33). Washington, DC: American Psychiatric Press.

Leichtentritt, J., & Shechtman, Z. (1998). Therapist, trainees, and child verbal response modes in child group therapy. *Group Dynamics, 2,* 36-47.

Lochman, J., Fitzgerald, D. P., & Whidby, J. M. (1999). Anger management with aggressive children. In C. E. Schaefer (Ed.), *Short-term psychotherapy groups for children* (pp. 301-350). Northvale, NJ: Aronson.

Lomonaco, S., Sceidlinger, S., & Aronson, S. (2000). Five decades of children's group treatment: An overview. *Journal of Child and Adolescent Group Therapy, 10,* 77-96.

Lusky, M. B., & Hayes, R. L. (2001). Collaborative consultation and program evaluation. *Journal of Counseling and Development, 79,* 26-38.

MacLennan, B. W. (2000). The future of adolescent psychotherapy groups in the new millennium. *Journal of Child and Adolescent Group Therapy, 10,* 169-179.

MacLennan, B. W., & Dies, K. G. (1992). *Group counseling and psychotherapy with adolescents.* New York: Columbia University Press.

McCallum, M. (1999, June). *Supportive therapy: Unique or common?* Paper presented at the plenary discussion of Society for Psychotherapy Research, Braga, Portugal.

Morganett, R. S. (1990). *Skills for living: Group counseling for young adolescents.* Champaign, IL: Research Press.

Morganett, R. S. (1994*). Skills for living: Group counseling activities for elementary students.* Champaign, IL: Research Press.

Morran, D. K., Robison, F. F., & Stockton, R. (1985). Feedback exchange in counseling groups: An analysis of message content and receiver acceptance as a function of leader versus member delivery, session, and valence. *Journal of Counseling Psychology, 32,* 57-67.

Nichols-Goldstein, N. (2001). The essence of effective leadership with adolescent groups: Regression in the service of the ego. *Journal of Child and Adolescent Group Therapy, 11,* 13-18.

Omizo, M. M., & Omizo, S. A. (1988). The effects of participation in group counseling sessions on self-esteem and locus of control among adolescents from divorced families. *School Counselor, 36,* 54-60.

O'Rourke, K., & Wortbyt, J. C. (1996). *Support groups for children.* Washington, DC: Accelerated Development.

Owense, P. C., & Kulic, K. R. (2001). What's needed now: Using groups for prevention. *Journal for Specialists in Group Work, 26,* 205-210.

Piaget, J. (1986). *The grasp of consciousness: Action and concept in the young child.* Cambridge, MA: Harvard University Press.

Piper, W. E., Joyce, A. S., McCallum, M., Azim, H. F., & Ogrodniczuk, J. S. (2002). *Interpretive and supportive psychotherapies.* Washington, DC: American Psychological Association.

Pollack, W. S. (1998). *Real boys.* New York: Penguin.

Pollock, K. M., & Kymissis, P. (2001). The future of adolescent group therapy. *Journal of Child and Adolescent Group Therapy, 11,* 3-12.

Prochaska, J. O. (1999). How do people change, and how can we change to help many more people. In M. A. Hubble, B. L. Duncan, & S. D. Miller (Eds.), *The heart & soul of change: What works in therapy* (pp. 227-258). Washington, DC: American Psychological Association.

Rose, S. R. (1998). *Group work with children and adolescents.* Thousand Oaks, CA: Sage.

Sanders, D. R., & Riester, A. E. (1996). School-based counseling groups for children of divorce: Effects on the self-concept of 5th grade children. *Journal of Child and Adolescent Group Therapy, 6,* 27-41.

Schaefer, C. E. (1999). *Short-term psychotherapy groups for children.* Northvale, NJ: Aronson.

Shechtman, Z. (1994). The effect of group psychotherapy on close same-sex friendships among preadolescent boys and girls. *Sex-Roles: A Research Journal, 30,* 829-834.

Shechtman, Z. (1997). Enhancing classroom climate and social acceptability at the elementary and secondary school levels. *Journal of Educational Research, 91,* 99-107.

Shechtman, Z. (1999). Low achieving elementary-school children. In C. E. Schaefer (Ed.), *Short-term psychotherapy groups for children* (pp. 79-106). Northvale, NJ: Aronson.

Shechtman, Z. (2001a). Prevention groups for angry and aggressive children. *Journal for Specialists in Group Work, 26,* 228-236.

Shechtman, Z. (2001b). Life Skills Training program: Outcomes and process. *Research Report.* Jerusalem, Israel: Ministry of Education (in Hebrew).

Shechtman, Z., & Bar-El, O. (1994). Group guidance and group counseling to foster self-concept and social status in adolescence. *Journal for Specialists in Group Work, 19,* 188-197.

Shechtman, Z., Bar-El, O., & Hadar, E. (1997). Therapeutic factors in counseling and psychoeducational groups for adolescents: A comparison. *Journal for Specialists in Group Work, 22,* 203-214.

Shechtman, Z., & Ben-David, M. (1999). Group and individual treatment of childhood aggression: A comparison of outcomes and process. *Group Dynamics, 3*(4), 1-12.

Shechtman, Z., Freedman, Y., Kashti, Y., & Sharabani, R. (2002). Group counseling to enhance adolescents' close friendship. *International Journal of Group Psychotherapy, 52,* 537-554

Shechtman, Z., Vurembrand, N., & Malajek, N. (1993). Development of self-disclosure in counseling and psychotherapy groups for children. *Journal for Specialists in Group Work, 18,* 189-199.

Shechtman, Z., & Yanuv, H. (2001). Interpretive interventions: Feedback, confrontation, and interpretation. *Group Dynamics, 5,* 124-135.

Silverman, W. K., Kurtines, W. M., Ginsburg, G. S., Weems, C. F., Lumpkin, P. W., & Carmichael, D. H. (1999). Treating anxiety disorders in children with cognitive-behavioral therapy: A randomized clinical trial. *Journal of Consulting and Clinical Psychology, 67,* 995-1003.

Slavson, S. R. (1945/1986). Differential methods of group therapy in relation to age levels. In A. E. Reister and I. A. Kraft (Eds.), *Child group psychotherapy: Future Tense* (pp. 9-28). Madison, CT: International Universities Press.

Smead, R. (1995). *Skills and techniques for group work with children and adolescents.* Champaign, IL: Research Press.

Snunit, M. (1999). *The soul bird.* New York: Hyperion.

Snyder, K. V., Kymissis, P., & Kessler, K. (1999). Anger management for adolescents: Efficacy of brief group therapy. *Journal of the American Academy of Child and Adolescent Psychiatry, 38,* 1409-1416.

Somer, E., Gilbar, O., & Dolgin, M. (1999). Siblings of children with cancer. In C. E. Schaefer (Ed.),

Short-term psychotherapy groups for children (pp. 59-77). Northvale, NJ: Aronson.

Spiegel, D. (2000). *Group therapy for cancer patients.* New York: Basic Books.

Yalom, I. D. (1995). *The theory and practice of group psychotherapy* (4th ed.). New York: Basic Books.

Weisz, J. R., Weiss, B., Alicke, M. D., & Klotz, M. L. (1987). Effectiveness of psychotherapy with children and adolescents: A meta-analysis for clinicians. *Journal of Consulting and Clinical Psychology, 55,* 542-549.

32

PRACTICE TRENDS IN WOMEN'S GROUPS

An Inclusive View

NATHALIE KEES

Colorado State University

NANCY LEECH

University of Colorado–Denver

Writing a chapter encompassing the complexities of women's groups is a difficult task. The potential for reinforcing stereotypes, universalizing, excluding, and overgeneralizing is ever present. There is no "typical" women's group. Women's groups are as diverse as the members who participate in them.

The goal of this chapter is to provide an inclusive view of women joining together in groups for individual growth, support, and empowerment as well as for social action and systemic change. The chapter includes the philosophical backgrounds of cultural, contextual, and feminist frameworks that serve as the foundation for this look at women's groups. It also focuses on current practice trends described in the women's group literature, including the importance of assessing the varied needs of women as members of groups, developing practical, comprehensive group programs to address these needs, and creating culturally meaningful approaches to working with women in groups.

A good deal of the women's group literature has been focused on addressing the needs of women with common histories and issues such as eating disorders, substance abuse, and sexual abuse. These types of issue-focused women's groups are described in separate chapters within this handbook, and the reader is referred to those chapters for additional information on women's groups.

While a diverse approach has been attempted in this chapter, it is important to remember that any author's standpoint is always but one perspective, regardless of how inclusive the attempt. Given that both authors are white Euro-American females, we have worked to expand our viewing point by looking at the group counseling literature through the varied lenses of race, ethnicity, class, age, ability, and sexual orientation, as well as gender, and through many years of personal and professional work in knowing, understanding, and appreciating difference.

PHILOSOPHICAL BACKGROUND

Cultural/Contextual Perspective

Understanding and appreciating the cultures and contexts within which we live is essential to developing an inclusive approach to working with women in groups (Grunebaum & Smith, 1996; Olarte, 1996). Helpful in creating this inclusive approach to counseling are three types of identities, individual, group, and universal, described by Sue and Sue (1990) as something counselors need to understand about themselves in order to be culturally skilled. Counselors must understand their own and their clients' unique characteristics, experiences, and beliefs, the beliefs and influences of the groups of which they are members, and the universal aspects of being human. This awareness becomes even more critical when working with diverse groups of women whose contexts will include personal and group histories of social and economic discrimination, oppression, and violence based on race, gender, age, ability, and sexual orientation (Avery, 1998; Olarte, 1996).

The cultural/contextual work of Linda James Myers (1988) expands Sue and Sue's concept of multiple identities by describing three truisms one needs to embrace simultaneously and with equal import to avoid perpetrating additional discrimination and oppression when working with any group or individual. These three truisms are:

1. All people are alike.

2. Groups of humans differ.

3. Each individual is unique.

While the concepts are simple, consistent implementation is difficult and requires constant vigilance. For most of us, the tendency is to hold one or two of these to be true at any time. Let us use the counseling profession as an example. For years, theory and research within the counseling profession have lived at number 1, All people are alike. This has typically meant all people are like the White and, until recently, mostly male undergraduate population upon which most counseling theory and research has been normed (Avery, 1998; Bernardez, 1996; Brown, 1990; Olarte, 1996). It is interesting that the use of the scientific method, based on control groups, limitations, and cautions about generalizing results beyond the population researched, has resulted in such widespread universalizing of results across genders, races, ethnic backgrounds, classes, sexual orientations, ages, and abilities. The more one breathes the air at the top of the cultural hierarchy of American society, the more difficult it is to realize that, yes, all people are alike in some ways, *and* individual and group differences exist and need to be given equal credence, value, and consideration (Bernardez, 1996; Comas-Diaz, 1991; Olarte, 1996).

Understanding the ways in which groups of humans differ is also essential to creating an inclusive view of women's groups. Resources in the women's mental health literature offer readers greater understanding of women's contextual frameworks. Maria Julia (2000) edited a recent collection of articles about understanding and working with women from various cultural backgrounds, including African American, Amish, Appalachian, Arab, Hispanic, Jewish, Native American, and Southeast Asian. The Boston Lesbian Psychologies Collective (1987) produced an earlier compilation of articles on lesbian and bisexual women's experiences. Collections such as these create greater awareness of clients' contextual experiences and enhance the counselor's ability to appreciate group differences. At the same time, it is important to be aware of the continuum of individual experiences, histories, and differences within any larger group context. Maintaining an equal appreciation for all three of Myers's truisms is difficult yet essential.

Feminist Perspective

Another of the philosophical foundations on which this chapter is based is the feminist perspective. Poet and writer Katha Pollitt described a feminist as one who can "answer the question 'Are women human?' with a yes. It is not about whether women are better than, worse than, or identical with men. . . . It's about justice, fairness, and access to the broad range of human experience. . . . It's about women having intrinsic value as persons, . . . human beings. . . . No more, no less" (as cited in Wood, 1999, p. 6). While it is beyond the scope of this chapter to cover feminist counseling theory in depth, a few guidelines pertaining to creating inclusive environments within women's groups is essential. These principles have been discussed in several sources (Avery, 1998; Brody, 1987; Brown, 1994; Brown & Ballou, 1992; Brown & Root, 1990; Cook, 1993; DeChant, 1996; Enns, 1997; Espin, 1993; Worrell & Johnson, 1997; Worrell & Remer, 1992) and are summarized here in relation to working with women in groups.

First, feminist group work is based on an egalitarian relationship. While there are inescapable power differentials between a group leader and group members, a feminist group leader will foster an awareness of these inherent imbalances and attempt not to create unnecessary power imbalances through actions such as withholding information about self or the group process, overdirecting the group, or overprescribing the direction for the group (Avery, 1998). Self-disclosure, mutual goal setting, shared decision making, and consensus building are some of the primary skills a feminist group therapist will use to create an egalitarian relationship within a group and between leader and members (Brody, 1987; Oakley, 1996). Thinking in terms of a group of experts, rather than the leader as "the expert," is an important philosophical perspective for feminist group work.

Feminist group work with women is phenomenological and is grounded in women's stories, lives, and experiences. Accepting as valid the personal truth of women's experiences is essential to effective feminist group work (Avery, 1998). An understanding of gender roles and stereotypes, as well as cultural differences in gender socialization, is also required. Efforts are made to educate leaders and members about these. Gender stereotypes are kept out of language and interactions as much as possible and are brought to the group's attention by both members and leaders (Reed & Garvin, 1996b). An example would be helping members overcome socialization that places women in a position of being less valued than men. Leaders will challenge members, and themselves, to explore ways in which they may have internalized this oppressive view, such as valuing themselves and relationships with women as less important than relationships with men (Bernardez, 1996).

An appreciation for different ways of knowing and being is also vital to the feminist approach to group work (Belenky, Clinchy, Goldberger, & Tarule, 1986; Goldberger, 1996). The values of the dominant American culture continue to favor science over intuition, thought over emotion, action over being, independence over interdependence, the individual over the family, and economic gain over just about everything else. Feminist group work equally values multiple ways of being and knowing and provides members with the understanding and means necessary to make as many conscious choices in one's life as possible (Bernardez, 1996; Rosenberg, 1996).

For example, after 15 years of conducting same-sex groups for women and men, Bernardez (1996) contends that both genders can benefit from mixed gender groups after appropriate same-sex group and/or individual work has been done to understand and ameliorate gender socialization issues common for males and females. The mixed gender group can then provide fertile ground for helping members, both male and female, appreciate multiple perspectives and approaches to life and share on common issues such as balancing work and family and increasing intimacy and closeness with people of both genders (Bernardez, 1996).

It is also important to remember that feminist group work is based not only on individual change but social action and systemic change as well (Brody, 1987; Reed & Garvin, 1996a). It is important for feminist group leaders and members to understand and acknowledge the systemic realities underlying many seemingly individual issues facing women, including issues of poverty, violence, social and economic discrimination based on race, gender, age, ability, and sexual orientation; issues related to body image and self-esteem; and the overdiagnosing of mental illness in women (Avery, 1998). Feminist group work focuses on understanding these systemic realities and working toward changing the systems within which women and men work and live. Feminist group leaders educate themselves and members on these issues within the group setting, empower members to become change agents, and work as catalysts for change themselves within the social and political systems in which they and their members work and live (Reed & Garvin, 1996a).

Finally, an inclusive approach to feminist group work acknowledges that gender is but one of the organizing principles in women's lives and that, for many women, it may not be the primary factor in understanding the intrapersonal, interpersonal, or societal issues they experience. As Brown (1990) stated, feminist theorists, researchers, and therapists "must cease insisting on the primacy of gender as *the* issue in our examinations of the lives of women of color, poor women, women from non-western cultures, and so on. . . . [F]or feminist women of color [for example] the requirement that sexism be chosen as the 'ultimate' oppression negates the validity of their internal realities" (p. 13). It is important that our research, theory, and practice of group work with women seeks to understand the point at which the various realities of women's lives intersect—where the effects of group membership by gender, race, ethnicity, age, class, sexual orientation, and ability intersect with the unique experiences of each individual woman as well as the universal realities of being a human being on this earth (Espin, 1993; Goldberger, 1996; Hertzberg, 1990; Olarte, 1996).

In accordance with feminist philosophy, a good deal of the research on feminist groups has been practice oriented, qualitative, and grounded in women's experiences. This research has investigated important aspects of group work such as the pros and cons of mixed gender or all-women's groups, the effects of the leader's gender on women's groups, the effects of leader self-disclosure on women's groups, stages in women's groups, and the validity of traditionally accepted group practices such as no member contact outside of group (Bernardez, 1996; Cunningham & Knight, 1996; DeChant, 1996; Kees, 1999; Kravetz & Marecek, 1996;

Rosenberg, 1996; Wright & Gould, 1996). While the outcomes of this research have been mixed and often limited in generalizability, it has provided an important foundation upon which future research will be built. What has been emphasized repeatedly in the feminist group research is that best practice in women's groups is contextual and must be based on the needs of group members. Group leaders must examine their own gender biases and the influences of their gender and their biases on the dynamics of the group. Group training programs must address these issues as well and should include training in feminist approaches to group work (DeChant, 1996).

There are many excellent resources on feminist counseling and psychotherapy. We recommend *Diversity and Complexity in Feminist Therapy*, edited by Laura S. Brown and Maria P. P. Root (1990), *Women and Group Psychotherapy*, edited by Betsy DeChant (1996), *Feminist Theories and Feminist Psychotherapies*, by Carolyn Zerbe Enns (1997), *Shaping the Future of Feminist Psychology: Education, Research, and Practice*, edited by Judith Worell and Norine G. Johnson (1997), and *Constructing Gender: Multicultural Perspectives in Working With Women*, edited by Maria Julia (2000).

PRACTICE TRENDS IN WOMEN'S GROUPS

In reviewing recent literature on women's groups, certain trends appear to be taking hold, while others, established early on in the history of women's groups, continue to be reinforced. Some of these trends are discussed below, and examples of the four types of groups outlined by the Association for Specialists in Group Work (ASGW) are provided. These include task, psychoeducational, counseling, and psychotherapy groups (ASGW, 2002). The support function of many of these groups is also addressed.

Understanding and Meeting Women's Needs

Focus Groups. On the basis of a review of the literature, an awareness of the importance of understanding and meeting the unique needs of women in groups is developing. Several practitioners and researchers are moving away from the prescriptive approach to designing women's groups and are beginning with a focus group process to allow for more complete understanding of the needs of each individual group and its members (DeFrancisco, 1996; Erwin & Stewart, 1997; Hodge & Casken, 1999; Rosen & Bezold, 1996).

The work of Hodge and Casken (1999) is an excellent example of the power of this type of task or focus group. In their 3-year project to develop "a culturally sensitive breast cancer educational program targeting American Indian women in California," a total of 65 women at six sites joined together in focus groups to answer some very basic and important questions: "How important do you think breast cancer is in your community? Is it a problem among Indian women? What are the barriers/facilitators to breast cancer screening? What are the cultural aspects surrounding breast cancer in terms of taboos and prohibitions? What beliefs do you hold about breast cancer, your risk, surgery, treatment, etc.?" (pp. 206-207). Sizes of the focus groups ranged from 5 to 18 participants. Focus groups were led by trained members of the American Indian communities and were held at Indian agencies in settings familiar and accessible to the participants. Focus group results were used to develop a questionnaire that was distributed to 352 American Indian women across four sites.

On the basis of the results of the focus groups, questionnaires, and the expressed needs and values of the women, educational materials and psychoeducational group workshops were developed from a culturally sensitive and gender-aware perspective. Rather than relying on written pamphlets and brochures, an educational video was produced that addressed issues such as "the importance of family and of health to the American Indian women in regard to the role they played as providers and caretakers for their immediate and extended families" (p. 211). Resource guides were developed at appropriate reading levels and used Native American artwork. Numerous barriers to breast cancer screening and treatment, such as the women's beliefs that breast cancer was not a major concern for them and fears

about screening and treatment procedures, were addressed in the materials and workshops. Women's beliefs about modesty, spiritual aspects of health, and a present-time orientation were just some of the many considerations.

Three hundred fifty-two women eventually participated in four Pathways to Health workshops. These 1-day psychoeducational groups provided information on risk factors, screening techniques, communication skills, treatment options, and patients' rights. Developed specifically for this population, a video, resource booklet, and patient's guide were used in the workshops. The workshops were held at Native American community sites and included Native American panel members and professionals. Workshop evaluations were reported as favorable but have not yet been published.

Comprehensive Approaches to Meeting Women's Needs in Groups. There is a growing realization that meeting the multiple needs of members is essential to the success of women's groups (Comas-Diaz, 1986; Hardman, 1997; Jarrett, Diamond, & El-Mohandes, 2000; Subramanian, Hernandez, & Martinez, 1995). These needs multiply, based on the number of ways, in addition to gender, each woman is targeted for oppression within our society. These include discrimination based on low income, age (including adolescent girls and elderly women), race and ethnicity, mental and chronic illnesses, different abilities, childhood trauma, and sexual orientation. Helping women group members meet their physiological needs, child care requirements, and transportation needs to and from group are some of the ways practitioner/researchers are improving the success of the groups they facilitate (Comas-Diaz, 1986; Hardman, 1997; Jarrett et al., 2000; Subramanian et al., 1995).

For example, in a project funded by the National Institutes of Health, Jarrett et al. (2000) used every means available to make sure that their group interventions with indigent African American mothers and their babies were successful. While control group members received standard social service support only, treatment group members received this standard support as well as weekly home visits for the first 4 months of their babies' lives. Control group members also received biweekly home visits and psychoeducational/support group interventions until the babies were a year old. The home visits, conducted by one of the group leaders and a parenting support specialist, gave participants 4 months to gain comfort with the program and its staff prior to the start of the psychoeducational/support group interventions.

To build trust and increase attendance for the groups, participants were given incentives such as toys, books, and relaxation tapes at every group session. On-site babysitting, transportation by taxi or hospital van, and meals were provided at each group session. The staff improved attendance by calling participants the day before the group and going to participants' homes the morning of group to help mothers organize and get ready to attend.

The group interventions consisted of (a) a parent support/counseling group and (b) a psychoeducational, developmental play group in which mothers interacted with their infants while learning about age-appropriate child behaviors, parenting techniques, and self-esteem and confidence building. The parent support/counseling group allowed mothers, without their infants, to explore their own experiences, beliefs, and struggles with parenting and to develop personal goals for change. Fifty-seven out of 62 mothers chose to participate in the psychoeducational/support group interventions and reported that they found the information shared about poverty and its effects on child development, coping with stress, self-esteem, and baby health care most helpful (Jarrett et al., 2000).

Cocreating Practical Solutions. Another trend in women's group literature is the movement away from process focused, unstructured groups toward a cocreation of real-life, practical solutions for women group members (Boudin, 1998; Brody, 1996; Hardman, 1997; Rife, 1997). One example of this was a 10-week psychoeducational/support group for prostituted women with children developed in London (Hardman, 1997). In an effort to overcome the systemic prejudices as well as internalized oppressions these women experienced, the group leaders worked very hard with members to establish a time-limited, solution-oriented group that met the needs of

all 23 members. For example, instead of the typical "condoms and crabs" focus of health care information, the women identified healthy eating, child health, insomnia, basic first aid, and menstruation as areas of greater concern (Hardman, 1997, p. 26). Unwilling to believe that these women "chose" prostitution, the leaders facilitated the members in cocreating plans for obtaining housing, legal advice, jobs, child care, parenting skills, counseling and therapy resources, and welfare benefits.

Unusual for a group with this population, absenteeism was low and all 23 women completed the program. At the end of the 10-week group, nine women were rehoused and no longer involved in prostitution. Twenty women were receiving a regular income from welfare benefits and all of the women had registered with the health care clinic. A second group began and, based on the evaluations of the first group, was extended to 15 weeks. A drop-in program was established to provide continuing support for previous members of the group.

Almost of equal importance were the attitude shifts of some of the social service workers who had believed that these women chose prostitution as a viable financial alternative. In the words of one social service team member, "I thought these women knew what they were getting into and should be prepared to live with the consequences. As a woman, I feel ashamed I have bought into the male myths that women actually seek out and enjoy prostitution" (Hardman, 1997, p. 30). The awareness that these women were the targets of multiple oppressions, including poverty, sexism, racism, and abuse, facilitated a shift in the workers' perceptions, thereby opening a window for the women members to view themselves differently as well.

These solution-oriented groups may be short-term or even single-session informational workshops as recommended by some authors (Gainor, 1992; Saxe & Johnson, 1999), or 3 to 5 years in duration, depending on the multiple needs of members and the number of nontherapeutic forces at work within the group (Berman-Rossi & Cohen, 1989). Adopting a very practical orientation for their work with homeless, mentally ill women, Berman-Rossi and Cohen (1989) created a "Dinner Group" in which members planned, shopped, prepared, and ate a meal together at a shelter most Sundays over a 5-year period. One of the most diverse, distrustful, and fiercely independent groups of women described in the literature, their refreshingly honest story is told from the perspectives of the students assigned to work with this task/ counseling group each year. It is a story of struggle and success.

While it took only 4 months for the women to master the logistics of planning, shopping, and preparing the food, Year 2 was still fraught with manipulations, power struggles, arguments, and even physical blows. It was not until Year 3 that the group began to develop cohesion, catalyzed by the loss of one member from stroke and the death of another member's husband. Although formal measures of cohesion were not used, the student leaders observed increases in cooperation and social communications between members, and the group began to function independently of the leaders. By Year 4, the group was able to spend an hour discussing an intragroup conflict, and by Year 5, the group began to use a consensus decision-making model more often and were able to work together with minimal leader intervention. Similar to Hardman's (1997) group, the leaders of the Dinner Group expressed a shift in their perceptions of the members as they began to trust the women's ability to take care of themselves and each other.

Using Culturally Meaningful Methodologies. A trend that is finding its way more often into the written record of women's groups is the use of culturally meaningful customs, languages, myths, and ceremonies to make group work personally relevant and impactful for women (Brown, Lipford-Sanders, & Shaw, 1995; Gloria, 1999; Hardin & Sukola, 1998; Heilbron & Guttman, 2000; Mahtani & Huq, 1993; Olarte, 1996; Williams, Frame, & Green, 1999). For example, using the Swahili word Kujichagulia, meaning self-determination, as the name for their psychotherapy/support group for African American women at a counseling center on a predominantly White college campus, Brown et al. (1995) created an Afrocentric atmosphere for their group based on valuing their "collective survival or sisterhood, emotional vitality, and a being orientation to time (importance placed on self as valuable because the person exists)" (p. 153). African American female role models were highlighted throughout the group, and members were encouraged to disclose their "secrets of the heart" concerning their experiences as African American women on a predominantly White campus.

The Kujichagulian groups are closed groups and meet for 2 hours a week over 10 weeks. The groups typically have 10 African American female students ranging in age from 21 to 42 years and are cofacilitated by African American female graduate students in counseling. Leaders have completed course work in group and multicultural counseling and are supervised by an African American female counseling professor. Gestalt therapy and role-playing techniques are used to challenge unresolved issues related to self-esteem, oppression, and family of origin. In addition to the benefits group members experience, the group also provides a diverse experience for counselors in training on a predominantly White campus.

Presenting a composite view of "Kujichagulian women" called "Keisha," Brown et al. (1995) described these women, who traditionally underutilize counseling services on White campuses, as experiencing hope, group cohesion and intimacy, empowerment, and support for personal as well as systemic change. Members expressed an increased connection to themselves and their African American sisters that, in turn, helped them overcome feelings of isolation and separateness within the larger campus community (Brown et al., 1995).

Hardin and Sukola (1998) also created a culturally sensitive counseling group by using storytelling and native myths to empower indigenous women in Guam dealing with abusive relationships and the societal expectations that kept them from leaving. Other authors have described culture-specific language, rituals, and ceremonies, their uses in groups, and their power for healing First Nations women (Heilbron & Guttman, 2000), African American women (Williams et al., 1999), Chicana women

(Gloria, 1999), lesbian women (Brody, 1996), and Euro-American women (Kees, 1999).

Personal Empowerment and Systemic Change

Throughout the history of women's groups, understanding the relationship between the personal empowerment of women, and creating social, political, or systemic change, has been an essential element in working with women in groups (Brody, 1987). Women's empowerment, either individually or in groups, has led to systemic change and, conversely, social reforms have had positive effects on the lives of women. In the words of feminist philosophers, "the personal is political" (Brody, 1987).

Excellent task group examples of this concept in action are the microfinancing or microcredit task groups being established around the globe (Parekh, 2000; Roberts, 2000; Wilentz, 2001). The creation of sources of small, low-interest business loans has allowed many people, including many women's groups in developing countries, to create sustainable means of economic support. Village Earth, based at Colorado State University, has taken this concept a step further and is working with women's social action groups in various countries, including the United States, to create their own savings and loan programs (Roberts, 2000). Rather than remaining dependent on lending institutions, women's groups in places such as the Rosebud Reservation in South Dakota and the villages of Nashik, India, are being helped to develop their own savings, investing, and loaning programs to establish businesses and economic viability (Parekh, 2000). "All Village Earth projects are developed on the premise that lack of access to resources is the primary obstacle to building a better life, and that poverty is a symptom rather than a cause of the problem" (Parekh, 2000, p. 1). The reciprocal interaction between personal empowerment and systemic change is one of the primary strengths of women's groups and is having an effect worldwide (Horne, 1999; Rogow, 2000; Tlakula, 1998).

CONCLUSION

The strength of women's groups is support. The literature tells us that women go to groups to regroup, to realize that they are not alone and that they are not crazy. They go to gain validation for their experience and to renew their energies so they can maintain in their regular lives. They gain information and potential solutions for often insoluble problems. They want a fair share of resources and they want to be seen as individuals worthy of equal respect and unprejudiced treatment. They learn that their individual experiences are often rooted in systemic problems. And they realize they can overcome early programming about who they should be.

We have learned much from the practice focus of women's group literature. Future research will hopefully expand on this understanding of women's experiences in groups with longitudinal studies, larger subject pools, comparative analyses, and controlled, experimental studies providing for more generalizability. In this way we may more fully answer the questions of what does work, what are the best practices for working with women in groups, and what implications might this have for group work theory and practice in general.

As stated above, women's groups are as diverse as the women who comprise them. It is the group leader's job to clear away any personal prejudices, to listen well to the needs of the members, and to cocreate experiences that will lead to individual as well as systemic change. More is certainly possible, but nothing less is expected.

REFERENCES

Association for Specialists in Group Work (2002). *Professional standards for the training of group workers.* Retrieved from http://asgw.educ.kent.edu/training_standards.htm.

Avery, L. (1998). A feminist perspective on group work with severely mentally ill women. *Women & Therapy, 21,* 1-14.

Belenky, M. F., Clinchy, B. M., Goldberger, N. R., & Tarule, J. M. (1986). *Women's ways of knowing.* New York: Basic Books.

Berman-Rossi, T., & Cohen, M. B. (1989). Group development and shared decision making working with homeless mentally ill women. *Social Work With Groups, 11,* 63-78.

Bernardez, T. (1996). Women's therapy groups as the treatment of choice. In B. DeChant (Ed.), *Women and group psychotherapy: Theory and practice* (pp. 242-262). New York: Guilford.

Boston Lesbian Psychologies Collective (Ed.). (1987). *Lesbian psychologies: Explorations & challenges.* Chicago: University of Illinois Press.

Boudin, K. (1998). Lessons from a mother's program in prison: A psychosocial approach supports women and their children. *Women & Therapy, 21,* 103-125.

Brody, R. (1987). *Women's therapy groups: Paradigms of feminist treatment.* New York: Springer.

Brody, R. (1996). Becoming visible: An art therapy support group for isolated low-income lesbians. *Art Therapy: Journal of the American Art Therapy Association, 13,* 20-30.

Brown, L. S. (1990). The meaning of a multicultural perspective for theory-building in feminist therapy. *Women & Therapy, 9,* 1-22.

Brown, L. S. (1994). *Subversive dialogues: Theory in feminist therapy.* New York: Basic Books.

Brown, L. S., & Ballou, M. (Eds.). (1992). *Personality and psychopathology: Feminist reappraisals.* New York: Guilford.

Brown, L. S., & Root, M. P. P. (Eds.). (1990). *Diversity and complexity in feminist therapy.* Binghamton, NY: Haworth.

Brown, S. P., Lipford-Sanders, J., & Shaw, M. (1995). *Kujichagulia*—Uncovering the secrets of the heart: Group work with African American women on predominantly white campuses. *Journal for Specialists in Group Work, 20,* 151-158.

Comas-Diaz, L. (1986). Puerto Rican alcoholic women: Treatment conditions. *Alcoholism Treatment Quarterly, 3,* 47-57.

Comas-Diaz, L. (1991). Feminism and diversity in psychology. *Psychology of Women Quarterly, 15,* 597-609.

Cook, E. P. (Ed.). (1993). *Women, relationships, and power: Implications for counseling.* Alexandria, VA: American Counseling Association.

Cunningham, J. M., & Knight, E. B. (1996). Mothers, models, and mentors: Issues in long-term group therapy for women. In B. DeChant (Ed.), *Women and group psychotherapy: Theory and practice* (pp. 284-299). New York: Guilford.

DeChant, B. (Ed.). (1996). *Women and group psychotherapy: Theory and practice.* New York: Guilford.

DeFrancisco, V. L. (1996). The world of designing women: A narrative account of focus group plans for a women's university. *Communication Education, 45,* 330-337.

Enns, C. E. (1997). *Feminist theories and feminist psychotherapies.* New York: Harrington Park.

Erwin, L., & Stewart, P. (1997). Gendered perspectives: A focus-group study of how undergraduate women negotiate their career aspirations. *Qualitative Studies in Education, 10,* 207-220.

Espin, O. M. (1993). Feminist therapy: Not for white women only. *Counseling Psychologist, 21,* 103-108.

Gainor, K. A. (1992). Internalized oppression as a barrier to effective group work with black women. *Journal for Specialists in Group Work, 17,* 235-242.

Gloria, A. M. (1999). Apoyando estudiantes Chicanas: Therapeutic factors in Chicana college student support groups. *Journal for Specialists in Group Work, 24,* 246-257.

Goldberger, N. (1996). Ways of knowing: Women's constructions of truth, authority, and self. In B. DeChant (Ed.), *Women and group psychotherapy: Theory and practice* (pp. 89-110). New York: Guilford.

Grunebaum, J., & Smith, J. M. (1996). Women in context(s): The social subtext of group psychotherapy. In B. DeChant (Ed.), *Women and group psychotherapy: Theory and practice* (pp. 50-88). New York: Guilford.

Hardin, A., & Sukola, K. R. (1998). Empowering abused women: Multi-cultural counseling techniques. In *Relating in a global community.* Proceedings of the International Conference on Counseling in the 21st Century (Sydney,

Australia). (ERIC Document Reproduction Service No. ED439385)

Hardman, K. L. J. (1997). A social work group for prostituted women with children. *Social Work With Groups, 20,* 19-31.

Heilbron, C. L., & Guttman, M. A. J. (2000). Traditional healing methods with First Nations women in group counselling. *Canadian Journal of Counselling, 34,* 3-13.

Hertzberg, J. F. (1990). Feminist psychotherapy and diversity: Treatment considerations from a self psychology perspective. *Women & Therapy, 9,* 275-297.

Hodge, F. S., & Casken, J. (1999). American Indian breast cancer project: Educational development and implementation. *American Indian Culture and Research Journal, 23,* 205-215.

Horne, S. (1999). From coping to creating change: The evolution of women's groups. *Journal for Specialists in Group Work, 24,* 231-245.

Jarrett, M. H., Diamond, L. T., & El-Mohandes, A. (2000). Group intervention as one facet of a multi-component intervention with high risk mothers and their babies. *Infants and Young Children, 13,* 15-24.

Julia, M. (Ed.). (2000). *Constructing gender: Multicultural perspectives in working with women.* Belmont, CA: Wadsworth.

Kees, N. L. (1999). Women together again: A phenomenological study of leaderless women's groups. *Journal for Specialists in Group Work, 24,* 288-305.

Kravetz, D., & Marecek, J. (1996). The personal is political: A feminist agenda for group psychotherapy research. In B. DeChant (Ed.), *Women and group psychotherapy: Theory and practice* (pp. 351-372). New York: Guilford.

Mahtani, A., & Huq, A. H. (1993). The use of a Western model across cultures. *British Journal of Guidance & Counselling, 21,* 35-40.

Myers, L. J. (1988). *Understanding an Afrocentric world view: Introduction to an optimal psychology.* Dubuque, IA: Kendall/Hunt.

Oakley, M. A. (1996). Short-term women's groups as spaces for integration. In B. DeChant (Ed.), *Women and group psychotherapy: Theory and practice* (pp. 263-283). New York: Guilford.

Olarte, S. W. (1996). Cross-cultural issues in group psychotherapy for women. In B. DeChant (Ed.), *Women and group psychotherapy: Theory and practice* (pp. 463-481). New York: Guilford.

Parekh, A. (2000, July). New Village Earth project in Nashik, India. *The Village Earth Connection.* Retrieved from http://villageearth.org.

Reed, B. G., & Garvin, C. D. (1996a). Feminist thought and group psychotherapy: Feminist principles as praxis. In B. DeChant (Ed.), *Women and group psychotherapy: Theory and practice* (pp. 15-49). New York: Guilford.

Reed, B. G., & Garvin, C. D. (1996b). Feminist psychodynamic group psychotherapy: The application of principles. In B. DeChant (Ed.), *Women and group psychotherapy: Theory and practice.* (pp. 127-156). New York: Guilford.

Rife, J. C. (1997). Group counseling model for helping older women secure employment. *Clinical Gerontologist, 18,* 43-47.

Roberts, J. (2000, July). Fundamental principles for designing a sustainable village-based development program. *The Village Earth Connection.* Retrieved from http://villageearth.org.

Rogow, D. (2000). *Alone you are nobody, together we float: The Manuela Ramos movement.* (ERIC Document Reproduction Service No. ED447265)

Rosen, K. H., & Bezold, A. (1996). Dating violence prevention: A didactic support group for young women. *Journal of Counseling and Development, 74,* 521-525.

Rosenberg, P. (1996). Comparative leadership styles of male and female therapists. In B. DeChant (Ed.), *Women and group psychotherapy: Theory and practice* (pp. 425-441). New York: Guilford.

Saxe, B. J., & Johnson, S. M. (1999). An empirical investigation of group treatment. *Journal of Child Sexual Abuse, 8,* 67-88.

Subramanian, K., Hernandez, S., & Martinez, A. (1995). Psychoeducational group work for low-income Latina mothers with HIV infection. *Social Work With Groups, 18,* 53-63.

Sue, D. W., & Sue, D. (1990). *Counseling the culturally different: Theory & practice* (2nd ed.). New York: Wiley.

Tlakula, M. (1998). The Elim Care group: Conflict in community development styles. *Community Development Journal, 33,* 157-164.

Wilentz, A. (2001, August). Jewel in the crown. *O: The Oprah Magazine,* 149-180.

Williams, C. B., Frame, M. W., & Green, E. (1999). Counseling groups for African American women: A focus on spirituality. *Journal for Specialists in Group Work, 24,* 260-273.

Wood, J. T. (1999). *Gendered Lives.* Belmont, CA: Wadsworth.

Worell, J., & Johnson, N. G. (Eds.). (1997). *Shaping the future of feminist psychology: Education, research, and practice.* Washington, DC: American Psychological Association.

Worell, J., & Remer, P. (1992). *Feminist perspectives in therapy: An empowerment model for women.* Chichester, England: Wiley.

Wright, F., & Gould, L. J. (1996). Research on gender-linked aspects of group behavior: Implications for group psychotherapy. In B. DeChant (Ed.), *Women and group psychotherapy: Theory and practice* (pp. 333-350). New York: Guilford.

33

COUNSELING MEN IN GROUPS

The Role of Myths, Therapeutic Factors, Leadership, and Rituals

MICHAEL P. ANDRONICO

Individual Practice, Somerset, New Jersey

*University of Medicine and Dentistry of
New Jersey, Robert Wood Johnson Medical School*

ARTHUR M. HORNE

University of Georgia

W orking with men in groups has been identified as one of the most powerful and effective means of addressing the issues being faced by men today (Andronico, 1996; Horne, Jolliff, & Roth, 1996; Jolliff & Horne, 1996; Rabinowitz, 2001). Men's groups may occur in many different formats, including task or work, psychoeducational/learning, support, counseling, and therapy groups, with each oriented to specific problems men bring to their groups. This chapter reviews several types of groups for men and addresses issues related to each approach.

WHAT ARE MEN'S PROBLEMS?

Men's problems range from stress from the current cultural milieu to specific concerns such as marital issues or work concerns. Groups address these problems, ranging from traditional counseling and psychotherapy groups to support groups and others such as the Million Man March, Promise Keeper rallies, sweat lodge groups, drumming events, and even more focused-agenda meetings such as groups seeking fathers' rights and gay rights groups. This chapter is on therapeutically oriented groups run by counselors or therapists, but it is important to be aware that there are many nontraditional or alternative models of groups operating to meet the needs that men have today, and that many—or even most—of these groups are led by facilitators who have not been trained in traditional counseling and therapy approaches.

Pleck (1995) posited that while there are essential differences in men and women and

456

some of the differences in behavior might be understood by biological explanations, gender roles are socially constructed. As the male gender role is socially constructed, it presents problems because gender norms are not always consistent, there is stress for men not adhering to the roles, and some of the behaviors expected are not psychologically healthy. Male gender role norms come from a variety of influences, including cultural, psychological, and political factors (Brooks & Silverstein, 1995). Brooks and Silverstein (1995) have proposed that the conflict—the gender role strain—that men experience is a culmination of experiences from a traditional patriarchal society and the learning of gender role expectations, but they believe men experience problems of role stress rather than gender identity.

There is considerable stress in the lives of men today. There is the changing role and influence of women in work, politics, and society in general; the highly competitive nature of the workplace; the extensive work hours and competitive demands that impact individuals, families, and groups; and while many traditional roles have changed, most men still feel the pressure of fulfilling the three P's: Provider, Protector, and Procreator.

In the 1970s, an increased emphasis on research of men's development began to occur, as well as enhanced attention on how to help men address the problems they were encountering. There was an examination of traditional role patterns, with suggestions that men could be living different lives (Goldberg, 1976; Pleck & Sawyer, 1980), and that the lives many were currently leading due to their adherence to traditional roles were, in fact, highly hazardous to the health of men. As a result of the popular books and increased research into men's issues, there is today a greater emphasis on men seeking treatment for their problems.

A number of authors have identified reasons why men are more reluctant than women to engage in the therapeutic process. Levant (1990) has indicated that the male role as traditionally developed requires independence, self-reliance, and a competitiveness and achievement orientation that makes therapy difficult. Brooks (1996) has described a number of reasons that therapy may be distasteful or rejected by men, including

that men are competitive, are used to being in charge, generally pay for products rather than processes, and have difficulty being emotive in relationships. Horne et al. (1996) added that there is often a male self-denial of problems; that men may become caught in a success trap in which it is difficult for those experiencing high rates of success to seek help; and therapy often requires suspending action for process, a difficult requirement for many men. Goldberg (1976) described in detail how therapy is an unmasculine experience. And yet, with all the restrictions for men entering therapy, group work is a viable alternative that provides an opportunity for men to obtain help with problems without having to experience the discomfort so many authors have identified as restricting men's participation in therapy (Andronico, 1996).

Group Processes That Facilitate Men's Participation in Groups

Conducting groups for men requires understanding the resistance and involves adapting the counseling or therapeutic experience to be inviting and encouraging rather than threatening and challenging. Men are used to working and playing in groups, both in the workplace and on the athletic field. An essential component of groups developed to address men's issues is attention to the elements of therapeutic factors defined by Yalom (1995). These specific therapeutic elements, and how they apply particularly to groups for men, are discussed next.

Instillation of Hope

Instillation of hope is crucial to the group process, for it is very important to anyone striving to attain a goal to believe that the goal is attainable. Yalom (1995) suggests that in any pregroup discussions and orientations, any potential positive effects and expectations be explicitly stated, for this helps to support optimism of the potential group member. The intake process must adhere to ethical guidelines that include not guaranteeing change or success, but must also present a reasonable hope for change and addressing problems.

Beyond the intake process, hope is developed through observing other members relate their positive experiences. When men see that others, working together in a group, have struggled with and resolved issues similar to theirs, the instillation of hope occurs and they become more optimistic. They see the therapeutic support that is available as a result of the group; men are able to free their energies from depression and pessimism to optimism and utilize these energies to resolve their issues. Those who have made the changes can feel good about their accomplishments, and those who need to make the change can see that it is possible. A specific concern often addressed in men's groups relates to those who have had poor or nonexistent relationships with their fathers. The presence and support of older men often instills hope in younger men, for there is an opportunity to symbolically, in a safe and supportive environment, satisfy their needs to have the good relationship they did not have with their own fathers.

Universality

When men feel alone, alienated, and miserable, it is helpful to realize that they are not alone and that other men have struggled and are still struggling with the same issues. In many cases, male socialization has focused upon competitiveness and the "rugged individualism" that our culture emphasizes. In helping men recognize that their concerns are not unique, but are part of the male experience shared by others in the group, there is a level of joining and cohesiveness that challenges the belief that they are alone.

Imparting Information

Several authors (Andronico, 1996; Jolliff & Horne, 1996) have identified the traditional process-oriented group as "unmasculine," for men have generally been socialized to action and problem solving. Yalom's (1995) inclusion of imparting information helps make group counseling and therapy particularly relevant to men's issues, for in men's groups, members learn a great deal from each other. As a function of group interaction, men learn about how other men cope with problems, which helps them to expand their repertoire of problem-solving behaviors.

When men struggle with their emotional issues, they often get into a rut and have trouble thinking outside the box. Men are often used to being problem solvers, but when their problem-solving skills in a particular area are severely limited due to heightened emotionality or defensiveness, their ability to be effective problem solvers erodes. Observing and listening to other men often helps them to discuss the situation in a more flexible and appropriate manner and widen their scope of problem-solving behaviors. Also, the group leader can stop when he thinks it is appropriate and give a brief didactic talk concerning the issue that is being discussed. In men's groups that have a more psychoeducational or counseling focus, the group focus is often on imparting information and the direct instruction of learning activities.

Altruism

Yalom (1995) relates the story of people in a room with a large pot of stew in the center of a round table with long-handled spoons. The people are able to reach the stew but, because of the long length of the handles, are unable to feed themselves. The solution to the problem is to end their own starvation by feeding each other. This process is a good analogy for men's groups as well, for men often derive great satisfaction not only in being helped but also by helping others. Many men who feel self-conscious, inept, or unfulfilled do not think of themselves as having much worth, but they increase their self-confidence when they realize that they can contribute to other people in positive ways. Participants often learn that "I have helped others" can be synonymous with "I am important enough that I can contribute to others."

Altruism helps build strong feelings of kinship and teamwork among the participants, along with a strong group spirit of cooperation. It is important that the leader recognize the power of men helping men and the altruistic factor that exists in teamwork, where the whole team benefits from the contributions of each of the members. For psychoeducational and counseling groups, the same impact is found, for as men help men deal with men's issues, their contributions to one another provide healing and growth opportunities for all the members.

The Corrective Recapitulation of the Primary Group

Traditional dynamic psychotherapy groups provide a very good stimulus for the reenactment of the primary family group. Group members can discuss in detail their reactions to those people who remind them of their family members. In the process of so doing, members also have the opportunity to expand their scope of responding to people with personalities similar to their family members. Because of gender socialization, men especially need and are receptive to expanding the scope of their social and emotional response repertoires.

Men's groups obviously do not include females. However, the opportunity is there to recapitulate many crucial relationships among male members. For example, often when there is a wide age range among male members of a men's group, there may be father-son types of intragroup transferences that occur. It is not unusual, for example, to hear one member say to another, "You remind me of my son. You often say that I was not a good enough father," or to have a younger man say to an older man something similar, such as "You were never satisfied with anything I did." This type of interaction or brother-to-brother interaction can help stimulate the feelings that are carried from childhood and give the group members an opportunity to resolve them by discussion, suggestions, and other means. The use of the group to address male developmental issues of the family is not restricted to psychotherapy groups, but may also be enacted during counseling groups, using the group members to help identify early family dynamics and then use the counseling problem-solving process to help establish more current and effective methods for addressing family problems in the here-and-now. Often there is transference to a member about female relationship issues, for example, the member does not listen, or perhaps the member does listen and is supportive like the mother or some other significant female in the member's life, which provides excellent material for group discussion.

Development of Socializing Techniques

Men in men's groups often say, "I come to these groups because I have had trouble all my life relating to men and I hope to be able to get along better with men in this group." Another common statement is "I came to this group to deal with my homophobia. I feel too upset when I get close to men." Group members have opportunities to talk about their feelings, discuss them, get input from others, and have opportunities to work more directly. For example, a man who is homophobic may, after discussing his increasing comfort of being close to men, be encouraged to sit closer to another man, may even sit with his arms around another man, and at other times hug. Of course, all of these interventions are calculated and must be appropriate to the situation, taking into consideration the readiness of the participants to perform these interventions and whether there are any sexual abuse issues.

In psychoeducational or counseling groups for men, much of the focus of the group is on socialization skills and the examination of beliefs and instilled behaviors that led to conflict with others or with difficulty being comfortable in social settings. Role plays, behavior rehearsals, and challenging of sexist thinking often facilitate the development of more effective interaction skills for men.

Imitative Behavior

During the course of the group, men often will say, "Now I know what it is like to be a man," or "It is so nice to be in this kind of a group, because Joe and Sam and Bill really have helped me to see how men behave." Another common statement is "I understand now that being a man is really being myself. You have helped me see this and I appreciate it." In all of these quotes, it is apparent that imitative behavior occurs in groups. It is helpful to learn from positive models rather than negative ones, and the models may be the group leader or other members of the group. Men who seek to find more of a personal identity in being male often encounter such experiences, and claim that this is one of the most important positive aspects of being in the group.

Interpersonal Learning

Yalom (1995) points out three factors emphasizing the importance of interpersonal learning:

1. The importance of interpersonal relationships

2. The corrective emotional experience

3. The group as a social microcosm

Many things occur in these three subfactors, but basically the men's group provides a stimulus to recognize men's feelings in interpersonal relationships and to see what each man's individual reaction to interpersonal relationships is in general and what his reaction is specific to individualized situations with particular individuals. Once a man begins to see that he has feelings or problems with certain kinds of people who exemplify certain kinds of behavior, then it is easier for him to recognize and understand his responses to these behaviors. For example, a man might recognize that he tends to withdraw and not assert himself with older aggressive men who remind him of his father. Once this is recognized, then the next step, the corrective emotional experience, has an opportunity to take place. What often occurs is that other men in the group might be supportive of him and encourage him to express himself directly to the person in more assertive ways. In addition, the men who remind the person of his father may also encourage him to speak more directly to them. For example, John was a man who had a very aggressive, critical father. John tended to defer to his father and never challenge him, withdrawing and not speaking when his father was around. In the course of the men's group, he recognized this pattern of behavior. It was helpful to have this process started by other people making the observation that "John, when Tom speaks, you tend to be quiet and almost never respond, whereas most of us do. Do you have any idea why that is?" John's response initially was "I don't know why, but I do feel uncomfortable when I hear Tom and Sam talk, so I keep quiet." The group then pursued this and said, "What is the difference between Tom and Tony and Bill?" Initially John said, "I don't know, but I feel comfortable with Tony and Bill, and I feel uncomfortable with Tom and Sam." The group leader suggested that John think about it and get back to it eventually. This intervention by the group leader was made to reduce the pressure that John was feeling to come up with an immediate answer. During the course of the

next few weeks, John began to identify more clearly that he thought that the people who reminded him of his father were more aggressive and more critical. This helped the other two people to recognize that there was a slight edge of criticism to their tone, and they thanked John for pointing that out and worked to diminish their negativity and critical outlook. The reactions of the two were surprising to John, who expected to be further criticized for speaking up and also for pointing out faults in them. As the group progressed, John became better able to assert himself in relationship to the other two people, and gradually he realized that he could do this with the encouragement of the group leader and the people of whom he was initially critical. This interpersonal learning was helpful to John, who reported to the group that he had become more assertive to people like his father because of the awareness and confidence he developed in his behavior.

The importance of the relationship of the therapist and patient or counselee is obvious in individual therapy. In the group, cohesiveness is analogous to the therapeutic relationship in individual therapy. The relationship of group members is as important, or even more so, as it is in individual therapy in the sense of creating good group cohesiveness, or of the group being "a team" or "a family." The relationship interactions are multiplied, perhaps by several fold, by the men in the groups. When men feel they are in a good group, they feel relaxed and more confident and they believe they can be more themselves and more self-availing. It is quite common to hear members say, "I really feel I can be myself, I can say what I want to say and still be accepted by you guys even if everything I say is not acceptable to everybody." These interactional processes that emanate from the cohesiveness of men's groups provide the opportunity for men to be open to learning from one another.

Catharsis

Like so many of the curative factors, catharsis is considered by many to be a necessary but not sufficient condition for personality change in men's therapy groups. This factor is much more important when people display strong emotions in the presence of symbolic characters in their lives as well as the important real people in the group (Andronico, 1998). One of the advantages of catharsis is that other men are able to witness the expression of feelings by other members of the group. In our society, it is often the men who tend to enforce the prohibition against strong feelings (other than anger) by men. The group setting provides the crucial opportunity for men to express their feelings and have them accepted and encouraged by other men.

The expression of emotion is often difficult, or perhaps even threatening, as so often men are taught to not be expressive of the emotions (and at times to not even know what feelings they are having). The group leader is able to provide an environment that is inviting of personal exploration of feelings, encourages the expression of those feelings, and provides support so that the feelings may be expressed without fear of rejection or reprisal, a most unusual circumstance in most men's lives. In the process of anger work, the male participants often get in touch with even deeper levels of emotion than they had been aware of, including recognition that the experiencing of anger is often the surface emotion covering deeper emotions, particularly shame and guilt. Without a safe and supportive environment, the expression of these emotions will not occur.

Existential Factors

The everyday concerns of existence such as death, isolation, freedom, and meaninglessness affect all human beings. Since men in our society usually struggle with a huge weight of responsibility, these existential issues are especially important to them. Men's groups, particularly discussion groups, offer the opportunity to deal with existential issues in conjunction with many other issues. In expressing their doubts, insecurities, and vulnerabilities, these existential issues are addressed.

MYTHS AND MISCONCEPTIONS ABOUT MEN'S GROUPS

While there is agreement that groups are a positive means for working with men and their issues (Rabinowitz, 2001), there are many misconceptions concerning the behavior of men in groups, particularly men's counseling/ therapy groups. Like many misconceptions, when these erroneous beliefs are held by a large group of people and spread, they assume the quality of a myth. Following are some misconceptions about men's groups and some clarification of why the beliefs or myths are erroneous. Many of the misconceptions came about from earlier writings about how therapy is an unmasculine activity (Goldberg, 1976; Hudson & Jacot, 1991; Kimmel, 1995), and a common belief among many therapists was that men would not engage well or benefit from traditional therapy (Rabinowitz, 2001).

Men Need Structure

One of the commonly assumed misconceptions is that a men's group needs a lot of structure (Jolliff & Horne, 1996). This assumes that men have difficulty and do not function well without a highly structured format, and that a lack of structure within the group will be stressful or uncomfortable. Given the variety of approaches to working with men in groups, it is difficult to form a generalization about structure in men's groups. The goals of the group help to determine what the structure of the group will be. Certain groups with specific goals, especially psychoeducational groups of 1-day, half-day, or even weekend duration, may be highly structured because of the nature of the group.

However, ongoing counseling or therapy groups where men get together to experience and express their feelings concerning their relationships with others and with the men in the group can often be quite unstructured and still be very effective (Andronico, 1996; Jolliff & Horne, 1996; Rabinowitz, 2001). Men often become very creative and develop their own structure to satisfy their particular needs. Some ongoing men's groups create structure through developing their own initial rituals (Andronico, 2001).

Even within the individualized structure of the group, men's groups often modify structures to meet their own needs. For example, one group had been discussing the importance of getting closer to and developing a newer appreciation of the beauty of nature. On a beautiful

Saturday morning, one of the group members said, "Why are we only talking about this? Maybe we can go into the park and experience the beauty of the day for half an hour and then come back to the office and discuss what our experiences were." The group readily agreed. When they returned, there was a lively discussion concerning their experiences. This discussion carried over into the following weeks.

In conducting groups for men, our experience is that two factors must be present in the group: an invitational approach and an assurance that the group will not use shame. A highly structured group appears to be less relevant for men than the engagement and support that is provided. When supervising trainees who are conducting men's groups, we often find that the need for structure is more a function of the inexperienced leader than of the members of the group.

Men Don't Emote

Behind this misconception is the assumption that men do not feel (Hudson & Jacot, 1991). One exception to this is the belief that men experience anger, an emotion that seems tied directly to the socialization of their gender role. Men do experience a wide range of feelings. Through various socialization and societal pressures, men learn not to express those feelings (Horne et al., 1996), and the socialization processes of children teach male social injunctions such as "Be a big wheel," "Don't be a sissy," "Give them hell," and "Be a sturdy oak" (Brannon, 1985).

Because of these injunctions, most men are in severe conflict concerning the expression of their wide range of feelings. Through the socialization process, men may get to the point where they suppress the expression of their feelings and stop experiencing many of their feelings. Those men who have not suppressed their own experience of their feelings often feel conflicted. Such conflict may be due to the fact that they are aware that they have strong feelings yet are told that there is something wrong with them if they do have these feelings. To ignore these social injunctions and to suppress their feelings leads to anxiety and then to a lack of practicing the experiencing and expressing of the feelings, even if they decide they want to express their feelings.

When men get together in groups, the idea of possessing a variety of different kinds of feelings is often one of the first subjects discussed. It is generally reassuring for men to discover that other men feel similarly in terms of inhibiting their feelings and not expressing them while at the same time having them.

Men often tend to be uncomfortable with their softer, more tender feelings (often called feminine feelings, though we disagree with this categorization, just as we reject the notion that when a woman expresses anger, she is being masculine). We find that even though men would like to discuss their feelings, especially their affectionate and more vulnerable feelings, they do not approach other men with these feelings for fear of being put down and otherwise shamed or humiliated (Horne et al., 1996; Hudson & Jacot, 1991). Often men think that they can only express personal feelings with women, or one woman in particular, often their girlfriends or wives. Our experience is that when men do get together in a group, they find comfort and much reassurance in being able to see that other men in the group are accepting their feelings. Once this happens, men tend to emote very deeply and consistently. Seeing others expressing their emotions becomes a permission-giving phenomenon to express these long suppressed feelings. Men tend to seize this permission and utilize it very effectively.

An example of using the group to facilitate male expression of feelings occurred in one of our groups:

Alex was still having trouble expressing his sadness over his father's death. In fact, Alex did not even mention to the group that his father had died three weeks ago because he knew it would only stimulate him to tear up. Derrick spoke to the group about his struggle with his wife. During Derrick's description of the problem, he broke down and began to cry. This was the first time anyone in the group had behaved in such a way. Toward the end of the session, Alex finally disclosed to the group, as he cried uncontrollably, that his father had died and he hoped to get support from the group. To his surprise, a number of the members were very supportive and shared their own experiences with the death of their relatives.

This illustrates the power of modeling and learning through observing the behavior of others. Some researchers believe that men seldom are exposed to other men expressing emotions other than anger and therefore never learned how to express such emotions when they experience them.

All Men's Groups
Are Really Anger Groups

This misconception is related to the myth discussed above, that men only have angry feelings. Given that misconception, it would follow logically that men's discussion groups would be filled with discussions of anger. This assumption, however, is inaccurate (Good & Sherrod, 2001).

It has been our experience that most men's groups address a wide range of feelings. Specific groups focus upon their stated themes, and so anger management groups concentrate on anger and how to deal with it. Other types of groups focus on issues specific to the group; for example, new fathers' groups or becoming a better father groups help men to improve their parenting skills. Aside from these specific topic- or theme-oriented groups, there are general men's discussion groups that have no specific focus. Men in these groups tend to display a wide range of feelings. Many men who are participating in a men's group for the first time are surprised at the amount of tenderness and warm nurturing feelings that other men discuss and display toward each other, especially the more experienced group members.

Fear and vulnerability, as well as shame, are often discussed in men's groups as well. These feelings center on men's own vulnerability as human beings and their fears of not being adequate in many areas of their lives. For example, one man in a workshop for expectant fathers hesitantly discussed his fears of not being able to adequately support his future daughter. Another member said, "I'm so happy to hear you say that. I feel the same way. In fact, all my life I've always felt carefree and confident. If I fail, I can pick myself up and go on. If I get hurt, so what, I'm strong and I can handle it. In fact, the main reason I was attracted to my wife was that she is so self-sufficient and independent.

But now, I am going to be a father and I feel I can't fail. I'm going to have a little helpless child depending upon me. I feel so vulnerable and under pressure!" A highly emotionally charged discussion followed that included many tears and reassuring hugs.

Men Are Too Competitive to Be
Supportive of Each Other in a Group

Men in general are socialized to be a "big wheel" (Brannon, 1985), which calls for high achievement and a competitive nature. Men, however, are socialized to work together on teams with common goals, such as athletic games and Boy Scout organizations. These activities, especially team sports, involve learning to work cooperatively and being supportive of one's teammates. Even in industrial settings where men are urged to achieve, much of what is necessary in attaining goals has to do with working together with other people on projects. Learning team methods and mutual cooperation is necessary for the achievement of these common goals, and men recognize that team effort works to achieve goals that individuals are not likely to accomplish.

Our experience is that during the course of men's discussion groups, men tend to be much more supportive and cooperative than many would assume, with competition playing a very small role. The absence of women in an all-male group is considered by many (Farrell, 1993; Hudson & Jacot, 1991) to be a very important factor. Often a man will make a statement such as "Now that I see that there are no women here that I have to prove myself to, I feel I can relax."

Men Aren't Interested in
Meeting With Other Men

The myth of the "loner" male who does everything by himself and does not need or want the support or companionship of other men is quite inaccurate, in our experience. Most men have a strong need to relate to others, especially other men. In a society that tends to discourage men from showing outward support for each other, this need has increased for many men because the opportunity for expression is rare (cf. Kimmel, 1995).

As society has changed in the last half century, a number of the societal structures that men used as opportunities to relate to each other have diminished, such as the all-male work setting as well as many other traditionally male experiences like the men's barbershop. Men gathered while waiting in a barbershop to talk in an informal manner without having to appear as if they were going out of their way to do this; they could speak without feeling ashamed or embarrassed. While the changing social structure includes greater involvement of mixed genders in various social settings, such as the workplace, unisex hair salons, and family activities or organized sports, males have often not replaced previous male-oriented settings with more current variations. The demise of the previous male bastions has not evolved into more socially endorsed male gatherings. What is mourned is not the loss of male power or male escapes, but the opportunity of men to gather and share.

Horne et al. (1996) and Jolliff and Horne (1996) have addressed this reduced opportunity for males to share time and experiences with one another in their chapters on males mentoring males. In their work, they have proposed that opportunities need to be offered for group mentoring, including men teaching men about effective nurturing, role modeling, initiating, mentoring, and eldering. As many traditional work and social activities of men have been reduced, there are often not enough opportunities developed, particularly in community and social settings for men to mentor other men.

Modern groups that have evolved to replace previous social gatherings include mythopoetic and male retreat models. The mythopoetic weekends that were given by Robert Bly (1990) and others, such as Michael Meade, James Hillman, and Joseph Campbell, attracted large gatherings of people for 1- or 2-day retreats. The Million Man March and the large football stadium meetings of the Promise Keepers are also indications of how important it is for males to gather together and relate with one another and to address spiritual needs. In those large gatherings, relating to other men is encouraged instead of discouraged. The proliferation of men's discussion groups also indicates that men do want and need to sit and talk with each other in groups in a structured setting that allows them to express their feelings and be supportive of themselves and each other.

Only Male Liberals Have a Need to Express Their Feelings With Other Men

Men who generally go for therapy are men who are fairly open-minded in their approach to dealing with problems (Brooks, 1996). This approach is usually regarded as being liberal in orientation, because males with a more conservative approach and attitude often do not seek therapy. Conservative men are then at times mistakenly regarded as not being interested in discussing their feelings, especially with other men. There are also those men who do not willingly seek therapy, but will go under pressure from their spouse, family, or legal system. Even these men will often benefit from participating in men's groups once they see the value of these discussions to others and they themselves feel safe.

The large numbers of men who have filled football stadiums to attend Promise Keepers is an example of the fact that these men, often conservative strict men, with very traditional and often a fundamentalist Christian point of view, do have a need to discuss their feelings and discuss them with other men. Even though the discussions in these types of gatherings are not typical of group counseling or therapy, these men do have a need to express their feelings to other men. It is likely that for attendees of such gatherings, there are needs to belong and be affirmed, particularly as men and by other men.

The Million Man March of minority men on Washington may also be regarded in the same way. There men were looking for a way to feel more connected to others, especially to men, and to feel more secure and adequate in their own eyes as well as the eyes of society. This gathering of men provided an opportunity to experience the connectedness, support, universality of the situation and to work toward solutions to the problems the men were encountering. The need to somehow feel better about themselves, feel more connected, less alienated, and certainly more adequate in society was evident in their gatherings. Men's counseling and therapy groups also offer at least a partial opportunity to satisfy some of these needs (Andronico, 2001).

How Groups Work Well

Individual work can be helpful, but men often feel self-conscious and risk feeling shame and humiliation when discussing their faults, insecurities, and vulnerabilities. This can sometimes be complicated by the client's competitive feelings. In groups, however, this is less likely to occur, or, when it does occur, it may be resolved by the group process.

Men are used to being with other men in groups with an external goal (e.g., Scouts, athletic teams, fraternities, military, university settings, AA groups and other 12-step programs, and industrial groups). They are often involved in activities that have goal-oriented tasks but involve very little face-to-face discussion. For example, in many athletic contests, the goal is to win the game. The means to achieve that goal may be to communicate in ways that show cooperation; however, the goal is not to communicate but to win. Men also may be involved in helping organizations such as the Kiwanis Club, the Lions Club, the Elks Club, and the Chamber of Commerce. The camaraderie that is involved and the cooperation in performing these tasks is significant and allows men to relate to each other more closely. However, the function of these organizations is to fix things about the society or in their communities. Men are socialized to work together in teams when there is a common task to be approached or problem to be resolved. Within the definition of these teams as helping groups or task-oriented groups, men are comfortable working together and can lower their defenses and feel comfortable in expressing their feelings.

One way of getting men into groups that are more task oriented rather than directly feeling oriented is through the use of psychoeducational groups (Andronico, 1996). Levant's (1996) chapter on a group for helping men to become better fathers is a good example of the initial focus being upon a goal (increasing fathering skills on the part of the men) and gradually transitioning to encouraging the men to express their own feelings concerning their role as fathers and their feelings about their own fathers. As the group progresses, the men become more comfortable with expressing their feelings.

Roles of the Leader

As in any type of group leadership, the roles the leader takes are determined by the goals of the group. Because there are many types of men's groups, it is difficult to talk about a rigid, stereotyped role of the leader. The following are more generic types of differences that are typical of leaders' roles in men's groups. They, of course, should be tailored to the specific goals and needs of each group. Numerous examples of specific roles for group leaders conducting groups with various presenting concerns are presented in Brooks and Good (2001).

Self-Disclosing. One aspect of the role of the leader is role modeling the particular image that the leader would like to portray. This involves self-disclosure on the part of the leader (Jolliff & Horne, 1996). It is important for members of the group to see that the leader still struggles with issues, even though he has addressed the concerns and explored his own masculinity and concerns related to being a male in today's society. Examples of how the leader has overcome some of his personal issues may be helpful to members of the group. The leader needs to be careful to model acceptance, hope, and encouragement rather than to use a condescending attitude. In this process, the timing and amount (depth and length) of disclosure used by the leader are important.

Structure. Many men's groups are of a shorter duration than ongoing psychotherapy groups; thus there may be a need to structure the focus of the group to have it move quickly (Jolliff & Horne, 1996; Rabinowitz, 2001). This is especially so in groups of 10-, 15-, or 20-session duration. It is also true in topic-focused groups such as How to Get Along Better in the Workplace or How to Improve Your Relationships With Women. In psychoeducational groups, the leader often needs to provide structure by arranging some educational materials for presentation at the beginning of each session. As the group progresses over time, the group leader may only need to provide 5 or 10 minutes of the session to get the group started on issues concerning the topic. The leader should then allow the group to participate in terms of freer or more open interaction. Beginning group leaders are often surprised at the creativity and wealth of talent that men display once they are given permission to express their feelings and have seen it modeled.

Different Forms of Men's Groups

Men's groups can have a variety of settings as well as lengths of time (Rabinowitz, 2001). They often meet weekly in a therapist's office, though some are offered as marathon groups going for a day or more or as a weekend retreat model. They can meet as an ongoing open-ended group, such as a group where a new member joins when another member finishes (Andronico, 1996). Groups can also be time limited with themes. Weekend groups such as the Somerset Men's Weekend (Andronico & Wissocki, 1996) usually meet in outdoor settings such as a retreat center. Such activities take advantage of the natural setting and have activities geared toward men getting in touch with nature and their own inner feelings, working toward integration and acceptance. Ongoing men's discussion groups may expand into a variety of activities, such as an ongoing group deciding to cease meeting with their group leader and meeting on their own.

The Role of Rituals in Men's Groups

Bernstein (1987) points out that groups in the past served the function of providing the indispensable setting for rituals and the rite of passage for men. This, he claims, played a crucial role in masculine individuation, which is now often replaced by inner symbols in men's psyche's such as dreams and obsessive behavior. Bernstein cites Henderson (1967), who puts forth three necessary conditions for male individuation:

1. Separation from the family of origin

2. Commitment to a "meaningful group" for an extended period of time

3. Freedom from becoming overly identified with the group, thus facilitating individuation

Many men's groups meet Henderson's (1967) three conditions for male individuation. Even though they are not specifically designed as male initiation, they symbolically or directly address these issues by helping a man to relate to the group of other men. This at least partly helps to support a man in individuating from his family of origin in an appropriate manner conducive to attaining maturity. It encourages a commitment to participate and help others and be helped by others. The group helps an individual to see his separateness from the group even though he is part of the group. This last step has to do with a more mature understanding that all people are different even though they may have commonalities.

Many men experience rituals in religious organizations, Scouts, and other childhood organizations. Rituals seem to provide men with significant meaning. Since many adult men have given up their institutional childhood religions, they often miss the value of rituals to help symbolically mark and emphasize a particular passage. By showing men that rituals can be used in nonreligious settings, men can become more comfortable responding to and integrating rituals. The concept of "sacred space" or ritual space often helps men in men's groups to recognize that this is not an ordinary experience that they are undergoing but one that is of particular value and meaning to them (Andronico, 2001). In an outdoor setting such as weekend retreats, symbols such as feathers, animal skulls, or antlers can often add an expansive dimension to the groups that men attend. It lends the feeling of belonging to a tribe, which enhances the concept of feeling that one is in a community. Native Americans call the burning of sage smudging. Smudging is commonly used in retreats in the outdoors when one is leaving the sacred space of the lodge or entering it. This ritual further emphasizes that this is an extraordinary rather than an ordinary event. and the men tend to be more focused and respectful of themselves and others during this event. In addition to smudging in the outdoors, some therapists use smudging as a way of entering the therapist's office.

Redundant drumming is another important part of the ritual in many men's groups. In the outdoors, some men's groups will have every man use a drum and drum together. However, it is not crucial that every man has a drum; some groups have one or two drums and men can alternate using them. Drumming can also be used as a marker when men are assigned a task to perform outdoors. The drum may be used in this situation as a symbol of their departure into the woods. Because some men go far distances from the cabin, the drums can be a way of calling them back when the activity is over.

An opening ritual common to many men's discussion groups is the 2-minute check-in. This is an opening ritual in which each member tells the others of their news since the last session and whether or not they wish to have more time to talk once the initial go-round or check-in is over. The talking stick is another ritualistic method; the groups that employ this talking stick give the stick to whoever wishes to speak. No one else is to talk until the speaker gives up the talking stick to the next speaker. This helps to prevent interruptions and maintain members' interest.

Diversity Among Men

There is a wide diversity among ethnic groups in terms of the ways that they react to certain issues and feelings, and the needs of the differing ethnic and racial groups have been expressed in a number of handbooks and reviews (Andronico, 1996; Brooks & Good, 2001; Horne & Kiselica, 1999). Culture influences the way that certain groups of men interact (e.g., African Americans, Latinos, Asians, gays). Rather than going into detail about each of these different ways of approaching community, it is important to understand and be able to differentiate between what is a cultural difference and tendency as opposed to an individual one. The group leader's role in connection with this is important. The group leader needs to be aware of his feelings and reactions, as well as being aware of differences among men, and to be accepting and tolerant of these differences. By role-modeling this acceptance, he helps the group members to expand their own tolerance and acceptance of differences among other people. It also helps the men to tolerate differences and feelings among themselves. Arcaya (1996), Sue et al. (1996), and Sutton (1996) have described a variety of differences within subgroups of men such as Hispanic, Asian, and African Americans. For leaders of men's groups, it is essential that they are familiar not only with effective processes of conducting groups in general but also how the issues of men require specialized focus, and beyond that, how the role of ethnicity influences the interpretation of men in groups. It is not possible to know every nuance and subtlety within every cultural and racial group, but it is important to have a generic idea as to what may motivate and offend certain groups of men, as well as how to focus the issues of men within the group setting, regardless of background and culture.

SUMMARY

Groups for men require that the group leader have experience in the various models of group work, including task or work groups, psychoeducational groups, counseling groups, and therapy groups. The leader must be current on issues of male development and changing social roles for men and the problems inherent in those shifting definitions today. There are a number of myths or misconceptions about why men do not work well in therapy, particularly in groups, but any barriers to effective treatment of men in groups may be addressed by understanding how groups can be used to facilitate growth rather than as an instrument of shame or coercion.

There has now been nearly two decades of research on men and male issues and how to address those in groups. Facilitators of men's groups need to be familiar not only with the theoretical underpinnings of the work with men, but also become acquainted with the specific techniques and skills necessary to effectively facilitate the growth and connection of men in groups, ranging from such broad issues as ethnicity, to specific skills such as the use of the talking stick in therapy. In this chapter, many excellent resources are referenced to guide the group practitioner, and the need for the services remains high.

REFERENCES

Andronico, M. P. (1996). *Men in groups: Insights, interventions, and psychoeducational work.*

Washington, DC: American Psychological Association.

Andronico, M. P. (1998). Resolving distortions of the self in group therapy via the chronological elevator and readmission therapy. *Journal of Redecision Therapy, 1,* 58-69.

Andronico, M. P. (2001). Mythopoetic and weekend retreats to facilitate men's growth. In G. R. Brooks & G. E. Good (Eds.), *The new handbook of psychotherapy and counseling with men* (pp. 664-682). San Francisco: Jossey-Bass.

Andronico, M. P., & Wissocki, G. (1996). The Somerset Institutes modern men's weekend. In M. P. Andronico (Ed.), *Men in groups: Insights, interventions, and psychoeducational work* (pp. 113-136). Washington, DC: American Psychological Association.

Arcaya, J. M. (1996). The Hispanic male in group psychotherapy. In M. P. Andronico (Ed.), *Men in groups: Insights, interventions, and psychoeducational work* (pp. 21-31). Washington, DC: American Psychological Association,.

Bernstein, J. S. (1987). The decline of rites of passage in our culture: The impact on masculine individuation. In L. C. Mahdi, S. Foster, & M. Little (Eds.), *Betwixt & between* (pp. 135-158). Chicago: Open Court.

Bly, R. (1990). *Iron John: A book about men.* Reading, MA: Addison-Wesley.

Brannon, R. (1985). A scale for measuring attitudes about masculinity. In A. Sargent (Ed.), *Beyond sex roles* (pp. 110-116). St. Paul, MN: West.

Brooks, G. R. (1996). Treatment for therapy-resistant men. In M. Andronico (Ed.), *Men in groups: Insights, interventions, and psychoeducational work* (pp. 7-19). Washington, DC: American Psychological Association.

Brooks, G. R., & Good, G. E. (2001). *The new handbook of psychotherapy and counseling with men.* San Francisco: Jossey-Bass.

Brooks, G. R., & Silverstein, L. B. (1995). Understanding the dark side of masculinity: An integrative systems model. In R. Levant & W. Pollack (Eds.), *A new psychology of men* (pp. 280-333). New York: Basic Books.

Farrell, W. T. (1993). *The myth of male power.* New York: Simon & Schuster.

Goldberg, H. (1976). *The hazards of being male.* New York: New American Library.

Good, G., & Sherrod, N. (2001). Men's problems and effective treatments: Theory and empirical

support. In G. Brooks & G. Good (Eds.), *The new handbook of psychotherapy and counseling with men.* (pp. 22-40). San Francisco: Jossey-Bass.

Henderson, J. (1967). *Thresholds of initiation.* Middletown, CT: Wesleyan University Press.

Horne, A., Jolliff, D., & Roth, E. (1996). Men mentoring men in groups. In M. Andronico (Ed.), *Men in groups: Insights, interventions, and psychoeducational work* (pp. 97-112). Washington, DC: American Psychological Association.

Horne, A., & Kiselica, M. (1999). *Handbook of counseling boys and adolescent males.* Thousand Oaks, CA: Sage.

Hudson, L., & Jacot, B. (1991). *The way men think.* New Haven, CT: Yale University Press.

Jolliff, D., & Horne, A. (1996). Group counseling for middle-class men. In M. Andronico (Ed.), *Men in groups: Insights, interventions, and psychoeducational work* (pp. 51-68). Washington, DC: American Psychological Association.

Kimmel, M. S. (1995). *The politics of manhood.* Philadelphia: Temple University Press.

Levant, R. F. (1990). Psychological services designed for men: A psychoeducational approach. *Psychotherapy, 27,* 309-315.

Levant, R. F. (1996). The male code and parenting: A psychoeducational approach. In M. Andronico (Ed.), *Men in groups: Insights, interventions, and psychoeducational work* (pp. 229-242). Washington, DC: American Psychological Association.

Pleck, J. H. (1995). The gender role strain paradigm: An update. In R. Levant & W. Pollack (Eds.), *A new psychology of men* (pp. 11-32). New York: Basic Books.

Pleck, J. H., & Sawyer, J. (1980). *Men and masculinity.* Englewood Cliffs, NJ: Prentice Hall.

Rabinowitz, F. (2001). Group therapy with men. In G. Brooks & G. Good (Eds.), *The new handbook of psychotherapy and counseling with men* (pp. 603-621). San Francisco: Jossey-Bass.

Sue, D. W., Ivey, A. E., & Pederson, P. B. (1996). *A theory of multicultural counseling and therapy.* Pacific Grove, CA: Brooks/Cole.

Sutton, A. (1996). African American men in group therapy. In M. P. Andronico (Ed.), *Men in groups: Insights, interventions, and psychoeducational work* (pp. 131-150). Washington, DC: American Psychological Association.

Yalom, I. D. (1995). *The theory and practice of group psychotherapy* (4th ed.). New York: Basic Books.

34

GROUP COUNSELING WITH OLDER ADULTS

DONNA A. HENDERSON

Wake Forest University

SAMUEL T. GLADDING

Wake Forest University

By the year 2030, the number of people aged 65 and older will constitute about 20% of the U.S. population (Administration on Aging, 1998). The existing mental health services for the elderly population are inadequate for this demand (Knight, 1996). Sadovy, Lazarus, Jarvik, and Grossberg (1996) estimated that approximately 2.7% of clinical services are provided to older adults, even though that group represents more than 11% of the population. Among other things, older adults may not seek mental health services because of cost, transportation difficulties, and other complications. Mental health professionals may fail to offer services because of the perception of poor prognosis for success, inadequate training, and stereotypes of older adults as lower status and unworthy recipients of treatment (Sarason & Sarason, 1996). Group work is one way to help bridge the gap between the mental health needs of a growing population of older people and the availability of essential services needed by them.

In order to make such a bridge possible, counselors must identify the special needs of elders and determine if they can be ameliorated through group activities. Schwiebert and Myers (2001) stated that recruiting, selecting, planning, and implementing groups with older people are essential components of working with them.

This chapter contains information counselors can use to lead effective groups with older adults. First, the chapter identifies the special needs of the elderly that support the efficacy of group counseling. Next, the discussion focuses on types of groups and the implementation of group work. Finally, the chapter explains the roles of the group leader and consider the strengths and limitations of groups.

SPECIAL NEEDS OF OLDER ADULTS IN GROUPS

Older adults have special needs that are developmental and situational in nature. One of these is the simple acceptance of moving from midlife to old age. Adults who are age 65 and older are considered "senior citizens" regardless of how they look, feel, or act, even though many have a quarter of their lives left to live (Cowley, 1997). Often, healthy older adults have difficulty accepting the labels they are given because of the incongruity of how they perceive themselves and how society as a whole views them.

In addition to this personal difficulty, Walsh (1988) acknowledges that married older people often have unique concerns. These concerns center around the fact that these couples usually experience increased marital satisfaction and intimacy and yet realize that they have only a limited time left to be a couple. Similarly, the elderly usually pay more attention to their religious and spiritual life and have a sense of well-being and meaningfulness (Levin, Taylor, & Chatters, 1994; McFadden & Atchley, 2001). Yet, they are acutely aware that they have a limited time left to live. Likewise, grandparenting and strong ties to their children provide other sources of enrichment and pleasure (Mead, 1972; Streib & Beck, 1981) but paradoxically with the realization that such joy will last for a limited time. Thus, with the positives of old age, including wisdom and integrity (Erikson, 1963), is the psychological paradox that these benefits of life are limited in a way unknown in earlier years.

Some other common physiological and psychological concerns that older adults share involve declines in health and overall functioning, loneliness, loss, fear, and hopelessness (Corey & Corey, 2002; France, 1984; Whitbourne, 2002). Feelings of worthlessness may result as older people lose control over their lives and their social position (Zarit, Pearlin, & Schaie, 2002). Older men may have trouble adapting to retirement. Age does not erase the complications that race, poverty, and gender may bring to life experiences. Himes, Hogan, and Eggebeen (1996) recognized that the poor and cultural minorities would continue to suffer discrimination and an inability to meet many of their basic needs during later life. The addition of ageism as a negative social force further complicates those difficulties and may tarnish any elder's sense of pride (Palmore, 1999). The loss of one's life partner may also cause difficulties for an older person. Yet another challenge to later years is facing one's own mortality. Some of these concerns may be best addressed in group counseling sessions.

BENEFITS OF GROUPS FOR OLDER ADULTS

Groups have a number of benefits for older adults. A primary thing groups may do is to promote mental health in older adults. For instance, Gatz (1989) identified the following as mechanisms of change that improve the mental health of elders: (a) fostering a sense of control, self-efficacy, and hope, (b) establishing relationships, (c) providing or clarifying a sense of meaning for the events of life, (d) promoting educational activities and the development of skills, and (e) finding new ways of coping. All of these may be goals of group activities with older adults.

Other advantages of group work with older people include reducing loneliness, increasing social interactions, and normalizing the process of aging (Schwiebert & Myers, 2001). Groups may also help aging adults overcome depression, anger, and loss of meaning that can be associated with the transitions of growing older (Blazer, 2002; Thomas & Martin, 1992). The very interpersonal nature of groups can be therapeutic for the elderly, particularly ones who are isolated and lonely.

TYPES OF GROUPS FOR OLDER ADULTS

Two types of groups for the elderly are those that focus on advocacy and those that focus on remediation (including prevention and psychoeducation).

Advocacy Groups

Advocacy groups provide an informal support system as well as coalitions to disseminate information. In the two most prominent of the advocacy groups for older adults, the members enroll themselves. Those two groups are the Gray Panthers and the American Association of Retired Persons (AARP). The Gray Panthers, organized both locally and nationally, address issues confronting seniors such as health care, jobs with a living wage, Social Security preservation, affordable housing, access to quality education, economic justice, the environment, peace, and challenging discrimination (Gray Panthers, 2003).

AARP is the largest nonprofit organization in the United States. This group is dedicated to the interests of mature Americans. It works in groups by advocacy, education, and community service activities (AARP, 2003). Many elders find meaning and services by belonging to these large and very powerful groups.

These two groups offer older adults several ways to participate in advocacy efforts that may increase the quality of life for the aging. From that participation, the members foster their sense of control and self-efficacy. Their cooperation with other members promotes relationships and helps them develop skills.

Remediation Groups

The major remedial groups for older people include those that are labeled (a) reality orientation, (b) remotivation therapy, (c) reminiscence focused, (d) topic-specific, and (e) member-specific (Beaver, 1983; Burnside, 1984; Capuzzi & Gross, 1980; Wellman & McCormack, 1984). The first three groups have been designed to help mentally impaired older people improve their living situation. The last two have a more psychoeducational, preventive nature (Myers, 1989).

Reality-Oriented Groups

Reality-oriented groups are designed for elders who have become disoriented to their surroundings. The groups emphasize members becoming more aware of their present environment in terms

of time, place, and people (Burnside, 1984). The goal of this type of group is to limit further deterioration (Thomas & Martin, 1992). Groups are limited to three or four participants when disorientation is severe. For less disoriented individuals, groups may include seven or eight people. As basic orientation to the surroundings is mastered, the members progress to more creative and practical activities (Capuzzi & Gross, 1980, 1990). The groups meet daily, usually in institutional settings, such as nursing homes. Sessions may include sensory training, group exercises, or practical skills (Taulbee, 1978). Group members may begin with information about time, date, place, and daily events. As these matters are mastered, topics may expand to include things like self-care, locating different objects in their living quarters, and social interactions with other group members. This process of becoming more oriented to their surroundings may also include the group participants being monitored and supported beyond the group sessions by the institutional staff who reinforce the skills being practiced.

As stated earlier, the reality-oriented groups focus on basic skills and education. Often minimal training in group dynamics is required for helping professionals to be leaders of reality-oriented groups. Leaders may be nursing staff, paraprofessionals, social workers, or counselors. The limited training of leaders may be one reason the empirical evidence for the success of this type of group is limited. Another reason may be the type of the clients who compose the groups (Zimpfer, 1987). Clients are selected based on their mental impairment interfering with everyday tasks. Potential group members are screened for cognitive functioning, sensory deficits, memory loss, mobility, and attention span (Thomas & Martin, 1992).

Remotivation Group

The goal of remotivation therapy groups is to help older clients become more invested in the present and future. Group members are those who have lost interest in any time period other than the past. Dennis (1978) recommended that participants be selected for their ability to relate to others, their willingness to join the group, and the lack of distorted memories. Groups are usually limited to 15 members. The group sessions focus on topics such as gardening, art, holidays, or other nonpathological topics. Group members are encouraged to respond appropriately to other members and to the materials that are presented. The goal is for the participants to gain more cognitive organization and to increase their socializing skills.

Remotivation groups follow five basic steps:

1. "The climate of acceptance": creating a warm, friendly relationship in the group

2. "A bridge to reality": reading, keeping up with current events, investigating ideas

3. "Sharing the world": developing an identified topic through leading questions, use of props, and planned activities

4. "An appreciation of the work of the world": encouraging the participants to think about themselves in terms of work or avocational interests

5. "The climate of appreciation": finding joy through the companionship of the group (Beaver, 1983, p. 240)

Burnside (1984) and Zimpfer (1987), in reviews of the literature, report positive empirical results for remotivation therapy groups. Members of such groups practice describing themselves realistically and concretely. In addition, they are stimulated to remember and relate to others accurately. Finally, through the group they are prepared for being involved in other group programs (Dennis, 1978).

Reminiscing Groups

Reminiscing groups originated in the 1960s and are based on the importance of "life review" (Butler, 1961; Ebersole, 1978; Garland & Garland, 2001). These groups are designed to help participants who are in later stages of life understand and appreciate more fully who they are and where they have been. Kennedy and Tanenbaum (2000) explained that rather than focusing on social skills, these groups aim at increasing life satisfaction. DeVries, Birren, and Deutchman (1995) suggest nine themes to guide reminiscing groups:

1. History of the major branching points in life

2. Family history

3. Career or major life work

4. The role of money in life

5. Health and body image

6. Loves and hates

7. Sexual identity, sex roles, and sexual experience

8. Experiences with ideas about death and dying and other losses

9. Influences, beliefs, and values that provide meaning in life

Individuals in these groups share memories, increase their personal integration, and become more aware of their lives and of others their age. According to Lewis and Butler (1984), the insight they gain helps the elders deepen their understanding of their finiteness and prepare for their death. These groups also provide opportunities for social intimacy (Singer, Tracz, & Dworkin, 1991). Other reported benefits include more positive moods, increased self-esteem, more life satisfaction, uncovered meaning of life, and enhanced feeling of competence and control (Goldwasser, Auerbach, & Harkins, 1987; Thomas & Martin, 1997).

Ebersole (1978) suggested that potential group members be told the purpose and format the reminiscing group will follow and members be allowed to make a commitment to be involved in the group. Participation should be voluntary, with each member's autonomy respected. Groups hold six to eight members and group sessions are held for approximately 1 hour, once or twice a week. Capuzzi and Gross (1990) assert that group members should be free to continue or leave the group after several sessions. Leaders may stimulate the group discussion by the use of mental imagery (Sherman, 1987), music, visual props, or objects that group members bring to the group (Gladding, 1998).

Memories provide ways to communicate with other group members at the same life stage.

All the group participants profit from the insights that occur as members review their lives. Members also benefit from increasing their interpersonal involvement and social skills. They may also integrate their life experiences and discover a greater acceptance about themselves. Like the remotivation groups, reminiscing groups can be springboards for other group experiences or the only group experience.

PREVENTIVE AND PSYCHOEDUCATIONAL GROUPS

Other psychoeducational and counseling groups for the elderly focus on the remediation of specific problems faced by the group, such as role changes, isolation, physical decline, and fear of the future (Alholtz, 1978; Weisman & Schwartz, 1989). Maynard (1980) described elderly clients who are referred to mental health services as often depressed, agitated and disruptive, or confused about their world.

Topic-Specific Groups

Topic-specific groups focus on a particular subject such as widowhood, bibliotherapy, sexuality, health, grandparenting, or the arts. Beaver (1983) notes that these psychoeducational groups are designed to improve the quality of daily life. The groups help the aged find more meaning in their worlds. The members establish a support group of people who have similar interests. The group leaders need knowledge of the subject being explored (Myers, 1989). Group membership is generally voluntary. Topic specific groups often result in improved self-esteem, enhanced skills, and encouragement from the social interaction (Burnside, 1984; Capuzzi & Gross, 1980; Vacha-Haase, Ness, Dannison, & Smith, 2000). Groups focusing on musical activities are helpful in encouraging movement, drawing out depressed or withdrawn clients, and increasing enjoyment and contentment (Burnside, 1978).

Member-Specific Groups

Member-specific groups focus more on specific transitions of the individual members such as grief, hospitalization, or institutionalized day care. These groups may be held for older adults or for members of their families (Capuzzi & Gross, 1980). The groups for the elderly aim at helping them recognize and face common concerns of aging such as loss of physical strength (Peck, 1968) or the effect of illnesses (Sullivan, Coffey, & Greenstein, 1987).

Schuster (1998) used therapeutic writing groups for residents in nursing homes. She found those in the writing group had a more positive identity and improved their family and social relationships. The group sessions included members sharing their writings to reveal their thoughts and feelings. Mazza and Vinton (1999) studied the prevalence of group work in nursing homes. They found that most of the 304 respondents offered educational, support, and therapy/counseling groups for their elderly residents.

Other benefits of member-specific groups besides those just mentioned include emotional adjustment to life stresses and personal problems (Bledsoe & Lutz-Ponder, 1986), decreased feelings of fear, loneliness, and anxiety (Capuzzi & Gross, 1990), and the advantages of shared concerns (Burnside, 1984).

IMPLEMENTING GROUPS FOR OLDER ADULTS

Groups for the elderly, as all other groups, should be thoughtfully proposed. Furr (2000) provides a framework of six steps for structuring groups for people of all ages. The first step includes a statement of purpose that explains the reason for the group. Next, goals are clearly established. Objectives that identify how the goals will be accomplished are then formulated. The further steps include organizing group content, designing exercises, and planning evaluation. Therapeutically oriented groups require pregroup screening. Group leaders may also want to plan a warm-up activity or brief introduction for the beginning of each group session to help group members, especially those who may be elderly or forgetful, understand the focus for the day (Capuzzi & Gross, 1980).

Some groups for the elderly are conducted in institutions; more often the groups are conducted on an outpatient or outreach basis (Gladding, 2002). Whatever the setting or focus, the following procedures guide the preparation of group work with the aged.

The physical environment of the meeting must be considered. The meeting room should be geared for function, comfort, and quiet. An ideal location would be a ground-floor room with upholstered chairs, good lighting, space for wheelchairs, close to a bathroom, and with a steady temperature around 75 degrees (Capuzzi & Gross, 1980; Hendrix & Sedgwick, 1989). The setting should accommodate members sitting in a close circle not only to aid the members who have hearing impairment but also to create a sense of cohesiveness (Stone & Waters, 1991).

People who are planning groups for the aged must give attention to scheduling. Groups scheduled for early evenings would be difficult to attend for the elderly who have problems with night driving or early bedtimes. To maximize participation, group leaders need to investigate the schedules of potential members and establish group meeting times around those schedules. Most groups for the elderly are arranged to be close-ended in order to build trust and to develop empathy (Capuzzi & Gross, 1980; Hendrix & Sedgwick, 1989). Groups in institutional settings or support groups may have an open-ended format (Folken, 1991; Yalom, 1995).

A third consideration is the physical ability of group members. A feeling of social isolation in the elderly may be exacerbated if they have physical disabilities or sensory impairments. Those difficulties may inhibit their participation in a group (Myers, 1990). Members who have limited sensory and mobility functions may need special treatment. A multimodal method that includes verbal and nonverbal ways of conveying information is one way to accommodate those needs. As an example, Yaretzky and Levinson (1996) described a process for using clay as a tool for group processing with the elderly. Technology may allow another way to decrease social isolation by elderly people participating in groups that meet via computer. Chapter 43 in this handbook discusses the use of online groups.

Burnside (1978) identifies other factors needing attention when planning a group for the elderly:

- Groups for older adults tend to have fewer members (four to eight people) than other groups because of scheduling problems and physical limitations such as hearing loss or a lack of physical mobility. Remotivation therapy groups that may have as many as 15 members are the exception.
- Physical environment is more important to the well-being of the group and its members than in other age-level groups. For some groups with older people, adding physical exercise to other group activities may be beneficial (Burlew, Jones, & Emerson, 1991).
- Elderly group members are encouraged to socialize outside the group setting.
- Themes across all groups for the elderly are growth and enhancement. With these groups, encouragement is more appropriate than confrontation.
- Older adults may be slower in trusting others than people in other age groups (Waters, McCarroll, & Penman, 1987). One reason for this distrust may be the belief that negative secrets should not be shared and that others cannot understand one's personal struggles.

ROLE OF THE LEADER IN GROUPS FOR OLDER ADULTS

Storandt (1983) stated that almost all major theoretical approaches may be used in working with the aged. The role of the leader in groups for the elderly depends on the theory followed, the type of group to be led, the leader's previous experience and abilities, and the readiness of the members. Prospective leaders can use the sets proposed by Hawkins (1983) for preparing to lead a group. These sets are basic but important.

Read. Leaders can study books and articles specific to the issues of the older adult in order to become more objective. Helpful information can be found in reviews of the literature on groups for the elderly in scholarly journals such as Myers, Poidevant, and Dean (1991).

Examine. Leaders also need to examine their own prejudices and stereotypes of the aged. Folken (1991) notes that leaders who grew up in a culture that valued youth or staying young may have difficulty in working with the elderly and their concerns. Leaders who have negative perceptions about older adults may be detrimental to the groups and should be replaced.

Meet. Leaders may identify their own perspective on the lives of older adults by remembering their experiences with the elderly within their own family of origin. Leaders can also learn about older people by visiting them.

Fantasize. Leaders can imagine their lives in the future and become more cognizant of their own hopes and fears.

Learn. Group leaders need to know about the social, educational, and political resources available to the elderly on the national, state, and local level.

Care. Leaders must have compassion for the elderly and must communicate that they care (Myers et al., 1991).

Leaders of groups for the elderly recognize that the pace of the groups may be slower and the goals more limited than for other groups. Myers et al. (1991) recommend that leaders compensate by being accepting, reminding group members of their positive changes, and encouraging continued participation. The key variables to effective group leadership with the elderly are the integration of one's own life, professional knowledge of aging, and familiarity with the group processes that will best help group relationships.

Strengths and Limitations of Groups for Older Adults

Older people who participate in groups receive many benefits. The increase in quantity and quality of interpersonal relationships are major benefits of the experience (Horswill, 1993). Other advantages are universality, experimentation, learning, and enhanced self-concept (Gladding, 2002; Yalom, 1995).

Through sharing in a group, members increase their awareness of personal needs, common concerns, individuality, and possibilities. They find support and reach resolutions to their concerns. Through sharing, the group members develop a sense of community and belongingness (Thomas, 1991). Gaining a sense of the universal nature of their issues is also a benefit of the group experience. Realizing that they are not the only ones concerned with body image, physical ailments, and fears of losing cognitive capacity can give comfort to members of groups (Hawkins, 1983). The atmosphere of universality contributes to wellness.

Another benefit of a group for the elderly is a forum for experimenting with different responses and new behaviors. Wrenn (1989) calls these opportunities "growing times," when new learning occurs individually and interpersonally. The process may involve an appreciation of past, present, or future encounters. Within a group, older individuals can try out a new response, fulfilling a sense of their ideal and a more positive view of themselves.

O'Brien, Johnson, and Miller (1979) identified that groups for older adults enhance self-concept. In groups, the elderly can be helped to focus on advantages of aging. They may find comfort in integrating different aspects of their lives. These reflections and continued involvement foster hope, the antithesis of depression. Members may then find ways to continue to be contributors to society.

Other benefits of groups for the elderly are the checks and balances of the group. Mardoyan and Weis (1981) explain that group members shift responsibility for growth from caretakers to group members. Group participants take control of their current lives and resolve past difficulties as best they can. The emphasis on growth comes from the interactions in the group. Elders learn to focus more on their choices, ways to optimize their opportunities, and ways to compensate for factors related to aging (Baltes & Baltes, 1990).

Some limitations of groups for older adults have also been identified. For instance, leaders may find the intensive labor and difficulty finding appropriate physical facilities taxing. The specialized skills and heightened sensitivities to life and death issues needed to lead groups with aging populations may be draining too. Leaders may also be frustrated by more limited goals of this age level as well as with members who may have more limited abilities in carrying out goals.

Finally, working with the caretakers of elderly group members may add stress to the leader's life because of the added physical effort usually needed to conduct such groups and because of the mental reminder through running the group that one may reach the age of those now in the group.

SUMMARY AND CONCLUSION

The elderly have unique concerns and potential. Their wealth of experiences, assets, and talents are too often overlooked. Working within groups provides a way to promote the positive aspects as well as to cope with the difficulties of aging. Group work with the aged has little history, although the research and approaches are becoming more refined (Myers, 1989; Myers et al., 1991). Combining children and the elderly in intergenerational group work (Pinquart, Wenzel, & Sorensen, 2000) is an example of one innovation in the field. Yet questions remain about the most effective ways of working with older adults.

Social connections and encouragement provided by groups help older adults integrate their lives, find support, and develop a sense of universality. Groups help battle loneliness and isolation, orient members to time and place, and provide opportunities for growth as well.

The leader's background and the participants' needs guide the arrangements for groups with the elderly. Many of the procedures for establishing groups mirror those found in working with other populations. However, group leaders must pay attention to time factors, group focus, and themes particular to aging. Horswill (1993) cautions leaders to include activities that will interest men and women, such as social and task-related opportunities. Whatever the challenges faced, leaders of groups for the elderly will discover they can promote positive interactions and development within the participants.

Helping older adults maintain their mental health, celebrate their lives, and enhance their current existence is rewarding for group leaders, members, and society. Group work of many types has a definite place in the lives of the elderly!

REFERENCES

Administration on Aging. (1998). *Profile of older Americans.* Washington, DC: Author.

Altholz, J. A. S. (1978). Group psychotherapy with the elderly. In I. M. Burnside (Ed.), *Working with the elderly: Group process and techniques* (pp. 354-370). North Scituate, MA: Duxbury.

American Association of Retired Persons. (2003). Retrieved from http://www.aarp.org/aarpfaq.html.

Baltes, P. B., & Baltes, M. M. (Eds.). (1990). *Successful aging: Perspectives from the behavioral sciences.* New York: Cambridge University Press.

Beaver, M. L. (1983). *Human service practice with the elderly.* Upper Saddle River, NJ: Prentice Hall.

Blazer, D. (2002). *Depression in late life* (3rd ed.). New York: Springer.

Bledsoe, N., & Lutz-Ponder, P. (1986). Group counseling with nursing home residents. *Journal for Specialists in Group Work, 11,* 37-41.

Burlew, L. D., Jones, J., & Emerson, P. (1991). Exercise and the elderly: A group counseling approach. *Journal for Specialists in Group Work, 16,* 152-158.

Burnside, I. M. (1978). Responsibilities of the preceptor. In I. M. Burnside (Ed.), *Working with the elderly: Group processes and techniques* (pp. 88-100). North Scituate, MA: Duxbury.

Burnside, I. M. (1984). *Working with the elderly: Group processes and techniques* (2nd ed.). Monterey, CA: Wadsworth.

Butler, R. N. (1961). The life review: An interpretation of reminiscence in the aged. *Psychiatry, 26,* 65-76.

Capuzzi, D., & Gross, D. (1980). Group work with the elderly: An overview for counselors. *Personnel and Guidance Journal, 59,* 206-211.

Capuzzi, D., & Gross, D. (1990). Recent trends in group work with elders. *Generations, 14,* 43-49.

Corey, M. S., & Corey, G. (2002). *Groups: Process and practice* (6th ed.). Pacific Grove, CA: Brooks/Cole.

Cowley, G. (1997, June 30). How to live to 100. *Newsweek,* 56-67.

Dennis, H. (1978). Remotivation therapy groups. In I. M. Burnside (Ed.), *Working with the elderly: Group processes and techniques* (pp. 219-235). North Scituate, MA: Duxbury.

DeVries, B., Birren, J. E., & Deutchman, D. E. (1995). Methods and uses of the guided autobiography. In

B. K. Haight & J. D. Webster (Eds.), *The art and science of reminiscing* (pp. 165-177). Philadelphia: Taylor & Francis.

Ebersole, P. P. (1978). A theoretical approach to the use of reminiscence. In I. M. Burnside (Ed.), *Working with the elderly: Group processes and techniques* (pp. 139- 154). North Scituate, MA: Duxbury.

Erikson, E. H. (1963). *Childhood and society* (2nd ed.). New York: Norton.

Folken, M. H. (1991). The importance of group support for widowed persons. *Journal for Specialists in Group Work, 16,* 172-177.

France, M. H. (1984). Responding to loneliness: Counselling the elderly. *Canadian Counsellor, 18,* 123-129.

Furr, S. (2000). Structuring psychoeducational groups. *Journal for Specialists in Group Work, 25,* 29-49.

Garland, J., & Garland, C. (2001). *Life review: The process of knowing yourself.* New York: Brunner-Routledge.

Gatz, M. (1989). Clinical psychology and aging. In M. Storandt & G. R. VandenBos (Eds.), *The adult years: Continuity and change.* Washington, DC: American Psychological Association.

Gladding, S. T. (1998). *Counseling as an art: The creative arts in counseling* (2nd ed.). Alexandria, VA: American Counseling Association.

Gladding, S. T. (2002). *Group work: A counseling specialty* (4th ed.). Upper Saddle River, NJ: Prentice Hall.

Goldwasser, A. N., Auerbach, S. M., & Harkins, S. W. (1987). Cognitive, affective, and behavioral effects of reminiscence group therapy on demented elderly. *International Journal of Aging and Human Development, 25,* 209-222.

Gray Panthers. (2003). Retrieved from http://www.graypanthers.org.

Hawkins, B. L. (1983). Group counseling as a treatment modality for the elderly: A group snapshot. *Journal for Specialists in Group Work, 8,* 186-193.

Hendrix, F. G., & Sedgwick, C. (1989). Group counseling with the elderly. In G. M. Gazda (Ed.), *Group counseling: A developmental approach* (pp. 195-211). Boston: Allyn & Bacon.

Himes, C. L., Hogan, D. P., & Eggebeen, D. J. (1996). Living arrangements of minority elders. *Journal of Gerontology, 51A,* 542-548.

Horswill, R. K. (1993). Are typical senior center group activities better suited for women than for men? *Journal for Specialists in Group Work, 18,* 45-48.

Kennedy, G. J., & Tanenbaum, S. (2000). Psychotherapy with older adults. *American Journal of Psychotherapy, 54,* 386-407.

Knight, B. G. (1996). *Psychotherapy with older adults* (2nd ed.). Newbury Park, CA: Sage.

Levin, J. S., Taylor, R. J., & Chatters, L. M. (1994). Race and gender differences in religiosity among older adults: Findings from four national surveys. *Journal of Gerontology, 49,* S137-S145.

Lewis, M. I., & Butler, R. N. (1984). Life-review therapy: Putting memories to work. In I. M. Burnside (Ed.), *Working with the elderly: Group processes and techniques* (2nd ed.) (pp. 50-59). Monterey, CA: Wadsworth.

Mardoyan, J. L., & Weis, D. M. (1981). The efficacy of group counseling with older adults. *Personnel and Guidance Journal, 60,* 161-163.

Maynard, P. E. (1980). Group counseling with the elderly. *Counseling and Values, 24,* 227-235.

Mazza, N., & Vinton, L. (1999). A nationwide study of group work in nursing homes. *Activities, Adaptation & Aging, 24,* 61-73.

McFadden, S. H., & Atchley, R. C. (2001). *Aging and the meaning of time.* New York: Springer.

Mead, M. (1972). *Blackberry winter.* New York: Morrow.

Myers, J. E. (1989). *Infusing gerontological counseling into counselor preparation.* Alexandria, VA: American Counseling Association.

Myers, J. E. (1990). Aging: An overview for mental health counselors. *Journal of Mental Health Counseling, 12,* 245-259.

Myers, J. E., Poidevant, J. M., & Dean, L. A. (1991). Groups for older persons and their caregivers: A review of the literature. *Journal for Specialists in Group Work, 16,* 197-205.

O'Brien, C. R., Johnson, J. L., & Miller, B. (1979). Counseling the aging: Some practical considerations. *Personnel and Guidance Journal, 57,* 288-291.

Palmore, E. B. (1999). *Ageism negative and positive* (2nd ed.). New York: Springer.

Peck, R. (1968). Psychological development in the second half of life. In B. Neugarten (Ed.), *Middle age and aging.* Chicago: University of Chicago Press.

Pinquart, M., Wenzel, S., & Sorensen, S. (2000). Changes in attitudes among children and elderly adults in intergenerational group work. *Educational Gerontology, 26,* 523-540.

Sadovy, J., Lazarus, I. W., Jarvik, L. E., & Grossber, G. T. (Eds.). (1996). *Comprehensive review of geriatric psychiatry* (2nd ed.). Washington, DC: American Psychiatric Press.

Sarason, I., & Sarason, B. (1996). *Abnormal psychology* (8th ed.). Upper Saddle River, NJ: Prentice Hall.

Schuster, E. (1998). A community bound by words: Reflections on a nursing home writing group. *Journal of Aging Studies, 12,* 137-147.

Schwiebert, V. L., & Myers, J. E. (2001). Counseling older adults. In E. R. Welfel & R. E. Ingersoll (Eds.), *The mental health desk reference.* New York: John Wiley.

Sherman, E. (1987). Reminiscence groups for community elderly. *Gerontologist, 27,* 569-572.

Singer, V. I., Tracz, S. M., & Dworkin, S. H. (1991). Reminiscence group therapy: A treatment modality for older adults. *Journal for Specialists in Group Work, 16,* 167-171.

Stone, M. L., & Waters, E. (1991). Accentuate the positive: A peer group counseling program for older adults. *Journal for Specialists in Group Work, 16,* 159-166.

Storandt, M. (1983). *Counseling and therapy with older adults.* Boston: Little, Brown.

Streib, G., & Beck, R. (1981). Older families: A decade review. *Journal of Marriage and the Family, 42,* 937- 956.

Sullivan, E. M., Coffey, J. F., & Greenstein, R. A. (1987). Treatment outcome in a group geropsychiatry program for veterans. *Gerontologist, 27,* 434-435.

Taulbee, L. R. (1978). Reality orientation: A therapeutic group activity for elderly persons. In I. M. Burnside (Ed.), *Working with the elderly: Group processes and techniques* (pp. 206-218). North Scituate, MA: Duxbury.

Thomas, M. C. (1991). Their past gives our present meaning: Their dreams are our future. *Journal for Specialists in Group Work, 16,* 132.

Thomas, M. C., & Martin, V. (1992). Training counselors to facilitate the transitions of aging through group work. *Counselor Education and Supervision, 32,* 51-60.

Thomas, M. C., & Martin, V. (1997). Helping older adults age with integrity, empowerment, and meaning through group counseling. In S. T. Gladding (Ed.), *New developments in group counseling* (pp. 43-45). Greensboro, NC: ERIC.

Vacha-Haase, T., Ness, C. M., Dannison, L., & Smith, A. (2000). Grandparents raising grandchildren: A psychoeducational group approach. *Journal for Specialists in Group Work, 25,* 67-78.

Walsh, F. (1988). The family in later life. In B. Carter & M. McGoldrick (Eds.), *The changing family life cycle* (2nd ed.) (pp. 311-332). New York: Gardner.

Waters, E., McCarroll, J., & Penman, N. (1987). *Training mental health workers for the elderly: An instructor's guide.* Rochester, MI: Continuum Center.

Weisman, C., & Schwartz, P. (1989). Worker expectations in group work with the frail elderly: Modifying the model for a better fit. *Social Work With Groups, 12,* 47-55.

Wellman, F. E., & McCormack, J. (1984). Counseling with older persons: A review of outcome research. *Counseling Psychologist, 12,* 81-93.

Whitbourne, S. K. (2002). *The aging individual* (2nd ed.). New York: Springer.

Wrenn, C. G. (1989). Preface. In J. E. Myers (Ed.), *Infusing gerontological counseling into counselor preparation* (pp. 9-15). Alexandria, VA: American Counseling Association.

Yalom, I. D.(1995). *The theory and practice of group psychotherapy* (4th ed.). New York: Basic Books.

Yaretzky, A., & Levinson, M. (1996). Clay as a therapeutic tool in group processing with the elderly. *American Journal of Art Therapy, 34,* 75-82.

Zarit, S. H., Pearlin, L. I., & Schaie, K. W. (2002). *Societal impacts on personal control in the elderly.* New York: Springer.

Zimpfer, D. G. (1987). Groups for the aging: Do they work? *Journal for Specialists in Group Work, 12,* 85-92.

Part VI

SPECIAL TOPIC GROUPS

Introduction

CYNTHIA R. KALODNER

This part, Special Topic Groups, includes examples of psychoeducational, counseling, and psychotherapy groups that address specific psychological concerns that affect millions of people. The goal of this part is to present readers with a continuum of different types of groups that are used to treat people with interpersonal and developmental issues such as grief, substance abuse, and depression. Each chapter in this part provides definitions and descriptions of the issues along with theoretical and empirical support for psychoeducational, counseling, and psychotherapy groups to treat the issue. The first chapter, by Cynthia R. Kalodner and Janelle W. Coughlin, describes psychoeducational and counseling groups used to prevent and treat eating disturbances. The second chapter, presented by Deborah A. Gerrity and Tricia L. Peterson, focuses on groups for females who have been sexually abused. In Chapter 37, Rebecca R. MacNair-Semands provides comprehensive coverage of the use of grief groups, while Chapter 38, written by Angie H. Rice, covers the group treatment of depression. In Chapter 39, Laurie B. Fleckenstein and Arthur M. Horne review anger management groups and provide a model for the use of these groups in the schools. In Chapter 40, Kathryn Kominars and Liane Dornheim provide background on the use of groups with people who abuse substances. In Chapter 41, Jonathan P. Schwartz and Michael Waldo review the literature on group counseling with men who have committed partner abuse. Chapter 42, by H. L. "Lee" Gillis and Michael A. Gass, explores how adventure-based groups provide a way to work with people that includes the use of active interventions.

35

PSYCHOEDUCATIONAL AND COUNSELING GROUPS TO PREVENT AND TREAT EATING DISORDERS AND DISTURBANCES

CYNTHIA R. KALODNER

Towson University

JANELLE W. COUGHLIN

Johns Hopkins University

Groups of various types are widely used to prevent and treat individuals with eating disorders and disturbances. Not only do groups provide cost-effective prevention and treatment that reaches large numbers of people (an important feature, since eating issues appear to be increasing for both men and women), they are a highly effective method of providing prevention and treatment (Fettes & Peters, 1992; Polivy & Federoff, 1997). The therapeutic factors of groups may be especially useful in helping clients work through issues typically associated with eating disorders. For example, the secret, shameful, and chronic nature of an eating disorder contributes to the client's sense of isolation, whereas groups offer the support of peers, multiple models of competency, reality testing, and opportunities for altruism (Oesterheld, McKenna, & Gould, 1987; Zimpfer, 1990). Groups reduce secrecy and shame associated with eating problems, supply a place for talking about the kinds of distorted beliefs and self-perceptions with others who are also facing eating disorders, and provide an interpersonal context to facilitate links between eating disorders and relationships (Laberg, Tornkvist, & Andersson, 2001).

Groups provide an opportunity for participants to challenge some of their unreasonably high standards and create self-expectations that are based on a less distorted view of reality. For example, many women with an eating disturbance hold perfectionistic ideals and accept the media's standards of beauty as their own. Groups also provide an interpersonal context to allow people to share perceptions with others who are also experiencing eating disorders. In addition, groups provide a forum for individuals with problematic eating behaviors and attitudes to explore their unrealistic self-expectations and belief systems (Laberg et al., 2001; Oesterheld et al., 1987) and to learn new behaviors, both interpersonal and eating related.

In a qualitative study of participants' reactions to group treatment for bulimia nervosa (BN), Laberg et al. (2001) interviewed seven participants who completed a cognitive-behavioral therapy group with an interpersonal focus. Many aspects of the group experience were noted as important to the members. Several were unique to groups, such as connecting with others who were struggling with the same problem, feeling the support from members of the group, and learning to trust each other. These qualitative data are important because they highlight that group treatment may work due to the unique approach associated with a group approach; these facets of therapy are not found in individual counseling. Participants indicated that learning that they were not the only ones living with an eating disorder provided some relief. They also noted that being treated in a group provided opportunities to develop outside relationships with group members and that these developed into friendships that continue to provide support for recovery.

In an attempt to identify those therapeutic factors that women with BN regard as most important in their experience of group therapy, Hobbs, Birtchnell, Harte, and Lacey (1989) questioned members of an all-female group, ranging in age from 21 to 30 years, who participated in an eclectic 10-week group counseling intervention. Participants rated self-understanding, vicarious learning, universality, and instillation of hope as the most valued therapeutic factors in the group experience. Again, these therapeutic factors are uniquely associated with group counseling or therapy and may not be relevant in individual counseling. Self-understanding was related to the content of group sessions and the emphasis

on increasing participants' awareness about behaviors, assumptions, motivations, and thoughts. The other three factors, vicarious learning, universality, and instillation of hope, are directly related to the experience of group treatment.

Meta-analyses of group treatments for bulimia support the effectiveness of group therapy (Fettes & Peters, 1992). On average, about 25% of participants were completely abstinent of bulimic symptoms after receiving at least 9 hours of group therapy, and this rate of abstinence was maintained for the year following treatment (Fettes & Peters, 1992). In addition, the average subject who participated in group therapy was better than 77% of the same subjects prior to treatment. They did not find that the type of treatment, gender of the therapist, or method of recruiting participants were associated with the strength of the outcome of treatment (Fettes & Peters, 1992).

This chapter includes a rationale for the use of groups to prevent eating disorders and as a treatment with people who have eating disorders and disturbances. Next, we present brief descriptions of the major eating disorders with a focus on the diagnostic issues that may be useful to consider when forming a group. We also discuss questions to guide the planning of psychoeducational, counseling, or psychotherapy groups for eating disorders, especially pertaining to screening potential members, leadership, and preparation for groups. This chapter also provides examples of psychoeducational groups focused on prevention or early intervention of eating problems and describes cognitive-behavioral and interpersonal therapy treatment groups. We discuss selected research related to eating disorders and eating disorders groups.

In regard to the types of groups defined by the Association for Specialists in Group Work (ASGW), the majority of research on groups for people with eating issues focuses on psychoeducational, counseling, and psychotherapy groups. Since many of the issues addressed in counseling groups overlap with the goals of psychotherapy groups, these groups are discussed together. The chapter closes with an introduction to using short stories in groups for individuals with eating problems (Van Lone, Kalodner, & Coughlin, 2002).

Definitions and Characteristics of Persons With Eating Disorders

Definitions

The term *eating disorders* refers to anorexia nervosa (AN), bulimia nervosa, and eating disorders not otherwise specified (EDNOS), a special category used for people who have eating disorders that meet most, but not all, of the criteria for AN or BN (APA, 2000). In addition to the three major types of eating disorders, there is a large group of people with eating disturbances who are dissatisfied with their body image and practice unhealthy eating practices, but do not fit the criteria for any eating disorder. People with eating disturbances may skip meals, restrict food choices to a few acceptable things, and avoid foods that contain fat. They may binge eat occasionally and self-induce vomiting but do not have an eating disorder. It has been suggested that eating disturbances occur in 19% to 23% of the general population (Mintz, O'Halloran, Mulholland, & Schneider, 1997; Mulholland & Mintz, 2001) and that such disturbances may progress into eating disorders.

AN is defined by a refusal to maintain a minimally normal body weight, an intense fear of weight gain, a disturbance in one's experience of one's own body weight, and an absence of at least three menstrual cycles (APA, 2000). Once a diagnosis of AN is ascertained, the individual is classified into one of two subtypes: the restricting type or the binge-eating/purging type. The restricting type has not engaged in binge-eating or purging behaviors during the current episode of AN, while the binge-eating/purging type has engaged in binge-eating or purging behaviors during the current episode of AN (APA, 2000).

BN is characterized as recurrent episodes of binge eating, engagement in compensatory behaviors to prevent weight gain, and a self-evaluation that is unduly influenced by body weight (APA, 2000). The purging subtype is assigned to individuals who engage in compensatory behaviors that include self-induced vomiting and/or misuse of diuretics, enemas, or laxatives, while those individuals who do not purge, but compensate by fasting or excessive exercise, are classified as the nonpurging type (APA, 2000).

EDNOS is a heterogeneous diagnostic category for individuals who have eating disorders but do not meet all the criteria for AN or BN (APA, 2000). A diagnosis of EDNOS does not imply minor clinical significance; instead, such a diagnosis is cause for serious concern and requires clinical treatment.

Demographics

The prevalence of AN and BN combined are reported as 0.5% to 1% and 1% to 3% of adolescent and young adult females respectively (APA, 2000). EDNOS are more prevalent, occurring in 4% to 6% of the general population (Herzog & Delinsky, 2001). Thus, the prevalence of EDNOS is approximately twice that of AN and BN. In addition, EDNOS is the appropriate diagnosis for more than 50% of patients with eating disorders who present for treatment (APA, 2000; Striegel-Moore & Smolak, 2001). Binge-eating disorder (BED), included in the *DSM-IV-TR* as an EDNOS, has a prevalence rate of 15% to 50% of participants in weight-control programs (with a mean of 30%; APA, 2000). Less is known about the prevalence of this disorder in the general population.

Cognitive, Behavioral, and Interpersonal Characteristics

AN, BN, EDNOS, and eating disturbances share certain diagnostic issues, such as dissatisfaction with body shape and weight and disturbances in eating behavior (see Kalodner & DeLucia-Waack, 2003). Fear about gaining weight and a negative attitude about weight and shape are also characteristic of those with eating disorders. Symptoms of eating disorders and disturbances are multifaceted in their cognitive (e.g., weight preoccupation, body dissatisfaction, drive for thinness, perfectionism, acceptance of cultural standards of thinness), affective (e.g., anxiety, feelings of ineffectiveness, low self-esteem, guilt), and behavioral components (e.g., purging, food restriction, binge eating, counting calories and fat, frequent weighing of self). These cognitive, affective, and behavioral components are influenced by interpersonal and sociocultural (e.g., the media, peers, family) factors. Given the complexity of eating disorder symptoms, different types of groups can be considered to address a given cluster of eating-related symptoms.

GENERAL GUIDELINES FOR FACILITATING PSYCHOEDUCATIONAL AND COUNSELING/THERAPY GROUPS

Planning Psychoeducational or Counseling/Therapy Groups

Psychoeducational and counseling/therapy groups have different formats, with different objectives and members with diverse needs; thus they require different planning. However, regardless of the type of group, group facilitators should ask organizing questions as they plan group interventions. For example, Who are the participants or members? What symptom(s) are being treated? What are the severity levels? Is this a prevention or treatment intervention? What is the intended outcome? How long are the group interventions? Are the goals realistic for the length of the group? The answers to these questions will allow leaders to consider the needs of the individuals being served and choose a group format that appropriately addresses these needs.

Psychoeducational groups focus on educating group members about an identified issue or risk factor that is associated with eating disorders and reducing the risk or occurrence of that cognitive, affective, or behavioral component. For example, the objectives of a psychoeducational program on the media and its impact on women might be to increase participants' awareness of the media's tendency to provide a distorted representation of women and to reduce participants' acceptance of societal standards of beauty (Coughlin & Kalodner, 2003). Polivy and Federoff (1997) asserted that psychoeducational groups may be less threatening than therapy and can be useful for people who have difficulty engaging in the therapy process and can prepare them for more intensive individual or group therapy.

Counseling and psychotherapy groups are often based on a particular theoretical model, such as cognitive-behavioral or interpersonal. Cognitive-behavioral counseling groups address symptom reduction through increasing participants' awareness of personal thoughts and feelings related to eating patterns and introducing strategies for changing their behaviors and belief systems. Interpersonal psychotherapy is based on the idea that understanding the interpersonal context (relationships that include family and friends) within which the eating disorder developed and has been maintained is necessary for persons to change their eating-disordered behavior (Fairburn, Welch, Doll, Davies, & O'Connor, 1997). Counseling groups based on the interpersonal therapy model provide opportunities for participants to adapt to and master interpersonal situations so the negative emotions that are associated with relationship problems.

Group size is dependent on the type and purpose of group. Psychoeducational groups may be larger than counseling groups, with numbers as few as 5 to more than 12 (Polivy & Federoff, 1997). Many school-based psychoeducational programs operate in classrooms and include more than 20 people. When groups include more interaction in addition to didactic presentations, the group size should be reduced to 5 to 10 participants (Polivy & Federoff, 1997).

Selection of Members for Psychoeducational and Counseling/Therapy Groups

There are differing opinions in the field of eating disorders related to selection of members for group counseling or psychotherapy; some believe that groups should be homogeneous with regard to eating disorder diagnosis, while others have used mixed groups including people with AN, BN, and EDNOS (Polivy & Federoff, 1997). For example, some (Hendren, Atkins, Sumner, & Barber, 1987; Piazza & Steiner-Adair, 1986) allow groups to consist of participants with all types of eating disorders, while others intentionally screen for a more homogeneous group of participants, such that groups consist of only persons with BN or AN (Hall, 1985; Romano, Quinn, & Halmi, 1994). In their recommendations for screening for cognitive-behavioral group psychotherapy for BN, Romano et al. (1994) suggest including only those individuals who meet all criteria for BN.

In their experience, including individuals who do not meet the specific frequency and duration criteria impedes group cohesion and commonality among group participants. In addition, there can be competition among group members when the groups are heterogeneous in terms of diagnosis, such that those with BN view those with AN as more successful at weight control. Although some researchers do not find low weight to be a contraindication to group treatment (Hendren et al., 1987), others have suggested that group participants who are severely underweight may be less appropriate for group treatment, given the likelihood that they may fail to comply with behavioral strategies, such as eating three meals per day and gradually increasing their exposure to feared or forbidden foods (Hall, 1985; Romano et al., 1994). Hall strongly asserted that groups with people who have AN can be extremely difficult, since people with AN can be quite withdrawn and have great difficulty identifying and expressing feelings.

Generally, it is best to avoid admitting group members who are not motivated and willing to commit to treatment (Romano et al., 1994). This is of particular relevance because lack of motivation and resistance to treatment are highly common among individuals with eating disorders and can lead to treatment attrition, failure, and relapse (Feld, Woodside, Kaplan, Olmsted, & Carter, 2001). Counseling and therapy groups generally exclude individuals who are (a) abusing alcohol or drugs, (b) psychotic, and/or (c) suicidal (Kirkley, Schneider, Agras, & Bachman, 1985; Telch, Agras, & Linehan, 2001). Individuals with personality disorders, in particular borderline personality disorder and thought disorders, should also be carefully considered prior to inclusion in group treatment for eating disorders (Hendren et al., 1987; Romano et al., 1994).

Although the majority of individuals with eating disorders tend to be female, males may also participate in psychoeducational groups and may present for treatment. Groups that include both males and females should be carefully considered, because mixing males and females can inhibit group participation. In a psychoeducational group described below (Phelps, Dempsey, Sapia, & Nelson, 1999),

experience suggested that the males included did not fully participate; thus the researchers recommended that future implementations of the program be devoted to female participants only. Likewise, many of the topics discussed in cognitive-behavioral eating disorder groups are gender specific (i.e., sociocultural issues). It is appropriate to avoid including both males and females when these topics will be part of the group intervention.

Preparation of Members for Groups

People with eating disorders are often ambivalent about participating in treatment (Feld et al., 2001), and thus recommendations about preparing them for groups may be helpful. People with eating disorders may present for treatment at the insistence of parents or other family members, friends, or physicians, and they may be resistant to change. Feld et al. (2001) compared people with eating disorders to those with addictions, indicating that both groups are often unmotivated to participate in counseling. It was this recognition that led to the development of the pretreatment motivational program, which has its roots in the addictions field. Feld et al. studied the effects of a pretreatment motivational enhancement therapy on individuals with eating disorders (AN, BN, and EDNOS). The intervention was four hour-long sessions that focused on "the benefits and costs of having an eating disorder; predicting life in 5 years with and without an eating disorder; and life values and goals in relation to an eating disorder" (p. 196), after which assessments of readiness to change and other psychological measures were collected. Participants were more motivated to change and viewed their behavior as a problem after the intervention. In addition, the sessions led to a decrease in depression, an increase in overall self-esteem, and a decrease in interpersonal distrust, which may indicate that the participants are better able to participate in a therapy experience. Most of the members entered a treatment program and indicated that the pretreatment motivation sessions positively influenced their decision to enter therapy.

Bowman and DeLucia-Waack (1996) also described the importance of preparation for group counseling, and Cummins (1996) adapted their multimedia model for potential members of an eating disorders group. Cummins indicated that preparation for group counseling is an especially important topic, because people may drop out if they are not prepared for this kind of therapeutic work. Her model includes cognitive, behavioral, and experiential components and includes reading information about group counseling, watching a videotape of a simulated eating disorders group, and then practicing responses such as self-disclosure and confrontation to vignettes. Though she does not present data demonstrating the effectiveness of this type of preparation, she indicated that attendance has increased and the dropout rate had decreased.

LEADER ISSUES

Although the gender of qualified therapists appears to be of less importance than the gender of group members (Romano et al., 1994), two female cotherapists seem to be more common than a male-female dyad. This may be because more female leaders have an interest in eating disorders and are beneficial for group members because the female coleaders may serve as healthy role models for girls and women who have eating disturbances. However, a male-female cotherapy pair can elicit important family issues and transference among group members. Moreno (1998) indicated that a male-female cotherapy team is ideal because it provides the opportunity for members to work out conflicts with both genders. However, he also indicated that in his psychodynamically oriented group, his comments were sometimes rejected, ridiculed, or ignored, while those made by the female coleader were accepted by the group. Moreno concluded that group therapy with people who have chronic eating disorders is difficult and that therapists are not advised to work alone. It is our experience that both males and females can effectively facilitate groups for eating disorders; instead, it is the presence of the universal therapeutic factors of group counseling and therapy (e.g., instillation of hope, group cohesion) that contribute more to the efficacy of groups for eating disorders.

It has been noted that counselors working with clients with eating disorders are impacted specifically in terms of their relationship with their food (DeLucia-Waack, 1999; Zerbe, 1993). Counselors of clients who have eating disorders are frequently influenced by the irrational and faulty belief systems of the clients; this means that working with people who have eating disorders may have an impact on the self-perceptions of the group leaders (Baumann, 1992; Zerbe, 1993). Furthermore, DeLucia-Waack indicates that working with clients with eating disorders may affect counselors' perceptions of themselves, which in turn affects their ability to serve as a reality check for their clients with eating disorders. This highlights the need for supervision for leaders of groups focused on eating disorders.

GUIDELINES FOR FACILITATING PSYCHOEDUCATIONAL GROUPS

Psychoeducational groups provide important information that can be used to prevent a person from developing an eating problem or assist someone who does have a problem by teaching about the issues related to eating problems and disorders. These groups often follow a lecture and discussion format and use structured material for the group meetings. Many are focused on prevention or early intervention. Through psychoeducation, people with eating disorders and those at risk of developing eating disorders are provided accurate information to challenge the misinformation and myths that those with eating problems may hold. These bits of misinformation may keep those who have an eating disorder from changing their behavior. Psychoeducational groups may also be used as an adjunct to counseling or psychotherapy for people with eating disorders. Psychoeducational programs are also a part of many treatment programs; cognitive-behavioral programs include psychoeducational components as part of treatment (Stein et al., 2001).

There are many references to the use of psychoeducational materials as part of a prevention or treatment program. Garner's (1997) chapter provides information about the breadth of issues that should be included in a psychoeducational intervention. An older manual (Davis et al., 1989) includes much of the same information structured for a weekly psychoeducational group. There are nine major topic areas included in psychoeducational programming for people who have an eating problem (Garner, 1997, p. 146):

1. Multiple causes of eating disorders

2. The cultural context for eating disorders

3. Set-point theory and the physiological regulation of weight

4. The effects of starvation on behavior

5. Restoring regular eating patterns

6. Vomiting, laxatives, and diuretics in controlling weight

7. Determining a healthy body weight

8. Physical complications

9. Relapse prevention techniques

In planning psychoeducational groups, the age and developmental level of the participants are considered. Most programs are developed for females at different stages of life, including the years of elementary school, middle school, high school, college, mid-20s, and older-ages. Examples of this type of psychoeducational group follow, and we provide additional resources on this topic at the end of this section.

A Prevention Program for Elementary School-Age Children

Eating Smart, Eating for Me (Smolak, 1999; Smolak, Levine, & Schermer, 1998) is an excellent example of a program designed to be used with children in elementary school. There are six goals of the program (Smolak et al., 1998, p. 153):

1. To explain the importance of proper nutrition, including that fat is a nutrient, and to explain how to use the USDA Food Guide Pyramid to achieve healthy nutrition.

2. To encourage healthy, moderate exercise on a regular basis

3. To teach students and parents about the diversity of body shapes

4. To encourage the development of a positive body image

5. To encourage healthy eating rather than caloric-restrictive dieting

6. To encourage critical evaluation of media messages about body shape and nutrition

This program has been the subject of several studies that were designed to assess the outcome of the prevention program with children aged 9 to 11. In a study published in 2001, Smolak and Levine found that 2 years after 289 students participated in the Eating Smart, Eating for Me program, they were more knowledgeable, used fewer unhealthy weight management techniques, and had higher body esteem than adolescents of the same age in a different school.

A Prevention Program Used With Middle School- and High School-Age Adolescents

A school-based eating disorder prevention program developed and tested in middle and high school is described by Phelps et al. (1999). This program contains six sessions that focus on sociocultural pressures, ways to enhance physical self-esteem, ideas to build personal competence, methods to reduce body dissatisfaction, and information about appropriate methods of weight control. In the final session, a person recovering from an eating disorder addresses the group and tells her story about how she developed her eating disorder and about her treatment.

In the middle school version, the first sessions focus on sociocultural pressures. An exercise that is helpful in the sociocultural area is looking critically at magazines and discussing the images and the weight-control messages that appear. The sessions focusing on physical self-esteem may allow participants to attend to the positive aspects of physical appearance. For example, they may be asked to find and comment on aspects of themselves that they do like, such as "I like my hair" or "I always liked my eyes." Physical fitness is described as healthy and strong, and participants are encouraged to find an activity that allows regular physical exercise. The sessions on building personal competence are focused on developing an internal locus of control. It can be hard for adolescents to make decisions without relying on group pressure, but developing strong personal values may be helpful in preventing eating problems. The sessions on body dissatisfaction are designed to normalize the natural weight gain during puberty through comparing photos of normal weight teenagers to models of extreme thinness. The sessions on weight control highlight the negative aspects of dieting and weight reduction such as "yo-yo" dieting and starvation. Set-point theory can be used to persuade participants that people have a bio-genetic disposition to a weight range that the body defends. In addition, these sessions may include information about healthy ways to control weight with a focus on moderate physical exercise and healthy eating. The food pyramid is a useful tool for addressing nutritional needs. The final session is one in which a person recovering from an eating disorder tells her story. This is usually engaging for adolescents, and they may be able to develop a deeper understanding of the serious nature of an eating disorder.

Phelps and her colleagues (1999) studied the effects of this program on 1,066 middle school girls and boys aged 11 to 15 and a smaller sample of 9th to 12th graders. Although the research did not find statistically significant changes in the middle school group, the researchers were encouraged by the nonsignificant reductions in current use and future intent to use dieting, excessive exercise, purging, and other unhealthy methods of weight control.

There are many resources that address the topic of prevention of eating disorders. Two excellent books, *Preventing Eating Disorders* (Piran, Levine, & Steiner-Adair, 1999) and *The Prevention of Eating Disorders* (Vandereycken & Noordenbos, 1998) provide the foundation for psychoeducational group-based prevention programs. In addition, chapters in two newer books (Striegel-Moore & Smolak, 2001; Thompson & Smolak, 2001) address prevention issues. In Piran, Levine, and Steiner-Adair's (1999) seminal textbook on prevention of eating disorders, there are examples of prevention programs for elementary and middle schools and programs used in high school and college settings.

GUIDELINES FOR FACILITATING COUNSELING AND PSYCHOTHERAPY GROUPS

In this section, we describe cognitive-behavioral and interpersonal counseling and therapy groups. These groups have been found to be effective treatments for BN, and there is continued study of their use with AN and EDNOS. Most researchers have concluded that cognitive-behavioral therapy is the most extensively researched and supported treatment for BN (Richards et al. 2000; Stein et al., 2001), and there have been a number of studies demonstrating the effectiveness of interpersonal psychotherapy (Fairburn et al., 1993; Wilfley et al., 1993).

Cognitive-Behavioral Counseling and Psychotherapy Groups

Cognitive-behavioral therapy (CBT) is a treatment of choice for BN; it is a gold standard, meaning that it may be the best treatment available for this disorder (Chambless et al., 1998; Stein et al., 2001; Wilson, Fairburn, & Agras, 1997). A 10-year follow-up of women treated with CBT (with or without an antidepressant) or a placebo indicated that participants who were treated with either CBT or an antidepressant had improved social adjustment compared to those who had only the placebo treatment (Keel, Mitchell, Davis, & Crow, 2002). CBT addresses symptom reduction through increasing participants' awareness of personal thoughts and feelings related to eating patterns and introducing strategies for changing their behaviors and belief systems. With modifications, CBT developed for BN may be used to treat EDNOS, especially BED. CBT has also been used to treat AN, though there is little research on this topic. The CBT program for AN contains some of the same components of the program for treatment of BN and addresses issues specific to AN, such as the effects of starvation and the need for weight gain (Bowers, 2001).

CBT has been used in individual and group settings for individuals with eating disorders. As will be seen in the material that follows, CBT as it is currently administered in a group format may not take full advantage of the power of the group. CBT uses a group format for presenting and processing information with a group of people, but may not be developed to enable group members to interact with each other in ways that may allow them to process their eating behaviors and the associated thoughts and feelings. In addition, most of the research that has been reported does not assess the role or power of the group; rather, the outcome assessment is tied to the symptoms of the eating disorder. This is unfortunate, since little is known about how the process works in groups. In the end, it is unclear how the interaction of the members of the group may be therapeutic in addition to the effects of the CBT itself. It would be useful to know if the treatment is effective because it is presented in a group format and uses the group as part of the treatment, rather than assuming that the group is simply individuals receiving the same treatment for the same presenting problem at the same time.

CBT generally includes three stages of treatment: establishing control over eating behaviors (Phase 1), identifying and modifying dysfunctional beliefs that contribute to maladaptive behaviors (Phase 2), and maintaining change (Phase 3) (Wilson et al., 1997). The first phase of CBT is generally more behavioral in nature, with the main goal of symptom reduction. One technique used in this phase of treatment is self-monitoring. Through daily log entries, eating patterns are identified by recording time and location of meals, quantity/type of food, circumstances surrounding the eating episode (e.g., individuals present, mood states), type of eating episode (e.g., binge, meal, snack), and any extreme weight control behaviors that were used (e.g., use of laxatives or purges). In Phase 1, behavior modification strategies are often introduced to encourage group participants to experiment with new eating behaviors. For example, in a group for individuals with BN, leaders may instruct participants to eat more regularly throughout the day, delay time between bingeing and vomiting, and practice relaxation between binge episodes and purge episodes. Relaxation exercises and stress management are an important part of this phase, providing group members with strategies for reducing anxiety when faced with urges to engage in extreme eating behaviors.

For example, group participants are taught to use relaxation exercises as they increase their exposure to feared, avoided, and "forbidden" foods. They are also instructed to use relaxation techniques after meals, to replace purging behaviors.

Phase 2 of cognitive-behavioral groups for eating disorders is more cognitive in nature, with an emphasis on challenging distorted beliefs about food, eating, weight, and body image (Wilson et al., 1997). The goal is to correct faulty reasoning and erroneous assumptions that serve to maintain dysfunctional eating behaviors. For example, the belief that "thinness leads to happiness" can be challenged and reconstructed to a more valid and logical statement that includes other factors that lead to happiness and reasons why thinness does not necessarily produce life satisfaction. Such statements can be discussed within the group, with an emphasis on elucidating the process by which distorted thinking leads to eating disorder symptoms. As group members learn to use cognitive techniques, they can challenge illogical and faulty statements that are revealed in the group and assist one another with creating more reality-based and logical belief systems. Group leaders may encourage members to identify and challenge these unhealthy thoughts when they hear them in the group, and members can also suggest other more positive self-statements.

In Phase 3, maintenance, group participants are encouraged to integrate and to apply the techniques covered in the first two stages of group while focusing on continued symptom reduction and reality-based thinking (Wilson et al., 1997). This stage, often referred to as relapse prevention, allows group members to prepare for setbacks that will occur. Group members can identify stressful situations that may trigger their urge to diet, binge, or purge while arming themselves with plans for managing such situations. In group sessions, visualization exercises can be used to prepare participants for potential events that might put them at risk for relapse. Group members can be encouraged to understand that lapses of dysfunctional eating behaviors are opportunities to learn, instead of indicators that they will never recover.

Dialectical behavior therapy (DBT), an intervention that evolved from cognitive-behavioral therapy (Linehan & Kehrer, 1993), has been suggested as a possible treatment for BED (Telch et al., 2001). DBT is a widely used intervention for the treatment of borderline personality disorder that involves analyzing and replacing dysfunctional behaviors with skillful behaviors (Linehan, 1993). It focuses on emotional regulation, with the primary objective being to teach clients skills to regulate negative emotions and manage emotional distress. Because it has been hypothesized that binge eating serves to temporarily relieve negative affect, this method of treatment has been considered in the treatment of BED (Polivy & Herman, 1985).

Telch et al. (2001) developed a 20-week treatment program that was adapted from Linehan's DBT for borderline personality disorder. Forty-four women who met diagnostic criteria for BED were assigned to either the DBT skills-training program or a wait-list control. Treatment involved an introduction to DBT, mindfulness skills, emotion regulation skills, distress tolerance skills, and a review. Results suggested that DBT is significantly more effective at reducing binge eating than no treatment. In fact, in the DBT group, 16 of 18 (89%) participants were abstinent from binge eating by the 20th week of treatment. This was very encouraging when considering that only 2 of 16 (12.5%) participants in the wait-list group had stopped bingeing. Among those who participated in the DBT group, 67% were abstinent at 3-month follow-up and 56% at 6-month follow-up. It is important to note that DBT, although derived from CBT, does not directly focus on eating behaviors. Instead, DBT focuses on affect and developing skills to manage extreme emotional states. Telch and colleagues suggest that DBT may be similar to interpersonal psychotherapy, an intervention that we discuss in the following section.

Interpersonal Counseling and Psychotherapy Groups

Interpersonal psychotherapy (IPT) is based on the idea that understanding the interpersonal context (relationships that include family and friends) from which the eating disorder developed and has been maintained is necessary for the person to change their eating-disordered behavior (Fairburn, 1997). The premise is that in order to help people stop their eating problems, it is necessary to find out and understand fully what is keeping the eating problems going. As an example, many binges are associated with an interpersonal trigger, such as an argument with a friend or family member, or feelings of loneliness. In IPT there is no attention or direct discussion about eating habits or behavior. Instead, the group leader helps the clients to study their past and present relationships and to understand how these relationships might be related to the eating disorder. Fairburn, the developer of this approach for use with eating disorders, has written and researched the use of IPT (Fairburn, 1997; Fairburn et al., 1993) and suggests that 15 to 20 sessions over 4 or 5 months is necessary to address eating disorders using this approach.

In the beginning of treatment, the therapist works to study four different histories: (1) the eating problem (how it started, dates of first binge and purge), (2) relationships (family, friends, peers), (3) other life events and relationships with others (might include a move, parental divorce, starting college), and (4) specific problems with self-esteem and depression. This information is used to create a life chart that shows how the eating problem, relationships, life events, and self-esteem/depression are related in the life of a person. The information obtained in the life chart forms the basis for the discussion in group sessions. There are four major interpersonal issues that arise in life charts. Presented in order of frequency in which they occur, they are interpersonal role disputes (64%), role transitions (36%), interpersonal deficits (16%), and grief (12%) (Fairburn, 1997).

In interpersonal psychotherapy, the goal is to resolve the individual's interpersonal problems by clarifying the problem in the relationship, considering the possibilities for changes, and helping the client to make positive changes in these relationships. For example, in the category of role transitions, the issue is usually one of establishing independence from parents. Other common transitions include beginning or ending college, changing jobs, getting married, or becoming a parent. Group therapists work with the members of the group to understand the changes that go along with these transitions in life. For individuals who are working to establish independence from parents, the group therapist might explore the kind of relationship the person wants to have with parents and help guide the development of healthy independence.

Less common problems are interpersonal deficits and grief. Interpersonal deficits refer to problems that an individual may have in developing and keeping relationships with people. Sometimes clients describe a history of being isolated and not having close friends. In this case, the group therapist helps the clients to understand the reason they might be having trouble forming or keeping relationships. Sometimes the relationship between the client and the group members and the group leaders can be used as a way to understand the development of important relationships. Grief is an issue that arises when someone important in the client's life has died. Facing the loss requires the client to express feelings about losing an important person and to adjust to life without the person who is gone. As the client becomes less focused on the past, it is easier to develop new interests and relationships.

During the group sessions focused on the interpersonal problems, few clients bring up their eating disorder. They rarely describe binge eating or purging, or body image issues. However, in the last few sessions, it is more common for clients to talk about their eating problems as they plan for the end of the group sessions. Therapists often tell clients that eating problems may be a kind of Achilles' heel, meaning that the eating problems may recur in times of emotional stress. Thus, the final sessions are planned to solidify the interpersonal changes that have been made during the process of psychotherapy and to reduce the risk of relapse.

Although studies of CBT have dominated the research literature, there have been a number of studies assessing the effectiveness of IPT for BN (Agras, Walsh, Fairburn, Wilson, & Kraemer, 2000; Fairburn et al., 1993; Fairburn, Norman, Welch, O'Connor, Doll, & Peveler, 1995). Research shows that IPT is an effective treatment for eating disorders. In an early study on the effectiveness of IPT, it was compared with cognitive-behavioral therapy and behavioral therapy in young women with bulimia (Fairburn et al., 1993); results indicated that both CBT and IPT were superior to treatment with only a behavioral component. Furthermore, CBT and IPT produced significant reductions in eating disordered behaviors. Although CBT was superior to IPT immediately following treatment, no significant differences were found between the two interventions 1 year after treatment. In a study that evaluated the longer-term effects of treatments for BN (CBT, behavioral, and IPT; Fairburn et al., 1995), those women who received CBT and IPT had significantly greater remission rates at 6-year follow-up than those who participated in the behavioral intervention. Furthermore, there were no significant differences in remission rates between those who participated in CBT and IPT at long-term follow-up. Similar to earlier findings, Agras et al. (2000) found that CBT was clinically and statistically superior to IPT immediately following treatment in reducing the behavioral symptoms of eating disorders (self-induced vomiting and dietary restraint). There were, however, no significant differences immediately following treatment in regard to weight and shape concerns, self-esteem, and interpersonal functioning. As in previous studies, when considering posttreatment status, no significant differences were detected between the two treatments. This suggests that, although CBT may be faster at reducing the behavioral symptoms associated with eating disorders, IPT is comparable to CBT when considering the posttreatment rates of recovery maintenance and remittance of symptoms.

Group IPT has been demonstrated to be an effective treatment for eating disorders (Wilfley et al., 1993). When group CBT and group IPT for individuals with nonpurging bulimia (i.e., binge eaters who did not purge to compensate for binges) were compared to wait-list controls, CBT group therapy and group IPT had similar effects on binge-eating behaviors. More specifically, both group treatments produced significant reductions in binge-eating behaviors at 6-month and 1-year follow-up. These results not only suggest that group IPT is an equally effective group treatment for the treatment of binge eating disorder, it emphasizes the importance of addressing social functioning and interpersonal issues in the group treatment of disordered eating behaviors.

Reiss (2002) provided a kind of integrative time-limited group therapy that merges aspects of CBT and IPT along with psychoeducation. She used the different approaches sequentially in her 12-session group, beginning with psychoeducation, then using CBT, and closing with an IPT kind of approach. In a pilot study of this type of group, 40 women who met the *DSM-IV-TR* criteria for BN were included in groups of 6 to 8 members. Of the 36 who completed the program, reductions in binge eating from an average of seven per week prior to therapy to four per week after therapy were shown.

Another integrative program called the Eating Disorders Contemplation Group (Tantillo, Bitter, & Adams, 2001) is a model based on CBT and focuses on the stages of change (Prochaska, Norcross, & DiClemente, 1994) and relational therapy based on the work of Jordan, Miller, and others from the Stone Center at Wellesley College (i.e., Jordan, Kaplan, Miller, Stiver, & Surrey, 1991). In their description of this treatment program, Tantillo et al. indicated that this integrated model works in a group approach because "the experience of mutuality in relationships fosters validation of the patients' strengths, problems, and present level of change. . . . [T]he opportunities to experience mutual relationships increase significantly in the context of group psychotherapy where patients are engaged with the group leader and peers" (p. 209). The authors indicated that they are continuing to collect data on the effectiveness of the group treatment; they have included a measure of mutuality, which will allow an assessment of the power of the group dynamics.

OTHER KINDS OF GROUP PSYCHOTHERAPY

Psychodynamic psychotherapy may be useful as an alternative treatment for eating disorders when cognitive-behavioral and interpersonal therapies prove ineffective. Although Moreno (1998) stated that there is a dearth of descriptive and controlled research on psychodynamic group therapy for people with eating disorders, he provided a case report of a group that he

conducted. The psychodynamic view of eating disorders is that binges may be used to help people deny or anesthetize uncomfortable emotions following interpersonal exchanges (Moreno). Psychodynamic therapy for eating disorders may take from 6 months to many years. It focuses on fostering an emotional experience that corrects underlying deficits in self-identity. After a group experience marked with difficulty (marginal institutional support, and participation, attendance, and commitment to the group were poor), Moreno concluded that thorough assessment and preparation of members might have avoided some of the major problems in this group. He also concluded that a multidimensional approach (including psychodynamic, cognitive, and behavioral procedures) should be used. Moreno's report is refreshing to read because it reviews the difficulties in doing this kind of work and highlights the need for well-trained coleaders. Group-oriented psychodynamic therapy may be used to help patients reexperience their past and examine ways to resolve these problems. However, this therapy for eating disorders has not been scientifically validated (Chambless et al., 1998).

Other therapies such as addiction-oriented, self-help, and support groups have been used for the treatment of eating disorders (Polivy & Federoff, 1997); however, they are less commonly represented in research on the topic of group treatment of eating disorders. There is tremendous variation on the kinds of groups offered and little evidence to indicate which kinds of groups are most beneficial with various kinds of eating problems.

A Creative Intervention Strategy: The Use of Short Stories in Eating Disorders Groups

Short stories may be used as an effective group-level intervention for people who have eating disturbances. Stories are especially useful in addressing disordered eating attitudes and behaviors because they allow group members to confront their eating problems in a nonthreatening way. Shifting the focus from the dysfunction of the individuals in the group to the dysfunctions of a neutral character in a story allows individuals to more openly process issues related to eating and body image disturbance. Short stories may be used in eating disorder-themed groups and in any other group in which eating disturbances are present among group members.

Individuals with eating disturbances tend to feel significant levels of shame and guilt (Burney & Irwin, 2000) and are often defensive and secretive regarding their eating attitudes and behaviors. Individuals with AN particularly are often withdrawn, anxious, rigid, egocentric, and have extreme difficulty in identifying and expressing feelings (Polivy & Federoff, 1997). Individuals who binge may have a difficult time disclosing their binge-eating behaviors. However, if the group leader presents a story that symbolically represents the act of binge eating (such as "all-or-nothing" behaviors), group members may identify the story and then they can participate and share with others in the group. Using a short story in groups may be an effective intervention because it allows members enough distance from a particular eating disturbance to feel comfortable engaging in the group process. Readers are encouraged to read stories that appear in every issue of *Eating Disorders: The Journal of Treatment and Prevention* to expand their repertoire of stories. For example, one study titled "Pulling Weeds and Planting Flowers" (Andersen, 1994) describes a person who is removing all the self-defeating behavior and learning to replace it with more healthy and adaptive behavior. Questions like Can we plant flowers at the same time we are pulling weeds? and Where do you think this group is right now in taking care of our gardens? can be used to raise a useful discussion about the destructive nature of eating-disordered behaviors. More information about how to use short stories in groups focused on eating disorders can be found in Van Lone, Kalodner, and Coughlin's (2002) article.

CAUTIONS

As with any kind of treatment, there are cautions to consider. Polivy and Federoff (1997) indicated that there is a risk that "patients will form a strong 'anorexic,' 'bulimic,' or 'eating disordered' identity" (p. 472), which may prevent them from attempting to recover. This means that the development of an identity of "me as a person with an eating disorder" may develop and be difficult to change. Polivy and Federoff also indicated that in a group setting, those who are more disturbed may undermine the progress of those with less severe disorders. It is also possible that those with less severe disturbances will consider themselves "not that bad" and inhibit their efforts to recover. They raise the commonly heard concern that individuals will teach each other symptoms and unhealthy practices and that some may become overly dependent on others. Leaders need to be aware of these possibilities and monitor the group for indications of these cautions.

Other issues that influence the type of treatment selected and the outcome of treatment are the co-occurring psychological problems, such as substance abuse/dependence, depression, and anxiety disorders (especially obsessive-compulsive disorder). These issues complicate treatment of the eating disorders. It is difficult to help a person with an eating disorder who is also dependent on alcohol or other drugs. Likewise, when a person has an eating disorder and depression or an anxiety disorder, the treatment must attend to both problems.

REMAINING ISSUES

It is difficult to assess the role of the group environment in the effectiveness of these interventions. Very few studies have included a measure of group cohesion or any other group variable. The focus in both the psychoeducational prevention and counseling and therapy treatment groups is on the outcome, tied to the symptoms of the eating problems, rather than the process by which the change occurs. The group appears to be a way to reach more people at the same time, a kind of issue of efficiency, rather than one that is based on using the power of the group to influence change. Future research using group treatment would benefit from an explicit use and evaluation of the effect of the group as part of the therapeutic approach. Research evaluating the effectiveness of groups should include a measure of group cohesion, in addition to outcome measures associated with eating disorders.

Another problem is the definition of the outcome of recovery. For BN, recovery is usually described in terms of reductions in the frequency or severity of binge eating, purging, or other problematic behaviors, or the proportion of people who stopped or reduced these behaviors. For AN, recovery is framed as the amount of weight gained or the proportion of individuals who achieved a weight that is a percentage of ideal weight. The return of menstruation in women is another outcome measure of the success of treatment. What is missed in this assessment of change is the change in attitudes about body image. In AN, this includes the "intense fear of gaining weight or becoming fat" and "disturbance in the way in which one's body weight or shape is experienced, undue influence of body weight or shape on self-evaluation, or denial of the seriousness of the current low body weight." In BN, this includes the notion that self-evaluation is unduly influenced by body shape and weight (APA, 2000). Also, associated issues, such as depression, anxiety, and other psychological adjustment, are rarely reported.

SUMMARY

Group work with individuals with eating disorders is hard work (Moreno, 1998) and requires careful planning, screening, and ongoing supervision (DeLucia-Waack, 1999). This chapter includes information that is useful in the planning of psychoeducational, counseling, or psychotherapy groups for eating disorders and provides examples of psychoeducational and cognitive-behavioral and interpersonal therapy groups focused on eating disorders. The reader is encouraged to read the sources cited in this chapter and seek supervision before embarking on a group program with this population.

REFERENCES

Agras, S. W., Walsh, T., Fairburn, C. G., Wilson, G. T., & Kraemer, H. C. (2000). A multicenter comparison of cognitive-behavioral therapy and interpersonal psychotherapy for bulimia nervosa. *Archives of General Psychiatry, 57,* 459-466.

American Psychiatric Association. (2000). *Diagnostic and statistical manual of mental disorders* (4th ed-TR.). Washington, DC: Author.

Andersen, A. (1994). Stories I tell my patients: Pulling weeds and planting flowers. *Eating Disorders: The Journal of Prevention and Treatment, 2,* 184-185.

Baumann, J. (1992). Reflections on groups psychotherapy with eating disorder patients. *Group Psychotherapy for Eating Disorders, 16,* 95-100.

Bowers, W. A. (2001). Basic priniciples for applying cognitive-behavioral therapy to anorexia nervosa. *Psychiatric Clinics of North America, 24,* 293-303.

Bowman, V. E., & DeLucia-Waack, J. L. (1996). Preparation for counseling revisited: New applications to meet the goals of brief counseling. *Crisis Intervention and Time Limited Treatment, 2,* 255-266.

Burney, J., & Irwin, H. J. (2000). Shame and guilt in women with eating-disordered symptomatology. *Journal of Clinical Psychology, 56,* 51-61.

Chambless, D. L., Baker, M. J., Baucom, D. H., Beutler, L. E., Calhoun, K. S., & Crits-Christoph, P., et al. (1998). Update on empirically validated therapies, II. *Clinical Psychologist, 51*(1), 3-16.

Coughlin, J. W., & Kalodner, C. R. (2003). *Media influences on eating disorders.* Manuscript submitted for publication.

Cummins, P. N. (1996). Preparing clients with eating disorders for group counseling: A multimedia approach. *Journal for Specialists in Group Work, 21,* 4-10.

Davis, R., Dearing, S., Faulkner, J., Jasper, K.,Olmsted, M. P., Rice, C., et al., (1989). The road to recovery: A manual for participants in the psychoeducation group for bulimia nervosa. In H. Harper-Giuffre & K. R. MacKenzie (Eds.), *Group psychotherapy for eating disorders* (Appendix). Washington, DC: American Psychiatric Association Press.

DeLucia-Waack, J. L. (1999). Supervision for counselors working with eating disorders groups: Countertransference issues related to body image, food, and weight. *Journal of Counseling and Development, 77,* 379-388.

Fairburn, C. G. (1997). Interpersonal psychotherapy for bulimia nervosa. In D. M. Garner & P. E. Garfinkel (Eds.), *Handbook of treatment for eating disorders* (2nd ed.) (pp. 25-33). New York: Guilford.

Fairburn, C. G., Jones, R., Peveler, R. C., Hope, R. A., & O'Connor, M. (1993). Psychotherapy and bulimia nervosa: The longer-term effects of interpersonal psychotherapy, behavior therapy, and cognitive behavior therapy. *Archives of General Psychiatry, 50,* 419-428.

Fairburn, C. G., Norman, P. A., Welch, S. L., O'Connor, M. E., Doll, H. A., & Peveler, R. C. (1995). A prospective study of outcome in bulimia nervosa and the long-term effects of three psychological treatments. *Archives of General Psychiatry, 52* , 304-312.

Fairburn, C. G., Welch, S. L., Doll, H. A., Davies, B. A., & O'Connor, M. E. (1997). Risk factors for bulimia nervosa: A community-based case-control study. *Archives of General Psychiatry, 54,* 509-517.

Feld, R., Woodside, D. B., Kaplan, A. S., Olmsted, M. P., & Carter, J. C. (2001). Pretreatment motivational enhancement therapy for eating disorders: A pilot study. *International Journal of Eating Disorders, 29,* 393-400.

Fettes, P. A., & Peters, J. M. (1992). A meta-analysis of group treatments for bulimia nervosa. *International Journal of Eating Disorders, 11,* 97-110.

Garner, D. M. (1997). Psychoeducational principles in treatment. In D. M. Garner & P. E. Garfinkel (Eds.), *Handbook of treatment for eating disorders* (2nd ed.) (pp. 145-177). New York: Guilford.

Hall, A. (1985). Group psychotherapy for anorexia nervosa. In D. M. Garner & P. E. Garfinkel (Eds.), *Handbook of psychotherapy for eating disorders* (pp. 213-239). Washington, DC: American Psychiatric Press.

Hendren, R. L., Atkins, D. M., Sumner, C. R., & Barber, J. K. (1987). Model for the group treatment of eating disorders. *International Journal of Group Psychotherapy, 37,* 589-602.

Herzog, D. B., & Delinsky, S. S. (2001). Classification of eating disorders. In R. H. Striegel-Moore & L. Smolak (Eds.), *Eating disorders: Innovative directions in research and practice* (pp. 31-50). Washington, DC: American Psychological Association.

Hobbs, M., Birtchnell, S., Harte, A., & Lacey, H. (1989). Therapeutic factors in short-term group therapy for women with bulimia. *International Journal of Eating Disorders, 8,* 623-633.

Jordan, J., Kaplan, A., Miller, J., Stiver, I., & Surrey, J. (1991). *Women's growth in connection:*

Writings from the Stone Center. New York: Guilford.

Kalodner, C. R., & DeLucia-Waack, J. L (2003). Theory and research on eating disorders and disturbances in women: Suggestions for practice. In M. Kopala and M. Keitel (Eds.), *Handbook of counseling women.* Thousand Oaks, CA: Sage.

Keel, P. K., Mitchell, J. E., Davis, T. L., & Crow, S. J. (2002). Long-term impact of treatment in women diagnosed with bulimia nervosa. *International Journal of Eating Disorders, 31,* 151-158.

Kirkley, B. G., Schneider, J. A., Agras, S., & Bachman, J. A. (1985). Comparison of two group treatments for bulimia. *Journal of Consulting & Clinical Psychology, 53,* 43-48.

Laberg, S., Tornkvist, A., & Andersson, G. (2001). Experiences of patients in cognitive behavioural group therapy: A qualitative study of eating disorders. *Scandinavian Journal of Behaviour Therapy, 30,* 161-178.

Linehan, M. M. (1993). *Cognitive-behavioral treatment of borderline personality disorder.* New York: Guilford.

Linehan, M. M., & Kehrer, C. A. (1993). Borderline personality disorder. In D. H. Barlow (Ed.), *Clinical handbook of psychological disorders: A step-by-step treatment manual* (pp. 396-441). New York: Guilford.

Mintz, L. B., O'Halloran, M. S., Mulholland, A. M., & Schneider, P. A. (1997). The questionnaire for eating disorder diagnoses: Reliability and validity of operationalizing *DSM-IV* criteria into a self-report format. *Journal of Counseling Psychology, 44,* 63-79.

Moreno, J. K. (1998). Long-term psychodynamic group psychotherapy for eating disorders: A descriptive case report. *Journal for Specialists in Group Work, 23,* 269-284.

Mulholland, A. M., & Mintz, L. B. (2001). Prevalence of eating disorders among African American women. *Journal of Counseling Psychology, 48,* 111-116.

Oesterheld, J. R., McKenna, M. S., & Gould, N. B. (1987). Group psychotherapy of bulimia: A critical review. *International Journal of Group Psychotherapy, 57,* 163-184.

Phelps, L., Dempsey, M., Sapia, J., & Nelson, L. (1999). The efficacy of a school-based eating disorder prevention program: Building physical self-esteem and personal competencies. In

N. Piran, M. P. Levine, & C. Steiner-Adair (Eds.), *Preventing eating disorders: A Handbook of interventions and special challenges* (pp. 163-174). Philadelphia: Taylor & Francis.

Piazza, E. A., & Steiner-Adair, C. (1986). Recent trends in group therapy for anorexia nervosa and bulimia. In F. E. F. Larocca (Ed.), *Eating disorders: Effective care and treatment* (pp. 25-51). New York: Wiley.

Piran, N., Levine, M. P., & Steiner-Adair, C. (1999). *Preventing eating disorders: A handbook of interventions and special challenges.* Philadelphia: Taylor & Francis.

Polivy, J., & Federoff, I. (1997). Group psychotherapy. In D. M. Garner & P. E. Garfinkel (Eds.), *Handbook of treatment for eating disorders* (2nd ed.) (pp. 462-475). New York: Guilford.

Polivy, J., & Herman, C. P. (1985). Dieting and binging: A causal analysis. *American Psychologist, 40,* 193-201.

Prochaska, J. O., Norcross, J. C., & DiClemente, C. C. (1994). *Changing for good.* New York: William Morrow.

Richards, P. S., Baldwin, B. M., Frost, H. A., Clark-Sly, J. B., Berrett, M. E., & Hardman, R. K. (2000). What works for treating eating disorders? Conclusions of 28 outcome reviews. *Eating Disorders: The Journal of Treatment and Prevention, 8,* 189-206.

Riess, H. (2002). Integrative time-limited group therapy for bulimia nervosa. *International Journal of Group Psychotherapy, 52,* 1-26.

Romano, S. J., Quinn, L., & Halmi, K. (1994) Cognitive-behavioral group psychotherapy for bulimia nervosa: Clinical considerations and group format. *Eating Disorders: The Journal of Treatment and Prevention, 2,* 31-41.

Smolak, L. (1999). Elementary school curriculum for the primary prevention of eating problems. In N. Piran, M. P. Levine, & C. Steiner-Adair (Eds.), *Preventing eating disorders: A handbook of interventions and special challenges* (pp. 87-104). Philadelphia: Taylor & Francis.

Smolak, L., Levine, M. P., & Schermer, F. (1998). Lessons from lessons: An evaluation of an elementary school prevention program. In W. Vandereycken & G. Noordenbos (Eds.), *The prevention of eating disorders* (pp. 137-172). New York: New York University Press.

Stein, R. I., Saelens, B. E., Dounchis, J. Z., Lewczyk, C. M., Swenson, A. K., & Wilfley, D. E. (2001). Treatment of eating disorders in women. *Counseling Psychologist, 29,* 695-732.

Striegel-Moore, R. H., & Smolak, L. (2001). Introduction. In R. H. Striegel-Moore & L. Smolak (Eds.), *Eating disorders: Innovative directions in research and practice* (pp. 3-7). Washington, DC: American Psychological Association.

Tantillo, M., Bitter, C. N., & Adams, B. (2001). Enhancing readiness for eating disorder treatment: A relational/motivational group model for change. *Eating Disorders: The Journal of Treatment and Prevention, 9,* 203-216.

Telch, C. F., Agras, W. S., & Linehan, M. M. (2001). Dialectical behavior therapy for binge eating disorder. *Journal of Consulting and Clinical Psychology, 69,* 1061-1065.

Thompson, J. K., & Smolak, L. (2001). *Body image, eating disorders, and obesity in youth.* Washington, DC: American Psychological Association.

Van Lone, J. L., Kalodner, C. R., & Coughlin, J. W. (2002). Using short stories to address eating disturbances in groups. *Journal for Specialists in Group Work, 27,* 59-77.

Vandereycken, W., & Noordenbos, G. (1998). *The prevention of eating disorders.* New York: New York University Press.

Wilfley, D. E., Agras, S. W., Telch, C. F., Rossiter, E. M., Schneider, J. A., Cole, A. B., et al. (1993). Group cognitive-behavioral therapy and group interpersonal psychotherapy for the non-purging bulimic individual: A controlled comparison. *Journal of Consulting & Clinical Psychology, 61,* 296-305.

Wilson, G. T., Fairburn, C. G., & Agras, W. S. (1997). Cognitive-behavioral therapy for bulimia nervosa. In D. M. Garner & P. E. Garfinkel (Eds.), *Handbook of treatment for eating disorders* (2nd ed.) (pp. 67-93). New York: Guilford.

Zerbe, K. J. (1993). Whose body is it anyway? Understanding and treating psychosomatic aspects of eating disorders. *Bulletin of the Menninger Clinic, 57,* 161-177.

Zimpfer, D. G. (1990). Group work for bulimia: A review of outcomes. *Journal for Specialists in Group Work, 15,* 239-251.

36

GROUPS FOR SURVIVORS OF CHILDHOOD SEXUAL ABUSE

DEBORAH A. GERRITY

University at Buffalo, SUNY

TRICA L. PETERSON

University at Buffalo, SUNY

INCIDENCE AND DEFINITIONS

In 1989, Goodwin and Talwar wrote that childhood sexual abuse (CSA) is "a condition that now occurs more frequently than does tonsillectomy" (p. 104). Research supports that between 16% (Russell, 1983) and 44% (Briere & Runtz, 1987) of American females and 5% to 16% (Finkelhor, 1993) of males were subjected to some form of sexual abuse as children. In a 1994 review of international studies, Finkelhor found that 7% to 36% of women and 3% to 29% of men had histories of CSA.

CSA is the sexual exploitation of a child by an older person for the adult's satisfaction while ignoring a child's (a) developmental immaturity, (b) inability to understand sexual behavior, (c) inability to give informed consent, and (d) lesser physical authority and status compared to the adult (Courtois, 1996). According to the National Clearinghouse on Child Abuse and Neglect Information (2002), "Sexual abuse includes fondling a child's genitals, intercourse, incest, rape, sodomy, exhibitionism, and commercial exploitation through prostitution or the production of pornographic materials" (p. 3). The majority of CSA is perpetrated by males who are family members or known by the child (Courtois, 1996; Finkelhor, 1993).

This chapter discusses group treatment for those who have experienced CSA. Psycho-educational, counseling, and therapy groups are discussed, although usually there are not clear demarcations in the literature between these types of groups because education is often mixed with counseling and therapy (Gerrity, 1998). The chapter is divided into groups for adolescents/adults and preadolescent children. Although most of the literature focuses on female survivors, the chapter includes some of the sparse information on male survivors.

ADVANTAGES AND INTEGRATION OF GROUP TREATMENT

CSA treatment is usually long term, multimodal, and multidimensional because of the pervasive effects of abuse, the compounded consequences due to delayed treatment of abuse, and the complexities of the posttraumatic responses (Courtois, 1996). Finkelhor (1986) identified four causes of the trauma: sexualization, stigmatization, betrayal, and powerlessness. Often, treatment resembles reparenting, with the goal being to help a client move from victim to survivor, gain hope, and individuate (Courtois, 1996). Therapists, therefore, have the dual task of assisting survivors in reviewing the abuse and working through the aftereffects.

Consistently throughout the literature, group treatment for CSA survivors has been highly recommended (Briere, 1996; Gonsiorek, Bera, & LeTourneau, 1994; Herman, 1992). Group interventions allow survivors to (a) normalize the aftereffects of abuse, (b) identify and develop a therapeutic relationship with other group members, (c) recognize universality, (d) break the secrecy and acknowledge their abuse, (e) experience a support network or surrogate family, (f) create a context and catalyst to explore and challenge emotions, beliefs, and childhood messages, (g) have a grief forum, (h) have a place to observe and explore interpersonal patterns and client dynamics, and (i) recognize ineffective and maladaptive dissociation (Briere, 1996; Courtois, 1996; Shaffer, Brown, & McWhirter, 1998).

Group advantages over individual therapy include "benefits of lessened isolation and stigmatization, reduced shame, . . . the opportunity to help as well as be helped—a process that supports self-esteem and lessens the sense of being a deviant, passive recipient of treatment" (Briere, 1996, p. 170). In addition, Talbot et al. (1998) related that therapy with a peer group helps lessen the perceived power of the authority figures (leaders) and helps break down resistance and regression that may occur in individual treatment. Forseth and Brown (1981) also stated that three quarters of programs offering treatment for abused children provided group interventions. Stalker and Fry (1999) compared 10 sessions of group versus individual treatment and found no differences between the treatments but significant improvements from pretest to posttest for both interventions. Since groups are more cost and time efficient, they may be the intervention of choice.

Therefore, group is widely accepted as a primary mode of therapy for CSA survivors. The specific type of group utilized (e.g., psychoeducational, counseling, therapy) is often dependent on the survivor's current stage of healing from the abuse. The specific interventions incorporated depend on the theoretical framework to which the therapists adhere.

THERAPEUTIC MODELS RELATED TO CSA GROUPS

Therapeutic models related to group interventions for sexual abuse populations come from several frameworks. Existential/process and feminist theories have particular relevance to this population. At the end of this section, Judith Herman's (1992) stage model is discussed as a way to decide which interventions are appropriate to which groups of survivors.

Existential/Process Groups. Yalom (1995) delineated group treatment that focuses on the process of interaction among group members in the here and now. He described therapeutic factors that contribute to the benefits of group therapy: vicarious learning (Friedrich, 1990; Homeyer, 1999), instillation of hope (Friedrich, 1990), universality (Friedrich, 1990; Homeyer, 1999), group cohesiveness (Friedrich, 1990; Homeyer, 1999), and catharsis (Friedrich, 1990). These factors are thought to provide members with opportunities to experience belonging, acceptance, self-analysis, and a release from negative feelings (Hansen, Hecht, & Futa, 1998). Randall (1995) compared the curative factors rankings across three female incest survivors groups. He found that cohesiveness, self-understanding, and family reenactment were the top three factors in the two long-term treatment groups. While family reenactment was not in the top rankings of the short-term group, both catharsis and existential learning were.

Feminist. Feminist theory states that each client is an expert on his or her own life and experiences and that egalitarian relationships among members and with leaders is crucial to healing (Courtois, 1999). Therefore, feminist group leaders try to break down power dynamics and increase autonomy and empowerment for group members. Leaders emphasize members' control from the start, giving information and reinforcing choices (Valente & Shuttleworth, 1997). The development of safety in the group and acknowledgment of the strength necessary to seek help are important. In addition, leaders give affirmation, answer questions, and offer reassurance. Through this, members are encouraged to recognize their ability to influence their own lives.

Feminists have supported group therapy as a strong, significant intervention for females who have been sexually abused (Rittenhouse, 1997). For women, relationships and intimacy facilitate maturation and development (Gilligan, 1982). "Because pain, terror, and shame have been linked with relating to important others, survivors find it hard to know whom to trust or how to behave in a trustworthy fashion" (Rittenhouse, 1997, p. 112). Courtois (1996) and Herman (1992) suggested that part of the healing from sexual trauma for women is learning to relate in a healthy manner and create supportive, nurturing connections with nonabusive others. This reduces isolation, shame, and guilt and teaches survivors ways to develop healthy judgments regarding whom to trust. Feminist therapists use the group to educate members about political and societal influences that contribute to their problems and to externalize the blame to those who had power in the abusive situation (Rittenhouse, 1997). Members are assisted in developing their own sense of self in relation to the group and then to also generalize that learning to the outside world.

Stage Model. Herman (1992) delineated the stages through which survivors need to progress to heal from the abuse. Because boundaries were violated, the needs of the child were dismissed, and trust was broken, survivors in the first stage need to learn to create safety and become aware of their own basic needs. In the second stage, they need to clarify and come to terms with the abuse experience. Finally, they need to integrate their abuse identity into who they are as complete and healthy individuals. Herman recommends specific types of groups suitable for each stage.

For CSA survivors who have not addressed safety and trust issues, the group should be cognitively oriented and structured. Psychoeducational groups best fit this stage because they allow the exchange of information on trauma aftereffects, symptom patterns, and self-care strategies. Groups should focus on strengths and coping abilities of the survivor while protecting against being overwhelmed. Group process is related to maintaining boundaries and offering support, not confrontation and interpersonal relating.

The second stage is for individuals who have established safety and a support network in their lives. These individuals have amassed the personal and interpersonal resources necessary to confront the reality of the abuse and its effect on their lives. Counseling and therapy groups address the issues with which individuals in the second stage need to work. Through telling the story of the abuse to a small group of others, it has the effect of "releasing her from her isolation with the perpetrator and readmitting the fullness of the larger world from which she has been alienated" (Herman, 1992, p. 222). Leaders need to actively structure the sessions and orient members to work with their memories. Members need to be committed to exploration and understand the goals of treatment. Time-limited groups work best for this stage, so that members realize that feelings will intensify during the group, but that there will be an end. Herman believes that the focus for this type of group is in the past, not on the present, and the goal is mastery over the content and memories of the abuse. The task is to remember and mourn.

Groups for the third stage address reconnection, and any type of group is appropriate. Counseling groups may address different coping styles, interpersonal functioning and relationships, and sexual dysfunction. Since dysfunctional styles of relating to others may take a long time to erase, open-ended therapy groups provide a safe place to practice relating to others in a healthy, consistent manner. The more competent survivors become in their interpersonal skills, the more they benefit from a diverse, heterogeneous group composition. At the beginning of this stage, the trauma is still a central part of the identity of the survivor, but by the end, it is integrated into the whole personality and does not define who he or she is.

Throughout the rest of the chapter, these theories are recognizable in the various models and process and outcome studies presented. Readers are encouraged to seek additional information on other prominent models of sexual abuse intervention, such as psychoanalytic (Frawley-O'Dea, 1997), attachment (Mitchum, 1987), cognitive processing (Chard, Weaver, & Resick, 1997; DiVitto, 1998), and social constructivist theories (Sheinberg, True, & Fraenkel, 1994).

CRITICAL THERAPEUTIC ISSUES

Leadership

The adoption of a therapeutic framework for developing CSA groups is only one of the issues that leaders face. It is imperative that leaders be cognizant of potential legal issues, sexual abuse aftereffects, and general group therapy techniques (Knight, 1997). Since group members may disclose continuing or current abuse of someone else in their family, knowledge of legal statutes regarding mandated reporting of abuse is critical. The aftereffects of CSA may be chronic or acute and/or appear and remit periodically and spontaneously. The abuse may affect children's abilities to learn and develop platonic and/or romantic relationships (Reeker, Ensing, & Elliot, 1997). CSA survivors are at risk of abusing others (Blount & Chandler, 1979), abusing themselves (Levenkron, 1998), and being in abusive relationships (Courtois, 1996). Chronic depression is the most common symptom. Generalized anxiety, fear, apprehension, anxiety attacks, sleep disturbance, nightmares, and various phobias, including agoraphobia, claustrophobia, and fear of the dark continue into adulthood (Courtois, 1996). Survivors frequently report self-loathing, emotional numbness, feelings of isolation, stigmatization, negative self-concept and self-esteem, and inability to trust. They may experience guilt, shame, betrayal, or lowered self-image because their body was aroused or climactic despite their efforts to control the sensations. Adult survivors often alternate between feeling helpless and powerless, and malignantly powerful (Weiner, 1988).

While some aspects of abuse transcend gender, male survivors do have some issues that are unique (Pescolido, 1988). A male survivor often confronts issues about his sexuality and masculinity (Friedrich, 1995) and may exhibit different behavior patterns than females in sexual abuse groups, such as increased sexual behavior (Friedrich, 1995) and aggression (Zamanian & Adams, 1997). "Whereas female victims often overcompensate for their fears of sexuality by becoming hypersexual, male victims can overcompensate by becoming hyperaggressive" (Goodwin & Talwar, 1989, p. 281).

"Since the abuse often occurred in what should be the safest of places—their homes and in intimate relationships—they [CSA survivors] are skeptical and suspicious about the therapist's promise of a safe atmosphere" (Buchele, 2000, p. 183). Leaders need to understand that when disclosing, group members may have two fears: (1) that others will see them as defective and (2) that there will be retribution for the disclosure. As group members share their stories, their isolation turns to a sense of affiliation, and they begin a trustful relationship with someone in authority. Leaders should expect members to vacillate between idealization and anger, both of which are directed at the leader in his or her role as the authority. It is the exploration of these transferences that assist group members in working through their trust and authority issues (Buchele, 2000). As the healing progresses for CSA survivors, they need to struggle with a loss of the central piece of their identity. For most of their life, the sexual abuse may have been a defining characteristic of who they are, and they may fear the emptiness and void left as they let go of this identity. Leaders are essential to helping members see that they are integrating the strengths from their previous identity into the growing identity of themselves as a whole individual.

Gartner (1997) describes the dynamic between patients and therapist as one in which the patient tries to re-create the abusive relationships with the therapist. One of the important lessons that the therapist can teach the patient is that it is possible to have a warm, caring relationship that does not include abuse or sex. Buchele (2000) discusses common countertransference issues that include dreading sessions; feeling unskilled and incompetent; wishing to rescue members; feeling voyeuristic; and experiencing anger, fascination, extreme frustration, and paranoia. Therapists who work with survivors may feel that they deserve special status and entitlement for working with this population. Reactions of shock and horror to the abuse details can cause a leader to hurry the member into awareness and insight without appropriately exploring affect and other after-effects (Gartner, 1997). Leaders need to be aware of their reactions to member stories and use them in a self-diagnostic manner. Leaders can experience a kind of secondary posttraumatic reaction (Figley, 1995). When leaders experience too much emotional reaction and the inability to stop the intrusion of thoughts, or desensitization and numbing, this suggests a need for intervention via supervision or counseling for themselves. Failure of group leaders to address these countertransferences can lead to retraumatization of group members (Figley, 1995).

One way to address transference issues is coleadership. Many authors agree that CSA groups should be co-led (Courtois, 1996; Douglas & Matson, 1989; Harris, 1998; Herman, 1992; Knight, 1997). The stress and risk of burnout is high; having another professional with whom to review personal reactions, group dynamics, and countertransference issues is valuable. In addition, coleaders can model healthy discussion and confrontation as they interact with each other within the group sessions (Herman, 1992).

Boundaries

Because boundaries have been transgressed for CSA survivors, many have few or poor boundaries (Mathews & Gerrity, 2002). CSA survivors also can be very skillful at pushing boundaries. Douglas and Matson (1989) stated that time boundaries are very difficult for leaders to enforce. There may be pressure on group leaders from members to interact outside of group in a social or mentoring relationship. This elicits concerns about dual relationships.

Depending on the theoretical framework and the types of groups being led, there is disagreement on another boundary issue: whether, and the degree to which, leaders should self-disclose (Gerrity & Mathews, 2003). Often leaders are asked by members whether they themselves are survivors. The question itself allows the leaders to explore with members in what ways this knowledge will be helpful to them. This can help members reflect on what they need for trust and safety and how leadership by a survivor or nonsurvivor might make a difference to them. Leaders should reflect on their self-disclosure before and after to assess its impact on the group and on individual members.

Memory Issues

Courtois (1999) stated that "more than 35 scientific studies . . . document various degrees of forgetting (or amnesia) for experience of CSA, . . . 4.5 percent to 68 percent [of CSA survivors] depending on the study" (p. 124). There is an ongoing debate about whether leaders should have group members describe their abuse experiences in detail. Turner (1993) says that shame and guilt are dispelled by publicly airing the secret, having others hear the story, and placing the responsibility on the perpetrator. Herman (1992) asserted, "[I]nvariably the group offers a fresh emotional perspective that provides a bridge to new memories" (p. 224).

However, Clancy, Schacter, McNally, and Pitman (2000) stated that "individuals who report frequent episodes of dissociation (disruptions in consciousness) may be especially likely to confuse the products of imagination and the products of perception" (p. 26). Courtois (1999) suggests that therapists should focus on the consequences of the trauma. It is important to help survivors stabilize aftereffects and empower them to function as healthy individuals who make meaning of their own history. Memories of abuse should be addressed as they occur naturally in treatment. Goals are to validate and normalize the experience, while moderating the intensity of the group. It is the responsibility of the therapist to remain objective and help members to tolerate ambiguity and doubts. Practitioners should rely on informed consent procedures that address risks and benefits of treatment, the treatment framework, roles, boundaries, limitations, safety issues, and treatment alternatives.

ORGANIZING A GROUP

Screening and Selection

Since group treatment is more intense than individual, and leaders and members have less capacity to control the speed and content of the group, it is important to choose members carefully. Herman (1992) stated, "Just as it is never safe to assume that a traumatized individual's family will be supportive, it is never safe to assume that a group of people will be able to rally and cohere simply because all of its members have suffered from the same terrible event" (p. 219). Leaders have different approaches to the selection, ranging from accepting all, to excluding those who are psychotic, suicidal, or have unstable life situations (actively abusing substances, homeless, active domestic violence, etc.; Douglas & Matson, 1989). For additional information on screening criteria for adults, see Briere (1996), Chard et al. (1997), Courtois (1996), Harris (1998), and Knight (1997).

Appropriate screening and selection of participants in CSA groups for children is also extremely vital (Friedrich, 1990). Attention is given to selecting children who are of similar developmental age and physical size (Jones, 2002). Likewise, children who have recently been abused are often treated in individual therapy before going into the group setting (Homeyer, 1999; Jones, 2002).

Another advantage of screening other than of choosing prospective members is that it gives the group leader(s) the opportunity to pretrain about the norms of the group, how to give and receive appropriate feedback, and the role of leaders and members. Palmer, Baker, and McGee (1997) found that a two-page pretraining essay given to selected members increased self-disclosure and cohesion in their incest survivor group.

Group Structure

Several different types of group therapy are currently being used in treatment, including support groups, short-term or time-limited groups, long-term or open-ended groups, and retreats (Courtois, 1996). Structure can be a very important tool in the intervention process, providing safety and allowing survivors to observe consistent, clear, and explicit boundaries regarding the therapeutic process. Most practitioners agree that a session should be at least 1½ to 2 hours long (Gerrity & Mathews, 2003). However, this can vary, based on the attention span of group members, types of activities employed, and the setting. The number of sessions may differ, based on the theoretical framework as well as the type of setting, the goals of the group, and whether the group is a psychoeducational, counseling, or therapy group.

Briere (1996) recommended that group members also participate in concurrent individual therapy due to their high levels of stress accruing from both their own memories and listening to the stories of other group members. Douglas and Matson (1989) stated that concurrent individual therapy helps with more disturbed clients and mediates the emotional turmoil of termination. It allows for a safe place to discuss issues that cannot be processed in the group, due to time concerns or individual needs (Harris, 1998; Shaffer et al., 1998).

ADOLESCENT AND ADULT GROUPS

Group models are categorized into psychoeducational, interpersonal/process, and other theoretical/mixed intervention groups. Most research studies are not specific to an intervention, and the majority of therapeutic effort has been directed toward the treatment needs of females, leaving practitioners of male sexual abuse groups without empirical guidance (Hack, Osachuk, & DeLuca, 1994). Pescolido (1988) described a deficiency in the literature regarding "the dynamics, the structure, and the process of treatment of male children who are sexually abused" (p. 103) that still exists in 2002. Of the studies that have been conducted on adult females, small samples and instruments with poor or no reliability and validity information are often utilized. Control groups with survivor members are not frequently used due to the ethical implications of withholding treatment from clients in need of services, and control groups containing nonabused members do not provide adequate information about the specific efficacy of group treatment for CSA survivors. In addition, few studies have included long-term follow-up measures, providing little information about the impact of group therapy on survivors' future experiences.

Marotta and Asner (1999) reviewed 21 studies of groups for adult female incest survivors. The majority of studies were descriptive or case studies, and only 3 used pretest-posttest designs. Studies were rated on research design with a score from 0 to 12, with 12 being most rigorous. The top three, Alexander, Neimeyer, and Follette (1989), Follette, Alexander, and Follette (1991), and Roberts and Lie (1989), scored 11, 11, and 10 respectively and are described later in this chapter (Alexander et al. and Follette et al. used the same sample). Other examples of groups discussed are from a variety of models, highlighting some more interesting designs. Table 36.1 provides a brief overview of research studies on group interventions, including goals, sample description, interventions, and outcomes.

Psychoeducation

Most psychoeducational groups are designed for children and are discussed later in the chapter. Those for adults are intended to work with survivors in the first of Herman's (1992) stages. The Women's Safety in Recovery (Talbot et al., 1998, 1999) groups are designed for individuals who are acutely ill. The goal is to educate members about trauma and self-care in order to establish safety and control. The groups are co-led by female and male leaders to model mixed gender cooperation and collaboration. They are open to new members and meet three times a week for 3 weeks, with each week covering a different topic. The week on control of

the body addresses physical health issues such as substance abuse, self-harming behaviors, sexuality, and distorted perceptions of the body. The control of the environment module focuses on judgments about safety, trustworthiness, and danger. The control of the emotions module addresses posttraumatic stress disorder, dissociation, anger, guilt, and interpersonal relationships while helping members identify their own triggers. Emotion-managing strategies such as social support, physical activity, psychotherapy, and relaxation techniques are planned. The program reduced negative emotions and improved patient functioning.

Interpersonal/Process Groups

Groups with interpersonal goals place emphasis on interactions between individual group members and between group members and leaders to help members learn and practice skills that can be applied outside the group. These groups (see Table 36.1: Alexander et al., 1989, 1991; Carver, Stalker, Stewart, & Abraham, 1989; Douglas & Matson, 1989; Follette et al., 1991; Hazzard, Rogers, & Angert, 1993; Herman & Schatzow, 1984; Longstreth, Mason, Schrieber, & Tsao-Wei, 1998; Lundqvist & Ojehagen, 2001; Neimeyer, Harter, & Alexander, 1991; Richter, Snider, & Gorey, 1997; Tsai & Wagner, 1978) tend not to have organized exercises and structured presentations, but focus mainly on the process of the group communication. On the basis of the above studies, these groups significantly decreased negative emotional impact, as well as increased self-esteem and improved social skills and interactions.

Pistorello and Follette (1998) found that CSA survivors with communication problems were more likely to have been abused at an earlier age. The most frequent themes related to relationship problems for survivors "revolved around sex-related (e.g., dissociation), survivor-specific (e.g., confusing partner and perpetrator), partner-specific (e.g., personal difficulties), relationship-specific (e.g., difficulty expressing emotion), and attitudinal (e.g., negative attitudes toward men) themes" (pp. 478-479). When tested with another set of four short-term groups, the predominant themes were emotional

(*Text continues on page 509*)

Table 36.1   Research on Groups for Survivors of Childhood Sexual Abuse

Study	Sample	# of Sessions	Interventions and/or Constructs	Outcomes[a]
Alexander et al. (1989, 1991)	65 adult females in 8 groups; Caucasian and Black	Co-led; 1.5 hrs/10 wks	Interpersonal transaction (IT) vs. process groups vs. wait list control	Both group formats had improved adjustment compared to wait list and maintained at 6 mo follow-up. IT group: less overall distress, less group conflict compared to process group. Process group: improved social adjustment compared to IT. Generally, women with no previous therapy experience preferred IT and those with experience preferred the process group.
Bagley and Young (1998)	Mothers: 29 CSA group tx vs. 28 CSA individual tx vs. 60 nonabused	1 hr/15 wks	Multimodal, eclectic	Group compared to individual decreased social isolation. Group pre to 6 yrs post: significant increase in self-esteem. Significant decreases in depression, suicidal ideation, suicide attempts, and social isolation. CSA still significantly less self-esteem and more symptoms than nonabused at 6 yrs.
Carver et al. (1989)	57 adult females	10-15 wks	Process-oriented; dropout characteristics; assessment, pretest and posttesting	Members who were employed, never hospitalized, and not in individual therapy were more likely to complete the group. All subscales but paranoid ideation on SCL-90 improved from pre to post but there were no significant changes in depression (Zung Self-Rating Depression Scale) or self-esteem (Texas Social Behavior Inventory). Group was rated as helpful, especially sharing, being understood, being with others and not feeling different, and breaking the secret. Members reported feeling more anger and less guilt and responsibility.
Chard et al. (1997)	15 women in 3 PTSD groups	1.5 hrs/17 wks (group) and individual 1 hr wks 1-8 and 17	Combined individual and group cognitive processing therapy: process feelings and cognitions, and practice skills; address memories, reconstruct, integrate and process the abuse, and future planning	Improvement in PTSD, global symptoms, and depression. At pretest, all had PTSD but none at posttest. Decreases in negative cognitions, and improvements in managing stress, relationships, and sexual functioning. Most helpful was normalizing and confrontation.

(Continued)

Table **36.1** (Continued)

Study	Sample	# of Sessions	Interventions and/or Constructs	Outcomes[a]
DeLuca, Boyes, Grayston, and Romano (1995)	35 girls, aged 7-12 yrs, 6-8 members per group	9-12 wk, 1.5 hrs, female co-leaders	Psychoeducational: activities addressing feelings toward offender, self-esteem, body image, sex education, abuse prevention	Increased self-esteem, decreased anxiety and behavior problems.
DiVitto (1998)	10 adult outpatients	8 weeks	Cognitive-behavioral; affect via a self-regulation group, increase constructive behavioral responses	Decreases in flashbacks, dissociation, suicidal ideation, self-harm, panic. Increases in rage and anger, identifying triggers of symptoms, and controlling behavior.
Douglas and Matson (1989)	8 women (20-30 yrs of age) male and female coleaders	Individual screening and group goal discussion/ 1.25 hrs x 10-wk group	Process: reduce isolation, guilt, and anger; break the secret; understand relationship between abuse and current problems; learn about sexual development, abuse, and safety for children; and provide support	Most highly rated contributions were from male therapist, followed by female therapist and other members. No reduction in general stress or improvement in general health.
Follette et al. (1991)	65 adult females in 8 groups; Caucasian and Black	Co-led; 1.5 hrs/10 wks	Interpersonal transaction (IT) vs. process groups vs. wait list control	Pretreatment adjustment was associated with marital adjustment and depression. Overall predictors of positive outcome included higher education, unmarried, less severity of abuse, and lower distress and depression.
Gilovich and Miller (1994)	89 Caucasian females (per group: 5-8 adolescents and 6-14 adults) ages 12-60	Weekend retreat, 4-5 facilitators per retreat	Mentoring and exploration; topics included sexuality, empowerment, identity, anger, self-abuse, safety, trust, shame, guilt, family	Self-report: adolescents identified with adult survivors, adults felt part of a group, all reevaluated culpability, gained hope and strength, grieved, experienced positive play, felt altruism and increased self-esteem. Problems included boundary issues, countertransference, and need for limit setting.
Hack, Osachuk, and DeLuca (1994)	6 boys aged 8-11 yrs.	12 wks, plus intake interview, 1.5 hrs	Psychoeducational: identify and label emotions, discussing blame, sex education	Decreased anxiety and depression, increased self-esteem, improved externalizing and internalizing behaviors as reported by caregivers.

(Continued)

Table 36.1 (Continued)

Study	Sample	# of Sessions	Interventions and/or Constructs	Outcomes[a]
Hazzard et al. (1993)	102 adult females, 92% Caucasian	1.5 hrs/1 yr, 4-10 members	Process-oriented; pretest and posttest	At pretest, trauma symptomology was related to number of abusers, dissociation to age at start of abuse, and overall distress to type of abuse. Group dropouts were more likely to have previous hospitalizations. Pre and post differences on increased locus of control and self-esteem, and decreased sexual avoidance and problems, trauma-related symptomatology, and overall psychopathology.
Herman and Schatzow (1984)	20 adult females	Co-led 3 grps w/ 5-7 members; 1.5 hrs/10 wks	Process-oriented telling of stories, setting goals, and action plans. Pre, post, and 6-mo follow-up	Most helpful was contact with other survivors. Improved self-esteem, decreased shame, guilt, isolation, and increased safety.
Hiebert-Murphy et al. (1992)	5 females, aged 7-9 yrs.	9 wks, plus intake interview, 90 minutes	Psychoeducational: discussion and activities regarding disclosure, labeling feelings, assertiveness self-esteem, sex education, peer relationships	Decrease in parent report of internalizing and externalizing behavior problems, no change in self-reported self-esteeem.
Longstreth et al. (1998)	19 women from 8 groups co-led by social workers	1.5 hrs/16 wks	Validation of abuse and responses to it; process-oriented psychotherapy	Increased self-image, coping techniques, relationships, and mothering. Improvement on all SCL-90-R symptoms, self-blame, and boundaries. At 1-yr follow-up only hostility was not different from pretest. No differences in use of medical services were found.
Lundqvist and Ojehagen (2001)	22 women in 5 groups	2 yrs	Psychodynamic; improvement of psychiatric symptoms and social functioning	Overall reduction in symptoms, higher appreciation of social interactions, improvement in social adjustment, ability to identify feelings and improve self-esteem. Most reported improvements in relationships with partners, children, and friends.
Morgan and Cummings (1999)	40 women in tx group vs. 40 non-tx	20 weeks	Relationship building and trauma processing (feminist/cognitive-behavioral); relaxation, imagery, support building, and discussions re: boundaries, PTSD, dissociation, relationships, and change	Significant deceases in depression, social maladjustment, self-blame, and PTSD. No differences on anger.

(Continued)

Table 36.1 (Continued)

Study	Sample	# of Sessions	Interventions and/or Constructs	Outcomes[a]
Naar et al. (1998)	6 women per group, ages 23-55	3 hrs/9 wks	Psychodrama; exploration of each member's personal stories	Qualitative descriptions of decrease in guilt, shame, and isolation.
Neimeyer et al. (1991)	49 adult females (abused by father or stepfather); 69% White, 27% Black; 4% Hispanic	Co-led by females; 8 grps; 1.5 hrs/10 wks	Effects of group (IT or process) participation; pre, post, and follow-up	Those who identified quickly with group leaders and members showed greatest improvement. Those polarizing therapists and members showed poor outcomes. Member polarization is predictive in early sessions but therapist polarization is predictive at both early and later sessions, and was predictive of psychiatric distress at follow-up.
Nelki and Watters (1989)	6 female children ages 4-8 yrs., male and female cotherapists	9 wks, 1 hour, parallel caregivers group	Psychoeducational and process: safety, secrets, disclosure, processing anger and responsibility	Increased confidence, decrease in reported behavioral problems from pre to post treatment.
Reeker and Ensing (1998)	19 children (5-8 yrs of age) in 4 mixed gender groups	12-wk curriculum ran twice	Psychoeducational: abuse prevention strategies, sexual education, placing blame for abuse, sharing feelings about abuse	Decrease in behavior problems, increased knowledge of sexual information and abuse prevention strategies, increased self-esteem.
Richter et al. (1997)	115 adult women, 4-10 members per group vs. wait list	1.5-2 hrs/15 wks	Problem-solving process group; recorded goals and monitored each other's progress; poetry, prose, bibliotherapy, and discussion exercises	Decrease in depression and increase in self-esteem; 6-mo follow-up found continued improvement.
Roberts and Lie (1989)	52 adult females	9 closed groups	Process with psychoeducational components	Pre, post, follow-up design with improvements in depression and perception of well-being.
Stauffer and Deblinger (1996)	19 nonoffending mothers and their 19 sexually abused children age 2-6 yrs in 6 groups	11 wks, 2-hr sessions, parallel mother and child groups	Cognitive-behavioral: body safety, communication, and coping skill development and behavior management techniques	Decrease in child sexualized behaviors, decrease in maternal general distress, increased appropriate maternal responses to child.

(Continued)

Table 36.1 (Continued)

Study	Sample	# of Sessions	Interventions and/or Constructs	Outcomes[a]
Talbot et al. (1998)	56 inpatient females, using male and female cotherapists	1 hr, 3 x wk for 3 wks	Women's Safety in Recovery (WSR) psychoeducation; control over the body; control over the environment; control over emotions	Reduction in interpersonal sensitivity, anxiety, hostility, phobic anxiety, and paranoid ideation.
Talbot et al. (1999)	43 adult inpatient females	Usual 20 hrs vs. WSR group: co-led, 1 hr 3 x/wk for 3 wks	Usual tx = group (nonabuse-related) and activity therapies vs. Women's Safety in Recovery (WSR) group with focus on abuse, safety, and control in a psychoeducational, mixed format	WSR had significantly greater reduction on global severity index, including interpersonal sensitivity, anxiety, hostility, phobic anxiety, and paranoid ideation. Sexual abuse issues were more thoroughly addressed (both patient and therapist reports).
Tsai and Wagner (1978)	23 adult females, ages 19-53	Co-led male and female; 10 grps w/4-6 members; 1.5 hrs/4 sessions	Process-oriented: telling story and discussing repercussions	At 6-mo follow-up, group was seen as helpful. Most helpful were sharing feelings, similar experiences, being understood, release of feelings, and learning what could be done. Members reported less guilt and more self-acceptance. Relationships with partners improved.
Westbury and Tutty (1999)	22 women tx groups vs. 10 wait list, all in concurrent individual tx	2.5 hrs/10-12 wks	Body-focused feminist; tell their story	Significant decreases in depression and anxiety.
Zlotnik et al. (1997)	48 women with PTSD; tx group vs. wait list control	2 hrs/15 wks	Affect management; psychoeducational, skill building, skill application, homework	~25% dropout for both tx and control groups related to high dissociation and PTSD. At end, only 13% of tx group and 59% of wait list still met PTSD criteria.

a. Only statistically significant findings are presented.

communication and intimacy, control issues within the relationship, lack of boundaries, blaming the survivor's history, and negative attitudes. The first two were found in half of the coded segments, suggesting that much of process group therapy centers on relationship concerns.

Alexander et al. (1989, 1991) compared time-limited interpersonal therapy groups to process groups and a wait list sample and found both treatment groups efficacious in treating social adjustment, depression, and general distress. The interpersonal transaction group included a new disclosure topic each week (e.g., feeling different, perceptions of self, helplessness, trust, family secrets). Members discussed the topic in pairs and then the group discussed the issue and found similarities and differences among members. In the process group, members shared their history and goals for the group. The rest of the group focus was on member interactions with each other, based on topics that members brought to the group. Follette et al. (1991), using the data from these groups, found that marital adjustment and depression were predictive of pretreatment adjustment. Less education, being married, high pretreatment distress, and depression were associated with poorer therapy outcomes. Also, type of abuse predicted treatment outcome, with those experiencing oral genital abuse or intercourse improving less than those experiencing other types of sexual abuse.

Friedman (1994) described a psychodynamic long-term therapy group for men. Group themes included group boundaries, safety, power and control, intimacy, shame/guilt, and the aftereffects of trauma. While not different from themes in groups for women, Friedman describes gender-related dynamics and conflicts related specifically to all male groups, in addition to concerns for members whose perpetrators were male.

Other Interventions

Other types of treatment include cognitive-behavioral, psychoanalytic, feminist, and mixed approaches. These groups have less structure than psychoeducational groups, are usually more structured than process groups, and often include a skill-building component. Overall, CSA groups that used other interventions have been successful in decreasing negative affect symptomology, increasing skills to identify triggers of negative emotions, and increasing self-esteem and self-worth. (See Table 36.1 for outcome research: Bagley & Young, 1998; Chard et al., 1997; DiVitto, 1998; Gilovich & Miller, 1994; Morgan & Cummings, 1999; Naar, Doreian-Michael, & Santhouse, 1998; Roberts & Lie, 1989; Stauffer & Deblinger, 1996; Westbury & Tutty, 1999; Zlotnik et al., 1997.)

Affect. Some groups are designed to specifically focus on certain types of affect. Groups with a focus on affect expression and regulation encourage survivors to fully experience their emotions and feelings in a healthy, stable manner. However, it is common for dissociative symptoms to present a barrier to the realization of this therapeutic goal. Therefore, these symptoms are often directly addressed in affect-oriented groups. While dissociation was useful at the time of the trauma, survivors tend not to learn how to manage and regulate feelings and often have pervasive numbing of all affect, marked emotionality, or intense swings between these two extremes. The impact can increase destructive patterns that lead to revictimization, personality disorders, and a host of other negative consequences.

Shaffer, Brown, and McWhirter (1998) used a four-phase plan to help address dissociative coping in the group context. The goal was for members to realize the triggers that led to dissociation and acquire methods of remaining present in the here and now, even when triggers were present. In the first phase, an atmosphere of safety, development of cohesiveness, and education about long-term effects of CSA and PTSD was fostered. Phase 2 dealt with feelings and dissociation by helping members to separate the past from the present, identify their triggers, and recognize ways to break through the dissociation. Homework and structured exercises were frequently used, and contact between members outside of group was considered very useful. In Phase 3, additional education and coping strategies, such as reframing, reemphasizing skills and concepts, and skill development, were important in enabling members to challenge faulty beliefs and thoughts. The fourth phase was devoted to farewell rituals, helping group members to consolidate gains made during group, and discussing ways of maintaining these gains after termination.

DiVitto (1998) related another approach to disrupt dissociative coping. A grounding box that included sensory stimuli was used to bring people back to the here and now: "Peppermint for taste, cinnamon and perfume for smell, and ice packs, and velvet and satin swatches for touch. Verbal redirection to open the eyes and look at the therapist stimulates sight. The patient is encouraged to use counting or poetry reciting, spoken out loud to stimulate hearing" (p. 82). Group members are encouraged to monitor dissociation in themselves and other members and assist each other in using the grounding box.

Cognitive-Behavioral. Survivor groups with cognitive and behavioral restructuring goals focus on changing how members think about their experiences and learning and practicing new skills. Chard et al. (1997) described a combined individual and group intervention based on cognitive processing theory (CPT). Individual therapy was designed to address the clients' memories of the abuse and help them reconstruct, integrate, and process the abuse experience. In the group, members were introduced to information processing theory, PTSD symptomatology, and family systems dynamics, and asked to reflect on positive and negative relationships and to focus on cognitive concepts by identifying antecedent events, beliefs, and consequences to those beliefs. The group focused on five main themes: safety, trust, power, esteem, and intimacy, with an emphasis on helping members see the impact that the trauma has had and how these issues interrelate to one another. In the final session, members identified social support networks and discussed how they will continue to improve their coping skills.

Mixed. Roberts and Lie's (1989) study is an example of a mixed approach. The 10-session groups started with experiential structured exercises to build cohesiveness and security. All sessions included beginning "check-ins," and the treatment entailed homework, creative drawing, relaxation training, and disclosure of abuse experiences while looking at a photo of the abuser. During the disclosure sessions (one per group member), the group discussed family system pathology, loss and grief, the inner child, and detailed memories. Participants reported significant reductions in depression and increases in self-assessment.

Maxine Harris and the Community Connections Trauma Work Group (CCTW) (1998) authored a practical guide to group treatment for a diverse socioeconomic population of women who had been abused. The women coming to their clinic frequently lacked financial, emotional, and support resources to sustain traditional treatment for CSA survivors. CCTW has nine foci: (1) basic education; (2) reframing of symptoms; (3) appreciation of problem-solving attempts; (4) basic skills in self-regulation, boundary maintenance, and communication; (5) female sexuality; (6) creating a healing community; (7) rediscover and reconnection of memory, feelings, and perceptions; (8) competence and resolution; and (9) trust own perceptions and receive validation from others.

Fallot, Freeman, Zazanis, and Dende (as cited in Harris, 1998) modified the CCTW model for male CSA survivors that meets 40 to 45 times. It is based on five themes essential to recovery and development for males: (1) self-esteem, (2) self-protection, (3) self-direction, (4) mutuality, and (5) responsibility. Eleven topics focus on men's issues (What is a man? culturally, personally, biologically), problem-solving styles, and friendships/relationships. The second segment is more focused on the trauma and recovery.

CHILDREN'S GROUPS

Although lacking a strong, empirical foundation, group therapy is the most widely used treatment modality with child survivors of sexual abuse (Friedrich, 1990; Hiebert-Murphy, DeLuca, & Runtz, 1992). At present, guidance for group development and technique application appears to be derived from case studies, descriptions of other groups, and anecdotal affirmations of therapeutic efficacy in the available literature.

Groups designed for preadolescent children differ considerably from adolescent and adult groups in terms of structure and content. Sexual abuse groups for children tend to be structured according to age and gender. Preschool groups provide services to children between the ages of 4 and 6 years and are usually either mixed gender (e.g., Grosz, Kempe, & Kelly, 2000) or only female (Pescolido & Petrella, 1986). Latency groups, ages 7 to 11, usually contain same-sex children (Friedrich, 1990). The topics addressed remain consistent, however, and often include a combination of feelings regarding abuse and the perpetrators (e.g., Berliner & Elliott, 1996; Grosz et al., 2000; Heiman & Ettin, 2001), feelings toward self (e.g., Grosz et al., 2000; Homeyer, 1999), sex education (e.g., Hack et al., 1994; Hyde, Bentovim, & Monck, 1995), sexual abuse prevention (e.g., Sirles, Walsma, Lytle-Barnaby, & Lander, 1988), court preparation (e.g., Berliner & Elliott, 1996; Heiman & Ettin, 2001), and identification of a support system (e.g., Berliner & Elliott, 1996; Heiman & Ettin, 2001).

Preschool-aged children are in Piaget's preoperational stage of cognitive development (Damon, Todd, & MacFarlane, 1987), making it difficult to understand abstract concepts (Burton, Rasmussen, Bradshaw, Christopherson, & Huke, 1998). Therefore, groups with preschool children use more concrete, action-oriented activities and interventions, whereas latency groups begin to shift the focus to discussing psychological concepts that are more abstract and may be less comprehensible to preschoolers (i.e., self-esteem).

Reeker, Ensing, and Elliot (1997) list several problems with the research literature: (a) few control groups due to ethical concerns that children receive services as soon as possible, (b) no comparisons between types of group treatment, (c) low sample sizes, and (d) heterogeneity of groups (age ranges, gender, length of sessions, duration). They applied a meta-analysis for the 15 group pre-post test outcome studies from 1987 to 1996 that treated children and adolescents ages 3 to 17 who had experienced sexual abuse. Overall, group treatment for children who were sexually abused was found to be efficacious and similar to other types of individual and group treatments for children and adolescents. Although not statistically significant, there was a trend for sexual abuse groups to be more effective with

females than males. There were no differences based on age. Constructs that were measured to ascertain outcomes included sexual abuse/prevention ($n = 1$), sexual behaviors ($n = 3$), self-esteem ($n = 10$), general distress ($n = 9$), internalizing symptoms ($n = 7$), and externalizing symptoms ($n = 5$). Reeker et al. recommended that future research include control groups and multiple treatments and continue to focus on the outcome variables above, especially prevention and sexual behaviors.

Stevenson (1999) analyzed the methodological structure and corresponding results reported in the available literature for children. It is difficult to determine which modality is most effective with this population, as studies with poor reliability and validity should not be utilized in meta-analyses. Evaluation of the small group of well-designed studies revealed several trends: (a) effective treatments for adults have similar efficacy with children, (b) treatment efficacy for children who have been sexually abused is about equal to children with other concerns, and (c) psychological treatment yields better results than no treatment.

A movement toward finding empirically validated treatments has also emerged (Hansen et al., 1998). Hansen et al. (1998) presented a structured group treatment protocol for use in latency-aged groups. A three-factor model of areas impacted by the abuse was created to focus therapeutic intervention on "the individual or 'self' (self-esteem, guilt, fears, etc.), relationships (peer, family), and sex (sexual knowledge, sexual abuse-specific knowledge)" (p. 153). Continued interest is quite likely in the quest to validate specific approaches to group therapy with CSA survivors.

Clinical Practice: Preschool-Aged Groups

Regardless of the specific approach adopted for preschool groups, much of the structure is similar across groups. As stated earlier, groups for children aged 4 to 6 years tend to be mixed gender or only female. Membership is usually limited to four to eight children who meet for 10 to 12 weekly sessions for 1 to 2 hours (e.g., Homeyer, 1999). While there is literature showing open groups for this age (Grosz et al., 2000), most preschool groups are closed and time limited (Berliner & Elliott, 1996), allowing group cohesion and safety to develop more quickly. Concrete language and experiential interventions are routinely utilized (Burton et al., 1998). In addition, most groups for this age range incorporate a snack and play time (e.g., Mitchum, 1987; Pescolido & Petrella, 1986) to provide a nurturing reprieve from intense feelings and to promote peer interaction.

While sexual abuse groups for preschool-aged children can take the form of counseling, psychoeducational, or therapy, counseling groups utilizing nondirective play therapy techniques are most common in the literature. Homeyer (1999) promoted play therapy as the most effective treatment for preschoolers who have been sexually abused because it is developmentally appropriate. Children in this age range most likely lack a framework to understand the trauma they have experienced, making verbal, emotional expression difficult. Play therapy allows emotional expression through the "language of play" (Homeyer, 1999, p. 299) that may even be more accurate than a child's verbal statements (Marvasti, 1988). In play therapy groups, children have access to a range of materials chosen to facilitate creative and expressive play (Jones, 2002). The purposeful lack of instruction regarding the correct manner in which to play with the materials allows the children to choose. Children are not pressured to verbalize frightening experiences and beliefs, but are encouraged to communicate those messages via different methods of play. Seipker (1985) described play therapy as being essential for preschool-aged children because it involved the "interpretation of the meanings and feeling of the play and behavior" (p. 36). As preschool children tend to act out their emotions rather than discuss them (Jones, 2002), nondirective play therapy can provide the therapist with an opportunity to receive, validate, and interpret the messages that the child is sending. Reflecting feeling to the child and interpreting the meaning behind it aids in the development of the therapeutic alliance between the child and therapist (Marvasti, 1988). Homeyer (1999) cautioned against therapists pushing an agenda, as it could create anxiety and distrust. Therapists are urged to trust that children will

deal with their concerns in the order most important to them.

Several behavior patterns commonly emerge within the play therapy group format. Children may exhibit aggression toward the therapist or peers, withdraw from the group, become hypervigilant, reenact the abusive situation, dissociate, or be unable to negotiate conflict with peers. Boundary issues may also be apparent, as children become regressive or nurturing and produce more sexualized behaviors (Jones, 2002). Although many sexual abuse groups for this age group incorporate an educational component, strictly psychoeducational group formats appear to be uncommon, which is not surprising, given the developmental limitations of preschool children. Most sexual abuse groups for preschool-aged children appear to infuse psychoeducational interventions (Pescolido & Petrella, 1986), structured weekly topics (Grosz et al., 2000), or a more directive stance (Damon et al., 1987) while incorporating some play therapy techniques. (See Table 36.1, Stauffer & Deblinger, 1996, for a manualized, cognitive-behavioral therapy group for preschool-aged children.)

Clinical Practice: Latency-Aged Groups

As with preschool-aged groups, the majority of latency-aged groups for children who have been sexually abused have a similar structure. Groups usually have between four and eight children, meet for 8 to 12 weeks, and last 1 to 2 hours. Due to developmental differences and variation in treatment concerns, latency-aged groups are generally same sex (Hiebert-Murphy et al., 1992) and contain more group discussion than preschool groups. The three areas most often targeted in these groups are feelings, social interactions, and abuse prevention education (Sirles et al., 1988). Many groups incorporate snack time (e.g., Reeker & Ensing, 1998), nondirective play therapy time (e.g., Hansen et al., 1998), and sharing time to discuss the previous week (e.g., Hiebert-Murphy et al., 1992).

Unlike preschool-aged groups, psychoeducational groups predominate for this age range, emphasizing cognitive and didactic areas (DeLuca, Boyes, Grayston, & Romano, 1995; Heiman & Ettin, 2001; Nelki & Watters, 1989) in a structured format. The rationale described by Sturkie (1983) for utilizing a structured group format was that it increased the ability of the group to cover all themes in a timely fashion, used relevant experiential games and exercises, provided less disruption in the group when there was an exchange of facilitators, and allowed for the training of graduate students in sexual abuse treatment.

Traditional, latency-aged groups are generally time limited and use a topical format that does not focus attention on group process issues (Friedrich, 1995; Heiman & Ettin, 2001). Recently, practitioners have begun incorporating various techniques into the group setting in order to assess the efficacy of an eclectic/integrative approach to sexual abuse treatment (Zaidi & Gutierrez-Kovner, 1995). Heiman and Ettin (2001) presented a short-term, structured group design that emphasized the utilization of group processes to maximize treatment efficacy. Corder, Haizlip, and DeBoer (1990) devised a group therapy program that encouraged members to develop defense mechanisms used by asymptomatic child survivors. Berman (1990) advocated for the use of a long-term, insight-oriented, structured group format as the primary therapeutic intervention for children, rather than group therapy remaining as a short-term addendum to individual therapy. While group therapy is widely accepted as the treatment of choice for children who have been sexually abused (Friedrich, 1990; Hiebert-Murphy et al., 1992), researchers and practitioners continue to explore alternative formatting and conceptualizations for group treatment.

Many therapists of children's groups offer parallel, nonoffending parents groups (Hansen et al., 1998; Hyde, Bentovim, & Monck, 1995). Therapists and researchers assert that parental support after disclosure of abuse is a major determinant of the impact the abuse has on the child and of the child's ability to progress in treatment (Stauffer & Deblinger, 1996). Parallel groups also assist in the child's treatment through alleviating parental resistance about discussing the abuse and by treating issues of isolation and guilt that may be present for nonoffending parents (Gaines, 1986). Additionally, nonoffending parents of children who have been sexually abused may often experience a number of other reactionary, psychological, and physiological symptoms (Stauffer & Deblinger, 1996).

CONCLUSIONS

Group leaders have a multitude of factors to take into consideration when leading CSA groups. Previous training in sexual abuse issues and group therapy interventions is necessary to appropriately address the needs of the group members. Other concerns, such as boundary and memory issues, must also be addressed in order to effectively manage the group experience as it unfolds. Extensive planning and organization is required to create an effective sexual abuse group. This chapter discusses a number of ways to conceptualize a CSA group. Clearly, there is no right way to resolve all of these issues, but group leaders need to be aware and carefully plan their group to maximize the therapeutic effect for members. Treatment needs and group goals and procedures also have to be adapted for various age groups. Most of the groups have a brief format and are designed for women and children who are fairly high functioning and have support networks. A few address the concerns and needs of inpatients and women with lower socioeconomic status. There are very few groups that have been designed for males, and no research studies were found addressing these groups.

REFERENCES

Alexander, P. C., Neimeyer, R. A., & Follette, V. M. (1991). Group therapy for women sexually abused as children: A controlled study and investigation of individual differences. *Journal of Interpersonal Violence, 6,* 218-231.

Alexander, P. C., Neimeyer, R. A., Follette, V. M., Moore, M. K., et al. (1989). A comparison of group treatments of women sexually abused as children. *Journal of Consulting & Clinical Psychology, 57,* 479-483.

Bagley, C., & Young, L. (1998). Long-term evaluation of group counseling for women with a history of CSA: Focus on depression, self-esteem, suicidal behaviors and social support. *Social Work With Groups, 21,* 63-73.

Berliner, L., & Elliott, D. M. (1996). Sexual abuse of children. In J. Briere, L. Berliner, J. A. Bulkey, C. Jenny, & T. Reid (Eds.), *The APSAC handbook on child maltreatment* (pp. 51-71). Thousand Oaks, CA: Sage.

Berman, P. (1990). Group therapy techniques for sexually abused preteen girls. *Child Welfare, 69,* 239-253.

Blount, H. R., & Chandler, T. A. (1979). Relationship between childhood abuse and assaultive behavior in adolescent male psychiatric patients. *Psychological Reports, 44,* 1126.

Briere, J. (1996). *Therapy for adults molested as children: Beyond survival.* New York: Springer.

Briere, J., & Runtz, M. (1987). Post sexual abuse trauma: Data and implications for clinical practice. *Journal of Interpersonal Violence, 2,* 367-379.

Buchele, B. J. (2000). Group psychotherapy for survivors of sexual and physical abuse. In Robert H. Klein and Victor L. Schermer (Eds.), *Group psychotherapy for psychological trauma* (pp. 170-187). New York: Guilford.

Burton, J. E., Rasmussen, L. A., Bradshaw, J., Chistopherson, B. J., & Huke, S. C. (1998). *Treating children with sexually abusive behavior problems.* New York: Haworth.

Carver, C. M., Stalker, C., Stewart, E., & Abraham, B. (1989). The impact of group therapy for adult survivors of childhood sexual abuse. *Canadian Journal of Psychiatry: Revue Canadienne de Psychiatrie, 34,* 753-758.

Chard, K. M., Weaver, T. L., & Resick, P. A. (1997). Adapting cognitive processing therapy for child sexual abuse survivors. *Cognitive & Behavioral Practice, 4,* 31-52.

Clancy, S. A., Schacter, D. L., McNally, R. J., & Pitman, R. K. (2000). False recognition in women reporting recovered memories of sexual abuse. *Psychological Science, 11,* 26-31.

Corder, B. F., Haizlip, T., & DeBoer, P. (1990). A pilot study for a structured, time-limited therapy group for sexually abused pre-adolescent children. *Child Abuse & Neglect, 14,* 243-251.

Courtois, C. A. (1996) *Healing the incest wound: Adult survivors in therapy.* New York: Norton.

Courtois, C. A. (1999). *Recollections of sexual abuse: Treatment principles and guidelines.* New York: Norton.

Damon, L., Todd, J., & MacFarlane, K. (1987). Treatment issues with sexually abused young children. *Child Welfare, 66,* 125-137.

DeLuca, R. V., Boyes, D. A., Grayston, A. D., & Romano, E. (1995). Sexual abuse: Effects of group therapy on pre-adolescent girls. *Child Abuse Review, 4,* 263-277.

DiVitto, S. (1998). Empowerment through self-regulation: Group approach for survivors of incest. *Journal of the American Psychiatric Nurses Association, 4*(3), 77-86.

Douglas, A., & Matson, I. C. (1989). An account of a time-limited therapeutic group in an NHS setting for women with a history of incest. *Group, 13,* 83-94.

Figley, C. R. (1995). Systemic traumatization: Secondary traumatic stress disorder in family therapists. In R. H. Mikesell, D. Lusterman, & S. H. MacDaniel (Eds.), *Integrating family therapy: Handbook of family psychology and systems theory.* Washington, DC: American Psychological Association.

Finkelhor, D. (1986). *A sourcebook on child sexual abuse.* Newbury Park, CA: Sage.

Finkelhor, D. (1993). Epidemiological factors in the clinical identification of child sexual abuse. *Child Abuse & Neglect, 17,* 67-70.

Follette, V. M., Alexander, P. C., & Follette, W. C. (1991). Individual predictors of outcome in group treatment for incest survivors. *Journal of Consulting & Clinical Psychology, 59,* 150-155.

Forseth, L. B., & Brown, A. (1981). A survey of intrafamilial sexual abuse treatment centers: Implications for intervention. *Child Abuse and Neglect, 5,* 177-186.

Frawley-O'Dea, M. (1997). Transference paradigms at play in psychoanalytically oriented group therapy with female adult survivors of childhood sexual abuse. *International Journal of Group Psychotherapy, 47,* 427-441.

Friedman, R. M. (1994). Psychodynamic group therapy for male survivors of sexual abuse. *Group, 18,* 225-234.

Friedrich, W. N. (1990). *Psychotherapy of sexually abused children and their families.* New York: Norton.

Friedrich, W. N. (1995). *Psychotherapy with sexually abused boys: An integrated approach.* Thousand Oaks, CA: Sage.

Gaines, T. (1986). Applications of child group psychotherapy. In A. E. Reister & I. A. Kraft (Eds.), *Child group psychotherapy: Future tense* (pp. 103-122). Madison, CT: International Universities Press.

Gartner, R. B. (1997). Considerations in the psychoanalytic treatment of men who were sexually abused as children. *Psychoanalytic Psychology, 14*(1), 13-41.

Gerrity, D. A. (1998). A classification matrix using goals and process dimensions: Issues for therapy groups. *Journal for Specialists in Group Work, 23,* 202-207.

Gerrity, D. A., & Mathews, L. (2003). Survey of childhood sexual abuse group leaders. Unpublished manuscript, University of Buffalo.

Gilligan, C. (1982). *In a different voice: Psychological theory and women's development.* Cambridge, MA: Harvard University Press.

Gilovich, K. D., & Miller, L. (1994). Combining adult and adolescent female incest survivors in a weekend retreat. *Journal of Child Sexual Abuse, 3,* 15-30.

Gonsiorek, J. C., Bera, W. H., & LeTourneau, D. (1994). *Male sexual abuse: A trilogy of intervention strategies.* Thousand Oaks, CA: Sage.

Goodwin, J. M., & Talwar, N. (1989). Group psychotherapy for victims of incest. *Psychiatric Clinics of North America, 12,* 279-293.

Grosz, C. A., Kempe, R. S., & Kelly, M. (2000). Extrafamilial sexual abuse: Treatment for child victims and their families. *Child Abuse & Neglect, 24*(1), 9-23.

Hack, T. F., Osachuk, T. A. G., & DeLuca, R. V. (1994). Group treatment for sexually abuse preadolescent boys. *Families in Society, 75,* 217-228.

Hansen, D. J., Hecht, D. B., & Futa, K. T. (1998). Child sexual abuse. In V. B. Van Hasselt & M. Hersen (Eds.), *Handbook of psychological treatment protocols for children and adolescents* (pp. 153-178). Mahwah, NJ: Lawrence Erlbaum.

Harris, M. (1998). *Trauma recovery and empowerment: A clinician's guide for working with women in groups.* New York: Free Press.

Hazzard, A., Rogers, J. H., & Angert, L. (1993). Factors affecting group therapy outcome for adult sexual abuse survivors. *International Journal of Group Psychotherapy, 43,* 453-468.

Heiman, M. L., & Ettin, M. F. (2001). Harnessing the power of the group for latency-aged sexual abuse victims. *International Journal of Group Psychotherapy, 51,* 265-282.

Herman, J. L. (1992). *Trauma and recovery.* New York: Basic Books.

Herman, J., & Schatzow, E. (1984). Time-limited group therapy for women with a history of incest.

International Journal of Group Psychotherapy, 34, 605-616

Hiebert-Murphy, D., DeLuca, R. V., & Runtz, M. (1992). Group treatment for sexually abused girls: Evaluating outcome. *Families in Society, 73,* 205-213.

Homeyer, L. E. (1999). Group play therapy with sexually abused children. In D. S. Sweeney & L. E. Homeyer (Eds.), *The handbook of group play therapy: How to do it, how it works, whom it's best for* (pp. 299-318). San Francisco: Jossey-Bass.

Hyde, C., Bentovim, A., & Monck, E. (1995). Some clinical and methodological implications of a treatment outcome study of sexually abused children. *Child Abuse & Neglect, 19,* 1387-1399.

Jones, K. D. (2002). Group play therapy with sexually abused preschool children: Group behaviors and interventions. *Journal for Specialists in Group Work, 27,* 377-389.

Knight, C. (1997). Critical roles and responsibilities of the leader of a therapy group for adult survivors of child sexual abuse. *Journal of Child Sexual Abuse, 6*(1), 21-37.

Levenkron, S. (1998). *Cutting: Understanding and overcoming self-mutilation.* New York: Norton.

Longstreth, G. F., Mason, C., Schrieber, I. G., & Tsao-Wei, D. (1998). Group psychotherapy for women molested in childhood: Psychological and somatic symptoms and medical visits. *International Journal of Group Psychotherapy, 48,* 533-541.

Lundquist, G., & Ojehagen, A. (2001). Childhood sexual abuse: An evaluation of a two-year group therapy in adult women. *European Psychiatry: The Journal of the Association of European Psychiatrists, 16*(1), 64-67.

Marotta, S. A., & Asner, K. K. (1999). Group psychotherapy for women with a history of incest: The research base. *Journal of Counseling & Development, 77,* 315-323.

Marvasti, J. A. (1988). Play therapy with sexually abused children. In S. M. Sgroi (Ed.), *Vulnerable populations* (pp. 1-41). New York: Lexington.

Mathews, L. L., & Gerrity, D. A. (2002). Therapists' use of boundaries in sexual abuse groups: An exploratory study. *Journal for Specialists in Group Work, 27,* 78-91.

Mitchum, N. T. (1987). Developmental play therapy: A treatment approach for child victims of molestation. *Journal of Counseling and Development, 65,* 320-321.

Morgan, T., & Cummings, A. L. (1999). Change experienced during group therapy by female survivors of childhood sexual abuse. *Journal of Consulting and Clinical Psychology, 67*, 28-36.

Naar, R., Doreian-Michael, C., & Santhouse, R. (1998). Short-term psychodrama with victims of sexual abuse. *International Journal for Action Methods, 51*, 75-82.

National Clearinghouse on Child Abuse and Neglect Information. (2002). Retrieved from http://www.calib.com/nccanch/statutes/index.cfm.

Neimeyer, R. A., Harter, S., & Alexander, P. C. (1991). Group perceptions as predictors of outcome in the treatment of incest survivors. *Psychotherapy Research, 1*, 148-158.

Nelki, J. S., & Watters, J. (1989). A group for sexually abused young children: Unraveling the web. *Child Abuse & Neglect, 13*, 369-377.

Palmer, K. D., Baker, R. C., & McGee, T. F. (1997). The effects of pretraining on group psychotherapy for incest-related issues. *International Group Psychotherapy, 47*, 71-89.

Pescolido, F. J. (1988). Sexual abuse of boys by males: Theoretical and treatment implications. In S. M. Sgroi (Ed.), *Vulnerable populations* (pp. 85-109). New York: Lexington.

Pescolido, F. J., & Petrella, D. M. (1986). The development, process, and evaluation of group psychotherapy with sexually abused preschool girls. *International Journal of Group Psychotherapy, 36*, 447-469.

Pistorello, J., & Follette, V. M. (1998). Childhood sexual abuse and couples' relationships: Female survivors' reports in therapy groups. *Journal of Marital & Family Therapy, 24*, 473-485.

Randall, D. A. (1995). Curative factor rankings for female incest survivor groups: A summary of three studies. *Journal for Specialists in Group Work, 20*, 232-239.

Reeker, J., & Ensing, D. (1998). An evaluation of a group treatment for sexually abused young children. *Journal of Child Sexual Abuse, 7*(2), 65-85.

Reeker, J., Ensing, D., & Elliott, R. (1997). A meta-analytic investigation of group treatment outcomes for sexually abused children. *Child Abuse & Neglect, 21*, 669-680.

Richter, N. L., Snider, E., & Gorey, K. M. (1997). Group work interventions with female survivors of childhood sexual abuse. *Research on Social Work Practice, 7*(1), 53-69.

Rittenhouse, J. (1997). Feminist principles in survivor's groups: Out-of-group contact. *Journal for Specialists in Group Work, 22*(2), 111-119.

Roberts, L., & Lie, G. (1989). A group therapy approach to the treatment of incest. *Social Work With Groups, 12*, 77-90.

Russell, D. E. (1983). The incidence and prevalence of intrafamilial and extrafamilial sexual abuse of female children. *Child Abuse & Neglect, 7*, 133-146.

Seipker, B. B. (1985). Children's and adolescents' group therapy literature. In B. B. Seipker & C. S. Kandaras (Eds.), *Group therapy with children and adolescents: A treatment manual.* New York: Human Sciences Press.

Shaffer, J., Brown, L. L., & McWhirter, J. J. (1998). Survivors of child sexual abuse and dissociative coping: Relearning in a group context. *Journal for Specialists in Group Work, 23*(1), 74-94.

Sheinberg, M., True, F., & Fraenkel, P. (1994). Treating the sexually abused child: A recursive, multimodal program. *Family Process, 33*, 263-276.

Sirles, E. A., Walsma, J., Lytle-Barnaby, R., & Lander, L. C. (1988). Group therapy techniques for work with child sexual abuse victims. *Social Work With Groups, 11*, 67-78.

Stalker, C. A., & Fry, R. (1999). A comparison of short-term group and individual therapy for sexually abused women. *Canadian Journal of Psychiatry, 44*(2), 168-174.

Stauffer, L. B., & Deblinger, E. (1996). Cognitive behavioral groups for nonoffending mothers and their young sexually abused children: A preliminary treatment outcome study. *Child Maltreatment, 1*(1), 65-80.

Stevenson, J. (1999). The treatment of the long-term sequelae of child abuse. *Journal of Child Psychology & Psychiatry, 40*(1), 89-111.

Sturkie, K. (1983). Structured group treatment for sexually abused children. *Health & Social Work, 8*(4), 299-308.

Talbot, N., Houghtalen, R. P., Cyrulik, S., Betz, A., Barkun, M., Duberstein, P. R., & Wynne, L. C. (1998). Women's safety in recovery: Group therapy for patients with a history of childhood sexual abuse. *Psychiatric Services, 49*, 213-217.

Talbot, N. L., Houghtalen, R. P., Duberstein, P. R., Cox, C., Giles, D. E., & Wynne, L. C. (1999). Effects of group treatment for women with a history of childhood sexual abuse. *Psychiatric Services, 50*, 686-692.

Tsai, M., & Wagner, N. N. (1978). Therapy groups for women sexually molested as children. *Archives of Sexual Behavior, 7,* 417-427.

Turner, S. (1993). Talking about sexual abuse: The value of short-term groups for women survivors. *Journal of Group Psychotherapy, Psychodrama & Sociometry, 46,* 110-121.

Valente, M., & Shuttleworth, A. (1997). The co-working relationship: Groupwork with women survivors of sexual abuse. *Child Abuse Review, 6,* 219-225.

Weiner, L. J. (1988). Issues in sex therapy with survivors of intrafamily sexual abuse. *Women & Therapy, 7,* 253-264.

Westbury, E., & Tutty, L. M. (1999). The efficacy of group treatment for survivors of childhood abuse. *Child Abuse & Neglect, 23*(1), 31-44.

Yalom, I. (1995). *The theory and practice of group psychotherapy* (4th ed.). New York: HarperCollins.

Zaidi, L. Y., & Gutierrez-Kovner, V. M. (1995). Group treatment of sexually abused latency-aged girls. *Journal of Interpersonal Violence, 10*(2), 215-227.

Zamanian, K., & Adams, C. (1997). Group psychotherapy with sexually abused boys: Dynamics and interventions. *International Journal of Group Psychotherapy, 47*(1), 109-126.

Zlotnick, C., Shea, T. M., Rosen, K., Simpson, E., Mulrenin, K., Begin, A., et al. (1997). An affect-management group for women with posttraumatic stress disorder and histories of childhood sexual abuse. *Journal of Traumatic Stress, 10,* 425-436.

37

THEORY, PRACTICE, AND RESEARCH OF GRIEF GROUPS

REBECCA R. MACNAIR-SEMANDS

University of North Carolina at Charlotte

Loss is a universal experience that involves anxiety, sadness, anger, emotional numbing, and guilt (Worden, 1991). The isolation that individuals experience after a significant death may be one of the most difficult challenges in life, particularly once support from family and community begins to wane. Bereavement seems to permeate every aspect of life and every corner of experience, including the core of self-identity (Moorey, 1995). However, our society inhibits experience and expression of emotions associated with bereavement, leading people to feel unprepared to cope with the profoundly traumatic event of death (Corazzini, 1980). Social support is known to help bereaved individuals (Gray, 1988), and thus professionals represent a necessary resource for supporting and intervening with grieving individuals (Keitel, Kopala, & Robin, 1998). Because mourning is both culturally determined and highly specific for individuals, professional support must be relevant to the customs and symbolic meanings of the bereaved.

Groups may be a preferred modality to counteract avoidance of death by providing a forum for talking about the death experience and the deceased (Keitel et al., 1998). Yalom and Vinogradov (1988) observed that despite the need for empirically supported grief treatments, many grief groups have been led by lay leaders or peers rather than trained professionals. Leaders of bereavement groups must be knowledgeable of the major tasks facing the bereaved to help members identify, understand, and master these tasks. In addition to the need for more empirically supported and professionally led grief group treatments, quality research examining existing grief groups is essential. Much of the grief group research has been beleaguered by methodological problems such as inadequate sample size, confounding variables, and the use of inexperienced leaders (Piper & McCallum, 1991).

Psychoeducational and counseling groups are perhaps the ideal environment for the bereaved to not only engage in cathartic experiences but also to learn to connect with new persons in an intimate manner. Osterweis, Soloman, and Green (1984) outlined the functions that grief groups can offer members, including the person-to-person exchange based on identification and reciprocity, access to a body of specialized information, the opportunity to share coping techniques, reinforcement for positive change, and an opportunity for education with other persons. Bereavement groups can create intimate relationships that have been described as acting as a bridge between the past and the future (Silverman, 1987). Burnell and Burnell (1989) stated that groups can effectively help the bereaved through the long, difficult phases of grief by providing opportunities to shift coping styles away from a preoccupation with the deceased and toward a reinvestment of interests, altruistic outreach, or other forms of productive coping styles.

Earlier theories on grief was based on a stage model, which holds that the bereaved go through phases of mourning. Bowlby (1961) first published his description of the phases of mourning in relation to attachment and separation: numbness, yearning, disorganization, and reorganization. Kübler-Ross (1969) later outlined the well-known stages used to identify grief: denial and isolation, anger, bargaining, depression, and acceptance. More recently, Sanders (1999) labeled her delineation of the phases of grief: shock, awareness of loss, conservation-withdrawal, healing, and renewal. However, leaders of grief groups use a framework of two broad phases of grief, described as the "fast pain" of initial shock, denial, and acute loss, followed by the "slow pain" of insidious and resistant discomfort related to the changes in lifestyle, social role, and self-image after a loss (Yalom & Vinogradov, 1988). Group leaders may facilitate work regarding Worden's (1991) four tasks of mourning as they respond and react to members: accepting the reality of the loss, working through the pain of grief, adjusting to an environment in which the deceased is missing, and emotionally relocating the deceased and moving on with life. It appears that working through the *tasks* of mourning within a broad framework of the *phases* of mourning that can incorporate members with diverse grief experiences may be the most effective for leaders.

Complicated grief is a term used when extenuating factors confound the process of grief, and thus the bereavement is more severe and longer lasting. Most researchers distinguish between normal grief reactions and complicated grief. Complicated bereavement of a variety of forms can be successfully treated in grief groups (Piper, 1994), and many of the groups discussed in this chapter were specifically designed for members experiencing complicated bereavement. Other research includes grief reactions typically termed *normal* grief, which generally denotes little disturbance of the normal progress toward the resolution of grief. Rando (1993) argues that, whether complicated or uncomplicated, the grief process is expected to be unique and idiosyncratic due to the multitude of factors that combine to determine reactions to loss.

This chapter reviews theoretical, practical, and research findings on group treatment of loss, with primary emphasis on counseling and therapy groups related to the actual death of a loved one. Research and practice involving selection of members, client preparation for group, dropout prevention, and norm-setting interventions are discussed. Practical guidelines and examples of grief group interventions are provided within a model of group culture building. The general interpersonal techniques of group treatment are demonstrated as they are tailored to specific issues of bereavement and personal change: establishing norms, encouraging processing, and making here-and-now interventions.

COUNSELING AND THERAPY GROUPS FOR LOSS

Counseling and therapy groups dealing with loss and death issues have been described through written descriptions with much greater frequency than they have been researched for effectiveness. Various theoretical approaches for both individual and group interventions have been recommended, including short-term psychoanalytic, interpersonal, cognitive-behavioral, gestalt, behavioral, and existential-humanistic.

Short-Term Psychoanalytic Grief Groups

The short-term psychoanalytic approach to grief group treatment (Piper, McCallum, &

Azim, 1992) has been the most thoroughly researched approach to date. The psychoanalytic grief group model has a solid theoretical base and a long history of methodological rigor due primarily to the work of Piper and his colleagues, who have been conducting a group program in Canada since 1986 for patients with complicated grief. Short-term psychoanalytic grief groups strive to maintain a clear and specific focus, emphasize awareness of the time limits, and focus on current relationships and behaviors (Piper et al., 1992). Leaders are encouraged to play an active role to encourage rapid cohesion in the group. Interpretive rather than supportive techniques are the focus of leadership, and transference issues are viewed as contributing to an overall demanding role required of group leaders. Psychoanalytic groups have been written about extensively in the literature, and thus are not reviewed in this chapter.

The Interpersonal Group Model

The interpersonal group psychotherapy approach to grief work (IPT-G) is best known for its tendency toward inclusiveness of difficult patients in group and as a useful modality for treatment of depression (MacKenzie & Grabovac, 2001). Perhaps the most complex written description of an interpersonal grief group treatment was put forth by Yalom and Vinogradov (1988). Four grief groups and control group members with long-term follow-up procedures were studied, and the authors described techniques and themes. Interpersonal techniques consisted of establishing norms, encouraging process review, and making here-and-now interventions. Existential themes of responsibility for oneself are central in such groups, with in-depth processing of complex questions of growth and identity. The groups were eight sessions long; members were constantly reminded of the number of remaining sessions to connect to the theme of loss.

In a similar interpersonal psychotherapy model (IPT) developed by Klerman, Weissman, Rounsaville, and Chevron (1984), difficulties are classified into four problem areas: grief, role disputes, role transitions, and interpersonal deficits. MacKenzie and Grabovac (2001) delineated that in such interpersonal group treatment, specific target goals are developed with each client and are the focus of the first group session. Prolonged discussion of symptoms in the group is discouraged. Relationship patterns are examined to develop an understanding of current relationship difficulties.

In interpersonal approaches specific to grief work, catharsis related to death is not in itself sufficient to treat complicated bereavement. The necessary next step is to alter interpersonal interactions and become open to developing new relationships to fill the empty space left by the lost loved one (Weissman, Markowitz, & Klerman, 2000). The two primary goals of the interpersonal grief approach are to facilitate the mourning process (encouraging thinking about the loss, discussing sequence and consequences of events around the death, and exploring associated feelings) and to help the bereaved reestablish interests and relationships.

The first major undertaking of group leaders is to elicit emotions related to the loss, with questions such as "What was [the person] like? What had you hoped to do together that you didn't get to do? How did you learn about [the person's] death?" (Weissman et al., 2000). Using this approach in a group context, clients are often reassured about anger, shame, guilt, and ambivalent feelings. The lost relationship is reconstructed verbally; normal ups and downs of the relationship are openly discussed to purposely reconstruct a realistic view of the deceased person. Lieberman established, for example, that ambivalence toward the deceased person is a central dynamic in the role of grief resolution and must be verbalized. It has been noted that the open and emotional nature of grief groups is strikingly different at the onset from the more guarded beginning typical of most therapy groups (Yalom & Vinogradov, 1988).

The second major task for group leaders, helping the members reestablish interests and relationships, may come less easily for members. Leaders using the interpersonal approach are active in guiding clients to become involved with activities such as organizations and dating. Clients described as *overgrieving* often see mourning as an expected role and a duty; they must be encouraged to return to satisfying activities or to develop new activities while challenging the belief that they are betraying the memory of the loved one (Weissman et al., 2000). Other difficult interpersonal dynamics that arise in grief groups can be handled effectively with an interpersonal approach, such as comparing losses, advice giving, moralist ideals, nonparticipation, content brought up at the end of group, content given to therapist outside of group, interrupting or dominating, inappropriate affect, overdisclosure, and critical styles of reacting to others (Worden, 1991).

Other Theoretical Approaches to Grief in a Group Setting

All of the major theoretical approaches focus on specific goals and themes in relation to grief work in a group setting. However, some authors have argued that certain approaches are less comprehensive or must be integrated in working with the bereaved. For example, Sanders (1999) puts forth that client-centered and psychoanalytic therapies are more suited for clients in the first phases of shock and awareness of loss. She notes that client-centered therapy focuses on empathy with the bereaved and thus may be a particularly good fit with grief in the early phases when safety needs are unmet and raw feelings are overwhelming. On the other hand, existential-humanistic therapies have been proposed as best suited to the middle phases of grief, as this approach typically involves taking greater responsibility for the outcome of grief and searching for meaning and purpose (Sanders, 1999). Finally, gestalt and behavior therapies are described as suited to the latter phases of healing, renewal, and reinvestment of energy.

Behavior therapy is one of the few approaches clearly outlining a particular exercise or technique found to be empirically supported, termed *guided mourning* (Mawson, Marks, Ramm, & Stern, 1981). Guided mourning exercises involve encouraging the group members to say good-bye by writing, visiting a cemetery, and generally reliving and expressing painful memories until the distress is diminished.

Cognitive-behavioral therapy (CBT) uses structure and agenda setting in groups, although grief groups from a cognitive approach are rarely put forth in the literature. Padesky and Greenberger (1995) describe that at the beginning of a group session, the group leaders and members list topics they wish to discuss. To set the agenda, the leaders search for common themes such as upsetting thoughts or memories that the group members share. A group member may have thoughts, for example, that it is too soon after a death to begin meeting new people. The leader might ask, "How many people are having this kind of thought?" If it is a common theme, the members decide whether to engage in an automatic thought record for this situation. After developing the agenda for the group session, CBT group leaders ask the group to name the emotional consequences of the target thought, such as "I feel guilty." CBT group therapy attempts to demonstrate to members that practically any thought has consequences and that to gain awareness of the process is to gain influence on it (White, 2000). Together, the members tap into personal resources and share alternative ways of challenging the distorted or unproductive thinking. The goal of this exercise is learning to identify the connection between automatic thoughts and feelings and how to test the accuracy of the thoughts.

Systematic desensitization and graded exposure techniques have also been developed to treat chronic grief, including elements of cognitive restructuring, stress management, and coping skills. Kavanagh (1990) proposes a model originally developed for individual treatment of chronic grief based on exploring the costs and benefits of change with the bereaved person, recognizing skills, and encouraging graded exposure to bereavement cues. Viewing the cognitive paradigm of chronic grief as a negative feedback system, this approach uses graduated reinvestment in roles and activities, and identifying and challenging negative thoughts for excessively negative cognitions. Using controlled distraction from emotions at times, this approach is in sharp contrast to the guided mourning interventions (Mawson et al., 1981).

SELECTION OF GROUP MEMBERS: SUGGESTIONS BASED ON EMPIRICAL FINDINGS

Can clients with different types of loss and grief come together successfully in a group? One of the most influential ways to create a healthy culture for grieving and healing is to select group members who have the capacity to develop effective group norms. Ideally, clients who are psychologically minded, open to feedback, and value emotional processing may quickly accept the values and norms of a grief group. However, client appropriateness is one of the most difficult criteria to judge at a pregroup screening, and thus screening measures are often needed to successfully predict group outcome (MacNair & Corazzini, 1994).

Grief group leaders typically select between six and eight members and hold weekly sessions for 60 to 90 minutes in length (Keitel et al., 1998). Worden (1991) recommends selecting only those clients whose loss occurred at least 6 weeks prior to the start of a grief group, proposing that the recency of a loss may lead to difficulty. Premature termination is a specific concern for grief-focused groups, with some dropout rates as high as 77% (Marmar, Horowitz, Weiss, Wilner, & Kaltreider, 1988). The desire to gain relief from pain may be offset by a strong avoidance of the process of discussing the loss with others. Although our current literature lacks research delineating the clear causes of such dropout rates in grief groups, other research has demonstrated that personal factors such as substance use, somatization, hostility, or social inhibition contributes to low attendance and dropout (MacNair & Corazzini, 1994; MacNair-Semands, 2001). Thus, prescreening members of grief groups can reduce inappropriate member referrals and protect group members from the pain and loss around member dropout, which can be such a poignant issue for the bereaved.

Due to the lack of empirical findings about selection criteria specific to grief groups, leaders look to the general group therapy selection research for practice guidelines. In grief groups as well as general therapy groups, writers have focused on exclusion criteria more than on inclusion criteria with little scientific basis (MacNair-Semands & Corazzini, 1996). Researchers examining the types of clients who tend to drop out of group treatment prematurely have warned against making wide-ranging exclusions of clients (MacNair & Corazzini, 1994; Woods & Melnick, 1979). Leaders of grief groups should also directly address with members the potential pitfalls of homogeneous groups, such as the members focusing on commonalities of symptoms rather than individual experiences, avoidance of responsibility for current dilemmas, and an assumption that those outside of group would not understand or relate (Yalom & Yalom, 1990). Leaders generally exclude members who are angry, uncooperative, or unwilling to agree to the group norms and rules.

GROUP MEMBER PREPARATION

In addition to selection criteria as a dropout prevention mechanism, intentional pregroup preparation and explicit written contracts have been put forth in the literature as ways to further clarify expectations of group members and teach group membership skills (MacKenzie, 1997; Piper et al., 1992). In an interpersonal grief group format, clients are typically prepared for group therapy by attempting to reduce rather than build anxiety. Clear guidelines are given through a discussion of handouts addressing effectiveness of group therapies, how to benefit most from group treatment, and expectations for confidentiality, attendance, and substance use (MacKenzie & Grabovac, 2001).

In preparing grief group members to respond to each other therapeutically, specific descriptions of member disclosure and beneficial ways of responding are given. Table 37.1 provides an example of verbal messages given in a pregroup session for grief group members. A specific written contract can be discussed in detail during the pregroup screening, and clients who are not willing to meet the contract are not accepted into the group. This contract may include attention to confidentiality and requirements for attendance and participation. MacKenzie (1997) and Piper et al. (1992) also provide examples of group contracts and handouts.

NORM SETTING FOR GRIEF GROUPS

Yalom and Vinogradov (1988) emphasized that establishing norms is an essential process in grief groups: expectations for the group include that

Table 37.1   Pregroup Training: Example for Interpersonal Grief Groups

1. Unexpressed feelings are a major reason why people experience difficulties when someone they love dies. Self-disclosure about your loss can affect how much you will be helped. You are responsible for getting what you need from group. We do not have a system of rotating talk-time in group. Do you think it may be difficult for you to jump in or talk in the group? If so, we can talk about how to do that, and how we can help you.

2. The first few groups will be focused on sharing your experience of loss as you establish trust with each other. Members usually work to talk personally and honestly and make a firm commitment to the group, which enhances the trust. If you are unsure about the amount you are revealing about yourself, please ask the group for feedback. You control what, how much, and when you share with the group.

3. We will help you focus on relationships with each other in this group, not just the losses you have outside of group. Forming relationships, being able to help someone else, and responding to each other in this group are some of the best ways to heal.

4. Members give feedback to each other by expressing their own feelings and reactions to each other's disclosures about loss. If a member discusses an emotionally difficult topic, try and make a verbal response directly to the person. In this safe place, grief group members can try out new ways of both reaching out and asking for help. Try to be honest and spontaneous—not just saying something nice or what you think they want to hear.

5. If you need support for your grief, let the group know. If you would like challenging about your style of interacting or avoidance of new growth experiences, let them know. It is important to tell the members what you want from them during the various tasks you face in grieving.

6. Most people are anxious about being able to talk about such a significant loss without losing control in the group. Almost without exception, within a few sessions of group, people find that they do begin to talk more openly—and when upset, are able to stop crying before the end of the group session.

7. Interacting in the grief group is quite different from other situations (leaving superficial small talk outside, etc.), and so we coach and train the members often at the beginning. Later in the group we will be less active and members will give each other the support and feedback needed to survive your loss.

they will explore painful issues in a safe and gentle environment and focus primarily on the future despite the loss experienced. MacKenzie (1983) and Yalom (1995) suggested that while the group members themselves directly create the climate and therapeutic factors in the group, the group leaders indirectly create this climate through a series of interactional dimensions. Instilling group norms is a social process, taught and facilitated from the start of the pregroup screening and continuing throughout the life of the group (MacNair-Semands, 1996).

Yalom and Vinogradov (1988) elaborated that in all bereavement groups, it is crucial to set the norm early with members that the group accept responsibility for its own direction. Building norms to enhance cohesiveness may be most significant in the first few sessions to illustrate the value of grieving in a group. Most therapeutic dropouts occur during the beginning of treatment (Klein & Carroll, 1986; Stone & Rutan, 1984; Weiner 1984). Piper, McCallum, Joyce, Rosie, and Ogrodniczuk (2001) recently found that over 70% of grief group dropouts left during the first third of therapy. Thus, promoting universality (i.e., a shared experience of loss) and cohesiveness are crucial at the start of group treatment for members to believe that they can help each other through a loss. Yalom and Vinogradov (1988) noted that of the 36 grief group clients studied there were only 2 clients, who later dropped out of group, who were truly unable to shed denial and admit the pervasiveness of their grief. Specific guidelines about group member attendance and participation contribute to cohesiveness and prevention of dropout early in the group process through a perceived level of commitment to the group.

It is important to know what a leader can do to influence group norms and group climate, particularly because group climate has a strong relationship with group member outcome (Kivlighan & Tarrant, 2001). Dies (1994) reviewed 135 group studies and found that leader structure, particularly providing meaningful concepts and building positive relationships with group members, is consistently related to group outcome in various forms of groups. The grief group climate emerges from norms for group interactions that influence cohesiveness and trust. Facilitating norm building in a grief group can lead to support, frank communication, and challenges to help members invest in new relationships and activities outside the group.

One important norm for grief groups relates to the use of structured exercises. Yalom and Vinogradov (1988) found that including structured exercises in the first group meeting were neither "successful nor necessary" in an interpersonal model. Group leaders found that imposition of structure was generally counterproductive, as members preferred and welcomed a simple forum where they could talk openly. A more important norm to set was to spend time in early sessions to review the process of the group. For example, members were asked in the second session to discuss feelings they had as they went home from the first session.

In examining norm setting, MacDevitt (1987) was the first researcher to specifically conceptualize how the therapeutic components of group are created and maintained at different stages of various groups. He emphasized (a) the leader's use of direct instruction, reinforcement, and modeling to build individual expectations and group norms, (b) focusing attention on different therapeutic factors at different developmental stages, and (c) helping the clients give meaning to the emotional experiences they have in the group, thus highlighting the cognitive dimension of their experiences. These components are particularly important in grief groups to promote cohesion and commitment.

CULTURE BUILDING THROUGH LEADERSHIP IN GRIEF GROUPS

Another helpful model for norm setting and culture building for grief groups comes from the organizational behavior literature. Schein (1985) proposed that leaders shape group culture through deliberate role modeling, teaching and coaching, attention to certain behaviors, and leader reinforcement. The model can be particularly useful in facilitating the tasks of mourning by building a culture of group norms through which material is processed. The following section provides practical examples of culture building in grief groups based on the Schein group leadership model.

What Leaders Attend to, Measure, and Control

Because the focus of group leader attention acts as a cue to therapeutic priorities and purpose, it is important for grief group leaders to consciously convey communication norms for the group to emulate.

Examples:

1. "What thoughts are you censoring right now, Leila? You have a painful look on your face and seem distant today." (group culture message: we speak about feelings out loud)

2. "The silence is quite loud today. After the intense emotion in the last session, I wonder why the group is hesitant to be vulnerable today?" (culture message: we actively process hesitation and resistance)

3. If the conversation in the group is superficial rather than therapeutic, both direct and indirect communication may be used. The leaders may shift position in the chair, scan the group visually, or directly ask the group the purpose of the topic. (culture message: we move to depth)

Leader Reactions to Critical Incidents and Crises

Because of the intensified emotional involvement during a crisis event, crises are pivotal in shaping grief group culture. Donigian and Hulse-Killacky (1999) describe critical incidents in groups as moments during the evolving life of a group that can either present potential barriers or opportunities for the group's growth. How group therapists manage such incidents will determine how the events influence group development. When group leaders design strategies of response to opportunities for critical incidents, timing and content must be considered (Cohen & Smith, 1976). Leader reactions to crises around grieving help group members learn both experientially and through observation of leader reactions to other members.

Example:

> "I am noticing that as Curtis is talking about feeling suicidal, the group is attempting to talk him out of his feelings." (culture message: intense feelings can be heard and contained in this group)

Deliberate Role Modeling, Teaching, and Coaching by the Leaders

Pretherapy training helps clients obtain the necessary schemata for group counseling so that experiential data make sense as they occur (Randall & Wodarski, 1989). However, leader behaviors eventually have more value than initial instruction. Explicit coaching and other informal messages may be the most powerful teaching mechanisms (Schein, 1985). Leaders typically teach members to discuss feelings, give direct feedback to each other, become aware of patterns of behavior, and use empathic communication with each other. Other teaching includes telling the members about the two tasks of termination from a grief group (Yalom & Vinogradov, 1988): dealing with the loss of the group (acknowledging the ending of the group, saying good-bye to each other, and facing feelings evoked by termination) and anticipating and preventing regret (work left undone in the group is discussed, and members are asked to take responsibility for keeping the group working until the very last minute).

Examples:

1. "Maybe you could ask the group for help, Angela." (culture message: awareness of pattern of behavior, withdrawal)

2. "We have 10 minutes left for today. As you think of leaving here, who will be disappointed that you did not talk more about your loss? Perhaps you can use some of the time remaining to meet your needs." (culture message: it will be more productive to process unspoken dynamics)

Criteria for the Allocation of Rewards in Group

Leaders must establish a reinforcement system that is compatible with certain assumptions and values related to group functioning. Grief group leaders who intentionally reinforce emotional openness often describe a more rapid level of disclosure from group members. Leaders can quickly communicate priorities and values by contingently reinforcing to the behaviors they want to increase.

Examples:

1. "Sam, I'm sure it was difficult for you to talk about [the topic] and you did a nice job expressing yourself." (culture message: we reinforce openness and vulnerability)

2. "Betty, I'm glad you brought up your suicidal thoughts at the beginning of group this time so we could have time to help you." (culture message: do not bring up important topics at the end of group without time to process)

THE EFFECTIVENESS OF GRIEF GROUPS: PRESENT AND FUTURE

Research with grief groups has illustrated that bereavement is complex, impinging on both the inner life as well as on external tasks and adjustments (Lieberman, 1993). After a dearth of research on grief groups, Piper, McCallum, and colleagues (1991, 1992) brought the field to a new level of understanding and rigor regarding psychoanalytically oriented short-term group therapy for loss (McCallum, Piper, & Morin, 1993). Among other findings, these researchers have demonstrated that participant positive affect increased with time in group therapy and was related to favorable outcome. Clients also reduced depressive symptoms, self-esteem, life satisfaction, autonomy, and target problems (McCallum, Piper, Azim, & Lakoff, 1991). Investigators used large sample sizes, actual clinical populations, standard forms of therapy, and random allocation assignment of patients to ensure quality results. Piper (1994) has thus provided evidence that time-limited group therapy is a treatment of choice for patients with pathological grief reactions. Other models of grief group treatment now must be studied with the rigor needed to fully understand client change.

Most existing studies have focused on the setting of study or population, rather than investigating theoretical approach and clinical outcome. Berch (1999) used a modified Solomon-Four group design to compare the coping abilities of hospice group treatment participants with a control group of nonparticipants. Bereavement groups yielded positive results on an adapted version of the Texas Revised Inventory of Grief (TRIG) in comparison to the control group, measured at 6 weeks after the death and again 6 months later. Studies exploring groups targeting typical adjustment to loss are important contributions to the literature, as such groups may be more prevalent than treatment interventions for complicated bereavement. Research on specific interventions are also helpful: Mawson et al. (1981) designed a study for bereaved persons using the *guided mourning* approach described earlier. Significant improvement was demonstrated in the guided mourning group compared to a group encouraging avoidance of such thoughts and memories.

Burlingame and Fuhriman (1990) argued that the next developmental step for the general short-term group literature is the systematic, empirical investigation of the components of short-term models, as well as the documentation of treatment processes related to outcome. The authors proposed that brief groups may too often emphasize a thematic focus rather than an interaction between specific content themes and process. For example, in a grief group the members may address loneliness without the leaders processing how the loneliness dynamic affects group interactions and group member relationships. Typically, the effect of such interactional relationships are unknown in these groups. A challenge in researching the beneficial components of any group is to find unifying common denominators in assessing these factors with different types of groups (MacNair-Semands, 2000).

PSYCHOEDUCATIONAL GROUPS AND TASK GROUPS

In 1992, the Association for Specialists in Group Work (ASGW) suggested that groups be categorized into four major modalities: task/work groups, guidance/psychoeducational groups, counseling/interpersonal problem solving, and psychotherapy/personality reconstruction (ASGW, 1992, p. 13). Although the task/work group category has not been applied to grief groups, the other categories do apply to grief groups with some overlap in group goals and processes. Grief groups are difficult to classify in such a system, as identified goals can be as diverse as moving through the acute emotional pain of loss, gaining understanding of the tasks of grieving, and making interpersonal progress by reinvesting in new relationships and activities. Schwab (1986) writes that the *populations* served by grief groups have most often been used as a classification system: for example, widows and widowers, parents who have lost a child, and individuals who have experienced a suicide. A brief review of several types of loss interventions follows.

Loss Related to HIV and Aging

Several groups have combined members who were HIV-seropositive with gay men suffering a recent loss of close friend or lover to HIV (Goodkin et al., 1997). A theoretical model for these groups integrates life stressor appraisals, social support, and active coping. The three-phase grief work microstructure includes a standardized bereavement group protocol presented within the framework of a theory-driven research model of life stressor response. In a 10-session semistructured model, three phases of grief are taught in the group: making contact, venting of emotion, and moving on. For example, the topic "managing distressing feelings and letting go" from the third phase of grief, moving on, contains a discussion of coping strategies. Management of stressors is integrated with the grief work focus.

Maasen (1998) also described the mourning process for gay men with multiple loss experiences, providing as many as 50 sessions of group counseling. Group members suffering from multiple loss experiences engaged in exploration of the tendency to act out rage toward the outside hostile world and processed psychological conflicts about being gay and HIV infected. Frost (1997) further examined grief issues specific to gay men and aging unrelated to personal HIV status, arguing that the group modality is the treatment of choice for aging gay men. Aging in gay men has been described as a complex phenomenon involving identity, self-esteem, internalized homophobia, stereotypes about older gay men, and the paucity of positive gay male role models to help direct development.

Grief Groups Within Substance Abuse Treatment

There is increasing evidence of a connection between the addicted person's loss of significant persons, unresolved grief, and substance abuse (Denny & Lee, 1984). Substance abusers often use substances to deny a loss and, additionally, may suffer losses because of the use of addictive substances. Attempting to sever a tie to an addictive substance is a substantial loss in itself (Martin & Privette, 1989), including the loss of the associated social environment. Martin and Privette note that group therapy promotes the grieving process of substance abusers; the focus may include identifying losses, understanding forms of denial, accepting loss, addressing personal limitations, and reinvesting energy. Common themes in such groups may include loss of children to foster care, death of children, and losses around rape, incest, or violence (McComish et al., 1999).

A brief group model has been found to be appropriate for abusers in residential treatment programs (Denny & Lee, 1984). Denny and Lee studied a five-session model that indicated that participants in a treatment group were significantly less depressed and better able to resolve painful feelings about losses than persons in the control group. Conscious attention and education about emotional numbness, guilt, anger, and loneliness can help group members resolve loss and put energies into relationships with

available persons. In longer or open-ended groups, it has been found that clients who attended a relatively few number of sessions remained in substance abuse treatment longer and experienced improvements in depressive symptoms, overall mood, and parenting attitudes and beliefs (McComish et al., 1999).

Cognitive-Existential Groups for Patients With Breast Cancer

Other groups with both psychoeducational and supportive bases include anticipatory grief and loss related to medical diagnoses. Themes such as death anxiety, living with uncertainty, understanding treatment, and forming the collaborative doctor-patient relationships all emerged in the Kissane et al. (1997) study of groups for breast cancer patients. Goals for members included developing a support network, improving problem solving, developing cognitive strategies to maximize coping, working through grief over losses related to health, enhancing a sense of mastery over life, and reevaluating future priorities.

Grief Groups for Women in Prison

Prison presents an unusual setting for mourning, as there is often no place to speak of grief, contributing to the possibility of developing complicated bereavement. Not only do women in prison deal with losses due to death of others and a new confinement, but some deal with mourning the loss of a person they murdered (Woolfenden, 1997). During this process, lack of emotional contact with loved ones, loss of a life with freedom, and lack of significant counseling services often contribute to prisoners developing mental health problems (Kupers, 1999). Being estranged from family and friends, oscillating between real grief and denial of death, and understanding ways of mourning in different cultures and religions are typically processed in prison groups. Woolfenden's (1977) results, similar to those of the Lieberman (1993) study, delineated that resolving ambivalent feelings about the deceased is crucial to healing.

Self-Help Grief Groups With a Psychoeducational Focus

Self-help bereavement groups have been described as poorly defined with limited empirical support (Lieberman, 1993). Most researched have been groups for spousal bereavement and child loss by parents, which often measured effectiveness around issues of anger, isolation, and guilt (Lieberman, 1983). These groups typically include components of learning about the common phases of grief and exposure to information about coping strategies. In addition, the less restrictive group norms in comparison to society (e.g., accepting both laughing and intense anger) are seen as beneficial aspects of such groups.

CONCLUSION

Information exists that delineates the core processes and practice techniques in short-term grief groups, such as the importance of addressing ambivalence about the deceased (Lieberman, 1993). The general interpersonal techniques used in group treatment—establishing norms, encouraging processing, and making here-and-now interventions—have been successfully adapted to bereavement (Yalom & Vinogradov, 1988). Leaders can facilitate the natural process of healing from grief by focusing on growth and existential issues within new relationships. Whereas the components of loss and pain are both crucial and important for growth, they are considered insufficient without a second component addressing growth and new relationships. Rather than overemphasizing the components of loss and pain, a group focus on new social and intimate relationships can help grief group members expand personal identity, address existential issues about death, and discover new personal resources and strengths. Yalom and Vinogradov warn that specific structured exercises, such as having members bring in photographs, should be cautiously used so as not to hamper the more spontaneous interactions and discussions we know are central to group treatment for loss. Other authors use structured exercises and specific group techniques by setting an agenda around specific

thoughts and feelings that are shared by many group members (Padesky & Greenberger, 1995), or with clients in specific phases of grief to prevent stagnation (e.g., guided mourning exercises).

Group therapy may be the treatment of choice for the bereaved (McCallum et al., 1993; Piper, 1994). However, there is continued need for empirically supported grief treatments and specific information about the relationship between process and outcome in grief groups. It appears that empirical evidence about intervention and outcome in grief group treatments has been derived from counseling and therapy groups, in comparison to the more descriptive and practical writing found in the literature about psychoeducational and support groups. Clinicians should have the ability not only to prevent co-morbid disorders and complicated bereavement for those with recent losses, but to more skillfully treat those experiencing complicated bereavement.

REFERENCES

Association for Specialists in Group Work. (1992). Association for Specialists in Group Work: Professional standards for training of group workers. *Journal for Specialists in Group Work, 17,* 12-19.

Berch, D. G. (1999). Group treatment in a hospice bereavement program. *Dissertation Abstracts International, 60,* 1289. (UMI No. 9923190)

Bowlby, J. (1961). Processes of mourning. *International Journal of Psycho-Analysis, 42,* 317-340.

Burlingame, G. M., & Fuhriman, A. (1990). Time-limited group therapy. *Counseling Psychologist, 18,* 93-118.

Burnell, G. M., & Burnell, A. L. (1989). The Compassionate Friends: A support group for bereaved parents. *Journal of Family Practice, 22,* 295-296.

Cohen, A. M., & Smith, R. D. (1976). *The critical incident in growth groups: Theory and technique.* La Jolla, CA: University Associates.

Corazzini, J. G. (1980). The theory and practice of loss therapy. In B. M. Schoenberg (Ed.), *Bereavement counseling: A multidisciplinary handbook* (pp. 71-85). Westport, CT: Greenwood Press.

Denny, G. M., & Lee, L. J. (1984). Grief work with substance abusers. *Journal of Substance Abuse Treatment, 1,* 249-254.

Dies, R. R. (1994). Therapist variables in group psychotherapy research. In A. Fuhriman & G. M. Burlingame (Eds.), *Handbook of group psychotherapy* (pp. 114-154). New York: Wiley.

Donigian, J., & Hulse-Killacky, D. (1999). *Critical incidents in group therapy* (2nd ed). Pacific Grove, CA: Brooks/Cole.

Frost, J. (1997). Group psychotherapy with the aging gay male: Treatment of choice. *Group, 21,* 267-285.

Goodkin, K., Burhkhalter, J., Tuttle, R., Blaney, N., Feaster, D., & Leeds, B. (1997). A research derived bereavement support group technique for the HIV-1 infected. *Omega, 34,* 279-300.

Gray, R. E. (1988). The role of school counselors with bereaved teenagers: With and without peer support groups. *School Counselor, 35,* 185-193.

Kavanagh, D. J. (1990). Towards a cognitive-behavioral intervention for adult grief reactions. *British Journal of Psychiatry, 157,* 373-383.

Keitel, M. A., Kopala, M., & Robin, L. (1998). Loss and grief groups. In K. Stoiber and T. Kratochwill (Eds.), *Handbook of group intervention for children and families* (pp. 159-171). Boston: Allyn & Bacon.

Kissane, D. W., Bloch, S., Miach, P., Smith, G. C., Seddon, A., & Keks, N. (1997). Cognitive-existential group therapy for patients with primary breast cancer. *Psycho-Oncology, 6,* 25-33.

Kivlighan, D. M., & Tarrant, J. M. (2001). Does group climate mediate the group leadership-group member outcome relationship? A test of Yalom's hypotheses about leadership priorities. *Group dynamics: Theory, research, and practice, 5,* 220-234.

Klein, R. H., & Carroll, R. A. (1986). Patient characteristics and attendance patterns in outpatient group psychotherapy. *International Journal of Group Psychotherapy, 36,* 115-132.

Klerman, G. L., Weissman, M., Rounsaville, B. J., & Chevron, E. (1984). *Interpersonal psychotherapy of depression.* New York: Basic Books.

Kübler-Ross, E. (1969). *On death and dying.* New York: Macmillan.

Kupers, T. (1999). *Prison madness: The mental health crisis behind bars and what we must do about it.* San Francisco: Jossey-Bass.

Lieberman, M. A. (1983). Comparative analysis of change mechanisms in groups. In H. H. Blumberg, A. P. Hare, V. Kent, & M. Davies (Eds.), *Small groups and social interaction* (pp. 239-252). London: Wiley.

Lieberman, M. A. (1993). A reexamination of adult life crises: Spousal loss in mid- and late life. In G. Pollock & S. Greenspan (Eds.), *The course of life* (Vol. 6) (pp. 69-110). Madison, WI: International Universities Press.

Maasen, T. (1998). Counselling gay men with multiple loss and survival problems: The bereavement group as a transitional object. *AIDS Care, 10 (Supp. 1),* S57-S63.

MacDevitt, J. W. (1987). Conceptualizing therapeutic components of group counseling. *Journal for Specialists in Group Work, 12,* 76-84.

MacKenzie, K. R. (1983). The clinical application of a group climate measure. In R. R. Dies & K. R. MacKenzie (Eds.), *Advances in group psychotherapy: Integrating research and practice* (pp. 159-170). Madison, CT: International Universities Press.

MacKenzie, K. R. (1997). *Time-managed group psychotherapy: Effective clinical applications.* Washington, DC: American Psychiatric Press.

MacKenzie, K. R., & Grabovac, A. D. (2001). Interpersonal psychotherapy group (IPT-G) for depression. *Journal of Psychotherapy Practice and Research, 10,* 46-51.

MacNair, R. R., & Corazzini, J. (1994). Client factors influencing group therapy dropout. *Psychotherapy, 31,* 352-361.

MacNair-Semands, R. R. (1996). Efficient therapy groups: Intervening to shape group norms. In S. T. Gladding (Ed.), *New developments in group counseling* (pp. 65-67). Greensboro, NC: ERIC/CASS.

MacNair-Semands, R. R. (2000). Examining the beneficial components of group: Commentary on Estabrooks & Carron (2000) and Terry et al. (2000). *Group Dynamics: Theory, Research, and Practice, 4,* 254-258.

MacNair-Semands, R. R. (2001, February). Assessment of group selection factors and therapeutic dynamics. In S. Taylor (Chair), *Current research in groups.* Symposium conducted at the American Group Psychotherapy Association Conference, Boston, MA.

MacNair-Semands, R. R. & Corazzini, J. (1996, August). *Developing effective group therapy programs at counseling centers.* Paper presented at the American Psychological Association Conference, Toronto, Ontario, Canada.

Marmar, C. R., Horowitz, M. J., Weiss, D. S., Wilner, N. R., & Kaltreider, N. B. (1988). A controlled trial of brief psychotherapy and mutual-help group treatment of conjugal bereavement. *American Journal of Psychiatry, 145,* 203-209.

Martin, S., & Privette, G. (1989). Process model of grief therapy in an alcohol treatment program. *Journal for Specialists in Group Work, 14,* 46-52.

Mawson, D., Marks, J. M., Ramm, L., & Stern, R. S. (1981). Guided mourning for morbid grief: A controlled study. *British Journal of Psychiatry, 138,* 185-193.

McCallum, M., Piper, W. E., Azim, H., & Lakoff, R. S. (1991). The Edmonton model of short-term group therapy for loss: An integration of theory, practice, and research. *Group Analysis, 24,* 375-388.

McCallum, M., Piper, W. E., & Morin, H. (1993) Affect and outcome in short-term group therapy for loss. *International Journal of Group Psychotherapy, 43,* 303-319.

McComish, J., Greenberg, R., Kent-Bryant, J., Chruscial, H., Ager, J., Hines, F., et al. (1999). Evaluation of a grief group for women in residential substance abuse treatment. *Substance Abuse, 20,* 45-58.

Moorey, J. (1995). *Living with grief and mourning.* New York: Manchester University Press.

Osterweis, M., Soloman, E., & Green, M. (Eds.). (1984). *Bereavement: Reactions, consequences and care* (Report by the Committee for the Study of Health Consequences of the Stress of Bereavement, Institute of Medicine, National Academy of Sciences). Washington, DC: National Academy Press.

Padesky, C. A., & Greenberger, D. (1995). *Clinician's guide to mind over mood.* New York: Guilford.

Piper, W. E. (1994). Brief intensive group psychotherapy for loss. In K. R. MacKenzie (Ed.), *Effective use of group therapy in managed care* (pp. 43-59). Washington, DC: American Psychiatric Press.

Piper, W. E., & McCallum, M. (1991). Group interventions for persons who have experienced loss: Description and evaluative research. *Group Analysis, 24,* 363-373.

Piper, W. E., McCallum, M., & Azim, H. (1992). *Adaptation to loss through short-term group psychotherapy.* New York: Guilford.

Piper, W. E., McCallum, M., Joyce, A. S., Rosie, J., & Ogrodniczuk, J. S. (2001). Patient personality and time-limited group psychotherapy for complicated grief. *International Journal of Group Psychotherapy, 51,* 525-552.

Randall, E., & Wodarski, J. S. (1989). Theoretical issues in clinical social group work. *Small Group Behavior, 20,* 475-499.

Rando, T. A. (1993). *Treatment of complicated mourning.* Champaign, IL: Research Press.

Sanders, C. M. (1999). *Grief: The mourning after.* New York: John Wiley.

Schein, E. H. (1985). *Organizational culture and leadership.* San Francisco: Jossey-Bass.

Schwab, R. (1986). Support groups for the bereaved. *Journal for Specialists in Group Work, 11,* 100-106.

Silverman, P. R. (1987). In search of new selves: Accommodating to widowhood. In L. A. Bond & B. M. Wagner (Eds.), *Families in transition: Primary prevention programs that work.* Beverly Hills, CA: Sage.

Stone, W. N., & Rutan, J. (1984). Duration of treatment in group psychotherapy. *International Journal of Group Psychotherapy, 34,* 93-109.

Taub, D. J. (1998). Promoting student development through psychoeducational groups: A perspective on the goals and process matrix. *Journal for Specialists in Group Work, 23,* 196-201.

Waldo, M., & Bauman, S. (1998). Regrouping the categorization of group work: A goals and process (GAP) matrix for groups. *Journal for Specialists in Group Work, 23,* 164-176.

Weiner, M. F. (1984). Outcome of psychoanalytically oriented group psychotherapy. *Group, 8*(2), 3-12.

Weissman, M. M., Markowitz, J. C., & Klerman, G. L. (2000). *Comprehensive guide to interpersonal psychotherapy.* New York: Basic Books.

White, J. R. (2000). Depression. In J. R. White & A. S. Freeman (Eds.), *Cognitive-behavioral group therapy for specific problems and populations.* Washington DC: American Psychological Association.

Woods, M., & Melnick, J. (1979). A review of group therapy selection criteria. *Small Group Behavior, 10,* 155-175.

Woolfenden, J. (1997). Open Space: A bereavement and loss group in a closed women's prison. *Psychodynamic Counselling, 3,* 77-82.

Worden, J. W. (1991). *Grief counseling and grief therapy: A handbook for the mental health practitioner* (2nd ed.). New York: Springer.

Yalom, I. (1995). *The theory and practice of group psychotherapy* (4th ed.). New York: Basic Books.

Yalom, I., & Vinogradov, S. (1988). Bereavement groups: Techniques and themes. *International Journal of Group Psychotherapy, 38,* 419-446.

Yalom, V., & Yalom, I. (1990). Brief interactive group psychotherapy. *Psychiatric Annals, 20,* 362-367.

38

GROUP TREATMENT OF DEPRESSION

ANGIE H. RICE

FamilyStrength

"Depression is a hole, a black pit, the midnight of the soul, where the ladder of hope cannot penetrate to lift the heart from despair and sadness."

—Depression group client

D epression is one of the most prevalent and potentially serious of all mental disturbances, with estimates that it afflicts from 8% to as much as 20% of the population with symptoms serious enough to warrant treatment (Wilfley, MacKenzie, Walsh, Ayers, & Weissman, 2000). As many as 1 in 50 persons is hospitalized due to depressive symptoms, suicidal ideation, or attempts, and 1 in 200 may commit suicide (Rush, 1982). Depression is the most common problem reported by the elderly and is a growing problem for children and adolescents, with suicide being the number two cause of death of teenagers (Leszcz, 1997; Levitt, Lubin, & Brooks, 1983). Moreover, depression has a high rate of recurrence, especially if left untreated, with 50% to 85% of persons who have experienced a depressive episode likely to have such episodes in the future (Lowry, 1992). Depression is a serious social and health problem, leading to reduced

quality of life, reduced productiveness, job and family disruptions, and possible death. However, appropriate treatment can help over 80% of persons suffering from depression (NIMH/DART, 1991).

This chapter covers background information and theoretical explanations of depression and various group interventions, along with research on treatment effectiveness and application of group treatment to different populations. Finally, planning and conducting groups for depression are highlighted.

SOCIOCULTURAL AND GENDER ASPECTS OF DEPRESSION

All societies report symptoms associated with depression. While there is no acceptable cross-cultural definition, and symptomatology varies somewhat as a function of ethnicity, cross-cultural studies indicate that African and Asian societies show greater complaints regarding bodily functions, loss of energy, and shame, or feelings of failure at not living up to the expectations of others and society. Guilt and feelings of wrongdoing are more associated with Western societies (Estin, 1999; Noh, Kasper, & Chen, 1998).).

Depression is reported to occur in women twice as often as in men, even in different cultures (Koss-Chioino, 1999; Weissman & Klermann, 1990). Various ideas have been set forth to explain the prevalence of depression in women. Biological factors such as hormonal processes have been thought to predispose women to depression, but there is no clear linkage. Environmental factors such as role restriction or role change, and other socialization processes, have also been implicated (Rothblum, 1982; Seligman, 1975). Social and interpersonal deficiencies such as a lack of intimate relationships, social isolation, the presence of young children in the home, or troubled marital relations have also been linked to women's increased rates (Brown & Harris, 1978). Both the inner and outer worlds of women seem to contribute to the vulnerability to depression.

Results of studies in regard to education, income, social class, and status are often confusing and contradictory. However, there does seem to be a positive correlation between less education, lower socioeconomic factors, and increased depression. Income has been found to have a curvilinear relationship to depression, with those at both the high and low ends of the income spectrum exhibiting increased levels of depression (Levitt, Lubin, & Brooks, 1983). It is clear that there are multiple causes of depression, with the following predisposing a person to depressive symptomatology: (a) genetic vulnerability, (b) developmental events (early loss and trauma), (c) psychosocial events (life changes and interpersonal difficulties), (d) personality traits, and (e) physiological stressors (health problems, lack of sleep). All these underscore the multifaceted and multidetermined nature of depression, and all can be addressed in group counseling and therapy formats.

DEPRESSIVE ILLNESSES

The *Diagnostic and Statistical Manual of Mental Disorders, 4th Edition,* describes a collection of behaviors and feelings that covers mood disturbance and somatic, behavioral, and cognitive functions (APA, 2000). Major depression is manifested by a combination of symptoms that may occur once, twice, or several times in a lifetime. These symptoms include dysphoria (depressed mood); anhedonia (loss of interest in pleasurable activities); loss of sexual drive; disturbances in appetite leading to weight gain or loss; sleep disturbances (hypersomnia or insomnia); psychomotor agitation or retardation; disturbances in cognitive functioning, including decreased attention and ability to think; indecisiveness; and suicidal ideation. In addition, there may be feelings of worthlessness, guilt, reproach, and loss of hope. A less severe but more long-term type of depression has been labeled dysthymia. While not as disabling as major depression, there is a chronic lowering of feelings of happiness, productivity, and energy. Bipolar disorder is a less prevalent form of depression that involves cycling from periods of depression to periods of mania, which may include inappropriate elation, irritability, or social behavior; increased agitation and activity in thoughts and actions; insomnia; and grandiose thinking or poor judgment. The heterogeneity of depressive disorders may best be understood as the result of the interactions between biological, psychological, and social factors.

THEORIES OF DEPRESSION

Given the multidetermined nature of depression, multiple theories of causality have been delineated to explain depressive illnesses. These theories can be classified into four general areas, each with their own way of explaining causal processes: (1) biological, (2) psychodynamic and interpersonal, (3) cognitive, and (4) behavioral. Each of these views has something to add to our understanding of the complex phenomenon of depression and can be useful in guiding the kinds of group treatment interventions that practitioners devise and employ. Psychoeducational groups can address biological and medication management issues, as well as social and interpersonal skills and behavioral and cognitive strategies for treating depression. Counseling and therapy groups can address these issues as well through mutual aid and support, interpersonal learning and feedback, and emotional release.

Biological Theory

The biological model assumes some aberration in bodily functions to be the causes of most, if not all, mental illnesses, including depression. The biological model seeks to understand the relationship between brain structures and functions and ensuing thoughts, feelings, and behaviors and is associated with pharmacological treatment (NIMH/DART, 1991). Medications play a crucial role in managing and treating depressive illnesses. Groups can be helpful in addressing issues of medication management, such as education regarding side effects and noncompliance. However, biological functions cannot be compartmentalized from human emotions, thoughts, and behaviors; all reciprocally affect each other and can be examined in counseling and therapy groups.

Psychodynamic Theory

Psychodynamic theory includes both intrapsychic and object relational views of depression. The intrapsychic view is a conflict model that focuses on drives and wishes and defenses against those drives and wishes. Blocks or traumas, particularly at the oedipal phase of development, were seen as setting the stage for later depression. Ego functions and object relations, or relations with significant others, both impact and shape one another. Early traumatic experiences, perceived losses, and impaired object relations may leave deficits in self-esteem and a concomitant vulnerability to depression. While there is little empirical evidence to support much of psychodynamic theory, it has continued to influence views on depression (Piper, McCallum, & Azim, 1992). This perhaps is due to certain recurrent

universal themes in the theory of love, loss, hate, vulnerability, happiness, and disappointment that speak to the human condition. These kinds of issues may be very appropriate for work in a group therapy setting, where interactions with others and the feelings associated with such interactions are open to examination, clarification, interpretation, and feedback regarding feelings and behaviors. Psychodynamic group therapy may not be applicable to everyone who suffers from depression. A certain amount of psychological mindedness and capacity for insight is needed (Piper et al., 1992). This type of therapy strives to strengthen a person's fundamental adaptive capacities and change personality structure rather than solely ameliorate symptoms. The idea is to help a person understand how past experiences lead to depressive feelings and influence the present. It is best suited for those suffering more long-term depression, or those with episodic depression and long-standing maladaptive personality problems (Bemporad, 1990). These long-standing patterns can be enacted and interpreted in the microcosm of the small group, and the insight received supported by group members.

Interpersonal Theory

Interpersonal theories encompass what happens both within and between individuals. Disrupted interpersonal relations are usually associated with clinical depression in some way. Groups, by their very nature, are interpersonal and provide an ideal setting for examining and working on personal relationships.

Research into the social and interpersonal origins of depression prompted the development of interpersonal psychotherapy for depression (Klerman, Weissman, Rounsaville, & Chevron, 1984/1994). The focus of treatment is on current interpersonal relations and four general problem areas: (1) grief reactions, (2) role disputes, (3) role transitions, and (4) interpersonal difficulties, such as marital disputes, lack of intimate personal relations, and social skills deficits (Weissman & Klerman, 1990). Research points to the efficacy of such treatment in individual therapy, and there is a growing body of literature pointing to the efficacy of this approach in groups (Levkovitz et al., 2000;

Lowry, 1992; Wilfley et al., 2000). Interpersonal theory has had a significant impact on the practice of psychotherapy, with attendance to interpersonal relations a significant part of most modern approaches.

Adaptation of this brief, focused individual therapy for use in groups addresses many of the interpersonal problems faced by persons with depression. The interpersonal skills that can be developed and refined in a group may be more easily transferred to a person's social milieu than those learned in individual therapeutic interaction. Group members can identify the problems common to many who suffer from depression, examine the interplay of these problems in their interpersonal relationships, and help break the patterns of isolation and self-stigmatization that contribute to maintaining depressive symptoms. Problems with grief and loss, role difficulties, and disrupted intimate relationships can all be examined in the here-and-now atmosphere. Maintaining a focus on individual goals while utilizing the unique therapeutic factors of groups is important. Use of individual interviews, focused interpersonal assessment inventories, explicit preparation for group work, and regular communication of group issues with members, plus maintaining a here-and-now interactional and interpersonal focus, are essential factors in employing interpersonal psychotherapy in groups (Wilfley et al., 2000).

Cognitive Theory

The cognitive view of depression posits that negative automatic thoughts mediate between experience and action, causing feelings and actions associated with depression. Patterns of dysfunctional or distorted thinking and unrealistic cognitive appraisals of events cause emotional disorders. Depressed persons possess a cognitive triad: (1) a negative view of the self, (2) a negative view of the world, and (3) a negative view of the future (Beck, 1987). Early life experiences engender negative self-concepts and thinking patterns, or schemas, which make persons vulnerable to later depressive episodes. These schemas influence how a person manages day-to-day living and social relationships. They can remain dormant until activated by some perceived trauma or loss.

Cognitive theory states that feelings are caused by thoughts, and negative feelings can be managed by changing an individual's schemas. Therefore, treatment involves cognitive restructuring by replacing schemas with more realistic ones. More positive "self-talk" will lead to more positive feelings and interactions with the social environment. A group is an ideal place to examine irrational beliefs and distorted thinking patterns and to practice changing these negative phenomena. Group members can help one another identify these patterns, devise more realistic and positive statements and patterns, and practice applying these in everyday living situations, through such interventions as verbal role plays and written exercises. This approach has considerable empirical validation and is clinically useful in treating depression in both individual and group settings (McDermut, Miller, & Brown, 2001; Rush, 1982).

Behavioral Theory

The behavioral view characterizes depression as a series of behaviors learned under the same conditions of reward and reinforcement as other behaviors. Several theoretical models have developed from this basic behavioral learning premise. Usually, a single symptom was selected as the core or center of depression, with other symptoms following or generalized as secondary effects. Various treatment approaches were developed to address the core symptom (Rehm, 1990). Reinforcement theory states that depression is a result of a loss or lack of positive reinforcement for behaviors that leads to a reduction in activities and level of functioning (Ferster, 1973). It is postulated that by increasing one's level of activity, especially pleasant events, one can reduce the levels of depression (Lewinsohn, Munoz, Youngren, & Zeiss, 1986). Depressed persons are also theorized as having a deficit or deficits in various skill areas, such as stress management and social skills, which contributes to reduced positive reinforcement. Social skills such as assertiveness training and communication skills are important in managing and negotiating human relationships. Relaxation and stress management skills are important in learning to manage stress, loss, and rejection (Lewinsohn, Steinmetz, Antonuccio, & Teri, 1985). Both the behavioral and cognitive approaches have empirical validation and have proven effective in treating cases of unipolar depression in both individual and group formats (Robinson, Berman, Neimeyer, & Haykel, 1990; Wierzbicki & Bartlett, 1987). Social skills training and increasing pleasurable activities can be carried out within the small group. Group members can identify both positive and negative social skills behavior and work to increase the amount of positive interactions through behavioral rehearsal. Members can decide upon and use reinforcement strategies such as token rewards in the group setting to increase positive social skills. Pleasurable social activities can also be identified, schedules for increasing such activities can be devised, and appropriate reward strategies developed by group members to aid one another in increasing pleasurable activities. Groups can even participate in such activities together, thus providing needed support and feedback to one another for these activities.

Cognitive-Behavioral Theory

Cognitive theory and behaviorism have evolved into what has been termed the cognitive-behavioral perspective, which is a melding of the two orientations. There is not one cognitive, or cognitive-behavior therapy, but there are common elements. The therapies are usually time limited, problem specific, ahistorical, active, and fairly structured. They are usually interested in the modification of cognitions, feelings, and behaviors and use behavior therapy procedures (Dobson, 2001). However, the approaches are diverse, with different emphases on various cognitive aspects and differing philosophical orientations. Different aspects of cognitive experience, such as beliefs, self-statements, and images, are emphasized in different approaches. There is differing emphasis on where to intervene in the cycle of cognition, affect, behavior, and the consequences of behavior. Different strategies are applied, such as (a) refuting irrational beliefs, changing automatic thoughts, or producing more adaptive behaviors, (b) different intervention styles, from highly directive to collaborative, and (c) differential use of behavior modification procedures.

There are three major classes of cognitive-behavior therapies, all amenable for use in a group format: (1) coping skills therapies, (2) problem-solving therapies, and (3) cognitive restructuring methods. Coping skills training deals with problems in which the person is largely reacting to events outside the self. The focus is on ways persons may decrease the influence of negative events through cognitions, or the actions persons may take to lessen the impact of negative events (Dobson, 2001). Groups are an ideal place for persons to identify problematic social situations, both through interaction with group members and specific examination of outside social situations within the group. Reality testing of these situations by using feedback from group members is important, as is rehearsal of more appropriate ways of interacting within the group setting. The coping skills approach teaches strategies that people can use independently in dealing with problems and for reducing anxiety and depression (Sank & Shaffer, 1984), including the use of assertiveness skills, relaxation skills, coping self-statements, and self-reinforcement to deal with stress and anxiety-producing situations and more healthy ways of self-talk (Dobson, 2001). Learning these skills facilitates the acquisition of emotionally expressive behaviors. Group members can assist one another in learning these skills. Behavioral goals include standing up for oneself, making requests and refusals, and appropriately expressing affection, anger, and sadness. Again, the group is an invaluable setting for examining and practicing these skills through imparting information, role play, and rehearsal. Teaching coping skills can lessen feelings of anxiety and depression and increase the sense of self-efficacy, particularly if practiced in a supportive group atmosphere.

Problem-solving therapies focus on facilitation of social competence through training in systematic problem solving (Dobson, 2001); it attempts to provide a structure for working on problems that resist ready solutions. Many of the steps identified in problem-solving therapies, particularly problem identification, goal formation, and the generation of alternative actions and evaluation of these alternatives, are fostered by group interaction.

Cognitive restructuring addresses disturbances created within a person, that is, dysfunctional thinking, negative thinking, and irrational beliefs that lead to dysfunctional moods (Dobson, 2001; Sank & Shaffer, 1984). Cognitive restructuring procedures often used in groups are (a) dispelling irrational beliefs, (b) relabeling or reframing, (c) corrective information, and (d) thought stopping (Rose, 1977). Members can explore their beliefs and alternatives to these beliefs. This can also be done with uncovering automatic thoughts, looking at distorted thinking patterns, and negative self-talk. The group serves an important function in examining and redefining these patterns that are so prevalent in depression. Part of group treatment is the discovery of inadequate or incorrect information and its correction; it is possible to deal with general information and topics without people admitting their ignorance and to receive information in specific areas.

GROUP TREATMENT OF DEPRESSION

Group therapy has become an accepted modality in the treatment of depression (Lewinsohn et al., 1985; McDermut et al., 2001). Depressed individuals may have little opportunity to encounter interpersonal experiences that will modify existing interpersonal beliefs and dysfunctional interpersonal behavior patterns. Group treatment may provide new experiences that will help modify these beliefs and related behavior patterns and give members an opportunity to try out new behaviors and coping skills. Besides economy and universality, there are several advantages to a group format. The educational or didactic nature of therapy, which frequently employs psychoeducational methods such as lectures, workshops, and bibliotherapy, lends itself to and may be more effective in a group (Ettin, Heiman, & Kopel, 1988). Moreover, in a group counseling setting, clients may be made more aware of maladaptive cognitions and behavior. Members share experiences and give honest appraisals and feedback to help correct inaccurate perceptions and promote more realistic behavior. Challenges to thinking and behavior are more effective and may be more accurate when they emanate from

several peers rather than the therapist alone (MacKenzie, 1997). The social environment of the small group makes generalization of learning to real-life situations more possible. In addition, some techniques such as modeling, rehearsal, role play, and the use of a buddy system almost require a group setting (Rose, 1977, 1989). The use of a buddy system may be particularly helpful in treating depression, as it reduces isolation and increases social support for depressed persons.

Short-Term Group Treatment

Most of the models in use for group treatment of depression can be classified as short term, or lasting less than 6 months (Rice, 1996). Part of the proliferation of such therapies or models is the recognition that much of therapeutic treatment is short term in nature if not by design. One study at a large university hospital setting found that over half the patients treated in group therapy were seen for 12 or fewer sessions (Klein & Carroll, 1986). In most short-term group experiences, the mean number of sessions appears to range between 12 and 15, with most held weekly and lasting for 1 to 1½ hours (Butcher & Koss, 1978; MacKenzie, 1997). It has also been demonstrated that most therapeutic improvement in group therapy occurs within the first 6 months of treatment, no matter the type of group, with smaller increments of change occurring thereafter (MacKenzie, 1997).

The conscious use of time puts the responsibility for action into the hands of each individual member and reduces dependency on the group. Reducing dependency and increasing personal action is important, as one of the reasons posited for depressive symptoms is learned helplessness (Seligman, 1975). Termination is a factor in treatment; helping people resolve endings and deal with issues of termination successfully can be very important, as people suffering from depression often have suffered multiple, unresolved losses (Piper et al., 1992). The implicit, and often explicit, message is that if gains are to be realized, participation in the group is essential, and it must be done before the group ends. Time is used as a boundary for structuring the group process; short-term treatment has limited and specific therapeutic goals. Neither extensive personality change/ reconstruction nor complete symptom remission are realistic goals for any short-term therapy; however, reducing levels of depressive sympto-motology is.

Effectiveness of Group Treatment

Research suggests that group interventions are effective in the alleviation of depressive symptoms (Robinson, Berman, Neimeyer, & Haykal, 1990). Measured by self-report inventories like the Beck Depression Inventory, mood, social isolation, and withdrawal are improved with group treatment. However, specific conclusions about the factors, such as therapeutic or curative factors, treatment or therapeutic relationship factors, or patient factors and characteristics that are responsible for this positive outcome, have not yet been elucidated, and more research needs to be done in this area (McDermut et al., 2001). Much of current research has shown a nonspecificity to treatment (Rehm, 1990). In other words, regardless of the type of therapy individuals receive, there tends to be improvement in depressive symptoms.

While most research efforts indicate that group treatment of depression is as effective as other treatment forms, some studies have shown an inconsistency of outcome between individual and group therapy (Mohr, Boudewyn, Goodkin, Bostrom, & Epstein, 2001; Steffen, Futterman, & Gallagher-Thompson, 1999), with some studies showing more improvement for group therapy, while others showed more improvement with individual therapy. Two such studies indicated that individual cognitive therapy was superior to group cognitive therapy (Wierzbicki & Bartlett, 1987). However, these two studies were conducted on mildly depressed patients and involved a duration of 6 weeks of treatment. There was a significant time by treatment interaction, which may indicate that for some patients suffering from milder forms of depression, brief individual treatment may be more effective in the initial stages. One meta-analytic study, based on 58 studies of psychotherapy for depression that included both individual and group therapy studies, found that once the influence of investigator allegiance to a particular therapeutic model

was removed, there was no evidence for the superiority of any one model over another, leading to a call for more research on the therapeutic mechanisms responsible for change rather than differences in effectiveness among treatment models (Robinson et al., 1990).

Studies with follow-up components have begun to show more long-term effectiveness of group treatments for depression (Porter, 2001). One study, which examined a combination of cognitive-behavioral group therapy and medication for the treatment of depression among HIV-positive gay men, demonstrated that depression levels were substantially lower at 1-year follow-up than at pretreatment. Self-reports indicated that the focus on cognitive restructuring had been especially valuable in alleviating depressive symptoms (Lee, Cohen, Hadley, & Goodwin, 1999). The literature shows beginning attempts to identify what components may be more effective in producing change, such as the use of homework and homework compliance, but these are as yet inconclusive (Rekart, 2001).

Studies on group behavioral therapy have shown the efficacy of this treatment orientation. Fuchs and Rehm (1977) used behavioral group therapy with a group of depressed women who were taught to monitor, evaluate, and reinforce behaviors that were considered nondepressive. A second group of subjects were assigned to nonspecific group therapy, and a third group was assigned to a wait-list control condition. Those in the behavioral intervention reported decreased depression levels at posttest and increased group interaction during group sessions over both the nonspecific group treatment and the wait-list control group. Hodgson (1981) used behavioral methods with a group of depressed college students to improve interaction skills, and compared this to another group that used behavioral methods to modify cognitions. Both groups showed improved levels of depression and interactive skills, with a slightly superior outcome for the behavioral skills group.

A sequence of two studies compared group behavioral, individual behavioral, and a nonspecific interpersonal group therapy in treating depressed clients (Shapiro, Sank, Schaffer, & Donovan, 1982). Both behavioral conditions used relaxation training and the teaching of assertiveness skills. In the first study, the group behavior therapy condition reduced levels of depression and increased relaxation and assertiveness skills. In the second study, subjects in all three treatment conditions showed improvement with no clear superiority to any condition. The lack of control groups in both studies, and the lack of differential treatment effects in the second study, leads to difficulty in drawing any conclusions regarding these results.

Covi and Lipman (1987) compared group behavioral, group behavioral with medication, and traditional group therapy. The groups were led by experienced therapists trained in the models. Interventions in the behavioral groups focused on increasing pleasant activities and identifying and reinforcing positive social skills. The more traditional group therapy focused on insight and interpretation of transferential material in the group. At the end of 15 weeks of treatment, the behavior group with medication showed the most improvement in depression as rated by both the Beck Depression Inventory and the Hamilton Rating Scale for Depression. These results continued at 9-month follow-up, with the traditional group therapy condition demonstrating little or no effect on levels of depression.

While there has been an explosion in the literature describing the differences in mental health problems of persons from different cultures and ethnicities, only one empirical study on group treatment for depression addressed a different cultural population. In a control group design, Comas-Diaz (1981) compared the effects of group behavioral therapy and cognitive-behavioral group therapy with depressed Puerto Rican women. The behavioral group condition used activity schedules, contracts, and rehearsal of social skills in meetings, while the cognitive-behavioral group focused on reinforcement of positive cognitions and reduction of negative ones. Members of both treatment conditions showed improvement at the conclusion of 5 weeks of treatment; at a follow-up assessment, the members of the group behavior condition showed greater improvements in depression levels.

The studies on behavioral, cognitive-behavioral, and cognitive group treatment of depression that have been highlighted have focused on increasing pleasant activities, improving social skills, increasing interpersonal skills, or challenging and changing negative cognitions and irrational beliefs. One of the difficulties of research into differential treatment effectiveness has been the lack of consistent differential effects across treatment conditions and groups. Several studies point to the fact that a majority of persons in all treatment conditions demonstrate clinical improvement from pretreatment to both posttreatment and follow-up. There may be common, nonspecific factors, such as assurance, attention, and assessment, that play an active role in any treatment and account for the gains shown by patients (Wollersheim & Wilson, 1991).

While most of the research done on group treatment of depression has involved cognitive or behavioral interventions, research on both individual and group treatment indicates that other therapeutic strategies, such as psychodynamic and interpersonal, are also effective in the treatment of depression. Unresolved grief and loss, and the underlying conflicts that accompany these, have been addressed in a psychodynamically oriented short-term group treatment program instituted at a large university hospital (Piper et al., 1992). These groups covered wide age ranges, with most suffering mild to moderate levels of depression. A large-scale controlled, clinical research evaluation of the treatment program revealed a strong treatment effect both statistically and clinically. Patients were experiencing clinically significant difficulties associated with loss and grief that were long-standing and often involved multiple losses. The treatment identified internal conflicts with the use of clarification and interpretation, and focused on group interaction. The study involved 16 therapy groups led by experienced therapists and 154 patients who were randomly assigned to immediate or delayed therapy. Multiple outcome measures and follow-up assessments were also used. The results of the study showed a strong treatment effect and also identified a patient personality characteristic, psychological mindedness (or the capacity to link current difficulties with unconscious conflicts), which was significantly related to success in the groups.

Although most of the studies have focused on milder forms of depression, a study of a psychoeducational group treatment by Antonuccio and associates (1984) showed that participants with chronic depression maintained treatment gains at a 9-month follow-up. This may be due to the teaching of skills that were useful and received positive reinforcement in the everyday environment of participants. A study of an integrated model of brief treatment with a community mental health population, many with long-standing moderate to severe levels of depressive symptomatology, revealed that group members improved significantly more than a wait-list control group from pre- to posttreatment (Rice, 2001). This structured treatment model integrated various theoretical and practice orientations into a unified approach using the interactional framework of the small group to help members achieve their goals in dealing with depression. Alternate treatment groups using brief supportive psychotherapy and a wait-list control group were compared to the structured treatment groups on six outcome measures. Findings indicated that members of the structured treatment groups improved significantly on four of the six measures of depression in relation to the wait-list control group. While there was no statistically significant difference between the structured treatment groups and the alternate groups on the outcome measures, members of the alternate groups improved on only one measure of depression. Group leadership and group process measures were also analyzed and found not to have any significant effects on outcomes. This model is one in a growing trend to synthesize contributions made by different theoretical orientations into effective clinical interventions (Leszcz, 1997; Rice, 1995).

Group Treatment of Depression With Various Populations

Group treatment of depression has been used with children, adolescents, adults, and the elderly in a variety of settings. The research literature on treatment of children and adolescents in groups is sparse, particularly in the area of depression. A review of empirical research on treating depressed children suggests a need for the integration of a variety of cognitive and behavioral approaches in both individual and group settings, along with parent involvement through education and family therapy (Stark, Napolitano, Swearer, & Schmidt, 1996). Research on group treatment of adolescents indicates that short-term group treatment is effective in a variety of situations (Clarke et al., 1992; Pearce, 2000). Depressed adolescents tend to show more cognitive distortions and less effective problem-solving styles than peers, with an inverse relationship between social skills knowledge and depression. Both behavioral and problem-solving approaches to social skills training have shown these groups to be more effective than a wait-list control group (Fine, Forth, Gilbert, & Haley, 1991). It is interesting to note that the problem-solving group, or what was termed therapeutic discussion group, showed greater improvement posttreatment than did the behaviorally oriented social skills group, but these differences did not exist at 6-month follow-up. This suggests that social skills learning continues to foster improvement after treatment has ended, but that initial improvement for depressed adolescents may be fostered more by self-disclosure and discussion.

A study by Corder, Whiteside, & Haizlip (1981) on adolescent group therapy, which used a more traditional supportive and insight-oriented framework, found that the most important therapeutic factors were self-disclosure and interpersonal interaction, with vicarious learning and insight seen as least helpful by the participants. The less disturbed the group members were, the more they seemed to value cognitive therapeutic factors and learning by interpersonal interaction. The more disturbed the group members, the more they valued support, acceptance, and the instillation of hope.

Another study on the treatment of depressed adolescent outpatients used an adaptation of the Coping With Depression course (Lewinsohn et al., 1986) and provided social skills training. These adolescents showed significant improvement over a wait-list control group, particularly when a parent involvement component was added, and the gains were maintained at a 2-year follow-up. Further analysis revealed that adolescents who were rated as not depressed after treatment showed a lower initial score on the Beck Depression Inventory, lower intake state anxiety, higher levels of enjoyment and pleasant activities, and more rational thinking styles with less cognitive distortions, mirroring findings with adult groups (Clarke et al., 1992).

Older adults are particularly vulnerable to depression, expressing the themes of physical, social, and emotional losses of aging and the developmental tasks of role changes and transitions, accepting increased dependence and loss, and confronting one's own mortality. Group work centered on loss and relationship needs and "reminiscence" work, or what Erikson termed "life review," has been shown to be helpful (Fielden, 1992). Life review activities, such as structured storytelling or creation of life books, can be successfully conducted in group settings. The aid and support of the group can assist members with behavioral components of therapy and reduce isolation. Group cognitive therapy has been shown to improve cognitive functioning and reduce social isolation by increasing or regaining lost social skills. Group members were also less likely to prematurely terminate treatment (Beutler, Scogin, Kirkish, & Schretlen, 1987). Persons working with the depressed elderly need to be more directive, open, empathic, and supportive in the use of past experiences to promote the understanding of present emotional distress (Fielden, 1992). Recent research has pointed to the importance of explicit, individualized goals that address elders' sense of hopelessness as being useful in treating late life depression (Klausner, Snyder, & Cheavens, 2000).

Some research indicates that those undergoing treatment with more insight-oriented therapy showed more depression after treatment and more relapses after 1 year than those patients having a more structured therapy approach with clearly defined goals (Fielden, 1992). A meta-analysis of 17 studies on the efficacy of psychosocial interventions revealed that treatment was better than a placebo or no treatment. Behavior therapy and cognitive-behavior therapy produced larger effect sizes than other forms such as reminiscence therapy or anger expression. Individual therapy seemed to produce better results than group therapy; however, the authors note that the attention-placebo effect was an important factor, and that due to the small sample size of the analysis, the results should be interpreted cautiously (Engels & Vermey, 1997).

Groups have also been instituted for persons with special needs or conditions, such as depressed caregivers, AIDS patients and other medical patients suffering from depression, or depressed psychiatric inpatients (Lee et al., 1999; Rekart, 2001; Steffen, Futterman, & Gallagher-Thompson, 1999). While most studies have involved evaluation of the effectiveness of group treatment of unipolar depression, several studies have been done on persons diagnosed with bipolar depression in conjunction with lithium medication (Van Gent & Zwart, 1993). These groups ranged in duration from 10 weeks to a year or more, with all having an emphasis on patient education, coping skills, and group support. Therapy groups have also been found useful for patients with both bipolar and thought disorders. The integration of psychoeducational, supportive, and interpersonal theories and techniques was found to be useful for patients with thought disorders (Kanas, 1999). The forgoing studies showed that group therapy was associated with improvements in functioning, psychosocial problem solving, and improved adherence to medication schedules and seemed to provide benefits to patients not evident with medication alone.

PLANNING AND CONDUCTING GROUPS

Selection of Members

Most persons seeking mental health services fall into two categories: those with more long-standing difficulties who are marginally functional in the community and those with more recent, acute onset of difficulties who suffer from such environmental stresses as economic difficulties, job loss, illness, family difficulties, and marital dissolution. Many of the latter may also have had long-standing difficulties but were able to cope with these until some crisis pushed them past the limits of their coping abilities. The clinical outcome of a therapy experience for persons with more long-standing difficulties will not be as great as for persons with more recent acute onset of difficulties (Budman & Bennett, 1983; MacKenzie, 1997).

Thus, selection criteria for any group should consider these variables. Early assessment of the client's difficulties, capacities, and motivation to engage in therapy is important in order to determine suitability for treatment and facilitate the adoption of appropriate treatment goals

Some authors advocate exclusion if the patient is psychotic, borderline, self-destructive, or violent (Budman & Bennett, 1983); others add inclusionary criteria of more acute onset of difficulties, being able to relate interpersonally with others, and not overly dependent or aggressive (Butcher & Koss, 1978). A study of referrals for group therapy in a large university hospital setting showed that the majority were for moderately to severely disturbed individuals, mostly single, White females from middle- and working-class backgrounds, university students, or poorly educated, unemployed minority clients (Klein & Carroll, 1986). More seriously disturbed, chronically ill, or less motivated patients also can benefit from group therapy; however, the goals of the group, its structural features, and the role and techniques of the therapist need to be tailored accordingly. Less attention to insight and more attention to support and structure are seen as helpful with these patients. Persons who are actively psychotic and unable to relate to others would not likely benefit from a group (Klein, 1985).

Composition

The composition of any group exerts a great deal of influence on subsequent group events and the ability of members to engage in the work of the group. Yalom (1995) advocates heterogeneity of patient characteristics, symptoms, and problems but homogeneity in regard to ego strength and capacity to tolerate anxiety. Other authors have also subscribed to the view that heterogeneity is desirable, stating that variety in personality and emotional problems tends to prevent reinforcement of and facilitate communication through the variety of problems (Poey, 1985).

Much recent literature supports the use of homogeneous groups, those organized around a focal problem or theme, particularly in regard to short-term treatment (Flowers & Booraem, 1991). In homogeneous groups, members share a sense of commonality that promotes the development of cohesion. It is easier to feel closer and less threatened by people who are perceived as having similar qualities and problems. This sense of commonality or similarity also promotes curative factors, such as vicarious and interpersonal learning, acceptance, universality, and the instillation of hope (Brabender, Albrecht, Sillitti, Cooper, & Kramer, 1983). For depression groups, it seems desirable to have homogeneity of problem type and heterogeneity of other patient characteristics.

Structure

Structure has been referred to as the activities and interventions of the leader, such as (a) pretherapy training; (b) structuring the interaction of the group in various ways, with direct interventions such as talking more, directing conversation, explicitly promoting positive therapeutic norms, modeling, and reinforcement; and (c) indirectly by structuring activities, such as exercises, role plays, didactic teaching, and creation of agendas for sessions in order to help members reach their goals (i.e., a psychoeducational approach). Findings from one study point to the possibility that it is structure, in the form and timing of leader interventions and learning experiences, rather than homogeneity that contributes to therapeutic outcome in short-term therapeutic groups (Flowers & Booraem, 1990). These structured intervention strategies have been successfully employed in groups for depression and have considerable empirical validation as to their effectiveness in treating depressive symptomotology (Rice, 1996).

Pretherapy Preparation

Pretherapy preparation is seen as contributing to the effectiveness of any therapeutic endeavor and is especially important for short-term group treatment (Poey, 1985). While there is no methodologically strong empirical evidence about the relationship between specific kinds of pretherapy training and specific therapeutic effects, present evidence supports the use of some form of training (Piper & Perrault, 1989). Pretherapy training can correct client misperceptions and facilitate the development of appropriate group norms that contribute to the ability of the group and individuals to work on goal attainment. This type of preparation may be particularly important, given the nature of depressive symptoms, which often makes it difficult for persons to concentrate, remember, and think effectively. Explanations of how the groups will work and what can be expected may need to be reiterated for members. Moreover, the social isolation and withdrawal can start to be alleviated through pretherapy training. Preparation of group members can be done individually, but some authors have found group training to be particularly helpful for preparation for group therapy (Budman & Bennett, 1983; Rose, 1989).

Leadership

As stated above, the group therapist or leader uses activities and interventions to structure group interaction to aid the development of a meaningful and positive therapeutic learning environment. In a thoughtful discussion of leadership in short-term therapeutic groups, Dies (1985) states that leaders must intervene actively to manage boundaries, maintain task focus, and regulate the intensity of emotional expression. This type of leadership may be especially important in depression groups due to the interpersonal nature of client problems, difficulties with self-esteem, and prevalence of negative thinking patterns and distortions. Leaders play a significant role in facilitating an open and supportive atmosphere within the group, which is so important for working with depression groups. The group leader actively intervenes to foster supportive interactions and make connections of similarities among group members. The leader also lessens the possibilities for confrontative exchanges, especially early in the group's development and with members who have more severe pathology. Research on groups in laboratory and training settings has shown that positive feedback is almost always rated as more desirable, having greater impact, and leading to greater intention to change than negative feedback, and that behaviorally oriented feedback is more effective than emotional feedback (Dies, 1983). Members suffering from depression need support and

encouragement from other members to institute changes in their lives, in addition to clarification about the things they may do to help alleviate their symptoms. The leader has a crucial role in modeling and reinforcing these types of interactions in groups.

SUMMARY AND CONCLUSIONS

Depression is a multifaceted and multidetermined mental health problem that causes a great deal of human suffering and loss to society. Group treatment has been found to be an effective psychosocial intervention for persons in a variety of settings who suffer from this difficulty. Research has demonstrated that when clients are specific about the problems or goals for therapy, disclose these problems in the group, and spend time discussing these with some reduction in emotional intensity, there tends to be therapeutic improvement. In other words, behaviorally specific messages delivered in a positive manner by group members regarding a goal the client has deemed important, and in which there is some emotional investment, has the potential to effect therapeutic change. Moreover, the use of structure in the form of leader interventions and activities fosters problem identification, positive interaction and catharsis, and rapid group cohesion that facilitates therapeutic improvement in depression groups.

When persons interact with one another in a supportive, caring environment, dynamic forces are released that contribute to personal change and growth. There is something unique to group interaction that helps unlock these forces for change, or therapeutic factors. While no specific studies have been undertaken to identify the therapeutic factors that operate in groups for depression, clinical judgment points to the factors of universality, acceptance, cohesiveness, and instillation of hope as being particularly relevant in combating the withdrawal, isolation, and sense of powerless and hopelessness so prevalent in depressive illnesses. The major challenge for clinicians is properly identifying depression and discovering what treatment options are most suitable for which persons. For many, groups may be the treatment of choice for managing the multifaceted nature of depression.

REFERENCES

American Psychiatric Association. (2000). *Diagnostic and statistical manual of mental disorders* (4th Ed-TR.). Washington, DC: American Psychiatric Association.

Antonuccio, D., Thompson, A., Chatham, P., Monagin, J., Tearman, B., & Aiger, B. (1984). An exploratory study: The psycho-educational group treatment of drug-refractory unipolar depression. *Journal of Behavioral Therapy and Experimental Psychiatry, 15,* 309-313.

Beck, A. T. (1987). Cognitive therapy. In J. K. Zeig (Ed.), *The evolution of psychotherapy.* New York: Brunner/Mazel.

Bemporad, J. R. (1990). Psychoanalytic therapy of depression. In B. B. Wolman & G. Stricker (Eds.), *Depressive disorders: Fact, theories, and treatment methods.* New York: John Wiley.

Beutler, L. E., Scogin, F., Kirkish, P., & Schretlen, D. (1987). Group cognitive therapy and alprazolam in the treatment of depression in older adults. *Journal of Consulting and Clinical Psychology, 55,* 550-556.

Brabender, V., Albrecht, E., Sillitti, J., Cooper, J., & Kramer, E. (1983). A study of curative factors in short-term group psychotherapy. *Hospital and Community Psychiatry, 34,* 643-644.

Brown, G. W., & Harris, T. (1978). *Social origins of depression.* New York: Free Press.

Budman S. H., & Bennett, M. J. (1983). Short-term group psychotherapy. In H. Kaplan & B. Sadock (Eds.), *Comprehensive group psychotherapy* (2nd ed.). Baltimore: Williams & Wilkins.

Butcher, J. N., & Koss, M. P., (1978). Research in brief and crisis-oriented psychotherapies. In A. E. Bergin & S. L. Garfield (Eds.), *Handbook of psychotherapy and behavior change.* New York: John Wiley.

Clarke, G., Hops, H., Lewinsohn, P. M., Andrews, J., Seeley, J. R., & Williams, J. (1992). Cognitive-behavioral group treatment of adolescent depression: Prediction of outcome. *Behavior Therapy, 23,* 341-354.

Comas-Diaz, L. (1981). Effects of cognitive and behavioral group treatment on the depressive symptomatology of Puerto Rican women. *Journal of Consulting and Clinical Psychology, 49,* 627-632.

Corder, B. F., Whiteside, R., & Haizlip, T. (1981). A study of curative factors in group psychotherapy with adolescents. *International Journal of Group Psychotherapy, 31,* 345-354.

Covi, L., & Lipman, R. S. (1987). Cognitive behavioral group psychotherapy combined with imipramine in major depression. *Psychopharmacology Bulletin, 23,* 173-176.

Dies, R. R. (1983). Clinical implications of research on leadership in short-term group psychotherapy. In R. R. Dies & K. R. MacKenzie (Eds.), *Advances in group psychotherapy: Integrating research and practice.* New York: International Universities Press.

Dies, R. R. (1985). Leadership in short-term group therapy: Manipulation or facilitation? *International Journal of Group Psychotherapy, 35,* 435-455.

Dobson, K. S. (2001). *Handbook of cognitive-behavioral therapies* (2nd ed.). New York: Guilford.

Engels, G. I., & Vermey, M. (1997). Efficacy of treatments of depression in elders: A quantitative analysis. *Journal of Clinical Geropsychology, 3,* 17-35.

Estin, P. J. (1999). Spotting depression in Asian patients. *RN, 62,* 39-41.

Ettin, M. F., Heiman, M., & Kopel, S. A. (1988). Group building: Developing protocols for psychoeducational groups. *Group, 12,* 205-225.

Ferster, C. B. (1973). A functional analysis of depression. *American Psychologist, 28,* 857-870.

Fielden, M. A. (1992). Depression in older adults: psychological and psychosocial approaches. *British Journal of Social Work, 22,* 291-307.

Fine, S., Forth, A., Gilbert, M., & Haley, G. (1991). Group therapy for adolescent depressive disorder: A comparison of social skills and therapeutic support. *Journal of the American Academy of Child and Adolescent Psychiatry, 3,* 79-85.

Flowers, J. V., & Booraem, C. D. (1990). Four studies toward an empirical foundation for group therapy. *Advances in group work research.* New York: Haworth.

Flowers, J. V., & Booraem, C. D. (1991). A psychoeducational group for clients with heterogeneous problems: Process and outcome. *Small Group Research, 22,* 258-273.

Fuchs, C. Z., & Rehm, L. P. (1977). A self control behavior therapy program for depression. *Journal of Consulting and Clinical Psychology, 45,* 206-215.

Hodgson, J. D. (1981). Cognitive versus behavioral-interpersonal approaches to group treatment of depressed college students. *Journal of Counseling Psychology, 28,* 243-249.

Kanas, N. (1999). Group therapy with schizophrenic and bipolar patients: Integrative approaches. In V. Schermer & M. Pines (Eds.), *Group psychotherapy of the psychoses: Concepts, interventions, and contexts.* International library of group analysis 2 (pp. 129-147). Bristol, PA: Jessica Kingsley Publishers.

Klausner, E. J., Snyder, C. R., & Cheavens, J. (2000). A hope-based group treatment for depressed older adult outpatients. In G. Williamson & D. Shaffer (Eds.). *Physical illness and depression in older adults: A handbook of theory, research, and practice* (pp. 295-310). New York: Kluwer Academic/ Plenum.

Klein, R. R. (1985). Some principles of short-term group therapy. *International Journal of Group Psychotherapy, 35,* 309-329.

Klein, R. R., & Carroll, R. A., (1986). Patient characteristics and attendance patterns in outpatient group psychotherapy. *International Journal of Group Psychotherapy, 36,* 115-132.

Klerman, G. L., Weissman, M. M., Rounsaville, B. J., & Chevron, M. S. (1984/1994). *Interpersonal psychotherapy of depression.* New York: Basic Books.

Koss-Chioino, J. D. (1999). Depression among Puerto Rican women: Culture, etiology, and diagnosis. *Hispanic Journal of Behavioral Sciences, 21,* 330-351.

Lee, M. R., Cohen, L., Hadley, S. W., & Goodwin, F. K. (1999). Cognitive-behavioral group therapy with medication for depressed gay men with AIDS or symptomatic HIV infection. *Psychiatric Services, 50,* 948-952.

Leszcz, M. (1997). Integrated group psychotherapy for the treatment of depression in the elderly. *Group, 21,* 89-113.

Levitt, E. E., Lubin, B., & Brooks, J. M. (1983). *Depression: Concepts, controversies, and some new facts* (2nd ed.). Hillsdale, NJ: Lawrence Erlbaum.

Levkovitz, Y., Shahar, G., Native, G., Hirsfeld, E., Treves, I., Krieger, I., et al. (2000). Group interpersonal psychotherapy for patients with major depression disorder-pilot study. *Journal of Affective Disorders, 60,* 191-195.

Lewinsohn, P. M., Munoz, R. F., Youngren, M. A., & Zeiss, A. M. (1986). *Control your depression.* New York: Prentice Hall.

Lewinsohn, P. M., Steinmetz, J. L., Antonuccio, D., & Teri, L. (1985). Group therapy for depression: The coping with depression course. *International Journal of Mental Health, 13,* 8-33.

Lowry, C. E. (1992, July). *New strategies in the assessment and treatment of depression.* Presentation at the 1992 World Assembly, National Association of Social Workers, Washington, DC.

MacKenzie, K. R. (1997). *Time managed group psychotherapy effective clinical applications.* Washington, DC: American Psychiatric Press.

McDermut, W., Miller, I. W., & Brown, R. A. (2001). The efficacy of group psychotherapy for depression: A meta-analysis and review of the empirical research. *Clinical Psychology: Science and Practice, 8,* 98-116.

Mohr, D. C., Boudewyn, A. C., Goodkin, D. E., Bostrom, A., & Epstein, L. (2001). Comparative outcomes for individual cognitive-behavior therapy, supportive-expressive group psychotherapy and sertraline for the treatment of depression in multiple sclerosis. *Journal of Clinical and Consulting Psychology, 69,* 942-950.

National Institute of Mental Health/Depression Awareness, Recognition, and Treatment Program. (1991). *Depression, what you need to know.* Rockville, MD: Department of Health and Human Services.

Noh, S., Kasper, V., & Chen, X. (1998). Measuring depression in Korean immigrants: Assessing validity of the translated Korean version of the CES-D scale. *Cross-Cultural Research: The Journal of Comparative Social Science, 32,* 358-377.

Pearce, J. C. (2000). The effect of cognitive-behavioral group counseling on adolescent depression, academic performance, and self-esteem. *Dissertations Abstracts International Section B: The Sciences and Engineering, 61*(3-B), 1648.

Piper, W. E., McCallum, M., & Azim, H. F. A. (1992). *Adaptation to loss through short-term group psychotherapy.* New York: Guilford.

Piper, W. E., & Perrault, E .L. (1989). Pre-therapy preparation for group members. *International Journal of Group Psychotherapy, 39,* 17-34.

Poey, K. (1985). Guidelines for the practice of brief, dynamic group therapy. *International Journal of Group Psychotherapy, 35,* 331-354.

Porter, J. F. (2001). Venture Behavioral Health Southwestern Michigan treatment of depression collaborative study: The effectiveness of behavioral activation group therapy and initial investigation. *Dissertation Abstracts International Section B: The Sciences and Engineering, 61*(9-B), 5001.

Rehm, L. P. (1990). Cognitive and behavioral theories. In B. B. Wolman & G. Stricker (Eds.), *Depressive disorders: Facts, theories, and treatment models.* New York: John Wiley.

Rekart, J. A. (2001). The effects of cognitive-behavioral group therapy, homework compliance, and quality of compliance with depressed patients. *Dissertation Abstracts International Sciences and Engineering, 61*(10-B), 5578.

Rice, A. H. (1995). Structured group treatment of depression. In K. R. MacKenzie (Ed.), *Effective use of groups in managed care.* Washington, DC: American Psychiatric Association.

Rice, A. H. (1996). *Structured group treatment of depression: An integrated social work model.* Ann Arbor, MI: UMI.

Rice, A. H. (2001). Evaluating brief structured group treatment of depression. *Research on Social Work Practice, 11,* 53-78.

Robinson, L. A., Berman, J. S., Neimeyer, R., & Haykal, S. (1990). Psychotherapy for the treatment of depression: A comprehensive review of controlled outcome research. *Psychological Bulletin, 108,* 30-49.

Rose, S. A. (1977). *Group therapy: A behavioral approach.* Englewood Cliffs, NJ: Prentice Hall.

Rose, S. (1989). *Working with adults in groups: Integrating cognitive-behavioral and small group strategies.* San Francisco: Jossey-Bass.

Rothblum, E. D. (1982). Women's socialization and the prevalence of depression: The feminine mistake. *Women and Therapy, 1,* 5-13.

Rush, A. J. (1982). *Short-term psychotherapies for depression.* New York: Guilford.

Sank, S. L., & Schaffer, C. S. (1984). *A therapist's manual for cognitive behavior therapy in groups.* New York: Plenum.

Seligman, M. E. P. (1975). *Helplessness: On depression, development and death.* San Francisco: Freeman.

Shapiro, J., Sank, L. I., Schaffer, C. S., & Donovan, D. C. (1982). Cost effectiveness of individual vs. group cognitive behavior therapy for problems of depression and anxiety in an HMO population. *Journal of Clinical Psychology, 38,* 674-677.

Stark, K. D., Napolitano, S., Swearer, S., Schmidt, K. (1996). Issue in the treatment of depressed children. *Applied and Preventive Psychology, 5,* 59-83.

Steffen, A. M., Futterman, A., & Gallagher-Thompson, D. (1999). Depressed caregivers: Comparative outcomes of two interventions. *Clinical Gerontologist, 19,* 3-15.

Van Gent, E. H., & Zwart, F. M. (1993). Ultra-short versus group therapy in addition to lithium. *Patient Education and Counseling, 21,* 135-141.

Weissman, M. M., and Klerman, G. L. (1990). Interpersonal psychotherapy for depression. In B. B. Wolman & G. Stricker (Eds.), *Depressive disorders: Facts, theories, and treatment models.* New York: John Wiley.

Wierzbicki, M., & Bartlett, T. S. (1987). The efficacy of group and individual cognitive therapy for mild depression. *Cognitive Therapy and Research, 11,* 337-342.

Wilfley, D., MacKenzie, K. R., Welch, R. R., Ayers, V. E., & Weissman, M. W. (2000). *Interpersonal psychotherapy for group.* New York: Basic Books.

Wollersheim, J. P., & Wilson, G. (1991). Group treatment of unipolar depression: A comparison of coping, supportive, bibliotherapy, and delayed treatment groups. *Professional Psychology: Research and Practice, 22,* 496-502.

Yalom, I. D. (1995). *The theory and practice of group psychotherapy* (4th ed.). New York: Basic Books.

39

ANGER MANAGEMENT GROUPS

LAURIE B. FLECKENSTEIN
University of Georgia

ARTHUR M. HORNE
University of Georgia

Three primary group modalities are relevant in the treatment of anger management. These modalities are psychoeducational, counseling, and therapy groups (Association for Specialists in Group Work [ASGW], 2000; Gazda, Ginter, & Horne, 2001). This chapter discusses anger management issues and reviews each of these three group interventions, including the definition of the group approach, leader and member roles, and methods of evaluating change. A case example of each of the group formats frames treatment points and treatment efficacy issues while illustrating differences between the three approaches.

DEVELOPMENTAL ISSUES
INFLUENCING TREATMENT APPROACH

Anger can be a problem at any stage of life including childhood. It is common for children to struggle as they learn the process of managing their feelings and emotional self-regulation. Children may experience anger problems in the context of everyday situations involving interactions with family members, teachers, and peers. They have not learned more appropriate, prosocial methods of handling discomforting internal or external situations; thus frustration and anger are not uncommon.

Similarly, adolescents may have learned that anger can be instrumental in helping them achieve goals or payoffs, at least in the short run. They may have learned to use anger as an effective form of manipulating others. Adults with anger control problems may have more entrenched difficulties with emotional regulation. The specific group intervention model is selected based on the developmental concerns as related to the client's presenting anger problem. Furthermore, the selection of the intervention is influenced by the extent of the problem, with less serious problems being best addressed via psychoeducational models. Furthermore, higher degrees of problematic anger conditions are addressed by counseling and severe anger behavior control problems are the focus of therapy groups (Gazda et al., 2001).

DECIDING ON GROUP TYPE

Choosing the appropriate type of group involves consideration of many different factors, including group members' developmental maturity, group members' history of anger problems, group size, leadership styles, and settings. These factors influencing recruitment, screening, and selection of members are explored using case examples for each group approach.

Psychoeducational Groups

Psychoeducational groups may be particularly effective when working with younger individuals, as this approach fits well with their educational experience within the school system. The focus of the process in these groups is on emotional and behavioral learning. Psychoeducational groups are particularly effective to aid children in developing behavioral and affective skills necessary for effective emotional management. Specifically, psychoeducational groups provide the opportunity for students to become familiar with the process of learning to understand the feelings of others (empathy training), identifying appropriate and inappropriate anger, and learning appropriate interpersonal behaviors to express anger without hurting others. The learning environment, experienced through the group, provides children with a practice group for the development of social skills and provides a powerful learning component, including skills training, behavioral rehearsal, and cognitive training information. Psychoeducational groups involve individuals in settings in which the group may be large and the backgrounds of participants diverse and variable. The structural component of psychoeducational groups fits well with the larger group atmosphere, as it focuses on working through lessons with less emphasis on self-disclosure. In fact, personal disclosure would be guarded against, as the group members' interests might be at risk with inappropriate self-disclosures in this larger group context.

Therapy skills are not necessary to conduct psychoeducational groups, which means individuals with varied backgrounds can act as group leaders. Teachers, school psychologists or social workers, other educators, or counselors may conduct psychoeducational groups. The important consideration for the leader is not whether the person is a trained counselor, but whether the person has adequate training in conducting groups. As is evident, there is a difference in teaching material to a class (education) and conducting a group in which the leader offers content but also utilizes the dynamics of the group and the interactions of the individuals within the group to facilitate the learning process for members. While teachers may be experts at content, they may not have the group facilitation skills necessary to have the experience be as powerful as desired if they lack specific training in group skills. As is evident from the different approaches to group work, to conduct psychoeducational groups one does not have to have therapy skills, but it is necessary to have a solid understanding of group process, group dynamics, and supervised experience in engaging group members in the learning process.

There are extensive descriptions of psychoeducational groups that have been developed to help young people learn to manage anger effectively, including programs by Smead (1990, 1994, 1999) and Goldstein (1999) and his associates (Goldstein, Glick, & Gibbs, 1998). Sample activities that they have developed include helping students become aware of others' anger by feeling charts, practicing understanding how others might feel, or taking on others' roles by assigning members of the group to role plays. Furthermore, students are encouraged to develop an understanding of the thought processes that lead to angry thinking and the self-talk necessary to bring change. An example of the social cognitive skills training of psychoeducational groups is illustrated in an activity developed by Meyer, Farrell, Northup, Kung, and Plybon (2000). As an activity in their 25-session program named RIPP (Responding in Peaceful and Powerful Ways), they introduce SCIDDLE, which stands for Stop, Calm down, Identify the problem and feelings, Decide what to do, Do it, Look back, and Evaluate the plan and outcome to see how it worked. The core components of anger management skills are included in this activity, such as helping students gain self-control, engage in problem solving and effective decision making, and the implementation and evaluation of carefully determined cognitive and behavioral strategies.

CASE EXAMPLE OF PSYCHOEDUCATIONAL GROUP

In this case example, components of an anger management group for elementary-aged students are highlighted. These students are involved in a classroom-based psychoeducational group approach. The class meets in a large group, and those present have varying degrees of anger problems. Despite some fluctuation, the leader's role frequently involves modeling new behaviors and leading group members in an educational manner through the development of new skills, and the leader actively encourages students to participate in interactive activities such as role plays and skill rehearsals.

Two anger-reduction interventions for children are utilized in the group format (Goldstein, Glick, Reiner, Zimmerman, & Coultry, 1987). The first is aimed at increasing prosocial awareness and behavior, because an aspect of anger control is being able to understand the perspective of others. Being skilled in recognizing the role that emotions play for oneself as well as others is important. Also, understanding the importance of prosocial awareness in groups, classrooms, and other gatherings of people is essential for developing appropriate social skills. The second part of the intervention, development of inhibition of anger outburst or aggressive reactivity, focuses on helping students learn to identify the ABCs of behavior. These ABCs refer to the circumstances leading to conflict (antecedents), how people behave given those antecedents (behaviors), and the impact that the behavior has on oneself and others (consequences). Thus, the elements of the SCIDDLE model are included in the Goldstein et al. (1987) program. Both elements are taught through having the leader provide an overview of the importance of cooperation and friendship, of getting along with others, and of being able to problem solve without resorting to violence or aggression. These activities are then discussed and role-played or rehearsed at each level (awareness, understanding others, problem solving, evaluating change).

Sample Psychoeducational Group Outline

1. Opening Session
   - Group interactively decides on group guidelines, rules, and expectations
   - The focus of the group is explained by the group leaders

2. Awareness of Proactive, Empathic Behavior: Defining Positive Group Participation
   - Leaders model and participants practice "I" statements
   - Discussion focuses on skills in listening to other group members

3. Awareness of Anger Response & Anger Triggers
   - Acknowledging when you are angry is explored as important
   - Developing an awareness of personal anger triggers
   - Recognizing how you react
   - Brainstorming alternative responses to anger triggers

4. Awareness of Attributional Bias
   - Exploration of alternative explanations
   - Awareness of how participants' attributions affect their responses
   - Skills in recognizing attributional bias in social interactions

(Continued)

Continued

5. Self-Regulatory Strategies
   - Development of self-statements to aid in coping with anger
   - Responding to failure or teasing
   - Dealing with being excluded

6. Calming Strategies
   - Deep breathing exercises
   - Calming imagery
   - Skills to help calm others

7. Anger Replacement
   - Developing negotiation skills
   - Learning preparatory skills for difficult interactions

8. Development of Conflict Resolution Plan
   - Individualized anger plans constructed and linked with anger triggers

9. Empathy Skills
   - Skills in recognizing and decoding others' emotions and feeling states
   - Empathizing with others

10. Practice Planning Skills
    - Use of role play to review skills and increase capacity to deal with anger problems that may arise in the future

The session outline provides a broad framework and general understanding of how the group is designed. Sessions and activities are created to develop prosocial skills as well as awareness of triggers and experiences of anger. These two components come together to create the backbone of the group and extend through the following case exemplars. Goldstein and colleagues (1987) noted that variability in presenting training stimuli would create greater positive transfer. Group activities are developed to create variability in order to increase generalizability. This includes having role plays in which participants engage in a number of activities (being assertive, problem solving, resolving conflict peacefully), in a number of settings (classroom, playground, neighborhood, department store), with a number of people (friends, strangers, bullies). Through varied practice, greater skill development occurs and generalizability to other settings is established.

PSYCHOEDUCATIONAL INTERVENTION: BUILDING ANGER AWARENESS

A key component of working on anger management involves recognition and skill in labeling the emotional experience of anger. Leaders encourage students to explore ways that they know they are experiencing anger. This could be done through activity sheets that encourage students to use expressive arts to explore their experience of anger (Newman, Horne, & Bartolomucci, 2000). These activities allow for exploration of the physiological arousal that is connected with the experience of anger, and they encourage students to understand their experiences and gain skills in labeling their emotional experience. Furthermore, they highlight the important role that recognition of emotion plays in deescalating angering situations.

An example of developing anger awareness is an activity called Feel the Heat. The group is given a silhouette of a body and they are asked to use colored pencils to mark on the silhouette where they feel anger when something happens they do not like. For most students, this is an activity that causes them to stop and examine where they do experience anger and to mark it on the drawing, thus helping them become aware of their responses to conflict. By sharing this activity within the group, members learn how others experience anger and how to identify when anger is developing and being experienced.

Psychoeducational Intervention: Anger Inhibition Activities

Recognizing various forms of anger and various outcomes can help individuals understand how to handle their anger. The treatment of anger problems may be enhanced by encouraging individuals to evaluate their anger based on outcomes, such as the cost of revenge (DiGiuseppe & Tafrate, 2001). Often the cost of "getting even" or seeking revenge is an escalation and continuation of the conflict. In helping participants evaluate anger outcomes, leaders actively encourage individuals to brainstorm new ideas and alternative behaviors. Members are encouraged to brainstorm solutions in small groups, as leaders circulate and encourage participants in the group discussions. To guide the discussion, individuals are given short vignettes in which the characters are faced with anger triggers. The use of stories provides a format for students to explore how the experience of anger can be channeled in a proactive, controlled way as well as a negative, hostile manner. Furthermore, the stories allow individuals to evaluate their own personal anger problems without disclosing a large amount of information, which would be problematic in a large group. The ability of individuals to engage on a personal level without disclosing to their own detriment in the classroom is an important aspect for consideration and may help the group leader develop appropriate anger interventions. During this phase of groups, the leader provides examples of stories

or references from children's books, fairy tales, and even current television shows. Leaders discuss short-term/long-term goals as well, with short-term goals being topics such as "get even, get revenge, make them pay" and long-term goals being "to get along, to have friends, to be liked."

Psychoeducational Activity: Problem-Solving Strategies

Since a skill deficit in problem solving may be driving anger problems, group members often benefit from explicit training in how to think through problem solving (DiGiuseppe, Deffenbacher, & Oetting, 2002). Leaders may provide vignette-driven examples. The participants work with leaders to come up with as many alternative problem-solving strategies as possible. Group leaders assist individuals in asking important questions when solving problems such as:

- What is the problem in the story?
- How might the character feel about the problem?
- What can the character do to change the problem?

In response to the problem of anger control problems in schools, resulting in violence and aggression, many schools have implemented psychoeducational group programs to prevent and reduce it. Unfortunately, little is known about their effectiveness, as few programs have been carefully evaluated and disseminated (U.S. Department of Health and Human Services, 2001), though several strategies have been used to address the problem of anger control and school violence. In a comprehensive review of the literature, Mytton and colleagues found only 16 studies that have evaluated the effect of an intervention for primary school children selected for displaying high levels of aggression and anger control problems. The results varied greatly among studies and, overall, showed only a modest reduction in aggression as a result of the intervention (Mytton,

DiGuiseppi, Gough, Taylor, & Logan, 2002), while Olweus and Limber (2002) reported between 15% and 35% reduction in problem aggressive behavior. Hinshaw (1996) also found that anger control training groups were moderately successful when working with children who had attention-deficit/hyperactivity disorders (ADHD) and anger control problem. The behaviors are "particularly refractory to all but the most powerful treatment strategies" (p. 303). Furthermore, he recommended that self-management treatments be combined with behavioral interventions for optimal results.

Other psychoeducational group approaches have resulted in curricula designed to prevent and reduce student aggression and anger problems. RIPP was evaluated twice in a sample of mostly African American sixth graders. Results of the first evaluation showed an overall increase in emotional control among boys but not among girls (Farrell & Meyer, 1997). Results of the second evaluation indicated an overall reduction of in-school suspensions, and this effect was maintained at a 12-month follow-up for boys but not for girls. Effects measured by self-reported prevalence of problem behaviors were not maintained at follow-up (Farrell, Meyer, & White, in press). When Second Step: A Violence Prevention Curriculum was evaluated among elementary school children, behavioral observations showed a significant reduction of fighting and aggression; however, no effect was observed on parent or teacher reports (Grossman et al., 1997). Two evaluations of a middle school version of the curriculum showed no lasting reduction of students' aggressive behaviors (Orpinas, Parcel, McAlister, & Frankowski, 1995; Orpinas et al., 2000). The evaluation of the Resolving Conflict Creatively Program (RCCP) in a large sample of elementary school children in New York City highlights the importance of dosage of implementation, because some intervention effect was observed among students who received more lessons of the curriculum compared to those who received few or no lessons (Aber, Jones, Brown, Chaudry, & Samples, 1998). Cooper, Lutenbacher, and Faccia (2000) reviewed two decades of publications on youth violence

prevention and concluded that only 15 studies had shown some reduction of students' aggression or delinquency rates. Another psychoeducational program developed for anger control and bullying problems, Bully Busting (Newman et al., 2000), found that more effective anger control was developed for younger children who bullied or were victims of bullying. However, older children had less success with the treatment (Orpinas, Horne, & Staniszewski, in press). In summary, while the research indicates there is some positive impact of psychoeducational training programs for anger management and aggression control, the power of the programs to be fully effective has not been established. It may be that the programs are most effective for preventing problems from developing, and may provide skills to average or moderately aggressive/hostile students, but a psychoeducational group intervention may not be powerful enough to stop fully established anger/violence problems (Orpinas, Horne, & Staniszewski, in press).

COUNSELING GROUPS

Psychoeducational groups are offered for participants without a specified problem, or as a prevention and early intervention to problem areas. Counseling groups, on the other hand, focus more on the concerns or problems participants have and address growth and development by helping participants address problems of adjustment or interpersonal conflict. This different focus results in a different approach to group work for anger management and reduction.

In group counseling the focus is on current problems and normal developmental issues, but becomes more problem focused. Group counseling is for a targeted problem group (those who have either self-identified or been referred for specific problems) rather than a universal group where students need assistance with skill development but not with specific personal problems. The climate and disclosure level of the group requires a smaller number of participants. These groups involve high levels of personal exploration and insight development, and group leaders may focus on the history of anger problems and the development of interpersonal difficulties.

DEVELOPING AN ALTERNATIVE RESPONSE

Anger management counseling groups target those who function satisfactorily in most areas of their lives but have difficulty managing their anger in their normal day-to-day lives. The groups focus on identifying specific areas of conflict and developing more adaptive and healthy relationships and general living experiences. To accomplish this, members explore their cognitive styles as well as their skills in interacting with others.

The group counseling approach is applied to anger problems using a case example focusing on an adolescent population. This self-regulation is developed through an understanding of what influences relate to a volatile anger response. This approach involves a multilevel focus, as participants engage in developing a deeper understanding of their anger. Group exercises focus on developing anger awareness from a physiological, cognitive, and emotional standpoint.

In exploring how group type and target population influence intervention modification, relaxation skill building is emphasized. One component of physiological awareness involves understanding the importance of relaxation skills that are used to assist the group members to recognize and choose appropriate responses to reach a desired physiological state. Relaxation training is presented early in group counseling, as it has been found to be an efficacious form of treatment for decreasing anger across populations (DiGiuseppe et al., 2002).

RELAXATION-BASED INTERVENTIONS

Relaxation continues to be an essential component in the treatment of anger (DiGuiseppe et al., 2002). As group members decrease their anxiety and develop better control of their stress responses, they become more adept at analyzing anger-provoking situations, evaluating their

array of behavioral choices, and determining courses of action that are nonreactive. In comparison to the relaxation training conducted with the psychoeducation group, relaxation training with counseling groups focuses on achieving greater insight and personal exploration rather than fundamentally focusing on controlling the physiological response of anger arousal. For instance, group members take part in activities brainstorming and logging personal ways that they might relax themselves, thus developing insights into self-calming and relaxation skills that fit best with their individual style. Instead of having members perform a relaxation exercise that is generalized for the whole group, leaders work to make the intervention centered on the needs of the member; for example, members decide whether progressive muscle relaxation and/or imaginal relaxation match best with their style. As an added component of the inductive focus of the group, group members share specific activities, mental imagery, or self-talk that they find to be relaxing and anger reducing. By sharing, members become involved in increasing their repertoire of self-control skills. In taking the step to understand what others do in response to anger arousal, group members enhance their range of skills in handling or inhibiting their anger response. One of the important components of this group would be the inductive focus and the open exchange of client-driven ideas.

Relaxation training materials are available from a number of programs, including Skill streaming the Elementary School Child (McGinnis & Goldstein, 1997), Bully Busters (Newman et al., 2000), and Skills for Living (Smead, 1990, 1994). Some have been demonstrated to be quite effective (Howard, Horne, & Jolliff, 2001; Newman & Horne, in press)

COGNITIVE FOCUS: REINTERPRETING ANGER-INDUCING SITUATIONS

Counseling groups implement activities that help members work though anger difficulties and evaluate their habitual response patterns to anger-provoking situations. Cognitive therapy has been linked with lowered trait anger and anger reactivity and is applicable to decreasing anger tendencies in provocative situations (Deffenbacher, Dahlen, Lynch, Morris, & Gowensmith, 2000). In group sessions, members explore and evaluate their cognitive schemas, thought patterns, and views on anger. Through this exploration, members develop insight into the background and pattern of responses they have and develop motivation to alter their anger explosions. This insight, combined with motivation, along with group support and practice of new skills, leads to the development of commitment to change and the beginning of skills training that facilitates the change. Interventions are aimed at increasing prosocial and socially adaptive views, and little time is focused on deconstructing hostile, inappropriate responses, such that a primary focus of the group is on aiding participants to construct internal dialogues that guide them in situations that previously led to anger problems. In the counseling group, members discuss specific situations that have triggered anger problems, discuss the thoughts that previously led to anger outbursts, and describe alternative, constructive self-talk. This serves as a pertinent time for the group leader to increase the involvement between group members while continuing to facilitate group members in developing alternative thought patterns and attributional styles surrounding anger triggers.

An example of how the group may facilitate the examination of functional and dysfunctional self-talk is to use the "big questions." The big questions are:

- What is my goal?
- What am I doing?
- Is what I'm doing helping me to achieve my goal?
- If not, what can I do differently?

The goal of anger management counseling groups is to help members learn to have healthier and more functional lives, so a goal of all members is to manage their anger and to engage in healthy responses to previously provoking circumstances. What they are often doing is engaging in anger-inducing thoughts, and that does not work to help them achieve their goals. What they can do differently is develop new self-talk that is more facilitative. This process can be accomplished in a counseling group by having members identify provoking situations from their personal lives, then using a two-columned activity sheet that lists the anger-provoking thoughts ("She shouldn't have done that," "He's trying to tick me off," "She's a dumb-ass") with more calming and functional thoughts ("I wish he hadn't done that, but he did, so now we have to deal with the problem," "She made a mistake and we need to figure out what to do about it," "He's doing the best he can right now and we need to work together to resolve this or I need to find other people to work with so that I don't keep having these frustrating [rather than angry] situations"). Practice of this activity, with group members facilitating the development of functional and dysfunctional thoughts and then role-playing the situations, is very powerful for facilitating change.

SOCIAL SKILL: BUILDING PRACTICAL STRATEGIES AT INCREASING PROSOCIAL INTERACTIONS

In counseling groups, members engage in discussions about their frustrations and their personal experiences in social situations that lead to anger problems. Thus, group members focus on helping each other to practice prosocial behavior to generalize from the group to life outside the group. To accomplish this, the development of appropriate and effective social skills is a focus of each counseling group session. Training in social skills includes modeling, behavioral rehearsal, and role plays. Group members use the big questions as they engage in these skills training activities in order to examine and evaluate their previous ways of managing anger problems versus using more effective prosocial approaches in anger-inducing interactions. Throughout group interactions, social skills are practiced to increase the generalization of skills from the group to life outside the group (DiGiuseppe et al., 2002; Gazda et al., 2001).

Sample Group Counseling Outline

1. Awareness of Anger
   - Individuals discuss the various ways in which they specifically have experienced anger and analyze how to distinguish healthy anger from destructive anger (Tangney, Wagner, Hill-Barlow, Marschall, & Gramzow, 1996).
   - The differences between healthy and destructive anger are examined. Healthy anger is based on constructive interactions such as maintaining a relationship, asserting one's needs, or making a change in the instigator's behavior. However, destructive anger is considered to be potentially harmful.
   - Individuals evaluate the function of their anger and replace anger responses with other responses to get needs met.
   - Group leaders work to connect with participants empathically while helping individuals develop insight and motivation to change destructive behaviors.

2. Progressive Muscle Relaxation Exercises
   - Participants are engaged in relaxation skills that enable them to self-calm and to choose appropriate responses to anger-invoking stimuli.
   - Leaders encourage individuals to explore new ways to have needs met in lieu of anger.

3. Imaginal and Cognitive Relaxation Strategies
   - Focus on developing a calming imaginal scene.
   - Participants share calming thoughts.
   - Leaders emphasize the importance of using these exercises when anger triggers occur between sessions.

4. Awareness of Self-Talk
   - Participants talk through thoughts and images that run through their minds when they are about to act explosively.
   - Individuals work in dyads or small groups to develop new self-talk that will calm and proactively direct energy stemming from anger.

5. Development of Self-Regulation Through Self-Talk
   - Participants use the self-talk skills from the prior session to develop self-talk to regulate their mood.
   - Leaders model how they change their self-talk by demonstrating for group.

6. Problem-Solving Skills Part I
   - Explore how problems can be examined from different perspectives.
   - Leaders use encouragement and open-ended questions to help participants gain awareness of goals and alternative problem-solving strategies.

7. Problem-Solving Skills Part II
   - As a lack of alternative problem skills may hinder participants, this session will work to cement skills from the prior session.
   - Members work in large groups and/or in dyads by recalling real events to which they needed to find an alternative solution in order not to get angry.
   - If group work is done in dyads, leaders should take care to ensure that the alternative solutions are prosocial and take others' feelings into account.

8. Communication Skills
   - Upon learning to alter their self-talk, individuals explore new ways to interact with others.
   - Leaders encourage individuals to practice skills through role plays.

Group Psychotherapy

When group members experience chronic or severe personal and interpersonal problems in their lives that are caused by cognitive distortions or ongoing patterns of dysfunctional behavior, then psychoeducational and counseling groups are not sufficient. Instead, group psychotherapy is called for, with the more intense focus that therapy brings for group members.

Here is an example of a psychotherapy group focused on adults with chronic and severe anger problems. This group focuses on heightening cognitive and emotional awareness. It emphasizes highly inductive, client-focused interventions that use group members' experiences. In addition, the group leaders' expertise is utilized to develop alternative cognitive and behavioral means to achieving goals. The inductive focus is linked with less resistance and stronger therapeutic alliances, which makes this approach appropriate for use with chronically angry clients (Deffenbacher, Thwaites, Wallace, & Oetting, 1994). Due to the inductive nature of this group, a structural outline is not easily applicable. Instead, specific issues are explained and they would then be tailored to the client's anger problem background.

In attempting to keep the group client-focused and inductive, members are encouraged to brainstorm alternative, nonviolent ways of dealing with feelings of anger. Leaders encourage group members to brainstorm and assist clients in developing ideas by asking open-ended questions. Group leaders avoid structured advising. As clients develop their own alternative methods and skills in dealing with anger, they are more likely to accept the skills. Furthermore, group members build a therapeutic alliance by working as a team to find alternative solutions. The alternative behaviors and skills can be experimented with as homework activities. Group members reinforce and assist each other to generalize the group experience to anger-inducing provocations outside of therapy. During this process, group leaders increase empathic awareness, as group members may neglect the feeling states of fellow group members.

Increasing Emotional Awareness

In working through issues of anger, group members develop emotional and cognitive awareness of anger triggers. After deciding what provokes the greatest anger response, individuals rank the triggers or anger-invoking scenarios in a hierarchy. In constructing this hierarchy, a few things are accomplished. First, group members build rapport by disclosing more about what triggers anger. Second, group leaders work with group members to develop insights about anger and interrelated issues. In determining the hierarchy, the group is encouraged to recognize multiple different emotional issues, along with issues surrounding anger. Leaders encourage group members to follow up with individuals and talk about emotional and cognitive insights surrounding emotionally difficult situations. By recognizing feelings of powerlessness or hopelessness that coexist with anger, the group members become oriented toward responding to their emotional needs and cognitively directing their energy toward proactive resolutions rather than responding with reactive anger.

Desensitization Interventions

Attempts at decreasing physiological arousal are especially important when dealing with individuals expressing intense anger or who have long-term anger difficulties (Biaggio, 1987). With this in mind, a core part of the psychotherapy group involves decreasing physiological arousal by increasing members' skill in self-calming. Self-calming is incorporated through the combination of behavioral and cognitive therapy. The combined approach may be particularly efficacious in decreasing anxiety along with anger problems (Hazaleus & Deffenbacher, 1986). As noted in earlier groups, relaxation training and desensitization continue to be important components used in coordination (DiGiuseppe, Deffenbacher, & Oetting, 2002). Members of the group may have chronic anger problems; thus, negative emotional arousal may be exhibited during group as well as outside of group. Therefore, self-calming may be beneficial in guiding group interactions as well as providing a skill base for handling anger outside of therapy.

Summary of Approaches to Group Work With Anger Management Problems

The selection of a psychoeducational, counseling, or therapy group for addressing anger management problems will be influenced by the purpose of the group (universal skill development, addressing current problems, providing therapy for long-standing or severe anger problems), focus of the intervention (universal intervention for all versus intensive training and therapy for a few), the developmental stage of the participants, and the skill and ability level of the group leader. Each of the three models of group work has been demonstrated to be highly effective with some people but less effective with others, again having the factors of change influencing the outcome.

Questions to Consider: Screening Prospective Group Members

The following questions examine the level of entrenchment surrounding anger problems and they help guide choices regarding group type and fit. Recall that psychoeducational groups aim at increasing skills, counseling groups aim to help those who are adequately functioning yet have some anger problems, and therapy groups target individuals with more deeply entrenched anger problems.

1. What is the frequency and intensity of anger problems? Does the individual report being motivated to change either dimension or both?

2. Is the experience of anger problems specific to certain triggers or viewed as more generalized?

3. What are the members' greatest fears and wishes for the group? How will the individual feel about having others challenge her or him?

4. If individuals seem like they may be reactive to challenges, will social skills training be beneficial as a precursor to group participation?

SETTING UP AN ANGER MANAGEMENT GROUP

Guiding Group Development

The screening questions are used to help the group leader determine who may be appropriate for what level of group. Most psychoeducational groups are provided to a universal population—that is, all members in a group receive the group intervention, and it is assumed that the group is used for prevention and early intervention of problems. The psychoeducational group, then, generally does not require screening, other than to have an awareness of any potential members who may be too disruptive to participate in the group presentation.

On the other hand, the group leader who will be conducting counseling groups will likely benefit from conducting intake interviews with potential counseling group members as a way of making certain that the group is not misrepresented to potential members and as a process to help participants clarify group goals, define any membership issues, understand the role of the leader, and help members understand the expectations for participation in the group. Expectations will include being willing to share concerns and problems and also to be available to be helpful to others in the group. Also, during the screening interview, it is important for the group leader to be sensitive to issues about whether members will be able to interact effectively with other potential members of the group and to assess the extent of possible anger control problems that might exist, as a way of ensuring the safety of other group members.

For group therapy, intake interviews are expected for screening purposes. Since the therapy group is most appropriate for participants with chronic and/or severe levels of anger control, it is essential that the leader become adept at identifying possible harm to self or others that can occur by members in the group. This can be done by evaluating the extent to which the problem is manageable within a group structure and identifying alternative referral sources for those individuals who may react strongly to challenges within the group context.

Effective Leadership

Leadership is a critical component in advancing the experience of group members in all three group styles. For each of the groups, though, a different level of skill in dealing with anger is necessary. For psychoeducational groups, the leader needs to be familiar with activities and programs that will help participants develop an understanding of the importance of anger control and activities for group members that lead to awareness of the importance of skills, to the actual development of anger management skills, and to appropriate interpersonal skills. The leader must be capable of demonstrating the interpersonal skills as well as each of the learning activities involved. For counseling groups, though, the leader will need to have expertise in the same areas as the leader of psychoeducational groups, but will also need to be comfortable dealing with the anger with which group members present as they interview for the group. For example, in group counseling, although the groups still have a prevention/early intervention focus looking at here-and-now issues, members join the group because they are having problems, either self-identified or other-referred. They have difficulty managing their anger, and the leader will have group counseling activities that bring the conflicts to the surface to be addressed, thus exposing the group to the potential of anger outbursts in the group. A leader who is uncomfortable encountering anger with groups should not be leading the group independently, but rather should cofacilitate the group with a leader who is comfortable confronting anger among members. For psychotherapy groups, there will certainly be the opportunity of encountering anger within the group, for by definition, members have chronic

and severe difficulties managing their anger, and groups that focus on the circumstances of the anger will certainly elicit it within the group setting. Leaders must not only be confident and skilled in the management of anger, but for the protection of group members they must also be capable of defusing anger that is harmfully expressed in groups.

For psychoeducational group leaders, skills are necessary for facilitating talk about anger and for directing skill development for enhancing interpersonal skills related to conflict. For group counselors, there is also a need to be able to facilitate the group interaction so that the power of the group is used to help individuals within the group getting benefit from the experiences, knowledge, and insight of the whole group. This involves a leader who is comfortable dealing with anger but who also knows how to move the group toward solutions for anger problems, who is able to build on the strength and resources of the membership to identify what is working and what is not, and then to use the group to find usable solutions. At the same time, the leader must be able to protect all members of the group from the harm that anger may bring if it is directed against members of the group. The leader of psychotherapy groups must have skills for engaging discussions of anger in a way that creates a safe environment for all group members and that helps members identify and recognize the underlying conflicts and personal anguish that result in the anger they experience. The leader must also find within the group the resources to find curative experiences for all members. This will occur through an invitational approach that incorporates the curative factors described in other chapters of this handbook.

Gazda et al. (2001) suggest several critical components of effective leadership that stand out as specifically important in working with clients who have anger problems. First, the leader's ability to extend warmth and empathy to each client is fundamentally important. Empathy with angry clients is a key component in the therapeutic alliance with angry clients. DiGiuseppe and Tafrate (2001) suggest that empathy may be particularly difficult when therapists are engaged with angry clients, as the anger may be turned to members of the group or to the group leader, thus requiring the leader to be comfortable managing the anger. Furthermore, the therapist may construe anger as a block to therapeutic progress, as the client may stop or slow down the impact of the group on the member, or even reduce the effectiveness of the work of the group for all members. Prochaska (2000; Prochaska, Norcross, & DiClement, 1994) has described six stages of readiness for change: *precontemplative,* in which individuals are not aware of a need for change; *contemplative,* for those who are aware that a problem exists but have not seriously considered any action; *preparation,* for those who recognize a need for change and are beginning to make plans to do some form of change; *action,* for those engaged in the process of making change; *maintenance,* for those who have made change and need support in maintaining the change that has occurred; and *termination,* for those who have no temptation to engage in the problem behavior. As group members pass through one stage, they enter the next level, but without development of empathy for the client's emotional experience, the therapeutic alliances are hindered. Without a healthy alliance, exploration and insight that might move the client to an action stage are less likely to occur. Therefore, while leader warmth and caring is an important variable in all groups, it may be of heightened importance in working with anger problems. It is essential that leaders be cognizant of how they respond to clients' anger. Without leader awareness of how clients' anger affects them, they are more likely to have difficulties in developing the therapeutic alliance, and thereby have difficulties in advancing therapeutic advancement in anger control.

Another group leader characteristic mentioned by Gazda and colleagues (2001) that is particularly pertinent in leading anger management groups is awareness in timing interventions. Leaders may need to spend time on members' resistance to taking responsibility for their anger. Individual group members may view their anger as functional and focus blame on others, and this is likely to be influenced by the individuals' stage of change and on members' ability to see the problem from others' perspectives.

Pretraining Techniques

Another leadership skill for anger groups is to use pregroup experiences effectively. Individuals with anger problems may have a deficit in skills to use when handling strong emotions such as sadness or disempowerment. It may be particularly important to use pretraining groups to help members develop communication strategies before involvement in the group process. This is important, as individuals might direct anger at other members of the group during sessions. When anger is vented toward group members, it is beneficial for group members to stop the cycle of anger that might develop.

Intake Interviews

Another leader skill involves carrying out explorative intake interviews. One primary purpose of the intake interview is to provide the leader with the opportunity to determine the suitability of the potential group member in relationship to the group type. While it may be advantageous to conduct intake interviews for all group types, it may be noted that most psychoeducational groups are considered generally applicable and do not involve intake interviews. Counseling groups, on the other hand, often do require intake interviews, and psychotherapy groups usually have such a requirement. In screening participants for counseling and psychotherapy groups, the leader needs to ascertain that the prospective member will be able to identify anger problems and move toward taking responsibility for anger outbursts. Furthermore, viable prospective group members must be willing to use the group to address needed changes and also be skilled in engaging other group members in their anger work.

Protecting Members

Once groups are initiated, the leader is responsible for the safety—both emotional and physical—of the group members. This requires that the leader be able to understand the individual characteristics of the members, often from information learned during intake interviews, and that the leader will be able to use this information to encourage exploration of problems, challenge growth and exploration by all, and still be aware of the interactional effect of each member on other members of the group. The leader characteristics described earlier—invitational, empathic, supportive—fit as leader skills, but also the leader needs to be able to direct the discussion so that there is growth of all and an absence of intimidation within the group.

Length of Group

The length of anger management groups is often determined by the setting and circumstances of the group. For example, the length of a term at school or the availability of the counselor or therapist determines the length of many counseling groups focusing on anger management. Ideally, length should be determined by the nature of the problem, but this is not always the case, for external factors such as availability of space or time may influence the group. The time that is available should be utilized effectively, and this may call for an emphasis on solution-focused, brief group work, as there is no certainty about how long members may be in a group. At youth detention centers, for example, it is not uncommon for members to be available for only a session or two before being moved on to another setting or being released to the community. In these situations, each session should have some focus on specific skills that may be taken away by the members as they leave the group. The programs mentioned earlier (Skillstreaming, Life Skills, Bully Busters) are particularly effective, as they have activities that identify anger control activities that may be incorporated into psychoeducational, counseling, and therapy groups and provide participants with specific skills regardless of the nature of the anger problem.

Conclusion

Group work for anger management has been found to be effective and powerful for eliciting change in children, adolescents, and adults. The extent of the problem, the developmental level of participants, the leader's expertise and comfort, and the referring agency's needs are integral in determining the particular approach taken. While considerable work has occurred examining skills development for children and adolescents, less work has occurred for adult groups, and most of the anger management group work that we have examined and evaluated has focused on skills training directed toward learning effective anger management through interpersonal skills development, problem solving, and personal self-talk.

References

Aber, J. L., Jones, S. M., Brown, J. L., Chaudry, N., & Samples, F. (1998). Resolving conflict creatively: Evaluating the developmental effects of a school-based violence prevention program in neighborhood and classroom context. *Developmental Psychopathology, 10,* 187-213.

Association for Specialists in Group Work. (2000). Professional standards for the training of group workers (Rev. ed.). Retrieved November 21, 2002, from http://asgw.educ.kent.edu/.

Biaggio, M. K. (1987). Clinical dimensions of anger management. *American Journal of Psychotherapy, 41*(3), 417-427.

Cooper, W. O., Lutenbacher, M., & Faccia, K. (2000). Components of effective youth violence prevention programs for 7- to 14-year-olds. *Archives of Pediatric Adolescent Medicine, 154,* 1134-1139.

Deffenbacher, J. L, Dahlen, E. R., Lynch, R. S., Morris, C. D., & Gowensmith, W. N. (2000). An application of Beck's cognitive therapy to general anger reduction. *Cognitive Therapy and Research, 24*(6), 689-697.

Deffenbacher, J. L., Thwaites, G. A., Wallace, T. L., & Oetting, E. R. (1994). Social skills and cognitive-relaxation approaches to general anger reduction. *Journal of Counseling Psychology, 41*(3), 386-396.

DiGiuseppe, R., & Tafrate, R. C. (2001). A comprehensive treatment model for anger disorders. *Psychotherapy, 38,* 262-271.

DiGiuseppe, R. A., Deffenbacher, J. L., & Oetting, E. R. (2002). Principles of empirically supported interventions applied to anger management. *Counseling Psychologist, 30*(2), 262-280.

Farrell, A. D., & Meyer, A. L. (1997). The effectiveness of a school-based curriculum for reducing violence among urban sixth-grade students. *American Journal of Public Health, 87,* 979-984.

Farrell, A. D., Meyer, A. L., & White, K. S. (In press). Evaluation of Responding In Peaceful and Positive Ways (RIPP): A school-based prevention program for reducing violence among urban adolescents. *Journal of Child Clinical Psychology.*

Gazda, G. M., Ginter, E. J., & Horne, A. M. (2001). *Group counseling and group psychotherapy: Theory and application.* Boston: Allyn & Bacon.

Goldstein, A. (1999). *Low-level aggression: First steps on the ladder to violence.* Champaign, IL: Research Press.

Goldstein, A., Glick, B., & Gibbs, J. (1998). *ART: Aggression Replacement Training; A comprehensive intervention for aggressive youth.* Champaign, IL: Research Press.

Goldstein, A. P., Glick, B., Reiner, S., Zimmerman, D., & Coultry, T. M. (1987). *Aggression Replacement Training: A comprehensive intervention for aggressive youth.* Champaign, IL: Research Press.

Grossman, D. C., Neckerman, H. J., Koepsell, T. D., Liu, P. Y., Asher, K. N., Beland, K., et al. (1997). Effectiveness of a violence prevention curriculum among children in elementary school: A randomized controlled trial. *Journal of the American Medical Association, 277,* 1605-1611.

Hazaleus, S. L., & Deffenbacher, J. L. (1986). Relaxation and cognitive treatments of anger. *Journal of Consulting and Clinical Psychology, 54*(2), 222-226.

Hinshaw, S. (1996). Enhancing social competence: Integrating self-management strategies with behavioral procedures for children with ADHD. In E. Hibbs & P. Jensen (Eds.), *Psychosocial treatments for child and adolescent disorders* (pp. 285-309). Washington, DC: American Psychological Association.

Howard, N., Horne, A., & Jolliff, D. (2001). Self-efficacy in a new training model for the prevention of bullying in schools. *Journal of Emotional Abuse, 2,* 181-191.

McGinnis, E., & Goldstein, A. (1997). *Skillstreaming the elementary school child* (2nd ed.). Champaign, IL: Research Press.

Meyer, A., Farrell, A., Northup, W., Kung, E., & Plybon, L. (2000). *Promoting nonviolence in early adolescence: Responding in peaceful and powerful ways.* New York: Kluwer.

Mytton, J. A., DiGuiseppi, C., Gough, D. A., Taylor, R. S., & Logan, S. (2002). School-based violence prevention programs: Systematic review of secondary prevention trials. *Archives of Pediatrics & Adolescent Medicine, 156,* 752-762.

Newman, D., & Horne, A. (In press). A psychoeducational intervention for reducing bullying behavior in middle school students. *Journal of Counseling and Development.*

Newman, D., Horne, A., & Bartolomucci, C. (2000). *Bully Busters: A teacher's manual for helping bullies, victims, and bystanders.* Champaign, IL: Research Press.

Olweus, D., & Limber, S. (2002). *Bullying prevention program* (Rep. No. Book 9). Boulder, CO: Center for the Study and Prevention of Violence, Institute of Behavioral Science, University of Colorado at Boulder.

Orpinas, P., Horne, A. & Staniszewski, D. (In press). School bullying: Changing the problem by changing the school. *School Psychology Review.*

Orpinas, P., Kelder, S., Frankowski, R., Murray, N., Zhang, Q., & McAlister, A. (2000). Outcome evaluation of a multi-component violence-prevention program for middle schools: The Students for Peace project. *Health Education Research, 15,* 45-58.

Orpinas, P., Parcel, G. S., McAlister, A., & Frankowski, R. (1995). Violence prevention in middle schools: A pilot evaluation. *Journal of Adolescent Health, 17,* 360-371.

Prochaska, J. O. (2000). *Changes at differing stages.* New York: John Wiley.

Prochaska, J. O., Norcross, J., & DiClement, C. C. (1994). *Changing for good.* New York: William Morrow.

Smead, R. (1990). *Skills for living: Group counseling activities for young adolescents* (Vol. 1). Champaign, IL: Research Press.

Smead, R. (1994). *Skills for living: Group counseling activities for elementary students.* Champaign, IL: Research Press.

Smead, R. (1999). *Skills for living: Group counseling activities for young adolescents* (Vol. 2). Champaign, IL: Research Press.

Tangney J. P., Wagner, P. E., Hill-Barlow, D., Marschall, D. E., & Gramzow, R. (1996).

Relation of shame and guilt to constructive versus destructive responses to anger across the lifespan. *Journal of Personality and Social Psychology 70*(4):797-809.

U.S. Department of Health and Human Services. (2001). *Youth violence: A report of the Surgeon General.* Rockville, MD: U.S. Department of Health and Human Services; Centers for Disease Control and Prevention, National Center for Injury Prevention; Substance Abuse and Mental Health Services Administration, Center for Mental Health Services; and National Institutes of Health, National Institute of Mental Health.

40

Group Approaches in Substance Abuse Treatment

Kathryn Kominars

Florida International University

Liane Dornheim

Florida International University

Substance abuse is a major public health problem in the United States. According to epidemiological studies, the lifetime prevalence is approximately 8% to 14% for alcohol dependence (American Psychological Association [APA], 2000). Fifteen percent of the population will experience a substance use disorder at one point in their lives, and an average of 20% of patients in general medical facilities and 35% in general psychiatric units will present with substance use disorders (Galanter & Kleber, 1999). Also, 29% of clients with a current mental health problem have a history of substance use disorder, and among some populations (e.g., those with schizophrenia), the percentages are even higher (Regier et al., 1990).

A National Household Survey on Drug Abuse conducted by the U.S. Department of Health and Human Services (2001) estimated that 3.1 million people aged 12 or older, or 1.4% of the population, received treatment for alcohol or drug abuse during the 12 months prior to the survey. Approximately 1.2 million individuals, or 38.7%, received treatment for both alcohol and drugs. Sixteen percent received treatment for drug abuse only. Thirty-two percent received treatment for alcohol only, and 13% reported receiving treatment without specifying their substance problem.

Historically, mental health professionals have not been on the front lines of treatment for substance use disorders (Polcin, 2000), leading to the proliferation of self-help groups such as Alcoholics Anonymous (AA) and the provision of treatment by paraprofessionals in specialized chemical dependency treatment programs (Khantzian, 1985). The development of these types of specialized treatment programs occurred because the traditional psychodynamic approach of treating substance abuse as merely a symptom of an underlying psychiatric disorder was ineffective (Polcin, 1997a). When mental health professionals began to address the needs of those with substance use disorders, they were faced with a multiplicity of self-help models without empirical evidence of efficacy (Shaffer, 1986). Fortunately, in recent empirical studies, several therapeutic approaches (cognitive-behavioral and motivational interviewing in combination with 12-step programs) specifically adapted to the needs of those with substance use disorders have been found to be effective (Miller & Brown, 1997; National Institute of Alcohol Abuse and Alcoholism, 1997; Ouimette, Finney, & Moos, 1997). However, with recent findings supporting a variety of different treatment combinations, mental health professionals still have the unenviable task of deciding which intervention strategy to use with each client.

Substance abuse treatment exists along a continuum of care that ranges from intensive residential programs to unstructured outpatient treatment. Major types of treatment options are social learning programs, therapeutic community treatment, methadone maintenance, and different variations of outpatient treatment. The group treatment approach has been the most popular intervention regarding substance abuse, and many assert that it is the treatment of choice (Flores & Mahon, 1993; Greif, 1996; Khantzian, Golden, & McCauliffe, 1999; Mahon & Flores,1992).

This chapter presents a summary of group approaches for substance abuse using psychoeducational, counseling, and psychotherapy interventions. Divided into separate sections for psychoeducation, counseling, and psychotherapy groups, the chapter includes discussion of relevant theory, recent research findings, and recommendations for different group approaches to substance abuse.

For the following discussion, the term *substance abuse* will be used to encompass both substance abuse and dependence as defined in the *DSM-IV-TR* (APA, 2000). Substance abuse is defined as a maladaptive pattern of substance use leading either to clinically significant impairment or distress (failure to fulfill major role obligations, substance use in situations where it poses a physical hazard, substance-related legal problems, and recurrent interpersonal problems), or to tolerance, withdrawal, and other physiological symptoms. Substance use is defined as consumption of alcohol and/or other drugs that have not been prescribed by a physician or are prescribed but abused. In this sense, abuse implies the use of alcohol and drugs beyond social and recreational purposes and in situations where the use is problematic and negative consequences ensue. Substance dependence includes behaviors found in substance abuse but adds a physiological dimension such as tolerance and withdrawal symptoms.

Group Processes and Clinical Practices

Using the categories developed by Stinchfield, Owen, and Winters (1994), group therapy can be either a primary treatment, a concurrent supplement to primary treatment, or a posttreatment supplement. Primary treatment, meaning an approach other than group therapy, can include inpatient detoxification, outpatient medical treatment such as antabuse, and/or individual approaches such as motivational interviewing to prepare participants for therapy, or individual psychotherapy. However, the group approach itself is considered standard practice in the treatment of substance abuse (Stinchfield et al., 1994). Whether group treatment is the primary treatment or used as an adjunct, groups can be either closed or open to new members, with the former being the exception rather than the rule (G. Skypek, personal communication, February 15, 2002). According to Stinchfield et al., outcome for group therapy as the primary treatment is mixed at best. They concluded that the preferable treatment approach includes a combination of group therapy, behavior modification training, and family involvement. With regard to group therapy as an adjunct to primary treatment, they concluded that group therapy as a concurrent treatment in a multimodal program is critical. However, it has to be consistent with the other treatment components in order to be beneficial for the participants. Regarding group therapy as aftercare, so far there is no empirical support that it alone adds to overall improvement (Stinchfield et al., 1994).

Composition of Groups

Groups can be heterogeneous on a number of dimensions, such as the type of substance that is abused as well as severity of use, level of psychosocial functioning of the members, prior treatment history, and co-morbidity. An argument can be made for and against the heterogeneity of group composition. However, published research only evaluates homogenous group composition with regard to the abused substances and the severity of abuse (Stinchfield et al., 1994). Requirements by third party payers, larger public policy priorities, and lack of evidence of efficacy of treatment approaches can be seen as important external variables or societal influences that have had an impact on the formation of heterogeneous groups.

Like group therapy in general, group therapy for substance abuse relies on the presence of therapeutic factors such as cohesion, trust, and imparting of information (Yalom, 1995). Vannicelli et al. (1982) identified three change factors—developing an understanding of commonality (universality) with others relative to the substance abuse, learning about attitudes and defenses pertaining to the substance abuse and related problems, and improving on communication strategies.

Therapeutic Considerations

While therapists have important roles as facilitators of these change factors, they may face regular challenges from group members as to their own competency, based on whether they share a common history of substance abuse aside from their clinical skills or training. Vannicelli (1991) emphasizes the importance of therapists' skill and technique in addressing predictable critical incidents. Often, a greater degree of therapist self-disclosure is sought or expected by substance abuse group members than is customarily encountered in therapy groups. Clinicians should be prepared to address demands or requests for personal information in a nondefensive, caring, and sensitive fashion (Greif, 1996). Treatment providers new to working with this population are advised to seek consultation and guidance in advance of such confrontations.

Clinicians need to develop realistic expectations for work with this population. There is likely to be a temptation to become overly focused on outcome after termination and take responsibility for numerous situational factors over which counselors have little or no influence

or control. For example, a client who is fired from his or her job, or whose spouse files for divorce after discharge from treatment, may be more likely to relapse than a client who is welcomed back to a supportive work environment and whose family situation is stable and supportive. Clinicians need to refrain from making a client's relapse a personal reflection on their clinical skills. Furthermore, clinicians need to assist group members to process other members' relapse constructively and realistically. Greif (1996) described specific strategies to avoid common mistakes for novice group therapists. He suggests that the group will stand or fall based on how successfully group rules are kept, thus supporting his assertion that group rules need to be revisited frequently and explicitly.

It is also important for clinicians to be prepared to cope with boundary challenges with regard to personal addiction and recovery history and invitations to become personally as well as professionally engaged in clients' recovery processes. It is particularly challenging for clinicians who attend 12-step programs to support their own recovery, to navigate boundary challenges when encountering their clients at 12-step meetings. This is especially difficult in small communities where the number of 12-step meetings may be limited. Whether dealing with clients in public or with requests to self-disclose in group, Greif (1996) writes that therapists who are either too withholding or too revealing, as a result of anxiety, may misperceive the group members' needs or inaccurately evaluate the group dynamics.

Another common pitfall, according to Greif (1996), is a lack of consistency between a group leader's theoretical approach and the agency style and/or philosophy or conflicts within the group leadership team itself. The needs of the group members fall between the cracks when group leaders are distracted by theoretical differences within the agency or treatment program or by conflicts related to cofacilitation priorities or approaches. Maintaining an ongoing accurate understanding of the level of the group's development is important because it affects the demands on and tasks of the clinician. In open groups with fluctuating group membership, it is essential to set aside preconceived notions of an organized and stable flow of group development and to continually integrate new members into the group. This integration needs to be framed, for those continuing in group, as an opportunity for their own growth, as a time for evaluation of the groups' achievements, and for recontracting for future work. Research regarding the efficacy of open versus closed groups has yet to be conducted.

Countertransference will provide excellent opportunities for clinicians to learn more about themselves, because working with people with substance abuse is likely to generate more direct attacks on their competence and leadership ability. Leaders sometimes try to overcome countertransference responses by subtly encouraging difficult members to leave the group or actively treating these members inappropriately by being overly solicitous, attentive, or harsh (Greif, 1996).

It is important for group facilitators, early in the process, to educate group members about norms (e.g., regular and timely attendance, maintenance of abstinence, respect toward others, the expectation of honest self-disclosure, the analysis of group processes) and the value of maintaining these norms for the benefit of the members and the group as a whole. Special emphasis and discussion of the challenges and application of confidentiality is advisable, and members should be instructed that breaches of confidentiality will be addressed within the group and that consequences will be forthcoming (Matano, Yalom, & Schwartz, 1997; Yalom, 1995).

Client Considerations

Other important therapeutic issues include maintaining the goal of abstinence once external pressures for abstinence abate, handling group members who continue to use substances during the course of treatment, and recognizing when the content of substance abuse-focused discussion (storytelling) serves as a method of avoidance of important group dynamics and processes. According to Stinchfield et al. (1994), the variability in retention rate is less related to the type of therapy than to the individual characteristics of the therapist. For group therapy, as with all other therapeutic modalities or theoretical orientations, the therapeutic alliance between therapist and client is an important predictor of treatment outcome.

However, Yalom (1974) suggests that therapists may need to make decisions about group composition based upon the necessity of preserving the group as a whole as opposed to the specific needs of the individual.

Stinchfield et al. (1994) reported that client characteristics seem to be the best predictor of treatment outcomes. Individuals with moderate symptom severity, without concurrent mental disorders, and with increased tolerance for anxiety seem to have the greatest treatment gains.

Some members (Vannicelli et al., 1991) may need to be educated that the expectations for participation in group therapy differ from peer support groups, with group therapy emphasizing the process and analysis of the group experience. Kanas (1982) suggested a three-phase model of intervention. The initial phase encompasses basic support, education about abstinence, and clear examples of denial and minimization of problematic behaviors. The second phase entails reflection and exploration of the nature and quality of a drug-free lifestyle and the processes of change needed to support ongoing abstinence. In the final stage, the emphasis is on addressing predisposing intrapsychic factors for substance abuse that also are seen as predisposing factors for relapse. Stinchfield et al. (1994) noted the many schools of thought that prioritize differently the specific issues addressed in group treatment. However, the formats for substance abuse groups are generally structured to address affect, cognitions, and behaviors, in different proportions according to theoretical orientation, in order to foster the development of a drug-free lifestyle.

OVERVIEW

It was not until 1993 that the American Psychological Association approved a Division for Addictions (i.e., Division 50). Margolis and Zweben (1998) reported that 90% of psychology graduate students indicated that they had no formal course work in the area of substance abuse.

Group approaches are popular in different types of formats like Alcoholics Anonymous, family groups, educational groups, psychodrama, insight groups, and motivational groups (Duckert,

Amundsen, & Johnson, 1992; Kadden, Carroll, Donovan, Cooney, Monti et al., 1992 ; Levine & Gallogly, 1985; Pfeiffer, Feuerlein, & Brenk-Schulte, 1991; Vannicelli, 1991). Even though therapists and clients in group therapy consider it useful and efficient, there is a lack of scientific evidence regarding its mechanisms of action. Several studies have noted how difficult it is to evaluate group therapy processes of change and efficacy (Besson, Barrias, Borg, & Verbanck, 1993; Sanderson, 1982) because of the wide variety of salient factors like attendance, group pressure, identification, learning processes, or complex combinations thereof (Loughlin, 1992; Lovett & Lovett, 1991) that are not clearly described or evaluated in the published literature. Length of treatment, leadership style, numbers and types of patients, and conditions facilitating treatment also make comparisons between empirical research difficult.

Psychoeducation

Psychoeducational groups are generally utilized as a first step to more comprehensive treatment programs intending to inform and teach about medical, behavioral, and psychological consequences of drug use/abuse (Nace, 1987). Many believe that this method will educate group members and lead them to make a commitment to treatment (Drake et al., 1991).

A review of recent literature (1994-2002) shows that psychoeducation groups are used with a variety of individuals (adolescents, adults, and "dual-diagnosis" adults). Most psychoeducational programs are substance abuse prevention-focused (often in schools) or relapse prevention-focused (in rehabilitation or hospital settings). Psychoeducational groups as a single intervention with substance-abusing individuals have not been studied. Psychoeducation components are embedded into multimodal programs for substance abuse. This accounts for the paucity of published research regarding the effectiveness of psychoeducational approaches to substance abuse.

Research Findings

Addington and el-Guebaly (1998) found that the combination of social support,

psychoeducation, and social skills training improved outcome in patients with schizophrenia and substance abuse problems with abstinence rates of 44% after a 6- to 12-month follow-up. Plasse (2000) studied mothers in substance abuse treatment (N = 7) while qualitatively examining their engagement in a 15-week psychoeducational parenting skills group. After interviews with women involved in the group, she concluded that there was evidence of conceptual learning that occurred in the context of caring interpersonal relationships. However, participants were at risk of losing custody of their children upon nonparticipation or relapse.

In a review, Pentz (1999) concluded that school-based psychoeducational programs delivered by teachers have very low overall effects and no effect at a 5-year follow-up. One exception to this study was an intervention that required 30 sessions of instruction (Botvin et al., 1995). This study consisted of a randomized trial involving 56 public schools and a total of 3,597 predominantly white 12th grade students, who represented 60% of the initial 7th grade sample. The intervention consisted of 15 classes in 7th grade, 10 booster sessions in 8th grade, and 5 booster sessions in 9th grade. The classes taught general life skills and skills for resisting social influences to use drugs. Unlike traditional prevention approaches, the program concentrated on immediate negative consequences of drug use and decreasing social acceptability of use. Only minimal information regarding long-term consequences of drug use was provided. Follow-up data were collected 6 years after baseline using surveys. There were significant reductions in both drug and polydrug use for the groups that received the prevention program relative to the controls. Stronger effects for students who received the complete version of the program were obtained. Botvin et al. (1995) attributed the results to the duration (over 3 years) and length of the intervention (30 hours), the use of 15 booster sessions, and the assessment of implementation fidelity. However, differences between group outcomes (control vs. psychoeducation) were small and most likely due to the power of the large sample size.

Another study focused on parent programming delivered as a part of a multicomponent school or community intervention. This program demonstrated some impact on parent substance use, communication styles, and participation in prevention of their children's substance use (Rohrbach et al., 1994). Effects of mass media programs, if not combined with other programs, have been limited, with the exception of some advertising campaigns aimed at high-risk youth in changing attitudes toward drug use (Lorsch et al., 1994). Social influence programs conducted in community settings are similar to school-based programs and have not produced, by themselves, long-term decreases in drug use (St. Pierre et al., 1992). With regard to alcohol use, Moyers and Hester (1999) concluded that there is insufficient evidence of effectiveness for psychoeducation (i.e., lectures/films, etc.) with alcohol-abusing patients. They also reported that the use of videotapes for the purpose of self-confrontation, with alcohol-abusing patients, have shown negative outcomes. This type of intervention tends to significantly increase dropout rates. Although clinicians confidently provide educational lectures and utilize films in their psychoeducation programs, Moyers and Hester (1999) report that the findings of controlled clinical research did not show the effectiveness of these psychoeducation interventions as the only mode of intervention.

Recommendations

Existing research suggests that short-term low-intensive interventions do not produce significant changes in substance use/abuse behavior. Psychoeducation may be better used for prevention, but substance abuse is complex and requires multimodal treatment of longer duration and intensity to produce significant changes.

Psychoeducational intervention for prevention purposes should be sufficiently intense in frequency and duration. The content of the psychoeducational program should be matched to the setting, needs, and motivation of attendees and the intended goals of the program. The treatment program should be designed differently, depending on the age of participants.

The content areas may include the following (Marlatt, 1985, 1998; Perkinson, 1997; Sobell & Sobell, 1993):

- Physiological and psychological effects of substance abuse in the present and over an extended period of time
- Data about differences in use patterns (occasional, binge, frequent, daily use)
- Information about standard drinks (beer, wine, distilled spirits) and blood alcohol data in connection with differing amounts of consumption in combination with differing physical characteristics and time of ingestion
- Information about drugs other than alcohol and their common physiological effects
- Impact of substance abuse on interpersonal functioning (children, family, friends, etc.)
- Impact on occupational functioning
- Impact on observable behavior (acting out, antisocial acts, etc.)
- Impact on mood states (increases in anxious and depressed affect states)
- Information about differences between abuse versus dependence, including information about withdrawal and tolerance
- Education about the recovery process (physical and psychological)
- Information about defense mechanisms (e.g., denial, minimization, rationalization)
- Information about community resources and additional sources of support for change (12-step programs, counseling and psychotherapy, medical intervention, outpatient and inpatient programs, etc.)

Ideally, psychoeducational programs provide information so that attendees may make informed decisions about substance use and abuse and the subsequent consequences. Goals of psychoeducational approaches can be multi-faceted and centered around educating and empowering the attendees to make responsible and informed choices. Such programs are developed by treatment providers and are not standardized or packaged for dissemination.

GROUP COUNSELING AND PSYCHOTHERAPY

Group counseling and *psychotherapy* are terms that are used interchangeably, and we will review the research together, because existing research does not distinguish between them. There are a number of populations whose treatment needs are being addressed with group psychotherapy. Review of the literature shows that recent empirical research has included group therapy with children, adolescents, and adults with simple and multiple substance abuse disorders. Studies have been conducted with individuals who have additional confounding conditions such as physical, emotional, and sexual abuse histories, diagnosed posttraumatic stress disorders, and delinquency. With regard to theoretical approach, aside from the disease and 12-step recovery approaches, cognitive-behavioral (Johnson, 2001), motivational interviewing (Foote et al., 1999; Jungerman, de Almeida, & Laranjeira, 2000; Velasquez, Maurer, Crouch, & DiClemente, 2001), and psychodynamic (Intxusta, 2001; Winship, 1999) approaches are notable additions to the research body. All approaches may include family and/or adjunct counseling.

In a review of 23 studies of family-based interventions for adolescent drug abusers, Cormack and Carr (2000) concluded that the use of systemic engagement procedures was effective for families who were reluctant to enter treatment. Also, both family therapy and multisystemic family therapy were effective. Multisystemic treatment (ranging from 12 to 36 sessions) was more effective than individual or group supportive counseling and parent education. Family therapy (ranging from 6 to 24 sessions) is more effective than individual interventions that focused on the adolescent only, such as supportive therapy or social skills training. In these studies, family therapy involved treating individual families. The multisystemic approach included a combination of individual counseling, family therapy, and psychoeducation for the adolescents and their parents. (There is an extensive body of literature that focuses on family therapy approaches to substance abuse that is beyond the scope of this chapter.)

Washington (1997) studied the effects of cognitive/didactic group counseling versus experiential group counseling on self-efficacy and perceptions of employability in chemically dependent women. Treatment consisted of 2½ hours-long group counseling sessions per week for 6 weeks. Participants were assessed 1 week before the group began and again 1 week after the sessions ended. Results indicated that the cognitive/didactic counseling groups yielded more positive results, on previously noted variables, than the less directive experiential group counseling approach.

Cohen and Tempier (1999) described an ongoing pilot project of group treatment for clients with long-term psychosis and polysubstance abuse. The program was based on psychoeducational and cognitive-behavioral approaches. Client-client interactions followed the constructive confrontational approach, with sessions ending by setting goals. Clients who were experiencing some success in treatment were called upon to act as role models and to assist other patients to overcome denial of problems related to substance abuse. Behavioral interventions such as relapse prevention strategies and cue identification as well as role playing, relaxation techniques, communication skills, and drug refusal skills were included in the multimodal program. In addition, psychoeducational activities and attendance at Alcoholics Anonymous and Narcotics Anonymous meetings were encouraged. According to their findings, positive outcomes were achieved from the process itself, in that the group became more cohesive and increased group attendance. While there is a great deal of anecdotal reports regarding the efficacy of these programs, empirical evidence is lacking.

Jungerman et al. (2000) studied the efficacy of a motivational interviewing approach to the treatment of drug-dependent adolescents and adults in Brazil. Treatment sessions (18 months) involved motivational discussion of pros and cons of drug use, high-risk situations, routines, stages of change, and availability of psychiatric support. The results of this study do not investigate whether there is an interaction effect between the motivational interview group approach, group cohesion, and increased attrition rates. However, it appears that attrition rates and curative factors of counseling groups are linked to the maintenance of abstinence as well as reduction of substance abuse. However, subsequent research has not been conducted to identify the underlying causal factors for this improvement.

Monras and Gual (2000) studied 329 alcohol-dependent clients in Spain who participated in outpatient psychotherapy groups over a 5-year period while comparing attrition and retention data. Regrettably, they did not report any specific theoretical orientation utilized in the five outpatient psychotherapy groups employed in their research. Successful retention in treatment and outcome over 2 years seemed to follow a series of phases where the first 3 months in group psychotherapy was crucial. To maximize involvement in therapy during the first months, they suggested that group leaders train participants in understanding group processes and the use of motivational techniques. Training group members in the skills that facilitate connection with others is likely to influence group cohesiveness.

Crits-Christoph et al. (2001) used data from the National Institute on Drug Abuse Collaborative Cocaine Treatment Study to examine the relative efficacy of four treatments for cocaine dependence on psychosocial and other problems. The 480 patients were randomly assigned to 6 months of treatment in individual cognitive therapy, individual psychodynamic therapy, or individual drug counseling (with additional group drug counseling) or to group drug counseling alone. No significant differences between treatments were found regarding psychiatric symptoms, employment, or medical, legal, interpersonal, or alcohol use problems. Accordingly, Crits-Christoph et al. concluded that individual therapy approaches were not superior to group approaches. Vasilakis (1997) evaluated postdischarge functioning of adolescent substance abusers, comparing their participation in individual and group therapy modalities. Although participant response indicated a positive overall experience, there was no difference in postdischarge level of functioning between the two interventions.

Kaminer and Burleson (1999) compared short-term cognitive-behavioral (CBT) in comparison with interactional (IT) group psychotherapies for dual-diagnosed adolescent substance abusers 3 and 15 months after treatment completion. At the 3-month follow-up, adolescents assigned to CBT demonstrated a significant reduction in severity of substance abuse compared to adolescents in the IT treatment. At the 15-month follow-up, no differential improvements related to therapy type could be discerned. However, participants in general maintained significant treatment gains in both CBT and IT group therapy approaches, and they both were associated with similar long-term outcomes.

Overall, studies evaluating the efficacy of group therapy compared to other treatment approaches have shown that patients who are in psychotherapy groups have better compliance rates (Avila-Escribano, Perez-Madruga, & Rodriguez-Treceno, 1994), have higher rates of abstinence (Avila-Escribano et al., 1994), improve on a number of variables related to living standards (Bowers & Al-Redha, 1990; Cooney, Kadden, Litt, & Getter, 1991; Getter, Litt, & Kadden, 1992; Hoffmann & Miller, 1993; Monras, Freixa, Martinez, & Bach, 1990), improve their transition from inpatient to outpatient treatment (Hanson, Foreman, Tomlin & Bright, 1994), and are more likely to return for aftercare (Verinis & Taylor, 1994). Information regarding success rates is presented in a comparative fashion between types of treatment without identifying effect sizes.

RECOMMENDATIONS

Ideally, goals of counseling groups for substance abuse guide the focus of the group. These goals include establishing abstinence, improving coping skills, gaining increased control over affect, and developing and maintaining healthy relationships. As Polcin (1997b) and Steigerwald and Stone (1999) pointed out, Alcoholics Anonymous can be conceptualized as a cognitive-behavioral approach helping members to learn specific cognitive and behavioral skills that support abstinence and prevent relapse. It has to be remembered that self-help groups, particularly based on the 12-step program of Alcoholics Anonymous, are recommended by a majority of chemical dependency treatment programs for substance use disorders in the United States (Montgomery, Miller, & Tonigan, 1995; Morgenstern, Labouvie, McCrady, Kahler, & Frey, 1997) and that Alcoholics Anonymous has become the most commonly utilized treatment (Weisner & Schmidt, 1995).

In addition to structuring groups to address the necessary content areas, it is also important to consider other factors when planning treatment. The population of individuals with substance abuse disorders is extremely diverse; it is advisable to integrate different treatment modalities and services. Polcin (1997a, 1997b) recommended developing a perspective encompassing professional treatment, self-help groups, and substance abuse programs to increase the likelihood of effectively addressing clients' needs. Also, Johnson and Chappel (1994) and Zweben (1995) recommended replacing obsolete treatment paradigms that focus on the presence or absence of a "disease of addiction." Instead, they suggested that treatment consist of cognitive restructuring that targets attitudinal changes toward substance use and adaptive strategies to maintain abstinence.

To date, findings are clear that motivational interviewing group therapy and cognitive-behavioral group therapy are both helpful for short-term and longer-term outcomes. (Note: Except for the single study conducted in Spain [Monras & Gual, 2000], there are no published reports on motivational group therapy in the current English literature. In the United States, the motivational approach is conducted with individuals instead of groups.) The first 3 months in treatment are crucial regarding retention as well as outcome success (Monras & Gual, 2000). Treatment of co-occurring diagnoses is essential (Cohen & Tempier, 1999; Kaminer & Burleson, 1999) as well as adjunctive services regarding substance abuse-related problems (employment, housing, legal medical, etc.) (Polcin, 1997a, 1997b).

Findings clearly show that more intensive and longer duration interventions are better. All findings are consistent that multimodal interventions are more effective than unimodal interventions. However, although multimodal treatments are recommended, there continues to be uncertainty as to the exact components of the multimodal treatment that contribute to successful outcomes.

Group Formation Considerations

Considerations such as screening, client selection, number of sessions, and length and duration of treatment sessions are not addressed in the empirical literature. For screening and selection purposes, we suggest attending to the diagnoses of group members, because polysubstance abuse may be more complex and resistant to intervention than abuse of a single substance, and the problems of those who abuse alcohol may be different from those of individuals who use illegal substances. It is beneficial to have homogeneous groups with regard to abuse and dependency, but the actual substance that is used may not be as important. With greater heterogeneity with regard to substances that have been abused, the group may be more interesting for the members, the degree of interpersonal learning may be increased, and misconceptions about others may be reduced. With regard to occupational and social functioning, severely impaired individuals may require significantly more adjunctive services and they may have more difficulty relating to others who are higher functioning and vice versa. Screening must evaluate whether prospective group members can understand and comply with group rules such as confidentiality, attendance, and abstinence requirements.

With regard to the number of individuals in a group, one should follow the general guidelines for psychoeducational, counseling, and psychotherapy groups that suggest larger groups for psychoeducational purposes and smaller groups (6-10) for counseling and psychotherapy formats. With regard to the question of an open versus closed group, a closed group is more cohesive and time does not need to be spent orienting new members once the group has started. However, an open group can take advantage of the increased member-to-member interpersonal learning that comes from the shared experiences of those with longer periods of abstinence.

The length of sessions should depend on the number of individuals in the group. There is no empirical support of specific guidelines for session length, but a rule of thumb is to structure the group to allow for at least 10 minutes per group member. This will allow for sufficient "air time" without creating a marathon experience.

The frequency and duration of the group depend on the setting. In an inpatient setting, often the structure and financial realities of the facility will have an impact on the type of treatment provided. With regard to the optimal frequency and length of treatment, the field is still at the beginning of the learning curve. However, AA and other 12-step programs are very helpful because, at a minimum, they can provide social support independent of financial contributions. When considering discharge decisions, a useful benchmark is that the person needs to have adaptive functioning in all major life areas. With regard to outpatient settings, more treatment over a longer time span is better, but how much is enough is still unclear.

CONCLUSIONS

Historically, treatment of substance abuse began with a psychodynamic approach followed by a combination of 12-step programs and medical interventions. Over time, more psychologically diverse approaches have been applied to the treatment of substance abuse. Common factors include collaborative therapeutic alliance, the artful balance of empathic support and confrontation, cognitive restructuring strategies, and education regarding strategies to achieve and maintain abstinence. Effective treatments focus on problem resolution without making assumptions of an underlying psychiatric condition or mental disorder. For example, examining defense mechanisms and other cognitive distortions is essential, but this must be done in a fashion that focuses on the substance abuse and not on a presumed underlying mental disorder. With the appropriate balance of empathic confrontation mixed with support, the client will be empowered to determine self-selected goals (abstinence vs. modified use). Professionals need to provide information, as well as input and feedback, regarding the likelihood of success in achieving these goals (abstinence or modification) as well as the potential consequences of failure.

Treatment should include cognitive restructuring (including the instillation of hope in the possibility of attaining abstinence) and other cognitive strategies that support an abstinence-based lifestyle. In addition, treatment should foster the increased capacity to successfully manage affect and the development of interpersonal skills that effectively support relationships like assertive communication skills and

appropriate conflict resolution skills. Education regarding effective use of relapse prevention strategies and the development of a supportive social network are also important components of treatment. Supportive services that address related problems such as housing, academic or vocational challenges, family system resistances to change, and legal and medical problems are likely to have a positive impact on outcome as well.

REFERENCES

Addington, J., & el-Guebaly, N. (1998). Group treatment for substance abuse in schizophrenia. *Canadian Journal of Psychiatry, 4,* 843-845.

American Psychiatric Association. (2000). *Diagnostic and statistical manual of mental disorders* (4th ed.-TR). Washington, DC: Author.

Avila-Escribano, J. J., Perez-Madruga, A., & Rodriguez-Treceno, M. (1994). Estudio de una muestra de pacientes alcoholicosdos anos despues de finalizarel tratamiento. *Actas Luso Esp. Neurol. Psiquiatr Cienc Afines,* 6-12.

Besson, J., Barrias, J., Borg, S., & Verbanck, P. (1993). Treatment evaluation of alcoholism: Non-pharmacological interventions. *Alcohol* (Supp.), *2,* 145-149.

Botvin, G. J., Baker, E., Dusenbury, L., et al. (1995). Long-term follow-up results of a randomized drug abuse prevention trial in a white middle-class population. *Journal of the American Medical Association, 273,* 1106-1112.

Bowers, T. G., & Al-Redha, M. R. (1990). A comparison of outcome with group/marital and standard/individual therapies with alcoholics. *Journal of Studies on Alcoholism, 1,* 301-309.

Cohen, D., & Tempier, R. (1999). Group treatment of substance abuse for patients with schizophrenia or related disorders. *Canadian Journal of Psychiatry, 44*(9), 928.

Cooney, N. L., Kadden, R. M., Litt, M. D., & Getter, H. (1991). Matching alcoholics to coping skills or interactional therapies: Two-year follow-up results. *Journal of Consulting and Clinical Psychology, 59,* 598-601.

Cormack, C., & Carr, A. (2000). Drug abuse. In A. Carr (Ed.), *What works with children and adolescents?: A critical review of psychological interventions with children, adolescents, and* their families (pp. 155-177). Florence, KY: Taylor & Francis/Routledge.

Crits-Christoph, P., Siqueland, L., McCalmont, E., Weiss, R., Gastfriend, D. R., Frank, A., et al. (2001). Impact of psychosocial treatments associated with problems of cocaine-dependent patients. *Journal of Counseling & Clinical Psychology, 69,* 825-830.

Drake, R. E, Antosca, L. M., Noordsy, D. L., et al. (1991). New Hampshire's specialized services for the dual diagnosed. In K. Monkoff & R. E. Drake (Eds.), *Dual diagnosis of major mental illness and substance disorder* (pp. 57-67). San Francisco: Jossey-Bass.

Duckert, F., Amundsen, A., & Johnson, J. (1992). What happens to drinking after therapeutic intervention? *British Journal of Addiction, 87,* 1457-1467.

Flores, P. J., & Mahon, L. (1993). The treatment of addiction in group psychotherapy. *International Journal of Group Psychotherapy, 43*(3), 143-156.

Foote, J., DeLuca, A., Maquara, S., Warner, A., Grand, A., Rosenblum, A., et al. (1999). A motivational treatment for chemical dependency. *Journal of Substance Abuse Treatment, 17*(3), 181-192.

Galanter, M., & Kleber, R. D. (1999). *Textbook of substance abuse treatment.* Washington DC: American Psychiatric Press.

Getter, H., Litt, M. D., & Kadden, R. M. (1992). Measuring treatment progress in coping skills and interactional group therapies for alcoholism. *International Journal of Group Psychotherapy, 42,* 419-430.

Greif, G. L. (1996). Ten common errors beginning substance abuse workers make in group treatment. *Journal of Psychoactive Drugs, 28*(3), 297-299.

Hanson, M., Foreman, L., Tomlin, W., & Bright, W. (1994). Facilitating problem drinking clients' transition from inpatient to outpatient care. *Health Social Work, 19,* 23-28.

Hoffmann, N. G., & Miller, N. S. (1993). Perspectives of effective treatment for alcohol and drug disorders. *Psychiatric Clinical North American, 16,* 127-140.

Intxusta, G. R. (2001). Treatment of drug addicts by a professional staff team using a therapeutic community approach. *Therapeutic Communities, 22*(1), 29-40.

Johnson, J. (2001). The effects of a brief cognitive-behavioral group intervention on the depression and hopelessness of drug-dependent, human immunodeficiency virus-positive women (immune deficiency). *Dissertation Abstract International, Section B: Sciences & Engineering, 62*(1-B), 551.

Johnson, N. P., & Chappel, J. N. (1994). Using AA and other 12-step programs more effectively. *Journal of Substance Abuse Treatment, 11,* 137-142.

Jungerman, F. S., de Almeida, R. A. M., & Laranjeira, R. (2000). Motivational groups: Descriptive study of a treatment for drug dependents. *Journal Brasileiro de Psiquiatria, 49*(3), 61-68.

Kadden, R., Carroll, K. M., Donovan, D., Cooney, N., Monti, P., Abrams, D., et al. (1992). *Cognitive-behavioral coping skills therapy manual: A clinical research guide for therapists treating individuals with alcoholic abuse and dependence.* Washington, DC: U.S. Government Printing Office.

Kadden, R. M., Litt, M. D., Cooney, N. I., & Busher, D. A. (1992). Relationship between role-play measures of coping skills and alcoholism treatment outcome. *Addictive Behavior, 17,* 425-437.

Kaminer, Y., & Burleson, J. A. (1999). Psychotherapies for adolescent substance abusers: 15-month follow-up. *American Journal on Addictions, 8*(2), 114-119.

Kanas, N. (1982). Alcoholism and group psychotherapy. In E. Kauffman & M. Pattison (Eds.), *Encyclopedic handbook of alcoholism* (pp. 1011-1021). New York: Gardner.

Khantzian, E. J. (1985). Psychotherapeutic interventions with substance abusers: The clinical context. *Journal of Substance Abuse Treatment, 2,* 83-85.

Khantzian, E. J., Golden, S. J., & McCauliffe, W. E. (1999). Group therapy. In M. Galanter & R. D. Kleber (Eds.), *Textbook of substance abuse treatment* (pp. 367-378). Washington DC: American Psychiatric Press.

Levine, B., & Gallogly, V. (1985). *Group therapy with alcoholics: Outpatient and inpatient approaches.* Beverly Hills, CA: Sage.

Lorch, E., Palmgreen, P., Donohew, L., et al. (1994). Program context, sensation seeking, and attention to televised anti-drug public service announcements. *Communication Research, 20,* 390-412.

Loughlin, N. (1992). A trial of the use of psychodrama for women with alcohol problems. *Nursing Practioner, 5,* 14-19.

Lovett, L., & Lovett, J. (1991). Group therapeutic factors on an alcoholic in-patient unit. *British Journal of Psychiatry, 59,* 365-370.

Mahon, L., & Flores, P. (1992). Group psychotherapy as the treatment of choice for individuals who grew up with alcoholic parents: A theoretical review. *Alcoholism Treatment Quarterly, 9,* 113-125.

Margolis, R. D., & Zweben, J. E. (1998). *Treating patients with alcohol and other drug problems: An integrated approach.* Washington, DC: APA.

Marlatt, G. A. (1985). Relapse prevention: Theoretical rationale and overview of the model. In G. A. Marlatt & J. R. Gordon Miller (Eds.), *Relapse prevention* (pp. 3-70). New York: Guilford.

Marlatt, G. A. (1998). Basic principles and strategies of harm reduction. In G. A. Marlatt (Ed.), *Harm reduction: Pragmatic strategies for managing high-risk behaviors* (pp. 49-66). New York: Guilford.

Matano, R. A., Yalom, I. D., & Schwartz, K. (1997). Interactive group therapy for substance abusers. In J. L. Spira (Ed.), *Group therapy for medically ill patients* (pp. 296-325). New York: Guilford.

Miller, W. R., & Brown, S. A. (1997). Why psychologists should treat alcohol and drug problems. *American Psychologist, 52,* 1269-1279.

Monras, M., Freixa, N., Martinez, M., & Bach, L. (1990). Abandono de la terapia grupal en pacientes alcoholicos. Seguimiento de diez grupos. *Adicciones, 2,* 93-104.

Monras, M., & Gual, A. (2000). Attrition in group therapy with alcoholics: A survival analysis. *Drug & Alcohol Review,* 55-63.

Montgomery, H. A., Miller, W. R., & Tonigan, J. S. (1995). Does Alcoholics Anonymous involvement predict treatment outcome? *Journal of Substance Abuse Treatment, 23,* 241-246.

Morgenstern, J., Labouvie, E., McCrady, B. S., Kahler, C. W., & Frey, R. M. (1997). Affiliation with Alcoholics Anonymous after treatment: A study of its therapeutic effects and mechanisms of action. *Journal of Consulting and Clinical Psychology, 65,* 768-777.

Moyers, T., & Hester, R. K. (1999). Outcome research: Alcoholism. In M. Galanter & R. D. Kleber (Eds.), *Textbook of substance abuse treatment* (pp. 129-134). Washington, DC: American Psychiatric Press.

Nace, E. P. (1987). *The treatment of alcoholism.* New York: Brunner & Mazel.

National Institute of Alcohol Abuse and Alcoholism Project MATCH Research Group. (1997). Matching alcoholism treatments to client heterogeneity: Project MATCH posttreatment drinking outcomes. *Journal of Studies on Alcohol, 90,* 1179-1188.

Ouimette, P. C., Finney, J. W., & Moos, R. H. (1997). Twelve-step and cognitive-behavioral treatment for substance abuse: A comparison of treatment effectiveness. *Journal of Consulting and Clinical Psychology, 65,* 230-240.

Pentz, M. A. (1999). Prevention. In M. Galanter & R. D. Kleber (Eds.), *Textbook of substance abuse treatment* (pp. 535-544). Washington DC: American Psychiatric Press.

Perkinson, R. R. (1997). *Chemical dependency counseling: A practical guide.* Thousand Oaks, CA: Sage.

Pfeiffer, W., Feuerlein, W., & Brenk-Schulte, E. (1991). The motivation of alcohol dependents to undergo treatment. *Drug & Alcohol Dependence, 29,* 87-95.

Plasse, B. R. (2000). Components of engagement: Women in a psychoeducational parenting skills group in substance abuse treatment. *Social Work With Groups, 22*(4), 33-50.

Polcin, D. L. (1997a). The etiology and diagnosis of alcohol dependence: Differences in the professional literature. *Psychotherapy, 34,* 297-306.

Polcin, D. L. (1997b). Combining cognitive-behavioral and 12-step approaches in the treatment of alcohol dependence. *California Therapist, 9*(2), 47-51.

Polcin, D. L. (2000). Professional counseling versus specialized programs for alcohol and drug abuse treatment. *Journal of Addictions & Offender Counseling, 21,* 2-11.

Regier, D. A., Farmer, M., Rae, D. S., Locke, B. Z., Keith, S. J., Judd, L., et al. (1990). Comorbidity of mental disorders with alcohol and other drug abuse. *Journal of the American Medical Association, 264,* 2511-2518.

Rohrbach, L. A., Hodgson, C. S., Broder, B. I., et al. (1994). Parental participation in drug abuse prevention: Results from the Midwestern Prevention Project. *Journal of Research on Adolescence, 4,* 295-317.

Sanderson, S. C. (1982). Group therapy with alcoholic clients: A review. *Advances in Alcohol & Substance Abuse, 2,* 23-40.

Shaffer, H. (1986). Observations on substance abuse theory. *Journal of Counseling and Development, 65,* 26-30.

Sobell, M. B., & Sobell, L. C. (1993). *Problem drinkers: Guided self-change treatment.* New York: Guilford.

Steigerwald F., & Stone, D. (1999). Cognitive restructuring and the 12-step program Alcoholics Anonymous. *Journal of Substance Abuse Treatment, 4,* 321-327.

Stinchfield, R., Owen, P. L., & Winters, K. C. (1994). Group therapy for substance abuse: A review of the empirical research. In A. Fuhriman and G. M. Burlingame (Eds.), *Handbook of group psychotherapy: An empirical and clinical synthesis* (pp. 458-488). New York: Wiley.

St. Pierre, T. L., Kaltreider, D. L., Mark, N. N., et al. (1992). Drug prevention in community setting: A longitudinal study of the relative effectiveness of a three-year primary prevention program in boys and girls clubs across the nation. *American Journal of Public Health, 60,* 76-78.

U.S. Department of Health and Human Services. (2001). National Household Survey on Drug Abuse (NHSDA). Retrieved from http://www.samhsa.gov/oas/oasftp.htm.

Vannicelli, M. (1982). Group psychotherapy with alcoholics: Special techniques. *Journal of Studies on Alcohol, 43,* 17-37.

Vannicelli, M. (1991). Dilemmas and countertransference considerations in group psychotherapy with adult children of alcoholics. *International Journal of Group Psychotherapy, 41,* 295-312.

Vasilakis, W. H. (1997). Comparison of the efficacy of various treatment modalities and their impact on level functioning in an outpatient adolescent program. *Dissertation Abstracts International, Section B: The sciences & Engineering. 57*(8-B), 5348.

Velasquez, M. M., Maurer, G. G., Crouch, C., & DiClemente, C. (2001). *Group treatment for substance abuse: A stages-of-change therapy manual.* New York: Guilford.

Verinis, J. S., & Taylor, J. (1994). Increasing alcohol patients' aftercare attendance. *International Journal of Addiction, 29,* 1487-1494.

Washington, O. (1997). The effects of cognitive/didactic and experiential group counseling on the self-efficacy and perceptions of employability of chemically dependent women. *Dissertation Abstracts International, 58*(3-B), 1552.

Weisner, C., & Schmidt, L. A. (1995). Expanding the frame of health services research in the drug abuse field. *Health Service Research, 30,* 707-726.

Winship, G. (1999). Group therapy in the treatment of drug addiction. In D. Waller & J. Mahoney (Eds.), *Treatment of addiction: Current issues for arts therapists* (pp. 46-58). Florence, KY: Taylor & Francis/ Routledge.

Yalom, I. (1995). *Theory and practice of group psychotherapy.* New York: Basic Books.

Zweben, J. E. (1995). Integrating psychotherapy and 12-step approaches. In A. M. Washton (Ed.), *Psychotherapy and substance abuse. A practitioner's handbook* (pp. 124-140). New York: Guilford.

41

Group Work
With Men Who Have
Committed Partner Abuse

Jonathan P. Schwartz

Louisiana Tech University

Michael Waldo

New Mexico State University

In this chapter, we provide a background on the prevalence of partner abuse and the history of partner abuse treatment and describe the characteristics of men involved in partner abuse. We discuss the implications of this information for group treatment for men who have committed partner abuse and the therapeutic factors available in groups and group developmental stages as they relate to partner abuse treatment. We describe three different formats for group treatment of abuse—psychoeducational, counseling, and therapy—and review outcome studies evaluating group treatment. Finally, we offer suggestions for future practice and research.

In this chapter, the term *partner abuse* is used to describe abuse in intimate relationships. This term is more inclusive than *spouse abuse*, and conveys the view that abuse is a behavior rather than a type of person, which is implied by

labels such as *batterers, perpetrators, offenders,* or *abusers*. The focus of the chapter is on group treatment specifically for heterosexual men who have engaged in abusive behavior toward an intimate partner. There is evidence that men, rather than women, are more likely to perpetuate partner abuse and do more physical damage when they are abusive (Stets & Straus, 1990). While there is a growing body of evidence that women are also involved in partner abuse and may have some of the same motivations and causes for engaging in abusive behavior as men (Hines & Malley-Morrison, 2001; Straus & Gelles, 1990), and there is also evidence in the literature that domestic violence occurs in same-sex relationships at the same rate as heterosexual relationships (Miller, Bobner, & Zarski, 2000), group treatment with these populations has not received the research attention. This chapter focuses on group treatment of heterosexual men who have committed partner abuse because this population has been the focus of the majority of group practice and research (Adams, 1994).

PARTNER ABUSE PREVALENCE AND HISTORY OF TREATMENT

Partner abuse is a prevalent and serious problem in our society. Approximately 8.7 million married couples experience physical violence every year within their relationships (Straus, 1999). It is estimated that between 21% and 34% of all adult women are physically assaulted by an intimate male (Browne, 1993). In addition to the physical injuries sustained in partner abuse incidents, victims often suffer from prolonged psychological and physical health problems (Campbell & Lewandowski, 1997; Stark & Flitcraft, 1996). For children who witness partner abuse, the result is often a variety of emotional and social problems (Margolin, 1998), including subsequent involvement with abuse as adults (Browne, 1993; Dutton, 1998). The last two surgeon generals of the United States as well as the Public Health Objectives for Healthy People 2000 have described family violence as an "epidemic" and have called for more efforts to treat and prevent violence (Poirier, 1997).

Historically, partner abuse was viewed as a private matter. Partner abuse only began to receive public attention in the 1970s in response to the active efforts of the women's movement (Hage, 2000). Now over 1,500 community-based programs exist providing shelters and counseling for domestic violence victims (Stark & Flitcraft, 1996). Police arrests and court action against men who abuse have risen in the last decade (Murphy, Musser, & Maton, 1998). The development of treatment for men who have committed partner abuse occurred because of the recognition that couples involved in partner violence often choose to remain together (Finn, 1985) and the belief that it is the individuals who perpetuates violence against their intimate partners who need to change (Waldo, 1986). The first program specifically designed for men who have committed partner abuse was opened in 1977 (Adams, 1994). There are now domestic violence offender treatment centers across the country as well as in various countries around the world (Gerlock, 1997), the majority of which were created as adjuncts to shelters and counseling centers for victims of domestic violence (Adams, 1994). The most effective interventions for men who have committed partner abuse have involved the interweaving of social services, counseling, and corrective efforts by police and the courts (Murphy et al., 1998).

Group work is a commonly accepted format for treatment of men who have committed partner abuse (Ceasar & Hamberger, 1989; Gondolf, 1997; Lawson et al., 2001). Groups initially focused on feminist-oriented consciousness raising. Later, cognitive-behavioral techniques were added to help men challenge sexist beliefs and develop nonsexist attitudes (Gondolf, 1997). The groups evolved into sociocultural/feminist-based programs that sought to both hold men accountable for their abuse and remove the stigma from women who were abused (Gondolf, 1997). It was also assumed that men helping men was the most effective way to combat domestic violence (Wexler, 1999). In the late 1980s, the prevalence of court-mandated counseling dramatically increased and diversified the group counseling approaches used by partner abuse programs (Finn, 1987; Gondolf, 1991). During this period, battered women's advocates and partner abuse program staff raised concerns regarding the quality of the varied group approaches being used (Gondolf, 1997). These concerns led to the development of standards for treatment that were adopted in 11 states (Gondolf, 1997). The standards mandate treating abuse as a tactic used by men to gain power and control in their relationship, specified the training needed to conduct groups, and set guidelines for prioritizing the safety of the person who was abused. The standards are not universally accepted. Professionals remain uncertain about the characteristics of men who have committed partner abuse and the best format for working with them in groups (Gondolf, 2000). The scientific study of domestic violence has been limited to the last 20 years, and systematic outcome research on group treatment of partner abuse has only begun to be conducted (Berns, Jacobson, & Gottman, 1999; Gondolf, 2000).

Understanding Men Who Have Committed Partner Abuse

It is important to understand the causes of partner abuse to inform and design appropriate treatments (Holtzworth-Munroe & Stuart, 1994; Waldo, 1987; Waltz, Babcock, Jacobson, & Gottman, 2000). For a thorough review of the literature on characteristics of men who commit partner abuse, see Jasinski and Williams (1998). Their review indicates that many issues contribute to partner abuse, suggesting the need for multifaceted treatment. There currently are no universally accepted typologies of men who commit partner abuse. Researchers have investigated societal influences and gender socialization, witnessing or experiencing violence in the family of origin, substance abuse, and personality or pathological characteristics as root causes of partner abuse by males (Fagan, 1990; Gortner, Gollan, & Jacobson, 1997; Hamberger & Hastings, 1986; Stith & Farley, 1993).

Societal Influences and Gender Socialization

Hypotheses that societal influences and gender socialization contribute to partner abuse have been made by a number of theorists and researchers. Feminist theory proposes that men are socialized to take a patriarchal role with women and control them through psychological and physical abuse (Dobash & Dobash, 1979; Hamberger & Hastings, 1986; Pence & Paymer, 1993; Walker, 1984). The portrayal of men's abuse of women in popular media, including music, television, and movies, has also been theorized to contribute to spouse abuse (Lore & Shultz, 1993). The feminist perspective has been supported by findings that men who approve of the use of violence toward women are more violent (Kaufman-Kantor, Janiski, & Aldorondo, 1994; Straus & Gelles, 1990). Also, research suggests that men who hold patriarchal ideologies have higher rates of abusive behavior (Stith & Farley, 1993). Although patriarchy has been identified as an important variable, it has not offered a comprehensive or sufficient explanation of the cause of abuse (Dutton, 1995; Gortner et al., 1997; O'Neil & Harway, 1997). Research has demonstrated that not all men who hold patriarchal ideologies are abusive (Dutton, 1995).

Another way of conceptualizing how male socialization contributes to abuse is through gender role conflict or stress theory. O'Neil, Good, and Holmes (1995) defined gender role conflict as a psychological state in which socialized gender roles have negative consequences on the person or others. Gender role conflict has been hypothesized to cause shame and powerlessness, and to be related to abusive behavior (Jennings & Murphy, 2000; O'Neil & Harway, 1997). In a study of men who were court-mandated to treatment for committing partner abuse, Schwartz, Merta, Waldo, and Bloom-Langell (1998) found that gender role conflicts, in particular gender role conflicts resulting in having difficulty forming relationships with other men, were related to abusive behavior. In addition, masculine gender role stress (cognitive appraisals of specific situations that may be perceived as stressful to their construct of masculinity) has been related to men's increased attribution of negative intent to their partners, expression of more irritation, anger, jealousy, endorsed aggressive responding, and increased reporting of abusive behavior (Copenhaver, Lash, & Eisler, 2000; Eisler, Franchina, Morre, Honeycutt, & Rhatigan, 2000). These findings suggest that gender role conflict and stress may be related to men committing partner abuse toward women.

Abusive Behavior in Family of Origin

Witnessing or experiencing abusive behavior in their families of origin has been related to men subsequently engaging in spouse abuse (Dutton, 1998; Gortner et al., 1997). Social learning theorists, such as Bandura (1973), suggest that children who witness violence in their family of origin demonstrate the influence of parental modeling when they exhibit violence as adults (Gortner et al., 1997). Witnessing or experiencing violence in the family of origin also has been hypothesized to have a detrimental effect on self-esteem, resulting in men being vulnerable to threats to their self-concept and depression

(Murray & Baxter, 1997). There is a higher rate of depression among men who have abused their partners (Pan, Neidig, & O'Leary, 1994). Dutton (1999) posited that witnessing or experiencing violence in the family of origin, feeling shamed, and having insecure attachments are traumas that can lead to personality disorders, primarily Borderline Personality Disorder. Borderline Personality Disorder and Antisocial Personality Disorder have consistently been found in men involved in partner abuse (Dutton, 1995; Gottman et al., 1995; Holtzworth-Munroe & Stuart, 1994).

The disruption of early relationships caused by experiencing or witnessing abuse as a child could also prevent men from developing working models of healthy relationships, and lead to their having difficulties with self-concept and intimacy in future relationships (Bowlby, 1988). Abusive men have been found to be more demanding of their partner, feel more threatened by their partner's independence, feel less power in their relationships, and lack the skills to communicate their needs (Babcock, Waltz, Jacobson, & Gottman 1993; Berns et al., 1999; Ehrensaft, Laughinrichse-Rohling, Heyman, O'Leary, & Lawrance, 1999). It has been suggested that childhood trauma from witnessing or experiencing child abuse could cause men to identify with the aggressor in order to feel more powerful, perpetrate the same trauma onto others in order to gain a sense of control over the trauma, and/or defend against painful memories through anger and aggression (Saunders, 1996).

Substance Abuse

Substance abuse, particularly alcohol abuse, has been linked to domestic violence (Fagan, 1990). Gorney (1989) found that 60% to 70% of violent men assault their partners while they are under the influence of alcohol. The relationship between substance abuse and partner abuse is complex, and the effects of substances are mediated by beliefs about the substance as well as the direct effect of the substance (Bushman & Cooper, 1990). Pence and Paymer (1993) point out that alcohol can be used to minimize and deny responsibility for abusive behavior.

Advantages of Group Work

Group work has a number of distinct advantages for helping men who have engaged in partner abuse. The therapeutic factors available in groups have the potential to simultaneously address the wide array of issues associated with partner abuse, making groups particularly useful when therapeutic gains need to be made in a variety of areas (e.g., addressing gender role socialization, understanding and managing difficult emotions, increasing self-esteem, changing beliefs, and learning new behaviors). Also, men who are court mandated for counseling may be uneasy about engaging in treatment and resist counselors' guidance (Waldo, 1987). Groups provide a reassuringly familiar environment for most men because they are like classes or other group settings in which men have been involved. Group dynamics generate peer influences that may be more compelling than the influence of therapists who are seen as aligned with the authority structures that mandated their referral. Also, group work is more economically efficient than other forms of treatment, which makes it more accessible to men in need of services.

THERAPEUTIC FACTORS IN GROUPS FOR MALES WHO HAVE COMMITTED PARTNER ABUSE

The therapeutic factors Yalom (1995) and others have identified have been the subject of extensive research on the effectiveness of group interventions, including groups for men being treated for domestic violence (Schwartz & Waldo, 1999). Each of the therapeutic factors offers potential benefits to men who have engaged in partner abuse, as follows:

Instillation of Hope. By the time men who have engaged in partner abuse reach treatment, they are often deeply discouraged. Their relationships with their partners, on whom they are likely to have been highly dependent (Dutton, 1995), are either at risk of being terminated or have ended. Men may also feel vulnerable in a group that may manifest itself as resistance (Stonsy, 1997). Groups can counter these negative emotions by instilling hope for a better future for group members. The fact that groups have been organized to help (instead of further punish) men who have been abusive sends the message that help is possible. The commitment, caring, and competence demonstrated by group leaders offers the men further reason to believe they will receive assistance. Perhaps most important, when men involved in partner abuse enter ongoing groups consisting of experienced members, they can see that other men have been dealing with the problems they have, and have been making progress. Instillation of hope motivates men to invest in their futures, take responsibility for their behaviors, and try to get the most out of treatment.

Universality. Men who are being treated for partner abuse often experience overwhelming shame and often respond to shame with denial (Dutton, 1995). They reject responsibility for the abuse, potentially sabotaging their treatment because they refuse to accept help or initiate changes to address a problem they claim they do not have (Pence & Paymer, 1993). Universality in groups helps members overcome denial. Because the group is organized for and made up by men who are dealing with the same problem, members recognize that they are not alone or unique. This discovery validates their essential commonality with other men and helps them see abuse as a problem to be overcome rather than hidden.

Catharsis. Men who engage in partner abuse have difficulty managing their emotions (Guerney, Waldo, & Firestone, 1987; Schwartz et al., 1998). Often they repress their sadness, fear, helplessness, and hurt, converting these feelings into anger or jealousy. Also, they typically do not express anger or jealousy when they first occur (Berns, Jacobson, & Gottman, 1999). Instead, they store these volatile feelings up until they reach a breaking point and explode (Holtzworth-Munroe & Stuart, 1994). When they see the negative consequences of their emotional outbursts, they become sadder, more fearful, helpless, and hurt, and also more cautious about experiencing and expressing emotions, resulting in more repression. When more anger and jealousy are generated, their feelings build up to higher and more dangerous levels

until the next explosion. A pattern of escalating emotional outbursts develops that can lead to an escalating cycle of violence (Walker, 1984). Catharsis can help break this cycle. Groups offer safe environments that encourage and accept emotional expression. Men benefit from the relief associated with emotional release, and have a reduced need to employ defenses against emotions. They also can gain understanding and acceptance of the feelings they have that come before anger (like hurt and fear), and develop appropriate means of communicating their feelings. These benefits help men end the destructive cycle of emotional outbursts.

Corrective Recapitulation of the Primary Family Group. Groups offer men a chance to correct the abusive pattern that many have experienced or witnessed in their family of origin (Dutton, 1999). Because groups have a leader (or leaders) who can symbolize parental authority, and members who can symbolize siblings, they re-enact some of the dynamics members experienced in their families earlier in their life. However, since groups are structured and emotionally healthy settings, they do not allow a replay of abuse. Instead, emotions are appropriately managed, and positive relationships are maintained between group members and the leaders. This allows for a corrective reworking of family dynamics the members previously experienced, helping them develop healthy internal models of family interaction that they can generalize to their relationships with their partners.

Cohesion. Many men who have committed partner abuse are isolated (Browne, Saunders, & Staecker, 1997). Their low self-esteem results in their being reluctant to establish relationships outside of the relationship they have with their partner (Goldstein & Rosenbaum, 1985; Holtzworth-Munroe & Stuart, 1994). Groups offer members an experience of closeness with other men. They can feel valued and accepted, which raises their self-esteem and reduces their dependence on their partner. Reduced dependence on their partner makes men less vulnerable to desperate possessiveness, which can trigger violent behavior. Cohesion can also motivate members to adhere to the group's goal of ending abuse, because they want to remain involved with a cohesive group and are likely to be terminated from the group if they abuse again.

Altruism. Participation in a group offers men a chance to help others. Focusing on other men's suffering can help men move past obsession with their own pain and anger (Berns et al., 1999). Group members' success at helping others can increase their sense of self-efficacy. Furthermore, offering advice to other members on how to avoid violence and improve their relationships makes it more likely the advice givers will follow the advice they are giving.

Interpersonal Learning. Relationships between men in groups become social microcosms of their lives outside of group. Aspects of men's interpersonal styles that cause problems in relationships outside of group (Dutton, 1999; Holtzworth-Munroe & Stuart, 1994) cause problems in the group as well. When problems arise in the group, other members give the members involved feedback about how they are coming across. The experience of receiving feedback can constitute a critical incident for group members. Feedback provides them with insight into their maladaptive relational patterns and offers them a corrective emotional experience in that they recognize that their destructive patterns are not necessary or desirable. Feedback about the way men interact with each other in the group can be more powerful than feedback about men's attitudes or reported behavior in relationships outside of group. This is because other members witnessed the interaction, reducing opportunities for distorted perceptions or reporting. In addition, the feedback is coming from other members who many men perceive to be less biased than their partners or counselors (Dutton, Ginkel, & Starzomski, 1995).

Imparting of Information. Most men who engage in partner abuse have had minimal exposure to information about domestic violence and how it can be prevented (Pence & Paymer, 1993). Group offers an ideal setting for men to learn new information and attitudes that can help them better understand how to live without violence. One of the most common statements made by men when assessing their group experience is "If only I had known all this 2 years ago!"

Imitative Behavior. Many men who have abused their partners witnessed or experienced abuse in their families of origin (Dutton, 1998). Group can help men overcome the negative effects of prior models by providing relevant positive models. The leaders serve as models because they have status in the group and are proficient in the skills they are sharing with group members. The effectiveness of the leaders as models is increased if members can see similarities between themselves and the leaders. Female/male coleadership can be particularly effective in modeling an equal relationship (Nosko & Wallace, 1997). Positive group members also serve as models for each other.

Development of Socializing Techniques. The family of origin experience of many men who have engaged in abuse provided them few opportunities to develop effective relationship skills. Instead, their families often reinforced the use of negative interaction patterns (Gortner et al., 1997). Groups offer numerous opportunities for members to practice new ways of relating. Once members have decided to develop new relationship skills (often in response to interpersonal learning in the group), have learned information about the skill and viewed it being modeled, they can practice it while interacting with other members during sessions. For example, a man who has received feedback that he is passive could learn about assertiveness, see it modeled by the leaders and other members, and then practice appropriate assertiveness during subsequent sessions. The leaders' and members' positive responses to his skill development reinforce his continued use of the skill, both in and outside of group. Assertiveness in his marital relationship could help him avoid developing a backlog of resentment that eventually explodes in an emotional outburst.

Existential Factors. Many men who are arrested for partner abuse fail to recognize their responsibility in perpetrating abuse. Instead of accepting responsibility, they blame their partner, her friends and relatives, the legal system, and a variety of other targets (Pence & Paymer, 1993). Men can be encouraged to recognize that they are choosing how they respond in group, which in turn can help them recognize the choices they made that led to abuse, their responsibility for those choices, and their responsibility for their choices in the future. Because their involvement in a group inevitably ends, groups also help men recognize that time and opportunities to change are limited. Recognizing these existential realities can motivate group members to take responsibility for choosing nonviolence with their partners.

GROUP STAGES

In addition to promoting the therapeutic factors described above (Waldo, 1985), Group Stages, the dynamics associated with developmental stages of groups have particular advantages for treatment of men who have engaged in partner abuse. Groups have been described as passing through developmental stages that have dynamic characteristics (Waldo, 1987). The dependency fostered by the Forming Stage of group encourages men to blend in, be cooperative, and have faith in treatment, promoting the therapeutic factors of universality and instillation of hope. The strong emotions that emerge during a groups Storming Stage can overcome the men's denial of feelings and give them an opportunity to manage their emotions appropriately, promoting the therapeutic factors of catharsis and corrective recapitulation of the primary family group. The warmth and caring generated between members during the Norming Stage of group helps promote the therapeutic factors of cohesion and altruism. After having passed through the Forming, Storming, and Norming Stages, groups reach the Performing Stage and are ready to work. It is at this stage that members are able to benefit from interpersonal learning generated by feedback, imparting of information, imitative learning, and trying new socializing techniques. When group members face terminating with the group (Adjourning Stage), they are forced to recognize the existential reality that while they may not have perceived themselves to have had a choice about entering the group, they did have a choice and responsibility to make good use of the sessions and their relationships with other members. They can see that these realities apply to their relationships outside the group as well. While they cannot control their partners, they do have choices in how they respond to them and responsibility for their choices. And like the group, those relationships are also ultimately time limited.

Types of Groups Applied to Partner Abuse Treatment

Three types of groups are discussed in this section: psychoeducational, counseling, and therapy. The discussion of the three types of groups is followed by a section on integrated treatment. When categorizing groups into one of these types, it should be recognized that groups rarely fit exclusively within one type (Waldo & Bauman, 1998). Therapy groups may include psychoeducational procedures, and psychoeducational groups may pursue therapeutic goals. Self-help groups may include both psychoeducational and therapy goals and processes. The problem of categorizing abuse treatment groups that are reported in the literature is further complicated by authors not having identified the specific group treatment approaches that were used (Gondolf, 1997). Because treatment of men who have engaged in partner abuse is focused on remediating a serious problem, abusive behavior, all group approaches to partner abuse may be considered to have a therapeutic goal. The categorization of groups offered below is based on the process typically employed in the group, as follows: psychoeducational groups are dominated by teaching; counseling groups focus on supportive interaction between group members; and therapy groups evoke self-exploration, personal disclosure, and in-depth analysis of intrapersonal problems.

Psychoeducational Groups

The predominant psychoeducational groups in partner abuse counseling are feminist/sociocultural educational groups and cognitive-behavioral/skill-based groups (Wexler, 2000). Many current partner abuse treatment models now combine these two (Ceasar & Hamberger, 1989; Ganley, 1989). Some combined groups emphasize sociocultural reorientation (Duluth Model, Pence, & Paymer, 1993), while others focus on cognitive-behavioral skills (Feminist Cognitive-Behavioral Treatment [FCBT], Saunders, 2000). For example, techniques such as time-out and positive self-talk were first introduced in anger management curriculums and are now often employed in feminist/sociocultural educational groups (Common Purpose, 1996). In this review, types of psychoeducational groups will be differentiated by their primary focus and approach as follows: the Duluth Model groups are feminist/sociocultural educational groups that focus on confronting men on their use of abuse to dominate women. Duluth Model groups integrate cognitive-behavioral approaches such as positive self-talk (Pence & Paymer, 1993). In contrast, FCBT groups primarily focus on increasing men's respect and equal treatment of women and employ a primarily cognitive-behavioral approach (Saunders, 2000).

Psychoeducational groups based on a feminist/sociocultural theoretical perspective are the most prevalent type of group today (Wexler, 1999). State guidelines for court-mandated domestic violence programs often include the feminist/sociocultural treatment model (Gondolf, 1997; Wexler, 1999). The Duluth (Pence & Paymer, 1993) and Emerge (Adams, Bancroft, German, & Sousa, 1992) programs are two of the most popular examples of this type of treatment model. Physical violence and other forms of abuse are viewed as tactics of maintaining power and control in intimate relationships (Adams et al., 1992; Pence & Paymer, 1993). Men involved in partner abuse are held responsible for their abuse and often encouraged to recognize violence as a method of coercion and intimidation (Adams et al., 1992; Pence & Paymer, 1993). Men are educated about male socialization, patriarchal beliefs are exposed, and minimization and denial of abuse are confronted by group leaders and group members (Pence & Paymer, 1993). The programs explicitly do not focus on providing therapy for group members (Common Purpose, 1996; Pence & Paymer, 1993).

Strengths cited for the feminist/sociocultural approach include encouraging men to take responsibility for their abusive behavior and maintaining an environment that challenges rather than colludes with men's attempts to minimize, deny, and blame others for their abusive behavior (Adams, 1994; Pence & Paymer, 1993). The view that violent behavior by men is learned and socially reinforced suggests the need for reeducation through group treatment (Dobash & Dobash, 1979). Feminist/sociocultural models provide reeducation on gender socialization that leads to the use of power and control abusively in relationships (Pence & Paymer, 1993).

Criticisms of the feminist/sociocultural approach include questioning the value of using extensive confrontation with men who are already experiencing shame (Browne et al., 1997; Dutton, 1998). It has been noted that empathetic group leaders of abuse treatment groups are more effective than confrontational ones and that a confrontational approach may exacerbate resistance (Murray & Baxter, 1997). Others state that failing to provide therapy for apparent psychological and emotional issues related to abusive behavior is problematic (Schwartz & Waldo, 1999; Wexler, 1999). Finally, it has been noted that these psychoeducational groups fail to consider other possible causes of abusive behavior besides social influences (Dutton, 1995).

There are limited outcome data on pure forms of the feminist/sociocultural educational groups. Sheppard (1992) conducted a 5-year follow-up study with 100 men who were mandated to a feminist/sociocultural educational group. Sheppard found a 40% recidivism rate. The number of sessions attended and completion of the treatment program did not predict recidivism. The characteristics of the men who committed partner abuse, such as chemical dependency issues, a history of abuse as children, and a history of criminal behavior, did predict recidivism. Petrik, Olson-Petrik, and Subotnik (1994) conducted a study on 26 men who completed treatment in feminist/sociocultural educational groups. They found that treatment failed to decrease the men's feeling of powerlessness or to increase their tolerance for being controlled. Gondolf (2000) completed a 30-month follow-up of 402 court-referred men in four cities who attended feminist/sociocultural educational groups. Forty-one percent of the men committed reassault during the 30-month follow-up period. Program dropouts were more likely to have recidivism of abuse than men who completed at least 3 months of treatment. Two major experimental studies using the Duluth Model that were conducted with random assignment to treatment and control groups (Davis, Taylor, & Maxwell, 1998; Feder & Forde, 2000) showed little to no program effects. In both studies, difficulties in implementing the random assignment of subjects, substantial dropout rates, and relatively low follow-up response rates limited confidence in the results (Gondolf, 2001). Finally, Edleson and Syers (1990) compared three treatment models, a feminist/sociocultural structured education model, a self-help model, and a combination of the two. They found that the educational model was more effective than the self-help model and combined model in reducing violence and terroristic threats at a 6-month follow-up.

Programs focused on skill-building or cognitive-behavioral approaches often include a combination of problem solving, anger management, interpersonal skills, stress management/ relaxation skills, and empathy (Saunders, 1996). Cognitive approaches target anger as the cause of aggression and focus on the role of cognitive distortions and irrational beliefs as leading to the arousal of anger (Saunders, 2000; Sonkin & Durphy, 1985). Behavioral approaches focus on interpersonal skills, specifically assertive communication (vs. aggressive or passive aggressive) to alleviate men's aggression (Holtzworth-Munroe, 1992; Saunders, 2000). Behavioral approaches take advantage of the group format by using role plays of anger management scenarios. These differ from feminist/sociocultural groups (Gondolf, 1990), because they focus on individual-level impulse control as opposed to societal-level gender issues. Cognitive-behavioral/skill-based approaches have been used in couples group counseling with violent couples sometimes following completion of group by the male partner (Gondolf, 1997; Guerney, Waldo, & Firestone, 1987). Couples counseling is controversial because of concerns that men will abuse women as a result of the joint sessions (Walker, 1984). The majority of conjoint group therapy for violent couples follows a cognitive-behavioral framework that is similar to anger management group formats for abusive men (Geffner, Mantooth, Franks, & Rao, 1989).

A strength noted for the cognitive-behavioral/ skill-building approach is that it teaches concrete skills that men can use to change their behavior (Lawson et al., 2001). In addition, this approach is based on empirically validated principles that have been used successfully to treat other aggressive behavior (Saunders, 2000). One criticism of this approach is the concern that a broader more comprehensive treatment may be needed to deal with the effects of the early traumas that many abusive men have experienced (Dutton, 1998; Wexler, 2000). Also, concerns have been raised that if this approach is not integrated with a feminist/sociocultural approach, there is a danger of ignoring the social reinforcement for partner abuse in society (Pence & Paymer, 1993; Saunders, 2000).

A number of outcome studies have investigated primarily cognitive-behavioral and skill-based groups. Two studies comparing cognitive-behavioral skill-based treatment approaches to no treatment found significantly reduced recidivism at follow-up for the treatment groups (Dutton, 1986; Waldo, 1988). Dutton found a 4% recidivism rate for those who completed treatment after 3 years of follow-up and a 40% recidivism rate for a comparable group that did not have treatment. Waldo found 0% recidivism after 1 year of follow-up for men who completed treatment as compared to 20% recidivism for those who were not referred to treatment and 20% recidivism for those who were referred but never engaged in treatment. Studies of cognitive-behavioral and skill-based groups with no comparison or control group demonstrated significant reductions in self and partner ratings of both physical and psychological abuse (Farley & Magill, 1988; Faulkner, Stoltenberg, Cogen, Nolder, & Sooter, 1992; Petrik et al., 1994; Waldo, 1986). In one of these studies, the men also showed significant improvements in their communication skills (Waldo, 1986). Saunders (1996) conducted a comparison study where men were randomly assigned to a Feminist Cognitive-Behavioral Treatment or a Process Psychodynamic Treatment. Men with dependent personalities had better outcomes in a Process Psychodynamic Treatment. Men with antisocial traits, substance abuse problems, and hypomania had better outcomes in the Feminist Cognitive-Behavioral Treatment group. These findings suggest that the Feminist Cognitive-Behavioral Treatment may provide the structure and skill training needed for antisocial, hypomanic, and substance abuse problem groups. Finally, Saunders found that the Feminist Cognitive-Behavioral Treatment led to increased relationship satisfaction, possibly due to the focus on communication skills.

Group Counseling

Group counseling for men who abuse their intimate partners is typically offered in minimally structured self-help groups. Members usually define the topics covered and former members often facilitate the meetings (Edleson & Syers, 1990). Goffman (1980) developed a self-help group titled Batterers Anonymous, which follows a 12-step model similar to Alcoholics Anonymous. The support and identification with other group members available in counseling groups have been hypothesized to be important factors in creating change in abusive men (Jennings, 1987; Waldo, 1987). The unstructured counseling group provides an environment that facilitates new skill development in an atmosphere where new skills can be practiced and transferred to the other environments (Gondolf, 1987; Jennings, 1987).

Jennings (1987) and Wexler (1999) cited the benefits of men helping other men overcome violence in an environment of support as a strength of self-help group counseling. Criticisms include a lack of focus on confrontation and education of men to take responsibility for their abusive behavior (Dobash & Dobash, 1979; Pence & Paymer, 1993).

There are few outcome studies on self-help counseling groups. In one outcome study, Edleson and Syers (1990) found that self-help groups were not as effective in reducing violence and terroristic threats at 6-month follow-up as feminist/sociocultural educational groups.

Therapy Groups

Theories that explain partner abuse as a reaction to childhood trauma led to the creation of a Process-Psychodynamic Treatment (PPT) model (Browne, Saunders, & Staecker, 1997; Jennings, 1987; Saunders, 1996). This is a minimally structured model that assumes that therapy happens through the process of supportive, nondidactic group relationships (Jennings, 1987). The leaders create a supportive environment, which decreases isolation and allows men to explore the childhood roots of sex-role expectations and shame-based behaviors, reexperience childhood traumas, grieve their losses, give up control over others, learn to empathize with others, increase their emotional investment in others' welfare, and increase their capacity to express feelings directly and responsibly (Browne et al., 1997).

Psychodynamic process groups are the most common types of therapy groups for men who have committed partner abuse. Other types of therapy groups focus on the attachment deficits of men involved in partner abuse. Self-psychology groups (Wexler, 1999) are based on the belief that men who have committed partner abuse did not have sufficient "mirroring self-objects" (p. 137). Treatment is focused on addressing psychological issues and offering respect for the group members' feelings of powerlessness and emotional injuries resulting from their primary relationships. The Compassion Workshop (Stonsy, 1995) is a therapy group format based on the idea that most men who have committed partner abuse cannot sustain attachments. Group activities and homework focus on developing compassion for the self. Finally, solution-focused therapy groups (Lee, Greene, Uken, Rheinscheld, & Sebold, 1997; O'Hanlon & Weiner-Davis, 1989) are based on focusing on the strengths and resources of the men rather than on problems and deficits.

Strengths cited for the therapy group approaches include the benefits men derive from creating relationships and learning to nurture one another (Jennings, 1987; Waldo, 1987). Jennings (1987) believes that therapy groups can help men develop self-help skills, learn tolerance and patience, feel emotional safety, and experience mutually supportive relationships. Therapy groups are also believed to aid men in the expression of shame and related emotions (Wallace & Nosco, 1993). Feldman and Ridley (1995) pointed out that most groups primarily focus on violent behavior, rather than broader issues, including self-esteem, personality disorders, and depression. Therapy groups are more likely than sociocultural psychoeducational groups or self-help counseling groups to address the attachment issues, relationship insecurities, and personality disorders that research suggests are related to abuse (Babcock et al., 1993; Dutton, 1999; Holtzworth-Munroe & Stuart, 1994). Browne et al. (1997) suggested that unstructured process groups can respond more flexibly to the needs of group members. Criticisms of the therapy group approach have been made by proponents of feminist/sociocultural groups. They believe that the psychodynamic groups create an atmosphere of collusion, rather than a group atmosphere that confronts abusive behavior (Pence & Paymer, 1993). Furthermore, concerns have been raised that a supportive and empathic group environment may reinforce rationalization of abusive behavior and that the therapy groups may take too long to change abusive behavior (Adams, 1994). There have been few outcome studies on therapy groups. In one study, Saunders (1996) found that men with dependent personalities had better outcomes in a Process-Psychodynamic Treatment group.

Integrated Treatment

A small number of studies have attempted to integrate group treatment approaches (Lawson et al., 2001; Saunders & Hanusa, 1986). Lawson et al. (2001) integrated feminist, cognitive-behavioral, and psychodynamic approaches. Saunders and Hanusa combined cognitive behavioral and counseling approaches. The potential strengths of integrated treatment approaches include the ability to address the multifaceted issues that contribute to abusive behavior by creating new treatment models based on existing research and theory (Carden, 1994; Lawson et al., 2001). Criticisms of integrated approaches are likely to focus on the lack of theoretical rational for integration (Gondolf, 1987). The two studies cited above evaluated integrated treatment approaches they employed and found them to be moderately successful in curtailing abuse and issues related to abusive behavior (Lawson

et al., 2001; Saunders & Hanusa, 1986). The idea of integrative treatment to deal with the multidimensional problem of partner abuse appears to be gaining in popularity in the literature (Carden, 1994; Gondolf, 1987; Lawson et al., 2001).

PROBLEMS WITH RESEARCH ON TREATMENT OF PARTNER ABUSE

There are two major problems that make conducting research with men who have abused their partners difficult: measurement problems and group attrition. There are three types of data that can be collected to assess the effectiveness of partner abuse treatment: self-report from the men, reports from the men's partners, and police/court information. There are problems with each of these sources of data (Gondolf, 1997). The motivation to stay out of trouble and not to violate probation may result in men and their partners not providing follow-up data or underreporting abuse (Edleson & Grusznski, 1988; Tolman & Bennet, 1990). The people most likely to be responding at follow-up are men with positive outcomes, potentially biasing results in a positive direction (Gondolf, 1997; Moffit et al., 1997). Furthermore, utilizing police or military arrest reports may underestimate actual recidivism rates due to inconsistencies in the responses to abuse by legal systems (Tolman & Bennet, 1990). Finally, few studies have used outcome measures other than incidents of physical violence. More comprehensive and detailed information could be gathered on psychological abuse, threats, and measures of successful behavior (positive caring behavior, increased communication, relationship equality) (Gondolf, 1997; Rosenfeld, 1992).

Second, it has been hard to evaluate the effectiveness of partner abuse treatment because of high attrition rates from groups (Hamberger, Lohr, & Gottlieb, 2000). A number of outcome studies have demonstrated that up to half the participants involved in group treatment drop out before the completion of the group (Edelson & Syers, 1990; Gondolf & Foster, 1991). High attrition results in a limited and potentially biased sample (Hamberger et al., 2000). Studies of men who drop out of group could help explain why they are dropping out and what can be done to influence them to stay.

SUGGESTIONS FOR PRACTICE AND RESEARCH

Additional work needs to be done on retaining men in partner abuse treatment groups. Evidence suggests that individuals who drop out of treatment have higher recidivism rates than those who complete treatment (Dutton, Bodnarchuk, Kropp, Hart, & Ogloff, 1997). Research has investigated client characteristics and system and treatment variables that affect completion, including age, education/employment, court-mandated status, ethnicity, and minority group status (Gondolf & Foster, 1991; Hamberger et al., 2000; Rondeau, Brodeur, Brochu, & Lemire, 2001; Tolman & Bennet, 1990; Williams & Becker, 1994). Hamberger et al. (2000) found that personality variables are particularly important, with paranoid personality characteristics predicting early dropout and borderline personality characteristics predicting late dropout. Studies have found that structured pregroup orientations can be successful in increasing completion rates (Tolman & Bhosley, 1990). Taft, Murphy, Elliott, and Morrel (2001) found success utilizing motivational enhancement therapy to reduce low session attendance and high dropout in group counseling for men involved in partner abuse. Rondeau et al. (2001) found that a therapeutic alliance between the client and therapist was the strongest variable in predicting if men would complete treatment. Taft et al. found that supportive and personalized communication from the therapist was especially effective in retention of minority group members. Williams and Becker (1994) suggest the need for partner abuse programs to improve their level of cultural competence and preparation for working with culturally diverse clients to reduce dropout rates among minority groups.

Additional work needs to be done addressing recidivism of partner abuse among those men who complete treatment (Holtzworth-Monroe, Beatty, & Anglin, 1995). There are problems with accurately measuring recidivism because of inconsistencies in reporting from legal systems, men and their partners minimizing, and group members not providing follow-up information (Edleson & Syers, 1990). Even though recidivism is probably underreported, Hamberger and Hastings (1990) found that between 25% and 50% of men who attended partner abuse treatment were reported in outcome studies to be violent during follow-up periods of 6 months and 2 years. Gondolf (2000) conducted a 30-month follow-up study of four treatment centers and found that the majority of recidivism happened in the first 6 months of treatment. Recidivism steadily decreased during the 30-month follow-up period. Gondolf also found that one fifth of the men repeatedly reassaulted their partners and accounted for most of the reported injuries. These findings suggest that treatment may have a cumulative impact and that the small minority of men who are the most violent may need alternative treatment.

To increase treatment completion and reduce recidivism, community court systems and treatment centers should hold men involved in partner abuse accountable through strong and consistent legal repercussions for failure to complete treatment and/or reoccurrence of abuse (Murphy, Musser, & Maton, 1998). Mandated long-term treatment in maintenance groups (similar to those used in substance abuse programs) would allow extended follow-up assessment and provide men with ongoing support (Myers & Salt, 2000). Communities need to carefully coordinate the activities of treatment programs, legal authorities, and police advocates (Murphy et al., 1998). It is also critically important for communities to focus on the safety of persons who were abused, providing them with counseling and support groups (Gerlock, 1997; Jacobson, 1994).

Finally, treatment and research could be advanced through improved assessment of the multifaceted causes of abusive behavior (Lawson et al., 2001). It is important to address those causes through treatment approaches that are most likely to meet the men's needs (Holtzworth-Munroe et al., 1995; Saunders, 1996). There is also a need for new and innovative treatment approaches.

Conclusions

Partner abuse appears to be a multifaceted problem, which calls for multifaceted approaches to treatment. Groups offer multiple benefits (including empirically identified therapeutic factors) that can address the multifaceted causes of abuse. There are no definitive findings on what kind of group is most effective (psychoeducational, counseling, therapy). Limited outcome research on group treatment has demonstrated positive results in reducing recidivism, but recidivism remains high. Limited research suggests that integrated approaches to treatment will be most effective (Lawson et al., 2001), and that matching the characteristics of men who have committed partner abuse to treatment approaches could increase treatment effectiveness (Saunders, 1996). There is also some evidence that recidivism rates could be further reduced by identifying the minority of men who are most violent and providing them with specialized services (including ongoing monitoring) (Gondolf, 2000).

References

Adams, D. (1994). *Historical timelines of institutional responses to battered women.* Cambridge, MA: Emerge.

Adams, D., Bancroft, L., German, T., & Sousa, C. (1992). *First stage groups for men who batter.* Cambridge, MA: Emerge.

Babcock, J. C., Waltz, J., Jacobson, N. S., & Gottman, J. M. (1993). Power and violence: The relation between communication patterns, power discrepancies, and domestic violence. *Journal of Consulting and Clinical Violence, 61,* 40-50.

Bandura, A. (1973). *Aggression: A social learning analysis.* Englewood Cliffs, NJ: Prentice Hall.

Berns, S. B., Jacobson, N. S., & Gottman, J. M. (1999). Demand-withdraw interaction in couples with a violent husband. *Journal of Consulting and Clinical Psychology, 67,* 666-674.

Bowlby, J. (1988). *A secure base: Parent-child attachment and healthy human development.* New York: Basic Books.

Browne, A. (1993). Violence against women by male partners: Prevalence, outcomes, and policy implications. *American Psychologist, 48,* 1077-1087.

Browne, K. O., Saunders, D. G., & Staecker, K. M. (1997). Process-psychodynamic groups for men who batter: A brief treatment model. *Families in Society, 78,* 265-271.

Bushman, B. J., & Cooper, H. M. (1990). Effects of alcohol on human aggression: An integrative research review. *Psychological Bulletin, 107,* 341-354.

Campbell, J. C., & Lewandowski, L. A. (1997). Mental and physical effects of intimate partner violence on women and children. *Psychiatric Clinics of North America, 20,* 353-374.

Carden, A. D. (1994). Wife abuse and the wife abuser: Review and recommendations. *Counseling Psychologist, 22,* 539-582.

Ceasar, P. L., & Hamberger, L. K. (1989). Introduction: Brief historical overview of interventions for wife abuse in the United States. In L. Ceasar & K. Hamberger (Eds.), *Treating men who batter.* New York: Springer.

Common Purpose. (1996). *Common Purpose training: Common Purpose training manual.* Boston: Author.

Copenhaver, M. M., Lash, S. J., & Eisler, R. M. (2000). Masculine gender-role stress, anger, and male intimate abusiveness: Implications for men's relationships. *Sex Roles: A Journal of Research, 42,* 405-414.

Davis, R., Taylor, B., & Maxwell, C. (1998). *Does batterer treatment reduce violence? A randomized experiment in Brooklyn.* Washington, DC: National Institute of Justice.

Dobash, R. E., & Dobash, R. (1979). *Violence against wives.* New York: Free Press.

Dutton, D. G. (1986). The outcome of court-mandated treatment for wife assault: A quasi-experimentawl evaluation. *Violence and Victims, 1,* 163-175.

Dutton, D. G. (1995). Trauma symptoms and PTSD-like profiles in perpetrators of intimate abuse. *Journal of Traumatic Stress, 8,* 299-316.

Dutton, D. G. (1998). *The abusive person.* New York: Guilford.

Dutton, D. G. (1999). Traumatic origins of intimate rage. *Aggression and Violent Behavior, 4,* 431-437.

Dutton, D. G., Bodnarchuk, M., Kropp, R., Hart, S. D, & Ogloff, J. R. P. (1997). Wife assault treatment and criminal recidivism: An 11-year follow-up. *International Journal of Offender Therapy and Comparative Criminology, 41,* 9-23.

Dutton, D. G., Ginkel, C. V., & Starzomski, A. (1995). The role of shame and guilt in the intergenerational transmission of abusiveness. *Violence and Victims, 10,* 121-131.

Edleson, J. L., & Grusznski, R. J. (1988). Treating men who batter: Four years of outcome data from the domestic abuse project. *Journal of Social Service Research, 12,* 3-22.

Edleson, J. L., & Syers, M. (1990). Relative effectiveness of group treatments for men who batter. *Social Work Research & Abstracts,* 10-17.

Ehrensaft, M. K., Langhinrichse-Rohling, J., Heyman, R. E., O'Leary, K. D., & Lawrance, E. (1999). Feeling controlled in marriage: A phenomenon specific to physically aggressive couples? *Journal of Family Psychology, 13,* 20-32.

Eisler, R. M., Franchina, J. J., Morre, M. T., Honeycutt, H. G., & Rhatigan, D. L. (2000). Masculine gender role stress and intimate abuse: Effects of gender relevance of conflict situations on men's attributions and affective responses. *Psychology of Men and Masculinity, 1,* 30-36.

Fagan, J. (1990). Intoxication and aggression. In M. Tonry & J. Q. Wilson (Eds.), *Drugs and crime* (pp. 241-320). Chicago: University of Chicago Press.

Farley, D., & Magill, J. (1988). An evaluation of a group program for men who batter. *Social Work With Groups, 11,* 53-65.

Faulkner, K., Stoltenberg, C. D., Cogen, R., Nolder, N., & Shooter, E. (1992). Cognitive-behavioral group treatment for male spouse abusers. *Journal of Family Violence, 7,* 37-55.

Feder, L., & Forde, D. (2000). *A test of the efficacy of court-mandated counseling for domestic violence offenders: The Broward experiment.* Washington, DC: National Institute of Justice.

Feldman, C. M., & Ridley, C. A. (1995). The etiology and treatment of domestic violence between adult partners. *Clinical Psychology, 2,* 317-348.

Finn, J. (1985). Men's domestic violence treatment groups: A statewide survey. *Social Work With Groups, 8,* 81-94.

Finn, J. (1987). Men's domestic violence treatment: The court referral component. *Journal of Interpersonal Violence, 2,* 154-165.

Ganley, A. L. (1989). Integrating feminist and social learning analyses of aggression. In P. L. Ceasar & L. K. Hamberger (Eds.), *Treating men who batter.* New York: Springer.

Geffner, R., Mantooth, C., Franks, D., & Rao, L. (1989). A psychoeducational, conjoint therapy approach to reducing family violence. In L. Ceasar & K. Hamberger (Eds.), *Treating men who batter* (pp. 103-133). New York: Springer.

Gerlock, A. A. (1997). New directions in the treatment of men who batter: A critical review of the literature. *Health Care for Women International, 18,* 481-493.

Goffman, J. M. (1980). *Batterers anonymous: Mutual support counseling for women-batterers.* Redlands, CA: Coalition for the Prevention of Abuse of Women and Children.

Goldstein, D., & Rosenbaum, A. (1985). An evaluation of the self-esteem of martially violent men. *Family Relations, 34,* 425-428.

Gondolf, E. W. (1987). Changing men who batter: A developmental model for integrated interventions. *Journal of Family Violence, 2,* 335-339.

Gondolf, E. W. (1990). An exploratory survey of court-mandated batterer programs. *Response to Victimization of Women and Children, 13,* 7-11.

Gondolf, E. W. (1991). A victim-based assessment of court-mandated counseling for batterers. *Criminal Justice Review, 16,* 214-226.

Gondolf, E. W. (1997). Batterer programs: What we know and need to know. *Journal of Interpersonal Violence, 12,* 83-98.

Gondolf, E. W. (2000). A 30-month follow-up of court-referred batterers in four cities. *International Journal of Offender Therapy and Comparative Criminology, 44,* 111-128.

Gondolf, E. W. (2001). Limitations of experimental evaluation of batterer programs. *Trauma, Violence, & Abuse, 2,* 79-88.

Gondolf, E. W., & Foster, R. A. (1991). Pre-program attrition in batterer programs. *Journal of Family Violence, 6,* 337-350.

Gorney, B. (1989). Domestic violence and chemical dependency: Dual problems, dual interventions. *Journal of Psychoactive Drugs, 21,* 229-238.

Gortner, E. T., Gollan, J. K., & Jacobson, N. S. (1997). Psychological aspects of perpetrators of domestic violence and their relationships with the victims. *Anger, Aggression, and Violence, 20,* 337-352.

Gottman, J. M., Jacobson, N. S., Rushe, R. H., Shortt, J. W., Babcock, J., La Taillade, J. J., et al. (1995). The relationship between heart rate reactivity, emotionally aggressive behavior, and generally violence in batterers. *Journal of Family Psychology, 9,* 227-248.

Guerney, B., Jr., Waldo, M., & Firestone, L. (1987). Wife-battering: A theoretical construct and case report. *American Journal of Family Therapy, 15,* 34-43.

Hage, S. M. (2000). The role of counseling psychology in preventing male violence against female intimates. *Counseling Psychologist, 28,* 797-828.

Hamberger, L. K., & Hastings, J. E. (1986). Personality correlates of men who abuse their partners: A cross validation study. *Journal of Family Violence, 1,* 323-341.

Hamberger, L. K., & Hastings, J. E. (1990). Recidivism following spouse abuse abatement counseling: Treatment program implications. *Violence and Victims, 5,* 157-170.

Hamberger, K. L., Lohr, M. J., & Gottlieb, M. (2000). Predictors of treatment dropout from a spouse abuse abatement program. *Behavior Modification, 24,* 528-552.

Hines, D. A., & Malley-Morrison, K. (2001). Psychological effects of partner abuse against men: A neglected area. *Psychology of Men and Masculinity, 2,* 75-85.

Holtzworth-Munroe, A. (1992). Social skill deficits in martially violent men: Interpreting the data using a social information processing model. *Clinical Psychology Review, 12,* 605-617.

Holtzworth-Munroe, A., Beatty, S. B., & Anglin, K. (1995). The assessment and treatment of marital violence: An introduction for the marital therapist. In N. S. Jacobson & A. S. Gurman (Eds.), *Clinical handbook of couple therapy* (pp. 317-339). New York: Guilford.

Holtzworth-Munroe, A., & Stuart, G. L. (1994). Typologies of male batterers: Three subtypes and the differences among them. *Psychological Bulletin, 116,* 476-497.

Jacobson, N. S. (1994). Rewards and dangers in researching domestic violence. *Family Process, Inc., 33,* 81-85.

Janiski, J. L., & Williams, L. M. (Eds.). (1998). *Partner violence: A comprehensive review of 20 years of research.* Thousand Oaks, CA: Sage.

Jennings, J. L. (1987). History and issues in the treatment of battering men: A case for unstructured group therapy. *Journal of Family Violence, 2,* 193-214.

Jennings, J. L., & Murphy, C. M. (2000). Male-male dimensions of male-female battering: A new look at domestic violence. *Psychology of Men and Masculinity, 1,* 21-29.

Kaufman-Kantor, G., Jasinski, J., & Aldorondo, E. (1994). Sociocultural status and incidence of marital violence in Hispanic families. *Violence and Victims, 9,* 207-222.

Lawson, M. D., Dawson, T. E., Kieffer, K. M., Perez, L. M., Burke, J., & Kier, F. J. (2001). An integrated feminist/cognitive-behavioral and psychodynamic group: Treatment model for men who abuse their partners. *Journal of Men & Masculinity, 2,* 88-99.

Lee, M., Greene, G., Uken, A., Rheinscheld, L., & Sebold, J. (1997) *Solution-focused brief treatment: A viable modality for treating domestic violence offenders.* Paper presented at the 5th International Family Violence Research Conference, Durham, NH.

Lore, R. K., & Shultz, L. A. (1993). Control of human aggression. *American Psychologist, 48,* 16-25.

Margolin, G. (1998). Effects of domestic violence on children. In P. Trickett & C. Schellenback (Eds.), *Violence against children in the family and the community* (pp. 57-101). Washington, DC: American Psychological Association.

Miller, A. J., Bobner, R. F., & Zarski, J. J. (2000). Sexual identity development: A base for work with same-sex couple partner abuse. *Contemporary Family Therapy: An International Journal, 22,* 189-200.

Moffit, T. E., Caspi, A., Krueger, R. F., Magdol, L., Margolin, G., Silva, P. A., et al. (1997). Do partners agree about abuse in their relationship? A psychometric evaluation of interpartner agreement. *Psychological Assessment, 9,* 47-56.

Murphy, C. M., Musser, P. H., & Maton, K. I. (1998). Coordinated community interventions for domestic abusers: Intervention system involvement and criminal recidivism. *Journal of Family Violence, 13,* 263-284.

Murray, C. M., & Baxter, V. A. (1997). Motivating batterers to change in the treatment context. *Journal of Interpersonal Violence, 12,* 607-613.

Myers, P. L., & Salt, N. R. (2000). *Becoming an addictions counselor.* Sudbury, MA: Jones & Bartlett.

Nosko, A., & Wallace, R. (1997). Female/male co-leadership in groups. *Social Works With Groups, 20,* 3-16.

O'Hanlon, W., & Weiner-Davis, M. (1989). *In search of solutions.* New York: Norton.

O'Neil, J. M., Good, G. E., & Holmes, S. (1995). Fifteen years of theory and research on men's gender role conflict. In R. Levant & W. Pollacks (Eds.), *The new psychology of men* (pp. 143-206). New York: Basic Books.

O'Neil, J. M., & Harway, M. (1997). A multivariate model explaining men's violence toward women. *Violence Against Women, 3,* 182-203.

Pan, H., Neidig, P., & O'Leary, D. (1994). Predicting mild and severe husband to wife physical aggression. *Journal of Consulting Clinical Psychology, 62,* 875-981.

Pence, E., & Paymer, M. (1993). *Educational groups for men who batter: The Duluth Model.* New York: Springer.

Petrik, N. D., Olson Petrik, R. E., & Subotnik, L. S. (1994). Powerlessness and the need to control: The male abuser's dilemma. *Journal of Interpersonal Violence, 9,* 278-285.

Poirier, L. (1997). The importance of screening for domestic violence abuse in all women. *Nurse Practitioner, 22,* 105-115.

Rondeau, G., Brodeur, N., Brochu, S., & Lemire, G. (2001). Dropout and completion of treatment among spouse abusers. *Violence and Victims, 16,* 127-143.

Rosenfeld, B. (1992). Court-ordered treatment of spouse abuse. *Clinical Psychology Review, 12,* 205-226.

Saunders, D. G. (1996). Feminist-cognitive-behavioral and process-psychodynamic treatments for men who batter: Interaction of abuser traits and treatment models. *Violence and Victims, 11,* 393-414.

Saunders, D. G. (2000). Feminist, cognitive and behavioral group interventions, for men who batter: An overview of rationale and method. In D. B. Wexler (Ed.), *Domestic violence 2000: An integrated skills program for men* (pp. 21-31). New York: Norton.

Saunders, D. G., & Hanusa, D. (1986). Cognitive-behavioral treatment of men who batter: The short-term effects of group therapy. *Journal of Family Violence, 1,* 357-372.

Schwartz, J. P., Merta, R., Waldo, M., & Bloom-Langell, J. (1998). *Measuring spouse abuse group outcomes using the gender role conflict scale.* Presentation in the *Gender-role conflict research: Expanding empirical research in men's studies* symposium at the American Psychological Association, San Francisco, CA.

Schwartz, J. P., & Waldo, M. (1999). Therapeutic factors in Duluth Model spouse abuser group treatment. *Journal for Specialists in Group Work, 24,* 197-207.

Sheppard, M. (1992). Predicting batterer recidivism five years after community intervention. *Journal of Family Violence, 7,* 167-178.

Sonkin, D. J., & Durphy, M. (1985). *Learning to live without violence* (2nd ed.). San Francisco: Volcano Press.

Stark, E., & Flitcraft, A. (1996). *Women at risk: Domestic violence and women's health.* Thousand Oaks, CA: Sage.

Stets, J. E., & Straus, M. A. (1990). Gender differences in reporting of marital violence and its medical and psychological consequences. In M. A. Straus & R. J. Gelles (Eds.), *Physical violence in American families: Risk factors and adaptations to violence in 8,145 families* (pp. 151-165). New Brunswick, NJ: Transaction.

Stith, S. M., & Farley, S. C. (1993). A predictive model of male spousal violence. *Journal of Family Violence, 8,* 183-201.

Stonsy, S. (1995). *Treating attachment abuse.* New York: Springer.

Stonsy, S. (1997). Group work with populations at risk. In G. L. Greif & P. H. Ephross (Eds.), *Violence: Victims and perpetrators.* New York: Oxford University Press.

Straus, M. A. (1999). The controversy over domestic violence by women. In X. B. Arriaga & S. Oskamp (Eds.), *Violence in intimate relationships* (pp. 17-44). Thousand Oaks, CA: Sage.

Straus, M. A., & Gelles, R. J. (1990). *Physical violence in American families: Risk factors and adaptations to violence in 8,145 families.* New Brunswick, NJ: Transaction.

Taft, C. T., Murphy, C. M., Elliott, J. D., & Morrel, T. M. (2001). Attendance-enhancing procedures in group counseling for domestic abusers. *Journal of Counseling Psychology, 48,* 51-60.

Tolman, R. M., & Bennett, L. W. (1990). A review of quantitative research on men who batter. *Journal of Interpersonal Violence, 5,* 87-118.

Tolman, R. M., & Bhosley, G. (1990). A comparison of two types of pregroup preparation for men who batter. *Journal of Social Service Research, 13,* 33-44.

Waldo, M. (1985). A curative factor framework for conceptualizing group counseling. *Journal of Counseling and Development, 64,* 52-58.

Waldo, M. (1986). Group counseling for military personnel who battered their wives. *Journal for Specialists in Group Work, 11,* 132-138.

Waldo, M. (1987). Also victims: Understanding and treating men arrested for spouse abuse. *Journal of Counseling and Development, 64,* 52-58.

Waldo, M. (1988). Counseling groups for wife abusers. *Journal of Mental Health Counseling, 10,* 37-45.

Waldo, M., & Bauman, S., (1998). Regrouping the categories of group work: A goals and process (GAP) matrix. *Journal for Specialists in Group Work, 23,* 164-176.

Walker, L. E. (1984). *Abused women and survivor therapy.* Washington, DC: American Psychological Association.

Wallace, B., & Nosko, A. (1993). Working with shame in the group treatment of male batterers. *International Journal of Group Therapy, 43,* 45-61.

Waltz, J., Babcock, J. C., Jacobson, N. S., & Gottman, J. M. (2000). Testing a typology of batterers. *Journal of Consulting and Clinical Psychology, 68,* 658-669.

Wexler, D. B. (1999). The broken mirror: A self psychological treatment perspective for relationship violence. *Journal of Psychotherapy Practice and Research, 8,* 129-141.

Wexler, D. B. (2000). *Domestic violence 2000: An integrated skills program for men.* New York: Norton.

Williams, O. J., & Becker, R. L. (1994). Domestic partner abuse treatment programs and cultural competence: The results of a national survey. *Violence and Victims, 9,* 287-296.

Yalom, I. D. (1995). *The theory and practice of group psychotherapy* (4th ed.). New York: Basic Books.

42

ADVENTURE THERAPY WITH GROUPS

H. L. "LEE" GILLIS

Georgia College & State University

MICHAEL A. GASS

University of New Hampshire

Slavson and Moreno, pioneers of group psychotherapy, used activities as a primary method of change in their group work (Scheidlinger, 1995). Gillis and Bonney (1989) noted that if adventure-based activities were known during Moreno's heyday, he would probably be an adventure therapist as well as a psychodramatist. While the activity base for group work was generally abandoned for many years for the extensive use of "talk therapies," it has been "rediscovered" by art, music, wilderness, recreation, and other experientially based group therapies. The purpose of this chapter is to introduce the concepts of adventure therapy and provide readers with a rationale for the use of adventure experiences in group therapy.

Gillis and Thomsen (1996) presented a global view of adventure therapy, placing it within the larger field of experiential therapies. In this view, adventure therapy is an active and experiential approach to group psychotherapy, utilizing an activity base (e.g., cooperative group games, ropes courses, outdoor pursuits, or wilderness expeditions), and employing real

and/or perceived risk (physical and psychological) as clinically significant agents to bring about desired change. Clients make meaning through insights that are expressed verbally, nonverbally, or unconsciously and lead to behavioral change. This is done from both verbal and nonverbal introductions prior to the experience as well as discussions following the experience (e.g., debriefings).

Advanced techniques of adventure therapists include the use of metaphor, where the reality of the adventure experience is linked with the clients' issues. The use of metaphor is rooted in the psychotherapy work of Milton Erickson (Haley, 1973). Bacon (1983) and Gass (1993) advanced the use of metaphors in the presentation of therapeutic adventure experiences. Most of the therapeutic interventions used by adventure therapists are grounded not only in Erickson's work but also in the experiential approaches of Moreno (Blatner & Blatner, 1988), Perls (1969), Satir (1972), and Whitaker (Whitaker & Keith, 1981). Thus, many of the origins of adventure therapy can be traced to the stress-challenge experiences associated with taking groups into wilderness environments for recreational purposes (Bacon & Kimball, 1989) and the activities associated with team building through the use of challenge course experiences (Rohnke, 1989; Schoel, Prouty, & Radcliffe, 1988).

The object of this chapter is to (a) present a brief history of adventure therapy, (b) provide examples of adventure activities used in group work, (c) outline the rationale behind adventure therapy processes, (d) present a case study depicting adventure therapy assessment techniques and interventions, (e) summarize the research supporting adventure therapy, and (f) discuss ethical guidelines and professional issues for those who use adventure therapy with groups.

BRIEF HISTORY OF AN ADVENTURE APPROACH TO GROUP WORK

Gillis and Ringer (1999) noted that adventure therapy has much of its documented history in the philosophies of experiential learning inherent in Outward Bound, a wilderness-based program teaching self-discipline and teamwork through adventure experiences (Bacon, 1983). Kurt Hahn, who helped shape the foundations of the Outward Bound movement, may be considered one of the first adventure therapists, due to his work with young soldiers in the 1940s and his attempts to develop within them a "will to live" through the use of challenging adventure experiences (Thomas, 1980). Kelly and Baer (1968) demonstrated that a 21-day standard Outward Bound course for groups of adjudicated youth was more effective in reducing recidivism and less costly than traditional treatment for adolescents in correctional programs. This finding alone led many states to invest in this therapeutic way of working with groups of youth in wilderness environments.

Davis-Berman and Berman (1994) documented the therapeutic use of the outdoors as early as the 1900s, when groups of hospitalized tuberculosis patients were taken out of doors to camp in tents on the hospital grounds as a way to quarantine them. These reports of dramatic physical and attitudinal improvements from the patients regarding the outdoor therapeutic experiences were like the tenting of the tuberculosis patients. Behavioral change was seen from the impact of the environment where the groups were conducted.

The field of therapeutic uses of adventure experiences, however, suffers from semantic confusion (Roland, Keene, Dubois, & Lentini, 1988). The multiplicity of terms used to define adventure therapy can include adventure therapy (Gass, 1993), adventure-based counseling (Maizell, 1988; Schoel et al., 1988), experiential-challenge (Roland, Summers, Freidman, Barton, & McCarthy, 1987), outdoor-adventure pursuits (Ewert, 1989), therapeutic adventure programs (Wichmann, 1991), therapeutic camping (Rice, 1988; Walton, 1985), and wilderness therapy (e.g., Bacon & Kimball, 1989; Davis-Berman & Berman, 1994; Levitt, 1982; Russell, 2001). For simplicity, we use the term *adventure therapy*.

ADVENTURE THERAPY SETTINGS

There are three primary locations in which adventure therapy operates: (1) on challenge/ ropes courses and through the initiative experiences associated with adventure therapy approaches, (2) in wilderness settings (e.g., Outward Bound, 20- to 60-day wilderness travel programs), and (3) through residential camping (e.g., stationary, primitive living programs) (Crisp, 1998; Gass, 1993). These adventure therapy group experiences are primarily characterized by the length of time involved and the type of programming used. In this chapter, we focus on the use of adventure therapy in traditional group work. However, readers should be aware that the other two approaches have demonstrated interesting and often effective psychotherapeutic approaches, particularly with youth at risk (e.g., Hattie, Marsh, Neill, & Richards, 1997).

Based on a survey of 47 programs, Gillis and colleagues (1991) identified adventure therapy programming in terms of the overall goals of programs and the characteristics of participants. Therapeutic programs were described as focusing primarily on educational or enrichment goals (i.e., where change was attained through a focus on generic issues of the target group) or on adjunctive parts of larger treatment systems (i.e., where change was achieved through adventure experiences in combination with other therapies), or were involved in primary therapy (i.e., where change was obtained solely through adventure experiences in lieu of other psychotherapies). Programs with enrichment goals were typically offered to a wider range of groups with (relatively) less specificity in treatment objectives, while primary therapy programs generally involved smaller, more dysfunctional groups with greater amounts of time spent in assessment and design of interventions.

An Adventure Experience

One adventure therapy experience that served as adjunctive therapy was Walk the Talk. It was developed for a coed relapse prevention group of adult substance abusers in the recovery process. The group was a traditional group for relapse prevention, and this activity was added during the last 45 minutes of a one time per week, 3-hour relapse group session with approximately 15 people. The title of the activity was selected to punctuate the experience's connection to what group members face once they leave the therapy room. Naming activities for clients to fit the objective of the experience is common practice for isomorphically framed adventure therapy experiences (i.e., experiences with parallel processes with treatment issues).

The experience presented emphasized the following treatment goals: (a) maintaining a drug-free lifestyle, (b) identifying, staying connected to, and having a strong focus on the elements maintaining abstinence, and (c) strengthening clients' resistance to the social pressures that tempt them to begin using drugs again.

The adventure experience used for the treatment objectives was the Stepping Stones activity (Gillis & Simpson, 1994; Rohnke & Butler, 1995). The equipment included (a) two ropes to mark the "beginning" and "finish" or "end" lines, (b) a flat, unobstructed distance of 60 to 100 feet, and (c) one prop per person on which words could be written. Examples of props could be rug pads, rubber or plastic circles, or paper plates about the same size as a client's foot. The objective is to get from one end line to the other without touching the ground in between the beginning and end lines. Group members are positioned behind the beginning line and provided with approximately 25 minutes

to get to the finish line. Anyone touching the ground between the lines was required to return back to the beginning. If at any time during the experience anyone lost physical contact with any prop, the group lost the use of that prop. For physical safety considerations, the group was told not to run, jump, or throw props. Participants could not climb on one another's backs to make it across to the finish line.

The presentation of the activity to the group was stated in a circle where everyone could see one another and the group leader. The leader said:

> It's been good to be together for the last couple of hours and share your triumphs as well as your concerns about your recovery process. And even though we've addressed some hard topics, it actually is almost too comfortable here in this room! I say this because while it's tough looking at the things we've addressed today, it is almost certainly going to be tougher for all of you when you step through the door of this room at the end of our group meeting. You know it is not a matter of **if** you will be tempted to use drugs again, but **when** you will face this decision. And this decision may not come from strangers, but a lot of times from people you know best and who may be close to you.
>
> One of the great things we have gone over in treatment were the qualities, commitments, and elements you feel will help you stay drug-free. And in our discussions, it seems the more committed and connected you stay to these elements or qualities, the more likely you are to make it back into this room next week drug-free.
>
> Here is what the final activity of our time here today is about: (1) how to make it back to this meeting next week drug-free, (2) how to stay connected to those things helping you maintain your abstinence, and (3) how to strengthen your resistance to the temptations that try to get you to use drugs again.
>
> Before we begin, I want you each to take a plate (prop) and write on the back of it one to three words describing a quality or element you think will help you stay drug-free over the next week if you stay connected to and focused on it. After you've done this, let's go around the circle and have each person share what they've written and briefly describe the reason why they feel staying

connected to and focused on this quality is so important.

(After everyone has shared their quality) Okay, please join me over here on this flat stretch of ground behind this line. Behind this line represents us right now in this room: confronting in some ways, but in others pretty safe and comfortable. The truth is we can't stay in this room forever! In 45 minutes or so we are all going to walk out that door and be in places over the next week that are going to challenge our abilities to stay drug-free. There is probably no better time than now to start practicing for those challenges. After explaining the rules of the activity, I am going to give you 5-7 minutes to plan and talk as a group on how you might want to consider going about this process.

Here's the deal. You need to get from this beginning line over across the line 90 feet away, just like you need to get from where you are today back to this room next week. As you go from line to line, you cannot touch the ground. If you do, you need to return to the beginning of this line. The only way you can cross from "today" to "next week" is by using your qualities (i.e., plates) as protection to step on and get across to the other line. As long as your foot remains on your plate and no other part of your body touches the ground (e.g., arm), you're fine.

You also must stay in constant contact with your resources. If at any time you lose connection with your plate, even for a split second, I (representing addiction) will get to take your resource from you. I may even tempt or trick you into giving it to me, so just as you need to be on a constant vigil throughout this coming week, you also need to have that level of attention to these qualities during the activity.

As a group, you have 25 minutes to get over the finish line. If anyone touches the ground between the ropes, they must return back to the beginning. At any time or instant a person loses physical contact with any resource, the group loses that prop to me. If there are no questions, your 5 minutes of planning begins. Good luck.

The group began the experience. Some members were diligent in literally hanging on to the paper plates with the recovery elements written on them. They also were incredibly attentive when placing their plates on the

ground to step on them. While slow but sure, individuals in this subgroup advanced slowly toward the end line with a few minor slip-ups along the way. Others were less diligent in paying attention to their task, and their progress was hampered by losing plates when they did not maintain physical contact and they became distracted by other group members' needs. Several members lost so many plates it became impossible for them to complete the task.

With this group, debriefing this experience focuses on (a) the therapeutic objectives of the activity (i.e., maintaining a drug-free lifestyle, (b) staying connected to abstinent behaviors, and (c) strengthening clients' resistance—and how they relate to the clients' coming week. Key to this process is punctuating the isomorphic (i.e., parallel) connections between the insights and learnings during the activity to the parallels existing within clients' lives. One reality is the literal "walking of their talk" of staying drug-free by being in contact with the very concepts they have identified as key elements of their sobriety. In a different yet important and similar reality, "walking of their talk" means staying drug-free by implementing these concepts in their lives for the coming week. Hence, successful resolution of adventure therapy experiences mirrors and provides guidance and meaning to a successful resolution of the therapeutic issues. This concept is critical to all successful adventure therapy frameworks.

A Rationale Behind Adventure Therapy

Based on over 30 years of evolving practices and research with adventure therapy, the following six points provide a generally accepted rationale to support the use of adventure therapy in groups:

1. *Multiple and corroborating representations of reality.* Using adventure experiences with clients often turns passive therapeutic analysis and interaction into active and multidimensional experiences. Didactic and verbal processes are augmented in adventure-based groups by concrete physical actions and experiences. Clients' behaviors are viewed from another perspective; they are asked to "walk" rather than merely "talk" their behaviors.

Therapeutic interaction becomes observed and holistic, involving physical and affective as well as cognitive interaction for the purposes of examining client patterns and beliefs.

As seen in the previous therapeutic experience, clients are literally on one level and figuratively on another level walking the talk of their therapeutic issue and potential resolutions to issue. As illustrated above, insight is received from personal actions, language, thoughts and belief systems, and feelings and perceptions.

2. *Contrasting experiences.* The unfamiliar adventure experience created provides a medium that is "contrasting" to a group member's current reality state. Contrast in adventure experiences is utilized by clients to see elements of their lives that tend to be overlooked and gain new perspectives. Group members' entry into a contrasting experience is often the first step toward reorganizing the meaning and direction of their life (Priest & Gass, 1997b; Walsh & Golins, 1976). It is important to remember that what is unfamiliar for one person may not be for another. Therapists using adventure experiences work to ensure that the quality of unfamiliarity is met to achieve the goals of this concept.

Obviously, most people don't go around stepping on plates or rug pads as part of their everyday life, let alone as a step in their recovery process. This "unfamiliar difference" provides the engaging contrast described earlier while still maintaining structural similarity for treatment effectiveness.

3. *Production of "eustress" as a motivational agent for change.* When properly implemented, adventure experiences introduce eustress, or the healthy use of stress, into the group member's system in a manageable yet challenging manner. This type of stress places individuals into situations where the use of certain positive problem-solving abilities (e.g., trust, cooperation, clear and effective communication) is necessary to reach a desired state of equilibrium. The process of striving to attain this state of equilibrium is sometimes referred to as "adaptive dissonance" (e.g., Priest & Gass, 1997b; Walsh & Golins, 1976), where group members must change their behaviors to achieve desired states. The adaptive processes

used to create change are often healthy and functional structural patterns for rectifying group members' dysfunctional behaviors. These patterns and processes (as seen in the case study to follow) often provide the processes and means for clients to achieve therapeutic objectives.

Combined with the activity's contrast is the appropriate use of physical and emotional eustress. This quality differentiates this therapeutic process from other experiential therapies, often serving as a catalyst in the client change process.

4. *Conflict resolution patterns to structurally implement change.* Adventure experiences are usually designed with internal mechanisms of resolvable conflict. These mechanisms use experiences that are organized, incremental, concrete, manageable, consequential, and holistic (Priest & Gass, 1997a; Walsh & Golins, 1976). Adventure experiences are organized to meet the needs of the group and are sequenced progressively (e.g., conducted incrementally in terms of complexity and consequence). Groups begin with easier tasks and gather senses of competency and mastery from accomplishing these tasks, and then attempt more difficult tasks with an established base of increased skills and confidence. Adventure experiences are concrete and easy to define in terms of content (e.g., tasks are easily recognizable and typically visually stimulating; tasks generally possess a definite beginning and end). While initially appearing insurmountable to many clients, adventure experiences can be managed or accomplished by groups with the resources they possess. Initially, resources and the method in which the resources need to be coordinated may be unclear to some groups, but their abilities to accomplish the task are based on their abilities to manage these resources with personal skills. Adventure experiences are consequential, and the results, positive or negative, generally have an immediate, nonarbitrary, and direct effect on clients. Adventure experiences address a variety of learning domains, including cognitive, social, emotional, and psychomotor learning. Combinations of these learning domains provide a holistic perspective on how to help clients change.

5. *Solution-oriented structures.* Entering therapy can be extremely threatening, heightening client defense mechanisms and resistance to change. Most adventure experiences possess the natural occurrence of solutions in their structure. With unfamiliar adventure experiences, group members are presented with opportunities to focus on their abilities rather than on their dysfunctions. This type of orientation diminishes initial defenses and leads to healthy change when combined with the successful completion of progressively difficult and rewarding tasks. Rather than being resistant in therapy, group members are challenged to stretch perceived limitations and discover untapped resources and strengths. Group member efforts are also framed by the therapist to center on the potential to achieve self-empowerment by establishing and maintaining functional change.

Walk the Talk engaged clients in their search for elements leading them to the successful resolution of issues concerning the maintenance of their sobriety. This search possessed elements related to the solution to this issue, not reasons why sobriety could not be achieved or maintained. Problems are not "ignored" in such a process, but handled in a way that focuses clients on their abilities to place themselves in situations where the problems don't exist or are not as strong in certain circumstances. Such a process leads to the engagement of resources and strengths, which often diminishes the problem focus even further.

6. *Changes in therapist's role.* Adventure therapy experiences change the role of therapists from passive and stationary to more active and mobile. Therapists are encouraged to actively design and frame adventure experiences around critical issues for group members, focusing on the development of specific treatment outcomes. When utilizing adventure experiences with groups, adventure-based therapists are removed from serving as the central vehicle of functional change. The "experience" takes on the central medium for orchestrating change, freeing therapists to take on a more "mobile" role (e.g., for supporting, joining, confronting) in the coconstruction of change processes with the group. Combined with the informal setting of adventure experiences, the dynamics of this approach removes many of the barriers limiting interaction. While still maintaining clear and appropriate boundaries, adventure therapists often become more approachable and achieve greater interaction with group members when compared to traditional group therapists.

Like other appropriate adventure therapy experiences, the Walk the Talk activity is so engaging that it often permits the therapists to step aside and observe behavior more closely, align themselves with certain belief systems at different times during the experience, and empower clients to take on more of a self-education process in the experience. Rather than the direct medium for change, this initiative takes this role and permits the therapist to achieve a more mobile, neutral, and curious state in the process.

All six of the components for how adventure therapy works exist in the Walk the Talk experience. The experience was (1) organized around treatment objectives, (2) sequenced or incremental in reference to the path clients would need to go through to make it back to the next meeting with their sobriety in place, (3) concrete in terms of substance abuse issues clients might face, (4) manageable when appropriate coping strategies were utilized, (5) consequential in relation to supporting functional strategies and providing valid feedback for negative decisions, and (6) holistic in terms of cognitive, social/emotional, and psychomotor learning. Each of these qualities contributed to the ability of the adventure therapy experience to assist the client achieve a more functional change process. These strategies can also be seen in the following example of a counseling group conducted in a traditional group room at a university counseling center that involved four single parents and their four adolescent sons

Another Example of Adventure Therapy Interventions

A group of single mothers with adolescent sons had responded to an announcement for an eight-session enrichment group focused on parenting. The group was conducted in a university counseling center and had progressed into the third session, using adventure experiences as a group warm-up as a technique to focus the group on parenting issues with their sons. To this point, the group sessions had centered on various aspects of living together more peacefully. In order to structurally represent the struggle many of these parents had described in previous sessions, an experience was introduced in this session requiring each parent-adolescent pair to face one another about 10 feet apart. A 15-foot piece of sturdy rope was placed between them, with each person holding onto the remaining 2 feet of rope at their end. The experience, titled Gotcha, was introduced, with the objective being to cause one's partner to fall off balance by manipulating the rope. After numerous times of literally being jerked around by her son, one mother dropped the rope in frustration, exclaiming *"This is exactly what goes on in my house every afternoon after school."* The son smiled sheepishly as if he had been "caught" in his after-school ritual of arguing with his mother, but he did not say a word.

Group therapists know that this mother and her son do not literally get out a piece of sturdy rope and jerk each other around every afternoon. However, for the mother, at some level of insight and knowledge, the feeling attached to the experience with the rope (figuratively) felt like what she experienced each day after school.

The experience led to some coaching by the group leader regarding the mother's strategy with the rope. She had been holding the rope tight in an attempt to resist her son and occasionally jerking the rope to try and overpower him. This strategy was not working, and she was experiencing the consequences of this interaction. With strategic intervention and her own insight, she found that when she gave her son some slack when he jerked, he literally was caught off balance. The mother's new actions with the rope led to a discussion among the other mothers as to how they could use different strategies to avoid after-school power struggles.

The goals for this therapeutic session were to redirect the interaction between parents and their adolescent sons by (a) providing an experience structurally paralleling the reality of the mother-son interaction, (b) offering new perspectives and potential solutions when new behaviors were tried, (c) creating a safe atmosphere for change offering similarities to as well

as contrast with the "normal" home environment while acknowledging and empathizing with the mother's and son's thoughts and feelings, (d) changing the parent-son interaction to be more functional and less dependent on the adolescents' abilities to win the power struggles, and (e) moving out of a traditional group therapist's role and being seen as more active and available by the parents and sons during the cocreation of the adventure experience.

Assessment Capabilities and Treatment Planning

One critical piece of utilizing adventure experiences in therapy room situations is to determine when one actually implements adventure experiences in a group session. The CHANGES model (Gass & Gillis, 1995b) is organized into interactive steps designed to acquire information for developing functional client change. The seven steps make up the acronym CHANGES: Context, Hypotheses, Action, Novelty, Generating, Evaluation, and Solutions.

1. *Context.* In preparing for the group experience, the therapist gathers all the information he or she can about the clients. Why has the client group entered into this experience? How long will they be involved? What are their stated goals as a group and as individuals?

2. *Hypotheses.* After gathering this assessment information, the adventure therapist establishes hypotheses about what behavior(s) might be expected from the group. These hypotheses are "tested" through engagement in carefully designed adventure experiences.

3. *Action.* Much of the material used for constructing change is obtained from the actions of group members as they involve themselves in adventure experiences. Kimball (1983) and Creal and Florio (1986) relate this process to the psychological concept of "projection." Based on this premise, group members project a clear representation of their behavior patterns, personalities, structure, and interpretation onto the adventure activities because they are usually unfamiliar with what is being asked of them in the experience.

4. *Novelty.* As noted above, actions that are unfamiliar or new to the group cause group members to struggle with the spontaneity of an adventure experience. As a result, group members do not always know how they are expected to act, and this prevents them from hiding behind a false or "social" self, leading them to show their true behaviors, and provides additional information to the group therapist.

5. *Generating.* By careful observation of the group member's responses to a multitude of "actions," the skilled adventure therapist identifies lifelong behavior patterns, dysfunctional ways of coping with stress, intellectual processes, conflicts, needs, and emotional responsiveness. When properly observed, recorded, and articulated, these data can be the basis for therapeutic goals (Kimball, 1983).

6. *Evaluation.* When information has been generated from observations of the group's behaviors, it can be compared with working hypotheses once again. Do group actions fit the working hypotheses? Are these hypotheses supported or refuted? What new knowledge now exists to revisit action, novelty, and generating in the next experience?

7. *Solutions.* Finally, and most important, when the evaluation provides a clear picture of the group's issues, it leads toward solutions of those issues. Integrating and interpreting information gathered in previous steps helps in making decisions about how to construct potential solutions to the groups' concerns.

The CHANGES model provides one useful way to acquire and organize information to systemically structure a change experience. One powerful technique for accessing the strength of adventure experiences is when group members are utilizing metacommunication patterns in their dialogue.

METACOMMUNICATION IN ADVENTURE-BASED GROUPS

The concept of metacommunication, eloquently outlined by such therapeutic pioneers as Bateson (1972), de Shazer (1982), Waltzlawick, Beavin, and Jackson (1967), and Waltzlawick, Weakland, and Fisch (1974), provides a clear understanding of how adventure experiences can heighten therapeutic effectiveness. In the group members' reality, there really are two meanings to words used in the adventure experience: one for the reality of the adventure experience and one for the group members' real-world reality. The joining of these two realities can be heard in their words. Such metacommunication provides a valuable link for group members reaching deep and valuable meaning in adventure experiences (e.g., Gass & Gillis, 1998; Gillis & Gass, 1993).

The case example presented represents how many who use adventure activities in group work fall into the "right" activity. However, it can serve as an example of how metacommunication works in adventure-based groups. When the mother experienced being jerked around by her son and expressed such to the group, she was joining two realities: the actual experience of the activity and the experience she had at home almost every day after school.

In the use of metacommunication to create an adventure experience, the adventure therapist, in listening to the mother in the example above describe her situation at home during the context phase of the CHANGES model, may have heard her say, "I feel like my son jerks me around all the time." Or she might comment to the group, "I feel like I am at the end of my rope." The skilled adventure therapist, listening to the mother's metacommunication, would then *hypothesize* about an *activity* that involved getting jerked around. Would this activity be *novel* enough to *generate* information in order to *evaluate* the mother-son relationship and begin to cocreate some *solutions* in their treatment plan? Once the mother was able to connect with the activity, the therapist could begin to offer metacommunication language, such as coaching her to give her son some slack (in order for him to lose his control of the after-school situation).

The key to a solution for the mother-son relationship was to have an activity that matched or was isomorphic with their home experience. In addition, the activity needed to offer strategies whereby the mother could engage in new behaviors (giving slack) more functional for her relationship with her son and offering a different outcome. This outcome of the activity (causing the other to fall off balance) needed to be a natural consequence of the adventure experience to have the greatest chance of leading to a more lasting behavioral change. The son would need to experience something familiar (jerking his mother around) and new (falling off balance) in order for a discussion to take place that could lead to an awareness that "things would be different after school."

Listening to common metacommunication from clients such as "get over," "give up," "stepped on," and "get around" helps create hypotheses for the group therapist about activities that will be most useful in connecting with group members' issues. Note that literal experiences where clients are put in dangerous or unethical situations are unnecessarily risky and unprofessional. There are numerous books offering adventure activities for recreational purposes (Rohnke, 1989; Rohnke & Butler, 1995) that have been adapted for therapeutic use due to the inherent structures of the activities that connect to the language of the group members. The language used by group members can help in the cocreation of powerful adventure experiences that can aid clients to walk their talk.

Research Supporting Adventure Therapy

The use of outdoor adventure experiences for therapeutic and counseling groups is documented with numerous clinical populations, such as parents and adolescents (Gillis & Gass, 1993), couples (Gillis & Lindsay, 1991), those treated for substance abuse (Gass & McPhee, 1990; Gillis & Simpson, 1994), adjudicated youth (Bacon & Kimball, 1989; Kelly & Baer, 1968; Kimball, 1983), and clients served in private practices (Berman & Davis-Berman, 1989) and psychiatric hospitals (Schoel et al., 1988, Stich & Senior, 1984; Stich & Sussman, 1981.

Cason and Gillis (1993), Ewert (1989), Gillis, (1992), and Gillis and Thomsen (1996) have provided reviews of research into adventure programming that include references to therapeutic populations. Many of these reviews indicate that there is a lack of research in the therapeutic use

of adventure. They are also critical of the experimental methodology used. Most studies lacked control groups, and few had any follow-up data. These earlier reviews agree with the findings of Hattie, Marsh, Neill, and Richards (1997) that globally measured self-esteem has been found to increase following participation in adventure-based groups, although the transfer of these changes to other settings has not been empirically validated. Note this study was based on 1,728 effect sizes from 96 different studies of adventure programs. The Hattie et al. (1997) meta-analysis of adventure education programs found the strongest effect sizes for constructs related to self-control: independence (0.47), confidence (0.33), self-efficacy (0.31), and self-understanding (0.34). Interestingly enough, these effects were found to increase when individual follow-up assessments were conducted. The authors note that "adventure programs appear to be most effective at providing participants with a sense of self-regulation" (p. 70). Such findings speak to the power of this group approach—even as a recreational and educational vehicle—in enhancing individual group members' ability for self-control in adventure therapy experiences.

Newes's (2001) recent critique of the literature specific to adventure therapy highlights the difficulty in empirically supporting adventure therapy. As Gillis and Thomsen (1996) noted, there is still no one clearly defined and researched method of conducting therapy with adventure activities; thus, the group therapist is left with little guidance for what type of adventure activity or setting is most effective with which client group. The researched programs offer confusing findings, since they utilize different adventure activities (wilderness expeditions versus ropes courses) and methods (educational, adjunctive, and primary), making comparisons among programs difficult. More troublesome is that the majority of research studies do not specify methodology (what they actually did that was considered therapeutic), so that the reader can determine if one program's findings can be compared with another's. There is no way to measure integrity of adventure therapy at this point in time. Newes (2001) provides some direction for researchers into adventure therapy, such as the use of dismantling and additive designs instead of comparative designs. Such direction is especially helpful to graduate students seeking different ways to improve and expand the use of adventure as a recognized treatment approach.

In addition to strengthening research methodologies, we support a focus on significant change events in adventure therapy. A database for collecting case studies and results of therapeutic interventions across different adventure therapy groups remains a dream. Adventure therapists tend to be doers and not writers. There are few practitioners evaluating programs in order to inform practice through research that is both clinically relevant and statistically accurate. Graduate students are encouraged to put their energies into this promising field of group work.

ETHICS IN USING ACTIVITIES IN GROUPS

Group workers are ethically bound to perform within their area of professional competence (ASGW, 2000). Physical activities, even the ones described in this chapter, have the potential to be dangerous in traditional group work settings (Gillis & Bonney, 1986). It is surprising to us that the classic "trust fall" is still listed in current editions of some group development textbooks (Johnson, 2001) without any disclaimers to its potential risk. Readers are advised to only do activities that they have been trained to facilitate or activities with which they have considerable experience. Adventure therapists share the goals of group counseling and other helping professions to "do no harm" and act responsibly and competently.

Not one group therapy "skill" is more important than the responsibility to competently conduct safe adventure practices. Adventure therapy is a field that utilizes powerful techniques that are often perceived as risky and can be dangerous. The reality is that people can be injured or die in this approach to therapy. Adventure therapists cannot afford to lose one life, nor can those who entrust us be fearful of our practices.

With the death of Aaron Bacon (a troubled adolescent whose parents enrolled him in an expedition-based wilderness program with questionable practices), a harsh light has shone on the unregulated growth of programs *claiming* to be operating by principles of adventure therapy or wilderness therapy (Morgenstern, 1995). Numerous questions are raised about the militaristic methods and survivalist mentality of such program philosophies. Competent and accredited programs have sought to distance themselves from the wilderness expedition programs masquerading as wilderness or adventure therapy (Russell, 2001). The field of adventure therapy must continue to educate the public as well as other mental health colleagues on how to distinguish competent programs from those that pretend to be such.

CURRENT ISSUES IN ADVENTURE THERAPY

In an article describing critical questions in adventure therapy, Itin (2001) identified many of the current issues facing adventure therapy. These issues include what type of educational degree an adventure therapist should have, whether a certification process is needed for those who wish to call themselves adventure therapists, whether recognized mental health practitioners must be involved in group work that is labeled "therapy," how the work of wilderness or adventure therapy is documented and evaluated, and how labels like "therapeutic adventure" and "adventure therapy" help distinguish or confuse the public about what is actually happening during the group experiences. All of these professional struggles might sound familiar to those who have been involved with group counseling and group therapy, because they are issues that many mental health professionals have gone through in the past 30 years.

Much of the debates in adventure therapy have taken place in forums and workshops held by members of the Therapeutic Adventure Professional Group (TAPG) of the Association for Experiential Education (AEE). This group is comprised of "those AEE members who use adventure-based practice and the philosophy of experiential education therapeutically within the fields of health, mental health, corrections, education, and other human service fields" (AEE Therapeutic Adventure Professional Group, 2003). The group has been in existence since the late 1970s and adopted a professional code of ethics in 1992, but has yet to agree on minimal competencies for who can call themselves an adventure therapist. The TAPG serves as both an entry point and a place for continuing education for the group practitioner interested in using adventure experiences in group work. As a professional group, TAPG also has helped launch an international conference on adventure therapy. The first of these conferences was held in Perth, Western Australia, in 1997, the second in Augsburg, Germany, in 2000, and the third in Victoria, British Columbia, in 2003. Group counselors interested in learning more about the use of adventure experiences in therapeutic settings are encouraged to join those of like mind in the TAPG and at international gatherings.

SUMMARY

In a time of increasing expectations, changing conditions, and growing complexity of group member issues, group counselors may be searching for therapeutic approaches and techniques that actively empower group members' lives. Adventure therapy offers a means to reach those ends through an approach to group work that provides a contrasting experience to "the problem," offers multiple and corroborating representations of reality, fosters the development of change through active eustress experiences, uses experiences that have internal mechanisms of resolvable conflict with structures focused on the production of solutions, and changes the role of the therapist to be more active and mobile. This approach to group work should be ventured into by those wanting to ethically and competently use experiences that enhance the therapeutic process and encourage positive and lasting change.

REFERENCES

AEE Therapeutic Adventure Professional Group (TAPG). (2003). Retrieved from http://www.geocities.com/aee_tapg/tapg.html.

Association for Experiential Education (AEE). (2003). Retrieved from www.aee.org.

Association for Specialists in Group Work. (2000). Association for Specialists in Group Work: Professional standards for the training of group workers. *Journal for Specialists in Group Work, 25*, 327-342

Bacon, S. (1983). *The conscious use of metaphor in Outward Bound.* Greenwich, Denver, CO: Outward Bound. (ERIC Document Reproduction Service No. ED296848)

Bacon, S. B., & Kimball, R. (1989). The wilderness challenge model. In R. D. Lyman, S. Prentice-Dunn, & S. Gabel (Eds.), *Residential and inpatient treatment of children and adolescents* (pp. 115-144). New York: Plenum.

Bateson, G. (1972). *Steps to an ecology of the mind.* New York: Ballantine.

Berman, D. S., & Davis-Berman, J. L. (1989). Wilderness therapy: A therapeutic adventure for adolescents. *Journal of Independent Social Work, 3*(3), 65-77.

Blatner A., & Blatner, A. (1988). *Foundations of psychodrama: History, theory, and practice.* New York: Springer.

Cason, D. R., & Gillis, H. L. (1993). A meta-analysis of adventure programming with adolescents. *Journal of Experiential Education, 17*(1).

Creal, R. S., & Florio, N. (1986). The family wilderness program: A description of the project and its ethical concerns. In M. Gass & L. Buell (Eds.), *Proceedings Journal for the 14th Annual AEE Conference: The season of ingenuity: Ethics in experiential education.* Boulder, CO: Association for Experiential Education.

Crisp, S. (1998). International models of best practice in wilderness and adventure therapy. In C. Itin (Ed.), *Exploring the boundaries of adventure therapy: International perspectives.* Boulder, CO: Association for Experiential Education.

Davis-Berman, J., & Berman, D. S. (1994). *Wilderness therapy: Foundations, theories and research.* Dubuque, IA: Kendall Hunt.

de Shazer, S. (1982). *Patterns of brief family therapy: An ecosystemic approach.* New York: Guilford.

Ewert, A. (1989). *Outdoor adventure pursuits: Foundations, models, and theories.* Worthington, OH: Publishing Horizons.

Gass, M. A. (Ed.). (1993). *Adventure therapy: Therapeutic applications of adventure programming.* Dubuque, IA: Kendall Hunt.

Gass, M. A., & Gillis, H. L. (1995b). Constructing solutions in adventure therapy. *Journal of Experiential Education, 1*(2), 63-69.

Gass, M., & McPhee, P. (1990). Emerging for recovery: A descriptive analysis of adventure therapy for substance abusers. *Journal of Experiential Education, 13*(2), 29-35.

Gass, M. A., & Gillis, H. L. (1998, November). *A room with a view: Adventure therapy programs in traditional office settings.* Paper presented at the Association for Experiential Education 26th Annual International Conference, Lake Tahoe, NV.

Gillis, H. L. (1992, January). *Therapeutic uses of adventure-challenge-outdoor-wilderness: theory and research.* In K. Henderson (Ed.), *Proceedings of coalition for education in the outdoors symposium.* Martinsville: Bradford Woods, Indiana University.

Gillis, H. L., & Bonney, W. C. (1986). Group counseling with couples or families: Adding adventure activities. *Journal for Specialists in Group Work, 11*(4), 213-220.

Gillis, H. L., & Bonney, W. C. (1989). Utilizing adventure activities with intact groups: A sociodramatic systems approach to consultation. *Journal of Mental Health Counseling, 11*(4), 345-358.

Gillis, H. L., & Gass, M. A. (1993). Bringing adventure into marriage and family therapy: An innovative experiential approach. *Journal of Marriage and Family Therapy, 19*(3), 273-286.

Gillis, H. L., Gass, M. A., Bandoroff, S., Rudolph, S., Clapp, C., & Nadler, R. (1991). Family adventure survey: Results and discussion. In C. Birmingham (Ed.), *Proceedings Journal of the 19th Annual AEE Conference* (pp. 29-39). Boulder, CO: Association for Experiential Education.

Gillis, H. L., & Lindsay, J. F. (1991, April). *Pairenting: Adventure-based counseling for parent and adolescent wellness.* Paper presented at the Annual Conference of the American Association of Counseling and Development, Reno, NV.

Gillis, H. L., & Simpson, C. A. (1994). *Working with substance abusing adolescents through Project Adventure.* [Addictions Looseleaf Notebook]. Aspen, CO: Love Publishing.

Gillis, H. L., & Thomsen, D. (1996). *A research update (1992-1995) of adventure therapy: Challenge activities and ropes courses, wilderness expeditions, & residential camping programs.* Paper presented at the *Coalition for education in the outdoors symposium*, Martinsville: Bradford Woods, Indiana University.

Gillis, H. L., & Ringer, T. M. (1999). Therapeutic adventure programs. In S. Priest & J. Miles (Ed.), *Adventure programming.* State College, PA: Venture.

Haley, J. (1973). *Uncommon therapy: The psychiatric techniques of Milton H. Erickson, M.S.* New York: Norton.

Hattie, J. A., Marsh, H. W., Neill, J. T., & Richards, G. E. (1997). Adventure education and Outward Bound: Out-of-class experiences that make a lasting difference. *Review of Educational Research, 67*, 43-87.

Itin, C. (2001). Adventure therapy: Critical questions. *Journal of Experiential Education, 24*(2), 80-84.

Johnson, D. (2001). *Reaching out* (7th ed.). Boston: Allyn & Bacon.

Kelly, F. J., & Baer, D. J. (1968). *Outward Bound schools as an alternative to institutionalization for adolescent delinquent boys.* Boston: Fandel.

Kimball, R. (1983). The wilderness as therapy. *Journal of Experiential Education, 5*(3), 6-9.

Maizell, R. S. (1988). Adventure-based counseling as a therapeutic intervention with court-involved adolescents. *Dissertation Abstracts International, 50*(06-B), 2628. (University Microfilms No. AAD89-21901)

Morgenstern, J. (1995, January 15). A death in the wilderness. *Los Angeles Times Magazine,* pp. 14-18.

Newes, S. L. (2001). Future directions in adventure-based therapy research: Methodological considerations and design suggestions. *Journal of Experiential Education, 24*(2), 92-99.

Perls, F. S. (1969). *Gestalt therapy verbatim.* Moab, UT: Real People Press.

Priest S., & Gass, M. A. (1997a). *Effective leadership in adventure programming.* Champaign, IL: Human Kinetics.

Priest, S., & Gass, M. A. (1997b). An examination of "problem-solving" versus "solution-oriented" facilitation styles in a corporate setting. *Journal of Experiential Education, 20*(1), 34-39.

Rice, S. (1988). A study of the impact of long-term therapeutic camping on self-concept development among troubled youth. *Dissertation Abstracts International, 49*(07-A), 1706. (University Microfilms No. AAD88-19365)

Rohnke, K. (1989). *Cowstails and cobras II: A guide to games, initiatives, ropes courses, and adventure curriculum.* Hamilton, MA: Project Adventure.

Rohnke, K., & Butler, S. (1995). *Quicksilver.* Dubuque, IA: Kendall-Hunt.

Roland, C., Keene, T., Dubois, M., & Lentini, J. (1988). Experiential challenge program development in the mental health setting. *Bradford Papers Annual* (Vol. 3). Martinsville, IN: Bradford Woods Outdoor Center.

Roland, C., Summers, S., Freidman, M., Barton, G., & McCarthy, K. (1987). Creation of an experiential challenge program. *Therapeutic Recreation Journal, 21*(2), 54-63.

Russell, K. (2001). What is wilderness therapy? *Journal of Experiential Education, 24*(2), 70-79.

Satir, V. (1972). *Peoplemaking.* Palo Alto, CA: Science and Behavior.

Scheidlinger, S. (1995). The small healing group: A historical overview. *Psychotherapy, 32*(4), 657-668

Schoel, J., Prouty, D., & Radcliffe, P. (1988). *Islands of healing: A guide to adventure-based counseling.* Hamilton, MA: Project Adventure.

Stich, T. F., & Senior, N. (1984). Adventure therapy: An innovative treatment for psychiatric patients. In B. Pepper and H. Ryglewicz (Eds.), *Advances in treating the young adult chronic patient* (pp. 103-108). San Francisco: Jossey-Bass.

Stich, T. F., & Sussman, L. R. (1981). *Outward Bound An adjunctive psychiatric therapy: Preliminary research findings.* (ERIC Document Reproduction Service No. ED239791)

Thomas, J. (1980). Sketch of a moving spirit: Kurt Hahn. *Journal of Experiential Education, 3*(1), 17-22.

Walsh, V., & Golins, G. (1976). *The exploration of the Outward Bound process.* Denver, CO: Colorado Outward Bound School.

Walton, R. A. (1985). Therapeutic camping with inpatient adolescents: A modality for training in interpersonal cognitive problem-solving skills (self-esteem residential treatment). *Dissertation Abstracts International, 47*(08-B), 3549. (University Microfilms No. AAD86-28822)

Waltzlawick, P., Beavin, J., & Jackson, D. (1967). *Pragmatics of human communication.* New York: Norton.

Waltzlawick, P., Weakland, J., & Fisch, R. (1974). *Change.* New York: Norton.

Whitaker, C. A., & Keith, D. V. (1981). Symbolic-experiential family therapy. In A. S. Gurman & D. P. Kniskern (Eds.), *Handbook of family therapy.* New York: Brunner/Mazel.

Wichmann, T. F. (1991). Of wilderness and circles: Evaluating a therapeutic model for wilderness adventure programs. *Journal of Experiential Education, 14*(2), 43-48.

Part VII

CRITICAL ISSUES AND EMERGING TOPICS

Introduction

DEBORAH A. GERRITY

I
t is difficult for a handbook to include a section with this focus because the topics that fall under this category, by their very nature, change in time. However, to not include this section would neglect the exciting and cutting-edge development of groups. Therefore, the editors do not claim that this section is all-encompassing. However, as a snapshot in time, at publication in 2003, the topics reflect the zeitgeist and provide a crucial glimpse into group interventions for the future.

Emerging issues, such as online and prevention groups, are beginning to get attention and appear to be a strong focus of the future. The practice and research literature are barely descriptive, and this is appropriate, as the subject of these chapters is new and just capturing the phenomenon is important. Page's "Online Group Counseling" covers the cutting-edge technology and its influence on mental health. There are numerous group interventions online, yet most are not influenced by mental health professionals. Page advocates that it is time for researchers and practitioners to get involved and influence this phenomenon. Conyne's "Prevention Groups" focuses on a topic that is as old as the field of mental health but has not received much attention until now. He relates what is known about prevention groups and discusses areas for future attention.

The chapters that focus on critical issues also emphasize both practice and research. Klaw and Humphreys's chapter, "The Role of Peer-Led Mutual Help Groups in Promoting Health and Well-Being," addresses ways mental health professionals can reach more people through consultation and research activities. While a myriad of groups exists in the self-help field, little research has been done, and mental health professionals have much to offer to support and improve these interventions. Piper and Ogrodniczuk's chapter, "Brief Group Therapy," discusses time-limited groups and their importance in the current health care world. There is a significant body of research that supports brief group therapy interventions. Finally, Burlingame, Fuhriman, and Johnson's chapter, "Current Status and Future Directions of Group Therapy Research," summarizes the state of group research currently and suggests areas for further development. It is a great resource for those professionals who endeavor to contribute to the growth of knowledge about group interventions.

This section fits well at the end of the handbook because it helps the reader to look to the future. Group interventions are constantly adapting to our ever-changing world, and group professionals are ever striving to meet these demands.

43

ONLINE GROUP COUNSELING

BETSY J. PAGE

Kent State University

The Internet is an information highway that extends to universities, community centers, public libraries, and schools as well as the homes of individuals. It opens the doors for rapid communication globally (Harris-Bowlsbey, 2000). It is gradually transforming how Americans meet health care needs, including mental health information and counseling (Bowman & Bowman, 1998).

This chapter examines the extent and nature of online group counseling. Possible types of online counseling groups and the use of technology in these groups are described. Literature related to potential benefits and problems of online group counseling is discussed as well as the role of the leader in such groups. Ethical codes and considerations for professionals wishing to refer members to online groups are discussed.

It is useful to consider the culture of the Internet, which values nonprofessional innovation, risk taking, freedom from rules and regulations, mutual assistance, and no cost or nonprofit alternatives. Many of these values are different from those of the mental health professions, which value professionalism, research-based practice, licenses, rules, regulations, minimization of risk, and often an expectation of profit. Considering the contrasting values, it should not be a surprise that online groups only partially mirror face-to-face groups. I encourage readers to approach the topic of online groups with an open mind, to learn about this domain of group work, to appreciate the potential for teaching and healing through online groups, and to make a commitment to engage in online group work. In the process of doing so, professionals can help address areas that may be justly criticized. A list of key terms related to online groups is included in an appendix to this chapter.

TYPES OF GROUPS

The Association for Specialists in Group Work (ASGW) (2000) has identified four types frequently used as a framework for conceptualizing groups: (1) task/work groups, (2) guidance/psychoeducational groups, (3) counseling/interpersonal problem-solving groups, and (4) psychotherapy/personality. One of the differences between face-to-face groups and online groups is that customary conceptual frameworks do not seem to be a good fit for the types of groups on the Internet. Group work online is influenced by the communications formats that technology provides. The processes of online groups reflect the experience and values of the Internet culture.

Online groups vary on several dimensions, including synchronicity and technology (Page et al., 2000). Members of synchronous groups log onto the Internet at the same time and interact in real time. In contrast, members of asynchronous groups access the group site at varied times to participate by posting text to the group site. Online groups interact through text, audio, video, or some combinations of these technologies. The vast majority of Internet sites providing online groups use a format in which members post messages sent through e-mail to a common site or message board. E-mail groups may be synchronous or asynchronous.

A third dimension in conceptualizing online groups is leadership. Many of the online groups are not conducted by mental health professionals. Leaders may conceptualize themselves as listserv owners, group facilitators, leaders of support groups, or hosts (Gary & Remolino, 2000). Their functions range from maintaining the technology to full professional leadership. Full professional leaders would carry out all the functions of leaders in face-to-face groups while using technology as a tool and helping members to use the technology with ease.

While the issues discussed in the group may be similar to those discussed in groups falling into ASGW's counseling and interpersonal problem-solving category, the groups generally describe themselves as self-help or support rather than counseling or therapy. The goals of many groups are to provide support, information, and community. This inconsistency in the use of terminology makes it difficult for the novice user to know what to expect from online groups. Inconsistent use of key words for online searches further confuses the situation. Searches of the Internet, conducted in September 2001, resulted in approximately 403,000 sites for "online group counseling," and 1,720,000 sites for "support groups online." The search terms do not denote distinct categories of groups, and the category in which a specific site is retrieved depended more on how the creator of the site titled it than the position of the group on a continuum from support to counseling.

One approach to comprehending the nature of specific groups might be first to conceptualize the position of the group on the continuum from support to counseling and then consider the purpose of the group in terms of the ASGW classifications (Gladding, 2003).

A Review of Selected Literature on Online Groups

Asynchronous Groups. Finn (1996) suggested that online groups in the 1990s parallel the encounter groups of the 1960s in that there is little research about a group process in which many people are participating. Little is known about online groups, and existing research addresses widely scattered topics (Meier, 2000; Winzelberg, 1997). Available information focuses primarily on text-based online groups.

The existing literature consists of scattered studies on groups with various topics and formats. The studies are perhaps uncoordinated first steps at investigating the phenomena of online groups. Finn (1996) investigated participation and potential benefits and difficulties of using computer-mediated self-help groups, particularly Recovery (a substance abuse recovery program). The groups use a bulletin board system (BBS). Exchange of postings among members may take 2 days (Sparks, 1992). Use of the BBS is extensive and increasing. Two thirds of the callers in the group studied by Finn (1996) made more than one call to the system in a month. Benefits of participating in the online group included meeting people in cyberspace, 24-hour availability of groups, availability of groups for people unable to attend face-to-face groups, and ability to engage in catharsis at any hour without disturbing the sleep of others. Dependency issues of members in early stages of recovery could be diffused among many members. Furthermore, reluctant members could gather information in a low-risk environment. One disadvantage of this technology is that sometimes the exchange of postings among members may take 2 days (Sparks, 1992) or they may not get a response. Another disadvantage was "flaming," or destructive interactions such as attacking another person and name calling. A second concern was that some members expressed a dependence on online communications, raising the possibility that they were becoming socially isolated. Finally, the exclusion of members who did not have access to technology was also a major concern.

King (1994) surveyed the members of an electronic support group (ESG) in which members posted text messages to a BBS. These electronic support groups were used to supplement attendance at Alcoholics Anonymous meetings. Reports of respondents ($n = 71$) indicated significant correlations between improvement in their recovery program and the number of hours a week the respondents used the electronic support group ($r = 0.46$), and the frequency it was used to seek advice ($r = 0.46$). Members also indicated that they contacted others from the ESG outside the group context. These outside contacts occurred by phone, postal service mail, or in person.

Weinberg, Schmale, Uken, and Wessel (1995) conducted a computer-mediated support group in which members participated through a BBS. Members were selected for the group by their oncologist and all had breast cancer. Researchers limited access to the group by assigning members a password. Furthermore, the researchers monitored the content of the postings and actively intervened to restore participation when a critical incident disrupted group participation. In general, benefits and concerns observed in these groups were similar to those observed in support groups conducted on public BBS. An additional benefit noted by Weinberg, Schmale et al. (1995) was that the computer record of postings can be printed out and studied. Loss of visual and auditory cues were one disadvantage. Technology problems causing difficulty operating the BBS or members to be cut off were concerns in this group. Weinberg, Uken, Schmale, and Adamek (1995) were able to document that participants' perceptions of helpfulness correlated with perceived presence of Yalom's therapeutic factors of instillation of hope ($r = 0.56$), group cohesion ($r = 0.65$), and universality ($r = 0.45$). These correlations should be considered preliminary indicators of the presence of Yalom's therapeutic factors, because the group was a small pilot study with six members.

Holden, Bearison, Rode, Kapoloff, and Rosenberg (2000) compared the effects of engaging with a computer network—STARBRIGHT World (SBW2)—to the general pediatric milieu (GPM) for reduction of pain intensity, pain aversiveness, and anxiety of hospitalized pediatric patients whose ages ranged from 7 to 18 years. SBW2 is a computer network linking 25 major medical centers in the United States, which allows users to communicate with other hospitalized children using e-mail, bulletin boards, chat rooms, and video conferencing. Interactive programs also allow exploration, seeking of information, and distraction from pain. Children ($n = 44$) reported less pain, pain aversiveness, and anxiety in the SBW2 condition than in the general pain milieu condition. The SBW2 system was used primarily for exploration/activities (68%) and for connecting with others (20%). On 65% of occasions, the children were engaged with the system while talking with others in the hospital room; on 28%, the children were videoconferencing.

Gary and Remolino (2000) described online text-based support groups for grief and loss that provided an atmosphere of safety, anonymity, and control for members to share their stories, pain, and healing processes. Nonprofessional hosts provided resources and made referrals as well as selected a weekly topic for the group and generally led the groups. Typical topics included phases and emotions of grief, terminal illnesses, and helping caregivers and grieving children. Gary and Remolino stated universality, increased access, and the ability to meet specialized needs (e.g., the increased use of online support groups following the shootings at Columbine High School) as the expected benefits of online groups for grief and loss. Anonymity breaches, decreased interpersonal feedback, and difficulties in crisis management were identified as limitations of this online support group format. In crisis situations in which members were unknown to hosts, the hosts (often nonprofessional leaders) were trained to deal with mental health crises by instructing members to log off the computer and dial 911.

Meier (2000) investigated the use of a 10-week listserv-based group to help practicing master's-level social workers ($n = 52$) from 11 different states explore job stress and coping issues. Members, most of whom were seasoned professionals, rated themselves as having good to excellent computer and Internet skills. Member participation levels were monitored as an indicator of group cohesion. In an effort to sustain a viable group, all members were asked to send at least one message weekly. The facilitator encouraged members to share goals, explore concerns, discuss the effects of technology on group process, and develop a satisfying group process. Members sent a total of 294 messages, 50% of which were sent by five members. While participation varied weekly, 78% of the members averaged at least one message a week.

Members responded to others and developed a group process norm in which subheadings were included in messages that indicated whether comments were for the entire group or for a specific member. Support and validation characterized about half the messages sent. However, content of some postings indicated that crises of emotionally needy members felt overwhelming to some of the other members.

Comparison of pre- and postgroup data indicated no significant changes in members' psychological strain, occupational stress, or coping resourcefulness. In the follow-up survey, about half the members felt their experiences were similar to others in the group, and 68% wanted the group to continue.

Winzelberg (1997) analyzed discourse contained in 306 messages posted to an ESG during 3 months of an online group for people with eating disorders, including anorexia nervosa and bulimia nervosa. Some of the members reported previous hospitalizations for eating disorders. Analysis of messages indicated that 10% of the members sent 63% of the messages and that frequent users were likely to respond to requests for support and information. Most participants posted one or two messages (69%). Personal disclosure, information, and support accounted for 70% of the messages. Messages posted between 6:00 P.M. and 7:00 A.M.—when professional help is least available—constituted two thirds of the messages.

Medical information exchanged in the group was generally accurate; however, 12% of the information provided was outside the range of acceptable medical and psychological care. An additional concern was the activity of members selling costly and potentially dangerous treatments.

Summary of Results and the Ongoing Debate. Some results were observed across multiple studies. The asynchronous groups were convenient for members. This resulted in use scattered across the 24 hours of the day, allowing members to read postings and to engage in catharsis at times of the day when little professional help would be available (Finn, 1996; Galinsky, Schopler, & Abell, 1997). All of these studies indicated that the asynchronous groups provided support for members. However, what is difficult to determine from the literature is what support, if any, the groups provided for members who were minimally active in the groups.

Some members contributed a high proportion of the postings. Content of the postings of the high users was generally supportive and often expressed specific support directed to individual members (Winzelberg, 1997).

Online group process used some of Yalom's (1995) therapeutic factors, particularly universality, cohesion, and the provision of hope (Gary & Remolino, 2000; Weinberg, Uken et al., 1995). In addition to providing support, participation in the online groups was related to positive outcomes—members in alcohol treatment programs progressed in their recovery programs, and pain symptoms were decreased in hospitalized children (Holden et al., 2000; King, 1994).

In addition to the positive aspects of group process and outcome described above, researchers noted several serious concerns. Galinsky et al. (1997) noted loss of nonverbal information, loss of information from voice tones, and problems recognizing and dealing with safety issues. Flaming, dependency of needy members, problems managing safety issues, and the provision by members of dangerously inaccurate medical and psychological information were issues difficult to address with the peer or nonprofessional leadership arrangements typical of most online groups (Finn, 1996; Gary & Remolino, 2000; Winzelberg, 1997).

The review of the literature on asynchronous groups presented problems and posed questions about interpretation of reported results that cannot be satisfactorily addressed. The existing literature can be described as sparse, largely descriptive in nature, and in an early stage of development. One problem related to the early developmental state of the research base on online groups is that there is insufficient information about what typical participation looks

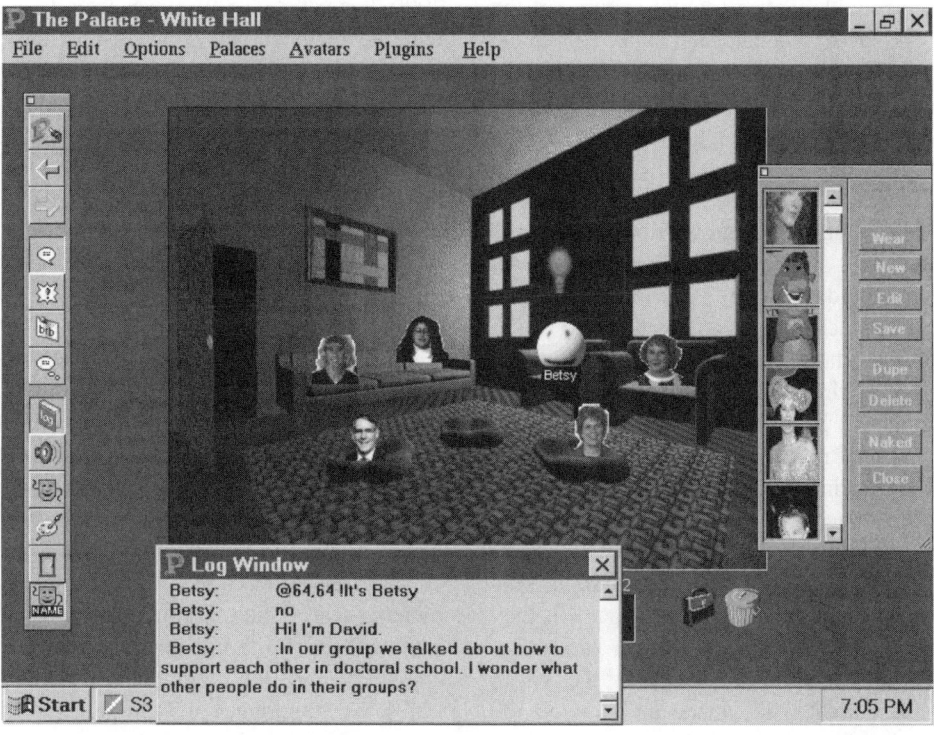

Figure 43.1   Virtual Group Using the Palace

like. For example, if a researcher reported that 60% of members posted a message to a group weekly, there is not enough existing literature to know whether that level of participation should be interpreted as high, average, low, or sufficient to reap the benefits. It is also not clear if lurkers who do not post messages to the group are being helped. No data are reported in professional literature that quantifies the number of people whose only participation is lurking, nor is there a definition indicating how many times a person must log on to the group without sending messages to be considered a lurker.

A second question is, Who is to decide what is acceptable? If a typical participation pattern in an online group is that a number of members contribute a weekly posting, a few members ask for specific information or help, and the bulk of the responses are from a small group of members, professional group leaders may consider this pattern unsatisfactory, while online group members may find the groups sufficiently helpful that they continue to engage in the group.

If group members report feeling connected to a group even when the group process can accurately be described as asynchronous and extended over time (quite different from group process in face-to-face groups), does the community of professional group leaders have the right to declare that face-to-face interaction is integral to professional group work?

Synchronous Groups. Page et al. (2000) investigated group process and member experience in a synchronous virtual support group conducted using The Palace, a software program that allows the creation of a virtual space in which members may interact. A virtual group room was created, including a door that could be locked to prevent persons other than the group members from entering the room (see Figure 43.1). A training session was conducted in a university computer lab to familiarize the members with the process of logging on to the group and using The Palace. The group met in a virtual room in which they represented themselves with avatars (digital pictures of the members' faces) that had been imported into the program. The leader helped members with technical issues and facilitated the group process. Members typed messages that appeared in the speech bubbles (as the speech of cartoon characters is represented). Members were able to move their avatars about the group room to express closeness to or distance from other members. All members could see where each member was in relation to other members as well as the nature and timing relative to group discussion of any movement within the group room.

Members organized interactions by developing a norm of placing a virtual light bulb over their heads to indicate that they wished to speak next. The Palace produced a log that was essentially a transcript of the group that members could consult to clarify who had spoken if several members spoke at the same time or if they could not remember what a member had said.

Members reported appreciating the visual cues possible in The Palace and missed the information that they would have received from voice tones and nonverbal behavior in a face-to-face group. At times, members felt the reflection forced on them by the need to type messages was useful in that typing messages was slower than speaking in a face-to-face group. Sometimes members had to wait while the person whose turn it was to speak typed a message. During this pause, members reflected on what others had said.

One of the major differences between the group conducted using The Palace and face-to-face groups is that technology affects multiple aspects of the group. Members with greater computer skills had an easier time logging on to the group at the start of sessions. Those who typed slowly found participation more difficult. The reliability of the functioning of technology also affected group process. In order for the group to run smoothly, the electricity, the desktop computers used by the members, the Palace server, and all LAN and Internet connections had to function correctly and without interruption. Problems with the functioning of the technology have the potential to create critical incidents in group process. During one session of the group, a problem arose when the Internet provider cut off one member (Delmonico et al.,

2000; Page et al., 2000). It was later determined that the member had connected to the group using a dial-in Internet provider. The member had been listening but not sending messages, and the dial-in service automatically disconnected her. This critical incident caused by an unexpected action of the technology has both similarities and differences from the situations in a face-to-face group in which a member drops out without telling the leader or the group. In the online group and in the face-to-face group, the leader has multiple concerns to address, including (a) the safety of the detached member, (b) the concerns of the remaining members for the detached member, (c) possible interpretation of remaining group members about why the other member is gone, and (d) decrease in trust in the group and its effects on group process. What differs between the two situations is that a member who is cut off from a group because of a technology issue did not make a conscious choice to leave the group. This situation illustrates the importance of adhering to requirements of ethics codes that extensive safety protocols be followed for online groups.

Page et al. (2003) investigated students' experience in a synchronous, audio-based online group. A group was created using PalTalk (www.paltalk.com), a program that can be downloaded without cost from the Internet. In the process of establishing a group, the group administrator (counselor educator) established a group name and administrator code number. To further increase privacy, the group was established as a locked group, requiring a password that was then issued by the administrator only to the group members. Five doctoral students in counselor education at a university in the Midwest volunteered to participate in four 1-hour groups. (The students chose mutually agreed upon nonconfidential discussion topics related to the supervision of counseling). After an initial training session that was conducted in person in the program office, students downloaded PalTalk into their own computers and established a late evening time for group. One student volunteered to set up the group and served as leader. The group functioned primarily as an audio-based group in which members could hear each other speaking in real time. PalTalk also allows text-based message transmission, which proved useful when audio quality was not satisfactory. After the group was completed, students filled out a questionnaire that included demographics, information about pregroup computer experience, and students' responses to their experiences in the group.

The students reported feeling that they were connected in the group and that the group promoted learning. They also indicated that the group was convenient. While the PalTalk program itself worked well, some students reported poor audio quality. This problem appeared to be due to poor quality of transmission on some rural phone lines.

There were a few similarities between the use of The Palace and PalTalk that may be useful for group leaders who are interested in synchronous online groups. First, students were satisfied with the online group experience. Second, the interactive group process flowed better—one person spoke at a time—when some commonly understood process was used to moderate group interaction—students using The Palace developed a process using a light bulb avatar, PalTalk has a built-in option in which a member can raise a hand avatar indicating he or she wishes to speak and receive the microphone avatar from the administrator, indicating he or she is the current speaker. And third, unexpected problems that affected connection or quality of connection occurred in both groups due to transmission lines.

SUMMARY

The cutting edge of current technology appears to be synchronous video groups. While this author was unable to locate research reports on video-based groups in the literature, there are video-based groups with high video and audio quality. Voice tones were clear, and nonverbal communication was as clear as it would be in a face-to-face group. The video-based groups were conducted using Polycoms connected through Internet2, a second-generation, "high speed Internet for use exclusively by government researchers and academic institutions" (T1 Glossary, 2000).

Quality connections were established between four locations: a university in the Midwest, two universities in the Southeast, and a university in Tokyo. While the use of Polycoms, which are somewhat expensive, and Internet2, which is currently available to institutions rather than individuals, limits current access to technology needed for these groups, it is important for readers of this chapter to know that high-tech and high-quality groups currently exist. First, the group process in high-quality video-based groups is similar to the process in face-to-face groups. This type of group addresses group workers' concerns about loss of voice tones and nonverbal information. Second, access to high-speed connections, including Internet2, is growing, and the price of technology continues to decrease, making the use of video-based groups a realistic possibility for more people. A list of universities currently connected to Internet2 is available on the Internet at http://members. internet2.edu/university/universities.cfm.

ETHICS AND ETHICAL QUESTIONS

Standards for the Ethical Practice of Internet Counseling (National Board for Certified Counselors [NBCC], 2001) and Ethical Standards for Internet On-line Counseling (American Counseling Association [ACA], 1999) provide some guidelines to consider; however, neither code specifically refers to groups. The American Psychological Association (APA) has issued a Statement on Services by Telephone, Teleconferencing, and Internet (American Psychological Association, 1997), but no set of standards or ethical codes is developed to address services provided over the Internet (online services). The primary advice presented by the APA statement is to practice within the area of one's competence. The NBCC and ACA codes identify the following points that can be considered in evaluating specific sites:

- Counseling requires secure sites, including servers and encrypted messages (ACA, 1999). Clients should be informed about the encryption methods to be used (NBCC, 2001).
- Nonsecure sites are appropriate to provide information and Internet links (ACA, 1999).
- All counselors and supervisors who have access to information from the site should be made known to the clients (ACA, 1999).

- Counselors should verify clients' identities (ACA, 1999). When such verification is difficult, code words or numbers should be used to address imposter concerns (NBCC, 2001).
- Counselors determine if clients are minors and, if so, obtain consent from parents or guardians (NBCC, 2001).
- Limits of confidentiality, including those due to the nature of technology used, should be made clear to clients and a waiver agreement signed (ACA, 1999).
- There must be plans for contacting the counselor in an emergency, accessing local counselors providing face-to-face care for emergencies, and hotline numbers should be provided (ACA, 1999; NBCC, 2001).
- Counselors inform clients how often e-mail will be checked by the Internet counselor when the counselor is providing asynchronous counseling (NBCC, 2001).
- Counselors explain to clients that technology failure is possible and what to do in the event of such a failure (NBCC, 2001).
- Counselors should advise clients regarding the keeping of records and the processes for transferring records electronically (ACA, 1999; NBCC, 2001).
- Counseling Web sites provide links to licensure and certification boards (NBCC, 2001).
- Counselors confirm that their liability insurance covers online counseling (ACA, 1999).
- Counselors abide by local licensure laws and codes as well as by local customs related to age of consent and child abuse reporting (ACA, 1999; NBCC, 2001).

While the intent of the requirement to abide by local laws, codes, and customs appears to be that the counselor should adhere to standards for professional practice in the client's locale, counselors also need to attend to laws and licensure requirements in their home state. Depending on the location of both counselor and client, additional national or international laws may also apply.

Questions about ethics of online groups exist at the most fundamental level. Given that the preponderance of groups describe themselves as self-help or support groups and are typically led by nonprofessionals, to which groups and in what manner do the ethical codes apply? What can professional group leaders in the mental heath professions and the licensure and certification boards do to clarify and improve the ethics of leading online groups in a worldwide electronic community?

Informed consent implies that leaders can explain to members what might be expected in the group. This is more difficult in online groups because the groups do not fall into neatly describable categories. Furthermore, how can the Internet and possible types of group work be explained to potential consumers, particularly when some consumers have little understanding of computer or Internet functioning?

Cautions in the ethical codes remind professionals to practice within their areas of competence. Universities provide initial professional training for most group leaders; however, current training standards fail to address training experiences for provision of groups through the Internet (CACREP, 2001). At this point in the development of the Internet and of groups on the Internet, professional counseling organizations may wish to address the need for standards directly. Careful consideration should be given to describing training experiences to be included in accreditation standards to promote competence in online groups.

REFERRING MEMBERS

Mental health professionals may wish to refer potential members to online groups. This referral process should include factors that counselors generally consider in referring members to face-to-face groups, such as member goals, the purpose of the group, the skill and experience of the leader with the issue that is of concern to the member, and the member's ability to access the group. In order to make a referral to a technology-based group, the referring counselor should also inquire about the quality of Internet connection that the potential member can access as well as the member's level of computer skill and comfort. The range of Internet connections may include (a) dial-in connections on ordinary phone lines, (b) dial-in connections on ISDN lines, (c) cable, DSL, LAN, or T1 connection, and (d) connection through Internet2. If the potential member has dial-in connections through ordinary phone lines, the member could participate in text-based groups. Groups based on synchronous audio discussions should be considered for dial-in Internet users only if the audio transmission is clear on the phone line because members of both telephone-based (Thomas & Urbano, 1993) and audio-based groups (Page, Jencius et al., 2003) report dissatisfaction with the group if sound quality is poor. Members with dial-in connections are unlikely to have connections with the bandwidth for groups containing video transmission and may find that only text-based groups work well using their equipment. Members who have access to high-speed connections may prefer groups that incorporate synchronous audio or audio-video interactions, as these types of groups provide more voice tones and other nonverbal communication information. The referring counselor should explain to the potential member that there is no such thing as absolute confidentiality in online groups and assist the member in acquiring information accurately describing the level of security, if any, available at the site.

The referring professional should also help the potential group member evaluate the cost of participating in online groups. Such costs may be weighed against the costs of face-to-face groups. Public access to computers and the Internet through public libraries or schools may be helpful to members who find the cost of computers prohibitive. There were no studies that compared the effectiveness of face-to-face groups with that of online groups. Therefore, it is not possible at this time to consider cost and effectiveness simultaneously in choosing the format of the group that is best for the potential member.

Mental health professionals seeking to refer clients to online groups may locate groups by searching sites on the Internet using a search engine such as Google (http://www.google.com/advanced_search). Prescreened sites can be placed into a word-processing file that can be saved as an html file, copied to a computer disk, and given to the client. The file on the disk will then provide active hyperlinks to the sites recommended to the member.

CONCLUSIONS AND ISSUES THAT REQUIRE CONTINUED ATTENTION

Four major conclusions should be considered when thinking about online groups. First, member participation in online groups is extensive. Many groups are available online and many people participate. It is possible to get some indication of the range of groups by visiting Google groups (http://groups.google.com/grphp?hl=en&ie=UTF80e=UTF8q=). Many of the groups that discuss mental health topics are listed in the index under "alt. Any conceivable topic." Second, the distinction between types of groups online may not be very meaningful. Professional leaders tend to associate specific types of groups with types of content and possibly processes. Many online groups mirror the Internet culture and are nonprofessional. The titles of the groups do not reflect the function or content of the groups; for example, some news groups may discuss depression. There is no quick way to easily identify groups led by professionals. This poses a problem with application of the ACA ethical codes that distinguish clear rules for counseling versus the provision of information on the Internet. Where do support groups, which are the predominant form of online groups, fit into this picture? Perhaps these groups challenge the helping professions to develop standards for ethical and effective conduct of support groups online when the groups are to be led by nonprofessionals. The challenge may be to provide basic training experiences in online group leadership, to own and administrate the servers, and to provide emergency support without changing the essential support rather than counseling focus of the support group.

While research is scant, the degree of member engagement in online groups indicates that the groups are helpful to many people. Finally, study of online groups is in the infancy stage. Researchers would do well to attend to the suggestions of Bednar and Kaul (1994) to pursue "careful observations, accurate description, and precise measurement" as a foundation for research in this promising frontier of group work (Bednar & Kaul, 1994, p. 633).

REFERENCES

American Counseling Association. (1999). Ethical standards for Internet on-line counseling. Retrieved June 4, 2002, from http://www.counseling.org/site/PageServer?pagename=resources_internet.

American National Standard for Telecommunications: Telecommunications Glossary 2000. (2000). *T1 Glossary 2000.* Retrieved June 4, 2002, from http://www.atis.org/tg2k/.

American Psychological Association. (1997). *APA statement on services provided by telephone, teleconferencing, and Internet.* Retrieved June 4, 2002, from http://www.apa.org/ethics/stmnt01.html.

Association for Specialists in Group Work. (2000, January). Professional standards for the training of group workers. Retrieved June 4, 2002, from http://www.asgw.org/training_standards.htm.

Bednar, R. L., & Kaul, T. J. (1994). Experiential group research: Can the cannon fire? In A. E. Bergin & S. L. Garfield (Eds.), *Handbook of psychotherapy and behavior change* (pp. 631-633). New York: John Wiley.

Bowman, R. L., & Bowman, V. E. (1998). Life on the electronic frontier: The application of technology to group work. *Journal for Specialists in Group Work, 23,* 428-445.

Council for Accreditation of Counseling and Related Educational Programs. (2001). *CACREP accreditation manual.* Alexandria, VA: Author.

Delmonico, D. L., Dannihirsh, C., Page, B., Walsh, J., L'Amoreaux, N. A., & Thompson, R. S. (2000). The Palace: Participant responses to a virtual support group. *Journal of Technology in Counseling, 1*(2). Available at http://jtc.colstate.edu/vol1_2/palace.htm.

Finn, F. (1996). Computer-based self-help groups: On-line recovery for additions. *Computers in Human Services, 13*(1), 21-41.

Galinsky, M. J., Schopler, J. H., & Abell, M. D. (1997). Connecting group members through telephone and computer groups. *Health and Social Work, 22,* 181-188.

Gary, J. M., & Remolino, L. (2000). Coping with loss and grief through on-line support groups. In J. W. Bloom & G. R. Walz (Eds.), *Cybercounseling and cyberlearning: Strategies and resources for the millennium* (pp. 95-114). Alexandria, VA: American Counseling Association.

Gladding, S. T. (2003). *Group work: A counseling specialty* (4th ed.). Upper Saddle River, NJ: Merrill.

Harris-Bowlsbey, J. (2000). The Internet: Blessing or bane for the counseling profession? In J. W. Bloom & G. R. Walz (Eds.). *Cybercounseling and cyberlearning: Strategies and resources for the millennium* (pp. 39-49). Alexandria, VA: American Counseling Association.

Holden, G., Bearison, D. J., Rode, D. C., Kapoloff, M. F., & Rosenberg, G. (2000). The effects of a computer network on pediatric pain and anxiety. In J. Finn & G. Holden (Eds.), *Human services online: A new arena for service delivery* (pp. 27-47). Binghamton, NY: Haworth.

King, S. (1994). Analysis of electronic support for recovering addicts. Interpersonal computing and technology: *An Electronic Journal for the 21st Century, 2*(3), 47-56.

Meier, A. (2000). Offering social support via the Internet: A case study of an online support group for social workers. In J. Finn & G. Holden (Eds.), *Human services online: A new arena for service delivery* (pp. 237-266). Binghamton, NY: Haworth.

National Board for Certified Counselors. (2001). *Standards for the ethical practice of Internet counseling.* Retrieved June 4, 2002, from http://www.nbcc.org/ethics/webethics.htm.

Page, B. J., Delmonico, D., Walsh, J., Danninhirsh, C., L'Amoreaux, N., Thompson, R., et al. (2000). Setting up on-line groups in The Palace. *Journal for Specialists in Group Work, 25,* 133-145.

Page, B. J., Jencius, M. J, Rehfuss, M. C., Foss, L. L., Petruzzi, M. L., et al. (2003). PalTalk on-line groups: Process and reflections on students' experience. *Journal for Specialists in Group Work, 28,* 35-41.

Sparks, S. (1992). Exploring electronic support groups. *American Journal of Nursing, 92,* 62-65.

Thomas, T., & Urbano, J. (1993). A telephone group support program for the visually-impaired elderly. *Clinical Gerontologist, 13*(2), 61-71.

T1 Glossary. (2000). Retrieved from http://www/atis.org/tg2k/_i2.html.

Weinberg, N., Schmale, J. D., Uken, J., & Wessel, K. (1995). Computer mediated support groups. *Social Work With Groups, 17*(4), 43-54.

Weinberg, N., Uken, J. S., Schmale, J., & Adamek, M. (1995). Therapeutic factors: Their presence in a computer mediated support group. *Social Work With Groups, 18*(4), 57-69.

Winzelberg, A. (1997). The analysis of an electronic support group for individuals with eating disorders. *Computers in Human Behavior, 13*(3), 393-407.

Yalom, I. D. (1995). *The theory and practice of group psychotherapy* (4th ed.). New York: Basic Books.

APPENDIX

Key Terms

Audio-based: Groups in which members communicate by speaking and hearing each other's voices

Cable: Type of Internet connection that offers transmission rates faster than Digital Subscriber Line (DSL) and slower than T-1 and can often be connected over the same cable that is used for cable TV

Cyberspace: Digital world constructed by computer networks, particularly the Internet (NETGOLS)

Dial-up networking: A service that allows remote users to dial into the network or the Internet (such as through a telephone or an ISDN connection)

DSL (Digital Subscriber Line): Uses conventional telecommunications voice lines to provide connections at data rates up to T-1 speeds

Flaming: Making an angry remark or message in a group

Host (administrator): The person who is in charge of the group in many online groups

Integrated Services Digital Network (ISDN): A switched telephone service that provides midband digital communication capabilities used for Internet connections and for remote access to LANs, as well as voice communication

Internet: A collection of computer networks that exchange information

Internet2 (I2): A second generation, high-speed Internet for use exclusively by government researchers and academic institutions

ISDN line (Integrated Services Digital Network): Contains two channels that yield a capacity of 128 kbps

LAN (Local Area Network): A system comprising multiple computers that are physically connected through network adapter cards and cabling

Listserv: A computer conferencing system in which messages are sent to and redistributed from a computer that acts as a server

Logon: The process of connecting to a computer network

Online: A computer user connected to a network

Polycom: A video conferencing unit that can be attached to a computer

T-1: A permanent private circuit that can be leased and has a bandwidth of 1.544 Mbps and connect to IP routers at both termination points

Text-based: Sending and receiving typed messages

Video conferencing: A process using a two-way electronic communications system that permits two or more persons in different locations to engage in the equivalent of face-to-face audio and video communications

Virtual: Referring to objects or activities that are in cyberspace

44

PREVENTION GROUPS

ROBERT K. CONYNE

University of Cincinnati

This chapter focuses on the joining of two powerful forces in mental health delivery: "prevention" and "groups." Each force is important in its own right.

Mental health practitioners need to become preventive in their work for many reasons, including (a) too few helpers exist to meet the burgeoning demand for remedial service (Albee, 1986), (b) seeking help for mental health problems is enshrouded in stigma for far too many (Surgeon General Report, 2001), and (c) a variety of health and mental health concerns can be avoided through carefully planned and delivered before-the-fact preventive interventions (Conyne, 1994; Romano & Hage, 2000).

Likewise, group methods are becoming an essential way to deliver the full range of mental health needs in contemporary America (ASGW, 2000, cited in Gazda et al., 2001; Trotzer, 1999), a point that this handbook clearly underscores. Groups are especially well suited to reach prevention goals. Drawn from the public health tradition, preventive services are intended to be applied within an "extra-individual" approach: in small groups, social systems, and populations. Groups provide a natural way for meeting mental health prevention goals.

This chapter has two purposes: (1) to draw a linkage between prevention and groups and (2) to encourage training, research, and practice in the use of groups for prevention. The chapter contains rationale documenting the importance of both groups and prevention and then it presents a definition for prevention groups. Although it is possible for any group work type (e.g., group counseling, group psychotherapy, task groups) to be used to accomplish prevention goals, it is the psychoeducational group that affords the "best fit," an assertion that is elaborated in the latter sections of this chapter through definition, best practice suggestions, and a case example.

WHY GROUPS?

Groups are efficacious. Research over the last 35 years demonstrates that groups are superior to no treatment and are at least comparable to individual counseling and therapy. In many cases, groups have been found to exceed the benefits of individual therapy (Toseland & Siporin, 1986) across an array of presenting problems and diagnoses (Fuhriman & Burlingame, 1994). In other cases, such as eating disorders (e.g., Hendren, Atkins, Sumner, Calvin, & Barber, 1987), group and individual therapeutic approaches can be combined to offer maximum efficacy. In still other instances, outpatient group therapy is not always the best choice for everyone, due to a myriad of circumstances, such as acute psychosis or sociopathy; in such cases, the group approach may be counterindicated in favor of an individual delivery of service (Piper, 1994). However, basic reviews of the efficaciousness of group approaches (see, e.g., Barlow, Burlingame, & Fuhriman, 2000; Bednar & Kaul, 1994; Burlingame, Kircher, & Taylor, 1994; Fuhriman & Burlingame, 2001; Horne & Rosenthal, 1997) allow mental health professionals to be confident in asserting generally that groups work. As stated by Barlow et al. (2000):

> With few exceptions (cf. Piper & McCallum, 1991), the general conclusion to be drawn from approximately 730 studies that span almost three decades is that the group format consistently produced positive effects with a number of disorders using a variety of treatment models. (P. 122)

Of course, groups also are efficient (e.g., Spitz, 1996). When several people can participate during the same time period with one (or two) group leaders, then the professional helper-to-client ratio improves in favor of efficient practice. This fact also can provide just the wrong reason for using groups, however. For instance, excessive emphasis on efficiency to the detriment of other considerations, such as failing to properly compose the group or ignoring member interaction and group process, can serve to impair a group's power and success.

A final point to be made about the value of groups has particular salience for prevention. The classical application of prevention, as mentioned above, is not done with one person at a time. Rather, the preventive intent, drawn from public health, is to affect large groupings—populations—if possible. For examples one need only to think in terms of population-level efforts to eliminate cholera, malaria, polio, and, more recently, with AIDS prevention. Using groups, then, is consonant with this historic approach to reach prevention goals while also providing mental health practitioners with a vehicle to impact greater numbers of people.

WHY PREVENTION?

The prevention of psychological distress and the promotion of mental health are critically important in contemporary society. As Albee (1986) warned, human psychological, emotional, and other needs far outstrip the available supply of professionally trained mental health care providers, especially if providers restrict their helping service to the individual, remedial, direct service pattern. If one considers the condition of depression as but one example, approximately 28% of the U.S. adult population meets full criteria for psychiatric diagnosis in any 1 year, with fewer than 33% of them receiving any mental health treatment. Even worse, with regard to children, only 6% of the 33% of children diagnosed with depression receive mental health treatment (Cardemil & Barber, 2001).

In practice, however, determining what prevention is and is not has proven to be difficult. In an attempt to clarify the historically used terminology of primary, secondary, and tertiary prevention, the Institute of Medicine (IOM) has described three categories of prevention programs: (1) *universal* programs (e.g., parent education for all parents in a school) that are intended for everyone, without any focus on risk, (2) *selective* programs (e.g., children of alcoholics group) that are intended for at-risk persons, and (3) *indicated* programs (e.g., crisis intervention for survivors of violent attack) that target those who presently display low levels of symptoms (Mrazek & Haggerty, 1994). Romano and Hage (2000), in their impressive review of prevention in counseling psychology, indicated that four major goals exist for engaging in prevention: (1) to increase use of systemic and integrative approaches, (2) to emphasize early prevention with children and youth, (3) to develop interventions that are sensitive to the range of diversity, and (4) to deliver training domains that support the science and practice of prevention (note: psychoeducational groups constitute one of these domains for prevention).

As prevention definitions and goals become clearer, evidence also is mounting to show that prevention works (Conyne & Horne, 2001; Durlak & Wells, 1997; Price, Cowen, Lorion, & Ramos-McKay, 1988; Romano & Hage, 2000). Well-documented mental health prevention programs point to success in such areas as disease prevention in communities (Maccoby & Altman, 1988), interpersonal cognitive problem solving with children (Shure & Spivack, 1988), substance abuse prevention with adolescents (Botvin, Schinke, & Orlandi, 1995), workplace sexual aggression prevention (Kagan, Kagan, & Watson, 1995), eating disorder prevention (Mussell, Binford, & Fulkerson, 2000), improvement of interpersonal relations with students (Brand, Lakey, & Berman, 1995), preventing male violence (Hage, 2000), and unemployment prevention with adults (Vinokur, Price, & Schul, 1995).

The Existing Paradigm in Mental Health Delivery: Individual, Remedial, Direct Service

Although critically important as a delivery mode (while occupying the undisputed position of a paradigm in the counseling profession, see Conyne, 1987), individual, remedial, direct service affords but a partial solution to the mental health needs of our populace. Exclusive reliance on this paradigm is an idea whose time has come and gone. It is unreflective of the disparity between gargantuan mental health needs and the circumscribed supply of trained professionals and is costly, time consuming, culture bound, and largely inaccessible to lower income groups, including many children and older people (Cowen & Work, 1988). There needs to be a paradigm expansion in counseling and mental health.

This paradigm expansion needs to include, but not be restricted to, individual-remedial-direct service. This expansion should emphasize health and prevention (in addition to reparation) and groups and communities (in addition to individuals). This direction is in keeping with "positive psychology" (Seligman, 1998; Seligman & Csikszentmihalyi, 2000; Snyder & Lopez, 2002), an emerging force within general psychology that has enjoyed a long heritage within counseling and counseling psychology.

Paradigm Expansion: Prevention Groups

Prevention groups are those groups that are used to accomplish prevention goals. They are used

with people before the fact, prior to the entrenchment of dysfunction. These groups can be used within the universal, selective, and indicated categories of prevention described earlier. As we see later, although any type of group can be used for prevention purposes, the most well suited for prevention are psychoeducational groups.

Prevention groups are key aspects of the paradigm expansion needed in counseling and mental health. Prevention groups are recognized as being cost effective, offering an abundance of therapeutic factors, and they provide an interpersonal context for realistic experimentation, social support, change, and application (Budman et al., 1988; Corey, 1995; Gladding, 1999; Horne & Rosenthal, 1997; Spitz, 1996; Trotzer, 1999; Yalom, 1995). In addition, prevention groups are an important means for optimizing human well-being (Conyne, 2003), a significant aspect of positive psychology (Seligman, 2002).

What Are Prevention Groups?

Groups for prevention are those that

[i]nvolve small numbers of members who are generally healthy or are at risk for the development of an identified physical or psychosocial dysfunction and who meet face-to-face with a trained group leader(s). Members interact with each other focusing on an appropriate blend of content (e.g., social skills development; psychoactive substance use and abuse information) and process (e.g., cognitive clarification, interpersonal feedback, consciousness raising, group decision making) consistent with the focus and structure of the group. The general purpose is to gain knowledge and skills that will empower them to avoid future harmful events and situations and to live their lives more meaningfully and productively. (Conyne & Wilson, 2001, p. 10)

Coordinated research teams from the University of Georgia and the University of Cincinnati decided to investigate the present status of prevention groups within the relevant professional literature, using the above definition of prevention groups as a guide. Extensive literature reviews of prevention through groups were conducted by the two teams, under the auspices of the Division of Group Psychology and Group Psychotherapy (Division 49) of the American Psychological Association. These reviews, from 1990 to 1997 and involving 25 scholarly journals, focused on children and early adolescents (Georgia) and on late adolescents and adults (Cincinnati). Results have been reported in several sources, including a special issue of the *Journal for Specialists in Group Work* (Conyne & Horne, 2001).

The review results showed clearly that prevention with groups that use interactive, participative methods to reach goals are more able to be successful than those that transmit information without harnessing group dynamics. At the same time, extensive reviews of prevention through groups (note: 11,622 studies published during the 1990s identified just 148 as meeting acceptable criteria) reveal that much more research needs to address the effectiveness of prevention groups.

Areas where prevention groups have been documented as being effective with late adolescents and adults include the prevention of (a) psychological disorders (e.g., substance abuse, sexual aggression, stress), (b) impairment in interpersonal relations (e.g., social skill development, marital communication), (c) failure in social and occupational roles (e.g., employment, parenting), (d) problems in task and work groups (e.g., teams, committees), and (e) physical disorders (e.g., lifestyle, sexually transmitted diseases, cardiovascular diseases). Prevention groups with children and early adolescents have shown most success in school settings, where academic (e.g., study skills), life transitions (e.g., children of divorce), and social skills (e.g., problem solving, coping) matters can most easily be addressed (see Conyne & Horne, 2001).

Psychoeducational Groups: Best Fit With Prevention

A range of group types is available for use by counselors and other helpers (ASGW, 2000, cited in Gazda et al., 2001; Conyne, Wilson, & Ward, 1997). These group work types are (a) task group facilitation (e.g., Fatout & Rose, 1995; Hulse-Killacky, Killacky, & Donigian, 2001), (b) psychoeducational groups (e.g.,

B. Brown, 1997; N. Brown, 1998), (c) counseling groups (e.g., Gladding, 1999; Trotzer, 1999), and (d) psychotherapy groups (e.g., Klein, Bernard, & Singer, 1992; Yalom, 1995). Prevention can be accomplished through using group work of any type, and, arguably perhaps, it should be a component of all group work.

Task groups, such as a neighborhood watch group, can plan and implement safety procedures that can lower the incidence of local crime. Counseling groups can help members turn increased awareness of an interpersonal problem, such as poor relationships with others, into interpersonal skills that can improve the formation of future relationships. Therapy groups can at times help members to avoid thoughts or behaviors that continually have proven to be dysfunctional, so that similar problems in the future might be lessened. Psychoeducational groups, however, are assuming increased importance as the desired group method for accomplishing prevention goals.

As noted earlier, psychoeducational groups for prevention are one of the eight major training domains that Romano and Hage (2000) identified for preparing counseling psychologists to assume a prevention agenda. Psychoeducational groups are directly relevant to prevention because they involve a clear focus on factors that are central to conducting prevention (ASGW, 1998, cited in Gazda et al., 2001; Conyne & Wilson, 1999; Ettin, Heiman, & Kopel, 1988; Hoyt, 1995; McKay & Paleg, 1992; Ward, 2000). These factors are summarized next.

Psychoeducational groups

• *Focus on normal human development and functioning and/or those at risk.* Psychoeducational groups can readily be focused on helping members to develop existing resources and to prevent maladaptive processes from occurring. As well, these groups can be used effectively with members who are at risk developmentally for the future manifestation of psychological, behavioral, educational, or emotional disturbance.

• *Set specific goals.* Goals are set clearly for the psychoeducational group experience. Examples include to become a more effective problem solver, to learn attending skills, or to prevent the onset of substance abuse.

• *Include structure.* The psychoeducational group process is not completely free flowing, but often incorporates the use of timed events and various structured experiences, such as dyads, skill training, and role playing.

• *Value efficiency.* Psychoeducational groups are time limited overall, and within each session attention is given to interacting within set timelines. Each session is formatted within the overall general plan of the group.

• *Enhance education.* Psychoeducational groups seek to teach members important information about a phenomenon of interest for the group (e.g., about stress in a stress prevention group). They are informative, and may include brief lecturettes and dissemination of relevant materials.

• *Develop skills.* Psychoeducational groups are intended to enhance specific skills of members. Attention during each session generally is given to training members in the acquisition, practice, and display of a skill or skill set. For example, in a stress prevention group, members might practice the skill set of relaxation and learn how to use relaxation in their lives to reduce stress.

• *Generate group member interaction in the here and now.* Psychoeducational groups are planned and conducted to elevate the importance of member-to-member interaction, set within a here-and-now (presentized) context. They are *not* centered on the one-way transmission of information or by a complete focus on skill training. The thoughts, feelings, and behavior of members are critically important.

• *Attend to psychological processes and group dynamics.* Psychoeducational groups harness member interaction and give attention to processes and dynamics occurring within the here-and-now group activities. The processing of meaning derived from these interactions and dynamics is a centrally important focus.

• *Emphasize application.* Psychoeducational groups are very concerned with how members will apply learning from the group to their everyday lives outside the group. Therefore, these groups frequently include specific attention to issues of transferability to ongoing life situations.

PREVENTION GROUP IMPLEMENTATION GUIDELINES

A general set of guidelines exists to guide the conduct of prevention groups (Conyne & Wilson, 1999). These guidelines emerge from the definition of prevention groups, cited earlier, and are adapted from the ASGW Best Practice Guidelines for Group Workers (ASGW, 1998, cited in Gazda et al., 2001), that are focused on the steps of Planning, Performing, and Processing.

To conduct a prevention group, the following steps can serve as a guide:

Planning Steps

• Conduct an ecological assessment, using various means (e.g., interviews, surveys, focus groups), to identify target population, setting, needs, and press. It is important that the group content and purpose fit the life situation of prospective members.

• Collaborate for planning with a set of people who represent the target and setting.

• Leaders should not design prevention groups in isolation, but work with cultural informants to coproduce a viable plan.

• Identify a generative body of knowledge that pertains to the emerging focal area.

• The professional literature contains descriptions of successful prevention groups and can serve as an external reference for idea generation (e.g., see Albee & Gullotta, 1997; Bloom, 1996; Price et al., 1988; Weissberg, Gullotta, Hampton, Ryan, & Adams, 1997).

• Determine collaboratively with members of the target population what is to be prevented (e.g., sexually transmitted diseases) and/or promoted (e.g., advocacy skills) through the group, and how evaluation will be accomplished. Many programs intending to be preventive have failed because this step was not adequately addressed. It is a key point, serving in many ways to distinguish prevention programs from others.

• Develop a written, detailed overall and session-by-session group plan that specifies such elements as group goals, group development model, recruitment, group setting, activities, strategies, resources, timelines, leader qualifications and responsibilities, and evaluation. Prevention groups generally follow the psychoeducational group format. Careful overall planning and session-by-session detailing is important.

• Include brevity and structure within the format, while orienting the group toward goal accomplishment. Prevention groups are usually concise and focused, with an emphasis from the start on goals to be reached.

Performing Steps

Attend to the balance to be achieved between information delivery, skill development, and group processes. Make sure group processes are harnessed. Many intended prevention groups become misbalanced, favoring the delivery of information and using a one-way style from the leader to members. While sometimes this approach may be useful (such as when part of a comprehensive treatment program), in a stand-alone prevention group it ignores a vitally important ingredient of all group work: promoting and learning from group interaction and processes.

Seek to enhance cohesion in the group, including selecting members who share a similar problem set. Prevention groups can benefit from membership that is homogeneous regarding the problem or issue constituting the focus of the group (e.g., substance abuse prevention). Heterogeneity for other characteristics can be intentionally selected for, or be trusted to develop from, the group composition itself as the group unfolds. A key is to design to promote cohesion.

Seek to approach skill development, as appropriate to the setting and population, through the use of a performance model that includes these steps: (a) present content to be learned, (b) describe relevant skill, (c) demonstrate skill, (d) practice, perhaps in pairs, (e) give performance feedback, (f) discuss application to real world settings, (g) retry skill, and (h) hold general processing discussion with entire group (Conyne & Wilson, 1999). An important goal of prevention groups generally is for members to enhance existing skills in the area of focus, such as in problem solving, and a systematic approach to training can be very useful.

Processing Steps

Include processing within each session and, for leaders, between sessions, to promote learning, make appropriate adaptations, and consider application to real-world settings and demands. As Lieberman, Yalom, and Miles (1973) clearly demonstrated, meaning attribution is a centrally important group leader function. Members need to be helped to translate the events and experiences of group life to personal meaning and application (Conyne, 1999).

Evaluate group process and outcomes (over time, if possible) to determine accomplishment of prevention goals. A criticism of all group work, and of prevention groups in particular, revolves around the lack of evaluation to demonstrate effectiveness. Include evaluation from the program's initial steps through formative evaluation measures and, at the end, through summative evaluation. As we have seen earlier, prevention groups can be effective. The challenge is to demonstrate that fact in ongoing practice.

BRIEF CASE EXAMPLE

A preventive, psychoeducational group was conducted to increase perceived social support among members (Brand, Lakey, & Berman, 1995). This prevention group was identified as "excellent" through the extensive reviews conducted by University of Cincinnati and University of Georgia researchers cited earlier (Conyne & Horne, 2001).

As discussed earlier, prevention groups are described with low frequency in the scholarly literature. Those reported usually are described only partially and tend to be flawed in some way, lacking some aspect of expected methodology (e.g., no control group) or of delivery (e.g., giving only minimal attention to group process). The Brand et al. (1995) preventive psychoeducational group intervention contained noticeable strengths while reiterating weaknesses that need to be shorn up in future groups. The brief description follows.

Fifty-one single adults (divorced, widowed, separated, never married) who were judged as being free from significant psychopathology (i.e., they were generally healthy) composed the study. The purpose was to increase perceived social support among participants who self-assessed their current level of social support as low (thus, this group would qualify as an "indicated" prevention group).

The group was set within an experimental design. Research participants were randomly assigned to four psychoeducational groups and one no treatment control group. Each group had 4 to 10 members. Group leaders were four doctoral-level and two master's-level graduate students. The groups were co-led. The coleaders were highly trained and closely supervised, more so than may be practiced in typical settings.

The psychoeducational group lasted for 13 weeks, with each weekly session lasting 3 hours. The first six sessions focused on skills training (e.g., positive assertions to self and others, conflict resolution strategies, active listening, making and refusing requests, expressing negative affect appropriately, and responding to criticism). The last seven sessions focused on cognitive restructuring (e.g., identifying and correcting dysfunctional attitudes occurring in relationships, positive self-statements, self-acceptance, and reconceptualizing negative thoughts and feelings). Most of each session was devoted to modeling, coaching, and rehearsing. Reading and homework were used throughout the group. While attention to group process was included, the intervention emphasized content.

Assessment was accomplished using standard testing measures in a pretest and a delayed posttest design (1 to 3 weeks following completion of the groups). Results showed no statistical differences between groups for social support from friends. However, the group intervention did significantly increase ($p = 0.01$) perceived support from family, with increases in self-cognition being larger than those for perceived support.

Although this effort possessed many assets, especially related to its experimental design

and its attempt to use the group method affect social support, which is an important component of healthy functioning, deficits were present in this otherwise admirable project. As is typical in most reports of group interventions, details about methodology were scant. More must be learned about the ongoing processes of involvement within and across group sessions. A second deficit is evident by the diminution of process in favor of content. This, too, is a frequent problem with prevention groups, as they continue to disproportionately emphasize information dissemination over interpersonal and group processes. Balance between content and process is needed in prevention groups, just as in any other type of group (Donigian & Hulse-Killacky, 1995).

SUMMARY

Prevention groups fit centrally within a paradigm expansion that is needed in mental health. Psychoeducational groups are emerging as an especially important prevention resource.

A growing number of acceptable examples of prevention groups, such as the one highlighted above, are appearing in the literature. Although most of these reported groups do not fulfill all desired research and practice criteria, they can serve as useful reference points for designing and delivering future prevention groups that may possess fewer deficits.

Considerably more attention, however, is needed in training programs, in service delivery, and in research projects to continue the evolution of prevention groups. It is hoped that the contents of this chapter might assist in guiding readers as they engage in this effort.

REFERENCES

Albee, G. (1986). Toward a just society: Lessons from observations on the primary prevention of psychopathology. *American Psychologist, 41*, 891-898.

Albee, G., & Gullotta, T. (Eds.). (1997). *Primary prevention works.* Thousand Oaks, CA: Sage.

Barlow, S., Burlingame, G., & Fuhriman, A. (2000). Therapeutic application of groups: From Pratt's "Thought Control Classes" to modern group psychotherapy. *Group Dynamics: Theory, Research, and Practice, 4,* 115-134.

Bednar, R., & Kaul, T. (1994). Experiential group research: Can the canon fire? In A. Bergin & S. Garfield (Eds.), *Handbook of psychotherapy and behavior change* (4th ed.) (pp. 631-667). New York: Wiley.

Bloom, M. (1996). *Primary preventive practices.* Thousand Oaks, CA: Sage.

Botvin, G., Schinke, S., & Orlandi, M. (Eds.). (1995). *Drug abuse prevention with multiethnic youth.* Thousand Oaks, CA: Sage.

Brand, E., Lakey, B., & Berman, S. (1995). A preventive, psychoeducational approach to increase perceived social support. *American Journal of Community Psychology, 23,* 117-135.

Brown, B. (1997). Psychoeducation group work. *Counseling and Human Development, 29,* 1-14.

Brown, N. (1998). *Psychoeducational groups.* Philadelphia: Accelerated Development.

Budman, S., Demby, A., Redondo, J., Hannan, M., Feldstein, M., Ringer, J., et al. (1988). Comparative outcomes in time-limited individual and group psychotherapy. *International Journal of Group Psychotherapy, 38,* 63-86.

Burlingame, G., Kircher, J., & Taylor, S. (1994). Methodological considerations in group psychotherapy research: Past, present, and future practices. In A. Fuhriman & G. Burlingame (Eds.), *Handbook of group psychotherapy: An empirical and clinical synthesis* (pp. 41-82). New York: Wiley.

Cardemil, E., & Barber, J. (2001). Building a model for prevention practice: Depression as an example. *Professional Psychology, Research and Practice, 32,* 392-401.

Conyne, R. (1987). *Primary preventive counseling: Empowering people and systems.* Muncie, IN: Accelerated Development.

Conyne, R. (1994). Preventive counseling. *Counseling and Human Development, 27,* 1-10.

Conyne, R. (1999). *Failures in group work: How we can learn from our mistakes.* Thousand Oaks, CA: Sage.

Conyne, R. (2003, August). Prevention groups as a means for optimizing well-being. In S. Barlow (Chair), *Thematic programming symposium: Optimizing well-being though group modalities.* Presented at the annual meeting of the American Psychological Association, Toronto, Ontario, Canada.

Conyne, R., & Horne, A. (Special Issue Eds.). (2001). Special Issue: The use of groups for prevention. *Journal for Specialists in Group Work, 26,* 205-292.

Conyne, R., & Wilson, F. R. (1999). *Psychoeducation group training program* (Video #14Y1812). New York: Insight Media.

Conyne, R., & Wilson, F. R. (2001). Division 49 position paper: Recommendations of the task force for the use of groups for prevention. *Group Psychologist, 11,* 10-11.

Conyne, R., Wilson, F. R., & Ward, D. (1997). *Comprehensive group work: What it means & how to teach it.* Alexandria, VA: American Counseling Association.

Corey, G. (1995). *Theory and practice of group counseling* (4th ed.). Pacific Grove, CA: Brooks/Cole.

Cowen, E., & Work, W. (1988). Resilient children, psychological wellness, and primary prevention. *American Journal of Community Psychology, 16,* 591-607.

Donigian, J., & Hulse-Killacky, D. (Chairs). (1995, January). *Effective group leadership: Balancing process and content.* Workshop presented at the Third National Conference of the Association for Specialists in Group Work, University of Georgia, Athens.

Durlak, J., & Wells, A. (1997). Primary prevention mental health programs for children and adolescents: A meta-analytic review. *American Journal of Community Psychology, 25,* 115-152.

Ettin, M., Heiman, M., & Kopel, S. (1988). Group building: Developing protocols for psychoeducational groups. *Group, 12,* 205-225.

Fatout, M., & Rose, S. (1995). *Task groups in the social services.* Thousand Oaks, CA: Sage.

Fuhriman, A., & Burlingame, G. (Eds.). (1994). *Handbook of group psychotherapy: An empirical and clinical synthesis.* New York: Wiley.

Fuhriman, A., & Burlingame, G. (2001). Group psychotherapy training and effectiveness. *International Journal of Group Psychotherapy, 51,* 399-416.

Gazda, G., Ginter, E., & Horne, A. (2001). *Group counseling and group psychotherapy: Theory and application.* Needham Heights, MA: Allyn & Bacon.

Gladding, S. (1999). *Group work: A counseling specialty* (3rd ed.). Upper Saddle River, NJ: Prentice Hall.

Hage, S. (2000). The role of counseling psychology in preventing male violence against female intimates. *Counseling Psychologist, 28,* 797-828.

Hendren, R., Atkins, D., Sumner, F., Calvin, R., & Barber, J. (1987). Model for the group treatment of eating disorders. *International Journal of Group Psychotherapy, 37,* 589-602.

Horne, A., & Rosenthal, R. (1997). Research in group work: How did we get where we are? *Journal for Specialists in Group Work, 22,* 228-240.

Hoyt, M. (1995). *Brief therapy and managed care: Readings for contemporary practice.* San Francisco: Jossey-Bass.

Hulse-Killacky, D., Killacky, J., & Donigian, J. (2001). *Making task groups work in your world.* Upper Saddle River, NJ: Merrill Prentice Hall.

Kagan, N., Kagan, H., & Watson, M. (1995). Stress reduction in the workplace: The effectiveness of psychoeducational programs. *Journal of Counseling Psychology, 42,* 71-78.

Klein, R., Bernard, H., & Singer, D. (Eds.). (1992). *Handbook of contemporary group psychotherapy.* Madison, CT: International Universities Press.

Lieberman, M., Yalom, I., & Miles, M. (1973). *Encounter groups: First facts.* New York: Basic Books.

Maccoby, N., & Altman, D. (1988). Disease prevention in communities: The Stanford Heart Disease Prevention Program. In R. Price, E. Cowen, R. Lorion, & J. Ramos-McKay (Eds.), *14 ounces of prevention: A casebook for practitioners* (pp. 165-174). Washington, DC: American Psychological Association.

McKay, M., & Paleg, K. (1992). *Focal group psychotherapy.* Oakland, CA: New Harbinger.

Mrazek, P., & Haggerty. R. (1994). *Reducing risks for mental disorders: Frontiers for preventive intervention research.* Washington, DC: National Academy Press.

Mussell, M., Binford, R., & Fulkerson, J. (2000). Eating disorders: Summary of risk factors, prevention programming, and prevention research. *Counseling Psychologist, 28,* 764-796.

Piper, W. (1994). Client variables. In A. Fuhriman & G. Burlingame (Eds.), *Handbook of group psychotherapy: An empirical and clinical synthesis* (pp. 83-113). New York: Wiley.

Piper, W., & McCallum, M. (1991). Group interventions for persons who have experienced loss: Description and evaluative research. *Group Analysis, 24,* 363-373.

Price, R., Cowen, E., Lorion, R., & Ramos-McKay, J. (Eds.). (1988). *14 ounces of prevention: A casebook for practitioners.* Washington, DC: American Psychological Association.

Romano, J., & Hage, S. (2000). Prevention and counseling psychology: Revitalizing commitments for the 21st century. In J. Romano & S. Hage (Special Section Editors), Prevention in counseling psychology. *Counseling Psychologist, 28,* 733-763.

Seligman, M. E. P. (1998). Building human strength: Psychology's forgotten mission. *APA Monitor, 29,* 2.

Seligman, M. (2002). *Authentic happiness: Using the new positive psychology to realize your potential for lasting fulfillment.* New York: Free Press.

Seligman, M. E. P., & Csikszentimihalyi, M. (2000). Positive psychology. *American Psychologist, 55,* 5-14.

Shure, M., & Spivack, G. (1988). Interpersonal cognitive problem solving. In R. Price, E. Cowen, R. Lorion, & J. Ramos-McKay (Eds.), *14 ounces of prevention: A casebook for practitioners* (pp. 69-82). Washington, DC: American Psychological Association.

Snyder, C. R., & Lopez, S. (Eds.). (2002). *Handbook of positive psychology.* New York: Oxford University Press.

Spitz, H. (1996). *Group psychotherapy and managed mental health care: A clinical guide for practitioners.* New York: Brunner/Mazel.

Surgeon General Report (2001). *A supplement to mental health (mental health: culture, race, and ethnicity): A report of the Surgeon General.* Washington, DC: U.S. Department of Health and Human Services.

Toseland, R., & Siporin, M. (1986). When to recommend group treatment. *International Journal of Group Psychotherapy, 36,* 172-201.

Trotzer, J. (1999). *The counselor and the group: Integrating theory, training, and practice.* Philadelphia: Taylor & Francis.

Vinokur, A., Price, R., & Schul, Y. (1995). Impact of the JOBS intervention on unemployed workers varying in risk for depression. *American Journal of Community Psychology, 23,* 39-74.

Ward, D. (2000). Special Issue: Psychoeducational group work. *Journal for Specialists in Group Work, 25,* 29-121.

Weissberg, R., Gullotta, T., Hampton, R., Ryan, B., & Adams, G. (1997). *Establishing preventive services.* Thousand Oaks, CA: Sage.

Yalom, I. (1995). *The theory and practice of group psychotherapy* (4th ed.). New York: Basic Books.

45

THE ROLE OF PEER-LED MUTUAL HELP GROUPS IN PROMOTING HEALTH AND WELL-BEING

ELENA KLAW

San Jose State University

KEITH HUMPHREYS

Stanford University

T he purpose of this chapter is to provide specialists in group interventions with cutting-edge information on theory, research, and practice related to peer-led mutual help groups. To do this, we review scholarly literature on the prevalence of mutual help groups, the characteristics of participants, and the effects of group participation on the health of members. Mutual help group research has a more than 20-year history and has been carefully reviewed in the past (Humphreys & Rappaport, 1994; Kurtz, 1997; Lieberman, 1986; Powell, 1987); the present chapter highlights selected examples of work from the field.

In light of available literature, and our own expertise working in a North American context, mutual help in the United States is presented as focal.

DEFINITIONS

The terms *self-help group* and *mutual help group* are synonyms and are used interchangeably in this chapter. Surgeon General C. Everett Koop's *Workshop on Self-Help and Public Health* (1990) defined self-helps group as "[s]elf-governing groups whose members share

Author's Note: Thanks go to Erin Petersen and Lynzey Baldwin for their help in preparing this manuscript. Preparation of this manuscript was funded in part by the Department of Veterans Affairs Mental Health Strategic Healthcare and by a grant from The California Wellness Foundation.

Table 45.1   Mutual Help Groups Addressing Prevalent Chronic Conditions and Leading Causes of Mortality

Prevalent Chronic Condition	*Example Group*
Arthritis	Young et Heart
Visual impairment	Council of Citizens With Low Vision Support Groups
Hearing impairment	Self-Help for Hard of Hearing People
Ischemic heart disease	Mended Hearts
Diabetes mellitus	Diabetics Anonymous
Malignant neoplasms	Make Today Count
Psychiatric disabilities	Recovery Inc.
Leading Cause of Mortality	*Example Group*
Tobacco	Nicotine Anonymous
Diet/Activity patterns	Overeaters Anonymous
Alcohol	Women for Sobriety
Microbial agents	Hepatitis B Foundation Support Groups
Toxic agents	Parents Against Lead
Firearms	Parents of Murdered Children
Sexual behavior	Blacks Educating Blacks About Sexual Health Issues
Motor vehicles	Mothers Against Drunk Driving
Illicit drug use	Narcotics Anonymous

a common health concern and give each other emotional support and material aid, charge either no fee or only a small fee for membership, and place a high value on experiential knowledge in the belief that it provides special understanding of a situation. In addition to providing mutual support for their members, such groups may also be involved in information, education, material aid, and social advocacy in their communities." Most self-help groups meet face-to-face, but a significant number have meetings using new technologies such as the Internet and teleconferencing (see Chapter 43, this volume).

Support groups organized and led by helping professionals are *not* considered self-help groups unless the helping professional personally shares the problem/concern of the group (e.g., a social worker who has cancer could lead a cancer self-help group) and relates as a peer

with group members (i.e., both gives and receives help and does not charge members a fee). Finally, in this chapter *self-help* refers only to community and Internet-based group activities and not to self-help books read in isolation by individuals.

THE STATUS AND SCOPE OF THE MUTUAL HELP GROUP MOVEMENT

In the United States alone, there are over 800 self-help organizations that address a plethora of health and social problems (White & Madara, 1998). Indeed, mutual help organizations exist for almost every major chronic condition and leading cause of mortality (McGinnis & Foege, 1993) in the United States (see Table 45.1).

A recent national survey indicated that a large number of Americans participate in mutual help

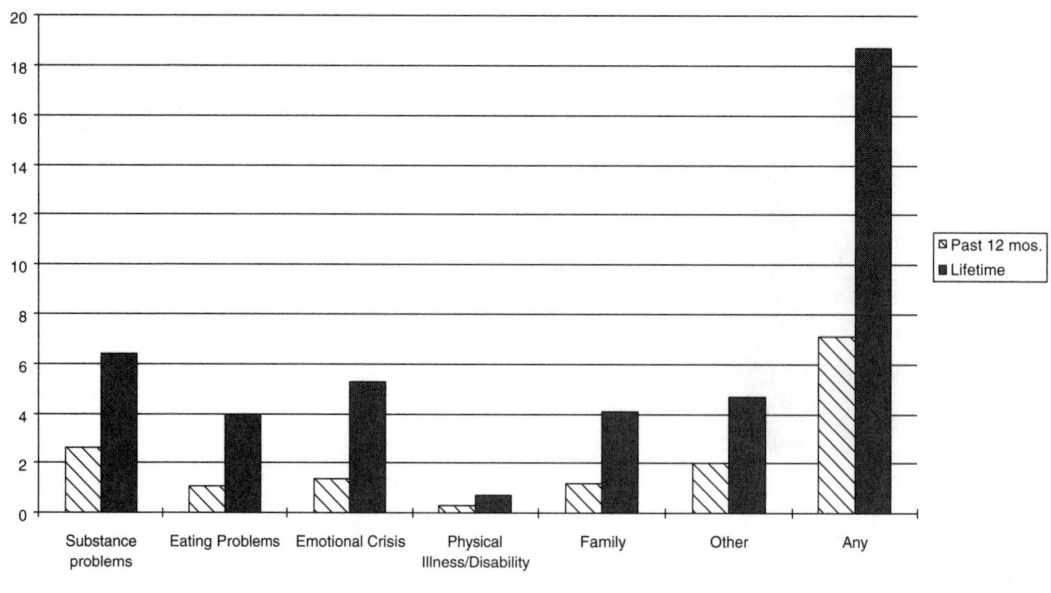

Figure 45.1   Lifetime and Past 12 Months Participation in Self-Help Groups

groups for a variety of health concerns (Kessler, Mickelson, & Zhao, 1997). As shown in Figure 45.1, approximately 7% of American adults (about 11 million people) participated in a mutual help group in the past year, and 18% have done so at some point in their lifetime.

The most common type of participation identified in the survey was for mutual help groups that address substance abuse and emotional problems. A key reason for this is that the largest and most attended mutual help organization is Alcoholics Anonymous (AA) (Weisner, Greenfield, & Room, 1995), which has approximately 1 million members in the United States. The importance of AA, other addiction groups (e.g., Women for Sobriety, Moderation Management), and mental health-related groups (e.g., Manic Depressive and Depressive Association) to the nation's de facto system of care has been well documented (Kessler et al., 1997; Room & Greenfield, 1993). Figure 45.2 illustrates this point using data from a national study of help-seeking for substance abuse and psychiatric concerns (Kessler et al., 1997). Impressively, Americans make more visits to mutual help groups for addiction and psychiatric problems than they do to the entire mental health specialty care sector (i.e., psychiatrists, psychologists, social workers, etc.).

Because they are so widely attended, addiction and mental health self-help groups are the best known. However, the self-help group movement is by no means limited to these sorts of groups. As was shown in Figure 45.1, millions of Americans participate in groups focused on chronic physical illnesses, disabilities, stigmatized statuses, and family problems (Davison, Pennebaker, & Dickerson, 2000). Furthermore, new self-help organizations are constantly coming into being in response to new health and social concerns, including latex allergies, postterrorist attack trauma (e.g., groups were formed after the terrorist attacks at the World Trade Center and in Oklahoma City), and adverse reactions to antidepressant medication (e.g., Prozac).

The national survey revealed some important facts about the characteristics of self-help group participants. First, with the exception of groups for eating problems (whose membership is composed almost entirely of Caucasian women), African Americans and Whites are equally likely to attend all types of self-help groups. Furthermore, individuals with low incomes ($0-$20,000/year) are more likely to participate than are middle-class and affluent individuals. Finally, individuals who are divorced or separated and have less social support are

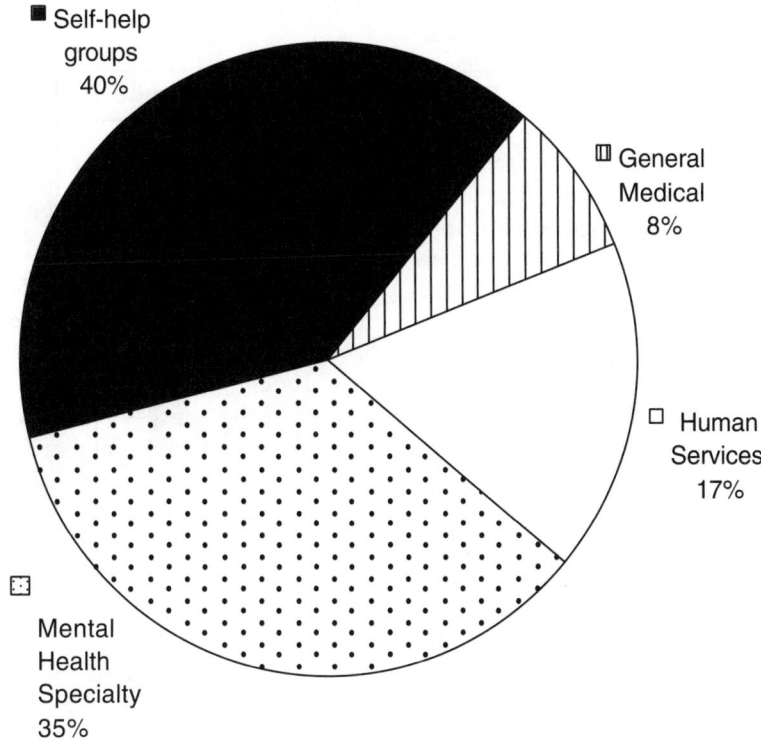

Figure 45.2   Help-Seeking Visits for Addiction and Psychiatric Problems by U.S. Adults

more likely to attend groups than are married individuals and individuals with extensive social support. Given these data, we may conclude that self-help groups have significant potential to benefit diverse racial groups and individuals with low financial and social resources.

In addition, Internet technology has greatly enhanced individuals' ability to exchange information and emotional support. Hundreds of online mutual help groups (OMHGs) for health and social problems have been formed in the past decade (Madara, 1999), and over 20 million Web pages now provide health-related information (Lawrence & Giles, 1999). With about 90 million Internet users in North America (Internet Society, 1999, cited in Kerlin, 1999) and more than 150 million worldwide (CommerceNet Consortium, 1999), online mutual aid networks have considerable potential to promote health, well-being, and empowerment. The Internet expands mutual help access to individuals

unable to attend face-to-face groups such as the mobility impaired, homebound, and chronically ill. It also provides a safe forum for those such as the socially phobic and individuals who represent minority segments of a given problem community (e.g., female problem drinkers) who might feel uncomfortable attending live meetings (Davison et al., 2000; Klaw, Huebsch, & Humphreys, 2000; Madara, 1999).

SIMILARITIES AND DIFFERENCES BETWEEN SELF-HELP GROUPS AND GROUP PSYCHOTHERAPY

Mental health professionals usually think of mutual help organizations as alternative forms of treatment for people with problems in living (Borkman, 1991; Rappaport, 1993). Although mutual aid offers many of the benefits associated with group psychotherapy, such as emotional support, role modeling, and instillation of hope (Davison et al., 2000; Yalom, 1995), mutual help groups differ from professional psychotherapy in several significant ways. Borkman (1991) outlines these distinctions in a special issue of *The American Journal of Community Psychology* focused on self-help. She notes, for example, that in the self-help context, a group member both provides and receives services. The term *prosumer* thus illustrates the nonhierarchical roles embodied in mutual help. Furthermore, mutual help involves reciprocal relationships that are neither mediated nor regulated by the exchange of money. In contrast to professionals' emphasis on service provision from experts who are designated by titles, training, and credentials, mutual help posits that individuals can come together voluntarily to take action toward resolving or addressing shared concerns (Borkman, 1991; Salem, Reischel, Gallacher, & Randall, 2000). As described by Salem and her colleagues (2000) in their study of Schizophrenics Anonymous, mutual help groups thereby offer an alternate referent community in which expertise and power is based on experience with the issue at hand. For individuals struggling with such stigmatized concerns as mental illness and addiction, the opportunity to help others may be unique. As described by Riessman and Carroll's (1995) helper therapy principle, the experience of providing help is associated with significant improvements in psychosocial adjustment (Roberts et al., 1999). Qualitative studies suggest that as experienced mutual help members internalize the empowering narratives of the group, they often undergo positive identity transformation (Humphreys, 2000; Kennedy & Humphreys, 1994; Klaw & Humphreys, 2000; Rappaport, 1993; Salem et al., 2000).

Social climate comparisons of mutual help and psychotherapy groups suggest the two modalities may differ significantly in process, even when they do not generate different outcomes (Toro, Rappaport, & Seidman, 1987; Toro et al., 1988). Mentally ill mutual help participants reported their groups had greater cohesion, more active leaders, and more of a task-focused orientation. Psychotherapy group participants, in contrast, perceived their groups as more encouraging of expressing negative feelings and more flexible in structure.

Specific Benefits of Self-Help Groups to Health and Well-Being

Self-help organizations can contribute to health and well-being through two main avenues:

1. *Independent, community-based self-help organizations can serve as an accessible, low-cost resource for managing illness and promoting health.*

Increasing access to health-promoting resources and reducing health disparities between individuals from different socioeconomic strata are key goals of public health, as reflected in the *Healthy People 2000* initiative (1990) and in the mission statements of many health-related foundations. Because self-help groups are typically free or nearly free of charge, they have significant potential to help society meet these goals. Despite their low cost, community-based self-help groups can produce impressive health outcomes.

For example, a prospective study of 201 alcohol-abusing individuals indicated that, over a 3-year period, individuals who attended AA decreased their daily alcohol intake by 75% and decreased their alcohol dependence symptoms (e.g., blackouts) by 71%. These positive outcomes were comparable to those of a comparison group that had sought treatment from a professional outpatient service provider (Humphreys & Moos, 1996). Most important, AA participants in this study consumed 45% less alcohol-related health care resources (almost $2,000 less per person) over time than did individuals who initially sought professional outpatient treatment. These results were replicated in a study of over 1,600 substance abuse patients.

Turning to a different type of self-help group, Marmar, Horowitz, and Weiss (1988) found evidence supporting the effectiveness of self-help groups for complicated conjugal bereavement. Treatment-seeking widows who had shown no evidence of spontaneous improvement within 4 months of bereavement ($n = 61$) were randomly assigned to either a bereavement self-help group or 12 sessions of professional psychotherapy. At

4-month follow-up, self-help group participants improved in a variety of psychiatric (e.g., depression, anxiety), social adjustment, and work functioning outcomes. Across outcome measures, the average degree of improvement experienced by self-help group participants was 21%, which was comparable to that experienced by the widows who had received professional psychotherapy.

In terms of chronic illness, mutual aid groups can increase participants' knowledge of their condition and improve their coping and self-care (Humphreys, 1997). For example, Hinrichsen, Revenson, and Shinn (1985) found that participation in Scoliosis Association self-help groups was associated with less shame about the condition, fewer psychosomatic symptoms, and a more positive life outlook. Similarly, African Americans with sickle-cell disease who became highly involved in mutual help groups (Nash & Kramer, 1993) experienced decreased emotional upset and reduced occupational and interpersonal impairment.

Mutual help groups also appear to be helpful in promoting weight loss, which is of tremendous importance in the United States, given the alarming statistic that one third of the nation's population is now overweight (Kuczmarski, Flegal, Campbell, & Johnson, 1994). A study of weight-loss mutual help groups in Norway found that participants lost an average of 14 pounds over 8 weeks, and that 85% of this weight loss was maintained a year later (Grimsmo, Helgesen, & Borchgrevink, 1981). The "staying power" of the effects of weight-loss mutual help groups stands in sharp contrast to the transient benefits of most diets undertaken in isolation by overweight individuals. Although the number of longitudinal studies examining the effects of mutual help group participation on health is currently small, the studies that have been done suggest that free, member-run self-help groups can produce positive health and social outcomes.

2. Self-help groups can enhance the quality of professionally run health promotion and health care programs.

Self-help groups that are integrated into professionally operated health interventions are different from independent, community-based groups in that they lose some of their grassroots flavor and self-direction. Nevertheless, studies (see Gilden, Hendryx, Clar, Casia, & Singh, 1992) suggest that self-help groups can be successfully incorporated into professional programs in a fashion that enhances outcomes with little additional cost. For example, Jason, Gruder, and Martino (1987) implemented a worksite smoking cessation program composed of a manual and a related television program. Twenty-one out of 43 companies were randomly assigned to have this intervention supplemented by employee-led self-help groups. Companies that had employee-led groups achieved average postintervention quit rates of 41% compared to 21% in companies without groups.

Turning from health promotion to health care, a controlled evaluation of self-help groups for parents of premature infants also reported positive results. Twenty-eight parents were randomly assigned to participate in a group co-led by a nurse and a mother who had successfully raised a premature infant. Parents in the experimental condition visited their infants more often (4.5 versus 3.1 times per week) and spent about 20% more time touching, talking to, and gazing at their infants during hospital visits than did controls ($n = 29$). Three months after the babies were discharged, self-help group participants also showed more involvement with their infant during feeding and reported greater confidence in raising their infant than did parents in the control condition (Minde et al., 1980).

Equally impressive outcomes have been found with discharged psychiatric inpatients. Patients randomly assigned to participate in a patient-operated mutual help network were half as likely to be rehospitalized within 10 months as were controls (Edmunson, Bedell, Archer, & Gordon, 1982). In addition, when patients assigned to the mutual help network were rehospitalized, their stays averaged only 7 days, compared to 25 days for controls. Similarly, a structured self-help format involving videotaped information and participant discussion was found to be equally effective in group cognitive-behavioral therapy in helping clients with Binge Eating Disorder (Peterson et al., 2001). Findings from these projects converge with those of studies of community-based self-help groups (Humphreys & Moos, 1996, 2001;

Kennedy, 1989), demonstrating that self-help groups not only promote positive outcomes but also may take a significant burden off the formal health care system.

SUMMARY OF BENEFITS OF SELF-HELP

Self-help groups are by no means a panacea for all the psychological, social, and health-related problems faced by individuals and communities. The evidence reviewed here, however, demonstrates the following:

- Self-help groups are a low-cost helping resource accessed by a diverse group of over 10 million Americans.
- Self-help group participation produces positive health outcomes and also may lower health care expenditures.
- Professionally operated health care and health promotion programs can be improved by integrating self-help approaches.

RECOMMENDATIONS FOR GROUP WORK SPECIALISTS

Given these benefits of self-help groups, expanding and supporting the self-help group movement is clearly an important mechanism for improving health and well-being. We now turn to recommendations for how this expansion and support could be accomplished and how mental health professionals might be involved.

The Role of Clinician Referrals

Clinicians can expand the range of patients they assist by becoming familiar with the broad array of options that exist for addressing psychological and health-related concerns. In addition to books and continuing education programs, the Internet can be a useful resource in this regard. For example, as noted on its Web site, www.selfhelpgroups.org, the American Self-Help Clearinghouse (White & Madara, 2001) provides an online searchable database of over 1,000 national and international self-help support groups for addictions, bereavement, health, mental health, disabilities, abuse, parenting, caregiver concerns, and other life stressors. The site also lists local self-help clearinghouses worldwide, research studies, information on starting face-to-face and online groups, and a registry for those interested in starting national or international self-help groups. Dr. John Grohol's Mental Health Page (Grohol, 2002) at http://www.psychcentral.com also provides a searchable index for a wide variety of mental health and support resources. In his book *The Insider's Guide to Mental Health Resources Online, 2000/2001 Edition,* Grohol explains and evaluates various search tools and databases, describes specific mental health sites, and provides advice on such topics as to how to research particular disorders, network with other professionals, and search for relevant grants.

Ethical Considerations in Providing Referrals to Self-Help

In their book *Community Psychology: A Common Sense Approach to Mental Health,* Scileppi, Teed, and Torres (2000, p. 118) note that professionals are bound by ethical principles to ensure that psychotherapy will first "do no harm." Thus, they admonish clinicians to only refer to self-help groups that are effective and therapeutic. On the basis of the framework they provide, issues that professionals might consider and discuss in making a referral include the training and expertise of group leadership, the group's adherence to confidentiality standards, and the available evidence of group outcomes. Of course, mutual help groups cannot be expected to work for everyone. Many mutual help group participants drop out shortly after becoming involved (Luke, Roberts, & Rappaport, 1993), and others find themselves unable to change problematic behaviors despite attending many meetings. Individuals struggling with substance abuse, for example, may try a variety of professional and mutual help approaches (e.g., AA, Moderation Management, Women for Sobriety, Rational Recovery) before achieving satisfying results (Kaskutas & Weisner, 1996; Klaw & Humphreys, 2000).

PROFESSIONAL MUTUAL HELP COLLABORATION

The number one recommendation put forth in the *Surgeon General's Workshop on Self-Help and Public Health* (1988) was to incorporate "information and experiential knowledge about self-help in the training and practices of professionals" (p. 32). Studies have suggested that students in both psychology and social work have positive attitudes toward collaborating with self-help organizations and desire further training in this area (Meissen, Mason, & Gleason, 1991). On the basis of a public health approach, community psychiatry has long recognized the key role of mutual-helpers in buffering stress, preventing mental illness, and providing crisis intervention (Caplan & Caplan, 2000). Challenges in professional collaboration with self-help abound, however, and certain settings such as highly structured residential treatment centers may be particularly inhospitable to a mutual help approach (Salem, Gant, & Campbell, 1998). First and foremost, professionals must resist the urge to "take over" (Rappaport, 1993). Instead, professionals must be willing to let the expressed needs of the group dictate their role.

FUTURE RESEARCH DIRECTIONS

Further research is needed to assess specific psychosocial outcomes associated with mutual help participation (Davison et al., 2000). Longitudinal investigations that compare the outcomes of different mutual help groups and contrast the effects of mutual help participation with the effects of professional group psychotherapy will be particularly valuable in identifying the distinct effects of each type of care over time. Among other issues, research in this area should address the health and health care utilization effects of group participation, the current location and prevalence of different types of groups, the needs of self-help groups, the effects of external assistance on groups, and the interplay of self-help groups and formal health care systems. To maximize the utility of research results, a variety of stakeholders (e.g., self-help group members, foundation staff, policy makers, academics) should be involved in defining the nature, process, and purposes of self-help group evaluation research projects (Chesler, 1991; Nelson, Ochocka, Griffin, & Lord, 1998; Powell & Cameron, 1991). As research regarding the effects of self-help participation becomes increasingly available, clinicians who refer patients for concurrent self-help involvement will play an important role in monitoring its impact and disseminating observations to the treatment community.

SUMMARY OF WAYS IN WHICH MENTAL HEALTH SPECIALISTS AND HEALTH CARE PROFESSIONALS CAN SUPPORT SELF-HELP

To conclude, there are many ways in which mental health specialists and other health care professionals can support mutual help. Below we provide a brief list of suggestions toward that end. We urge professionals to contact individual mutual help groups to explore opportunities for fruitful ongoing collaboration.

Ways to Support Mutual Help

- Make literature about mutual help available in your waiting room or office.
- Refer clients to mutual help groups that are relevant to their concerns.
- Provide mutual help groups with access to resources such as office space and photocopying facilities.
- Provide mutual help groups with consultation regarding the focal concern of the group.
- Advise mutual help group participants in conducting research regarding the group's functioning and its effects.

REFERENCES

Borkman, T. J. (1991). Introduction to the special issue. *American Journal of Community Psychology, 19*(5), 643-651.

Caplan, G., & Caplan, R. (2000). Principles of community psychiatry. *Community Mental Health Journal, 36*(1), 7-24.

Chesler, M. A. (1991). Participatory action research with self-help groups: An alternative paradigm for inquiry and action. *American Journal of Community Psychology, 19*(5), 757-769.

CommerceNet Consortium. (1999). *CommerceNet/ Nielsen Internet demographics survey.* Retrieved from www.commerce.net/information/surveys.

Davison, K. P., Pennebaker, J. W., & Dickerson, S. S. (2000). Who talks? The social psychology of illness support groups. *American Psychologist, 55*(2), 205-217.

Edmunson, E. D., Bedell, J. R., Archer, R. P., & Gordon, R. E. (1982). Integrating skill building and peer support in mental health treatment: The early intervention and community network development projects. In A. M. Jeger and R. S. Slotnick (Eds.), *Community mental health and behavioral ecology* (pp. 127-139). New York: Praeger.

Gilden, J. L., Hendryx, M. S., Clar, S., Casia, C., & Singh, S. P. (1992). Diabetes support groups improve health care of older diabetic patients. *Journal of the American Geriatrics Society, 40,* 147-150.

Grimsmo, A., Helgesen, G., & Borchgrevink, C. (1981). Short-term and long-term effects of lay groups on weight reduction. *British Medical Journal, 283*(6299), 1093-1095.

Grohol, J. (2001). *The insider's guide to mental health resources online, 2000/2001 edition.* New York: Guilford.

Grohol, J. (2002). *Psych Central: Dr. John Grohol's mental health page.* Retrieved from http://www.psychcentral.com.

Healthy people 2000: National health promotion and disease prevention objectives. (1990). Washington, DC: U.S. Department of Health and Human Services.

Hinrichsen, G. A., Revenson, T. A., & Shinn, M. (1985). Does self-help help? An empirical investigation of scoliosis peer support groups. *Journal of Social Issues, 41*(1), 65-87.

Humphreys, K. (1997). Individual and social benefits of self-help groups. *Social Policy, 27,* 12-19.

Humphreys, K. (2000). Community narratives and personal stories in Alcoholics Anonymous. *Journal of Community Psychology, 28,* 495-506.

Humphreys, K., & Moos, R. (1996). Reduced substance abuse-related health care costs among voluntary participants in Alcoholics Anonymous. *Psychiatric Services, 47,* 709-713.

Humphreys, K., & Moos, R. (2001). Can encouraging substance abuse patients to participate in self-help groups reduce demand for health care? A quasi-experimental study. *Alcoholism: Clinical and Experimental Research, 25*(5), 711-716.

Humphreys, K., & Rappaport, J. (1994). Researching self-help/mutual aid groups and organizations: Many roads, one journey. *Applied and Preventive Psychology, 3,* 217-231.

Jason, L. A., Gruder, C. L., & Martino, S. (1987). Work site group meetings and the effectiveness of a televised smoking cessation intervention. *American Journal of Community Psychology, 15,* 57-72.

Kaskutas, L. A., & Weisner, C. (1996). *Alcoholics Anonymous involvement at treatment intake among African Americans and Caucasians.* Paper presented at the annual meeting of the Research Society on Alcoholism, Washington, DC.

Kennedy, M. (1989). *Psychiatric rehospitalization of GROWers.* Paper presented at the biennial conference of the Society for Community Research and Action, East Lansing, MI.

Kennedy, M., & Humphreys, K. (1994). Understanding worldview transformation in members of mutual help organizations. *Prevention in Human Services, 11*(1), 181-198.

Kerlin, S. (1999). *Scott Kerlin's virtual learning organization.* Retrieved from http://www.teleport.com/~skerlin.

Kessler, R. C., Mickelson, K. D., & Zhao, S. (1997). Patterns and correlates of self-help group membership in the United States. *Social Policy, 27,* 27-46.

Klaw, E., Huebsch, P. D., & Humphreys, K. (2000). Communication patterns in an on-line group for problem drinkers. *Journal of Community Psychology, 28*(5), 535-546.

Klaw, E., & Humphreys, K. (2000). Life stories of Moderation Management mutual help group members. *Contemporary Drug Problems, 27,* 779-803.

Kuczmarski, R. J., Flegal, K. M., Campbell, S. M., & Johnson, C. L. (1994). Increasing prevalence of overweight among US adults: The National Health and Nutrition Examination surveys, 1960 to 1991. *Journal of the American Medical Association, 272*(3), 205-211.

Kurtz, L. F. (1997). *Self-help and support groups.* Thousand Oaks, CA: Sage.

Lawrence, S., & Giles, L. G. (1999). Accessibility of information on the web. *Nature, 400*(8), 107-109.

Lieberman, M. (1986). Self-help groups and psychiatry. *Annual Review of Psychiatry, 5,* 744-760.

Luke, D. A., Roberts, L., & Rappaport, J. (1993). Individual, group context, and individual-group fit predictors of self-help group attendance. *Journal of Applied Behavioral Science, 29*(2), 216-238.

Madara, E. J. (1999). From church basements to world wide web sites: The growth of self-help support groups online. *International Journal of Self Help & Self Care, 1*(1), 37-48.

Marmar, C. R., Horowitz, M. J., & Weiss, D. S. (1988). A controlled trial of brief psychotherapy and mutual-help group treatment of conjugal bereavement. *American Journal of Psychiatry, 145,* 203-209.

McGinnis, J. M., & Foege, W. H. (1993). Actual causes of deaths in the United States. *JAMA: The Journal of the American Medical Association, 270,* 2207-2212.

Meissen, G. L., Mason, W. C., & Gleason, D. F. (1991). Understanding the attitudes and intentions of future professionals toward self-help. *American Journal of Community Psychology, 19*(5), 699-709.

Minde, K., Shosenberg, N., Marton, P., Thompson, J., Ripley, J., & Burns, S. (1980). Self-help groups in a premature nursery. *Journal of Pediatrics, 96(5),* 933-940.

Nash, K., & Kramer, K. D. (1993). Self-help for sickle cell disease in African-American communities. *Journal of Applied Behavioral Science, 29,* 202-215.

Nelson, G., Ochocka, J., Griffin, K., & Lord, J. (1998). "Nothing about me, without me": Participatory action research with self-help/mutual aid organizations for psychiatric consumer/survivors. *American Journal of Community Psychology, 26*(6), 881-908.

Peterson, C. B., Mitchell, J. E., Engbloom, S., Nugent, S., Mussell, M. P., Crow, S. J., et al. (2001). Self-help versus therapist-led group cognitive-behavioral treatment of binge eating disorder at follow-up. *International Journal of Eating Disorders, 30,* 363-374.

Powell, T. J. (1987). *Self-help organizations and professional practice.* Silver Spring, MD: NASW.

Powell, T. J., & Cameron, M. C. (1991). Self-help research and the public health system. *American Journal of Community Psychology, 19*(5), 797-805.

Rappaport, J. (1993). Narrative studies, personal stories, and identity development in the mutual help context. *Journal of Applied Behavioral Science, 29*(2), 239-256.

Riessman, F., & Carroll, D. (1995). *Redefining self-help.* San Francisco: Jossey-Bass.

Roberts, L. J., Salem, D., Rappaport, J., Toro, P., Luke, D., & Seidman, E. (1999). Giving and receiving help: Interpersonal transactions in mutual-help meetings and psychosocial adjustment of members. *American Journal of Community Psychology, 27*(3), 841-868.

Room, R., & Greenfield, T. (1993). Alcoholics Anonymous, other 12-step movements and psychotherapy in the U.S. population, 1990. *Addiction, 88,* 555-562.

Salem, D. A., Gant, L., & Campbell, R. (1998). The initiation of mutual-help groups within residential treatment settings. *Community Mental Health Journal, 34*(4), 419-429.

Salem, D. A., Reischel, T. M., Gallacher, F., & Randall, K. W. (2000). The role of referent and expert power in mutual help. *American Journal of Community Psychology, 28*(3), 303-325.

Scileppi, J. A., Teed, E. L., & Torres, R. D. (2000). *Community psychology: A common sense approach to mental health.* Upper Saddle River, NJ: Prentice Hall.

Surgeon General's workshop on self-help and public health. (1988). Special report (DHHS Publication No. 224-250.) Washington, DC: U.S. Government Printing Office.

Surgeon General's workshop on self-help and public health. (1990). Washington, DC: Bureau of Maternal and Child Health and Resource Development, U.S. Department of Health and Human Services.

Toro, P. A., Rappaport, J., & Seidman, E. (1987). Social climate comparisons of mutual help and psychotherapy groups. *Journal of Consulting and Clinical Psychology, 55*(3), 430-431.

Toro, P. A., Zimmerman, M. A., Seidman, E., Reischl, T., Rappaport, J., Luke, D., & Roberts, L. (1988). Professionals in mutual help groups: Impact on social climate and members' behavior. *Journal of Consulting and Clinical Psychology, 56*(4), 631-632.

Weisner, C., Greenfield, T., and Room, R. (1995). Trends in the treatment of alcohol problems in the U.S. general population, 1979 though 1990. *American Journal of Public Health, 85,* 55-60.

White, B. J., & Madara, E. (Eds.). (2001). *Self-help sourcebook online.* Retrieved from http://www.selfhelpgroups.org.

White, B. J., & Madara, E. J. (1998). *The self-help sourcebook: Your guide to community and online support groups* (6th ed.). Denville, NJ: American Self-Help Clearinghouse.

Yalom, I. D. (1995). *The theory and practice of group psychotherapy* (4th ed.). New York: Harper Collins.

46

BRIEF GROUP THERAPY

WILLIAM E. PIPER

University of British Columbia

JOHN S. OGRODNICZUK

University of British Columbia

The topic of this chapter is brief group therapy (BGT). Thus, this chapter focuses on a specific form of one of the four types of groups (task, psychoeducational, counseling, therapy) emphasized by the Association for Specialists in Group Work (2002). *Brief* is a relative term that generally refers to durations of 2 to 6 months. However, most forms of BGT last only 2 to 3 months and involve between 8 and 12 weekly sessions. BGT also tends to be time limited, which means that both the client and therapist know the duration of the group prior to its onset. Historically, brief individual therapy arose in the 1970s and early 1980s as an innovative alternative to long-term individual therapy. Following this development, BGT evolved similarly as an innovative alternative to long-term group therapy. Today, there is considerable interest in the various applications and benefits of BGT.

There are three salient reasons for providing BGT: (1) there is considerable evidence of its efficacy (effectiveness) and applicability over a broad range of problems, (2) there is considerable evidence of its cost-efficiency, and (3) there is evidence to suggest that it may be the treatment of choice for certain types of client problems.

However, there are also reasons that deter clients and therapists from participating in BGT. These include (a) client and therapist resistance to group therapy, (b) therapist administrative time, (c) therapist lack of training, (d) therapist resentment of health care reform, and (e) treatment limitations in achieving certain outcomes.

Perhaps the most powerful factor in overcoming client and therapist resistance and reluctance to participate in BGT is the continued demonstration of its favorable outcomes. There are a number of steps that therapists can take to facilitate favorable outcomes. These involve (a) careful selection of clients, (b) careful preparation of clients, (c) creation of homogeneous compositions, and (d) focusing. The next sections of this chapter elaborate on the reasons for providing BGT, the reasons that deter clients and therapists from BGT, and the steps the therapist can take to optimize favorable outcomes.

Subsequently, two examples of promising new applications are described.

REASONS FOR PROVIDING BRIEF GROUP THERAPY

Efficacy and Applicability

In 1980, Smith, Glass, and Miller published an extensive review of 475 controlled studies of psychotherapy outcome. They concluded that therapy is effective and there are minimal differences in effectiveness among different types of therapy. Almost half of the studies involved group therapy and most were brief (average duration = 11 weeks). In their 1994 book, Fuhriman and Burlingame discussed an additional 22 reviews of the group literature. They concluded that group therapy consistently produced positive effects with diverse disorders. Most of the group therapies were also brief. Reviewing 48 research reports of group therapy for depression (average sessions = 11.7), McDermut, Miller, and Brown (2001) found considerable evidence for its efficacy. In an even more recent review of the literature based on 107 studies and 14 meta-analytic reviews, Burlingame, MacKenzie, and Strauss (2004) provided another strong endorsement of the efficacy of group therapy.

More specific to BGT, Piper and Joyce (1996) published a review of the efficacy of time-limited group therapies (average duration = 10 weeks). They covered a wide range of problems, including lifestyle difficulties; medical conditions; mood, anxiety, eating, and personality disorders; traumatic experiences; and anger control. The groups represented a diverse set of theoretical orientations. Of the studies that included a therapy versus control condition, 96% provided evidence of greater benefit for therapy on a wide range of outcome criteria. In general, the many reviews of the literature are consistent in providing a strong endorsement for the efficacy and applicability of BGT.

Cost-Efficiency

Each of the above reviews also compared the efficacy of group therapy and individual therapy. Some reviews (e.g., McRoberts, Burlingame, & Hoag, 1998) have focused specifically on this comparison. The McRoberts et al. (1998) review was unable to focus on the comparison between BGT and long-term group therapy, given that the average number of sessions for the group therapies in the 23 studies of their review was only 16. Essentially, it was a review of BGT. The reviewers concluded that the two types of therapy (individual and group) had nearly equivalent positive results. In the current era of health care reform, there is strong pressure on clinicians to use the most cost-efficient treatments. Given that group therapy is as efficacious as individual therapy and requires less therapist time, it appears to be the more cost-efficient treatment.

Treatment of Choice

For certain types of problems (e.g., complicated grief, trauma reactions, adjustment problems, and existential concerns), the specific features of BGT, in particular its time limitations, provide unique opportunities for therapeutic understanding and change. The authors have had considerable experience providing BGT to clients with complicated grief following death losses (Piper, McCallum, & Azim, 1992; Piper, McCallum, Joyce, Rosie, & Ogrodniczuk, 2001). Limited time for the therapy group is a particularly relevant issue for clients with complicated grief. In addition, common events such as client lateness to sessions, absenteeism, and dropping out often trigger feelings and conflicts similar to the reactions that clients had experienced toward people whom they were losing and people whom they eventually lost. Termination of the group, as well, provides an opportunity for clients to examine their reactions to an immediate loss, compare them to previous reactions, and attempt adaptive reactions. In BGT for complicated grief, the therapist can use these natural events productively.

REASONS THAT DETER CLIENTS AND THERAPISTS FROM BRIEF GROUP THERAPY

Resistance to Group Therapy

Despite the evidence for efficacy, applicability, and cost efficiency, group therapy is not readily embraced. Many clients prefer individual therapy, and a number of aspects of the group therapy situation make it seem more intimidating. Compared to individual therapy, clients often experience a sense of less control in a group because many people influence the flow of events. There can also be a diminished sense of individuality. The client must accept that he or she is part of a group. There is also the potential for less complete understanding of events that transpire in a group session. There is less privacy, clients are continually exposed, and confidentiality is impossible to guarantee. There is also a diminished sense of safety for many clients in a group because criticism can come from many directions. Thus, issues related to loss of control, individuality, understanding, privacy, and safety often lead to greater client apprehension about participating in group therapy.

Required Administrative Time

Groups are more complicated to organize than individual therapy. An entire set of clients must be assembled to begin at the same time. This requires a substantial number of referrals that may be difficult to achieve. The homogeneous nature of most brief therapy groups further restricts the number of clients who are eligible and thus exacerbates this problem. Because of the group situation, difficulties with individual clients may affect other clients. The latter may choose to leave the group rather than continue to experience the difficulties. If one or more clients change their minds about participating before the group begins, the onset of the group can be delayed. If one or more clients leave the group prematurely, this can trigger a chain reaction of dropouts, which threatens the viability of the group. Conducting BGT means that these administrative procedures and experiences are repeated more often.

Therapist Training

Unfortunately, many therapists have not received formal training in group therapy, particularly BGT, in graduate or postgraduate programs. Even if a therapist is trained in long-term group therapy, BGT makes unique demands and requires additional skills. If therapists do not feel prepared or skillful when conducting BGT, it is not surprising when they do not readily embrace it. The same issues regarding loss of control, individuality, understanding, privacy, and safety that concern clients also concern therapists, particularly if they lack sufficient training.

Resentment About Health Care Reform

In North America, there have been many negative reactions to health care reform, in particular to procedures required by managed care companies. Such companies often engage in close monitoring of therapists' activities. Sometimes therapists feel that their professional autonomy and judgment are being usurped by rigid administrative policies. Doubts concerning whether they will be reimbursed fully for their services and whether their group therapy skills are valued create additional concerns for therapists. Clearly, if therapists believe that the use of BGT is part of an effort to reduce costs at the expense of quality of care, it will not be well received.

Limitations of Brief Group Therapy

Clinicians often raise the legitimate question, What can be accomplished for my client in a group that lasts only a short time? In a long-term group, clients can work over an extended period of time toward changing interpersonal patterns that took a long time to develop. Eventually, all clients become the focus of the therapist's attention. In the case of BGT, the nature of the therapist's attention to individuals is less certain. It is clear that the benefits of BGT should not be oversold. To do so would diminish its credibility. Although there is extensive evidence of its efficacy from reviews of the research literature, as cited above, it should not be promoted as a cure-all or as a means of bringing about lasting personality change. An example involves efficacy studies of BGT for clients experiencing complicated grief (Piper et al., 1992; Piper et al., 2001). Considerable improvements were found for loss-specific symptoms and general psychiatric symptoms. In contrast, improvements involving interpersonal distress, social (role) dysfunction, and interpersonal dependency were relatively small. This suggests that interpersonal traits are not likely to change after 12 sessions of group therapy. Similarly, it would be unrealistic to expect BGT to bring about significant characterological changes in clients who have personality disorders. Much can be accomplished in BGT, but not everything.

FACILITATIVE THERAPIST PROCEDURES

Careful Selection of Clients

Therapists should choose clients who possess characteristics that optimize their chances of working, remaining, and benefiting. For BGT, this requires clients who are suitable for brief therapy *and* group therapy. In regard to brief therapy, this means clients who have a focal problem and who can engage quickly in the therapeutic process. In regard to group therapy, this means clients who are capable of working in a group situation, that is, clients who can tolerate social anxiety and work collaboratively. Other desirable characteristics for psychotherapy in general, such as realistic expectations and motivation to change, have been recommended. It is also clear that some desirable characteristics are specific to the particular theoretical and technical orientation of the treatment. In studies of BGT for clients with complicated grief, Piper et al. (2001) identified two client personality characteristics that are related to favorable outcomes: psychological mindedness and quality of object relations. Psychological mindedness refers to the ability to understand problems in psychological terms, and quality of object relations refers to the lifelong pattern of relationships with others, ranging from primitive to mature. Given the psychodynamic theoretical orientation and the interpretive or supportive technical orientations of the forms of BGT that were studied, these findings are meaningful. In BGT of different theoretical and technical orientations (e.g., cognitive-behavioral group therapy involving homework assignments), other client personality characteristics (e.g., conscientiousness) may be more important.

Careful Preparation of Clients

One method of reducing patient resistance and risk of failure is pretherapy training (PT).

PT refers to any procedure conducted prior to therapy that attempts to prepare clients for the task of working in a therapy group. The ultimate objectives of pretherapy training include facilitating attendance, retention, desirable group process, and favorable outcome. Immediate objectives include creating accurate expectations about desirable client behavior, customary therapist roles, typical therapy events, and realistic outcomes; reducing anxiety; establishing positive bonds; and increasing participation, self-disclosure, and interpersonal feedback. In most cases, pretherapy training occurs as a natural part of initial interviews between client and therapist. Research reviews (Piper & Perrault, 1989; Yalom, 1995) suggest that pretherapy training is a good investment of resources.

Creation of Homogeneous Compositions

Most brief therapy groups are composed of clients who share similar characteristics. The most salient is usually the common problem that brought the clients to treatment (e.g., depression or complicated grief). Other common characteristics include historical events in the clients' lives (e.g., trauma or loss), and long-standing conflicts (e.g., dependence vs. independence). Client commonalities facilitate two therapeutic factors (cohesion and universality) that are frequently cited in the literature as important to the outcome of group therapy (Yalom, 1995). Cohesion refers to the set of affective bonds that unite members of the group. Universality is the sense that others in the group share one's problems and circumstances. Because of limited time, it is important that BGT clients get off to a quick start. The common characteristics work to accelerate involvement and productive work. We have often been impressed with how quickly clients in short-term loss groups, when there are multiple commonalities, become affectively involved and disclose private material.

Consistent Focusing

Also because of the limited time in BGT, therapists cannot be passive. Although clients often get off to a quick start, they can become bogged down due to the sensitive nature of the material that is discussed and the work that is required to bring about change. The therapist must keep the group on task. This is usually referred to as maintaining a focus. The focus is usually related to the commonalities that were used to compose the group. In addition, the focus can address content themes and client roles that emerge in the group. Focus on themes and roles can alleviate resistance and provide a lively forum to enhance understanding and change. Skill as a therapist requires familiarity with common client characteristics and group processes. The therapist must be well primed to recognize and work with the commonalities as they emerge. For example, in BGT for compli- cated grief, the therapist can routinely expect to encounter themes related to trust, survivor guilt, mortality, and termination. When subtle refer- ences to such themes are made, the therapist should not hesitate to focus on associated con- flicts. Consistent focusing is demanding but necessary in BGT.

NEW APPLICATION: BRIEF GROUP THERAPY WITH MEDICALLY ILL CLIENTS

An area of recent expansion is the delivery of psychosocial interventions to the medically ill, thus broadening the reach of BGT beyond tradi- tional clients with psychiatric conditions. Generally, medically ill clients differ in that their focus of concern, at least initially, is on learning about a specific disease or medical procedure. However, many also struggle with emotionally laden issues, including those related to body image, sexuality, self-esteem, and existential factors. There is a large popula- tion of medically ill clients for whom specific psychological interventions may be useful.

Group therapy may be the most powerful psychosocial intervention for clients with med- ical illnesses (Spira, 1997). Groups are appeal- ing because they help normalize clients' concerns, decrease isolation, and provide a sup- port network of peers (Simonton & Sherman, 2000). Groups are often perceived as less stig- matizing than individual therapy. As well, they are well suited to the types of issues that med- ically ill clients often want to address (e.g., education and coping skills). The efficiency of BGT makes it a desirable adjunct to medical

treatments (Leszcz & Goodwin, 1998). Therapy groups have been developed for a myriad of medical conditions, including AIDS/HIV (Kelly, 1998), diabetes (Francis, Grogan, & Hardy, 1990), coronary artery disease (Linden, Stossel, & Maurice, 1996), and multiple sclero- sis (Mohr & Goodkin, 1999).

The most prevalent use is with clients who have cancer (Spiegel & Classen, 2000). Being diagnosed with cancer confronts the individual with life's fragility. Fears of death, recurrence, disability, and loss of functioning are common. Denial is a frequent defense that is fraught with danger if it leads to avoiding needed medical and emotional support (Benioff & Vinogradov, 1993). Among clients with breast cancer, it has been estimated that 22% to 50% meet criteria for depression (Newport & Nemeroff, 1998), 3% to 19% meet criteria for posttraumatic stress disorder (Cordova et al., 1995), and 33% meet criteria for acute stress disorder (McGarvey, Canterbury, & Cohen, 1998).

The need for intervention has led to the devel- opment of a wide variety of therapy groups. Spira (1997) and Simonton and Sherman (2000) have identified three basic types of groups: (1) informational education, (2) acquisition of coping strategies, and (3) social and emotional support. Combinations are also common.

Education groups are often quite brief (one to four meetings) and lecture oriented, with inter- action often limited to questions addressed to the leader. Education groups focus on informa- tion only or information plus simple skill devel- opment. Content includes information about their disease, treatments, rehabilitative options following surgery, and preventive measures. Occasionally, skills are also taught, such as relaxation or breast self-exam.

The most common type of group teaches active coping strategies that focus on specific concerns for improving daily functioning. The concerns are about communication issues, diet and exercise, pain and nausea, anxious behav- iors, and so on. Such groups are usually short term (6 to 10 meetings) and commonly use a cognitive-behavioral orientation. Because the groups focus on education and psychological issues (e.g., anxiety and pain), they are often referred to as psychoeducational groups. The topics usually focus more on learning skills than challenging cognitive distortions. For example, these groups are more likely to focus on progressive muscle relaxation, imagery techniques, breathing meditation, and problem solving rather than on how certain cognitive styles (e.g., a tendency to ruminate) may contribute to feeling distressed. By actively practicing new coping strategies in the group, clients ideally incorporate these changes in their everyday lives.

Clients with more advanced disease, or those having difficulty adjusting to a life-threatening illness, can benefit from therapy focusing on social and emotional support. These groups are more interpersonally oriented than the other groups described above and are psychotherapeutic in nature. Many of these groups are brief, ranging in duration from 3 to 4 months, although some are long term, lasting up to and over 1 year. The groups provide an opportunity for clients to form intimate bonds, thus creating an environment in which clients are able to discuss virtually any issue of personal concern related to having cancer. The clients are quite active, with the therapists typically taking a more passive role, only intervening to keep the clients on track, facilitate interactions, and make interpretations.

There are basic principles to which therapists should attend in any type of group for clients with cancer. Familiarity and comfort with medical terminology is essential (Leszcz, 1998). Straker (1998) has also highlighted other issues. For example, he recommends that therapists should be familiar with the phases of cancer illness and the challenges presented to the client. Clients need to be evaluated initially on the basis of their presenting psychiatric symptoms as well as their physical health and stage of disease. The shifting nature of the disease requires that the therapist be flexible. Insight-oriented therapy may have to give way to crisis intervention and support, or clients who first present for crisis intervention or supportive therapy may later require insight-oriented therapy. The therapist must also be flexible in regard to the need for medication or for referral for other therapies, such as behavior therapy for conditioned nausea. Therapists also need to be aware of quality of life issues and focus on continuity of care. Finally, special attention is required in dealing with the therapist's own feelings in order to be able to engage the client in an empathic, helpful manner.

The reported benefits of group therapy for medical illnesses include extending survival times for clients and improving psychosocial functioning. The most well-known study of survival outcome was that of Spiegel and colleagues (Spiegel, Bloom, & Yalom, 1981; Spiegel, Bloom, Kraemer, & Gottheil, 1989). They identified a significant survival effect in women with metastatic breast cancer who were treated for 1 year with weekly, supportive-expressive group therapy compared to women who did not participate in group therapy. Although not BGT, the study highlights the potentially powerful effect of group therapy. Spiegel's conclusions were subsequently supported by Fawzy et al. (1993), who studied a brief group intervention for patients with malignant melanoma. Their 6-week intervention incorporated health education, stress management, coping skills training, and supportive psychotherapy. Despite the promising results of these earlier studies, more recent studies have failed to find significant effects of group therapy on survival rates (Blake-Mortimer, Gore-Felton, Kimerling, Turner-Cobb, & Spiegel, 1999; Leszcz & Goodwin, 1998). The positive effect of group therapy on psychosocial functioning has been reported more consistently in the literature (Fawzy & Fawzy, 1998; Sheard & Maguire, 1999; Spiegel et al., 1999). Many of these studies used BGT (e.g., Wellisch et al., 1999). There are also many clinical descriptions of brief group therapies for cancer patients (e.g., Edelman and Kidman, 1999). Overall, there is strong evidence for the effectiveness of group therapy for clients with cancer.

New Application: Combining Brief Group Therapies

There is evidence that many clients with personality disorders respond well to group therapy and that it may be more effective than individual therapy (Budman, Demby, Soldz, & Merry, 1996; MacKenzie, 2001; Munroe-Blum & Marziali, 1995). Because personality disorders are revealed through interactions with others, therapy in a group context provides a unique opportunity to examine their core features. Advantages of group therapy have been noted

(Budman et al., 1996; MacKenzie, 2001). The group situation is particularly conducive to clients who are threatened by the intimacy of the individual therapy situation or who react negatively to authority figures.

Although group therapy has been demonstrated to be effective, most approaches have involved long-term treatment (MacKenzie, 2001). Concern over the spiraling cost of health services argues against this approach. The option of BGT arises. However, no single BGT is likely to meet the diverse needs of clients with personality disorders. Clients often have a number of affective, cognitive, and behavioral impairments. As emphasized earlier in this chapter, there are limitations to the types of outcomes that can be expected from any one type of BGT. Furthermore, many clients meet criteria for between three and six personality disorders (Dolan, Evans, & Norton, 1995). Such clients need diverse and intensive interventions to address their problems. It is possible that a combination of types of BGT could address this need. However, to be efficient, a large number of clients would have to be treated. A treatment approach that provides multiple types of BGT to large groups of clients is day treatment.

Day treatment is an ambulatory treatment approach that offers intensive and structured treatment within a stable therapeutic milieu. Day treatment programs often incorporate several small and large groups and generally treat about 20 to 45 clients at any one time. Clients typically participate in a variety of brief therapy groups several hours each weekday for several months. The therapy groups draw from different technical orientations. Behavioral and cognitive interventions can be used in structured, skills-oriented groups, while dynamic interventions can be used in unstructured, insight-oriented groups. Family and couple interventions may also be used. The combination of different groups in day treatment is congruent with contemporary arguments for combined treatments that can address the multiple domains of pathology exhibited by clients with personality disorders (Livesley, 2001).

There are a number of features of day treatment that tend to make it effective for clients with personality disorders (Piper & Rosie, 1998). First, there is the intensity of the group experience. Clients spend a considerable amount of time participating in a number of different groups each day. Second, the groups vary in size, structure, objectives, and processes. Such diversity provides a comprehensive approach to treatment. Third, the system of groups is integrated and synergistic. Clients are expected to bring up important material and events that occurred in previous groups during current groups. In this way, they are encouraged to think in terms of the total system. Fourth, clients benefit from working with multiple staff and a large number of peers. Emotionally inhibited clients can benefit from observing emotionally expressive clients and vice versa. Fifth, day treatment capitalizes on the traditional characteristics of a therapeutic community (democratization, permissiveness, communalism, reality confrontation). These features serve to strengthen cohesion, which helps retain clients in treatment. Time-limited programs provide an additional benefit. There is a clear sense that much needs to be done in a limited and relatively short period of time. This puts pressure on clients and staff to work hard.

A well-developed model for short-term day treatment is the program in Edmonton, Canada, that has treated a large number of clients with personality disorders for over 30 years (Piper, Rosie, Joyce, & Azim, 1996). The day treatment program is an ongoing, structured therapeutic milieu with an emphasis on dynamic group psychotherapy. Patients are invited to participate in the program for a time-limited period of 18 weeks. There are generally 35 patients attending. Two or three patients enter treatment on the Monday of a given week, and two or three patients are discharged per week. Patients meet for 7 hours per day, 5 days per week. The program is divided into three phases: beginning, middle, and termination. Each phase is 6 weeks long. Each patient passes through each phase in sequence. The program consists of a variety of small and large groups. No individual therapy is offered. The Edmonton Day Treatment program is not unique in its structure or emphasis on treating patients with personality disorders. Many similar programs exist in other countries, most notably the United Kingdom and Norway. In fact, the successful program established by Sigmund Karterud and colleagues in Oslo,

Norway, was developed using the Edmonton program as the prototype.

Some groups are attended by all patients for the duration of their stay in the program. These include the daily large psychotherapy group, the weekly government group, the weekly social outing, the weekly recreation group, and the weekly patient evaluation groups. Most of the patients also attend the exercise group twice weekly, although some opt for the relaxation training group instead during the middle phase. Several other groups are attended by only 8 to 10 patients and are either specific to only one of the three phases or to two of the phases. Thus, the small groups are quite brief, lasting only 6 or 12 weeks. The allocation of patients to groups is such that every patient is in a group with every other patient and staff member at least once in a given day. There is ample time in a given week for patients from different phases to interact. Only the large psychotherapy group is conducted daily. All other groups are conducted only once or twice each week.

A research group conducted a controlled trial of the Edmonton Day Treatment program (Piper, Rosie, Azim, & Joyce, 1993). The prospective trial used a randomized treatment-versus-control (delayed treatment) design. Sixty matched pairs of clients (N = 120) completed the treatment and control conditions. Findings revealed that treated clients evidenced significantly better outcomes than control clients on seven variables: social dysfunction, family dysfunction, interpersonal behavior, mood level, life satisfaction, self-esteem, and severity of disturbance associated with individual goals of treatment. Benefits were maintained over an 8-month follow-up period. Overall, the study supports the efficacy of a short-term, intensive day treatment program for clients who manifest significant difficulties associated with personality disorders.

Other efficacy studies of day treatment for clients with personality disorders have been reviewed by Ogrodniczuk and Piper (2001). Programs of varying lengths (4-8 months) and orientations have been investigated by different research groups. All found that day treatment led to significant reductions in psychiatric symptomatology and improvements in social and interpersonal functioning, and life satisfaction. In addition, preliminary evidence provided by Krawitz (1997) suggests that short-term day treatment may lead to a reduction of future health services costs. There is growing empirical support for the combination of brief group therapies, in the form of a day treatment program, to address the various therapeutic needs of clients with personality disorders.

CONCLUSION

This chapter has emphasized many promising aspects of BGT. Although BGT is not a panacea, there is considerable evidence of its efficacy and cost-efficiency in treating a diverse range of clients. A number of facilitative therapist procedures are available. Promising new applications involve BGT for clients with medical illnesses and combinations of BGT for clients with personality disorders. Future research will likely identify other applications. The field will also benefit from future research that provides information about which types of BGT are most useful with what types of problems.

REFERENCES

Association for Specialists in Group Work. (2002). *Professional standards for the training of group workers.* Retrieved from http:// asgw.educ.kent. edu/training_standards.htm.

Benioff, L. R., & Vinogradov, S. (1993). Group psychotherapy with cancer patients and the terminally ill. In H. I. Kaplan & B. J. Sadock (Eds.), *Comprehensive group psychotherapy* (3rd ed.) (pp. 477-489). Baltimore: Williams & Wilkins.

Blake-Mortimer, J., Gore-Felton, C., Kimerling, R., Turner-Cobb, J. M., & Spiegel, D. (1999). Improving the quality and quantity of life among patients with cancer: A review of the effectiveness of group psychotherapy. *European Journal of Cancer, 35,* 1581-1586.

Budman, S. H., Cooley, S., Demby, A., Koppenaal, G., Koslof, J., & Powers, T. (1996). A model of time-effective group psychotherapy for patients with personality disorders: The clinical model. *International Journal of Group Psychotherapy, 46,* 329-355.

Budman, S. H., Demby, A., Soldz, S., & Merry, J. (1996). Time-limited group psychotherapy for patients with personality disorders: Outcomes and dropouts. *International Journal of Group Psychotherapy, 46,* 357-377.

Burlingame, G. M., MacKenzie, K. R., & Strauss, B. (2004). Small group treatment: Evidence for effectiveness and mechanisms of change. In M. Lambert (Ed.), *Handbook of psychotherapy and behaviour change* (5th ed.) (pp. 647-696). New York: Wiley.

Cordova, M. J., Andrykowski, M. A., Redd, W. H., Kenady, D. E., McGrath, P. C., & Sloan, D. A. (1995). Frequency and correlates of posttraumatic stress disorder-like symptoms after treatment for breast cancer. *Journal of Consulting and Clinical Psychology, 63,* 981-986.

Dolan, B., Evans, C., & Norton, K. (1995). Multiple Axis-II diagnoses of personality disorder. *British Journal of Psychiatry, 166,* 107-112.

Edelman, S., & Kidman, A. D. (1999). Description of a group cognitive behaviour therapy programme with cancer patients. *Psycho-Oncology, 8,* 306-314.

Fawzy, F. I., & Fawzy, N. W. (1998). Group therapy in the cancer setting. *Journal of Psychosomatic Research, 45,* 191-200.

Fawzy, F. I., Fawzy, N. W., Hyun, C. S., Elashoff, R., Guthrie, D., Fahey, J. L., et al. (1993). Malignant melanoma: Effects of an early structured psychiatric intervention, coping, and affective state of recurrence and survival 6 years later. *Archives of General Psychiatry, 50,* 681-689.

Francis, G. L., Grogan, D., & Hardy, L. (1990). Group psychotherapy in the treatment of adolescent and preadolescent military dependents with recurrent diabetic ketoacidosis. *Military Medicine, 155,* 351-354.

Fuhriman, A., & Burlingame, G. M. (1994). Group psychotherapy: Research and practice. In A. Fuhriman & G. M. Burlingame (Eds.), *Handbook of group psychotherapy: An empirical and clinical synthesis* (pp. 3-40). New York: Wiley.

Kelly, J. A. (1998). Group psychotherapy for persons with HIV and AIDS-related illnesses. *International Journal of Group Psychotherapy, 48,* 143-162.

Krawitz, R. (1997). A prospective psychotherapy outcome study. *Australian and New Zealand Journal of Psychiatry, 31,* 465-473.

Leszcz, M. (1998). Introduction to special issue on group psychotherapy for the medically ill. *International Journal of Group Psychotherapy, 48,* 137-141.

Leszcz, M., & Goodwin, P. J. (1998). The rationale and foundations of group psychotherapy for women with metastatic breast cancer. *International Journal of Group Psychotherapy, 48,* 245-273.

Linden, W., Stossel, C., & Maurice, J. (1996). Psychosocial interventions for patients with coronary artery disease: A meta-analysis. *Archives of Internal Medicine, 156,* 745-752.

Livesley, W. J. (2001). A framework for an integrated approach to treatment. In W. J. Livesley (Ed.), *Handbook of personality disorders* (pp. 570-600). New York: Guilford.

MacKenzie, K. R. (2001). Group psychotherapy. In W. J. Livesley (Ed.), *Handbook of personality disorders* (pp. 497-526). New York: Gulford.

McDermut, W., Miller, I. W., & Brown, R. A. (2001). The efficacy of group psychotherapy for depression: A meta-analysis and review of the empirical research. *Clinical Psychology: Science and Practice, 8,* 98-116.

McGarvey, E. L., Canterbury, R. J., & Cohen, R. B. (1998). Evidence of acute stress disorder after diagnosis of cancer. *Southern Medical Journal, 91,* 864-866.

McRoberts, C., Burlingame, G. M., & Hoag, M. J. (1998). Comparative efficacy of individual and group psychotherapy: A meta-analytic perspective. *Group Dynamics: Theory, Research, and Practice, 2,* 101-117.

Mohr, D. C., & Goodkin, D. E. (1999). Treatment of depression in multiple sclerosis: Review and meta-analysis. *Clinical Psychology: Science and Practice, 6,* 1-9.

Munroe-Blum, H., & Marziali, E. (1995). A controlled trial of short-term group treatment for borderline personality disorder. *Journal of Personality Disorder, 9,* 190-198.

Newport, D. J., & Nemeroff, C. B. (1998). Assessment and treatment of depression in the cancer patient. *Journal of Psychosomatic Research, 45,* 215-237.

Ogrodniczuk, J. S., & Piper, W. E. (2001). Day treatment for personality disorders: A review of research findings. *Harvard Review of Psychiatry, 9,* 105-117.

Piper, W. E., & Joyce, A. S. (1996). A consideration of factors influencing the utilization of time-limited, short-term group therapy. *International Journal of Group Psychotherapy, 46,* 311-328.

Piper, W. E., McCallum, M., & Azim, H. F. A. (1992). *Adaptation to loss through short-term group psychotherapy.* New York: Guilford.

Piper, W. E., McCallum, M., Joyce, A. S., Rosie, J. S., & Ogrodnniczuk, J. S. (2001). Patient personality and time-limited psychotherapy for complicated grief. *International Journal of Group Psychotherapy, 51,* 525-552.

Piper, W. E., & Perrault, E. L. (1989). Pretherapy preparation for group members. *International Journal of Group Psychotherapy, 39,* 17-34.

Piper, W. E., & Rosie, J. S. (1998). Group treatment of personality disorders: The power of the group in the intensive treatment of personality disorders. *In Session: Psychotherapy in Practice, 4,* 19-34.

Piper, W. E., Rosie, J. S., Azim, H. F. A., & Joyce, A. S. (1993). A randomized trial of psychiatric day treatment for patients with affective and personality disorders. *Hospital and Community Psychiatry, 44,* 757-763.

Piper, W. E., Rosie, J. S., Joyce, A. S., & Azim, H. F. A. (1996). *Time-limited day treatment for personality disorders.* Washington, DC: American Psychological Association.

Sheard, T., & Maquire, P. (1999). The effect of psychological interventions on anxiety and depression in cancer patients: Results of two meta-analyses. *British Journal of Cancer, 80,* 1770-1780.

Simonton, S., & Sherman, A. (2000). An integrated model of group treatment for cancer patients. *International Journal of Group Psychotherapy, 50,* 487-506.

Smith, M., Glass, G., & Miller, T. (1980). *The benefits of psychotherapy.* Baltimore: John Hopkins University Press.

Spiegel, D., Bloom, J. R., Kraemer, H. C., & Gottheil, E. (1989). Effect of psychosocial treatment on survival of patients with metastatic breast cancer. *Lancet, 2,* 888-901.

Spiegel, D., Bloom, J. R., & Yalom, I. D. (1981). Group support for patients with metastatic cancer. *Archives of General Psychiatry, 38,* 527-533.

Spiegel, D., & Classen, C. (2000). *Group therapy for cancer patients: A research-based handbook of psychosocial care.* New York: Basic Books.

Spiegel, D., Morrow, G. R., Classen, C., Raubertas, R., Stott, P. B., Mudaliar, N., et al. (1999). Group psychotherapy for recently diagnosed breast cancer patients: A multicenter feasibility study. *Psycho-Oncology, 8,* 482-493.

Spira, J. L. (1997). Understanding and developing psychotherapy groups for medically ill patients. In J. L. Spira (Ed.), *Group therapy for medically ill patients* (pp. 3-54). New York: Guilford.

Straker, N. (1998). Psychodynamic psychotherapy for cancer patients. *Journal of Psychotherapy Practice and Research, 7,* 1-9.

Wellisch, D. K., Hoffman, A., Goldman, S., Hammerstein, J., Klein, K., & Bell, M. (1999). Depression and anxiety symptoms in women at high risk for breast cancer: Pilot study of a group intervention. *American Journal of Psychiatry, 156,* 1644-1645.

Yalom, I. D. (1995). *The theory and practice of group psychotherapy* (4th ed.). New York: Basic Books.

47

CURRENT STATUS AND FUTURE DIRECTIONS OF GROUP THERAPY RESEARCH

GARY M. BURLINGAME

Brigham Young University

ADDIE J. FUHRIMAN

Brigham Young University

JENNIFER JOHNSON

Brigham Young University

Group interventions, broadly conceived, comprise groups that vary widely in format and objectives. Coyne, Wilson, and Ward (1997) described a classification system endorsed by the Association of Specialists in Group Work (ASGW) to capture and order this diversity through four general types of groups: psychoeducation, counseling, psychotherapy, and task. More specifically, they describe the typical psychoeducational group as focusing on developing members' cognitive, affective, or behavior skills through a structured and sequenced set of procedures and exercises within and across group sessions. Counseling groups are traditionally aimed at enhancing members'

interpersonal potential and increasing their intrapersonal growth. The usual focus of psychotherapy groups is on alleviating psychopathology through interaction among group members and group leaders. Psychotherapy groups can be further distinguished by the formal change theory that guides treatment (cognitive, psychodynamic, humanistic, etc.). Finally, task groups are generally developed to achieve one of two broad purposes: (1) to serve organizational needs, through vehicles such as committees or other administrative groups or (2) to serve member or client needs through means such as teams, treatment conferences, and social action groups (Toseland, Rivas, & Chapman, 1984).

A common theme across all four types of groups is the differential use of the group ecosystem to advance the work of the group and its members. In general, ecosystems are defined by the group properties that have been related to productive outcomes. For instance, therapy groups that produce an enduring sense of belonging among members (i.e., cohesion) have been linked to better individual member outcomes. Understandably, conceptual models of ecosystems vary, depending on the type of group and the writer's perspective. For instance, task group ecosystem definitions are dominated by social psychology and organizational behavior terms that have less utility for therapeutic groups. The most mature conceptual and empirical ecosystem models are found in the psychotherapy group literature. Accordingly, much of the research in this chapter focuses on psychotherapy or counseling groups, with a modicum of attention being given to psychoeducational groups.

The research trail of group psychotherapy presents a panorama of activity and focus that illustrates the conceptual, empirical, and clinical discoveries that have come to define the character of group therapy. Both the focus and the findings of studies throughout the history of group psychotherapy research have been directed by *when* and *where* studies occurred—the point-in-time and the setting defining the specific contribution of the research. Moreover, the methodology that drives the research has also evolved over the years, moving from individual outcome studies and process studies to process-outcome studies and, most recently, to long-term programmatic research. This empirical trail has allowed the field to establish not only that group psychotherapy works but, more specifically, with whom and under what conditions.

To provide a context for the meaning and significance of the current research in group therapy, and to be able to forecast the future of group therapy, the chapter will briefly describe the topics past researchers and clinicians deemed important to pursue and what they discovered in that inquiry. Hopefully, this will produce a better grasp on the breadth and depth of specific research topics as they have emerged over time.

Topical themes in the early years (prior to 1960) focused on models and approaches, the therapeutic relationship, curative factors such as cohesion and catharsis, and the ecosystem (e.g., interpersonal feedback, group norms, group development; cf. Burlingame, Fuhriman, & Johnson, 2002). For the most part, populations and settings investigated were people who were mentally ill, children, adolescents, the family, and the elderly. In later years, researchers focused more on homogeneous client populations, client and leader variables, the effects of structure (e.g., format, size, norms), therapeutic factors or mechanisms (a continuing interest in curative processes), and personal, member-to-member, and group-as-a-whole dynamics. Regarding these last dynamics, it is noted that the members' interaction with one another is an important consideration, as well as their individual dynamics.

Each decade of research activity has added to previous work, providing the field with growing confidence about the overall efficacy of group work (Barlow, Burlingame, & Fuhriman, 2000; Bretz, Heekerens, & Schmitz, 1994; Fuhriman & Burlingame, 1994; Tschuschke, 1999). Reviewers of outcome research on group therapy during the 1960s concluded that patient change occurred in 45% of the reviewed studies (Mann, 1966; see also Anderson, 1968). For instance, Mann concluded that "group psychotherapy does, indeed, produce objectively measurable changes in attitude, personality, and behavior" (p. 145).

The 1970s found additional success, suggesting that group was effective when compared to control groups and that group treatment had comparable results to individual and alternative psychological treatments. It remained unclear, though, regarding treatment effects with specific psychological disorders. The 1980s revealed that group therapy had significant improvement over inert comparison groups and was comparable or superior to other active treatment protocols. It is important to note that these protocols considered group as primary treatment rather than secondary or auxiliary. There was also some indication that combined individual and group treatments result in superior outcomes. Meta-analyses conducted during this decade showed that group treatment appeared to be most successful in studies that highlighted the *unique* properties of group processes and treatment, such as cohesion, member-member interactions, group development, group norms, universality, and interpersonal learning (cf. Fuhriman & Burlingame, 1994). This nascent understanding began to raise the possibility of matching specific patients with specific models of group treatment.

The most reliable harbinger of a future journey is the imprint and direction left by our most recent travels. The trail leading into the new millennium—research of the 1990s—is qualitatively distinct from the preceding decades in at least four ways. First, a large number of researchers took the path of testing treatment protocols for specific patient populations. Others began to carefully track the interaction between treatment protocols and the unique process features of group treatment using complex programs of research. A third trail resulted in the use of more sophisticated research designs and statistical models buttressed by a fourth, the development of promising new measures to strengthen our knowledge base. Illustrations of each are offered as useful milestones to guide our research journey into the new millennium.

POPULATION-SPECIFIC RESEARCH

Prior to the 1990s, the aggregate research needed to support the disorder- and patient-specific group models found in this book simply did not exist. Prior to this time period, the modal study treated heterogeneous patient populations, described only by such terms as *inpatients, outpatients,* or *college students.* This nonspecific nomenclature left the clinician with few guidelines when faced with running a group composed of patients suffering from obsessive-compulsive disorder or caretakers of those suffering from Alzheimer's disease. However, by the mid-1980s, investigators focused their efforts on the needs of specific populations. One result of this maturity of focus is that we can now talk about empirically supported group treatments for a large number of specific disorders. However, treatment protocols are often initially developed for the individual format and then modified for the group format (Wilfley, Frank, Welch, Spurrell, & Rounsaville, 1998).

To illustrate, great progress has been made on developing efficacious group treatments for anxiety disorders. Well-controlled studies of cognitive-behavioral group treatment (CBGT) for patients with agoraphobia and panic disorders (Lidren et al., 1994; Telch, et al., 1993; Telch, Schmidt, Jamimez, Jacquin, & Harrington, 1995) show both clinically and statistically significant improvement in anxiety, fear, depression, frequency and severity of panic attacks, agoraphobic avoidance, and catastrophic cognitions. As many as 81% of the patients were improved by the end of treatment in these studies. Significant strides also have been made in the group treatment of social phobia. Heimberg and colleagues have been a dominant force in this line of research, developing and refining a CBGT protocol for the past 15 years. They report reductions in social phobic anxiety, depression, and catastrophic cognitions, with gains maintained at 6-month and 5-year follow-up (Heimberg et al., 1990; Heimberg, Salzman, Holt, & Blendell, 1993). A missing component in investigations of CBGT is the recognition and incorporation of small group processes (e.g., therapeutic interaction, interpersonal feedback, support). For instance, in several studies, the effects of active treatment were rivaled by placebo attention groups that relied solely on patients gathering together to interact in an unstructured supportive climate (cf. Burlingame, MacKenzie, & Strauss, 2003). In other words, the "horse race" between groups guided by leaders using formal change theories (e.g., CBT, IPT) and unstructured "discussion" groups resulted in a tie. One explanation for the success of the placebo groups is that they incorporated therapeutic features inherent in the group format, such as mutual support or a sense of universality among group members. A more careful understanding of the role of small group processes is a critical clarification needed in future research.

Other populations have also received empirical attention in the group literature. For instance, the elderly are a rapidly increasing proportion of the North American and European population, and the group literature has, to some extent, kept up with this demographic development. A variety of group protocols for the elderly have been designed to improve mood, reduce anxiety, teach problem-solving skills, facilitate the sharing of memories and feelings, and increase self-esteem and life satisfaction. Mixed treatment gains have been associated with these protocols, although treatment effectiveness appears to be independent of client age, gender, or length and setting of treatment (Burlingame et al., 2003; Gorey & Cryns, 1991; Scogin & McElreath, 1994). Group treatments for elders will continue to be a burgeoning research topic in the future. However, to rectify past problems, researchers are admonished to use more rigorous comparative designs rather than simply reaffirming post-treatment gains (see Chapter 34 in this handbook on groups for the elderly).

Research on group treatment for the severely and persistently mentally ill also demands further attention. For instance, group-based treatments of schizophrenia have been revitalized as researchers have uncovered the marginal effect of medication on negative symptoms. For instance, there has been an increased attention given to psychoeducational group treatment focusing on improving social skills (Liberman et al., 1993), neurocognitive rehabilitation (Spaulding, Reed, Sullivan, Richardson, & Weiler, 1999), and psychoeducational protocols focusing on the management of negative symptoms (McFarlane, Link, Dushay, Marchal, & Crilly, 1995; McFarlane, Lukens et al., 1995). Promising developments have begun to show that the skills learned in psychoeducational group treatment for clients with schizophrenia may generalize to later community functioning (Liberman et al., 1998). This is welcome news because of the difficulty that these patients face in successfully reintegrating into communities and living independent lives. However, more of this groundbreaking research is needed in the future.

COMPLEX, PROGRAMMATIC LINES OF RESEARCH

Another pathway traversed in the 1990s was the development and/or maturation of research teams conducting long-term programmatic work. We define research programs as complex when they test relationships among pretherapy characteristics of the patients (ie., moderator variables), group process patterns believed to moderate change, formal change theories (e.g., psychodynamic or interpretive models), and multivariate outcomes. The complexity of simultaneously testing such relationships often required serial investigations that built upon each other in a systematic way, replicating previous studies and answering questions raised in those studies. Interestingly, while cognitive-behavioral models dominated the aforementioned population-specific literature, the majority of the complex studies focus on psychodynamic group models.

Piper and colleagues on the Vancouver/ Edmonton team have pursued one of the most progressive and comprehensive programs of group research. One dimension that made this particular line of research so strong and informative is that it first showed that group treatment worked, and then identified specific components of the treatment and patient presentation that predicted patient improvement (see Ogrodniczak, Piper, McCallum, Joyce, & Rosie, 2002; Piper, Rosie, Joyce, & Azim, 1996). For instance, they investigated how characteristics of the group members, the group structure, and leadership led to improved therapeutic results in their population of interest. Their research found that patients who varied along the dimensions of psychological mindedness and capacity for interpersonal relationships differentially responded to the supportive and the interpretive group approaches. Tests of the effectiveness of an interpretive group treatment of pathological grief for clients with different characteristics (Piper, McCallum, & Azim, 1992) led to the inclusion of a supportive model that appeared to be more beneficial for particular patients.

Another example of a complex, programmatic line of research is the work done by Marziali and Munroe-Blum (1994) on interpersonal group treatment of borderline personality disorder. Controlled and uncontrolled studies report systematic reductions in depression and suicidal tendencies and increases in interpersonal functioning, life satisfaction, and adjustment (Munroe-Blum & Marziali, 1995) using their treatment model. In addition, these authors' examination of process variables and mechanisms of change further contributed to our understanding of treatment effects with this difficult population.

A final example of complex programs is the Heimberg team that developed one of the few CBGT models and empirically tested the differential effectiveness of specific treatment interventions in the model. For instance, group-based exposure and cognitive restructuring interventions (components of the treatment protocol) were experimentally manipulated by this team to determine their independent effect on improvement of social phobia symptoms (Hope, Heimberg, & Bruch, 1995). This research not only demonstrated that group treatment for social phobia is effective, but also articulated which components of treatment were most important. As expected, both CBGT and exposure-alone clients improved more than the wait-list patients on measures of anxiety, social phobia, and behavioral performance. Surprisingly, the exposure-alone clients achieved more broad-based change on measures of social phobia and cognition. Although they proffered alternative explanations, the authors suggested that "the experiential learning that accompanies exposure may provide ample evidence [for patients] to counter dysfunctional beliefs without direct intervention" (p. 648). Such complex lines of research provide information on which parts of treatment are the most helpful and for whom.

The bad news is that complex programs of research are a rare occurrence in the existing literature. The good news is that a few complex programs have begun, providing models for future researchers to follow. We strongly encourage research in this direction, since such models seem most likely to provide us a comprehensive understanding of the mechanisms responsible for successful group treatment.

SOPHISTICATED RESEARCH DESIGNS AND STATISTICAL MODELS

An important trajectory set in the 1990s was the more consistent application of traditionally strong research designs. Historically, our literature has been evaluated as soft on methodology (Bednar & Kaul, 1994; Burlingame, Kircher, & Taylor, 1994). While rigor improved in a traditional sense (multiple outcome and process measures, larger samples with random assignment), recent studies also incorporate actual clinical cases instead of college student volunteers and experienced therapists rather than graduate students. In addition, more of the recent studies used therapy manuals and checked for treatment fidelity. Finally, the increased use of

long-term follow-up helped test the durability of group treatment effects. Unfortunately, these improvements are unevenly applied across the literature (cf. Burlingame et al., 2003). In short, there are some populations where the empirical literature is still "methodologically soft."

The standard for current published studies is to provide detailed information on the basics of the treatments, patients, leaders, and procedures involved. Unfortunately, even the most basic information is often missing (cf. Strauss, Burlingame, & MacKenzie, 2001) in our literature, making interpretation and replication of studies difficult. The future inquirer must provide information on the presence and effect of attrition, results at both the group and individual level, information about clinically significant change, and the information required to compute effect sizes (i.e., means and variances).

While the most important contribution to solid research is the use of well-known principles of good research design, novel statistical techniques can sometimes provide information that previously has not been accessible. For example, a few recent studies have used time series analyses to study cause-and-effect relationships. While such methods are not new, their applications to group therapy are infrequent. For instance, Hurley (1997) used sequential measurement of self- and other-acceptance to show cause-and-effect relationships of these with leader and group climate measures. Brossart, Patton, and Wood (1998) illustrated how Tuckerized Growth Curve Analysis (TCGA) could be used to plot changes in individual group members over time. TCGA may be particularly useful for group psychotherapy research because it allows researchers to analyze individuals in a group without being constrained by statistical limitations. This kind of analysis removes the limitations of previous analyses that collapsed individual differences, either by taking means or by having the "group-as-a-whole" rated. Having information on individual differences will allow researchers and theoreticians to make inroads into important group constructs such as cohesion and outcome prediction. Our enthusiasm for the utility of the method is tempered by the apparent complexity of the analysis. Other intriguing kinds of analyses (e.g., nonlinear dynamical analyses) have begun to fall by the wayside in the group literature because of the complexity of performing and interpreting them (cf. Burlingame & Fuhriman, 1994; Burlingame & Hope, 1997).

PROMISING MEASUREMENT INSTRUMENTS

In a recent review of the cohesion literature, 21 separate measures of cohesion were uncovered (Burlingame et al., 2002). Having so many instruments measuring the same construct ensures competing findings (DeLucia-Waack, 1997). However, a few instruments are emerging as standards in the 1990s. Instead of a host of measures being used in one or two isolated studies, a few measures with good psychometric properties are being used by many different investigators. These practices will invariably result in an accumulation of knowledge that will enable comparisons across different patient populations and treatment protocols. We highlight two measures representing reputable process and outcome instruments that are making such inroads. For a thorough overview of group measurement instruments, see Chapter 9 in this volume.

The most frequently used process instrument in the group literature is the Group Climate Questionnaire (GCQ) (MacKenzie, 1983). This instrument has good psychometric properties and has been made extremely popular by its ease of use (12-question self-report measure). The widespread use of the GCQ has begun to bridge formerly separate aspects of the literature. For example, bridges between alliance and outcome (MacKenzie, 1997), other process variables and outcome (Braaten, 1990; MacKenzie, Dies, Coche, Rutan, & Stone, 1987; MacKenzie & Tschuschke, 1993), group stages (Brossart et al., 1998), and patient variables affecting social perception in groups (Kivlighan & Angelone, 1992) have all been made with the GCQ. While its ease of use makes it a prime candidate for a position in a core process battery (cf. Burlingame et al., 2003), it is not without its critics (see Hurley & Brooks, 1987, 1988).

The Outcome Questionnaire (OQ) (Lambert et al., 1996) and its child/adolescent counterpart (Y-OQ) (Burlingame, Wells, & Lambert, 1996) are multiple-choice, self-report instruments that assess client symptoms in common areas of concern (intrapsychic discomfort, interpersonal functioning, and social role performance). Like the GCQ, the use of these two instruments has grown exponentially over the past decade. They correlate well with other well-known symptom measures and have been shown to be sensitive to small changes in patient well-being (Burlingame et al., 2001; Vermeersch, Lambert, & Burlingame, 2000).

The importance of having a common outcome measure cannot be underestimated. For instance, these two instruments have been applied with a variety of patients, treatment models, and settings, generating over 20 published reports with findings that can be directly compared. In spite of the progress that has been made on a few fronts, further efforts directed toward building consensus on core process and outcome measures are needed. While more refined and frequently used measures have been developed, much is left to discover regarding the similarities and differences in the underlying constructs being assessed. Confidence in inferences from research on group outcomes and processes is directly tied to the rigor and standardization of measurement protocols. A core set of brief paper-and-pencil process measures would help to unify the literature and would increase knowledge overlap between investigations. In this vein, the American Group Psychotherapy Association has recently formed a task force to recommend a core set of outcome and process instruments. The continued development of observational measures that allow for more than one method of assessing group process would allow researchers to be more confident in their conclusions.

FUTURE CONSIDERATIONS

The review of group psychotherapy research over the past 40 years demonstrates the direction that future research must take in order to best serve clinicians and practitioners in the field. That direction can best be understood within the context of H. E. Durkin's (1972) observation of groups: "[O]rganized complexities . . . are the product of the dynamic interaction among their parts rather than the sum of their absolute characteristics. Neither the resultant whole nor its new characteristics can be explained by the nature of the parts themselves" (p. 161). This *iterative, dynamic,* and *holistic* nature of the group presents as a prototype for group therapy research in the future. It is becoming increasingly clear that research paradigms designed to capture the efficacy and efficiency of group therapy must likewise embrace these three characteristics (i.e., *iterative, dynamic,* and *holistic* nature of the group). Indeed, research must measure, and hence understand, the interactive, connected, and holistic processes of group and then link these with long-term outcome. This is evident in the call (Burlingame et al., 2002) to understand specificity (e.g., patient characteristics, treatment protocol), relationships (e.g., cohesion, intragroup dynamics), and complexity (e.g., patient × treatment × time, ecosystem). These highlight the necessity of withdrawing from research on singular events, measures, and conditions and advancing inquiry into multiple interactive parts and multifaceted relationships that change over the course of time.

The interest in long-term, programmatic research during the past decade is heartening, particularly as it has explored not only outcome but complex, interactive therapeutic processes as well. The demonstrated success of group therapy and its predicted increase in the future (Fuhriman & Burlingame, 2001; Taylor et al., 2001) demand that we continue such research efforts. Group therapy protocols designed for specific clientele and specific problem focus continue to proliferate. Groups are being designed and implemented to help patients and their families cope with such problems as medical (e.g., cancer, heart, paralysis), catastrophic trauma (e.g., war, flood, fire), violence (e.g., spouse and child abuse, criminal acts), loss (e.g., death, employment, divorce, abandonment), and drug dependency (e.g., drug, alcohol, medication abuse). Research has the daunting task of tracking the effectiveness of such specific treatment and the means whereby it is accomplished. Burlingame et al. (2003) conceptualized the critical components that contribute to the effectiveness of group treatment. These factors, each of which is a study in and of itself, include formal change theory, small group process, the group leader, the patient, and structural factors (e.g., size, setting, sessions). Understanding their role, potency,

and relationship in treatment will require us to be more strategic in implementing our research methodologies. The days of a singular, end-of-treatment measurement regime are over. What is required now and in the future are multi-measure strategies that capture the contribution of member, leader, technique, and process to individual and group change. These measures must have a valid and reliable history and must also be grounded in the context of group treatment (versus individual). The community and systemic features of group push us further to include qualitative methodologies with our quantitative techniques. The intricacies of process and response and the vital linkages occurring during change may more effectively be disclosed through additional in-depth interviewing and on-site observation.

Recent advances in outcomes management methods further illustrate the importance of measuring individual × therapist × therapeutic strategy (Brown, Burlingame, Lambert, Jones, & Vaccaro, 2001). For instance, outcome management methods track outcomes (improvement or deterioration) over time and compare a patient's progress to published norms. Such methods could be applied to track the progress of group members over time and allow researchers to look at patterns of symptom reduction with different kinds of clients, therapies, and therapists. The implications of outcomes management methods are enormous for group therapy research, particularly given the demand for short-term, structured group treatment by managed care providers (Taylor et al., 2001). The need for such research is further heightened by the findings regarding the training of group psychotherapists by the various health care professions (i.e., psychiatry, psychology, social work). More specifically, Fuhriman and Burlingame (2001) found that the training of mental health professionals is not well calibrated with research and economics. They note that research on the effectiveness of our pedagogy is nonexistent, our practice is not in line with either the perceived demand or the empirical literature, our training requirements are not in alignment with predicted market demands, nor are the health care disciplines calibrated with one another in their educational efforts (Fuhriman & Burlingame, 2001; Taylor et al., 2001). The linkage of who is being trained, how they are being trained, and the effect of such training on patient outcome has yet to be determined, but is sorely needed.

The time has never been better for group psychotherapy research. Indeed, we are realizing the results of good group psychotherapy research during a time of increased use of group therapy. Nevertheless, challenges still confront us, such as linking outcome with process, training with practice, practice with research, and facilitating the application of research results by clinicians in the field.

REFERENCES

Anderson, A. (1968). Group counseling. *Review of Educational Research, 33,* 209-226.

Barlow, S. H., Burlingame, G. M., & Fuhriman, A. (2000). Therapeutic application of groups: From Pratt's "Thought Control Classes" to modern group psychotherapy. *Group Dynamics: Theory, Research, and Practice, 4,* 115-134.

Bednar, R. L., & Kaul, T. J. (1994). Experiential group research: Can the cannon fire? In A. E. Bergin & S. L. Garfield (Eds.), *Handbook of psychotherapy and behavior change* (4th ed.) (pp. 631-663). New York: Wiley.

Braaten, L. J. (1990). The different patterns of group climate and critical incidents in high and low cohesion sessions of group psychotherapy. *International Journal of Group Psychotherapy, 40*(4), 477-493.

Bretz, H. J., Heerkerens, H.-P., & Schmitz, B. (1994). Eine Metanalyse zur Eirksamkeit von Gestalttherapie [Metanalytical assessment of the effectiveness of Gestalt therapy]. *Zeitschrift für Klinische Psychologie, Psychiatrie und Psychotherapie, 42,* 241-260.

Brossart, D., Patton, M., & Wood, P. (1998). Assessing group process: An illustration using Tuckerized growth curves. *Group Dynamics: Theory, Research, and Practice, 2*(1), 3-17.

Brown, G. S., Burlingame, G. M., Lambert, M. J., Jones, E., & Vaccaro, J. (2001). Pushing the quality envelope: A new outcomes management system. *Psychiatric Services, 52,* 925-934.

Burlingame, G., & Fuhriman, A. (1994). Epilogue. In A. Fuhriman & G. Burlingame (Eds.), *Handbook of group psychotherapy: An empirical and clinical synthesis* (pp. 559-562). New York: Wiley.

Burlingame, G. M., Fuhriman, A., & Johnson, J. (2002). Cohesion in group psychotherapy. In J. Norcross (Ed.), *A guide to psychotherapy relationships that work* (pp. 71-81). Oxford, UK: Oxford University Press.

Burlingame, G. M., & Hope, C. (1997). Dynamic system theory and social psychology: Promises and pitfalls. *Psychological Inquiry, 8*(2), 104-110.

Burlingame, G. M., Kircher, J. C., & Taylor, S. (1994). Methodological considerations in group psychotherapy research: Past, present, and future practices. In A. Fuhriman & G. M. Burlingame (Eds.), *Handbook of group psychotherapy: An empirical and clinical synthesis* (pp. 41-80). New York: Wiley.

Burlingame, G. M., MacKenzie, K. R., & Strauss, B. (2003). Small group treatment: Evidence for effectiveness and mechanisms of change. In M. J. Lambert (Ed.), *Handbook of psychotherapy and behavior change* (5th ed.). (pp. 647-696). New York: Wiley.

Burlingame, G. M., Mosier, J. I., Wells, M. G., Atkin, Q. G., Lambert, M. J., Whoolery, M., et al. (2001). Tracking the influence of mental health treatment: The development of the Youth Outcome Questionnaire. *Clinical Psychology & Psychotherapy, 8,* 361-379.

Burlingame, G. M., Wells, M. G., & Lambert, M. J. (1996). *Youth Outcome Questionnaire.* Stevenson, MD: American Professional Credentialing Services.

Conyne, R. K., Wilson, F. R., & Ward, D. E. (1997). *Comprehensive group work: What it means and how to teach it.* Alexandria, VA: American Counseling Association.

DeLucia-Waack, J. L. (1997). Measuring the effectiveness of group work: A review and analysis of process and outcome measures. *Journal for Specialists in Group Work, 22(*4), 277-293.

Durkin, H. E. (1972). General systems theory and group therapy: An introduction. *International Journal of Group Psychotherapy, 22,* 159-166.

Fuhriman, A., & Burlingame, G. M. (1994). Group psychotherapy: Research and practice. In A. Fuhriman & G. M. Burlingame (Eds.), *Handbook of group psychotherapy: An empirical and clinical synthesis* (pp. 3-40). New York: Wiley

Fuhriman, A., & Burlingame, G. (2001). Group psychotherapy training and effectiveness. *International Journal of Group Psychotherapy, 51*(3), 399-416.

Gorey, K. M., & Cryns, A. G. (1991). Group work as interventive modality with the older depressed client: A meta-analytic review. *Journal of Gerontological Social Work, 16*(1-2), 137-157.

Heimberg, R. G., Dodge, C. S., Hope, D. A., Kennedy, C. R., Zollo, L. J., & Becker, R. J. (1990). Cognitive behavioral group treatment for social phobia: Comparison with a credible placebo control. *Cognitive Therapy and Research, 14,* 1-23.

Heimberg, R. G., Salzman, D., Holt, C. S., & Blendell, K. (1993). Cognitive behavioral group treatment for social phobia: Effectiveness at five-year follow-up. *Cognitive Therapy & Research, 17,* 325-339.

Hope, D. A., Heimberg, R. G., & Bruch, M. A. (1995). Dismantling cognitive-behavioral group therapy for social phobia. *Behavior Research and Therapy, 33,* 637-650.

Hurley, J. (1997). Interpersonal theory and measures of outcome and emotional climate in 111 personal development groups. *Group Dynamics: Theory, Research, and Practice, 1*(1), 86-97.

Hurley, J., & Brooks, L. (1987). Brief reports group climate's principal dimension: Affiliation. *International Journal of Group Psychotherapy, 37*(3), 441-448.

Hurley, J., & Brooks, L. (1988). Primacy of affiliativeness in ratings of group climate. *Psychological Reports, 62,* 123-133.

Kivlighan, D. M., Jr., & Angelone, E. O. (1992). Interpersonal problems: Variables influencing participants perception of group climate. *Journal of Counseling Psychology, 39,* 468-472.

Lambert, M. J., Hansen, N. B., Umphress, V., Lunnen, K., Okiishi, J., Burlingame, G., et al. (1996). *Administration and scoring manual for the OQ 45.2.* Stevenson, MD: American Professional Credentialing Services.

Liberman, R. P., Wallace, C. J., Blackwell, G., Eckman, T. A., Vaccaro, J. V., & Kuehnel, T. G. (1998). Innovations in skills training for the seriously mentally ill: The UCLA social and independent living skills (SILS) modules. *Innovations and Research, 2*(2), 43-59.

Liberman, R. P., Wallace, C. J., Blackwell, G., Kopelowicz, A., Vaccaro, J. V., & Mintz, J. (1993). Skills training versus psychosocial occupational therapy for persons with persistent schizophrenia. *American Journal of Psychiatry, 155*(8), 1087-1091.

Lidren, D. M., Watkins, P. L., Gould, R. A., Clum, G. A., Asterino, M., & Tullock, H. L. (1994). A comparison of bibliotherapy and group therapy in the treatment of panic disorder. *Journal of Consulting and Clinical Psychology, 62,* 865-869.

MacKenzie, K. R. (1983). The clinical application of group measure. In R. R. Dies & K. R. MacKenzie (Eds.), *Advances in group psychotherapy: Integrating research and practice* (pp. 159-170). New York: International Universities Press.

MacKenzie, K. R. (1997). *Time-managed group psychotherapy: Effective clinical applications.* Washington, DC: American Psychiatric Press.

MacKenzie, K. R., Dies, R. R., Coche, E., Rutan, J. S., & Stone, W. N. (1987). An analysis of AGPA Institute groups. *International Journal of Group Psychotherapy, 37*(1), 55-74.

MacKenzie, K. R., & Tschuschke, V. (1993). Relatedness, group work, and outcome in long-term inpatient psychotherapy groups. *Journal of Psychotherapy: Practice and Research, 2,* 147-156.

Mann, J. (1966). Evaluation of group psychotherapy. In J. Moreno (Ed.), *The international handbook of group psychotherapy.* New York: Philosophical Library.

Marziali, E., & Munroe-Blum, H. (1994). *Interpersonal group psychotherapy for borderline personality disorder.* New York: Basic Books.

McFarlane, W. R., Link, B., Dushay, R., Marchal, J., & Crilly, J. (1995). Psychoeducational multiple family groups: Four-year relapse outcome in schizophrenia. *Family Process, 34,* 127-144.

McFarlane, W. R., Lukens, E., Link, B., Dushay, R., Deakins, S. A., Newmark, M., et al. (1995). Multiple-family groups and psychoeducation in the treatment of schizophrenia. *Archives of General Psychiatry, 52,* 679-687.

Munroe-Blum, H., & Marziali, E. (1995). A controlled trial of short-term group treatment for borderline personality disorder. *Journal of Personality Disorder, 9,* 190-198.

Ogrodniczak, J., Piper, W. E., McCallum, M., Joyce, A. S., & Rosie, J. S. (2002). Patient personality and time-limited group psychotherapy for complicated grief. *International Journal of Group Psychotherapy, 52*(4), 511-553.

Piper, W. E., McCallum, M., & Azim, H. F. A. (1992). *Adaptation to loss through short-term group psychotherapy.* New York: Guilford.

Piper, W. E., Rosie, J. S., Joyce, A. S., & Azim, H. F. A. (1996). *Time-limited treatment for personality disorders*. Washington, DC: American Psychological Association.

Scogin, F., & McElreath, L. (1994). Efficacy of psychosocial treatments for geriatric depression: A quantitative review. *Journal of Consulting and Clinical Psychology, 62*(1), 69-74.

Spaulding, W. D., Reed, D., Sullivan, M., Richardson, C., & Weiler, M. (1999). Effects of cognitive treatment in psychiatric rehabilitation. *Schizophrenia Bulletin, 25*(4), 657-676.

Strauss, B., Burlingame, G. M., & MacKenzie, K. R. (2001). Wer, was, wann, wo, wie? Minimalanforderugen für die Veröffentlichung gruppentherapiebezogener Forshungsergebnisse. *Gruppenpsychotherapie und Gruppendynamik, 37,* 207-213.

Taylor, N. T., Burlingame, G. M., Fuhriman, A., Kristensen, K. B., Johansen, J., & Dahl, D. (2001). A survey of mental health care provider and managed care organization attitudes toward, familiarity with, and use of group interventions. *International Journal of Group Psychotherapy, 51*(2), 243-263.

Telch, M. J., Lucasm, J. A., Schmidt, N. B., Hanna, H. H., Jaimez, T. L., & Lucas, R. A. (1993). Group cognitive behavioral treatment of panic disorder. *Behavioral Research and Therapy, 31,* 279-288.

Telch, M. J., Schmidt, N. B., Jamimez, T. L., Jacquin, K. M., & Harrington, P. J. (1995). Impact of cognitive behavioral treatment on quality of life in panic disorder patients. *Journal of Consulting and Clinical Psychology, 63*(5), 823-830.

Toseland, R. W., Rivas, R. F., & Chapman, D. (1984). An evaluation of decision-making methods in task groups. *Social Work, 29*(4), 339-349.

Tschuschke, V. (1999). Gruppentherapie versus Einzeltherapie-gleich wirksam? [Group versus individual psychotherapy: Equally effective?]. *Gruppenpsychotherapie und Gruppendynamik, 35,* 257-274.

Vermeesch D. A., Lambert M. J., & Burlingame G. M. (2000). Outcome Questionnaire: Item sensitivity to change. *Journal of Personality Assessment, 74*(2), 242-261.

Wilfley, D. E., Frank, M. A., Welch, R., Spurrell, E. B., & Rounsaville, B. J. (1998). Adapting interpersonal psychotherapy to a group format (IPT-G) for binge eating disorder: Toward a model for adapting empirically supported treatments. *Psychotherapy Research, 8*(4), 379-391.

Conclusions

General Comments

As we began to plan and organize this handbook, we were energized and overwhelmed by the number of topics and issues that we wanted to address. As we finish this process, our feelings have not changed. We are still both energized and overwhelmed, but for very different reasons. The energy comes from the realization than there are many people committed to advancing the field of groups, both group practitioners and researchers, and that much has been accomplished in terms of theory, research, and practice in this area. However, the overwhelmed feeling comes from the realization that much of what has been written in the field of groups is based on theory and counseling practice. Research has been conducted in some areas and with certain types of groups, but there is still much more that we need to know about how to effectively facilitate groups.

Part I, Current and Historical Perspectives on the Field of Group Counseling and Psychotherapy looks back at the winding road that group counseling and psychotherapy has traveled. Groups are widely practiced as a therapeutic intervention with research supporting their efficacy. Research in areas like group process, therapeutic factors, and leadership behavior has improved as methodology, statistical analyses, and measurement instruments have become more sophisticated.

Part II, Best Practices in Groups, provides the most up-to-date information about how to conduct group counseling and psychotherapy effectively. The training of group leaders as well as specific interventions are highlighted, including the choice of activities and leader interventions, how to process group events, selection of assessment instruments, supervision, and ethical considerations.

Several themes emerge from Part III, Multicultural Groups. One is that group leader competence is critical, specifically multicultural group counseling skills. In addition, knowledge of other cultural worldviews and values and how these may inhibit or increase a potential group member's willingness to participate and behavior in group is essential. Each chapter on specific cultural groups identified cultural values, beliefs, or behaviors that may conflict with a traditional Western view of group counseling as well as aspects of each culture that promote acceptance of groups. Acculturation was also noted as an important variable in predicting the behavior of potential group members. Effective groups must help members to understand themselves and others as individuals within the context of their culture and choose interventions and methods of change based on the interplay between the individuals and their worldviews.

Part IV, Groups Across Settings, includes examples of psychoeducational, counseling, and psychotherapy groups in a variety of settings. This part presents readers with a look at the various settings within which a variety of different types of groups are used. From the schools to the Veteran's Administration, from college counseling centers to correctional facilities, and from the workplace to private practice, groups are well utilized in a variety of settings for people of diverse ages with different presenting problems. The setting typically determines the type of groups that fit best with the needs of the participants. While psychoeducational groups are used in each of these settings, counseling and psychotherapy groups are used more often in college/university counseling centers, private practice, and community mental health centers than in the workplace (which focuses on task groups). The breadth of the impact of group interventions across settings is impressive.

Groups Across the Life Span, Part V, emphasizes and describes the commonalities and differences in groups by age and gender. There is support for conducting groups that are homogeneous in age and gender because of the impact of cognitive development and different life tasks across age groups on the purpose and content of the group. The structure of the group, types of exercises, focus on process versus content, and group goals are all determined by the abilities and needs of the group members.

Part VI, Special Topic Groups, includes examples of psychoeducational, counseling, and psychotherapy groups that address specific psychological concerns that affect millions of people. Focusing on different types of groups used to treat people with interpersonal and developmental issues, including grief, substance abuse, depression, eating disorders, and others, this part provides the reader with hands-on strategies for developing a group on these topics, along with theoretical and empirical support for psychoeducational, counseling, and psychotherapy groups to treat the issue.

The goal for Part VII, Critical Issues and Emerging Topics, was to capture the zeitgeist at the end of the 20th and beginning of the 21st centuries. It is difficult to grasp the cutting edge of a field that is actively growing and changing. However, the chapters in this part give a significant glimpse into the evolution of the field. The overall theme of these chapters is that there is a growing need for counseling and supportive services, and that group interventions are an integral part of the services that mental health professionals provide. However, online groups and mutual support groups are frequently not administered by professionals. More involvement, research, and cooperation by group specialists are needed to reach a much wider population of individuals. Preventative and brief interventions can be effective and may ameliorate problems before they become more serious. There is also a call for deepening the focus of research to cover a comprehensive set of variables, link process with outcome, increase sample sizes, and apply the findings to practice and training of group specialists.

Across all of these chapters, there are three major themes. With regard to practice, new and innovative techniques need to be encouraged and continue to be developed. Systematic descriptions of interventions that have been proven effective have begun to be published, but there is much room for innovation and growth in the field. In regard to research, more studies are needed with larger samples, rigorous designs, and diverse populations. As for training and continuing education, the field needs to provide students with the building blocks and foundation to lead groups and also provide education opportunities through professional organizations to continue to develop practitioner skills and add competencies in additional areas.

ENDING COMMENTS

Our hope is that this book will serve as a reference for both group counselors and researchers alike. We have tried to provide a theoretical context along with guidelines and suggestions based on group counseling practice. In addition, whenever possible, suggestions for psychoeducational groups as well as counseling and therapy groups have been included as an acknowledgment of the importance of education and prevention in the counseling field. Wherever possible, relevant research has been described to aid group practitioners in selecting effective interventions. Our scope has been wide, including groups across the life span, in different settings, and with different therapeutic goals. This book is a testament to the educators, practitioners, and researchers in the realm of group practice. It is with pride that we realize that as we write this conclusion, new and evolving developments are occurring in this vibrant and growing field.

Appendix A

ASSOCIATION FOR SPECIALISTS IN GROUP WORK

Professional Standards for the Training of Group Workers

Revision Approved by the Executive Board, January 22, 2000

PREPARED BY F. ROBERT WILSON AND LYNN S. RAPIN, CO-CHAIRS, AND LYNN HALEY-BANEZ, MEMBER, ASGW STANDARDS COMMITTEE

CONSULTANTS: ROBERT K. CONYNE AND DONALD E. WARD

PREAMBLE

For nearly two decades, the Association for Specialists in Group Work (herein referred to as ASGW or as the Association) has promulgated professional standards for the training of group workers. In the early 1980s, the Association published the ASGW Training Standard for Group Counselors (1983), which established nine knowledge competencies, seventeen competencies, and clock-hour baselines for various aspects of supervised clinical experience in group counseling. The focus on group counseling embodied in these standards mirrored the general conception of the time that whatever counselors did with groups of individuals should properly be referred to as group counseling.

New ground was broken in the 1990 revision of the ASGW Professional Standards for the Training of Group Workers with (a) the articulation of the term, *group work,* to capture the variety of ways in which counselors work with groups, (b) differentiation of core training, deemed essential for all counselors, from specialization training required of those intending to engage in group work as part of their professional practice, and (c) the differentiation among four distinct group work specializations: task and work group facilitation, group psychoeducational, group counseling, and group psychotherapy.

Over the ten years in which these standards have been in force, commentary and criticism has been elicited through discussion groups at various regional and national conferences and through published analyses in the Association's journal, the *Journal for Specialists in Group Work.*

In this Year-2000 revision of the ASGW Professional Standards for the Training of Group Workers, the foundation established by the 1990 training standards has been preserved and refined by application of feedback received through public discussion and scholarly debate.

The Year-2000 revision maintains and strengthens the distinction between core and specialization training with requirements for core training and aspirational guidelines for specialization training. Further, the definitions of group work specializations have been expanded and clarified. Evenness of application of training standards across the specialization has been assured by creating a single set of guidelines for all four specializations with specialization specific detail being supplied where necessary. Consistent with both the pattern for training standards established by the Council for Accreditation of Counseling and Related Educational Program accreditation standards and past editions of the ASGW training standard, the Year-2000 revision address both content and clinical instruction. Content instruction is described in terms of both course work requirements and knowledged object while clinical instruction is articulated in experiential requirements and skill objectives. This revision of the training standards was informed by and profits from the seminal ASGW Best Practice Guidelines (1998) and the ASGW Principles for Diversity-Competent Group Workers (1999).

Although each of these documents have their own form of organization, all address the group work elements of planning, performing, and processing and the ethical and diversity competent treatment of participants in group activities.

PURPOSE

The purpose of the Professional Standards for the Training of Group Workers is to provide guidance to counselor training programs in the construction of their curricula for graduate programs in counseling (e.g., master's, specialist, and doctoral degrees and other forms of advanced graduate study). Specifically, core standards express the Association's view on the minimum training in group work all programs in counseling should provide for all graduates of their entry level, master's degree programs in counseling, and specialization standards provide a framework for documenting the training philosophy, objectives, curriculum, and outcomes for each declared specialization program.

Core Training in Group Work. All counselors should possess a set of core competencies in general group work. The Association for Specialists in Group Work advocates for the incorporation of core group work competencies as part of required entry-level training in all counselor preparation programs. The Association's standards for core training are consistent with and provide further elaboration of the standards for accreditation of entry-level counseling programs identified by the Council for Accreditation of Counseling and Related Educational Programs (CACREP, 1994). Mastery of the core competencies detailed in the ASGW training standards will prepare the counselor to understand group process phenomena and to function more effectively in groups in which the counselor is a member. Mastery of basic knowledge and skill in group work provides a foundation which specialty training can extend but does not qualify one to independently practice any group work specialty.

Specialist Training in Group Work. The independent practice of group work requires training beyond core competencies. ASGW advocates that independent practitioners of group work must possess advanced competencies relevant to the particular kind of group work practice in which the group work student wants to specialize (e.g., facilitation of task groups, group psychoeducational, group counseling, or group psychotherapy). To encourage program creativity in development of specialization training, the specialization guidelines do not prescribe minimum trainee competencies. Rather, the guidelines establish a framework within which programs can develop unique training experiences utilizing scientific foundations and best practices to achieve their training objectives. In providing these guidelines for specialized training, ASGW makes no presumption that a graduate program in counseling must provide training in a group work specialization nor that adequate training in a specialization can be accomplished solely within a well-rounded master's degree program in counseling. To provide adequate specialization training, completion of post-master's options such as certificates of post-master's study or doctoral degrees may be required. Further, there is no presumption that an individual who may have received adequate training in a given declared specialization will be prepared to function effectively with all group situations in which the graduate may want to or be required to work. It is recognized that the characteristics of specific client populations and employment settings vary widely. Additional training beyond that which was acquired in a specific graduate program may be necessary for optimal, diversity-competent, group work practice with a given population in a given setting.

DEFINITIONS

Group Work: is a broad professional practice involving the application of knowledge and skill in group facilitation to assist an interdependent collection of people to reach their mutual goals which may be interpersonal, interpersonal, or work-related. The goals of the group may include the accomplishment of tasks related to work, education, personal development, personal and interpersonal problem solving, or remediation of mental and emotional disorders.

Core Training in Group Work: includes knowledge, skills, and experiences deemed necessary for general competency for all master's degree-prepared counselors. ASGW advocates for all counselor preparation programs to provide core training in group work regardless of whether the program intends to prepare trainees for independent practice in a group work specialization. Core training in group work is considered a necessary prerequisite for advanced practice in group work.

Specialization Training in Group Work: includes knowledge, skills, and experiences deemed necessary for counselors to engage in independent practice of group work. Four areas of advanced practice, referred to as specializations, are identified: Task Group Facilitation, Group Psychoeducational, Group Counseling, and Group Psychotherapy. This list is not presumed to be exhaustive and while there may be no sharp boundaries between the specializations, each has recognizable characteristics that have professional utility. The definitions for these group work specializations have been built upon the American Counseling Association's model definition of counseling (adopted by the ACA Governing Council in 1997), describing the methods typical of the working stage of the group being defined and the typical purposes to which those methods are put and the typical populations served by those methods. Specialized training presumes mastery of prerequisite core knowledge, skills, and experiences.

Specialization in Task and Work Group Facilitation:

- The application of principles of normal human development and functioning
- through group based educational, developmental, and systemic strategies
- applied in the context of here-and-now interaction
- that promote efficient and effective accomplishment of group tasks
- among people who are gathered to accomplish group task goals.

Specialization in Psychoeducational Group Leadership:

- The application of principles of normal human development and functioning
- through group-based educational and developmental strategies
- applied in the context of here-and-now interaction
- that promote personal and interpersonal growth and development and the prevention of future difficulties
- among people who may be at risk for the development of personal or interpersonal problems or who seek enhancement of personal qualities and abilities.

Specialization in Group Counseling:

- The application of principles of normal human development and functioning
- through group-based cognitive, affective, behavioral, or systemic intervention strategies
- applied in the context of here-and-now interaction
- that address personal and interpersonal problems of living and promote personal and interpersonal growth and development
- among people who may be experiencing transitory maladjustment, who are at risk for the development of personal or interpersonal problems, or who seek enhancement of personal qualities and abilities.

Specialization in Group Psychotherapy:

- The application of principles of normal and abnormal human development and functioning
- through group-based cognitive, affective, behavioral, or systemic intervention strategies
- applied in the context of negative emotional arousal
- that address personal and interpersonal problems of living, remediate perceptual and cognitive distortions or repetitive patterns of dysfunctional behavior, and promote personal and interpersonal growth and development
- among people who may be experiencing severe and/or chronic maladjustment.

CORE TRAINING STANDARDS

I. Coursework and Experiential Requirements

A. Coursework Requirements. Core training shall include at least one graduate course in group work that addresses such as but not limited to scope of practice, types of group work, group development, group process and dynamics, group leadership, and standards of training and practice for group workers.

B. Experiential Requirements. Core training shall include a minimum of 10 clock hours (20 clock hours recommended) of observation of and participation in a group experience as a group member and/or as a group leader.

II. Knowledge and Skill Objectives

A. Nature and Scope of Practice

1. *Knowledge Objectives.* Identify and describe:
   a. the nature of group work and the various specializations within group work
   b. theories of group work including commonalties and distinguishing characteristics among the various specializations within group work
   c. research literature pertinent to group work and its specializations

2. *Skill Objectives.* Demonstrate skill in:
   a. preparing a professional disclosure statement for practice in a chosen area of specialization
   b. applying theoretical concepts and scientific findings to the design of a group and the interpretation of personal experiences in a group

B. Assessment of Group Members and the Social Systems in Which They Live and Work

1. *Knowledge Objectives.* Identify and describe:
   a. principles of assessment of group functioning in group work
   b. use of personal contextual factors (e.g., family-of-origin, neighborhood-of-residence, organizational membership, cultural membership) in interpreting behavior of members in a group

2. *Skill Objectives.* Demonstrate skill in:
   a. observing and identifying group process
   b. observing the personal characteristics of individual members in a group
   c. developing hypotheses about the behavior of group members
   d. employing contextual factors (e.g., family of origin, neighborhood of residence, organizational membership, cultural membership) in interpretation of individual and group data

C. Planning Group Interventions

1. *Knowledge Objectives.* Identify and describe:
   a. environmental contexts, which affect planning for group interventions
   b. the impact of group member diversity (e.g., gender, culture, learning style, group climate preference) on group member behavior and group process and dynamics in group work
   c. principles of planning for group work

2. *Skill Objectives.* Demonstrate skill in:
   a. collaborative consultation with targeted populations to enhance ecological validity of planned group interventions
   b. planning for a group work activity including such aspects as developing overarching purpose, establishing goals and objectives, detailing methods to be used in achieving goals and objectives, determining methods for outcome assessment, and verifying ecological validity of plan

D. Implementation of Group Interventions

1. *Knowledge Objectives.* Identify and describe:
   a. principles of group formation including recruiting, screening, and selecting group members
   b. principles for effective performance of group leadership functions
   c. therapeutic factors within group work and when group work approaches are indicated and contraindicated
   d. principles of group dynamics including group process components, developmental stage theories, group member roles, group member behaviors

2. *Skill Objectives.* Demonstrate skill in:
   a. encouraging participation of group members
   b. attending to, describing, acknowledging, confronting, understanding, and responding empathetically to group member behavior
   c. attending to, acknowledging, clarifying, summarizing, confronting, and responding empathetically to group member statements
   d. attending to, acknowledging, clarifying, summarizing, confronting, and responding empathetically to group themes
   e. eliciting information from and imparting information to group members
   f. providing appropriate self-disclosure
   g. maintaining group focus; keeping a group on task
   h. giving and receiving feedback in a group setting

E. Leadership and Co-Leadership

1. *Knowledge Objectives.* Identify and describe:
   a. group leadership styles and approaches
   b. group work methods including group worker orientations and specialized group leadership behaviors
   c. principles of collaborative group processing

2. *Skill Objectives.* To the extent opportunities for leadership or co-leadership are provided, demonstrate skill in:
   a. engaging in reflective evaluation of one's personal leadership style and approach
   b. working cooperatively with a co-leader and/or group members
   c. engaging in collaborative group processing

F. Evaluation

1. *Knowledge Objectives.* Identify and describe:
   a. methods for evaluating group process in group work
   b. methods for evaluating outcomes in group work

2. *Skill Objectives.* Demonstrate skill in:
   a. contributing to evaluation activities during group participation
   b. engaging in self-evaluation of personally selected performance goals

G. Ethical Practice, Best Practice, Diversity-Competent Practice

1. *Knowledge Objectives.* Identify and describe:
   a. ethical considerations unique to group work
   b. best practices in group work
   c. diversity competent group work

2. *Skill Objectives.* Demonstrate skill in:
   a. evidencing ethical practice in planning, observing, and participating in group activities
   b. evidencing best practice in planning, observing, and participating in group activities
   c. evidencing diversity-competent practice in planning, observing, and participating in group activities

SPECIALIZATION GUIDELINES

I. Overarching Program Characteristics

A. The program has a clearly specified philosophy of training for the preparation of specialists for independent practice of group work in one of the forms of group work recognized by the Association (i.e., task and work group facilitation, group psychoeducational, group counseling, or group psychotherapy).

1. The program states an explicit intent to train group workers in one or more of the group work specializations.

The program states an explicit philosophy of training, based on the science of group work, by which it intends to prepare students for independent practice in the declared specialization(s).

B. For each declared specialization, the program specifies education and training objectives in terms of the competencies expected of students completing the specialization training. These competencies are consistent with

1. the program's philosophy and training model,

2. the substantive area(s) relevant for best practice of the declared specialization area, and standards for competent, ethical, and diversity sensitive practice of group work

C. For each declared specialization, the program specifies a sequential, cumulative curriculum, expanding in breadth and depth, and designed to prepare students for independent practice of the specialization and relevant credentialing.

D. For each declared specialization, the program documents achievement of training objectives in terms of student competencies.

II. Recommended Coursework and Experience

A. *Coursework.* Specialization training may include coursework that provides the student with a broad foundation in the group work domain in which the student seeks specialized training:

1. *Task/Work Group Facilitation:* coursework includes but is not limited to organizational development, management, and consultation, theory and practice of task/work group facilitation

2. *Group Psychoeducational:* coursework includes but is not limited to organizational development, school and community counseling/ psychology, health promotion, marketing, program development and evaluation, organizational consultation, theory and practice of group psychoeducation

3. *Group Counseling:* coursework includes but is not limited to normal human development, health promotion, theory and practice of group counseling

4. *Group Psychotherapy:* coursework includes but is not limited to normal and abnormal human development, assessment and diagnosis of mental and emotional disorders, treatment of psychopathology, theory and practice of group psychotherapy

B. *Experience.* Specialization training includes

1. *Task/Work Group Facilitation:* a minimum of 30 clock hours (45 clock hours recommended) supervised practice facilitating or conducting an intervention with a task or work group appropriate to the age and clientele of the group leader's specialty area (e.g., school counseling, student development counseling, community counseling, mental health counseling)

2. *Group Psychoeducational:* a minimum of 30 clock hours (45 clock hours recommended) supervised practice conducting a psychoeducational group appropriate to the age and clientele of the group leader's specialty area (e.g., school counseling, student development counseling, community counseling, mental health counseling)

3. *Group Counseling:* a minimum of 45 clock hours (60 clock hours recommended) supervised practice conducting a counseling group appropriate to the age and clientele of the group leader's specialty area (e.g., school counseling, student development counseling, community counseling, mental health counseling)

4. *Group Psychotherapy:* a minimum of 45 clock hours (60 clock hours recommended) supervised practice conducting a psychotherapy group appropriate to the age and clientele of the group leader's specialty area (e.g., mental health counseling)

III. Knowledge and Skill Elements

In achieving its objectives, the program has and implements a clear and coherent curriculum plan that provides the means whereby all students can acquire and demonstrate substantial understanding of and competence in the following areas:

A. Nature and Scope of Practice

The program states a clear expectation that its students will limit their independent practice of group work to those specialization areas for which they have been appropriately trained and supervised.

B. Assessment of Group Members and the Social Systems in Which They Live and Work

All graduates of specialization training will understand and demonstrate competence in the use of assessment instruments and methodologies for assessing individual group member characteristics and group development, group dynamics, and process phenomena relevant for the program's declared specialization area(s). Studies should include but are not limited to:

1. methods of screening and assessment of populations, groups, and individual members who are or may be targeted for intervention

2. methods for observation of group member behavior during group interventions

3. methods of assessment of group development, process, and outcomes

C. Planning Group Interventions

All graduates of specialization training will understand and demonstrate competence in planning group interventions consistent with the program's declared specialization area(s). Studies should include but are not limited to:

1. establishing the overarching purpose for the intervention

2. identifying goals and objectives for the intervention

3. detailing methods to be employed in achieving goals and objectives during the intervention

4. selecting methods for examining group process during group meetings, between group sessions, and at the completion of the group intervention

5. preparing methods for helping members derive meaning from their within-group experiences and transfer within-group learning to real-world circumstances

6. determining methods for measuring outcomes during and following the intervention

7. verifying ecological validity of plans for the intervention

D. Implementation of Group Interventions

All graduates of specialization training will understand and demonstrate competence in implementing group interventions consistent with the program's declared specialization area(s). Studies should include but are not limited to:

1. principles of group formation including recruiting, screening, selection, and orientation of group members

2. standard methods and procedures for group facilitation

3. selection and use of referral sources appropriate to the declared specialization

4. identifying and responding constructively to extra-group factors which may influence the success of interventions

5. applying the major strategies, techniques, and procedures

6. adjusting group pacing relative to the stage of group development

7. identifying and responding constructively to critical incidents

8. identifying and responding constructively to disruptive members

9. helping group members attribute meaning to and integrate and apply learning

10. responding constructively to psychological emergencies

11. involving group members in within-group session processing and ongoing planning

E. Leadership and Co-Leadership

All graduates of specialization training will understand and demonstrate competence in pursuing personal competence as a leader and in selecting and managing the interpersonal relationship with a co-leader for group interventions consistent with the program's declared specialization area(s). Studies should include but are not limited to:

1. characteristics and skills of effective leaders

2. relationship skills required of effective co-leaders

3. processing skills required of effective co-leaders

F. Evaluation

All graduates of specialization training will understand and demonstrate competence in evaluating group interventions consistent with the program's declared specialization area(s). Studies should include but are not limited to methods for evaluating participant outcomes and participant satisfaction.

G. Ethical Practice, Best Practice, Diversity-Competent Practice

All graduates of specialization training will understand and demonstrate consistent effort to comply with principles of ethical, best practice, and diversity-competent practice of group work consistent with the program's declared specialization area(s). Studies should include but are not limited to:

1. ethical considerations unique to the program's declared specialization area

2. best practices for group work within the program's declared specialization area

3. diversity issues unique to the program's declared specialization area

IMPLEMENTATION GUIDELINES

Implementation of the Professional Standards for the Training of Group Workers requires a commitment by a program's faculty and a dedication of program resources to achieve excellence in preparing all counselors at core competency level and in preparing counselors for independent practice of group work. To facilitate implementation of the training standards, the Association offers the following guidelines.

Core Training in Group Work

Core training in group work can be provided through a single, basic course in group theory and process. This course should include the elements of content instruction detailed below and may also include the required clinical instruction component.

Content Instruction

Consistent with accreditation standards (CACREP, 1994; Standard II.J.4), study in the area of group work should provide an understanding of the types of group work (e.g., facilitation of task groups, psychoeducational groups, counseling groups, psychotherapy groups); group development, group dynamics, and group leadership styles; and group leadership methods and skills. More explicitly, studies should include, but not be limited to, the following:

- principles of group dynamics including group process components, developmental stage theories, and group member's roles and behaviors;

- group leadership styles and approaches including characteristics of various types of group leaders and leadership styles;

- theories of group counseling including commonalties, distinguishing characteristics, and pertinent research and literature;

- group work methods including group leader orientations and behaviors, ethical standards, appropriate selection criteria and methods, and methods of evaluating effectiveness;

- approaches used for other types of group work, including task groups, prevention groups, support groups, and therapy groups; and,

- skills in observing member behavior and group process, empathic responding, confronting, self-disclosing, focusing, protecting, recruiting and selecting members, opening and closing sessions, managing, explicit and implicit teaching, modeling, giving and receiving feedback.

Clinical Instruction

Core group work training requires a minimum of 10 clock hours of supervised practice (20 clock hours of supervised practice is recommended). Consistent with CACREP standards for accreditation, the supervised experience provides the student with direct experiences as a participant in a small group, and may be met either in the basic course in group theory and practice or in a specially conducted small group designed for the purpose of meeting this standard (CACREP, 1994; Standard II.D). In arranging for and conducting this group experience, care must be taken by program faculty to assure that the ACA ethical standard for dual relationships and ASGW standards for best practice are observed.

Specialist Training in Group Work

Though ASGW advocates that all counselor training programs provide all counseling students with core group work training, specialization training is elective. If a counselor training program chooses to offer specialization training (e.g., task group facilitation, group psychoeducational, group counseling, group psychotherapy), ASGW urges institutions to develop their curricula consistent with the ASGW standards for that specialization.

Content Instruction

Each area of specialization has its literature. In addition to basic course work in group theory and process, each specialization requires additional coursework providing specialized knowledge necessary for professional application of the specialization:

• **Task Group Facilitation:** course work in such areas as organization development, consultation, management, or sociology so students gain a basic understanding of organizations and how task groups function within them.

• **Group Psychoeducation:** course work in community psychology, consultation, health promotion, marketing, and curriculum design to prepare students to conduct structured consciousness-raising and skill training groups in such areas as stress management, wellness, anger control and assertiveness training, and problem solving.

• **Group Counseling:** course work in normal human development, family development and family counseling, assessment and problem identification of problems in living, individual counseling, and group counseling, including training experiences in personal growth or counseling group.

• **Group Psychotherapy:** coursework in abnormal human development, family pathology and family therapy, assessment and diagnosis of mental and emotional disorders, individual therapy, and group therapy, including training experiences in a therapy group.

Clinical Instruction

For Task Group Facilitation and Group Psychoeducational, group specialization training recommends a minimum of 30 clock hours of supervised practice (45 clock hours of supervised practice is strongly suggested). Because of the additional difficulties presented by Group Counseling and Group Psychotherapy, a minimum of 45 clock hours of supervised practice is recommended (60 clock hours of supervised practice is strongly suggested). Consistent with CACREP standards for accreditation, supervised experience should provide an opportunity for the student to perform under supervision a variety of activities that a professional counselor would perform in conducting group work consistent with a given specialization (i.e., assessment of group members and the social systems in which they live and work, planning group interventions, implementing group interventions, leadership and co-leadership, and within-group, between-group, and end-of-group processing and evaluation).

In addition to courses offering content and experience related to a given specialization, supervised clinical experience should be obtained in practical and internship experience.

Following the model provided by CACREP for master's practical, we recommend that one quarter of all required supervised clinical experience be devoted to group work:

• **Master's Practicum:** At least 10 clock hours of the required 40 clock hours of direct service should be spent in supervised leadership or co-leadership experience in group work, typically in Task Group Facilitation, Group Psychoeducational, or Group Counseling (at the master's practicum level, experience in Group Psychotherapy would be unusual) (CACREP, 1994; Standard III.H.1).

• **Master's Internship:** At least 60 clock hours of the required 240 clock hours of direct services should be spent in supervised leadership or co-leadership in group work consistent with the program's specialization offering(s) (i.e., in Task Group Facilitation, Group Psychoeducational, Group Counseling, or Group Psychotherapy).

- **Doctoral Internship:** At least 150 clock hours of the required 600 clock hours of direct service should be spent in supervised leadership or co-leadership in group work consistent with the program's specialization offering(s) (i.e., in Task Group Facilitation, Group Psychoeducational, Group Counseling, or Group Psychotherapy).

REFERENCES

Association for Specialists in Group Work. (1998). ASGW Best Practice Guidelines. *Journal for Specialists in Group Work, 23,* 237-244.

Association for Specialists in Group Work. (1999). ASGW Principles for Diversity-Competent Group Workers. *Journal for Specialists in Group Work, 24,* 7-14.

Association for Specialists in Group Work. (1983). *ASGW Professional Standards for Group Counseling.* Alexandria, VA: Author.

Association for Specialists in Group Work. (1990). *Professional Standards for the Training of Group Workers.* Alexandria, VA: Author.

Council for Accreditation of Counseling and Related Educational Programs (CACREP) (1994). *CACREP Accreditation Standards and Procedures Manual.* Alexandria, VA: Author.

Appendix B

ASSOCIATION FOR SPECIALISTS IN GROUP WORK

Principles for Diversity-Competent Group Workers

Approved by the Executive Board, August 1, 1998

PREPARED BY LYNN HALEY-BANEZ, SHERLON PACK-BROWN, AND BOGUSIA MOLINA

CONSULTANTS: MICHAEL D'ANDREA, PATRICIA ARRENDONDO, NILOUFER MERCHANT, AND SANDRA WATHEN

PREAMBLE

The Association for Specialists in Group Work (ASGW) is committed to understanding how issues of diversity affect all aspects of group work. This includes but is not limited to: training diversity-competent group workers; conducting research that will add to the literature on group work with diverse populations; understanding how diversity affects group process and dynamics; and assisting group facilitators in various settings to increase their awareness, knowledge, and skills as they relate to facilitating groups with diverse memberships.

As an organization, ASGW has endorsed this document with the recognition that issues of diversity affect group process and dynamics, group facilitation, training, and research. As an organization, we recognize that racism, classism, sexism, heterosexism, ableism, and so forth, affect everyone. As individual members of this organization, it is our personal responsibility to address these issues through awareness, knowledge, and skills. As members of ASGW, we need to increase our awareness of our own biases, values, and beliefs and how they impact the groups we run. We need to increase our awareness of our group members' biases, values, and beliefs and how they also impact and influence group process and dynamics. Finally, we need to increase our knowledge in facilitating, with confidence, competence, and integrity, groups that are diverse on many dimensions.

DEFINITIONS

For the purposes of this document, it is important that the language used is understood. Terms such as "dominant," "nondominant," and "target" persons and/or populations are used to define a person or groups of persons who historically, in the United States, do not have equal access to power, money, certain privileges (such as access to mental health services because of financial constraints, or the legal right to marry, in the case of a gay or lesbian couple), and/or the ability to influence or initiate social policy because of unequal representation in government and politics. These terms are not used to denote a lack of numbers in terms of representation in the overall U.S. population. Nor are these terms used to continue to perpetuate the very biases and forms of oppression, both overt and covert, that this document attempts to address.

For the purposes of this document, the term "disabilities" refers to differences in physical, mental, emotional, and learning abilities and styles among people. It is not meant as a term to define a person, such as a learning disabled person, but rather in the context of a person with a learning disability.

Given the history and current cultural, social, and political context in which this document is written, the authors of this document are limited to the language of this era. With this in mind, we have attempted to construct a "living document" that can and will change as the sociopolitical and cultural context changes.

THE PRINCIPLES

I. Awareness of Self

A. Attitudes and Beliefs

1. Diversity-competent group workers demonstrate movement from being unaware to being increasingly aware and sensitive to their own race, ethnic and cultural heritage, gender, socioeconomic status (SES), sexual orientation, abilities, and religion and spiritual beliefs, and to valuing and respecting differences.

2. Diversity-competent group workers demonstrate increased awareness of how their own race, ethnicity, culture, gender, SES, sexual orientation, abilities, and religion and spiritual beliefs are impacted by their own experiences and histories, which in turn influence group process and dynamics.

3. Diversity-competent group workers can recognize the limits of their competencies and expertise with regard to working with group members who are different from them in terms of race, ethnicity, culture (including language), SES, gender, sexual orientation, abilities, religion, and spirituality and their beliefs, values, and biases. (For further clarification on limitations, expertise, and type of group work, refer to the training standards and best practice guidelines, Association for Specialists in Group Work, 1998; and the ethical guidelines, American Counseling Association, 1995.)

4. Diversity-competent group workers demonstrate comfort, tolerance, and sensitivity with differences that exist between themselves and group members in terms of race, ethnicity, culture, SES, gender, sexual orientation, abilities, religion, and spirituality and their beliefs, values, and biases.

B. Knowledge

1. Diversity-competent group workers can identify specific knowledge about their own race, ethnicity, SES, gender, sexual orientation, abilities, religion, and spirituality, and how they personally and professionally affect their definitions of "normality" and the group process.

2. Diversity-skilled group workers demonstrate knowledge and understanding regarding how oppression in any form—such as, racism, classism, sexism, heterosexism, ableism, discrimination, and stereotyping—affects them personally and professionally.

3. Diversity-skilled group workers demonstrate knowledge about their social impact on others. They are knowledgeable about communication style differences, how their style may inhibit or foster the group process with members who are different from themselves along the different dimensions of diversity, and how to anticipate the impact they may have on others.

C. Skills

1. Diversity-competent group workers seek out educational, consultative, and training experiences to improve their understanding and effectiveness in working with group members who self-identify as Indigenous Peoples, African Americans, Asian Americans, Hispanics, Latinos/Latinas, gays, lesbians, bisexuals, or transgendered persons and persons with physical, mental/emotional, and/or learning disabilities, particularly with regard to race and ethnicity. Within this context, group workers are able to recognize the limits of their competencies and: (a) seek consultation, (b) seek further training or education, (c) refer members to more qualified group workers, or (d) engage in a combination of these.

2. Group workers who exhibit diversity competence are constantly seeking to understand themselves within their multiple identities (apparent and unapparent differences), for example, gay, Latina, Christian, working-class and female, and are constantly and actively striving to unlearn the various behaviors and processes they covertly and overtly communicate that perpetuate oppression, particularly racism.

II. Group Worker's Awareness of Group Member's Worldview

A. Attitudes and Beliefs

1. Diversity-skilled group workers exhibit awareness of any possible negative emotional reactions toward Indigenous Peoples, African Americans, Asian Americans, Hispanics, Latinos/Latinas, gays, lesbians, bisexuals, or transgendered persons and persons with physical, mental/emotional, and/or learning disabilities that they may hold. They are willing to contrast in a nonjudgmental manner their own beliefs and attitudes with those of Indigenous Peoples, African Americans, Asian Americans, Hispanics, Latinos/Latinas, gays, lesbians, bisexuals, or transgendered persons and persons with physical, mental/emotional, and/or learning disabilities who are group members.

2. Diversity-competent group workers demonstrate awareness of their stereotypes and preconceived notions that they may hold toward Indigenous Peoples, African Americans, Asian Americans, Hispanics, Latinos/Latinas, gays, lesbians, bisexuals, or transgendered persons and persons with physical, mental/emotional, and/or learning disabilities.

B. Knowledge

1. Diversity-skilled group workers possess specific knowledge and information about Indigenous Peoples, African Americans, Asian Americans, Hispanics, Latinos/Latinas, gays, lesbians, bisexuals, and transgendered people and group members who have mental/emotional, physical, and/or learning disabilities with whom they are working. They are aware of the life experiences, cultural heritage, and sociopolitical background of Indigenous Peoples, African Americans, Asian Americans, Hispanics, Latinos/Latinas, gays, lesbians, bisexuals, or transgendered persons and group members with physical, mental/emotional, and/or learning disabilities. This particular knowledge-based competency is strongly linked to the various racial/minority and sexual identity development models available in the literature (Atkinson, Morten, & Sue, 1993; Cass, 1979; Cross, 1995; D'Augelli & Patterson, 1995; Helms, 1992).

2. Diversity-competent group workers exhibit an understanding of how race, ethnicity, culture, gender, sexual identity, different abilities, SES, and other immutable personal characteristics may affect personality formation, vocational choices, manifestation of psychological disorders, physical "dis-ease" or somatic symptoms, help-seeking behavior(s), and the appropriateness or inappropriateness of the various types of and theoretical approaches to group work.

3. Group workers who demonstrate competency in diversity in groups understand and have the knowledge about sociopolitical influences that impinge upon the lives of Indigenous Peoples, African Americans, Asian Americans, Hispanics, Latinos/Latinas, gays, lesbians, bisexuals, or transgendered persons and persons with physical, mental/emotional, and/or learning disabilities. Immigration issues, poverty, racism, oppression, stereotyping, and/or powerlessness adversely impacts many of these individuals and therefore impacts group process or dynamics.

C. Skills

1. Diversity-skilled group workers familiarize themselves with relevant research and the latest findings regarding mental health issues of Indigenous Peoples, African Americans, Asian Americans, Hispanics, Latinos/Latinas, gays, lesbians, bisexuals, or transgendered persons and persons with physical, mental/emotional, and/or learning disabilities. They actively seek out educational experiences that foster their knowledge and understanding of skills for facilitating groups across differences.

2. Diversity-competent group workers become actively involved with Indigenous Peoples, African Americans, Asian Americans, Hispanics, Latinos/Latinas, gays, lesbians, bisexuals, or transgendered persons and persons with physical, mental/emotional, and/or learning disabilities outside of their group work/counseling setting (community events, social and political functions, celebrations, friendships, neighborhood groups, etc.) so that their perspective of minorities is more than academic or experienced through a third party.

III. Diversity-Appropriate Intervention Strategies

A. Attitudes and Beliefs

1. Diversity-competent group workers respect clients' religious and/or spiritual beliefs and values, because they affect worldview, psychosocial functioning, and expressions of distress.

2. Diversity-competent group workers respect indigenous helping practices and respect Indigenous Peoples, African Americans, Asian Americans, Hispanics, Latinos/Latinas, gays, lesbians, bisexuals, or transgendered persons and persons with physical, mental/emotional, and/or learning disabilities and can identify and utilize community intrinsic help-giving networks.

3. Diversity-competent group workers value bilingualism and sign language and do not view another language as an impediment to group work.

B. Knowledge

1. Diversity-competent group workers demonstrate a clear and explicit knowledge and understanding of generic characteristics of group work and theory and how they may clash with the beliefs, values, and traditions of Indigenous Peoples, African Americans, Asian Americans, Hispanics, Latinos/Latinas, gays, lesbians, bisexuals, or transgendered persons and persons with physical, mental/emotional, and/or learning disabilities.

2. Diversity-competent group workers exhibit an awareness of institutional barriers that prevent Indigenous Peoples, African Americans, Asian Americans, Hispanics, Latinos/Latinas, gays, lesbians, bisexuals, or transgendered members and members with physical, mental/emotional, and/or learning disabilities from actively participating in or using various types of groups, that is, task groups, psychoeducational groups, counseling groups, and psychotherapy groups or the settings in which the services are offered.

3. Diversity-competent group workers demonstrate knowledge of the potential bias in assessment instruments and use procedures and interpret findings, or actively participate in various types of evaluations of group outcome or success, keeping in mind the linguistic, cultural, and other self-identified characteristics of the group member.

4. Diversity-competent group workers exhibit knowledge of the family structures, hierarchies, values, and beliefs of Indigenous Peoples, African Americans, Asian Americans, Hispanics, Latinos/Latinas, gays, lesbians, bisexuals, or transgendered persons and persons with physical, mental/emotional, and/or learning disabilities. They are knowledgeable about the community characteristics and the resources in the community as well as about the family.

5. Diversity-competent group workers demonstrate an awareness of relevant discriminatory practices at the social and community level that may be affecting the psychological welfare of persons and access to services of the population being served.

C. Skills

1. Diversity-competent group workers are able to engage in a variety of verbal and nonverbal group-facilitating functions, dependent upon the type of group (task, counseling, psychoeducational, psychotherapy), and the multiple, self-identified status of various group members (such as Indigenous Peoples, African Americans, Asian Americans, Hispanics, Latinos/Latinas, gays, lesbians, bisexuals, or transgendered persons and persons with physical, mental/emotional, and/or learning disabilities). They demonstrate the ability to send and receive both verbal and nonverbal messages accurately, appropriately, and across/between the differences represented in the group. They are not tied down to one method or approach to group facilitation and recognize that helping styles and approaches may be culture-bound. When they sense that their group facilitation style is limited and potentially inappropriate, they can anticipate and ameliorate its negative impact by drawing upon other culturally relevant skill sets.

2. Diversity-competent group workers have the ability to exercise institutional intervention skills on behalf of their group members. They can help a member determine whether a "problem" with the institution stems from the oppression of Indigenous Peoples, African Americans, Asian Americans, Hispanics, Latinos/Latinas, gays, lesbians, bisexuals, or transgendered persons and persons with physical, mental/emotional, and/or learning disabilities, such as in the case of developing or having a "healthy" paranoia, so that group members do not inappropriately personalize problems.

3. Diversity-competent group workers do not exhibit a reluctance to seek consultation with traditional healers and religious and spiritual healers and practitioners in the treatment of members who are self-identified Indigenous Peoples, African Americans, Asian Americans, Hispanics, Latinos/Latinas, gays, lesbians, bisexuals, and transgendered persons and/or group members with mental/emotional, physical, and/or learning disabilities when appropriate.

4. Diversity-competent group workers take responsibility for interacting in the language requested by the group member(s) and, if not feasible, make an appropriate referral. A serious problem arises when the linguistic skills of a group worker and a group member or members, including sign language, do not match. The same problem occurs when the linguistic skills of one member or several members do not match. This being the case, the group worker should (a) seek a translator with cultural knowledge and appropriate professional background, and (b) refer to a knowledgeable, competent bilingual group worker or a group worker competent or certified in sign language. In some cases, it may be necessary to have a group for group members of similar languages or to refer the group member for individual counseling.

5. Diversity-competent group workers are trained and have expertise in the use of traditional assessment and testing instruments related to group work, such as in screening potential members, and they also are aware of the cultural bias/limitations of these tools and processes. This allows them to use the tools for the welfare of diverse group members following culturally appropriate procedures.

6. Diversity-competent group workers attend to as well as work to eliminate biases, prejudices, oppression, and discriminatory practices. They are cognizant of how sociopolitical contexts may affect evaluation and provision of group work and should develop sensitivity to issues of oppression, racism, sexism, heterosexism, classism, and so forth.

7. Diversity-competent group workers take responsibility in educating their group members to the processes of group work, such as goals, expectations, legal rights, sound ethical practice, and the group worker's theoretical orientation with regard to facilitating groups with diverse membership.

CONCLUSION

This document is the "starting point" for group workers as we become increasingly aware, knowledgeable, and skillful in facilitating groups whose memberships represent the diversity of our society. It is not intended to be a "how to" document. It is written as a call to action and/or a guideline and represents ASGW's commitment to moving forward with an agenda for addressing and understanding the needs of the populations we serve. As a "living document," the Association for Specialists in Group Work acknowledges the changing world in which we live and work and therefore recognizes that this is the first step in working with diverse group members with competence, compassion, respect, and integrity. As our awareness, knowledge, and skills develop, so too will this document evolve. As our knowledge as a profession grows in this area and as the sociopolitical context in which this document was written changes, new editions of these Principles for Diversity-Competent Group Workers will arise. The operationalization of this document (article in process) will begin to define appropriate group leadership skills and interventions as well as make recommendations for research in understanding how diversity in group membership affects group process and dynamics.

REFERENCES

American Counseling Association. (1995). *Code of ethics and standards.* Alexandria, VA: Author.

Association for Multicultural Counseling and Development. (1996). *Multicultural competencies.* Alexandria, VA: American Counseling Association.

Association for Specialists in Group Work. (1991). Professional standards for training of group workers. *Together, 20,* 9-14.

Association for Specialists in Group Work. (1998). Best practice guidelines. *Journal for Specialists in Group Work, 23,* 237-244.

Atkinson, D. R., Morten, G., & Sue, D. W. (Eds.). (1993). *Counseling American minorities* (4th ed.). Madison, WI: Brown & Benchmark.

Cass, V. C. (1979). Homosexual identity formation: A theoretical model. *Journal of Homosexuality, 4,* 219-236.

Cross, W. E. (1995). The psychology of Nigrescence: Revising the cross model. In J. G. Ponterotto, J. M. Casas, L. A. Suzuki, & C. M. Alexander (Eds.), *Handbook of multicultural counseling* (pp. 93-122). Thousand Oaks, CA: Sage.

D'Augelli, A. R., & Patterson, C. J. (Eds.). (1995). *Lesbian, gay and bisexual identities over the lifespan.* New York: Oxford University Press.

Helms, J. E. (1992). *A race is a nice thing to have.* Topeka, KS: Context Communications.

Appendix C

ASSOCIATION FOR SPECIALISTS IN GROUP WORK

Best Practice Guidelines

Approved by the Executive Board, March 29, 1998

PREPARED BY LYNN S. RAPIN AND LINDA KEEL,
ASGW ETHICS COMMITTEE CO-CHAIRS

PREAMBLE

The Association for Specialists in Group Work (ASGW) is a division of the American Counseling Association whose members are interested in and specialize in group work. We value the creation of community; service to our members, clients, and the profession; and value leadership as a process to facilitate the growth and development of individuals and groups.

The Association for Specialists in Group Work recognizes the commitment of its members to the Code of Ethics and Standards of Practice (as revised in 1995) of its parent organization, the American Counseling Association, and nothing in this document shall be construed to supplant that code. These Best Practice Guidelines are intended to clarify the application of the ACA Code of Ethics and Standards of Practice to the field of group work by defining Group Workers' responsibility and scope of practice involving those activities, strategies and interventions that are consistent and current with effective and appropriate professional ethical and community standards. ASGW views ethical process as being integral to group work and views Group Workers as ethical agents. Group Workers, by their very nature in being responsible and responsive to their group members, necessarily embrace a certain potential for ethical vulnerability. It is incumbent upon Group Workers to give considerable attention to the intent and context of their actions because the attempts of Group Workers to influence human behavior through group work always have ethical implications. These Best Practice Guidelines address Group Workers' responsibilities in planning, performing and processing groups.

SECTION A: BEST PRACTICE IN PLANNING

A.1. Professional
Context and Regulatory Requirements

Group Workers actively know, understand and apply the ACA Code of Ethics and Standards of Best Practice, the ASGW Professional Standards for the Training of Group Workers, these ASGW Best Practice Guidelines, the ASGW diversity competencies, the ACA Multicultural Guidelines, relevant state laws, accreditation requirements, relevant National Board for Certified Counselors Codes and Standards, their organization's standards, and insurance requirements impacting the practice of group work.

A.2. Scope of Practice and
Conceptual Framework

Group Workers define the scope of practice related to the core and specialization competencies defined in the ASGW Training Standards. Group Workers are aware of personal strengths and weaknesses in leading groups. Group Workers develop and are able to articulate a general conceptual framework to guide practice and a rationale for use of techniques that are to be used. Group Workers limit their practice to those areas for which they meet the training criteria established by the ASGW Training Standards.

A.3. Assessment

a. *Assessment of self.* Group Workers actively assess their knowledge and skills related to the specific group(s) offered. Group Workers assess their values, beliefs and theoretical orientation and how these impact upon the group, particularly when working with a diverse and multicultural population.
b. *Ecological assessment.* Group Workers assess community needs, agency or organization resources, sponsoring organization mission, staff competency, attitudes regarding group work, professional training levels of potential group leaders regarding group work; client attitudes regarding group work, and multicultural and diversity considerations. Group Workers use this information

as the basis for making decisions related to their group practice, or to the implementation of groups for which they have supervisory, evaluation, or oversight responsibilities.

A.4. Program Development and Evaluation

a. *Group Workers identify the type(s) of group(s) to be offered and how they relate to community needs.*
b. *Group Workers concisely state in writing the purpose and goals of the group.* Group Workers also identify the role of the group members in influencing or determining the group goals.
c. *Group Workers set fees consistent with the organization's fee schedule, taking into consideration the financial status and locality of prospective group members.*
d. *Group Workers choose techniques and a leadership style appropriate to the type(s) of group(s) being offered.*
e. *Group Workers have an evaluation plan consistent with regulatory, organization and insurance requirements, where appropriate.*
f. *Group Workers take into consideration current professional guidelines when using technology, including but not limited to Internet communication.*

A.5. Resources

Group Workers coordinate resources related to the kind of group(s) and group activities to be provided, such as: adequate funding; the appropriateness and availability of a trained coleader; space and privacy requirements for the type(s) of group(s) being offered; marketing and recruiting; and appropriate collaboration with other community agencies and organizations.

A.6. Professional Disclosure Statement

Group Workers have a professional disclosure statement which includes information on confidentiality and exceptions to confidentiality, theoretical orientation, information on the nature, purpose(s) and goals of the group, the group services that can be provided, the role and responsibility of group members and leaders,

Group Workers' qualifications to conduct the specific group(s), specific licenses, certifications and professional affiliations, and address of licensing/credentialing body.

A.7. Group and Member Preparation

a. *Group Workers screen prospective group members if appropriate to the type of group being offered.* When selection of group members is appropriate, Group Workers identify group members whose needs and goals are compatible with the goals of the group.

b. *Group Workers facilitate informed consent.* Group Workers provide in oral and written form to prospective members (when appropriate to group type): the professional disclosure statement; group purpose and goals; group participation expectations including voluntary and involuntary membership; role expectations of members and leader(s); policies related to entering and exiting the group; policies governing substance use; policies and procedures governing mandated groups (where relevant); documentation requirements; disclosure of information to others; implications of out-of-group contact or involvement among members; procedures for consultation between group leader(s) and group member(s); fees and time parameters; and potential impacts of group participation.

c. *Group Workers obtain the appropriate consent forms for work with minors and other dependent group members.*

d. *Group Workers define confidentiality and its limits (for example, legal and ethical exceptions and expectations; waivers implicit with treatment plans, documentation and insurance usage).* Group Workers have the responsibility to inform all group participants of the need for confidentiality, potential consequences of breaching confidentiality and that legal privilege does not apply to group discussions (unless provided by state statute).

A.8. Professional Development

Group Workers recognize that professional growth is a continuous, ongoing, developmental process throughout their career.

a. *Group Workers remain current and increase knowledge and skill competencies through activities such as continuing education, professional supervision, and participation in personal and professional development activities.*

b. *Group Workers seek consultation and/or supervision regarding ethical concerns that interfere with effective functioning as a group leader.* Supervisors have the responsibility to keep abreast of consultation, group theory, process, and adhere to related ethical guidelines.

c. *Group Workers seek appropriate professional assistance for their own personal problems or conflicts that are likely to impair their professional judgment or work performance.*

d. *Group Workers seek consultation and supervision to ensure appropriate practice whenever working with a group for which all knowledge and skill competencies have not been achieved.*

e. *Group Workers keep abreast of group research and development.*

A.9. Trends and Technological Changes

Group Workers are aware of and responsive to technological changes as they affect society and the profession. These include but are not limited to changes in mental health delivery systems; legislative and insurance industry reforms; shifting population demographics and client needs; and technological advances in Internet and other communication and delivery systems. Group Workers adhere to ethical guidelines related to the use of developing technologies.

Section B: Best Practice in Performing

B.1. Self-Knowledge

Group Workers are aware of and monitor their strengths and weaknesses and the effects these have on group members.

B.2. Group Competencies

Group Workers have a basic knowledge of groups and the principles of group dynamics, and are able to perform the core group competencies, as described in the ASGW Professional Standards for the Training of

Group Workers. Additionally, Group Workers have adequate understanding and skill in any group specialty area chosen for practice (psychotherapy, counseling, task, psychoeducational, as described in the ASGW Training Standards).

B.3. Group Plan Adaptation

a. *Group Workers apply and modify knowledge, skills and techniques appropriate to group type and stage, and to the unique needs of various cultural and ethnic groups.*
b. *Group Workers monitor the group's progress toward the group goals and plan.*
c. *Group Workers clearly define and maintain ethical, professional, and social relationship boundaries with group members as appropriate to their role in the organization and the type of group being offered.*

B.4. Therapeutic Conditions and Dynamics

Group Workers understand and are able to implement appropriate models of group development, process observation and therapeutic conditions.

B.5. Meaning

Group Workers assist members in generating meaning from the group experience.

B.6. Collaboration

Group Workers assist members in developing individual goals and respect group members as co-equal partners in the group experience.

B.7. Evaluation

Group Workers include evaluation (both formal and informal) between sessions and at the conclusion of the group.

B.8. Diversity

Group Workers practice with broad sensitivity to client differences including but not limited to ethnic, gender, religious, sexual, psychological maturity, economic class, family history, physical characteristics or limitations, **and** geographic location. Group Workers continuously seek information regarding the cultural issues of the diverse population with whom they are working both by interaction with participants and from using outside resources.

B.9. Ethical Surveillance

Group Workers employ an appropriate ethical decision-making model in responding to ethical challenges and issues and in determining courses of action and behavior for self and group members. In addition, Group Workers employ applicable standards as promulgated by ACA, ASGW, or other appropriate professional organizations.

Section C: Best Practice in Group Processing

C.1. Processing Schedule

Group Workers process the workings of the group with themselves, group members, supervisors or other colleagues, as appropriate. This may include assessing progress on group and member goals, leader behaviors and techniques, group dynamics and interventions; developing understanding and acceptance of meaning. Processing may occur both within sessions and before and after each session, at time of termination, and later follow up, as appropriate.

C.2. Reflective Practice

Group Workers attend to opportunities to synthesize theory and practice and to incorporate learning outcomes into ongoing groups. Group Workers attend to session dynamics of members and their interactions and also attend to the relationship between session dynamics and leader values, cognition and affect.

C.3. Evaluation and Follow-Up

a. *Group Workers evaluate process and outcomes.* Results are used for ongoing program planning, improvement and revisions of current group and/or to contribute to professional research literature. Group Workers follow all applicable policies and standards in using group material for research and reports.

b. *Group Workers conduct follow-up contact with group members, as appropriate, to assess outcomes or when requested by a group member(s).*

C.4. Consultation and Training With Other Organizations

Group Workers provide consultation and training to organizations in and out of their setting, when appropriate. Group Workers seek out consultation as needed with competent professional persons knowledgeable about group work.

Reprinted with permission from Association for Specialists in Group Work.

Author Index

Subject Index